808.82
W 43

DRAMA IN THE MODERN WORLD

PLAYS AND ESSAYS

Alternate Edition

DRAMA IN THE MODERN WORLD

PLAYS AND ESSAYS

Alternate Edition

SAMUEL A. WEISS

University of Illinois, Chicago Circle

054154

D. C. HEATH AND COMPANY

Lexington, Massachusetts   Toronto   London

International Standard Book Number: 0-669-83121-2

Library of Congress Catalog Card Number: 73-9350

PREFACE

Like its predecessor, the alternate edition of *Drama in the Modern World* offers a selection of outstanding plays from the modern repertory, accompanied by critical materials that illuminate the playwrights or the particular works. Fourteen of the fifteen plays are new, and in addition to the usual stage plays this edition includes a radio play, a cinema script, and a modern Peking Opera. No attempt is made to preempt the reader's or teacher's role by lengthy editorial commentary. On the contrary, the editor's introductions are brief and sufficient to orient the reader without prejudicing his responses.

Inevitably, the established masters appear again, but in fresh selections. Tastes differ, and in choosing new plays by these dramatists, I have turned to what for many are their greatest, or among their greatest, achievements. Thus readers will welcome Ibsen's *The Master Builder* and Shaw's *Heartbreak House* as infrequently anthologized masterworks altogether deserving of attention. Strindberg's *A Dream Play*, Chekhov's *Three Sisters*, Pirandello's *Henry IV*, and O'Neill's *The Hairy Ape* may perhaps be more demanding than corresponding selections in the earlier edition, but they are great and indeed favorite works. Synge is here represented by *Riders to the Sea*, which adumbrates issues of language, content, and theme central to evolving modern drama. And Lorca and Brecht appear with examples of their best work: *Blood Wedding* and *Mother Courage*.

A newcomer to the selection of older masters is Arthur Schnitzler, the unduly neglected Austrian playwright, whose *La Ronde* (*Reigen*) is a unique, incisive, and entertaining portrait of egoistic and exploitative sexuality in a world of heedless values, game-playing, and loveless adventure. Notorious in its own day, *La Ronde* is a masterpiece of social and psychological insight that offers an exceptional opportunity to explore the sensitive and troubling area of sexual values.

Of more recent playwrights, Ionesco appears in a new selection: *Jack or the Submission*. Samuel Beckett is again represented with his radio play *All That*

Fall. This non-stage form may initiate discussion of modern technology affecting dramatic art and can be explored in juxtaposition to Sergei Eisenstein's cinema script *Ivan the Terrible*, Part I, an extraordinary amalgam of cinematic and literary poetry. Another variant dramatic form, virtually unknown in the West until quite recently, is the modern revolutionary Peking Opera, here represented by *The Red Lantern*, a vivid realization of the genre. These were chosen in order to avoid the parochialism that focuses on the Western stageplay to the exclusion of other forms and other cultures. Finally, *No Place to Be Somebody* introduces the lyrical, many-colored voice of Charles Gordone, who blazed onto the stage in 1969 with his long-pondered play about black and white America.

All but three of the accompanying essays are new to this edition and are chosen for their interest, readability, and liveliness. Michael Meyer offers a fascinating collation of documents on Ibsen and Emilie Bardach; Frederic Morton conjures up Schnitzler's Vienna in its Hapsburgian decadence; Gorky unforgettably recalls Chekhov; Valency, Brustein, Barea, and Ivor Montagu comment in depth on their subjects; Synge, Shaw, and Brecht speak for themselves, as do—in revealing interviews—O'Neill and Beckett. Ionesco debates with Tynan in a superbly balanced contest; Walter Kerr reviews Charles Gordone in an example of glittering journalistic skill; and Chairman Mao, redoubtable poet and politician, discusses the principles of revolutionary art.

The arrangement of the plays is essentially chronological. The main exception is Eisenstein's *Ivan the Terrible*. Placed after Beckett's radio play, it joins the Peking Opera as a non-Western, but also variant, dramatic form. Still *Ivan* can be read along with Brecht's *Mother Courage* as a contrasting example of Marxian historical drama appearing in the forties.

Dates for plays in the introductions refer to final year of composition unless otherwise indicated.

The appended Bibliography has been carefully updated and revised, and a section on reference works has been added.

S.A.W.

CONTENTS

DRAMA IN THE MODERN WORLD

PLAYS AND ESSAYS

Alternate Edition

Henrik
Ibsen
1828–1906

Ibsen was born in the town of Skien in southern Norway, into a merchant family that suffered a humiliating bankruptcy when he was eight. Thus he experienced the destructive effects of narrow provincial values early in life, and throughout his career he was to inveigh against stultifying convention and to champion the rebellious spirit. At fifteen he left his family and moved to Grimstad, a neighboring small town where he was apprenticed to a pharmacist; there, at eighteen, he fathered an illegitimate child. At Grimstad, too, Ibsen found provincial life intolerable and expressed his revolt in wild and riotous pranks. Finally he set out for Christiania to study medicine, but his bent for philosophy and literature soon won out. Caught up in the revolutionary currents of 1848, he had written a verse drama, *Catiline*, idealizing the Roman traitor as a champion of liberty. He now joined a liberal weekly and a secret revolutionary group, but renounced political activity when the group's leaders were seized and imprisoned. A turning point in his life came when he was invited to become stage manager of the state theatre in Bergen, and from 1851 to 1862 he was associated with theatres in Bergen and Christiania, producing, directing, and writing. In 1864, however, he became depressed and embittered by Norway's failure to defend Denmark against Prussia, and left for a self-imposed exile in Rome. Not until 1891 did he return to Norway. In Italy he wrote his finest poetic dramas, *Brand* (1866) and *Peer Gynt* (1867). But it was his realistic prose plays in which he grappled with contemporary social and moral issues that made a profound impression on European culture and drama; he was hailed as a liberator by some and denounced as a subverter of morality by others. Ibsen struck out against hypocrisy and social conformity and called for creative self-realization in such plays as *A Doll's House* (1879), *Ghosts* (1881), and *An Enemy of the People* (1882). He met the central issue of the individual in society with a slashing attack on the "compact majority." Yet he recognized the limits of his own iconoclasm, as is evident in the subtle studies of neurotic idealists and destructive pseudo-Ibsenites in

The Wild Duck (1884), *Rosmersholm* (1886), and *Hedda Gabler* (1890). With *The Master Builder* (1892) Ibsen turned to the tragedy of the aging artist. A deepening note of frustration and failure now entered his work; his plays withdrew into ever more obscure symbolism, dealing with autobiographical and metaphysical matters. He died in 1906, after a series of strokes had broken his once-powerful mind.

THE MASTER BUILDER

A drama in three acts

HENRIK IBSEN

Translated by Arvid Paulson

PERSONS IN THE PLAY

HALVARD SOLNESS, a builder
ALINE SOLNESS, his wife
DOCTOR HERDAL, their physician
KNUT BROVIK, a former architect now in the employ of Solness
RAGNAR BROVIK, his son, a draftsman

KAJA FOSLI, niece of Knut Brovik; a bookkeeper
HILDE WANGEL, a young woman of about twenty-three
SEVERAL LADIES
TOWNSPEOPLE

[The action takes place at the home of HALVARD SOLNESS and his wife on the outskirts of a city in Norway.]

ACT I

[THE SETTING.—A plainly furnished workroom in the house of HALVARD SOLNESS. On the right is a folding door leading to the rest of the rooms on that floor. In the rear, a doorway leads to the draftsmen's office. Downstage, right, a desk with books, papers, and writing materials. On the upstage side of the door, a stove. In the upstage corner, on the left, a sofa with a table and a couple of chairs. A decanter of water and glasses on the table. Downstage, left, a smaller table, a rocking chair and an armchair. On the table in the draftsmen's office and on the tables in the corner, as well as on the desk, are lamps that are lighted.

In the draftsmen's office KNUT BROVIK and his son RAGNAR, both seated, are working on construction plans and calculations. At the high desk in the workroom, KAJA FOSLI stands writing in the main ledger.

KNUT BROVIK is a slightly built elderly man. His hair and beard are white. He is dressed in a neat though rather threadbare black coat and wears a somewhat faded white necktie, and spectacles.

RAGNAR BROVIK is a blond young man in his thirties; he has a slight stoop, and is scrupulously dressed.

KAJA FOSLI is a slender young woman in her early twenties; she is frail and appears to be delicate in health. She is carefully dressed and wears a green eyeshade.

When the curtain rises, all three are seen busy at work, and they continue working for some moments in silence.]

KNUT BROVIK [rises suddenly from the drawing table as if in agony. He is breathing heavily and with difficulty as he walks to the door opening]. Oh, I can't stand this much longer!

KAJA [goes over to him]. I'm afraid you are not feeling well tonight, Uncle . . . ?

BROVIK. I seem to be getting worse with every day.

RAGNAR [has risen and comes up to his father]. I really think you ought to go home, Father. Go home—and try to get some sleep . . .

BROVIK [impatiently]. And go to bed, you mean? Do you want me to suffocate?

KAJA. Then why don't you go out and get a little fresh air, Uncle?

RAGNAR. Yes, do that, Father. I'll go with you.

BROVIK [vehemently]. I will not leave until he comes back! I must tell him to-night—I must speak with . . . [with suppressed resentment and indignation] . . . with him—the master builder!

KAJA [anxiously]. Oh no, Uncle—please let that wait!

RAGNAR. Yes, let that wait, Father! It's better!

BROVIK [breathing with difficulty]. Hah! Hah! I'm afraid there isn't much time left for me to wait . . .

KAJA [listening]. Sh! I hear him coming on the stairs . . .

[All three resume working. There is a silence. Then HALVARD SOLNESS enters from the hall. He is a man well along in years, strong and healthy, with close-cropped curly hair, a dark mustache, and thick eyebrows. He is dressed in a grayish green coat with a high collar and broad lapels, and on his head he wears a soft gray felt hat. His coat is buttoned, and he carries a couple of portfolios under his arm.]

SOLNESS [at the door; he points toward the draftsmen's room and asks KAJA in a whisper]. Have they gone?

KAJA [in a low voice, shaking her head]. No. [She removes her eyeshade.]

[SOLNESS walks across the room, throws his hat on a chair, lays the portfolio on the table by the sofa and again approaches the desk. KAJA keeps writing in the ledger but she shows signs of uneasiness and nervousness.]

SOLNESS [aloud]. What is it you are entering in the ledger, Miss Fosli?

KAJA [with a start]. Oh, it's only something that . . .

SOLNESS. Let me see, Miss Fosli. [He leans over her, pretending to be looking at the ledger, and whispers to her.] Kaja!

KAJA [in a subdued voice, while continuing to write]. Yes?

SOLNESS. Why do you always remove your eyeshade when I come in?

KAJA [as before]. Why? Because I look so horrid with it on.

SOLNESS [with a smile]. And that you don't want, do you?

KAJA [looking at him out of the corner of her eye]. Not for anything in the world! And least of all in your eyes!

SOLNESS [lightly stroking her hair]. Poor, poor little Kaja!

KAJA [bending low over the ledger]. Sh! They'll hear you!

[SOLNESS walks casually across the room toward the left, turns and stops in the doorway to the drafting room.]

SOLNESS. Has anyone been here to see me?

RAGNAR [rises]. Yes, the young people who want to have a villa built out at Lövstrand.

SOLNESS [with a growl]. Oh, those two? Well—they'll have to wait! I haven't made up my mind yet about the design.

RAGNAR [approaching him; somewhat hesitantly]. They were so anxious to see the preliminary sketches as soon as possible.

SOLNESS [again with a growl]. Yes, of course, of course! That's what they all want!

BROVIK [looks up]. They just can't wait—they are terribly anxious to move into a house of their own, they said. Terribly anxious . . .

SOLNESS. Why, certainly, certainly. It's the same old story! And so they take the first thing that comes along. And what do they get? A house with four walls—a place where they can eat and sleep—but not a home. No, thank you! No—let them go to someone else. Tell them that when they come here again.

BROVIK [pushes his spectacles up on his brow and gazes at him shocked]. To someone else? Do you really mean that you would want to turn away a client?

SOLNESS [impatiently]. Yes, of course, damn it! If it comes to that, I would rather do that than build something haphazardly. And besides, I know nothing about these people.

BROVIK. They are reliable people. Ragnar knows them. They are friends of his. They are very reliable.

SOLNESS. Oh, reliable! Reliable! I have never implied that they are not reliable!

Good Lord! Don't even you understand what I mean any more? [*Irascibly.*] I don't know these people! I want to have nothing to do with them. Let them go to whomever they want! I am not interested!

BROVIK [*rises*]. Are you quite serious when you say that?

SOLNESS [*sullenly*]. I am—yes. For once.

[*He walks across the room.* BROVIK *exchanges a glance with* RAGNAR *who makes a deprecatory gesture.* BROVIK *then goes into the workroom.*]

BROVIK [*to* SOLNESS]. May I speak with you for a moment?

SOLNESS. Certainly.

BROVIK [*to* KAJA]. Go into the other room for a minute, Kaja.

KAJA [*disturbed*]. Oh but, Uncle . . .

BROVIK. Do as I say, child. And close the door after you. [KAJA *hesitates but goes into the draftsmen's room with an anxious look and with a pleading glance at* BROVIK. *She closes the door after her.* BROVIK *speaks in a subdued tone of voice.*] I don't want the poor children to know how ill I really am.

SOLNESS. Yes—you do look a little feeble of late.

BROVIK. It'll soon be over for me. My strength is leaving me—little by little.

SOLNESS. Sit down for a minute.

BROVIK. Thank you. May I?

SOLNESS [*moves the armchair and beckons to* BROVIK *to sit down*]. There—there you are. Sit down now. Well?

BROVIK [*has seated himself with some difficulty*]. Well—it's about Ragnar I want to speak with you. He is my greatest worry. I don't know what will become of him . . .

SOLNESS. Your son stays with me, of course. He can stay here as long as he likes.

BROVIK. But that is exactly what he doesn't want to do. He doesn't feel he can—not any longer.

SOLNESS. Well, if I may say so, he earns a good salary here. But if he is not satisfied with what he gets, I have no objection to increasing his . . .

BROVIK. No, no, it's not a question of money! But what he would like is, of course, to get a chance to work for himself.

SOLNESS [*without looking at* BROVIK]. Do you think Ragnar is sufficiently qualified for that?

BROVIK. No—that is just what worries me most. I have come to have doubts about my boy. And you have never given him the slightest encouragement—not with a word even. Still, I think, he must have ability. I just can't think otherwise.

SOLNESS. Yes, but he has learned comparatively little. He has no thorough experience—except as a draftsman.

BROVIK [*looks at him with concealed hatred and says hoarsely*]. Experience! Had you had any experience when I took you to work for me? Yet you went into business for yourself in spite of it, didn't you? [*He breathes heavily.*] And you kept going up in the world—and drove not only me but a lot of others to the wall.

SOLNESS. Well, I had luck on my side, you see.

BROVIK. You are right. Luck was with you—in whatever you did. For that reason alone, you can't have the heart to let me go to my grave without having had the satisfaction of seeing my son successful in life. And then—I did want to see them married also—before I leave this world.

SOLNESS [*in a sharp tone*]. Is it she who is so eager to marry?

BROVIK. It isn't so much Kaja. But Ragnar keeps talking about it continuously. [*Pleadingly.*] You must—you must help him to get some work of his own now! I want to see my boy do something of his own, you hear!

SOLNESS [*irritated*]. What the devil do you expect me to do? Get a commission for him from someone on the moon?

BROVIK. He has a chance to get a commission right now. Quite an important one at that.

SOLNESS [*with a start; disturbed*]. Has he?

BROVIK. Yes—if you will give your approval.

SOLNESS. What sort of project is it?

BROVIK [*with some hesitation*]. He has a chance to get that contract to build the villa out at Lövstrand.

SOLNESS. That one! You know very well I am building that myself!

BROVIK. Oh—but you no longer are interested in it.

SOLNESS [flares up]. Not interested! I —not interested! Who has the audacity to say that?

BROVIK. You just said so a moment ago.

SOLNESS. Oh, pay no attention to what I say. And you say Ragnar has a chance to get the contract for that house?

BROVIK. Yes, you see, he knows the family. And—just to amuse himself—he has drawn some preliminary sketches and made some estimates. He has made a complete set of drawings.

SOLNESS. And the drawings? Are they satisfied with them? Are they?

BROVIK. Yes, and if you would only look them over and approve them, then . . .

SOLNESS. Then they will give Ragnar the commission for the villa?

BROVIK. They admired all his innovations—thought his design was something new in architecture, they said.

SOLNESS. Oho! Something new! Not the old-fashioned kind of rubbish that I build, eh?

BROVIK. They thought it was unusual and different.

SOLNESS [with suppressed anger]. So that's the reason they came while I was out? It was Ragnar they wanted to see!

BROVIK. They came here for the purpose of seeing you. They wanted to see if they couldn't persuade you to withdraw . . .

SOLNESS [in a rage]. Withdraw? I— withdraw?

BROVIK. Yes—if you approved of Ragnar's sketches . . .

SOLNESS. I withdraw? Withdraw—for the sake of your son?

BROVIK. They meant—to cancel the agreement.

SOLNESS. Oh, it's the same thing! [With an embittered smile.] So-o! Halvard Solness—Halvard Solness is beginning to go downhill, is he? To make room for those who are younger—perhaps even for the very young. Yes—make room! Make room! Make room!

BROVIK. Good Lord! Isn't there room here for more than one builder?

SOLNESS. Oh—there is not too much room here. But be that as it may, I shall never retire! I shall never step aside for anyone! Not voluntarily! I'll never do that—never!

BROVIK [gets up out of the chair with difficulty]. So you want me to die without peace in my heart? All my hopes gone? Without trust and belief in Ragnar? Without having seen a single work of his come to life? Is that what you want?

SOLNESS [turns half-aside, muttering]. H'm! Stop asking all these questions!

BROVIK. Yes, give me your answer to that! Am I to go out of this life so impoverished?

SOLNESS [seems to struggle with himself; finally he says in a low but firm voice]. You may go out of this life as best you can!

BROVIK. So be it. [He goes upstage.]

SOLNESS [follows him in near desperation]. Don't you understand—I can't do otherwise! I am made that way. And I can't change—I can't change my nature!

BROVIK. No, no—I imagine you can't. [He reels and stops at the table by the sofa.] Will you let me have a glass of water?

SOLNESS [pours him a glass and hands it to him]. Here you are.

BROVIK. Thank you. [He drinks, then puts the glass on the table. SOLNESS goes over and opens the door leading to the draftsmen's room.]

SOLNESS. Ragnar! Come over here! You had better see that your father gets home.

[RAGNAR rises swiftly from his seat. He and KAJA come into the workroom.]

RAGNAR. What is wrong, Father?

BROVIK. Take hold of me by the arm— and let us leave.

RAGNAR. Yes. And you, too, Kaja. Put your things on.

SOLNESS. Miss Fosli will have to stay a little longer. She will be with you in a moment or two. I have a letter to dictate to her.

BROVIK [with a glance at SOLNESS]. Good night. Sleep well—if you can . . .

SOLNESS. Good night.

[BROVIK and RAGNAR leave through the hall door. KAJA goes over to her desk. SOLNESS stands with head bent on the left, near the armchair.]

KAJA [hesitantly]. You have a letter you want me to . . .

SOLNESS [shortly]. No, of course not. No. [He gives her a blustering look.] Kaja!

KAJA [frightened; in a low voice]. Yes?

SOLNESS [pointing to a spot on the floor in a commanding manner]. Come here—immediately!

KAJA [hesitantly]. Yes.

SOLNESS [as before]. Closer!

KAJA [does as he says]. What do you want me to do?

SOLNESS [gazes at her for a moment]. Is it you I have to thank for this?

KAJA. No, no—you mustn't think that I . . .

SOLNESS. But you do want to get married? Don't you?

KAJA [in a suppressed tone of voice]. Ragnar and I have been engaged for four or five years. And so I . . .

SOLNESS. And so you think you have been engaged long enough? Is that what you think?

KAJA. Ragnar and Uncle keep saying I ought to get married. And I have to do what they want.

SOLNESS [in a gentler tone]. You really are quite fond of Ragnar, too, aren't you, Kaja?

KAJA. I was very fond of Ragnar at one time—before I came here—to you.

SOLNESS. But now you no longer are? Not at all?

KAJA [passionately stretching out her arms to him, her hands clasped]. Why, you know that I now care for only one—one only—and for no one else in the whole world! And I shall never care for anyone else!

SOLNESS. Yes, you say that now! And still you want to leave me. And then I'll be left to cope with everything by myself.

KAJA. Why couldn't I keep on here with you even if Ragnar . . .

SOLNESS [rejecting the suggestion]. No, no—that's entirely out of the question! If Ragnar should leave and go into business for himself, he will need you.

KAJA [wringing her hands]. Oh! I don't see how I can leave you! I just can't—I don't think I ever could!

SOLNESS. Well, then see that Ragnar gets rid of this foolish notion of his. Go ahead and marry him! By all means, do! [In a changed tone.] Well, well—I mean, persuade him to stay with me—where he has a secure position. And then I can keep you with me also, Kaja dear.

KAJA. Oh yes! If that could be done—oh, how wonderful it would be!

SOLNESS [taking her head in his hands, he whispers]. For I can't be without you, Kaja! I can't be without you for a single day!

KAJA [enraptured; nervously]. Oh God! God!

SOLNESS [kisses the top of her head]. Kaja—Kaja!

KAJA [sinks to the floor]. Oh, how good you are to me! I can't find words to tell you how good you are!

SOLNESS [quickly; frightened]. Get up! Quick—get up! I think someone is coming!

[He helps her to her feet, and she totters to her desk. MRS. SOLNESS enters from the door on the left. She is an emaciated and careworn woman, with traces of former beauty. She wears her still blondish hair in ringlets and is fashionably dressed in black. She is rather slow in speech and has a mournful, plaintive voice.]

MRS. SOLNESS [in the doorway]. Halvard!

SOLNESS [turns around]. Oh, it's you, my dear?

MRS. SOLNESS [with a glance at KAJA]. I'm afraid I am disturbing you.

SOLNESS. Not at all. Miss Fosli has a short letter to write—that is all.

MRS. SOLNESS. Yes—so I see.

SOLNESS. Was it anything special you wanted, Aline?

MRS. SOLNESS. I only wanted to tell you that Doctor Herdal is inside—in the corner room. Wouldn't you like to come in and keep us company?

SOLNESS [looks at her suspiciously]. H'm. Is it absolutely necessary that he have a talk with me?

MRS. SOLNESS. No, it's not so very necessary. He just dropped by to see me. But he thought—since he was here—he would like to have a chat with you, too.

SOLNESS [with a placid smile]. I suppose he would, yes. Well—you have to ask him to wait a while.

MRS. SOLNESS. You will come in, then, won't you?

SOLNESS. Perhaps. After a while—after a while, my dear. In a little while.

MRS. SOLNESS [again with a glance at KAJA]. Well—only don't forget now, Halvard. [She walks slowly to the door, left, goes out and closes the door after her.]

KAJA [in a subdued voice]. Oh God! Oh God! I'm quite sure Mrs. Solness suspects something!

SOLNESS. Why, no—not at all. At any rate, not any more so than usual. But it's probably best that you go now, Kaja.

KAJA. Yes, yes, now I must go.

SOLNESS [with severity]. And be sure to settle that other matter for me, do you hear!

KAJA. Oh, if it depended upon me alone—then . . .

SOLNESS. I want it settled, I say! And by tomorrow!

KAJA [filled with anxiety]. If I can't do it any other way, I'll be glad to break off our engagement.

SOLNESS [excitedly]. Break off your engagement? Have you gone clean out of your mind? Break off your engagement!

KAJA [in despair]. Yes—rather that— for I must stay here with you—I must! I can't leave you! I can't! I can't!

SOLNESS [flaring up]. But—what the devil . . . What about Ragnar? It's mostly because of Ragnar that I . . .

KAJA [gazes at him, frightened]. Is it for Ragnar's sake that you primarily . . . ?

SOLNESS. Why, no—of course not! You misunderstand me completely! It's you, of course, I want—you, Kaja, more than anything! And that's the very reason I want you to persuade Ragnar to remain here with me also . . . There—there, now . . . Go home now . . .

KAJA. Yes, yes . . . Good night.

SOLNESS. Good night. [As she is about to leave.] Oh, by the way, are Ragnar's drawings in there? [He points to the drafting room.]

KAJA. Yes—I didn't see him take them with him.

SOLNESS. Then look and see if you can find them for me. I might take a glance at them nevertheless.

KAJA [beaming]. Oh yes, I wish you would!

SOLNESS. I will, for your sake, Kaja dear. Now, hurry up and find them for me, do you hear!

[KAJA runs into the drafting room where she anxiously rummages in the table drawer. She brings a portfolio to SOLNESS.]

KAJA. Here are the drawings—all of them.

SOLNESS. Good. Put them on the table over there.

KAJA [lays the portfolio on the table]. Well—good night, then. [In a pleading voice.] You will think of me—you will give me a kind thought, won't you?

SOLNESS. I always do. Good night, dear little Kaja. [With a glance in the direction of the door on the left.] Be on your way now!

[MRS. SOLNESS and DOCTOR HERDAL enter through the door, left. DOCTOR HERDAL is a plump, elderly gentleman with a round, beardless face, light, thinning hair, and a self-satisfied look. He wears gold-rimmed spectacles.]

MRS. SOLNESS [in the doorway]. Halvard—I can't detain the doctor any longer.

SOLNESS. Well, then—come in here.

MRS. SOLNESS [to KAJA, who is putting out the light in the lamp on the desk]. Did you get the letter written, Miss Fosli?

KAJA [confused]. The letter?

SOLNESS. Yes—it was only a short letter.

MRS. SOLNESS. It must have been very short.

SOLNESS. You may go now, Miss Fosli. And be sure to be on time in the morning.

KAJA. Yes, I'll be on time. Good night, Mrs. Solness.

[She leaves through the hall door.]

MRS. SOLNESS. You are fortunate, Halvard, to have found a girl like her.

SOLNESS. Yes, indeed. She is of use to me in more ways than one.

MRS. SOLNESS. Yes, I see she is.

DOCTOR HERDAL. Is she good at bookkeeping also?

SOLNESS. Well—she has learned a good deal about it during these two years she has been here. And she is always eager to do whatever she is asked to do. She is so willing.

MRS. SOLNESS. Yes—and that must be very gratifying to you . . .

SOLNESS. It is, indeed—especially when one is not used to anything like that.

MRS. SOLNESS [gently reproaching him]. How can you say that, Halvard?

SOLNESS. No, no—I didn't mean that, Aline dear. Please forgive me.

MRS. SOLNESS. Don't mention it. Well, Doctor Herdal, then you'll come back later and have tea with us, won't you?

DOCTOR HERDAL. Yes, as soon as I have made my sick call, I'll come back.

MRS. SOLNESS. That's very good of you, Doctor.

[She goes out through the door on the left.]

SOLNESS. Are you in a great hurry, Doctor?

DOCTOR HERDAL. No, not at all.

SOLNESS. You have time for a little chat, then?

DOCTOR HERDAL. Gladly.

SOLNESS. Let us sit down then. [He gestures to DOCTOR HERDAL to seat himself in the rocking chair. He himself sits down in the armchair. SOLNESS looks at him searchingly.] Tell me—did you notice anything special about Aline?

DOCTOR HERDAL. You mean now—just now when she was in here?

SOLNESS. Yes—her attitude toward me. Did you notice it?

DOCTOR HERDAL [with a smile]. Well —hell, I couldn't help noticing that your wife . . . H'm.

SOLNESS. What?

DOCTOR HERDAL. That your wife is not particularly fond of that Miss Fosli.

SOLNESS. Is that all? Yes, I have noticed that myself.

DOCTOR HERDAL. And that's only natural.

SOLNESS. What?

DOCTOR HERDAL. That she shouldn't relish your having another woman with you every day of the week.

SOLNESS. Yes, yes—you may be right in that. And Aline, too, for that matter. But—but I can't do anything about that.

DOCTOR HERDAL. Couldn't you replace her with a man?

SOLNESS. And have to take the first one that comes along? No, thank you— What good would that do me?

DOCTOR HERDAL. But as long as your wife . . . You know how delicate her health is—and as long as she can't tolerate this sort of thing . . .

SOLNESS. For God's sake, I can't help that. . . . I shouldn't have said that—but I must have Kaja Fosli—I must have her here with me. I have to have her. I can't have anyone else.

DOCTOR HERDAL. No one else?

SOLNESS [curtly]. No one else.

DOCTOR HERDAL [moving closer to SOLNESS]. My dear Mr. Solness, listen to me now. May I be permitted to ask you a question—in strictest confidence?

SOLNESS. By all means, do.

DOCTOR HERDAL. You know that women at times have a damned uncanny intuition, don't you?

SOLNESS. So they have, I admit, but . . .

DOCTOR HERDAL. Well—listen to me now. Since your wife can't bear this Kaja Fosli . . .

SOLNESS. Well, what then?

DOCTOR HERDAL. Hasn't she some little cause—however slight it may be—for feeling as she does about Miss Fosli?

SOLNESS [gazes at him for a moment, then gets up]. Oho!

DOCTOR HERDAL. Don't be offended now! Tell me—hasn't she?

SOLNESS [curtly, determinedly]. No.

DOCTOR HERDAL. None? Not even the slightest?

SOLNESS. It all stems from her suspiciousness.

DOCTOR HERDAL. I know there have been other women in your life.

SOLNESS. So there have.

DOCTOR HERDAL. And you were quite smitten by one or two of them.

SOLNESS. Oh yes, I will admit I was.

DOCTOR HERDAL. But in your relations with Miss Fosli—there has been no such feeling?

SOLNESS. No. None whatever—as far as I am concerned.

DOCTOR HERDAL. But what about her?

SOLNESS. I don't think you have any right to ask such a question, Doctor Herdal.

DOCTOR HERDAL. It was because of your wife's suspicions that I asked.

SOLNESS. Yes, of course. Of course. And, as far as Aline's intuition—as you call it—is concerned—well, she has, I admit, been proved right—to a certain extent.

DOCTOR HERDAL. There! There you see!

SOLNESS [sits down]. Doctor Herdal, I am going to tell you a curious story—if you care to listen . . .

DOCTOR HERDAL. I like to hear curious stories.

SOLNESS. Very well, then. You remember no doubt that—after Knut Brovik had failed in his business—I took the old man and his son to work for me.

DOCTOR HERDAL. Yes, I seem to recollect that you did.

SOLNESS. For both are really capable men, you know. Each one has his own particular capabilities. But then the son, Ragnar, hit upon the idea to go and get engaged. And was anxious to get married, of course, and to go into the building business for himself. For that is all these young people think of . . .

DOCTOR HERDAL [with a laugh]. Yes—they all have that bad habit—wanting to be together.

SOLNESS. Well, then—but that certainly would not have been to my interest, for Ragnar, especially, was useful to me. And the old man, too, for that matter. Knut Brovik is extremely good at calculations of strains and tensions and cubage—and all that damned sort of thing, you know.

DOCTOR HERDAL. Oh well, that's part of the business, isn't it?

SOLNESS. Yes, of course, yes. But Ragnar was determined he would start in business for himself. He had his mind set on that.

DOCTOR HERDAL. Yet he is still with you.

SOLNESS. Well, I'll tell you the rest. One day she, Kaja Fosli, came in to see Ragnar and the old man about something. It was the first time she came to the office. And when I saw how madly in love with each other they seemed to be, this thought suddenly occurred to me: if I could get her to work for me here, perhaps I could get Ragnar to remain here also.

DOCTOR HERDAL. That was a fair enough supposition to make.

SOLNESS. Yes. But I never even broached the idea at that time—not by a word. I just stood there, looking at her— and I hoped—I hoped that I might persuade her to work for me. I spoke a few kind words to her—about this and that—and then she left.

DOCTOR HERDAL. And so?

SOLNESS. Well, the next day, toward evening, after old Brovik and Ragnar had left the office, she came back. And she acted as if I had made her a promise.

DOCTOR HERDAL. A promise? What kind of promise?

SOLNESS. A promise to do precisely what she now came to ask for—to give her employment—the very thing I so fervently had wished for—yet had never said a word about.

DOCTOR HERDAL. That's really quite remarkable.

SOLNESS. Yes, isn't it? And she wanted to know what she was to do and if she could start in to work the very next morning, and so forth.

DOCTOR HERDAL. Don't you think she did it so she could be near young Brovik?

SOLNESS. That was what I thought at first. But I found out differently. From the moment she came here to work, she seemed to turn away from him almost entirely.

DOCTOR HERDAL. And turn to you?

SOLNESS. Yes—altogether. I have noticed especially that whenever I look at her and her back is turned to me, she is conscious of my glances. She shakes and she trembles whenever I am near her. How do you explain that?

DOCTOR HERDAL. H'm. That's easy enough to explain.

SOLNESS. Well—but what about her thinking that I had told her what I had merely hoped and wished for—without uttering a word about it—something I had kept entirely to myself? What do you say about that, Doctor Herdal? Can you explain that?

DOCTOR HERDAL. No, I don't propose to enter into a conjecture on that score.

SOLNESS. I might have known it. That's why I have never wanted to speak about it before. But it is getting to be damned annoying, you understand. Every day I have to keep up the deceit and act as if I . . . And I can't help feeling I am being unfair to the poor girl. [With vehemence.] However, there is nothing I can do about it! For if she leaves—then Ragnar will leave with her.

DOCTOR HERDAL. But have you never told your wife how it all started?

SOLNESS. No.

DOCTOR HERDAL. Why in the world don't you?

SOLNESS [with an intent look at DOCTOR HERDAL, he says in a subdued tone of voice]. Because I seem to derive a kind of pleasing, satisfying self-torment by letting Aline inflict this injustice upon me . . .

DOCTOR HERDAL [with a shake of the head]. To save my soul, I don't understand a word of what you just said.

SOLNESS. Oh, don't you see? It's like a small payment on an immense, monstrous debt.

DOCTOR HERDAL. That you owe your wife?

SOLNESS. Yes. And it helps to relieve my mind, you understand. I can breathe a little freer, easier, for a while.

DOCTOR HERDAL. No, by God, I don't understand you.

SOLNESS [interrupts him; gets up]. Well, well, well—let's not talk any more about it then. [He walks across the floor; then comes back and stops at the table. He looks at DOCTOR HERDAL with a sly smile.] I suppose you think you have ferreted me out completely now, Doctor?

DOCTOR HERDAL [with a touch of annoyance]. Ferreted you out? There again I fail to understand what you mean, Mr. Solness.

SOLNESS. Oh—don't hesitate to speak out. I have noticed it quite plainly, you see!

DOCTOR HERDAL. What is it you have noticed?

SOLNESS [in a subdued voice; deliberately]. That you come around here for the purpose of keeping an eye on me secretly.

DOCTOR HERDAL. Do I? Why on earth should I do that?

SOLNESS. Because you think that I . . . [Flaring up.] Hell and damnation! Because you think the same thing about me that Aline does!

DOCTOR HERDAL. And what does she think?

SOLNESS [again in control of himself]. She seems to think that I am—that I am —well . . . sick.

DOCTOR HERDAL. Sick? You sick? She has never even mentioned a word to me about it. What does she think could be wrong with you, my dear Mr. Solness?

SOLNESS [leaning over the back of the chair, he whispers to DOCTOR HERDAL]. Aline has got the idea that I am mad. She does—really.

DOCTOR HERDAL [rising]. But my dear, dear Mr. Solness!

SOLNESS. Yes—that's what she thinks —upon my soul, she does! And she has persuaded you to believe the same! Oh yes, I assure you, Doctor, I notice it all too well by the way you behave. And I am not so easy to deceive, let me tell you.

DOCTOR HERDAL [looks at him with astonishment]. Never, Mr. Solness, never has such a thought come into my mind.

SOLNESS [with a smile of distrust]. Is that true? You really mean it?

DOCTOR HERDAL. Yes—never! Nor does your wife think such a thing, I am quite sure. I could almost take an oath on that.

SOLNESS. Well, I think you had best dispense with that. For in a way, you see —in a way she may have certain grounds for thinking something of that sort.

DOCTOR HERDAL. Well, now I think I must tell you that you . . .

SOLNESS [interrupts him with a sweeping gesture]. Now, now, my dear Doctor, let us not discuss this matter any further. It is best that we each keep our own opinions to ourselves. [Assuming a tone of quiet amusement.] But tell me, Doctor . . . H'm.

DOCTOR HERDAL. Eh?

SOLNESS. Since you don't think that I am—that I am sick—in the head—mad —whatever you choose to call it . . .

DOCTOR HERDAL. Well—what then? What do you mean?

SOLNESS. Then you probably think I must be a very happy man, don't you?

DOCTOR HERDAL. Could it be that you are not?

SOLNESS [with a laugh]. No, no! Of course not! For God's sake! But think! To be Halvard Solness—Halvard Solness, the master builder! That is something to be proud of!

DOCTOR HERDAL. Yes, if I may say so, I think you have been extraordinarily lucky.

SOLNESS [repressing a wry smile]. So I have. I have no complaint to make there.

DOCTOR HERDAL. Your luck began when that old robber's castle of timber burned down. That certainly was a piece of good fortune for you.

SOLNESS [with a serious expression]. That was Aline's old family home. You must not forget that.

DOCTOR HERDAL. Yes, that must have been a great blow to her.

SOLNESS. She has never gotten over it —never to this day—although it is now more than twelve years ago.

DOCTOR HERDAL. But what happened afterward probably caused her even greater sorrow.

SOLNESS. One thing followed upon another.

DOCTOR HERDAL. But you—you used it as a ladder to success, and climbed to the top as a result of it—you, a poor lad from the country. And now you have reached the top in your profession! Oh yes, Mr. Solness, you certainly have been in luck.

SOLNESS [with a timid look at him]. Yes—but you see that is exactly what frightens me—frightens me no end—and constantly.

DOCTOR HERDAL. Frightens you? Does it frighten you to have luck on your side?

SOLNESS. Yes—every minute of the day! I am afraid—afraid that some day my luck will run out, you understand.

DOCTOR HERDAL. What nonsense! What do you think could change your luck?

SOLNESS [with firm conviction]. The younger generation!

DOCTOR HERDAL. Pshaw! The younger generation! You are not as old as that, you know. Oh no—I am convinced you have never been so solidly entrenched as you are today.

SOLNESS. The day will come when things will change. I feel it will come— that my luck is about to change. Someone will suddenly take up the challenge with the cry: "Step aside! Make room for me!" And all the others will join in the assault and they will shriek and threaten: "Make room! Make room!" Yes—you will see, Doctor, that it won't be long before the younger generation will come knocking at my door ...

DOCTOR HERDAL [with a laugh]. Well, good Lord, what of it?

SOLNESS. What of it, you say? Why— that will be the end of Master Builder Solness ...

[There is a knock at the door, right.]

SOLNESS [with a start]. What was that? Did you hear?

DOCTOR HERDAL. It was a knock.

SOLNESS [in a loud voice]. Come in!

[HILDE WANGEL enters through the door from the hall. She is a young woman of average height, lithe and of delicate build; her face is slightly tanned by the sun. She is dressed in hiking clothes, her skirt tucked up at the back. She wears a loose, turned-down collar and a small sailor's hat. A knapsack is slung across her back on a strap; similarly a blanket. She carries a long alpenstock. She approaches SOLNESS, her eyes radiant with happiness.]

HILDE WANGEL. Good evening!

SOLNESS [looks at her dubiously]. Good evening ...

HILDE [with a laugh]. Why, I don't believe you even recognize me!

SOLNESS. No—to be quite frank—I—I don't for the moment ...

DOCTOR HERDAL [steps up to her]. But I do, Miss ...

HILDE [beaming]. Why, yes—it was you who ...

DOCTOR HERDAL. Why, of course, it's I. [To SOLNESS.] We met at a lodge up in the mountains this summer. [To HILDE.] What happened to the rest of the young women?

HILDE. Oh, they took off in a different direction—they went west.

DOCTOR HERDAL. I'm afraid they didn't like that we made so much noise that night.

HILDE. No, I don't think they did, as a matter of fact.

DOCTOR HERDAL [pointing a finger at her]. And to tell the truth, I'm inclined to believe that you tried to flirt with us a little, didn't you?

HILDE. Well, isn't there more fun in that than to sit and knit socks with a lot of females?

DOCTOR HERDAL [with a laugh]. I am in complete accord with you on that score.

SOLNESS. You just came to town this evening, did you?

HILDE. Yes, I just arrived.

DOCTOR HERDAL. Alone? Quite alone, Miss Wangel?

HILDE. Yes—quite alone!

SOLNESS. Wangel? Is your name Wangel?

HILDE [looks at him, surprised and amused]. Why, of course, that's my name.

SOLNESS. Could it be that your father is the district physician at Lysanger?

HILDE [as before]. Yes—who else could be my father?

SOLNESS. Oh—so then we have met each other at Lysanger. The summer I spent up there erecting a tower for the old church.

HILDE [a little more seriously]. Yes, that was the time.

SOLNESS. But that's many years ago.

HILDE [looking at him with steady eyes]. It is exactly ten years today.

SOLNESS. And at that time you were a mere child, weren't you?

HILDE [casually]. I was at least twelve —or thirteen.

DOCTOR HERDAL. Is this the first time you have been here in town, Miss Wangel?

HILDE. Yes, it is.

SOLNESS. And perhaps you don't know anybody here?

HILDE. Only you. Well—and your wife.

SOLNESS. Oh, so you know her, too?

HILDE. Only slightly. We spent a few days together at the sanitarium . . .

SOLNESS. Ah—up there.

HILDE. She said she would be glad to see me if I should ever come here. [With a smile.] But her invitation was entirely superfluous.

SOLNESS. I have never heard her mention anything about that.

[HILDE puts away her alpenstock at the stove, unbuckles her strap and places the knapsack and blanket on the sofa. DOCTOR HERDAL tries to help her. SOLNESS stands watching her. HILDE goes up to him.]

HILDE. Well—and now I am going to ask you to put me up for the night.

SOLNESS. That can certainly be arranged.

HILDE. But I have nothing to wear except what I have on. Oh yes, I have a set of underwear in my knapsack, but that will have to be washed—it's frightfully soiled.

SOLNESS. Oh well, don't worry about that. Let me go in and tell my wife that you . . .

DOCTOR HERDAL. And I'll have to go and see my sick patient now.

SOLNESS. Yes, do that. And when you have been to see him, you are coming back here, aren't you?

DOCTOR HERDAL [jestingly, with a glance at HILDE]. You may be damned sure I'll be back! [He laughs.] You prophesied correctly, Mr. Solness!

SOLNESS. What do you mean?

DOCTOR HERDAL. The younger generation did come knocking at your door!

SOLNESS [with animation]. So it did, yes—but not exactly as I expected.

DOCTOR HERDAL. No—I can't deny you are right. [He goes out through the hall.]

SOLNESS [opens the door on the left and calls into the adjoining room]. Aline! Won't you come in here, please. There is an acquaintance of yours here—a Miss Wangel.

MRS. SOLNESS [appears in the doorway]. Who do you say it is? [She sees HILDE.] Oh, it is you, Miss Wangel . . . [She goes up to HILDE and shakes her hand.] So you did come to our town after all!

SOLNESS. Miss Wangel has only just arrived. She would like to spend the night here with us.

MRS. SOLNESS. With us? Why, certainly, she may.

SOLNESS. That will give her a chance to have her clothes put in order, you understand.

MRS. SOLNESS. I'll help you in any way I can. That's no more than I should do. I suppose your trunk will arrive later?

HILDE. I have no trunk.

MRS. SOLNESS. Well, you can get along with the clothes you have with you, no doubt. But now you have to be satisfied with talking to my husband for a few minutes while I go and see about getting a room ready for you.

SOLNESS. Why couldn't we put her in one of the children's rooms? They always stand ready, you know.

MRS. SOLNESS. Yes—yes, there you will have ample room. [To HILDE.] Now sit down and rest yourself a bit.

[She goes out, left. HILDE, her hands clasped behind her back, starts to walk about in the room, curiously looking at everything. SOLNESS stands by the table, downstage; he follows her with his eyes. HILDE stops and looks at him.]

HILDE. Have you more than one nursery room in the house?

SOLNESS. We have three.

HILDE. For heaven's sake! Then I suppose you have a disgusting lot of children?

SOLNESS. No—we have no children. But now you will have to be the child in the house, while you stay here.

HILDE. Yes—for tonight. And I won't do any crying. I'll try to sleep like a good baby.

SOLNESS. Yes, I imagine you are terribly tired.

HILDE. Not at all! But then again—it's so indescribably delightful to be lying in bed dreaming.

SOLNESS. Do you often dream at night?

HILDE. Why, yes. Almost every night.

SOLNESS. What do you dream about most?

HILDE. I won't tell you—not tonight. Some other time, perhaps. [HILDE again starts walking about in the room. She finally stops at the high desk and rummages among the books and papers.]

SOLNESS [goes up to her]. Are you looking for something in particular?

HILDE. No, I am merely taking a look at all these things. [She turns to him.] Perhaps you don't want me to?

SOLNESS. I have no objection.

HILDE. Are you the one who does all the writing in this large ledger?

SOLNESS. No, that's done by the bookkeeper.

HILDE. A female?

SOLNESS [with a smile]. Yes, she is a woman.

HILDE. And you keep a woman here with you?

SOLNESS. Yes.

HILDE. Is she married? Is she?

SOLNESS. No, she is not.

HILDE. Oh—I see!

SOLNESS. But I think it won't be long before she will marry.

HILDE. That will be a good thing—for her.

SOLNESS. But it won't do me much good, for then I'll have no one to help me.

HILDE. But you can find someone else who is just as good, can't you?

SOLNESS. Perhaps you would like to remain here—and take care of the big ledger?

HILDE [looks him up and down]. Oh, so that's what you would like! No, thank you—that's the last thing I would do! [Again she saunters about the room, then seats herself on the rocking chair. SOLNESS goes over to the table. HILDE concludes her retort.] For there are other things to do here, I imagine, than that sort of thing. [She looks at him and smiles.] Wouldn't you say so?

SOLNESS. You are quite right. The first thing you'll do, I suppose, is to make a visit to the shops and dress yourself up in grand style.

HILDE [merrily]. No—I think I won't bother with that.

SOLNESS. You don't say?

HILDE. No—because I have spent all the money I had with me, you see.

SOLNESS [laughs]. In short: no trunk—and no money!

HILDE. Neither. But, pish! It doesn't bother me!

SOLNESS. Now—I could like you for that! I really could!

HILDE. Only for that?

SOLNESS. For that—and for other reasons, too. [He seats himself in the armchair.] Is your father still living?

HILDE. Yes, Father is still living.

SOLNESS. And now, perhaps, you intend to study here in town?

HILDE. No—that would be the last thing I would do.

SOLNESS. But you do intend to stay here for a while, don't you?

HILDE. That remains to be seen. [She starts rocking and keeps regarding him, half seriously, half smiling a quizzical smile. Then she removes her hat and places it on the table in front of her.] Master Builder Solness?

SOLNESS. Yes?

HILDE. Are you very forgetful?

SOLNESS. Forgetful? No—I don't think I am.

HILDE. Then don't you want to talk to me about what happened up there?

SOLNESS [is momentarily taken aback]. Up there at Lysanger? [Indifferently.] Well, I don't know that we have anything to talk about that happened up there?

HILDE [gazes at him reproachfully]. How can you say a thing like that?

SOLNESS. Well, then, why don't you tell me?

HILDE. When the tower had been erected, there was a great celebration in town . . .

SOLNESS. Yes—I'll never forget that day!

HILDE [with a smile]. You'll never forget? That's very nice of you!

SOLNESS. Nice?

HILDE. Music was played at the graveyard—next to the church. Many, many hundreds were there—all of us girls from school were dressed in white—and each one carried a flag. . . .

SOLNESS. Yes, yes, those flags—I remember them well.

HILDE. And then you climbed straight up the scaffolding—all the way to the very top! And in your hand you had an enormous wreath—and you hung that wreath high up on the weathervane . . .

SOLNESS [brusquely interrupting]. In those days I would do that. It's an old tradition.

HILDE. It was so fantastically exciting to be standing down below and looking up at you at the top of the spire. Suppose he should fall from that height! He—the master builder himself!

SOLNESS [as if trying to divert her]. Yes, yes, yes—that could easily have happened, by God, for one of those devilish little brats, all dressed in white, carried on so noisily and kept screaming to me . . .

HILDE [radiantly happy]. "Hurrah for Master Builder Solness!" Yes . . .

SOLNESS. . . . and she kept waving her flag, swinging it in all directions, until I . . . until I almost became dizzy.

HILDE [in a slower tempo; with seriousness]. That devilish little brat—that—was I . . .

SOLNESS [staring at her fixedly]. Now I am sure it was you. It could not have been anyone but you.

HILDE [again with animation]. Oh, it was so frightfully thrilling—and something so beautiful! I couldn't believe that there could be another man in the whole world who could build a tower that high. And then—to see you stand up there, at the very top of the spire, full of life and without the slightest trace of fear or of dizziness—that—that was enough to make one dizzy looking at it!

SOLNESS. But how could you be so sure that it didn't affect . . .

HILDE [rejecting the thought]. You—never! Shame on you! Couldn't I feel it inside me! Besides, how could you ever have sung, standing up there, if your head had been swimming!

SOLNESS [looks at her in wonder]. Sung? Did I sing?

HILDE. Why, of course you sang!

SOLNESS [shaking his head]. I never sang a note in my life!

HILDE. Oh yes—that day you sang! It was the voice of an angel coming from above.

SOLNESS [puzzled]. This is—this is all very strange to me . . .

HILDE [after a brief silence, she looks at him and says in a subdued tone of voice]. But then—then came the most stirring thing of all . . .

SOLNESS. The most stirring?

HILDE [radiating animation]. Do I have to remind you of that?

SOLNESS. Well—yes . . . Do tell me a little about that also?

HILDE. You do remember that a big banquet was given in your honor at the club, don't you?

SOLNESS. Oh yes. That must have been the same afternoon—for I left the following morning.

HILDE. And after the affair at the club you were invited to spend the evening at our home.

SOLNESS. You are right, Miss Wangel, quite right. It's remarkable how well you remember every trivial little thing!

HILDE. Trivial little thing! Well, you are a fine one! Perhaps you call it a trivial thing, too, that I was alone in the living room when you arrived?

SOLNESS. So-o? Were you?

HILDE [without answering him]. You didn't call me a devilish brat that time.

SOLNESS. No, I suppose I didn't.

HILDE. You told me I looked pretty in my white dress—that I looked like a little princess.

SOLNESS. No doubt you did, Miss Wangel. And on that day I was, of course, in an especially animated and lively mood.

HILDE. And you also said that when I had grown up I would be your princess.

SOLNESS [with a chuckle]. Oh, you don't say! Did I say that, too?

HILDE. Yes, you did. And when I asked you how long I would have to wait, you said you would return in ten years—that you would come as a troll and carry me off—to Spain, or some other far-away country. And there you were to buy me a kingdom. That's what you promised me.

SOLNESS [as before]. Well—after a good dinner one often feels one can afford to be bountiful. Did I really promise all that?

HILDE [with a quiet smile]. Yes—and you also told me what our kingdom was to be named.

SOLNESS. What was its name to be?

HILDE. You said it was to be called the Kingdom of Appelsinia.

SOLNESS. Well—that was certainly an appetizing name.

HILDE. It didn't appeal to me at all. It almost sounded to me as if you said it in jest—to make fun of me.

SOLNESS. That was far from my intention.

HILDE. Yes—I would like to believe you were not jesting—particularly when I think of what you did afterward . . .

SOLNESS. What in all the world did I do then?

HILDE. Why, you don't mean to tell me you don't remember that either! You certainly couldn't have forgotten that!

SOLNESS. Well—well, if you will just help me a little, perhaps . . . perhaps I will . . .

HILDE [her eyes firmly fixed on him]. You took hold of me and kissed me, Mr. Solness.

SOLNESS [his mouth wide open, he gets up]. I did!

HILDE. So you did, yes. You took me in your arms—and you leaned over me— and you kissed me! Over and over again!

SOLNESS. Now, now, my dear, dear Miss Wangel!

HILDE [rises]. You certainly don't want to deny that, do you?

SOLNESS. I most certainly do!

HILDE [with a scornful look at him]. Oh, you do! [She turns and walks slowly over to the stove. There she remains standing motionless, her hands clasped behind her back. There is a brief silence. Then SOLNESS circumspectly moves up behind her.]

SOLNESS. Miss Wangel . . . ? [HILDE stands silent and motionless.] Now don't stand there as if carved in stone! All this that you just told me must have been something you dreamt. [He places his hand on her arm.] Now—look here . . . [HILDE makes an impatient movement with her arm. SOLNESS, as if struck by a sudden idea.] Oh . . . Wait a moment! There is something mysterious, something baffling at the bottom of all this, you may be sure. [HILDE is motionless as before. SOLNESS, in a subdued yet emphatic voice.] I must have had some such thoughts in my mind. I must have wanted such a thing to happen—desired it to come about—had a yearning for it . . . and so . . . Couldn't that be a possible explanation, eh? [HILDE remains silent. SOLNESS shows signs of impatience.] Oh well . . . Damn it! I suppose I did do it, then!

HILDE [moves her hand slightly but does not look at him]. Then you do admit it?

SOLNESS. Yes—anything you like.

HILDE. You admit that you embraced me?

SOLNESS. Yes, yes!

HILDE. And leaned over me?

SOLNESS. As far as you say!

HILDE. And kissed me?

SOLNESS. Yes—that, too.

HILDE. Over and over again?

SOLNESS. As many times as you like.

HILDE [turning quickly toward him, she again radiates happiness]. Well! You see—at last I got you to confess!

SOLNESS [with a faint smile on his lips]. And to think I could have forgotten anything like that!

HILDE [again sulking a little, she walks away from him]. Oh, I suppose you have kissed a great many in your day!

SOLNESS. Oh! You mustn't think that of me . . . [HILDE seats herself in the armchair. SOLNESS stands by the rocking chair, supporting himself against it. He regards HILDE intently.] Miss Wangel . . .

HILDE. Yes?

SOLNESS. How was it now? What came of all this—this episode between us?

HILDE. Nothing! That was the end of it. You know that as well as I! For just then the rest of our guests came—and then . . . Ugh!

SOLNESS. Oh, yes, of course—the other guests arrived! How could I have forgotten that, too?

HILDE. Oh, you haven't forgotten anything, I am sure. You are only a little ashamed of yourself. One doesn't forget moments like that so easily.

SOLNESS. No, it would seem so.

HILDE [again animated, she looks at him]. And perhaps you have also forgotten the day and the month it happened?

SOLNESS. What day?

HILDE. What day was it that you hung the wreath on the church spire? Well? Answer me quickly now!

SOLNESS. H'm. Upon my soul, I have forgotten what day it was. All I know is that it was ten years ago—some time in the fall.

HILDE [nodding her head slowly]. It was ten years ago. On the nineteenth of September.

SOLNESS. Quite right—I should say it was about that time of year. So you remember that, too? [He interrupts himself.] But wait a moment! Why yes! Today is the nineteenth of September.

HILDE. Yes, so it is. And the ten years have now passed! And you never came as you had promised!

SOLNESS. Promised? You mean as I scared you, frightened you—when I said I would come as a troll.

HILDE. I never thought of that as anything so frightening.

SOLNESS. Well, perhaps I just tried to play a little trick on you.

HILDE. So that was all you wanted—to deceive me?

SOLNESS. Well—or to have a little fun with you, then. So help me God, I have no recollection of it. But I dare say, that was all it was. Why, you were only a child at that time.

HILDE. Oh—I don't think I was such a child! Not the kind of spoiled brat you think I am!

SOLNESS [looks at her searchingly]. Have you really been thinking all these years that I would return to you?

HILDE [hiding a half-tantalizing smile]. I most certainly have! I have been expecting you!

SOLNESS. Expecting me to come and take you from your home and carry you away with me?

HILDE. Yes—like a troll.

SOLNESS. And make you a princess?

HILDE. That's what you promised me, wasn't it?

SOLNESS. And give you a kingdom also?

HILDE [looking up at the ceiling]. And why not? It need not necessarily be one of those existing, ordinary kingdoms . . .

SOLNESS. But some other kind of kingdom that would be just as good?

HILDE. Yes—at least as good. [Gazes at him for a moment.] If you could build the highest church tower in the world, I thought to myself, then you could surely also build a kingdom of one kind or another.

SOLNESS [shaking his head]. I just can't make you out, Miss Wangel.

HILDE. Can't you? It seems to me it is all so very simple.

SOLNESS. No—I just can't convince myself that you really mean all that you tell me, or if you are only jesting . . .

HILDE [with a smile]. That I, too, am jesting, you mean—with you?

SOLNESS. Just that, yes. Each of us jesting—each in his turn. [He regards her.] Were you aware that I was a married man?

HILDE. Yes. I knew that from the beginning. Why do you ask?

SOLNESS [casually]. Oh—oh, I was just wondering. [Looking at her earnestly, he says in a low voice.] Why have you come here?

HILDE. I have come to demand my kingdom—now that the time is up.

SOLNESS [with an involuntary smile]. Well, you are a strange one, you are!

HILDE [gleefully]. Come, bring me my kingdom, Master Builder! [She raps on the table.] My kingdom on the table!

SOLNESS [moving the rocking chair closer to her, he sits down]. Seriously speaking—why did you come here? What exactly do you mean to do here?

HILDE. Well, first of all, I intend to go looking at all that you have built.

SOLNESS. Then you will have enough to do—more than enough.

HILDE. I know. You have erected a lot of buildings.

SOLNESS. That I have, yes—especially during the past few years.

HILDE. Church towers, too? Many such spires that are so fabulously high?

SOLNESS. No—I am not building any more church towers—or any more churches either, for that matter.

HILDE. Then what do you build now?

SOLNESS. Homes—homes for human beings.

HILDE [thoughtfully]. Why couldn't you—why couldn't you build some kind of church tower as a part of those houses?

SOLNESS [startled]. What exactly do you mean by that?

HILDE. I mean—something that points straight up—straight up into the sky—into the free air—and with a weather-vane at a dizzying height.

SOLNESS [cogitating]. How strange that you should mention that—for that is what I have always thought of doing . . .

HILDE [impatiently]. But why don't you do it, then?

SOLNESS [shaking his head]. Why, people don't want anything like that.

HILDE. Imagine it! That they can be so stupid!

SOLNESS [in a lighter vein]. But now I am building myself a new home—just beyond this one.

HILDE. For yourself?

SOLNESS. Yes. It is almost finished. And that house has a tower!

HILDE. A high tower?

SOLNESS. Yes.

HILDE. Very high?

SOLNESS. People will probably say it is much too high. Too high for a home at least.

HILDE. I want to see that tower the first thing in the morning!

SOLNESS [resting his head in his hand, he regards her fixedly]. Tell me, Miss Wangel . . . What is your name? I mean your first name.

HILDE. My name is Hilde, of course.

SOLNESS [as before]. Hilde? Oh?

HILDE. Have you no memory? You called me Hilde that day—the day you were so naughty.

SOLNESS. Did I? Did I really?

HILDE. But that day you called me little Hilde. And I didn't like that a bit.

SOLNESS. So-o? You didn't like to be called little Hilde, Miss Hilde?

HILDE. No—not at a moment like that. But Princess Hilde . . . that, on the other hand, would sound rather nice, I think.

SOLNESS. Yes, it would. Princess Hilde of—of . . . What was the name we were to give to our kingdom?

HILDE. Ugh! That silly kingdom! I want to have nothing to do with it! I want another kingdom—an entirely different one!

SOLNESS [who has been leaning back in his chair, keeps regarding her]. Isn't it strange? Now that I think of it, I am beginning to realize why I have been going about here all these years, worrying and tormenting myself, trying to think of . . . h'm . . .

HILDE. Of what?

SOLNESS. Of an adventure of some sort that I had a vague idea of having experienced in the past. But I never did discover what it was . . .

HILDE. You should have tied a knot in your handkerchief, Mr. Solness.

SOLNESS. Then I would only have gone about wondering why the knot was there.

HILDE. Oh well, there are trolls like that in the world, too.

SOLNESS [getting up slowly]. It's a blessing that you came to me just now.

HILDE [looking deep into his eyes]. A blessing, you say?

SOLNESS. Yes—I've been living here in loneliness—looking at everything helplessly. [In a more subdued tone of voice.] I am going to confide something to you, Hilde . . . I am beginning to be afraid—yes, terribly afraid of the younger generation.

HILDE [making light of his fears]. Nonsense! Why should you be afraid of youth?

SOLNESS. Yes—I mean just that! And that's the reason I have isolated myself—locked myself in . . . [with an air of mystery]. I tell you that before long the younger generation will come pounding at my door and break it down! Then they will have a foothold and gain the upper hand!

HILDE. Then, instead, why don't you open the door to the younger generation?

SOLNESS. Open the door?

HILDE. Yes—let them come in—accept them with your blessing and good will.

SOLNESS. No, no, no! You don't understand! The younger generation will mean ostracism for me—and recrimination. Youth is the vanguard of the changing times—the banner of a new day, so to speak.

HILDE [rises and looks at him, then says with a quiver]. Can you use me for anything, Mr. Solness?

SOLNESS. Yes, now I most certainly

can! For you also come waving a new banner, as it were! Thus: youth pitted against youth!

[DOCTOR HERDAL enters from the hall.]

DOCTOR HERDAL. So you and Miss Wangel are still here?

SOLNESS. Yes—we have had much to talk about, we two.

HILDE. Yes, both old and new.

DOCTOR HERDAL. You don't say!

HILDE. Oh, we have had such a wonderful time. Mr. Solness has the most extraordinary memory—for everything. Even the most minute details he remembers—without any prodding whatsoever.

[MRS. SOLNESS enters through the door on the left.]

MRS. SOLNESS. Now your room is ready for you, Miss Wangel.

HILDE. Oh, that's very nice of you. I appreciate it.

SOLNESS [to MRS. SOLNESS]. One of the nursery rooms?

MRS. SOLNESS. Yes—the room in the middle. But first, I think, we'll have something to eat.

SOLNESS [with a nod to HILDE]. So tonight Hilde is to sleep in the children's room . . .

MRS. SOLNESS [looking at him]. Hilde?

SOLNESS. Yes, Miss Wangel's name is Hilde. I knew her when she was a little child.

MRS. SOLNESS. Oh, did you? Well, will you please step inside then—everything is ready. [She takes DOCTOR HERDAL's arm and goes out with him through the door on the left. Meanwhile HILDE has been gathering up her equipment.]

HILDE [softly and rapidly to SOLNESS]. Was it true what you said a moment ago? You can find use for me, can you?

SOLNESS [taking her belongings from her]. It is for you I have been most lonely.

HILDE [looks at him with happy wonderment]. What a wonderful, heavenly world we live in!

SOLNESS [tensely]. You mean . . .

HILDE. I have now found my kingdom!

SOLNESS [instinctively]. Hilde!

HILDE [again with a quiver on her lips]. Almost found it—was what I wanted to say.

[She goes out to the left. SOLNESS follows her.]

ACT II

[THE SETTING.—A small, handsomely furnished drawing room in the home of MR. and MRS. SOLNESS.

In the rear, a glass door opens up onto a veranda and garden. On the right, a small door in the corner between two walls; it is covered with wallpaper. There are also doors on each side of the room, right and left. Downstage, left, a high mirror with a console table at the foot of it. Also on the left, a cut-off corner with a projecting bay window, in which are flower pots on stands. There is an abundance of plants and flowers throughout the room. On the right, downstage, a sofa with a table and chairs. A little farther upstage, a bookcase. On the floor, set away from the bay window, a small table and a couple of chairs.

It is mid-morning.

SOLNESS sits at the small table with RAGNAR BROVIK's opened portfolio before him. He turns over the drawings and scrutinizes some of them.

MRS. SOLNESS, carrying a water can, moves noiselessly about the room, looking after her flowers and watering them. As in Act I, she is wearing a black dress. Her hat, coat, and parasol lie on a chair over by the mirror.

SOLNESS glances at her occasionally in an unobtrusive manner. Neither one speaks.

KAJA FOSLI enters quietly through the door on the right.]

SOLNESS [turns his head and says casually]. Oh, it's you?

KAJA. I just wanted to let you know that I am here.

SOLNESS. Yes, yes—that's good. How about Ragnar? Isn't he here, too?

KAJA. No, not yet. He had to stay and wait for the doctor. But he will soon be here. And he wants to know . . .

SOLNESS. How is the old man's condition today?

KAJA. Not good—not good at all. He asked to be excused—he must stay in bed today.

SOLNESS. Why, certainly—let him by all means stay in bed. But now you must get to your work.

KAJA [stopping at the door]. Do you want to speak with Ragnar when he comes?

SOLNESS. No—there is nothing special I have to talk to him about.

[KAJA goes out, right. SOLNESS continues to look at the drawings.]

MRS. SOLNESS [over by the flower pots]. You'll see that he will soon be dead, too.

SOLNESS [gives her a look]. He, too? Who is the other one?

MRS. SOLNESS [does not answer him]. Yes, yes, old Brovik—he will die, too, Halvard. You'll see ...

SOLNESS. Aline dear—don't you think you ought to go out for a little walk?

MRS. SOLNESS. Yes, I really think I should. [She keeps on attending to her flowers and plants.]

SOLNESS [poring over the drawings]. Is she still sleeping?

MRS. SOLNESS [looking at him]. Is it Miss Wangel you are sitting there thinking about?

SOLNESS [with indifference]. I just happened to think of her.

MRS. SOLNESS. Miss Wangel has been up since early morning.

SOLNESS. Has she, really?

MRS. SOLNESS. When I was in her room she was busy looking after her clothes. [She goes over to the mirror and slowly starts putting on her hat.]

SOLNESS [after a brief silence]. Well, at last we found use for the nursery, Aline.

MRS. SOLNESS. Yes, we did.

SOLNESS. And I think that's better than to let the children's rooms stand empty all the time, don't you think?

MRS. SOLNESS. Yes, you are right. There is an emptiness here—an awful emptiness.

SOLNESS [closes the portfolio and gets up. He goes over to MRS. SOLNESS]. But you'll see, Aline, that from now on things will be better and much more pleasant. Life will be easier, more comfortable for us—especially for you.

MRS. SOLNESS [with a look at him]. From now on?

SOLNESS. Yes, you may be sure of that, Aline.

MRS. SOLNESS. Do you mean—because she is here?

SOLNESS [controls himself]. I mean, of course—when we have moved into our new house.

MRS. SOLNESS [taking her coat]. Oh, you think so, Halvard? You think that will change things, do you?

SOLNESS. I can't help thinking it will. And I am sure you must think the same, don't you?

MRS. SOLNESS. I think neither one way nor another about the new house.

SOLNESS [dejectedly]. I am disappointed to hear you talk that way, when you know it was really for you—for your sake—I built the house. [He tries to help her on with her coat. MRS. SOLNESS rejects the gesture.]

MRS. SOLNESS. I am afraid you do altogether too much for my sake.

SOLNESS [with a sign of vehemence]. No, no—and you must not say anything like that, Aline—absolutely not! I can't bear to hear you say such things!

MRS. SOLNESS. Well, then I shan't say anything more, Halvard!

SOLNESS. But I stand by what I said. You'll see that you will have it better over in the new house.

MRS. SOLNESS. God! Better for me ... ?

SOLNESS [eagerly]. Yes—yes! Of that you may be sure. And, you will see—in that house you will have so many, many things that will remind you of your old home ...

MRS. SOLNESS. Of my father's and my mother's home—that burned down—burned to ashes ...

SOLNESS [in a subdued voice]. Yes, yes, poor Aline! That was a hard blow for you!

MRS. SOLNESS [whimpering]. You may build as much as you like, Halvard—but you will never build another home, a real home, for me!

SOLNESS [pacing across the room]. Well, then—let us for God's sake talk about it no more!

MRS. SOLNESS. For that matter—we never do talk about it. You always are evasive about it ...

SOLNESS. Evasive? Why should I be evasive? What reason would I have to avoid the subject?

MRS. SOLNESS. Oh yes—I understand you all too well, Halvard. You want to spare me, of course—and make apologies for me—always—whenever you can.

SOLNESS [with astonishment]. For you, Aline? Is it you—is it yourself you are talking about, Aline?

MRS. SOLNESS. Yes, of course, I am talking about myself.

SOLNESS [involuntarily; to himself]. That, too!

MRS. SOLNESS. As far as the old house is concerned—well, what happened I suppose was meant to happen. Good heavens! Once misfortune strikes, why . . .

SOLNESS. Yes, you are right. There is an old saying: No one should be blamed when misfortune strikes.

MRS. SOLNESS. But the horrible misfortune that the fire brought upon us—that is what I can never get over!

SOLNESS [excitedly]. Stop thinking about that, Aline!

MRS. SOLNESS. No, I will never stop thinking of that. And for once I will speak about it also! For I don't think I can endure the memory of it any longer —and I shall never be able to forgive myself for what happened!

SOLNESS [ejaculates]. Forgive—yourself?

MRS. SOLNESS. Yes—for I had a duty not only to you but to our little ones. I should have shown some strength. I should not have let the grief over that terrible misfortune affect me so deeply that I was overcome by fright when I saw my old home go up in flame. [Wringing her hands.] Oh, if I had only been strong, Halvard!

SOLNESS [moved, he goes up close to her and says gently]. Aline—I want you to promise me that you will never again think any such thoughts. Will you promise me that?

MRS. SOLNESS. Oh God! Promise! It's so easy to promise, isn't it?

SOLNESS [clenching his hands, he paces the floor]. Oh! This continuous despair, these lamentations! Never a ray of sunshine! Not even so much as a gleam of light in this home of ours!

MRS. SOLNESS. We have no home, Halvard.

SOLNESS. No—you are quite right. [With heavy heart.] And God knows if you are not right in saying it won't be any better when we move into the new house.

MRS. SOLNESS. It never will. It will be just as empty there—just as desolate— as it is here.

SOLNESS [flaring up]. Then why in the world did we ever build it? Tell me that if you can.

MRS. SOLNESS. No, you have to find the answer to that yourself.

SOLNESS [giving her a suspicious glance]. What do you mean by that, Aline?

MRS. SOLNESS. What do I mean?

SOLNESS. Yes—what the hell . . . ! You said it so strangely—as if you were trying to insinuate something.

MRS. SOLNESS. Nothing of the kind, I can assure you.

SOLNESS [goes up closer to her]. Oh, thank you! I know all about that! I have both eyes and ears, Aline. Don't forget that!

MRS. SOLNESS. I have no idea what you are alluding to. What is it?

SOLNESS [stands facing her]. Don't you try to read some veiled, underhand meaning into everything I say, however innocent it may be?

MRS. SOLNESS. You say I do? You really think I do?

SOLNESS [with a laugh]. Ho-ho-ho! But I presume that is only to be expected— since you are burdened with a sick husband . . .

MRS. SOLNESS [with anxiety]. Sick? Are you sick, Halvard?

SOLNESS [in a fury]. Half-demented, then! Crazy! Call it what you will!

MRS. SOLNESS [groping for the back of a chair to support herself, she sits down]. Halvard—for God's sake!

SOLNESS. But you are both wrong— both you and the doctor. There is nothing the matter with me, as you seem to think! [He paces the floor. MRS. SOLNESS follows him anxiously with her eyes. After a few moments he calms down and goes up to her.] No, indeed, there is nothing wrong with me at all.

MRS. SOLNESS. Why, of course not! But what is it, then, that so preys upon your mind?

SOLNESS. It is my guilt that haunts me —my frightful, unspeakable guilt! Many a time I have been on the verge of breaking at the thought of the debt I owe.

MRS. SOLNESS. Debt, you say? Why— you don't owe anything to anyone, Halvard!

SOLNESS [softly, moved]. I owe an enormous debt to you—to you, Aline— to you!

MRS. SOLNESS. What is back of all this? You may as well tell me now.

SOLNESS. I am not keeping anything from you! I have never harmed you in any way—never intentionally, at least! And yet—yet I feel weighted down by a heart-sickening sense of having done some wrong . . .

MRS. SOLNESS. Some wrong? Toward me?

SOLNESS. Yes—toward you!

MRS. SOLNESS. Then you are sick—after all—Halvard!

SOLNESS [in a dull tone]. I'm afraid I am—or nearly so. [Glances at the door, left, which is being opened, and his mood changes.] There! Now we'll have some sunshine.

[HILDE WANGEL enters. She is now carefully groomed. Her skirt is no longer pinned up at the back.]

HILDE. Good morning, Mr. Solness!

SOLNESS [with a nod]. Did you sleep well?

HILDE. Wonderfully well—like a babe in its cradle. Oh! I lay in bed, stretching myself like a—like a princess!

SOLNESS [with a slight smile]. You were comfortable, in other words.

HILDE. I was, indeed.

SOLNESS. And I dare say you dreamed?

HILDE. I certainly did—but what I dreamt was ghastly.

SOLNESS. Oh?

HILDE. Yes—I dreamt I was falling from a terrible height—from a steep mountain cliff. Don't you ever have dreams like that?

SOLNESS. Oh yes—once in a while I do.

HILDE. It's really terribly exciting—to be hurtling through the air like that—falling—falling . . .

SOLNESS. It makes me feel as if my blood turned to ice.

HILDE. Do you pull your legs up under you while you are falling through the air, do you?

SOLNESS. Yes—as high as I can.

HILDE. I do the same.

MRS. SOLNESS [takes her parasol]. I think I'd best be on my way to town now, Halvard. [To HILDE.] And while I am there, I'll try to find a few things that you may have use for.

HILDE [throws her arms round MRS. SOLNESS's neck]. Oh, dearest, sweetest Mrs. Solness! You are really much too kind!

MRS. SOLNESS [frees herself from the embrace and draws away from HILDE]. It is not kindness. It is merely an obligation, a duty, that's all. And that is why I am glad to do it.

HILDE [hurt; she pouts]. As a matter of fact, I don't see why I shouldn't go into town myself—now that I look somewhat more decent. What do you think?

MRS. SOLNESS. Quite frankly, I think more than one person would turn around and take a second look at you.

HILDE [making light of the remark]. Pooh! Is that all? Why, wouldn't that be fun?

SOLNESS [in a dark, unpleasant mood]. Yes—but people might get the idea that you also were demented, don't you see?

HILDE. Demented? Are there so many demented people in this town?

SOLNESS [pointing to his forehead]. You see one here, at least, who is.

HILDE. You—Mr. Solness?

MRS. SOLNESS. Ugh! But Halvard dear, now you . . .

SOLNESS. Haven't you noticed it by now?

HILDE. No, to tell the truth, I haven't. [She stops to think, then laughs a little.] Yes—come to think of it, there is one thing I have noticed . . .

SOLNESS. You hear that, Aline?

MRS. SOLNESS. And what may that be, Miss Wangel?

HILDE. Oh, I can't tell you that . . .

SOLNESS. Oh, please tell us!

HILDE. No, thank you—I am not that crazy.

MRS. SOLNESS. When you and Miss Wangel are alone, I think she will tell you, Halvard.

SOLNESS. Oh—you think she will?

MRS. SOLNESS. Oh, I am quite certain she will. After all, you know her quite well—you have known her since she was a child, you tell me.

[She goes out through the door on the right.]

HILDE [after a few moments]. Your wife does not like me, does she?

SOLNESS. Does she give you that impression?

HILDE. Can't you see that yourself?

SOLNESS [evasively]. Aline has grown

to be terribly shy of people during the past few years.

HILDE. Oh, she has grown shy also?

SOLNESS. But once you really learn to know her, you'll find she is kind and good in every way—so genuinely good . . .

HILDE [impatiently]. But if she is so kind—why did she have to talk about duty the way she did?

SOLNESS. About duty?

HILDE. Yes, you heard her say that she would go out and buy some things for me—because it was her duty. That's what she said! And I can't stand hearing that ugly, disgusting word duty!

SOLNESS. Why don't you like it?

HILDE. Because it sounds so cold and sharp! It has such a biting sound! Duty—duty! Doesn't it affect you the same way? Don't you think it has a sort of biting sound?

SOLNESS. H'm. I have never given it any particular thought.

HILDE. Oh yes! And if she is as kind as you say she is—why would she say such a thing?

SOLNESS. But, good Lord, what would you want her to say, then?

HILDE. She might have said that she did it because she had taken such a tremendous liking to me. She might have said something of that sort—something with warmth in it—something from the heart, don't you understand?

SOLNESS [regards her]. Is that what you would like?

HILDE. Yes—exactly. [She walks about the room, stops at the bookcase and looks at the books in it.] You have a great many books, haven't you?

SOLNESS. Oh yes—I have collected quite a few.

HILDE. Have you read all of them?

SOLNESS. I tried to—in years past. Do you read much?

HILDE. No, never! Not any more. It seems so futile.

SOLNESS. That's the way I feel about it, too.

[HILDE moves about a little, stops at the small table, opens the portfolio and rummages through it.]

HILDE. Did you draw these sketches?

SOLNESS. No, a young draftsman I employ, did them.

HILDE. Someone you yourself taught?

SOLNESS. Oh well—no doubt he has learned something from me, too.

HILDE [seats herself]. Then I imagine he must be a very clever young man? [She looks at one of the drawings for some moments.] He is, isn't he?

SOLNESS. Oh, not especially. For my purpose, he . . .

HILDE. Oh yes! He must be exceptionally clever!

SOLNESS. Is that the impression you get from looking at his drawings?

HILDE. Pooh! No—not from these lines and curves! But if he has been your apprentice, then he must be . . .

SOLNESS. Oh, for that reason . . . There are many in this town who have been apprenticed to me. And yet they haven't amounted to much.

HILDE [shaking her head, she looks at him]. I can't for the life of me understand how you can be so stupid.

SOLNESS. Stupid? You think I am so terribly stupid, do you?

HILDE. Yes, that's just what I think you are, if you spend so much time teaching all these young men, and . . .

SOLNESS [taken aback]. Well—why shouldn't I?

HILDE [gets up; she is serious, yet smiling]. Pshaw! Oh no, Mr. Solness! What good does that do? You should be the only one who should be allowed to build—you, and only you. You should do it all yourself! Now I have told you!

SOLNESS [instinctively]. Hilde!

HILDE. Well?

SOLNESS. Where in all the world did you get this idea of yours?

HILDE. Do you think it's such a wildly insane idea, do you?

SOLNESS. No, I wouldn't say it is. But now I want to tell you something.

HILDE. What?

SOLNESS. I have been going about here day in and day out in my loneliness, quietly playing with the very same idea.

HILDE. Yes, there is logic in it, it seems to me.

SOLNESS [gives her a searching look]. And I shouldn't be surprised if you had noticed that I . . .

HILDE. No, I haven't as a matter of fact—not in the slightest.

SOLNESS. But a little while ago you

made the remark you thought I was . . . that I was rather odd, didn't you? Particularly in one respect?

HILDE. Oh, I was thinking of quite another matter.

SOLNESS. Of what?

HILDE. Oh, what difference does it make, Mr. Solness?

SOLNESS [takes a few steps across the floor]. Well, well—just as you like. [He stops at the bay window.] Come over here! I want to show you something.

HILDE [approaches him]. What is it?

SOLNESS. Do you see—over there—in the garden?

HILDE. Yes?

SOLNESS [points into the distance]. Just beyond the big stone pit . . .

HILDE. You mean the new house?

SOLNESS. The one under construction, yes. It's almost completed.

HILDE. I see it has a very high tower.

SOLNESS. The scaffolding has not been removed yet.

HILDE. Is that your new home?

SOLNESS. Yes.

HILDE. And that's the house you will soon be moving into?

SOLNESS. Yes.

HILDE [regards him]. Are there nursery rooms in that house also?

SOLNESS. Three of them—exactly as here.

HILDE. And yet—no children.

SOLNESS. There never will be any.

HILDE [with a half-smile]. Well—don't you think I was right in what I said, then?

SOLNESS. What did you say?

HILDE. That you are, after all, a little mad.

SOLNESS. So that was what you had in your mind, was it?

HILDE. Yes—I was thinking of the nursery room I slept in—and the other nursery rooms that are empty.

SOLNESS [in a suppressed voice]. We have had children—Aline and I.

HILDE [looking tensely at him]. Have you?

SOLNESS. Two little boys—born the same day.

HILDE. Oh—twins, then.

SOLNESS. Yes, twins. It is now eleven or twelve years ago . . .

HILDE [prudently]. And now both your sons are . . . Are they both . . . ? Are they both dead?

SOLNESS [quietly moved]. We kept them only three weeks—not quite that long, even. [In an outburst of emotion.] Oh, Hilde! I can't tell you what it means to have you here with me! For at last I have someone I can talk with!

HILDE. You mean you can't talk with —with her?

SOLNESS. Not about that—not the way I would like to—not the way I need to . . . [Gloomily.] And for that matter— not about anything else either!

HILDE [in an undertone]. Was that the only thing you had in mind when you said you needed me? Was that all?

SOLNESS. I suppose that was the reason —at any rate, it was yesterday. But today I am no longer quite so certain . . . [He breaks off.] Come over here, Hilde, and let us sit down. Sit on the sofa—where you can see the garden. [HILDE sits down in the corner of the sofa. SOLNESS places a chair close by her.] Would you care to listen to what I have to say?

HILDE. Yes—I am terribly eager to hear all about it.

SOLNESS [seats himself]. Then I shall tell you everything.

HILDE. Now I sit facing both you and the garden, Master Builder Solness—so tell me your story—quickly!

SOLNESS [pointing toward the bay window]. Up there—on that height over there—where you now see the new house being built . . .

HILDE. Yes?

SOLNESS. . . . there is where Aline and I lived the first years of our marriage. In those days an old house that had been her mother's, stood on the height. We inherited it from her—together with the great garden that belonged to the property.

HILDE. Did that house also have a tower?

SOLNESS. No—there was no tower. It looked like nothing so much as an enormous wooden box—a dark, ugly pile of lumber. But inside it was comfortable enough—and peaceful—despite its outward appearance.

HILDE. And then, I suppose, you finally tore it down, didn't you?

SOLNESS. No—it burned down.

HILDE. Burned to the ground?

SOLNESS. Yes.

HILDE. Did you consider it a great misfortune that it did?

SOLNESS. That depends upon how you look at it. That fire turned out to be my good fortune—as a builder . . .

HILDE. Oh, but . . . ?

SOLNESS. Our two little boys had just been born . . .

HILDE. Yes—those poor little twins . . .

SOLNESS. They were so strong and healthy; and we watched them grow from day to day . . .

HILDE. Yes—babies do grow fast in their first days.

SOLNESS. You never saw a more beautiful sight than when Aline lay in her bed with those two little ones! And then— then came the night of the fire!

HILDE [tensely]. Just how did it happen? Tell me! Was anyone lost in the fire?

SOLNESS. No—no one died. Everybody was brought from the house safely.

HILDE. Well, then—what . . .

SOLNESS. Aline, still convalescing, was so terribly shaken by fright: not only from hearing the fire alarm, but from the shock of being carried out with the little ones under such frightening circumstances—into the cold of the night! For they had to be carried out just as they were—all three—she and her babies . . .

HILDE. You mean it proved too much for them?

SOLNESS. No—the little ones withstood the ordeal, but Aline came down with fever, and it affected her milk. And she insisted upon nursing the babies herself. She said it was her duty as a mother. And so our little ones—they . . . [Clenching his fist.] They . . . Oh!

HILDE. And they didn't have the resistance to overcome it?

SOLNESS. No—they never did. That is how we lost them.

HILDE. It must have been a terrible shock for you.

SOLNESS. It was a shock for me—but ten times more so for Aline. [He clenches his hands.] Oh! Why must anything like that happen in this world? [Tersely, firmly.] At the same time I lost them, I lost the desire to build churches.

HILDE. Perhaps you didn't even want to build the spire on the church in my town?

SOLNESS. No, I didn't. I recall how relieved I was, and how it eased my mind to have that tower finished.

HILDE. I know you were glad it was done.

SOLNESS. And today I don't build any more temples! And I never will! Never! Neither temples nor church towers!

HILDE [with a slow nod]. Nothing but houses for people to live in.

SOLNESS. Only homes that human beings can live in, Hilde.

HILDE. But homes with towers—high towers, ending in a spire . . .

SOLNESS. Preferably that. [In a lighter vein.] Well—as I just said—that fire was the beginning of my good fortune. It established me as a builder.

HILDE. Why don't you call yourself an architect as the others do?

SOLNESS. I am not sufficiently qualified for that. All that I know I have learned through experience.

HILDE. But you climbed to the top nevertheless.

SOLNESS. After the fire, yes. I divided almost the entire garden into dwelling lots. And there I had an opportunity to build exactly what I wanted—and the way I wanted. And soon everything began to come my way.

HILDE [with a searching look at him]. I am sure you must be an extremely happy man, Mr. Solness—a man who has been so successful.

SOLNESS [his face darkens]. Happy? That's what they all think. And now you say the same.

HILDE. Yes—and I think you should be happy. If only you could stop thinking about your sons, you would . . .

SOLNESS [slowly]. My two little ones . . . It is not so easy to forget them, Hilde.

HILDE [with a slight hesitation]. Does their memory still haunt you—after all these years?

SOLNESS [gazing fixedly at her, he does not answer]. A happy man, did you say?

HILDE. Yes—aside from this grief— aren't you otherwise happy?

SOLNESS [keeps gazing at her]. When I told you this about the fire—h'm . . .

HILDE. Yes?

SOLNESS. Didn't something occur to you? I mean—something in particular?

HILDE [*trying to think*]. No, I have absolutely no idea what you have in mind?

SOLNESS [*with suppressed emphasis*]. Had it not been for that fire, I may not have had the opportunity to build homes for people—for human beings. Comfortable, decent homes, full of light, where parents and children could live in security, and with a genuine feeling of happiness for being born into this world. And—most important of all—with a feeling of neighborliness, of belonging—belonging to each other—not only in a larger sense but in little things as well.

HILDE [*eagerly*]. Well—but doesn't that give you great happiness—to be able to erect such beautiful homes?

SOLNESS. But think of the price—the frightful price I have had to pay in order to obtain the opportunity!

HILDE. Isn't it exactly this that you ought to try to overcome?

SOLNESS. No. In order to build homes for others I had to give up for all time the thought of having a home of my own. By that I mean a home with children.

HILDE [*cautiously*]. You say, for all time. But was that necessary?

SOLNESS [*with a slow nod*]. That is the price I have had to pay for this happiness of mine which people are always talking about. [*Breathing heavily.*] Such happiness—h'm—such happiness is not to be bought cheaply, Hilde.

HILDE [*as before*]. But don't you think there might still be a chance that . . .

SOLNESS. Never—never in the world! That, too, is a result of the fire—of Aline's illness afterward.

HILDE [*gazes at him with an indefinable expression*]. And still you build all these nursery rooms!

SOLNESS [*earnestly*]. Haven't you noticed, Hilde, that there is something alluring about trying to do the impossible—something that keeps enticing, attracting us?

HILDE [*pondering*]. The impossible? [*With animation.*] Oh yes—yes! Have you noticed that, too?

SOLNESS. Yes, I have.

HILDE. Then, I suppose you, too, have something of the troll in you?

SOLNESS. Troll?

HILDE [*in a suppressed voice, with emotion*]. Well—what would you call it, then?

SOLNESS [*getting up*]. Oh well, perhaps you are right. [*With vehemence.*] But how can I help being a troll—the way things always turn out for me—no matter what I do?

HILDE. I don't understand you.

SOLNESS [*subdued, with deep emotion*]. I want you to pay attention to what I now tell you, Hilde. All I have managed to accomplish—all I have built for comfort and security and created in beauty—yes, and I dare say, even in grandeur . . . [*With clenched fists.*] Oh! It is too horrible to think of!

HILDE. What is it you can't bear to think of?

SOLNESS. That all this I now have to take into account and weigh carefully, and pay for in full—not with money but with human happiness. And not my own happiness only, but the happiness of others as well. Yes, yes—you see what I mean, Hilde! That is the price I have had to pay for the position I hold in my profession—and that others have had to pay. And day in and day out I am reminded of the price that must be paid —over and over again—and ever again!

HILDE [*gets up and gazes intently at him*]. You are undoubtedly thinking of —of her now.

SOLNESS. Yes. Primarily of Aline. For Aline—*she* had *her* mission in life, too— and hers was quite as important as mine. [*With trembling voice.*] But her calling in life was sacrificed, thwarted—was all in vain, in order that I might climb step by step to some kind of grand and glorious victory. And I must tell you, by the way, that Aline also had a gift for building.

HILDE. She had? A gift for building?

SOLNESS [*shaking his head*]. Not for building towers and spires and the kind of things I build.

HILDE. What kind then?

SOLNESS [*softly, moved*]. She had a gift for building the souls of little children, Hilde, to develop them so that they became as strong and healthy in mind as in body; so that they would grow into mature, upright human beings. This was what Aline had a gift for. And now that gift of hers has wasted away because of not being used. She will never be able to use it again; it has been lost forever. It is like the barren ruins after a fire.

HILDE. Yes, but even if that were the case . . .

SOLNESS. It is! It is! I know that is what has happened!

HILDE. But certainly you are not to be blamed for it.

SOLNESS [his eyes fixed on her, he nods slowly]. Well—you see—that is the terrible question. That is the never-ending doubt that gnaws my conscience night and day.

HILDE. But why do you let it?

SOLNESS. Well—suppose . . . suppose the blame were mine—or partially mine . . .

HILDE. Yours? For the fire, you mean?

SOLNESS. For everything—all of it! And perhaps—perhaps entirely innocently.

HILDE [gazes at him, troubled and confused]. Oh, Mr. Solness—when you say a thing like that, then you really must be sick.

SOLNESS. H'm. I am afraid I am. I never stop thinking about it.

[RAGNAR BROVIK cautiously opens the small door in the corner, right. HILDE walks toward the center of the stage.]

RAGNAR [on seeing HILDE]. Oh—pardon me, Mr. Solness. [He is about to leave.]

SOLNESS. No, no—don't go! We must come to some sort of understanding.

RAGNAR. Oh yes! I would like it if we could.

SOLNESS. I hear your father's condition has not improved.

RAGNAR. Father is failing rapidly. That's why I want to ask you—ask you from the bottom of my heart—if you please won't write something—just a few words—to show you have confidence in me—on one of my drawings . . . Something for Father—before he . . .

SOLNESS [vehemently]. Stop talking to me about those drawings of yours!

RAGNAR. Have you looked at them?

SOLNESS. Yes, I have.

RAGNAR. And you mean they are not good enough? Then I suppose I am not worth much either?

SOLNESS [evading the question]. You stay with me, Ragnar, and you will have things your own way. And then you can marry Kaja, and you'll have nothing to worry about. You may even find happiness. But give up the thought of starting in business for yourself.

RAGNAR. Well—well . . . I guess I'll have to go home and tell Father what you said . . . I promised him I would. So this is what you want me to tell Father —before he passes away?

SOLNESS [as in pain, with a groan]. Tell him—tell him whatever you like. No—I think you had best tell him nothing! [In an outburst.] I can't act any other way than I do, Ragnar!

RAGNAR. May I at least take home the drawings with me?

SOLNESS. Yes, take them with you—by all means! They are lying there on the table.

RAGNAR [goes to the table]. Thank you.

HILDE [placing a hand on the portfolio]. No, no—leave them here!

SOLNESS. But why?

HILDE. Because I would like to look at them.

SOLNESS. But you already . . . [To RAGNAR.] Well, then—leave them here.

RAGNAR. Certainly, just as you say.

SOLNESS. And now—don't delay—go home to your father.

RAGNAR. Yes—I had better be going.

SOLNESS [as if in agony]. Ragnar—you must never ask anything of me that I can't do! Is that clear, Ragnar? You must never do that!

RAGNAR. No, no . . . I'm sorry. [He bows and goes out through the door in the corner. HILDE goes and sits down on a chair by the mirror.]

HILDE [with an angry look at SOLNESS]. You were downright contemptible and selfish just now.

SOLNESS. So—you think so, too?

HILDE. Yes, you were terribly mean— you certainly were. You were hard—and cruel—and evil.

SOLNESS. Oh, but you don't realize the position I am in.

HILDE. That doesn't matter. No—you should never act like that—not you!

SOLNESS. You said yourself a moment ago that only I should be allowed to build.

HILDE. I may say such things—but not you. It is not for you to say them.

SOLNESS. If you please, I have a right

to say them. Haven't I paid dearly to get where I am?

HILDE. Oh well—you have had to sacrifice what you call domestic comfort—and things of that sort.

SOLNESS. And my peace of mind as well!

HILDE [gets up]. Peace of mind! [Ardently.] Yes, yes, you are quite right! Poor Mr. Master Builder! You imagine yourself to be . . .

SOLNESS [with a quiet chuckle]. Please sit down again, Hilde, then I'll tell you something that will make you laugh.

HILDE [sits down in anticipation]. Well?

SOLNESS. It seems like such a ridiculously small matter—for, you see, the story has to do with nothing but a crack in a chimney pipe.

HILDE. Is that all? Nothing else?

SOLNESS. No—not to begin with. [He moves a chair close to HILDE and sits down.]

HILDE [impatiently tapping her knee]. Now—let's hear about the crack in the chimney pipe!

SOLNESS. I had noticed that little crack in the pipe for some time—long before the fire. Every time I went to the attic I made it a point to see if it was still there.

HILDE. And was it?

SOLNESS. Yes. And no one but I knew about it.

HILDE. And you told no one?

SOLNESS. No—I told no one.

HILDE. And you never thought of repairing it?

SOLNESS. I thought about it—but that was all. Every time I thought I would do something about it, it was as if a hand had held me back. And I said to myself: Not today—tomorrow! And so nothing was ever done about it.

HILDE. But why didn't you repair it immediately?

SOLNESS. Because a thought took hold of me and I became obsessed with it. I thought: perhaps by means of that small crack in the chimney pipe I could swing myself up to the top—as a builder.

HILDE [looking into space]. That must have been exciting!

SOLNESS. Not only exciting—almost irresistible! And I couldn't resist it! It seemed to me so very easy and simple at the time. I wanted it to happen on some morning, just before noon, during the winter. I was to be out driving in the sleigh and Aline was to be with me; the servants would be at home and would have built blazing fires in the stoves and fireplaces . . .

HILDE. Naturally—it would have had to be horribly cold, freezing weather that day . . .

SOLNESS. Frightfully cold. And, of course, the servants would want to have the house warm and comfortable for Aline when she returned.

HILDE. And I imagine she is rather sensitive to the cold . . .

SOLNESS. Yes, she is. And on our way home, we were to have seen the smoke . . .

HILDE. Only the smoke?

SOLNESS. That is the first thing I thought we would have seen. That is the way I had hoped it would happen . . . But by the time we arrived at the garden gate, the old wooden crate was a mass of roaring flames, ablaze from top to bottom.

HILDE. Heavens! What a pity it didn't go according to your plan!

SOLNESS. You may well say that, Hilde.

HILDE. Oh but, Mr. Solness! Are you so absolutely certain that the fire started only because of that little crack in the chimney pipe?

SOLNESS. No, I am not. On the contrary, I am almost certain that that crack had nothing whatever to do with the fire.

HILDE. What's that you say?

SOLNESS. It was clearly brought out that the fire began in a clothes closet—in an entirely different part of the house.

HILDE. Then why all this twaddle about that crack in the chimney pipe?

SOLNESS. Do you mind if I talk to you a little longer, Hilde?

HILDE. No—if you stop talking nonsense!

SOLNESS. I'll try. [He moves his chair closer to her.] Don't you believe as I do, Hilde, that there are certain chosen people who through some act of grace have been given the ability and the power to wish for something so doggedly, to hope and yearn and crave for something so fervently that they—in the end—are given what they want? Don't you?

HILDE [with an indefinable expression

in her eyes]. If there are, then we'll find out one of these days if *I* am one of the chosen.

SOLNESS. It is not by oneself *alone* that great achievements are made. Oh no! The fellow servants and fellow helpers—they must do their share, too, if the wish is to come true. But they will not come of their own free will. One has to call to them persistently and urge them on. And the wish has to come from the depths of the heart, you understand.

HILDE. What do you mean by fellow servants and fellow helpers?

SOLNESS. Let's talk about that some other time. Let us go back to what we were talking about—the fire.

HILDE. Don't you think that fire would have occurred—even if you had not wished for it to happen?

SOLNESS. If old Brovik had owned the house, it would never in the world have burned down so conveniently. Of that I am certain. He has neither the ability nor the power to summon either helpers or servants. [*He rises in a state of agitation.*] Now you see, Hilde, that—after all—I am the one who is responsible for the death of my little boys. And is it not my fault, too, that Aline never had an opportunity to be what she should have been —and which she so fervently wanted to be?

HILDE. Well, but since it was the helpers and the servants who . . .

SOLNESS. Who called for the helpers and the servants? I did! And they came! And they carried out my will! [*With growing emotion.*] And this is what people generally call having good fortune! But let me tell you what that sort of luck feels like! It is like having a raw, festering wound in my chest—and the servants and the helpers have to go out and bring back pieces of flesh and skin—which they have cut from other people—to fill up the wound. But the wound will not heal! It will never heal! Never! Oh, if you only knew how painful it is—how it burns and stings . . .

HILDE [*observing him closely*]. You are sick, Mr. Solness. Very sick, I am afraid.

SOLNESS. Why don't you say mad? That's what you mean, isn't it?

HILDE. No, I don't think you are lacking in sanity.

SOLNESS. In what, then? Speak out!

HILDE. I wonder whether you were not born with a squeamish conscience?

SOLNESS. A squeamish conscience? What in hell is that?

HILDE. I mean that there is something utterly wrong with your conscience. It is weak. It is not made of iron. It can't support a heavy load—can't even lift it.

SOLNESS [*grumbling*]. H'm! May I ask what sort of conscience you would like me to have, then?

HILDE. I would like you to have a conscience that was—that was really strong —robust—immutable.

SOLNESS. So? Immutable? Oh? Is that the kind of conscience you have, I wonder?

HILDE. Yes, I believe I have. I have never known it to be otherwise.

SOLNESS. I imagine it has never been really put to the test, either.

HILDE [*with quivering lips*]. Oh—I didn't find it so very easy to leave my father, whom I love dearly.

SOLNESS. Why—for a month or two . . .

HILDE. I don't think I'll ever go home again.

SOLNESS. Never? Why did you leave?

HILDE [*half seriously, half in jest*]. Now, have you forgotten again that the ten years are up?

SOLNESS. Tell me! Was there anything wrong at home? Was there? Eh?

HILDE [*with complete seriousness*]. It was this yearning within me that kept tempting me and drove me to come here. It kept intriguing me—attracting me . . .

SOLNESS [*eagerly*]. There we have it! There we have it, Hilde! You have something of the troll in you, too—just as I have in me. For it is the troll in us, you see, that keeps calling for those powers we lack ourselves. And whether we want to or not, we give in.

HILDE. I almost believe you are right, Mr. Solness.

SOLNESS [*walking about the floor*]. Oh —the world is full of demons that we are not aware of, Hilde.

HILDE. Demons, too?

SOLNESS [*stops walking about*]. Yes. Good demons and evil demons! Blond demons and swarthy demons! If only we could know whether we are in the grip of the fair or the swarthy ones! [*He starts pacing the floor again.*] Yes—then it would be simple enough!

HILDE [*keeps following him with her eyes*]. Or—if we had a really healthy conscience, exuberantly healthy, and had the courage to do what we most wanted to do.

SOLNESS [*comes to a halt by the console table*]. In that respect, I believe most everyone else is as much of a weakling as I am.

HILDE. That may well be.

SOLNESS [*leaning against the table*]. In the old sagas . . . Have you ever read any of the old sagas?

HILDE. Oh yes! In the past—when I enjoyed reading—then I . . .

SOLNESS. In the sagas there are tales about vikings who sailed to foreign lands and burned and plundered, killed men, and . . .

HILDE. . . . and captured women . . .

SOLNESS. . . . took them aboard their ships . . .

HILDE. . . . and sailed back to their homeland with them . . .

SOLNESS. . . . and behaved like the most wicked of trolls toward them.

HILDE [*looking into space with a half-veiled gaze*]. Oh, that must have been exciting!

SOLNESS [*with a short, croaking laugh*]. To capture women?

HILDE. To be captured!

SOLNESS [*looks at her for a moment*]. Oh, indeed!

HILDE [*abruptly*]. But just why did you bring this up about the vikings, Mr. Solness?

SOLNESS. Because these men—they had a robust conscience, they had! When they returned from their seafaring, they ate and drank lustily—and they were as merry and happy as children. And what about the women? They were loath to part from their men. Can you understand that, Hilde?

HILDE. I can understand those women completely.

SOLNESS. Oho! Perhaps you would act exactly as they did?

HILDE. Why not?

SOLNESS. You would live with a savage brute, a fiend like that—of your own free will, would you?

HILDE. If I really were in love with a brute like that—yes.

SOLNESS. Do you really mean you could fall in love with such a man?

HILDE. Good heavens! One never knows whom one will fall in love with— and once in love, there is no help for it, is there?

SOLNESS [*looks at her thoughtfully*]. No . . . No—I presume the troll in us is to blame for that, too.

HILDE [*with a slight chuckle*]. Not to mention all those blessed demons that you are on such good terms with—both the fair and the swarthy!

SOLNESS [*quietly, warmly*]. And here is a wish that the demons will choose kindly for you, Hilde.

HILDE. They have already made their choice for me—once for all.

SOLNESS [*gazes at her with feeling*]. Hilde! You are like some wild bird of the forests.

HILDE. I am nothing of the kind. I don't go hiding myself under the bushes.

SOLNESS. No, no. I think you have probably something of the bird of prey in you.

HILDE. Rather that—perhaps. [*With great vehemence.*] And why not a bird of prey? Why shouldn't I, too, go hunting down my victim—and make a capture if it pleases me—if I can only get my claws into it and get the best of it—and tame it?

SOLNESS. Hilde! Do you know what you are?

HILDE. Yes. I am one of those strange birds, of course.

SOLNESS. No. You are like the dawn of a new day! When I look upon you, I have a feeling as though I were watching a rising sun.

HILDE. Tell me, Mr. Solness—are you certain you have never called to me— from the depths of your heart, as you said?

SOLNESS [*gently, slowly*]. I almost believe—I must have.

HILDE. What did you want with me?

SOLNESS. Hilde . . . you are Youth, Hilde.

HILDE [*smiles*]. Youth! Youth—that you are in such fear of!

SOLNESS [*with a slow nod*]. And which I deep down in my heart have such fearful yearning for . . .

[HILDE *gets up, goes over to the small*

table and picks up RAGNAR's *portfolio which she hands to* SOLNESS.]

HILDE. These were the drawings that you . . .

SOLNESS [*curtly, with a deprecatory gesture*]. Put those drawings back! I have looked enough at them!

HILDE. Yes—but you want to write something on them for him, don't you?

SOLNESS. Write something on them? Never in this world!

HILDE. But you know the poor old man is dying! You can do that much for him before he dies, can't you? It will make both him and the son so happy. And perhaps it will help the son to get the contract for that house.

SOLNESS. Yes—that is exactly what would happen! He has made sure of that —that young whippersnapper!

HILDE. But, heavens—if that is so— why couldn't you tell a little white lie— for once?

SOLNESS. A lie? [*In a rage.*] Hilde! Don't come near me with those damned drawings!

HILDE [*hugging the portfolio*]. Well, well, well! You don't have to bite me! You talk about trolls! It seems to me you behave like a troll yourself! [*Looking about the room.*] Where is your pen and ink?

SOLNESS. I don't keep any in here.

HILDE [*walks toward the door*]. But the young lady in the office—she must have some . . .

SOLNESS. Stay here, Hilde! You say— you want me to tell a lie. Oh well—for the sake of the old man I imagine I could. For I did break him once—I put him out of business.

HILDE. Him also?

SOLNESS. I had to make way for myself. But that son of his, Ragnar—he must not—under any circumstance—get ahead.

HILDE. But you don't expect him to, poor fellow, if—as you say—he has so little talent . . .

SOLNESS [*coming close to her, he gazes at her and whispers*]. If Ragnar Brovik should get ahead, he will put me out of business—ruin me—just as I ruined his father.

HILDE. Put you out of business? You think he could do that?

SOLNESS. You may be sure he could!

He is the younger generation that stands waiting to rap at my door and break in. And that would be the end of Halvard Solness, the master builder.

HILDE [*with a look of quiet reproach*]. And yet you would bar him from coming in! For shame, Master Builder Solness!

SOLNESS. I have lost enough of my heart's blood during these years of struggle. And I am afraid the helpers and the servants no longer pay any heed to me.

HILDE. Then there is nothing for you to do but to rely on yourself, and yourself only.

SOLNESS. That would be hopeless, Hilde. Another day is coming—and with it, sooner or later, a change. And then retribution will be inevitable.

HILDE [*in agony, she covers her ears with her hands*]. Don't speak like that! Why do you torment me? Why do you try to rob me of what to me is dearer than life itself?

SOLNESS. And what is that?

HILDE. To see you as a man of greatness. To see you—carrying a wreath in your hand—high, high up—at the pinnacle of a church spire! [*Again calm.*] Well—get out your pencil, then! You have a pencil, haven't you?

[SOLNESS *takes a pencil from his vest pocket.*]

HILDE [*laying the portfolio on the table by the sofa*]. Good. Now let us sit down here—Master Builder Solness. [SOLNESS *sits down at the table.* HILDE, *standing behind him, leans over the back of the chair.*] And now we'll write on the drawings. Let's write something very nice— something warm and sincere—for that bad fellow Ro-ar—or whatever his name is. [SOLNESS *writes a few lines, turns his head and gazes at her.*]

SOLNESS. Tell me something, Hilde . . .

HILDE. Yes?

SOLNESS. If you really had been waiting for me these ten years . . .

HILDE. Yes?

SOLNESS. . . . then why didn't you write to me? And I could have written back to you.

HILDE [*spontaneously*]. No, no, no! That is exactly what I didn't want.

SOLNESS. Why not?

HILDE. I was afraid that everything

would go up in smoke ... But we were to write something on the drawings, you know, Mr. Solness ...

SOLNESS. So we were, yes.

HILDE [leaning over him while he is writing]. What you are writing sounds so warm—as if coming from the heart. ... Oh, how I hate this Roald.

SOLNESS [while writing]. Have you ever really loved anyone, Hilde?

HILDE [in a severe tone of voice]. What did you say?

SOLNESS. Have you ever loved anyone?

HILDE. You mean—anyone else, don't you?

SOLNESS [looks up at her]. Anyone else —yes. Have you—during all these years —these ten years? Have you?

HILDE. Oh—perhaps I have. When I was really angry with you because you never came back.

SOLNESS. Then there have been others ...

HILDE. Only intermittently. Just for a week or so. Good heavens, Mr. Solness, you can't be innocent about such things.

SOLNESS. Hilde—why, exactly, did you come here?

HILDE. Don't waste time talking nonsense! While you are chattering away, the poor old man may be dying!

SOLNESS. Answer me, Hilde. What is it you want of me?

HILDE. I want my kingdom.

SOLNESS. H'm. ... [He gives a casual glance in the direction of the door, right, and then continues to write on the drawings. MRS. SOLNESS enters, carrying several packages.]

MRS. SOLNESS. I brought home with me a few things for you, Miss Wangel. I bought some other things, too; they will be delivered later. They were too big to carry.

HILDE. Oh—how very, very nice you are to me!

MRS. SOLNESS. It is nothing but my duty, that's all.

SOLNESS [reading over what he has written]. Aline!

MRS. SOLNESS. Yes?

SOLNESS. Did you notice if she—if the bookkeeper was in the office?

MRS. SOLNESS. Yes—of course she was there.

SOLNESS [putting the drawings in the portfolio]. H'm. ...

MRS. SOLNESS. She was standing at her high desk, where she always stands— when I pass through the office.

SOLNESS [rising]. Then I'll just go in and give her the portfolio and tell her to ...

HILDE [takes the portfolio from him]. Oh no—let me have that pleasure. [She walks toward the door but suddenly turns.] What is her name?

SOLNESS. Her name is Miss Fosli.

HILDE. Faugh! That sounds so stiff and cold! I mean her first name.

SOLNESS. Kaja—I believe that's her name.

HILDE [opens the door to the office and calls out]. Kaja! Come in here! Hurry! Mr. Solness would like to talk to you.

[KAJA FOSLI comes in and remains standing just inside the doorway. She looks at SOLNESS in a frightened manner.]

KAJA. Here I am.

HILDE [hands her the portfolio]. Here you are, Kaja. You can take these home with you, for now Mr. Solness has written his recommendation on them.

KAJA. Oh, at last!

SOLNESS. Bring them to old Brovik as quickly as you can.

KAJA. I'll bring them to him immediately.

SOLNESS. Yes, do that. And now Ragnar will have his chance to build.

KAJA. Oh! Will you let him come and thank you for all that you ... ?

SOLNESS [in a hard tone]. I don't want any thanks! Tell him that from me!

KAJA. Yes—I will ...

SOLNESS. And you can also tell him that I shan't need him any more. And the same applies to you.

KAJA [almost inaudibly, in a trembling voice]. To me—too?

SOLNESS. From now on you will have other things to think about and to look after. And that is quite as it should be. Well—take the drawings home now, Miss Fosli. And don't delay, do you hear!

KAJA [as before]. Yes, Mr. Solness. [She goes out.]

MRS. SOLNESS. She has the eyes of a hypocrite!

SOLNESS. She! That poor little creature!

MRS. SOLNESS. Oh—don't worry, I am not blind, Halvard. Are you really letting them go?

SOLNESS. Yes.

MRS. SOLNESS. Her, too?

SOLNESS. Wasn't that what you wanted?

MRS. SOLNESS. But how will you be able to get along without her? Oh well, I suppose you have someone else to take her place, Halvard.

HILDE [gaily]. Well, I certainly am not made to stand at that high desk.

SOLNESS. Well, well, well, Aline—I'll manage somehow. All I want you to be concerned about now is our new home. We have to get ready to move. And the sooner, the better. This evening we are hanging the wreath . . . [Turns to HILDE.] . . . at the top of the tower—at the very top of it! What do you say to that, Miss Hilde?

HILDE [riveting her eyes upon him radiantly]. Oh! It will be wonderfully exciting to see you so high up in the air again!

SOLNESS. Me?

MRS. SOLNESS. Why, whatever put such an idea into your head, Miss Wangel? My husband—who is subject to spells of dizziness!

HILDE. Dizziness! Why—he is nothing of the kind!

MRS. SOLNESS. Oh yes—he most certainly is!

HILDE. But I have seen him myself— at the very top of a high church tower!

MRS. SOLNESS. Yes, I have heard such talk—but it couldn't possibly be so!

SOLNESS [vehemently]. Not possible! Not possible, you say? But no matter what you say I have done it!

MRS. SOLNESS. Why—how can you say such a thing, Halvard? You can't even bear to go out on the terrace on the second floor! You have always been that way!

SOLNESS. Perhaps you will think differently when you see me this evening.

MRS. SOLNESS [with sudden fear]. Oh, no, no! May God help me, if I should ever see you do a thing like that! Then I will have to send a message to the doctor immediately. And he will put a stop to it.

SOLNESS. Why, Aline . . . !

MRS. SOLNESS. Yes, yes—for you are sick, Halvard! What you are saying proves it! Oh, God! Oh, God!

[She hastens out, left.]

HILDE [regarding SOLNESS tensely.] Is this true, or isn't it?

SOLNESS. That I suffer from dizziness?

HILDE. That my Master Builder cannot —that he has not the courage to climb as high as he builds?

SOLNESS. Is that what you think?

HILDE. Yes.

SOLNESS. I begin to think there isn't anything about me that you haven't found out.

HILDE [gazing toward the bay window]. Up there, then! All the way to the top!

SOLNESS [coming closer to her]. I would have you live in the topmost room in the tower, Hilde. There you could live like a princess.

HILDE [with a tone between seriousness and jesting]. Well, that's what you promised me, wasn't it?

SOLNESS. Did I really do that?

HILDE. Why, Mr. Solness! Didn't you say I was to be a princess—and that I would be given a kingdom? And then you . . . Well!

SOLNESS [circumspectly]. Are you sure you haven't dreamt all this—that it is not some sort of illusion—something you have conjured up in your mind—which has become an obsession?

HILDE [evasively]. You mean to say you didn't promise?

SOLNESS. I really don't know what I did . . . [In a softer tone.] But one thing I am sure of now—that I . . .

HILDE. That you . . . ? Out with it— quick!

SOLNESS. That I ought to have done it!

HILDE [with an exclamation; happily, animatedly]. There is nothing about you that is dizzy!

SOLNESS. This evening we will hang the wreath at the top of the tower—Princess Hilde.

HILDE [with a touch of bitterness]. Above your new home, yes!

SOLNESS. Above the new house—that will never be home to me!

[He leaves through the door which leads to the garden.]

HILDE [pensively gazing into space, she whispers to herself so that one hears only the words]. . . . frightfully exciting!

ACT III

[THE SETTING.—A broad, spacious terrace on the second floor of HALVARD SOL-

NESS's house. A part of the house with a door leading to the terrace can be seen on the right; on the left is seen the balustrade. In the rear, at the end of the terrace, steps lead down to the garden below. The branches of tall old trees in the garden overhang the terrace and stretch toward the house. Far over to the left can be seen the lower part of the new villa between the trees; also a portion of its tower, enclosed by scaffolding. The garden is hemmed in by an old wooden fence at the rear. Beyond the fence, a road with small, low houses in dilapidated condition.

It is evening. There are sunlit clouds in the sky. On the terrace, a garden bench is placed along the wall of the house, and in front of the bench a longish table. On the far side of the table, an armchair and some taborets. All the pieces of furniture are of basket weave.

MRS. SOLNESS, wrapped in a big white shawl of crape, sits resting in the armchair; she is gazing fixedly toward the left. Soon after, HILDE WANGEL comes up the steps that lead from the garden. She is dressed as in the preceding act and wears a hat. On her bosom she has a small bouquet of tiny flowers of a common variety.]

MRS. SOLNESS [slightly turning her head]. So you have been walking about in the garden, Miss Wangel, have you?

HILDE. Yes, I have been looking around down there.

MRS. SOLNESS. And found a few flowers, too, I see.

HILDE. Yes! There are more than enough of these—in among the bushes.

MRS. SOLNESS. Oh, are there really? At this time of year? Well, it's so seldom I go down into the garden.

HILDE [coming closer]. You mean that? Don't you go down there every day?

MRS. SOLNESS [with a weary smile]. I don't go anywhere—any more.

HILDE. Oh, but don't you go down once in a while and take in all the beautiful things that are there?

MRS. SOLNESS. It has all become so remote to me—all of it—that I am almost afraid to look at it again.

HILDE. Your own garden!

MRS. SOLNESS. I don't feel it is mine any longer.

HILDE. Oh! How can you . . .

MRS. SOLNESS. Yes, yes! It is not my garden. It is not what it was when my father and mother were alive. They have taken away so much of it. It makes me feel sad, Miss Wangel. Think of it! They have divided it up into parcels and built houses for all sorts of strange people—people I don't know—and who sit at their windows and stare at me!

HILDE [cheerfully]. Mrs. Solness . . .

MRS. SOLNESS. Yes?

HILDE. Will you let me stay with you here for a while?

MRS. SOLNESS. Gladly—if you would really like to.

[HILDE moves one of the taborets over to MRS. SOLNESS and sits down at her side.]

HILDE. Ah! Now I can sit here and really sun myself like a cat.

MRS. SOLNESS [placing her hand lightly on the back of HILDE's neck]. How nice of you to want to sit with me. I thought you were going inside to my husband.

HILDE. Why should I want to go in to him?

MRS. SOLNESS. To help him—I suppose.

HILDE. No, thank you. Besides—he is not at home. He is over at the villa with the workmen. But he looked so ferocious that I didn't dare talk to him!

MRS. SOLNESS. Oh, he is really so very gentle and soft at heart . . .

HILDE. He!

MRS. SOLNESS. You don't know him yet, Miss Wangel—really know him.

HILDE [with a warm look at her]. Does it make you happy to be moving into your new house?

MRS. SOLNESS. I should be, I suppose—for it's what Halvard wants, you see . . .

HILDE. Oh, but why should you be happy simply because he wants it?

MRS. SOLNESS. Yes, yes, Miss Wangel. For you know it's my duty to bow to his wishes. But it's oftentimes difficult to persuade the mind to obey.

HILDE. Yes, I should think it would be.

MRS. SOLNESS. I can assure you it is. Especially for anyone with as many faults as I have. Then it . . .

HILDE. Anyone who has been through all that you have been through . . .

MRS. SOLNESS. How can you know?

HILDE. Your husband told me.

MRS. SOLNESS. He hardly ever talks to me about that. Yes . . . believe me, I have had more than my share of misfortune in life.

HILDE [looks at her sympathetically and nods slowly]. Poor Mrs. Solness! First you had the fire . . .

MRS. SOLNESS [with a sigh]. Yes. I lost everything!

HILDE. And what followed—was a still greater misfortune.

MRS. SOLNESS [with a questioning look]. Still greater?

HILDE. A greater misfortune than anything else.

MRS. SOLNESS. Just what—do you mean?

HILDE [gently]. When you lost your little ones . . .

MRS. SOLNESS. Oh—the little ones—yes. Well, that—that was something very different. That was an act of Providence. And we must bow before His will and be grateful for what He sends us.

HILDE. Do you really accept that?

MRS. SOLNESS. Not always, I am sorry to say, even though I know it is my duty. But, somehow, I can't always live up to it.

HILDE. No, no—that's quite understandable.

MRS. SOLNESS. Time and time again I have to remind myself that it was sent to me as a rightful punishment.

HILDE. Because of what?

MRS. SOLNESS. Because I failed to be strong in my hour of trial.

HILDE. But I can't understand how . . .

MRS. SOLNESS. Oh, Miss Wangel—don't let us speak any more about my little boys! We must be happy for them! For where they are now, they are at peace! No—it's the little things we lose in life, which leave a hurt deep in our hearts. The loss of things which to others seem meaningless and insignificant . . .

HILDE [putting her arm on MRS. SOLNESS's knee, she looks up at her with a warm expression in her eyes]. Dear Mrs. Solness! Do tell me what these little things are that you are alluding to!

MRS. SOLNESS. As I said—they were just little things. All the family portraits hanging on the walls—they were all destroyed. All the old silk gowns—they

burned up. And they had been handed down in the family from generation to generation. The whole of my mother's and grandmother's collection of lace was burned—and all the jewelry was lost in the fire, too! [Sadly.] And think of it! All the dolls!

HILDE. The dolls?

MRS. SOLNESS [with a sob in her throat]. I had nine lovely dolls . . .

HILDE. And they went, too?

MRS. SOLNESS. They were all lost. Oh! It was hard to take! So hard!

HILDE. Had you saved all your dolls? Had you put them all away—I mean all those you had from the time you were a little girl?

MRS. SOLNESS. Not put them away! They lived with me—every one of them!

HILDE. You mean—even after you were grown up?

MRS. SOLNESS. Yes—long after that.

HILDE. Even after you were married?

MRS. SOLNESS. Oh yes, yes! And when he wasn't there to see it, I . . . But the poor things were burned in the fire. And no one even thought of saving them! Oh, I can't tell you how pathetic it all seems! Oh, you mustn't laugh at me, Miss Wangel!

HILDE. I am not laughing.

MRS. SOLNESS. For you see, they had a spark of life in them, too. I carried them under my heart—like little unborn babies . . .

[DOCTOR HERDAL, his hat in his hand, comes out on the terrace through the door and discovers MRS. SOLNESS and HILDE.]

DOCTOR HERDAL. So-o, Mrs. Solness, you are sitting out here on the terrace trying to catch cold, are you?

MRS. SOLNESS. I thought it was so nice and warm out here today.

DOCTOR HERDAL. Yes, yes. But you sent a message to me . . . Is there anything wrong here?

MRS. SOLNESS [rising]. Yes, there is something I must talk to you about.

DOCTOR HERDAL. I am at your service. Perhaps we had best go inside, then we . . . [To HILDE.] Dressed for mountain climbing today again, Miss Wangel?

HILDE [rising; with a playful expression]. Oh yes! In full attire, with war paint and everything! But today I am not doing any climbing and risking my neck! You and I, Doctor—we'll remain below, away from all danger, and just look on, won't we?

DOCTOR HERDAL. What are we to look at?

MRS. SOLNESS [alarmed; softly to HILDE]. Sh! Sh! For Heaven's sake! He is coming! Oh, please try to get that wild notion out of his head! And let us two be friends, Miss Wangel! Can't we be friends?

HILDE [throws her arms impulsively round MRS. SOLNESS's neck]. Oh, if we only could!

MRS. SOLNESS [gently freeing herself]. There, there, there! Here he comes, Doctor . . . Let me have a few words with you . . .

DOCTOR HERDAL. You mean—concerning him?

MRS. SOLNESS. Yes, of course—it's about him. Let's go inside—quickly.

[She and DOCTOR HERDAL go inside. A moment later, SOLNESS enters by the steps leading from the garden. A serious expression comes over HILDE's countenance.]

SOLNESS [glances toward the door which is being closed cautiously from the inside]. Have you noticed, Hilde, that the moment I appear, she disappears?

HILDE. I have noticed that your entrance always acts as a cue for her exit.

SOLNESS. Perhaps you are right. But I can't help that. [He regards HILDE intently.] You look as if you were freezing, Hilde.

HILDE. I have only just come up from the grave.

SOLNESS. What do you mean by that?

HILDE. I am afraid the frigidity has affected me.

SOLNESS [slowly]. I think I understand . . .

HILDE. Just why did you come here?

SOLNESS. I saw you from over by the new house.

HILDE. But then you saw her, too, didn't you?

SOLNESS. I knew she would leave the moment I came.

HILDE. Does it hurt you to have her avoid you like that?

SOLNESS. I should say it gives me a sense of relief.

HILDE. Not to have to be with her every minute, you mean?

SOLNESS. Yes.

HILDE. So that you won't have to see how hard she takes the loss of her little sons?

SOLNESS. Yes—mostly because of that. [HILDE walks to the far end of the terrace, her hands behind her back, and then stops by the balustrade, where she stands looking out over the garden. After a brief pause, SOLNESS speaks again.] Did you talk with her long? [HILDE stands motionless; she does not answer.] Did you talk long, I asked? [HILDE remains silent.] What did she talk about, Hilde? [HILDE still does not reply.] Poor Aline! I presume she talked about our little boys? [HILDE shudders nervously and gives a few quick nods.] She will never get over it—she never will! [Walks up to HILDE.] Now you stand there again like a statue—just as you did last evening.

HILDE [turns and regards him with a wide open, serious look]. I am going away.

SOLNESS [in a sharp tone]. Going away?

HILDE. Yes.

SOLNESS. Oh—but you can't—I won't let you!

HILDE. What is there for me to do after this?

SOLNESS. All you have to do is to stay!

HILDE [looking him up and down]. Oh, thank you! I dare say it wouldn't stop at that!

SOLNESS [without thinking]. So much the better!

HILDE [with vehement emphasis]. I could never harm anyone I know! I can't deprive her of what is hers.

SOLNESS. Who says you should?

HILDE [persistently]. A stranger—yes! For that is an entirely different matter. Someone I have never met—yes. But someone I have come to know—oh, no —never! Never! Ugh!

SOLNESS. Well—but I have never said that you should, have I?

HILDE. Oh, Mr. Solness, you know very well how it would end! And that is why I am leaving.

SOLNESS. But what will become of me, if you should go? What will then be left for me to live for?

HILDE [with an impenetrable expression in her eyes]. Why should you be concerned about yourself? You have your duties and obligations toward her. Live for them!

SOLNESS. It's much too late. These—these powers. These—these . . .

HILDE. Demons?

SOLNESS. Yes—demons! And the troll within me . . . They have drained her of her lifeblood. [With an agonized laugh.] They did it in order to bring me material success! Success! [Gloomily.] And now she is no longer living—and I am the cause of it! And I am chained to a living corpse! [In frantic agony.] I—I, who need joy more than anything else in this life!

[HILDE walks around the table, then sits down on the bench, resting her elbows on top of the table and her head in her hands. She sits gazing at him for a moment.]

HILDE. What do you intend to build next, Master Builder?

SOLNESS [shaking his head]. I don't think I'll be building very much more after this, Hilde.

HILDE. No snug, happy homes for parents and their children?

SOLNESS. Heaven knows whether there will be much use for any such homes in the future.

HILDE. Poor Master Builder! And you have dedicated your life to just that these ten long years!

SOLNESS. Yes—I have, Hilde.

HILDE [in an outburst]. Oh, how ridiculous it all seems—how thoroughly ridiculous—this whole thing!

SOLNESS. Which thing?

HILDE. Not to have the courage to grasp your own happiness—your happiness in life! And merely because someone stands in the way—and because you happen to know that person!

SOLNESS. A person you have no right to push aside and dishonor . . .

HILDE. I just wonder whether one hasn't the right, after all, to do so. Yet, even so . . . Oh—if one could only sleep it all away! [She lays her arms flat on the table, rests one cheek against them, and closes her eyes. SOLNESS turns his armchair so that he sits close to the table.]

SOLNESS. Were you happy in your home—up there with your father, Hilde?

HILDE [she answers, motionless, as if half-asleep]. All I had there was a cage.

SOLNESS. And you have no desire to go back?

HILDE [as before]. A bird of the forests can't be caged in.

SOLNESS. They would much rather be free and able to hunt in the open . . .

HILDE [still motionless]. The bird of prey likes best to hunt . . .

SOLNESS. Oh! If we only had the viking spirit in life today . . .

HILDE [she opens her eyes and speaks in her usual voice, but does not move]. And that other thing—what was it you called it?

SOLNESS. A robust conscience.

[HILDE sits up on the bench. He eyes again radiate happiness. She nods to him.]

HILDE. I know what you will build next, Mr. Solness.

SOLNESS. Then you know more than I do, Hilde.

HILDE. Yes—builders are so stupid.

SOLNESS. And what will I build?

HILDE [again with a nod]. The castle.

SOLNESS. What castle?

HILDE. Don't you know? My castle, of course.

SOLNESS. Oh? Now you want a castle?

HILDE. If you don't mind—you owe me a kingdom—don't you?

SOLNESS. Yes, I just now hear you say I do.

HILDE. And, as you owe me a kingdom, you must also owe me a castle. The two go together, you must know!

SOLNESS [becoming more and more animated]. Yes—they usually do, yes.

HILDE. Very well. Then go ahead and build it for me. And don't procrastinate!

SOLNESS [with a laugh]. This very minute, you mean?

HILDE. Exactly! For the ten years are up now. And I don't care to wait any longer. Therefore—let us have the castle, Mr. Master Builder!

SOLNESS. It is certainly no laughing matter to be in debt to you, Hilde.

HILDE. You should have thought of that before. Now it is too late. Therefore . . . [She raps on the table.] . . . my castle—on the table with it! It is my castle—and I don't want to wait for it!

SOLNESS [*he leans over toward her, now more in earnest, and rests his arms on the table*]. What had you thought this castle of yours should look like, Hilde?

[*Her expression gradually becomes more and more puzzling. It seems as though she were gazing into the innermost recesses of her soul. Her words come slowly.*]

HILDE. My castle must be situated away up high—at the very top of a mountain crest. It must be open to light and air on all sides so that I can gaze far into the distance in all directions.

SOLNESS. And you will want a high tower on it, I imagine?

HILDE. And at the very top there shall be a balcony. And there I shall stand and . . .

SOLNESS [*instinctively clutching at his forehead*]. I don't see how you can ever stand looking down from that balcony at such a dizzying height!

HILDE. Oh—yes! That is exactly why I want to be up there—so that I can look down upon the people below—the ones who build temples—and homes—homes for fathers and mothers and their little children. And I shall invite you to come and look down with me from there.

SOLNESS [*in a suppressed tone of voice*]. Will the Master Builder be permitted to come and see the princess?

HILDE. If the Master Builder would like to—yes.

SOLNESS [*in a softer, still more subdued voice*]. Then I think he will come.

HILDE [*with a nod*]. The Master Builder will come.

SOLNESS. And yet he will never build again—poor Master Builder!

HILDE [*animatedly*]. Oh yes—yes! We two shall build together. And we will build the loveliest—the most beautiful thing there is in all the world!

SOLNESS [*excitedly*]. Hilde—tell me—what that might be!

[HILDE *looks at him with a smile, shaking her head a little. Then she purses her lips and speaks as if to a child.*]

HILDE. Builders are really exceedingly —exceedingly stupid people.

SOLNESS. Why, of course, they are stupid. Of couse they are. But tell me what it is, then—this that is to be the most beautiful thing in the world and which you and I are to build together . . .

HILDE [*after a brief silence, with an indefinable expression in her eyes*]. Castles in the air!

SOLNESS. Castles in the air?

HILDE [*with a nod*]. Yes—castles in the air! Do you know what such a castle in the air is called?

SOLNESS. Well—you say it is more beautiful than anything else in the world . . .

HILDE [*rises in a temper; with a deprecating gesture*]. Why, certainly—certainly! Castles in the air—they are so convenient to fall back upon, to take refuge in. And so easy to build, too . . . [*She gives him a scornful look.*] . . . especially for such builders as have a—a dizzy conscience.

SOLNESS [*gets up*]. From this day on, Hilde, you and I will build together.

HILDE [*with a smile, tinged with doubt*]. A real castle in the air?

SOLNESS. Yes—on a rockbed foundation.

[RAGNAR BROVIK *enters from the house. He carries a large green wreath, studded with flowers, and decorated with ribbons.*]

HILDE [*bursts out happily*]. The wreath! Oh! This is going to be awfully exciting!

SOLNESS [*with astonishment*]. How is it that you are bringing the wreath, Ragnar?

RAGNAR. I had promised the foreman I would.

SOLNESS [*relieved*]. Oh. Then your father is getting better?

RAGNAR. No.

SOLNESS. Didn't what I wrote help to put new life into your father?

RAGNAR. It came too late.

SOLNESS. Too late!

RAGNAR. When Kaja came with the drawings, he was already unconscious. He had had a stroke.

SOLNESS. Then you must go home to him and—and look after him!

RAGNAR. He doesn't need me now.

SOLNESS. But you should be there just the same, don't you think?

RAGNAR. She is at his bedside.

SOLNESS [*a little hesitantly*]. Kaja?

RAGNAR [*with a dark look at him*]. Yes —Kaja, yes.

SOLNESS. Go home to them, Ragnar.

They both need you. And let me have the wreath.

RAGNAR [suppressing a sarcastic smile]. You don't mean that you yourself—that you intend to . . .

SOLNESS. I'll take it down there myself. [Takes the wreath from RAGNAR.] And you go home now. We don't need you today.

RAGNAR. I am aware you don't need me any more. But today I am staying.

SOLNESS. Well, then—do . . . if that's what you want.

HILDE [by the balustrade]. Master Builder—here is where I want to stand and watch you.

SOLNESS. Watch me?

HILDE. It will be frightfully exciting!

SOLNESS [in an undertone]. Let's talk about that between ourselves later, Hilde.

[Carrying the wreath, he goes down the steps that lead into the garden, is seen walking through it and then disappears out of sight. HILDE watches him for a few moments, then turns to RAGNAR.]

HILDE. It seems to me you could at least have thanked him.

RAGNAR. Thanked him? Should I have thanked him?

HILDE. Yes, you certainly should have!

RAGNAR. If I were to thank anyone, I imagine it should be you.

HILDE. How can you talk like that?

RAGNAR [without retorting to her]. But be on your guard, Miss Wangel! For you don't know him yet as he really is.

HILDE [passionately]. Oh—I know him better than any of you!

RAGNAR [with an embittered laugh]. And you think I should thank him! Thank him for holding me back year after year! For sowing a doubt in my father's mind and making him lose faith in me. For making me doubt myself . . . And why did he do it? Because . . .

HILDE [as if sensing the truth]. Because of what? Tell me quickly!

RAGNAR. So that he could keep her with him!

HILDE [with a sudden movement toward him]. The girl at the high desk?

RAGNAR. Yes.

HILDE [threateningly, with clenched fist]. It is not true! You are lying!

RAGNAR. I didn't want to believe it, either—until today—when she told me herself.

HILDE [as if beside herself]. What did she say? I want to know—this minute—this very minute!

RAGNAR. She said that he had taken complete possession of her—body and soul—her mind—her heart! She tells me she can never be away from him, never escape from him—that she has to be wherever he is . . .

HILDE [her eyes flashing]. She won't be allowed to!

RAGNAR [as if trying to explore what is in her mind]. Who will not allow her?

HILDE [spontaneously]. He won't allow her either!

RAGNAR. No, of course not! I understand it all now! From now on she would only be—be in the way.

HILDE. You understand nothing—if you talk like that! But now I shall tell you why he was so anxious to keep his hold on her.

RAGNAR. Why was he so anxious?

HILDE. Because he was afraid of losing you.

RAGNAR. Did he tell you that?

HILDE. No. But that was the reason. It couldn't be anything else. [Savagely.] I want it—I want that to be the reason!

RAGNAR. However—the moment you arrived—he let her go.

HILDE. It was you—it was you he let go! You don't really think he would care for a young woman like her, do you?

RAGNAR [reflecting]. You don't think he could have been afraid of me, do you?

HILDE. He afraid! I wouldn't be so conceited as to think that, if I were you.

RAGNAR. But I don't doubt he realized long ago that I, too, had capabilities. Afraid of me, yes! For that is just what he is: a coward!

HILDE. He—a coward! You are not really trying to make me believe that!

RAGNAR. He is a coward in some ways —he is—the great Master Builder! He robs people of their happiness in life— just as he crushed my father's happiness and mine. When it comes to doing that —then he shows no fear. But—when it comes to climbing an ordinary scaffolding —he would probably pray to God to deliver him from that!

HILDE. Oh—if you had only seen him

as I once saw him—high up in the air—
at a dizzying height!

RAGNAR. And you have!

HILDE. I most certainly have! Oh, he
was so full of courage and spirit—so fear-
less—where he stood at the top of the
spire and hung the wreath upon the
weathervane!

RAGNAR. I have heard that he was reckless enough to do it once—just one
single time in his life. We younger ones
have often wondered about that. But no
power on earth seems to be able to get
him to do it again!

HILDE. He will today!

RAGNAR [sarcastically]. You don't really
believe that?

HILDE. You will see!

RAGNAR. We shall never see it—
neither you nor I!

HILDE [in a violent, unruly outburst].
I want him to do it! I want to see it! I
must see it!

RAGNAR. But you won't! He hasn't the
courage. It's a weakness with him—a
defect, he has—the great Master Builder!

[MRS. SOLNESS comes out on the terrace from the house. She looks
around.]

MRS. SOLNESS. He isn't here. Where
can he be?

RAGNAR. Mr. Solness is over at the villa
with the workmen.

HILDE. He took the wreath with him
when he left here.

MRS. SOLNESS [terrified]. He took the
wreath with him! Oh God! Oh, my God!
Brovik—you must go over and talk to
him! Get him to come back up here!

RAGNAR. Shall I say that you would
like to speak with him, Mrs. Solness?

MRS. SOLNESS. Yes, yes, dear Brovik—
do that. No, no—don't say that I would
like him to come . . . Tell him there is
somebody here who . . . And tell him to
come at once.

RAGNAR. Very well, Mrs. Solness, I'll
tell him. [He goes down the flight of
steps that leads to the garden and then
disappears through the garden.]

MRS. SOLNESS. Oh, Miss Wangel, I
can't tell you how concerned I am about
him.

HILDE. But is this anything to be so
terribly afraid of?

MRS. SOLNESS. Oh but—don't you understand? Suppose he should really go

through with it! Suppose he actually gets
the notion to climb the scaffolding!

HILDE [full of excitement]. Do you
think he will?

MRS. SOLNESS. Oh, one never knows
what he might take into his head to do.
He is likely to do anything.

HILDE. Aha! Perhaps you even think
that he is a little . . .

MRS. SOLNESS. I don't know what to
think about him any more. Doctor
Herdal has just told me all sorts of
things; and when I add them all up together with certain remarks I have heard
him make . . .

[DOCTOR HERDAL looks out through
the door.]

DOCTOR HERDAL. Won't he be here
soon?

MRS. SOLNESS. Yes, he ought to be
here shortly. At any rate, I have sent
word to him.

DOCTOR HERDAL [coming up to her].
But I think you should go inside, Mrs.
Solness.

MRS. SOLNESS. Oh no, oh no! I want to
stay out here and wait for Halvard.

DOCTOR HERDAL. Yes, but some ladies
have come to call on you . . .

MRS. SOLNESS. Oh heavens! That, too!
And at a time like this!

DOCTOR HERDAL. They are anxious to
see the ceremony.

MRS. SOLNESS. Well, well—then I
imagine I'll have to go in to them—for it
is my duty, of course.

HILDE. Why couldn't you just ask
them to leave?

MRS. SOLNESS. Oh—no! That wouldn't
do! Absolutely not! As long as they are
here, it is my duty to receive them. But
you remain here for a while . . . and detain him when he comes.

DOCTOR HERDAL. And try to hold him
up here! Keep talking to him as long as
you can.

MRS. SOLNESS. Yes, do that, dear Miss
Wangel. Don't let him get away—be
sure to keep him here.

HILDE. Don't you think you are the
right person to do that?

MRS. SOLNESS. Oh God—yes, it's my
duty, of course. But when one has so
many other duties here and there, one
can't . . .

DOCTOR HERDAL [looking toward the
garden]. He is coming!

MRS. SOLNESS. And just as I have to go inside!

DOCTOR HERDAL [to HILDE]. Don't tell him I am here.

HILDE. Don't worry! I am quite sure I can find something else to talk to him about.

MRS. SOLNESS. And don't let him get away from you. But I think you can hold him better than anyone else.

[MRS. SOLNESS and DOCTOR HERDAL go inside. HILDE remains standing on the terrace. SOLNESS comes up the flight of steps leading from the garden.]

SOLNESS. I understand there is someone here who wants to see me.

HILDE. So there is, Master Builder Solness. It is I.

SOLNESS. Oh, it's you Hilde. I was afraid it might be Aline and the Doctor.

HILDE. You seem to be rather frightened of them. Are you?

SOLNESS. Is that what you think?

HILDE. Yes, and I also hear you are afraid of crawling up one of those scaffoldings.

SOLNESS. Well—that's an entirely different matter.

HILDE. But you are afraid! Aren't you?

SOLNESS. Yes—I am.

HILDE. Afraid of falling down and killing yourself?

SOLNESS. No—that's not the reason.

HILDE. Of what are you afraid, then?

SOLNESS. I have a fear of—of retribution, Hilde.

HILDE. Retribution? [She shakes her head.] That you will have to explain . . .

SOLNESS. Sit down—and I will tell you something.

HILDE. Yes—tell me—I can't wait . . . [She sits down on one of the taborets near the balustrade and looks at him expectantly. SOLNESS throws his hat on the table.]

SOLNESS. I believe you know that my very first building contracts had to do with churches.

HILDE [with a nod]. Yes, I know . . .

SOLNESS. For, you see, I was brought up in a devoutly pious home on a farm in the country. And so it seemed natural to me that building churches was the noblest occupation to choose.

HILDE. Yes, I understand . . .

SOLNESS. And I think I can truthfully say that I built these humble little places of worship with such honesty and devotion that—that . . .

HILDE. . . . that? Go on!

SOLNESS. Well—that I felt that He should have been pleased with me.

HILDE. He? Which he?

SOLNESS. He—to whom they were dedicated, of course. He—to whose glory and praise they were erected . . .

HILDE. Oh, I see! And are you so certain that—that He wasn't pleased with you—as you say?

SOLNESS [with scorn]. He—pleased with me! How can you ask such a question, Hilde? He—who let the troll in me take possession and run riot at will! He—who sent the trolls to be at my beck and call, to serve me night and day—all these—these . . .

HILDE. The demons?

SOLNESS. Yes—both kinds. Oh yes—I found out soon enough that He was not pleased with me. [Mysteriously.] You know—it was really because of that He let the old house burn down.

HILDE. Was that the reason?

SOLNESS. Why, yes—don't you see? What He wanted was to make me a great builder of churches—a master builder—so that I could erect still loftier, more glorious temples to His honor. In the beginning I did not grasp just what was in His mind. Then, suddenly, I realized.

HILDE. When was that?

SOLNESS. It was when I was building the church tower at Lysanger.

HILDE. I thought so.

SOLNESS. You see, Hilde—up there I was among strangers, and I spent my time alone—by myself. And I had time to ponder; and I kept brooding, and probing myself. It was then it suddenly became clear to me why He had taken my little ones from me. He took them because He was afraid I would be more attached to them than to the mission He had given me. Nothing—neither happiness nor love—was to stand in the way of that mission, you understand. I was to devote my entire life to building for Him—and to nothing else. [With a laugh.] But I soon made an end of that.

HILDE. How? What did you do?

SOLNESS. First I searched my soul through and through, probed myself thoroughly . . .

HILDE. Then what did you do?

SOLNESS. Then—I did *the impossible.* I as well as He!

HILDE. The impossible?

SOLNESS. I had never before had the courage to climb to any great height—I always faltered when I looked down below. But that day I overcame my fear—and did the impossible!

HILDE [*jumps to her feet*]. Yes—yes —that day you did!

SOLNESS. And as I stood up there, at the very top, and placed the wreath on the weathervane, I spoke to Him and said: "Now listen to me, Omnipotent One! From this day on I will be a free and independent builder—no less free and independent than You are. I want to be just as independent in my work as You are in Your domain. I will never again build temples for You—nothing but homes for human beings.

HILDE [*with wide open, shining eyes*]. That must have been the singing I heard in the air!

SOLNESS. But my refusal brought grist to His mill afterward.

HILDE. I am afraid I don't understand?

SOLNESS [*with a disheartened glance at* HILDE]. This work of putting up homes for people—it just isn't worth the trouble, Hilde.

HILDE. Is that how you feel about it now?

SOLNESS. Yes—I see it now. People don't make use of them—don't use them as homes—nor for happiness. And I myself wouldn't have made much use of such a home either, if I had had one. [*With a quiet, embittered laugh.*] As I now look back on it all—of what benefit have my efforts been? Nothing ever built —*really* built. And no effort, no sacrifice made for achieving real building. Nothing! Nothing! I have accomplished nothing!

HILDE. And so you will never build anything from now on?

SOLNESS [*with a sudden animation*]. Yes—Now I am really going to begin to build!

HILDE. What do you plan to build? What? Tell me quickly!

SOLNESS. I will build the only refuge in which human happiness can find a haven . . . *That* is what I will build now.

HILDE [*with a firm look at him*]. Master Builder—you are speaking about our castles in the air now, aren't you?

SOLNESS. Our castles in the air, yes.

HILDE. I am afraid you would have a dizzy spell before they were halfway up.

SOLNESS. Not if you were by my side and held me by the hand, Hilde.

HILDE [*with a touch of suppressed indignation*]. I only? Will there not be others who come along?

SOLNESS. What others do you mean?

HILDE. Oh—she . . . that Kaja who stands at the high desk. Poor girl! Don't you think you would like to have her come along, too?

SOLNESS. Oho! So it was about her Aline sat and talked to you, was it?

HILDE. Is it true, or isn't it?

SOLNESS. I am not going to answer that question! You must have absolute and undivided confidence in me!

HILDE. For ten years I have believed in you uncompromisingly, completely!

SOLNESS. You must continue to have faith in me!

HILDE. Then let me see you high in the air—free and reckless—recklessly free!

SOLNESS [*with heavy heart*]. Oh, Hilde! I can't be doing that at just any time!

HILDE [*fervently*]. I want you to do it! I want you to do it! [*Imploringly.*] Just this one time, Master Builder! Do the *impossible* once more!

SOLNESS [*looking deep into her eyes*]. If I should do it, Hilde—then I will stand up there and speak to Him as I did the time before.

HILDE [*with growing excitement*]. What will you be saying to Him?

SOLNESS. I will say to Him: Listen to me, Almighty Lord! You may now judge me according to Your will. But from this day on, I shall build only the fairest thing in all the universe . . .

HILDE [*with exaltation*]. Yes—yes— yes . . .

SOLNESS. . . . and I shall build it in partnership with a princess whom I love . . .

HILDE. Yes, do tell Him that! Tell Him that!

SOLNESS. Yes—and then I will say to Him: Now I shall go down and hold her in my embrace and I shall kiss her . . .

HILDE. More than once! Many times! Say that to Him!

SOLNESS. Many, many times I will tell him!

HILDE. And after that?

SOLNESS. Then I shall wave my hat—and come down to earth again—and do what I told Him I would do.

HILDE [with outstretched arms]. Now I see you once more as I did at that time—when there was singing in the air!

SOLNESS [looks at her with head bowed]. Hilde! How did you ever become the way you are?

HILDE. Whatever did you do to me to make me what I am?

SOLNESS [spontaneously and firmly]. The princess shall have her castle.

HILDE [jubilantly clapping her hands]. Oh! Master Builder! My beautiful, beautiful castle! Our castle in the air!

SOLNESS. Built on a rockbed foundation!

[Meantime a crowd has been gathering on the road outside the garden. The people are, however, only barely visible between the trees. From the vicinity of the new villa in the distance can be heard music played by a brass band. MRS. SOLNESS, wearing a fur neckpiece, DOCTOR HERDAL, carrying her white shawl over his arm, and SEVERAL LADIES come out on the terrace. At the same time, RAGNAR BROVIK enters by the steps from the garden.]

MRS. SOLNESS [to RAGNAR]. Is there to be music also?

RAGNAR. Yes. It's the band of the Building Workers' Union. [To SOLNESS.] The foreman asked me to tell you that he is ready to go up with the wreath.

SOLNESS [taking his hat]. Very well, I'll go over there myself.

MRS. SOLNESS [showing anxiety]. What do you have to do over there?

SOLNESS [brusquely]. I should be over there with the men.

MRS. SOLNESS. Well, but—but down below, Halvard—only below!

SOLNESS. Isn't that what I always do—stay below? [He goes down the steps and disappears through the garden. MRS. SOL-NESS calls after him, standing by the balustrade.]

MRS. SOLNESS. And do ask the man to be careful when he goes up the scaffolding! Will you promise me that, Halvard?

DOCTOR HERDAL [to MRS. SOLNESS]. Now you see I was right! He has put this crazy notion out of his head.

MRS. SOLNESS. Oh! I am so relieved! Two men have already fallen down—and both were killed instantly. [Turning to HILDE.] Oh, Miss Wangel—let me thank you for holding on to him so conscientiously. I don't think I could ever have done it.

DOCTOR HERDAL [jovially]. Yes, yes, Miss Wangel—you know how to keep your hold on a man, if you really make up your mind, I dare say.

[MRS. SOLNESS and DOCTOR HERDAL go over to the LADIES who are standing close to the steps and are looking out over the garden. HILDE remains at the balustrade, in the foreground. RAGNAR walks over to her.]

RAGNAR [suppressing a laugh, he says slowly, in an undertone]. Miss Wangel—do you see all those young people out there on the road?

HILDE. Yes.

RAGNAR. They are my friends—my fellow apprentices and workers. They have come to watch their master.

HILDE. Why should they want to watch him, I wonder?

RAGNAR. They are looking forward to seeing him lose courage and back down, afraid to climb as high as his own house.

HILDE. So that's what they have come for, these fellows?

RAGNAR [full of indignation and sarcasm]. He has kept us down for so long now; and this time we will see that he, too, is kept down.

HILDE. You will not see it! Not this time!

RAGNAR [with a smile]. You don't say! What will we see?

HILDE. High up—high up at the top of the weathervane you will see him!

RAGNAR [with a laugh]. He—at the top of the tower! You don't really believe that?

HILDE. He is determined to get to the top! So you will see him there—naturally!

RAGNAR. He is determined, you say. I can believe that! But he can't—and never will! His head would be swirling long, long before he was halfway up. He'd have to crawl down again on his hands and knees.

DOCTOR HERDAL [pointing in the direction of the new villa]. Look! There goes the foreman up the ladder!

MRS. SOLNESS. And the wreath—he has to carry that, too . . . Oh! I do hope he doesn't slip!

RAGNAR [staring in disbelief, he cries out]. But it is not . . . It is . . .

HILDE [bursts out jubilantly]. It's the Master Builder himself!

MRS. SOLNESS [with a shriek of terror]. Yes—it is Halvard! Oh, heavenly Father! Halvard! Halvard!

DOCTOR HERDAL. Quiet! Don't scream that way!

MRS. SOLNESS [almost beside herself]. I must go to him! I must make him come down!

DOCTOR HERDAL [holding her back]. Don't move—stand absolutely still—all of you! Don't make a sound!

HILDE [motionless, she follows SOLNESS with her eyes]. He is going up—step by step! Higher—higher—and still higher! Look! Look!

RAGNAR [breathlessly]. He can't go much higher—he will have to turn back —or he will . . .

HILDE. He keeps climbing . . . now he will soon have reached the top . . .

MRS. SOLNESS. Oh—I shall die of fright —I can't bear to look at him!

DOCTOR HERDAL. You shouldn't be watching him, then.

HILDE. Now he has reached the top of the scaffolding! He is at the top!

DOCTOR HERDAL. No one move! Do you hear!

HILDE [quietly exulting, with fervor]. At last! At last! Now I see him again— magnificent and free in spirit!

RAGNAR [nearly speechless]. But this is . . . Why—this is . . .

HILDE. This is the way I have seen him these ten years! See how sure of himself he is! This is what I call exciting, thrilling! Look at him! Now he is hanging the wreath on the weathervane!

RAGNAR. This is like looking at something that is wholly impossible.

HILDE. What he is doing is just that: the impossible! [Again she has that indefinable expression in her eyes.] Do you see someone else up there with him?

RAGNAR. There is no one else up there.

HILDE. Yes—there is someone up there he is quarreling with.

RAGNAR. You are wrong.

HILDE. And you don't hear the singing in the air, either?

RAGNAR. You are hearing the wind up in the tree tops . . .

HILDE. I hear singing—mighty, wonderful singing. [Cries out in wild, uninhibited exultation and joy.] Look! Look! Now he is waving his hat! He is waving to us! Oh—but wave—wave back to him! For now it is done! [She snatches the white shawl from DOCTOR HERDAL, waves it in the air and cries aloud to SOLNESS.] Hurrah for Master Builder Solness!

DOCTER HERDAL. Stop it! Stop it! For God's sake!

[THE LADIES on the terrace wave their handkerchiefs, and cheering is heard from the crowd on the road. Suddenly there is a silence and the people on the road give a shriek of horror. Hurtling through the air and falling among the trees can faintly be seen a body, together with planks, débris, etc., from the scaffolding.]

MRS. SOLNESS and THE LADIES. He is falling! He is falling!

[MRS. SOLNESS totters and falls over in a faint. Confused and amidst outcries, THE LADIES come to her rescue. The crowd outside storms into the garden, breaking down the fence. DOCTOR HERDAL likewise hastens into the garden. There is a brief pause.]

HILDE [her eyes staring fixedly on the tower, she says as if turned to stone]. My Master Builder!

RAGNAR [trembling, he supports himself against the balustrade]. There can't be anything left of him! He must have died instantaneously!

ONE OF THE LADIES [while MRS. SOLNESS is being carried into the house]. Run for the doctor . . . bring him back . . .

RAGNAR. I can't move . . .

SECOND LADY. Then call to someone— to bring him back.

RAGNAR [in an effort to call out]. How is he? Is he still alive?

A VOICE [*from down in the garden*]. Halvard Solness is dead.

OTHER VOICES [*from somewhat closer*]. His head is completely crushed! He fell on a rock!

HILDE [*turns to* RAGNAR *and says in a quiet voice*]. Now I no longer see *him* up there . . .

RAGNAR. This is horrible! But it was too much for him.

HILDE [*as if in quiet triumph over something lost*]. But he did reach the top —the very top! And I heard harps in the air . . . [*She waves the shawl in the air and screams out with wild intensity.*] My —my Master Builder!

Michael Meyer

IBSEN AND EMILIE BARDACH

Ibsen wrote *The Master Builder* in Christiania in 1892, at the age of sixty-four. It was the first play he had written in Norway since *The Pretenders* in 1863.

The previous summer, he had left his home in Munich for a holiday to the North Cape. While he was there, he decided to stay in Christiania over the winter; and in fact he stayed for the remaining fifteen years of his life.

There were several reasons for this decision to settle again in his native country after twenty-seven years abroad. He told Georg Brandes that it would be more convenient for him financially, but Fru Ibsen later said she thought it was because he wanted to die in Norway. During his visit in 1885 he had been unwell, and had then spoken of settling there; and in the beginning of 1890 he had a severe attack of influenza, which may have helped to remind him that he was no longer young. Moreover, he still had the obsessive longing for the sea which had twice recently driven him northwards (in 1885 and 1887), and a further factor was that his son Sigurd was now very active in Norwegian politics, and was being spoken of as a likely Foreign Minister as soon as Norway should obtain her independence from Sweden. Ibsen was very devoted to his son, and although he himself did not nowadays take much interest in politics he found himself acclaimed by both the right and the left wing parties. Life in Norway had seemed insufferable to him when he had been impoverished and unsuccessful; now that he was a national hero, it held certain attractions. So he stayed.

Departing from his usual routine of writing only during the summer and autumn, he began work on a new play that March (1892). Before the spring was over, however, he scrapped everything he had written, and did not start again until August. He finished his new draft some time in October, and *The Master Builder* was published by Gyldendals of Copenhagen on December 12, 1892. People everywhere were puzzled by it, as they had been puzzled by his two preceding plays, *The Lady from the Sea* and *Hedda Gabler*, but for a different reason. Some new element had entered into Ibsen's work; it had been perceptible in *Hedda Gabler*, but in *The Master Builder* it was more than perceptible; it stuck out for all to see. Put bluntly, *The Master Builder* seemed primarily to be a play about sex; one did not need to wait for Freud to be made uneasy by all that talk about the beauty of towers and spires. People speculated as to what new influence could have entered into the old man's life to turn his thoughts so sharply in this direction, and not until after Ibsen's death in 1906 was the answer given.

In that year, Georg Brandes published a series of letters which Ibsen had written between October 1889 and December 1890 (i.e., eighteen to twelve months before he began *The Master Builder*) to a young Austrian girl named Emilie Bardach. These revealed that, in the summer of 1889, when Ibsen was sixty-one and Emilie was eighteen, they had met at Gossensass in the Austrian Tyrol and that some kind of infatuation had resulted; whether mutual or one-sided was not quite clear. They had corresponded for over a year, and then Ibsen, gently but firmly, had told her not to write to him any more.

SOURCE: From the introduction to "The Master Builder" from the book *When We Dead Awaken and Three Other Plays*, Vol. 1, by Henrik Ibsen, translation by Michael Meyer. Copyright © 1960 by Michael Meyer. Reprinted by permission of Doubleday & Company, Inc.

At about the time these letters appeared, a friend of Ibsen's, the German literary historian Julius Elias, published an account of a conversation he had had with Ibsen about Emilie Bardach which seemed to put the incident into proportion. This conversation had taken place in Berlin in February 1891, over lunch, while Ibsen was waiting for a train:

An expansive mood came over Ibsen and, chuckling over his champagne glass, he said: "Do you know, my next play is already hovering before me—in general outline, of course. One thing I can see clearly, though—an experience I once had myself—a female character. Very interesting—very interesting." Then he related how he had met in the Tyrol a Viennese girl of very remarkable character, who had at once made him her confidant. The gist of it was that she was not interested in the idea of marrying some decently brought up young man; most likely she would never marry. What tempted, fascinated, and delighted her was to lure other women's husbands away from them. She was a demonic little wrecker; she often seemed to him like a little bird of prey, who would gladly have included him among her victims. He had studied her very, very closely. But she had had no great success with him. "She did not get hold of me, but I got hold of her —for my play. Then I fancy she consoled herself with someone else."

This seemed to settle the matter. Ibsen's version of Emilie's character, or Elias's report of it, received general acceptance, and Emilie Bardach went down to history, while she was still a young woman (she survived into the Second World War) as a predatory little monster, more or less identical with the character of Hilde Wangel which Ibsen based on her. In 1923, however, two remarkable articles entitled "Ibsen and Emilie Bardach" were published in the American *Century Magazine*. The author was Basil King, an Ibsen enthusiast; in 1908, he had met Emilie, then a woman of thirty-seven, "gentle of manner, soft of voice, dressed with the distinction of which Viennese women have long possessed the art . . . going to Paris for the spring, to London for the season, and often to Scotland for country-house gatherings." She allowed King to see, and later to quote from, the diary she had kept during the time she had known and corresponded with Ibsen. These articles caused no particular sensation at the time, interest in Ibsen being rather low during the early twenties; there seems, however, no reason to doubt the authenticity of the diary extracts, and they go much further than Ibsen's account of the incident to explain the stormy and dynamic quality of his last five plays, after the comparative optimism of *The Lady from the Sea*.

Ibsen had come to Gossensass in July of 1889. He had holidayed there on several previous occasions, but this was his first visit for five years, and the town had decided to celebrate his return by naming his old lookout on the hill the Ibsenplatz. There was a festal procession, and Ibsen, despite the steep ascent, climbed at the head of it and "received with friendliness and dignity all the homage that was accorded him." Emilie Bardach wrote in her diary (August 5, 1889):

The weather is very bad and we cannot make any excursions. The day of the Ibsen fete has been the only fine one; but I washed my hair and could not go. After the concert, however, I made his acquaintance in a way quite delightful.

There was a valley on the outskirts of the town named the Pflerschtal, with a stream flowing through it, and a view of mountains and glaciers. While walking here, Ibsen saw a girl seated on a bench with a book. He came and sat beside her, and learned her name, her parentage, her home residence, and the fact that in Gossensass they lived so near together that his windows looked into hers. A few days later she ran into him at a dull birthday party. "It is a pity," she noted, "that German gives him so much difficulty, as apart from that we understand each other so well."

She fell ill and, a few days later, Ibsen came to see her, climbing over the garden gate to do so. "He remained with me a long while, and was both kind and sympathetic." A little later: "We talk a great deal together. His ardour ought to make me feel proud." Then:

Ibsen has begun to talk to me quite seriously about myself. He stayed a long time with me on Saturday, and also again this evening. Our being so much together cannot but have some powerful influence over me. He puts such strong feeling into what he says to me. His words often give me a sensation of terror and cold. He talks about the most serious things in life, and believes in me so much. He expects from me much, much more than, I am afraid, he will ever find. Never in his whole life, he says, has he felt so much joy in knowing anyone. He never admired anyone as he admires me. But all in him is truly good and noble. What a pity it is that I cannot remember all his words! He begs me so intensely to talk freely to him, to be absolutely frank with him, so that we may become fellow-workers together.

Next she writes:

Mama has just gone out, so that I have the room to myself. At last I am free to put down the incredible things of these recent days. How poor and insufficient are the words! Tears say these things better. Passion has come when it cannot lead to anything, when both of us are bound by so many ties. Eternal obstacles! Are they in my will? Or are they in the circumstances? . . . How could I compare anything else that has happened to an outpouring like this? It could never go so far, and yet . . . !

She swings off on to Baron A., the only lover who afforded a standard of comparison.

But how much calmer he was!—how inarticulate!—beside this volcano, so terribly beautiful! Yesterday afternoon, we were alone together at last. Oh, the words!—if only they could have stamped themselves on my heart more deeply and distinctly! All that has been offered me before was only the pretense at love. This is the true love, the ideal, he says, to which without knowing it he gave himself in his art. At last he is a real poet through pain and renunciation. And yet he is glad of having known me—the most beautiful! the most wonderful! Too late! How small I seem to myself that I cannot spring to him!

Neither Ibsen's wife nor Emilie's mother suspected what was afoot. But:

The obstacles!—how they grow more numerous, the more I think of them!

The difference of age!—his wife!—his son!—all that there is to keep us apart! Was it inevitable? Could I have foreseen it? Could I have prevented it? When he talks to me as he does, I often feel that I must go far away from here—far away!—and yet I suffer at the thought of leaving him. I suffer most from his impatience, his restlessness. I begin to feel it now even when we are in the salon, quite apart from each other.

It all came to me so suddenly! I noticed first how he began to change his regular ways of life, but I didn't know what it meant. Of course—I was flattered at his sympathy, and at being distinguished among the many who surround him, eager for a word.

An early snowstorm came, and the guests at Gossensass began to leave. Emilie realised they would soon have to part.

And I have nothing to give him, not even my picture, when he is giving me so much. But we both feel it is best to remain outwardly as strangers. His wife shows me much attention. Yesterday I had a long talk with his son.

I am reading Ibsen's *Love's Comedy*, but if anyone comes I am seen holding Beaconsfield's *Endymion* in my hands. Nearly everyone has gone. The days we have still to spend here can now be counted. I don't think about the future. The present is too much. We had a long talk together in the forenoon, and after lunch he came again and sat with me. What am I to think? He says it is to be my life's aim to work with him. We are to write to each other often; but what am I to write?

Ibsen confided his feelings to two ladies. One fainted; another described the scene to Emilie as "beautiful and terrible as an Alpine thunderstorm. She wonders that I do not lose my head. She says that she herself would have been absolutely overcome. This consoles me. I do not seem so weak."

Did something happen between Ibsen and Emilie on September 19, and if so was it anything like what Hilde Wangel describes as having happened between her and Solness on another September 19? Nearly forty years later, in 1927, Emilie told A. E. Zucker that Ibsen had never kissed her; perhaps, with Ibsen as with Solness, these things only happened in his mind. Next day, September 20, he wrote in Emilie's album: "*Hohes, schmerzliches Glück—um das Unerreichbare zu ringen!*"—— "High and painful fate—to struggle for the unattainable!"

A week later, on September 27, Emilie noted in her diary:

> Our last day at Gossensass. Then nothing but memory will remain. Two weeks ago, memory seemed to Ibsen so beautiful, and now—— He says that tomorrow he will stand on the ruins of his happiness. These last two months are more important in his life than everything that has gone before. Am I unnatural in being so terribly quiet and normal? . . . Last evening when Mama went to talk to his wife he came over and sat at our table. We were quite alone. He talked about his plans. I alone am in them—I, and I again. I feel quieter because he is quieter, though yesterday he was terrible.

That night, at 3 A.M., the express from Verona to Vienna passed through Gossensass, and Ibsen left on it. The same night, Emilie wrote in her diary:

> He means to possess me. This is his absolute will. He intends to overcome all obstacles. I do what I can to keep him from feeling this, and yet I listen as he describes what is to lie before us —going from one country to another— I with him—enjoying his triumphs together . . . Our parting was easier than I had feared.

Emilie told Zucker in 1927 that Ibsen had, in Gossensass, "spoken to her of the possibility of a divorce and of a subsequent union with her, in the course of which they were to travel widely and see the world." The last entry in her diary would seem to bear this out. Once back in Munich, however, Ibsen seemed to resign himself to the impossibility of going through with such a plan. Perhaps he feared the scandal; perhaps he felt a duty towards his sickly and aging wife, who had stood so firmly by him during the long years of failure; perhaps he reflected that the difference of forty-three years between their ages was too great; perhaps, away from Gossensass, he felt old. Probably he felt all these things. At any rate, his letters from Munich to her in Vienna are no more than those of an affectionate old man to a charming school-girl (though we must bear in mind that he is writing in a foreign language which "gives him much difficulty," that he was always an extremely inhibited letter-writer, and that he must have been very careful not to commit himself on paper).

> München, Maximilianstrasse 32.
> October 7, 1889.
>
> With my whole heart I thank you, my beloved Fraulein, for the dear and delightful letter which I received on the last day of my stay at Gossensass, and have read over and over again.
>
> There the last autumn week was a very sad one, or it was so to me. No more sunshine. Everything—gone. The few remaining guests could give me no compensation for the brief and beautiful end-of-summer life. I went to walk in the Pflerschthal. There there is a bench where two can commune together. But the bench was empty, and I went by without sitting down. So, too, the big salon was waste and desolate. . . . Do you remember the big, deep bay-window on the right from the verandah? What a charming niche! The flowers and plants are still there, smelling so sweetly—but how empty— how lonely—how forsaken!
>
> We are back here at home—and you in Vienna. You write that you feel surer of yourself, more independent, happier. How glad I am of these words! I shall say no more.
>
> A new poem begins to dawn in me. I want to work on it this winter, transmuting into it the glowing inspiration of the summer. But the end may be disappointment. I feel it. It is my way. I told you once that I only corresponded by telegraph. So take this letter as it is. You will know what it means. A thousand greetings from your devoted— H. I.

The "poem" may have been *Hedda Gabler*, which he was to write the following year, or it may have been *The Master Builder* itself. He did not in fact write the latter until three years later, but he may have conceived it at this early stage and then, deliberately, put it aside until he could consider it with more detachment.

Emilie's diary, October 8, 1889:

> A few words before I go to bed. I have good news. Today, at last, came Ibsen's long-expected letter. He wants me to read between the lines. But do not the lines themselves say enough?

This evening I paid grandmama a quite unpleasant visit. The weather is hot and stuffy and so is papa's mood. In other days, this would have depressed me; but now I have something to keep me up.

We do not know how she replied to Ibsen, for he did not preserve her letters. On October 15, however, he writes again:

I receive your letter with a thousand thanks—and have read it, and read it again. Here I sit as usual at my desk, and would gladly work, but cannot do so.

My imagination is ragingly at work, but always straying to where in working hours it should not. I cannot keep down the memories of the summer, neither do I want to. The things we have lived through I live again and again—and still again. To make of them a poem is for the time being impossible.

For the time being?

Shall I ever succeed in the future? And do I really wish that I could and would so succeed?

For the moment, at any rate, I cannot—or so I believe. That I feel—that I know.

And yet it must come. Decidedly it must come. But will it? or can it?

Ah, dear Fräulein!—but forgive me! —you wrote so charmingly in your last —no, no! God forbid!—in your previous letter you wrote so charmingly: "I am not Fräulein for you"——So, dear Child—for that you surely are for me —tell me—do you remember that once we talked about Stupidity and Folly— or, more correctly, I talked about it; and you took up the role of teacher, and remarked, in your soft, musical voice, and with your far-away look, that there is always a difference between Stupidity and Folly.... Well, then, I keep thinking over and over again: Was it a Stupidity or was it a bit of Folly that we should have come together? Or was it both a Stupidity and a bit of Folly? Or was it neither?

I believe the last is the only supposition that would stand the test. It was a simple necessity of nature. It was equally our fate.... Your always devoted H. I.

On receipt of this letter, Emilie wrote in her diary:

I left it unopened till I had finished everything, and could read it quietly. But I was not quiet after reading it. Why does he not tell me of something to read which would feed my

mind, instead of writing in a way to inflame my already excited imagination? I shall answer very soberly.

Ibsen to Emilie, October 29, 1889:

I have been meaning every day to write you a few words, but I wanted to enclose the photograph. This is still unfinished, and my letter must go off without it....

How charmingly you write! Please keep sending me a few lines, whenever you have a half hour not good for anything else.

So you leave my letters unopened till you are alone and quite undisturbed! Dear Child! I shall not try to thank you. That would be superfluous. You know what I mean.

Don't be uneasy because just now I cannot work. In the back of my mind, I am working all the time. I am dreaming over something which, when it has ripened, will become a poem.

Someone is coming. Can write no further. Next time a longer letter. Your truly devoted H. I.

Emilie's diary:

I wrote to him on Monday, very late at night. Though I was tired, I did not want to put off doing so, because I had to thank him for the books I received on Sunday. The same evening I had read Rosmersholm, parts of which are very fine. I have to make so many duty calls, but this and a great many other things I can stand better than I used to. They are only the outward things; my inner world is something very different. Oh, the terror and beauty of having him care about me as he never cared about anyone else! But when he is suffering he calls it hohes, schmerzliches Glück—high, and painful fate!

Ibsen to Emilie, November 19, 1889:

At last I can send you the new picture. I hope you may find it a better likeness than the one you have already. A German sketch of my life will appear within a few days, and you will receive it at once. Read it when you have the time. It will tell you my story up to the end of last year.

Heartfelt thanks for your dear letter; but what do you think of me for not having answered it earlier? And yet— you know it well—you are always in my thoughts, and will remain there. An active exchange of letters is on my side

an impossibility. I have already said so.
Take me as I am. . . .

I am greatly preoccupied with the
preparations for my new work. Sit tight
at my desk the whole day. Go out only
toward evening. I dream and remember
and write. To dream is fine; but the
reality at times can be still finer. Your
most devoted H. I.

On the back of the photograph stood
the inscription: "An die Maisonne eines
Septemberlebens [To the May sun of a
September life]."

Ibsen to Emilie, December 6, 1889:

Two dear, dear letters have I had
from you, and answered neither till now.
What do you think of me? But I cannot find the quiet necessary to writing
you anything orderly or straightforward.
This evening I must go to the theatre
to see An Enemy of the People. The
mere thought of it is a torture. Then,
too, I must give up for the time being
the hope of getting your photograph.
But better so than to have an unfavour-
able picture. Besides, how vividly your
dear, serene features remain with me in
my memory! The same enigmatic princess stands behind them. But the enigma itself? One can dream of it, and
write about it—and that I do. It is
some little compensation for the unattainable—for the impenetrable reality.
In my imagination I always see you
wearing the pearls you love so much.
In this taste for pearls I see something
deeper, something hidden. I often think
of it. Sometimes I think I have found
the interpretation—and then again not.
Next time I shall try to answer some
of your questions; but I myself have
so many questions to ask you. I am
always doing it—inwardly—inaudibly.
Your devoted H. I.

In her diary, Emilie repeats his words:
"It is some little compensation for the
unattainable, for the impenetrable reality."

Ibsen to Emilie, December 22, 1889:

How shall I thank you for your dear
and delightful letter? I simply am not
able to, not at least as I should like.
The writing of letters is always hard for
me. I think I have told you so already,
and you will in any case have noticed it
for yourself.

I read your letter over and over, for
through it the voice of the summer
awakens so clearly. I see—I go through
again—the things we lived together. As

a lovely creature of the summer, dear
Princess, I have known you, as a being
of the season of butterflies and wild
flowers. How I should like to see you as
you are in winter! I am always with you
in spirit. I see you in the Ring Strasse,
light, quick, poised like a bird, gracious
in velvet and furs. In soirées, in society,
I also see you, and especially at the
theatre, leaning back, a tired look in
your mysterious eyes. I should like, too,
to see you at home, but here I don't
succeed, as I haven't the data. You have
told me so little of your home-life—
almost nothing definite. As a matter of
fact, dear Princess, in many important details we are strangers to each
other. . . .

More than anything I should like to
see you at home on Christmas night,
where I suppose you will be. As to what
happens to you there, I have no clear
idea. I only imagine—to myself.

And then I have a strange feeling
that you and Christmas don't go well
together. But who knows? Perhaps you
do. In any case accept my heartfelt
wishes and a thousand greetings. Your
always devoted H. I.

Ibsen to Emilie, December 30, 1889:

Your lovely and charming picture,
so speakingly like, has given me a
wholly indescribable joy. I thank you
for it a thousand times, and straight
from the heart. How you have brought
back, now in midwinter, those brief
sunny summer days!

So, too, I thank you from the heart
for your dear, dear letter. From me you
must expect no more than a few words.
I lack the time, and the necessary quiet
and solitude, to write to you as I should
like. . . .

Ibsen to Emilie, January 16, 1890:

How sorry I am to learn that you,
too, have been ill. But what do you
think? I had a strong presentiment that
it was so. In my imagination I saw you
lying in bed, pale, feverish, but sweet
and lovely as ever. . . . How thankful I
am that I have your charming picture!

Ibsen to Emilie, February 6, 1890:

Long, very long, have I left your last,
dear letter—read and read again—without an answer. Take today my heartfelt
thanks for it, but given in very few
words. Henceforth, till we see each
other face to face, you will hear little
from me, and very seldom. Believe me,
it is better so. It is the only right thing.

It is a matter of conscience with me to end our correspondence, or at least to limit it. You yourself should have as little to do with me as possible. With your young life you have other aims to follow, other tasks to fulfil. And I—I have told you so already—can never be content with a mere exchange of letters. For me it is only half the thing; it is a false situation. Not to give myself wholly and without reserve makes me unhappy. It is my nature. I cannot change it. You are so delicately subtle, so instinctively penetrating, that you will easily see what I mean. When we are again together, I shall be able to explain it all more fully. Till then, and always, you will be in my thoughts. You will be so even more when we no longer have to stop at this wearisome halfway-house of correspondence. A thousand greetings. Your H. I.

For four days after the reception of this letter, there is no entry in Emilie's diary. Then she writes of balls, singing lessons, domestic duties; then suddenly: "What is my inner life after Ibsen's letter? I wrote at once and henceforth will be silent, silent." Ten days later: "Will he never write any more? I cannot think about it. Who could? And yet, not to do so is in his nature. In his very kindness there is often cruelty."

For seven months he did not write to her. During this time he was struggling with *Hedda Gabler*. On June 29, he wrote to the Swedish poet, Carl Snoilsky, that he had been hoping to spend the summer in the Tyrol but had encountered difficulties in the writing of his new play and did not want to leave Munich until he had overcome them. He had in fact been planning to return to Gossensass, and from the references in his letters to "when we are together again" I think it is fair to assume that he hoped to meet Emilie there (we must remember that her parents knew nothing of her feelings for Ibsen). It is interesting to note that, in the first draft of *Hedda Gabler*, in the scene where Hedda is showing Løvborg the photographs from her honeymoon, the dialogue runs as follows:

> HEDDA. What was this little country town called?
> TESMAN. What? Let me think. Oh, that's Gossensass, on the Brenner Pass. We stayed a day there——

HEDDA. Yes, and met all those amusing people.

In his final draft, Ibsen struck out all mention of Gossensass, and the dialogue reads:

> HEDDA. Do you remember that little country town?
> TESMAN. Oh, that one below the Brenner Pass? That was where we stayed the night.

King observes: "Though in that play [i.e., *Hedda Gabler*] there is no outward trace of Emilie Bardach or Gossensass, both must be present as vital forces.... It is safe to say that to the girl in Vienna *Hedda Gabler* owes much of its marvellous *élan*. She was not in it, but she was behind it, as, according to her English biographer [Edmund Gosse] she was to be behind everything else for the rest of the poet's life."

In September, Ibsen broke his silence to write Emilie a letter of sympathy on the bereavement of her father, with some news of himself and his family, but no more. On December 30, he writes briefly to thank her for a Christmas present:

> *I have duly received your dear letter, as well as the bell with the beautiful picture. I thank you for them, straight from the heart. My wife finds the picture very pretty. But I beg you, for the time being, not to write to me again. When conditions have changed, I will let you know. I shall soon send you my new play. Accept it in friendship—but in silence. How I should love to see you and talk with you again! A Happy New Year to you and to Madame your mother. Your always devoted H. I.*

She did not write to him again, nor did the meeting to which they had both looked forward so eagerly ever take place. For seven years there was no contact between them. Then, on his seventieth birthday, an occasion of great celebration in Scandinavia, she sent him a telegram of congratulation. His letter of reply was the last message that passed between them:

> *Christiania, March 15, 1898.*
> *Herzlich liebes Fräulein!*
> *Accept my most deeply felt thanks for your message. The summer in Gossensass was the happiest, the most lovely, in my whole life.*
> *I scarcely dare to think of it—and*

yet I must think of it always——— Always!

Your truly devoted H. I.

It is against this background that we must read *The Master Builder*. Other elements, of course, intrude into it. He had returned to Norway by the time he began to write it, and he took pains to make Hilde almost ostentatiously Norwegian in her speech and manners. He had by this time struck up a friendship with a young Norwegian pianist, Hildur Andersen, the daughter of old friends from his Bergen days. She seems to have had many of the qualities which he admired in Emilie, notably the combination of eagerness and sensitivity, and it may be that her name, Hildur, caused him to remember the Hilde whom he had created as a minor character in *The Lady from the Sea* and whom he now resurrected, ten years older, to play a more important role. Aline Solness is plainly based on Ibsen's wife, and the relationship between the Solnesses bears an uncomfortable resemblance to that which appears to have existed at this time in the Ibsen household. Shortly after their return to Norway, Ibsen's mother-in-law, Magdalene Thoresen, wrote in a letter: "They live splendidly, and have an elegant home, though all is pretty much in philistine style. They are two lonely people—each for himself—each absolutely for himself."

A few months before Ibsen began *The Master Builder*, the young novelist Knut Hamsun had delivered three lectures in Christiania on the decadence of modern literature. In them, he had particularly attacked the "Big Four" of Norwegian literature, Ibsen, Bjørnson, Lie, and Kielland. An invitation was sent to Ibsen and, to the consternation of those present, he attended all three lectures, sitting in seat number one in the front row. He is reported to have sat "quiet and serious, with unmoved countenance.... His strong blue eyes did not leave the speaker for a minute." It may well have been the memory of Hamsun's invective that suggested Solness's fear of "youth banging on the door." In passing, one may note that in the course of his lectures Hamsun had insisted on the necessity of probing into the dark and unconscious

corners of the human mind, and that Ibsen, in *The Master Builder* and the three plays which followed, was to do just this—he had already begun to do so in *The Lady from the Sea*.

The character of Solness was the closest thing to a self-portrait that Ibsen had yet attempted, though he was to follow it with two more in *John Gabriel Borkman* and *When We Dead Awaken*. He admitted in a speech a few years later that Solness "is a man who is somewhat related to me." Ibsen had long regarded himself as a builder, and his plays as works of architecture. As early as 1858, in a poem entitled "Building Plans," he had compared the artist to a master builder, and when Erik Werenskiold, seeing him looking at some new buildings in Christiania, asked him: "You are interested in architecture?" Ibsen replied: "Yes; it is, as you know, my own trade." Ibsen, like Solness, had always had a fear of looking down from a great height, or into a deep chasm, and this had become worse as he had grown older. Solness's ruthlessness, his readiness to sacrifice the happiness of those nearest him for the sake of his ambition, his longing for and fear of youth, and the conflict in him between aesthetic and ethical demands—all these were Ibsen's too. Moreover, during Ibsen's last years in Munich, we are told that he continually raised the subject of hypnotism, of how one human being could gain power over the mind of another, and how unexpressed wishes sometimes translated themselves into actions. This curiosity, too, had already manifested itself in *The Lady from the Sea*.

A word about trolls. Solness's repeated references to them are meaningless unless one has a clear understanding of what the word means. The great Norwegian scholar, Professor Francis Bull, defined them admirably in a lecture delivered at Oxford in 1954:

> Trolls—what are they? The word cannot be translated at all! The trolls are supernatural beings, akin to the enemies of the gods in the heathen world, and very well known in Norwegian fairy tales and folklore. They are supposed to live in the woods and mountains, and you must not imagine them in the shape of little goblins; they

look more like Polyphemus and Cyclops in the Odyssey—huge, clumsy and ugly.... [They] may be said to represent the evil forces in Nature, at first only as incarnations of frightening sounds and visions from without, but in more recent literature gradually taken in a wider sense, embodying or symbolizing those powers of evil, hidden in the soul of man, which may at times suddenly suppress his conscious will and dominate his actions. A great Norwegian novelist and friend of Ibsen has written two volumes of short stories and fairy tales, simply called *Trolls*, starting with this declaration: "That there are trolls in Man, everybody knows who has any insight into such things."...In...*The Master Builder*, which is very much the author's personal confession, Solness, half in joke and half in earnest and remorse, tells about his devils or trolls; in a way they serve him, but by ever pandering to his evil instincts and desires they have come to be really his rulers—mysterious powers that make him afraid of himself.

Ever since childhood, Ibsen had been fascinated by towers. In the memoirs of his childhood and youth which he had compiled a few years previously, to help Henrik Jaeger in the writing of his authorised biography, Ibsen had mentioned that the house in which he was born "stood exactly opposite the front of the church, with its high flight of steps and its conspicuous tower from which the watchman used to proclaim the hour at night." A poodle also lived in the tower; it "had fiery red eyes, but was rarely visible. Indeed, so far as I know, he was never seen but once." One New Year's morning, just as the watchman shouted "One" through the opening in the front of the tower, the poodle appeared behind him and looked at him with his fiery eyes, whereupon the watchman fell down into the market place and was killed. "From that night, the watchman never calls 'One' from the church tower at Skien." It was from the opening in this tower, Ibsen continues, that he received "the first conscious and permanent impression on my mind. My nurse one day took me up the tower and allowed me to sit on the ledge outside. ...I perfectly recollect how amazed I was at looking down on the tops of the hats of the people below." His mother

happened to look up from her window, saw him there, shrieked, and fainted "as people used to do in those days.... As a boy, I never went across the market place without looking up at the tower window. I always felt as though the opening and the church poodle were some special concern of mine."

In a letter written to his sister Hedvig on March 13, 1891 (when he was already planning *The Master Builder*), Ibsen recalled that "the house where I was born and lived the first years of my childhood, and the church, the old church with its christening-angel under the roof, are now burned down. All that my earliest memories are associated with —it was all burned." These feelings are strongly echoed in Solness's account of the burning of his wife's family home; and the christening-angel (which was lowered when a child was to be christened) may be the original of Aline's dolls.

Shortly before he left Munich that summer, Ibsen heard the legend of the master builder who had built St. Michael's Church there, and had thrown himself down from the tower of the church because he was afraid the roof would not hold. Ibsen said he thought the legend must have arisen in Scandinavia, and when the others observed that every famous cathedral in Germany had the same legend, he replied that this must be because people felt instinctively that a man could not build so high without paying the penalty for his hubris.

The publication of *The Master Builder* was eagerly awaited throughout Europe. English, French, and German translations appeared almost simultaneously with the original, the German translation being by Ibsen's son, Sigurd. Translations into Russian, Dutch, Polish, and Bohemian followed shortly afterwards. Great arguments developed as to the meaning of the play. As one contemporary put it: "While one person sees Solness as Ibsen himself, another sees him as Bjørnson, a third as a symbol of the right wing party, a fourth as a symbol of the left and its leader; a fifth sees Solness as a symbol of Man rising in rebellion against God; a sixth sees the play as a conflict between youth and the older generation." Some sought to identify Solness with Bismarck, while the *Saturday Review* in London decided that he was meant as a portrait of Mr. Gladstone, and that the play was full of references to the Irish question. Ibsen, when asked which of these interpretations was true, answered that the play merely portrayed people whom he had known and that he could not understand what everyone was arguing about.

The Master Builder received its first performance at Trondheim in January 1893, after the usual public reading in London to secure performing copyright.

Before the end of the month, it had also been staged in Bergen, Copenhagen, Gothenburg, Stockholm, Abo, Helsingfors, and Berlin. London and Chicago saw it in February, and Rome in April. It has remained one of Ibsen's most admired and most frequently performed plays.

In 1908, in Munich, Emilie Bardach saw *The Master Builder* for the first time. After the performance, she commented: "I didn't see myself, but I saw him. There is something of me in Hilde; but in Solness, there is little that is not Ibsen."

August
Strindberg
1849–1912

From his birth, Strindberg's existence seems to have been haunted. His father, a bankrupt Stockholm manufacturer of aristocratic descent, and his mother, an ex-barmaid, had lived together without benefit of marriage until shortly before August was born. His home life was one of poverty, overcrowding, and neglect, tinctured with the religious fanaticism of his grandmother. The death of his mother when August was thirteen and his father's rapid remarriage further aggravated Strindberg's hypersensitivity. In later years he was obsessed with a savage antifeminism, hating women yet hopelessly dependent on them. His instability became apparent early in his life. Beginning as a lay preacher, he then turned to private tutoring; discharged as a tutor, he enrolled in the University at Upsala. Here financial difficulties forced his withdrawal, and he became a public-school teacher. He took to alcohol, and further instability followed as he tried first the study of medicine, then acting, and finally writing. Success with a verse drama earned him a University scholarship, but he failed his examinations; he returned to Stockholm and a variety of odd jobs. In 1875 he began an affair with an older married woman, Baroness Wrangel, who obtained a divorce and married Strindberg. This, the first of his three tormented marriages, ended in divorce fourteen years later. A second marriage failed, and Strindberg now began to suffer from delusions of persecution and grandeur. He was already famous as the author of plays, novels, and stories and had written his powerful realistic dramas depicting the deadly struggle between men and women: *The Father* (1887), *Miss Julie* (1888), and *Creditors* (1888). For a period Strindberg was genuinely insane, but friendly care led to his recovery, and he returned to writing in another great burst of energy. In plays such as *To Damascus* (Parts I, II—1898; Part III—1904), *A Dream Play* (1902), and *The Ghost Sonata* (1907), Strindberg turned from realism to experimental techniques of symbolism. His misfortunes continued as his third marriage ended in divorce and his attempt to run a theatre failed. In 1911 he discovered that he had cancer. His countrymen now rallied to him with a celebration for his sixty-third birthday, and when he died the following year they honored him with a great public demonstration. In his stormy voyage from aggressive materialism to chastened mysticism, Strindberg spanned the polarities of modern consciousness. So, too, in his esthetic transition from naturalism to symbolism, he bridged the divergent tendencies of modern art. And while seeking a measure of integration for his warring sexual, social, and intellectual drives in submission to higher powers, Strindberg never lost sight of human suffering and injustice in a riddling universe.

A DREAM PLAY

AUGUST STRINDBERG

Translated by Arvid Paulson

THE AUTHOR'S PREFACE

As in his previous dream play, *To Damascus*, the author has in *A Dream Play* attempted to reproduce the detached and disunited—although apparently logical—form of dreams. Anything is apt to happen, anything seems possible and probable. Time and space do not exist. On a flimsy foundation of actual happenings, imagination spins and weaves in new patterns: an intermingling of remembrances, experiences, whims, fancies, ideas, fantastic absurdities and improvisations, and original inventions of the mind.

The personalities split, take on duality, multiply, vanish, intensify, diffuse and disperse, and are brought into a focus. There is, however, one single-minded consciousness that exercises a dominance over the characters: the dreamer's. There are for the dreamer no secrets, no inconsequences, no scruples, no laws. He neither pronounces judgment nor exonerates; he merely narrates.

Since dreams most frequently are filled with pain, and less often with joy, a note of melancholy and a compassion for all living things runs through the limping story. Sleep, the liberator, often appears as a tormentor, a torturer, but when the agony is most oppressive the awakening rescues the sufferer and reconciles him to reality. No matter how agonizing reality may be, it will at this moment be welcomed cheerfully as a release from the painful dream.

CHARACTERS

THE VOICE OF INDRA	THE POET
THE DAUGHTER OF INDRA	HE
THE GLAZIER	SHE
THE OFFICER	THE PENSIONER
THE FATHER	THE ELDERLY DANDY
THE MOTHER	THE OLD FLIRT
LINA	HER LOVER [THE MAJOR]
THE PORTRESS	THE THREE SERVANT MAIDS
THE BILLPOSTER	PLAIN-LOOKING EDITH
THE SINGER	EDITH'S MOTHER
A WOMAN'S VOICE [VICTORIA]	ALICE
THE BALLET GIRL	THE TEACHER
THE CHORIST	THE NAVAL OFFICER
THE PROMPTER	SEVERAL BOY PUPILS
THE POLICEMAN	THE HUSBAND
THE ATTORNEY	THE WIFE
KRISTIN	THE BLIND MAN
THE QUARANTINE MASTER	FIRST COAL HEAVER

SOURCE: From *Eight Expressionist Plays* by August Strindberg, translated by Arvid Paulson. Copyright © 1972 by Arvid Paulson, and published by New York University Press. Reprinted by permission of the New York University Press.

SECOND COAL HEAVER
THE GENTLEMAN
THE LADY
THE LORD CHANCELLOR
THE DEAN OF THEOLOGY
THE DEAN OF PHILOSOPHY

THE DEAN OF MEDICINE
THE DEAN OF JURISPRUDENCE
THE SHIP'S CREW
MEMBERS OF THE OPERA COMPANY
CLERKS, HERALDS, DANCING GIRLS,
  MEN AND WOMEN, AND OTHERS

[Prologue. The background represents cloud banks shaped like disintegrating slate cliffs, dotted with castles and fortified strongholds.

The constellations Leo, Virgo, and Libra can be discerned in the firmament. In their midst the planet Jupiter is visible, shining with a bright light.

The DAUGHTER OF INDRA stands on the topmost cloud.]

VOICE OF INDRA [heard from above]. Where are you Daughter . . . where?

DAUGHTER OF INDRA. Here, Father . . . here!

VOICE OF INDRA. You've lost your way, my child! Take care—you're sinking. . . .
How did you stray?

DAUGHTER OF INDRA. I followed in the path of lightning from the ether
and used a cloud as travel coach. . . .
The cloud, however, sank—and now we're falling. . . .
Oh, tell me, lofty Father Indra, to what regions
I have come. And why so sultry here, so hard to breathe?

VOICE OF INDRA. You've left the second world and come into the third one—
you've passed the star of morning, and from Çukra you now enter
the atmosphere of Earth; there you will see
the Scales, the seventh house of planet Sun,
where Çukra stands on guard at the autumnal equinox—
when day and night are equal in duration.

DAUGHTER OF INDRA. You spoke of Earth. . . . Is that the dreary planet whose darkness is lit up by Mother Moon?

VOICE OF INDRA. It is the heaviest and densest
of the spheres that sail in space.

DAUGHTER OF INDRA. And do the sun's rays never reach it?

VOICE OF INDRA. Oh yes, it gets some sun, but not at all times. . . .

DAUGHTER OF INDRA. There is a rift now in the cloud—and I can see below—

VOICE OF INDRA. What do you see, my child?

DAUGHTER OF INDRA. I see . . . that there is beauty—the woods are green—
the water's blue—and snowcapped mountains—yellow fields. . . .

VOICE OF INDRA. A beauty such as only Brahma could create. . . .
yet it has once had even greater beauty
when Time was born, long, long ago. . . .
Then something happened—
its destined orbit was disturbed, or maybe something else;
revolt bred crime that had to be suppressed. . . .

DAUGHTER OF INDRA. Now I can hear sounds from down below. . . .
What kind of beings live upon that planet?

VOICE OF INDRA. Descend and see. . . .
I will not slander these poor children of Creation;
and what you now can hear is their tongue.

DAUGHTER OF INDRA. It sounds as though. . . . It has a ring that is not happy.

VOICE OF INDRA. I feared so!—Their mother-tongue is discontent!
Yes—I fear that the people of the Earth are hard to please, a most ungrateful race. . . .

DAUGHTER OF INDRA. Speak not unkindly. . . . Now I hear joyous cries—
and shooting—thunder—I see lightning. . . .
Now bells are ringing, fires burning—
and voices—thousands upon thousands—
sing praise and thanks to the celestial. . . .
[There is a silence.]
You judge them much too harshly, Father. . . .

VOICE OF INDRA. Descend, then, and

when you have learned, have seen,
and heard,
return and tell me if they've cause to
grumble and complain,
to be lamenting and bewailing constantly.
DAUGHTER OF INDRA. I'll go then—
down to them ... but won't you,
Father, come with me?
VOICE OF INDRA. No, no—I cannot
breathe down there.
DAUGHTER OF INDRA. The cloud is sinking. ... Oh, how close it is. ... It's
stifling here.
This is not air I'm breathing ... it is
smoke and moisture. ...
It weighs me down—it drags me downward, downward;
I feel a tilting, turning motion—
the third world truly can't be said to be
the best. ...
VOICE OF INDRA. No, it is not the best
—yet not the worst;
its name is Dust, it rotates like the rest
of them—
that's why the people there are prone to
dizziness,
a thing between plain foolishness and
madness. ...
Take courage now, my child, for this is
but a test, a trial.
DAUGHTER OF INDRA [kneels as the
cloud descends]. I am sinking ...

[Outside the growing garden. The background represents giant hollyhocks in
bloom. The flowers are of various colors:
white, pink, crimson, sulfur-yellow and
bluish-purple. Above their tops is seen
the gilded roof of a castle; its apex is a
flower bud resembling a crown. At the
foot of the foundation walls of the castle,
hay and straw heaped up in stacks. These
cover litter cast out from the stable.
The wings, which remain unchanged
throughout the play, are stylized frescoes:
a blending of interior, architecture and
landscape.
The GLAZIER and the DAUGHTER OF IN-
DRA are seen entering.]

DAUGHTER OF INDRA. The castle is
steadily growing up from the earth. ...
Can you see how it has grown since last
year?
GLAZIER [to himself]. I have never seen
this castle before—have never heard of a
castle that could grow—but ... [To the
DAUGHTER OF INDRA, with sincere conviction.] Yes—it has grown six feet. ...
That's because of the manure ... and if
you take a good look, you will see that a
wing has sprouted on the side where the
sun shines.
DAUGHTER OF INDRA. Don't you think
it will come out in bloom soon, now that
it is past midsummer?
GLAZIER. You see the flower up there,
don't you?
DAUGHTER OF INDRA. Yes—I see it!
[She claps her hands joyfully.] Tell me,
Father, why is it that flowers rise up out
of dirt?
GLAZIER [with piety]. Because they do
not thrive in dirt. That is why they are
anxious to reach the light, so that they
may blossom and die.
DAUGHTER OF INDRA. Do you know
who lives in the castle?
GLAZIER. I did know once but have
forgotten.
DAUGHTER OF INDRA. I believe someone
is imprisoned there ... he must be waiting for me to set him free.
GLAZIER. And at what cost?
DAUGHTER OF INDRA. One never bar-
gains when it comes to duty. Let us enter
the castle.
GLAZIER. Yes—let us go in.

[They go toward the rear, which slowly
opens, dividing itself in two parts that
disappear in the wings.
The scene is now a plain, naked room.
A table and a few chairs are the only
furnishings in it.
On one of the chairs is seated the OF-
FICER, attired in a bizarre, yet modern,
uniform. He is rocking back and forth
in his chair while striking the table with
his saber.]

DAUGHTER OF INDRA [goes over to the
OFFICER and gently takes the saber from
his hand]. You mustn't do that! You
mustn't do that!
OFFICER. Agnes dear, let me keep the
saber!
DAUGHTER OF INDRA. No, you will
break the table! [to the GLAZIER]. Go
down to the harness room now and put
in the pane. We'll see each other later.
[The GLAZIER leaves.]
DAUGHTER OF INDRA. You are a pris-

oner in your own house. I have come to set you free.

OFFICER. I have been waiting for you to come, although I was never certain you *would* come.

DAUGHTER OF INDRA. The castle is a stronghold—it has seven walls—but . . . it will be done!—Do you wish to be free, or don't you?

OFFICER. To tell the truth, I don't know. Whatever I choose, it will mean suffering. Every joy in life has to be paid for with double its worth of sorrow. Living here is hard enough, but if I have to buy back my precious freedom, I shall have to suffer threefold. . . . Agnes, I'd rather endure life as it is here, if I may only see you.

DAUGHTER OF INDRA. What do you see in me?

OFFICER. In you I see beauty—which is the harmony of the universe. Only in the solar system's motion, in the exquisite, inspiring chords of a stringed instrument, in the vibrations of light do I find delineated anything resembling the beauty of your figure. . . . You are a child of celestial spheres—

DAUGHTER OF INDRA. And so are you!

OFFICER. Why, then, must I tend horses, look after stables, and see that the litter is removed?

DAUGHTER OF INDRA. That you may wish to get away from it all!

OFFICER. I wish to—but it is so hard to do!

DAUGHTER OF INDRA. But we owe it to ourselves to seek freedom in light, don't we? It is a duty we have—

OFFICER. Duty? Life has never recognized its duties to me!

DAUGHTER OF INDRA. You feel that life has been unjust to you, then?

OFFICER. Yes—it has been unjust. . . .

[*Voices can now be heard behind the screen or partition which is drawn aside in the next moment.*

The OFFICER *and the* DAUGHTER OF INDRA *glance in that direction. Then they remain motionless in position, gesture, and expression. Seated at a table is the* MOTHER. *She is sickly. Before her is a lighted taper. Now and then she prunes the wick with a pair of snuffers. Piled on the table are some shirts which she has just finished making and which she is now marking with quill and ink. On the right stands a dark, wooden wardrobe.*]

FATHER [*hands her a cape of silk. Then he speaks to her gently.*] Don't you want it?

MOTHER. A silken cape for me, my dear? What use would it be to me, when I am going to die soon?

FATHER. Do you really believe what the doctor says?

MOTHER. That, too . . . but most of all I believe the voice inside me. [*Her hand fumbles toward her heart.*]

FATHER [*with sorrow in his voice*]. Then you are really seriously—? And first, last, and always you are thinking of your children. . . .

MOTHER. Haven't they been everything to me—my life, my very reason for living, my happiness, my sorrows?

FATHER. Kristina! Forgive me—for all I have failed in!

MOTHER. Forgive you? For what? . . . But forgive me, my dearest! We have both tormented each other—and why? That's something we cannot explain . . . there was no other way out, I suppose! Now here is the children's new linen. . . . Be sure to see that they change twice a week, Wednesdays and Saturdays, and that Louise washes them—their whole bodies. . . . Are you going out?

FATHER. I have to be at the teachers' staff meeting at eleven.

MOTHER. Will you ask Alfred to come in to me, before you leave?

FATHER [*points to the* OFFICER]. But, dearest, he is standing right here!

MOTHER. To think that my eyes should be failing me, too . . . yes, darkness is setting in. [*She snuffs out the taper.*] Alfred, come here! [*The* FATHER *disappears through the wall. As he leaves, he nods good-by. The* OFFICER *steps over to the* MOTHER.] Who is that girl there?

OFFICER [*in a whisper*]. Why, it's Agnes!

MOTHER [*in a similar tone of voice*]. Oh, it's Agnes, is it? Have you heard what they are saying? That she is the daughter of the God Indra, and that she pleaded with him to come down to Earth in order to see how human beings really live and behave. But don't mention this to anyone. . . .

OFFICER. A child of heaven, that's what she is!

MOTHER [in a louder voice]. Alfred, my darling, I shall soon be leaving you and the rest of the children. But before I go, I want to leave a thought with you. to be remembered all through your life!

OFFICER [sadly]. Speak, Mother—

MOTHER. Just these words: Never quarrel with God!

OFFICER. What do you mean, Mother?

MOTHER. You must not go about feeling that life has wronged and cheated you.

OFFICER. But when people treat me unjustly . . .

MOTHER. You are alluding to the time when you were unfairly punished for having taken a coin that later was found elsewhere?

OFFICER. Yes! That piece of injustice has distorted the purpose of my life ever since—

MOTHER. Perhaps it has! But go and look in the wardrobe now—

OFFICER [shamefaced]. So you know, then! It's—is it . . . ?

MOTHER. The Swiss Family Robinson —for which—

OFFICER. Don't say it—don't—

MOTHER. —for which your brother was punished . . . and which you had torn the leaves out of—and hidden!

OFFICER. To think that this old wardrobe should still be here—after twenty years. . . . After the many times we have moved! And my mother died ten years ago!

MOTHER. Well, what has that to do with it? You just have to ask questions about everything. That's why you ruin for yourself the best that life has to give! —Ah, there is Lina!

LINA [enters]. I want to thank you ever so much, ma'am, but I can't go to the christening after all.

MOTHER. Why not, my child?

LINA. I have nothing to wear.

MOTHER. I'll lend you my cape here.

LINA. Dear me—no, that wouldn't do!

MOTHER. I don't see why not! I shall never again be going to another party.

OFFICER. What would Father say? He gave it to you, didn't he?

MOTHER. Oh, what petty minds.

FATHER [puts his head inside the door]. Are you letting the maid use the cape I gave you?

MOTHER. Don't say things like that! Remember that I, too, was a servant girl once. . . . Why do you want to be insulting to an innocent young girl?

FATHER. And why should you offend me, your husband?

MOTHER. Oh, this life of ours! When you do something out of the goodness of your heart there is always someone who finds it ugly and bad. And if you do something good for one person, then someone else feels hurt. Oh, this life!

[She trims the taper, so that it goes out. The scene is now in darkness, and the partition is pushed back into its previous position.]

DAUGHTER OF INDRA. Humanity is to be pitied!

OFFICER. Is that what you think?

DAUGHTER OF INDRA. Yes. Life is hard —but love conquers all! Come—and see! [They walk toward the rear.]

[The alley outside the opera house. The backdrop is now raised. One sees a different background, representing a dilapidated, ancient fireproof wall. In its center is a gate opening onto a path that terminates at a green, sun-lit space, featuring a blue aconite, or monk's hood, of giant proportions.

On the right, close by the gate, sits the PORTRESS. She wears a shawl wrapped round her head and shoulders, and she is busy crocheting a star-studded bedspread.

On the other side of the gate, left, there is a small billboard, which the BILL-POSTER is in the throes of cleaning. Nearby stands a dip-net on a pole painted green. Farther to the left is a door with an air-hole shaped like a four-leaf clover.

To the right of the gate stands a dwarfed lime tree. Its trunk is jet-black, and it bears few leaves. These are pale-green in color. Nearby is seen an opening, leading to the basement.]

DAUGHTER OF INDRA [steps over to the PORTRESS]. You haven't finished the star-covered bedspread, have you?

PORTRESS. No, my dear little friend. Twenty-six years is not a long time for a work like this!

DAUGHTER OF INDRA. And he never came back—your lover?

PORTRESS. No—but that was not *his* fault. He *had* to go away . . . poor man. . . . It's thirty years ago now!

DAUGHTER OF INDRA [to the BILL-POSTER]. She used to be in the ballet, didn't she? In there at the Opera?

BILLPOSTER. She was the best one they had there. . . . But when he went away, it was as if he had taken her dancing feet with him—and it was not long before her career was ended.

DAUGHTER OF INDRA. People do nothing but complain. You see it in their eyes—and the lament is in their voices, too. . . .

BILLPOSTER. I don't think I complain very much. Certainly not now that I have got myself a dip-net and a green fish-chest!

DAUGHTER OF INDRA. And that makes you happy?

BILLPOSTER. Yes, it makes me very happy! I have dreamed of it since I was a lad! And now my dream has come true! —I know I am past fifty, of course. . . .

DAUGHTER OF INDRA. Fifty years for a dip-net and a fish-chest.

BILLPOSTER. A *green* fish-chest—a green one. . . .

DAUGHTER OF INDRA [to the PORTRESS]. If you will let me have your shawl now, I'd like to sit here and watch the human children. . . . But you must stand behind me and help me a little! [She is given the shawl and takes the PORTRESS' seat by the gate.]

PORTRESS. Today is the last day of the season, and then the Opera will be closed. Today they will know whether they have been re-engaged.

DAUGHTER OF INDRA. What about those who are not engaged?

PORTRESS. Oh, may God forgive me—I hate to look at them. . . . I cover my face with my shawl—I—

DAUGHTER OF INDRA. Poor human beings!

PORTRESS. Look! Here is one of them! . . . She is not among the chosen!—See how she is crying.

[The SINGER enters from the left. She hastens out through the gate, hold-ing a handkerchief to her eyes. She stops momentarily on the path outside the gate and presses her head against the wall. Then she leaves quickly.]

DAUGHTER OF INDRA. Man is to be pitied! . . .

PORTRESS. But here—here you see what a happy human being looks like! [The OFFICER enters through the gate. He is dressed in a redingote and top hat; in his hand he carries a bouquet of roses. He radiates joy and buoyant happiness.] He is engaged to be married to Miss Victoria—

OFFICER [stands downstage, looks up above and sings]. Victoria!

PORTRESS. Miss Victoria will be here in a moment.

OFFICER. Good! The carriage is waiting—the table is set—the champagne is on ice. . . . I'd like to embrace you ladies. [He embraces the DAUGHTER OF INDRA and the PORTRESS. Then he sings out again.] Victoria!

WOMAN'S VOICE [sings back from above]. Here I am!

OFFICER [starts to pace]. Oh well . . . I shall wait!

DAUGHTER OF INDRA. Do you know me?

OFFICER. No—I know only one woman—Victoria! For seven years I have been waiting for her here—waiting—waiting . . . at noon of day when the sun's rays touch the chimney-stacks, and in the evening when the dusk of night sets in. . . . Look—here you can see the imprint of my steps on the walk—the faithful lover's steps. . . . Hurray! She is mine! [He sings.] Victoria! [This time there is no reply.] Well—she is dressing. [To the BILLPOSTER.] There is your dip-net, I see! Everybody at the Opera is mad about dip-nets—or I should say, fish! Because the fish are mute—and therefore can't sing. . . . How much does a gadget like that cost?

BILLPOSTER. It's rather expensive.

OFFICER [sings]. Victoria! [He shakes the lime tree.] See! It's getting green again! For the eighth time! [He sings out.] Victoria! . . . Now she is arranging her hair. [To the DAUGHTER OF INDRA.] My sweet lady, please let me go upstairs and fetch my bride!

PORTRESS. No one is allowed to go backstage.

OFFICER. For seven years I have been coming here! Seven times three hundred and sixty-five makes two thousand five hundred and fifty-five! [*He halts and pokes at the door with the four-leaf clover.*] And I have looked at this door two thousand five hundred and fifty-five times without being able to figure out where it leads! And that clover leaf, which is supposed to let in light! For whom is it to let in light? Is anybody in there, eh? Does anybody live in there?

PORTRESS. I don't know anything about it! I've never seen it opened.

OFFICER. It looks like a door to a pantry. I saw one like it when I was four and went visiting with our maid one Sunday afternoon! She took me from one family to another—to chat with the servants there—but we never went beyond the kitchen. And I had to sit wedged between the water barrel and a keg of salt. I have seen a multitude of kitchens in my days, and the pantry was invariably in the servants' hall outside the kitchen and always had small round holes bored in the door —holes shaped like a four-leaf clover. . . . But why should they have a pantry at the Opera, when they haven't any kitchen there! [*He sings.*] Victoria!—Tell me, my dear lady—she couldn't have gone out any other way, could she?

PORTRESS. No—there is no other way.

OFFICER. Oh well, then I am bound to see her. [*Artists come rushing out. The* OFFICER *scrutinizes each and every one.*] Now she simply must be here before much longer! Oh, madam! That blue aconite out there! I've seen that flower there since I was a child. . . . Is it the same flower? . . . I recall being in a parsonage out in the country when I was seven. . . . The aconite has two doves—two blue doves underneath its hood . . . and then a bee came flying and crept into the hood. I thought to myself: now I'll catch you . . . and I cupped my hands round the flower. But the bee stung my hand right through the petals, and I started to cry. Then the pastor's wife came and put some wet earth on it to ease the pain . . . and then we had wild strawberries and cream for supper. . . . I think it's already getting dark. [*To the* BILLPOSTER.] Where are you going now?

BILLPOSTER. I am going home for supper.

OFFICER [*running his hand across his eyes*]. Supper? At this time of day?—Oh, please, may I go in and make a brief telephone call to "the growing castle"? May I?

DAUGHTER OF INDRA. What business could you have there?

OFFICER. I want to tell the Glazier to put in the storm windows. Soon we'll have winter—and I suffer so terribly from the cold!

[*He goes inside to the* PORTRESS.]

DAUGHTER OF INDRA. Who is Miss Victoria?

PORTRESS. She is his sweetheart.

DAUGHTER OF INDRA. There is truth in your answer. What she is to us and to others, means nothing to him. Only what she is to *him* is what she *really* is! [*There is a sudden, stark darkness.*]

PORTRESS [*lights her lantern*]. It is getting dark early today.

DAUGHTER OF INDRA. To the gods the years are as minutes.

PORTRESS. And to us humans a minute may seem like a year!

OFFICER [*comes out again. He is covered with dust, and the roses are withered*]. She hasn't come yet?

PORTRESS. No.

OFFICER. But she will, I am sure!—She will come! [*He starts to pace.*] Yes, perhaps I had best cancel the dinner—since it is already a little late. . . . Yes, yes, that's what I'll do! [*He goes inside again to telephone.*]

PORTRESS [*to the* DAUGHTER OF INDRA]. May I have my shawl now?

DAUGHTER OF INDRA. No—you take it easy for a while, my dear. I'll take care of your duties! I want to learn all I can about life and human beings. . . . I want to see if life is really so hard as they say it is.

PORTRESS. But one never gets a moment of rest here. Day and night, one never gets a chance to shut an eye.

DAUGHTER OF INDRA. No sleep—even at night?

PORTRESS. Well, yes—if you can manage it with the bell cord round your wrist . . . for there are watchmen on the stage all through the night—and they are relieved every three hours.

DAUGHTER OF INDRA. But that's torture!

PORTRESS. You may think so, but the rest of us are only too glad to get a position like this. If you only knew how envious people are of me.

DAUGHTER OF INDRA. Envious! They are envious of the tortured!

PORTRESS. Yes. But let me tell you something that is harder to bear than all the night vigil and all the drudgery, harder than the draft and cold and dampness—and that is to have to receive the confidences of all the unfortunates here—as I have to do.... They all come to me! Why? Perhaps in the wrinkles of my face they read the runes of past suffering. Perhaps that is what persuades them to confide to me their secrets.... That shawl, my dear, holds agonies and disappointments, secrets and confidences—my own and theirs—of the past thirty years!

DAUGHTER OF INDRA. It is heavy, and it burns like nettle.

PORTRESS. Wear it then, if you like.... And if you should find it too heavy for you, just call me and I'll come and relieve you.

DAUGHTER OF INDRA. Good-bye. What you can do, I should be able to do.

PORTRESS. We'll see! ... Only treat my poor young friends kindly—and never lose patience with them when they come with their complaints!

[She disappears down the walk.]

[The stage grows completely dark. During the darkness, there is a change of season: the lime tree now has lost its leaves; the blue aconite has withered. When daylight has returned, the verdure in the perspective of the walk has changed into autumn brown.

The OFFICER appears again, coming out when the stage is lighted. His hair is now gray, likewise his beard. His clothes are shabby, his collar wilted and soiled. All that remains of the bouquet of roses is the forked stems—no leaves, no petals are left. He walks to and fro.]

OFFICER. Judging by what I see, summer is gone and fall is near. I can see it by the lime tree there—and the monk's hood! [He commences his walk again.] But autumn is spring for me, for that's when the Opera opens again! And that's when she'll be here! Dear madam, will you allow me to sit down for a little while?

DAUGHTER OF INDRA [gets up from her chair and offers it to the OFFICER]. Sit here, my friend . . . I'll stand.

OFFICER [seats himself]. If I could only get a little sleep, too! That would be still better. [He dozes momentarily, and then suddenly gets up with a start and begins to pace back and forth. He stops before the door with the four-leaf clover and pokes at it.] This door—it just won't give me any peace! What is behind it? There must be something! [Faint music is heard from above, in dance tempo.] So! They've started rehearsals again! [The stage is now lighted by fits and starts, as by a flashing light.] What's the meaning of this? [He accentuates the words as the lights go on and off.] Light and dark; dark and light. . . .

DAUGHTER OF INDRA [imitates him]. Day and night; night and day. . . . A merciful Providence desires to shorten your waiting. That is why the days fly, ever pursuing the nights!

[It again grows light on the stage. The BILLPOSTER enters with his dip-net and billposting material.]

OFFICER. So—it's you—with your dip-net. . . . Did you have a good catch?

BILLPOSTER. Yes, I should say I did! It was a warm summer, and a little long. . . . The net wasn't bad—but not as good as I had expected it to be. . . .

OFFICER [accentuates the words]. Not as good as I had expected it to be! That is very well put! Nothing is as I expected it to be! . . . Because the thought is greater than the deed—higher than anything material. [He starts to pace again, beating the bouquet against the wall so that the last remaining petals and leaves fall off.]

BILLPOSTER. Hasn't she come down yet?

OFFICER. No, not yet, but she won't be long now!—Have you any idea what is behind that door?

BILLPOSTER. No, I have never seen that door open.

OFFICER. I am going in to telephone for a locksmith to come and open it. [He goes inside. The BILLPOSTER puts up a bill; then he goes toward the right.]

DAUGHTER OF INDRA. What was wrong with the dip-net?

BILLPOSTER. What was wrong? Well, there wasn't anything wrong with it exactly—but it wasn't precisely what I had expected it to be.... So my first joy turned into disappointment, you might say....

DAUGHTER OF INDRA. What had you expected when you bought the dip-net?

BILLPOSTER. What I'd expected? Why —I don't know....

DAUGHTER OF INDRA. Let me tell you then! You had expected it to be what it turned out *not* to be. You wanted it to be green, but *not*—the green you got!

BILLPOSTER. You put your finger on it, lady! You know everything! That's why they all come to you with their troubles. ... I wish you would listen to *me*, too, some time....

DAUGHTER OF INDRA. I will be happy to. Come and tell me, pour out your heart to me. [*She goes into her room. The* BILLPOSTER *remains outside and talks to her through the wicket.*]

[*Again the stage is in complete darkness. Then it grows light, and the lime tree can be seen, its leaves now green; the aconite is blooming again, and the sun shines on the verdure in the space at the end of the walk, in the background.*

The OFFICER *comes out. He is now an old, white-haired man. His clothes are in rags, his shoes worn. He still carries the stems that are left of the bouquet of roses. He walks to and fro, moving like a man who has aged considerably. Then he stops and studies the bill that has just been posted. A* BALLET GIRL *comes from the left.*]

OFFICER. Has Miss Victoria left yet?

BALLET GIRL. No, she has not.

OFFICER. Then I'll wait! No doubt she'll be down soon?

BALLET GIRL [*with a serious expression on her face*]. No doubt she will!

OFFICER. Don't go away yet, and you'll see what is behind this door. I've just sent for the locksmith!

BALLET GIRL. It will really be interesting to see that door opened. That door and the growing castle! Do you know the growing castle?

OFFICER. Do I!—Haven't I been a prisoner there!

BALLET GIRL. You don't say? Was that you? But tell me—why did they have so many horses there?

OFFICER. Why—it was a stable castle—

BALLET GIRL [*painfully touched*]. How stupid of me! I should have known....

[*A* CHORIST *enters from the left.*]

OFFICER. Has Miss Victoria left yet?

CHORIST [*in a serious voice*]. No! She hasn't left! She never leaves!

OFFICER. That's because she loves me! ... Don't leave now before the locksmith comes to open the door here.

CHORIST. Oh—are they going to open the door? Oh, that will be fun to see!— I just want to ask the Portress a question.

[*The* PROMPTER *enters from the left.*]

OFFICER. Has Miss Victoria left yet?

PROMPTER. No, not as far as I know.

OFFICER. There you see! Didn't I say that she would be waiting for me!—But don't go! The door is to be opened.

PROMPTER. Which door?

OFFICER. Is there more than one door?

PROMPTER. Oh, I know. The one with the clover leaf! Then I certainly want to stay! I just want to have a word with the Portress. [*The* BALLET GIRL, *the* CHORIST, *and the* PROMPTER *group themselves beside the* BILLPOSTER *outside the* PORTRESS' *window. They take turns speaking with the* DAUGHTER OF INDRA. *The* GLAZIER *enters through the gate.*]

OFFICER. Are you the locksmith?

GLAZIER. No, the locksmith couldn't come. But I guess I can do the job, even though I am a glazier.

OFFICER. Certainly—but have you your diamond with you?

GLAZIER. Of course! A glazier without a diamond! What do you think?

OFFICER. Never mind!—Let's get to work! [*He claps his hands. All gather round the door.* CHORISTS *dressed as Mastersingers, and* BALLET GIRLS, *attired as the dancers in Aïda, enter from the left. They join the others.*] Locksmith—or glazier ... do your duty! [*The* GLAZIER *steps to the door with his diamond in his hand.*] A moment like this does not come often in a man's life. For this reason, my good friends, stop to think ... think carefully....

POLICEMAN [*enters*]. In the name of the law, I forbid you to open that door!

OFFICER. Oh heavens, what a fuss there is whenever anybody tries to do something great and new! But we shall take this matter to court! I'll see a lawyer! Then we'll find out what the law says! I'm going to the Attorney!

[*Without lowering the curtain, the scene changes to an attorney's office. The gate remains in its place, functioning now as the entrance wicket in the railing that extends from left to right, clear across the stage.*

The PORTRESS' *room serves as the* ATTORNEY'S *private compartment, the front partition having been removed. The lime tree, now barren, serves as a hat and coat rack. The billboard is covered with official and legal notices and court decisions. The door with the clover leaf now hides bookshelves on which documents are piled.*

The ATTORNEY, *in evening dress with tails and white tie, sits at a writing desk littered with legal papers and documents, right, in back of the railing. His face speaks of untold sufferings. It is chalkwhite and wrinkled, with shadows of bluish purple. He is ugly, and his countenance reflects all the crimes and vices with which he has been forced to come in contact.*

His two clerks are both infirm: one has lost an arm, the other one is minus an eye.

The ones who collected to view the opening of the door remain on the stage; they now seem to be waiting to gain admittance to the ATTORNEY. *They appear to have been waiting forever.*

The DAUGHTER OF INDRA, *wearing the* PORTRESS' *shawl, stands downstage, as does the* OFFICER.]

ATTORNEY [*steps forward to the* DAUGHTER OF INDRA]. Tell me, my sister, may I have that shawl? I'll hang it inside until I can make a fire in the stove—then I'll burn it with all its sorrows and miseries. . . .

DAUGHTER OF INDRA. Not yet, my brother! First I want to have it completely filled! And above all, I want it to absorb all your agonies—all the confidences about crime and vice, about revilement and slander, about things wrongly gained. . . .

ATTORNEY. My dear little friend—for that your shawl would not be big enough! Look at these walls. . . . Even the wallpaper seems to have been soiled by every kind of sin! Take a look at these papers, which are filled with stories of wrongs, written by me! Look at me!

—Among those who come here you will never find a human being with a smile on his face—here you see only vicious glances, clenched fists, and teeth ready to bite! And they all squirt their anger and their envy, and spit their suspicions over me. . . . See. . . . Look at my hands! They are black—and can never be washed clean! You see how cracked and bleeding they are! I can never wear a suit of clothes more than a day or two before it stinks of other people's crimes. . . . Sometimes I have the place fumigated with sulfur—but it doesn't help much. . . . I sleep in the back room, and whenever I dream, I dream about crime. . . . Just now I have a murder case before the court. . . . That's bad enough—but do you know what is worse—the very worst?—Having to separate a married couple!—I feel as if I heard a cry from the bowels of the earth and from the heavens—a voice crying treason—treason against the source of life, against the well-spring of everything that's good, against love itself. . . . And you'll find that after reams and reams of paper have been scribbled full of mutual accusations . . . and then a sympathetic person takes one of them aside for a heart-to-heart talk, and asks—with a pinch of the ear, or with a smile—this simple question: What is it that you really have against your husband?—or your wife, as the case may be—then he—or she—stands mute, can't find an answer, doesn't know the cause of it all! I can remember once when . . . yes, I think the trouble was caused by a salad . . . another time it was caused by a mere word—generally such trouble is caused by nothing but trifles. . . . But the suffering, the torture! That's what I have to bear! Look at my face! Do you think I could ever win a woman's love with a face such as mine—a criminal's face? And do you think anybody would care to be a friend of mine—I, who have to collect debts and accounts and liabilities for everybody in the city? —To be a human being is hard!

DAUGHTER OF INDRA. Man is to be pitied!

ATTORNEY. Indeed, man is! And how people manage to live is a puzzle to me! They marry on an income of two thousand a year—when they need four thousand. . . . And so they have to borrow, of course! They all borrow! And then they muddle along and zigzag through life for the rest of their days until they die. . . . And then it's discovered there is nothing left but debts! Who is it who pays in the end? Well—who knows. . . .

DAUGHTER OF INDRA. He who feeds the birds!

ATTORNEY. Well—but if He who feeds the birds would only come to Earth and see what we poor human creatures have to go through—then, perhaps, He would show compassion. . . .

DAUGHTER OF INDRA. Man is, indeed, to be pitied!

ATTORNEY. Man is, indeed! [He turns to the OFFICER.] What is it you wish?

OFFICER. I simply wish to know whether Miss Victoria has left yet.

ATTORNEY. No, she has not, you can rest assured of that. . . . But why are you poking at my closet there?

OFFICER. Why, the door looks exactly like . . .

ATTORNEY. Oh no—oh no—oh no. . . .
[Church bells are heard ringing.]

OFFICER. Is there a funeral in the city?

ATTORNEY. No, today is university graduation day. They are conferring doctors' degrees. They are conferring the degree of doctor of laws on me today. Wouldn't you, too, like to have a degree conferred on you and receive the laurel wreath?

OFFICER. Why, I have no objection. At least it would be a kind of distraction.

ATTORNEY. Well, then, let's get ready for the solemnity without delay. . . . But you must first go home and dress for the occasion!
[The OFFICER leaves.]

[The scene is darkened, and the setting is changed into the chancel of a church.

The railing now functions as the balustrade; the billboard serves as an announcement board for the hymns to be sung at the occasion; the ATTORNEY's desk is the pulpit of the presiding functionary; the door with the clover leaf is the entrance to the vestry.

The CHORISTS from Die Meistersinger function as heralds with staffs. The BALLET GIRLS carry laurel wreaths. The others act as spectators.

The backdrop is raised, baring the new background representing the pipes of a huge organ. The instrument itself with the keyboard is below. On it, above, is the organist's mirror. The music swells from the organ.

On each side are representatives of the four faculties: Philosophy, Theology, Medicine, and Jurisprudence.

The scene is empty for a few moments. The HERALDS enter from the left. The BALLET GIRLS follow, carrying the laurel wreaths, which they hold high before them. Three Conferees enter in turn, one after the other, from the right. Each one is crowned with a wreath; after which they go out, left.

The ATTORNEY steps forward to receive his wreath. The BALLET GIRLS turn their backs on him, refusing to present him with a wreath, and leave. The ATTORNEY, visibly affected, supports himself against a temple column. All withdraw, leaving the ATTORNEY alone on the stage. The DAUGHTER OF INDRA enters. She wears a white veil over her shoulders and head.]

DAUGHTER OF INDRA. Now, you see, I have washed the shawl. . . . But why are you standing here? Didn't you get your wreath?

ATTORNEY. No—I was not considered worthy of it.

DAUGHTER OF INDRA. Why not? Because you have been championing the poor, spoken a good word for the wicked, lightened the burden for the guilty, obtained another chance for the condemned? Oh, humanity! . . . Men are no angels—they are to be pitied!

ATTORNEY. You must not speak badly about human beings. . . . Isn't it my duty to plead for them?

DAUGHTER OF INDRA [supports herself against the organ]. Why do they always abuse their friends?

ATTORNEY. They don't know any better.

DAUGHTER OF INDRA. Then let us show them the light. . . . Will you help? Shall we—together—

ATTORNEY. They do not care to be enlightened. . . . Oh, that the gods in heaven would hear the weeping of our sorrow.

DAUGHTER OF INDRA. I shall reach their ears. [She seats herself at the organ.] Do you know what I see in the mirror here?

The world as it *should* be—as it *really is!* Because as it is now, it is upside down!

ATTORNEY. How did it come to be turned upside down?

DAUGHTER OF INDRA. When the copy was made...

ATTORNEY. You put your finger on what is wrong! The copy...I always sensed that the replica was faulty! When I recalled the original, I became dissatisfied with the world. And I was called an ingrate, hard to please; I was told I was looking at things through the devil's eyes, and much more in that vein.

DAUGHTER OF INDRA. Yes, isn't it a mad world! Look at the four faculties here! The government—whose duty it is to preserve society—pays their salaries, all four of them. Theology, the science of God, is constantly attacked and ridiculed by Philosophy, which declares itself to be the cornerstone of all wisdom. And Medicine, which is forever at odds with Philosophy, contradicts Theology's claim to be a science and calls it mere superstition. And yet the four are part of the same academic council—whose duty it is to teach respect for the university! Wouldn't you call this madness? And woe be to him who first recovers his reason and sanity!

ATTORNEY. The first ones to realize it are the theologians. As a preparatory study they take philosophy. Philosophy teaches them that theology is nonsense. Then, when they study theology, they are taught that philosophy is nonsense! Isn't that madness?

DAUGHTER OF INDRA. Then there is jurisprudence—the servant of all, except the toilers—

ATTORNEY. Justice, which—in the name of the law—can mark a man for life! Justice—which so often makes a mockery of justice!

DAUGHTER OF INDRA. What a sorry mess you have made for yourselves, you children of humanity! For that's what you all are—children!—Come here, and I shall give you a wreath—one that will be more appropriate for you! [*She places a wreath of thorns on his head*] and now I shall play for you. [*She sits down at the keyboard of the organ. But instead of hearing organ music, one hears human voices.*]

VOICES OF CHILDREN. Eternal One! Eternal One! [*The last note is sustained.*]

VOICES OF WOMEN. Be merciful, O God! [*The last note is similarly held.*]

VOICES OF MEN [*tenors*]. Save us, for Your mercy's sake! [*Again the last note is held.*]

VOICES OF MEN [*basses*]. Spare Your children, O Lord, and let not Your wrath descend upon us!

ALL. Be merciful, O God! Hear us! Take pity upon us mortals!—Eternal One, why are You afar from us? We cry out of the depths to You: Have mercy upon us, God Eternal! Make not the burden of Your children too heavy! Hear us! Hear us!

[*The scene grows dark. The* DAUGHTER OF INDRA *rises, goes toward the* ATTORNEY. *Through effects of lighting, the organ is transformed into Fingal's Cave. The backwash of the sea can be seen against the basalt pillars, and the sounds of waves and wind can be heard in harmonious blending.*]

ATTORNEY. Where are we, sister?

DAUGHTER OF INDRA. What do you hear?

ATTORNEY. I hear the dripping of water.

DAUGHTER OF INDRA. It is tears...the tears of mankind. What else do you hear?

ATTORNEY. I hear sighing....I hear whining and wailing.

DAUGHTER OF INDRA. This is as far as the plaints of mortals reach...and no farther. But why this eternal wailing? Is there nothing in life to rejoice over?

ATTORNEY. Yes—that . . . which is sweeter than anything...and yet more bitter than anything: love—a wife and a home: the most sublime and the most hollow!

DAUGHTER OF INDRA. I would like to submit myself to the test.

ATTORNEY. With me?

DAUGHTER OF INDRA. With you!—You know the pitfalls and the stumbling blocks....Let us stay clear of them.

ATTORNEY. I am poor...

DAUGHTER OF INDRA. What does it matter? All that matters is that we love each other! A little beauty does not have to be bought.

ATTORNEY. I have dislikes and aversions. They may be your likes and sympathies.

DAUGHTER OF INDRA. We have to modify and compromise, give way to each other.

ATTORNEY. And if we tire of each other?

DAUGHTER OF INDRA. When the child comes, it will bring a joy that will be ever young!

ATTORNEY. And you—you will have me, poor and ugly as I am, scorned and despised, disdained and rejected?

DAUGHTER OF INDRA. Yes. Let us unite our destinies.

ATTORNEY. So be it.

[The ATTORNEY's *living quarters. A starkly simple room behind the* ATTORNEY's *office. On the left, a large double bed with curtains around it; close by, a window.*

On the right, a parlor stove with cooking utensils. KRISTIN *is busy pasting paper strips, or tape, along the openings between the windows and the casement.*

There is a door, rear, leading to the law office. It is open, and beyond it can be seen men and women, all visibly poor, waiting to see the ATTORNEY.]

KRISTIN. I paste, I paste!

DAUGHTER OF INDRA [*sits by the stove. She looks pale and worn*]. You are shutting out the air! I am stifling!

KRISTIN. I have just one little leaky spot left now . . .

DAUGHTER OF INDRA. Air! Air!—I can't breathe here . . .

KRISTIN. I paste, I paste!

ATTORNEY. That's right, Kristin. . . . Heat costs money!

DAUGHTER OF INDRA. Oh, I feel as if my jaws were glued together.

ATTORNEY [*standing in the doorway, holding a document in his hand*]. Is the little one asleep?

DAUGHTER OF INDRA. Yes, at last!

ATTORNEY [*gently*]. Its continual crying drives away my clients.

DAUGHTER OF INDRA [*in a mild tone of voice*]. What is there we can do about it?

ATTORNEY. Nothing!

DAUGHTER OF INDRA. We must try to find a roomier place to live.

ATTORNEY. We can't afford it.

DAUGHTER OF INDRA. Will you let me open the window? The air here is foul! It suffocates me!

ATTORNEY. Then the heat will escape, and we'll freeze.

DAUGHTER OF INDRA. This is horrible! Will you let us scrub the floor in the office?

ATTORNEY. You are not strong enough to do that! I haven't the strength either! And Kristin must finish the pasting. She has to paste strips throughout the house, from top to bottom—every crack and crevice—in the ceilings, the walls, and the floors.

DAUGHTER OF INDRA. I foresaw that we might be poor, but I was not prepared for this filth and dirt.

ATTORNEY. Poverty is a kin of squalor.

DAUGHTER OF INDRA. This is worse than I had thought!

ATTORNEY. There are others who are worse off. We still have some food in the house.

DAUGHTER OF INDRA. But what kind of food?

ATTORNEY. Cabbage is cheap. And it is nourishing and good.

DAUGHTER OF INDRA. Yes—if you like cabbage! To me it is distasteful!

ATTORNEY. You never complained before.

DAUGHTER OF INDRA. I tried to sacrifice my own preferences out of love for you!

ATTORNEY. Then I must make a sacrifice of what I like, too. We each must sacrifice something.

DAUGHTER OF INDRA. What shall we eat, then? Fish?—But you don't like fish!

ATTORNEY. And it's expensive, too.

DAUGHTER OF INDRA. This is more wretched than I thought it would be.

ATTORNEY [*in a gentle voice*]. Now you see how hard it is. . . . And the child was to be the bond between us—our blessing! The child turns out to be our undoing.

DAUGHTER OF INDRA. Beloved! I shall die in here—in this air! All I ever see is the view of the yard in the back! I hear nothing but crying children, and lie without sleep for hours! I hear the people outside, whining without end, bickering with each other, accusing each other. . . . There is nothing left for me but death!

ATTORNEY. My poor little flower, who is without light—without air—

DAUGHTER OF INDRA. And you say there are those who have it worse than we?

ATTORNEY. I am one of the few envied ones in our street.

DAUGHTER OF INDRA. If I could only have some beauty in my home, things might not seem so bad.

ATTORNEY. I know ... you mean a flower—above all a heliotrope. But that would cost as much as six bottles of milk or half a bushel of potatoes.

DAUGHTER OF INDRA. I'll gladly go without food if I can only have a flower.

ATTORNEY. But there is one kind of beauty one doesn't have to pay for! Its lack in the home is more painful than anything else to a man with a feeling for beauty. . . .

DAUGHTER OF INDRA. What is that?

ATTORNEY. If I should tell you, you'll be angry with me.

DAUGHTER OF INDRA. Haven't we agreed never to get angry?

ATTORNEY. So we have. Everything can be overlooked, Agnes, except a short-tempered, sharp, curt tone of voice. Have you ever heard such a tone of voice? Or haven't you?

DAUGHTER OF INDRA. Such a tone will never be used by either of us.

ATTORNEY. Never as far as I am concerned!

DAUGHTER OF INDRA. You can tell me now!

ATTORNEY. Well—when I come into a room, the first thing I look at is the curtains—to see how they are draped in the sash. [He goes over to the window and adjusts the curtains.] If they hang like a rope or a rag, then I don't remain long in that house. . . . Next I take a glance at the chairs. If they are placed where they should be placed, I stay. [He moves a chair back against the wall.] And finally I look at the candles in their holders. If they are askew—then the whole house is awry. [He puts straight a candle on the bureau.] It is this kind of beauty that cannot be bought, my dearest.

DAUGHTER OF INDRA [with bent head]. Don't be short-tempered, Axel—

ATTORNEY. I wasn't short-tempered!

DAUGHTER OF INDRA. Yes, you were.

ATTORNEY. Now, what in hell . . .

DAUGHTER OF INDRA. What kind of language is that?

ATTORNEY. Forgive me, Agnes! But I have suffered as much from your disorderliness as you have suffered from dirt and filth. And I haven't dared offer my help to keep the house in order for fear that you would be angry. You would think I was reproaching you. Ugh! Don't you think we ought to stop bickering?

DAUGHTER OF INDRA. It is a hardship to be married. . . . A greater test than anything else! One has to be an angel. . . .

ATTORNEY. I think you are right.

DAUGHTER OF INDRA. I feel as if I were beginning to hate you!

ATTORNEY. That would be the end for us! Let us never feel hatred for each other! I vow I shall never again remark upon the disorderliness in our home—even though it tortures me!

DAUGHTER OF INDRA. And I shall eat cabbage, even if I suffer agony.

ATTORNEY. A married life of common pain and deprivation! What is pleasure to one is pain to another.

DAUGHTER OF INDRA. Men are to be pitied!

ATTORNEY. You've come to realize it now?

DAUGHTER OF INDRA. I have ... but in the name of Heaven, let us stay clear of the rocks, now that we know their dangers.

ATTORNEY. Yes, let us try. . . . We are both good, and we are intelligent. We both have forbearance, and have learned to forgive.

DAUGHTER OF INDRA. Why shouldn't we pass over all trifles with a smile?

ATTORNEY. We can! And only we can do it. . . . Let me tell you—I read today in the Morning . . . By the way, where is the newspaper?

DAUGHTER OF INDRA [embarrassed]. Which newspaper?

ATTORNEY [in a biting tone]. Do I keep more than one? Do I?

DAUGHTER OF INDRA. Smile now, and don't speak harshly. . . . I used it to start the fire with.

ATTORNEY [bursts out violently]. Hell and damnation!

DAUGHTER OF INDRA. Smile ... smile! I burned it because it ridiculed what to me is holy!

ATTORNEY. And to me—unholy! Cha! [He strikes his fist against the palm of his hand, incontrollably.] I'll keep smiling until my molars show. . . . I'll be lenient and forgiving, and suppress my opinions, and say yes to everything and anything, and be a sneak and a hypocrite! So, you have burned my newspaper, eh? [He rearranges the curtain round the bed.] Now you see—I am rearranging things again, and that will make you angry. Agnes, this just cannot go on!

DAUGHTER OF INDRA. No, it can't.

ATTORNEY. And yet we must endure it. It isn't our vows and promises that matter so much as our child!

DAUGHTER OF INDRA. You are right! It's the child that matters!—that matters most! . . . Oh! Oh! . . . We must keep going. . . .

ATTORNEY. Now I must go out to my clients. You hear how they chatter, impatient to tear at each other, aching to see the other fellow getting fined and imprisoned! They are lost souls.

DAUGHTER OF INDRA. These poor, poor people. . . . And this incessant pasting! [She bends her head in silent despair.]

KRISTIN. I paste . . . I paste. . . .

[The ATTORNEY stands at the door, nervously squeezing and turning the doorknob.]

DAUGHTER OF INDRA. Oh! The screech from that knob! It makes me feel as if you were squeezing my heart . . .

ATTORNEY. I turn and twist, I turn and twist . . .

DAUGHTER OF INDRA. Please—please don't!

ATTORNEY. I turn and twist . . .

DAUGHTER OF INDRA. Don't! . . .

ATTORNEY. I . . .

OFFICER [turns the knob from within the office]. Allow me . . .

ATTORNEY [lets go the knob]. Certainly . . . seeing that you have a doctor's degree . . .

OFFICER. Now I have all of life before me! All roads are open to me! I have reached my Parnassus, have won the laurel wreath, gained fame and immortality! The world is mine!

ATTORNEY. And what are you going to live on?

OFFICER. Live on?

ATTORNEY. You must have a place to live in, you must have food, clothes . . .

OFFICER. There is always a way out, so long as you have someone to love you.

ATTORNEY. I can well imagine! I can well . . . Paste, Kristin! Paste until they can't breathe any longer!

[Goes out backward, nodding.]

KRISTIN. I paste, I paste—until they can't breathe. . . .

OFFICER [to the DAUGHTER OF INDRA]. Will you come with me now?

DAUGHTER OF INDRA. This very moment! But where?

OFFICER. To Faircove! Where it is summer, where the sun is shining—where there is youth, where there are children and flowers, singing and dancing, gaiety and exuberant life!

DAUGHTER OF INDRA. Then I would like to go there!

OFFICER. Come, then!

ATTORNEY [enters again]. Now I return to my first hell. This was the second—the more terrible one! The sweeter the hell, the more horrible! . . . Now look here—she has dropped hairpins on the floor again! [He picks up the hairpins.]

OFFICER. Imagine, he has discovered the hairpins, too!

ATTORNEY. Too? Look at this one! It has two prongs, yet it is one pin. Two—yet only one! If I straighten it, then it is one; if I bend it, it becomes two—yet without ceasing to be one! That means that the two are one! But if I should break it—like this—then the two are two. [He breaks the hairpin in two and throws away the pieces.]

OFFICER. He has seen all that! But before breaking, the prongs must diverge. If they converge—they will hold.

ATTORNEY. And if they are parallel, they will never meet—and then they will neither break nor hold anything.

OFFICER. The hairpin is the most perfect among created things! A straight line that equals two parallel lines!

ATTORNEY. A lock that shuts while it is open—

OFFICER. —for, while open, it shuts in a braid of hair that remains outside while it is shut in . . .

ATTORNEY. Much like this door! When I close it . . . I open—the way out—for you, Agnes.

[He withdraws, closing the door after him.]

DAUGHTER OF INDRA. And now?

[*Foulgut. There is a change of scenery. The bed with the curtains is transformed into a tent; the stove remains. The backdrop is raised; and one sees now in the background a beautiful, wooded shore with flags flying from its jetties, to which white sailboats are moored. Some of the boats have their sails hoisted, others have dropped sails. Small Italian villas, pavilions, kiosks, and marble statues can be discerned along the shore, between the treetops.*

On the left, downstage, is a hillside, scorched by fire and with patches of red heather; here and there a smoky, blackened white tree stub and several pigpens and outhouses, painted red.

Below is an open-air gymnasium for the rehabilitation of physically handicapped and other ailing persons, where patients go through a routine of exercises on apparatuses resembling instruments of torture.

On the right in the foreground are visible some of the open sheds of the quarantine station, supplied with fireplaces, furnaces, and piping conduits.

Between the shore in the background and the landscape in the foreground is a narrow strait.

The QUARANTINE MASTER, *dressed as a blackamoor, is walking along the shore. The* OFFICER *steps up to him. They shake hands.*]

OFFICER. Well, if it isn't Ordström! So you've landed out here?

QUARANTINE MASTER. So I have, as you see!

OFFICER. Can this be Faircove?

QUARANTINE MASTER. No—Faircove is across the strait. This is Foulgut.

OFFICER. Then we have come to the wrong place!

QUARANTINE MASTER. We?—Won't you introduce me?

OFFICER. No, that wouldn't do! [*In an undertone.*] Do you know who she is? She is the Daughter of Indra.

QUARANTINE MASTER. The Daughter of Indra? I thought she was the Daughter of Varuna himself! Well, aren't you surprised to see my face black?

OFFICER. My dear boy! When one has reached fifty, one ceases to be surprised at anything!—I immediately took it for

granted that you were going to a masquerade ball this afternoon.

QUARANTINE MASTER. You are quite right. And I hope you will both come with me.

OFFICER. And why not? . . . For I can't say—I can't say that this place seems especially inviting. . . . What kind of people live here anyway?

QUARANTINE MASTER. Here is where the sick live . . . over there are the healthy.

OFFICER. Then you have nothing but poor people here, I suppose?

QUARANTINE MASTER. On the contrary . . . here is where you find the rich! Take a look at that one on the rack there. He has stuffed himself with goose liver and truffles and consumed so much burgundy that his feet have curled into knots.

OFFICER. Into knots?

QUARANTINE MASTER. Yes, he has developed knotted feet. And that one over there—on that guillotine—has swallowed so much brandy that his spine has to be mangled out!

OFFICER. Will that really help?

QUARANTINE MASTER. For the rest, all who have some sort of misery that they wish to hide, live on this side! For instance—do you see the man coming here? [*An* ELDERLY DANDY *is pushed on the stage in a wheelchair. He is accompanied by a woman of sixty, an emaciated ugly* OLD FLIRT, *dressed in latest fashion. She is being attended by her* LOVER, *a man of about forty.*]

OFFICER. It's the Major! He went to school with us, didn't he?

QUARANTINE MASTER. Yes—Don Juan! You can see, can't you, that he is still in love with that old spook-face next to him! He doesn't even see how she has aged—that she is ugly, faithless, and cruel!

OFFICER. Well—that's what love does! But I never thought that such a fickle fellow as he used to be could fall in love so deeply, so seriously!

QUARANTINE MASTER. You look at things in a very sympathetic way, I must say.

OFFICER. I have been in love myself—with Victoria . . . and I am still waiting—waiting for her to come.

QUARANTINE MASTER. Oh, it's you—

it's you who are waiting for her in the passageway.

OFFICER. Yes—I am the fellow. . . .

QUARANTINE MASTER. Tell me—have you got that door opened yet?

OFFICER. No—the matter is still before the court. . . . The Billposter is out fishing with his dip-net, of course—and that's what's delaying the testimony. . . . Meantime the Glazier has been putting in the windows in the castle—it has now grown half a story higher. . . . This has been an exceptionally good year—warm and wet.

QUARANTINE MASTER. But you haven't had it as hot as I have had it here, that's certain!

OFFICER. How hot do you keep your ovens, may I ask?

QUARANTINE MASTER. When we fumigate suspected cholera cases, we run it up to 108 degrees Fahrenheit.

OFFICER. Is the cholera rampant again?

QUARANTINE MASTER. Didn't you know?

OFFICER. Yes, of course, I know—but I forget so frequently things I should remember. . . .

QUARANTINE MASTER. I often wish I could forget, too, especially myself. That's one reason why I like to disguise myself and go to masquerade balls and take part in theatricals.

OFFICER. What have you been doing these many years?

QUARANTINE MASTER. If I told anyone, people would say I was boasting. And if I should say nothing, I would be called a hypocrite!

OFFICER. Is that why you have blackened your face?

QUARANTINE MASTER. Yes—I've made myself a little blacker than I really am!

OFFICER. Who is that man coming here?

QUARANTINE MASTER. Oh, he is a poet. . . . He is coming to get his mud bath. . . . [*The* POET *enters. His eyes are turned heavenward. He is carrying a bucket of mud.*]

OFFICER. In Heaven's name! Why don't you give him a sun bath—or an air bath—instead?

QUARANTINE MASTER. Oh no—he is forever flitting about in loftier regions—and so gets homesick for the mud occasionally. . . . Wallowing about in the slime and dirt toughens the skin. Look at the pigs! And once he is toughened, he is immune to the stings of the horseflies.

OFFICER. This is a strange world! So full of contradictions!

POET [*ecstatically*]. Out of clay the god Ptah created man, on a potter's wheel, or lathe . . . [*Skeptically.*] out of clay or something else—whatever it was! [*Ecstatically.*] Out of clay the sculptor creates his more or less immortal masterpieces . . . [*Skeptically.*] most of the time nothing but rubbish [*Ecstatically.*] Out of clay are manufactured the wares and utensils—so absolutely necessary in a household—which we commonly call pottery, earthenware, dishes, and so forth . . . [*Skeptically.*] anyhow, what do I care *what* they are called! [*Ecstatically.*] That much for clay! When the clay is oozy, or thin, in liquid form, it's called mud. And that's what I want! [*He calls.*] Lina! [*Lina enters with a bucket.*] Lina, show yourself to Miss Agnes!—She knew you ten years ago when you were a young girl, full of joy—and, we might say, pretty. . . . But take a look at Lina now —after five children, drudgery, baby-cries, lack of nourishment, and cruel treatment! You can see how all that was lovely has vanished—that happiness is gone! And all the while she was trying to exercise her duties—duties which ought to have given her an inner satisfaction that would have shown in her face! Her face would have had a pleasing symmetry, her eyes would have shone with warmth and gentleness . . .

QUARANTINE MASTER [*covers the* POET's *mouth with his hand*]. Keep your mouth shut! Will you keep your mouth shut!

POET. That's what they all say! And if I keep silent, they say: Why don't you say something? Oh, these unpredictable mortals!

DAUGHTER OF INDRA [*goes over to* LINA]. Tell me what troubles you!

LINA. I wouldn't dare! It would only make things worse for me!

DAUGHTER OF INDRA. Who is so cruel to you?

LINA. I wouldn't dare say. . . . I would only suffer for it. . . .

POET. Well, never mind . . . but I shall —even if the blackamoor should threaten to knock all my teeth out! ... I am not afraid to say that we don't always get justice here!—Agnes, daughter of the gods, do you hear the music and dancing up there on the hillside?—Then listen to what I have to say! It is all for Lina's sister, who has come home from the city, where she went astray—you know what I mean. ... Now they are killing the fatted calf for her—but Lina, who stayed at home—she has to carry the slops to the swine and feed them!

DAUGHTER OF INDRA. Bear in mind: there is rejoicing in that home not alone because the misguided child has come back to her parents, but all the more because she has abandoned the path of evil!

POET. But why not then give a ball and a banquet every evening in the week for the blameless toiler who never strayed from the straight and narrow path? Why not do that? No—that they would never do! But when Lina has a moment to herself, she has to go to a prayer meeting and hear herself reproached for not being perfect!—Do you call that justice—do you?

DAUGHTER OF INDRA. I find it hard to answer your questions because they—because there are so many unforeseen, so many different angles to take into consideration. ...

POET. That is just what Harun the Just, the caliph, realized while he sat tranquilly on his throne. There he sat, away on high, without any knowledge of how the mortals fared below. ... Finally the complaints reached his ear. One day he descended, and in disguise he mingled unrecognized with the crowds. He wanted to find out what sort of justice was being meted out to his subjects.

DAUGHTER OF INDRA. But I am not Harun the Just!

OFFICER. Let us talk about something else. ... Here comes some visitors. ... [A white, dragonlike boat with sails of light blue on a gilded yard and with gilded mast glides slowly into the strait from the right. A rosy red pennant flies from the masthead. HE and SHE are seated aft by the rudder, their arms entwined around each other.] There—there you see perfect happiness, boundless bliss, triumphant young love. ...

[The scene gradually grows light. HE stands up in the boat and sings.]

HE. Hail, hail, fairest cove
where in youth I spent my springtime ...
where in rosy colors I dreamt youth's
    sweet dreams.
Here I come to you again—
though not, as then, alone!
Greet her, you sea and sky,
you bays and groves—
greet her. ...
My love, my bride,
my life, my sun!

[The flags flowing from the slips and jetties at Faircove are dipped in salute; white handkerchiefs are waved from the cottages and the shore, and soft music from harps and violins is heard.]

POET. Behold the shining light that radiates from them! Hear the music floating over the water!—The god of love ... Eros!

OFFICER. It's Victoria!

QUARANTINE MASTER. Well—what of it?

OFFICER. It's his Victoria! My Victoria is still mine! And I won't let anybody see her. ... Now—you hoist the quarantine flag, and I shall pull in the net! [The QUARANTINE MASTER waves a yellow flag. The OFFICER pulls at a rope, causing the boat to turn toward Foulgut.] Hold on there! [HE and SHE suddenly become aware of the dread features of the locality and express their horror audibly.]

QUARANTINE MASTER. Well, well—this takes the wind out of your sails, doesn't it? But they all have to come here—all who come from cholera-infested localities.

POET. Imagine speaking in that manner—doing such a thing to two human beings who are in love! Don't you touch them! Don't soil their great love! It would be a crime—nothing short of high treason! ... Woe unto us! All that was once beautiful must be dragged down—dragged into the mud and mire! [HE and SHE step ashore. They now look shamefaced and sad.]

HE. Why should we have to suffer this grief? What have we done?

QUARANTINE MASTER. You needn't necessarily have done anything, even if you are pricked by life's little barbs.

SHE. That is how long happiness and joy last!

HE. How long do we have to stay here?

QUARANTINE MASTER. Forty days and forty nights.

SHE. Then let us rather die!

HE. To have to live here—among fire-scorched hills and pigsties! Oh!

POET. Love conquers all—even sulfur fumes and carbolic acid!

QUARANTINE OFFICER [makes a fire in the oven. Blue sulfur flames break out.] Now I have started the fire and am burning the sulfur. . . . Will you please step inside. . . .

SHE. Oh! My blue dress will be discolored. . . .

QUARANTINE MASTER. It will turn white—and so will your red roses. . . .

HE. And your cheeks, too, before the forty days are over!

SHE [to the OFFICER]. That will make you glad!

OFFICER. No, that's not true! . . . It's true that your happiness became the source of my unhappiness—but . . . that doesn't matter now. I have received my degree and have now a tutoring position across the strait . . . yes, yes—yes, yes—and in the fall I'll be teaching school. . . . I'll be teaching the boys the same lessons I learned in my long childhood, and all through my youth—and now I'll be teaching these same lessons throughout my manhood—and finally, the very same lessons till I am an old man and ready to die: How much is two times two?—How many times two is four? . . . until I'm pensioned off and have nothing to do except to wait around for the meals to be served, and for the newspapers! . . . And at last I am brought to the crematorium and burned to ashes. . . . Is there nobody here who is entitled to a pension? I think it's about the worst next to "two times two is four"! And to start going to school all over again, after being given a doctor's degree—and to have to ask the same questions over and over again until you die! [An aged gentleman, his hands on his back, is seen passing.] See—there you have a pensioner who is waiting for nothing but the end. . . . I think he must be an army captain who couldn't make the grade—or he may have been a clerk of the supreme court who failed to be appointed to a judgeship. Many are called, but few are chosen. . . . He is impatiently waiting for his breakfast. . . .

PENSIONER. No—for the newspaper! The Morning News!

OFFICER. And he is only fifty-four years old. . . . He might be waiting for his meals and his newspaper twenty-five years from now! Isn't it frightful?

PENSIONER. What is it that isn't frightful? Tell me, tell me, tell me!

OFFICER. Well, let him answer who can! . . . Now I am going to teach boys that two times two is four—and how many times four can be evenly divided by two. [He scratches his head in desperation.] And Victoria—whom I loved and therefore wished the greatest happiness in the world. . . . Now she has found her happiness—the greatest for her . . . and I suffer . . . I suffer . . . suffer!

SHE. Do you think I can be happy when I see you suffer? How can you think that? Perhaps it will lessen the pain for you to know that I am being incarcerated here for forty days and forty nights? Does that lighten the pain?

OFFICER. Yes—and no! How can I be happy, while you suffer? Oh . . .

HE. And do you think my happiness can be built on your misery and pain?

OFFICER. We are all to be pitied!

ALL [they lift their hands toward the sky and utter a dissonant cry of anguish]. Oh! . . .

DAUGHTER OF INDRA. Eternal One, hear their cry! Life is misery! Men are to be pitied!

ALL [as before]. Oh! . . .

[Faircove. For a moment the stage is dark. During this period, those on the stage disappear or change position. When the stage is light again, the shore at Foulgut can be seen dimly in the background. The strait flows between Foulgut and Faircove; the latter is visible in the foreground. The body of water and Faircove are bathed in light. On the left, a corner of the main pavilion or casino. Through its open windows can be seen a couple, dancing. On a wooden crate outside stand three servant maids with their arms round each other's waists. They are watching the dancers inside. On the terrace stand a piano with open keyboard and a bench. Seated on the latter is PLAIN-LOOKING EDITH. She is bareheaded and seems depressed; she has a mass of tousled hair, and sad eyes.

On the right is a yellow frame house. Two children in summer dress are playing ball outside. On the downstage side of the strait is a jetty with sailboats tied up to it. In the rear, flags and pennants fly from the jetty's flagpoles. In the stream is anchored a white navy brig with gunports.

The entire scene is in winter dress, and both the ground and the barren trees are covered with snow.

The DAUGHTER OF INDRA and the OFFICER enter.]

DAUGHTER OF INDRA. Here is peace and happiness. Here you can relax. Drudgery is banished. Every day is a day of enjoyment. People are dressed as for a holiday. Music and dancing from early morn. [To the SERVANT MAIDS.] Why don't you go inside and join in the dancing?

ONE OF THE SERVANT MAIDS. We?

OFFICER. Can't you see they are servants?

DAUGHTER OF INDRA. I forgot!—But why is Edith sitting there by herself? Why isn't she dancing? [EDITH buries her face in her hands.]

OFFICER. You shouldn't have asked her that! She has been sitting there for three hours, and no one has asked her to dance. . . .

[He goes into the yellow house on the right.]

DAUGHTER OF INDRA. What cruelty there can be in pleasure!

EDITH'S MOTHER [comes out from the casino. She is dressed in a low-necked dress. She goes directly over to EDITH]. Why don't you go inside as I told you!

EDITH. Because—I can't put myself on exhibition! I can't force people to dance with me, can I? I know I am not pretty to look at! That's why nobody wants to dance with me . . . and I wish you would stop reminding me of it. . . . [She starts to play on the piano Johann Sebastian Bach's Toccata con Fuga, No. 10. At first the music from within is heard faintly; then it increases in sound as if it were trying to drown out Bach's Toccata. EDITH, however, persists and the dance finally stops. Guests at the casino appear in the doorway, fascinated by her playing. They all stand silent, in rapt attention.]

NAVAL OFFICER [puts his arm round the waist of ALICE, one of the guests, and leads her down toward the jetty]. Come quickly!

[EDITH breaks off her playing abruptly, rises and follows them, agonized, with her eyes. She remains standing as if she had turned into stone.]

[The façade of the yellow house is now removed, revealing a classroom in a school. One sees three rows of benches, seated on which are a number of boy pupils. Among them is the OFFICER. He seems to be ill at ease, restless, and worried. Facing the pupils stands the TEACHER; he is wearing spectacles, and in his hand he has a piece of chalk and a rattan cane.]

TEACHER [to the OFFICER]. Well, my boy, can you tell me now what two times two makes? [The OFFICER remains seated. He racks his brain without being able to give the answer.] Stand up when you are asked a question!

OFFICER [painfully affected, he rises]. Two . . . times two. . . . Let me see . . . it's . . . two two . . .

TEACHER. Oho! You haven't studied your lesson!

OFFICER [ashamed]. Yes, I have—but . . . I know the answer—but I can't tell you. . . .

TEACHER. You are trying to get out of answering! You know the answer—but you can't tell me! Perhaps you want me to help you! [He pulls the OFFICER's hair.]

OFFICER. Oh, this is terrible—terrible!

TEACHER. Yes, isn't it! A big boy like you—so completely lacking in ambition. . . .

OFFICER [tortured]. A big boy! Yes—I am big—bigger than the other boys here. . . . I'm a grown man—have been through school. [He searches his mind; he seems to be recovering his memory.] I have been given a doctor's degree, haven't I?—Then why am I sitting here? Haven't I been given a degree?

TEACHER. Of course you have . . . but you see, you have to sit here to mature. You have to mature—isn't that so?

OFFICER [runs his hand over his forehead]. Yes, of course . . . you are right—we have to mature. . . . Two times two—

is two . . . and I'll prove it by a demonstration in analogy—the highest form of reasoning that exists. Now listen to me! —One times one is one; isn't it? Therefore two times two is two! For what applies in one case must of necessity apply in another.

TEACHER. Your conclusion is in complete conformity with good logic—but the answer is wrong!

OFFICER. What is right according to logic can't be wrong! Let's put it to the test. One divided by one gives one—and so two divided by two must give two.

TEACHER. Entirely correct according to the conclusion arrived at by analogy. But what does one times three make?

OFFICER. Three!

TEACHER. Consequently two times three should also make three, shouldn't it?

OFFICER [ponders the question]. No— that can't be right . . . it can't be—unless . . . [He sits down in despair.] Yes, I see I am not mature yet!

TEACHER. No—you are not! Not by any means!

OFFICER. But how long will I have to sit here, then?

TEACHER. How long?—Do you believe in the existence of time and space?— Suppose that time does exist—then you should be able to tell me what it is. What is time?

OFFICER. Time? [He reflects.] I can't say exactly what it is—but I know very well what it is. . . . Consequently, why can't I know what two times two makes, without being able to say it? Can you tell me what time is, Teacher?

TEACHER. Of course I can!

ALL THE PUPILS [in chorus]. Tell us, then!

TEACHER. Time—let me see! [He stands immobile, one finger on his nose.] While we are talking, time flies . . . therefore it is something that flies . . . while I talk . . .

A PUPIL [stands up]. Now you are talking, Teacher, and while you are talking, I fly . . . consequently I am time!

[He runs out.]

TEACHER. Absolutely correct according to the laws of logic!

OFFICER. But in that case the laws of logic are ridiculous—for Nils, who just skipped class, can't possibly be time. . . .

TEACHER. What you say is also quite in accordance with the laws of logic, except that it's silly. . . .

OFFICER. Then all logic must be silly!

TEACHER. It really seems so. . . . But if logic is asinine, then the whole world must be crazy . . . and then the devil himself wouldn't want to stay here and teach you any more idiotic stupidities!—If anybody cares to treat me to a good stiff drink, I wouldn't mind taking you for a swim!

OFFICER. I would call this a posterus prius, or—the world turned upside down. I always thought the swim came first and the drink afterward. You old fogy!

TEACHER. I warn you not to get a swelled head, Doctor!

OFFICER. Call me Major, if you please! I am an army officer—and I haven't the faintest idea why I am sitting her taking scoldings like any schoolboy. . . .

TEACHER [pointing his finger at him]. We have to learn—to mature!

QUARANTINE MASTER [enters]. The quarantine is now in effect!

OFFICER. Oh, there you are! Can you imagine—he made me sit among the young lads in this classroom, despite my degree as a doctor of philosophy!

QUARANTINE MASTER. Well, why didn't you get up and leave?

OFFICER. Leave, you say. . . . Well I don't know. . . . It isn't so easy as you think. . . .

TEACHER. No—you are quite right! You just try!

OFFICER [to the QUARANTINE MASTER]. Save me! Save me from his staring eyes!

QUARANTINE MASTER. Just come with me!—Come and join in the dance . . . we have to dance before the plague breaks out—we simply must!

OFFICER. Is the brig sailing?

QUARANTINE MASTER. Yes, that's the first thing we must do—get the brig away from here!—There'll be much weeping, of course. . . .

OFFICER. There always is, whenever that brig comes here—and whenever it leaves!—Let us go. . . . [They go out. The TEACHER, in pantomime, continues calmly with his teaching.]

[The SERVANT MAIDS, who have been standing outside the casino win-

*dows, now drag themselves mourn-
fully down to the jetty.* EDITH, *who
has remained standing like a statue
by the piano, follows them.*]

DAUGHTER OF INDRA [*to the* OFFICER].
Is there then not one person who is
happy in this paradise?

OFFICER. Yes—there is a couple that
have just been married. . . . Let's listen to
them and watch them. [*The two newly-
married enter.*]

HUSBAND [*to his* WIFE]. My bliss is so
boundless that I could die happy this moment. . . .

WIFE. Why should you wish to die?

HUSBAND. Because at the core of happiness lies the seed of unhappiness. . . .
Happiness devours itself as fire does! The
flame can't burn eternally—it is doomed
to die. . . . This foreknowledge of the
finality of things annihilates bliss at its
very apex.

WIFE. Then let us die together—this
very moment!

HUSBAND. Die . . . together. . . . Come!
I am frightened of happiness and its
treachery! . . .

[*They disappear toward the sea.*]

DAUGHTER OF INDRA [*to the* OFFICER].
Life is misery! Man is to be pitied!

OFFICER. Look at this man coming
here! He is the most envied of the humans in this community! [*The* BLIND
MAN *enters. He is being led by another
man.*] He is the owner of hundreds of
Italian villas here. He owns all these
coves and bays, shores and woods, the
fish in the water, the birds in the air, and
the game in the woods. These, close to a
thousand human beings, are his tenants
—and the sun rises over his holdings by
the sea and sets over his properties inland. . . .

DAUGHTER OF INDRA. And does he complain also?

OFFICER. Yes—and with good reason.
. . . He can't see. . . .

QUARANTINE MASTER. He is blind!

DAUGHTER OF INDRA. And he is the
most envied of all. . . .

OFFICER. Now he is watching the brig
sail away. . . . His son is aboard. . . .

BLIND MAN. I may not see—but I can
hear! I can hear the claws of the anchor
grappling with the mud at the bottom of
the sea . . . exactly as when one extracts

a fishhook from a fish and the heart is
dragged out at the same time. . . . My son
—my only child—is leaving for strange
lands across the wide open seas . . . and I
can only be with him in my thoughts. . . .
Now I hear the cable screech and groan
. . . and . . . I hear something flutter and
flap in the wind—like wet wash on a
clothes line. . . . It might be wet handkerchiefs hung up to dry. . . . And I hear
weeping and sobbing—as when people
can't control their feelings. . . . I can't tell
whether it's the small waves lapping
against the seams of the ship, or whether
it's the young girls on the shore—the
ones who are being abandoned and who
are disconsolate. . . . I once asked a little
boy why the sea was so salty. . . . The
child's father was away on a long voyage.
. . . Without a moment's hesitation he
answered: The sea is salty because seamen cry so often. Why do seamen cry so
much? I asked. Because they always have
to leave their homes; that's why they always have to hang their handkerchiefs on
the masts to dry! . . . And why do human
beings cry when they feel sorrow? I asked
again. Why! said he, that's because the
windows of the eyes have to be washed
now and then so that we can see more
clearly. . . .

[*The brig has now set sail and is slowly
gliding off. The girls on shore wave
their handkerchiefs and some of
them wipe their eyes. From the signal rack on the foremast is then
hoisted the signal "yes": a red ball
on a white field. In answer to it*
ALICE *exultantly waves her handkerchief.*]

DAUGHTER OF INDRA [*to the* OFFICER].
What's the meaning of that flag?

OFFICER. It carries the message "yes."
It's the lieutenant's way of reaffirming
his love—in red—like the crimson blood
of a heart—against the sky-blue canvas of
heaven. . . .

DAUGHTER OF INDRA. How would they
signal the word "no"?

OFFICER. It would be blue as the ran-
cid blood in blue veins. . . . But just see
how Alice almost leaps with joy!

DAUGHTER OF INDRA. And Edith is
weeping!

BLIND MAN. To meet and to part . . .
to part and to meet. . . . That is life. . . .

I met her—his mother. . . . And then she left me—and I was left our son. . . . Now he has left me. . . .

DAUGHTER OF INDRA. But he will come back. . . .

BLIND MAN. Who is that speaking to me? I have heard that voice before—in my dreams—in my youth—when the holidays of summer came—when first I was married—when my child was brought into the world—whenever life smiled upon me, I heard that voice—like the soughing of the south wind—like the voice of harps from ethereal worlds; as I feel the angels would have sung their greeting on the night of His birth. [*The* ATTORNEY *enters. He steps over to the* BLIND MAN *and whispers in his ear.*] You don't say?

ATTORNEY. Yes—believe me! [*He turns to the* DAUGHTER OF INDRA.] Now you have seen many things—but you have not met with the worst. . . .

DAUGHTER OF INDRA. And the worst is . . .

ATTORNEY. To go back, to go over again, to recapitulate! To have to learn the same lesson over and over again! Come!

DAUGHTER OF INDRA. Where are we going?

ATTORNEY. To your duties!

DAUGHTER OF INDRA. And what are they?

ATTORNEY. Whatever you are in dread of! Whatever you have no desire to do, yet must do! It means—to deny yourself things you desire—to sacrifice—to go through hardships and deprivations—in brief, everything that lacks joy and beauty—everything that is vile, loathsome, and painful. . . .

DAUGHTER OF INDRA. Are no duties pleasant, then?

ATTORNEY. Yes—when they are done—when they are fulfilled!

DAUGHTER OF INDRA. And then they no longer exist. . . . Duty, then, is always something odious. . . . Is there nothing that is joyful and pleasant here?

ATTORNEY. Pleasures are sin.

DAUGHTER OF INDRA. Sin?

ATTORNEY. Something to be punished. yes! If I enjoy myself day and night, I suffer the agonies of hell and have a bad conscience the day after.

DAUGHTER OF INDRA. How strange!

ATTORNEY. I wake up in the morning with a headache—and at once the iteration, the recapitulation begins! But it is always a perverted recapitulation! What seemed beautiful and delightful and witty the night before seems to me the next morning ugly and loathsome and stupid. Pleasure seems decayed; joy disintegrated. What people like to call success invariably turns out to be the cause of their next setback. Every success I have achieved during my life has turned into some failure for me. People have an instinctive fear and envy of seeing others get along. They feel that fate is unjust when it favors someone else; and so they try to restore the balance by placing obstacles in the way of others. To be talented is dangerous to one's life: one runs the risk of starving to death!—But you must return to your duties—or I shall bring suit against you. . . . I'll take it through every court, from the lowest to the highest.

DAUGHTER OF INDRA. I have to go back to the stove and the cooking, the cabbage, and the baby's clothes? . . .

ATTORNEY. Yes, you must! We have a big wash today—all the handkerchiefs have to be washed.

DAUGHTER OF INDRA. Oh, must I do this again . . . again . . .

ATTORNEY. Life is one long stretch of repetitions. . . . Look at the schoolmaster in there! Yesterday he was given a degree, was given the laurel wreath and a salute of guns, reached his Parnassus, and was embraced by the monarch. . . . And today he is back in school again, asking for an answer to what two times two makes . . . and he'll be asking that question until his dying day. . . . But—come back to your home, come back to me!

DAUGHTER OF INDRA. I would rather die!

ATTORNEY. Die? No—you must not think of that! First of all, it is a disgrace—a disgrace so great that your body would be abused and subjected to insults; and secondly, you would find no rest in the hereafter. . . . It is a mortal sin!

DAUGHTER OF INDRA. It is not easy to be a human!

ALL. How true!

DAUGHTER OF INDRA. I will not return

with you to humiliation and dirt—I
yearn to go back up there, from where I
came ... but ... first the door must be
opened so that I may learn the secret
within. ... It is my will that the door be
opened!

ATTORNEY. To learn that secret you
must retrace your steps, travel the road
back, all the way, and suffer through all
the vexations and adversities, repetitions,
restraints, and circumlocutions that go
with a lawsuit. ...

DAUGHTER OF INDRA. So be it ... but
first I shall go to some lonely spot out in
the wilderness and find my own self
again. ... We shall see each other in the
future. [To the POET.] Follow me! [Cries
of anguish and pain are heard distantly:
"O woe! O woe! O woe!"] Did you hear
that?

ATTORNEY. That came from the lost
souls over at Foulgut. ...

DAUGHTER OF INDRA. Why is their anguish today louder than usual?

ATTORNEY. Because the sun is shining
here, because there is youth and dancing
here, because there is music in the air.
... It is then that they feel their pains
and afflictions so much more deeply.

DAUGHTER OF INDRA. We must set
them free!

ATTORNEY. You may try!—Once there
was a man who sought to liberate ... He
was hanged on a cross. ...

DAUGHTER OF INDRA. Who hanged
him?

ATTORNEY. The self-righteous, the sanc-
timonious! ...

DAUGHTER OF INDRA. Who are they?

ATTORNEY. Don't you know who the
self-righteous are? You will soon learn to
know them!

DAUGHTER OF INDRA. Was it they who
refused you your degree?

ATTORNEY. Yes!

DAUGHTER OF INDRA. Then I know
who they are. ...

[A beach on the Mediterranean. On the
right, in the foreground, is a white wall.
Protruding above it are orange trees, laden
with fruit. In the background are villas
and the casino with its terraced approach.

On the left, a big pile of coal and two
wheelbarrows.

In the background, to the left, can be
discerned a faint and limited view of the
blue sea. Two COAL HEAVERS, naked to
the waist and black of body, face, and
hands from handling the coal, sit on the
wheelbarrows. Their faces show despair
and agony.

The DAUGHTER OF INDRA and the AT-
TORNEY are visible in the background.]

DAUGHTER OF INDRA. This is paradise!

FIRST COAL HEAVER. This is hell!

SECOND COAL HEAVER. Nearly eighty-
seven degrees in the shade!

FIRST COAL HEAVER. What do you say
about a dip in the sea?

SECOND COAL HEAVER. And get the police on us! Don't you know you can't
bathe here?

FIRST COAL HEAVER. How about picking an orange from one of the trees?

SECOND COAL HEAVER. No—we'll have
the police on us. ...

FIRST COAL HEAVER. But I can't work
in this heat. ... I'm quitting right now.

SECOND COAL HEAVER. If you do, the
police will be after you. ... [There is a
silence.] And furthermore—you wouldn't
be able to buy yourself food. ...

FIRST COAL HEAVER. No food? We,
who work harder than anyone else—we
get the least to eat! The rich, on the
other hand, who do nothing, get all they
want! ... Don't you think one can truthfully say that this is unrighteous and unjust?—I wonder what the Daughter of
the Gods has to say about it?

DAUGHTER OF INDRA. I am at a loss for
a reply!—But tell me—what have you
done to make you so grimy? Why are you
having such a hard life?

FIRST COAL HEAVER. What we have
done? It was our lot to be born of poor
parents—and not too respectable at that.
... We may have been convicted a couple of times, too. ...

DAUGHTER OF INDRA. Convicted?

FIRST COAL HEAVER. Yes! The unpun-
ished lounge up there in the casino, feasting on eight-course dinners and wine.

DAUGHTER OF INDRA [to the ATTOR-
NEY]. Can this really be true?

ATTORNEY. Broadly speaking, yes. ...

DAUGHTER OF INDRA. You mean to say
that every mortal, if given his just de-
serts, would—at some time or other—
have been condemned to prison?

ATTORNEY. Yes.

DAUGHTER OF INDRA. Even you?

ATTORNEY. Yes—even I!

DAUGHTER OF INDRA. Is it true that the poor cannot go bathing in the sea here?

ATTORNEY. Yes—not even with their clothes on! The only ones who escape being fined are the ones who try to drown themselves. . . . But I have heard that they are given a good thrashing by the police. . . .

DAUGHTER OF INDRA. But isn't there some place on the outskirts of the community, out in the country, where they can go bathing?

ATTORNEY. There is no such facility here—all the properties are fenced in.

DAUGHTER OF INDRA. But I mean—on the free, open shore beyond. . . .

ATTORNEY. Nothing is free here. It all belongs to somebody.

DAUGHTER OF INDRA. Even the sea— the great, open sea? . . .

ATTORNEY. Yes—even the sea! You can't go sailing the sea and put into port without being duly registered and charged for it. A nice state of affairs, isn't it?

DAUGHTER OF INDRA. This is no paradise. . . .

ATTORNEY. No—this is not paradise!

DAUGHTER OF INDRA. Why, then, do people do nothing to improve their lot?

ATTORNEY. People do try, of course! But the ones who do try—the reformers —end in a prison or a madhouse. . . .

DAUGHTER OF INDRA. Who has them put in prison?

ATTORNEY. All the righteous, the respectable people. . . .

DAUGHTER OF INDRA. And who sends them to the madhouse?

ATTORNEY. Their own anguish . . . despair over the hopelessness of their struggle.

DAUGHTER OF INDRA. Has the thought not occurred to anyone that things—for reasons not known—must remain as they are?

ATTORNEY. Yes—to them who are well off! They always think that way!

DAUGHTER OF INDRA. That the world is as it should be? . . .

FIRST COAL HEAVER. Nevertheless— aren't we the very foundations of society? —If we didn't deliver the coal, you would have no fire in the kitchen range, or in the fireplaces in the rest of the house— you would have no coal for your factories. The lights in the streets, in the homes and the shops would go out, you would freeze in darkness! That's why we sweat like hell to see that you get the black coal. . . . And what do you give us in return?

ATTORNEY [to the DAUGHTER OF INDRA]. Help them! [There is a silence.] Things can't be the same for all—I understand ᴛʜat . . . but why should the gap be so great? [The GENTLEMAN and the LADY walk across the stage.]

LADY. Will you come with me and play a game?

GENTLEMAN. No, I have to take a walk —otherwise I'll have no appetite for dinner. . . .

FIRST COAL HEAVER. No appetite for dinner? . . .

SECOND COAL HEAVER. No appetite! . . . [Several CHILDREN enter. They scream, frightened when they see the two COAL HEAVERS.]

FIRST COAL HEAVER. They scream when they see us! They scream. . . .

SECOND COAL HEAVER. Hell and damnation!—I'm afraid we'll have to drag out the scaffolds soon and operate on this carcass. . . .

FIRST COAL HEAVER. Yes, damn it, I say the same! [He spits contemptuously.]

ATTORNEY [to the DAUGHTER OF INDRA]. There is no question—something is wrong. . . . Yet people are not too bad . . . but it's . . .

DAUGHTER OF INDRA. But—what?

ATTORNEY. It's their superiors—those who have the authority. . . .

DAUGHTER OF INDRA [hides her face]. This is not paradise!

[She leaves.]

COAL HEAVERS. No—it's not paradise! It's hell—that's what it is!

[Fingal's Cave. Languishing great green waves roll into the cave. In the foreground a red alarm buoy rocks to and fro on the waves; it emits no sound, however, except at such times as indicated in the play. Music of the winds and the waves. The DAUGHTER OF INDRA and the POET are visible when the curtain rises.]

POET. Where have you brought me?

DAUGHTER OF INDRA. Far from the murmur and moans and laments of the children of humanity, to the farthest end of the seven seas—to this grotto, which

has been given the name of Indra's Ear
because it is here that the Master of the
Heavens is said to listen to the complaints of the mortals. . . .

POET. Here?—How can . . .

DAUGHTER OF INDRA. Can't you see
that this grotto is built like a sea shell?
You can see it, can't you? And don't you
know that your own ear is built like a
shell? You know it—but you haven't
given thought to it. [She picks up a sea
shell on the shore.] When you were a
child, don't you remember holding a sea
shell to your ear, listening—listening to
its singing? . . . You heard the ripple of
your heart's blood, the hum of your brain
thinking, the snapping of thousands of
tiny little wornout fibres inside the tissues
of your body, didn't you? All that you
heard in such a little sea shell. . . . Imagine then what sounds you will hear in
this enormous ear!

POET [listens]. I hear nothing but the
whisper of the wind. . . .

DAUGHTER OF INDRA. Then let me interpret what it tells me. . . . Listen to the
wailing of the winds. [She recites to soft
music.]

Born beneath the firmament of heaven,
Indra's flashing lightning soon pursued us
to the earth of dust below. . . .
Litter of pasture fields soiled our feet;
we were forced to endure
the dust of highways,
the smoke of cities,
and evil-smelling breaths,
the odors of wines and cooking. . . .
Finally we fled to the open sea
to take breath and fill our lungs
with fresh air, to flap our wings
and cleanse and bathe our feet.
Indra, Lord of the Heavens,
hear us! . . .
Hear our sighs! . . .
Unclean is the Earth,
life there is miserable;
mankind is not wicked—
yet it can't be called good.
People live as best they can,
for each passing day.
Sons of the Dust, they trudge through
    dust;
born out of dust,
they return to dust.
Feet they were given to move with,
wings were denied them. . . .

Laden with dust they are. . . .
Are they to be blamed—
or are You?

POET. And then I heard one time . . .

DAUGHTER OF INDRA. Hush! The winds
are still singing. [She continues, to soft
music.]

We, the winds, the sons of Air,
Scatter abroad the wails of humans. . . .
Did you hear us
on autumn nights—
whining in the chimneys,
rattling the stove shutters,
or stealing through leaky windows,
whilst the rain wept tears on the roof
    tiles? . . .
Or in wintry night,
in snow-clad woods of pine? . . .
Have you heard moaning and bewailing
in sails and rigging
upon the windswept sea? . . .
It is we—we, the winds—
sons of the Air! . . .
And we've learned these sounds of pain
from anguished human breasts,
which we have pierced and invaded—
on sickbeds, on battlefields . . .
but mostly when babes
whimper at childbirth
and utter cries
of painful anguish at being born. . . .
It is we—winds of the Air—
hissing and whining!
Woe! Woe! Woe!

POET. It seems as if I once . . .

DAUGHTER OF INDRA. Hush! The waves
are singing. [She again recites to subdued
music.]

It is we, the billowy waves,
that cradle the winds
to their sleep! . . .
Green are the cradles we rock,
watery are we and salty;
we leap like fiery flames—
watery flames we are. . . .
Burning and quenching,
bathing and cleansing,
begetting, conceiving. . . .
We—the billowy waves
that cradle them, rock them
into sleep!

Treacherous and faithless waves. . . . All

on earth that is not burned, falls victim to the sea. . . . Look here. [*She points to a heap of debris.*] Look what the sea has plundered and destroyed. . . . All that remains of the sunken ships is the figurehead—and their name-boards: *Justice, Friendship, Golden Peace,* and *Hope.* . . . This is all that remains of Hope—of inconstant and capricious Hope! Railings and rowlocks and bailers! And look here: a lifebuoy—that saved *itself,* but let men in distress go down!

POET [*searching in the pile of debris*]. Here is the name-board of the good ship *Justice*—the very same ship that sailed from Faircove with the Blind Man's son aboard! It was lost, then! And so is Alice's betrothed, with whom poor Edith was so hopelessly in love.

DAUGHTER OF INDRA. The Blind Man? Faircove? Could I have been dreaming? And Alice's fiancé, ugly Edith, Foulgut with its quarantine, its sulfur and carbolic acid, the university ceremony in the church, the Attorney's office, the Portress's cubicle at the Opera, and Victoria, the growing castle and the Officer . . . I have dreamed it all. . . .

POET. I have lived it in my imagination. . . .

DAUGHTER OF INDRA. You know what poetry and imagination are, then. . . .

POET. I know what dreams are. . . . But what is poetry?

DAUGHTER OF INDRA. It is not reality. . . . It is more than reality. It is not dreaming—but dreams come alive, envisioned. . . .

POET. And the children of humanity think that we poets only like to play, are mere jesters—that we merely fabricate, make believe!

DAUGHTER OF INDRA. And that may be a good thing, my friend. Else the world would lie fallow and be barren for lack of care and cultivation. Everybody would be lying on his back, gazing at the sky; and nobody would touch a hoe or a pickax, a shovel or a plow.

POET. And you say this—you, Indra's daughter, who hail from realms above? . . .

DAUGHTER OF INDRA. You reproach me justly. . . . I have dwelt too long down here, wallowing in the mud like you. . . . My thoughts no longer take flight—their wings are weighted down by clay—the mud sticks to their feet! And I myself . . .

[*She raises her arms.*] I myself keep sinking . . . sinking . . . Help me, O Father, God of the Heavens! [*There is a silence.*] No longer can I hear His voice! The ether no longer carries the sound from His lips to my ear—the silvery thread has snapped. . . . Woe to me, I am earthbound!

POET. When will you ascend? Is the time near?

DAUGHTER OF INDRA. When I have shed this mortal guise and it has burned to dust . . . for all the water of the sea cannot make me clean. . . . Why do you ask?

POET. Because I have a favor to beseech of you: a prayer, a fervent supplication. . . .

DAUGHTER OF INDRA. What is it you desire?

POET. A prayer of all mankind—to the ruler of the universe—framed in words by a dreamer . . .

DAUGHTER OF INDRA. And by whom do you wish it to be given to Him? . . .

POET. By Indra's daughter!

DAUGHTER OF INDRA. Have you committed it to memory—this petition?

POET. Yes, I know it by heart.

DAUGHTER OF INDRA. Then speak it!

POET. I'd rather you did!

DAUGHTER OF INDRA. Where may I read the words?

POET. In my mind—and also here. [*He hands her a scroll.*]

DAUGHTER OF INDRA [*accepts the scroll, but speaks without glancing at it*]. Then I shall give voice to your prayer. . . .

"Why must you be born in anguish,
child of mankind? Why must mothers
suffer birth pains when you bring her
the most precious of all gifts:
motherhood, life's greatest blessing?
Why must you to life awaken? . . .
Why do you salute the sunlight
with a cry of pain and mean ill-temper?
Why do you not smile on dawning life,
mortal child, since human happiness
has been promised as your birthright?
Why must we be born like beasts—
we, descendants of both gods and mortals?—
Better guise could have been given us than this
wretched body spun of blood and slime . . .

and why must this image of the gods
shed teeth?"

Silence, rash one! Blame the image—not
the Maker!
No man yet has solved life's riddle!

"Started thus, the pilgrimage begins
over stones and thorns and thistles. . . .
Should it lead across a beaten path,
you will find the road forbidden;
and if you should pluck a flower,
you'd be held for trespass—and for thiev-
ing also;
if a field should stop you from advancing
and you take a short cut through it,
you will trample down the farmer's crops;
others do the same to you,
equalizing thus the damage!—
Every moment that gives joy
brings to others only grief;
your own sorrow spreads, however,
not much gladness anywhere:
thus it's sorrow after sorrow! . . .
So the pilgrimage goes on—
even death brings gain to others!"

Is it this way, you—the son of Dust—
mean to come before the Great Almighty? . . .

POET. How could I, the Son of dust,
find such chaste, ethereal words
that they'd soar to realms beyond?
Child of Gods, will you translate
all our sorrows into speech
that will reach immortal ears?

DAUGHTER OF INDRA. I will.
POET [points to the buoy]. What is
that floating there?—Is it a buoy?
DAUGHTER OF INDRA. Yes.
POET. It looks like a lung with an
Adam's apple.
DAUGHTER OF INDRA. It is the watch-
man of the seas. When there is danger
ahead, it utters a warning.
POET. It looks as if the sea were rising
and the waves were growing restless and
ever higher. . . .
DAUGHTER OF INDRA. So it does. . . .
POET. Woe! What do I see? A ship—
just outside—close by the reef. . . .
DAUGHTER OF INDRA. What ship can
that be?
POET. I believe it is the eternal ghost
ship. . . .

DAUGHTER OF INDRA. The ghost ship?
What ship is that?
POET. The Flying Dutchman. . . .
DAUGHTER OF INDRA. Oh, I know. . . .
Why is he being punished so cruelly, and
why doesn't he ever put ashore?
POET. Because he had seven unfaithful
wives.
DAUGHTER OF INDRA. Why should he
be punished for that?
POET. He was condemned by all the
righteous-minded. . . .
DAUGHTER OF INDRA. How strange this
world is!—But can't he ever be freed
from the curse?
POET. Freed?—One has to be careful
not to set people free. . . .
DAUGHTER OF INDRA. Why?
POET. Because . . . No, it's not the Flying Dutchman! It's just an ordinary ship
in distress!—Why doesn't the buoy cry
out a warning now?—Look, the sea is
rising, the waves are growing higher and
higher. . . . Soon we shall be marooned in
the cave!—The ship's bell is clanging
now . . . before long there'll be another
figurehead floating on the water. . . . Cry
out your warning, buoy! Do your duty,
watchman! [The buoy emits a four-tone
chord of fifths and sixths, resembling the
sound of a foghorn.] The crew are signal-
ing and waving to us—and we ourselves
are perishing. . . .
DAUGHTER OF INDRA. Is it not your
wish to be set free?
POET. Why, certainly! Of course I wish
to be set free . . . but not at this moment
—and not through water!
CREW [singing in quartet]. Christ
Kyrie! [Cries and shouts from the ship.]
POET. Now they are shouting—and the
sea roars—and no one can hear them. . . .
CREW [singing as before]. Christ Kyrie!
DAUGHTER OF INDRA. Who is that coming there?
POET. Walking on the waters? There
is only one who walks on the waters. And
it is not Peter the Rock, for he sank like
a stone. [A white light appears on the
surface of the water in the distance.]
CREW. Christ Kyrie!
DAUGHTER OF INDRA. Is that He?
POET. It is He—who was crucified. . . .
DAUGHTER OF INDRA. Why . . . tell me
. . . why was He crucified?
POET. Because He wished to set
free . . .

DAUGHTER OF INDRA. I have forgotten who . . . who crucified Him.

POET. All the righteous-minded. . . .

DAUGHTER OF INDRA. What a strange world!

POET. The sea is rising! Darkness is coming upon us! The storm is increasing! [*The* CREW *gives out a scream of terror.*] The men are screaming, horror-stricken at the sight of their Saviour! . . . and now —and now they are jumping overboard out of fear. [*The* CREW *screams anew with fear.*] They cry from fear of dying! They come into the world crying and go out crying! [*The rolling, surging waves keep increasing in height and volume and threaten to drown the two in the grotto.*]

DAUGHTER OF INDRA. If I were only certain that it is a ship. . . .

POET. To tell the truth . . . I don't believe it is a ship . . . it is a two-story house with trees before it . . . and . . . a telephone tower—a tower reaching to the skies. . . . It is the Babel's Tower of our times sending messages by wire to higher regions—communicating with the dwellers there. . . .

DAUGHTER OF INDRA. My child, the thoughts of mankind need no wires for transmission! The prayers of the pious reach to the far ends of the universe. . . . No—it cannot be a Tower of Babel . . . for if you wish to assail the heavens, you must do so by prayer. . . .

POET. No, it is no house—and no telephone tower. . . . You can see that, can't you?

DAUGHTER OF INDRA. Then what do you see?

POET. I see a vast snow-covered space —a drill ground. . . . The winter sun is peeking out from behind a church on a hillside, and its tower casts a long shadow over the snow. . . . Now I see a company of soldiers marching across the open field. . . . They march straight to the tower, march up the spire. . . . Now they have reached the cross, but I have a foreboding that the first one who steps on the weathercock at the pinnacle will die. . . . Now they are close to the top—a corporal is at the head of his men. . . . Aha! A cloud comes sweeping across the field . . . it blots out the sun . . . now everything has disappeared . . . the moisture of the cloud has put out the sun's fire! The sunlight created the shadow picture of

the tower, but the shadow picture of the cloud disembodied the shadow image of the tower. . . .

[*While the preceding dialogue is being spoken, the setting is being shifted: it now shows again the alley outside the Opera.*]

DAUGHTER OF INDRA [*to the* PORTRESS]. Has the Lord Chancellor arrived yet?

PORTRESS. No.

DAUGHTER OF INDRA. Have the Deans come?

PORTRESS. No.

DAUGHTER OF INDRA. Then please call them at once . . . the door is about to be opened!

PORTRESS. Is it so important?

DAUGHTER OF INDRA. Yes, it is. People have become excited. . . . They have a notion that the solution to the riddle of the world is being hidden in there!—So please call the Lord Chancellor and the Deans of the Faculties at once! [*The* PORTRESS *blows a whistle.*] And don't forget the Glazier with his diamond! If he doesn't come, we'll have to call it off!

[*People of the Opera enter from the right, as in the earlier scenes. The* OFFICER *enters from the rear. He is dressed in a redingote and top hat and carries a bouquet of roses. He is radiantly happy.*]

OFFICER. Victoria!

PORTRESS. Miss Victoria will be down in a moment!

OFFICER. Splendid! The carriage is waiting, the table is set, the champagne is on ice. . . . Let me embrace you, madam! [*He embraces the* PORTRESS.] Victoria!

WOMAN'S VOICE [*sings out from above*]. Here I am!

OFFICER [*starts to pace*]. Good! I'll be waiting!

POET. It seems to me as if I had experienced all this once before. . . .

DAUGHTER OF INDRA. I also!

POET. Perhaps I have dreamed it!

DAUGHTER OF INDRA. Or lived it in your imagination—in a poem?

POET. Perhaps even that. . . .

DAUGHTER OF INDRA. Now you know what poetry is. . . .

POET. Now I know what dreams are. . . .

DAUGHTER OF INDRA. I feel as if we

have spoken these very words once before
—but in some other place. . . .

POET. Therefore you can easily conceive what reality is. . . .

DAUGHTER OF INDRA. Or dreams!

POET. Or the imagery of poetry! [The
LORD CHANCELLOR and the DEANS of the
theological, philosophical, medical, and
law faculties enter.]

LORD CHANCELLOR. It is about that
door, of course!—What does the Dean of
Theology think about the matter?

DEAN OF THEOLOY. I don't think. I believe—credo . . .

DEAN OF PHILOSOPHY. I hold the view
that . . .

DEAN OF MEDICINE. I know . . .

DEAN OF JURISPRUDENCE. I hold a
doubt until I have seen the evidence and
heard the testimony!

LORD CHANCELLOR. Now they'll start
wrangling again! . . . Well, let's first hear
what Theology has to say!

DEAN OF THEOLOGY. I believe that this
door should not be opened for the reason
that it has been place there to conceal
dangerous truths . . .

DEAN OF PHILOSOPHY. Truth is never
dangerous!

DEAN OF MEDICINE. What is truth?

DEAN OF JURISPRUDENCE. That which
can be proved by two witnesses.

DEAN OF THEOLOGY. A shyster lawyer
can prove anything—with two false witnesses!

DEAN OF PHILOSOPHY. Truth is wisdom; and wisdom plus knowledge is
philosophy itself. . . . Philosophy is the
science of sciences, the supreme knowledge, and all the other sciences are
merely its handmaids.

DEAN OF MEDICINE. There is only one
science: natural science! Philosophy is no
science. It's nothing but empty speculation!

DEAN OF THEOLOGY. Bravo!

DEAN OF PHILOSOPHY [to the DEAN OF
THEOLOGY.] You shout bravo. What
about yourself? You are the archenemy
of all knowledge. You are the very an-
tithesis of science—you are full of obscurity and vagueness. . . .

DEAN OF MEDICINE. Bravo!

DEAN OF THEOLOGY [to the DEAN OF
MEDICINE]. You shout bravo—you who
can't see any further than your nose,

when you look through your microscope
—you, who only put faith in your de-
ceptive senses: your eye, for example,
which may be farsighted, nearsighted,
blind, dim-sighted, cross-eyed, one-eyed,
color-blind, red-blind, green-blind . . .

DEAN OF MEDICINE. Dolt! Idiot!

DEAN OF THEOLOGY. Fool! Ass! [They
fly at each other.]

LORD CHANCELLOR. Calm yourselves!
Are you two crows trying to peck each
other's eyes out?

DEAN OF PHILOSOPHY [to the CHAN-
CELLOR and the DEANS OF JURISPRU-
DENCE and PHILOSOPHY]. If I had to
choose between those two, Theology and
Medicine, I would choose—neither!

DEAN OF JURISPRUDENCE. And if I had
to sit in judgment over you three, I
would—find you all guilty!—You don't
seem to find a single point on which
you can agree! Neither now nor in the
past!—But let's get back now to the case
in hand! What is the Lord Chancellor's
opinion regarding this door and its
opening?

LORD CHANCELLOR. Opinion? I have
no opinions. I have merely been appointed by the government to make sure
that you don't break each other's arms
and legs during Council meetings—for
the edification of the students! My
opinion . . . No, no! I stay away from
anything that has to do with opinions.
. . . There was a time when I had an
opinion or two, but it didn't take long to
put an end to them. . . . Opinions are
quickly proved to be erroneous—by one's
opponents, of course!—Could we proceed with the opening of the door now
—even at the risk of discovering some
dangerous truths behind it?

DEAN OF JURISPRUDENCE. What is
truth? What is truth?

DEAN OF THEOLOGY. I am the truth
and the life . . .

DEAN OF PHILOSOPHY. I am the core
of all knowledge . . .

DEAN OF MEDICINE. I am the exact
science . . .

DEAN OF JURISPRUDENCE. I doubt! . . .
[They fly at each other.]

DAUGHTER OF INDRA. Shame on you,
you teachers of the young!

DEAN OF JURISPRUDENCE. Mr. Lord
Chancellor! As the representative of the

government, as the head of the body of instructors in this university, it is your duty to bring this woman before a court of justice for her offensive demeanor. She has dared to tell you to be ashamed of yourselves! This is an insult! She has —in a scoffing, sneering manner—sarcastically labeled you the teachers of the young. . . . This is nothing short of slander!

DAUGHTER OF INDRA. I pity the young!

DEAN OF JURISPRUDENCE. She feels sorry for the young! Isn't that the same as an accusation against us?—Lord Chancellor, prosecute her without a moment's delay!

DAUGHTER OF INDRA. Yes—I accuse you, all of you, of sowing doubt and dissension in the minds of the young.

DEAN OF JURISPRUDENCE. Listen to her! She is herself casting doubt on our authority, inveigling the young! And what is more, she accuses us of creating doubts! I ask of all the righteous-minded: Is not this a criminal offense?

ALL THE RIGHTEOUS-MINDED. It is indeed a criminal offense!

DEAN OF JURISPRUDENCE. All the righteous-minded have judged you!—Now leave—leave in peace with what you have gained from us—or else . . .

DAUGHTER OF INDRA. What I have gained from you?—Or else—or else what?

DEAN OF JURISPRUDENCE. Or you will be stoned!

POET. Or crucified. . . .

DAUGHTER OF INDRA [to the POET]. I shall go. . . . Follow me, and you shall learn the riddle.

POET. Which riddle?

DAUGHTER OF INDRA. What did he mean when he spoke of my gain?

POET. Probably nothing. What he said was what we call fatuous prattle. He just talked.

DAUGHTER OF INDRA. It was this that hurt me more than anything.

POET. That's probably why he said it. People are like that. . . .

ALL THE RIGHTEOUS-MINDED. Hurrah! The door has been opened!

LORD CHANCELLOR. What was behind it?

GLAZIER. I don't see anything. . . .

LORD CHANCELLOR. You can't see any-thing? No, of course, you can't! Deans! What was hidden behind the door?

DEAN OF THEOLOGY. Nothing! That is the solution of the riddle of the world. . . . In the beginning God created heaven and earth out of nothing . . .

DEAN OF PHILOSOPHY. Out of nothing comes nothing . . .

DEAN OF MEDICINE. Nothing but nonsense—and that's nothing!

DEAN OF JURISPRUDENCE. I doubt. It is a clear case of fraud. I appeal to all the righteous-minded!

DAUGHTER OF INDRA [to the POET]. Who are the righteous-minded?

POET. Well—tell me that—whoever can! All the righteous-minded are usually only one person. Today it may be I and my followers—tomorrow it may be you and yours. It is a position one is chosen for—or rather, one chooses oneself!

ALL THE RIGHTEOUS-MINDED. We have been deceived, defrauded!

LORD CHANCELLOR. Who has deceived you?

ALL THE RIGHTEOUS-MINDED. The Daughter of Indra!

LORD CHANCELLOR. Will the Daughter of Indra please tell us why she was so anxious to have this door opened?

DAUGHTER OF INDRA. No, my friends . . . for if I did tell you, you would not believe me. . . .

DEAN OF MEDICINE. But there is nothing in there!

DAUGHTER OF INDRA. You speak the truth—yet you do not understand it.

DEAN OF MEDICINE. She is talking nonsense, rubbish!

ALL. Nonsense! Rubbish!

DAUGHTER OF INDRA [to the POET]. They are to be pitied! . . .

POET. Are you speaking seriously?

DAUGHTER OF INDRA. I am always in earnest.

POET. Do you feel pity for the self-righteous, too?

DAUGHTER OF INDRA. I think I pity them most. . . .

POET. And the four faculties?

DAUGHTER OF INDRA. Yes, and not least them. Four heads, four minds—and all part of one body! Who created this monster?

ALL. She hasn't answered the Lord Chancellor's question. . . .

LORD CHANCELLOR. Then flog her!

DAUGHTER OF INDRA. I have already answered.

LORD CHANCELLOR. Listen—she is answering back! ...

ALL. Beat her! Flog her! She is answering back. ...

DAUGHTER OF INDRA. Whether she answers or doesn't answer, strike her, beat her! [*To the* POET.] Come with me, Seer, and then I shall answer the riddle—but far away from here—out in the wilderness—where no one can hear us, no one can see us. [*The* ATTORNEY *appears. He takes hold of the* DAUGHTER OF INDRA *by the arm.*]

ATTORNEY. Have you forgotten your duties?

DAUGHTER OF INDRA. Oh God! No! —But I have other duties, higher duties, to perform. ...

ATTORNEY. And your child?

DAUGHTER OF INDRA. My child. What more?

ATTORNEY. Your child is crying for you. ...

DAUGHTER OF INDRA. My child! Woe to me! I am earth-bound! ... And this pain in my breast, this dread, this anguish! ... What is it?

ATTORNEY. And you don't know? ...

DAUGHTER OF INDRA. No!

ATTORNEY. It is remorse—the pangs of conscience. ...

DAUGHTER OF INDRA. Alas, is that my grieving conscience?

ATTORNEY. Yes!—Remorse sets in after every duty that has been neglected; after every pleasure indulged in, however innocent—if there *is* such a thing as an innocent pleasure; after every suffering inflicted upon others.

DAUGHTER OF INDRA. And is there no remedy for it?

ATTORNEY. Yes, there is a remedy— and only one! By fulfilling one's duties without hesitation. ...

DAUGHTER OF INDRA. You look like a demon when you utter the word *duty!*— But I—I have not *one* duty—my duties are twofold—What am I to do?

ATTORNEY. You fulfill one at at time.

DAUGHTER OF INDRA. Then the highest duty first ... and so: will you look after my child while I fulfill my duty? ...

ATTORNEY. Your child will miss you, and will suffer. ... Can you endure knowing that someone will suffer for your sake?

DAUGHTER OF INDRA. Now there is struggle in my soul ... it seems to be cleaving in two—each part pulling away from the other. ...

ATTORNEY. It is a mere sample of the disharmony that exists in life! Now you know how it feels! ...

DAUGHTER OF INDRA. Oh! How it tugs and tears at my heart!

POET. If you knew ... if you only suspected how much grief and devastation I have caused by fulfilling my calling— and note that I use the word calling, which is a higher, more sublime duty— then you would not touch my hand!

DAUGHTER OF INDRA. What have you done, then?

POET. I was an only son. My father cherished the hope that I would some day take over his business. But I ran away from business school. My father took it so to heart that he died. My mother, who was deeply religious, wanted me to be religious, too. I *could* not. ... She disowned me. I had a friend who helped me through hard and trying days. This friend behaved like a tyrant toward those whose cause I had taken upon myself. I was compelled to strike down my friend and benefactor in order to save my soul! Ever since, I have had no peace. Now I am called scum, offal, infamous and lacking in honor!—And this despite the fact that my conscience tells me: "You were in the right!" For in the next moment it tells me: "You did wrong!"— That is the way life is. ...

DAUGHTER OF INDRA. Come away with me—out into the wilderness!

ATTORNEY. What about your child?

DAUGHTER OF INDRA [*indicates all those who are present*]. These are my children! Individually they are good—but as soon as they get together with one another, they quarrel and become demons. ... Farewell!

[*Outside the castle. The setting is the same as in the first scene in the early part of the play. Now, however, the ground, facing the foundation walls of the castle, is covered with flowers: blue monk's hood, or aconite.*

Topmost on the roof of the castle, on its lantern, is seen a chrysanthemum bud about to open its petals. The castle windows are illuminated with tapers.

The DAUGHTER OF INDRA *and the* POET *appear on the stage.*]

DAUGHTER OF INDRA. The moment for my ascent to the ether is not far off. . . . I shall have the help of fire. . . . It is this severance from Earth that you call death, and that you humans look forward to with fear. . . .

POET. Fear of the unknown . . .

DAUGHTER OF INDRA. That you have within you . . .

POET. Who has? . . .

DAUGHTER OF INDRA. All of you! Why do you put no faith in your prophets?

POET. Prophets have always been disbelieved! Why? . . . And—"if God has spoken, why will not men believe?" . . . Nothing can stand up against His Omnipotence. . . .

DAUGHTER OF INDRA. Have you always doubted?

POET. No—many a time I have felt certainty beyond doubt . . . but then it slipped away . . . like a dream on waking. . . .

DAUGHTER OF INDRA. It is not easy to be a mortal. . . .

POET. You have come to realize—and admit it?

DAUGHTER OF INDRA. I do. . . .

POET. Tell me—did not Indra once send His son down to Earth to probe the plaints and charges of mankind?

DAUGHTER OF INDRA. So He did—yes! —And how was He received?

POET. How did He fulfill His mission? —to answer with another question. . . .

DAUGHTER OF INDRA. And may I answer with still another?—Was not Man helped by His stay on Earth? Answer me truthfully!

POET. Helped?—Yes—in a measure . . . yet very little. . . . But instead of asking questions—will you not explain the riddle to me?

DAUGHTER OF INDRA. Yes—but how can it be of help to you? You will not believe me!

POET. I shall believe you, for I know who you are. . . .

DAUGHTER OF INDRA. Then I shall tell you. . . . In the early morning of Time —before the sun was born—Brahma, the divine force of all living things, allowed himself to be tempted by Maya, the Mother of the Universe, to propagate himself. This meeting of the divine primal force with the earth matter, constituted the fall of heaven into sin. Thus the universe, mankind, existence are merely a phantom, a dream, an illusion . . .

POET [*ecstatically*]. My dream!

DAUGHTER OF INDRA. A dream of truth! . . . But Brahma's offspring seek to free themselves from the earth matter through self-denial and suffering. . . . Thus suffering becomes the liberator. However, this yearning for suffering comes into conflict with the craving and the desire to find enjoyment—and love! Do you now understand what love is, with its mixture of the greatest in enjoyment and the greatest in suffering, the sweetest and the bitterest? Can you now understand what woman is? Woman—through whom sin and death came into being? . . .

POET. I can. . . . And where is the end?

DAUGHTER OF INDRA. You know the end. . . . The struggle between the pain that follows enjoyment and the pleasure that we take in suffering: between the penitent's torment and torture and the sensualist's dissipations. . . .

POET. And therefore strife?

DAUGHTER OF INDRA. Struggle between opposites produces energy—just as fire and water generate steam.

POET. But peace—and rest?

DAUGHTER OF INDRA. Hush! You must ask no more questions; and I must speak no more! . . . The altar is already adorned for the sacrifice: the flowers stand on guard, the tapers are lighted, white sheets are hung in the windows, twigs of spruce have been spread in the gateway. . . .

POET. You speak as calmly as though suffering did not exist for you!

DAUGHTER OF INDRA. As though it did not exist! . . . I have suffered all your sufferings hundredfold, for my sensibilities are so much more receptive. . . .

POET. Tell me your sorrows!

DAUGHTER OF INDRA. Could you, Poet, lay bare your own, frankly, candidly? Could your words, even once, for a fleeting moment, impart the full and true meaning of your thoughts?

POET. No—you are right! I have always seemed to myself a mere deaf-mute! The crowd always listened admiringly to my outpourings, but I could find them only hollow and empty. And so, you see, I felt ashamed when people acclaimed me and paid me homage. . . .

DAUGHTER OF INDRA. And yet you wish me to . . . Look me in the eye!

POET. I cannot endure your gaze!

DAUGHTER OF INDRA. How would you then be able to endure my words if I were to speak in my celestial tongue?

POET. But before you go, tell me what you suffered most from down here!

DAUGHTER OF INDRA. From being— from living—from feeling one's sight weakened by an eye, one's hearing impaired by an ear, and my thoughts—my luminous, enlightening, ethereal thoughts —bound up in a labyrinth of coiled slime! You have seen a brain, haven't you?—with its crooked, crawling, worming tracks and passages. . . .

POET. I have—and that's what makes all the righteous-minded think so crookedly. . . .

DAUGHTER OF INDRA. Malicious—always malicious! But you are all the same!

POET. How could we be otherwise?

DAUGHTER OF INDRA. Now I shake the dust off my feet—the dust, the earth, the clay. . . .

[She removes her shoes and casts them in the fire.]

PORTRESS [enters. She places her shawl on the fire]. You don't mind if I burn my shawl, too?

[She leaves.]

OFFICER [enters]. And here are my roses—with nothing but the thorns left. . . .

[He, too, offers them to the flames.]

BILLPOSTER [enters]. The posters you may have—but the dip net—never! . . .

[He throws the posters into the fire.]

GLAZIER [enters]. Take the diamond that opened the door! Farewell!

[He rushes out, after having sacrificed his diamond.]

ATTORNEY [enters]. And here is the dossier containing the minutes of the great dispute concerning the pope's beard or the diminishing water supply in the sources of the Ganges River.

[He sacrifices the documents to the flames; then he leaves.]

QUARANTINE MASTER [comes in]. Here is my contribution: the black mask which changed me into a blackamoor against my will. . . .

[He throws the mask into the fire.]

VICTORIA [enters]. I offer you my beauty—my sorrow!

[She leaves.]

BLIND MAN [enters. He thrusts his hand into the fire]. Having no eye to sacrifice, I give my hand!

DON JUAN [enters in his wheelchair. He is followed by SHE and the LOVER (THE MAJOR)]. Make haste, make haste! Life is short!

[He leaves together with the others.]

POET. I have read somewhere that when the end is near, all of life passes before us in one long cavalcade. . . . Is this the end for you?

DAUGHTER OF INDRA. Yes—it is the end! Farewell!

POET. Then speak a word before we part!

DAUGHTER OF INDRA. No—that I cannot! Could your words, do you think, truly image your thoughts?

DEAN OF THEOLOGY [enters. He is in a raging temper]. God has disavowed me —I am persecuted by man—the government has deserted me—and I am the scorn of my colleagues! How can I keep my faith, when no one else has faith? How can I defend a God who does not defend his own? . . . It's rubbish—that's all it is!

[He flings a book into the fire and struts out.]

POET [snatches the book from the flames]. Do you know what he threw into the fire?—A martyrology! A calendar with a martyr for each day of the year. . . .

DAUGHTER OF INDRA. A martyr?

POET. Yes—one who has suffered and been tortured to death for the sake of his faith! And can you tell me why? Do you believe that all who endure pain, suffer? And that all who are put to death, feel pain? Isn't it through suffering we gain redemption from sin—and doesn't death give us deliverance and set us free?

KRISTIN [enters, carrying her strips of paper]. I paste—I paste—until every nook and cranny has been pasted over. . . .

POET. And if there were a cleft in heaven itself, you would try to patch it with your tape. . . . Go away!

KRISTIN. Are there no double windows in the castle?

POET. No! That is one place where you won't find any!

KRISTIN [turns to leave]. Well, then I'll be going!

DAUGHTER OF INDRA. My life on earth is ending—it is time to leave. . . .

Farewell, you mortal child, you poet-dreamer,
who—better than the rest—has learned to live. . . .
Borne upon wings, you soar to heights beyond this earth,
yet sometimes fall into the mire,
but don't get caught in it—you merely graze it!

Now that I leave, the loss of what has been,
what I have loved, and the remorse for things left undone,
arises in me, as—when parting from one's friends—
one says Godspeed to them, and to the places one holds dear. . . .

Oh! In this moment I can feel the utter pain of being,
of living, and of being mortal. . . .
One misses even what was once disdained
and feels a guilt for wrongs that one did never do. . . .
One longs to leave—yet yearns to stay. . . .
Thus in a tug of war the heart is torn in twain
and feelings rent asunder by the beasts
of conflict, indecision, and disharmony. . . .
Farewell! And tell your earth-kin I shall never
forget them where I go—and I shall bring
their plaint to Indra—in your name. . . .
Farewell! . . .

[She enters the castle. Music is heard. The background is illuminated by the flames from the burning castle and reveals a wall of human faces—faces that are searching and inquiring, sorrowful and grief-stricken, tortured by agony and anguish. As the castle burns, the flower bud on the rooftop opens into a chrysanthemum of giant proportions.]

Maurice Valency

STRINDBERG

Like *Peer Gynt, Lucky Per's Journey,* and *To Damascus, A Dream Play* traces the steps of a mythical journey. The plot —if it can be called a plot—is rudimentary, another and more abstract version of the narrative which underlies the action of *To Damascus. A Dream Play* develops the situation of a lady who becomes, presumably, the mistress of an officer, through whom she meets a lawyer, who marries her. She bears him a child. But in time she finds life with the lawyer unendurable, and she sets off with her first love on a long journey which she does not enjoy, but in the course of which she meets a poet, whom she finds congenial. The lawyer now attempts to assert his conjugal rights, whereupon the lady puts an end to her troubles by withdrawing from the world. Such, at least, are the bones of the action; and seldom has a plot had less relation to a play.

Though *A Dream Play* in many ways recalls *To Damascus,* the narrative patterns necessarily differ a good deal. *To Damascus*—the story of a man hunted by God—belongs to the tradition of the medieval chase-allegory, and, very properly, has a medieval coloring. *A Dream Play* belongs to the *topos* of the visitor from another sphere. Since, in this play, the Daughter of Indra is on a sightseeing tour of the Christian world, she grows and develops, but she maintains her identity from beginning to end; she is, essentially, a constant in variable circumstances, and in this she somewhat resembles the Unknown in the earlier play. She is, however, unlike the Unknown, fundamentally an observer, and her perceptions are therefore much more objective than would be the case were she the primary subject of the action as he is. Nevertheless, in a general way, it is as if in *A Dream Play* the story of *To Damascus,* or something near it, were told from the viewpoint of the Lady.

The play, we are told in the foreword, is intended to produce on the stage the effect of a dream. Its shapes arise out of chaos half formed, with wisps of chaos, so to speak, still clinging to them. In its effects of abstraction and its bizarre groupings, it clearly announces the art of the twentieth century; yet its subject matter and its mood are unmistakably romantic. It is, moreover, as I have suggested, only seemingly amorphous. Its episodes are grouped quite systematically within the rigid frame that encloses them. It has a beginning, middle, and end; and its conclusion follows from the *données* of its beginning in a way that is by no means characteristic of dreams. Beyond doubt it was a brilliantly revolutionary departure in its day, far ahead of the theatre of its time. It is only when we compare it with more completely developed examples of the genre it inaugurated—the brothel scene in *Ulysses,* for example—that its connections with the romantic tradition of the nineteeneth century become apparent.

It is customary to say that in this play Strindberg explored the workings of the subconscious during sleep, but it must be obvious that the unconscious elements of *A Dream Play* do not come into consciousness here any more readily than they would in any other play. *A Dream Play* is a play, not a dream. It is a montage of scenes in prose and verse composed in accordance with a conscious artistic aim, and for a wholly rational purpose. The play has therefore the enigmatic character of a work of art, and not at all the enigmatic character of a dream, and while much of its beauty,

SOURCE: From *The Flower and the Castle* by Maurice Valency. Copyright © 1963 by Maurice Valency. (Footnotes omitted.) Reprinted with permission of The Macmillan Company.

and its power, are derived from what is suggested by and to the unconscious, on the whole it is directed to the intellectual faculty and is meant to be understood.

Within the mythological frame which Strindberg imposed upon it, *A Dream Play* consists of a series of vignettes abstracted from the autobiographical sources which customarily provided him with his subject matter. It is, like *To Damascus*, essentially a personal statement, the complete comprehension of which would entail an impossibly intimate knowledge of the author's life and works. Consequently, although it has been the subject of the most careful study, much of the detail remains, and very likely will always remain, puzzling. Underlying the entire conception is the Brahmanic myth of self-sacrifice, to which Strindberg gave a vaguely Christian tone. As he understood the myth, the diversification of Brahma was the result of a sexual act, a seduction, and in the union of Brahma with Maya, the world mother, was figured the primal union of spirit and matter, corresponding to the creation of the world.

The Daughter's name, Agnes, was doubtless suggested by Agni the fire-god and heavenly messenger, often associated mythologically with Indra, the principal god of the Vedas, lord of the sky and the lightning, and dispenser of the fructifying rain. The Daughter's incarnation in *A Dream Play*, and her life on earth, is a species of sacrifice in the course of which she experiences all the evil she can bear in order to carry to her heavenly father a full report of the miseries of mankind. Through Agnes, Strindberg once more rationalizes the desire for suffering as a spiritual yearning for deliverance. The Daughter says, in words which come somewhat closer to Hartmann's *Philosophy of the Unconscious* than to the Upanishads:

> But in order to be freed from the earthly element, the descendants of Brahma sought renunciation and suffering ... And so you have pain as the deliverer ... But this yearning for pain comes in conflict with the longing for joy and love ... now you understand what love is: the highest joy in the greatest suffering, the most beautiful in the most bitter!

Strindberg's position in *A Dream Play* is thus entirely consistent with his earlier views on the subject of pain and pleasure. Deliverance is a matter of freeing the spirit from its material involvements. This necessitates suffering. Pleasure binds us to the flesh; pain liberates us from it. It was through woman that the spirit was first entangled in matter, and it is through her that it is trapped in the flesh forever in the irresistible process of reproduction. But woman, who seduces the spirit through joy, also chastens it through suffering, and thus she teaches us the way of renunciation by which the spirit may be freed from the misery of being. Meanwhile the lot of mankind is pitiable, for man is continually torn between the craving for joy, which enslaves him, and the desire for suffering, which liberates him from the flesh. Such, according to the Daughter, is the answer to the riddle of life—as much of it, at least, as the Poet is privileged to hear.

There is nothing to indicate that Strindberg's acquaintance with the complexities of Eastern philosophy was other than superficial; but it was amply sufficient to support the poetic groundwork of *A Dream Play*. The Daughter's explanation of the riddle of the universe is based on the fundamental myth of *atma-yajna*, the act of self-sacrifice through which God brought the world into existence, and through which man eventually resumes his godhead. In the beginning, according to the myth, the Consciousness behind the universe, in the guise of Brahma, created the world by an act of self-forgetting, or self-dismemberment, through which the One became many. The diverse universe was the result. But this diversity of nature is only a seeming, *maya*. Accordingly, all attempts at definition and classification are merely an expression of the viewpoint of the beholder. In reality, there is only the flux of being; the forms exist only with relation to one another; and the play of contraries is simply the result of a poetic fiction, since order would be meaningless without disorder, and good would have no special character without evil.

The play of God does not go on eternally; only for countless *kalpas* of time: ultimately, the God comes to himself

again, but only to forget himself once
more in the endless game of improvisation. In the meantime, the individual
consciousness, "that which knows" in
each mind, is none other than God himself, the primal consciousness, and each
individual life is a role in which the
mind of God is absorbed in the course
of the play which is our reality. Thus, the
one divine actor plays all the parts, and
when the play of existence comes to an
end, the individual consciousness awakens to its own divinity.

The sacrificial act by which God gives
birth to the world, and by which men
in turn reintegrate themselves into God,
involves the giving up of the individual
life. This act is the same whether it be
considered from the standpoint of creation or of cessation. For Strindberg this
act had an erotic connotation. He sym-
bolized it through the Growing Castle,
where life begins and, in its flowering,
ends. The Swedenborgian influence is
seen in the manner in which the correspondence is indicated between the
dream of man and the dream of God, the
micro-macrocosmic relation. In Strindberg's play, the dreamer—with relation
to his dream—is Brahma; and his single
consciousness becomes multiple as he
bodies forth through his fancy the dream-
characters who live their independent
lives while his mind is absorbed in them,
and yet have no being aside from his.

The dreamer's personal experience,
moreover, has universal character. In his
dream, all begins and ends, and begins
again through the Growing Castle,
which endlessly initiates the cycle of
birth-and-death, samsara. In the Maha-
yana scriptures, the castle is sometimes
used as a symbol for the personality, the
ego, in which the individual fortifies himself against the external world, isolating
himself in the belief that there is a
sacred difference between one individual
and another, while the truth is that there
are no individuals; and the external
world is merely the externalization of
mind, which casts its shadow, as the
French symbolists would say, in order to
see itself.

The characters of A Dream Play thus
stand in a complex relationship to one
another. They are at the same time different and the same, many and one. In
To Damascus, which makes use of a
similar relationship for symbolic purposes,
these identities are rationalized in
metaphysical terms, though even there
we are aware of the psychological undercurrent as one by one the personalities
of the Unknown are integrated into his
single person until at the end only the
Tempter remains unresolved. In A
Dream Play, the identification is wholly
psychological—all the characters, and all
their experiences, are manifestations of
the personality of the dreamer, from
whose sole consciousness they derive their
being, and whose fantasy is their life.

Aside from the Daughter of Indra, A
Dream Play has four principal characters:
the Officer, the Lawyer, the Quarantine
Master, and the Poet. Whatever else
they may be or represent, these characters, evidently, are four aspects of the
author, the dreamer, and in their com-
posite life is indicated his manifold nature. Moreover, since Strindberg cherished the idea that men lead several
lives simultaneously, the four characters
are thought of sometimes as four independent personages, sometimes as a single individual, depending on the circumstances. It is much the same in To
Damascus. Here, the Officer represents
the romantic hero, the Lawyer is the
bickering husband, the Quarantine Master, the merciless critic, while the Poet
is the lover of beauty in his creative
aspect, and is consequently more closely
identified with the author, as dreamer,
than the others, since A Dream Play, in
a strict sense, is the Poet's dream.

To the Daughter of Indra, however,
the dream gives a degree of autonomy
that the other characters have not. She is
the subject of all the dreamer's experience, the mirror which reflects his consciousness, and she is also, like the Lady
in To Damascus, the woman he has
endlessly wooed and lost. In that play,
the Unknown has relations with the Lady
in her various guises, chiefly, but not exclusively, as himself; but in A Dream
Play the dreamer wins and loses her as
Officer, Lawyer, and Poet in turn: he
experiences her from every angle. Ultimately, of course, she too is an aspect of
the dreamer; but, it is implied, an aspect

of his truest and inmost self, which is conversant with God.

It is consistent with this idea that the Daughter is the only personage who develops organically in the course of the action; and this action is, on the whole, her biography. In the beginning she is relatively innocent, eager to experience life, energetic, and full of curiosity. At the end, she is weary and heavy with suffering, but yet as knowing and as fierce as Beatrice in the *Purgatorio*, whom she recalls:

DAUGHTER: . . . Look into my eyes.
POET: I cannot endure your gaze.
DAUGHTER: How then will you endure my words, if I speak in my own language?

In keeping with its dream-like character, the action of *A Dream Play* involves a wealth of detail, not all of which comes into focus, and not all of which admits of a ready interpretation. The Daughter of Indra is first seen outside the Growing Castle in which the Officer is found imprisoned. She appears in the company of the Glazier (*Glasmäster*), whom she calls father. There is no certain way to identify the Glazier, whose diamond is capable of opening all doors, including the doors of the castle. Possibly this character was suggested by Baudelaire's prose-poem *Le Mauvais Vitrier*; possibly, Strindberg had in mind the great Leverrier, director of the Paris Observatoire; there are certainly other, and perhaps better, possibilities.

With the Growing Castle, we are on safer ground. The figure appears to have been suggested by the vaulted roof of the cavalry barracks, with its crown-shaped cupola, which Strindberg could see above the treetops from the window of his study at Karlavägen 40 in Stockholm. In *A Dream Play* the castle grows quite appropriately out of the heaps of manure and straw that accumulate around stables, and, since it is a growing thing, it is topped by a blossom. The symbol of the flower, rooted in the soil and aspiring to the heavens, was a favorite figure with Strindberg: in *The Ghost Sonata*, there is the shallot which grows out of the lap of Buddha. The phallic character of this symbol need hardly be pointed out; doubtless Strindberg intended to suggest

through it the reproductive process by which through pain the material world little by little becomes spirit.

In the interior of the castle, the restive Officer somewhat hesitantly permits the Daughter to draw him into the outer world, in order that he may see how, in spite of the pitiable condition of mankind, love conquers all. The allusion is clear in this scene to the role of Harriet Bosse in drawing Strindberg from his self-imposed seclusion, and the feelings of guilt and impotent fury which his seclusion involved. Having liberated the Officer, the Daughter passes, without any transition, from the castle to the stage-door corridor of the opera. There is a giant monkshood growing behind the gate; for Strindberg, the monkshood, with its charming blue flower and its deadly root, was a symbol of worldly desire. The Officer appears, top-hatted and frock-coated, bearing a bouquet of roses: he has come to wait for his beloved Victoria. He has been waiting for her to come out, we learn, for seven years, and while he waits, he is overcome with a longing to see what lies beyond the mysterious clover-leaf door which opens off the theatre alley. The tempo of the action is suddenly accelerated. Day follows night, flash upon flash. The Officer comes and goes. His hair grows white. His clothes become shabby. His roses wilt. Victoria never comes out. The Officer preserves his good humor; he does not despair, but at last he insists on having the mysterious door opened, behind which, he is told, is the answer to the riddle of life. He sends for a locksmith. Instead, the Glazier comes with his diamond. He is about to open the door with this instrument when a policeman commands him to stop in the name of the law. The Officer resolves that the law which forbids us to know the riddle of life must be changed, and he dashes off, in the company of the Daughter of Indra, to find a lawyer.

The opera corridor now literally dissolves into the law office. The clover-leaf door, which remains on the stage as a visible reminder of the unsolved enigma of existence, thus becomes the door to the Lawyer's document file. For a time, the Officer gives place to the

Lawyer as the focus of attention, and the Daughter becomes the principal witness of the Lawyer's pain. Like the Lady of *To Damascus II*, the Lawyer has grown hideous because of the evil absorbed from his clients. The law office suddenly turns into a church; the clover-leaf door becomes the entrance to the vestry; and the Lawyer, who is passed over in the conferring of degrees which takes place in the church, is crowned not with laurel but with thorns. The Daughter sits at the organ, from which she elicits screams of human pain; then the organ turns into the resonant wall of Fingal's grotto, which is called the ear of the world. In this symbolic setting, the Daughter joins her destiny to that of the Lawyer, so that she may experience with him the supreme joy of life, which is love and marriage. The scene at once dissolves into the squalid apartment which they share, and in which the Daughter has so far savored the joys of marriage that when the Officer comes to her rescue, she gladly goes away with him.

The Officer means to take the Daughter to the beautiful seaside resort of Fairhaven. Instead, they land at Shamestrand. There they meet the Quarantine Master. In this worthy, whom the Officer greets as "old chatterbox" (*Ordström*: literally, word-stream), we are invited to recognize Strindberg in person. He is in blackface, because, as he says, he finds it best to show himself to the world a shade blacker than he is; and he tells us that it is in order to forget himself that he has taken up masquerade and play-acting. Now the Poet appears, his eyes on the heavens, and a bucket of mud in his hand, and gradually the suggestion takes form that it is essentially he who is the dreamer whose dream we are witnessing. There ensues an interlude in which a pair of lovers, one of whom is the Officer's beloved Victoria, are mercilessly fumigated by the Quarantine Master, in spite of the Poet's protests.

The symbolism once again grows transparent. The fumigation scene is evidently intended to represent comically the inner conflict of the dreamer in his trinary capacity as hero, critic, and poet. As the hero of the play, he recognizes his lost love, and he feels jealousy; as poet, he feels compassion; but in his capacity

as national watchman, it is his duty to apply the severest measures to prevent the spread of the disease of love. While the lovers go sadly into the quarantine shed to be purified of passion, the Officer prepares to take up the hated profession of schoolmaster in order to support his mistress. Accompanied by the Daughter, he enters Fairhaven, the earthly paradise, a rich resort where a ball is constantly in progress. As it turns out, nobody is happy in Fairhaven; and the Officer suffers deep and undeserved humiliation as a student in the very school where he meant to teach.

The dream now becomes fragmentary. The cry of human anguish swells higher, and the Daughter, utterly weary, and faced with the obligation of returning to the Lawyer's home, yearns mightily for the peace of the upper world. To be rid of the Lawyer, and his domestic entanglements, however, she must retrace her steps until she is once again her own true self. She begins the backward journey in the company of the Poet. They find themselves first in a Mediterranean resort where two coal heavers demonstrate how society makes a hell of paradise. Then they are once again in the marine grotto, and the play begins to unwind. The Poet presents the Daughter with a petition for the lord of the universe. From the grotto they witness a shipwreck at sea: Christ himself appears on the waters, but his appearance merely serves to inspire the mariners with terror. While these visions appear and dissolve, the ship's mast turns into a tree, the cave turns into the opera house corridor, and now the Daughter summons the chancellor and the faculties of the university to witness the opening of the door which conceals the secret of the universe.

Time rolls back. The Officer appears, young and fresh, with his bouquet of roses for Victoria. Before the assembled faculties, constantly at odds with each other, the Glazier solemnly springs the lock with his diamond. The door swings open: there is nothing behind it. The university faculties grow angry. They threaten to stone the Daughter. But by now the Daughter has recovered herself sufficiently so that she offers to reveal the secret to the Poet if he will come with her into the wilderness. The Lawyer opposes this, asserting his claims and the needs of his child. It is in vain. The corridor scene turns back into the Growing Castle. The Daughter reveals to the Poet the secret of the origin of pain, the nature of love, and the source of power; but she stops short of the ultimate answer, and the riddle remains unsolved as she shakes the dust of the world from her feet and prepares to enter the fire which will make her one with the air. The flame springs up spontaneously. While the characters of the play appear one by one and cast into the flames the poor things they have prized on earth, the Daughter speaks her farewell to mankind:

DAUGHTER: . . . Oh, now I know the
whole of the pain of
existence.
This, then, it is to be a
human being . . .
To regret even what one
never valued,
and feel remorse for what
one never did . . .
To wish to go, and to wish
to stay,
Thus the heart is cleft this
way and that . . .
. . . Farewell!

She enters the castle. Silhouetted against the wall of human faces, the castle burns, and as the flames rise high, the chrysanthemum bud that tops it bursts into flower. . . .

Arthur
Schnitzler
1862–1931

Arthur Schnitzler, Austrian playwright, story-writer, and essayist, was born in Vienna, the son of an eminent Jewish doctor. Following his father's profession, Schnitzler, like Chekhov, became a practicing physician, but his enduring interest was literature. As the product of upper-bourgeois Vienna, Schnitzler experienced the easygoing, hedonistic life of the Austrian capital during its imperial decline. His upper-class characters are clever and sophisticated, pursuing amorous adventure, yet troubled with melancholy, introspection, and fear of death. In *Anatol* (1893) Schnitzler pictured an urbane man-about-town entangled in love affairs leading to disillusionment. The failure of decadent aristocracy to confront reality on the eve of revolution is the subject of *The Green Cockatoo* (1898); anti-Semitism, then rife in Austria, motivates his play *Professor Bernhardi* (1912). But while dealing with social problems, Schnitzler's special talent lay in the graceful, skeptically ironic, and humorous penetration of the human psyche beset with sexual complexities, self-indulgent, deluded, and weak. *Light-o'-Love* (*Liebelei*, 1894) shows the disastrous consequences of aristocratic frivolity. His story *Leutnant Gustl* (1901) examined critically false conceptions of honor and was denounced by nationalistic and anti-Semitic circles as affronting the Austrian army. But riotous scandal was caused by *La Ronde* (*Reigen*, 1897). Privately printed at first, it was violently attacked when issued in 1903 and banned as obscene in Germany. Riots broke out when it was produced in Berlin and Munich after the First World War, and its Viennese premiere in 1921 was the pretext for stormy outrages by proto-Nazis who invaded the theatre. In *La Ronde* Schnitzler captured the spirit of fin-de-siècle Vienna in a series of sexual escapades linking dancers in a round of promiscuous love that is deceiving and empty. It portrays a world morally bankrupt, if charming; and when the Hapsburg Empire collapsed after the First World War, a sterner, more demanding note came into Schnitzler's work. The triumph of Nazism drove Schnitzler's plays from the German stage. By then he and the "old Vienna" he had depicted were dead.

LA RONDE

ARTHUR SCHNITZLER

Translated by Carl Richard Mueller

CAST OF CHARACTERS

THE PROSTITUTE   THE HUSBAND
THE SOLDIER   THE SWEET YOUNG THING
THE PARLOR MAID   THE POET
THE YOUNG GENTLEMAN   THE ACTRESS
THE YOUNG WIFE   THE COUNT

Time: The eighteen-nineties

Place: Vienna

SCENE ONE

THE PROSTITUTE AND THE SOLDIER

[Late evening. On the Augarten Bridge. The SOLDIER comes along whistling, on his way home.]

PROSTITUTE. Hey there, honey. Come here. [The SOLDIER turns around to look, then continues on.]

PROSTITUTE. Don't you want to come with me?

SOLDIER. You talking to me?

PROSTITUTE. Sure, who else? Hey, come on. I live right around here.

SOLDIER. I haven't got time. I've got to get back to the barracks!

PROSTITUTE. You'll get back to the barracks okay. It's nicer here with me.

SOLDIER [near her]. You think so?

PROSTITUTE. Psst! A policeman could come by anytime.

SOLDIER. You're crazy! A policeman! Anyway, I'm armed!

PROSTITUTE. Come on, what do you say?

SOLDIER. Cut it out. I haven't got any money.

PROSTITUTE. I don't need money.

SOLDIER [stops; they are at a street light.] You don't need money? Who the hell are you?

PROSTITUTE. It's these civilians that got to pay. A guy like you can get it free anytime he wants.

SOLDIER. I think you must be the one Huber was talking about.

PROSTITUTE. I don't know any Huber.

SOLDIER. Sure, you're the one. You know—the coffee-house in Schiff Gasse? He went home with you from there.

PROSTITUTE. I've gone home with more guys than him from that coffee-house. Eh! Eh!

SOLDIER. Okay, let's go, let's go.

PROSTITUTE. What's the matter, you can't wait now?

SOLDIER. Well, what's there to wait for? And I got to be back at the barracks by ten.

PROSTITUTE. How long you been in?

SOLDIER. None of your business! You live far?

PROSTITUTE. About ten minutes' walk.

SOURCE: La Ronde by Arthur Schnitzler, translated by Carl Richard Mueller, copyright 1964, reprinted by permission of the translator. Inquiries concerning use of this translation should go to C. R. Mueller, Theater Arts Department, University of California, Los Angeles.

SOLDIER. Hell, that's too far. Give me a kiss.

PROSTITUTE [kisses him]. I figure that's the best part of it when you really like a guy.

SOLDIER. Oh, yeah? Hell, I can't go with you, it's too far.

PROSTITUTE. Well then, why not come tomorrow afternoon?

SOLDIER. Great. What's the address?

PROSTITUTE. Ah, but you won't come.

SOLDIER. If I promise?

PROSTITUTE. Hey, you know what? If you don't want to go all the way home with me tonight—what about—over there?—

[She points toward the Danube.]

SOLDIER. What's over there?

PROSTITUTE. It's nice and quiet there, too. Nobody around at this time of night.

SOLDIER. Ah, that's no good.

PROSTITUTE. Everything I got's good. Come on, stay awhile with me. Who knows, we might be dead tomorrow.

SOLDIER. All right, come on—but make it quick!

PROSTITUTE. Careful, it's awful dark over here. One slip and you'll end up in the Danube.

SOLDIER. That might be the best bet after all.

PROSTITUTE. Psst, not so fast. We'll come to a bench soon.

SOLDIER. You're right at home, uh?

PROSTITUTE. I'd like one like you for a sweetheart.

SOLDIER. I'd only make you jealous.

PROSTITUTE. I could take care of that.

SOLDIER. Ha—

PROSTITUTE. Not so loud. Sometimes these policemen get lost down here. Who'd ever think us in the middle of Vienna?

SOLDIER. Come over here, come on.

PROSTITUTE. What's the matter with you, if we slip we end up in the river.

SOLDIER [takes hold of her]. There, that's better—

PROSTITUTE. You just hold tight.

SOLDIER. Don't worry . . .

* * *

PROSTITUTE. It would have been better on the bench.

SOLDIER. Hell, what's the difference!—Well, come on, get up.

PROSTITUTE. What are you running for?

SOLDIER. I've got to get back to the barracks, I'll be late as it is.

PROSTITUTE. Hey, uh, what's your name?

SOLDIER. What's it to you what my name is!

PROSTITUTE. My name's Leocadia.

SOLDIER. Ha!—Who ever heard of a name like that!

PROSTITUTE. You!

SOLDIER. Well, what do you want?

PROSTITUTE. Well, uh, how about a little something for the janitor?

SOLDIER. Ha! What do you think I am! So long! Leocadia . . .

PROSTITUTE. Tightwad! Son-of-a-bitch!

[He has disappeared.]

SCENE TWO

THE SOLDIER AND
THE PARLOR MAID

[The Prater. Sunday evening. A path leading from the Wurstelprater, an amusement park, out into the dark avenues. The confused sounds of the park are still audible, along with the music of the Fünfkreuzertanz, a banal polka, played by a brass band. The SOLDIER. The PARLOR MAID.]

PARLOR MAID. Why did we have to leave just now?

[The soldier laughs stupidly; he is embarrassed.]

PARLOR MAID. It was so nice in there. And I just love to dance.

[The soldier takes her by the waist.]

PARLOR MAID [letting him]. But we're not dancing now. Why are you holding me so tight?

SOLDIER. What's your name? Kathi?

PARLOR MAID. You must have Kathi on the brain!

SOLDIER. I know, I know, don't tell me . . . Marie.

PARLOR MAID. Oh, it's so dark here. I'm going to be afraid.

SOLDIER. As long as I'm here you don't have to be afraid. You just leave it to me!

PARLOR MAID. But where are we going

now? There are no people around. Come
on, let's go back!—And it's so dark!

SOLDIER [draws on his Virginia cigar,
making the tip glow red]. How's that for
light? Haha! Oh, you beautiful . . .

PARLOR MAID. Hey, what are you doing. If I had only known!

SOLDIER. I'll be damned if you aren't
the softest one of the bunch, Fräulein
Marie.

PARLOR MAID. I suppose you tried
them all.

SOLDIER. You notice things like that,
dancing. You notice a lot of things! Ha!

PARLOR MAID. You sure danced more
with that pie-faced blonde than with me.

SOLDIER. She's a friend of a friend of
mine.

PARLOR MAID. The Corporal with the
turned-up moustache?

SOLDIER. No, the civilian at the table
with me earlier, the one with the big
mouth.

PARLOR MAID. Oh, I remember. He
sure is fresh.

SOLDIER. Did he do anything to you?
I'll teach him a . . . What did he do to
you?

PARLOR MAID. Oh, nothing—I only
watched him with the others.

SOLDIER. Tell me something, Fräulein
Marie . . .

PARLOR MAID. You'll burn me with
that cigar.

SOLDIER. Sorry!—Fräulein Marie, why
are we being so formal?

PARLOR MAID. Because we aren't well
acquainted yet.

SOLDIER. A lot of people who can't
stand each other aren't as formal as we
are.

PARLOR MAID. The next time maybe,
when we . . . oh, Herr Franz—

SOLDIER. So you *do* know my name.

PARLOR MAID. But, Herr Franz . . .

SOLDIER. Just call me Franz, Fräulein
Marie.

PARLOR MAID. Then don't be so fresh
—Come on, what if somebody sees us!

SOLDIER. So let them look. They
couldn't see two feet in front of their
own faces out here.

PARLOR MAID. But, Herr Franz, where
are you taking me?

SOLDIER. Look there—two more just
like us.

PARLOR MAID. Where? I can't see a
thing.

SOLDIER. There—right in front of us.

PARLOR MAID. Why did you say 'two
just like us'?

SOLDIER. Well, what I meant was, they
like each other, too.

PARLOR MAID. Oh, be careful there!
What is it? I almost fell.

SOLDIER. Just the railing around the
grass.

PARLOR MAID. Stop pushing me like
that, I'll fall.

SOLDIER. Psst, not so loud.

PARLOR MAID. I'm really going to
scream in a minute.—Why, what are
you doing . . . why . . .

SOLDIER. There's not a soul in sight
out here.

PARLOR MAID. Then let's go back
where there are.

SOLDIER. What do we need people
for, Marie . . . what we need is . . . come
on . . . come on.

PARLOR MAID. Oh, but, Herr Franz,
please, for Heaven's sake, listen to me,
if I'd only . . . known . . . oh . . . oh . . .
yes! . . .

* * *

SOLDIER [blissfully]. My God, don't . . .
don't stop . . . ah . . .

PARLOR MAID. . . . I can't even see your
face.

SOLDIER. My God—my face . . .

* * *

SOLDIER. Well, are you going to lay
there all night, Fräulein Marie?

PARLOR MAID. Please, Franz, help me.

SOLDIER. Oh, come on.

PARLOR MAID. Oh, God, Franz.

SOLDIER. Well, what's all this with
Franz all of a sudden?

PARLOR MAID. You're a terrible man,
Franz.

SOLDIER. Sure, sure. Hey, wait for me.

PARLOR MAID. Why did you let go of
me?

SOLDIER. Do you mind if I light my
cigar again?

PARLOR MAID. It's so dark.

SOLDIER. It'll be light again tomorrow.

PARLOR MAID. At least tell me if you
like me.

SOLDIER. What's the matter, Fräulein Marie, didn't you feel anything? Ha!

PARLOR MAID. Where are we going?

SOLDIER. Back.

PARLOR MAID. Please, not so fast!

SOLDIER. What's the matter now? Do you think I like walking in the dark?

PARLOR MAID. Tell me, Franz, do you like me?

SOLDIER. But I just told you I liked you!

PARLOR MAID. Don't you want to give me a kiss?

SOLDIER [kindly]. There . . . Listen— you can hear the music again now.

PARLOR MAID. You mean you want to go back dancing again?

SOLDIER. Sure, why not?

PARLOR MAID. Well, Franz, I've got to go home. They'll be angry with me as is, my mistress is such a . . . she'd rather we never go out.

SOLDIER. All right, then, go home.

PARLOR MAID. Well, I was thinking, Herr Franz, that you would walk home with me.

SOLDIER. Walk home with you? Ah!

PARLOR MAID. Well, you see, it's always so lonely walking home alone.

SOLDIER. Where do you live?

PARLOR MAID. Not at all far—in Porzellan Gasse.

SOLDIER. I see! We've got quite a walk ahead of us . . . but it's too early now . . . I want to have some fun. I've got a late pass tonight . . . I don't have to be back before twelve. I'm going to dance some more.

PARLOR MAID. Sure, I know. Now it's the blonde's turn, with the pie-face!

SOLDIER. Ha!—She's no pie-face.

PARLOR MAID. Oh, God, why are men so terrible. I'll bet you treat them all that way.

SOLDIER. Oh, I wouldn't say that!

PARLOR MAID. Franz, please, not tonight again—stay with me tonight, won't you?

SOLDIER. All right, all right. But I'm still going back in dancing.

PARLOR MAID. I wouldn't dance with another soul tonight!

SOLDIER. We're almost there.

PARLOR MAID. Where?

SOLDIER. The Swoboda! We made good time. Listen, they're still playing

it . . . tatatatum tatatatum . . . [He sings along.] . . . Okay, if you want to wait for me, I'll take you home . . . if not . . . so long!

PARLOR MAID. I'll wait.

[They enter the dance hall.]

SOLDIER. I'll tell you what, Fräulein Marie, why not buy yourself a glass of beer? [Turning to a blonde as she dances past in the arms of a young man.] May I have this dance?—

SCENE THREE

THE PARLOR MAID AND THE YOUNG GENTLEMAN

[A hot summer afternoon. His parents are already off to the country. The cook is having her day off. The PARLOR MAID is in the kitchen writing a letter to the SOLDIER who is her lover. A bell rings from the room of the YOUNG GENTLEMAN. She rises and goes to the room of the YOUNG GENTLEMAN. The YOUNG GENTLEMAN is lying on the divan, smoking and reading a French novel.]

PARLOR MAID. Did the young gentleman ring?

YOUNG GENTLEMAN. Oh, yes, Marie, yes, I, uh, rang. Yes, now what was it I . . . ? Oh, yes, of course, the blinds, would you let them down, Marie? It's cooler with the blinds down . . . yes . . .

[The PARLOR MAID goes to the window and lowers the blinds.]

YOUNG GENTLEMAN [continues reading]. What are you doing, Marie? Oh, yes. Well, now it's too dark to read, isn't it?

PARLOR MAID. The young gentleman is always so studious.

YOUNG GENTLEMAN [ignores this genteelly]. There, that's fine.

[MARIE goes out. The YOUNG GENTLEMAN tries to continue reading; soon, however, he drops his book and rings again. The PARLOR MAID appears.]

YOUNG GENTLEMAN. Oh, Marie . . . what I wanted to say was . . . uh . . . would you have any cognac in the house?

PARLOR MAID. Yes, but it would be locked up.

YOUNG GENTLEMAN. Well, who has the key?

PARLOR MAID. Lini has the key.

YOUNG GENTLEMAN. Who is Lini?

PARLOR MAID. The cook, Herr Alfred.

YOUNG GENTLEMAN. Well then, tell Lini to do it.

PARLOR MAID. Yes, but she's on her day off.

YOUNG GENTLEMAN. I see . . .

PARLOR MAID. Shall I run down to the café for the young gentleman?

YOUNG GENTLEMAN. No, no . . . it's warm enough as is. I don't think I'll need the cognac. But, Marie, you might bring me a glass of water. And, Marie—let it run so it will be nice and cold.—

[The PARLOR MAID goes off. The YOUNG GENTLEMAN watches her leave. At the door she turns around to him—the YOUNG GENTLEMAN looks into space. The PARLOR MAID turns the handle on the tap and lets the water run. Meanwhile she goes into her little room, washes her hands, and arranges her curls in front of the mirror. Then she brings the YOUNG GENTLEMAN his glass of water. She goes to the divan. The YOUNG GENTLEMAN raises up half-way, the PARLOR MAID hands him the glass of water, their fingers touch.]

YOUNG GENTLEMAN. Thank you.— Well, what is it?—Be careful; put the glass back on the saucer . . . [He lies down again and stretches himself out.] What time is it?

PARLOR MAID. Five o'clock, sir.

YOUNG GENTLEMAN. Oh, five o'clock.— Good.

[The PARLOR MAID goes out; she turns around at the door; the YOUNG GENTLEMAN has followed her with his eyes; she notices this and smiles. The YOUNG GENTLEMAN remains on the divan for a while, then rises suddenly. He walks as far as the door, then comes back, lies down again on the divan. He tries to continue reading. After a few moments he rings again. The PARLOR MAID appears with a smile which she does not try to hide.]

YOUNG GENTLEMAN. Oh, Marie, what I meant to ask you—did Doctor Schueller come by this morning?

PARLOR MAID. No, there was no one here this morning.

YOUNG GENTLEMAN. How strange. You're sure he didn't come? Would you know him if you saw him?

PARLOR MAID. Yes. He's the tall man with the black beard.

YOUNG GENTLEMAN. That's right. Was he here?

PARLOR MAID. No, sir, there was no one here.

YOUNG GENTLEMAN [having decided]. Come here, Marie.

PARLOR MAID [steps a bit closer]. Yes, sir?

YOUNG GENTLEMAN. Closer . . . there . . . why . . . I always thought . . .

PARLOR MAID. What is it, sir?

YOUNG GENTLEMAN. I thought . . . I always thought . . . About that blouse . . . What's it made of . . . Well, come on, come closer. I won't bite.

PARLOR MAID [goes to him]. What about my blouse? Doesn't the young gentleman like it?

YOUNG GENTLEMAN [takes hold of her blouse and pulls her down to him]. Blue? It's quite a lovely blue, isn't it? [Simply.] You're very nicely dressed, Marie.

PARLOR MAID. Oh, but the young gentleman . . .

YOUNG GENTLEMAN. Why, what is it? [He has opened her blouse. Pertinently.] You have such lovely white skin, Marie.

PARLOR MAID. The young gentleman flatters me.

YOUNG GENTLEMAN [kisses her breast]. That can't hurt you, can it?

PARLOR MAID. No.

YOUNG GENTLEMAN. It's your sighing! Why are you sighing so, Marie?

PARLOR MAID. Oh, Herr Alfred . . .

YOUNG GENTLEMAN. And what nice slippers you have on . . .

PARLOR MAID. . . . But . . . Herr Alfred . . . what if someone rings!

YOUNG GENTLEMAN. Who'd ring at a time like this?

PARLOR MAID. But doesn't the young gentleman . . . look . . . how light it is . . .

YOUNG GENTLEMAN. You needn't be ashamed in front of me. You needn't be ashamed in front of anyone . . . not as lovely as you are. My God, Marie, you're so . . . Even your hair smells wonderful.

PARLOR MAID. Herr Alfred . . .

YOUNG GENTLEMAN. Don't be so silly, Marie . . . I've seen you—look quite different. One night just after I came home I went to the kitchen for a glass of water; the door to your room was open . . . well . . .

PARLOR MAID [hides her face]. Oh, God, I never thought you would do such a terrible thing, Herr Alfred!

YOUNG GENTLEMAN. I saw everything, Marie . . . here . . . and here . . . and here . . . and—

PARLOR MAID. Oh, Herr Alfred!

YOUNG GENTLEMAN. Come here, come here . . . come . . . there, that's right . . .

PARLOR MAID. But someone might ring!

YOUNG GENTLEMAN. Now you stop that . . . we simply won't answer . . .

* * *

[The bell rings.]

YOUNG GENTLEMAN. Goddamn! . . . Couldn't he make a little more noise!— He probably rang earlier and we didn't hear it.

PARLOR MAID. Oh, I was listening the whole time.

YOUNG GENTLEMAN. Well, go and see who it is—through the peep-hole.

PARLOR MAID. Herr Alfred . . . you're . . . no . . . you're a terrible man.

YOUNG GENTLEMAN. Please, go see who it is . . .

[The PARLOR MAID goes out. The YOUNG GENTLEMAN opens the blinds.]

PARLOR MAID [appears again]. He must have left again. There's no one there now. It might have been Doctor Schueller.

YOUNG GENTLEMAN [unfavorably moved]. That will be all.

[The PARLOR MAID draws nearer to him.]

YOUNG GENTLEMAN [avoids her]. Oh, Marie—I'm going to the coffee-house now.

PARLOR MAID [tenderly]. So soon . . . Herr Alfred?

YOUNG GENTLEMAN [sternly]. I'm going to the coffee-house now. If Doctor Schueller should call—

PARLOR MAID. He won't come anymore today.

YOUNG GENTLEMAN [more sternly]. If Doctor Schueller should call, I'll . . . I'll be in the coffee-house. [He goes into the other room.]

[The PARLOR MAID takes a cigar from the smoking table, puts it in her pocket and goes off.]

SCENE FOUR

THE YOUNG GENTLEMAN AND THE YOUNG WIFE

[Evening. A salon in the house on Schwind Gasse, furnished with cheap elegance. The YOUNG GENTLEMAN has just entered, and, while still wearing his topcoat and with hat still in his hand, lights the candles. He then opens the door to the adjoining room and looks in. The light from the candles in the salon falls across the inlaid floor to the four-poster against the back wall. The reddish glow from a fireplace in the corner of the room diffuses itself on the curtains of the bed. The YOUNG GENTLEMAN also inspects the bedroom. He takes an atomizer from the dressing-table and sprays the pillows on the bed with a fine mist of violet perfume. He then goes through both rooms with the atomizer, pressing continuously on the little bulb, until both rooms smell of violet. He then removes his topcoat and hat, sits in a blue velvet armchair, and smokes. After a short while he rises again and assures himself that the green shutters are down: Suddenly he goes back into the bedroom, opens the drawer of the night-table. He feels around in it for a tortoise-shell hairpin. He looks for a place to hide it, then finally puts it in the pocket of his topcoat. Then he opens a cabinet in the salon, removes a tray with a bottle of cognac on it and two small liqueur glasses which he places on the table. He goes to his overcoat and removes a small white package from the pocket. He opens it and places it beside the cognac, returns to the cabinet, and takes out two small plates and eating utensils. From the

small package he takes a marron glacé
and eats it. He then pours himself a cognac and drinks it. He looks at his watch.
He paces the room, back and forth.—
He stops in front of the large wall mirror
and combs his hair and his small moustache with a pocket comb. He now goes
to the door of the hallway and listens.
Not a sound. The bell rings. The YOUNG
GENTLEMAN starts suddenly. He then
seats himself in the armchair and rises
only when the door is opened and the
YOUNG WIFE enters. She is heavily veiled,
closes the door behind her, remains
standing there for a moment while she
brings her left hand to her heart as
though to master an overwhelming emotion. The YOUNG GENTLEMAN goes to her,
takes her left hand in his and imprints
a kiss on the white black-trimmed glove.]

YOUNG GENTLEMAN [softly]. Thank
you.

YOUNG WIFE. Alfred—Alfred!

YOUNG GENTLEMAN. Come in, gracious
lady . . . come in, Frau Emma.

YOUNG WIFE. Please, leave me alone
here for a while—please . . . please, Alfred! [Still standing at the door.]

[The YOUNG GENTLEMAN stands in
front of her, holding her hand.]

YOUNG WIFE. Where am I?

YOUNG GENTLEMAN. With me.

YOUNG WIFE. This house is a fright,
Alfred.

YOUNG GENTLEMAN. But why? It's a
very distinguished house.

YOUNG WIFE. I passed two gentlemen
on the stairs.

YOUNG GENTLEMAN. Did you know
them?

YOUNG WIFE. I'm not sure. But it's
possible.

YOUNG GENTLEMAN. My dear lady,
you must know your own friends.

YOUNG WIFE. I couldn't see a thing.

YOUNG GENTLEMAN. Even if they had
been your best friends—they could never
have recognized you. With that veil on I
would never have recognized you myself,
unless I knew.

YOUNG WIFE. There are two of them.

YOUNG GENTLEMAN. Won't you come
in? And you must at least take your hat
off.

YOUNG WIFE. Oh, but, Alfred, I

couldn't possibly! I told you before I
came: five minutes . . . no, not a moment
longer . . . I assure you—

YOUNG GENTLEMAN. Well, at least your
veil.

YOUNG WIFE. There are two of them.

YOUNG GENTLEMAN. Well, yes, then
both veils . . . but at least let me see you.

YOUNG WIFE. Do you really love me,
Alfred?

YOUNG GENTLEMAN [deeply hurt].
Emma—how can you . . .

YOUNG WIFE. It's so warm in here.

YOUNG GENTLEMAN. Well, you still
have on your fur cape—you're sure to
catch a cold.

YOUNG WIFE [finally enters the room
and throws herself into the armchair].
I'm dead tired.

YOUNG GENTLEMAN. May I? [He takes
off her veils; takes the pin out of her hat,
and places the hat, the pin, and the veils
to the side. The YOUNG WIFE does not
stop him. The YOUNG GENTLEMAN stands
in front of her, shakes his head.]

YOUNG WIFE. What's the matter?

YOUNG GENTLEMAN. You have never
been so lovely.

YOUNG WIFE. Why, what do you
mean?

YOUNG GENTLEMAN. Alone . . . alone
with you—Emma—[He kneels beside
her armchair, takes her hands in his and
covers them with kisses.]

YOUNG WIFE. And now . . . now I must
go. I've done all you asked of me.

[The YOUNG GENTLEMAN lets his head
sink onto her lap.]

YOUNG WIFE. You promised me to be
good.

YOUNG GENTLEMAN. Yes.

YOUNG WIFE. I'm about to suffocate in
this room.

YOUNG GENTLEMAN [rises]. You still
have your fur cape on.

YOUNG WIFE. Here, put it beside my
hat.

YOUNG GENTLEMAN [takes off her cape
and places it beside the other things on
the divan]. There.

YOUNG WIFE. And now—adieu—

YOUNG GENTLEMAN. Emma—Emma!

YOUNG WIFE. Those five minutes are
long past.

YOUNG GENTLEMAN. Not a single minute has gone by!

YOUNG WIFE. Now, Alfred, for once I want you to tell me exactly what time it is.

YOUNG GENTLEMAN. It's a quarter to seven, exactly.

YOUNG WIFE. I should have been at my sister's long ago.

YOUNG GENTLEMAN. Your sister can see you anytime.

YOUNG WIFE. Oh, God, Alfred, why did you ever mislead me into this?

YOUNG GENTLEMAN. Because I ... worship you, Emma.

YOUNG WIFE. How many others have you told that to?

YOUNG GENTLEMAN. Since I first saw you, no one.

YOUNG WIFE. What a frivolous woman I've become! If anyone had told me of this ... even just a week ago ... even yesterday ...

YOUNG GENTLEMAN. And it was the day before yesterday that you promised me ...

YOUNG WIFE. You tormented me so. But I didn't want to do it. God as my witness, I didn't want to do it ... Yesterday I was firmly resolved ... Do you know that yesterday evening I wrote you a long letter?

YOUNG GENTLEMAN. I didn't receive it.

YOUNG WIFE. I tore it up. Oh, how I wish now I'd sent you the letter!

YOUNG GENTLEMAN. It's better this way.

YOUNG WIFE. Oh, no, it's disgraceful ... of me. I don't even understand myself. Adieu, Alfred, you must let me go.

[*The* YOUNG GENTLEMAN *embraces her and covers her face with passionate kisses.*]

YOUNG WIFE. Is this how you ... keep your promise?

YOUNG GENTLEMAN. Just one more kiss ... just one.

YOUNG WIFE. And the last. [*He kisses her; she returns the kiss; their lips remain locked together for a long while.*]

YOUNG GENTLEMAN. Shall I tell you something, Emma? I know now, for the first time, what happiness is.

[*The* YOUNG WIFE *sinks back into the armchair.*]

YOUNG GENTLEMAN [*sits on the arm of the chair, places his arm lightly about her neck*].... or better still, I know now what happiness *could* be.

[*The* YOUNG WIFE *sighs deeply. The* YOUNG GENTLEMAN *kisses her again.*]

YOUNG WIFE. Alfred, Alfred, what are you making of me!

YOUNG GENTLEMAN. Tell me now ... it's not really so uncomfortable here, is it? And we're so safe here, too. It's a thousand times more wonderful than our meetings in the open.

YOUNG WIFE. Oh, please, don't remind me of it.

YOUNG GENTLEMAN. I will think of those meetings with a great deal of joy. Every moment that I've been able to spend with you will be with me forever!

YOUNG WIFE. Do you still remember the Industrial Ball?

YOUNG GENTLEMAN. Do I remember it? I sat beside you during supper, quite close beside you. Your husband ordered champagne ... [*The* YOUNG WIFE *looks protestingly at him.*] I was only going to mention the champagne. Emma, would you like a glass of cognac?

YOUNG WIFE. Just a drop, but I'd like a glass of water first.

YOUNG GENTLEMAN. Yes ... Well now, where is the—ah, yes ... [*He pushes back the doors and enters the bedroom. The* YOUNG WIFE *watches him. The* YOUNG GENTLEMAN *enters with a decanter of water and two drinking glasses.*]

YOUNG WIFE. Where were you?

YOUNG GENTLEMAN. In the ... the next room. [*Pours a glass of water.*]

YOUNG WIFE. I want to ask you something now, Alfred—and promise me you will tell me the truth.

YOUNG GENTLEMAN. I promise.

YOUNG WIFE. Has there ever been another woman in these rooms?

YOUNG GENTLEMAN. Well, Emma— this house is twenty years old!

YOUNG WIFE. You know what I mean, Alfred ... with you!

YOUNG GENTLEMAN. With me—here —Emma!—It's not at all nice that you should think of such a thing.

YOUNG WIFE. Then you ... how shall I say it ... But no, I'd rather not ask you. It's better if I don't. I'm the one to blame. Nothing goes unavenged.

YOUNG GENTLEMAN. What is it? I don't understand! What doesn't go unavenged?

YOUNG WIFE. No, no, no, I mustn't

come to myself, or I'll sink into the earth in shame.

YOUNG GENTLEMAN [*with the decanter of water in hand, shakes his head sadly*]. Emma, if you only knew how you're hurting me.

[*The* YOUNG WIFE *pours herself a glass of cognac.*]

YOUNG GENTLEMAN. I want to tell you something, Emma. If you are ashamed to be here—if I mean absolutely nothing to you—if you are unable to feel that for me you are all the joy in the world—then I think you had best leave.

YOUNG WIFE. Yes, I'll do exactly that.

YOUNG GENTLEMAN [*taking her by the hand*]. But if you are able to realize that I cannot live without you, that to kiss your hand means for me more than the endearments of all the women of the world . . . Emma, I'm not like these other young people who know how to court women—perhaps I'm too naive . . . I . . .

YOUNG WIFE. And what if you *were* like these other young people?

YOUNG GENTLEMAN. Then you wouldn't be here—because you aren't like other women.

YOUNG WIFE. How do you know?

YOUNG GENTLEMAN [*has pulled her to the divan, seated himself close beside her*]. I have thought a great deal about you. I know that you are unhappy.

[*The* YOUNG WIFE *is pleased.*]

YOUNG GENTLEMAN. Life is so empty, so futile—and then—so short—so terribly short! There's only one happiness . . . to find another person who will love you.

[*The* YOUNG WIFE *has taken a candied pear from the table and puts it into her mouth.*]

YOUNG GENTLEMAN. Give me half!

[*She proffers it to him with her lips.*]

YOUNG WIFE [*takes hold of his hands which threaten to go astray*]. What are you doing, Alfred . . . is this the way you keep your promise?

YOUNG GENTLEMAN [*swallowing the pear, then more boldly*]. Life is so short.

YOUNG WIFE [*weakly*]. But that's no reason to—

YOUNG GENTLEMAN [*mechanically*]. Oh, but it is.

YOUNG WIFE [*more weakly*]. Now you see, Alfred, and you promised to be good . . . And it's so light . . .

YOUNG GENTLEMAN. Come, come, my only, only . . . [*He lifts her from the sofa.*]

YOUNG WIFE. What are you doing?

YOUNG GENTLEMAN. It's not at all light in there.

YOUNG WIFE. You mean there's another room?

YOUNG GENTLEMAN [*takes her with him*]. A beautiful room . . . and very dark.

YOUNG WIFE. But I'd rather stay here.

[*The* YOUNG GENTLEMAN *is already through the doorway with her, into the bedroom, and begins to unbutton her blouse.*]

YOUNG WIFE. You're so . . . oh, God, what are you making of me!—Alfred!

YOUNG GENTLEMAN. I worship you, Emma!

YOUNG WIFE. Please, wait, can't you at least wait . . . [*Weakly.*] Go on, I'll call you.

YOUNG GENTLEMAN. Please let me—let me—let me help you.

YOUNG WIFE. You're tearing my clothes.

YOUNG GENTLEMAN. Don't you wear a corset?

YOUNG WIFE. I never wear a corset. And neither does Dusé. But you can unbutton my shoes.

[*The* YOUNG GENTLEMAN *unbuttons her shoes, kisses her feet.*]

YOUNG WIFE [*has slipped into bed*]. Oh, I'm so cold.

YOUNG GENTLEMAN. You'll be warm enough soon.

YOUNG WIFE [*laughing softly*]. Do you think so?

YOUNG GENTLEMAN [*unfavorably moved, to himself*]. She shouldn't have said that. [*He undresses in the dark.*]

YOUNG WIFE [*tenderly*]. Come, come, come!

YOUNG GENTLEMAN [*suddenly in a better mood*]. Right away—

YOUNG WIFE. I smell violets.

YOUNG GENTLEMAN. It's you who smell that way . . . Yes—[*to her*]—it's you.

YOUNG WIFE. Alfred . . . Alfred!!!!

YOUNG GENTLEMAN. Emma . . .

* * *

YOUNG GENTLEMAN. It's obvious I love you too much . . . I feel like I've lost my senses.

YOUNG WIFE. . . .

YOUNG GENTLEMAN. These past days I've felt like I were going mad. I knew it would happen.

YOUNG WIFE. Don't worry about it.

YOUNG GENTLEMAN. Of course not. It's natural for a man to . . .

YOUNG WIFE. No . . . no . . . You're all excited. Calm yourself now . . .

YOUNG GENTLEMAN. Are you familiar with Stendhal?

YOUNG WIFE. Stendhal?

YOUNG GENTLEMAN. His *Psychology of Love?*

YOUNG WIFE. No, why do you ask?

YOUNG GENTLEMAN. There's a story in it that's very significant.

YOUNG WIFE. What kind of story is it?

YOUNG GENTLEMAN. There's a large crowd of cavalry officers that's gotten together—

YOUNG WIFE. And?

YOUNG GENTLEMAN. And they tell about their love affairs. And each one reports that with the woman he loves most, that is, most passionately . . . that he, that they—well, to come to the point, that the same thing happened to each of them that happened to us just now.

YOUNG WIFE. I see.

YOUNG GENTLEMAN. I find that very characteristic.

YOUNG WIFE. Yes.

YOUNG GENTLEMAN. Oh, I'm not through yet. One of them claims that it never happened to him in his entire life. But, Stendhal adds—he was a notorious braggart.

YOUNG WIFE. I see.

YOUNG GENTLEMAN. Still, it does give one a jolt, that's the stupid thing about it, even if it doesn't mean anything.

YOUNG WIFE. Of course. And besides, don't forget you promised me to be good.

YOUNG GENTLEMAN. Don't laugh, it doesn't help matters any.

YOUNG WIFE. Oh, but I'm *not* laughing. What you said about Stendhal is really very interesting. I always thought it only happened to older men . . . or with very . . . well, you understand, with men who have lived a great deal . . .

YOUNG GENTLEMAN. What are you talking about! That has nothing to do with it. Besides I forgot to tell you the nicest of all of Stendhal's stories. One of the cavalry officers even tells how he spent three nights—or was it six, I don't remember—with a woman he had wanted for weeks on end—*désirée*, you understand—and all they did during those nights was cry with happiness . . . both of them . . .

YOUNG WIFE. Both of them?

YOUNG GENTLEMAN. Yes. Isn't that remarkable? I find it so understandable—especially when you're in love.

YOUNG WIFE. But surely there must be many who *don't* cry.

YOUNG GENTLEMAN [*nervously*]. Surely . . . that was an exceptional case, too.

YOUNG WIFE. Oh—I thought Stendhal said that *all* cavalry officers cry under the circumstances.

YOUNG GENTLEMAN. There now, you see, you're making fun of me.

YOUNG WIFE. What are you talking about! Don't be so childish, Alfred!

YOUNG GENTLEMAN. It makes me nervous, that's all . . . and I have the feeling that you can think of *nothing else.* That's what embarrasses me most.

YOUNG WIFE. I'm not thinking about it at *all.*

YOUNG GENTLEMAN. Oh, yes, you are. If only I were convinced that you love me.

YOUNG WIFE. What more proof can you want?

YOUNG GENTLEMAN. You see . . . ? You're always making fun of me.

YOUNG WIFE. What do you mean? Come here, give me your sweet little head.

YOUNG GENTLEMAN. I like that.

YOUNG WIFE. Do you love me?

YOUNG GENTLEMAN. Oh, I'm so happy!

YOUNG WIFE. But you needn't cry, too.

YOUNG GENTLEMAN [*pulling himself from her, highly irritated*]. Again, again! And I begged you so.

YOUNG WIFE. All I said was you shouldn't cry.

YOUNG GENTLEMAN. You said: "You needn't cry, *too!*"

YOUNG WIFE. You're nervous, my sweet.

YOUNG GENTLEMAN. I know that.

YOUNG WIFE. But you shouldn't be. I find it rather nice that . . . that we . . . well, that we, so to speak, are good . . . comrades . . .

YOUNG GENTLEMAN. You're at it again!

YOUNG WIFE. Don't you remember! That was one of our first talks together. We wanted to be good comrades, nothing more. Oh, that was a lovely time ... it was at my sister's, the big ball in January, during the quadrille ... Oh, for God's sake, I should have been gone long ago ... my sister's waiting for me —what will she say ... Adieu, Alfred ...

YOUNG GENTLEMAN. Emma! Are you going to leave me this way?

YOUNG WIFE. Yes—just like that!

YOUNG GENTLEMAN. Just five more minutes ...

YOUNG WIFE. All right. Just five more minutes. But you must promise me ... not to move. All right? ... I'll give you another kiss when I leave. Psst ... quiet ... don't move, I said, or I shall get up at once, my sweet ... sweet ...

YOUNG GENTLEMAN. Emma ... my dearest ...

*   *   *

YOUNG WIFE. My dear Alfred—

YOUNG GENTLEMAN. It's Heaven to be with you.

YOUNG WIFE. But now I really must go.

YOUNG GENTLEMAN. Oh, let your sister wait.

YOUNG WIFE. I must get home. It's far too late for my sister. What time is it?

YOUNG GENTLEMAN. Well, how am I to find that out?

YOUNG WIFE. You'll have to look at your watch.

YOUNG GENTLEMAN. But my watch is in my waistcoat.

YOUNG WIFE. Then get it.

YOUNG GENTLEMAN [gets up with a mighty push]. Eight.

YOUNG WIFE [rises quickly]. Oh, my God! ... Quick, Alfred, give me my stockings. What am I to tell him? They're sure to be waiting for me at home ... Eight o'clock ... !

YOUNG GENTLEMAN. When will I see you again?

YOUNG WIFE. Never.

YOUNG GENTLEMAN. Emma! Don't you love me anymore?

YOUNG WIFE. That's why. Give me my shoes.

YOUNG GENTLEMAN. Never again? Here are your shoes.

YOUNG WIFE. There's a buttonhook in my bag. Please hurry, I beg of you ...

YOUNG GENTLEMAN. Here's the buttonhook.

YOUNG WIFE. Alfred, this can cost both of us our necks.

YOUNG GENTLEMAN [quite unfavorably moved]. Why's that?

YOUNG WIFE. Well, what shall I answer him when he asks me: Where have you been?

YOUNG GENTLEMAN. At your sister's.

YOUNG WIFE. If only I could lie.

YOUNG GENTLEMAN. You'll simply have to.

YOUNG WIFE. All this for someone like you! Oh, come here ... let me kiss you again. [She embraces him.]—And now— leave me alone, go in the other room. I can't dress myself with you here.

[The YOUNG GENTLEMAN goes into the salon and dresses himself. He eats some of the pastry and drinks a glass of cognac.]

YOUNG WIFE [calls after a while]. Alfred!

YOUNG GENTLEMAN. My sweet.

YOUNG WIFE. I think it better that we didn't cry.

YOUNG GENTLEMAN [smiling not without pride]. How can one be so flippant—

YOUNG WIFE. What do you think will happen—if just by chance we should meet again one day at a party?

YOUNG GENTLEMAN. By chance?—One day? Surely you'll be at Lobheimer's tomorrow, won't you?

YOUNG WIFE. Why, yes. And you?

YOUNG GENTLEMAN. Of course. May I ask you for the cotillion?

YOUNG WIFE. Oh, but I can't go! What can you be thinking of!—Why I would ... [She enters the salon fully dressed, takes a chocolate pastry.] ... sink into the earth.

YOUNG GENTLEMAN. Well, then, tomorrow at Lobheimer's, that will be lovely.

YOUNG WIFE. No, no ... I'll excuse myself; absolutely—

YOUNG GENTLEMAN. Then the day after tomorrow ... here.

YOUNG WIFE. What are you talking about?

YOUNG GENTLEMAN. At six . . .

YOUNG WIFE. Are there carriages here on the corner?—

YOUNG GENTLEMAN. As many as you like. The day after tomorrow, then, here, at six. Say yes, my dearest, sweetest . . .

YOUNG WIFE. . . . We'll talk about that tomorrow during the cotillion.

YOUNG GENTLEMAN [embraces her]. My angel.

YOUNG WIFE. Don't muss my hair again.

YOUNG GENTLEMAN. Tomorrow at Lobheimer's, then, and the day after tomorrow, here in my arms.

YOUNG WIFE. Goodbye . . .

YOUNG GENTLEMAN [suddenly troubled again]. But what will you tell him—today?

YOUNG WIFE. You mustn't ask . . . you mustn't ask . . . it's too terrible to think about.—Why do I love you so!—Adieu. —If I meet anyone on the stairs again, I'll have a stroke.—Ha!

[The YOUNG GENTLEMAN kisses her hand once again. The YOUNG WIFE goes off. The YOUNG GENTLEMAN stays behind alone. Then he sits on the divan.]

YOUNG GENTLEMAN [smiles and says to himself]. At last an affair with a respectable woman.

SCENE FIVE

THE YOUNG WIFE AND
THE HUSBAND

[A comfortable bedroom. It is 10:30 P.M. The YOUNG WIFE is reading in bed. The HUSBAND enters the bedroom in his bathrobe.]

YOUNG WIFE [without looking up]. Have you stopped working?

HUSBAND. Yes. I'm too tired. And besides . . .

YOUNG WIFE. Well?

HUSBAND. Suddenly at my writing table I felt very lonely. I felt a longing for you.

YOUNG WIFE [looks up]. Really?

HUSBAND [sits beside her on the bed].

Don't read anymore tonight. You'll ruin your eyes.

YOUNG WIFE [closes the book]. What is it?

HUSBAND. Nothing, my child. I'm in love with you! But of course you know that!

YOUNG WIFE. One might almost forget it at times.

HUSBAND. At times one has to forget it.

YOUNG WIFE. Why?

HUSBAND. Because marriage would be imperfect otherwise. It would . . . how shall I say it . . . it would lose its sanctity.

YOUNG WIFE. Oh . . .

HUSBAND. Believe me—it's true . . . If during these last five years we hadn't forgotten at times that we are in love with one another—well, perhaps we wouldn't be.

YOUNG WIFE. That's beyond me.

HUSBAND. The matter is simply this: we have had perhaps twelve love affairs with one another . . . Wouldn't you say so?

YOUNG WIFE. I haven't kept count!—

HUSBAND. If we had fully experienced our first love affair to its logical end, if from the beginning I had surrendered myself involuntarily to my passion for you, then we would have ended the same as every other pair of lovers. We would have been through with one another.

YOUNG WIFE. Oh . . . is that what you meant.

HUSBAND. Believe me—Emma—in the early days of our marriage I was afraid it would turn out that way.

YOUNG WIFE. Me, too.

HUSBAND. You see? Wasn't I right? That's why I think it well, for short periods of time, to live together merely as good friends.

YOUNG WIFE. I see.

HUSBAND. That way we can always experience new honeymoons with one another, simply because I never let our honeymoons . . .

YOUNG WIFE. Last for months.

HUSBAND. Right.

YOUNG WIFE. And now . . . would you say another of these periods of friendship has come to an end?

HUSBAND [tenderly pressing her to him]. It just might be.

YOUNG WIFE. But just suppose that . . . that it were different with me.

HUSBAND. But it's *not* different. You are the cleverest, most enchanting creature there is. I'm very fortunate to have found you.

YOUNG WIFE. It's really very nice this way you ... court me ... from time to time.

HUSBAND [*has also gone to bed*]. For a man who's been around a bit in the world—come, lay your head on my shoulder—well, marriage is something far more mysterious than it is for a young girl out of a good family. You come to us pure and ... at least to a certain degree, ignorant, and therefore you have a far clearer conception of the nature of love than we.

YOUNG WIFE [*laughing*]. Oh!

HUSBAND. Of course. Because we're completely confused, made insecure by the various experiences we are forced into before marriage. You women hear a great deal and know far too much, in fact you even read too much, but you have no proper conception of what we men have to experience. What is commonly called love is made absolutely repellent to us; for, after all, what are those creatures on whom we are so dependent!

YOUNG WIFE. Yes, what are they?

HUSBAND [*kisses her on the forehead*]. Be glad, my sweet, that you have never had to become aware of such relationships. Besides that, they're mostly pitiable creatures—so let us not cast stones!

YOUNG WIFE. I'm sorry—but this pity —it doesn't seem to me quite properly placed.

HUSBAND [*with gentle mildness*]. They deserve it. You young girls from good families, who enjoyed the protection of your parents until a bridegroom came along to ask for your hand—you know nothing of the misery that drives most of these poor creatures into the arms of sin.

YOUNG WIFE. So they all sell themselves?

HUSBAND. I wouldn't want to say *that*. And I'm not talking only about material misery. There is also such a thing—I might say—as moral misery; a faulty comprehension of what is proper, and especially of what is noble.

YOUNG WIFE. But why are they pitiable?—They seem to be doing rather well.

HUSBAND. You have rather strange notions, my child. You oughtn't to forget that such creatures as they are destined by nature to sink deeper and deeper. There's no end to it.

YOUNG WIFE [*snuggling close to him*]. It sounds rather nice.

HUSBAND [*rather pained*]. How can you talk like that, Emma! I should think that for a respectable woman there could be nothing more repulsive than a woman who is not ... respectable.

YOUNG WIFE. Of course, Karl, of course. I only said it. But tell me more. I like it when you talk this way. Tell me more.

HUSBAND. About what?

YOUNG WIFE. Well—about these creatures.

HUSBAND. What are you talking about!

YOUNG WIFE. Don't you remember when we were first married, I always begged you to tell me something of your youth?

HUSBAND. Why should that interest you?

YOUNG WIFE. Well, aren't you my husband? And isn't it rather unfair that I should know absolutely nothing about your past?

HUSBAND. Surely you can't think me so tactless as to—That will do, Emma ... it would be an absolute profanation.

YOUNG WIFE. Nevertheless ... who knows how many other women you've held in your arms, just like you're holding me now.

HUSBAND. Women, perhaps—but not like you.

YOUNG WIFE. But you must answer me one question ... otherwise ... otherwise ... there will be no honeymoon.

HUSBAND. You have a way of talking that ... don't forget you're a mother ... that our little girl is sleeping right in there ...

YOUNG WIFE [*snuggling close to him*]. But I'd like a boy, too.

HUSBAND. Emma!

YOUNG WIFE. Oh, don't be that way ... Of course I'm your wife ... but I'd like sometimes to be your mistress, too.

HUSBAND. Would you really?

YOUNG WIFE. Well—but first my question.

HUSBAND [*accommodating*]. Well?

YOUNG WIFE. Was there . . . was there ever a . . . a married woman among them?

HUSBAND. What's that?—How do you mean?

YOUNG WIFE. You know what I mean.

HUSBAND [mildly disturbed]. What makes you ask?

YOUNG WIFE. I wondered whether . . . that is—I know there are such women . . . yes. But did you ever . . .

HUSBAND [seriously]. Do you know such a woman?

YOUNG WIFE. Well, I'm not really sure.

HUSBAND. Is there such a woman among your female friends?

YOUNG WIFE. How can I possibly say yes or no to such a thing and—and be certain?

HUSBAND. Perhaps one of your friends . . . well, people talk a great deal . . . women, when they get together—did one of them confess?

YOUNG WIFE [uncertainly]. No.

HUSBAND. Have you ever suspected that any of your friends . . .

YOUNG WIFE. Suspect . . . oh . . . suspect . . .

HUSBAND. Then you have.

YOUNG WIFE. Of course not, Karl, absolutely not. Now that I think about it —I wouldn't suppose them capable of it.

HUSBAND. Not even one of them?

YOUNG WIFE. No—not my friends.

HUSBAND. Promise me something, Emma.

YOUNG WIFE. Well?

HUSBAND. That you will have nothing to do with a woman of whom you have the slightest suspicion that she . . . whose life is not completely above reproach.

YOUNG WIFE. I have to promise you a thing like that?

HUSBAND. Of course I know you would never seek out such acquaintances. But it could just by chance happen that . . . Well, it's not uncommon that such women whose reputations aren't exactly the best seek out the companionship of respectable women, partly as a relief for them, and partly—how shall I say it— partly as a longing for virtue.

YOUNG WIFE. I see.

HUSBAND. Yes. I believe it's quite true, what I've just said. A longing for virtue. One thing you can believe for certain, that all of these women are very unhappy.

YOUNG WIFE. Why?

HUSBAND. How can you even ask? Emma!—How can you?—Just imagine the kind of existence these women lead! Full of lies, viciousness, vulgarity, and full of danger.

YOUNG WIFE. Why, of course. You're quite right.

HUSBAND. Absolutely.—They pay for their bit of happiness . . . their bit of . . .

YOUNG WIFE. Pleasure.

HUSBAND. Why pleasure? How do you come to call it pleasure?

YOUNG WIFE. Well—there must be something to recommend it—or they wouldn't do it.

HUSBAND. It has nothing to recommend it . . . mere intoxication.

YOUNG WIFE [reflectively]. Mere intoxication.

HUSBAND. No, it's not even intoxication. But it is bought at a high price, that is for certain!

YOUNG WIFE. Then you . . . then you must have known it at first hand?

HUSBAND. Yes, Emma.—It is my saddest recollection.

YOUNG WIFE. Who is it? Tell me! Do I know her?

HUSBAND. How can you think such a thing?

YOUNG WIFE. Is it long past? Was it very long before you married me?

HUSBAND. Don't ask me. Please, don't ask me.

YOUNG WIFE. But, Karl!

HUSBAND. She's dead.

YOUNG WIFE. Seriously?

HUSBAND. Yes . . . I know it sounds ridiculous, but I have the feeling that all these women die young.

YOUNG WIFE. Did you love her very much?

HUSBAND. One doesn't love a liar.

YOUNG WIFE. Then why . . .

HUSBAND. Intoxication . . .

YOUNG WIFE. Then it does have something to . . .

HUSBAND. Don't talk about it, please. It's all long past. I have loved only one woman—and you are that woman. One can love only purity and truth.

YOUNG WIFE. Karl!

HUSBAND. How secure, how happy I

feel in these arms. Why didn't I know you as a child? I am sure I wouldn't have looked at other women.

YOUNG WIFE. Karl!

HUSBAND. How beautiful you are! . . . beautiful! . . . come here . . . [He puts out the light.]

* * *

YOUNG WIFE. Do you know what I can't help thinking about tonight?

HUSBAND. About what, my sweet?

YOUNG WIFE. About . . . about . . . about Venice.

HUSBAND. That first night . . .

YOUNG WIFE. Yes . . . it was so . . .

HUSBAND. What—? Tell me!

YOUNG WIFE. Do you love me like that now?

HUSBAND. Just like that.

YOUNG WIFE. Oh . . . if you would always . . .

HUSBAND [in her arms]. What?

YOUNG WIFE. Dear Karl!

HUSBAND. What did you mean to say? If I would always . . . ?

YOUNG WIFE. Yes.

HUSBAND. Well, what would happen if I would always . . . ?

YOUNG WIFE. Then I would always know that you love me.

HUSBAND. Yes. But you must know that already. One can't always be the loving husband, at times one must venture out into the hostile world, he must fight and struggle for an existence! You must never forget that, my child! In marriage everything has its place—that's the beauty of it all. There aren't many couples five years later who can remember their . . . their Venice.

YOUNG WIFE. Of course.

HUSBAND. And now . . . good night, my child.

YOUNG WIFE. Good night!

SCENE SIX

THE HUSBAND AND
THE SWEET YOUNG THING

[A private room in the Riedhof Restaurant. Comfortable, modest elegance.

The gas stove is burning.—On the table are the remains of a meal, meringues with whipped cream, fruit, cheese.

The HUSBAND smokes a Havana cigar; he leans in the corner of the divan. The SWEET YOUNG THING sits beside him on a chair and spoons the whipped cream out of a bowl, which she sucks up with great pleasure.]

HUSBAND. Taste good?

SWEET YOUNG THING [not letting herself be disturbed]. Oh!

HUSBAND. Would you like another?

SWEET YOUNG THING. No, I've had too much already.

HUSBAND. You're out of wine. [He pours her some.]

SWEET YOUNG THING. No . . . I'll just let it sit there, sir.

HUSBAND. You said "sir" again.

SWEET YOUNG THING. Did I?—Well, I guess I just always forget—don't I, sir?

HUSBAND. Karl!

SWEET YOUNG THING. What?

HUSBAND. "Don't I, Karl?" not "Don't I, sir?"!—Come, sit over here, by me.

SWEET YOUNG THING. Just a minute . . . I'm not through yet.

[The HUSBAND rises, places himself behind the chair and embraces her, while turning her head toward him.]

SWEET YOUNG THING. What is it?

HUSBAND. I'd like a kiss.

SWEET YOUNG THING [gives him a kiss]. You're a very forward man, sir—I mean, Karl.

HUSBAND. Are you just discovering that?

SWEET YOUNG THING. Oh, no, I knew that before . . . on the street.—You certainly must have a nice impression of me, sir.

HUSBAND. Karl!

SWEET YOUNG THING. Karl.

HUSBAND. Why?

SWEET YOUNG THING. That I came here with you so easily—to a private room and . . .

HUSBAND. Well, I wouldn't say it was that easy.

SWEET YOUNG THING. But you have such a nice way of asking.

HUSBAND. Do you think so?

SWEET YOUNG THING. And after all, what's the difference?

HUSBAND. Of course.

SWEET YOUNG THING. What's the difference if we go for a walk or . . .

HUSBAND. Oh, it's much too cold for a walk.

SWEET YOUNG THING. Of course it's too cold.

HUSBAND. And it *is* nice and warm here, isn't it?

[*He has seated himself again, puts his arms around the* SWEET YOUNG THING *and pulls her to his side.*]

SWEET YOUNG THING [*weakly*]. Oh!—

HUSBAND. Tell me now . . . you've noticed me before, haven't you?

SWEET YOUNG THING. Naturally. In Singer Strasse.

HUSBAND. I don't mean today. But yesterday and the day before yesterday, when I followed you.

SWEET YOUNG THING. A lot of people follow me.

HUSBAND. I can well imagine. But did you notice me?

SWEET YOUNG THING. Do you know what happened to me the other day? My cousin's husband followed me in the dark without recognizing me.

HUSBAND. Did he speak to you?

SWEET YOUNG THING. Don't be silly! Do you think everyone is as forward as you?

HUSBAND. It happens.

SWEET YOUNG THING. Naturally it happens.

HUSBAND. What did you do?

SWEET YOUNG THING. Why, nothing. —I simply didn't answer.

HUSBAND. Hm . . . but you answered me.

SWEET YOUNG THING. Well, are you sorry I did?

HUSBAND [*kisses her violently*]. Your lips taste like whipped cream.

SWEET YOUNG THING. Yes, they're always sweet.

HUSBAND. How many other men have told you that?

SWEET YOUNG THING. How many others! The way you talk!

HUSBAND. Be honest for once. How many other men have kissed that mouth of yours?

SWEET YOUNG THING. Are you asking me? You'd never believe it if I told you!

HUSBAND. And why shouldn't I?

SWEET YOUNG THING. Guess!

HUSBAND. Well, let's say—but you mustn't be angry . . .

SWEET YOUNG THING. Why should I be angry?

HUSBAND. Well then, let's say—twenty.

SWEET YOUNG THING [*pulling away from him*]. Well—why didn't you say a hundred right off?

HUSBAND. I was only guessing.

SWEET YOUNG THING. It wasn't a very good one.

HUSBAND. Well then, ten.

SWEET YOUNG THING [*insulted*]. Sure! a girl who lets herself be approached on the street and goes right to a private room!

HUSBAND. Don't be so childish. What's the difference between running around the streets or sitting in a room . . . ? Here we are in a restaurant. The waiter could come in any time—there's nothing to it.

SWEET YOUNG THING. That's what I thought, too.

HUSBAND. Have you ever been in a private room in a restaurant before?

SWEET YOUNG THING. Well, if you want me to be honest about it: yes.

HUSBAND. There, you see, I like the way you answered that: at least you're honest about it.

SWEET YOUNG THING. But not the way you think. It was with a friend of mine and her husband, during the Fasching Carnival last year.

HUSBAND. It wouldn't exactly be a tragedy if sometime you had been . . . well, with your lover—

SWEET YOUNG THING. Naturally it wouldn't have been a tragedy. But I don't have a lover.

HUSBAND. Now really!

SWEET YOUNG THING. Believe me, I haven't.

HUSBAND. Are you trying to tell me that I'm the . . .

SWEET YOUNG THING. The what?—It's just that I don't have one . . . well, for the last six months, I mean.

HUSBAND. I see.—But before that? Who was it?

SWEET YOUNG THING. You're awfully inquisitive.

HUSBAND. I'm inquisitive because I love you.

SWEET YOUNG THING. Do you mean it?

HUSBAND. Of course. Surely you must have noticed. But tell me about it. [*presses her close to him*].

SWEET YOUNG THING. What do you want me to tell you?

HUSBAND. Why must I always beg you? I'd like to know who it was.

SWEET YOUNG THING [*laughing*]. Oh, just a man.

HUSBAND. Well—well—who was he?

SWEET YOUNG THING. He looked a little bit like you.

HUSBAND. Oh?

SWEET YOUNG THING. If you hadn't looked so much like him—

HUSBAND. What then?

SWEET YOUNG THING. Why ask, if you already know . . .

HUSBAND [*understands*]. Then that's why you let me talk to you?

SWEET YOUNG THING. Well, I suppose.

HUSBAND. I really don't know now whether to be happy or angry.

SWEET YOUNG THING. If I were in your place, I'd be happy.

HUSBAND. Well, yes.

SWEET YOUNG THING. And even the way you talk reminds me of him . . . the way you look at a person . . .

HUSBAND. What was he?

SWEET YOUNG THING. And your eyes—

HUSBAND. What was his name?

SWEET YOUNG THING. No, you mustn't look at me that way, please.

[*The* HUSBAND *embraces her. A long passionate kiss.*]

HUSBAND. Where are you going?

SWEET YOUNG THING. It's time to go home.

HUSBAND. Not yet.

SWEET YOUNG THING. No, I really must get home. What do you think my mother will say!

HUSBAND. You live with your mother?

SWEET YOUNG THING. Naturally I live with my mother. Where did you think?

HUSBAND. I see—with your mother. Do you live alone with her?

SWEET YOUNG THING. Yes, of course, alone! Five of us! Two brothers and two more sisters.

HUSBAND. Why do you sit so far away from me? Are you the eldest?

SWEET YOUNG THING. No, I'm the second. Kathi comes first, she works, in a flower shop. And then I come next.

HUSBAND. Where do you work?

SWEET YOUNG THING. I stay home.

HUSBAND. All the time.

SWEET YOUNG THING. *Somebody* has to stay home.

HUSBAND. Of course. Yes—and what do you tell your mother when you—come home so late?

SWEET YOUNG THING. It doesn't happen often.

HUSBAND. Then today for example. Won't your mother ask?

SWEET YOUNG THING. Naturally she'll ask. I can be quiet as a mouse when I come home, but she'll hear me every time.

HUSBAND. Then, what will you tell her?

SWEET YOUNG THING. Well, I'll say I went to the theatre.

HUSBAND. And she'll believe you?

SWEET YOUNG THING. Well, why *shouldn't* she believe me? I go to the theatre quite often. Just last Sunday I went to the Opera with my girlfriend and her husband and my elder brother.

HUSBAND. Where did you get the tickets?

SWEET YOUNG THING. My brother's a barber!

HUSBAND. Oh, a barber—you mean a theatrical barber.

SWEET YOUNG THING. Why are you questioning me?

HUSBAND. It interests me, that's all. And what is your other brother?

SWEET YOUNG THING. He's still in school. He wants to be a teacher. Imagine . . . a teacher!

HUSBAND. And then you have still a younger sister?

SWEET YOUNG THING. Yes, she's a little brat, you have to keep an eye on her. You have no idea how a girl can be ruined at school! Why, just the other day I found her out with a boy.

HUSBAND. What?

SWEET YOUNG THING. Yes! With a boy from the school across from us; she went out walking with him at half-past seven in Strozzi Gasse. The little brat!

HUSBAND. And what did you do about it?

SWEET YOUNG THING. Well, she got a spanking!

HUSBAND. Are you that strict?

SWEET YOUNG THING. If *I'm* not, who *will* be? My elder sister works, my mother does nothing but nag;—everything lands on *me*.

HUSBAND. My God, but you're sweet! [*Kisses her and grows more tender.*] You remind me of someone, too.

SWEET YOUNG THING. Oh?—Who?

HUSBAND. Of no one in particular . . . perhaps—perhaps of my youth. Come, my child, have some wine!

SWEET YOUNG THING. How old are you? My goodness . . . I don't even know your name.

HUSBAND. Karl.

SWEET YOUNG THING. Not really! Your name is Karl?

HUSBAND. Was his name Karl, too?

SWEET YOUNG THING. No, I don't believe it, it's a miracle . . . it's an absolute —why, those eyes . . . that look . . . [*Shakes her head.*]

HUSBAND. And still you haven't told me who he was!

SWEET YOUNG THING. He was a terrible man—that's for sure, or else he wouldn't have walked out on me.

HUSBAND. Did you love him very much?

SWEET YOUNG THING. Of course I loved him very much.

HUSBAND. I know his kind—he was a lieutenant.

SWEET YOUNG THING. No, he wasn't a soldier. They wouldn't take him. His father had a house in . . . but why do you want to know all this?

HUSBAND [*kisses her*]. Do you know your eyes are grey? At first I thought they were black.

SWEET YOUNG THING. Well, aren't they pretty enough for you?

[*The* HUSBAND *kisses her eyes.*]

SWEET YOUNG THING. No, no—I can't stand that . . . oh, please—oh, God . . . no, let me up . . . just for a moment—please.

HUSBAND [*ever more tenderly*]. Oh, no, no.

SWEET YOUNG THING. Please, Karl, please . . .

HUSBAND. How old are you?—Eighteen? Hm?

SWEET YOUNG THING. Nineteen.

HUSBAND. Nineteen . . . and how old am *I*?

SWEET YOUNG THING. You're . . . thirty . . .

HUSBAND. And a little more.—But let's not talk about that.

SWEET YOUNG THING. He was thirty-two when I first got to know him.

HUSBAND. How long ago was that?

SWEET YOUNG THING. I don't remember . . . You know, I think there was something in that wine.

HUSBAND. What makes you think so?

SWEET YOUNG THING. I'm all . . . well, you know—my head's turning.

HUSBAND. Just hold tight to me. There . . . [*He presses her to him and grows increasingly more tender, she scarcely repulses him.*] You know something, my sweet, I think we could go now.

SWEET YOUNG THING. Yes . . . home.

HUSBAND. Not home exactly . . .

SWEET YOUNG THING. What do you mean? . . . Oh, no, oh, no . . . I won't go anywhere, what are you thinking of—

HUSBAND. Now, just listen to me, child, the next time we meet, we'll arrange it so that . . . [*He has sunk to the floor, his head in her lap.*] Oh, that's nice, oh, that's so nice.

SWEET YOUNG THING. What are you doing? [*She kisses his hair.*] You know, I think there was something in that wine —I'm so . . . sleepy . . . whatever will happen to me if I can't get up? But, but, look here, but, Karl . . . what if someone comes in . . . oh, please . . . the waiter.

HUSBAND. No waiter . . . 'll come in here. . . if he knows . . . what's . . .

* * *

[*The* SWEET YOUNG THING *leans, with her eyes closed, in the corner of the divan. The* HUSBAND *walks back and forth in the small room after lighting a cigarette. A long silence.*]

HUSBAND [*looks at the* SWEET YOUNG THING *for a long while; to himself*]. Who knows what kind of person she really is —Damn! . . . It happened so quickly . . . It wasn't very careful of me . . . Hm . . .

SWEET YOUNG THING [*without opening her eyes*]. There must have been something in the wine.

HUSBAND. Really? Why?

SWEET YOUNG THING. Otherwise . . .

HUSBAND. Why blame it all on the wine?

SWEET YOUNG THING. Where are you? Why are you way over there? Come over here by me.

[*The* HUSBAND *goes to her, sits down.*]

SWEET YOUNG THING. Tell me, do you really like me?

HUSBAND. You should know that . . . [He quickly interrupts himself.] Of course.

SWEET YOUNG THING. You know . . . I still . . . Come on now, tell me the truth, what was in the wine?

HUSBAND. What do you think I am . . . a poison-mixer?

SWEET YOUNG THING. I just don't understand it. I'm not that way . . . We've only known each other for . . . I tell you, I'm just not like that . . . I swear to God —and if you believe that of me—

HUSBAND. There now, what are you worrying about! I don't think anything bad of you. I only think that you like me.

SWEET YOUNG THING. Yes . . .

HUSBAND. And besides, when two young people are alone together in a room, having dinner and drinking wine . . . there needn't be anything at all in the wine . . .

SWEET YOUNG THING. I was just talking.

HUSBAND. Yes, but why?

SWEET YOUNG THING [somewhat obstinately]. Because I was ashamed of myself.

HUSBAND. That's ridiculous. There's no reason for it. And besides, I reminded you of your first lover.

SWEET YOUNG THING. Yes.

HUSBAND. Your first.

SWEET YOUNG THING. Why, yes . . .

HUSBAND. Now I'd be interested in knowing who the others were.

SWEET YOUNG THING. There were no others.

HUSBAND. That's not true, it can't be true.

SWEET YOUNG THING. Come on, please, don't pester me.—

HUSBAND. Cigarette?

SWEET YOUNG THING. No, thank you.

HUSBAND. Do you know what time it is?

SWEET YOUNG THING. What?

HUSBAND. Half-past eleven.

SWEET YOUNG THING. Really?

HUSBAND. Well, uh . . . what about your mother? She's used to it, uh?

SWEET YOUNG THING. You really want to send me home already?

HUSBAND. But, just a while ago you . . .

SWEET YOUNG THING. How you've changed. Wat have I done to you?

HUSBAND. Child, what's the matter, what are you taking about?

SWEET YOUNG THING. It was the look in your eyes, I swear, otherwise you'd have had to . . . a lot of men have begged me to go to private rooms like this with them.

HUSBAND. Well, would you like to . . . come here again soon . . . or somewhere else, too—

SWEET YOUNG THING. I don't know.

HUSBAND. What does that mean: I don't know?

SWEET YOUNG THING. Well then, why did you ask?

HUSBAND. All right, when? I just want to explain that I don't live in Vienna. I come here now and then for a few days.

SWEET YOUNG THING. Go on, you aren't Viennese?

HUSBAND. Oh, I'm from Vienna. But I don't live right in town . . .

SWEET YOUNG THING. Where?

HUSBAND. Why, what difference can that make?

SWEET YOUNG THING. Don't worry, I won't come looking for you.

HUSBAND. My God, if it will make you happy, come anytime you like. I live in Graz.

SWEET YOUNG THING. Seriously?

HUSBAND. Well, yes, why should that surprise you?

SWEET YOUNG THING. You're married, aren't you?

HUSBAND [greatly surprised]. Why do you say that?

SWEET YOUNG THING. It just seemed that way to me.

HUSBAND. And that wouldn't bother you?

SWEET YOUNG THING. Well, of course I'd rather you were single.—But you are married!

HUSBAND. You must tell me what makes you think so!

SWEET YOUNG THING. When a man says he doesn't live in Vienna and hasn't always got time—

HUSBAND. That's not so improbable.

SWEET YOUNG THING. I don't believe him.

HUSBAND. And it wouldn't give you a bad conscience to make a married man be unfaithful to his . . .

SWEET YOUNG THING. My God, your wife probably does the same thing!

HUSBAND [highly indignant]. I forbid

you to say such a thing! Such remarks
are . . .

SWEET YOUNG THING. I thought you
said you had no wife.

HUSBAND. Whether I have or not—one
doesn't make such remarks. [*He has
risen.*]

SWEET YOUNG THING. Karl, now, Karl,
what's the matter? Are you angry? Look,
I really *didn't* know that you were married. I only said it. Come on, be nice
again.

HUSBAND [*comes to her after a few
seconds*]. You're really such strange creatures, you . . . women. [*He becomes tender again at her side.*]

SWEET YOUNG THING. No . . . please . . .
besides, it's too late—

HUSBAND. All right, now listen to
me. Let's talk together seriously for once.
I want to see you again, see you
often.

SWEET YOUNG THING. Really?

HUSBAND. But if so, then it will be
necessary . . . well, I must be able to depend on you. I can't be careful *all* the
time.

SWEET YOUNG THING. Oh, I can take
care of myself.

HUSBAND. You're . . . well, I can't say
inexperienced—but you're young—and
—men in general are an unscrupulous
lot.

SWEET YOUNG THING. Oh, Lord!

HUSBAND. I don't necessarily mean that
in a moral sense.—But, you understand
what I mean.

SWEET YOUNG THING. Tell me, what do
you really think of me?

HUSBAND. Well—if you *do* want to
love me—only me—then I think we can
arrange something—even if I *do* usually
live in Graz. A place like this, where
someone could come in at any moment,
just isn't right.

[*The* SWEET YOUNG THING *snuggles
close to him.*]

HUSBAND. The next time . . . we'll get
together somewhere else, all right?

SWEET YOUNG THING. Yes.

HUSBAND. Where we can't be disturbed.

SWEET YOUNG THING. Yes.

HUSBAND [*embraces her passionately*].
We'll talk the rest over walking home.
[*Rises, opens the door.*] Waiter . . . the
check!

SCENE SEVEN

THE SWEET YOUNG THING
AND THE POET

[*A small room furnished in comfortable
good taste. The drapes keep it in semi-
darkness. Red curtains. A large writing
table upon which paper and books lie
about. An upright piano against the wall.
The* SWEET YOUNG THING *and the* POET
enter together. The POET *locks the door.*]

POET. There, my sweet [*kisses her*].

SWEET YOUNG THING [*in hat and cape*].
Oh! Isn't this nice! But you can't see
anything!

POET. Your eyes have to get used to
this semi-darkness.—These sweet eyes!—
[*Kisses her eyes.*]

SWEET YOUNG THING. I'm afraid my
sweet little eyes won't have time for that.

POET. Why not?

SWEET YOUNG THING. Because I'm going to stay here just one minute.

POET. Won't you take your hat off?

SWEET YOUNG THING. For one minute?

POET [*removes the pin from her hat
and places the hat at a distance*]. And
your cape—

SWEET YOUNG THING. What are you
doing?—I have to leave right away.

POET. But you must rest first! We've
been walking for three hours.

SWEET YOUNG THING. We were in a
carriage.

POET. Yes, on the way home—but in
Weidling-am-Bach we walked for a full
three hours. So why don't you sit down,
my child . . . wherever you like;—here at
the writing table;—but no, it's not comfortable enough. Sit here on the divan.—
There [*He urges her down onto the divan.*] If you're very tired you can even lie
down. [*He makes her lie down on the
divan.*] There, your little head on the
pillow.

SWEET YOUNG THING [*laughing*]. But
I'm not tired at all!

POET. You just think so. There—and
if you're sleepy you can sleep a bit. I shall
be quite still. Besides, I can play a lullaby
for you . . . one of my own. [*Goes to the
piano.*]

SWEET YOUNG THING. One of your own?

POET. Yes.

SWEET YOUNG THING. Why, Robert, I thought you were a doctor.

POET. How so? I told you I was a writer.

SWEET YOUNG THING. Writers are always doctors.

POET. No, not all. Myself for example. But why did you think of that?

SWEET YOUNG THING. Well, because you said the piece you were going to play was your own.

POET. Well . . . perhaps it isn't my own. But that's unimportant. Isn't it? It never really matters who does a thing—as long as it's beautiful—isn't that right?

SWEET YOUNG THING. Of course . . . as long as it's beautiful—that's the main thing!

POET. Do you know what I meant when I said that?

SWEET YOUNG THING. What you meant?

POET. Yes, what I just said.

SWEET YOUNG THING [sleepily]. Oh . . . of course.

POET [rises, goes to her and strokes her hair]. You didn't understand a word of it.

SWEET YOUNG THING. Go on, I'm not that stupid.

POET. Of course you're that stupid. And that's why I love you. It's a wonderful thing for a woman to be stupid. I mean, in your way.

SWEET YOUNG THING. Why are you making fun of me?

POET. You angel, you sweet little angel! Do you like lying on a soft Persian rug?

SWEET YOUNG THING. Oh, yes. Go on, why don't you play the piano?

POET. No, I'd rather be here with you. [He strokes her.]

SWEET YOUNG THING. Say, why don't you turn on the light?

POET. Oh, no . . . This twilight is very comforting. We spent the whole day bathed in sunlight. And now, you might say, we've just climbed from the bath and are about to wrap the . . . the twilight around us like a bathrobe—[He laughs.] —or, no—that should be put differently . . . Wouldn't you say so?

SWEET YOUNG THING. I don't know.

POET [gently moving from her]. How divine this stupidity can be! [Takes out a notebook and writes down a few words.]

SWEET YOUNG THING. What are you doing? [Turning towards him.] What are you writing?

POET [softly]. Sun, bath, twilight, robe . . . there . . . [Pockets the notebook. Out loud.] Nothing . . . Tell me now, my sweet, would you like something to eat or drink?

SWEET YOUNG THING. I'm not really thirsty. But I'm hungry.

POET. Hm . . . I'd rather you were thirsty. I have some cognac at home, but I'll have to go out for the food.

SWEET YOUNG THING. Can't you send out for it?

POET. That will be difficult—the maid's not around anymore—well, all right—I'll go myself . . . what would you like?

SWEET YOUNG THING. Oh, I don't think it'll be worth it—I have to be getting home anyway.

POET. Child, you mustn't think such a thing. But I'll tell you what: when we leave, let's go somewhere and have supper.

SWEET YOUNG THING. Oh, no. I don't have time. And besides, where would we go? We might meet friends.

POET. Have you that many friends?

SWEET YOUNG THING. It's bad enough if even one of them sees us.

POET. What do you mean "bad enough"?

SWEET YOUNG THING. Well, what would happen do you think if my mother heard about it?

POET. We could go somewhere where no one could see us; there are restaurants with private rooms, you know.

SWEET YOUNG THING [singing]. "Oh, take me to supper in a private room!"

POET. Have you ever been to one of those private rooms?

SWEET YOUNG THING. Well, to tell you the truth—yes.

POET. And who was the fortunate gentleman?

SWEET YOUNG THING. Oh, it's not what you're thinking . . . I was there once with my girl-friend and her husband. They took me along.

POET. I see. And you expect me to believe that?

SWEET YOUNG THING. I didn't ask you to believe it!

POET [close to her]. Are you blushing? It's too dark in here! I can't even make out your features. [He touches her cheek *with his hand.*] But I recognize you this way, too.

SWEET YOUNG THING. Just be careful you don't confuse me with someone else.

POET. How strange! I can't remember anymore what you look like.

SWEET YOUNG THING. Thanks!

POET [*seriously*]. Isn't that uncanny! I can't even picture you.—In a certain sense I've forgotten you.—And if I couldn't recognize you by the tone of your voice either . . . what would you be? —Near and far at the same time . . . uncanny.

SWEET YOUNG THING. Go on, what are you talking about—?

POET. Nothing, my angel, nothing. Where are your lips . . . [*He kisses her.*]

SWEET YOUNG THING. Don't you want to turn on the light?

POET. No . . . [*He grows very tender.*] Tell me, do you love me?

SWEET YOUNG THING. Very . . . oh, very much!

POET. Have you ever loved anyone else as much as me?

SWEET YOUNG THING. I already told you—no.

POET [*sighs*]. But . . . [*He sighs.*]

SWEET YOUNG THING. Well—he was my fiancé.

POET. I'd rather you didn't think about him.

SWEET YOUNG THING. Go on . . . what are you doing . . . look . . .

POET. We can imagine ourselves now in a castle in India.

SWEET YOUNG THING. I'm sure they couldn't be as bad there as you are.

POET. What nonsense! What a divine thing you are! If only you could guess what you mean to me.

SWEET YOUNG THING. Well?

POET. Stop pushing me away like that all the time; I'm not doing anything to you—yet.

SWEET YOUNG THING. You know what? —my corset hurts.

POET [*simply*]. Take it off.

SWEET YOUNG THING. Well—but you mustn't be bad if I do.

POET. No.

[*The* SWEET YOUNG THING *has risen and removes her corset in the dark.*]

POET [*in the meanwhile sits on the divan*]. Say, aren't you at all interested in knowing my last name?

SWEET YOUNG THING. Sure, what is it?

POET. I'd rather not tell you my name, but what I call myself.

SWEET YOUNG THING. What's the difference?

POET. Well, the name I write under.

SWEET YOUNG THING. Oh, you don't write under your real name?

[*The* POET *is close to her.*]

SWEET YOUNG THING. Oh . . . go on! . . . no.

POET. What a wonderful fragrance rises from you. How sweet it is. [*He kisses her breasts.*]

SWEET YOUNG THING. You're tearing my blouse.

POET. Here . . . let me . . . it's so unnecessary.

SWEET YOUNG THING. But, Robert!

POET. And now—enter our Indian castle.

SWEET YOUNG THING. Tell me first if you really love me.

POET. But I worship you. [*Kisses her passionately.*] I worship you, my sweet, my springtime . . . my . . .

SWEET YOUNG THING. Robert . . . Robert . . .

* * *

POET. That was unearthly bliss . . . I call myself . . .

SWEET YOUNG THING. Robert . . . my Robert!

POET. I call myself Biebitz.

SWEET YOUNG THING. Why do you call yourself Biebitz?

POET. My name isn't Biebitz—I just call myself that . . . well, don't you recognize the name?

SWEET YOUNG THING. No.

POET. You don't know the name Biebitz? Oh, how divine you are! Really? You're just saying that now, aren't you?

SWEET YOUNG THING. I swear, I never heard of it!

POET. Don't you go to the theatre?

SWEET YOUNG THING. Oh, yes—just recently I went with . . . with the uncle of a girl-friend of mine, and the girl-friend— we went to the Opera—*Cavalleria Rusticana.*

POET. Hm, then you don't go to the Burg Theatre.

SWEET YOUNG THING. Nobody gives me tickets for there.

POET. One day soon I'll send you a ticket.

SWEET YOUNG THING. Oh, please! But don't forget! And to something funny.

POET. I see . . . to something funny . . . you wouldn't want to see anything sad?

SWEET YOUNG THING. Not really.

POET. Not even if it's a play by me?

SWEET YOUNG THING. Oh! . . . a play by you? You write for the theatre?

POET. Excuse me, may I light a candle? I haven't seen you since you became my love.—Angel! [*He lights a candle.*]

SWEET YOUNG THING. No, don't, I'm ashamed. At least give me a cover.

POET. Later! [*He approaches her with the candle and looks at her for a long while.*]

SWEET YOUNG THING [*covers her face with her hands*]. Robert, you mustn't!

POET. You're beautiful. You are Beauty. Perhaps you are even Nature herself. You are sacred simplicity.

SWEET YOUNG THING. Oh! You're dripping on me! Look at that, why can't you be careful!

POET [*places the candle aside*]. You are what I have sought for for a long time. You love only me, you would love me even if I worked in a shop as an assistant. That's very comforting. I must confess to you that up to this moment I have harbored a certain suspicion. Tell me, honestly, didn't you have even the slightest idea that I was Biebitz?

SWEET YOUNG THING. Look, I don't know what you want with me, but I don't know any Biebitz.

POET. Oh, fame, fame! No, forget what I said, even forget the name I told you. I'm Robert to you, that's all. I was only joking. [*Lightly.*] I'm not even a writer, I'm a shop assistant, and in the evening I play the piano for folk singers.

SWEET YOUNG THING. Now you've *really* got me mixed up . . . oh, and the way you look at a person. What is it, what's the matter?

POET. It's very strange—it's almost never happened to me before, my sweet, but I could almost cry. You move me very deeply. We'll stay together for now. We'll love each other very much.

SWEET YOUNG THING. Did you mean that about the folk singers?

POET. Yes, but no more questions. If you really love me, then you will have no

question. Tell me, could you be free for a couple of weeks?

SWEET YOUNG THING. How do you mean "free"?

POET. Well, away from home.

SWEET YOUNG THING. Oh!! How could I do *that!* What would my mother say? And then, well, without me around the house everything would go wrong.

POET. I thought it might be nice to be alone with you somewhere where there's solitude, in the woods, surrounded by Nature, for a few weeks . . . to live there with you. Nature . . . surrounded by Nature . . . And then one day just to say goodby—to part from one another without knowing where.

SWEET YOUNG THING. You're already talking about saying goodby! And I thought you loved me so.

POET. That's *why*—[*Bends down to her and kisses her on the forehead.*] You precious creature!

SWEET YOUNG THING. Yes, hold me tight, I'm so cold.

POET. It's about time you were getting dressed. Wait, I'll light a few more candles for you.

SWEET YOUNG THING [*rises*]. But don't look.

POET. No. [*At the window.*] Tell me, child, are you happy?

SWEET YOUNG THING. How do you mean?

POET. I mean, in general, are you happy?

SWEET YOUNG THING. It could be better.

POET. You don't understand. You've told me enough about the conditions at home. I know that you're no princess. I mean, when you set all that aside, do you feel alive? Do you really feel you're living?

SWEET YOUNG THING. Got a comb?

POET [*goes to the dressing-table, gives her a comb, then looks at her*]. My God, but you're charming!

SWEET YOUNG THING. Now . . . don't!

POET. Come on, stay a while longer, stay, I'll get something for supper, and—

SWEET YOUNG THING. But it's much too late.

POET. It's not even nine.

SWEET YOUNG THING. Oh, well then, I've got to hurry.

POET. When will we see each other again?

SWEET YOUNG THING. Well, when do you *want* to see me again?

POET. Tomorrow.

SWEET YOUNG THING. What day is tomorrow?

POET. Saturday.

SWEET YOUNG THING. Oh, I can't tomorrow, I have to take my little sister to see our guardian.

POET. Sunday, then ... hm ... Sunday ... on Sunday ... I must explain something to you.—I am not Biebitz, but Biebitz is a friend of mine. I'll introduce you sometime. There's a play of his next Sunday; I'll send you some tickets and come to get you at the theatre. And you must tell me what you think of the play. All right?

SWEET YOUNG THING. And now all this about Biebitz!—I really must be stupid!

POET. I'll know you fully only when I know what you thought about the play.

SWEET YOUNG THING. There ... I'm ready.

POET. Come, my sweet. [*They go out.*]

SCENE EIGHT

THE POET AND THE ACTRESS

[*A room in a country inn. It is an evening in spring; the moon shines across the hills and the meadows. The windows are open. Complete silence. The* POET *and the* ACTRESS *enter; as they enter the candle in the* POET'S *hand goes out.*]

POET. Oh!

ACTRESS. What is it?

POET. The candle.—But we don't need it. Look, it's light enough. Wonderful!

[*The* ACTRESS *suddenly sinks to her knees beside the window, her hands folded.*]

POET. What's the matter?

[*The* ACTRESS *is silent.*]

POET [*goes to her*]. What are you doing?

ACTRESS [*indignant*]. Can't you see I'm praying?

POET. Do you believe in God?

ACTRESS. Of course—do you think I'm as mean as all that!

POET. I see!

ACTRESS. Come here to me, kneel down beside me. For once in your life you can pray, too. You won't lose any jewels out of your precious crown.

[*The* POET *kneels beside her and puts his arms around her.*]

ACTRESS. Libertine!—[*He rises.*] And do you know to whom I was praying?

POET. God, I suppose.

ACTRESS [*with great scorn*]. Of course! Of course! I was praying to you.

POET. Why did you look out the window then?

ACTRESS. Suppose *you* tell *me* where you've *brought* me, you abductor!

POET. But, child, it was all your idea. You wanted to go to the country. You wanted to come here.

ACTRESS. Well, wasn't I right?

POET. Of course, it's charming here. When you think it's only two hours from Vienna—and all this absolute solitude. What wonderful country!

ACTRESS. Yes, isn't it. If you had any talent you could write some poetry here.

POET. Have you been here before?

ACTRESS. Been here before? Ha! I lived here for years!

POET. With whom?

ACTRESS. Why, with Fritz, of course.

POET. I see!

ACTRESS. Oh, how I worshipped that man!

POET. Yes, you've told me.

ACTRESS. Well—I'm sorry—I can leave if I bore you!

POET. Bore me? You have no idea what you mean to me. You're a world in yourself. You're Divinity, you're Spirit. You are ... you are sacred simplicity itself. Yes, you ... But you mustn't talk about Fritz now.

ACTRESS. Yes, that was a mistake! Well!

POET. I'm glad you see that.

ACTRESS. Come here, give me a kiss! [*The* POET *kisses her.*]

ACTRESS. But now it's time we said goodnight! Goodbye, my sweet!

POET. How do you mean that?

ACTRESS. I'm going to bed!

POET. Yes—that's fine, but what do you mean goodnight ... where am *I* supposed to sleep?

ACTRESS. Surely there must be other rooms in the house.

POET. But the others have no attraction for me. What do you say I light a candle?

ACTRESS. Yes.

POET [he lights the candle on the night-table]. What a pretty room ... and how pious these people are. Nothing but holy pictures. It might be interesting to spend some time among these people. It's quite another world. We really know so little about our fellow men.

ACTRESS. Don't talk so silly, and hand me my pocketbook from the table, will you?

POET. Here, my only love!

[The ACTRESS takes a small, framed picture from her pocketbook and places it on the night-table.]

POET. What's that?

ACTRESS. A picture of the Madonna.

POET. Do you always have it with you?

ACTRESS. It's my talisman. Go on now, Robert!

POET. You must be joking! Don't you want me to help you?

ACTRESS. No, I want you to go.

POET. And when shall I come back?

ACTRESS. In ten minutes.

POET [kisses her]. Goodbye!

ACTRESS. Where will you go?

POET. I'll walk back and forth in front of your window. I'm very fond of walking outdoors at night. I get my best ideas that way. And especially when I'm near you, surrounded with my longing for you ... wafted along by your art.

ACTRESS. You're talking like an idiot ...

POET [painfully]. There are women who might have said ... like a poet.

ACTRESS. Go on now. But don't you start anything with the waitress.—

[The POET goes out. The ACTRESS undresses. She hears the POET as he goes down the wooden stairs and as he walks back and forth in front of her window. As soon as she is undressed she goes to the window, looks down and sees him standing there; she calls down to him in a whisper.]

ACTRESS. Come!

[The POET hurries upstairs, rushes to her. She has in the meanwhile gone to bed and put out the candle; he locks the door.]

ACTRESS. There now, you sit down here next to me and tell me a story.

POET [sits down beside her on the bed]. Shall I close the window? Aren't you cold?

ACTRESS. Oh, no!

POET. What shall I tell you?

ACTRESS. Well, to whom are you being unfaithful at this very moment?

POET. Unfortunately I'm not being unfaithful—yet.

ACTRESS. You mustn't worry about it, because I'm deceiving someone, too.

POET. I can imagine.

ACTRESS. Who do you think?

POET. Well, child, I haven't any idea.

ACTRESS. Just guess.

POET. Let me see ... Well, your producer.

ACTRESS. My dear, I'm not a chorus girl.

POET. It was only a guess.

ACTRESS. Guess again.

POET. One of the actors then ... Benno—

ACTRESS. Ha! That man never looked at a woman ... didn't you know? That man's having an affair with his postman!

POET. You must be joking!

ACTRESS. Why don't you kiss me!

[The POET embraces her.]

ACTRESS. Why, what are you doing?

POET. Why must you torture me this way?

ACTRESS. May I suggest something, Robert? Why don't you come to bed with me?

POET. Accepted!

ACTRESS. Quickly, quickly!

POET. If it had been up to me, I'd long ago have ... You hear that?

ACTRESS. What?

POET. The crickets chirping outside.

ACTRESS. You're mad, child, there are no crickets here.

POET. Don't you hear them?

ACTRESS. Come here, why are you taking so long?

POET. Here I am. [Goes to her.]

ACTRESS. There now, you lie there quietly now ... now ... I said quietly.

POET. What do you mean quietly!

ACTRESS. You mean you'd like to have an affair with me?

POET. I thought you'd already have guessed.

ACTRESS. A great many men have wanted to . . .

POET. But at the moment the chances seem to be more in *my* favor.

ACTRESS. Come, my cricket! I shall call you my cricket from now on.

POET. I like that . . .

ACTRESS. Well—who am I deceiving?

POET. Who? Me, perhaps . . . ?

ACTRESS. My dear child, are you sure you're all right?

POET. Or someone . . . you've never even seen . . . someone you don't know, someone—destined for you, but you've never found him . . .

ACTRESS. Why must you talk so silly!

POET. . . . Isn't it strange . . . even you—and one would have thought.—But no, it would be depriving you of all that's best about you if one . . . Come, come—come . . .

* * *

ACTRESS. This is so much nicer than acting in those idiotic plays . . . don't you think so?

POET. Well, I think it's nice that you have the chance to play in reasonable plays now and then.

ACTRESS. You arrogant dog, do you mean *your* play?

POET. Of course!

ACTRESS [*seriously*]. It's a magnificent play!

POET. There, you see!

ACTRESS. Yes, Robert, you're a great genius!

POET. Now that you have the chance why not tell me why you cancelled your performance the day before yesterday. And don't tell me you were ill.

ACTRESS. No, I wanted to antagonize you.

POET. But why? What did I do to you?

ACTRESS. You were arrogant.

POET. In what way?

ACTRESS. Everyone at the theatre thinks so.

POET. I see.

ACTRESS. But I told them: That man has every right to be arrogant.

POET. And what did they say to that?

ACTRESS. What *should* they have said? I never speak to them.

POET. Is that right?

ACTRESS. They would all like to poison me. But they'll never succeed.

POET. Don't think about other people now. Be happy that we're here together, and tell me you love me.

ACTRESS. Do you need even *more* proof?

POET. You don't prove such things.

ACTRESS. How nice! What more do you want?

POET. How many others have you tried to prove it to this way? Did you love them all?

ACTRESS. No. I've loved only one.

POET [*embracing her*]. My . . .

ACTRESS. Fritz.

POET. My name is Robert. What can I *possibly* mean to you if you can think of Fritz at a time like *this!*

ACTRESS. You are a whim.

POET. Thanks for telling me.

ACTRESS. Tell me, aren't you proud?

POET. What's there to make me proud?

ACTRESS. I think you have good reason to be.

POET. Oh, because of *that!*

ACTRESS. Of course, because of that, my little cricket!—And what about the chirping? Are they still chirping outside?

POET. Certainly. Can't you hear them?

ACTRESS. Of course, I hear them. But those are frogs you hear.

POET. You're mistaken: frogs croak.

ACTRESS. That's right, they're croaking.

POET. But not here, my child, they're chirping.

ACTRESS. You are the stubbornnest man I have ever come across. Give me a kiss, my little frog!

POET. Please, don't call me that. It makes me nervous.

ACTRESS. Well, what *shall* I call you?

POET. I have a name, don't I? Robert.

ACTRESS. But that's too silly.

POET. But I would *rather* you call me by my proper name.

ACTRESS. Kiss me, then—Robert.—Oh! [*She kisses him.*] Are you happy now, my little frog? Hahahaha.

POET. Do you mind if I light a cigarette?

ACTRESS. I'll have one, too.

[*He takes the cigarette case from the night-table, takes out two cigarettes, lights both, and hands her one.*]

ACTRESS. Incidentally, you said nothing about my performance last night.

POET. Performance?

ACTRESS. Really . . . !

POET. Oh! That one! I wasn't at the theatre.

ACTRESS. You must like to joke.

POET. Why, no. After your cancellation the day before yesterday I assumed you wouldn't be in full possession of your powers, so I thought I'd rather forgo it.

ACTRESS. You missed something.

POET. Oh?

ACTRESS. I was sensational. The audience turned pale.

POET. Could you really see them?

ACTRESS. Benno said: My child, you were a goddess!

POET. Hm! And so ill the day before.

ACTRESS. That's right, and I was, too. And do you know why? Out of longing for you.

POET. A little while ago you said you cancelled out because you wanted to antagonize me.

ACTRESS. What do you know of my love for you! All this leaves you cold. I had a fever for nights on end. Over a hundred and five!

POET. That's quite a temperature for just a whim.

ACTRESS. You call that a whim? Here I am dying of love for you, and you call it a whim—!

POET. And what about Fritz?

ACTRESS. Fritz? . . . Don't talk to me about that terrible creature!—

SCENE NINE

THE ACTRESS AND THE COUNT

[*The bedroom of the* ACTRESS. *Very sumptuously decorated. It is twelve noon, the blinds are still down, a candle burns on the small night-table, the* ACTRESS *lies in her canopied bed. Numerous newspapers are strewn across the bed cover.*

The COUNT *enters in the uniform of a Captain of the Dragoons. He remains standing at the door.*]

ACTRESS. Oh, Herr Count.

COUNT. Your dear mother gave me permission, or I should never have—

ACTRESS. Please, do come in.

COUNT. I kiss your hand. Excuse me— when one enters directly from the street . . . the fact is I still can't see a thing. Ah, yes . . . here we are—[*at the bed*]—I kiss your hand.

ACTRESS. Won't you have a seat, Herr Count.

COUNT. Your mother said that you weren't feeling well, Fräulein. I do hope it's nothing serious.

ACTRESS. Nothing serious? I was on the verge of death!

COUNT. Good heavens, is that possible?

ACTRESS. In any case I think it very nice of you to have troubled yourself on my account.

COUNT. On the verge of death! And last night you played like a goddess.

ACTRESS. Yes, it was rather a triumph, wasn't it?

COUNT. Colossal! The audience was absolutely carried away. And I won't even tell you what I thought.

ACTRESS. Thank you for the lovely flowers.

COUNT. Don't mention it.

ACTRESS [*indicates with her eyes a large basket of flowers sitting on a small table at the window*]. There they are.

COUNT. Yesterday you were absolutely overwhelmed with flowers and garlands.

ACTRESS. They are all still in my dressing room. I brought only your basket with me.

COUNT [*kisses her hand*]. That was very sweet of you. [*The* ACTRESS *suddenly takes his hand and kisses it.*] But, my dear!

ACTRESS. Don't be afraid, Herr Count, that doesn't oblige you in any way.

COUNT. What an extraordinary creature you are . . . one might almost say an enigma.— [*Pause*].

ACTRESS. Fräulein Birken might be easier to . . . solve.

COUNT. Oh, little Birken is no problem, although . . . but of course I know her only superficially.

ACTRESS. Ha!

COUNT. Believe me. But you are a problem. A kind that I have always longed for. I never realized until last night, when I saw you act for the first time, what an extraordinary pleasure I had let slip from me.

ACTRESS. Is that possible?

COUNT. Yes. You see, I find it rather difficult to get to the theatre. I'm accustomed to dining late . . . so that when I *do* arrive the best part of the play has already gone by.

ACTRESS. From now on you must eat earlier.

COUNT. Yes, I've considered that. Or perhaps not dining at all. Actually dining is no pleasure for me anymore.

ACTRESS. What does a young old man like you take pleasure in?

COUNT. I often ask myself the same question! But I am not an old man. There must be another reason.

ACTRESS. Do you think so?

COUNT. Yes. For example, Louie says I'm a philosopher. What he means, Fräulein, is that I think too much.

ACTRESS. Think . . . yes, well that *is* a misfortune.

COUNT. I have too much time on my hands, and so I think. But then, you see, I thought that if they were to transfer me to Vienna things might be different. There's amusement and stimulation here. But the fact is, it's not much different here than it was there.

ACTRESS. Where is "there"?

COUNT. Why, in Hungary . . . the small towns where I was generally stationed.

ACTRESS. Whatever did you do in Hungary?

COUNT. Well, I just told you, Fräulein, the Army.

ACTRESS. Well then why did you stay so *long* in Hungary?

COUNT. That's the way it happens.

ACTRESS. That must be enough to drive one mad.

COUNT. Why do you say that? Of course there's more to do there than here. Such things as training recruits, breaking in the horses . . . and then, too, the region isn't all as bad as they say. It's really quite lovely, the low-lying plains—and those sunsets . . . It's a pity I'm not a painter; I've often thought that if I were, I should paint it. There was one young man in the regiment, his name was Splany, he could have done it. —But why am I telling you all these dull stories, Fräulein?

ACTRESS. Oh, please, I'm terribly amused.

COUNT. You know, Fräulein, it's quite easy talking to you. Louie told me it would be. And that's something you don't often find.

ACTRESS. Well, in Hungary, I suppose not.

COUNT. And definitely not in Vienna! People are the same everywhere. The only difference is that where there are more people, the crowds are larger. Tell me, Fräulein, are you fond of people?

ACTRESS. Fond? I hate them! I can't *look* at a human being! I *never* see them! I am always alone, no one ever enters this house.

COUNT. You see, I was right when I thought you a misanthrope! It happens often where artists are concerned. When one exists in those higher regions . . . well, it's alright for you, at least you know why you're living!

ACTRESS. Whoever told you that? I have no idea why I'm living!

COUNT. But I beg to differ—you're famous—celebrated . . .

ACTRESS. Is that what you call happiness?

COUNT. Happiness? I'm sorry, but there is no such thing as happiness. Most of the things that people talk about so freely don't really exist . . . love, for example. It's the same there, too.

ACTRESS. You're quite right.

COUNT. Pleasure . . . intoxication . . . fine, there's nothing to say against them . . . they are something positive. If I take pleasure in something, fine, at least I *know* I take pleasure in it. Or else I feel myself intoxicated, excellent. That's positive, too. And when it's past, well then, it's past.

ACTRESS [*grandly*]. It's past!

COUNT. But as soon as one fails to, how shall I say it, as soon as one fails to live for the moment, and starts thinking about the future or the past . . . well, then it's all over with. The future . . . is sad . . . the past is uncertain. In short, it only confuses one. Am I right?

ACTRESS [*nods, her eyes large*]. You have gone to the heart of the matter.

COUNT. So you see, my dear madam, once you have perceived the truth of this, it really makes little difference whether you live in Vienna or in Pussta or even in Steinamanger. For example . . . excuse me, where can I put my cap? . . . Oh, thank you . . . now what were we talking about?

ACTRESS. Steinamanger.

COUNT. Ah, yes. It's just as I said, the difference is very slight. It's all the same to me whether I spend my evenings at the Casino or at the Club.

ACTRESS. And how does all this relate to love?

COUNT. If one believes in it, he'll always find someone around to love him.

ACTRESS. Fräulein Birken, for example.

COUNT. Really, my dear, I don't know why you always seem to return to poor little Birken.

ACTRESS. She's your mistress, isn't she?

COUNT. Whoever said that?

ACTRESS. Everyone knows.

COUNT. Except me. Isn't that remarkable!

ACTRESS. You even fought a duel for her sake!

COUNT. Perhaps I was even killed and didn't notice.

ACTRESS. Yes, Count, you are a man of honor. Won't you sit closer?

COUNT. May I?

ACTRESS. Here. [*She draws him to her and runs her fingers through his hair.*] I knew you would come today!

COUNT. How?

ACTRESS. I knew yesterday at the theatre.

COUNT. Could you see me from the stage?

ACTRESS. My dear man, couldn't you tell that I was playing for no one but you?

COUNT. How can that be?

ACTRESS. I felt like I was walking on air when I saw you in the first row!

COUNT. Walking on air? On my account? I had no idea you even saw me!

ACTRESS. You know, you can drive a woman to desperation with your "dignity."

COUNT. Fräulein!

ACTRESS. "Fräulein"!—At least take off your sabre!

COUNT. If I may. [*He unbuckles the belt and leans it against the bed.*]

ACTRESS. And now kiss me.

[*The* COUNT *kisses her, she does not let loose of him.*]

ACTRESS. Oh, how I wish I had never seen you!

COUNT. It's much better like this!—

ACTRESS. Count, you are a *poseur*!

COUNT. I? How so?

ACTRESS. How happy do you think many a man would be to find himself in your place right now!

COUNT. But I *am* happy. Very.

ACTRESS. I thought there was no happiness. Why are you looking at me that way? I do believe you are afraid of me, Herr Count!

COUNT. As I said, madam, you are a problem.

ACTRESS. Oh, don't bother me with your philosophizing . . . come here. And now, ask me for something. You can have anything you like. You're far too handsome.

COUNT. If I have your permission then —[*kissing her hand*]—I will return tonight.

ACTRESS. Tonight? . . . But I'll be playing.

COUNT. After the theatre.

ACTRESS. Is that all you're asking for?

COUNT. I shall ask for everything else *after* the theatre.

ACTRESS [*offended*]. And you'll have to ask for a long time, you miserable *poseur*.

COUNT. Well, you see, you see, we've been so open with one another up till now. I would really find all that so much nicer *after* the theatre . . . more comfortable than now. Well, I have the feeling that a door could open on us at any moment . . .

ACTRESS. The door doesn't open from the outside.

COUNT. Don't you feel it would be careless to spoil something at the start, something that might quite possibly turn out to be beautiful?

ACTRESS. "Quite possibly"!

COUNT. To be quite honest, I find love in the morning really rather ghastly.

ACTRESS. Well—you are easily the most insane man I have ever met!

COUNT. I'm not talking about just *any* woman . . . after all, in general it scarcely matters. But women like you . . . no, call me a fool a hundred times over if you like . . . women like you . . . aren't to be had before breakfast. And so . . . you see . . .

ACTRESS. My God, but you're sweet!

COUNT. You do see what I mean, don't you. The way I see it . . .

ACTRESS. *Tell* me how you see it!

COUNT. I thought that . . . I would wait

for you after the theatre in a carriage, and then we could drive somewhere together and have supper—

ACTRESS. I am not Fräulein Birken.

COUNT. I didn't say you were. It's that one must be in the mood. And I always find myself in the mood after supper. It's always nicer that way, when after supper you drive home together, and then . . .

ACTRESS. And then what?

COUNT. Well, then . . . then it simply depends on how things develop.

ACTRESS. Sit closer to me. Closer.

COUNT [sitting on the bed]. I must say there's a lovely aroma coming from your pillows—mignonette, isn't it?

ACTRESS. Don't you find it terribly hot in here?

[The COUNT bends down and kisses her throat.]

ACTRESS. Oh, but, my dear Count, that's not on your program.

COUNT. Who says so? I have no program.

[The ACTRESS draws him to her.]

COUNT. Yes, it is warm.

ACTRESS. Isn't it? And so dark, as though it were evening . . . [Pulls him to her.] It is evening . . . it's night.—Close your eyes if it's too light for you. Come! Come!

[The COUNT no longer resists.]

* * *

ACTRESS. What was that about being in the mood, you poseur?

COUNT. You're a little devil.

ACTRESS. What a thing to say!

COUNT. Well then, an angel.

ACTRESS. You should have been an actor! Really! You understand women! Do you know what I shall do now?

COUNT. Well?

ACTRESS. I shall tell you that I will never see you again.

COUNT. But why?

ACTRESS. No, no. You're too danger-ous for me! You'd drive a woman mad. There you are, standing in front of me now, as though nothing had happened.

COUNT. But . . .

ACTRESS. I beg you to remember, Herr Count, that I have just been your mis-tress.

COUNT. I shall never forget it!

ACTRESS. And what about tonight?

COUNT. How do you mean that?

ACTRESS. Well—you were going to wait for me after the theatre?

COUNT. Yes, fine, what about tomor-row?

ACTRESS. What do you mean 'tomor-row'? We were talking about tonight.

COUNT. But that wouldn't make sense.

ACTRESS. You old fool!

COUNT. Don't misunderstand. I mean it more, how shall I say, from the spiritual standpoint.

ACTRESS. What's your soul got to do with it?

COUNT. Believe me, that's part of it, too. I find it completely false that the two can be kept apart.

ACTRESS. Don't bother me with your philosophizing. When I want that, I'll read books.

COUNT. One doesn't learn from books.

ACTRESS. I agree! That's why you should wait for me this evening. We'll come to some agreement about the soul, you scoundrel!

COUNT. Well then, with your permis-sion, I shall have my carriage waiting—

ACTRESS. . . . After the theatre.

COUNT. Of course. [He buckles on his sabre.]

ACTRESS. What are you doing?

COUNT. I think it's time I were going. For a formal call I think I've overstayed my time a bit.

ACTRESS. But tonight it won't be a for-mal call.

COUNT. Really?

ACTRESS. You let me take care of that. And now give me another kiss, my little philosopher. Here, you seducer, you . . . sweet child, you slave-dealer, you polecat . . . you . . . [After having kissed him vigorously several times, she pushes him vigorously from her.] Count, it was a great honor!

COUNT. I kiss your hand, Fräulein! [At the door.] Au revoir!

ACTRESS. Adieu, Steinamanger!

SCENE TEN

THE COUNT AND THE PROSTITUTE

[Morning, around six o'clock. A miser-able little room with one window; the *dirty yellow blinds are down; worn green curtains on the window. A chest-of-drawers with a few photographs on it and a conspicuously tasteless, cheap woman's hat. A number of cheap Japanese fans behind the mirror. On the table, covered over with a reddish cloth, stands a kerosene lamp, still feebly alight and emitting its odor, with a yellow paper lampshade. Beside it is a jug with left-over beer and a half empty glass. On the floor beside the bed there is a disarray of woman's clothing, as though they had rapidly been thrown down. The* PROSTITUTE *is asleep in the bed; she breathes quietly. Fully dressed on the divan lies the* COUNT *in his overcoat, his hat on the floor at the head of the divan.]*

COUNT [*moves, rubs his eyes, rises quickly, remains sitting, looks around*]. How did I get ... Oh yes ... then I did go home with that female ... [*He rises quickly, sees her bed.*] And here she is ... The things that happen to a man my age! I can't remember ... did they carry me up here? No ... I saw—I came into the room ... yes, I was still awake ... or ... or is it that this room reminds me of somewhere else?—My God, yes, yes ... I saw it yesterday all right ... [*Looks at his watch.*] Hm! Yesterday! A couple hours ago, that's when I saw it—But I knew that something had to happen ... I felt it ... yesterday when I started drinking, I felt that something ... And what *did* happen?—Nothing ... Or did I ... ? My God ... not for ... not for ten years has anything happened to me that I haven't remembered. Well, in any case I was drunk. If only I could remember when I got that way.—At least I remember when I went into that whores' café with Louie and ... no, no ... it was after we left Sacher's ... and then on the way ... Yes, that's right, I was driving along with Louie ... But what am I wracking my brains for! It doesn't matter. Just see that you get out of here. [*Gets up; the lamp shakes.*] Oh! [*He looks at the sleeping girl.*] At least *she's* sleeping soundly. I don't remember a thing, but I'll put the money on the night-table ... and good-bye ... [*He stands looking at her a long while.*] If only one didn't know what she is! [*He looks at her thoughtfully for a long while.*] I've known a lot of her kind that didn't look so virtuous even in their sleep. My God ... Louie would say I'm philosophizing ... but it's true, it seems to me Sleep washes away all differences—like his brother, Death.—Hm, I wish I knew whether ... no, I'd remember that. No, no, I came straight in and fell onto the divan ... and nothing happened ... Isn't it remarkable how sometimes all women look alike.—Well, time to go. [*He is about to leave.*] Oh, I forgot. [*He takes out his wallet and is about to remove a bill.*]

PROSTITUTE [*wakes up*]. What! ... who's here so early? [*recognizing him*]. Hello!

COUNT. Good morning. Sleep well?

PROSTITUTE [*stretches herself*]. Oh! Come here. Give me a little kiss.

COUNT [*bends down to her, considers, pulls up*]. I was just going ...

PROSTITUTE. Going?

COUNT. It's about time.

PROSTITUTE. You want to go like this?

COUNT [*almost embarrassed*]. Well ...

PROSTITUTE. All right, so long; come back some other time.

COUNT. Yes. Goodbye. Won't you give me your hand? [*The* PROSTITUTE *extends her hand from under the cover.*]

COUNT [*takes the hand and kisses it mechanically, becomes aware of himself, laughs*]. Like a princess. After all, if one saw only ...

PROSTITUTE. What are you looking at me like that for?

COUNT. If one saw only that little head, like now ... when they wake one looks as innocent as the next ... my God, one could imagine all sorts of things, if only it didn't smell so of kerosene ...

PROSTITUTE. Yes, that lamp's always a bother.

COUNT. How old are you?

PROSTITUTE. Guess.

COUNT. Twenty-four.

PROSTITUTE. Sure, sure.

COUNT. You mean you're older?

PROSTITUTE. I'm going on twenty.

COUNT. And how long have you ...

PROSTITUTE. How long have I been in the business? A year.

COUNT. You started early.

PROSTITUTE. Better early than too late.

COUNT [*sits down on the bed*]. Tell me something, are you really happy?

PROSTITUTE. What?

COUNT. Well, what I mean is, how are you getting on?

PROSTITUTE. Oh, right now I'm doing all right.

COUNT. I see.—Tell me, didn't it ever occur to you that you could become something else?

PROSTITUTE. Like what?

COUNT. Well . . . you're really quite a lovely girl. You could have a lover, for example.

PROSTITUTE. What makes you think I don't have one?

COUNT. Yes, of course—what I meant was one who, you know, one who would support you, so that you wouldn't have to go around with just anyone who came along.

PROSTITUTE. I *don't* go around with just anyone. Thank God I'm not that hard up. I pick and choose.

[*The* COUNT *looks around the room.*]

PROSTITUTE [*noticing this*]. Next month we're moving into town. Spiegel Gasse.

COUNT. We? Who do you mean?

PROSTITUTE. Why, the madam and the couple other girls who still live here.

COUNT. There are others living here?

PROSTITUTE. Next door . . . can't you hear? . . . that's Milli, she was in the café, too.

COUNT. Someone's snoring.

PROSTITUTE. That's Milli all right! She'll snore like that all day long till ten at night. Then she gets up and goes to the café.

COUNT. That must be a terrible life.

PROSTITUTE. Sure. The madam gets fed up enough, too. I'm out on the street everyday by noon.

COUNT. What do you do on the street at noon?

PROSTITUTE. What do you think I do? I walk my beat.

COUNT. Oh, I see . . . of course . . . [*He rises, takes out his wallet, and places a bill on the night-table.*] Goodbye.

PROSTITUTE. Going so soon?—So long. —Come back again soon. [*Turns on her side.*]

COUNT [*stops again*]. Say, tell me something; does it really mean anything to you anymore?

PROSTITUTE. What?

COUNT. I mean, there's no enjoyment in it for you anymore?

PROSTITUTE [*yawns*]. I'm sleepy.

COUNT. It makes no difference whether a man is young or old . . .

PROSTITUTE. Why are you asking all this?

COUNT. . . . Well—[*Suddenly struck by an idea.*] My God, now I remember who you remind me of, it's . . .

PROSTITUTE. I remind you of someone?

COUNT. It's unbelieveable, unbelieveable! Please, now, don't say a word, just for a moment . . . [*Looks at her.*] The same face exactly, the same face exactly. [*He kisses her suddenly on the eyes.*]

PROSTITUTE. Say . . .

COUNT. My God, what a pity that you . . . that you aren't something else . . . you could really be a success.

PROSTITUTE. You're just like Franz.

COUNT. Who is Franz?

PROSTITUTE. A waiter at the café.

COUNT. How am I like Franz?

PROSTITUTE. He's always saying I could be a success, and that I should get married.

COUNT. Why don't you?

PROSTITUTE. No, thanks . . . no, I don't want to get married, not for all the money in the world. Later, maybe.

COUNT. Your eyes . . . it's your eyes that . . . Louie would say I'm a fool—but I do want to kiss your eyes, just once more . . . there . . . and now, goodbye, now I really must go.

PROSTITUTE. So long . . .

COUNT [*at the door*]. Say . . . tell me . . . doesn't it surprise you that . . .

PROSTITUTE. That what?

COUNT. That I want nothing of you?

PROSTITUTE. A lot of men aren't in the mood for it in the morning.

COUNT. Yes, I suppose . . . [*To himself.*] How silly of me to want her to be surprised . . . Well, goodbye . . . [*He is at the door.*] Still, it does annoy me. I know that girls like this do it only for the money . . . but why did I say: 'girls like this'? . . . it's nice at least that . . . that she doesn't pretend, that should be some satisfaction . . . [*To her.*] Say—I'll tell you what . . . I'll come back again soon.

PROSTITUTE [*with her eyes closed*]. Good.

COUNT. When are you at home?

PROSTITUTE. I'm always in. Just ask for Leocadia.

COUNT.   Leocadia . . . Good.—Well

then, goodbye. [*At the door.*] I can still feel that wine. Isn't it remarkable . . . here I am with one of her kind, and I did nothing more than kiss her eyes, just because she reminded me of someone . . . [*Turns to her again.*] Say, Leocadia, does it happen often that a man leaves you . . . like this?

PROSTITUTE. Like what?

COUNT. Like me.

PROSTITUTE. In the morning?

COUNT. No . . . I wondered whether it happened often that a man comes to you . . . and doesn't ask for anything.

PROSTITUTE. No, that never happened to me.

COUNT. What do you mean? Do you think I don't like you?

PROSTITUTE. Why shouldn't you like me? You liked me well enough last night.

COUNT. And I like you now, too.

PROSTITUTE. But you liked me better last night.

COUNT. Why do you say *that?*

PROSTITUTE. Why all the silly questions?

COUNT. Last night . . . yes, well, didn't I fall onto the divan right away?

PROSTITUTE. Sure you did . . . with me.

COUNT. With you?

PROSTITUTE. Sure, don't you remember?

COUNT. You mean I . . . that we . . . yes . . .

PROSTITUTE. But you went right to sleep.

COUNT. Right to sleep . . . I see . . . So that's the way it was . . .

PROSTITUTE. Sure, lovey. You must have had a real load on, not to remember.

COUNT. I see . . . —Still . . . there *is* a faint resemblance . . . So long . . . [*He listens.*] What's that noise?

PROSTITUTE. The parlor maid's up already. Why not give her a little something on the way out. The door's open, so you'll save on the janitor.

COUNT. Of course. [*In the entrance hall.*] Well . . . it would have been beautiful even if I had only kissed you on the eyes. That would almost have been an adventure in itself . . . Well, I suppose it wasn't meant to be. [*The* PARLOR MAID *stands at the door, holding it open for him.*] Oh—here you are . . . Good night.—

PARLOR MAID. Good morning.

COUNT. Yes, of course . . . good morning . . . good morning.

Frederic Morton

SCHNITZLER'S *YOUTH IN VIENNA*

Arthur Schnitzler's plays and fiction are the definitive genre pictures of fin-de-siècle Vienna. And since many of the best captions to those pictures were supplied by his contemporary, the aphorist Karl Kraus, it's hard to start talking about one without thinking of the other—of one aphorism in particular. "Vienna," said Karl Kraus, "is the laboratory of the apocalypse."

Such labs tend to have lush furnishings. I know because I spent my Austrian childhood, in the thirties, among the chipped monuments left over from the last experiment, the Hapsburg self-destruction via World War I. I also know because I live in New York where right this moment they're building still more cloud-high things that might become the ultimate props for the ultimate Götterdämmerung. And it comes to me that what we have in this book isn't just autobiography. Schnitzler does more than look back on the years of his youth from the 1860's to the 1880's in Vienna. Yes, he evokes a world long gone, where you could pick up a girl in a horse-tramway. But he also suggests how a world goes—it goes not all that gently, into not such a good night—and therefore he breathes a whiff of today's news. His canvas is gorgeously antique, dimly familiar, and it may be, God help us, faintly clairvoyant.

Schnitzler spent his childhood in a great empire a shade past its halcyon days, which means in the prime years of its myth. The good Emperor Franz Joseph had been mounted on his throne for enough decades to become his own statue, yet he had decades to go before he or the throne grew feeble. The monarchy reached from the Swiss Alps through the German-speaking heartlands to Hungary, Bohemia, southern Poland, down to the minarets of the eastern Balkans. It was a cornucopia of races, tongues, costumes and customs, all lavished around Vienna which during the very period of Schnitzler's youth ripened into the sumptuous *Alt Wien* that still exercises the world's nostalgia today.

When Schnitzler was born in 1862 the medieval walls of the capital were being demolished. Throughout his school and university years and the time he served as an intern and as young army doctor, there rose on the site of those walls—rose like a mirage—the masterpiece of Imperial Vienna. Round the city's ancient core the Ringstrasse rose up in festoons of marble munificence: neo-gothic Votive Cathedral, renaissance university, neo-gothic City Hall, renaissance museums, Grecian-columned Parliament, renaissance Opera, all huge jewels set in flower-studded and tree-shaded promenades. It was (and is) a unique five miles of gracefully orchestrated majesty. And even before the Ring was finished, the city burst across it toward the Vienna Woods, unfolding the wine gardens, the inns, the mixture of royalty and *Gemütlichkeit*, the sense of a courtier people delighting and perfecting their pastoral in the foothills of the Alps. Somehow that aura has not yielded to the gas stations built there since.

In Schnitzler's youth Vienna was the earth emporium of culture, comparable to New York in the century to come. Beethoven's body had lain in state not many blocks from where Schnitzler's father was to set up his clinic. Mozart, of course, had long gone to his pauper's grave, but Brahms, Bruckner, Mahler and Hugo Wolf were alive and fertile. And, starting from Vienna, the waltz conquered the world, as shockingly and thor-

SOURCE: From Foreword by Frederic Morton to Arthur Schnitzler's *My Youth in Vienna*. English translation copyright © 1970 by Holt, Rinehart and Winston. Introduction copyright © 1970 by Frederic Morton.

oughly as generations later rock-and-roll would conquer it, starting from New York.

The waltz, like rock, represented a liberation from the linear—in this case from the minuet; like rock it was accused of being a too bald erotic confrontation; like rock it obliterated tame beginning-middle-end steps and swept into the ecstatic infinity and renewability of sheer rhythm. For these among other reasons the Johann Strausses, father and son, became the first global pop-music stars. Composer-conductor-performers, they wielded charismatic violin bows; they ignited riots as well as raptures. In this sense the Beatles are but latter-day Strausses at best, if you consider that the fame of the two Johanns traveled across continents without benefit of media.

Schnitzler's quasi Bar Mitzvah[1] came close on the heels of the première of *Die Fledermaus* by Strauss junior, the operetta par excellence of all time. And the very lives of the Strausses, father and son, personified Schnitzler's obsession with the intertwisting of canker and rose. Johann Strauss senior, "magician of the lilt," was a pitiful, driven neurotic. It was said of him that "he died like a dog and was buried like a king." Johann Strauss junior, even more renowned, a still more glistening and triumphant sower of joy across the world, suffered even more from depression and nervous exhaustion, from recurrent despair. "His biography," writes a Viennese critic, "is a case history."

The Strauss irony was endemic to the glitter of the Hapsburg lands. It afflicted many of Schnitzler's boulevardier figures. In these recollections it's mixed into every bit of local color. Here is the hidden, yet almost axiomatic, prevalence of syphilis in all layers of society, particularly among the dashing and the fashionable; the anti-Semitism among Vienna's best-educated classes which was part of a general racist exasperation; the etiquette—exquisite far beyond the occidental norm—which was designed not to express but to hide the morals underneath. Characteristic is an episode in which young Arthur and his pal, both hand-kissing cavaliers, escort home the lovely mistress of a Hungarian aristocrat—and then with the girl's full acquiescence cast lots as to which of the two would jump into bed with her.

Here are oblique but graphic glimpses of how an empire began to fester just as its image flowered most gaily. No other city even approached Vienna's contrapuntal loveliness—palatial core balanced against the bucolic idyl of the vines. Yet the nexus between the two consisted of long stretches of new slum. It was the bill the city had to pay for industrialization which in turn paid for the myth's spectacular staging.

Franz Joseph's realm was like a pageant of ambivalences, exemplified by the literal duality of the crown. The Emperor of Austria doubled as King of Hungary. This made Hungary an autonomous domain and was hailed as a model of intranational accommodation. In practice, their autonomy let the Hungarian nobles exploit their peasants; it allowed them to oppress the huge Slav minorities within their lands and to provide a vicious example for their counterparts in other ethnic regions. Universities thrived all over the Empire, in Prague, in Budapest, in Vienna, but they only served to articulate through their students the clashing demands of awakened nationalisms. The vitality of the Austro-Hungarian idea withered even as its splendors and ceremonies flourished. It was a fairyland with a squalid underbelly and all its roads led —at least metaphorically—to Mayerling.[2]

In the popular fancy and therefore in the movies, Crown Prince Rudolph died together with Mary Vetsera for the sake of their impossible great love. Actually Franz Joseph's son—talented, drug-ridden, alcoholic, demoralized, a veritable prince of alienation—asked Vetsera to join him in suicide only after some chorus girls had turned down the honor. His motive was agony; hers the ultimate in social climbing. She crashed history as the leading lady of the Archduke's despair. That macabre tryst took place on January 30, 1889. A few weeks later there

---

[1] Traditional Jewish confirmation at thirteen—Ed.
[2] Famous for the double suicide of Prince Rudolph and Mary Vetsera—Ed.

was born, a few express stops away in Upper Austria, a baby boy named Adolf Hitler.

No, the center wouldn't hold. With surprising speed, radiance turned to phosphorescence. As usual, the forces of the future attacked just where the present century made its most spectacular stand. (Again imperial Austria seems to prefigure imperial America.) Since nothing energizes the arts like change, the Vienna of young Schnitzler vibrated with esthetic insurgencies. Arnold Schoenberg and Alban Berg broke the great molds of Beethoven and Brahms. And as they composed atonal music so Adolf Loos created a-traditional, anti-ornamental, anti-Ringstrasse architecture. His work, no less than Berg's and Schoenberg's, touched off demonstrations. In painting, the new Austrian impressionists ostentatiously marked their mutiny against the academics and the romantics by terming their movement (and their joint gallery) "The Secession." But the ultimate subversive intellectual enterprise took place in the study of the man who called Schnitzler "my Doppelgänger" [3]—Sigmund Freud.

Of course Freud and Schnitzler were contemporaries, fellow Jews, fellow students in the same university, fellow physicians, fellow devotees of hypnotism in their early careers, and fellow explorers of the erotic in their lifeworks. But their Doppelgänger-dom rests most significantly on the fact that both focused on the tension between man's inner motives and the choreography of his adjustments, between the instinctual core and the acquired façade. In 1893 Freud published his first important paper with psychoanalytic implications ("On the Psychical Mechanisms of Hysterical Phenomena"). The same year Schnitzler had his first première, the production of Farewell Supper at the Stadttheater in Bad Ischl. And when Freud brought out his Psychopathology of Everyday Life in 1904, the book version of Schnitzler's La Ronde had just been banned in Germany, almost by way of illustrating Freud's title.

It's obvious from these dates that most of the important Schnitzler canon came into being after the 1880's; that is, after this autobiography ends. Yet the Schnitzlerian leitmotif is foreshadowed here by his fascination with his own love affairs. Already he displays a cool, alert astonishment at his most headlong emotions, the kind of astonishment which is the writer's greatest engine and which later powered Schnitzler's investigations into the dramaturgy of sex, from the blush of infatuation to post-coital politesse.

In the seven one-acters of the Anatol cycle we have seven episodes from a philanderer's life, showing that all his deceptions are matched in smoothness by his self-deceptions. In La Ronde, Schnitzler's other cyclical masterpiece (are these structures sardonic echoes of the Ringstrasse?), ten affairs succeed each other. Their participants, from very different walks of life, keep changing partners until the male of the last scene makes love to the woman of the first. By the time the circle is closed, Schnitzler has paraded past us a whole spectrum of decent lies dressing up sex as if in a fashion show of straitjackets. And strangely, hauntingly, the pose that insists on decorating lust with love accomplishes in the end not decoration but debasement. "Oh, Alt Wien!"

Civilization is a lie the brain forces on the flesh: that theme also informs Schnitzler's prose. In Lieutenant Gustl a gutsy young officer of the Imperial Army finds himself pressed to the edge of suicide because a common baker has insulted him. In Fräulein Else a young girl must expose herself naked to a lecher who otherwise won't save her father from bankruptcy. Both novellas, done in virtuoso stream-of-consciousness style, wring fresh, evergreen anguish out of rotogravure plights. Both Gustl and Else suffer in order not to betray a life style, when in fact the life style is betraying them.

But the most memorable Schnitzler character is das süsse Mädel, the Sweet Girl, who in one guise or another appears not only in these reminiscences but in Anatol, in Liebelei, and other plays frequently revived today. The Sweet Girl's secret lies in her very vulnerability. Because of it she is no sooner bedded than betrayed. But because of it she also fascinates her betrayers—and us. In her will-

---

[3] Double—Ed.

ingness to be victimized there is an innocence and an odd strength, a dumb
sensuous faith which none of her seducers
can tap no matter how furiously they
thrust themselves through her. For they,
the smoothies, swingers before their time,
are really the empties; they have given up
on the world, while for the Sweet Girl
the world continues sweetly—at least for
a while. Such faith scrapes the jadedness
off our nerve ends, it even attunes us,
perversely, to the possibility of renewal.
At his best Schnitzler talked not just
about old Vienna but about the aging of
any culture; about the late, the very late,
the maybe too late hour in search of
dawn. Which may be our time of night
right now.

ANTON CHEKHOV 1860–1904

"... To judge between good and bad, between successful and unsuccessful, would need the eye of God," Chekhov wrote. Yet it would be false to suppose that this kindliest of writers was indifferent to human weakness or considered vulgarity and idleness on a par with sensitivity and hard work. Responsibilities settled early upon Chekhov when his father, facing the bankruptcy of his shop, escaped to Moscow with his family, leaving Anton in Taganrog to complete his preparatory studies. When some years later Chekhov joined his family in Moscow, he found it necessary not only to finance his medical studies at the University but to support the family as well. To do so he took to writing brief comic sketches which he published under pseudonyms. In 1884 he received his medical degree and thereafter devoted himself to his two callings, medicine ("my lawful spouse") and literature ("my mistress"). He had also contracted tuberculosis, the disease that was to cut his life short. The success of his first volume of stories gave Chekhov the freedom to write more seriously, and there followed the great tales which establish him as the unsurpassed master of the short story. After writing some short farces for vaudeville performance, Chekhov tried a full-length play, *Ivanov* (1887). It was a failure, and Chekhov was so discouraged that not until 1896 did he attempt another play, *The Sea Gull*. It too failed, and Chekhov vowed never again to write for the theatre; but the founding of the Moscow Art Theatre by Nemirovitch-Dantchenko and Constantin Stanislavsky induced him to change his mind. To the Moscow Art Theatre we owe the successful revival of *The Sea Gull* and Chekhov's succeeding masterpieces: *Uncle Vanya* (1897), *The Three Sisters* (1900), and *The Cherry Orchard* (1904). Chekhov knew well the ineffectual lives of the unproductive classes and the ignorance that prevailed over much of Russia. He wrote about the loneliness of his characters, their unfulfilled or wasted lives, their follies, strivings, dreams, and frustrations, with rare compassion and humor. To escape stagnation through purposeful labor was Chekhov's guiding principle. In addition to his literary work, he continued to practice medicine, studied peasant life, and investigated the barbarous conditions in Russian prisons in the hope of aiding those who suffered. His health soon failed, however, and he died at the early age of forty-four in Germany where he had gone for a cure. His body was returned to Russia in a boxcar inadvertently marked "fresh oysters" and was beside that of his father. In 1933 Chekhov's coffin was exhumed and reburied in a plot devoted to actors from the Moscow Art Theatre, whose symbol to this day is the seagull.

THE THREE SISTERS

ANTON CHEKHOV

Translated by Elizaveta Fen

CHARACTERS

PROZOROV, Andrey Serghyeevich
NATASHA [Natalia Ivanovna], his fiancée,
    afterwards his wife
OLGA [Olga Serghyeevna, Olia] ⎫
MASHA [Maria Serghyeevna]   ⎬ his
IRENA [Irena Serghyeevna]   ⎭ sisters
KOOLYGHIN, Fiodor Ilyich, master at the
    High School for boys, husband of
    Masha
VERSHININ, Alexandr Ignatyevich, Lieu-
    tenant-Colonel, Battery Commander
TOOZENBACH, Nikolai Lvovich, Baron,
    Lieutenant in the Army

SOLIONY, Vassily Vassilich, Captain
CHEBUTYKIN, Ivan Romanych, Army
    Doctor
FEDOTIK, Aleksey Petrovich, Second Lieu-
    tenant
RODÉ, Vladimir Karlovich, Second Lieu-
    tenant
FERAPONT [Ferapont Spiridonych], an old
    porter from the County Office
ANFISA, the Prozorovs' former nurse, an
    old woman of 80

Scene: The action takes place in a county town

ACT I

[A drawing-room in the Prozorovs'
house; it is separated from a large ballroom[1] at the back by a row of columns.
It is midday; there is cheerful sunshine
outside. In the ballroom the table is
being laid for lunch. OLGA, wearing the
regulation dark-blue dress of a secondary
school mistress, is correcting her pupils'
work, standing or walking about as she
does so. MASHA, in a black dress, is sitting reading a book, her hat on her lap.
IRENA, in white, stands lost in thought.]

OLGA. It's exactly a year ago that
Father died, isn't it? This very day, the
fifth of May—your Saint's day, Irena. I
remember it was very cold and it was
snowing. I felt then as if I should never
survive his death; and you had fainted
and were lying quite still, as if you were

dead. And now—a year's gone by, and
we talk about it so easily. You're wearing
white, and your face is positively radiant. . . .
[A clock strikes twelve.]
The clock struck twelve then, too. [A
pause.] I remember when Father was
being taken to the cemetery there was a
military band, and a salute with rifle
fire. That was because he was a general,
in command of a brigade. And yet there
weren't many people at the funeral. Of
course, it was raining hard, raining and
snowing.
IRENA. Need we bring up all these
memories?
[Baron TOOZENBACH, CHEBUTYKIN and
SOLIONY appear behind the columns
by the table in the ballroom.]
OLGA. It's so warm to-day that we can
keep the windows wide open, and yet
there aren't any leaves showing on the

SOURCE: From Plays by Anton Chekhov, translated by Elizaveta Fen. Copyright © 1951, 1954,
by Elizaveta Fen. Reprinted by permission of Penguin Books, Ltd.
[1] A large room, sparsely furnished, used for receptions and dances in Russian houses. (Translator's
notes.)

birch trees. Father was made a brigadier eleven years ago, and then he left Moscow and took us with him. I remember so well how everything in Moscow was in blossom by now, everything was soaked in sunlight and warmth. Eleven years have gone by, yet I remember everything about it, as if we'd only left yesterday. Oh, Heavens! When I woke up this morning and saw this flood of sunshine, all this spring sunshine, I felt so moved and so happy! I felt such a longing to get back home to Moscow!

CHEBUTYKIN [to TOOZENBACH]. The devil you have!

TOOZENBACH. It's nonsense, I agree.

MASHA [absorbed in her book, whistles a tune under her breath].

OLGA. Masha, do stop whistling! How can you? [A pause.] I suppose I must get this continual headache because I have to go to school every day and go on teaching right into the evening. I seem to have the thoughts of someone quite old. Honestly, I've been feeling as if my strength and youth were running out of me drop by drop, day after day. Day after day, all these four years that I've been working at the school....I just have one longing and it seems to grow stronger and stronger....

IRENA. If only we could go back to Moscow! Sell the house, finish with our life here, and go back to Moscow.

OLGA. Yes, Moscow! As soon as we possibly can.

[CHEBUTYKIN and TOOZENBACH laugh.]

IRENA. I suppose Andrey will soon get a professorship. He isn't likely to go on living here. The only problem is our poor Masha.

OLGA. Masha can come and stay the whole summer with us every year in Moscow.

MASHA [whistles a tune under her breath].

IRENA. Everything will settle itself, with God's help. [Looks through the window.] What lovely weather it is to-day! Really, I don't know why there's such joy in my heart. I remembered this morning that it was my Saint's day, and suddenly I felt so happy, and I thought of the time when we were children, and Mother was still alive. And then such wonderful thoughts came to me, such wonderful stirring thoughts!

OLGA. You're so lovely to-day, you really do look most attractive. Masha looks pretty to-day, too. Andrey could be good-looking, but he's grown so stout. It doesn't suit him. As for me, I've just aged and grown a lot thinner. I suppose it's through getting so irritated with the girls at school. But to-day I'm at home, I'm free, and my headache's gone, and I feel much younger than I did yesterday. I'm only twenty-eight, after all....I suppose everything that God wills must be right and good, but I can't help thinking sometimes that if I'd got married and stayed at home, it would have been a better thing for me. [A pause.] I would have been very fond of my husband.

TOOZENBACH [to SOLIONY]. Really, you talk such a lot of nonsense, I'm tired of listening to you. [Comes into the drawing-room.] I forgot to tell you: Vershinin, our new battery commander, is going to call on you to-day. [Sits down by the piano.]

OLGA. I'm very glad to hear it.

IRENA. Is he old?

TOOZENBACH. No, not particularly. Forty, forty-five at the most. [Plays quietly.] He seems a nice fellow. Certainly not a fool. His only weakness is that he talks too much.

IRENA. Is he interesting?

TOOZENBACH. He's all right, only he's got a wife, a mother-in-law and two little girls. What's more, she's his second wife. He calls on everybody and tells them that he's got a wife and two little girls. He'll tell you about it, too, I'm sure of that. His wife seems to be a bit soft in the head. She wears a long plait like a girl, she is always philosophizing and talking in high-flown language, and then she often tries to commit suicide, apparently just to annoy her husband. I would have run away from a wife like that years ago, but he puts up with it, and just grumbles about it.

SOLIONY [enters the drawing-room with CHEBUTYKIN]. Now I can only lift sixty pounds with one hand, but with two I can lift two hundred pounds, or even two hundred and forty. So I conclude from that that two men are not just twice as strong as one, but three times as strong, if not more.

CHEBUTYKIN [reads the paper as he comes in]. Here's a recipe for falling hair

... two ounces of naphthaline, half-a-bottle of methylated spirit ... dissolve and apply once a day.... [*Writes it down in a notebook.*] Must make a note of it. [*To* SOLIONY.] Well, as I was trying to explain to you, you cork the bottle and pass a glass tube through the cork. Then you take a pinch of ordinary powdered alum, and ...

IRENA. Ivan Romanych, dear Ivan Romanych!

CHEBUTYKIN. What is it, my child, what is it?

IRENA. Tell me, why is it I'm so happy to-day? Just as if I were sailing along in a boat with big white sails, and above me the wide, blue sky, and in the sky great white birds floating around?

CHEBUTYKIN [*kisses both her hands, tenderly*]. My little white bird!

IRENA. You know, when I woke up this morning, and after I'd got up and washed, I suddenly felt as if everything in the world had become clear to me, and I knew the way I ought to live. I know it all now, my dear Ivan Romanych. Man must work by the sweat of his brow whatever his class, and that should make up the whole meaning and purpose of his life and happiness and contentment. Oh, how good it must be to be a workman, getting up with the sun and breaking stones by the roadside—or a shepherd—or a schoolmaster teaching the children—or an engine-driver on the railway. Good Heavens! it's better to be a mere ox or horse, and work, than the sort of young woman who wakes up at twelve, and drinks her coffee in bed, and then takes two hours dressing.... How dreadful! You know how you long for a cool drink in hot weather? Well, that's the way I long for work. And if I don't get up early from now on and really work, you can refuse to be friends with me any more, Ivan Romanych.

CHEBUTYKIN [*tenderly*]. So I will, so I will....

OLGA. Father taught us to get up at seven o'clock and so Irena always wakes up at seven—but then she stays in bed till at least nine, thinking about something or other. And with such a serious expression on her face, too! [*Laughs.*]

IRENA. You think it's strange when I look serious because you always think of me as a little girl. I'm twenty, you know!

TOOZENBACH. All this longing for work. ... Heavens! how well I can understand it! I've never done a stroke of work in my life. I was born in Petersburg, an unfriendly, idle city—born into a family where work and worries were simply unknown. I remember a valet pulling off my boots for me when I came home from the cadet school.... I grumbled at the way he did it, and my mother looked on in admiration. She was quite surprised when other people looked at me in any other way. I was so carefully protected from work! But I doubt whether they succeeded in protecting me for good and all—yes, I doubt it very much! The time's come: there's a terrific thundercloud advancing upon us, a mighty storm is coming to freshen us up! Yes, it's coming all right, it's quite near already, and it's going to blow away all this idleness and indifference, and prejudice against work, this rot of boredom that our society is suffering from. I'm going to work, and in twenty-five or thirty years' time every man and woman will be working. Every one of us!

CHEBUTYKIN. I'm not going to work.

TOOZENBACH. You don't count.

SOLIONY. In twenty-five years' time you won't be alive, thank goodness. In a couple of years you'll die from a stroke—or I'll lose my temper with you and put a bullet in your head, my good fellow. [*Takes a scent bottle from his pocket and sprinkles the scent over his chest and hands.*]

CHEBUTYKIN [*laughs*]. It's quite true that I never have done any work. Not a stroke since I left the university. I haven't even read a book, only newspapers. [*Takes another newspaper out of his pocket.*] For instance, here.... I know from the paper that there was a person called Dobroliubov, but what he wrote about I've not the faintest idea.... God alone knows.... [*Someone knocks on the floor from downstairs.*] There! They're calling me to come down: there's someone come to see me. I'll be back in a moment.... [*Goes out hurriedly, stroking his beard.*]

IRENA. He's up to one of his little games.

TOOZENBACH. Yes. He looked very solemn as he left. He's obviously going to give you a present.

IRENA. I do dislike that sort of thing. . . .

OLGA. Yes, isn't it dreadful? He's always doing something silly.

MASHA. "A green oak grows by a curving shore, And round that oak hangs a golden chain" . . . [Gets up as she sings under her breath.]

OLGA. You're sad to-day, Masha.

MASHA [puts on her hat, singing].

OLGA. Where are you going?

MASHA. Home.

IRENA. What a strange thing to do.

TOOZENBACH. What! Going away from your sister's party?

MASHA. What does it matter? I'll be back this evening. Good-bye, my darling. [Kisses IRENA.] And once again—I wish you all the happiness in the world. In the old days when Father was alive we used to have thirty or forty officers at our parties. What gay parties we had! And to-day—what have we go to-day? A man and a half, and the place is as quiet as a tomb. I'm going home. I'm depressed to-day, I'm sad, so don't listen to me. [Laughs through her tears.] We'll have a talk later, but good-bye for now, my dear. I'll go somewhere or other. . . .

IRENA [displeased]. Really, you are a . . .

OLGA [tearfully]. I understand you, Masha.

SOLIONY. If a man starts philosophizing, you call that philosophy, or possibly just sophistry, but if a woman or a couple of women start philosophizing you call that . . . what would you call it, now? Ask me another!

MASHA. What are you talking about? You are a disconcerting person!

SOLIONY. Nothing.

"He had no time to say 'Oh, oh!'
   Before that bear had struck him
      low" . . .

[A pause.]

MASHA [to OLGA, crossly]. Do stop snivelling!

[Enter ANFISA and FERAPONT, the latter carrying a large cake.]

ANFISA. Come along, my dear, this way. Come in, your boots are quite clean. [To IRENA.] A cake from Protopopov, at the Council Office.

IRENA. Thank you. Tell him I'm very grateful to him. [Takes the cake.]

FERAPONT. What's that?

IRENA [louder]. Tell him I sent my thanks.

OLGA. Nanny, will you give him a piece of cake? Go along, Ferapont, they'll give you some cake.

FERAPONT. What's that?

ANFISA. Come along with me, Ferapont Spiridonych, my dear. Come along. [Goes out with FERAPONT.]

MASHA. I don't like that Protopopov fellow, Mihail Potapych, or Ivanych, or whatever it is. It's best not to invite him here.

IRENA. I haven't invited him.

MASHA. Thank goodness.

[Enter CHEBUTYKIN, followed by a soldier carrying a silver samovar. Murmurs of astonishment and displeasure.]

OLGA [covering her face with her hands]. A samovar! But this is dreadful! [Goes through to the ballroom and stands by the table.]

IRENA. My dear Ivan Romanych, what are you thinking about?

TOOZENBACH [laughs]. Didn't I tell you?

MASHA. Ivan Romanych, you really ought to be ashamed of yourself!

CHEBUTYKIN. My dear, sweet girls, I've no one in the world but you. You're dearer to me than anything in the world! I'm nearly sixty, I'm an old man, a lonely, utterly unimportant old man. The only thing that's worth anything in me is my love for you, and if it weren't for you, really I would have been dead long ago. [To IRENA.] My dear, my sweet little girl, haven't I known you since the very day you were born? Didn't I carry you about in my arms? . . . didn't I love your dear mother?

IRENA. But why do you get such expensive presents?

CHEBUTYKIN [tearfully and crossly]. Expensive presents! . . . Get along with you! [To the orderly.] Put the samovar over there. [Mimics IRENA.] Expensive presents!

[The orderly takes the samovar to the ballroom.]

ANFISA [crosses the drawing-room]. My dears, there's a strange colonel just arrived. He's taken off his coat and he's coming up now. Irenushka, do be nice and polite to him, won't you? [*In the doorway.*] And it's high time we had lunch, too.... Oh, dear! [*Goes out.*]

TOOZENBACH. It's Vershinin, I suppose. [*Enter* VERSHININ.]

TOOZENBACH. Lieutenant-Colonel Vershinin!

VERSHININ [*to* MASHA *and* IRENA]. Allow me to introduce myself—Lieutenant-Colonel Vershinin. I'm so glad, so very glad to be here at last. How you've changed! Dear, dear, how you've changed!

IRENA. Please, do sit down. We're very pleased to see you, I'm sure.

VERSHININ [*gaily*]. I'm so glad to see you, so glad! But there were three of you, weren't there?—three sisters. I remember there were three little girls. I don't remember their faces, but I knew your father, Colonel Prozorov, and I remember he had three little girls. Oh, yes, I saw them myself. I remember them quite well. How time flies! Dear, dear, how it flies!

TOOZENBACH. Alexandr Ignatyevich comes from Moscow.

IRENA. From Moscow? You come from Moscow?

VERSHININ. Yes, from Moscow. Your father was a battery commander there, and I was an officer in the same brigade. [*To* MASHA.] I seem to remember your face a little.

MASHA. I don't remember you at all.

IRENA. Olia, Olia! [*Calls toward the ballroom.*] Olia, do come!

[OLGA *enters from the ballroom.*]

IRENA. It seems that Lieutenant-Colonel Vershinin comes from Moscow.

VERSHININ. You must be Olga Serghyeevna, the eldest. And you are Maria. ... And you are Irena, the youngest....

OLGA. You come from Moscow?

VERSHININ. Yes. I studied in Moscow and entered the service there. I stayed there quite a long time, but then I was put in charge of a battery here—so I moved out here, you see. I don't really remember you, you know, I only remember that there were three sisters. I remember your father, though, I remember him very well. All I need to do is to close my eyes and I can see him standing there as if he were alive. I used to visit you in Moscow.

OLGA. I thought I remembered everybody, and yet...

VERSHININ. My Christian names are Alexandr Ignatyevich.

IRENA. Alexandr Ignatyevich, and you come from Moscow! Well, what a surprise!

OLGA. We're going to live there, you know.

IRENA. We hope to be there by the autumn. It's our home town, we were born there.... In Staraya Basmannaya Street.

[*Both laugh happily.*]

MASHA. Fancy meeting a fellow townsman so unexpectedly! [*Eagerly.*] I remember now. Do you remember, Olga, there was someone they used to call "the lovesick Major"? You were a Lieutenant then, weren't you, and you were in love with someone or other, and everyone used to tease you about it. They called you "Major" for some reason or other.

VERSHININ [*laughs*]. That's it, that's it. ... "The lovesick Major," that's what they called me.

MASHA. In those days you only had a moustache.... Oh, dear, how much older you look! [*Tearfully.*] How much older!

VERSHININ. Yes, I was still a young man in the days when they called me "the lovesick Major." I was in love then. It's different now.

OLGA. But you haven't got a single grey hair! You've aged, yes, but you're certainly not an old man.

VERSHININ. Nevertheless, I'm turned forty-two. Is it long since you left Moscow?

IRENA. Eleven years. Now what are you crying for, Masha, you funny girl?... [*Tearfully.*] You'll make me cry, too.

MASHA. I'm not crying. What was the street you lived in?

VERSHININ. In the Staraya Basmannaya.

OLGA. We did, too.

VERSHININ. At one time I lived in the Niemietzkaya Street. I used to walk from there to the Krasny Barracks, and I remember there was such a gloomy bridge I had to cross. I used to hear the noise of the water rushing under it. I remember how lonely and sad I felt there. [*A pause.*] But what a magnificently wide river you have here! It's a marvellous river!

OLGA. Yes, but this is a cold place. It's

cold here, and there are too many mosquitoes.

VERSHININ. Really? I should have said you had a really good healthy climate here, a real Russian climate. Forest, river . . . birch-trees, too. The dear, unpretentious birch-trees—I love them more than any of the other trees. It's nice living here. But there's one rather strange thing, the station is fifteen miles from the town. And no one knows why.

SOLIONY. I know why it is. [*Everyone looks at him.*] Because if the station were nearer, it wouldn't be so far away, and as it is so far away, it can't be nearer. [*An awkward silence.*]

TOOZENBACH. You like your little joke, Vassily Vassilich.

OLGA. I'm sure I remember you now. I know I do.

VERSHININ. I knew your mother.

CHEBUTYKIN. She was a good woman, God bless her memory!

IRENA. Mama was buried in Moscow.

OLGA. At the convent of Novo-Dievichye.

MASHA. You know, I'm even beginning to forget what she looked like. I suppose people will lose all memory of us in just the same way. We'll be forgotten.

VERSHININ. Yes, we shall all be forgotten. Such is our fate, and we can't do anything about it. And all the things that seem serious, important and full of meaning to us now will be forgotten one day— or anyway they won't seem important any more. [*A pause.*] It's strange to think that we're utterly unable to tell what will be regarded as great and important in the future and what will be thought of as just paltry and ridiculous. Didn't the great discoveries of Copernicus—or of Columbus, if you like—appear useless and unimportant to begin with?—whereas some rubbish, written up by an eccentric fool, was regarded as a revelation of great truth? It may well be that in time to come the life we live to-day will seem strange and uncomfortable and stupid and not too clean, either, and perhaps even wicked. . . .

TOOZENBACH. Who can tell? It's just as possible that future generations will think that we lived our lives on a very high plane and remember us with respect. After all, we no longer have tortures and public executions and invasions, though there's still a great deal of suffering!

SOLIONY [*in a high-pitched voice as if calling to chickens*]. Cluck, cluck, cluck! There's nothing our good Baron loves as much as a nice bit of philosophizing.

TOOZENBACH. Vassily Vassilich, will you kindly leave me alone? [*Moves to another chair.*] It's becoming tiresome.

SOLIONY [*as before*]. Cluck, cluck, cluck! . . .

TOOZENBACH [*to* VERSHININ]. The suffering that we see around us—and there's so much of it—itself proves that our society has at least achieved a level of morality which is higher. . . .

VERSHININ. Yes, yes, of course.

CHEBUTYKIN. You said just now, Baron, that our age will be called great; but people are small all the same. . . . [*Gets up.*] Look how small I am.

[*A violin is played off stage.*]

MASHA. That's Andrey playing the violin; he's our brother, you know.

IRENA. We've got quite a clever brother. . . . We're expecting him to be a professor. Papa was a military man, but Andrey chose an academic career.

OLGA. We've been teasing him to-day. We think he's in love, just a little.

IRENA. With a girl who lives down here. She'll be calling in to-day most likely.

MASHA. The way she dresses herself is awful! It's not that her clothes are just ugly and old-fashioned, they're simply pathetic. She'll put on some weird-looking, bright yellow skirt with a crude sort of fringe affair, and then a red blouse to go with it. And her cheeks look as though they've been scrubbed, they're so shiny! Andrey's not in love with her—I can't believe it; after all, he has got some taste. I think he's just playing the fool, just to annoy us. I heard yesterday that she's going to get married to Protopopov, the chairman of the local council. I thought it was an excellent idea. [*Calls through the side door.*] Andrey, come here, will you? Just for a moment, dear.

[*Enter* ANDREY.]

OLGA. This is my brother, Andrey Serghyeevich.

VERSHININ. Vershinin.

ANDREY. Prozorov. [*Wipes the perspiration from his face.*] I believe you've been appointed battery commander here?

OLGA. What do you think, dear? Alexandr Ignatyevich comes from Moscow.

ANDREY. Do you, really? Congratulations! You'll get no peace from my sisters now.

VERSHININ. I'm afraid your sisters must be getting tired of me already.

IRENA. Just look, Andrey gave me this little picture frame to-day. [*Shows him the frame.*] He made it himself.

VERSHININ [*looks at the frame, not knowing what to say*]. Yes, it's . . . it's very nice indeed. . . .

IRENA. Do you see that little frame over the piano? He made that one, too.

[ANDREY *waves his hand impatiently and walks off.*]

OLGA. He's awfully clever, and he plays the violin, and he makes all sorts of things, too. In fact, he's very gifted all round. Andrey, please, don't go. He's got such a bad habit—always going off like this. Come here!

[MASHA *and* IRENA *take him by the arms and lead him back, laughing.*]

MASHA. Now just you come here!

ANDREY. Do leave me alone, please do!

MASHA. You are a silly! They used to call Alexandr Ignatyevich "the lovesick Major," and he didn't get annoyed.

VERSHININ. Not in the least.

MASHA. I feel like calling you a "lovesick fiddler."

IRENA. Or a "lovesick professor."

OLGA. He's fallen in love! Our Andriusha's in love!

IRENA [*clapping her hands*]. Three cheers for Andriusha! Andriusha's in love!

CHEBUTYKIN [*comes up behind* ANDREY *and puts his arms round his waist*]. "Nature created us for love alone." . . . [*Laughs loudly, still holding his paper in his hand.*]

ANDREY. That's enough of it, that's enough. . . . [*Wipes his face.*] I couldn't get to sleep all night, and I'm not feeling too grand just now. I read till four o'clock, and then I went to bed, but nothing happened. I kept thinking about one thing and another . . . and it gets light so early; the sun just pours into my room. I'd like to translate a book from the English while I'm here during the summer.

VERSHININ. You read English, then?

ANDREY. Yes. My father—God bless his memory—used to simply wear us out with learning. It sounds silly, I know, but I must confess that since he died I've begun to grow stout, as if I'd been physically relieved of the strain. I've grown quite stout in a year. Yes, thanks to Father, my sisters and I know French and German and English, and Irena here knows Italian, too. But what an effort it all cost us!

MASHA. Knowing three languages in a town like this is an unnecessary luxury. In fact, not even a luxury, but just a sort of useless encumbrance . . . it's rather like having a sixth finger on your hand. We know a lot of stuff that's just useless.

VERSHININ. Really! [*Laughs.*] You know a lot of stuff that's useless! It seems to me that there's no place on earth, however dull and depressing it may be, where intelligence and education can be useless. Let us suppose that among the hundred thousand people in this town, all of them, no doubt, very backward and uncultured, there are just three people like yourselves. Obviously, you can't hope to triumph over all the mass of ignorance around you; as your life goes by, you'll have to keep giving in little by little until you get lost in the crowd, in the hundred thousand. Life will swallow you up, but you'll not quite disappear, you'll make some impression on it. After you've gone, perhaps six more people like you will turn up, then twelve, and so on, until in the end most people will have become like you. So in two or three hundred years life on this old earth of ours will have become marvellously beautiful. Man longs for a life like that, and if it isn't here yet, he must imagine it, wait for it, dream about it, prepare for it, he must know and see more than his father and his grandfather did. [*Laughs.*] And you're complaining because you know a lot of stuff that's useless.

MASHA [*takes off her hat*]. I'll be staying to lunch.

IRENA [*with a sigh*]. Really, someone should have written all that down.

[ANDREY *has left the room, unnoticed.*]

TOOZENBACH. You say that in time to come life will be marvellously beautiful. That's probably true. But in order to share in it now, at a distance so to speak, we must prepare for it and work for it.

VERSHININ [*gets up*]. Yes. . . . What a

lot of flowers you've got here! [*Looks round.*] And what a marvellous house! I do envy you! All my life I seem to have been pigging it in small flats, with two chairs and a sofa and a stove which always smokes. It's the flowers that I've missed in my life, flowers like these! ... [*Rubs his hands.*] Oh, well, never mind!

TOOZENBACH. Yes, we must work. I suppose you're thinking I'm a sentimental German. But I assure you I'm not— I'm Russian. I don't speak a word of German. My father was brought up in the Greek Orthodox faith. [*A pause.*]

VERSHININ [*walks up and down the room*]. You know, I often wonder what it would be like if you could start your life over again—deliberately, I mean, consciously.... Suppose you could put aside the life you'd lived already, as though it was just a sort of rough draft, and then start another one like a fair copy. If that happened, I think the thing you'd want most of all would be not to repeat yourself. You'd try at least to create a new environment for yourself, a flat like this one, for instance, with some flowers and plenty of light.... I have a wife, you know, and two little girls; and my wife's not very well, and all that.... Well, if I had to start my life all over again, I wouldn't marry.... No, no!

[*Enter* KOOLYGHIN, *in the uniform of a teacher.*]

KOOLYGHIN [*approaches* IRENA]. Congratulations, dear sister—from the bottom of my heart, congratulations on your Saint's day. I wish you good health and everything a girl of your age ought to have! And allow me to present you with this little book.... [*Hands her a book.*] It's the history of our school covering the whole fifty years of its existence. I wrote it myself. Quite a trifle, of course—I wrote it in my spare time when I had nothing better to do—but I hope you'll read it nevertheless. Good morning to you all! [*To* VERSHININ.] Allow me to introduce myself. Koolyghin's the name; I'm a master at the secondary school here. And a town councillor. [*To* IRENA.] You'll find a list in the book of all the pupils who have completed their studies at our school during the last fifty years. *Feci quod potui, faciant meliora potentes.* [*Kisses* MASHA.]

IRENA. But you gave me this book last Easter!

KOOLYGHIN [*laughs*]. Did I really? In that case, give it me back—or no, better give it to the Colonel. Please do take it, Colonel. Maybe you'll read it some time when you've nothing better to do.

VERSHININ. Thank you very much. [*Prepares to leave.*] I'm so very glad to have made your acquaintance....

OLGA. You aren't going, are you? ... Really, you mustn't.

IRENA. But you'll stay and have lunch with us! Please do.

OLGA. Please do.

VERSHININ [*bows*]. I see I've intruded on your Saint's day party. I didn't know. Forgive me for not offering you my congratulations. [*Goes into the ballroom with* OLGA.]

KOOLYGHIN. To-day is Sunday, my friends, a day of rest; let us rest and enjoy it, each according to his age and position in life! We shall have to roll up the carpets and put them away till the winter.... We must remember to put some naphthaline on them, or Persian powder.... The Romans enjoyed good health because they knew how to work *and* how to rest. They had *mens sana in corpore sano.* Their life had a definite shape, a form.... The director of the school says that the most important thing about life is form.... A thing that loses its form is finished—that's just as true of our ordinary, everyday lives. [*Takes* MASHA *by the waist and laughs.*] Masha loves me. My wife loves me. Yes, and the curtains will have to be put away with the carpets, too.... I'm cheerful to-day, I'm in quite excellent spirits. ... Masha, we're invited to the director's at four o'clock to-day. A country walk has been arranged for the teachers and their families.

MASHA. I'm not going.

KOOLYGHIN [*distressed*]. Masha, darling, why not?

MASHA. I'll tell you later.... [*Crossly.*] All right, I'll come, only leave me alone now.... [*Walks off.*]

KOOLYGHIN. And after the walk we shall all spend the evening at the director's house. In spite of weak health, that man is certainly sparing no pains to be sociable. A first-rate, thoroughly enlightened man! A most excellent person! After the conference yesterday he said to me: "I'm tired, Fiodor Ilyich. I'm tired!" [*Looks at the clock, then at his watch.*] Your clock is seven minutes fast. Yes, "I'm tired," he said.

[*The sound of the violin· is heard off stage.*]

OLGA. Will you all come and sit down, please! Lunch is ready. There's a pie.

KOOLYGHIN. Ah, Olga, my dear girl! Last night I worked up to eleven o'clock, and I felt tired, but to-day I'm quite happy. [*Goes to the table in the ballroom.*] My dear Olga!

CHEBUTYKIN [*puts the newspaper in his pocket and combs his beard*]. A pie? Excellent!

MASHA [*sternly to* CHEBUTYKIN]. Remember, you mustn't take anything to drink to-day. Do you hear? It's bad for you.

CHEBUTYKIN. Never mind. I've got over that weakness long ago! I haven't done any heavy drinking for two years. [*Impatiently.*] Anyway, my dear, what does it matter?

MASHA. All the same, don't you dare to drink anything. Mind you don't now! [*Crossly, but taking care that her husband does not hear.*] So now I've got to spend another of these damnably boring evenings at the director's!

TOOZENBACH. I wouldn't go if I were you, and that's that.

CHEBUTYKIN. Don't you go, my dear.

MASHA. Don't go, indeed! Oh, what a damnable life! It's intolerable.... [*Goes into the ballroom.*]

CHEBUTYKIN [*follows her*]. Well, well! ...

SOLIONY [*as he passes* TOOZENBACH *on the way to the ballroom*]. Cluck, cluck, cluck!

TOOZENBACH. Do stop it, Vassily Vassilich. I've really had enough of it....

SOLIONY. Cluck, cluck, cluck! ...

KOOLYGHIN [*gaily*]. Your health, Colonel! I'm a schoolmaster ... and I'm quite one of the family here, as it were. I'm Masha's husband. She's got a sweet nature, such a very sweet nature!

VERSHININ. I think I'll have a little of this dark vodka. [*Drinks.*] Your health! [*To* OLGA.] I do feel so happy with you people!

[*Only* IRENA *and* TOOZENBACH *remain in the drawing-room.*]

IRENA. Masha's a bit out of humour to-day. You know, she got married when she was eighteen, and then her husband seemed the cleverest man in the world to her. It's different now. He's the kindest of men, but not the cleverest.

OLGA [*impatiently*]. Andrey, will you please come?

ANDREY [*off stage*]. Just coming. [*Enters and goes to the table.*]

TOOZENBACH. What are you thinking about?

IRENA. Oh, nothing special. You know, I don't like this man Soliony, I'm quite afraid of him. Whenever he opens his mouth he says something silly.

TOOZENBACH. He's a strange fellow. I'm sorry for him, even though he irritates me. In fact, I feel more sorry for him than irritated. I think he's shy. When he's alone with me, he can be quite sensible and friendly, but in company he's offensive and bullying. Don't go over there just yet, let them get settled down at the table. Let me stay beside you for a bit. Tell me what you're thinking about. [*A pause.*] You're twenty ... and I'm not thirty yet myself. What years and years we still have ahead of us, a whole long succession of years, all full of my love for you! ...

IRENA. Don't talk to me about love, Nikolai Lvovich.

TOOZENBACH [*not listening*]. Oh, I long so passionately for life, I long to work and strive so much, and all this longing is somehow mingled · with my love for you, Irena. And just because you happen to be beautiful, life appears beautiful to me! What are you thinking about?

IRENA. You say that life is beautiful. Maybe it is—but what if it only seems to be beautiful? Our lives, I mean the lives of us three sisters, haven't been beautiful up to now. The truth is that life has been stifling us, like weeds in a garden. I'm afraid I'm crying.... So unnecessary.... [*Quickly dries her eyes and smiles.*] We must work, work! The reason we feel depressed and take such a gloomy view of life is that we've never known what it is to make a real effort.

We're the children of parents who despised work. . . .

[*Enter* NATALIA IVANOVNA. *She is wearing a pink dress with a green belt.*]

NATASHA. They've gone in to lunch already. . . . I'm late. . . . [*Glances at herself in a mirror, adjusts her dress.*] My hair seems to be all right. . . . [*Catches sight of* IRENA.] My dear Irena Serghyeevna, congratulations! [*Gives her a vigorous and prolonged kiss.*] You've got such a lot of visitors. . . . I feel quite shy. . . . How do you do, Baron?

OLGA [*enters the drawing-room*]. Oh, there you are, Natalia Ivanovna! How are you, my dear?

[*They kiss each other.*]

NATASHA. Congratulations! You've such a lot of people here, I feel dreadfully shy. . . .

OLGA. It's all right, they're all old friends. [*Alarmed, dropping her voice.*] You've got a green belt on! My dear, that's surely a mistake!

NATASHA. Why, is it a bad omen, or what?

OLGA. No, but it just doesn't go with your dress . . . it looks so strange. . . .

NATASHA [*tearfully*]. Really? But it isn't really green, you know, it's a sort of dull colour. . . . [*Follows* OLGA *to the ballroom.*]

[*All are now seated at the table; the drawing-room is empty.*]

KOOLYGHIN. Irena, you know, I do wish you'd find yourself a good husband. In my view it's high time you got married.

CHEBUTYKIN. You ought to get yourself a nice little husband, too, Natalia Ivanovna.

KOOLYGHIN. Natalia Ivanovna already has a husband in view.

MASHA [*strikes her plate with her fork*]. A glass of wine for me, please! Three cheers for our jolly old life! We keep our end up, we do!

KOOLYGHIN. Masha, you won't get more than five out of ten for good conduct!

VERSHININ. I say, this liqueur's very nice. What is it made of?

SOLIONY. Black beetles!

IRENA. Ugh! ugh! How disgusting!

OLGA. We're having roast turkey for dinner to-night, and then apple tart. Thank goodness, I'll be here all day to-day . . . this evening, too. You must all come this evening.

VERSHININ. May I come in the evening, too?

IRENA. Yes, please do.

NATASHA. They don't stand on ceremony here.

CHEBUTYKIN. "Nature created us for love alone." . . . [*Laughs.*]

ANDREY [*crossly*]. Will you stop it, please? Aren't you tired of it yet?

[FEDOTIK *and* RODÉ *come in with a large basket of flowers.*]

FEDOTIK. Just look here, they're having lunch already!

RODÉ [*in a loud voice*]. Having their lunch? So they are, they're having lunch already.

FEDOTIK. Wait half a minute. [*Takes a snapshot.*] One! Just one minute more! . . . [*Takes another snapshot.*] Two! All over now.

[*They pick up the basket and go into the ballroom where they are greeted uproariously.*]

RODÉ [*loudly*]. Congratulations, Irena Serghyeevna! I wish you all the best, everything you'd wish for yourself! Gorgeous weather to-day, absolutely marvellous. I've been out walking the whole morning with the boys. You do know that I teach gym at the high school, don't you? . . .

FEDOTIK. You may move now, Irena Serghyeevna, that is, if you want to. [*Takes a snapshot.*] You do look attractive to-day. [*Takes a top out of his pocket.*] By the way, look at this top. It's got a wonderful hum.

IRENA. What a sweet little thing!

MASHA. "A green oak grows by a curving shore, And round that oak hangs a golden chain." . . . A green chain around that oak. . . . [*Peevishly.*] Why do I keep on saying that? Those lines have been worrying me all day long!

KOOLYGHIN. Do you know, we're thirteen at table?

RODÉ [*loudly*]. You don't really believe in these old superstitions, do you? [*Laughter.*]

KOOLYGHIN. When thirteen people sit down to table, it means that some of them are in love. Is it you, by any chance, Ivan Romanych?

CHEBUTYKIN. Oh, I'm just an old sinner. . . . But what I can't make out is why Natalia Ivanovna looks so embarrassed.

[*Loud laughter.* NATASHA *runs out into the drawing-room,* ANDREY *follows her.*]

ANDREY. Please, Natasha, don't take any notice of them! Stop . . . wait a moment. . . . Please!

NATASHA. I feel so ashamed. . . . I don't know what's the matter with me, and they're all laughing at me. It's awful of me to leave the table like that, but I couldn't help it. . . . I just couldn't. . . . [*Covers her face with her hands.*]

ANDREY. My dear girl, please, please don't get upset. Honestly, they don't mean any harm, they're just teasing. My dear, sweet girl, they're really good-natured folks, they all are, and they're fond of us both. Come over to the window, they can't see us there. . . . [*Looks round.*]

NATASHA. You see, I'm not used to being with a lot of people.

ANDREY. Oh, how young you are, Natasha, how wonderfully, beautifully young! My dear, sweet girl, don't get so upset! Do believe me, believe me. . . . I'm so happy, so full of love, of joy. . . . No, they can't see us here! They can't see us! How did I come to love you, when was it? . . . I don't understand anything. My precious, my sweet, my innocent girl, please—I want you to marry me! I love you, I love you as I've never loved anybody. . . . [*Kisses her.*]

[*Enter two officers and, seeing* NATASHA *and* ANDREY *kissing, stand and stare in amazement.*]

ACT II

[*The scene is the same as in Act I. It is eight o'clock in the evening. The faint sound of an accordion is heard coming from the street.*

The stage is unlit. Enter NATALIA IVANOVNA *in a dressing-gown, carrying a candle. She crosses the stage and stops by the door leading to* ANDREY'S *room.*]

NATASHA. What are you doing, Andriusha? Reading? It's all right, I only wanted to know. . . . [*Goes to another door, opens it, looks inside and shuts it again.*] No one's left a light anywhere. . . .

ANDREY [*enters with a book in his hand*]. What is it, Natasha?

NATASHA. I was just going round to see if anyone had left a light anywhere. It's carnival week, and the servants are so excited about it . . . anything might happen! You've got to watch them. Last night about twelve o'clock I happened to go into the dining-room, and—would you believe it?—there was a candle alight on the table. I've not found out who lit it. [*Puts the candle down.*] What time is it?

ANDREY [*glances at his watch*]. Quarter past eight.

NATASHA. And Olga and Irena still out. They aren't back from work yet, poor things! Olga's still at some teachers' conference, and Irena's at the post office. [*Sighs.*] This morning I said to Irena: "Do take care of yourself, my dear." But she won't listen. Did you say it was a quarter past eight? I'm afraid Bobik is not at all well. Why does he get so cold? Yesterday he had a temperature, but today he feels quite cold when you touch him. . . . I'm so afraid!

ANDREY. It's all right, Natasha. The boy's well enough.

NATASHA. Still, I think he ought to have a special diet. I'm so anxious about him. By the way, they tell me that some carnival party's supposed to be coming here soon after nine. I'd rather they didn't come, Andriusha.

ANDREY. Well, I really don't know what I can do. They've been asked to come.

NATASHA. This morning the dear little fellow woke up and looked at me, and then suddenly he smiled. He recognized me, you see. "Good morning, Bobik," I said, "good morning, darling precious!" And then he laughed. Babies understand everything, you know, they understand us perfectly well. Anyway, Andriusha, I'll tell the servants not to let that carnival party in.

ANDREY [*irresolutely*]. Well . . . it's really for my sisters to decide, isn't it? It's their house, after all.

NATASHA. Yes, it's their house as well. I'll tell them, too. . . . They're so kind. . . . [*Walks off.*] I've ordered sour milk for supper. The doctor says you ought to eat nothing but sour milk, or you'll never get any thinner. [*Stops.*] Bobik feels cold. I'm afraid his room is too cold for him. He ought to move into a warmer room, at least until the warm weather comes. Irena's room, for instance —that's just a perfect room for a baby: it's dry, and it gets the sun all day long. We must tell her: perhaps she'd share Olga's room for a bit.... In any case, she's never at home during the day, she only sleeps there.... [*A pause.*] Andriusha, why don't you say anything?

ANDREY. I was just day-dreaming.... There's nothing to say, anyway....

NATASHA. Well.... What was it I was going to tell you? Oh, yes! Ferapont from the Council Office wants to see you about something.

ANDREY [*yawns*]. Tell him to come up.

[NATASHA *goes out.* ANDREY, *bending over the candle which she has left behind, begins to read his book. Enter* FERAPONT *in an old shabby overcoat, his collar turned up, his ears muffled in a scarf.*]

ANDREY. Hullo, old chap! What did you want to see me about?

FERAPONT. The chairman's sent you the register and a letter or something. Here they are. [*Hands him the book and the letter.*]

ANDREY. Thanks. That's all right. Incidentally, why have you come so late? It's gone eight already.

FERAPONT. What's that?

ANDREY [*raising his voice*]. I said, why have you come so late? It's gone eight already.

FERAPONT. That's right. It was still daylight when I came first, but they wouldn't let me see you. The master's engaged, they said. Well, if you're engaged, you're engaged. I'm not in a hurry. [*Thinking that* ANDREY *has said something.*] What's that?

ANDREY. Nothing. [*Turns over the pages of the register.*] Tomorrow's Friday, there's no meeting, but I'll go to the office just the same ... do some work. I'm so bored at home! ... [*A pause.*] Yes, my dear old fellow, how things do change, what a fraud life is! So strange! To-day I picked up this book, just out of boredom, because I hadn't anything to do. It's a copy of some lectures I attended at the University.... Good Heavens! Just think—I'm secretary of the local council now, and Protopopov's chairman, and the most I can ever hope for is to become a member of the council myself! I—a member of the local council! I, who dream every night that I'm a professor in Moscow University, a famous academician, the pride of all Russia!

FERAPONT. I'm sorry, I can't tell you. I don't hear very well.

ANDREY. If you could hear properly I don't think I'd be talking to you like this. I must talk to someone, but my wife doesn't seem to understand me, and as for my sisters ... I'm afraid of them for some reason or other, I'm afraid of them laughing at me and pulling my leg.... I don't drink and I don't like going to pubs, but my word! how I'd enjoy an hour or so at Tyestov's, or the Great Moscow Restaurant! Yes, my dear fellow, I would indeed!

FERAPONT. The other day at the office a contractor was telling me about some business men who were eating pancakes in Moscow. One of them ate forty pancakes and died. It was either forty or fifty, I can't remember exactly.

ANDREY. You can sit in some huge restaurant in Moscow without knowing anyone, and no one knowing you; yet somehow you don't feel that you don't belong there.... Whereas here you know everybody, and everybody knows you, and yet you don't feel you belong here, you feel you don't belong at all.... You're lonely and you feel a stranger.

FERAPONT. What's that? [*A pause.*] It was the same man that told me—of course, he may have been lying—he said that there's an enormous rope stretched right across Moscow.

ANDREY. Whatever for?

FERAPONT. I'm sorry, I can't tell you. That's what he said.

ANDREY. What nonsense! [*Reads the book.*] Have you ever been to Moscow?

FERAPONT [*after a pause*]. No. It wasn't God's wish. [*A pause.*] Shall I go now?

ANDREY. Yes, you may go. Good-bye. [FERAPONT *goes out.*] Good-bye. [*Reading.*] Come in the morning to take some letters.... You can go now. [*A pause.*] He's gone. [*A bell rings.*] Yes, that's how it is.... [*Stretches and slowly goes to his room.*]

[*Singing is heard off stage; a nurse is*

putting a baby to sleep. Enter
MASHA *and* VERSHININ. *While they
talk together, a maid lights a lamp
and candles in the ballroom.*]

MASHA. I don't know. [*A pause.*] I
don't know. Habit's very important, of
course. For instance, after Father died,
for a long time we couldn't get accustomed to the idea that we hadn't any or-
derlies to wait on us. But, habit apart, I
think it's quite right what I was saying.
Perhaps it's different in other places, but
in this town the military certainly do
seem to be the nicest and most generous
and best-mannered people.

VERSHININ. I'm thirsty. I could do
with a nice glass of tea.

MASHA [*glances at her watch*]. They'll
bring it in presently. You see, they married me off when I was eighteen. I was
afraid of my husband because he was a
school-master, and I had only just left
school myself. He seemed terribly learned
then, very clever and important. Now it's
quite different, unfortunately.

VERSHININ. Yes. . . . I see. . . .

MASHA. I don't say anything against
my husband—I'm used to him now—but
there are such a lot of vulgar and unpleasant and offensive people among the
other civilians. Vulgarity upsets me, it
makes me feel insulted, I actually suffer
when I meet someone who lacks refinement and gentle manners, and courtesy.
When I'm with the other teachers, my
husband's friends, I just suffer.

VERSHININ. Yes, of course. But I
should have thought that in a town like
this the civilians and the army people
were equally uninteresting. There's nothing to choose between them. If you talk
to any educated person here, civilian or
military, he'll generally tell you that he's
just worn out. It's either his wife, or his
house, or his estate, or his horse, or something. . . . We Russians are capable of
such elevated thoughts—then why do we
have such low ideals in practical life?
Why is it, why?

MASHA. Why?

VERSHININ. Yes, why does his wife
wear him out, why do his children wear
him out? And what about *him* wearing
out his wife and children?

MASHA. You're a bit low-spirited to-
day, aren't you?

VERSHININ. Perhaps. I haven't had any

dinner to-day. I've had nothing to eat
since morning. One of my daughters is a
bit off colour, and when the children are
ill, I get so worried. I feel utterly con-
science-stricken at having given them a
mother like theirs. Oh, if only you could
have seen her this morning! What a
despicable woman! We started quarrelling at seven o'clock, and at nine I just
walked out and slammed the door. [*A
pause.*] I never talk about these things
in the ordinary way. It's a strange thing,
but you're the only person I feel I dare
complain to. [*Kisses her hand.*] Don't be
angry with me. I've nobody, nobody but
you. . . . [*A pause.*]

MASHA. What a noise the wind's making in the stove! Just before Father died
the wind howled in the chimney just like
that.

VERSHININ. Are you superstitious?

MASHA. Yes.

VERSHININ. How strange. [*Kisses her
hand.*] You really are a wonderful creature, a marvellous creature! Wonderful,
marvellous! It's quite dark here, but I can
see your eyes shining.

MASHA [*moves to another chair*].
There's more light over here.

VERSHININ. I love you, I love you, I
love you. . . . I love your eyes, I love your
movements. . . . I dream about them. A
wonderful, marvellous being!

MASHA [*laughing softly*]. When you
talk to me like that, somehow I can't
help laughing, although I'm afraid at the
same time. Don't say it again, please.
[*Half-audibly.*] Well, no . . . go on. I
don't mind. . . . [*Covers her face with
her hands.*] I don't mind. . . . Someone's
coming. . . . Let's talk about something
else. . . .

[*Enter* IRENA *and* TOOZENBACH *through
the ballroom.*]

TOOZENBACH. I have a triple-bar-
relled name—Baron Toozenbach-Krone-
Alschauer—but actually I'm a Russian. I
was baptized in the Greek-Orthodox
faith, just like yourself. I haven't really
got any German characteristics, except
maybe the obstinate patient way I keep
on pestering you. Look how I bring you
home every evening.

IRENA. How tired I am!

TOOZENBACH. And I'll go on fetching
you from the post office and bringing you
home every evening for the next twenty

years—unless you send me away. . . .
[*Noticing* MASHA *and* VERSHININ, *with pleasure.*] Oh, it's you! How are you?

IRENA. Well, here I am, home at last! [*To* MASHA.] A woman came into the post office just before I left. She wanted to send a wire to her brother in Saratov to tell him her son had just died, but she couldn't remember the address. So we had to send the wire without an address, just to Saratov. She was crying and I was rude to her, for no reason at all. "I've no time to waste," I told her. So stupid of me. We're having the carnival crowd to-day, aren't we?

MASHA. Yes.

IRENA [*sits down*]. How nice it is to rest! I am tired!

TOOZENBACH [*smiling*]. When you come back from work, you look so young, so pathetic, somehow. . . . [*A pause.*]

IRENA. I'm tired. No, I don't like working at the post office, I don't like it at all.

MASHA. You've got thinner. . . . [*Whistles.*] You look younger, too, and your face looks quite boyish.

TOOZENBACH. It's the way she does her hair.

IRENA. I must look for another job. This one doesn't suit me. It hasn't got what I always longed for and dreamed about. It's the sort of work you do without inspiration, without even thinking.

[*Someone knocks at the floor from below.*]

That's the Doctor knocking. [*To* TOOZENBACH.] Will you answer him, dear? . . . I can't. . . . I'm so tired.

TOOZENBACH [*knocks on the floor*].

IRENA. He'll be up in a moment. We must do something about all this. Andrey and the Doctor went to the club last night and lost at cards again. They say Andrey lost two hundred roubles.

MASHA [*with indifference*]. Well, what are we to do about it?

IRENA. He lost a fortnight ago, and he lost in December, too. I wish to goodness he'd lose everything we've got, and soon, too, and then perhaps we'd move out of this place. Good Heavens, I dream of Moscow every night. Sometimes I feel as if I were going mad. [*Laughs.*] We're going to Moscow in June. How many months are there till June? . . . February, March, April, May . . . nearly half-a-year!

MASHA. We must take care that Natasha doesn't get to know about him losing at cards.

IRENA. I don't think she cares.

[*Enter* CHEBUTYKIN. *He has been resting on his bed since dinner and has only just got up. He combs his beard, then sits down at the table and takes out a newspaper.*]

MASHA. There he is. Has he paid his rent yet?

IRENA [*laughs*]. No. Not a penny for the last eight months. I suppose he's forgotten.

MASHA [*laughs*]. How solemn he looks sitting there!

[*They all laugh. A pause.*]

IRENA. Why don't you say something, Alexandr Ignatyevich?

VERSHININ. I don't know. I'm just longing for some tea. I'd give my life for a glass of tea! I've had nothing to eat since morning. . . .

CHEBUTYKIN. Irena Serghyeevna!

IRENA. What is it?

CHEBUTYKIN. Please come here. Venez ici! [IRENA *goes over to him and sits down at the table.*] I can't do without you.

[IRENA *lays out the cards for a game of patience.*]

VERSHININ. Well, if we can't have any tea, let's do a bit of philosophizing, anyway.

TOOZENBACH. Yes, let's. What about?

VERSHININ. What about? Well . . . let's try to imagine what life will be like after we're dead, say in two or three hundred years.

TOOZENBACH. All right, then. . . . After we're dead, people will fly about in balloons, the cut of their coats will be different, the sixth sense will be discovered, and possibly even developed and used, for all I know. . . . But I believe, life itself will remain the same; it will still be difficult and full of mystery and full of happiness. And in a thousand years' time people will still be sighing and complaining: "How hard this business of living is!"—and yet they'll still be scared of death and unwilling to die, just as they are now.

VERSHININ [*after a moment's thought*]. Well, you know . . . how shall I put it? I think everything in the world is bound to change gradually—in fact, it's changing before our very eyes. In two or three hundred years, or maybe in a thousand years —it doesn't matter how long exactly— life will be different. It will be happy. Of course, we shan't be able to enjoy that future life, but all the same, what we're living for now is to create it, we work and . . . yes, we suffer in order to create it. That's the goal of our life, and you might say that's the only happiness we shall ever achieve.

MASHA [laughs quietly].

TOOZENBACH. Why are you laughing?

MASHA. I don't know. I've been laughing all day to-day.

VERSHININ [to TOOZENBACH]. I went to the same cadet school as you did but I never went on to the Military Academy. I read a great deal, of course, but I never know what books I ought to choose, and probably I read a lot of stuff that's not worth anything. But the longer I live the more I seem to long for knowledge? My hair's going grey and I'm getting on in years, and yet how little I know, how little! All the same, I think I do know one thing which is not only true but also most important. I'm sure of it. Oh, if only I could convince you that there's not going to be any happiness for our own generation, that there mustn't be and won't be. . . . We've just got to work and work. All the happiness is reserved for our descendants, our remote descendants. [A pause.] Anyway, if I'm not to be happy, then at least my children's children will be.

[FEDOTIK and RODÉ enter the ballroom; they sit down and sing quietly, one of them playing on a guitar.]

TOOZENBACH. So you won't even allow us to dream of happiness! But what if I am happy?

VERSHININ. You're not.

TOOZENBACH [flinging up his hands and laughing]. We don't understand one another, that's obvious. How can I convince you?

MASHA [laughs quietly].

TOOZENBACH [holds up a finger to her]. Show a finger to her and she'll laugh! [To VERSHININ.] And life will be just the same as ever not merely in a couple of hundred years' time, but in a million years. Life doesn't change, it always goes on the same; it follows its own laws, which don't concern us, which we can't discover anyway. Think of the birds that migrate in the autumn, the cranes, for instance: they just fly on and on. It doesn't matter what sort of thoughts they've got in their heads, great thoughts or little thoughts, they just fly on and on, not knowing where or why. And they'll go on flying no matter how many philosophers they happen to have flying with them. Let them philosophize as much as they like, as long as they go on flying.

MASHA. Isn't there some meaning?

TOOZENBACH. Meaning? . . . Look out there, it's snowing. What's the meaning of that? [A pause.]

MASHA. I think a human being has got to have some faith, or at least he's got to seek faith. Otherwise his life will be empty, empty. . . . How can you live and not know why the cranes fly, why children are born, why the stars shine in the sky! . . . You must either know why you live, or else . . . nothing matters . . . everything's just wild grass. . . . [A pause.]

VERSHININ. All the same, I'm sorry my youth's over.

MASHA. "It's a bore to be alive in this world, friends," that's what Gogol says.

TOOZENBACH. And I feel like saying: it's hopeless arguing with you, friends! I give you up.

CHEBUTYKIN [reads out of the paper]. Balsac's marriage took place at Berdichev.[1]

IRENA [sings softly to herself].

CHEBUTYKIN. Must write this down in my notebook. [Writes.] Balsac's marriage took place at Berdichev. [Reads on.]

IRENA [playing patience, pensively]. Balsac's marriage took place at Berdichev.

TOOZENBACH. Well, I've thrown in my hand. Did you know that I'd sent in my resignation, Maria Serghyeevna?

MASHA. Yes, I heard about it. I don't see anything good in it, either. I don't like civilians.

TOOZENBACH. Never mind. [Gets up.] What sort of a soldier do I make, anyway? I'm not even good-looking. Well, what does it matter? I'll work. I'd like to do such a hard day's work that when I

[1] A town in Western Russia well known for its almost exclusively Jewish population.

came home in the evening I'd fall on my bed exhausted and go to sleep at once. [Goes to the ballroom.] I should think working men sleep well at nights!

FEDOTIK [to IRENA]. I've got you some coloured crayons at Pyzhikov's, in Moscow Street. And this little penknife, too. . . .

IRENA. You still treat me as if I were a little girl. I wish you'd remember I'm grown up now. [Takes the crayons and the penknife, joyfully.] They're awfully nice!

FEDOTIK. Look, I bought a knife for myself, too. You see, it's got another blade here, and then another . . . this thing's for cleaning your ears, and these are nail-scissors, and this is for cleaning your nails. . . .

RODÉ [in a loud voice]. Doctor, how old are you?

CHEBUTYKIN. I? Thirty-two.

[Laughter.]

FEDOTIK. I'll show you another kind of patience. [Sets out the cards.]

[The samovar is brought in, and AN-FISA attends to it. Shortly afterwards NATASHA comes in and begins to fuss around the table.]

SOLIONY [enters, bows to the company and sits down at the table].

VERSHININ. What a wind, though!

MASHA. Yes. I'm tired of winter! I've almost forgotten what summer is like.

IRENA [playing patience]. I'm going to go out. We'll get to Moscow!

FEDOTIK. No, it's not going out. You see, the eight has to go on the two of spades. [Laughs.] That means you won't go to Moscow.

CHEBUTYKIN [reads the paper]. Tzitzikar. Smallpox is raging. . . .

ANFISA [goes up to MASHA]. Masha, the tea's ready, dear. [To VERSHININ.] Will you please come to the table, your Excellency? Forgive me, your name's slipped my memory. . . .

MASHA. Bring it here, Nanny. I'm not coming over there.

IRENA. Nanny!

ANFISA. Comi-ing!

NATASHA [to SOLIONY]. You know, even tiny babies understand what we say perfectly well! "Good morning, Bobik," I said to him only to-day, "Good morning, my precious!"—and then he looked at me in such a special sort of way. You may

say it's only a mother's imagination, but it isn't, I do assure you. No, no! He really is an extraordinary child!

SOLIONY. If that child were mine, I'd cook him up in a frying pan and eat him. [Picks up his glass, goes into the drawing-room and sits down in a corner.]

NATASHA [covers her face with her hands]. What a rude, ill-mannered person!

MASHA. People who don't even notice whether it's summer or winter are lucky! I think I'd be indifferent to the weather if I were living in Moscow.

VERSHININ. I've just been reading the diary of some French cabinet minister—he wrote it in prison. He got sent to prison in connection with the Panama affair. He writes with such a passionate delight about the birds he can see through the prison window—the birds he never even noticed when he was a cabinet minister. Of course, now he's released he won't notice them any more. . . . And in the same way, you won't notice Moscow once you live there again. We're not happy and we can't be happy: we only want happiness.

TOOZENBACH [picks up a box from the table]. I say, where are all the chocolates?

IRENA. Soliony's eaten them.

TOOZENBACH. All of them?

ANFISA [serving VERSHININ with tea]. Here's a letter for you, Sir.

VERSHININ. For me? [Takes the letter.] From my daughter. [Reads it.] Yes, of course. . . . Forgive me, Maria Serghyeevna, I'll just leave quietly. I won't have any tea. [Gets up, agitated.] Always the same thing. . . .

MASHA. What is it? Secret?

VERSHININ [in a low voice]. My wife's taken poison again. I must go. I'll get away without them seeing me. All this is so dreadfully unpleasant. [Kisses MASHA's hand.] My dear, good, sweet girl. . . . I'll go out this way, quietly. . . . [Goes out.]

ANFISA. Where's he off to? And I've just brought him some tea! What a queer fellow!

MASHA [flaring up]. Leave me alone! Why do you keep worrying me? Why don't you leave me in peace? [Goes to the table, cup in hand.] I'm sick and tired of you, silly old woman!

ANFISA. Why. . . . I didn't mean to offend you, dear.

ANDREY'S VOICE [off stage]. Anfisa!

ANFISA [mimics him]. Anfisa! Sitting there in his den! . . . [Goes out.]

MASHA [by the table in the ballroom, crossly]. Do let me sit down somewhere! [Jumbles up the cards laid out on the table.] You take up the whole table with your cards! Why don't you get on with your tea?

IRENA. How bad-tempered you are, Mashka!

MASHA. Well, if I'm bad-tempered, don't talk to me, then. Don't touch me!

CHEBUTYKIN [laughs]. Don't touch her! . . . Take care you don't touch her!

MASHA. You may be sixty, but you're always gabbling some damn nonsense or other, just like a child. . . .

NATASHA [sighs]. My dear Masha, need you use such expressions? You know, with your good looks you'd be thought so charming, even by the best people—yes, I honestly mean it—if only you wouldn't use these expressions of yours! Je vous prie, pardonnez moi, Marie, mais vous avez des manières un peu grossières.

TOOZENBACH [with suppressed laughter]. Pass me . . . I say, will you please pass me. . . . Is that cognac over there, or what? . . .

NATASHA. Il parait que mon Bobik déjà ne dort pas. . . . I think he's awake. He's not been too well to-day. I must go and see him . . . excuse me. [Goes out.]

IRENA. I say, where has Alexandr Ignatyevich gone to?

MASHA. He's gone home. His wife's done something queer again.

TOOZENBACH [goes over to SOLIONY with a decanter of cognac]. You always sit alone brooding over something or other—though what it's all about nobody knows. Well, let's make it up. Let's have cognac together. [They drink.] I suppose I'll have to play the piano all night to-night—a lot of rubbishy tunes, of course. . . . Never mind!

SOLIONY. Why did you say "let's make it up"? We haven't quarrelled.

TOOZENBACH. You always give me the feeling that there's something wrong between us. You're a strange character, no doubt about it.

SOLIONY [recites]. "I am strange, but who's not so? Don't be angry, Aleko!"

TOOZENBACH. What's Aleko got to do with it? . . . [A pause.]

SOLIONY. When I'm alone with somebody I'm all right, I'm just like other people. But in company, I get depressed and shy, and . . . I talk all sorts of nonsense. All the same, I'm a good deal more honest and well-intentioned than plenty of others. I can prove I am.

TOOZENBACH. You often make me angry because you keep on pestering me when we're in company—but all the same, I do like you for some reason. . . . I'm going to get drunk to-night, whatever happens! Let's have another drink!

SOLIONY. Yes, let's. [A pause.] I've never had anything against you personally, Baron. But my temperament's rather like Lermontov's. [In a low voice.] I even look a little like Lermontov, I've been told. . . . [Takes a scent bottle from his pocket and sprinkles some scent on his hands.]

TOOZENBACH. I have sent in my resignation! Finished! I've been considering it for five years, and now I've made up my mind at last. I'm going to work.

SOLIONY [recites]. "Don't be angry, Aleko. . . . Away, away with all your dreams!"

[During the conversation ANDREY enters quietly with a book in his hand and sits down by the candle.]

TOOZENBACH. I'm going to work!

CHEBUTYKIN [comes into the drawing-room with IRENA]. And the food they treated me to was the genuine Caucasian stuff: onion soup, followed by chehartma—that's a meat dish, you know.

SOLIONY. Chereshma isn't meat at all; it's a plant, something like an onion.

CHEBUTYKIN. No-o, my dear friend. Chehartma isn't an onion, it's roast mutton.

SOLIONY. I tell you chereshma is a kind of onion.

CHEBUTYKIN. Well, why should I argue about it with you? You've never been to the Caucasus and you've never tasted chehartma.

SOLIONY. I haven't tasted it because I can't stand the smell of it. Chereshma stinks just like garlic.

ANDREY. [imploringly]. Do stop it, friends! Please stop it!

TOOZENBACH. When's the carnival crowd coming along?

IRENA. They promised to be here by nine—that means any moment now.

TOOZENBACH [*embraces* ANDREY *and sings*]. "Ah, my beautiful porch, my lovely new porch, my . . ."[2]

ANDREY [*dances and sings*]. "My new porch all made of maplewood. . . ."

CHEBUTYKIN [*dances*]. "With fancy carving over the door. . . ."

[*Laughter.*]

TOOZENBACH [*kisses* ANDREY]. Let's have a drink, the devil take it! Andriusha, let's drink to eternal friendship. I'll come with you when you go back to Moscow University.

SOLIONY. Which university? There are two universities in Moscow.

ANDREY. There's only one.

SOLIONY. I tell you there are two.

ANDREY. Never mind, make it three. The more the merrier.

SOLIONY. There are two universities in Moscow.

[*Murmurs of protest and cries of "Hush!"*]

There are two universities in Moscow, an old one and a new one. But if you don't want to listen to what I'm saying, if my conversation irritates you, I can keep silent. In fact I can go to another room. . . . [*Goes out through one of the doors.*]

TOOZENBACH. Bravo, bravo! [*Laughs.*] Let's get started, my friends, I'll play for you. What a funny creature that Soliony is! . . . [*Sits down at the piano and plays a waltz.*]

MASHA [*dances alone*]. The Baron is drunk, the Baron is drunk, the Baron is drunk. . . .

[*Enter* NATASHA.]

NATASHA [*to* CHEBUTYKIN]. Ivan Romanych! [*Speaks to him, then goes out quietly.* CHEBUTYKIN *touches* TOOZENBACH *on the shoulder and whispers to him.*]

IRENA. What is it?

CHEBUTYKIN. It's time we were going. Good-night.

IRENA. But really. . . . What about the carnival party?

ANDREY [*embarrassed*]. The carnival party's not coming. You see, my dear, Natasha says that Bobik isn't very well, and so . . . Anyway, I don't know . . . and certainly don't care. . . .

IRENA [*shrugs her shoulders*]. Bobik's not very well! . . .

MASHA. Never mind, we'll keep our end up! If they turn us out, out we must go! [*To* IRENA.] It isn't Bobik who's not well, it's her. . . . There! . . . [*Taps her forehead with her finger.*] Petty little bourgeois housewife!

[ANDREY *goes to his room on the right.* CHEBUTYKIN *follows him. The guests say good-bye in the ballroom.*]

FEDOTIK. What a pity! I'd been hoping to spend the evening here, but of course, if the baby's ill. . . . I'll bring him some toys to-morrow.

RODÉ [*in a loud voice*]. I had a good long sleep after lunch to-day on purpose, I thought I'd be dancing all night. I mean to say, it's only just nine o'clock.

MASHA. Let's go outside and talk it over. We can decide what to do then.

[*Voices are heard saying "Good-bye! God bless you!" and* TOOZENBACH *is heard laughing gaily. Everyone goes out.* ANFISA *and a maid clear the table and put out the lights. The nurse sings to the baby off stage. Enter* ANDREY, *wearing an overcoat and hat, followed by* CHEBUTYKIN. *They move quietly.*]

CHEBUTYKIN. I've never found time to get married, somehow . . . partly because my life's just flashed past me like lightning, and partly because I was always madly in love with your mother and she was married. . . .

ANDREY. One shouldn't marry. One shouldn't marry because it's so boring.

CHEBUTYKIN. That may be so, but what about loneliness? You can philosophize as much as you like, dear boy, but loneliness is a dreadful thing. Although, really . . . well, it doesn't matter a damn, of course! . . .

ANDREY. Let's get along quickly.

CHEBUTYKIN. What's the hurry? There's plenty of time.

ANDREY. I'm afraid my wife may try to stop me.

CHEBUTYKIN. Ah!

ANDREY. I won't play cards to-night, I'll just sit and watch. I'm not feeling too well. . . . What ought I to do for this breathlessness, Ivan Romanych?

CHEBUTYKIN. Why ask me, dear boy? I can't remember—I simply don't know.

ANDREY. Let's go through the kitchen.

[2] A traditional Russian dance-song.

[*They go out. A bell rings. The ring is repeated, then voices and laughter are heard.*]

IRENA [*coming in*]. What's that?

ANFISA [*in a whisper*]. The carnival party.

[*The bell rings again.*]

IRENA. Tell them there's no one at home, Nanny. Apologize to them.

[*ANFISA goes out. IRENA walks up and down the room, lost in thought. She seems agitated. Enter SOLIONY.*]

SOLIONY [*puzzled*]. There's no one here. . . . Where is everybody?

IRENA. They've gone home.

SOLIONY. How strange! Then you're alone here?

IRENA. Yes, alone. [*A pause.*] Well . . . good-night.

SOLIONY. I know I behaved tactlessly just now, I lost control of myself. But you're different from the others, you stand out high above them—you're pure, you can see where the truth lies. . . . You're the only person in the world who can possibly understand me. I love you. . . . I love you with a deep, infinite . . .

IRENA. Do please go away. Good-night!

SOLIONY. I can't live without you. [*Follows her.*] Oh, it's such a delight just to look at you! [*With tears.*] Oh, my happiness! Your glorious, marvellous, entrancing eyes—eyes like no other woman's I've ever seen. . . .

IRENA [*coldly*]. Please stop it, Vassily Vassilich!

SOLIONY. I've never spoken to you of my love before . . . it makes me feel as if I were living on a different planet. . . . [*Rubs his forehead.*] Never mind! I can't force you to love me, obviously. But I don't intend to have any rivals—successful rivals, I mean. . . . No, no! I swear to you by everything I hold sacred that if there's anyone else, I'll kill him. Oh, how wonderful you are!

[*Enter NATASHA carrying a candle.*]

NATASHA [*pokes her head into one room, then into another, but passes the door leading to her husband's room*]. Andrev's reading in there. Better let him read. Forgive me, Vassily Vassilich, I didn't know you were here. I'm afraid I'm not properly dressed.

SOLIONY. I don't care. Good-bye. [*Goes out.*]

NATASHA. You must be tired, my poor dear girl. [*Kisses IRENA.*] You ought to go to bed earlier.

IRENA. Is Bobik asleep?

NATASHA. Yes, he's asleep. But he's not sleeping peacefully. By the way, my dear, I've been meaning to speak to you for some time but there's always been something . . . either you're not here, or I'm too busy. . . . You see, I think that Bobik's nursery is so cold and damp. . . . And your room is just ideal for a baby. Darling, do you think you could move into Olga's room?

IRENA [*not understanding her*]. Where to?

[*The sound of bells is heard outside, as a "troika" is driven up to the house.*]

NATASHA. You can share a room with Olia for the time being, and Bobik can have your room. He is such a darling! This morning I said to him: "Bobik, you're my very own! My very own!" And he just gazed at me with his dear little eyes. [*The door bell rings.*] That must be Olga. How late she is!

[*A maid comes up to NATASHA and whispers in her ear.*]

NATASHA. Protopopov! What a funny fellow! Protopopov's come to ask me to go for a drive with him. In a troika! [*Laughs.*] Aren't these men strange creatures! . . .

[*The door bell rings again.*]

Someone's ringing. Shall I go for a short drive? Just for a quarter of an hour? [*To the maid.*] Tell him I'll be down in a minute. [*The door bell rings.*] That's the bell again. I suppose it's Olga. [*Goes out.*]

[*The maid runs out; IRENA sits lost in thought. Enter KOOLYGHIN and OLGA, followed by VERSHININ.*]

KOOLYGHIN. Well! What's the meaning of this? You said you were going to have a party.

VERSHININ. It's a strange thing. I left here about half an hour ago, and they were expecting a carnival party then.

IRENA. They've all gone.

KOOLYGHIN. Masha's gone, too? Where has she gone to? And why is Protopopov waiting outside in a troika? Who's he waiting for?

IRENA. Please don't ask me questions. I'm tired.

KOOLYGHIN. You . . . spoilt child!

OLGA. The conference has only just

ended. I'm quite worn out. The head-mistress is ill and I'm deputizing for her. My head's aching, oh, my head, my head. . . . [Sits down.] Andrey lost two hundred roubles at cards last night. The whole town's talking about it. . . .

KOOLYGHIN. Yes, the conference ex-hausted me, too. [Sits down.]

VERSHININ. So now my wife's taken it into her head to try to frighten me. She tried to poison herself. However, every-thing's all right now, so I can relax, thank goodness. . . . So we've got to go away? Well, good-night to you, all the best. Fiodor Illych, would you care to come along with me somewhere or other? I can't stay at home to-night, I really can't. . . . Do come!

KOOLYGHIN. I'm tired. I don't think I'll come. [Gets up.] I'm tired. Has my wife gone home?

IRENA. I think so.

KOOLYGHIN [kisses IRENA's hand]. Good-night. We can rest to-morrow and the day after to-morrow, two whole days! Well, I wish you all the best. [Going out.] How I long for some tea! I reckoned on spending the evening in congenial company, but—o, fallacem hominum spem! Always use the accusative case in exclamations.

VERSHININ. Well, it looks as if I'll have to go somewhere by myself.

[Goes out with KOOLYGHIN, whistling.]

OLGA. My head aches, oh, my head. . . . Andrey lost at cards . . . the whole town's talking. . . . I'll go and lie down. [Going out.] To-morrow I'm free. Heavens, what a joy! To-morrow I'm free, and the day after to-morrow I'm free. . . . My head's aching, oh, my poor head. . . .

IRENA [alone]. They've all gone. No one's left.

[Someone is playing an accordion in the street. The nurse sings in the next room.]

NATASHA [crosses the ballroom, wearing a fur coat and cap. She is followed by the maid]. I'll be back in half an hour. I'm just going for a little drive. [Goes out.]

IRENA [alone, with intense longing]. Moscow! Moscow! Moscow!

ACT III

[A bedroom now shared by OLGA and IRENA. There are two beds, one on the right, the other on the left, each screened off from the center of the room. It is past two o'clock in the morning. Off stage the alarm is being sounded on account of a fire which has been raging for some time. The inmates of the house have not yet been to bed. MASHA is lying on a couch, dressed, as usual, in black. OLGA and AN-FISA come in.]

ANFISA. Now they're sitting down there, under the stairs. . . . I keep telling them to come upstairs, that they shouldn't sit down there, but they just cry. "We don't know where our Papa is," they say, "perhaps he's got burned in the fire." What an idea! And there are people in the yard, too . . . half dressed. . . .

OLGA [takes a dress out of a wardrobe]. Take this grey frock, Nanny. . . . And this one. . . . This blouse, too. . . . And this skirt. Oh, Heavens! what is happening! Apparently the whole of the Kirsanovsky Street's been burnt down. . . . Take this . . . and this, too. . . . [Throws the clothes into ANFISA's arms.] The poor Vershinins had a fright. Their house only just es-caped being burnt down. They'll have to spend the night here . . . we mustn't let them go home. Poor Fedotik's lost every-thing, he's got nothing left. . . .

ANFISA. I'd better call Ferapont, Oliushka, I can't carry all this.

OLGA [rings]. No one takes any notice when I ring. [Calls through the door.] Is anyone there? Will someone come up, please!

[A window, red with the glow of fire, can be seen through the open door. The sound of a passing fire engine is heard.]

How dreadful it all is! And how tired of it I am! [Enter FERAPONT.] Take this downstairs please. . . . The Kolotilin girls are sitting under the stairs . . . give it to them. And this, too. . . .

FERAPONT. Very good, Madam. Mos-cow was burned down in 1812 just the same. Mercy on us! . . . Yes, the French were surprised all right.

OLGA. Go along now, take this down.

FERAPONT. Very good. [Goes out.]

OLGA. Give it all away, Nanny, dear. We won't keep anything, give it all away. . . . I'm so tired, I can hardly keep on my feet. We mustn't let the Vershinins go home. The little girls can sleep in the drawing-room, and Alexandr Ignatyevich can share the downstairs room with the Baron. Fedotik can go in with the Baron, too, or maybe he'd better sleep in the ballroom. The doctor's gone and got drunk—you'd think he'd done it on purpose; he's so hopelessly drunk that we can't let anyone go into his room. Vershinin's wife will have to go into the drawing-room, too.

ANFISA [wearily]. Don't send me away, Oliushka, darling! Don't send me away!

OLGA. What nonsense you're talking, Nanny! No one's sending you away.

ANFISA [leans her head against OLGA's breast]. My dearest girl! I do work, you know, I work as hard as I can. . . . I suppose now I'm getting weaker, I'll be told to go. But where can I go? Where? I'm eighty years old. I'm over eighty-one!

OLGA. You sit down for a while, Nanny. . . . You're tired, you poor dear. . . . [Makes her sit down.] Just rest a bit. You've turned quite pale.

[Enter NATASHA.]

NATASHA. They're saying we ought to start a subscription in aid of the victims of the fire. You know—form a society or something for the purpose. Well, why not? It's an excellent idea! In any case it's up to us to help the poor as best we can. Bobik and Sofochka are fast asleep as if nothing had happened. We've got such a crowd of people in the house; the place seems full of people whichever way you turn. There's 'flu about in the town. . . . I'm so afraid the children might catch it.

OLGA [without listening to her]. You can't see the fire from this room; it's quiet in here.

NATASHA. Yes. . . . I suppose my hair is all over the place. [Stands in front of the mirror.] They say I've got stouter, but it's not true! I'm not a bit stouter. Masha's asleep . . . she's tired, poor girl. . . . [To ANFISA, coldly.] How dare you sit down in my presence? Get up! Get out of here! [ANFISA goes out. A pause.] I can't understand why you keep that old woman in the house.

OLGA [taken aback]. Forgive me for saying it, but I can't understand how you . . .

NATASHA. She's quite useless here. She's just a peasant woman, her right

place is in the country. You're spoiling her. I do like order in the home, I don't like having useless people about. [Strokes OLGA's cheek.] You're tired, my poor dear! Our headmistress is tired! You know, when my Sofochka grows up and goes to school, I'll be frightened of you.

OLGA. I'm not going to be a head-mistress.

NATASHA. You'll be asked to, Olechka. It's settled.

OLGA. I'll refuse. I couldn't do it. . . . I wouldn't be strong enough. [Drinks water.] You spoke so harshly to Nanny just now. . . . You must forgive me for saying so, but I just can't stand that sort of thing . . . it made me feel quite faint. . . .

NATASHA [agitated]. Forgive me, Olia, forgive me. I didn't mean to upset you.

[MASHA gets up, picks up a pillow and goes out in a huff.]

OLGA. Please try to understand me, dear. . . . It may be that we've been brought up in a peculiar way, but anyway I just can't bear it. When people are treated like that, it gets me down, I feel quite ill. . . . I simply get un-nerved. . . .

NATASHA. Forgive me, dear, forgive me! . . . [Kisses her.]

OLGA. Any cruel or tactless remark, even the slightest discourtesy, upsets me. . . .

NATASHA. It's quite true, I know I often say things which would be better left unsaid—but you must agree with me, dear, that she'd be better in the country somewhere.

OLGA. She's been with us for thirty years.

NATASHA. But she can't do any work now, can she? Either I don't understand you, or you don't want to understand me. She can't work, she just sleeps or sits about.

OLGA. Well, let her sit about.

NATASHA [in surprise]. What do you mean, let her sit about? Surely she is a servant! [Tearfully.] No, I don't understand you, Olia! I have a nurse for the children and a wet nurse and we share a maid and a cook. Whatever do we want this old woman for? What for?

[The alarm is sounded again.]

OLGA. I've aged ten years to-night.

NATASHA. We must sort things out,

Olia. You're working at your school, and I'm working at home. You're teaching and I'm running the house. And when I say anything about the servants, I know what I'm talking about. . . . That old thief, that old witch must get out of this house to-morrow! . . . [*Stamps her feet.*] How dare you vex me so? How dare you? [*Recovering her self-control.*] Really, if you don't move downstairs, we'll always be quarrelling. This is quite dreadful!

[*Enter* KOOLYGHIN.]

KOOLYGHIN. Where's Masha? It's time we went home. They say the fire's getting less fierce. [*Stretches.*] Only one block got burnt down, but to begin with it looked as if the whole town was going to be set on fire by that wind. [*Sits down.*] I'm so tired, Olechka, my dear. You know, I've often thought that if I hadn't married Masha, I'd have married you, Olechka. You're so kind. I'm worn out. [*Listens.*]

OLGA. What is it?

KOOLYGHIN. The doctor's got drunk just as if he'd done it on purpose. Hopelessly drunk. . . . As if he'd done it on purpose. [*Gets up.*] I think he's coming up here. . . . Can you hear him? Yes, he's coming up. [*Laughs.*] What a fellow, really! . . . I'm going to hide myself. [*Goes to the wardrobe and stands between it and the wall.*] What a scoundrel!

OLGA. He's been off drinking for two years, and now suddenly he goes and gets drunk. . . . [*Walks with* NATASHA *towards the back of the room.*]

[CHEBUTYKIN *enters; walking firmly and soberly he crosses the room, stops, looks round, then goes to the wash-stand and begins to wash his hands.*]

CHEBUTYKIN [*glumly*]. The devil take them all . . . all the lot of them! They think I can treat anything just because I'm a doctor, but I know positively nothing at all. I've forgotten everything I used to know. I remember nothing, positively nothing. . . . [OLGA *and* NATASHA *leave the room without his noticing.*] The devil take them! Last Wednesday I attended a woman at Zasyp. She died, and it's all my fault that she did die. Yes. . . . I used to know a thing or two twenty-five years ago, but now I don't remember anything. Not a thing! Per-

haps I'm not a man at all, but I just imagine that I've got hands and feet and a head. Perhaps I don't exist at all, and I only imagine that I'm walking about and eating and sleeping. [*Weeps.*] Oh, if only I could simply stop existing! [*Stops crying, glumly.*] God knows. . . . The other day they were talking about Shakespeare and Voltaire at the club. . . . I haven't read either, never read a single line of either, but I tried to make out by my expression that I had. The others did the same. How petty it all is! How despicable! And then suddenly I thought of the woman I killed on Wednesday. It all came back to me, and I felt such a swine, so sick of myself that I went and got drunk. . . .

[*Enter* IRENA, VERSHININ *and* TOOZENBACH. TOOZENBACH *is wearing a fashionable new civilian suit.*]

IRENA. Let's sit down here for a while. No one will come in here.

VERSHININ. The whole town would have been burnt down but for the soldiers. They're a fine lot of fellows! [*Rubs his hands with pleasure.*] Excellent fellows! Yes, they're a fine lot!

KOOLYGHIN [*approaches them*]. What's the time?

TOOZENBACH. It's gone three. It's beginning to get light.

IRENA. Everyone's sitting in the ballroom and nobody thinks of leaving. That man Soliony there, too. . . . [*To* CHEBUTYKIN.] You ought to go to bed, Doctor.

CHEBUTYKIN. I'm all right. . . . Thanks. . . . [*Combs his beard.*]

KOOLYGHIN [*laughs*]. Half seas over, Ivan Romanych! [*Slaps him on the shoulder.*] You're a fine one! *In vino veritas*, as they used to say in Rome.

TOOZENBACH. Everyone keeps asking me to arrange a concert in aid of the victims of the fire.

IRENA. Well, who'd you get to perform in it?

TOOZENBACH. It could be done if we wanted to. Maria Serghyeevna plays the piano wonderfully well, in my opinion.

KOOLYGHIN. Yes, wonderfully well!

IRENA. She's forgotten how to. She hasn't played for three years . . . or maybe it's four.

TOOZENBACH. Nobody understands music in this town, not a single person. But

I do—I really do—and I assure you quite definitely that Maria Serghyeevna plays magnificently. She's almost a genius for it.

KOOLYGHIN. You're right, Baron. I'm very fond of Masha. She's such a nice girl.

TOOZENBACH. Fancy being able to play so exquisitely, and yet having nobody, nobody at all, to appreciate it!

KOOLYGHIN [sighs]. Yes. . . . But would it be quite proper for her to play in a concert? [A pause.] I don't know anything about these matters, my friends. Perhaps it'll be perfectly all right. But you know, although our director is a good man, a very good man indeed, and most intelligent, I know that he does hold certain views. . . . Of course, this doesn't really concern him, but I'll have a word with him about it, all the same, if you like.

CHEBUTYKIN [picks up a china clock and examines it].

VERSHININ. I've got my clothes in such a mess helping to put out the fire, I must look like nothing on earth. [A pause.] I believe they were saying yesterday that our brigade might be transferred to somewhere a long way away. Some said it was to be Poland, and some said it was Cheeta, in Siberia.

TOOZENBACH. I heard that, too. Well, the town will seem quite deserted.

IRENA. We'll go away, too!

CHEBUTYKIN [drops clock and breaks it]. Smashed to smithereens!

[A pause. Everyone looks upset and embarrassed.]

KOOLYGHIN [picks up the pieces]. Fancy breaking such a valuable thing! Ah, Ivan Romanych, Ivan Romanych! You'll get a bad mark for that!

IRENA. It was my mother's clock.

CHEBUTYKIN. Well, supposing it was. If it was your mother's, then it was your mother's. Perhaps I didn't smash it. Perhaps it only appears that I did. Perhaps it only appears to us that we exist, whereas in reality we don't exist at all. I don't know anything, no one knows anything. [Stops at the door.] Why are you staring at me? Natasha's having a nice little affair with Protopopov, and you don't see it. You sit here seeing nothing, and meanwhile Natasha's having a nice little affair with Protopopov.

. . . [Sings.] Would you like a date? . . . [Goes out.]

VERSHININ. So. . . . [Laughs.] How odd it all is, really. [A pause.] When the fire started, I ran home as fast as I could. When I got near, I could see that our house was all right and out of danger, but the two little girls were standing there, in the doorway in their night clothes. Their mother wasn't there. People were rushing about, horses, dogs . . . and in the kiddies' faces I saw a frightened, anxious, appealing look, I don't know what! . . . My heart sank when I saw their faces. My God, I thought, what will these children have to go through in the course of their poor lives? And they may live a long time, too! I picked them up and ran back here with them, and all the time I was running, I was thinking the same thing: what will they have to go through? [The alarm is sounded. A pause.] When I got here, my wife was here already . . . angry, shouting!

[Enter MASHA carrying a pillow; she sits down on the couch.]

VERSHININ. And when my little girls were standing in the doorway with nothing on but their night clothes, and the street was red with the glow of the fire and full of terrifying noises, it struck me that the same sort of thing used to happen years ago, when armies used to make sudden raids on towns, and plunder them and set them on fire. . . . Anyway, is there any essential difference between things as they were and as they are now? And before very long, say, in another two or three hundred years, people may be looking at our present life just as we look at the past now, with horror and scorn. Our own times may seem uncouth to them, boring and frightfully uncomfortable and strange. . . . Oh, what a great life it'll be then, what a life! [Laughs.] Forgive me, I'm philosophizing my head off again . . . but may I go on, please? I'm bursting to philosophize just at the moment. I'm in the mood for it. [A pause.] You seem as if you've all gone to sleep. As I was saying: what a great life it will be in the future! Just try to imagine it. . . . At the present time there are only three people of your intellectual calibre in the whole of this town, but future generations will be more productive of people like you. They'll go on producing more and more of the same sort until at last the time will come when everything will be just as you'd wish it yourselves. People will live their lives in your way, and then even you may be outmoded, and a new lot will come along who will be even better than you are.... [Laughs.] I'm in quite a special mood to-day. I feel full of a tremendous urge to live.... [Sings.]

"To Love all ages are in fee,
The passion's good for you and me." ...
[Laughs.]

MASHA [sings]. Tara-tara-tara. . . .
VERSHININ. Tum-tum. . . .
MASHA. Tara-tara . . .
VERSHININ. Tum-tum, tum-tum. . . .
[Laughs.]
[Enter FEDOTIK.]
FEDOTIK [dancing about]. Burnt, burnt! Everything I've got burnt!
[All laugh.]
IRENA. It's hardly a joking matter. Has everything really been burnt?
FEDOTIK [laughs]. Everything, completely. I've got nothing left. My guitar's burnt, my photographs are burnt, all my letters are burnt. Even the little note-book I was going to give you has been burnt.
[Enter SOLIONY.]
IRENA. No, please go away, Vassily Vassilich. You can't come in here.
SOLIONY. Can't I? Why can the Baron come in here if I can't?
VERSHININ. We really must go, all of us. What's the fire doing?
SOLIONY. It's dying down, they say. Well, I must say it's a peculiar thing that the Baron can come in here, and I can't. [Takes a scent bottle from his pocket and sprinkles himself with scent.]
VERSHININ. Tara-tara.
MASHA. Tum-tum, tum-tum.
VERSHININ [laughs, to SOLIONY]. Let's go to the ballroom.
SOLIONY. Very well, we'll make a note of this. "I hardly need to make my moral yet more clear: That might be teasing geese, I fear!" [3] [Looks at TOOZENBACH.] Cluck, cluck, cluck! [Goes out with VERSHININ and FEDOTIK.]
IRENA. That Soliony has smoked the

room out.... [Puzzled.] The Baron's asleep. Baron! Baron!
TOOZENBACH [waking out of his doze]. I must be tired. The brick-works.... No, I'm not talking in my sleep, I really do intend to go to the brick-works and start working there quite soon. I've had a talk with the manager. [To IRENA, tenderly.] You are so pale, so beautiful, so fascinating.... Your pallor seems to light up the darkness around you, as if it were luminous, somehow.... You're sad, you're dissatisfied with the life you have to live.... Oh, come away with me, let's go away and work together!
MASHA. Nikolai Lvovich, I wish you'd go away.
TOOZENBACH [laughs]. Oh, you're here, are you? I didn't see you. Kisses IRENA's hand.] Good-bye, I'm going. You know as I look at you now, I keep thinking of the day—it was a long time ago, your Saint's day—when you talked to us about the joy of work.... You were so gay and high-spirited then.... And what a happy life I saw ahead of me! Where is it all now? [Kisses her hand.] There are tears in your eyes. You should go to bed, it's beginning to get light ... it's almost morning.... Oh, if only I could give my life for you!
MASHA. Nikolai Lvovich, please go away! Really now. . . .
TOOZENBACH. I'm going. [Goes out.]
MASHA. [lies down]. Are you asleep, Fiodor?
KOOLYGHIN. Eh?
MASHA. Why don't you go home?
KOOLYGHIN. My darling Masha, my sweet, my precious Masha. . . .
IRENA. She's tired. Let her rest a while, Fyedia.
KOOLYGHIN. I'll go in a moment. My wife, my dear, good wife! . . . How I love you! . . . only you!
MASHA. [crossly]. Amo, amas, amat, amamus, amatis, amant!
KOOLYGHIN [laughs]. Really, she's an amazing woman!—I've been married to you for seven years, but I feel as if we were only married yesterday. Yes, on my word of honour, I do! You really are amazing! Oh, I'm so happy, happy, happy!

---

[3] From Krylov's fable Geese (translated by Bernard Pares).

MASHA. And I'm so bored, bored, bored! [*Sits up.*] I can't get it out of my head. . . . It's simply disgusting. It's like having a nail driven into my head. No, I can't keep silent about it any more. It's about Andrey. . . . He's actually mortgaged this house to a bank, and his wife's got hold of all the money—and yet the house doesn't belong to him, it belongs to all four of us! Surely, he must realize that, if he's got any honesty.

KOOLYGHIN. Why bring all this up, Masha? Why bother about it now? Andriusha owes money all round. . . . Leave him alone.

MASHA. Anyway, it's disgusting. [*Lies down.*]

KOOLYGHIN. Well, we aren't poor, Masha. I've got work, I teach at the county school, I give private lessons in my spare time. . . . I'm just a plain, honest man. . . . *Omnia mea mecum porto*, as they say.

MASHA. I don't ask for anything, but I'm just disgusted by injustice. [*A pause.*] Why don't you go home, Fiodor?

KOOLYGHIN [*kisses her*]. You're tired. Just rest here for a while. . . . I'll go home and wait for you. . . . Go to sleep. [*Goes to the door.*] I'm happy, happy, happy! [*Goes out.*]

IRENA. The truth is that Andrey is getting to be shallow-minded. He's aging and since he's been living with that woman he's lost all the inspiration he used to have! Not long ago he was working for a professorship, and yet yesterday he boasted of having at last been elected a member of the County Council. Fancy him a member, with Protopopov as chairman! They say the whole town's laughing at him, he's the only one who doesn't know anything or see anything. And now, you see, everyone's at the fire, while he's just sitting in his room, not taking the slightest notice of it. Just playing his violin. [*Agitated.*] Oh, how dreadful it is, how dreadful, how dreadful! I can't bear it any longer, I can't, I really can't! . . .

[*Enter* OLGA. *She starts arranging things on her bedside table.*]

IRENA [*sobs loudly*]. You must turn me out of here! Turn me out; I can't stand it any more!

OLGA [*alarmed*]. What is it? What is it, darling?

IRENA [*sobbing*]. Where. . . . Where has it all gone to? Where is it? Oh, God! I've forgotten. . . . I've forgotten everything . . . there's nothing but a muddle in my head. . . . I don't remember what the Italian for "window" is, or for "ceiling." . . . Every day I'm forgetting more and more, and life's slipping by, and it will never, never come back. . . . We shall never go to Moscow. . . . I can see that we shall never go. . . .

OLGA. Don't, my dear, don't. . . .

IRENA [*trying to control herself*]. Oh, I'm so miserable! . . . I can't work, I won't work! I've had enough of it, enough! . . . First I worked on the telegraph, now I'm in the County Council office, and I hate and despise everything they give me to do there. . . . I'm twenty-three years old, I've been working all this time, and I feel as if my brain's dried up. I know I've got thinner and uglier and older, and I find no kind of satisfaction in anything, none at all. And the time's passing . . . and I feel as if I'm moving away from any hope of a genuine, fine life, I'm moving further and further away and sinking into a kind of abyss. I feel in despair, and I don't know why I'm still alive, why I haven't killed myself. . . .

OLGA. Don't cry, my dear child, don't cry. . . . It hurts me.

IRENA. I'm not crying any more. That's enough of it. Look, I'm not crying now. Enough of it, enough! . . .

OLGA. Darling, let me tell you something. . . . I just want to speak as your sister, as your friend. . . . That is, if you want my advice. . . . Why don't you marry the Baron?

IRENA [*weeps quietly*].

OLGA. After all, you do respect him, you think a lot of him. . . . It's true, he's not good-looking, but he's such a decent, clean-minded sort of man. . . . After all, one doesn't marry for love, but to fulfil a duty. At least, I think so, and I'd marry even if I weren't in love. I'd marry anyone that proposed to me, as long as he was a decent man. I'd even marry an old man.

IRENA. I've been waiting all this time, imagining that we'd be moving to Moscow, and I'd meet the man I'm meant for there. I've dreamt about him and I've loved him in my dreams. . . . But it's all turned out to be nonsense... nonsense....

OLGA [*embracing her*]. My darling sweetheart, I understand everything perfectly. When the Baron resigned his commission and came to see us in his civilian clothes, I thought he looked so plain that I actually started to cry.... He asked me why I was crying.... How could I tell him? But, of course, if it were God's will that he should marry you, I'd feel perfectly happy about it. That's quite a different matter, quite different!

[NATASHA, *carrying a candle, comes out of the door on the right, crosses the stage and goes out through the door on the left without saying anything.*]

MASHA [*sits up*]. She goes about looking as if she'd started the fire.

OLGA. You're silly, Masha. You're the stupidest person in our family. Forgive me for saying so.

[*A pause.*]

MASHA. My dear sisters, I've got something to confess to you. I must get some relief, I feel the need of it in my heart. I'll confess it to you two alone, and then never again, never to anybody! I'll tell you in a minute. [*In a low voice.*] It's a secret, but you'll have to know everything. I can't keep silent any more. [*A pause.*] I'm in love, in love.... I love that man. ... You saw him here just now... Well, what's the good? ... I love Vershinin....

OLGA [*goes behind her screen*]. Don't say it. I don't want to hear it.

MASHA. Well, what's to be done? [*Holding her head.*] I thought he was queer at first, then I started to pity him ... then I began to love him ... love everything about him—his voice, his talk, his misfortunes, his two little girls....

OLGA. Nevertheless, I don't want to hear it. You can say any nonsense you like, I'm not listening.

MASHA. Oh, you're stupid, Olia! If I love him, well—that's my fate! That's my destiny.... He loves me, too. It's all rather frightening, isn't it? Not a good thing, is it? [*Takes* IRENA *by the hand and draws her to her.*] Oh, my dear! ... How are we going to live through the rest of our lives? What's going to become of us? When you read a novel, everything in it seems so old and obvious, but when you fall in love yourself, you suddenly discover that you don't really know anything, and you've got to make your own decisions.... My dear sisters, my dear sisters! ... I've confessed it all to you, and now I'll keep quiet.... I'll be like that madman in the story by Gogol —silence ... silence! ...

[*Enter* ANDREY *followed by* FERAPONT.]

ANDREY [*crossly*]. What do you want? I don't understand you.

FERAPONT [*stopping in the doorway, impatiently*]. I've asked you about ten times already, Andrey Serghyeevich.

ANDREY. In the first place, you're not to call me Andrey Serghyeevich—call me "Your Honour."

FERAPONT. The firemen are asking Your Honour if they may drive through your garden to get to the river. They've been going a long way round all this time —it's a terrible business!

ANDREY. All right. Tell them it's all right. [FERAPONT *goes out.*] They keep on plaguing me. Where's Olga? [OLGA *comes from behind the screen.*] I wanted to see you. Will you give me the key to the cupboard? I've lost mine. You know the key I mean, the small one you've got....

[OLGA *silently hands him the key.* IRENA *goes behind the screen on her side of the room.*]

ANDREY. What a terrific fire! It's going down though. That Ferapont annoyed me, the devil take him! Silly thing he made me say.... Telling him to call me "Your Honour"! ... [*A pause.*] Why don't you say anything, Olia? [*A pause.*] It's about time you stopped this nonsense ... sulking like this for no reason whatever.... You here, Masha? And Irena's here, too. That's excellent! We can talk it over then, frankly and once for all. What have you got against me? What is it?

OLGA. Drop it now, Andriusha. Let's talk it over to-morrow. [*Agitated.*] What a dreadful night!

ANDREY [*in great embarrassment*]. Don't get upset. I'm asking you quite calmly, what have you got against me? Tell me frankly.

VERSHININ'S VOICE [*off stage*]. Tumtum-tum!

MASHA [*in a loud voice, getting up*].

Tara-tara-tara! [*To* OLGA.] Good-bye, Olia, God bless you! [*Goes behind the screen and kisses* IRENA.] Sleep well. . . . Good-bye, Andrey. I should leave them now, they're tired . . . talk it over to-morrow. . . . [*Goes out.*]

OLGA. Really, Andriusha, let's leave it till to-morrow. . . . [*Goes behind the screen on her side of the room.*] It's time to go to bed.

ANDREY. I only want to say one thing, then I'll go. In a moment. . . . First of all, you've got something against my wife, against Natasha. I've always been conscious of it from the day we got married. Natasha is a fine woman, she's honest and straightforward and high-principled. . . . That's my opinion. I love and respect my wife. You understand that I respect her, and I expect others to respect her, too. I repeat: she's an honest, high-principled woman, and all your grievances against her—if you don't mind my saying so—are just imagination, and nothing more. . . . [*A pause.*] Secondly, you seem to be annoyed with me for not making myself a professor, and not doing any academic work. But I'm working in the Council Office, I'm a member of the County Council, and I feel my service there is just as fine and valuable as any academic work I might do. I'm a member of the County Council, and if you want to know, I'm proud of it! [*A pause.*] Thirdly . . . there's something else I must tell you. . . . I know I mortgaged the house without asking your permission. . . . That was wrong, I admit it, and I ask you to forgive me. . . . I was driven to it by my debts. . . . I'm in debt for about thirty-five thousand roubles. I don't play cards any more, I've given it up long ago. . . . The only thing I can say to justify myself is that you girls get an annuity, while I don't get anything . . . no income, I mean. . . . [*A pause.*]

KOOLYGHIN [*calling through the door*]. Is Masha there? She's not there? [*Alarmed.*] Where can she be then? It's very strange. . . . [*Goes away.*]

ANDREY. So you won't listen? Natasha is a good, honest woman, I tell you. [*Walks up and down the stage, then stops.*] When I married her, I thought we were going to be happy, I thought we should all be happy. . . . But . . . oh, my

God! . . . [*Weeps.*] My dear sisters, my dear, good sisters, don't believe what I've been saying, don't believe it. . . . [*Goes out.*]

KOOLYGHIN [*through the door, agitated*]. Where's Masha? Isn't Masha here? Extraordinary! [*Goes away.*]

[*The alarm is heard again. The stage is empty.*]

IRENA [*speaking from behind the screen*]. Olia! Who's that knocking on the floor?

OLGA. It's the doctor, Ivan Romanych. He's drunk.

IRENA. It's been one thing after another all night. [*A pause.*] Olia! [*Peeps out from behind the screen.*] Have you heard? The troops are being moved from the district . . . they're being sent somewhere a long way off.

OLGA. That's only a rumour.

IRENA. We'll be left quite alone then. . . . Olia!

OLGA. Well?

IRENA. Olia, darling, I do respect the Baron. . . . I think a lot of him, he's a very good man. . . . I'll marry him, Olia, I'll agree to marry him, if only we can go to Moscow! Let's go, please do let's go! There's nowhere in all the world like Moscow. Let's go, Olia! Let's go!

ACT IV

[*The old garden belonging to the Prozorovs' house. A river is seen at the end of a long avenue of fir-trees, and on the far bank of the river a forest. On the right of the stage there is a verandah with a table on which champagne bottles and glasses have been left. It is midday. From time to time people from the street pass through the garden to get to the river. Five or six soldiers march through quickly.*

CHEBUTYKIN, *radiating a mood of benevolence which does not leave him throughout the act, is sitting in a chair in the garden. He is wearing his army cap and is holding a walking stick, as if ready to be called away at any moment.* KOOLYGHIN, *with a decoration round his neck and with his moustache shaved off,* TOOZENBACH *and* IRENA *are standing on the verandah saying good-bye to* FEDOTIK *and*

RODÉ, *who are coming down the steps. Both officers are in marching uniform.*]

TOOZENBACH [*embracing* FEDOTIK]. You're a good fellow, Fedotik; we've been good friends! [*Embraces* RODÉ.] Once more, then.... Good-bye, my dear friends!

IRENA. Au revoir!

FEDOTIK. It's not "au revoir." It's good-bye. We shall never meet again!

KOOLYGHIN. Who knows? [*Wipes his eyes, smiling.*] There! you've made me cry.

IRENA. We'll meet some time.

FEDOTIK. Perhaps in ten or fifteen years' time. But then we'll hardly know one another.... We shall just meet and say, "How are you?" coldly.... [*Takes a snapshot.*] Wait a moment.... Just one more, for the last time.

RODÉ [*embraces* TOOZENBACH]. We're not likely to meet again.... [*Kisses* IRENA's *hand.*] Thank you for everything ... everything!

FEDOTIK [*annoyed*]. Do just wait a second!

TOOZENBACH. We'll meet again if we're fated to meet. Do write to us. Be sure to write.

RODÉ [*glancing round the garden*]. Good-bye, trees! [*Shouts.*] Heigh-ho! [*A pause.*] Good-bye, echo!

KOOLYGHIN. I wouldn't be surprised if you got married out there, in Poland.... You'll get a Polish wife, and she'll put her arms round you and say: Kohane![4] [*Laughs.*]

FEDOTIK [*glances at his watch*]. There's less than an hour to go. Soliony is the only one from our battery who's going down the river on the barge. All the others are marching with the division. Three batteries are leaving to-day by road and three more to-morrow—then the town will be quite peaceful.

TOOZENBACH. Yes, and dreadfully dull, too.

RODÉ. By the way, where's Maria Serghyeevna?

KOOLYGHIN. She's somewhere in the garden.

FEDOTIK. We must say good-bye to her.

RODÉ. Good-bye. I really must go, or

I'll burst into tears. [*Quickly embraces* TOOZENBACH *and* KOOLYGHIN, *kisses* IRENA's *hand.*] Life's been very pleasant here....

FEDOTIK [*to* KOOLYGHIN]. Here's something for a souvenir for you—a note-book with a pencil.... We'll go down to the river through here. [*They go off, glancing back.*]

RODÉ [*shouts*]. Heigh-ho!

KOOLYGHIN [*shouts*]. Good-bye!

[*At the back of the stage* FEDOTIK *and* RODÉ *meet* MASHA, *and say good-bye to her; she goes off with them.*]

IRENA. They've gone.... [*Sits down on the bottom step of the verandah.*]

CHEBUTYKIN. They forgot to say good-bye to me.

IRENA. Well, what about you?

CHEBUTYKIN. That's true. I forgot, too. Never mind, I'll be seeing them again quite soon. I'll be leaving to-morrow. Yes ... only one more day. And then, in a year's time I'll be retiring. I'll come back here and finish the rest of my life near you. There's just one more year to go and then I get my pension.... [*Puts a newspaper in his pocket and takes out another.*] I'll come back here and lead a reformed life. I'll be a nice, quiet, well-behaved little man.

IRENA. Yes, it's really time you reformed, my dear friend. You ought to live a different sort of life, somehow.

CHEBUTYKIN. Yes.... I think so, too. [*Sings quietly.*] Tarara-boom-di-ay.... I'm sitting on a tomb-di-ay....

KOOLYGHIN. Ivan Romanych is incorrigible! Incorrigible!

CHEBUTYKIN. Yes, you ought to have taken me in hand. You'd have reformed me!

IRENA. Fiodor's shaved his moustache off. I can't bear to look at him.

KOOLYGHIN. Why not?

CHEBUTYKIN. If I could just tell you what your face looks like now—but I daren't.

KOOLYGHIN. Well! Such are the conventions of life! *Modus vivendi,* you know. The director shaved his moustache off, so I shaved mine off when they gave me an inspectorship. No one likes it, but personally I'm quite indifferent. I'm content. Whether I've got a moustache or

[4] A Polish word meaning "beloved."

not, it's all the same to me. [*Sits down.*]

ANDREY [*passes across the back of the stage pushing a pram with a child asleep in it*].

IRENA. Ivan Romanych, my dear friend, I'm awfully worried about something. You were out in the town garden last night—tell me what happened there?

CHEBUTYKIN. What happened? Nothing. Just a trifling thing. [*Reads his paper.*] It doesn't matter anyway.

KOOLYGHIN. They say that Soliony and the Baron met in the town garden outside the theatre last night and . . .

TOOZENBACH. Don't please! What's the good? . . . [*Waves his hand at him deprecatingly and goes into the house.*]

KOOLYGHIN. It was outside the theatre. . . . Soliony started badgering the Baron, and he lost patience and said something that offended him.

CHEBUTYKIN. I don't know anything about it. It's all nonsense.

KOOLYGHIN. A school-master once wrote "nonsense" in Russian over a pupil's essay, and the pupil puzzled over it, thinking it was a Latin word. [*Laughs.*] Frightfully funny, you know! They say that Soliony's in love with Irena and that he got to hate the Baron more and more. . . . Well, that's understandable. Irena's a very nice girl. She's a bit like Masha, she tends to get wrapped up in her own thoughts. [*To* IRENA.] But your disposition is more easy-going than Masha's. And yet Masha has a very nice disposition, too. I love her, I love my Masha.

[*From the back of the stage comes a shout: "Heigh-ho!"*]

IRENA. [*starts*]. Anything seems to startle me to-day. [*A pause.*] I've got everything ready, too. I'm sending my luggage off after lunch. The Baron and I are going to get married to-morrow, and directly afterwards we're moving to the brick-works, and the day after to-morrow I'm starting work at the school. So our new life will begin, God willing! When I was sitting for my teacher's diploma, I suddenly started crying for sheer joy, with a sort of feeling of blessedness. . . . [*A pause.*] The carrier will be coming for my luggage in a minute. . . .

KOOLYGHIN. That's all very well, but somehow I can't feel that it's meant to be serious. All ideas and theories, but nothing really serious. Anyway, I wish you luck from the bottom of my heart.

CHEBUTYKIN [*moved*]. My dearest girl, my precious child! You've gone on so far ahead of me, I'll never catch you up now. I've got left behind like a bird which has grown too old and can't keep up with the rest of the flock. Fly away, my dears, fly away, and God be with you! [*A pause.*] It's a pity you've shaved off your moustache, Fiodor Illyich.

KOOLYGHIN. Don't keep on about it, please! [*Sighs.*] Well, the soldiers will be leaving to-day, and everything will go back to what it was before. Anyway, whatever they say, Masha is a good, loyal wife. Yes, I love her dearly and I'm thankful for what God has given me. Fate treats people so differently. For instance, there's an excise clerk here called Kozyrev. He was at school with me and he was expelled in his fifth year because he just couldn't grasp the *ut consecutivum*. He's dreadfully hard up now, and in bad health, too, and whenever I meet him, I just say to him: "Hullo, *ut consecutivum!*" "Yes," he replies, "that's just the trouble—*consecutivum*" . . . and he starts coughing. Whereas I—I've been lucky all my life. I'm happy, I've actually been awarded the order of Saint Stanislav, second class—and now I'm teaching the children the same old *ut consecutivum*. Of course, I'm clever, cleverer than plenty of other people, but happiness does not consist of merely being clever. . . .

[*In the house someone plays "The Maiden's Prayer."*]

IRENA. To-morrow night I shan't have to listen to "The Maiden's Prayer." I shan't have to meet Protopopov. . . . [*A pause.*] By the way, he's in the sitting-room. He's come again.

KOOLYGHIN. Hasn't our headmistress arrived yet?

IRENA. No, we've sent for her. If you only knew how difficult it is for me to live here by myself, without Olia! She lives at the school now; she's the headmistress and she's busy the whole day. And I'm here alone, bored, with nothing to do, and I hate the very room I live in. So I've just made up my mind—if I'm really not going to be able to live in Moscow, that's that. It's my fate, that's all. Nothing can be done about it. It's

God's will, everything that happens, and that's the truth. Nikolai Lvovich proposed to me. . . . Well, I thought it over, and I made up my mind. He's such a nice man, it's really extraordinary how nice he is. . . . And then suddenly I felt as though my soul had grown wings, I felt more cheerful and so relieved somehow that I wanted to work again. Just to start work! . . . Only something happened yesterday, and now I feel as though something mysterious is hanging over me. . . .

CHEBUTYKIN. Nonsense!

NATASHA [speaking through the window]. Our headmistress!

KOOLYGHIN. Our headmistress has arrived! Let's go indoors.

[Goes indoors with IRENA.]

CHEBUTYKIN [reads his paper and sings quietly to himself]. Tarara-boom-di-ay. . . . I'm sitting on a tomb-di-ay. . . .

[MASHA walks up to him; ANDREY passes across the back of the stage pushing the pram.]

MASHA. You look very comfortable sitting here. . . .

CHEBUTYKIN. Well, why not? Anything happening?

MASHA [sits down]. No, nothing. [A pause.] Tell me something. Were you in love with my mother?

CHEBUTYKIN. Yes, very much in love.

MASHA. Did she love you?

CHEBUTYKIN [after a pause]. I can't remember now.

MASHA. Is my man here? Our cook Marfa always used to call her policeman "my man." Is he here?

CHEBUTYKIN. Not yet.

MASHA. When you have to take your happiness in snatches, in little bits, as I do, and then lose it, as I've lost it, you gradually get hardened and bad-tempered. [Points at her breast.] Something's boiling over inside me, here. [Looking at ANDREY, who again crosses the stage with the pram.] There's Andrey, our dear brother. . . . All our hopes are gone. It's the same as when thousands of people haul a huge bell up into a tower. Untold labour and money is spent on it, and then suddenly it falls and gets smashed. Suddenly, without rhyme or reason. It was the same with Andrey. . . .

ANDREY. When are they going to settle down in the house? They're making such a row.

CHEBUTYKIN. They will soon. [Looks at his watch.] This is an old-fashioned watch: it strikes. . . . [Winds his watch which then strikes.] The first, second and fifth batteries will be leaving punctually at one o'clock. [A pause.] And I shall leave to-morrow.

ANDREY. For good?

CHEBUTYKIN. I don't know. I may return in about a year. Although, God knows . . . it's all the same. . . .

[The sounds of a harp and a violin are heard.]

ANDREY. The town will seem quite empty. Life will be snuffed out like a candle. [A pause.] Something happened yesterday outside the theatre; everybody's talking about it. I'm the only one that doesn't seem to know about it.

CHEBUTYKIN. It was nothing. A lot of nonsense. Soliony started badgering the Baron, or something. The Baron lost his temper and insulted him, and in the end Soliony had to challenge him to a duel. [Looks at his watch.] I think it's time to go. . . . At half-past twelve, in the forest over there, on the other side of the river. . . . Bang-bang! [Laughs.] Soliony imagines he's like Lermontov. He actually writes poems. But, joking apart, this is his third duel.

MASHA. Whose third duel?

CHEBUTYKIN. Soliony's.

MASHA. What about the Baron?

CHEBUTYKIN. Well, what about him? [A pause.]

MASHA. My thoughts are all in a muddle. . . . But what I mean to say is that they shouldn't be allowed to fight. He might wound the Baron or even kill him.

CHEBUTYKIN. The Baron's a good enough fellow, but what does it really matter if there's one Baron more or less in the world? Well, let it be! It's all the same. [The shouts of "Ah-oo!" and "Heigh-ho!" are heard from beyond the garden.] That's Skvortsov, the second, shouting from the boat. He can wait.

ANDREY. I think it's simply immoral to fight a duel, or even to be present at one as a doctor.

CHEBUTYKIN. That's only how it seems. . . . We don't exist, nothing exists, it only seems to us that we do. . . . And what difference does it make?

MASHA. Talk, talk, nothing but talk all day long! ... [Starts to go.] Having to live in this awful climate with the snow threatening to fall at any moment, and then on the top of it having to listen to all this sort of talk. ... [Stops.] I won't go into the house, I can't bear going in there. ... Will you let me know when Vershinin comes? ... [Walks off along the avenue.] Look, the birds are beginning to fly away already! [Looks up.] Swans or geese. ... Dear birds, happy birds. ... [Goes off.]

ANDREY. Our house will seem quite deserted. The officers will go, you'll go, my sister will get married, and I'll be left alone in the house.

CHEBUTYKIN. What about your wife?

[Enter FERAPONT with some papers.]

ANDREY. My wife is my wife. She's a good, decent sort of woman ... she's really very kind, too, but there's something about her which pulls her down to the level of an animal ... a sort of mean, blind, thick-skinned animal—anyway, not a human being. I'm telling you this as a friend, the only person I can talk openly to. I love Natasha, it's true. But at times she appears to me so utterly vulgar, that I feel quite bewildered by it, and then I can't understand why, for what reasons I love her—or, anyway, did love her.

CHEBUTYKIN [gets up]. Well, dear boy, I'm going away to-morrow and it may be we shall never see each other again. So I'll give you a bit of advice. Put on your hat, take a walking stick, and go away. ... Go away, and don't ever look back. And the further you go, the better.

[SOLIONY passes across the back of the stage accompanied by two officers. Seeing CHEBUTYKIN, he turns towards him, while the officers walk on.]

SOLIONY. It's time, Doctor. Half past twelve already. [Shakes hands with ANDREY.]

CHEBUTYKIN. In a moment. Oh, I'm tired of you all. [To ANDREY.] Andriusha, if anyone asks for me, tell them I'll be back presently. [Sighs.] Oh-ho-ho!

SOLIONY. "He had no time to say 'Oh, oh!' Before that bear had struck him low." ...

[Walks off with him.] What are you groaning about, old man?

CHEBUTYKIN. Oh, well!

SOLIONY. How do you feel?

CHEBUTYKIN [crossly]. Like a last year's bird's-nest.

SOLIONY. You needn't be so agitated about it, old boy. I shan't indulge in anything much, I'll just scorch his wings a little, like a woodcock's. [Takes out a scent bottle and sprinkles scent over his hands.] I've used up a whole bottle to-day, but my hands still smell. They smell like a corpse. [A pause.] Yes. ... Do you remember that poem of Lermontov's?

"And he, rebellious, seeks a storm,
As if in storms there were tranquillity." ...

CHEBUTYKIN. Yes.

"He had no time to say 'Oh, oh!'
Before that bear had struck him low."

[Goes out with SOLIONY. Shouts of "Heigh-ho!" and "Ah-oo!" are heard. Enter ANDREY and FERAPONT.]

FERAPONT. Will you sign these papers, please?

ANDREY [with irritation]. Leave me alone! Leave me alone, for Heaven's sake. [Goes off with the pram.]

FERAPONT. Well, what am I supposed to do with the papers then? They are meant to be signed, aren't they? [Goes to back of stage.]

[Enter IRENA and TOOZENBACH, the latter wearing a straw hat. KOOLYGHIN crosses the stage, calling: "Ah-oo! Masha! Ah-oo!"]

TOOZENBACH. I think he's the only person in the whole town who's glad that the army is leaving.

IRENA. That's quite understandable, really. [A pause.] The town will look quite empty.

TOOZENBACH. My dear, I'll be back in a moment.

IRENA. Where are you going?

TOOZENBACH. I must slip back to the town, and then ... I want to see some of my colleagues off.

IRENA. It's not true. ... Nikolai, why are you so absent-minded to-day? [A *pause*.] What happened outside the theatre last night?

TOOZENBACH [*with a movement of impatience*]. I'll be back in an hour. . . . I'll be back with you again. [*Kisses her hands*.] My treasure! . . .[*Gazes into her eyes*.] It's five years since I first began to love you, and still I can't get used to it, and you seem more beautiful every day. What wonderful, lovely hair! What marvellous eyes! I'll take you away tomorrow. We'll work, we'll be rich, my dreams will come to life again. And you'll be happy! But—there's only one "but," only one—you don't love me!

IRENA. I can't help that! I'll be your wife, I'll be loyal and obedient to you, but I can't love you. . . . What's to be done? [*Weeps*.] I've never loved anyone in my life. Oh, I've had such dreams about being in love! I've been dreaming about it for ever so long, day and night . . . but somehow my soul seems like an expensive piano which someone has locked up and the keys got lost. [*A pause*.] Your eyes are so restless.

TOOZENBACH. I was awake all night. Not that there's anything to be afraid of in my life, nothing threatening. . . . Only the thought of that lost key torments me and keeps me awake. Say something to me. . . . [*A pause*.] Say something!

IRENA. What? What am I to say? What?

TOOZENBACH. Anything.

IRENA. Don't, my dear, don't. . . . [*A pause*.]

TOOZENBACH. Such trifles, such silly little things sometimes become so important suddenly, for no apparent reason! You laugh at them, just as you always have done, you still regard them as trifles, and yet you suddenly find they're in control, and you haven't the power to stop them. But don't let us talk about all that! Really, I feel quite elated. I feel as if I was seeing those fir-trees and maples and birches for the first time in my life. They all seem to be looking at me with a sort of inquisitive look and waiting for something. What beautiful trees—and how beautiful, when you think of it, life ought to be with trees like these! [*Shouts of "Ah-oo! Heigh-ho!" are heard*.] I must go, it's time. . . . Look at that dead tree, it's all dried-up, but it's still swaying in the wind along with the others. And in the same way, it seems to me that, if I die, I shall still have a share in life somehow or other. Goodbye, my dear. . . . [*Kisses her hands*.] Your papers, the ones you gave me, are on my desk, under the calendar.

IRENA. I'm coming with you.

TOOZENBACH [*alarmed*]. No, no! [*Goes off quickly, then stops in the avenue*.] Irena!

IRENA. What?

TOOZENBACH [*not knowing what to say*]. I didn't have any coffee this morning. Will you tell them to get some ready for me? [*Goes off quickly*.]

[IRENA *stands, lost in thought, then goes to the back of the stage and sits down on a swing. Enter* ANDREY *with the pram;* FERAPONT *appears*.]

FERAPONT. Andrey Serghyeech, the papers aren't mine, you know, they're the office papers. I didn't make them up.

ANDREY. Oh, where has all my past life gone to?—the time when I was young and gay and clever, when I used to have fine dreams and great thoughts, and the present and the future were bright with hope? Why do we become so dull and commonplace and uninteresting almost before we've begun to live? Why do we get lazy, indifferent, useless, unhappy? . . . This town's been in existence for two hundred years; a hundred thousand people live in it, but there's not one who's any different from all the others! There's never been a scholar or an artist or a saint in this place, never a single man sufficiently outstanding to make you feel passionately that you wanted to emulate him. People here do nothing but eat, drink and sleep. . . . Then they die and some more take their places, and they eat, drink and sleep, too,—and just to introduce a bit of variety into their lives, so as to avoid getting completely stupid with boredom, they indulge in their disgusting gossip and vodka and gambling and law-suits. The wives deceive their husbands, and the husbands lie to their wives, and pretend they don't see anything and don't hear anything. . . . And all this overwhelming vulgarity and pettiness crushes the children and puts out any spark they might have in them, so that they, too, become miserable, half-dead creatures, just like one another and just like their parents! . . . [To FERAPONT, crossly.] What do you want?

FERAPONT. What? Here are the papers to sign.

ANDREY. What a nuisance you are!

FERAPONT [hands him the papers]. The porter at the finance department told me just now . . . he said last winter they had two hundred degrees of frost in Petersburg.

ANDREY. I hate the life I live at present, but oh! the sense of elation when I think of the future! Then I feel so light-hearted, such a sense of release! I seem to see light ahead, light and freedom. I see myself free, and my children, too,—free from idleness, free from kvass, free from eternal meals of goose and cabbage, free from after-dinner naps, free from all this degrading parasitism! . . .

FERAPONT. They say two thousand people were frozen to death. They say everyone was scared stiff. It was either in Petersburg or in Moscow, I can't remember exactly.

ANDREY [with sudden emotion, tenderly]. My dear sisters, my dear good sisters! [Tearfully.] Masha, my dear sister! . . .

NATASHA [through the window]. Who's that talking so loudly there? Is that you, Andriusha? You'll wake Sofochka. Il ne faut pas faire du bruit, la Sophie est dormie déjà. Vous êtes un ours. [Getting angry.] If you want to talk, give the pram to someone else. Ferapont, take the pram from the master.

FERAPONT. Yes, Madam. [Takes the pram.]

ANDREY [shamefacedly]. I was talking quietly.

NATASHA [in the window, caressing her small son]. Bobik! Naughty Bobik! Aren't you a naughty boy!

ANDREY [glancing through the papers]. All right, I'll go through them and sign them if they need it. You can take them back to the office later. [Goes into the house, reading the papers.]

[FERAPONT wheels the pram into the garden.]

NATASHA [in the window]. What's Mummy's name, Bobik? You darling! And who's that lady? Auntie Olia. Say: "Hullo, Auntie Olia."

[Two street musicians, a man and a girl, enter and begin to play on a violin and a harp; VERSHININ, OLGA and ANFISA come out of the house and listen in silence for a few moments; then IRENA approaches them.]

OLGA. Our garden's like a public road; everybody goes through it. Nanny, give something to the musicians.

ANFISA [giving them money]. Go along now, God bless you, good people! [The musicians bow and go away.] Poor, homeless folk! Whoever would go dragging round the streets playing tunes if he had enough to eat? [To Irena.] How are you Irenushka? [Kisses her.] Ah, my child, what a life I'm having! Such comfort! In a large flat at the school with Oliushka —and no rent to pay, either! The Lord's been kind to me in my old age. I've never had such a comfortable time in my life, old sinner that I am! A big flat, and no rent to pay, and a whole room to myself, with my own bed. All free. Sometimes when I wake up in the night I begin to think, and then—Oh, Lord! Oh, Holy Mother of God!—there's no one happier in the world than me!

VERSHININ [glances at his watch]. We shall be starting in a moment, Olga Serghyeevna. It's time I went. [A pause.] I wish you all the happiness in the world . . . everything. . . . Where's Maria Serghyeevna?

IRENA. She's somewhere in the garden. I'll go and look for her.

VERSHININ. That's kind of you. I really must hurry.

ANFISA. I'll come and help to look for her. [Calls out.] Mashenka, ah-oo! [Goes with IRENA towards the far end of the garden.] Ah-oo! Ah-oo!

VERSHININ. Everything comes to an end. Well, here we are—and now it's going to be "good-bye." [Looks at his watch.] The city gave us a sort of farewell lunch. There was champagne, and the mayor made a speech, and I ate and listened, but in spirit I was with you here. . . . [Glances round the garden.] I've grown so . . . so accustomed to you.

OLGA. Shall we meet again some day, I wonder?

VERSHININ. Most likely not! [A pause.] My wife and the two little girls will be staying on here for a month or two. Please, if anything happens, if they need anything. . . .

OLGA. Yes, yes, of course. You needn't worry about that. [A pause.] To-morrow there won't be a single officer or soldier in the town. . . . All that will be just a memory, and, of course, a new life will begin for us here. . . . [A pause.] Nothing ever happens as we'd like it to. I didn't want to be a headmistress, and yet now I am one. It means we shan't be going to live in Moscow. . . .

VERSHININ. Well. . . . Thank you for everything. Forgive me if ever I've done anything. . . . I've talked a lot too much, far too much. . . . Forgive me for that, don't think too unkindly of me.

OLGA [wipes her eyes]. Now . . . why is Masha so long coming?

VERSHININ. What else can I tell you now it's time to say "good-bye"? What shall I philosophize about now? . . . [Laughs.] Yes, life is difficult. It seems quite hopeless for a lot of us, just a kind of impasse. . . . And yet you must admit that it is gradually getting easier and brighter, and it's clear that the time isn't far off when the light will spread everywhere. [Looks at his watch.] Time, it's time for me to go. . . . In the old days the human race was always making war, its entire existence was taken up with campaigns, advances, retreats, victories. . . . But now all that's out of date, and in its place there's a huge vacuum, clamouring to be filled. Humanity is passionately seeking something to fill it with and, of course, it will find something some day. Oh! If only it would happen soon! [A pause.] If only we could educate the industrious people and make the educated people industrious. . . . [Looks at his watch.] I really must go. . . .

OLGA. Here she comes!

[Enter MASHA.]

VERSHININ. I've come to say good-bye. . . .

[OLGA walks off and stands a little to one side so as not to interfere with their leave-taking.]

MASHA [looking into his face]. Good-bye! . . . [A long kiss.]

OLGA. That'll do, that'll do.

MASHA [sobs loudly].

VERSHININ. Write to me. . . . Don't forget me! Let me go . . . it's time. Olga Serghyeevna, please take her away . . . I must go . . . I'm late already. . . . [Deeply moved, kisses OLGA's hands, then embraces MASHA once again and goes out quickly.]

OLGA. That'll do, Masha! Don't, my dear, don't. . . .

[Enter KOOLYGHIN.]

KOOLYGHIN [embarrassed]. Never mind, let her cry, let her. . . . My dear Masha, my dear, sweet Masha. . . . You're my wife, and I'm happy in spite of everything. . . . I'm not complaining, I've no reproach to make—not a single one. . . . Olga here is my witness. . . . We'll start our life over again in the same old way, and you won't hear a word from me . . . not a hint. . . .

MASHA [suppressing her sobs]. "A green oak grows by a curving shore, And round that oak hangs a golden chain." . . . "A golden chain round that oak." . . . Oh, I'm going mad. . . . By a curving shore . . . a green oak. . . .

OLGA. Calm yourself, Masha, calm yourself. . . . Give her some water.

MASHA. I'm not crying any more. . . .

KOOLYGHIN. She's not crying any more . . . she's a good girl.

[The hollow sound of a gun-shot is heard in the distance.]

MASHA. "A green oak grows by a curving shore, And round that oak hangs a golden chain." . . . A green cat . . . a green oak . . . I've got it all mixed up. . . . [Drinks water.] My life's messed up. . . . I don't want anything now. . . . I'll calm down in a moment . . . it doesn't matter. . . . What is "the curving shore"? Why does it keep coming into my head all the time? My thoughts are all mixed up.

[Enter IRENA.]

OLGA. Calm down, Masha. That's right . . . good girl! . . . Let's go indoors.

MASHA [irritably]. I'm not going in there! [Sobs, but immediately checks herself.] I don't go into that house now, and I'm not going to. . . .

IRENA. Let's sit down together for a moment, and not talk about anything. I'm going away to-morrow, you know. . . . [A pause.]

KOOLYGHIN. Yesterday I took away a false beard and a moustache from a boy in the third form. I've got them here. [Puts them on.] Do I look like our German teacher? . . . [Laughs.] I do, don't I? The boys are funny.

MASHA. It's true, you do look like that German of yours.

OLGA. [laughs]. Yes, he does.

[MASHA cries.]

IRENA. That's enough, Masha!

KOOLYGHIN. Very much like him, I think!

[Enter NATASHA.]

NATASHA [to the maid]. What? Oh, yes. Mr. Protopopov is going to keep an eye on Sofochka, and Andrey Serghyeevich is going to take Bobik out in the pram. What a lot of work these children make! . . . [To IRENA.] Irena, you're really leaving to-morrow? What a pity! Do stay just another week, won't you? [Catching sight of KOOLYGHIN, shrieks; he laughs and takes off the false beard and moustache.] Get away with you! How you scared me! [To IRENA.] I've grown so accustomed to you being here. . . . You mustn't think it's going to be easy for me to be without you. I'll get Andrey and his old violin to move into your room: he can saw away at it as much as he likes there. And then we'll move Sofochka into his room. She's such a wonderful child, really! Such a lovely little girl! This morning she looked at me with such a sweet expression, and then she said: "Ma-mma!"

KOOLYGHIN. It's quite true, she is a beautiful child.

NATASHA. So to-morrow I'll be alone here. [Sighs.] I'll have this fir-tree avenue cut down first, then that maple tree over there. It looks so awful in the evenings. . . . [To IRENA.] My dear, that belt you're wearing doesn't suit you at all. Not at all in good taste. You want something brighter to go with that dress. . . . I'll tell them to put flowers all round here, lots of flowers, so that we get plenty of scent from them. . . . [Sternly.] Why is there a fork lying on this seat? [Going into the house, to the maid.] Why is that fork left on the seat there? [Shouts.] Don't answer me back!

KOOLYGHIN. There she goes again.

[A band plays a military march off stage; all listen.]

OLGA. They're going.

[Enter CHEBUTYKIN.]

MASHA. The soldiers are going. Well. . . . Happy journey to them! [To her husband.] We must go home. . . . Where's my hat and cape? . . .

KOOLYGHIN. I took them indoors. I'll bring them at once.

OLGA. Yes, we can go home now. It's time.

CHEBUTYKIN. Olga Serghyeevna!

OLGA. What is it? [A pause.] What?

CHEBUTYKIN. Nothing. . . . I don't know quite how to tell you. . . . [Whispers into her ear.]

OLGA [frightened]. It can't be true!

CHEBUTYKIN. Yes . . . a bad business. . . . I'm so tired . . . quite worn out. . . . I don't want to say another word. . . . [With annoyance.] Anyway, nothing matters! . . .

MASHA. What's happened?

OLGA [puts her arms round IRENA]. What a dreadful day! . . . I don't know how to tell you, dear. . . .

IRENA. What is it? Tell me quickly, what is it? For Heaven's sake! . . . [Cries.]

CHEBUTYKIN. The Baron's just been killed in a duel.

IRENA [cries quietly]. I knew it, I knew it. . . .

CHEBUTYKIN [goes to the back of the stage and sits down]. I'm tired. . . . [Takes a newspaper out of his pocket.] Let them cry for a bit. . . . [Sings quietly to himself.] Tarara-boom-di-ay, I'm sitting on a tomb-di-ay. . . . What difference does it make? . . .

[The three sisters stand huddled together.]

MASHA. Oh, listen to that band! They're leaving us . . . one of them's gone for good . . . for ever! We're left alone . . . to start our lives all over again. We must go on living . . . we must go on living. . . .

IRENA [puts her head on OLGA's breast]. Some day people will know why such things happen, and what the purpose of all this suffering is. . . . Then there won't be any more riddles. . . . Meanwhile we must go on living . . . and working. Yes, we must just go on working! To-morrow I'll go away alone and teach in a school somewhere; I'll give my life to people who need it. . . . It's autumn now, winter will soon be here, and the snow will cover everything . . . but I'll go on working and working! . . .

OLGA [puts her arms round both her sisters]. How cheerfully and jauntily that band's playing—really I feel as if I wanted to live! Merciful God! The years will pass, and we shall all be gone for good and quite forgotten. . . . Our faces and our voices will be forgotten and people won't even know that there were once three of us here. . . . But our sufferings may mean happiness for the people who come after us. . . . There'll be a time when peace and happiness reign in the world, and then we shall be remembered kindly and blessed. No, my dear sisters, life isn't finished for us yet! We're going to live! The band is playing so cheerfully and joyfully—maybe, if we wait a little longer, we shall find out why we live, why we suffer. . . . Oh, if we only knew, if only we knew!

[*The music grows fainter and fainter.* KOOLYGHIN, *smiling happily, brings out the hat and the cape.* ANDREY *enters; he is pushing the pram with* BOBIK *sitting in it.*]

CHEBUTYKIN [*sings quietly to himself*]. Tarara-boom-di-ay. . . . I'm sitting on a tomb-di-ay. . . . [*Reads the paper.*] What does it matter? Nothing matters!

OLGA. If only we knew, if only we knew! . . .

Maxim Gorky

ANTON CHEKHOV

He once invited me to visit him in the village of Kuchuk-Koi, where he had a tiny plot of ground and a white, two-storey house. He showed me over his "estate," talking animatedly all the time:

> If I had lots of money I would build a sanitorium here for sick village teachers. A building full of light, you know, very light, with big windows and high ceilings. I'd have a splendid library, all sorts of musical instruments, an apiary, a vegetable garden, an orchard. I'd have lectures on agronomy, meteorology, and so on—teachers ought to know everything, old man—everything!

He broke off suddenly, coughed, cast an oblique glance at me, and smiled his sweet, gentle smile, a smile which had an irresistible charm, forcing one to follow his words with the keenest attention.

> Does it bore you to listen to my dreams? I love talking about this. If you only knew the absolute necessity for the Russian countryside of good, clever, educated teachers! In Russia we have simply got to create exceptional conditions for teachers, and that as soon as possible, since we realize that unless the people get an all-round education the state will collapse like a house built from insufficiently baked bricks. The teacher must be an actor, an artist, passionately in love with his work, and our teachers are navvies, half-educated individuals, who go to the village to teach children about as willingly as they would go to exile. They are famished, downtrodden, they live in perpetual fear of losing their livelihood. And the teacher ought to be the first man in the village, able to answer all the questions put to him by the peasants, to instil in the peasants a respect for his power worthy of attention and respect, whom no one will

dare to shout at . . . to lower his dignity, as in our country everybody does—the village policeman, the rich shopkeeper, the priest, the school patron, the elder and that official who, though he is called a school inspector, busies himself, not over the improvement of conditions for education, but simply and solely over the carrying out of district circulars to the letter. It's absurd to pay a niggardly pittance to one who is called upon to educate the people—to educate the people, mind! It is intolerable that such a one should go about in rags, shiver in a damp, dilapidated school, be poisoned by fumes from badly ventilated stoves, be always catching cold, and by the age of thirty be a mass of disease—laryngitis, rheumatism, tuberculosis. It's a disgrace to us! For nine or ten months in the year our teachers live the lives of hermits, without a soul to speak to, they grow stupid from loneliness, without books or amusements. And if they venture to invite friends to come and see them, people think they are disaffected —that idiotic word with which cunning folk terrify fools. . . . All this is disgusting . . . a kind of mockery of human beings doing a great and terribly important work. I tell you, when I meet a teacher I feel quite awkward in front of him—for his timidity, and his shabbiness. I feel as if I myself were somehow to blame for the teacher's wretched state—I do, really!

Pausing for a moment, he threw out his arm and said softly:

"What an absurd, clumsy country our Russia is!"

A shadow of profound sorrow darkened his fine eyes, and a fine network of wrinkles showed at the corners, deepening his glance. He looked around him and began making fun of himself.

"There you are—I've treated you to a

SOURCE: From *Literary Portraits* in *On Literature* by Maxim Gorky. Moscow: Foreign Languages Publishing House, n.d.

full-length leading article from a liberal newspaper. Come on, I'll give you some tea as a reward for your patience. . . ."

This was often the way with him. One moment he would be talking with warmth, gravity and sincerity, and the next, he would be laughing at himself and his own words. And beneath this gentle, sorrowful laughter could be felt the subtle scepticism of a man who knew the value of words, the value of dreams. There was a shade of his attractive modesty, his intuitive delicacy in this laughter, too.

We walked back to the house in silence. It was a warm, bright day; the sound of waves sparkling in the vivid rays of the sun, could be heard. In the valley, a dog was squealing its delight about something. Chekhov took me by the arm and said slowly, his speech interrupted by coughs:

"It's disgraceful and very sad, but it is true—there are many people who envy dogs. . . ."

And then he added, laughing:

"Everything I say today sounds senile —I must be getting old." . . .

It seems to me that in the presence of Anton Pavlovich everyone felt an unconscious desire to be simpler, more truthful, more himself, and I had many opportunities of observing how people threw off their attire of grand bookish phrases, fashionable expressions, and all the rest of the cheap trifles with which Russians, in their anxiety to appear Europeans, adorn themselves, as savages deck themselves with shells and fishes' teeth. Anton Pavlovich was not fond of fishes' teeth and cocks' feathers; all that is tawdry, tinkling, alien, donned by human beings for the sake of an "imposing appearance," embarrassed him, and I noticed that whenever he met with one of these dressed-up individuals he felt an overmastering impulse to free him from his ponderous and superfluous trappings, distorting the true face and living soul of his interlocutor. All his life Anton Pavlovich lived the life of the soul, was always himself, inwardly free, and took no notice of what some expected, and others—less delicate—demanded of Anton Chekhov. He did not like conversations on "lofty" subjects—conversations which Russians,

in the simplicity of their hearts, find so amusing, forgetting that it is absurd, and not in the least witty, to talk about the velvet apparel of the future, while not even possessing in the present a decent pair of trousers.

Of a beautiful simplicity himself, he loved all that was simple, real, sincere, and he had a way of his own of making others simple. . . .

He had the art of exposing vulgarity everywhere, an art which can only be mastered by one whose own demands on life are very high, and which springs from the ardent desire to see simplicity, beauty and harmony in man. He was a severe and merciless judge of vulgarity.

Someone said in his presence that the editor of a popular magazine, a man perpetually talking about the necessity for love and sympathy for others, had insulted a railway guard without the slightest provocation, and was in the habit of treating his subordinates roughly.

"Naturally," said Anton Pavlovich, with a grim chuckle. "He's an aristocrat, a cultivated man . . . he went to a seminary. His father went about in bast shoes, but *he* wears patent leather boots."

And the tone in which these words were spoken at once dismissed the "aristocrat" as a mediocre and ridiculous individual.

"A very gifted person," he said of a certain journalist. "His writing is always so lofty, so humane . . . saccharine. He calls his wife a fool in front of people. His servants sleep in a damp room, and they all develop rheumatism. . . ."

"Do you like So-and-So, Anton Pavlovich?"

"Oh, yes. A nice man," replies Anton Pavlovich, coughing. "He knows everything. He reads a lot. He took three books of mine and never returned them. A bit absent-minded, tells you one day that you're a fine fellow, and the next tells someone else that you stole the black silk socks with blue stripes of your mistress's husband." . . .

A subtle mockery almost always twinkled gently in his grey mournful eyes, but occasionally these eyes would become cold, keen, harsh, and at such moments a hard note would creep into the smooth, cordial tones of his voice, and then I felt that this modest, kindly man could stand up against any hostile force, stand up firmly, without knuckling under to it.

It sometimes seemed to me that there was a shade of hopelessness in his attitude to others, something akin to a cold, still despair.

"The Russian is a strange being," he said once.

He is like a sieve, he can hold nothing for long. In his youth he crams himself eagerly with everything that comes his way, and by the time he is thirty nothing is left of it all but a heap of colourless rubbish. If one wants to lead a good life, a human life, one must work. Work with love and with faith. And we don't know how to do that in our country. An architect, having built two or three decent houses, sits down to play cards for the rest of his life or hangs about the backstage of a theatre. As soon as a doctor acquires a practice he stops keeping up with science, never reads anything but *Novosti Terapii* (*Therapeutical News*) and by the age of forty is firmly convinced that all diseases come from colds. I have never met a single official who had even the slightest idea of the significance of his work—they usually dig themselves in in the capital, or some provincial town, and invent papers which they dispatch to Zmiyev and Smorgon for fulfilment. And whose freedom of movement is impeded in Zmiyev or Smorgon by these documents the official no more cares than an atheist does about the torments of hell. Having made a name by a successful defence the barrister ceases to bother about the defence of truth and does nothing but defend the rights of property, put money on horses, eat oysters, and pass himself off as a connoisseur of all the arts. An actor, having performed two or three parts with fair success, no longer learns his parts, but puts on a top hat and considers himself a genius. Russia is a land of greedy idlers. People eat and drink enormously, love to sleep in the daytime, and snore in their sleep. They marry for the sake of order in their homes, and take a mistress for the sake of social prestige. Their psychology is a dog's psychology. Beat them and they squeal meekly and sneak off to their kennels. Caress them, and they lie on their backs with their paws up, wagging their tails.

A cold, sorrowful contempt underlay these words. But while despising, he could pity, and when anyone was abused in his presence, Anton Pavlovich was sure to stick up for him.

"Come now! He's an old man, he's seventy. . . ."

Or:

"He's still young, it's just his stupidity. . . ."

And when he spoke like this I could see no signs of disgust in his face. . . .

When one is young, vulgarity seems to be simply amusing and insignificant, but it gradually surrounds the individual, its grey mist creeping into his brains and blood, like poison or charcoal fumes, till he becomes like an old tavern-sign, eaten up with rust—there seems to be something depicted on it, but what, it is impossible to make out.

From the very first Anton Pavlovich managed to reveal, in the grey ocean of vulgarity, its tragically sombre jokes. One only has to read his "humorous" stories carefully, to realize how much that was cruel was seen and shamefacedly concealed by the author in comic narrative and situations.

He had an almost virginal modesty, he could never bring himself to challenge people loudly and openly: "Be more decent—can't you!" vainly trusting that they would themselves realize the urgent necessity for being more decent. Detesting all that was vulgar and unclean, he described the seamy side of life in the lofty language of the poet, with the gentle smile of the humorist, and the bitter inner reproach beneath the polished surface of his stories is scarcely noticeable. . . .

No one ever understood the tragic nature of life's trifles so clearly and intuitively as Chekhov did, never before has a writer been able to hold up to human beings such a ruthlessly truthful picture of all that was shameful and pitiable in the dingy chaos of middle-class life.

His enemy was vulgarity. All his life he fought against it, held it up to scorn, depicted it with a keen impartial pen, discovering the fungus of vulgarity even where, at first glance, everything seemed to be ordered for the best, the most convenient, and even brilliant. And vulgarity got back on him with an ugly trick when his dead body—the body of a poet—was sent to Moscow in an oyster wagon.

This dingy green wagon strikes me as the broad triumphant grin of vulgarity at its weary foe, and the innumerable "reminiscences" of the yellow press—mere hypocritical grief, behind which I seem to feel the cold, stinking breath of that very vulgarity which secretly rejoiced in the death of its enemy.

Reading the works of Chekhov makes one feel as if it were a sad day in late autumn, when the air is transparent, the bare trees stand out in bold relief against the sky, the houses are huddled together, and people are dim and dreary. Everything is so strange, so lonely, motionless, powerless. The remote distances are blue and void, merging with the pale sky, breathing a dreary cold on the half-frozen mud. But the mind of the author, like the autumn sunshine, lights up the well-trodden roads, the crooked streets, the dirty, cramped houses in which pitiful "little" people gasp out their lives in boredom and idleness, filling their dwellings with a meaningless, drowsy bustle. There goes "the darling," as nervous as a little grey mouse, a sweet, humble woman, who loves so indiscriminately and so slavishly. Strike her a blow on the cheek and she will not even dare, meek slave, to cry out. Beside her stands the melancholy Olga from *The Three Sisters*; she, too, is capable of loving and submits patiently to the whims of the depraved, vulgar wife of her fainéant brother; the lives of her sisters fall in ruins around her and she only cries, incapable of doing anything about it, while not a single living, strong word of protest against vulgarity is formed within her.

And there go the tearful Ranevskaya and the rest of the former owners of *The Cherry Orchard*—selfish as children, and flabby as old people. They, who should have been dead long ago, whine and snivel, blind to what is going on around them, comprehending nothing, parasites unable to fasten their suckers into life again. The worthless student Trofimov holds forth eloquently on the need for working, and fritters away his time, amusing himself by dull-witted taunts at Varya, who works unceasingly for the welfare of the idlers.

Vershinin (the hero of *The Three Sisters*) dreams of the good life to come in three hundred years, and in the meantime does not notice that everything around him is falling to pieces, that before his very eyes Solyony is ready, out of boredom and stupidity, to kill the pitiable Baron Tusenbach.

A long procession of slaves to love, to their own stupidity and laziness, to their greed for earthly blessings passes before the reader's eyes. Here are the slaves to the obscure fear of life, moving in vague anxiety and filling the air with inarticulate ravings about the future, feeling that there is no place for them in the present. . . .

Sometimes the report of a gun is heard from the grey mass—this is Ivanov or Treplev, who, having suddenly discovered the only thing to do, has given up the ghost.

Many of them indulge in beautiful dreams of the glorious life to come in two hundred years, and nobody thinks of asking the simple question: who is to make it glorious, if we do nothing but dream?

And now a great, wise man passes by this dull, dreary crowd of impotent creatures, casting an attentive glance on them all, these dreary inhabitants of his native land, and says, with his sad smile, in tones of gentle but profound reproach, with despairing grief on his face and in his heart, in a voice of exquisite sincerity:

"What a dull life you lead, gentlemen!"

I have never met anyone who felt the importance of work as the basis of culture so profoundly and diversely as A. P. This feeling showed itself in all the trifles of his home life, in the selection of things for the home, in that love for things in themselves, and, while quite untainted by the desire to collect, he never wearied of admiring them as the product of man's creative spirit. He loved building, planting gardens, adorning the earth, he felt the poetry of work. With what touching care he watched the growth of the fruit-trees and shrubs he had himself planted. In the midst of the innumerable cares connected with the building of his house at Autko, he said:

"If everyone in the world did all he was capable of on his own plot of land, what a beautiful world it would be!" . . .

He spoke little and reluctantly about his literary work. I had almost said with the same virginal reserve with which he spoke about Lev Tolstoi. Very occasionally, when in spirits, he would relate the plot of a story, chuckling—it was always a humorous story.

> I say, I'm going to write a story about a schoolmistress, an atheist—she adores Darwin, is convinced of the necessity for fighting the prejudices and superstitions of the people, and herself goes to the bath-house at midnight to scald a black cat to get a wishbone for attracting a man and arousing his love —there is such a bone, you know. . . .

He always spoke of his plays as "amusing," and really seemed to be sincerely convinced that he wrote "amusing plays." No doubt Savva Morozov was repeating Chekhov's own words when he stubbornly maintained: "Chekhov's plays must be produced as lyrical comedies." . . .

His disease sometimes called into being a hypochondriac, or even a misanthropical, mood. At such times he would be extremely critical, and very hard to get on with.

One day, lying on the sofa, giving dry coughs, and playing with the thermometer, he said:

"To live simply to die is by no means amusing, but to live with the knowledge that you will die before your time, that really is idiotic. . . ."

Another time, seated at the open window and gazing out into the distance, at the sea, he suddenly said peevishly:

> We are accustomed to live in hopes of good weather, a good harvest, a nice love-affair, hopes of becoming rich or getting the office of chief of police, but I've never noticed anyone hoping to get wiser. We say to ourselves: it'll be better under a new tsar, and in two hundred years it'll be still better, and nobody tries to make this good time come tomorrow. On the whole, life gets more and more complex every day and moves on at its own sweet will, and people get more and more stupid, and

get isolated from life in ever-increasing numbers.

After a pause he added, wrinkling up his forehead:

"Like crippled beggars in a religious procession."

He was a doctor, and the illness of a doctor is always worse than the illnesses of his patients. The patients only feel, but the doctor, as well as feeling, has a pretty good idea of the destructive effect of the disease on his constitution. This is a case in which knowledge brings death nearer. . . .

I once heard Tolstoi praise a story of Chekhov's—*The Darling*, I think it was.

"It's like lace woven by a virtuous maiden," he said. "There used to be girl lace-makers in the old days, who, their whole lives long, wove their dreams of happiness into the pattern. They wove their fondest dreams, their lace was saturated with vague, pure aspirations of love." Tolstoi spoke with true emotion, with tears in his eyes.

But that day Chekhov had a temperature, and sat with his head bent, vivid spots of colour on his cheeks, carefully wiping his pince-nez. He said nothing for some time, and at last, sighing, said softly and awkwardly: "There are misprints in it."

Much could be written of Chekhov, but this would require close, precise narration, and that is what I'm no good at. He should be written about as he himself wrote *The Steppe*, a fragrant, open-air, very Russian story, pensive and wistful. A story for one's self.

It does one good to remember a man like that, it is like a sudden visitation of cheerfulness, it gives a clear meaning to life again.

Man is the axis of the Universe.

And his vices, you ask, his shortcomings?

We all hunger for the love of our fellow creatures, and when one is hungry, even a half-baked loaf tastes sweet.

George
Bernard
Shaw
1856–1950

As pamphleteer, wit, controversialist, critic, and playwright, Shaw challenged cant and convention throughout a long lifetime of activity. Shaw was born in Dublin into an impecunious Irish Protestant family with pretensions to gentility; his father was an alcoholic ex-civil servant, his mother a musician. After some perfunctory schooling he was apprenticed to a Dublin real-estate agent, but in 1876 he moved to London, where his mother had been living for some time. There followed years of unemployment, study, and unsuccessful novel-writing. Influenced by Henry George and Karl Marx, Shaw threw himself into the Socialist movement. He helped to found the Fabian Society, and turned to pamphleteering and speech making. In 1885 he found a job as a music critic and later also wrote drama and art criticism. He championed the music of Wagner and the drama of Ibsen, and finally offered to write a play for the Independent Theatre. His play *Widowers' Houses*, written when he was thirty-six, provoked a storm of comment, and Shaw's career as a dramatist was launched. Among his subjects for bold and iconoclastic treatment were conventional religious thinking (*Androcles and the Lion*, 1912, and *Back to Methuselah*, 1921), relations between the sexes (*Mrs. Warren's Profession*, 1893; *Candida*, 1894; *Man and Superman*, 1903), romantic military heroics (*Arms and the Man*, 1894), poverty, war, and politics (*Major Barbara*, 1905; *Heartbreak House*, 1913–1916; *The Apple Cart*, 1929), and the great man (*Caesar and Cleopatra*, 1898; *Saint Joan*, 1923). Shaw brought to his dramatic work a wide knowledge of comic techniques, an acute and fearlessly independent intellect, a precise and scintillating prose style, and a profound moral sense that sought through laughter and logic to expel human folly and cowardice. Personally timid ("he was always afraid of intimacy—physical, emotional, and spiritual," wrote his friend R. Ellis Roberts), Shaw fought his own nature and donned a mask of aggressive cockiness and occasional clowning. The world saw him as jaunty, confident, and unafraid up to his death at the age of ninety-four.

HEARTBREAK HOUSE

A fantasia in the Russian manner on English themes

GEORGE BERNARD SHAW

ACT I

[The hilly country in the middle of the north edge of Sussex, looking very pleasant on a fine evening at the end of September, is seen through the windows of a room which has been built so as to resemble the after part of an old-fashioned high-pooped ship with a stern gallery; for the windows are ship built with heavy timbering, and run right across the room as continuously as the stability of the wall allows. A row of lockers under the windows provides an unupholstered window-seat interrupted by twin glass doors, respectively halfway between the stern post and the sides. Another door strains the illusion a little by being apparently in the ship's port side, and yet leading, not to the open sea, but to the entrance hall of the house. Between this door and the stern gallery are bookshelves. There are electric light switches beside the door leading to the hall and the glass doors in the stern gallery. Against the starboard wall is a carpenter's bench. The vice has a board in its jaws; and the floor is littered with shavings, overflowing from a waste-paper basket. A couple of planes and a centrebit are on the bench. In the same wall, between the bench and the windows, is a narrow doorway with a half door, above which shews that it is a shelved pantry with bottles and kitchen crockery.

On the starboard side, but close to the middle, is a plain oak drawing-table with drawing-board, T-square, straightedges, set squares, mathematical instruments, saucers of water color, a tumbler of dis-colored water, Indian ink, pencils, and brushes on it. The drawing-board is set so that the draughtsman's chair has the window on its left hand. On the floor at the end of the table, on his right, is a ship's fire bucket. On the port side of the room, near the bookshelves, is a sofa with its back to the windows. It is a sturdy mahogany article, oddly upholstered in sailcloth, including the bolster, with a couple of blankets hanging over the back. Between the sofa and the drawing-table is a big wicker chair, with broad arms and a low sloping back, with its back to the light. A small but stout table of teak, with a round top and gate legs, stands against the port wall between the door and the bookcase. It is the only article in the room that suggests (not at all convincingly) a woman's hand in the furnishing. The uncarpeted floor of narrow boards is caulked and holystoned like a deck.

The garden to which the glass doors lead dips to the south before the landscape rises again to the hills. Emerging from the hollow is the cupola of an observatory. Between the observatory and the house is a flagstaff on a little esplanade, with a hammock on the east side and a long garden seat on the west.

A YOUNG LADY, gloved and hatted, with a dust coat on, is sitting in the window-seat with her body twisted to enable her to look out at the view. One hand props her chin: the other hangs down with a volume of the Temple Shakespear in it, and her finger stuck in the page she has been reading.

A clock strikes six.

The YOUNG LADY *turns and looks at her watch. She rises with an air of one who waits and is almost at the end of her patience. She is a pretty girl, slender, fair, and intelligent looking, nicely but not expensively dressed, evidently not a smart idler.*

With a sigh of weary resignation she comes to the draughtsman's chair; sits down; and begins to read Shakespear. Presently the book sinks to her lap; her eyes close; and she dozes into a slumber.

An elderly WOMANSERVANT *comes in from the hall with three unopened bottles of rum on a tray. She passes through and disappears in the pantry without noticing the* YOUNG LADY. *She places the bottles on the shelf and fills her tray with empty bottles. As she returns with these, the* YOUNG LADY *lets her book drop, awakening herself, and startling the* WOMANSERVANT *so that she all but lets the tray fall.*]

THE WOMANSERVANT. God bless us! [*The* YOUNG LADY *picks up the book and places it on the table.*] Sorry to wake you, miss, I'm sure; but you are a stranger to me. What might you be waiting here for now?

THE YOUNG LADY. Waiting for somebody to shew some signs of knowing that I have been invited here.

THE WOMANSERVANT. Oh, youre invited, are you? And has nobody come? Dear! dear!

THE YOUNG LADY. A wild-looking old gentleman came and looked in at the window; and I heard him calling out 'Nurse: there is a young and attractive female waiting in the poop. Go and see what she wants.' Are you the nurse?

THE WOMANSERVANT. Yes, miss: I'm Nurse Guinness. That was old Captain Shotover, Mrs Hushabye's father. I heard him roaring; but I thought it was for something else. I suppose it was Mrs Hushabye that invited you, ducky?

THE YOUNG LADY. I understood her to do so. But really I think I'd better go.

NURSE GUINNESS. Oh, dont think of such a thing, miss. If Mrs Hushabye has forgotten all about it, it will be a pleasant surprise for her to see you, wont it?

THE YOUNG LADY. It has been a very unpleasant surprise to me to find that nobody expects me.

NURSE GUINNESS. Youll get used to it, miss: this house is full of surprises for them that dont know our ways.

CAPTAIN SHOTOVER [*looking in from the hall suddenly: an ancient but still hardy man with an immense white beard, in a reefer jacket with a whistle hanging from his neck*]. Nurse: there is a hold-all and a handbag on the front steps for everybody to fall over. Also a tennis racquet. Who the devil left them there?

THE YOUNG LADY. They are mine, I'm afraid.

THE CAPTAIN [*advancing to the drawing-table*]. Nurse: who is this misguided and unfortunate young lady?

NURSE GUINNESS. She says Miss Hessy invited her, sir.

THE CAPTAIN. And had she no friend, no parents, to warn her against my daughter's invitations? This is a pretty sort of house, by heavens! A young and attractive lady is invited here. Her luggage is left on the steps for hours; and she herself is deposited in the poop and abandoned, tired and starving. This is our hospitality. These are our manners. No room ready. No hot water. No welcoming hostess. Our visitor is to sleep in the toolshed, and to wash in the duck-pond.

NURSE GUINNESS. Now it's all right, Captain: I'll get the lady some tea; and her room shall be ready before she has finished it. [*To the* YOUNG LADY.] Take off your hat, ducky; and make yourself at home. [*She goes to the door leading to the hall.*]

THE CAPTAIN [*as she passes him*]. Ducky! Do you suppose, woman, that because this young lady has been insulted and neglected, you have the right to address her as you address my wretched children, whom you have brought up in ignorance of the commonest decencies of social intercourse?

NURSE GUINNESS. Never mind him, doty. [*Quite unconcerned, she goes out into the hall on her way to the kitchen.*]

THE CAPTAIN. Madam: will you favor me with your name? [*He sits down in the big wicker chair.*]

THE YOUNG LADY. My name is Ellie Dunn.

THE CAPTAIN. Dunn! I had a boatswain whose name was Dunn. He was originally a pirate in China. He set up as a ship's chandler with stores which I have every reason to believe he stole from me. No doubt he became rich. Are you his daughter?

ELLIE [indignant]. No: certainly not. I am proud to be able to say that though my father has not been a successful man, nobody has ever had one word to say against him. I think my father is the best man I have ever known.

THE CAPTAIN. He must be greatly changed. Has he attained the seventh degree of concentration?

ELLIE. I dont understand.

THE CAPTAIN. But how could he, with a daughter! I, madam, have two daughters. One of them is Hesione Hushabye, who invited you here. I keep this house: she upsets it. I desire to attain the seventh degree of concentration: she invites visitors and leaves me to entertain them. [NURSE GUINNESS returns with the tea-tray, which she places on the teak table.] I have a second daughter who is, thank God, in a remote part of the Empire with her numskull of a husband. As a child she thought the figure-head of my ship, the Dauntless, the most beautiful thing on earth. He resembled it. He had the same expression: wooden yet enterprising. She married him, and will never set foot in this house again.

NURSE GUINNESS [carrying the table, with the tea-things on it, to ELLIE's side]. Indeed you never were more mistaken. She is in England this very moment. You have been told three times this week that she is coming home for a year for her health. And very glad you should be to see your own daughter again after all these years.

THE CAPTAIN. I am not glad. The natural term of the affection of the human animal for its offspring is six years. My daughter Ariadne was born when I was forty-six. I am now eighty-eight. If she comes, I am not at home. If she wants anything, let her take it. If she asks for me, let her be informed that I am extremely old, and have totally forgotten her.

NURSE GUINNESS. Thats no talk to offer to a young lady. Here, ducky, have some tea; and dont listen to him. [She pours out a cup of tea.]

THE CAPTAIN [rising wrathfully]. Now before high heaven they have given this innocent child Indian tea: the stuff they tan their own leather insides with. [He seizes the cup and the tea-pot and empties both into the leathern bucket.]

ELLIE [almost in tears]. Oh, please! I am so tired. I should have been glad of anything.

NURSE GUINNESS. Oh, what a thing to do! The poor lamb is ready to drop.

THE CAPTAIN. You shall have some of my tea. Do not touch that fly-blown cake: nobody eats it here except the dogs. [He disappears into the pantry.]

NURSE GUINNESS. Theres a man for you! They say he sold himself to the devil in Zanzibar before he was a captain; and the older he grows the more I believe them.

A WOMAN'S VOICE [in the hall]. Is anyone at home? Hesione! Nurse! Papa! Do come, somebody; and take in my luggage. [Thumping heard, as of an umbrella, on the wainscot.]

NURSE GUINNESS. My gracious. It's Miss Addy, Lady Utterword, Mrs Hushabye's sister: the one I told the Captain about. [Calling.] Coming, miss, coming.

[She carries the table back to its place by the door, and is hurrying out when she is intercepted by LADY UTTERWORD, who bursts in much flustered. LADY UTTERWORD, a blonde, is very handsome, very well dressed, and so precipitate in speech and action that the first impression (erroneous) is one of comic silliness.]

LADY UTTERWORD. Oh, is that you, Nurse? How are you? You dont look a day older. Is nobody at home? Where is Hesione? Doesnt she expect me? Where are the servants? Whose luggage is that on the steps? Where's papa? Is everybody asleep? [Seeing ELLIE.] Oh! I beg your pardon. I suppose you are one of my nieces. [Approaching her with outstretched arms.] Come and kiss your aunt, darling.

ELLIE. I'm only a visitor. It is my luggage on the steps.

NURSE GUINNESS. I'll go get you some fresh tea, ducky. [She takes up the tray.]

ELLIE. But the old gentleman said he would make some himself.

NURSE GUINNESS. Bless you! he's forgotten what he went for already. His mind wanders from one thing to another.

LADY UTTERWORD. Papa, I suppose?

NURSE GUINNESS. Yes, miss.

LADY UTTERWORD [vehemently]. Dont be silly, nurse. Dont call me Miss.

NURSE GUINNESS [placidly]. No, lovey. [She goes out with the tea-tray.]

LADY UTTERWORD [sitting down with a flounce on the sofa]. I know what you must feel. Oh, this house, this house! I come back to it after twenty-three years; and it is just the same: the luggage lying on the steps, the servants spoilt and impossible, nobody at home to receive anybody, no regular meals, nobody ever hungry because they are always gnawing bread and butter or munching apples, and, what is worse, the same disorder in ideas, in talk, in feeling. When I was a child I was used to it: I had never known anything better, though I was unhappy, and longed all the time—oh, how I longed!—to be respectable, to be a lady, to live as others did, not to have to think of everything for myself. I married at nineteen to escape from it. My husband is Sir Hastings Utterword, who has been governor of all the crown colonies in succession. I have always been the mistress of Government House. I have been so happy: I had forgotten that people could live like this. I wanted to see my father, my sister, my nephews and nieces (one ought to, you know), and I was looking forward to it. And now the state of the house! the way I'm received! the casual impudence of that woman Guinness, our old nurse! really Hesione might at least have been here: some preparation might have been made for me. You must excuse my going on in this way; but I am really very much hurt and annoyed and disillusioned: and if I had realized it was to be like this, I wouldnt have come. I have a great mind to go away without another word. [She is on the point of weeping.]

ELLIE [also very miserable]. Nobody has been here to receive me either. I thought I ought to go away too. But how can I, Lady Utterword? My luggage is on the steps; and the station fly has gone.

[The CAPTAIN emerges from the pantry with a tray of Chinese lacquer and a very fine tea-set on it. He rests it provisionally on the end of the table; snatches away the drawing-board, which he stands on the floor against the table legs; and puts the tray in the space thus cleared. ELLIE pours out a cup greedily.]

THE CAPTAIN. Your tea, young lady. What! another lady! I must fetch another cup. [He makes for the pantry.]

LADY UTTERWORD [rising from the sofa, suffused with emotion]. Papa! Dont you know me? I'm your daughter.

THE CAPTAIN. Nonsense! my daughter's upstairs asleep. [He vanishes through the half door.]

[LADY UTTERWORD retires to the window to conceal her tears.]

ELLIE [going to her with the cup]. Dont be so distressed. Have this cup of tea. He is very old and very strange: he has been just like that to me. I know how dreadful it must be: my own father is all the world to me. Oh, I'm sure he didnt mean it.

[The CAPTAIN returns with another cup.]

THE CAPTAIN. Now we are complete. [He places it on the tray.]

LADY UTTERWORD [hysterically]. Papa: you cant have forgotten me. I am Ariadne. I'm little Paddy Patkins. Wont you kiss me? [She goes to him and throws her arms round his neck.]

THE CAPTAIN [woodenly enduring her embrace]. How can you be Ariadne? You are a middle-aged woman: well preserved, madam, but no longer young.

LADY UTTERWORD. But think of all the years and years I have been away, papa. I have had to grow old, like other people.

THE CAPTAIN [disengaging himself]. You should grow out of kissing strange men: they may be striving to attain the seventh degree of concentration.

LADY UTTERWORD. But I'm your daughter. You havnt seen me for years.

THE CAPTAIN. So much the worse! When our relatives are at home, we have to think of all their good points or it would be impossible to endure them. But when they are away, we console ourselves for their absence by dwelling on their vices. That is how I have come to think my absent daughter Ariadne a perfect fiend; so do not try to ingratiate yourself here by impersonating her. [He walks firmly away to the other side of the room.]

LADY UTTERWORD. Ingratiating myself

indeed! [*With dignity.*] Very well, papa. [*She sits down at the drawing-table and pours out tea for herself.*]

THE CAPTAIN. I am neglecting my social duties. You remember Dunn? Billy Dunn?

LADY UTTERWORD. Do you mean that villainous sailor who robbed you?

THE CAPTAIN [*introducing* ELLIE]. His daughter. [*He sits down on the sofa.*]

ELLIE [*protesting*]. No—

[NURSE GUINNESS *returns with fresh tea.*]

THE CAPTAIN. Take that hogwash away. Do you hear?

NURSE. Youve actually remembered about the tea! [*To* ELLIE.] O, miss, he didnt forget you after all! You have made an impression.

THE CAPTAIN [*gloomily*]. Youth! beauty! novelty! They are badly wanted in this house. I am excessively old. Hesione is only moderately young. Her children are not youthful.

LADY UTTERWORD. How can children be expected to be youthful in this house? Almost before we could speak we were filled with notions that might have been all very well for pagan philosophers of fifty, but were certainly quite unfit for respectable people of any age.

NURSE. You were always for respectability, Miss Addy.

LADY UTTERWORD. Nurse: will you please remember that I am Lady Utterword, and not Miss Addy, nor lovey, nor darling, nor doty? Do you hear?

NURSE. Yes, ducky: all right, I'll tell them all they must call you my lady. [*She takes her tray out with undisturbed placidity.*]

LADY UTTERWORD. What comfort? what sense is there in having servants with no manners?

ELLIE [*rising and coming to the table to put down her empty cup*]. Lady Utterword: do you think Mrs Hushabye really expects me?

LADY UTTERWORD. Oh, dont ask me. You can see for yourself that Ive just arrived; her only sister, after twenty-three years absence! and it seems that *I* am not expected.

THE CAPTAIN. What does it matter whether the young lady is expected or not? She is welcome. There are beds: there is food. I'll find a room for her myself. [*He makes for the door.*]

ELLIE [*following him to stop him*]. Oh please—[*He goes out.*] Lady Utterword: I dont know what to do. Your father persists in believing that my father is some sailor who robbed him.

LADY UTTERWORD. You had better pretend not to notice it. My father is a very clever man; but he always forgot things; and now that he is old, of course he is worse. And I must warn you that it is sometimes very hard to feel quite sure that he really forgets.

[MRS HUSHABYE *bursts into the room tempestuously, and embraces* ELLIE. *She is a couple of years older than* LADY UTTERWORD *and even better looking. She has magnificent black hair, eyes like the fishpools of Heshbon, and a nobly modelled neck, short at the back and low between her shoulders in front. Unlike her sister she is uncorseted and dressed anyhow in a rich robe of black pile that shews off her white skin and statuesque contour.*]

MRS HUSHABYE. Ellie, my darling, my pettikins [*kissing her*]: how long have you been here? Ive been at home all the time: I was putting flowers and things in your room; and when I just sat down for a moment to try how comfortable the armchair was I went off to sleep. Papa woke me and told me you were here. Fancy you finding no one, and being neglected and abandoned. [*Kissing her again.*] My poor love! [*She deposits* ELLIE *on the sofa. Meanwhile* ARIADNE *has left the table and come over to claim her share of attention.*] Oh! youve brought someone with you. Introduce me.

LADY UTTERWORD. Hesione: is it possible that you dont know me?

MRS HUSHABYE [*conventionally*]. Of course I remember your face quite well. Where have we met?

LADY UTTERWORD. Didnt Papa tell you I was here? Oh! this is really too much. [*She throws herself sulkily into the big chair.*]

MRS HUSHABYE. Papa!

LADY UTTERWORD. Yes: Papa. Our papa, you unfeeling wretch. [*Rising angrily.*] I'll go straight to a hotel.

MRS HUSHABYE [*seizing her by the*

shoulders]. My goodness gracious goodness, you dont mean to say that youre Addy!

LADY UTTERWORD. I certainly am Addy; and I dont think I can be so changed that you would not have recognized me if you had any real affection for me. And Papa didnt think me even worth mentioning!

MRS HUSHABYE. What a lark! Sit down. [*She pushes her back into the chair instead of kissing her, and posts herself behind it.*] You do look a swell. Youre much handsomer than you used to be. Youve made the acquaintance of Ellie of course. She is going to marry a perfect hog of a millionaire for the sake of her father, who is as poor as a church mouse; and you must help me to stop her.

ELLIE. Oh please, Hesione.

MRS HUSHABYE. My pettikins, the man's coming here today with your father to begin persecuting you; and everybody will see the state of the case in ten minutes; so whats the use of making a secret of it?

ELLIE. He is not a hog, Hesione. You dont know how wonderfully good he was to my father, and how deeply grateful I am to him.

MRS HUSHABYE [*to* LADY UTTERWORD]. Her father is a very remarkable man, Addy. His name is Mazzini Dunn. Mazzini was a celebrity of some kind who knew Ellie's grandparents. They were both poets, like the Brownings; and when her father came into the world Mazzini said 'Another soldier born for freedom!' So they christened him Mazzini; and he has been fighting for freedom in his quiet way ever since. Thats why he is so poor.

ELLIE. I am proud of his poverty.

MRS HUSHABYE. Of course you are, pettikins. Why not leave him in it, and marry someone you love?

LADY UTTERWORD [*rising suddenly and explosively*]. Hesione: are you going to kiss me or are you not?

MRS HUSHABYE. What do you want to be kissed for?

LADY UTTERWORD. I dont want to be kissed; but I do want you to behave properly and decently. We are sisters. We have been separated for twenty-three years. You ought to kiss me.

MRS HUSHABYE. Tomorrow morning, dear, before you make up. I hate the smell of powder.

LADY UTTERWORD. Oh! you unfeeling —[*She is interrupted by the return of the* CAPTAIN.]

THE CAPTAIN [*to* ELLIE]. Your room is ready. [ELLIE *rises.*] The sheets were damp; but I have changed them. [*He makes for the garden door on the port side.*]

LADY UTTERWORD. Oh! What about my sheets?

THE CAPTAIN [*halting at the door*]. Take my advice: air them; or take them off and sleep in blankets. You shall sleep in Ariadne's old room.

LADY UTTERWORD. Indeed I shall do nothing of the sort. That little hole! I am entitled to the best spare room.

THE CAPTAIN [*continuing unmoved*]. She married a numskull. She told me she would marry anyone to get away from home.

LADY UTTERWORD. You are pretending not to know me on purpose. I will leave the house.

[MAZZINI DUNN *enters from the hall. He is a little elderly man with bulging credulous eyes and an earnest manner. He is dressed in a blue serge jacket suit with an unbuttoned mackintosh over it, and carries a soft black hat of clerical cut.*]

ELLIE. At last! Captain Shotover: here is my father.

THE CAPTAIN. This! Nonsense! not a bit like him. [*He goes away through the garden, shutting the door sharply behind him.*]

LADY UTTERWORD. I will not be ignored and pretended to be somebody else. I will have it out with papa now, this instant. [*To* MAZZINI.] Excuse me. [*She follows the* CAPTAIN *out, making a hasty bow to* MAZZINI, *who returns it.*]

MRS HUSHABYE [*hospitably, shaking hands*]. How good of you to come, Mr Dunn! You dont mind papa, do you? He is as mad as a hatter, you know, but quite harmless, and extremely clever. You will have some delightful talks with him.

MAZZINI. I hope so. [*To* ELLIE.] So here you are, Ellie dear. [*He draws her arm affectionately through his.*] I must thank you, Mrs Hushabye, for your kindness to my daughter. I'm afraid she would have had no holiday if you had not in-vited her.

MRS HUSHABYE. Not at all. Very nice of her to come and attract young people to the house for us.

MAZZINI [smiling]. I'm afraid Ellie is not interested in young men, Mrs Hush-abye. Her taste is on the graver, solider side.

MRS HUSHABYE [with a sudden rather hard brightness in her manner]. Wont you take off your overcoat, Mr Dunn? You will find a cupboard for coats and hats and things in the corner of the hall.

MAZZINI [hastily releasing ELLIE]. Yes —thank you—I had better—[He goes out.]

MRS HUSHABYE [emphatically]. The old brute!

ELLIE. Who?

MRS HUSHABYE. Who! Him. He. It. [Pointing after MAZZINI.] 'Graver, solider tastes,' indeed!

ELLIE [aghast]. You dont mean that you were speaking like that of my father!

MRS HUSHABYE. I was. You know I was.

ELLIE [with dignity]. I will leave your house at once. [She turns to the door.]

MRS HUSHABYE. If you attempt it, I'll tell your father why.

ELLIE [turning again]. Oh! How can you treat a visitor like this, Mrs Hush-abye?

MRS HUSHABYE. I thought you were going to call me Hesione.

ELLIE. Certainly not now!

MRS HUSHABYE. Very well: I'll tell your father.

ELLIE [distressed]. Oh!

MRS HUSHABYE. If you turn a hair—if you take his part against me and against your own heart for a moment, I'll give that born soldier of freedom a piece of my mind that will stand him on his selfish old head for a week.

ELLIE. Hesione! My father selfish! how little you know—

[She is interrupted by MAZZINI, who returns, excited and perspiring.]

MAZZINI. Ellie: Mangan has come: I thought youd like to know. Excuse me, Mrs Hushabye: the strange old gentle-man—

MRS HUSHABYE. Papa. Quite so.

MAZZINI. Oh, I beg your pardon: of course: I was a little confused by his

manner. He is making Mangan help him with something in the garden; and he wants me too—

[A powerful whistle is heard.]

THE CAPTAIN'S VOICE. Bosun ahoy! [The whistle is repeated.]

MAZZINI [flustered]. Oh dear! I believe he is whistling for me. [He hurries out.]

MRS HUSHABYE. Now my father is a wonderful man if you like.

ELLIE. Hesione: listen to me. You dont understand. My father and Mr Mangan were boys together. Mr Ma—

MRS HUSHABYE. I dont care what they were: we must sit down if you are going to begin as far back as that. [She snatches at ELLIE's waist, and makes her sit down on the sofa beside her.] Now, pettikins: tell me all about Mr Mangan. They call him Boss Mangan, dont they? He is a Napoleon of industry and disgustingly rich, isnt he? Why isnt your father rich?

ELLIE. My poor father should never have been in business. His parents were poets; and they gave him the noblest ideas; but they could not afford to give him a profession.

MRS HUSHABYE. Fancy your grandpar-ents, with their eyes in fine frenzy rolling! And so your poor father had to go into business. Hasnt he succeeded in it?

ELLIE. He always used to say he could succeed if he only had some capital. He fought his way along, to keep a roof over our heads and bring us up well; but it was always a struggle: always the same difficulty of not having capital enough. I don't know how to describe it to you.

MRS HUSHABYE. Poor Ellie! I know. Pulling the devil by the tail.

ELLIE [hurt]. Oh no. Not like that. It was at least dignified.

MRS HUSHABYE. That made it all the harder, didnt it? I shouldnt have pulled the devil by the tail with dignity. I should have pulled hard—[between her teeth] hard. Well? Go on.

ELLIE. At last it seemed that all our troubles were at an end. Mr Mangan did an extraordinarily noble thing out of pure friendship for my father and respect for his character. He asked him how much capital he wanted, and gave it to him. I dont mean that he lent it to him, or that he invested it in his business. He just simply made him a present of it. Wasnt that splendid of him?

MRS HUSHABYE. On condition that you married him?

ELLIE. Oh no, no, no. This was when I was a child. He had never even seen me: he never came to our house. It was absolutely disinterested. Pure generosity.

MRS HUSHABYE. Oh! I beg the gentleman's pardon. Well, what became of the money?

ELLIE. We all got new clothes and moved into another house. And I went to another school for two years.

MRS HUSHABYE. Only two years?

ELLIE. That was all; for at the end of two years my father was utterly ruined.

MRS HUSHABYE. How?

ELLIE. I don't know. I never could understand. But it was dreadful! When we were poor my father had never been in debt. But when he launched out into business on a large scale, he had to incur liabilities. When the business went into liquidation he owed more money than Mr Mangan had given him.

MRS HUSHABYE. Bit off more than he could chew, I suppose.

ELLIE. I think you are a little unfeeling about it.

MRS HUSHABYE. My pettikins: you mustnt mind my way of talking. I was quite as sensitive and particular as you once; but I have picked up so much slang from the children that I am really hardly presentable. I suppose your father had no head for business, and made a mess of it.

ELLIE. Oh, that just shews how entirely you are mistaken about him. The business turned out a great success. It now pays forty-four per cent after deducting the excess profits tax.

MRS HUSHABYE. Then why arnt you rolling in money?

ELLIE. I dont know. It seems very unfair to me. You see, my father was made bankrupt. It nearly broke his heart, because he had persuaded several of his friends to put money into the business. He was sure it would succeed; and events proved that he was quite right. But they all lost their money. It was dreadful. I dont know what we should have done but for Mr Mangan.

MRS HUSHABYE. What! Did the Boss come to the rescue again, after all his money being thrown away?

ELLIE. He did indeed, and never uttered a reproach to my father. He bought what was left of the business—the buildings and the machinery and things—from the official trustee for enough money to enable my father to pay six and eightpence in the pound and get his discharge. Everyone pitied papa so much, and saw so plainly that he was an honorable man, that they let him off at six-and-eightpence instead of ten shillings. Then Mr Mangan started a company to take up the business, and made my father a manager in it to save us from starvation; for I wasnt earning anything then.

MRS HUSHABYE. Quite a romance. And when did the Boss develop the tender passion?

ELLIE. Oh, that was years after, quite lately. He took the chair one night at a sort of people's concert. I was singing there. As an amateur, you know: half a guinea for expenses and three songs with three encores. He was so pleased with my singing that he asked might he walk home with me. I never saw anyone so taken aback as he was when I took him home and introduced him to my father: his own manager. It was then that my father told me how nobly he had behaved. Of course it was considered a great chance for me, as he is so rich. And —and—we drifted into a sort of understanding—I suppose I should call it an engagement—[She is distressed and cannot go on.]

MRS HUSHABYE [rising and marching about]. You may have drifted into it; but you will bounce out of it, my pettikins, if I am to have anything to do with it.

ELLIE [hopelessly]. No: it's no use. I am bound in honor and gratitude. I will go through with it.

MRS HUSHABYE [behind the sofa, scolding down at her]. You know, of course, that it's not honorable or grateful to marry a man you dont love. Do you love this Mangan man?

ELLIE. Yes. At least—

MRS HUSHABYE. I dont want to know about 'the least': I want to know the worst. Girls of your age fall in love with all sorts of impossible people, especially old people.

ELLIE. I like Mr Mangan very much; and I shall always be—

MRS HUSHABYE [impatiently complet-

ing the sentence and prancing away intolerantly to starboard]. —grateful to him for his kindness to dear father. I know. Anybody else?

ELLIE. What do you mean?

MRS HUSHABYE. Anybody else? Are you in love with anybody else?

ELLIE. Of course not.

MRS HUSHABYE. Humph! [*The book on the drawing-table catches her eye. She picks it up, and evidently finds the title very unexpected. She looks at Ellie, and asks, quaintly.*] Quite sure youre not in love with an actor?

ELLIE. No, no. Why? What put such a thing into your head?

MRS HUSHABYE. This is yours, isnt it? Why else should you be reading Othello?

ELLIE. My father taught me to love Shakespear.

MRS HUSHABYE [*flinging the book down on the table*]. Really! your father does seem to be about the limit.

ELLIE [*naïvely*]. Do you never read Shakespear, Hesione? That seems to me so extraordinary. I like Othello.

MRS HUSHABYE. Do you indeed? He was jealous, wasn't he?

ELLIE. Oh, not that. I think all the part about jealousy is horrible. But dont you think it must have been a wonderful experience for Desdemona, brought up so quietly at home, to meet a man who had been out in the world doing all sorts of brave things and having terrible adventures, and yet finding something in her that made him love to sit and talk with her and tell her about them?

MRS HUSHABYE. Thats your idea of romance, is it?

ELLIE. Not romance, exactly. It might really happen.

[ELLIE*'s eyes shew that she is not arguing, but in a daydream.* MRS HUSHABYE, *watching her inquisitively, goes deliberately back to the sofa and resumes her seat beside her.*]

MRS HUSHABYE. Ellie darling: have you noticed that some of those stories that Othello told Desdemona couldnt have happened?

ELLIE. Oh no. Shakespear thought they could have happened.

MRS HUSHABYE. Hm! Desdemona thought they could have happened. But they didnt.

ELLIE. Why do you look so enigmatic about it? You are such a sphinx: I never know what you mean.

MRS HUSHABYE. Desdemona would have found him out if she had lived, you know. I wonder was that why he strangled her!

ELLIE. Othello was not telling lies.

MRS HUSHABYE. How do you know?

ELLIE. Shakespear would have said if he was. Hesione: there are men who have done wonderful things: men like Othello, only, of course, white, and very handsome, and—

MRS HUSHABYE. Ah! Now we're coming to it. Tell me all about him. I knew there must be somebody, or youd never have been so miserable about Mangan: youd have thought it quite a lark to marry him.

ELLIE [*blushing vividly*]. Hesione: you are dreadful. But I dont want to make a secret of it, though of course I dont tell everybody. Besides, I dont know him.

MRS HUSHABYE. Dont know him! What does that mean?

ELLIE. Well, of course I know him to speak to.

MRS HUSHABYE. But you want to know him ever so much more intimately, eh?

ELLIE. No no: I know him quite—almost intimately.

MRS HUSHABYE. You dont know him; and you know him almost intimately. How lucid!

ELLIE. I mean that he does not call on us. I—I got into conversation with him by chance at a concert.

MRS HUSHABYE. You seem to have rather a gay time at your concerts, Ellie.

ELLIE. Not at all: we talk to everyone in the green-room waiting for our turns. I thought he was one of the artists: he looked so splendid. But he was only one of the committee. I happened to tell him that I was copying a picture at the National Gallery. I make a little money that way. I cant paint much; but as it's always the same picture I can do it pretty quickly and get two or three pounds for it. It happened that he came to the National Gallery one day.

MRS HUSHABYE. One student's day. Paid sixpence to stumble about through a crowd of easels, when he might have come in next day for nothing and found the floor clear! Quite by accident?

ELLIE [triumphantly]. No. On purpose. He liked talking to me. He knows lots of the most splendid people. Fashionable women who are all in love with him. But he ran away from them to see me at the National Gallery and persuade me to come with him for a drive round Richmond Park in a taxi.

MRS HUSHABYE. My pettikins, you have been going it. It's wonderful what you good girls can do without anyone saying a word.

ELLIE. I am not in society, Hesione. If I didnt make acquaintances in that way I shouldnt have any at all.

MRS HUSHABYE. Well, no harm if you know how to take care of yourself. May I ask his name?

ELLIE [slowly and musically]. Marcus Darnley.

MRS HUSHABYE [echoing the music]. Marcus Darnley! What a splendid name!

ELLIE. Oh, I'm so glad you think so. I think so too; but I was afraid it was only a silly fancy of my own.

MRS HUSHABYE. Hm! Is he one of the Aberdeen Darnleys?

ELLIE. Nobody knows. Just fancy! He was found in an antique chest—

MRS HUSHABYE. A what?

ELLIE. An antique chest, one summer morning in a rose garden, after a night of the most terrible thunderstorm.

MRS HUSHABYE. What on earth was he doing in the chest? Did he get into it because he was afraid of the lightning?

ELLIE. Oh no, no: he was a baby. The name Marcus Darnley was embroidered on his babyclothes. And five hundred pounds in gold.

MRS HUSHABYE [looking hard at her]. Ellie!

ELLIE. The garden of the Viscount—

MRS HUSHABYE.—de Rougemont?

ELLIE [innocently]. No: de Larochejaquelin. A French family. A vicomte. His life has been one long romance. A tiger—

MRS HUSHABYE. Slain by his own hand?

ELLIE. Oh no: nothing vulgar like that. He saved the life of the tiger from a hunting party: one of King Edward's hunting parties in India. The King was furious: that was why he never had his military services properly recognized. But he doesnt care. He is a Socialist and despises rank, and has been in three revolutions fighting on the barricades.

MRS HUSHABYE. How can you sit there telling me such lies? You, Ellie, of all people! And I thought you were a perfectly simple, straightforward good girl.

ELLIE [rising, dignified but very angry]. Do you mean to say you don't believe me?

MRS HUSHABYE. Of course I dont believe you. Youre inventing every word of it. Do you take me for a fool?

[ELLIE stares at her. Her candor is so obvious that MRS HUSHABYE is puzzled.]

ELLIE. Goodbye, Hesione. I'm very sorry. I see now that it sounds very improbable as I tell it. But I cant stay if you think that way about me.

MRS HUSHABYE [catching her dress]. You shant go. I couldnt be so mistaken: I know too well what liars are like. Somebody has really told you all this.

ELLIE [flushing]. Hesione: dont say that you dont believe him. I couldnt bear that.

MRS HUSHABYE [soothing her]. Of course I believe him, dearest. But you should have broken it to me by degrees. [Drawing her back to the seat.] Now tell me all about him. Are you in love with him?

ELLIE. Oh no, I'm not so foolish. I dont fall in love with people. I'm not so silly as you think.

MRS HUSHABYE. I see. Only something to think about—to give some interest and pleasure to life.

ELLIE. Just so. Thats all, really.

MRS HUSHABYE. It makes the hours go fast, doesnt it? No tedious waiting to go to sleep at nights and wondering whether you will have a bad night. How delightful it makes waking up in the morning! How much better than the happiest dream! All life transfigured! No more wishing one had an interesting book to read, because life is so much happier than any book! No desire but to be alone and not to have to talk to anyone: to be alone and just think about it.

ELLIE [embracing her]. Hesione: you are a witch. How do you know? Oh, you are the most sympathetic woman in the world.

MRS HUSHABYE [caressing her]. Pettikins, my pettikins: how I envy you! and how I pity you!

ELLIE. Pity me! Oh, why?

[A very handsome man of fifty, with mousquetaire moustaches, wearing a rather dandified curly brimmed hat, and carrying an elaborate walking-stick, comes into the room from the hall, and stops short at sight of the women on the sofa.]

ELLIE [seeing him and rising in glad surprise]. Oh! Hesione: this is Mr Marcus Darnley.

MRS HUSHABYE [rising]. What a lark! He is my husband.

ELLIE. But how—[She stops suddenly; then turns pale and sways.]

MRS HUSHABYE [catching her and sitting down with her on the sofa]. Steady, my pettikins.

THE MAN [with a mixture of confusion and effrontery, depositing his hat and stick on the teak table]. My real name, Miss Dunn, is Hector Hushabye. I leave you to judge whether that is a name any sensitive man would care to confess to. I never use it when I can possibly help it. I have been away for nearly a month; and I had no idea you knew my wife, or that you were coming here. I am none the less delighted to find you in our little house.

ELLIE [in great distress]. I dont know what to do. Please, may I speak to papa? Do leave me. I cant bear it.

MRS HUSHABYE. Be off, Hector.

HECTOR. I—

MRS HUSHABYE. Quick, quick. Get out.

HECTOR. If you think it better— [He goes out, taking his hat with him but leaving the stick on the table.]

MRS HUSHABYE [laying ELLIE down at the end of the sofa]. Now, pettikins, he is gone. Theres nobody but me. You can let yourself go. Dont try to control yourself. Have a good cry.

ELLIE [raising her head]. Damn!

MRS HUSHABYE. Splendid! Oh, what a relief! I thought you were going to be broken-hearted. Never mind me. Damn him again.

ELLIE. I am not damning him: I am damning myself for being such a fool. [Rising.] How could I let myself be taken in so? [She begins prowling to and fro, her bloom gone, looking curiously older and harder.]

MRS HUSHABYE [cheerfully]. Why not, pettikins? Very few young women can resist Hector. I couldnt when I was your age. He is really rather splendid, you know.

ELLIE [turning on her]. Splendid! Yes: splendid looking, of course. But how can you love a liar?

MRS HUSHABYE. I dont know. But you can, fortunately. Otherwise there wouldnt be much love in the world.

ELLIE. But to lie like that! To be a boaster! a coward!

MRS HUSHABYE [rising in alarm]. Pettikins: none of that, if you please. If you hint the slightest doubt of Hector's courage, he will go straight off and do the most horribly dangerous things to convince himself that he isnt a coward. He has a dreadful trick of getting out of one third-floor window and coming in at another, just to test his nerve. He has a whole drawerful of Albert Medals for saving people's lives.

ELLIE. He never told me that.

MRS HUSHABYE. He never boasts of anything he really did: he cant bear it; and it makes him shy if anyone else does. All his stories are made-up stories.

ELLIE [coming to her]. Do you mean that he is really brave, and really has adventures, and yet tells lies about things that he never did and that never happened?

MRS HUSHABYE. Yes, pettikins, I do. People don't have their virtues and vices in sets: they have them anyhow: all mixed.

ELLIE [staring at her thoughtfully]. Theres something odd about this house, Hesione, and even about you. I dont know why I'm talking to you so calmly. I have a horrible fear that my heart is broken, but that heartbreak is not like what I thought it must be.

MRS HUSHABYE [fondling her]. It's only life educating you, pettikins. How do you feel about Boss Mangan now?

ELLIE [disengaging herself with an expression of distaste]. Oh, how can you remind me of him, Hesione?

MRS HUSHABYE. Sorry, dear. I think I hear Hector coming back. You dont mind now, do you, dear?

ELLIE. Not in the least. I am quite cured.

[MAZZINI DUNN and HECTOR come in from the hall.]

HECTOR [as he opens the door and

allows MAZZINI *to pass in*]. One second more, and she would have been a dead woman!

MAZZINI. Dear! dear! what an escape! Ellie, my love: Mr Hushabye has just been telling me the most extraordinary—

ELLIE. Yes: I've heard it. [*She crosses to the other side of the room.*]

HECTOR [*following her*]. Not this one: I'll tell it to you after dinner. I think youll like it. The truth is, I made it up for you, and was looking forward to the pleasure of telling it to you. But in a moment of impatience at being turned out of the room, I threw it away on your father.

ELLIE [*turning at bay with her back to the carpenter's bench, scornfully self-possessed*]. It was not thrown away. He believes it. I should not have believed it.

MAZZINI [*benevolently*]. Ellie is very naughty, Mr Hushabye. Of course she does not really think that. [*He goes to the bookshelves, and inspects the titles of the volumes.*]

[BOSS MANGAN *comes in from the hall, followed by the* CAPTAIN. MANGAN, *carefully frock-coated as for church or for a directors' meeting, is about fifty-five, with a careworn, mistrustful expression, standing a little on an entirely imaginary dignity, with a dull complexion, straight, lustreless hair, and features so entirely commonplace that it is impossible to describe them.*]

CAPTAIN SHOTOVER [*to* MRS HUSHABYE, *introducing the newcomer*]. Says his name is Mangan. Not ablebodied.

MRS HUSHABYE [*graciously*]. How do you do, Mr Mangan?

MANGAN [*shaking hands*]. Very pleased.

CAPTAIN SHOTOVER. Dunn's lost his muscle, but recovered his nerve. Men seldom do after three attacks of delirium tremens. [*He goes into the pantry.*]

MRS HUSHABYE. I congratulate you, Mr Dunn.

MAZZINI [*dazed*]. I am a lifelong teetotaler.

MRS HUSHABYE. You will find it far less trouble to let papa have his own way than try to explain.

MAZZINI. But three attacks of delirium tremens, really!

MRS HUSHABYE [*to* MANGAN]. Do you know my husband, Mr Mangan [*She indicates* HECTOR.]

MANGAN [*going to* HECTOR, *who meets him with outstretched hand*]. Very pleased. [*Turning to* ELLIE.] I hope, Miss Ellie, you have not found the journey down too fatiguing. [*They shake hands.*]

MRS HUSHABYE. Hector: shew Mr Dunn his room.

HECTOR. Certainly. Come along, Mr Dunn. [*He takes* MAZZINI *out.*]

ELLIE. You havnt shewn me my room yet, Hesione.

MRS HUSHABYE. How stupid of me! Come along. Make yourself quite at home, Mr Mangan. Papa will entertain you. [*She calls to the* CAPTAIN *in the pantry.*] Papa: come and explain the house to Mr Mangan.

[*She goes out with* ELLIE. *The* CAPTAIN *comes from the pantry.*]

CAPTAIN SHOTOVER. Youre going to marry Dunn's daughter. Dont. Youre too old.

MANGAN [*staggered*]. Well! Thats fairly blunt, Captain.

CAPTAIN SHOTOVER. It's true.

MANGAN. She doesnt think so.

CAPTAIN SHOTOVER. She does.

MANGAN. Older men than I have—

CAPTAIN SHOTOVER [*finishing the sentence for him*]. —made fools of themselves. That, also, is true.

MANGAN [*asserting himself*]. I dont see that this is any business of yours.

CAPTAIN SHOTOVER. It is everybody's business. The stars in their courses are shaken when such things happen.

MANGAN. I'm going to marry her all the same.

CAPTAIN SHOTOVER. How do you know?

MANGAN [*playing the strong man*]. I intend to. I mean to. See? I never made up my mind to do a thing yet that I didnt bring it off. Thats the sort of man I am; and there will be a better understanding between us when you make up your mind to that, Captain.

CAPTAIN SHOTOVER. You frequent picture palaces.

MANGAN. Perhaps I do. Who told you?

CAPTAIN SHOTOVER. Talk like a man, not like a movy. You mean that you make a hundred thousand a year.

MANGAN. I dont boast. But when I meet a man that makes a hundred thousand a year, I take off my hat to that man, and stretch out my hand to him and call him brother.

CAPTAIN SHOTOVER. Then you also make a hundred thousand a year, hey?

MANGAN. No. I cant say that. Fifty thousand, perhaps.

CAPTAIN SHOTOVER. His half brother only. [He turns away from MANGAN with his usual abruptness, and collects the empty tea-cups on the Chinese tray.]

MANGAN [irritated]. See here, Captain Shotover. I dont quite understand my position here. I came here on your daughter's invitation. Am I in her house or in yours?

CAPTAIN SHOTOVER. You are beneath the dome of heaven, in the house of God. What is true within these walls is true outside them. Go out on the seas; climb the mountains; wander through the valleys. She is still too young.

MANGAN [weakening]. But I'm very little over fifty.

CAPTAIN SHOTOVER. You are still less under sixty. Boss Mangan: you will not marry the pirate's child. [He carries the tray away into the pantry.]

MANGAN [following him to the half door]. What pirate's child? What are you talking about?

CAPTAIN SHOTOVER [in the pantry]. Ellie Dunn. You will not marry her.

MANGAN. Who will stop me?

CAPTAIN SHOTOVER [emerging]. My daughter. [He makes for the door leading to the hall.]

MANGAN [following him]. Mrs Hushabye! Do you mean to say she brought me down here to break it off?

CAPTAIN SHOTOVER [stopping and turning on him]. I know nothing more than I have seen in her eye. She will break it off. Take my advice: marry a West Indian negress: they make excellent wives. I was married to one myself for two years.

MANGAN. Well, I am damned!

CAPTAIN SHOTOVER. I thought so. I was, too, for many years. The negress redeemed me.

MANGAN [feebly]. This is queer. I ought to walk out of this house.

CAPTAIN SHOTOVER. Why?

MANGAN. Well, many men would be offended by your style of talking.

CAPTAIN SHOTOVER. Nonsense! It's the other sort of talking that makes quarrels. Nobody ever quarrels with me.

[A GENTLEMAN, whose firstrate tailoring and frictionless manners proclaim the wellbred West Ender, comes in from the hall. He has an engaging air of being young and unmarried, but on close inspection is found to be at least over forty.]

THE GENTLEMAN. Excuse my intruding in this fashion; but there is no knocker on the door; and the bell does not seem to ring.

CAPTAIN SHOTOVER. Why should there be a knocker? Why should the bell ring? The door is open.

THE GENTLEMAN. Precisely. So I ventured to come in.

CAPTAIN SHOTOVER. Quite right. I will see about a room for you. [He makes for the door.]

THE GENTLEMAN [stopping him]. But I'm afraid you don't know who I am.

CAPTAIN SHOTOVER. Do you suppose that at my age I make distinctions between one fellowcreature and another? [He goes out. MANGAN and the newcomer stare at one another.]

MANGAN. Strange character, Captain Shotover, sir.

THE GENTLEMAN. Very.

CAPTAIN SHOTOVER [shouting outside]. Hesione: another person has arrived and wants a room. Man about town, well dressed, fifty.

THE GENTLEMAN. Fancy Hesione's feelings! May I ask are you a member of the family?

MANGAN. No.

THE GENTLEMAN. I am. At least a connexion.

[MRS HUSHABYE comes back.]

MRS HUSHABYE. How do you do? How good of you to come!

THE GENTLEMAN. I am very glad indeed to make your acquaintance, Hesione. [Instead of taking her hand he kisses her. At the same moment the CAPTAIN appears in the doorway.] You will excuse my kissing your daughter, Captain, when I tell you that—

CAPTAIN SHOTOVER. Stuff! Everyone kisses my daughter. Kiss her as much as you like. [He makes for the pantry]

THE GENTLEMAN. Thank you. One

moment. Captain. [*The* CAPTAIN *halts and turns. The* GENTLEMAN *goes to him affably.*] Do you happen to remember— but probably you dont, as it occurred many years ago—that your younger daughter married a numskull.

CAPTAIN SHOTOVER. Yes. She said she'd marry anybody to get away from this house. I should not have recognized you: your head is no longer like a walnut. Your aspect is softened. You have been boiled in bread and milk for years and years, like other married men. Poor devil! [*He disappears into the pantry.*]

MRS HUSHABYE [*going past* MANGAN *to the* GENTLEMAN *and scrutinizing him*]. I dont believe you are Hastings Utterword.

THE GENTLEMAN. I am not.

MRS HUSHABYE. Then what business had you to kiss me?

THE GENTLEMAN. I thought I would like to. The fact is, I am Randall Utterword, the unworthy younger brother of Hastings. I was abroad diplomatizing when he was married.

LADY UTTERWORD [*dashing in*]. Hesione: where is the key of the wardrobe in my room? My diamonds are in my dressing-bag: I must lock it up— [*Recognizing the stranger with a shock.*] Randall: how dare you? [*She marches at him past* MRS HUSHABYE, *who retreats and joins* MANGAN *near the sofa.*]

RANDALL. How dare I what? I am not doing anything.

LADY UTTERWORD. Who told you I was here?

RANDALL. Hastings. You had just left when I called on you at Claridge's; so I followed you down here. You are looking extremely well.

LADY UTTERWORD. Dont presume to tell me so.

MRS HUSHABYE. What is wrong with Mr Randall, Addy?

LADY UTTERWORD [*recollecting herself*]. Oh, nothing. But he has no right to come bothering you and papa without being invited. [*She goes to the window-seat and sits down, turning away from them ill-humoredly and looking into the garden, where* HECTOR *and* ELLIE *are now seen strolling together.*]

MRS HUSHABYE. I think you have not met Mr Mangan, Addy.

LADY UTTERWORD [*turning her head and nodding coldly to* MANGAN]. I beg

your pardon. Randall: you have flustered me so: I made a perfect fool of myself.

MRS HUSHABYE. Lady Utterword. My sister. My younger sister.

MANGAN [*bowing*]. Pleased to meet you, Lady Utterword.

LADY UTTERWORD [*with marked interest*]. Who is that gentleman walking in the garden with Miss Dunn?

MRS HUSHABYE. I don't know. She quarrelled mortally with my husband only ten minutes ago; and I didn't know anyone else had come. It must be a visitor. [*She goes to the window to look.*] Oh, it is Hector. Theyve made it up.

LADY UTTERWORD. Your husband! That handsome man?

MRS HUSHABYE. Well, why shouldnt my husband be a handsome man?

RANDALL [*joining them at the window*]. One's husband never is, Ariadne. [*He sits by* LADY UTTERWORD, *on her right.*]

MRS HUSHABYE. One's sister's husband always is, Mr Randall.

LADY UTTERWORD. Dont be vulgar, Randall. And you, Hesione, are just as bad.

[ELLIE *and* HECTOR *come in from the garden by the starboard door.* RANDALL *rises.* ELLIE *retires into the corner near the pantry.* HECTOR *comes forward; and* LADY UTTERWORD *rises looking her very best.*]

MRS HUSHABYE. Hector: this is Addy.

HECTOR [*apparently surprised*]. Not this lady.

LADY UTTERWORD [*smiling*]. Why not?

HECTOR [*looking at her with a piercing glance of deep but respectful admiration, his moustache bristling*]. I thought— [*Pulling himself together.*] I beg your pardon, Lady Utterword. I am extremely glad to welcome you at last under our roof. [*He offers his hand with grave courtesy.*]

MRS HUSHABYE. She wants to be kissed, Hector.

LADY UTTERWORD. Hesione! [*But she still smiles.*]

MRS HUSHABYE. Call her Addy; and kiss her like a good brother-in-law; and have done with it. [*She leaves them to themselves.*]

HECTOR. Behave yourself, Hesione. Lady Utterword is entitled not only to hospitality but to civilization.

LADY UTTERWORD [*gratefully*]. Thank

you, Hector. [*They shake hands cordially.*]

[MAZZINI DUNN *is seen crossing the garden from starboard to port.*]

CAPTAIN SHOTOVER [*coming from the pantry and addressing* ELLIE]. Your father has washed himself.

ELLIE [*quite self-possessed*]. He often does, Captain Shotover.

CAPTAIN SHOTOVER. A strange conversion! I saw him through the pantry window.

[MAZZINI DUNN *enters through the port window door, newly washed and brushed, and stops, smiling benevolently, between* MANGAN *and* MRS HUSHABYE.]

MRS HUSHABYE [*introducing*]. Mr. Mazzini Dunn, Lady Ut—oh, I forgot: youve met. [*Indicating* ELLIE.] Miss Dunn.

MAZZINI [*walking across the room to take* ELLIE'S *hand, and beaming at his own naughty irony*]. I have met Miss Dunn also. She is my daughter. [*He draws her arm through his caressingly.*]

MRS HUSHABYE. Of course: how stupid! Mr Utterword, my sister's—er—

RANDALL [*shaking hands agreeably*]. Her brother-in-law, Mr Dunn. How do you do?

MRS HUSHABYE. This is my husband.

HECTOR. We have 'met, dear. Dont introduce us any more. [*He moves away to the big chair, and adds.*] Wont you sit down, Lady Utterword? [*She does so very graciously.*]

MRS HUSHABYE. Sorry. I hate it: it's like making people shew their tickets.

MAZZINI [*sententiously*]. How little it tells us, after all! The great question is, not who we are, but what we are.

CAPTAIN SHOTOVER. Ha! What are you?

MAZZINI [*taken aback*]. What am I?

CAPTAIN SHOTOVER. A thief, a pirate, and a murderer.

MAZZINI. I assure you you are mistaken.

CAPTAIN SHOTOVER. An adventurous life; but what does it end in? Respectability. A ladylike daughter. The language and appearance of a city missionary. Let it be a warning to all of you. [*He goes out through the garden.*]

DUNN. I hope nobody here believes that I am a thief, a pirate, or a murderer.

Mrs Hushabye: will you excuse me a moment? I must really go and explain. [*He follows the* CAPTAIN.]

MRS HUSHABYE [*as he goes*]. It's no use. Youd really better— [*But* DUNN *has vanished.*] We had better all go out and look for some tea. We never have regular tea; but you can always get some when you want: the servants keep it stewing all day. The kitchen veranda is the best place to ask. May I shew you? [*She goes to the starboard door.*]

RANDALL [*going with her*]. Thank you, I dont think I'll take any tea this afternoon. But if you will shew me the garden—?

MRS HUSHABYE. Theres nothing to see in the garden except papa's observatory, and a gravel pit with a cave where he keeps dynamite and things of that sort. However, it's pleasanter out of doors; so come along.

RANDALL. Dynamite! Isnt that rather risky?

MRS HUSHABYE. Well, we dont sit in the gravel pit when theres a thunderstorm.

LADY UTTERWORD. Thats something new. What is the dynamite for?

HECTOR. To blow up the human race if it goes too far. He is trying to discover a psychic ray that will explode all the explosives at the will of a Mahatma.

ELLIE. The Captain's tea is delicious, Mr Utterword.

MRS HUSHABYE [*stopping in the doorway*]. Do you mean to say that youve had some of my father's tea? that you got round him before you were ten minutes in the house?

ELLIE. I did.

MRS HUSHABYE. You little devil! [*She goes out with* RANDALL.]

MANGAN. Wont you come, Miss Ellie?

ELLIE. I'm too tired. I'll take a book up to my room and rest a little. [*She goes to the bookshelf.*]

MANGAN. Right. You cant do better. But I'm disappointed. [*He follows* RANDALL *and* MRS HUSHABYE.]

[ELLIE, HECTOR, *and* LADY UTTERWORD *are left.* HECTOR *is close to* LADY UTTERWORD. *They look at* ELLIE, *waiting for her to go.*]

ELLIE [*looking at the title of a book*]. Do you like stories of adventure, Lady Utterword?

LADY UTTERWORD [*patronizingly*]. Of course, dear.

ELLIE. Then I'll leave you to Mr Hushabye. [*She goes out through the hall.*]

HECTOR. That girl is mad about tales of adventure. The lies I have to tell her!

LADY UTTERWORD [*not interested in* ELLIE]. When you saw me what did you mean by saying that you thought, and then stopping short? What did you think?

HECTOR [*folding his arms and looking down at her magnetically*]. May I tell you?

LADY UTTERWORD. Of course.

HECTOR. It will not sound very civil. I was on the point of saying 'I thought you were a plain woman.'

LADY UTTERWORD. Oh for shame, Hector! What right had you to notice whether I am plain or not?

HECTOR. Listen to me, Ariadne. Until today I have seen only photographs of you; and no photograph can give the strange fascination of the daughters of that super-natural old man. There is some damnable quality in them that destroys men's moral sense, and carries them beyond honor and dishonor. You know that, dont you?

LADY UTTERWORD. Perhaps I do, Hector. But let me warn you once for all that I am a rigidly conventional woman. You may think because I'm a Shotover that I'm a Bohemian, because we are all so horribly Bohemian. But I'm not. I hate and loathe Bohemianism. No child brought up in a strict Puritan household ever suffered from Puritanism as I suffered from our Bohemianism.

HECTOR. Our children are like that. They spend their holidays in the houses of their respectable schoolfellows.

LADY UTTERWORD. I shall invite them for Christmas.

HECTOR. Their absence leaves us both without our natural chaperons.

LADY UTTERWORD. Children are certainly very inconvenient sometimes. But intelligent people can always manage, unless they are Bohemians.

HECTOR. You are no Bohemian; but you are no Puritan either: your attraction is alive and powerful. What sort of woman do you count yourself?

LADY UTTERWORD. I am a woman of the world, Hector; and I can assure you that if you will only take the trouble always to do the perfectly correct thing, and to say the perfectly correct thing, you can do just what you like. An ill-conducted, careless woman gets simply no chance. An ill-conducted, careless man is never allowed within arm's length of any woman worth knowing.

HECTOR. I see. You are neither a Bohemian woman nor a Puritan woman. You are a dangerous woman.

LADY UTTERWORD. On the contrary, I am a safe woman.

HECTOR. You are a most accursedly attractive woman. Mind: I am not making love to you. I do not like being attracted. But you had better know how I feel if you are going to stay here.

LADY UTTERWORD. You are an exceedingly clever lady-killer, Hector. And terribly handsome. I am quite a good player, myself, at that game. Is it quite understood that we are only playing?

HECTOR. Quite. I am deliberately playing the fool, out of sheer worthlessness.

LADY UTTERWORD [*rising brightly*]. Well, you are my brother-in-law. Hesione asked you to kiss me. [*He seizes her in his arms, and kisses her strenuously.*] Oh! that was a little more than play, brother-in-law. [*She pushes him suddenly away.*] You shall not do that again.

HECTOR. In effect, you got your claws deeper into me than I intended.

MRS HUSHABYE [*coming in from the garden*]. Dont let me disturb you: I only want a cap to put on daddiest. The sun is setting; and he'll catch cold. [*She makes for the door leading to the hall.*]

LADY UTTERWORD. Your husband is quite charming, darling. He has actually condescended to kiss me at last. I shall go into the garden: it's cooler now. [*She goes out by the port door.*]

MRS HUSHABYE. Take care, dear child. I dont believe any man can kiss Addy without falling in love with her. [*She goes into the hall.*]

HECTOR [*striking himself on the chest*]. Fool! Goat!

[MRS HUSHABYE *comes back with the Captain's cap.*]

HECTOR. Your sister is an extremely enterprising old girl. Wheres Miss Dunn!

MRS HUSHABYE. Mangan says she has

gone up to her room for a nap. Addy wont let you talk to Ellie: she has marked you for her own.

HECTOR. She has the diabolical family fascination. I began making love to her automatically. What am I to do? I cant fall in love; and I cant hurt a woman's feelings by telling her so when she falls in love with me. And as women are always falling in love with my moustache I get landed in all sorts of tedious and terrifying flirtations in which I'm not a bit in earnest.

MRS HUSHABYE. Oh, neither is Addy. She has never been in love in her life, though she has always been trying to fall in head over ears. She is worse than you, because you had one real go at least, with me.

HECTOR. That was a confounded madness. I cant believe that such an amazing experience is common. It has left its mark on me. I believe that is why I have never been able to repeat it.

MRS HUSHABYE [laughing and caressing his arm]. We were frightfully in love with one another, Hector. It was such an enchanting dream that I have never been able to grudge it to you or anyone else since. I have invited all sorts of pretty women to the house on the chance of giving you another turn. But it has never come off.

HECTOR. I dont know that I want it to come off. It was damned dangerous. You fascinated me; but I loved you; so it was heaven. This sister of yours fascinates me; but I hate her; so it is hell. I shall kill her if she persists.

MRS HUSHABYE. Nothing will kill Addy: she is as strong as a horse. [Releasing him.] Now I am going off to fascinate somebody.

HECTOR. The Foreign Office toff? Randall?

MRS HUSHABYE. Goodness gracious, no! Why should I fascinate him?

HECTOR. I presume you dont mean the bloated capitalist, Mangan?

MRS HUSHABYE. Hm! I think he had better be fascinated by me than by Ellie. [She is going into the garden when the CAPTAIN comes in from it with some sticks in his hand.] What have you got there, daddiest?

CAPTAIN SHOTOVER. Dynamite.

MRS HUSHABYE. Youve been to the gravel pit. Dont drop it about the house: theres a dear. [She goes into the garden, where the evening light is now very red.]

HECTOR. Listen, O sage. How long dare you concentrate on a feeling without risking having it fixed in your consciousness all the rest of your life?

CAPTAIN SHOTOVER. Ninety minutes. An hour and a half. [He goes into the pantry.]

[HECTOR, left alone, contracts his brows, and falls into a day-dream. He does not move for some time. Then he folds his arms. Then, throwing his hands behind him, and gripping one with the other, he strides tragically once to and fro. Suddenly he snatches his walking-stick from the teak table, and draws it; for it is a sword-stick. He fights a desperate duel with an imaginary antagonist, and after many vicissitudes runs him through the body up to the hilt. He sheathes his sword and throws it on the sofa, falling into another reverie as he does so. He looks straight into the eyes of an imaginary woman; seizes her by the arms; and says in a deep and thrilling tone 'Do you love me!' The CAPTAIN comes out of the pantry at this moment; and HECTOR, caught with his arms stretched out and his fists clenched, has to account for his attitude by going through a series of gymnastic exercises.]

CAPTAIN SHOTOVER. That sort of strength is no good. You will never be as strong as a gorilla.

HECTOR. What is the dynamite for?

CAPTAIN SHOTOVER. To kill fellows like Mangan.

HECTOR. No use. They will always be able to buy more dynamite than you.

CAPTAIN SHOTOVER. I will make a dynamite that he cannot explode.

HECTOR. And that you can, eh?

CAPTAIN SHOTOVER. Yes: when I have attained the seventh degree of concentration.

HECTOR. Whats the use of that? You never do attain it.

CAPTAIN SHOTOVER. What then is to be done? Are we to be kept for ever in the mud by these hogs to whom the universe is nothing but a machine for greasing their bristles and filling their snouts?

HECTOR. Are Mangan's bristles worse than Randall's lovelocks?

CAPTAIN SHOTOVER. We must win powers of life and death over them both. I refuse to die until I have invented the means.

HECTOR. Who are we that we should judge them?

CAPTAIN SHOTOVER. What are they that they should judge us? Yet they do, unhesitatingly. There is an enmity between our seed and their seed. They know it and act on it, strangling our souls. They believe in themselves. When we believe in ourselves, we shall kill them.

HECTOR. It is the same seed. You forget that your pirate has a very nice daughter. Mangan's son may be a Plato: Randall's a Shelley. What was my father?

CAPTAIN SHOTOVER. The damndest scoundrel I ever met. [*He replaces the drawing-board; sits down at the table; and begins to mix a wash of color.*]

HECTOR. Precisely. Well, dare you kill his innocent grandchildren?

CAPTAIN SHOTOVER. They are mine also.

HECTOR. Just so. We are members one of another. [*He throws himself carelessly on the sofa.*] I tell you I have often thought of this killing of human vermin. Many men have thought of it. Decent men are like Daniel in the lion's den: their survival is a miracle; and they do not always survive. We live among the Mangans and Randalls and Billie Dunns as they, poor devils, live among the disease germs and the doctors and the lawyers and the parsons and the restaurant chefs and the tradesmen and the servants and all the rest of the parasites and blackmailers. What are our terrors to theirs? Give me the power to kill them; and I'll spare them in sheer—

CAPTAIN SHOTOVER [*cutting in sharply*]. Fellow feeling?

HECTOR. No. I should kill myself if I believed that. I must believe that my spark, small as it is, is divine, and that the red light over their door is hell fire. I should spare them in simple magnanimous pity.

CAPTAIN SHOTOVER. You cant spare them until you have the power to kill them. At present they have the power to kill you. There are millions of blacks over the water for them to train and let loose on us. Theyre going to do it. Theyre doing it already.

HECTOR. They are too stupid to use their power.

CAPTAIN SHOTOVER [*throwing down his brush and coming to the end of the sofa*]. Do not deceive yourself: they do use it. We kill the better half of ourselves every day to propitiate them. The knowledge that these people are there to render all our aspirations barren prevents us having the aspirations. And when we are tempted to seek their destruction they bring forth demons to delude us, disguised as pretty daughters, and singers and poets and the like, for whose sake we spare them.

HECTOR [*sitting up and leaning towards him*]. May not Hesione be such a demon, brought forth by you lest I should slay you?

CAPTAIN SHOTOVER. That is possible. She has used you up, and left you nothing but dreams, as some women do.

HECTOR. Vampire women, demon women.

CAPTAIN SHOTOVER. Men think the world well lost for them, and lose it accordingly. Who are the men that do things? The husbands of the shrew and of the drunkard, the men with the thorn in the flesh. [*Walking distractedly away towards the pantry.*] I must think these things out. [*Turning suddenly.*] But I go on with the dynamite none the less. I will discover a ray mightier than any X-ray: a mind ray that will explode the ammunition in the belt of my adversary before he can point his gun at me. And I must hurry. I am old: I have no time to waste in talk. [*He is about to go into the pantry, and* HECTOR *is making for the hall, when* HESIONE *comes back.*]

MRS HUSHABYE. Daddiest: you and Hector must come and help me to entertain all these people. What on earth were you shouting about?

HECTOR [*stopping in the act of turning the doorhandle*]. He is madder than usual.

MRS HUSHABYE. We all are.

HECTOR. I must change. [*He resumes his door opening.*]

MRS HUSHABYE. Stop, stop. Come back,

both of you. Come back. [*They return, reluctantly.*] Money is running short.

HECTOR. Money! Where are my April dividends?

MRS HUSHABYE. Where is the snow that fell last year?

CAPTAIN SHOTOVER. Where is all the money you had for that patent lifeboat I invented?

MRS HUSHABYE. Five hundred pounds; and I have made it last since Easter!

CAPTAIN SHOTOVER. Since Easter! Barely four months! Monstrous extravagance! I could live for seven years on £500.

MRS HUSHABYE. Not keeping open house as we do here, daddiest.

CAPTAIN SHOTOVER. Only £500 for that lifeboat! I got twelve thousand for the invention before that.

MRS HUSHABYE. Yes, dear; but that was for the ship with the magnetic keel that sucked up submarines. Living at the rate we do, you cannot afford life-saving inventions. Cant you think of something that will murder half Europe at one bang?

CAPTAIN SHOTOVER. No. I am ageing fast. My mind does not dwell on slaughter as it did when I was a boy. Why doesnt your husband invent something? He does nothing but tell lies to women.

HECTOR. Well, that is a form of invention, is it not? However, you are right: I ought to support my wife.

MRS HUSHABYE. Indeed you shall do nothing of the sort: I should never see you from breakfast to dinner. I want my husband.

HECTOR [*bitterly*]. I might as well be your lapdog.

MRS HUSHABYE. Do you want to be my breadwinner, like the other poor husbands?

HECTOR. No, by thunder! What a damned creature a husband is anyhow!

MRS HUSHABYE [*to the* CAPTAIN]. What about that harpoon cannon?

CAPTAIN SHOTOVER. No use. It kills whales, not men.

MRS HUSHABYE. Why not? You fire the harpoon out of a cannon. It sticks in the enemy's general; you wind him in; and there you are.

HECTOR. You are your father's daughter, Hesione.

CAPTAIN SHOTOVER. There is something in it. Not to wind in generals: they are not dangerous. But one could fire a grapnel and wind in a machine gun or even a tank. I will think it out.

MRS HUSHABYE [*squeezing the* CAPTAIN's *arm affectionately*]. Saved! You are a darling, daddiest. Now we must go back to these dreadful people and entertain them.

CAPTAIN SHOTOVER. They have had no dinner. Dont forget that.

HECTOR. Neither have I. And it is dark: it must be all hours.

MRS HUSHABYE. Oh, Guinness will produce some sort of dinner for them. The servants always take jolly good care that there is food in the house.

CAPTAIN SHOTOVER [*raising a strange wail in the darkness*]. What a house! What a daughter!

MRS HUSHABYE [*raving*]. What a father!

HECTOR [*following suit*]. What a husband!

CAPTAIN SHOTOVER. Is there no thunder in heaven?

HECTOR. Is there no beauty, no bravery, on earth?

MRS HUSHABYE. What do men want? They have their food, their firesides, their clothes mended, and our love at the end of the day. Why are they not satisfied? Why do they envy us the pain with which we bring them into the world, and make strange dangers and torments for themselves to be even with us?

CAPTAIN SHOTOVER [*weirdly chanting*].
I built a house for my daughters,
  and opened the doors thereof,
That men might come for their choosing, and their betters spring from
  their love;
But one of them married a numskull;

HECTOR [*taking up the rhythm*].
          The other a liar wed;

MRS HUSHABYE [*completing the stanza*].
And now must she lie beside him,
  even as she made her bed.

LADY UTTERWORD [*calling from the garden*]. Hesione! Hesione! Where are you?

HECTOR. The cat is on the tiles.

MRS HUSHABYE. Coming, darling, coming. [*She goes quickly into the garden.*]
[*The* CAPTAIN *goes back to his place at the table.*]

HECTOR [*going into the hall*]. Shall I turn up the lights for you?

CAPTAIN SHOTOVER. No. Give me deeper darkness. Money is not made in the light.

ACT II

[*The same room, with the lights turned up and the curtains drawn.* ELLIE *comes in, followed by* MANGAN. *Both are dressed for dinner. She strolls to the drawing-table. He comes between the table and the wicker chair.*]

MANGAN. What a dinner! I dont call it a dinner: I call it a meal.

ELLIE. I am accustomed to meals, Mr Mangan, and very lucky to get them. Besides, the Captain cooked some macaroni for me.

MANGAN [*shuddering liverishly*]. Too rich: I cant eat such things. I suppose it's because I have to work so much with my brain. Thats the worst of being a man of business: you are always thinking, thinking, thinking. By the way, now that we are alone, may I take the opportunity to come to a little understanding with you?

ELLIE [*settling into the draughtsman's seat*]. Certainly. I should like to.

MANGAN [*taken aback*]. Should you? That surprises me; for I thought I noticed this afternoon that you avoided me all you could. Not for the first time either.

ELLIE. I was very tired and upset. I wasnt used to the ways of this extraordinary house. Please forgive me.

MANGAN. Oh, thats all right: I dont mind. But Captain Shotover has been talking to me about you. You and me, you know.

ELLIE [*interested*]. The Captain! What did he say?

MANGAN. Well, he noticed the difference between our ages.

ELLIE. He notices everything.

MANGAN. You dont mind, then?

ELLIE. Of course I know quite well that our engagement—

MANGAN. Oh! you call it an engagement.

ELLIE. Well, isnt it?

MANGAN. Oh, yes, yes: no doubt it is

if you hold to it. This is the first time youve used the word; and I didnt quite know where we stood: thats all. [*He sits down in the wicker chair; and resigns himself to allow her to lead the conversation.*] You were saying—?

ELLIE. Was I? I forget. Tell me. Do you like this part of the country? I heard you ask Mr Hushabye at dinner whether there are any nice houses to let down here.

MANGAN. I like the place. The air suits me. I shouldnt be surprised if I settled down here.

ELLIE. Nothing would please me better. The air suits me too. And I want to be near Hesione.

MANGAN [*with growing uneasiness*]. The air may suit us; but the question is, should we suit one another? Have you thought about that?

ELLIE. Mr Mangan: we must be sensible, mustnt we? It's no use pretending that we are Romeo and Juliet. But we can get on very well together if we choose to make the best of it. Your kindness of heart will make it easy for me.

MANGAN [*leaning forward, with the beginning of something like deliberate unpleasantness in his voice*]. Kindness of heart, eh? I ruined your father, didnt I?

ELLIE. Oh, not intentionally.

MANGAN. Yes I did. Ruined him on purpose.

ELLIE. On purpose!

MANGAN. Not out of ill-nature, you know. And youll admit that I kept a job for him when I had finished with him. But business is business; and I ruined him as a matter of business.

ELLIE. I dont understand how that can be. Are you trying to make me feel that I need not be grateful to you, so that I may choose freely?

MANGAN [*rising aggressively*]. No. I mean what I say.

ELLIE. But how could it possibly do you any good to ruin my father? The money he lost was yours.

MANGAN [*with a sour laugh*]. Was mine! It is mine, Miss Ellie, and all the money the other fellows lost too. [*He shoves his hands into his pockets and shews his teeth.*] I just smoked them out like a hive of bees. What do you say to that? A bit of a shock, eh?

ELLIE. It would have been, this morning. Now! you cant think how little it matters. But it's quite interesting. Only, you must explain it to me. I dont understand it. [*Propping her elbows on the drawing-board and her chin on her hands, she composes herself to listen with a combination of conscious curiosity with unconscious contempt which provokes him to more and more unpleasantness, and an attempt at patronage of her ignorance.*]

MANGAN. Of course you dont understand: what do you know about business? You just listen and learn. Your father's business was a new business; and I dont start new businesses: I let other fellows start them. They put all their money and their friends' money into starting them. They wear out their souls and bodies trying to make a success of them. Theyre what you call enthusiasts. But the first dead lift of the thing is too much for them; and they havnt enough financial experience. In a year or so they have either to let the whole show go bust, or sell out to a new lot of fellows for a few deferred ordinary shares: that is, if theyre lucky enough to get anything at all. As likely as not the very same thing happens to the new lot. They put in more money and a couple of years more work; and then perhaps they have to sell out to a third lot. If it's really a big thing the third lot will have to sell out too, and leave their work and their money behind them. And thats where the real business man comes in: where I come in. But I'm cleverer than some: I dont mind dropping a little money to start the process. I took your father's measure. I saw that he had a sound idea, and that he would work himself silly for it if he got the chance. I saw that he was a child in business, and was dead certain to outrun his expenses and be in too great a hurry to wait for his market. I knew that the surest way to ruin a man who doesnt know how to handle money is to give him some. I explained my idea to some friends in the city, and they found the money; for I take no risks in ideas, even when theyre my own. Your father and the friends that ventured their money with him were no more to me than a heap of squeezed lemons. Youve been wasting your gratitude: my kind heart is all rot. I'm sick of it. When I see your father beam-

ing at me with his moist, grateful eyes, regularly wallowing in gratitude, I sometimes feel I must tell him the truth or burst. What stops me is that I know he wouldnt believe me. He'd think it was my modesty, as you did just now. He'd think anything rather than the truth, which is that he's a blamed fool, and I am a man that knows how to take care of himself. [*He throws himself back into the big chair with large self-approval.*] Now what do you think of me, Miss Ellie?

ELLIE [*dropping her hands*]. How strange! that my mother, who knew nothing at all about business, should have been quite right about you! She always said—not before papa, of course, but to us children—that you were just that sort of man.

MANGAN [*sitting up, much hurt*]. Oh! did she? And yet she'd have let you marry me.

ELLIE. Well, you see, Mr Mangan, my mother married a very good man—for whatever you may think of my father as a man of business, he is the soul of goodness—and she is not at all keen on my doing the same.

MANGAN. Anyhow, you dont want to marry me now, do you?

ELLIE [*very calmly*]. Oh, I think so. Why not?

MANGAN [*rising aghast*]. Why not!

ELLIE. I dont see why we shouldnt get on very well together.

MANGAN. Well, but look here, you know— [*He stops, quite at a loss.*]

ELLIE [*patiently*]. Well?

MANGAN. Well, I thought you were rather particular about people's characters.

ELLIE. If we women were particular about men's characters, we should never get married at all, Mr Mangan.

MANGAN. A child like you talking of 'we women'! What next! Youre not in earnest?

ELLIE. Yes I am. Arnt you?

MANGAN. You mean to hold me to it?

ELLIE. Do you wish to back out of it?

MANGAN. Oh no. Not exactly back out of it.

ELLIE. Well?

[*He has nothing to say. With a long whispered whistle, he drops into the wicker chair and stares before him like a beggared gambler. But a cunning look soon comes into his face. He leans over towards her on his right elbow, and speaks in a low steady voice.*]

MANGAN. Suppose I told you I was in love with another woman!

ELLIE [*echoing him*]. Suppose I told you I was in love with another man!

MANGAN [*bouncing angrily out of his chair*]. I'm not joking.

ELLIE. Who told you I was?

MANGAN. I tell you I'm serious. Youre too young to be serious; but youll have to believe me. I want to be near your friend Mrs Hushabye. I'm in love with her. Now the murder's out.

ELLIE. I want to be near your friend Mr Hushabye. I'm in love with him. [*She rises and adds with a frank air.*] Now we are in one another's confidence, we shall be real friends. Thank you for telling me.

MANGAN [*almost beside himself*]. Do you think I'll be made a convenience of like this?

ELLIE. Come, Mr. Mangan! you made a business convenience of my father. Well, a woman's business is marriage. Why shouldnt I make a domestic convenience of you?

MANGAN. Because I dont choose, see? Because I'm not a silly gull like your father. Thats why.

ELLIE [*with serene contempt*]. You are not good enough to clean my father's boots, Mr Mangan; and I am paying you a great compliment in condescending to make a convenience of you, as you call it. Of course you are free to throw over our engagement if you like; but, if you do, youll never enter Hesione's house again: I will take care of that.

MANGAN [*gasping*]. You little devil, youve done me. [*On the point of collapsing into the big chair again he recovers himself.*] Wait a bit, though: youre not so cute as you think. You cant beat Boss Mangan as easy as that. Suppose I go straight to Mrs Hushabye and tell her that youre in love with her husband.

ELLIE. She knows it.

MANGAN. You told her!!!

ELLIE. She told me.

MANGAN [*clutching at his bursting temples*]. Oh, this is a crazy house. Or else I'm going clean off my chump. Is she

making a swop with you—she to have your husband and you to have hers?

ELLIE. Well, you dont want us both, do you?

MANGAN [*throwing himself into the chair distractedly*]. My brain wont stand it. My head's going to split. Help! Help me to hold it. Quick: hold it: squeeze it. Save me. [*Ellie comes behind his chair; clasps his head hard for a moment; then begins to draw her hands from his forehead back to his ears.*] Thank you. [*Drowsily.*] Thats very refreshing. [*Waking a little.*] Dont you hypnotize me, though. Ive seen men made fools of by hypnotism.

ELLIE [*steadily*]. Be quiet. Ive seen men made fools of without hypnotism.

MANGAN [*humbly*]. You dont dislike touching me, I hope. You never touched me before, I noticed.

ELLIE. Not since you fell in love naturally with a grown-up nice woman, who will never expect you to make love to her. And I will never expect him to make love to me.

MANGAN. He may, though.

ELLIE [*making her passes rhythmically*]. Hush. Go to sleep. Do you hear? You are to go to sleep, go to sleep, go to sleep; be quiet, deeply deeply quiet; sleep, sleep, sleep, sleep, sleep.

[*He falls asleep.* ELLIE *steals away; turns the light out; and goes into the garden.*

NURSE GUINNESS *opens the door and is seen in the light which comes in from the hall.*]

GUINNESS [*speaking to someone outside*]. Mr Mangan's not here, ducky: theres no one here. It's all dark.

MRS HUSHABYE [*without*]. Try the garden. Mr Dunn and I will be in my boudoir. Shew him the way.

GUINNESS. Yes, ducky. [*She makes for the garden door in the dark; stumbles over the sleeping* MANGAN; *and screams.*] Ahoo! Oh Lord, sir! I beg your pardon, I'm sure: I didnt see you in the dark. Who is it? [*She goes back to the door and turns on the light.*] Oh, Mr Mangan, sir, I hope I havnt hurt you plumping into your lap like that. [*Coming to him.*] I was looking for you, sir. Mrs Hushabye says will you please— [*Noticing that he remains quite insensible.*] Oh, my good

Lord, I hope I havnt killed him. Sir! Mr Mangan! Sir! [*She shakes him; and he is rolling inertly off the chair on the floor when she holds him up and props him against the cushion.*] Miss Hessy! Miss Hessy! Quick, doty darling. Miss Hessy! [MRS HUSHABYE *comes in from the hall, followed by* MAZZINI DUNN.] Oh, Miss Hessy, Ive been and killed him.

[MAZZINI *runs round the back of the chair to* MANGAN's *right hand, and sees that the nurse's words are apparently only too true.*]

MAZZINI. What tempted you to commit such a crime, woman?

MRS HUSHABYE [*trying not to laugh*]. Do you mean you did it on purpose?

GUINNESS. Now is it likely I'd kill any man on purpose. I fell over him in the dark; and I'm a pretty tidy weight. He never spoke nor moved until I shook him; and then he would have dropped dead on the floor. Isnt it tiresome?

MRS HUSHABYE [*going past the nurse to* MANGAN's *side, and inspecting him less credulously than* MAZZINI]. Nonsense! he is not dead: he is only asleep. I can see him breathing.

GUINNESS. But why wont he wake?

MAZZINI [*speaking very politely into* MANGAN's *ear*]. Mangan! My dear Mangan! [*He blows into* MANGAN's *ear.*]

MRS HUSHABYE. Thats no good. [*She shakes him vigorously.*] Mr Mangan: wake up. Do you hear? [*He begins to roll over.*] Oh! Nurse, nurse: he's falling: help me.

[*Nurse Guinness rushes to the rescue. With* MAZZINI's *assistance,* MANGAN *is propped safely up again.*]

GUINNESS [*behind the chair; bending over to test the case with her nose*]. Would he be drunk, do you think, pet?

MRS HUSHABYE. Had he any of papa's rum?

MAZZINI. It cant be that: he is most abstemious. I am afraid he drank too much formerly, and has to drink too little now. You know, Mrs Hushabye, I really think he has been hypnotized.

GUINNESS. Hip no what, sir?

MAZZINI. One evening at home, after we had seen a hypnotizing performance, the children began playing at it; and Ellie stroked my head. I assure you I went off dead asleep; and they had to send for a professional to wake me up after I had slept eighteen hours. They had to carry me upstairs; and as the poor children were not very strong, they let me slip; and I rolled right down the whole flight and never woke up. [*Mrs Hushabye splutters.*] Oh, you may laugh, Mrs Hushabye; but I might have been killed.

MRS HUSHABYE. I couldnt have helped laughing even if you had been, Mr. Dunn. So Ellie has hypnotized him. What fun!

MAZZINI. Oh no, no, no. It was such a terrible lesson to her: nothing would induce her to try such a thing again.

MRS HUSHABYE. Then who did it? *I* didnt.

MAZZINI. I thought perhaps the Captain might have done it unintentionally. He is so fearfully magnetic: I feel vibrations whenever he comes close to me.

GUINNESS. The Captain will get him out of it anyhow, sir: I'll back him for that. I'll go fetch him. [*She makes for the pantry.*]

MRS HUSHABYE. Wait a bit. [*To* MAZZINI.] You say he is all right for eighteen hours?

MAZZINI. Well, *I* was asleep for eighteen hours.

MRS HUSHABYE. Were you any the worse for it?

MAZZINI. I dont quite remember. They had poured brandy down my throat, you see; and—

MRS HUSHABYE. Quite. Anyhow, you survived. Nurse, darling: go and ask Miss Dunn to come to us here. Say I want to speak to her particularly. You will find her with Mr Hushabye probably.

GUINNESS. I think not, ducky: Miss Addy is with him. But I'll find her and send her to you. [*She goes out into the garden.*]

MRS HUSHABYE [*calling* MAZZINI's *attention to the figure on the chair*]. Now, Mr Dunn, look. Just look. Look hard. Do you still intend to sacrifice your daughter to that thing?

MAZZINI [*troubled*]. You have completely upset me, Mrs Hushabye, by all you have said to me. That anyone could imagine that I—I, a consecrated soldier of freedom, if I may say so—could sacrifice Ellie to anybody or anyone, or that I should ever have dreamed of forcing her inclinations in any way, is a most painful blow to my—well, I suppose you would say to my good opinion of myself.

MRS HUSHABYE [*rather stolidly*]. Sorry.

MAZZINI [*looking forlornly at the body*]. What is your objection to poor Mangan, Mrs Hushabye? He looks all right to me. But then I am so accustomed to him.

MRS HUSHABYE. Have you no heart? Have you no sense? Look at the brute! Think of poor weak innocent Ellie in the clutches of this slavedriver, who spends his life making thousands of rough violent workmen bend to his will and sweat for him: a man accustomed to have great masses of iron beaten into shape for him by steam-hammers! to fight with women and girls over a halfpenny an hour ruthlessly! a captain of industry, I think you call him, dont you? Are you going to fling your delicate, sweet, helpless child into such a beast's claws just because he will keep her in an expensive house and make her wear diamonds to shew how rich he is?

MAZZINI [*staring at her in wide-eyed amazement*]. Bless you, dear Mrs Hushabye, what romantic ideas of business you have! Poor dear Mangan isnt a bit like that.

MRS HUSHABYE [*scornfully*]. Poor dear Mangan indeed!

MAZZINI. But he doesnt know anything about machinery. He never goes near the men: he couldnt manage them: he is afraid of them. I never can get him to take the least interest in the works: he hardly knows more about them than you do. People are cruelly unjust to Mangan: they think he is all rugged strength just because his manners are bad.

MRS HUSHABYE. Do you mean to tell me he isnt strong enough to crush poor little Ellie?

MAZZINI. Of course it's very hard to say how any marriage will turn out; but speaking for myself, I should say that he wont have a dog's chance against Ellie. You know, Ellie has remarkable strength of character. I think it is because I taught her to like Shakespear when she was very young.

MRS HUSHABYE [*contemptuously*]. Shakespear! The next thing you will tell me is that you could have made a great deal more money than Mangan. [*She retires to the sofa, and sits down at the port end of it in the worst of humors.*]

MAZZINI [*following her and taking the other end*]. No: I'm no good at making money. I dont care enough for it, somehow. I'm not ambitious! that must be it. Mangan is wonderful about money: he thinks of nothing else. He is so dreadfully afraid of being poor. I am always thinking of other things: even at the works I think of the things we are doing and not of what they cost. And the worst of it is, poor Mangan doesnt know what to do with his money when he gets it. He is such a baby that he doesnt know even what to eat and drink: he has ruined his liver eating and drinking the wrong things; and now he can hardly eat at all. Ellie will diet him splendidly. You will be surprised when you come to know him better: he is really the most helpless of mortals. You get quite a protective feeling towards him.

MRS HUSHABYE. Then who manages his business, pray?

MAZZINI. I do. And of course other people like me.

MRS HUSHABYE. Footling people, you mean.

MAZZINI. I suppose youd think us so.

MRS HUSHABYE. And pray why dont you do without him if youre all so much cleverer?

MAZZINI. Oh, we couldnt: we should ruin the business in a year. I've tried; and I know. We should spend too much on everything. We should improve the quality of the goods and make them too dear. We should be sentimental about the hard cases among the workpeople. But Mangan keeps us in order. He is down on us about every extra halfpenny. We could never do without him. You see, he will sit up all night thinking of how to save sixpence. Wont Ellie make him jump, though, when she takes his house in hand!

MRS HUSHABYE. Then the creature is a fraud even as a captain of industry.

MAZZINI. I am afraid all the captains of industry are what you call frauds, Mrs. Hushabye. Of course there are some manufacturers who really do understand their own works; but they dont make as high a rate of profit as Mangan does. I assure you Mangan is quite a good fellow in his way. He means well.

MRS HUSHABYE. He doesn't look well. He is not in his first youth, is he?

MAZZINI. After all, no husband is in his first youth for very long. Mrs Hushabye. And men cant afford to marry in their first youth nowadays.

MRS HUSHABYE. Now if *I* said that, it would sound witty. Why cant you say it wittily? What on earth is the matter with you? Why dont you inspire everybody with confidence? with respect?

MAZZINI [*humbly*]. I think that what is the matter with me is that I am poor. You dont know what that means at home. Mind: I dont say they have ever complained. Theyve all been wonderful: theyve been proud of my poverty. Theyve even joked about it quite often. But my wife has had a very poor time of it. She has been quite resigned—

MRS HUSHABYE [*shuddering involuntarily*]!!

MAZZINI. There! You see, Mrs. Hushabye. I dont want Ellie to live on resignation.

MRS HUSHABYE. Do you want her to have to resign herself to living with a man she doesnt love?

MAZZINI [*wistfully*]. Are you sure that would be worse than living with a man she did love, if he was a footling person?

MRS HUSHABYE [*relaxing her contemptuous attitude, quite interested in MAZZINI now*]. You know, I really think you must love Ellie very much; for you become quite clever when you talk about her.

MAZZINI. I didnt know I was so very stupid on other subjects.

MRS HUSHABYE. You are, sometimes.

MAZZINI [*turning his head away; for his eyes are wet*]. I have learnt a good deal about myself from you, Mrs Hushabye; and I'm afraid I shall not be the happier for your plain speaking. But if you thought I needed it to make me think of Ellie's happiness you were very much mistaken.

MRS HUSHABYE [*leaning towards him kindly*]. Have I been a beast?

MAZZINI [*pulling himself together*]. It doesnt matter about me, Mrs Hushabye. I think you like Ellie; and that is enough for me.

MRS HUSHABYE. I'm beginning to like you a little. I perfectly loathed you at first. I thought you the most odious, self-satisfied, boresome elderly prig I ever met.

MAZZINI [*resigned, and now quite cheerful*]. I daresay I am all that. I never have been a favorite with gorgeous women like you. They always frighten me.

MRS HUSHABYE [*pleased*]. Am I a gorgeous woman, Mazzini? I shall fall in love with you presently.

MAZZINI [*with placid gallantry*]. No you wont, Hesione. But you would be quite safe. Would you believe it that quite a lot of women have flirted with me because I am quite safe? But they get tired of me for the same reason.

MRS HUSHABYE [*mischievously*]. Take care. You may not be so safe as you think.

MAZZINI. Oh yes, quite safe. You see, I have been in love really: the sort of love that only happens once. [*Softly.*] Thats why Ellie is such a lovely girl.

MRS HUSHABYE. Well, really, you are coming out. Are you quite sure you wont let me tempt you into a second grand passion?

MAZZINI. Quite. It wouldnt be natural. The fact is, you dont strike on my box, Mrs Hushabye; and I certainly dont strike on yours.

MRS HUSHABYE. I see. Your marriage was a safety match.

MAZZINI. What a very witty application of the expression I used! I should never have thought of it.

[ELLIE *comes in from the garden, looking anything but happy.*]

MRS HUSHABYE [*rising*]. Oh! here is Ellie at last. [*She goes behind the sofa*].

ELLIE [*on the threshold of the starboard door*]. Guinness said you wanted me: you and papa.

MRS HUSHABYE. You have kept us waiting so long that it almost came to— well, never mind. Your father is a very wonderful man [*she ruffles his hair affectionately*]: the only one I ever met who could resist me when I made myself really agreeable. [*She comes to the big chair, on* MANGAN's *left.*] Come here. I have something to shew you. [ELLIE *strolls listlessly to the other side of the chair.*] Look.

ELLIE [*contemplating* MANGAN *without interest*]. I know. He is only asleep. We had a talk after dinner; and he fell asleep in the middle of it.

MRS HUSHABYE. You did it, Ellie. You put him asleep.

MAZZINI [*rising quickly and coming to the back of the chair*]. Oh, I hope not. Did you, Ellie?

ELLIE [*wearily*]. He asked me to.

MAZZINI. But it's dangerous. You know what happened to me.

ELLIE [*utterly indifferent*]. Oh, I daresay I can wake him. If not, somebody else can.

MRS HUSHABYE. It doesnt matter, anyhow, because I have at last persuaded your father that you dont want to marry him.

ELLIE [*suddenly coming out of her listlessness, much vexed*]. But why did you do that, Hesione? I do want to marry him. I fully intend to marry him.

MAZZINI. Are you quite sure, Ellie? Mrs Hushabye has made me feel that I may have been thoughtless and selfish about it.

ELLIE [*very clearly and steadily*]. Papa. When Mrs Hushabye takes it on herself to explain to you what I think or dont think, shut your ears tight; and shut your eyes too. Hesione knows nothing about me: she hasnt the least notion of the sort of person I am, and never will. I promise you I wont do anything I dont want to do and mean to do for my own sake.

MAZZINI. You are quite, quite sure?

ELLIE. Quite, quite sure. Now you must go away and leave me to talk to Mrs Hushabye.

MAZZINI. But I should like to hear. Shall I be in the way?

ELLIE [*inexorable*]. I had rather talk to her alone.

MAZZINI [*affectionately*]. Oh, well, I know what a nuisance parents are, dear. I will be good and go. [*He goes to the garden door.*] By the way, do you remember the address of that professional who woke me up? Dont you think I had better telegraph to him.

MRS HUSHABYE [*moving towards the sofa*]. It's too late to telegraph tonight.

MAZZINI. I suppose so. I do hope he'll wake up in the course of the night. [*He goes out into the garden.*]

ELLIE [*turning vigorously on HESIONE the moment her father is out of the room*]. Hesione: what the devil do you mean by making mischief with my father about Mangan?

MRS HUSHABYE [*promptly losing her temper*]. Dont you dare speak to me like that, you little minx. Remember that you are in my house.

ELLIE. Stuff! Why dont you mind your own business? What is it to you whether I choose to marry Mangan or not?

MRS HUSHABYE. Do you suppose you can bully me, you miserable little matrimonial adventurer?

ELLIE. Every woman who hasnt any money is a matrimonial adventurer. It's easy for you to talk: you have never known what it is to want money; and you can pick up men as if they were daisies. I am poor and respectable—

MRS HUSHABYE [*interrupting*]. Ho! respectable! How did you pick up Mangan? How did you pick up my husband? You have the audacity to tell me that I am a—a—a—

ELLIE. A siren. So you are. You were born to lead men by the nose: if you werent, Marcus would have waited for me, perhaps.

MRS HUSHABYE [*suddenly melting and half laughing*]. Oh, my poor Ellie, my pettikins, my unhappy darling! I am so sorry about Hector. But what can I do? It's not my fault: I'd give him to you if I could.

ELLIE. I dont blame you for that.

MRS HUSHABYE. What a brute I was to quarrel with you and call you names! Do kiss me and say youre not angry with me.

ELLIE [*fiercely*]. Oh, dont slop and gush and be sentimental. Dont you see that unless I can be hard—as hard as nails—I shall go mad. I dont care a damn about your calling me names: do you think a woman in my situation can feel a few hard words?

MRS HUSHABYE. Poor little woman! Poor little situation!

ELLIE. I suppose you think youre being sympathetic. You are just foolish and stupid and selfish. You see me getting a smasher right in the face that kills a whole part of my life: the best part that can never come again; and you think you can help me over it by a little coaxing and kissing. When I want all the strength I can get to lean on: something iron, something stony, I dont care how cruel it is, you go all mushy and want to slobber over me. I'm not angry; I'm not unfriendly; but for God's sake do pull yourself together; and dont think that because youre on velvet and always have been, women who are in hell can take it as easily as you.

MRS HUSHABYE [*shrugging her shoulders*]. Very well. [*She sits down on the sofa in her old place.*] But I warn you that when I am neither coaxing and kissing nor laughing, I am just wondering how much longer I can stand living in this cruel, damnable world. You object to the siren: well, I drop the siren. You want to rest your wounded bosom against a grindstone. Well [*folding her arms*], here is the grindstone.

ELLIE [*sitting down beside her, appeased*]. Thats better: you really have the trick of falling in with everyone's mood; but you dont understand, because you are not the sort of woman for whom there is only one man and only one chance.

MRS HUSHABYE. I certainly dont understand how your marrying that object [*indicating* MANGAN] will console you for not being able to marry Hector.

ELLIE. Perhaps you dont understand why I was quite a nice girl this morning, and am now neither a girl nor particularly nice.

MRS HUSHABYE. Oh yes I do. It's because you have made up your mind to do something despicable and wicked.

ELLIE. I dont think so, Hesione. I must make the best of my ruined house.

MRS HUSHABYE. Pooh! Youll get over it. Your house isnt ruined.

ELLIE. Of course I shall get over it. You dont suppose I'm going to sit down and die of a broken heart, I hope, or be an old maid living on a pittance from the Sick and Indigent Roomkeepers' Association. But my heart is broken, all the same. What I mean by that is that I know that what has happened to me with Marcus will not happen to me ever again. In the world for me there is Marcus and a lot of other men of whom one is just the same as another. Well, if I cant have love, thats no reason why I should have poverty. If Mangan has nothing else, he has money.

MRS HUSHABYE. And are there no young men with money?

ELLIE. Not within my reach. Besides, a young man would have the right to expect love from me, and would perhaps leave me when he found I could not give it to him. Rich young men can get rid of their wives, you know, pretty cheaply. But this object, as you call him, can expect nothing more from me than I am prepared to give him.

MRS HUSHABYE. He will be your owner, remember. If he buys you, he will make the bargain pay him and not you. Ask your father.

ELLIE [*rising and strolling to the chair to contemplate their subject*]. You need not trouble on that score, Hesione. I have more to give Boss Mangan than he has to give me: it is I who am buying him, and at a pretty good price too, I think. Women are better at that sort of bargain than men. I have taken the Boss's measure; and ten Boss Mangans shall not prevent me doing far more as I please as his wife than I have ever been able to do as a poor girl. [*Stooping to the recumbent figure.*] Shall they, Boss? I think not. [*She passes on to the drawing-table, and leans against the end of it, facing the windows.*] I shall not have to spend most of my time wondering how long my gloves will last, anyhow.

MRS HUSHABYE [*rising superbly*]. Ellie: you are a wicked sordid little beast. And to think that I actually condescended to fascinate that creature there to save you from him! Well, let me tell you this: if you make this disgusting match, you will never see Hector again if I can help it.

ELLIE [*unmoved*]. I nailed Mangan by telling him that if he did not marry me he should never see you again. [*She lifts herself on her wrists and seats herself on the end of the table.*]

MRS HUSHABYE [*recoiling*]. Oh!

ELLIE. So you see I am not unprepared for your playing that trump against me. Well, you just try it: thats all. I should have made a man of Marcus, not a household pet.

MRS HUSHABYE [*flaming*]. You dare!

ELLIE [*looking almost dangerous*]. Set him thinking about me if you dare.

MRS HUSHABYE. Well, of all the impudent little fiends I ever met! Hector says there is a certain point at which the only answer you can give to a man who breaks all the rules is to knock him down. What would you say if I were to box your ears?

ELLIE [*calmly*]. I should pull your hair.

MRS HUSHABYE [*mischievously*]. That wouldnt hurt me. Perhaps it comes off at night.

ELLIE [*so taken aback that she drops off the table and runs to her*]. Oh, you dont mean to say, Hesione, that your beautiful black hair is false?

MRS HUSHABYE [*patting it*]. Dont tell Hector. He believes in it.

ELLIE [*groaning*]. Oh! Even the hair that ensnared him false! Everything false!

MRS HUSHABYE. Pull it and try. Other women can snare men in their hair; but I can swing a baby on mine. Aha! you cant do that, Goldylocks.

ELLIE [*heartbroken*]. No. You have stolen my babies.

MRS HUSHABYE. Pettikins; dont make me cry. You know, what you said about my making a household pet of him is a little true. Perhaps he ought to have waited for you. Would any other woman on earth forgive you?

ELLIE. Oh, what right had you to take him all for yourself! [*Pulling herself together.*] There! You couldnt help it: neither of us could help it. He couldnt help it. No: dont say anything more; I cant bear it. Let us wake the object. [*She begins stroking* MANGAN's *head, reversing the movement with which she put him to sleep.*] Wake up, do you hear? You are to wake up at once. Wake up, wake up, wake—

MANGAN [*bouncing out of the chair in a fury and turning on them*]. Wake up! So you think Ive been asleep, do you? [*He kicks the chair violently out of his way, and gets between them.*] You throw me into a trance so that I cant move hand or foot—I might have been buried alive! it's a mercy I wasnt—and then you think I was only asleep. If youd let me drop the two times you rolled me about, my nose would have been flattened for life against the floor. But Ive found you all out, anyhow. I know the sort of people I'm among now. Ive heard every word youve said, you and your precious father, and [*to* MRS HUSHABYE] you too. So I'm

an object, am I? I'm a thing, am I? I'm a fool that hasnt sense enough to feed myself properly, am I? I'm afraid of the men that would starve if it werent for the wages I give them, am I? I'm nothing but a disgusting old skinflint to be made a convenience of by designing women and fool managers of my works, am I? I'm—

MRS HUSHABYE [*with the most elegant aplomb*]. Sh-sh-sh-sh-sh! Mr Mangan: you are bound in honor to obliterate from your mind all you heard while you were pretending to be asleep. It was not meant for you to hear.

MANGAN. Pretending to be asleep! Do you think if I was only pretending that I'd have sprawled there helpless, and listened to such unfairness, such lies, such injustice and plotting and backbiting and slandering of me, if I could have up and told you what I thought of you! I wonder I didnt burst.

MRS HUSHABYE [*sweetly*]. You dreamt it all, Mr Mangan. We were only saying how beautifully peaceful you looked in your sleep. That was all, wasnt it, Ellie? Believe me, Mr Mangan, all those unpleasant things came into your mind in the last half second before you woke. Ellie rubbed your hair the wrong way; and the disagreeable sensation suggested a disagreeable dream.

MANGAN [*doggedly*]. I believe in dreams.

MRS HUSHABYE. So do I. But they go by contraries, dont they?

MANGAN [*depths of emotion suddenly welling up in him*]. I shant forget, to my dying day, that when you gave me the glad eye that time in the garden, you were making a fool of me. That was a dirty low mean thing to do. You had no right to let me come near you if I disgusted you. It isn't my fault if I'm old and havnt a moustache like a bronze candlestick as your husband has. There are things no decent woman would do to a man—like a man hitting a woman in the breast.

[HESIONE, *utterly shamed, sits down on the sofa and covers her face with her hands.* MANGAN *sits down also on his chair and begins to cry like a child.* ELLIE *stares at them.* MRS HUSHABYE, *at the distressing sound he makes, takes down her hands and looks at him. She rises and runs to him.*]

MRS HUSHABYE. Dont cry: I cant bear it. Have I broken your heart? I didnt know you had one. How could I?

MANGAN. I'm a man aint I?

MRS HUSHABYE [half coaxing, half rallying, altogether tenderly]. Oh no: not what I call a man. Only a Boss: just that and nothing else. What business has a Boss with a heart?

MANGAN. Then youre not a bit sorry for what you did, nor ashamed?

MRS HUSHABYE. I was ashamed for the first time in my life when you said that about hitting a woman in the breast, and I found out what I'd done. My very bones blushed red. Youve had your revenge, Boss. Arnt you satisfied?

MANGAN. Serve you right! Do you hear? Serve you right! Youre just cruel. Cruel.

MRS HUSHABYE. Yes: cruelty would be delicious if one could only find some sort of cruelty that didnt really hurt. By the way [sitting down beside him on the arm of the chair], whats your name? It's not really Boss, is it?

MANGAN [shortly]. If you want to know, my name's Alfred.

MRS HUSHABYE [springing up]. Alfred!! Ellie: he was christened after Tennyson!!!

MANGAN [rising]. I was christened after my uncle, and never had a penny from him, damn him! What of it?

MRS HUSHABYE. It comes to me suddenly that you are a real person: that you had a mother, like anyone else. [Putting her hands on his shoulders and surveying him.] Little Alf!

MANGAN. Well, you have a nerve.

MRS HUSHABYE. And you have a heart, Alfy, a whimpering little heart, but a real one. [Releasing him suddenly.] Now run and make it up with Ellie. She has had time to think what to say to you, which is more than I had. [She goes out quickly into the garden by the port door.]

MANGAN. That woman has a pair of hands that go right through you.

ELLIE. Still in love with her, in spite of all we said about you?

MANGAN. Are all women like you two? Do they never think of anything about a man except what they can get out of him? You werent even thinking that about me. You were only thinking whether your gloves would last.

ELLIE. I shall not have to think about that when we are married.

MANGAN. And you think I am going to marry you after what I heard there!

ELLIE. You heard nothing from me that I did not tell you before.

MANGAN. Perhaps you think I cant do without you.

ELLIE. I think you would feel lonely without us all now, after coming to know us so well.

MANGAN [with something like a yell of despair]. Am I never to have the last word?

CAPTAIN SHOTOVER [appearing at the starboard garden door]. There is a soul in torment here. What is the matter?

MANGAN. This girl doesnt want to spend her life wondering how long her gloves will last.

CAPTAIN SHOTOVER [passing through]. Dont wear any. I never do. [He goes into the pantry.]

LADY UTTERWORD [appearing at the port garden door, in a handsome dinner dress]. Is anything the matter?

ELLIE. This gentleman wants to know is he never to have the last word?

LADY UTTERWORD [coming forward to the sofa]. I should let him have it, my dear. The important thing is not to have the last word, but to have your own way.

MANGAN. She wants both.

LADY UTTERWORD. She wont get them, Mr Mangan. Providence always has the last word.

MANGAN [desperately]. Now you are going to come religion over me. In this house a man's mind might as well be a football. I'm going. [He makes for the hall, but is stopped by a hail from the CAPTAIN, who has just emerged from his pantry.]

CAPTAIN SHOTOVER. Whither away, Boss Mangan?

MANGAN. To hell out of this house: let that be enough for you and all here.

CAPTAIN SHOTOVER. You were welcome to come: you are free to go. The wide earth, the high seas, the spacious skies are waiting for you outside.

LADY UTTERWORD. But your things, Mr Mangan. Your bags, your comb and brushes, your pyjamas—

HECTOR [who has just appeared in the port doorway in a handsome Arab cos-

tume]. Why should the escaping slave take his chains with him?

MANGAN. Thats right, Hushabye. Keep the pyjamas, my lady; and much good may they do you.

HECTOR [*advancing to* LADY UTTER-WORD'*s left hand*]. Let us all go out into the night and leave everything behind us.

MANGAN. You stay where you are, the lot of you. I want no company, especially female company.

ELLIE. Let him go. He is unhappy here. He is angry with us.

CAPTAIN SHOTOVER. Go, Boss Mangan; and when you have found the land where there is happiness and where there are no women, send me its latitude and longitude; and I will join you there.

LADY UTTERWORD. You will certainly not be comfortable without your luggage, Mr Mangan.

ELLIE [*impatient*]. Go, go: why dont you go? It is a heavenly night: you can sleep on the heath. Take my waterproof to lie on: it is hanging up in the hall.

HECTOR. Breakfast at nine, unless you prefer to breakfast with the Captain at six.

ELLIE. Good night, Alfred.

HECTOR. Alfred! [*He runs back to the door and calls into the garden.*] Randall: Mangan's Christian name is Alfred.

RANDALL [*appearing in the starboard doorway in evening dress*]. Then Hesione wins her bet.

[MRS HUSHABYE *appears in the port doorway. She throws her left arm round* HECTOR'*s neck; draws him with her to the back of the sofa; and throws her right arm round* LADY UTTERWORD'*s neck.*]

MRS HUSHABYE. They wouldnt believe me, Alf.

[*They contemplate him.*]

MANGAN. Is there any more of you coming in to look at me, as if I was the latest thing in a menagerie.

MRS HUSHABYE. You are the latest thing in this menagerie.

[*Before Mangan can retort, a fall of furniture is heard from upstairs; then a pistol shot, and a yell of pain. The staring group breaks up in consternation.*]

MAZZINI'S VOICE [*from above*]. Help! A burglar! Help!

HECTOR [*his eyes blazing*]. A burglar!!!

MRS HUSHABYE. No, Hector: youll be shot. [*But it is too late: he has dashed out past* MANGAN, *who hastily moves towards the bookshelves out of his way.*]

CAPTAIN SHOTOVER [*blowing his whistle*]. All hands aloft! [*He strides out after* HECTOR.]

LADY UTTERWORD. My diamonds! [*She follows the* CAPTAIN.]

RANDALL [*rushing after her*]. No, Ariadne. Let me.

ELLIE. Oh, is papa shot? [*She runs out.*]

MRS HUSHABYE. Are you frightened, Alf?

MANGAN. No. It aint my house, thank God.

MRS HUSHABYE. If they catch a burglar, shall we have to go into court as witnesses, and be asked all sorts of questions about our private lives?

MANGAN. You wont be believed if you tell the truth.

[MAZZINI, *terribly upset, with a duelling pistol in his hand, comes from the hall, and makes his way to the drawing-table.*]

MAZZINI. Oh, my dear Mrs Hushabye, I might have killed him. [*He throws the pistol on the table and staggers round to the chair.*] I hope you wont believe I really intended to.

[HECTOR *comes in, marching an old and villainous looking man before him by the collar. He plants him in the middle of the room and releases him.*

ELLIE *follows, and immediately runs across to the back of her father's chair, and pats his shoulders.*]

RANDALL [*entering with a poker*]. Keep your eye on this door, Mangan. I'll look after the other. [*He goes to the starboard door and stands on guard there.*]

[LADY UTTERWORD *comes in after* RANDALL, *and goes between* MRS HUSHABYE *and* MANGAN.

NURSE GUINNESS *brings up the rear, and waits near the door, on* MANGAN'*s left.*]

MRS HUSHABYE. What has happened?

MAZZINI. Your housekeeper told me there was somebody upstairs, and gave me a pistol that Mr. Hushabye had been practising with. I thought it would frighten him; but it went off at a touch.

THE BURGLAR. Yes, and took the skin

off my ear. Precious near took the top off my head. Why dont you have a proper revolver instead of a thing like that, that goes off if you as much as blow on it?

HECTOR. One of my duelling pistols. Sorry.

MAZZINI. He put his hands up and said it was a fair cop.

THE BURGLAR. So it was. Send for the police.

HECTOR. No, by thunder! It was not a fair cop. We were four to one.

MRS HUSHABYE. What will they do to him?

THE BURGLAR. Ten years. Beginning with solitary. Ten years off my life. I shant serve it all: I'm too old. It will see me out.

LADY UTTERWORD. You should have thought of that before you stole my diamonds.

THE BURGLAR. Well, youve got them back, lady: havnt you? Can you give me back the years of my life you are going to take from me?

MRS HUSHABYE. Oh, we cant bury a man alive for ten years for a few diamonds.

THE BURGLAR. Ten little shining diamonds! Ten long black years!

LADY UTTERWORD. Think of what it is for us to be dragged through the horrors of a criminal court, and have all our family affairs in the papers! If you were a native, and Hastings could order you a good beating and send you away, I shouldn't mind; but here in England there is no real protection for any respectable person.

THE BURGLAR. I'm too old to be giv a hiding, lady. Send for the police and have done with it. It's only just and right you should.

RANDALL [who has relaxed his vigilance on seeing the burglar so pacifically disposed, and comes forward swinging the poker between his fingers like a well-folded umbrella]. It is neither just nor right that we should be put to a lot of inconvenience to gratify your moral enthusiasm, my friend. You had better get out, while you have the chance.

THE BURGLAR [inexorably]. No. I must work my sin off my conscience. This has come as a sort of call to me. Let me spend the rest of my life repenting in a cell. I shall have my reward above.

MANGAN [exasperated]. The very burglars cant behave naturally in this house.

HECTOR. My good sir: you must work out your salvation at somebody else's expense. Nobody here is going to charge you.

THE BURGLAR. Oh, you wont charge me, wont you?

HECTOR. No. I'm sorry to be inhospitable; but will you kindly leave the house?

THE BURGLAR. Right. I'll go to the police station and give myself up. [He turns resolutely to the door; but HECTOR stops him.]

HECTOR.⎫ ⎧Oh no. You mustnt do that.

RANDALL. ⎪ No, no. Clear out, man, cant you; and dont be a fool.

MRS HUSHABYE. ⎪ Dont be so silly. Cant you repent at home?

LADY UTTERWORD. You will have to do as you are told.

THE BURGLAR. It's compounding a felony, you know.

MRS HUSHABYE. This is utterly ridiculous. Are we to be forced to prosecute this man when we dont want to?

THE BURGLAR. Am I to be robbed of my salvation to save you the trouble of spending a day at the sessions? Is that justice? Is it right? Is it fair to me?

MAZZINI [rising and leaning across the table persuasively as if it were a pulpit desk or a shop counter]. Come, come! let me shew you how you can turn your very crimes to account. Why not set up as a locksmith? You must know more about locks than most honest men?

THE BURGLAR. Thats true, sir. But I couldnt set up as a locksmith under twenty pounds.

RANDALL. Well, you can easily steal twenty pounds. You will find it in the nearest bank.

THE BURGLAR [horrified]. Oh what a thing for a gentleman to put into the head of a poor criminal scrambling out of the bottomless pit as it were! Oh, shame on you, sir! Oh, God forgive you! [He throws himself into the big chair and covers his face as if in prayer.]

LADY UTTERWORD. Really, Randall!

HECTOR. It seems to me that we shall

have to take up a collection for this in-opportunely contrite sinner.

LADY UTTERWORD. But twenty pounds is ridiculous.

THE BURGLAR [looking up quickly]. I shall have to buy a lot of tools, lady.

LADY UTTERWORD. Nonsense: you have your burgling kit.

THE BURGLAR. Whats a jemmy and a centrebit and an acetylene welding plant and a bunch of skeleton keys? I shall want a forge, and a smithy, and a shop, and fittings. I cant hardly do it for twenty.

HECTOR. My worthy friend, we havnt got twenty pounds.

THE BURGLAR [now master of the situation]. You can raise it among you, cant you?

MRS HUSHABYE. Give him a sovereign, Hector; and get rid of him.

HECTOR [giving him a pound]. There! Off with you.

THE BURGLAR [rising and taking the money very ungratefully]. I wont promise nothing. You have more on you than a quid: all the lot of you, I mean.

LADY UTTERWORD [vigorously]. Oh, let us prosecute him and have done with it. I have a conscience too, I hope; and I do not feel at all sure that we have any right to let him go, especially if he is going to be greedy and impertinent.

THE BURGLAR [quickly]. All right, lady, all right. I've no wish to be anything but agreeable. Good evening, ladies and gentlemen; and thank you kindly.

[He is hurrying out when he is con-fronted in the doorway by CAPTAIN SHOTOVER.]

CAPTAIN SHOTOVER [fixing the BURGLAR with a piercing regard]. Whats this? Are there two of you?

THE BURGLAR [falling on his knees be-fore the CAPTAIN in abject terror]. Oh my good Lord, what have I done? Dont tell me it's your house Ive broken into, Captain Shotover.

[The CAPTAIN seizes him by the collar; drags him to his feet; and leads him to the middle of the group, HECTOR falling back beside his wife to make way for them.]

CAPTAIN SHOTOVER [turning him to-wards ELLIE]. Is that your daughter? [He releases him.]

THE BURGLAR. Well, how do I know,

Captain? You know the sort of life you and me has led. Any young lady of that age might be my daughter anywhere in the wide world, as you might say.

CAPTAIN SHOTOVER [to MAZZINI]. You are not Billy Dunn. This is Billy Dunn. Why have you imposed on me?

THE BURGLAR [indignantly to MAZZINI]. Have you been giving yourself out to be me? You, that nigh blew my head off! Shooting yourself, in a manner of speak-ing!

MAZZINI. My dear Captain Shotover, ever since I came into this house I have done hardly anything else but assure you that I am not Mr William Dunn, but Mazzini Dunn, a very different person.

THE BURGLAR. He dont belong to my branch, Captain. Theres two sets in the family: the thinking Dunns and the drinking Dunns, each going their own ways. I'm a drinking Dunn: he's a think-ing Dunn. But that didnt give him any right to shoot me.

CAPTAIN SHOTOVER. So youve turned burglar, have you?

THE BURGLAR. No, Captain: I wouldnt disgrace our old sea calling by such a thing. I am no burglar.

LADY UTTERWORD. What were you do-ing with my diamonds?

GUINNESS. What did you break into the house for if youre no burglar?

RANDALL. Mistook the house for your own and came in by the wrong window, eh?

THE BURGLAR. Well, it's no use my telling you a lie: I can take in most cap-tains, but not Captain Shotover, because he sold himself to the devil in Zanzibar, and can divine water, spot gold, explode a cartridge in your pocket with a glance of his eye, and see the truth hidden in the heart of man. But I'm no burglar.

CAPTAIN SHOTOVER. Are you an honest man?

THE BURGLAR. I dont set up to be bet-ter than my fellow-creatures, and never did, as you well know, Captain. But what I do is innocent and pious. I en-quire about for houses where the right sort of people live. I work it on them same as I worked it here. I break into the house; put a few spoons or diamonds in my pocket; make a noise; get caught; and take up a collection. And you wouldnt believe how hard it is to get caught when youre actually trying to. I have knocked over all the chairs in a room without a soul paying any attention to me. In the end I have had to walk out and leave the job.

RANDALL. When that happens, do you put back the spoons and diamonds?

THE BURGLAR. Well, I dont fly in the face of Providence, if thats what you want to know.

CAPTAIN SHOTOVER. Guinness: you remember this man?

GUINNESS. I should think I do, seeing I was married to him, the blackguard!

[exclaiming together]

HESIONE. }{ Married to him!
LADY UTTERWORD. }{ Guinness!!

THE BURGLAR. It wasnt legal. Ive been married to no end of women. No use coming that over me.

CAPTAIN SHOTOVER. Take him to the forecastle. [He flings him to the door with a strength beyond his years.]

GUINNESS. I suppose you mean the kitchen. They wont have him there. Do you expect servants to keep company with thieves and all sorts?

CAPTAIN SHOTOVER. Land-thieves and water-thieves are the same flesh and blood. I'll have no boatswain on my quarter-deck. Off with you both.

THE BURGLAR. Yes, Captain. [He goes out humbly.]

MAZZINI. Will it be safe to have him in the house like that?

GUINNESS. Why didnt you shoot him, sir? If I'd known who he was, I'd have shot him myself. [She goes out.]

MRS HUSHABYE. Do sit down, everybody. [She sits down on the sofa.]

[They all move except ELLIE. MAZZINI resumes his seat. RANDALL sits down in the window seat near the starboard door, again making a pendulum of his poker, and studying it as Galileo might have done. HECTOR sits on his left, in the middle. MANGAN, forgotten, sits in the port corner. LADY UTTERWORD takes the big chair. CAPTAIN SHOTOVER goes into the pantry in deep abstraction. They all look after him; and LADY UTTERWORD coughs unconsciously.]

MRS HUSHABYE. So Billy Dunn was poor nurse's little romance. I knew there had been somebody.

RANDALL. They will fight their battles over again and enjoy themselves immensely.

LADY UTTERWORD [irritably]. You are not married; and you know nothing about it, Randall. Hold your tongue.

RANDALL. Tyrant!

MRS HUSHABYE. Well, we have had a very exciting evening. Everything will be an anticlimax after it. We'd better all go to bed.

RANDALL. Another burglar may turn up.

MAZZINI. Oh, impossible! I hope not.

RANDALL. Why not? There is more than one burglar in England.

MRS HUSHABYE. What do you say, Alf?

MANGAN [huffily]. Oh, I dont matter. I'm forgotten. The burglar has put my nose out of joint. Shove me into a corner and have done with me.

MRS HUSHABYE [jumping up mischievously, and going to him]. Would you like a walk on the heath, Alfred? With me?

ELLIE. Go, Mr. Mangan. It will do you good. Hesione will soothe you.

MRS HUSHABYE [slipping her arm under his and pulling him upright]. Come, Alfred. There is a moon: it's like the night in Tristan and Isolde. [She caresses his arm and draws him to the port garden door.]

MANGAN [writhing but yielding]. How you can have the face—the heart— [He breaks down and is heard sobbing as she takes him out.]

LADY UTTERWORD. What an extraordinary way to behave! What is the matter with the man?

ELLIE [in a strangely calm voice, staring into an imaginary distance]. His heart is breaking: that is all. [The CAPTAIN appears at the pantry door, listening.] It is a curious sensation: the sort of pain that goes mercifully beyond our powers of feeling. When your heart is broken, your boats are burned: nothing matters any more. It is the end of happiness and the beginning of peace.

LADY UTTERWORD [suddenly rising in a rage, to the astonishment of the rest]. How dare you?

HECTOR. Good heavens! Whats the matter?

RANDALL [in a warning whisper]. Tch—tch—tch! Steady.

ELLIE [surprised and haughty]. I was

not addressing you particularly, Lady Utterword. And I am not accustomed to be asked how dare I.

LADY UTTERWORD. Of course not. Anyone can see how badly you have been brought up.

MAZZINI. Oh, I hope not, Lady Utterword. Really!

LADY UTTERWORD. I know very well what you meant. The impudence!

ELLIE. What on earth do you mean?

CAPTAIN SHOTOVER [advancing to the table]. She means that her heart will not break. She has been longing all her life for someone to break it. At last she has become afraid she has none to break.

LADY UTTERWORD [flinging herself on her knees and throwing her arms round him]. Papa: dont say you think Ive no heart.

CAPTAIN SHOTOVER [raising her with grim tenderness]. If you had no heart how could you want to have it broken, child?

HECTOR [rising with a bound]. Lady Utterword: you are not to be trusted. You have made a scene. [He runs out into the garden through the starboard door.]

LADY UTTERWORD. Oh! Hector, Hector! [She runs out after him.]

RANDALL. Only nerves, I assure you. [He rises and follows her, waving the poker in his agitation.] Ariadne! Ariadne! For God's sake be careful. You will— [He is gone.]

MAZZINI [rising]. How distressing! Can I do anything, I wonder?

CAPTAIN SHOTOVER [promptly taking his chair and setting to work at the drawing-board]. No. Go to bed. Goodnight.

MAZZINI [bewildered]. Oh! Perhaps you are right.

ELLIE. Goodnight, dearest. [She kisses him.]

MAZZINI. Goodnight, love. [He makes for the door, but turns aside to the bookshelves.] I'll just take a book. [He takes one.] Goodnight. [He goes out, leaving ELLIE alone with the CAPTAIN.]

[The CAPTAIN is intent on his drawing.
ELLIE, standing sentry over his chair,
contemplates him for a moment.]

ELLIE. Does nothing ever disturb you, Captain Shotover?

CAPTAIN SHOTOVER. Ive stood on the bridge for eighteen hours in a typhoon. Life here is stormier; but I can stand it.

ELLIE. Do you think I ought to marry Mr Mangan?

CAPTAIN SHOTOVER [never looking up]. One rock is as good as another to be wrecked on.

ELLIE. I am not in love with him.

CAPTAIN SHOTOVER. Who said you were?

ELLIE. You are not surprised?

CAPTAIN SHOTOVER. Surprised! At my age!

ELLIE. It seems to me quite fair. He wants me for one thing: I want him for another.

CAPTAIN SHOTOVER. Money?

ELLIE. Yes.

CAPTAIN SHOTOVER. Well, one turns the cheek: the other kisses it. One provides the cash: the other spends it.

ELLIE. Who will have the best of the bargain, I wonder?

CAPTAIN SHOTOVER. You. These fellows live in an office all day. You will have to put up with him from dinner to breakfast; but you will both be asleep most of that time. All day you will be quit of him; and you will be shopping with his money. If that is too much for you, marry a seafaring man: you will be bothered with him only three weeks in the year, perhaps.

ELLIE. That would be best of all, I suppose.

CAPTAIN SHOTOVER. It's a dangerous thing to be married right up to the hilt, like my daughter's husband. The man is at home all day, like a damned soul in hell.

ELLIE. I never thought of that before.

CAPTAIN SHOTOVER. If youre marrying for business, you cant be too businesslike.

ELLIE. Why do women always want other women's husbands?

CAPTAIN SHOTOVER. Why do horse-thieves prefer a horse that is broken-in to one that is wild?

ELLIE [with a short laugh]. I suppose so. What a vile world it is!

CAPTAIN SHOTOVER. It doesnt concern me. I'm nearly out of it.

ELLIE. And I'm only just beginning.

CAPTAIN SHOTOVER. Yes; so look ahead.

ELLIE. Well, I think I am being very prudent.

CAPTAIN SHOTOVER. I didnt say prudent. I said look ahead.

ELLIE. Whats the difference?

CAPTAIN SHOTOVER. It's prudent to gain the whole world and lose your own soul. But dont forget that your soul sticks to you if you stick to it; but the world has a way of slipping through your fingers.

ELLIE [wearily, leaving him and beginning to wander restlessly about the room]. I'm sorry, Captain Shotover; but it's no use talking like that to me. Old-fashioned people are no use to me. Old-fashioned people think you can have a soul without money. They think the less money you have, the more soul you have. Young people nowadays know better. A soul is a very expensive thing to keep: much more so than a motor car.

CAPTAIN SHOTOVER. Is it? How much does your soul eat?

ELLIE. Oh, a lot. It eats music and pictures and books and mountains and lakes and beautiful things to wear and nice people to be with. In this country you cant have them without lots of money: that is why our souls are so horribly starved.

CAPTAIN SHOTOVER. Mangan's soul lives on pigs' food.

ELLIE. Yes: money is thrown away on him. I suppose his soul was starved when he was young. But it will not be thrown away on me. It is just because I want to save my soul that I am marrying for money. All the women who are not fools do.

CAPTAIN SHOTOVER. There are other ways of getting money. Why dont you steal it?

ELLIE. Because I dont want to go to prison.

CAPTAIN SHOTOVER. Is that the only reason? Are you quite sure honesty has nothing to do with it?

ELLIE. Oh, you are very very old-fashioned, Captain. Does any modern girl believe that the legal and illegal ways of getting money are the honest and dishonest ways? Mangan robbed my father and my father's friends. I should rob all the money back from Mangan if the police would let me. As they wont, I must get it back by marrying him.

CAPTAIN SHOTOVER. I cant argue: I'm too old: my mind is made up and finished. All I can tell you is that, old-fashioned or new-fashioned, if you sell yourself, you deal your soul a blow that all the books and pictures and concerts and scenery in the world wont heal. [He gets up suddenly and makes for the pantry.]

ELLIE [running after him and seizing him by the sleeve]. Then why did you sell yourself to the devil in Zanzibar?

CAPTAIN SHOTOVER [stopping, startled]. What?

ELLIE. You shall not run away before you answer. I have found out that trick of yours. If you sold yourself, why shouldnt I?

CAPTAIN SHOTOVER. I had to deal with men so degraded that they wouldnt obey me unless I swore at them and kicked them and beat them with my fists. Foolish people took young thieves off the streets; flung them into a training ship where they were taught to fear the cane instead of fearing God; and thought theyd made men and sailors of them by private subscription. I tricked these thieves into believing I'd sold myself to the devil. It saved my soul from the kicking and swearing that was damning me by inches.

ELLIE [releasing him]. I shall pretend to sell myself to Boss Mangan to save my soul from the poverty that is damning me by inches.

CAPTAIN SHOTOVER. Riches will damn you ten times deeper. Riches wont save even your body.

ELLIE. Old-fashioned again. We know now that the soul is the body, and the body the soul. They tell us they are different because they want to persuade us that we can keep our souls if we let them make slaves of our bodies. I am afraid you are no use to me, Captain.

CAPTAIN SHOTOVER. What did you expect? A Savior, eh? Are you old-fashioned enough to believe in that?

ELLIE. No. But I thought you were very wise, and might help me. Now I have found you out. You pretend to be busy, and think of fine things to say, and run in and out to surprise people by saying them, and get away before they can answer you.

CAPTAIN SHOTOVER. It confuses me to be answered. It discourages me. I cannot bear men and women. I have to run away.

I must run away now. [*He tries to.*]

ELLIE [*again seizing his arm*]. You shall not run away from me. I can hypnotize you. You are the only person in the house I can say what I like to. I know you are fond of me. Sit down. [*She draws him to the sofa.*]

CAPTAIN SHOTOVER [*yielding*]. Take care: I am in my dotage. Old men are dangerous: it doesnt matter to them what is going to happen to the world.

[*They sit side by side on the sofa. She leans affectionately against him with her head on his shoulder and her eyes half closed.*]

ELLIE [*dreamily*]. I should have thought nothing else mattered to old men. They cant be very interested in what is going to happen to themselves.

CAPTAIN SHOTOVER. A man's interest in the world is only the overflow from his interest in himself. When you are a child your vessel is not yet full; so you care for nothing but your own affairs. When you grow up, your vessel overflows; and you are a politician, a philosopher, or an explorer and adventurer. In old age the vessel dries up: there is no overflow: you are a child again. I can give you the memories of my ancient wisdom: mere scraps and leavings; but I no longer really care for anything but my own little wants and hobbies. I sit here working out my old ideas as a means of destroying my fellow-creatures. I see my daughters and their men living foolish lives of romance and sentiment and snobbery. I see you, the younger generation, turning from their romance and sentiment and snobbery to money and comfort and hard common sense. I was ten times happier on the bridge in the typhoon, or frozen into Arctic ice for months in darkness, than you or they have ever been. You are looking for a rich husband. At your age I looked for hardship, danger, horror, and death, that I might feel the life in me more intensely. I did not let the fear of death govern my life; and my reward was, I had my life. You are going to let the fear of poverty govern your life; and your reward will be that you will eat, but you will not live.

ELLIE [*sitting up impatiently*]. But what can I do? I am not a sea captain: I cant stand on bridges in typhoons, or go slaughtering seals and whales in Greenland's icy mountains. They wont let women be captains. Do you want me to be a stewardess?

CAPTAIN SHOTOVER. There are worse lives. The stewardesses could come ashore if they liked; but they sail and sail and sail.

ELLIE. What could they do ashore but marry for money? I dont want to be a stewardess: I am too bad a sailor. Think of something else for me.

CAPTAIN SHOTOVER. I cant think so long and continuously. I am too old. I must go in and out. [*He tries to rise.*]

ELLIE [*pulling him back*]. You shall not. You are happy here, arnt you?

CAPTAIN SHOTOVER. I tell you it's dangerous to keep me. I cant keep awake and alert.

ELLIE. What do you run away for? To sleep?

CAPTAIN SHOTOVER. No. To get a glass of rum.

ELLIE [*frightfully disillusioned*]. Is that it? How disgusting! Do you like being drunk?

CAPTAIN SHOTOVER. No: I dread being drunk more than anything in the world. To be drunk means to have dreams; to go soft; to be easily pleased and deceived; to fall into the clutches of women. Drink does that for you when you are young. But when you are old: very very old, like me, the dreams come by themselves. You dont know how terrible that is: you are young: you sleep at night only, and sleep soundly. But later on you will sleep in the afternoon. Later still you will sleep even in the morning; and you will awake tired, tired of life. You will never be free from dozing and dreams: the dreams will steal upon your work every ten minutes unless you can awaken yourself with rum. I drink now to keep sober; but the dreams are conquering: rum is not what it was: I have had ten glasses since you came; and it might be so much water. Go get me another: Guinness knows where it is. You had better see for yourself the horror of an old man drinking.

ELLIE. You shall not drink. Dream. I like you to dream. You must never be in the real world when we talk together.

CAPTAIN SHOTOVER. I am too weary to resist or too weak. I am in my second childhood. I do not see you as you really are. I cannot remember what I really am. I feel nothing but the accursed happiness I have dreaded all my life long: the happiness that comes as life goes, the happiness of yielding and dreaming instead of resisting and doing, the sweetness of the fruit that is going rotten.

ELLIE. You dread it almost as much as I used to dread losing my dreams and having to fight and do things. But that is all over for me: my dreams are dashed to pieces. I should like to marry a very old, very rich man. I should like to marry you. I had much rather marry you than marry Mangan. Are you very rich?

CAPTAIN SHOTOVER. No. Living from hand to mouth. And I have a wife somewhere in Jamaica: a black one. My first wife. Unless she's dead.

ELLIE. What a pity! I feel so happy with you. [She takes his hand, almost unconsciously, and pats it.] I thought I should never feel happy again.

CAPTAIN SHOTOVER. Why?

ELLIE. Dont you know?

CAPTAIN SHOTOVER. No.

ELLIE. Heartbreak. I fell in love with Hector, and didnt know he was married.

CAPTAIN SHOTOVER. Heartbreak? Are you one of those who are so sufficient to themselves that they are only happy when they are stripped of everything, even of hope?

ELLIE [gripping the hand]. It seems so; for I feel now as if there was nothing I could not do, because I want nothing.

CAPTAIN SHOTOVER. Thats the only real strength. Thats genius. Thats better than rum.

ELLIE [throwing away his hand]. Rum! Why did you spoil it?

[HECTOR and RANDALL come in from the garden through the starboard door.]

HECTOR. I beg your pardon. We did not know there was anyone here.

ELLIE [rising]. That means that you want to tell Mr Randall the story about the tiger. Come, Captain: I want to talk to my father; and you had better come with me.

CAPTAIN SHOTOVER [rising]. Nonsense! the man is in bed.

ELLIE. Aha! Ive caught you. My real father has gone to bed; but the father you

gave me is in the kitchen. You knew quite well all along. Come. [She draws him out into the garden with her through the port door.]

HECTOR. Thats an extraordinary girl. She has the Ancient Mariner on a string like a Pekinese dog.

RANDALL. Now that they have gone, shall we have a friendly chat?

HECTOR. You are in what is supposed to be my house. I am at your disposal.

[HECTOR sits down in the draughtsman's chair, turning it to face RANDALL, who remains standing, leaning at his ease against the carpenter's bench.]

RANDALL. I take it that we may be quite frank. I mean about Lady Utterword.

HECTOR. You may. I have nothing to be frank about. I never met her until this afternoon.

RANDALL [straightening up]. What! But you are her sister's husband.

HECTOR. Well, if you come to that, you are her husband's brother.

RANDALL. But you seem to be on intimate terms with her.

HECTOR. So do you.

RANDALL. Yes; but I am on intimate terms with her. I have known her for years.

HECTOR. It took her years to get to the same point with you that she got to with me in five minutes, it seems.

RANDALL [vexed]. Really, Ariadne is the limit. [He moves away huffishly towards the windows.]

HECTOR [coolly]. She is, as I remarked to Hesione, a very enterprising woman.

RANDALL [returning, much troubled]. You see, Hushabye, you are what women consider a good-looking man.

HECTOR. I cultivated that appearance in the days of my vanity; and Hesione insists on my keeping it up. She makes me wear these ridiculous things [indicating his Arab costume] because she thinks me absurd in evening dress.

RANDALL. Still, you do keep it up, old chap. Now, I assure you I have not an atom of jealousy in my disposition—

HECTOR. The question would seem to be rather whether your brother has any touch of that sort.

RANDALL. What! Hastings! Oh, dont

trouble about Hastings. He has the gift of being able to work sixteen hours a day at the dullest detail, and actually likes it. That gets him to the top wherever he goes. As long as Ariadne takes care that he is fed regularly, he is only too thankful to anyone who will keep her in good humor for him.

HECTOR. And as she has all the Shotover fascination, there is plenty of competition for the job, eh?

RANDALL [angrily]. She encourages them. Her conduct is perfectly scandalous. I assure you, my dear fellow, I havnt an atom of jealousy in my composition; but she makes herself the talk of every place she goes to by her thoughtlessness. It's nothing more: she doesnt really care for the men she keeps hanging about her; but how is the world to know that? It's not fair to Hastings. It's not fair to me.

HECTOR. Her theory is that her conduct is so correct—

RANDALL. Correct! She does nothing but make scenes from morning til night. You be careful, old chap. She will get you into trouble: that is, she would if she really cared for you.

HECTOR. Doesnt she?

RANDALL. Not a scrap. She may want your scalp to add to her collection; but her true affection has been engaged years ago. You had really better be careful.

HECTOR. Do you suffer much from this jealousy?

RANDALL. Jealousy! I jealous! My dear fellow, havnt I told you that there is not an atom of—

HECTOR. Yes. And Lady Utterword told me she never made scenes. Well, dont waste your jealousy on my moustache. Never waste jealousy on a real man: it is the imaginary hero that supplants us all in the long run. Besides, jealousy does not belong to your easy man-of-the-world pose, which you carry so well in other respects.

RANDALL. Really, Hushabye, I think a man may be allowed to be a gentleman without being accused of posing.

HECTOR. It is a pose like any other. In this house we know all the poses: our game is to find out the man under the pose. The man under your pose is apparently Ellie's favorite, Othello.

RANDALL. Some of the games in this house are damned annoying, let me tell you.

HECTOR. Yes: I have been their victim for many years. I used to writhe under them at first; but I became accustomed to them. At last I learned to play them.

RANDALL. If it's all the same to you, I had rather you didnt play them on me. You evidently dont quite understand my character, or my notions of good form.

HECTOR. Is it your notion of good form to give away Lady Utterword?

RANDALL [a childishly plaintive note breaking into his huff]. I have not said a word against Lady Utterword. This is just the conspiracy over again.

HECTOR. What conspiracy?

RANDALL. You know very well, sir. A conspiracy to make me out to be pettish and jealous and childish and everything I am not. Everyone knows I am just the opposite.

HECTOR [rising]. Something in the air of the house has upset you. It often does have that effect. [He goes to the garden door and calls LADY UTTERWORD with commanding emphasis.] Ariadne!

LADY UTTERWORD [at some distance]. Yes.

RANDALL. What are you calling her for? I want to speak—

LADY UTTERWORD [arriving breathless]. Yes. You really are a terribly commanding person. Whats the matter?

HECTOR. I do not know how to manage your friend Randall. No doubt you do.

LADY UTTERWORD. Randall: have you been making yourself ridiculous, as usual? I can see it in your face. Really, you are the most pettish creature.

RANDALL. You know quite well, Ariadne, that I have not an ounce of pettishness in my disposition. I have made myself perfectly pleasant here. I have remained absolutely cool and imperturbable in the face of a burglar. Imperturbability is almost too strong a point of mine. But [putting his foot down with a stamp, and walking angrily up and down the room] I insist on being treated with a certain consideration. I will not allow Hushabye to take liberties with me. I will not stand your encouraging people as you do.

HECTOR. The man has a rooted delusion that he is your husband.

LADY UTTERWORD. I know. He is jealous. As if he had any right to be! He compromises me everywhere. He makes scenes all over the place. Randall: I will not allow it. I simply will not allow it. You had no right to discuss me with Hector. I will not be discussed by men.

HECTOR. Be reasonable, Ariadne. Your fatal gift of beauty forces men to discuss you.

LADY UTTERWORD. Oh indeed! what about your fatal gift of beauty?

HECTOR. How can I help it?

LADY UTTERWORD. You could cut off your moustache: I cant cut off my nose. I get my whole life messed up with people falling in love with me. And then Randall says I run after men.

RANDALL. I—

LADY UTTERWORD. Yes you do: you said it just now. Why cant you think of something else than women? Napoleon was quite right when he said that women are the occupation of the idle man. Well, if ever there was an idle man on earth, his name is Randall Utterword.

RANDALL. Ariad—

LADY UTTERWORD [overwhelming him with a torrent of words]. Oh yes you are: it's no use denying it. What have you ever done? What good are you? You are as much trouble in the house as a child of three. You couldnt live without your valet.

RANDALL. This is—

LADY UTTERWORD. Laziness! You are laziness incarnate. You are selfishness itself. You are the most uninteresting man on earth. You cant even gossip about anything but yourself and your grievances and your ailments and the people who have offended you. [Turning to HECTOR.] Do you know what they call him, Hector?

[speaking together]

HECTOR.   ⎱ ⎰Please dont tell me.
RANDALL.   ⎰ ⎱I'll not stand it—

LADY UTTERWORD. Randall the Rotter: that is his name in good society.

RANDALL [shouting]. I'll not bear it, I tell you. Will you listen to me, you infernal— [He chokes.]

LADY UTTERWORD. Well: go on. What were you going to call me? An infernal what? Which unpleasant animal is it to be this time?

RANDALL [foaming]. There is no animal in the world so hateful as a woman

can be. You are a maddening devil. Hushabye: you will not believe me when I tell you that I have loved this demon all my life; but God knows I have paid for it. [He sits down in the draughtsman's chair, weeping.]

LADY UTTERWORD [standing over him with triumphant contempt]. Cry-baby!

HECTOR [gravely, coming to him]. My friend: the Shotover sisters have two strange powers over men. They can make them love; and they can make them cry. Thank your stars that you are not married to one of them.

LADY UTTERWORD [haughtily]. And pray, Hector—

HECTOR [suddenly catching her round the shoulder; swinging her right round him and away from RANDALL; and gripping her throat with the other hand]. Ariadne: if you attempt to start on me, I'll choke you: do you hear? The cat-and-mouse game with the other sex is a good game; but I can play your head off at it. [He throws her, not at all gently, into the big chair, and proceeds, less fiercely but firmly.] It is true that Napoleon said that woman is the occupation of the idle man. But he added that she is the relaxation of the warrior. Well, I am the warrior. So take care.

LADY UTTERWORD [not in the least put out, and rather pleased by his violence]. My dear Hector: I have only done what you asked me to do.

HECTOR. How do you make that out, pray?

LADY UTTERWORD. You called me in to manage Randall, didnt you? You said you couldnt manage him yourself.

HECTOR. Well, what if I did? I did not ask you to drive the man mad.

LADY UTTERWORD. He isnt mad. Thats the way to manage him. If you were a mother, youd understand.

HECTOR. Mother! What are you up to now?

LADY UTTERWORD. It's quite simple. When the children got nerves and were naughty, I smacked them just enough to give them a good cry and a healthy nervous shock. They went to sleep and were quite good afterwards. Well, I cant smack Randall: he is too big; so when he gets nerves and is naughty, I just rag him till he cries. He will be all right now.

Look: he is half asleep already [*which is quite true*].

RANDALL [*waking up indignantly*]. I'm not. You are most cruel, Ariadne. [*Sentimentally.*] But I suppose I must forgive you, as usual. [*He checks himself in the act of yawning.*]

LADY UTTERWORD [*to* HECTOR]. Is the explanation satisfactory, dread warrior?

HECTOR. Some day I shall kill you, if you go too far. I thought you were a fool.

LADY UTTERWORD [*laughing*]. Everybody does, at first. But I am not such a fool as I look. [*She rises complacently.*] Now, Randall: go to bed. You will be a good boy in the morning.

RANDALL [*only very faintly rebellious*]. I'll go to bed when I like. It isnt ten yet.

LADY UTTERWORD. It is long past ten. See that he goes to bed at once, Hector. [*She goes into the garden.*]

HECTOR. Is there any slavery on earth viler than this slavery of men to women?

RANDALL [*rising resolutely*]. I'll not speak to her tomorrow. I'll not speak to her for another week. I'll give her such a lesson. I'll go straight to bed without bidding her goodnight. [*He makes for the door leading to the hall.*]

HECTOR. You are under a spell, man. Old Shotover sold himself to the devil in Zanzibar. The devil gave him a black witch for a wife; and these two demon daughters are their mystical progeny. I am tied to Hesione's apron-string; but I'm her husband; and if I did go stark staring mad about her, at least we became man and wife. But why should you let yourself be dragged about and beaten by Ariadne as a toy donkey is dragged about and beaten by a child? What do you get by it? Are you her lover?

RANDALL. You must not misunderstand me. In a higher sense—in a Platonic sense—

HECTOR. Psha! Platonic sense! She makes you her servant; and when pay-day comes round, she bilks you: that is what you mean.

RANDALL [*feebly*]. Well, if I dont mind, I dont see what business it is of yours. Besides, I tell you I am going to punish her. You shall see: *I* know how to deal with women. I'm really very sleepy. Say goodnight to Mrs Hushabye for me,

will you, like a good chap. Goodnight. [*He hurries out.*]

HECTOR. Poor wretch! Oh women! women! women! [*He lifts his fists in invocation to heaven.*] Fall. Fall and crush. [*He goes out into the garden.*]

ACT III

[*In the garden,* HECTOR, *as he comes out through the glass door of the poop, finds* LADY UTTERWORD *lying voluptuously in the hammock on the east side of the flagstaff, in the circle of light cast by the electric arc, which is like a moon in its opal globe. Beneath the head of the hammock, a campstool. On the other side of the flagstaff, on the long garden seat,* CAPTAIN SHOTOVER *is asleep, with* ELLIE *beside him, leaning affectionately against him on his right hand. On his left is a deck chair. Behind them in the gloom,* HESIONE *is strolling about with* MANGAN. *It is a fine still night, moonless.*]

LADY UTTERWORD. What a lovely night! It seems made for us.

HECTOR. The night takes no interest in us. What are we to the night? [*He sits down moodily in the deck chair.*]

ELLIE [*dreamily, nestling against the* CAPTAIN]. Its beauty soaks into my nerves. In the night there is peace for the old and hope for the young.

HECTOR. Is that remark your own?

ELLIE. No. Only the last thing the Captain said before he went to sleep.

CAPTAIN SHOTOVER. I'm not asleep.

HECTOR. Randall is. Also Mr Mazzini Dunn. Mangan too, probably.

MANGAN. No.

HECTOR. Oh, you are there. I thought Hesione would have sent you to bed by this time.

MRS HUSHABYE [*coming to the back of the garden seat, into the light, with* MANGAN]. I think I shall. He keeps telling me he has a presentiment that he is going to die. I never met a man so greedy for sympathy.

MANGAN [*plaintively*]. But I have a presentiment. I really have. And you wouldnt listen.

MRS HUSHABYE. I was listening for something else. There was a sort of splendid drumming in the sky. Did none of you hear it? It came from a distance and then died away.

MANGAN. I tell you it was a train.

MRS HUSHABYE. And I tell you, Alf, there is no train at this hour. The last is nine fortyfive.

MANGAN. But a goods train.

MRS HUSHABYE. Not on our little line. They tack a truck on to the passenger train. What can it have been, Hector?

HECTOR. Heaven's threatening growl of disgust at us useless futile creatures. [*Fiercely.*] I tell you, one of two things must happen. Either out of that darkness some new creation will come to supplant us as we have supplanted the animals, or the heavens will fall in thunder and destroy us.

LADY UTTERWORD [*in a cool instructive manner, wallowing comfortably in her hammock*]. We have not supplanted the animals, Hector. Why do you ask heaven to destroy this house, which could be made quite comfortable if Hesione had any notion of how to live? Dont you know what is wrong with it?

HECTOR. We are wrong with it. There is no sense in us. We are useless, dangerous, and ought to be abolished.

LADY UTTERWORD. Nonsense! Hastings told me the very first day he came here, nearly twentyfour years ago, what is wrong with the house.

CAPTAIN SHOTOVER. What! The numskull said there was something wrong with my house!

LADY UTTERWORD. I said Hastings said it; and he is not in the least a numskull.

CAPTAIN SHOTOVER. Whats wrong with my house?

LADY UTTERWORD. Just what is wrong with a ship, papa. Wasnt it clever of Hastings to see that?

CAPTAIN SHOTOVER. The man's a fool. Theres nothing wrong with a ship.

LADY UTTERWORD. Yes there is.

MRS HUSHABYE. But what is it? Dont be aggravating, Addy.

LADY UTTERWORD. Guess.

HECTOR. Demons. Daughters of the witch of Zanzibar. Demons.

LADY UTTERWORD. Not a bit. I assure you, all this house needs to make it a sensible, healthy, pleasant house, with good appetites and sound sleep in it, is horses.

MRS HUSHABYE. Horses! What rubbish!

LADY UTTERWORD. Yes: horses. Why have we never been able to let this house? Because there are no proper stables. Go anywhere in England where there are natural, wholesome, contented, and really nice English people; and what do you always find? That the stables are the real centre of the household; and that if any visitor wants to play the piano the whole room has to be upset before it can be opened, there are so many things piled on it. I never lived until I learned to ride; and I shall never ride really well because I didnt begin as a child. There are only two classes in good society in England: the equestrian classes and the neurotic classes. It isn't mere convention: everybody can see that the people who hunt are the right people and the people who dont are the wrong ones.

CAPTAIN SHOTOVER. There is some truth in this. My ship made a man of me; and a ship is the horse of the sea.

LADY UTTERWORD. Exactly how Hastings explained your being a gentleman.

CAPTAIN SHOTOVER. Not bad for a numskull. Bring the man here with you next time: I must talk to him.

LADY UTTERWORD. Why is Randall such an obvious rotter? He is well bred; he has been at a public school and a university; he has been in the Foreign Office; he knows the best people and has lived all his life among them. Why is he so unsatisfactory, so contemptible? Why cant he get a valet to stay with him longer than a few months? Just because he is too lazy and pleasure-loving to hunt and shoot. He strums the piano, and sketches, and runs after married women, and reads literary books and poems. He actually plays the flute; but I never let him bring it into my house. If he would only— [*She is interrupted by the melancholy strains of a flute coming from an open window above. She raises herself indignantly in the hammock.*] Randall: you have not gone to bed. Have you been listening? [*The flute replies pertly:*]

How vulgar! Go to bed instantly, Randall: how dare you? [*The window is slammed down. She subsides.*] How can anyone care for such a creature!

MRS HUSHABYE. Addy: do you think Ellie ought to marry poor Alfred merely for his money?

MANGAN [*much alarmed*]. Whats that? Mrs Hushabye: are my affairs to be discussed like this before everybody?

LADY UTTERWORD. I dont think Randall is listening now.

MANGAN. Everybody is listening. It isnt right.

MRS HUSHABYE. But in the dark, what does it matter? Ellie doesnt mind. Do you, Ellie?

ELLIE. Not in the least. What is your opinion, Lady Utterword? You have so much good sense.

MANGAN. But it isnt right. It— [MRS HUSHABYE *puts her hand on his mouth.*] Oh, very well.

LADY UTTERWORD. How much money have you, Mr Mangan?

MANGAN. Really— No: I cant stand this.

LADY UTTERWORD. Nonsense, Mr Mangan! It all turns on your income, doesnt it?

MANGAN. Well, if you come to that, how much money has she?

ELLIE. None.

LADY UTTERWORD. You are answered, Mr Mangan. And now, as you have made Miss Dunn throw her cards on the table, you cannot refuse to shew your own.

MRS HUSHABYE. Come, Alf! out with it! How much?

MANGAN [*baited out of all prudence*]. Well, if you want to know, I have no money and never had any.

MRS HUSHABYE. Alfred: you mustnt tell naughty stories.

MANGAN. I'm not telling you stories. I'm telling you the raw truth.

LADY UTTERWORD. Then what do you live on, Mr Mangan?

MANGAN. Travelling expenses. And a trifle of commission.

CAPTAIN SHOTOVER. What more have any of us but travelling expenses for our life's journey?

MRS HUSHABYE. But you have factories and capital and things?

MANGAN. People think I have. People think I'm an industrial Napoleon. Thats why Miss Ellie wants to marry me. But I tell you I have nothing.

ELLIE. Do you mean that the factories are like Marcus's tigers? That they dont exist?

MANGAN. They exist all right enough. But theyre not mine. They belong to syndicates and shareholders and all sorts of lazy good-for-nothing capitalists. I get money from such people to start the factories. I find people like Miss Dunn's father to work them, and keep a tight hand so as to make them pay. Of course I make them keep me going pretty well; but it's a dog's life; and I dont own anything.

MRS HUSHABYE. Alfred, Alfred: you are making a poor mouth of it to get out of marrying Ellie.

MANGAN. I'm telling the truth about my money for the first time in my life; and it's the first time my word has ever been doubted.

LADY UTTERWORD. How sad! Why dont you go in for politics, Mr Mangan?

MANGAN. Go in for politics! Where have you been living? I am in politics.

LADY UTTERWORD. I'm sure I beg your pardon. I never heard of you.

MANGAN. Let me tell you, Lady Utterword, that the Prime Minister of this country asked me to join the Government without even going through the nonsense of an election, as the dictator of a great public department.

LADY UTTERWORD. As a Conservative or a Liberal?

MANGAN. No such nonsense. As a practical business man. [*They all burst out laughing.*] What are you all laughing at?

MRS HUSHABYE. Oh, Alfred, Alfred!

ELLIE. You! who have to get my father to do everything for you!

MRS HUSHABYE. You! who are afraid of your own workmen!

HECTOR. You! with whom three women have been playing cat and mouse all the evening!

LADY UTTERWORD. You must have given an immense sum to the party funds, Mr Mangan.

MANGAN. Not a penny out of my own pocket. The syndicate found the money: they knew how useful I should be to them in the Government.

LADY UTTERWORD. This is most interesting and unexpected, Mr Mangan. And what have your administrative achievements been, so far?

MANGAN. Achievements? Well, I dont know what you call achievements; but Ive jolly well put a stop to the games of the other fellows in the other departments. Every man of them thought he was going to save the country all by himself, and do me out of the credit and out of my chance of a title. I took good care that if they wouldnt let me do it they shouldnt do it themselves either. I may not know anything about my own machinery; but I know how to stick a ramrod into the other fellow's. And now they all look the biggest fools going.

HECTOR. And in heaven's name, what do you look like?

MANGAN. I look like the fellow that was too clever for all the others, dont I? If that isnt a triumph of practical business, what is?

HECTOR. Is this England, or is it a madhouse?

LADY UTTERWORD. Do you expect to save the country, Mr Mangan?

MANGAN. Well, who else will? Will your Mr Randall save it?

LADY UTTERWORD. Randall the Rotter! Certainly not.

MANGAN. Will your brother-in-law save it with his moustache and his fine talk.

HECTOR. Yes, if they will let me.

MANGAN [*sneering*]. Ah! Will they let you?

HECTOR. No. They prefer you.

MANGAN. Very well then, as youre in a world where I'm appreciated and youre not, youd best be civil to me, hadnt you? Who else is there but me?

LADY UTTERWORD. There is Hastings. Get rid of your ridiculous sham democracy; and give Hastings the necessary powers, and a good supply of bamboo to bring the British native to his senses: he will save the country with the greatest ease.

CAPTAIN SHOTOVER. It had better be lost. Any fool can govern with a stick in his hand. *I* could govern that way. It is not God's way. The man is a numskull.

LADY UTTERWORD. The man is worth all of you rolled into one. What do you say, Miss Dunn?

ELLIE. I think my father would do very well if people did not put upon him and cheat him and despise him because he is so good.

MANGAN [*contemptuously*]. I think I see Mazzini Dunn getting into parliament or pushing his way into the Government. Weve not come to that yet, thank God! What do you say, Mrs Hushabye?

MRS HUSHABYE. Oh, *I* say it matters very little which of you governs the country so long as we govern you.

HECTOR. We? Who is we, pray?

MRS HUSHABYE. The devil's granddaughters, dear. The lovely women.

HECTOR [*raising his hands as before*]. Fall, I say; and deliver us from the lures of Satan!

ELLIE. There seems to be nothing real in the world except my father and Shakespear. Marcus's tigers are false; Mr Mangan's millions are false; there is nothing really strong and true about Hesione but her beautiful black hair; and Lady Utterword's is too pretty to be real. The one thing that was left to me was the Captain's seventh degree of concentration; and that turns out to be—

CAPTAIN SHOTOVER. Rum.

LADY UTTERWORD [*placidly*]. A good deal of my hair is quite genuine. The Duchess of Dithering offered me fifty guineas for this [*touching her forehead*] under the impression that it was a transformation; but it is all natural except the color.

MANGAN [*wildly*]. Look here: I'm going to take off all my clothes. [*He begins tearing off his coat.*]

[*in consternation*]

LADY UTTERWORD. Mr Mangan!
CAPTAIN SHOTOVER. Whats that?
HECTOR. Ha! ha! Do. Do.
ELLIE. Please dont.

MRS HUSHABYE [*catching his arm and stopping him*]. Alfred: for shame! Are you mad?

MANGAN. Shame! What shame is there in this house? Let's all strip stark naked. We may as well do the thing thoroughly when we're about it. Weve stripped ourselves morally naked: well, let us strip ourselves physically naked as well, and see how we like it. I tell you I cant bear this. I was brought up to be respectable. I dont mind the women dyeing their hair and the men drinking: it's human nature.

But it's not human nature to tell every-body about it. Every time one of you opens your mouth I go like this [*he cowers as if to avoid a missile*] afraid of what will come next. How are we to have any self-respect if we dont keep it up that we're better than we really are?

LADY UTTERWORD. I quite sympathize with you, Mr Mangan. I have been through it all; and I know by experience that men and women are delicate plants and must be cultivated under glass. Our family habit of throwing stones in all di-rections and letting the air in is not only unbearably rude, but positively danger-ous. Still, there is no use catching physi-cal colds as well as moral ones; so please keep your clothes on.

MANGAN. I'll do as I like: not what you tell me. Am I a child or a grown man? I wont stand this mothering tyranny. I'll go back to the city, where I'm respected and made much of.

MRS HUSHABYE. Goodbye, Alf. Think of us sometimes in the city. Think of Ellie's youth!

ELLIE. Think of Hesione's eyes and hair!

CAPTAIN SHOTOVER. Think of this gar-den in which you are not a dog barking to keep the truth out!

HECTOR. Think of Lady Utterword's beauty! her good sense! her style!

LADY UTTERWORD. Flatterer. Think, Mr Mangan, whether you can really do any better for yourself elsewhere: that is the essential point, isnt it?

MANGAN [*surrendering*]. All right: all right. I'm done. Have it your own way. Only let me alone. I dont know whether I'm on my head or my heels when you all start on me like this. I'll stay. I'll marry her. I'll do anything for a quiet life. Are you satisfied now?

ELLIE. No. I never really intended to make you marry me, Mr Mangan. Never in the depths of my soul. I only wanted to feel my strength: to know that you could not escape if I chose to take you.

MANGAN [*indignantly*]. What! Do you mean to say you are going to throw me over after my acting so handsome?

LADY UTTERWORD. I should not be too hasty, Miss Dunn. You can throw Mr Mangan over at any time up to the last moment. Very few men in his position go bankrupt. You can live very comfortably

on his reputation for immense wealth.

ELLIE. I cannot commit bigamy, Lady Utterword.

[*exclaiming all together*]

MRS HUSHABYE.	Bigamy! What-ever on earth are you talk-ing about, Ellie?
LADY UTTERWORD.	Bigamy! What do you mean, Miss Dunn?
MANGAN.	Bigamy! Do you mean to say youre married al-ready?
HECTOR.	Bigamy! This is some enigma.

ELLIE. Only half an hour ago I became Captain Shotover's white wife.

MRS HUSHABYE. Ellie! What nonsense! Where?

ELLIE. In heaven, where all true mar-riages are made.

LADY UTTERWORD. Really, Miss Dunn! Really, papa!

MANGAN. He told me I was too old! And him a mummy!

HECTOR [*quoting Shelley*].

Their altar the grassy earth outspread,
And their priest the muttering wind.

ELLIE. Yes: I, Ellie Dunn, give my broken heart and my strong sound soul to its natural captain, my spiritual husband and second father.

[*She draws the* CAPTAIN's *arm through hers, and pats his hand. The* CAP-TAIN *remains fast asleep.*]

MRS HUSHABYE. Oh, thats very clever of you, pettikins. Very clever. Alfred: you could never have lived up to Ellie. You must be content with a little share of me.

MANGAN [*sniffing and wiping his eyes*]. It isnt kind— [*His emotion chokes him.*]

LADY UTTERWORD. You are well out of it, Mr Mangan. Miss Dunn is the most conceited young woman I have met since I came back to England.

MRS HUSHABYE. Oh, Ellie isnt con-ceited. Are you, pettikins?

ELLIE. I know my strength now, Hesione.

MANGAN. Brazen, I call you. Brazen.

MRS HUSHABYE. Tut tut, Alfred: dont

be rude. Dont you feel how lovely this marriage night is, made in heaven? Arnt you happy, you and Hector? Open your eyes: Addy and Ellie look beautiful enough to please the most fastidious man: we live and love and have not a care in the world. We women have managed all that for you. Why in the name of common sense do you go on as if you were two miserable wretches?

CAPTAIN SHOTOVER. I tell you happiness is no good. You can be happy when you are only half alive. I am happier now I am half dead than ever I was in my prime. But there is no blessing on my happiness.

ELLIE [her face lighting up]. Life with a blessing! that is what I want. Now I know the real reason why I couldnt marry Mr Mangan: there would be no blessing on our marriage. There is a blessing on my broken heart. There is a blessing on your beauty, Hesione. There is a blessing on your father's spirit. Even on the lies of Marcus there is a blessing; but on Mr Mangan's money there is none.

MANGAN. I dont understand a word of that.

ELLIE. Neither do I. But I know it means something.

MANGAN. Dont say there was any difficulty about the blessing. I was ready to get a bishop to marry us.

MRS HUSHABYE. Isnt he a fool, pettikins?

HECTOR [fiercely]. Do not scorn the man. We are all fools.

[MAZZINI, in pyjamas and a richly colored silk dressing-gown, comes from the house, on LADY UTTERWORD's side.]

MRS HUSHABYE. Oh! here comes the only man who ever resisted me. Whats the matter, Mr Dunn? Is the house on fire?

MAZZINI. Oh no: nothing's the matter; but really it's impossible to go to sleep with such an interesting conversation going on under one's window, and on such a beautiful night too. I just had to come down and join you all. What has it all been about?

MRS HUSHABYE. Oh, wonderful things, soldier of freedom.

HECTOR. For example, Mangan, as a practical business man, has tried to un-

dress himself and has failed ignominiously; whilst you, as an idealist, have succeeded brilliantly.

MAZZINI. I hope you dont mind my being like this, Mrs Hushabye. [He sits down on the campstool.]

MRS HUSHABYE. On the contrary, I could wish you always like that.

LADY UTTERWORD. Your daughter's match is off, Mr Dunn. It seems that Mr Mangan, whom we all supposed to be a man of property, owns absolutely nothing.

MAZZINI. Well of course I knew that, Lady Utterword. But if people believe in him and are always giving him money, whereas they dont believe in me and never give me any, how can I ask poor Ellie to depend on what I can do for her?

MANGAN. Dont you run away with this idea that I have nothing. I—

HECTOR. Oh, dont explain. We understand. You have a couple of thousand pounds in exchequer bills, 50,000 shares worth tenpence a dozen, and half a dozen tabloids of cyanide of potassium to poison yourself with when you are found out. Thats the reality of your millions.

MAZZINI. Oh no, no, no. He is quite honest: the businesses are genuine and perfectly legal.

HECTOR [disgusted]. Yah! Not even a great swindler!

MANGAN. So you think. But Ive been too many for some honest men for all that.

LADY UTTERWORD. There is no pleasing you, Mr Mangan. You are determined to be neither rich nor poor, honest nor dishonest.

MANGAN. There you go again. Ever since I came into this silly house I have been made to look like a fool, though I'm as good a man in this house as in the city.

ELLIE [musically]. Yes: this silly house, this strangely happy house, this agonizing house, this house without foundations. I shall call it Heartbreak House.

MRS HUSHABYE. Stop, Ellie; or I shall howl like an animal.

MANGAN [breaks into a low snivelling]!!!

MRS HUSHABYE. There! you have set Alfred off.

ELLIE. I like him best when he is howling.

CAPTAIN SHOTOVER. Silence! [MANGAN *subsides into silence.*] I say, let the heart break in silence.

HECTOR. Do you accept that name for your house?

CAPTAIN SHOTOVER. It is not my house: it is only my kennel.

HECTOR. We have been too long here. We do not live in this house: we haunt it.

LADY UTTERWORD [*heart torn*]. It is dreadful to think how you have been here all these years while I have gone round the world. I escaped young; but it has drawn me back. It wants to break my heart too. But it shant. I have left you and it behind. It was silly of me to come back. I felt sentimental about papa and Hesione and the old place. I felt them calling to me.

MAZZINI. But what a very natural and kindly and charming human feeling, Lady Utterword!

LADY UTTERWORD. So I thought, Mr Dunn. But I know now that it was only the last of my influenza. I found that I was not remembered and not wanted.

CAPTAIN SHOTOVER. You left because you did not want us. Was there no heartbreak in that for your father? You tore yourself up by the roots; and the ground healed up and brought forth fresh plants and forgot you. What right had you to come back and probe old wounds?

MRS HUSHABYE. You were a complete stranger to me at first, Addy; but now I feel as if you had never been away.

LADY UTTERWORD. Thank you, Hesione; but the influenza is quite cured. The place may be Heartbreak House to you, Miss Dunn, and to this gentleman from the city who seems to have so little self-control; but to me it is only a very ill-regulated and rather untidy villa without any stables.

HECTOR. Inhabited by—?

ELLIE. A crazy old sea captain and a young singer who adores him.

MRS HUSHABYE. A sluttish female, trying to stave off a double chin and an elderly spread, vainly wooing a born soldier of freedom.

MAZZINI. Oh, really, Mrs Hushabye—

MANGAN. A member of His Majesty's Government that everybody sets down as a nincompoop: dont forget him, Lady Utterword.

LADY UTTERWORD. And a very fascinating gentleman whose chief occupation is to be married to my sister.

HECTOR. All heartbroken imbeciles.

MAZZINI. Oh no. Surely, if I may so so, rather a favorable specimen of what is best in our English culture. You are very charming people, most advanced, unprejudiced, frank, humane, unconventional, democratic, free-thinking, and everything that is delightful to thoughtful people.

MRS HUSHABYE. You do us proud, Mazzini.

MAZZINI. I am not flattering, really. Where else could I feel perfectly at ease in my pyjamas? I sometimes dream that I am in very distinguished society, and suddenly I have nothing on but my pyjamas! Sometimes I havnt even pyjamas. And I always feel overwhelmed with confusion. But here, I dont mind in the least: it seems quite natural.

LADY UTTERWORD. An infallible sign that you are not now in really distinguished society, Mr. Dunn. If you were in my house, you would feel embarrassed.

MAZZINI. I shall take particular care to keep out of your house, Lady Utterword.

LADY UTTERWORD. You will be quite wrong, Mr Dunn. I should make you very comfortable; and you would not have the trouble and anxiety of wondering whether you should wear your purple and gold or your green and crimson dressing-gown at dinner. You complicate life instead of simplifying it by doing these ridiculous things.

ELLIE. Your house is not Heartbreak House: is it, Lady Utterword?

HECTOR. Yet she breaks hearts, easy as her house is. That poor devil upstairs with his flute howls when she twists his heart, just as Mangan howls when my wife twists his.

LADY UTTERWORD. That is because Randall has nothing to do but have his heart broken. It is a change from having his head shampooed. Catch anyone breaking Hastings' heart!

CAPTAIN SHOTOVER. The numskull wins, after all.

LADY UTTERWORD. I shall go back to my numskull with the greatest satisfaction when I am tired of you all, clever as you are.

MANGAN [*huffily*]. I never set up to be clever.

LADY UTTERWORD. I forgot you, Mr Mangan.

MANGAN. Well, I dont see that quite, either.

LADY UTTERWORD. You may not be clever, Mr Mangan; but you are successful.

MANGAN. But I dont want to be regarded merely as a successful man. I have an imagination like anyone else. I have a presentiment—

MRS HUSHABYE. Oh, you are impossible, Alfred. Here I am devoting myself to you; and you think of nothing but your ridiculous presentiment. You bore me. Come and talk poetry to me under the stars. [*She drags him away into the darkness.*]

MANGAN [*tearfully, as he disappears*]. Yes: it's all very well to make fun of me; but if you only knew—

HECTOR [*impatiently*]. How is all this going to end?

MAZZINI. It wont end, Mr Hushabye. Life doesnt end: it goes on.

ELLIE. Oh, it cant go on forever. I'm always expecting something. I dont know what it is; but life must come to a point sometime.

LADY UTTERWORD. The point for a young woman of your age is a baby.

HECTOR. Yes, but damn it, I have the same feeling; and I cant have a baby.

LADY UTTERWORD. By deputy, Hector.

HECTOR. But I have children. All that is over and done with for me: and yet I too feel that this cant last. We sit here talking, and leave everything to Mangan and to chance and to the devil. Think of the powers of destruction that Mangan and his mutual admiration gang wield! It's madness: it's like giving a torpedo to a badly brought up child to play at earthquakes with.

MAZZINI. I know. I used often to think about that when I was young.

HECTOR. Think! Whats the good of thinking about it? Why didnt you do something?

MAZZINI. But I did. I joined societies and made speeches and wrote pamphlets. That was all I could do. But, you know, though the people in the societies thought they knew more than Mangan, most of them wouldnt have joined if they had known as much. You see they had never had any money to handle or any men to manage. Every year I expected a revolution, or some frightful smash-up: it seemed impossible that we could blunder and muddle on any longer. But nothing happened, except, of course, the usual poverty and crime and drink that we are used to. Nothing ever does happen. It's amazing how well we get along, all things considered.

LADY UTTERWORD. Perhaps, somebody cleverer than you and Mr Mangan was at work all the time.

MAZZINI. Perhaps so. Though I was brought up not to believe in anything, I often feel that there is a great deal to be said for the theory of an overruling Providence, after all.

LADY UTTERWORD. Providence! I meant Hastings.

MAZZINI. Oh, I beg your pardon, Lady Utterword.

CAPTAIN SHOTOVER. Every drunken skipper trusts to Providence. But one of the ways of Providence with drunken skippers is to run them on the rocks.

MAZZINI. Very true, no doubt, at sea. But in politics, I assure you, they only run into jellyfish. Nothing happens.

CAPTAIN SHOTOVER. At sea nothing happens to the sea. Nothing happens to the sky. The sun comes up from the east and goes down to the west. The moon grows from a sickle to an arc lamp, and comes later and later until she is lost in the light as other things are lost in the darkness. After the typhoon, the flying-fish glitter in the sunshine like birds. It's amazing how they get along, all things considered. Nothing happens, except something not worth mentioning.

ELLIE. What is that, O Captain, my captain?

CAPTAIN SHOTOVER [*savagely*]. Nothing but the smash of the drunken skipper's ship on the rocks, the splintering of her rotten timbers, the tearing of her rusty plates, the drowning of the crew like rats in a trap.

ELLIE. Moral: dont take rum.

CAPTAIN SHOTOVER [*vehemently*]. That is a lie, child. Let a man drink ten barrels of rum a day, he is not a drunken skipper until he is a drifting skipper.

Whilst he can lay his course and stand on his bridge and steer it, he is no drunkard. It is the man who lies drinking in his bunk and trusts to Providence that I call the drunken skipper, though he drank nothing but the waters of the River Jordan.

ELLIE. Splendid! And you havnt had a drop for an hour. You see you dont need it: your own spirit is not dead.

CAPTAIN SHOTOVER. Echoes: nothing but echoes. The last shot was fired years ago.

HECTOR. And this ship we are all in? This soul's prison we call England?

CAPTAIN SHOTOVER. The captain is in his bunk, drinking bottled ditch-water; and the crew is gambling in the forecastle. She will strike and sink and split. Do you think the laws of God will be suspended in favor of England because you were born in it?

HECTOR. Well, I dont mean to be drowned like a rat in a trap. I still have the will to live. What am I to do?

CAPTAIN SHOTOVER. Do? Nothing simpler. Learn your business as an Englishman.

HECTOR. And what may my business as an Englishman be, pray?

CAPTAIN SHOTOVER. Navigation. Learn it and live; or leave it and be damned.

ELLIE. Quiet, quiet; youll tire yourself.

MAZZINI. I thought all that once, Captain; but I assure you nothing will happen.

[A dull distant explosion is heard.]

HECTOR [starting up]. What was that?

CAPTAIN SHOTOVER. Something happening. [He blows his whistle.] Breakers ahead!

[The light goes out.]

HECTOR [furiously]. Who put that light out? Who dared put that light out?

NURSE GUINNESS [running in from the house to the middle of the esplanade]. I did, sir. The police have telephoned to say we'll be summoned if we dont put that light out: it can be seen for miles.

HECTOR. It shall be seen for a hundred miles. [He dashes into the house.]

NURSE GUINNESS. The rectory is nothing but a heap of bricks, they say. Unless we can give the rector a bed he has nowhere to lay his head this night.

CAPTAIN SHOTOVER. The Church is on the rocks, breaking up. I told him it would unless it headed for God's open sea.

NURSE GUINNESS. And you are all to go down to the cellars.

CAPTAIN SHOTOVER. Go there yourself, you and all the crew. Batten down the hatches.

NURSE GUINNESS. And hide beside the coward I married! I'll go on the roof first. [The lamp lights up again.] There! Mr Hushabye's turned it on again.

THE BURGLAR [hurrying in and appealing to NURSE GUINNESS]. Here: wheres the way to that gravel pit? The boot-boy says theres a cave in the gravel pit. Them cellars is no use. Wheres the gravel pit, Captain?

NURSE GUINNESS. Go straight on past the flagstaff until you fall into it and break your dirty neck. [She pushes him contemptuously towards the flagstaff, and herself goes to the foot of the hammock and waits there, as it were by ARIADNE's cradle.]

[Another and louder explosion is heard. The burglar stops and stands trembling.]

ELLIE [rising]. That was nearer.

CAPTAIN SHOTOVER. The next one will get us. [He rises.] Stand by, all hands, for judgment.

THE BURGLAR. Oh my Lordy God! [He rushes away frantically past the flagstaff into the gloom.]

MRS HUSHABYE [emerging panting from the darkness]. Who was that running away? [She comes to ELLIE.] Did you hear the explosions? And the sound in the sky: it's splendid: it's like an orchestra: it's like Beethoven.

ELLIE. By thunder, Hesione: it is Beethoven.

[She and HESIONE throw themselves into one another's arms in wild excitement. The light increases.]

MAZZINI [anxiously]. The light is getting brighter.

NURSE GUINNESS [looking up at the house]. It's Mr Hushabye turning on all the lights in the house and tearing down the curtains.

RANDALL [rushing in in his pyjamas, distractedly waving a flute]. Ariadne: my soul, my precious, go down to the cellars: I beg and implore you, go down to the cellars!

LADY UTTERWORD [*quite composed in her hammock*]. The governor's wife in the cellars with the servants! Really, Randall!

RANDALL. But what shall I do if you are killed?

LADY UTTERWORD. You will probably be killed, too, Randall. Now play your flute to shew that you are not afraid; and be good. Play us Keep the home fires burning.

NURSE GUINNESS [*grimly*]. Theyll keep the home fires burning for us: them up there.

RANDALL [*having tried to play*]. My lips are trembling. I cant get a sound.

MAZZINI. I hope poor Mangan is safe.

MRS HUSHABYE. He is hiding in the cave in the gravel pit.

CAPTAIN SHOTOVER. My dynamite drew him there. It is the hand of God.

HECTOR [*returning from the house and striding across to his former place*]. There is not half light enough. We should be blazing to the skies.

ELLIE [*tense with excitement*]. Set fire to the house, Marcus.

MRS HUSHABYE. My house! No.

HECTOR. I thought of that; but it would not be ready in time.

CAPTAIN SHOTOVER. The judgment has come. Courage will not save you; but it will shew that your souls are still alive.

MRS HUSHABYE. Sh-sh! Listen: do you hear it now? It's magnificent.

[*They all turn away from the house and look up, listening.*]

HECTOR [*gravely*]. Miss Dunn: you can do no good here. We of this house are only moths flying into the candle. You had better go down to the cellar.

ELLIE [*scornfully*]. I dont think.

MAZZINI. Ellie, dear, there is no disgrace in going to the cellar. An officer would order his soldiers to take cover. Mr Hushabye is behaving like an amateur. Mangan and the burglar are acting very sensibly; and it is they who will survive.

ELLIE. Let them. I shall behave like an amateur. But why should you run any risk?

MAZZINI. Think of the risk those poor fellows up there are running!

NURSE GUINNESS. Think of them, indeed, the murdering blackguards! What next?

[*A terrific explosion shakes the earth. They reel back into their seats, or clutch the nearest support. They hear the falling of the shattered glass from the windows.*]

MAZZINI. Is anyone hurt?

HECTOR. Where did it fall?

NURSE GUINNESS [*in hideous triumph*]. Right in the gravel pit: I seen it. Serve un right! I seen it. [*She runs away towards the gravel pit, laughing harshly.*]

HECTOR. One husband gone.

CAPTAIN SHOTOVER. Thirty pounds of good dynamite wasted.

MAZZINI. Oh, poor Mangan!

HECTOR. Are you immortal that you need pity him? Our turn next.

[*They wait in silence and intense expectation.* HESIONE *and* ELLIE *hold each other's hand tight.*

A distant explosion is heard.]

MRS HUSHABYE [*relaxing her grip*]. Oh! they have passed us.

LADY UTTERWORD. The danger is over, Randall. Go to bed.

CAPTAIN SHOTOVER. Turn in, all hands. The ship is safe. [*He sits down and goes asleep.*]

ELLIE [*disappointedly*]. Safe!

HECTOR [*disgustedly*]. Yes, safe. And how damnably dull the world has become again suddenly! [*He sits down.*]

MAZZINI [*sitting down*]. I was quite wrong, after all. It is we who have survived; and Mangan and the burglar—

HECTOR. —the two burglars—

LADY UTTERWORD. —the two practical men of business—

MAZZINI. —both gone. And the poor clergyman will have to get a new house.

MRS HUSHABYE. But what a glorious experience! I hope theyll come again tomorrow night.

ELLIE [*radiant at the prospect*]. Oh, I hope so.

[*Randall at last succeeds in keeping the home fires burning on his flute.*]

George Bernard Shaw

HEARTBREAK HOUSE
AND HORSEBACK HALL

WHERE HEARTBREAK HOUSE STANDS

Heartbreak House is not merely the name of the play which follows this preface. It is cultured, leisured Europe before the war. When the play was begun not a shot had been fired; and only the professional diplomatists and the very few amateurs whose hobby is foreign policy even knew that the guns were loaded. A Russian playwright, Tchekov, had produced four fascinating dramatic studies of Heartbreak House, of which three, *The Cherry Orchard, Uncle Vanya,* and *The Seagull,* had been performed in England. Tolstoy, in his *Fruits of Enlightenment,* had shewn us through it in his most ferociously contemptuous manner. Tolstoy did not waste any sympathy on it: it was to him the house in which Europe was stifling its soul; and he knew that our utter enervation and futilization in that overheated drawing-room atmosphere was delivering the world over to the control of ignorant and soulless cunning and energy, with the frightful consequences which have now overtaken it. Tolstoy was no pessimist: he was not disposed to leave the house standing if he could bring it down about the ears of its pretty and amiable voluptuaries; and he wielded the pickaxe with a will. He treated the case of the inmates as one of opium poisoning, to be dealt with by seizing the patients roughly and exercising them violently until they were broad awake. Tchekov, more of a fatalist, had no faith in these charming people extricating themselves. They would, he thought, be sold up and sent adrift by the bailiffs; therefore he had no scruple in exploiting and even flattering their charm.

THE INHABITANTS

Tchekov's plays, being less lucrative than swings and round-abouts, got no further in England, where theatres are only ordinary commercial affairs, than a couple of performances by the Stage Society. We stared and said, 'How Russian!' They did not strike me in that way. Just as Ibsen's intensely Norwegian plays exactly fitted every middle and professional class suburb in Europe, these intensely Russian plays fitted all the country houses in Europe in which the pleasures of music, art, literature, and the theatre had supplanted hunting, shooting, fishing, flirting, eating and drinking. The same nice people, the same utter futility. The nice people could read; some of them could write; and they were the only repositories of culture who had social opportunities of contact with our politicians, administrators, and newspaper proprietors, or any chance of sharing or influencing their activities. But they shrank from that contact. They hated politics. They did not wish to realize Utopia for the common people: they wished to realize their favorite fictions and poems in their own lives; and, when they could, they lived without scruple on incomes which they did nothing to earn. The women in their girlhood made themselves look like variety theatre stars, and settled down later into the types of beauty imagined by the previous generation of painters. They took the only part of our society in which there was leisure for high culture, and made it an economic, political, and, as far as practicable, a moral vacuum; and as Nature, abhorring the vacuum, immediately filled it up with sex and with all sorts of refined pleasures, it was a very delightful place at its best for moments of relaxation. In other moments it was disastrous. For prime ministers and their like, it was a veritable Capua.

HORSEBACK HALL

But where were our front benchers to nest if not here? The alternative to Heartbreak House was Horseback Hall, consisting of a prison for horses with an annex for the ladies and gentlemen who rode them, hunted them, talked about them, bought them and sold them, and gave nine-tenths of their lives to them, dividing the other tenth between charity, churchgoing (as a substitute for religion), and conservative electioneering (as a substitute for politics. It is true that the two establishments got mixed at the edges. Exiles from the library, the music room, and the picture gallery would be found languishing among the stables, miserably discontented; and hardy horsewomen who slept at the first chord of Schumann were born, horribly misplaced, into the garden of Klingsor; but sometimes one came upon horsebreakers and heartbreakers who could make the best of both worlds. As a rule, however, the two were apart and knew little of one another; so the prime minister folk had to choose between barbarism and Capua. And of the two atmospheres it is hard to say which was the more fatal to statesmanship.

REVOLUTION ON THE SHELF

Heartbreak House was quite familiar with revolutionary ideas on paper. It aimed at being advanced and freethinking, and hardly ever went to church or kept the Sabbath except by a little extra fun at week-ends. When you spent a Friday to Tuesday in it you found on the shelf in your bedroom not only the books of poets and novelists, but of revolutionary biologists and even economists. Without at least a few plays by myself and Mr Granville Barker, and a few stories by Mr H. G. Wells, Mr Arnold Bennett, and Mr John Galsworthy, the house would have been out of the move-

ment. You would find Blake among the poets, and beside him Bergson, Butler, Scott Haldane, the poems of Meredith and Thomas Hardy, and, generally speaking, all the literary implements for forming the mind of the perfect modern Socialist and Creative Evolutionist. It was a curious experience to spend Sunday in dipping into these books, and on Monday morning to read in the daily paper that the country had just been brought to the verge of anarchy because a new Home Secretary or chief of police, without an idea in his head that his great-grandmother might not have had to apologize for, had refused to 'recognize' some powerful Trade Union, just as a gondola might refuse to recognize a 20,000-ton liner.

In short, power and culture were in separate compartments. The barbarians were not only literally in the saddle, but on the front bench in the House of Commons, with nobody to correct their incredible ignorance of modern thought and political science but upstarts from the counting-house, who had spent their lives furnishing their pockets instead of their minds. Both, however, were practiced in dealing with money and with men, as far as acquiring the one and exploiting the other went; and although this is as undesirable an expertness as that of the medieval robber baron, it qualifies men to keep an estate or a business going in its old routine without necessarily understanding it, just as Bond Street tradesmen and domestic servants keep fashionable society going without any instruction in sociology.

THE CHERRY ORCHARD

The Heartbreak people neither could nor would do anything of the sort. With their heads as full of the Anticipations of Mr H. G. Wells as the heads of our actual rulers were empty even of the anticipations of Erasmus or Sir Thomas More, they refused the drudgery of politics, and would have made a very poor job of it if they had changed their minds. Not that they would have been allowed to meddle anyhow, as only through the accident of being a hereditary peer can anyone in these days of Votes for Everybody get into parliament if handicapped by a serious modern cultural equipment; but if they had, their habit of living in a vacuum would have left them helpless and ineffective in public affairs. Even in private life they were often helpless wasters of their inheritance, like the people in Tchekov's *Cherry Orchard*. Even those who lived within their incomes were really kept going by their solicitors and agents, being unable to manage an estate or run a business without continual prompting from those who have to learn how to do such things or starve.

From what is called Democracy no corrective to this state of things could be hoped. It is said that every people has the Government it deserves. It is more to the point that every Government has the electorate it deserves; for the orators of the front bench can edify or debauch an ignorant electorate at will. Thus our democracy moves in a vicious circle of reciprocal worthiness and unworthiness.

NATURE'S LONG CREDITS

Nature's way of dealing with unhealthy conditions is unfortunately not one that compels us to conduct a solvent hygiene on a cash basis. She demoralizes us with long credits and reckless overdrafts, and then pulls us up cruelly with catastrophic bankruptcies. Take, for example, common domestic sanitation. A whole city generation may neglect it utterly and scandalously, if not with absolute impunity, yet without any evil consequences that anyone thinks of tracing to it. In a hospital two generations of medical students may tolerate dirt and carelessness, and then go out into general practice to spread the doctrine that fresh air is a fad, and sanitation an imposture set up to make profits for plumbers. Then suddenly Nature takes her revenge. She strikes at the city with a pestilence and at the hospital with an epidemic of hospital gangrene, slaughtering right and left until the innocent young have paid for the guilty old, and the account is balanced. And then she goes to sleep again and gives another period of credit, with the same result.

This is what has just happened in our political hygiene. Political science has been as recklessly neglected by Governments and electorates during my lifetime as sanitary science was in the days of Charles the Second. In international relations diplomacy has been a boyishly lawless affair of family intrigues, commercial and territorial brigandage, torpors of pseudo-goodnature produced by laziness, and spasms of ferocious activity produced by terror. But in these islands we muddled through. Nature gave us a longer credit than she gave to France or Germany or Russia. To British centenarians who died in their beds in 1914, any dread of having to hide underground in London from the shells of an enemy seemed more remote and fantastic than a dread of the appearance of a colony of cobras and rattlesnakes in Kensington Gardens. In the prophetic works of Charles Dickens we were warned against many evils which have since come to pass; but of the evil of being slaughtered by a foreign foe on our own doorsteps there was no shadow. Nature gave us a very long credit; and we abused it to the utmost. But when she struck at last she struck with a vengeance. For four years she smote our firstborn and heaped on us plagues of which Egypt never dreamed. They were all as preventible as the great Plague of London, and came solely because they had not been prevented. They were not undone by winning the war. The earth is still bursting with the dead bodies of the victors.

THE WICKED HALF CENTURY

It is difficult to say whether indifference and neglect are worse than false doctrine; but Heartbreak House and Horseback Hall unfortunately suffered from both. For half a century before the war civilization had been going to the devil very precipitately under the influence of a pseudo-science as disastrous as the blackest Calvinism. Calvinism taught that as we are predestinately saved or damned, nothing that we do can alter our destiny. Still, as Calvinism gave the individual no clue as to whether he had drawn a lucky number or an unlucky one, it left him a fairly strong interest in encouraging his hopes of salvation and allaying his fear of damnation by behaving as one of the elect might be expected to behave rather than as one of the reprobate. But in the middle of the nineteenth century naturalists and physicists assured the world, in the name of Science, that salvation and damnation are all nonsense, and that predestination is the central truth of religion, inasmuch as human beings are produced by their environment, their sins and good deeds being only a series of chemical and mechanical reactions over which they have no control. Such figments as mind, choice, purpose, conscience, will, and so forth, are, they taught, mere illusions, produced because they are useful in the continual struggle of the human machine to maintain its environment in a favourable condition, a process incidentally involving the ruthless destruction or subjection of its competitors for the supply (assumed to be limited) of subsistence available. We taught Prussia this religion; and Prussia bettered our instruction so effectively that we presently found ourselves confronted with the necessity of destroying Prussia to prevent Prussia destroying us. And that has just ended in each destroying the other to an extent doubtfully reparable in our time.

It may be asked how so imbecile and dangerous a creed ever came to be accepted by intelligent beings. I will answer that question more fully in my next volume of plays, which will be entirely devoted to the subject. For the present I will only say that there were better reasons than the obvious one that such sham science as this opened a scientific career to very stupid men, and all the other careers to shameless rascals, provided they were industrious enough. It is true that this motive operated very powerfully; but when the new departure in scientific doctrine which is associated with the name of the great naturalist Charles Darwin began, it was not only a reaction against a barbarous pseudo-evangelical teleology intolerably obstructive to all scientific progress, but was accompanied, as it happened, by discoveries of extraordinary interest in physics, chemistry, and that lifeless method of evolution which its investigators called Natural Selection. Howbeit, there was only one result possible in the ethical sphere, and that was the banishment of conscience from human affairs, or, as Samuel Butler vehemently put it, 'of mind from the universe.'

HYPOCHONDRIA

Now Heartbreak House, with Butler and Bergson and Scott Haldane alongside Blake and the other major poets on its shelves (to say nothing of Wagner and the tone poets), was not so completely blinded by the doltish materialism of the laboratories as the uncultured world outside. But being an idle house it was a hypochondriacal house, always running after cures. It would stop eating meat, not on valid Shelleyan grounds, but in order to get rid of a bogey called Uric Acid; and it would actually let you pull all its teeth out to exorcize another demon named Pyorrhea. It was superstitious, and addicted to table-rapping, materialization séances, clairvoyance, palmistry, crystal-gazing and the like to such an extent that it may be doubted whether ever before in the history of the world did soothsayers, astrologers, and unregistered therapeutic specialists of all sorts flourish as they did during this half century of the drift to the abyss. The registered doctors and surgeons were hard put to it to compete with the unregistered. They were not clever enough to appeal to the imagination and sociability of the Heartbreakers by the arts of the actor, the orator, the poet, the winning conversationalist. They had to fall back coarsely on the terror of infection and death. They prescribed inoculations and operations. Whatever part of a human being could be cut out without necessarily killing him they cut out; and he often died (unnecessarily of course) in consequence. From such trifles as uvulas and tonsils they went on to ovaries and appendices until at last no one's inside was safe. They explained that the human intestine was too long, and that nothing could make a child of Adam healthy except short circuiting the pylorus by cutting a length out of the lower intestine and fastening it directly to the stomach. As their mechanist theory taught them that medicine was the business of the chemist's laboratory, and surgery of the carpenter's shop, and also that Science (by which they meant their practices) was so important that no consideration for the interests of any individual creature, whether frog or philosopher, much less the vulgar commonplaces of sentimental ethics, could weigh for a moment against the remotest off-change of an addition to the body of scientific knowledge, they operated and vivisected and inoculated and lied on a stupendous scale, clamoring for and actually acquiring such legal powers over the bodies of their fellow-citizens as neither king, pope, nor parliament dare ever have claimed. The Inquisition itself was a Liberal institution compared to the General Medical Council.

THOSE WHO DO NOT KNOW HOW TO LIVE MUST MAKE A MERIT OF DYING

Heartbreak House was far too lazy and shallow to extricate itself from this palace of evil enchantment. It rhapsodized about love; but it believed in cruelty. It was afraid of the cruel people; and it saw that cruelty was at least effective. Cruelty did things that made money, whereas Love did nothing but prove the soundness of Larochefoucauld's saying that very few people would fall in love if they had never read about it. Heartbreak House, in short, did not know how to live, at which point all that was left to it was the boast that at least it knew how to die: a melancholy accomplishment which the outbreak of war presently gave it practically unlimited opportunities of displaying. Thus were the firstborn of Heartbreak House smitten; and the young, the innocent, the hopeful expiated the folly and worthlessness of their elders.

WAR DELIRIUM

Only those who have lived through a first-rate war, not in the field, but at home, and kept their heads, can possibly understand the bitterness of Shakespear and Swift, who both went through this experience. The horror of Peer Gynt in the madhouse, when the lunatics, exalted by illusions of splendid talent and visions of a dawning millennium, crowned him as their emperor, was tame in comparison. I do not know whether anyone really kept his head completely except those who had to keep it because they had to conduct the war at first hand. I should not have kept my own (as far as I did keep it) if I had not at once understood that as a scribe and speaker I too was under the most serious public obligation to keep my grip on realities; but this did not save me from a considerable degree of hyperaesthesia. There were of course some happy people to whom the war meant nothing: all political and general matters lying outside their little circle of interest. But the ordinary war-conscious civilian went mad, the main symptom being a conviction that the whole order of nature had been reversed. All foods, he felt, must now be adulterated. All schools must be closed. No advertisements must be sent to the newspapers, of which new editions must appear and be bought up every ten minutes. Travelling must be stopped, or, that being impossible, greatly hindered. All pretences about fine art and culture and the like must be flung off as an intolerable affectation; and the picture galleries and museums and schools at once occupied by war workers. The British Museum itself was saved only by a hairsbreadth. The sincerity of all this, and of much more which would not be believed if I chronicled it, may be established by one conclusive instance of the general craziness. Men were seized with the illusion that they could win the war by giving away money. And they not only subscribed millions to Funds of all sorts with no discoverable object, and to ridiculous voluntary organizations for doing what was plainly the business of the civil and military authorities, but actually handed out money to any thief in the street who had the presence of mind to pretend that he (or she) was 'collecting' it for the annihilation of the enemy. Swindlers were emboldened to take offices; label themselves Anti-Enemy Leagues; and simply pocket the money that was heaped on them. Attractively dressed young women found that they had nothing to do but parade the streets, collecting-box in hand, and live gloriously on the profits. Many months elapsed before, as a first sign of returning sanity, the police swept an Anti-Enemy secretary into prison *pour encourager les autres*, and the passionate penny collecting of the Flag Days was brought under some sort of regulation.

MADNESS IN COURT

The demoralization did not spare the Law Courts. Soldiers were acquitted, even on fully proved indictments for wilful murder, until at last the judges and magistrates had to announce that what was called the Unwritten Law, which meant simply that a soldier could do what he liked with impunity in civil life, was not the law of the land, and that a Victoria Cross did not carry with it a perpetual plenary indulgence. Unfortunately the insanity of the juries and magistrates did not always manifest itself in indulgence. No person unlucky enough to be charged with any sort of conduct, however reasonable and salutary, that did not smack of war delirium had the slightest chance of acquittal. There was in the country, too, a certain number of people who had conscientious objections to war as criminal or unchristian. The Act of Parliament introducing Compulsory Military Service thoughtlessly exempted these persons, merely requiring them to prove the genuineness of their convictions. Those who did so were very ill-advised from the point of view of their own personal interest; for they were persecuted with savage logicality in spite of the law; whilst those who made no pretence of having any objection to war at all, and had not only had military training in Officers' Training Corps, but had proclaimed on public occasions that they were perfectly ready to engage in civil war on behalf of their political opinions, were allowed the benefit of the Act on the ground that they did not approve of this particular war. For the Christians there was no mercy. In cases where the evidence as to their being killed by ill treatment was so unequivocal that the verdict would certainly have been one of wilful murder had the prejudice of the coroner's jury been on the other side, their tormentors were gratuitously declared to be blameless. There was only

one virtue, pugnacity: only one vice, pacifism. That is an essential condition of war; but the Government had not the courage to legislate accordingly; and its law was set aside for Lynch law.

The climax of legal lawlessness was reached in France. The greatest Socialist statesman in Europe, Jaurès, was shot and killed by a gentleman who resented his efforts to avert the war. M. Clemenceau was shot by another gentleman of less popular opinions, and happily came off no worse than having to spend a precautionary couple of days in bed. The slayer of Jaurès was recklessly acquitted: the would-be slayer of M. Clemenceau was carefully found guilty. There is no reason to doubt that the same thing would have happened in England if the war had begun with a successful attempt to assassinate Keir Hardie, and ended with an unsuccessful one to assassinate Mr Lloyd George.

THE LONG ARM OF WAR

The pestilence which is the usual accompaniment of war was called influenza. Whether it was really a war pestilence or not was made doubtful by the fact that it did its worst in places remote from the battle-fields, notably on the west coast of North America and in India. But the moral pestilence, which was unquestionably a war pestilence, reproduced this phenomenon. One would have supposed that the war fever would have raged most furiously in the countries actually under fire, and that the others would be more reasonable. Belgium and Flanders, where over large districts literally not one stone was left upon another as the opposed armies drove each other back and forward over it after terrific preliminary bombardments, might have been pardoned for relieving their feelings more emphatically than by shrugging their shoulders and saying 'C'est la guerre.' England, inviolate for so many centuries that the swoop of war on her homesteads had long ceased to be more credible than a return of the Flood, could hardly be expected to keep her temper sweet when she knew at last what it was to hide in cellars and underground railway stations, or lie quaking in bed, whilst bombs crashed, houses crumbled, and aircraft guns distributed shrapnel on friend and foe alike until certain shop windows in London, formerly full of fashionable hats, were filled with steel helmets. Slain and mutilated women and children, and burnt and wrecked dwellings, excuse a good deal of violent language, and produce a wrath on which many suns go down before it is appeased. Yet it was in the United States of America, where nobody slept the worse for the war, that the war fever went beyond all sense and reason. In European Courts there was vindictive illegality: in American Courts there was raving lunacy. It is not for me to chronicle the extravagances of an Ally: let some candid American do that. I can only say that to us sitting in our gardens in England, with the guns in France making themselves felt by a throb in the air as unmistakeable as an audible sound, or with tightening hearts studying the phases of the moon in London in their bearing on the chances whether our houses would be standing or ourselves alive next morning, the newspaper accounts of the sentences American Courts were passing on young girls and old men alike for the expression of opinions which were being uttered amid thundering applause before huge audiences in England, and the more private records of the methods by which the American War Loans were raised, were so amazing that they would put the guns and the possibilities of a raid clean out of our heads for the moment.

THE RABID WATCHDOGS OF LIBERTY

Not content with these rancorous abuses of the existing law, the war maniacs made a frantic rush to abolish all constitutional guarantees of liberty and well-being. The ordinary law was superseded by Acts under which newspapers were seized and their printing machinery destroyed by simple police raids à la Russe, and persons arrested and shot without any pretence of trial by jury or publicity of procedure or evidence. Though it was urgently necessary that production should be increased by the most scientific organization and economy of labor, and though no fact was better established than that excessive duration and intensity of toil reduces production heavily instead of increasing it, the factory laws were suspended, and men and women recklessly overworked until the loss of their efficiency became too glaring to be ignored. Remonstrances and warnings were met either with an accusation of pro-Germanism or the formula, 'Remember that we are at war now.' I have said that men assumed that war had reversed the order of nature, and that all was lost unless we did the exact opposite of everything we had found necessary and beneficial in peace. But the truth was worse than that. The war did not change men's minds in any such impossible way. What really happened was that the impact of physical death and destruction, the one reality that every fool can understand, tore off the masks of education, art, science, and religion from our ignorance and barbarism, and left us glorying grotesquely in the licence suddenly accorded to our vilest passions and most abject terrors. Ever since Thucydides wrote his history, it has been on record that when the angel of death sounds his trumpet the pretences of civilization are blown from men's heads into the mud like hats in a gust of wind. But when this scripture was fulfilled among us, the shock was not the less appalling because a few students of Greek history were not surprised by it. Indeed these students threw themselves into the orgy as shamelessly as the illiterate. The Christian priest joining in the war dance without even throwing off his cassock first, and the respectable school governor expelling the German professor with insult and bodily violence, and declaring that no English child should ever again be taught the language of Luther and Goethe, were kept in countenance by the most impudent repudiations of every decency of civilization and every lesson of political experience on the part of the very persons who, as university professors, historians, philosophers, and men of science, were the accredited custodians of culture. It was crudely natural, and perhaps necessary for recruiting purposes, that German militarism and German dynastic ambition should be painted by journalists and recruiters in black and red as European dangers (as in fact they are), leaving it to be inferred that our own militarism and our own political constitution are millennially democratic (which they certainly are not); but when it came to frantic denunciations of German chemistry, German biology, German poetry, German music, German literature, German philosophy, and even German engineering, as malignant abominations standing towards British and French chemistry and so forth in the relation of heaven to hell, it was clear that the utterers of such barbarous ravings had never really understood or cared for the arts and sciences they professed and were profaning, and were only the appallingly degenerate descendants of the men of the seventeenth and eighteenth centuries who, recognizing no national frontiers in the great realm of the human mind, kept the European comity of that realm loftily and even ostentatiously above the rancors of the battle-field. Tearing the Garter from the Kaiser's leg, striking the German dukes from the roll of our peerage, changing the King's illustrious and historically appropriate surname for that of a traditionless locality, was not a very dignified business; but the erasure of German names from the British rolls of science and learning was a confession that in England the little respect paid to science and learning is only an affectation which hides a savage contempt for both. One felt that the figure of St George and the Dragon on our coinage should be replaced by that of the soldier driving his spear through Archimedes. But by that time there was no coinage: only paper money in which ten shillings called itself a pound as confidently as the people who were disgracing their country called themselves patriots.

THE SUFFERINGS OF THE SANE

The mental distress of living amid the obscene din of all these carmagnoles and corobberies was not the only burden that lay on sane people during the war. There was also the emotional strain, complicated by the offended economic sense, produced by the casualty lists. The stupid, the selfish, the narrow-minded, the callous and unimaginative were spared a great deal. 'Blood and destruction shall be so in use that mothers shall but smile when they behold their infants quartered by the hands of war,' was a Shakespearean prophecy that very nearly came true; for when nearly every house had a slaughtered son to mourn, we should all have gone quite out of our senses if we had taken our own and our friends' bereavements at their peace value. It became necessary to give them a false value; to proclaim the young life worthily and gloriously sacrificed to redeem the liberty of mankind, instead of to expiate the heedlessness and folly of their fathers, and expiate it in vain. We had even to assume that the parents and not the children had made the sacrifice, until at last the comic papers were driven to satirize fat old men, sitting comfortably in club chairs, and boasting of the sons they had 'given' to their country.

No one grudged these anodynes to acute personal grief; but they only embittered those who knew that the young men were having their teeth set on edge because their parents had eaten sour political grapes. Then think of the young men themselves! Many of them had no illusions about the policy that led to the war: they went clear-sighted to a horribly repugnant duty. Men essentially gentle and essentially wise, with really valuable work in hand, laid it down voluntarily and spent months forming fours in the barrack yard, and stabbing sacks of straw in the public eye, so that they might go out to kill and maim men as gentle as themselves. These men, who were perhaps, as a class, our most efficient soldiers (Frederick Keeling, for example), were not duped for a moment by the hypocritical melodrama that consoled and stimulated the others. They left their creative work to drudge at destruction, exactly as they would have left it to take their turn at the pumps in a sinking ship. They did not, like some of the conscientious objectors, hold back because the ship had been neglected by its officers and scuttled by its wreckers. The ship had to be saved, even if Newton had to leave his fluxions and Michael Angelo his marbles to save it; so they threw away the tools of their beneficent and ennobling trades, and took up the bloodstained bayonet and the murderous bomb, forcing themselves to pervert their divine instinct for perfect artistic execution to the effective handling of these diabolical things, and their economic faculty for organization to the contriving of ruin and slaughter. For it gave an ironic edge to their tragedy that the very talents they were forced to prostitute made the prostitution not only effective, but even interesting; so that some of them were rapidly promoted, and found themselves actually becoming artists in war, with a growing relish for it, like Napoleon and all the other scourges of mankind, in spite of themselves. For many of them there was not even this consolation. They 'stuck it,' and hated it, to the end.

EVIL IN THE THRONE OF GOOD

This distress of the gentle was so acute that those who shared it in civil life, without having to shed blood with their own hands, or witness destruction with their own eyes, hardly cared to obtrude their own woes. Nevertheless, even when sitting at home in safety, it was not easy for those who had to write and speak about the war to throw away their highest conscience, and deliberately work to a standard of inevitable evil instead of to the ideal of life more abundant. I can answer for at least one person who found the change from the wisdom of Jesus and St Francis to the morals of Richard III and the madness of Don Quixote extremely irksome. But that change had to be made; and we are all the worse for it, except those for whom it was not really a change at all, but only a relief from hypocrisy.

Think, too, of those who, though they had neither to write nor to fight, and had no children of their own to lose, yet knew the inestimable loss to the world of four years of the life of a generation wasted on destruction. Hardly one of the epoch-making works of the human mind might not have been aborted or destroyed by taking their authors away from their natural work for four critical years. Not only were Shakespears and Platos being killed outright; but many of the best harvests of the

survivors had to be sown in the barren soil of the trenches. And this was no mere British consideration. To the truly civilized man, to the good European, the slaughter of the German youth was as disastrous as the slaughter of the English. Fools exulted in 'German losses.' They were our losses as well. Imagine exulting in the death of Beethoven because Bill Sykes dealt him his death blow!

STRAINING AT THE GNAT AND SWALLOWING THE CAMEL

But most people could not comprehend these sorrows. There was a frivolous exultation in death for its own sake, which was at bottom an inability to realize that the deaths were real deaths and not stage ones. Again and again, when an air raider dropped a bomb which tore a child and its mother limb from limb, the people who saw it, though they had been reading with great cheerfulness of thousands of such happenings day after day in their newspapers, suddenly burst into furious imprecations on 'the Huns' as murderers, and shrieked for savage and satisfying vengeance. At such moments it became clear that the deaths they had not seen meant no more to them than the mimic deaths of the cinema screen. Sometimes it was not necessary that death should be actually witnessed: it had only to take place under circumstances of sufficient novelty and proximity to bring it home almost as sensationally and effectively as if it had been actually visible.

For example, in the spring of 1915 there was an appalling slaughter of our young soldiers at Neuve Chapelle and at the Gallipoli landing. I will not go so far as to say that our civilians were delighted to have such exciting news to read at breakfast. But I cannot pretend that I noticed either in the papers, or in general intercourse, any feeling beyond the usual one that the cinema show at the front was going splendidly, and that our boys were the bravest of the brave. Suddenly there came the news that an Atlantic liner, the Lusitania, had been torpedoed, and that several well-known first class passengers, including a famous theatrical manager and the author of a popular farce, had been drowned, among others. The others included Sir Hugh Lane; but as he had only laid the country under great obligations in the sphere of the fine arts, no great stress was laid on that loss.

Immediately an amazing frenzy swept through the country. Men who up to that time had kept their heads now lost them utterly. 'Killing saloon passengers! What next?' was the essence of the whole agitation; but it is far too trivial a phrase to convey the faintest notion of the rage which possessed us. To me, with my mind full of the hideous cost of Neuve Chapelle, Ypres, and the Gallipoli landing, the fuss about the Lusitania seemed almost a heartless impertinence, though I was well acquainted personally with the three best-known victims, and understood, better perhaps than most people, the misfortune of the death of Lane. I even found a grim satisfaction, very intelligible to all soldiers, in the fact that the civilians who found the war such splendid British sport should get a sharp taste of what it was to the actual combatants. I expressed my impatience very freely, and found that my very straightforward and natural feeling in the matter was received as a monstrous and heartless paradox. When I asked those who gaped at me whether they had anything to say about the holocaust of Festubert, they gaped wider than before, having totally forgotten it, or rather, having never realized it. They were not heartless any more than I was; but the big catastrophe was too big for them to grasp, and the little one had been just the right size for them. I was not surprised. Have I not seen a public body for just the same reason pass a vote for £30,000 without a word, and then spend three special meetings, prolonged into the night, over an item of seven shillings for refreshments?

LITTLE MINDS AND BIG BATTLES

Nobody will be able to understand the vagaries of public feeling during the war unless they bear constantly in mind that the war in its entire magnitude did not exist for the average civilian. He could not conceive even a battle, much less a campaign. To the suburbs the war was nothing but a suburban squabble. To the miner and navvy it was only a series of bayonet fights between German champions and English ones. The enormity of it was quite beyond most of us. Its episodes had to be reduced to the dimensions of a railway accident or a shipwreck before it could produce any effect on our minds at all. To us the ridiculous bombardments of Scarborough and Ramsgate were colossal tragedies, and the battle of Jutland a mere ballad. The words 'after thorough artillery preparation' in the news from the front meant nothing to us; but when our seaside trippers learned that an elderly gentleman at breakfast in a week-end marine hotel had been interrupted by a bomb dropping into his egg-cup, their wrath and horror knew no bounds. They declared that this would put a new spirit into the army, and had no suspicion that the soldiers in the trenches roared with laughter over it for days, and told each other that it would do the blighters at home good to have a taste of what the army was up against. Sometimes the smallness of view was pathetic. A man would work at home regardless of the call 'to make the world safe for democracy.' His brother would be killed at the front. Immediately he would throw up his work and take up the war as a family blood feud against the Germans. Sometimes it was comic. A wounded man, entitled to his discharge, would return to the trenches with a grim determination to find the Hun who had wounded him and pay him out for it.

It is impossible to estimate what proportion of us, in khaki or out of it, grasped the war and its political antecedents as a whole in the light of any philosophy of history or knowledge of what war is. I doubt whether it was as high as our proportion of higher mathematicians. But there can be no doubt that it was prodigiously outnumbered by the comparatively ignorant and childish. Remember that these people had to be stimulated to make the sacrifices demanded by the war, and that this could not be done by appeals to a knowledge which they did not possess, and a comprehension of which they were incapable. When the armistice at last set me free to tell the truth about the war at the following general election, a soldier said to a candidate whom I was supporting 'If I had known all that in 1914, they would never have got me into khaki.' And that, of course, was precisely why it had been necessary to stuff him with a romance that any diplomatist would have laughed at. Thus the natural confusion of ignorance was increased by a deliberately propagated confusion of nursery bogey stories and melodramatic nonsense, which at last overreached itself and made it impossible to stop the war before we had not only achieved the triumph of vanquishing the German army and thereby overthrowing its militarist monarchy, but made the very serious mistake of ruining the centre of Europe, a thing that no sane European State could afford to do.

THE DUMB CAPABLES AND THE NOISY INCAPABLES

Confronted with this picture of insensate delusion and folly, the critical reader will immediately counterplead that England all this time was conducting a war which involved the organization of several millions of fighting men and of the workers who were supplying them with provisions, munitions, and transport, and that this could not have been done by a mob of hysterical ranters. This is fortunately true. To pass from the newspaper offices and political platforms and club fenders and suburban drawing-rooms to the Army and the munition factories was to pass from Bedlam to the busiest and sanest of workaday worlds. It was to rediscover England, and find solid ground for the faith of those who still believed in her. But a necessary condition of this efficiency was that those who were efficient should give all their time to their business and leave the rabble raving to its heart's content. Indeed the raving was useful to the efficient, because, as it was always wide of the mark, it often distracted attention very conveniently from operations that would have been defeated or hindered by publicity. A precept which I endeavored vainly to popularize early in the war, 'If you have anything to do go and do it: if

not, for heaven's sake get out of the way,' was only half carried out. Certainly the capable people went and did it; but the incapables would by no means get out of the way: they fussed and bawled and were only prevented from getting very seriously into the way by the blessed fact that they never knew where the way was. Thus whilst all the efficiency of England was silent and invisible, all its imbecility was deafening the heavens with its clamor and blotting out the sun with its dust. It was also unfortunately intimidating the Government by its blusterings into using the irresistible powers of the State to intimidate the sensible people, thus enabling a despicable minority of would-be lynchers to set up a reign of terror which could at any time have been broken by a single stern word from a responsible minister. But our ministers had not that sort of courage: neither Heartbreak House nor Horseback Hall had bred it, much less the suburbs. When matters at last came to the looting of shops by criminals under patriotic pretexts, it was the police force and not the Government that put its foot down. There was even one deplorable moment, during the submarine scare, in which the Government yielded to a childish cry for the maltreatment of naval prisoners of war, and, to our great disgrace, was forced by the enemy to behave itself. And yet behind all this public blundering and misconduct and futile mischief, the effective England was carrying on with the most formidable capacity and activity. The ostensible England was making the empire sick with its incontinences, its ignorances, its ferocities, its panics, and its endless and intolerable blarings of Allied national anthems in season and out. The esoteric England was proceeding irresistibly to the conquest of Europe.

THE PRACTICAL BUSINESS MEN

From the beginning the useless people set up a shriek for 'practical business men.' By this they meant men who had become rich by placing their personal interests before those of the country, and measuring the success of every activity by the pecuniary profit it brought to them and to those on whom they depended for their supplies of capital. The pitiable failure of some conspicuous samples from the first batch we tried of these poor devils helped to give the whole public side of the war an air of monstrous and hopeless farce. They proved not only that they were useless for public work, but that in a well-ordered nation they would never have been allowed to control private enterprise.

HOW THE FOOLS SHOUTED THE WISE MEN DOWN

Thus, like a fertile country flooded with mud, England shewed no sign of her greatness in the days when she was putting forth all her strength to save herself from the worst consequences of her littleness. Most of the men of action, occupied to the last hour of their time with urgent practical work, had to leave to idler people, or to professional rhetoricians, the presentation of the war to the reason and imagination of the country and the world in speeches, poems, manifestos, picture posters, and newspaper articles. I have had the privilege of hearing some of our ablest commanders talking about their work; and I have shared the common lot of reading the accounts of that work given to the world by the newspapers. No two experiences could be more different. But in the end the talkers obtained a dangerous ascendancy over the rank and file of the men of action; for though the great men of action are always inveterate talkers and often very clever writers, and therefore cannot have their minds formed for them by others, the average man of action, like the average fighter with the bayonet, can give no account of himself in words even to himself, and is apt to pick up and accept what he reads about himself and other people in the papers, except when the writer is rash enough to commit himself on technical points. It was not uncommon during the war to hear a soldier, or a civilian engaged on war work, describing events within his own experience that reduced to utter absurdity the ravings and maunderings of his daily paper, and yet echo the opinions of that paper like a parrot. Thus, to escape from the prevailing confusion and folly it was not enough to seek the company of the ordinary man of action: one had to get into contact with the master spirits. This was a privilege which only a handful of people could enjoy. For the unprivileged citizen there was no escape. To him the whole country seemed mad, futile, silly, incompetent, with no hope of victory except the hope that the enemy might be just as mad. Only by very resolute reflection and reasoning could he reassure himself that if there was nothing more solid beneath these appalling appearances the war could not possibly have gone on for a single day without a total breakdown of its organization.

THE MAD ELECTION

Happy were the fools and the thoughtless men of action in those days. The worst of it was that the fools were very strongly represented in parliament, as fools not only elect fools, but can persuade men of action to elect them too. The election that immediately followed the armistice was perhaps the maddest that has ever taken place. Soldiers who had done voluntary and heroic service in the field were defeated by persons who had apparently never run a risk or spent a farthing that they could avoid, and who even had in the course of the election to apologize publicly for bawling Pacifist or Pro-German at their opponent. Party leaders seek such followers, who can always be depended on to walk tamely into the lobby at the party whip's orders, provided the leader will make their seats safe for them by the process which was called, in derisive reference to the war rationing system, 'giving them the coupon.' Other incidents were so grotesque that I cannot mention them without enabling the reader to identify the parties, which would not be fair, as they were no more to blame than thousands of others who must necessarily be nameless. The general result was patently absurd; and the electorate, disgusted at its own work, instantly recoiled to the opposite extreme, and cast out all the coupon candidates at the earliest bye-elections by equally silly majorities. But the mischief of the general election could not be undone; and the Government had not only to pretend to abuse its European victory as it had promised, but actually to do it by starving the enemies who had thrown down their arms. It had, in short, won the election by pledging itself to be thriftlessly wicked, cruel, and vindictive; and it did not find it as easy to escape from this pledge as it had from nobler ones. The end, as I write, is not yet; but it is clear that this thoughtless savagery will recoil on the heads of the Allies so severely that we shall be forced by the sternest necessity to take up our share of healing the Europe we have wounded almost to death instead of attempting to complete her destruction.

THE YAHOO AND THE ANGRY APE

Contemplating this picture of a state of mankind so recent that no denial of its truth is possible, one understands Shakespear comparing Man to an angry ape, Swift describing him as a Yahoo rebuked by the superior virtue of the horse, and Wellington declaring that the British can behave themselves neither in victory nor defeat. Yet none of the three had seen war as we have seen it. Shakespear blamed great men, saying that 'Could great men thunder as Jove himself does Jove would ne'er be quiet; for every pelting petty officer would use his heaven for thunder: nothing but thunder.' What would Shakespear have said if he had seen something far more destructive than thunder in the hand of every village laborer, and found on the Messines Ridge the craters of the nineteen volcanoes that were let loose there at the touch of a finger that might have been a child's finger without the result being a whit less ruinous? Shakespear may have seen a Stratford cottage struck by one of Jove's thunderbolts, and have helped to extinguish the lighted thatch and clear away the bits of the broken chimney. What would he have said if he had seen Ypres as it is now, or returned to Stratford, as French peasants are returning to their homes today, to find the old familiar signpost in-

scribed 'To Stratford, 1 mile,' and at the end of the mile nothing but some holes in the ground and a fragment of a broken churn here and there? Would not the spectacle of the angry ape endowed with powers of destruction that Jove never pretended to, have beggared even his command of words?

And yet, what is there to say except that war puts a strain on human nature that breaks down the better half of it, and makes the worse half a diabolical virtue? Better for us if it broke it down altogether; for then the warlike way out of our difficulties would be barred to us, and we should take greater care not to get into them. In truth, it is, as Byron said, 'not difficult to die,' and enormously difficult to live: that explains why, at bottom, peace is not only better than war, but infinitely more arduous. Did any hero of the war face the glorious risk of death more bravely than the traitor Bolo faced the ignominious certainty of it? Bolo taught us all how to die: can we say that he taught us all how to live? Hardly a week passes now without some soldier who braved death in the field so recklessly that he was decorated or specially commended for it, being haled before our magistrates for having failed to resist the paltriest temptations of peace, with no better excuse than the old one that 'a man must live.' Strange that one who, sooner than do honest work, will sell his honor for a bottle of wine, a visit to the theatre, and an hour with a strange woman, all obtained by passing a worthless cheque, could yet stake his life on the most desperate chances of the battle-field! Does it not seem as if, after all, the glory of death were cheaper than the glory of life? If it is not easier to attain, why do so many more men attain it? At all events it is clear that the kingdom of the Prince of Peace has not yet become the kingdom of this world. His attempts at invasion have been resisted far more fiercely than the Kaiser's. Successful as that resistance has been, it has piled up a sort of National Debt that is not the less oppressive because we have no figures for it and do not intend to pay it. A blockade that cuts off 'the grace of our Lord' is in the long run less bearable than the blockades which merely cut off raw materials; and against that blockade our Armada is impotent. In the blockader's house, he has assured us, there are many mansions; but I am afraid they do not include either Heartbreak House or Horseback Hall.

PLAGUE ON BOTH YOUR HOUSES!

Meanwhile the Bolshevist picks and petards are at work on the foundations of both buildings; and though the Bolshevists may be buried in the ruins, their deaths will not save the edifices. Unfortunately they can be built again. Like Doubting Castle, they have been demolished many times by successive Greathearts, and rebuilt by Simple, Sloth, and Presumption, by Feeble Mind and Much Afraid, and by all the jurymen of *Vanity Fair*. Another generation of 'secondary education' at our ancient public schools and the cheaper institutions that ape them will be quite sufficient to keep the two going until the next war.

For the instruction of that generation I leave these pages as a record of what civilian life was during the war: a matter on which history is usually silent. Fortunately it was a very short war. It is true that the people who thought it could not last more than six months were very signally refuted by the event. As Sir Douglas Haig has pointed out, its Waterloos lasted months instead of hours. But there would have been nothing surprising in its lasting thirty years. If it had not been for the fact that the blockade achieved the amazing feat of starving out Europe, which it could not possibly have done had Europe been properly organized for war, or even for peace, the war would have lasted until the belligerents were so tired of it that they could no longer be compelled to compel themselves to go on with it. Considering its magnitude, the war of 1914–18 will certainly be classed as the shortest in history. The end came so suddenly that the combatants literally stumbled over it; and yet it came a full year later than it should have come if the belligerents had not been far too afraid of one another to face the situation sensibly. Germany, having failed to provide for the war she began, failed again to surrender before she was dangerously exhausted. Her op-

ponents, equally improvident, went as much too close to bankruptcy as Germany to starvation. It was a bluff at which both were bluffed. And, with the usual irony of war, it remains doubtful whether Germany and Russia, the defeated, will not be the gainers; for the victors are already busy fastening on themselves the chains they have struck from the limbs of the vanquished.

HOW THE THEATRE FARED

Let us now contract our view rather violently from the European theatre of war to the theatre in which the fights are sham fights, and the slain, rising the moment the curtain has fallen, go comfortably home to supper after washing off their rosepink wounds. It is nearly twenty years since I was last obliged to introduce a play in the form of a book for lack of an opportunity of presenting it in its proper mode by a performance in a theatre. The war has thrown me back on this expedient. *Heartbreak House* has not yet reached the stage. I have withheld it because the war has completely upset the economic conditions which formerly enabled serious drama to pay its way in London. The change is not in the theatres nor in the management of them, nor in the authors and actors, but in the audiences. For four years the London theatres were crowded every night with thousands of soldiers on leave from the front. These soldiers were not seasoned London playgoers. A childish experience of my own gave me a clue to their condition. When I was a small boy I was taken to the opera. I did not then know what an opera was, though I could whistle a good deal of opera music. I had seen in my mother's album photographs of all the great opera singers, mostly in evening dress. In the theatre I found myself before a gilded balcony filled with persons in evening dress whom I took to be the opera singers. I picked out one massive dark lady as Alboni, and wondered how soon she would stand up and sing. I was puzzled by the fact that I was made to sit with my back to the singers instead of facing them. When the curtain went up, my astonishment and delight were unbounded.

THE SOLDIER AT THE THEATRE FRONT

In 1915 I saw in the theatres men in khaki in just the same predicament. To everyone who had my clue to their state of mind it was evident that they had never been in a theatre before and did not know what it was. At one of our great variety theatres I sat beside a young officer, not at all a rough specimen, who, even when the curtain rose and enlightened him as to the place where he had to look for his entertainment, found the dramatic part of it utterly incomprehensible. He did not know how to play his part of the game. He could understand the people on the stage singing and dancing and performing gymnastic feats. He not only understood but intensely enjoyed an artist who imitated cocks crowing and pigs squeaking. But the people who pretended that they were somebody else, and that the painted picture behind them was real, bewildered him. In his presence I realized how very sophisticated the natural man has to become before the conventions of the theatre can be easily acceptable, or the purpose of the drama obvious to him.

Well, from the moment when the routine of leave for our soldiers was established, such novices, accompanied by damsels (called flappers) often as innocent as themselves, crowded the theatres to the doors. It was hardly possible at first to find stuff crude enough to nurse them on. The best music-hall comedians ransacked their memories for the oldest quips and the most childish antics to avoid carrying the military spectators out of their depth. I believe that this was a mistake as far as the novices were concerned. Shakespear, or the dramatized histories of George Barnwell, Maria Martin, or the Demon Barber of Fleet Street, would probably have been quite popular with them. But the novices were only a minority after all. The cultivated soldier, who in time of peace would look at nothing theatrical except the most advanced post-Ibsen plays in the most artistic settings, found himself, to his own astonishment, thirsting for silly jokes, dances, and brainlessly sensuous exhibitions of pretty girls. The author of some of the most grimly serious plays of our time told me that after enduring the trenches for months without a glimpse of the female of his species, it gave him an entirely innocent but delightful pleasure merely to see a flapper. The reaction from the battle-field produced a condition of hyperaesthesia in which all the theatrical values were altered. Trivial things gained intensity and stale things novelty. The actor, instead of having to coax his audiences out of the boredom which had driven them to the theatre in an ill humor to seek some sort of distraction, had only to exploit the bliss of smiling men who were no longer under fire and under military discipline, but actually clean and comfortable and in a mood to be pleased with anything and everything that a bevy of pretty girls and a funny man, or even a bevy of girls pretending to be pretty and a man pretending to be funny, could do for them.

Then could be seen every night in the theatres old-fashioned farcical comedies, in which a bedroom, with four doors on each side and a practicable window in the middle, was understood to resemble exactly the bedroom in the flats beneath and above, all three inhabited by couples consumed with jealousy. When these people came home drunk at night; mistook their neighbors' flats for their own; and in due course got into the wrong beds, it was not only the novices who found the resulting complications and scandals exquisitely ingenious and amusing, nor their equally verdant flappers who could not help squealing in a manner that astonished the oldest performers when the gentleman who had just come in drunk through the window pretended to undress, and allowed glimpses of his naked person to be descried from time to time. Men who had just read the news that Charles Wyndham was dying, and were thereby sadly reminded of *Pink Dominos* and the torrent of farcical comedies that followed it in his heyday until every trick of that trade had become so stale that the laughter they provoked turned to loathing: these veterans also, when they returned from the field, were as much pleased by what they knew to be stale and foolish as the novices by what they thought fresh and clever.

COMMERCE IN THE THEATRE

Wellington said that an army moves on its belly. So does a London theatre. Before a man acts he must eat. Before he performs plays he must pay rent. In London we have no theatres for the welfare of the people: they are all for the sole purpose of producing the utmost obtainable rent for the proprietor. If the twin flats and twin beds produce a guinea more than Shakespear, out goes Shakespear, and in come the twin flats and the twin beds. If the brainless bevy of pretty girls and the funny man outbid Mozart, out goes Mozart.

UNSER SHAKESPEAR

Before the war an effort was made to remedy this by establishing a national theatre in celebration of the tercentenary of the death of Shakespear. A committee was formed; and all sorts of illustrious and influential persons lent their names to a grand appeal to our national culture. My play, *The Dark Lady of The Sonnets*, was one of the incidents of that appeal. After some years of effort the result was a single handsome subscription from a German gentleman. Like the celebrated swearer in the anecdote when the cart containing all his household goods lost its tailboard at the top of the hill and let its contents roll in ruin to the bottom, I can only say, 'I cannot do justice to this situation,' and let it pass without another word.

THE HIGHER DRAMA
PUT OUT OF ACTION

The effect of the war on the London theatres may now be imagined. The beds and the bevies drove every higher form of art out of it. Rents went up to an unprecedented figure. At the same time prices doubled everywhere except at the theatre payboxes, and raised the expenses of management to such a degree that unless the houses were quite full every night, profit was impossible. Even bare solvency could not be attained without a very wide popularity. Now what had made serious drama possible to a limited extent before the war was that a play could pay its way even if the theatre were only half full until Saturday and three-quarters full then. A manager who was an enthusiast and a desperately hard worker, with an occasional grant-in-aid from an artistically disposed millionaire, and a due proportion of those rare and happy accidents by which plays of the higher sort turn out to be potboilers as well, could hold out for some years, by which time a relay might arrive in the person of another enthusiast. Thus and not otherwise occurred that remarkable revival of the British drama at the beginning of the century which made my own career as a playwright possible in England. In America I had already established myself, not as part of the ordinary theatre system, but in association with the exceptional genius of Richard Mansfield. In Germany and Austria I had no difficulty: the system of publicly aided theatres there, Court and Municipal, kept drama of the kind I dealt in alive; so that I was indebted to the Emperor of Austria for magnificent productions of my works at a time when the sole official attention paid me by the British Court was the announcement to the English-speaking world that certain plays of mine were unfit for public performance, a substantial set-off against this being that the British Court, in the course of its private playgoing, paid no regard to the bad character given me by the chief officer of its household.

Howbeit, the fact that my plays effected a lodgment on the London stage, and were presently followed by the plays of Granville Barker, Gilbert Murray, John Masefield, St John Hankin, Laurence Housman, Arnold Bennett, John Galsworthy, John Drinkwater, and others which would in the nineteenth century have stood rather less chance of production at a London theatre than the Dialogues of Plato, not to mention revivals of the ancient Athenian drama, and a restoration to the stage of Shakespear's plays as he wrote them, was made economically possible solely by a supply of theatres which could hold nearly twice as much money as it cost to rent and maintain them. In such theatres work appealing to a relatively small class of cultivated persons, and therefore attracting only from half to three-quarters as many spectators as the more popular pastimes, could nevertheless keep going in the hands of young adventurers who were doing it for its own sake, and had not yet been forced by advancing age and responsibilities to consider the commercial value of their time and energy too closely. The war struck this foundation away in the manner I have just described. The expenses of running the cheapest west-end theatres rose to a sum which exceeded by twenty-five per cent the utmost that the higher drama can, as an ascertained matter of fact, be depended on to draw. Thus the higher drama, which has never really been a commercially sound speculation, now became an impossible one. Accordingly, attempts are being made to provide a refuge for it in suburban theatres in London and repertory theatres in the provinces. But at the moment when the army has at last disgorged the survivors of the gallant band of dramatic pioneers whom it swallowed, they find that the economic conditions which formerly made their work no worse than precarious now put it out of the question altogether, as far as the west end of London is concerned.

CHURCH AND THEATRE

I do not suppose many people care particularly. We are not brought up to care; and a sense of the national importance of the theatre is not born in mankind: the natural man, like so many of the soldiers at the beginning of the war, does not know what a theatre is. But please note that all these soldiers who did not know what a theatre was, knew what a church was. And they had been taught to respect churches. Nobody had ever warned them against a church as a place where frivolous women paraded in their best clothes; where stories of improper females like Potiphar's wife, and erotic poetry like the Song of Songs, were read aloud; where the sensuous and sentimental music of Schubert, Mendelssohn, Gounod, and Brahms was more popular than severe music by greater composers; where the

prettiest sort of pretty pictures of pretty saints assailed the imagination and senses through stained-glass windows; and where sculpture and architecture came to the help of painting. Nobody ever reminded them that these things had sometimes produced such developments of erotic idolatory that men who were not only enthusiastic amateurs of literature, painting, and music, but famous practitioners of them, had actually exulted when mobs and even regular troops under express command had mutilated church statues, smashed church windows, wrecked church organs, and torn up the sheets from which the church music was read and sung. When they saw broken statues in churches, they were told that this was the work of wicked godless rioters, instead of, as it was, the work partly of zealots bent on driving the world, the flesh, and the devil out of the temple, and partly of insurgent men who had become intolerably poor because the temple had become a den of thieves. But all the sins and perversions that were so carefully hidden from them in the history of the Church were laid on the shoulders of the Theatre: that stuffy, uncomfortable place of penance in which we suffer so much inconvenience on the slenderest chance of gaining a scrap of food for our starving souls. When the Germans bombed the Cathedral of Rheims the world rang with the horror of the sacrilege. When they bombed the Little Theatre in the Adelphi, and narrowly missed bombing two writers of plays who lived within a few yards of it, the fact was not even mentioned in the papers. In point of appeal to the senses no theatre ever built could touch the fane at Rheims: no actress could rival its Virgin in beauty, nor any operatic tenor look otherwise than a fool beside its David. Its picture glass was glorious even to those who had seen the glass of Chartres. It was wonderful in its very grotesques: who would look at the Blondin Donkey after seeing its leviathans? In spite of the Adam-Adelphian decoration on which Miss Kingston had lavished so much taste and care, the Little Theatre was in comparison with Rheims the gloomiest of little conventicles: indeed the cathedral must, from the Puritan point of view, have debauched a million voluptuaries for every one whom the Little Theatre had sent home thoughtful to a chaste bed after Mr Chesterston's *Magic* or Brieux's *Les Avariés*. Perhaps that is the real reason why the Church is lauded and the Theatre reviled. Whether or no, the fact remains that the lady to whose public spirit and sense of the national value of the theatre I owed the first regular public performance of a play of mine had to conceal her action as if it had been a crime, whereas if she had given the money to the Church she would have worn a halo for it. And I admit, as I have always done, that this state of things may have been a very sensible one. I have asked Londoners again and again why they pay half a guinea to go to a theatre when they can go to St Paul's or Westminster Abbey for nothing. Their only possible reply is that they want to see something new and possibly something wicked; but the theatres mostly disappoint both hopes. If ever a revolution makes me Dictator, I shall establish a heavy charge for admission to our churches. But everyone who pays at the church door shall receive a ticket entitling him or her to free admission to one performance at any theatre he or she prefers. Thus shall the sensuous charms of the church service be made to subsidize the sterner virtue of the drama.

THE NEXT PHASE

The present situation will not last. Although the newspaper I read at breakfast this morning before writing these words contains a calculation that no less than twenty-three wars are at present being waged to confirm the peace, England is no longer in khaki; and a violent reaction is setting in against the crude theatrical fare of the four terrible years. Soon the rents of theatres will once more be fixed on the assumption that they cannot always be full, nor even on the average half full week in and week out. Prices will change. The higher drama will be at no greater disadvantage than it was before the war; and it may benefit, first, by the fact that many of us have been torn from the fools' paradise in which the theatre formerly traded, and thrust upon the sternest realities and necessities until we have lost both faith in and patience with the theatrical pretences that had no root either in reality or necessity; second, by the startling change made by the war in the distribution of income. It seems only the other day that a millionaire was a man with £50,000 a year. Today, when he has paid his income tax and super tax, and insured his life for the amount of his death duties, he is lucky if his net income is £10,000, though his nominal property remains the same. And this is the result of a Budget which is called 'a respite for the rich.' At the other end of the scale millions of persons have had regular incomes for the first time in their lives; and their men have been regularly clothed, fed, lodged, and taught to make up their minds that certain things have to be done, also for the first time in their lives. Hundreds of thousands of women have been taken out of their domestic cages and tasted both discipline and independence. The thoughtless and snobbish middle classes have been pulled up short by the very unpleasant experience of being ruined to an unprecedented extent. We have all had a tremendous jolt; and although the widespread notion that the shock of the war would automatically make a new heaven and a new earth, and that the dog would never go back to his vomit nor the sow to her wallowing in the mire, is already seen to be a delusion, yet we are far more conscious of our condition than we were, and far less disposed to submit to it. Revolution, lately only a sensational chapter in history or a demagogic claptrap, is now a possibility so imminent that hardly by trying to suppress it in other countries by arms and defamation, and calling the process anti-Bolshevism, can our Government stave it off at home.

Perhaps the most tragic figure of the day is the American President who was once a historian. In those days it became his task to tell us how, after that great war in America which was more clearly than any other war of our time a war for an idea, the conquerors, confronted with a heroic task of reconstruction, turned recreant, and spent fifteen years in abusing their victory under cover of pretending to accomplish the task they were doing what they could to make impossible. Alas! Hegel was right when he said that we learn from history that men never learn anything from history. With what anguish of mind the President sees that we, the new conquerors, forgetting everything we professed to fight for, are sitting down with watering mouths to a good square meal of ten years revenge upon and humiliation of our prostrate foe, can only be guessed by those who know, as he does, how hopeless is remonstrance, and how happy Lincoln was in perishing from the earth before his inspired messages became scraps of paper. He knows well that from the Peace Conference will come, in spite of his utmost, no edict on which he will be able, like Lincoln, to invoke 'the considerate judgment of mankind, and the gracious favor of Almighty God.' He led his people to destroy the militarism of Zabern; and the army they rescued is busy in Cologne imprisoning every German who does not salute a British officer; whilst the Government at home, asked whether it approves, replies that it does not propose even to discontinue this Zabernism when the Peace is concluded, but in effect looks forward to making Germans salute British officers until the end of the world. That is what war makes of men and women. It will wear off; and the worst it threatens is already proving impracticable; but before the humble and contrite heart ceases to be despised, the President and I, being of the same age, will be dotards. In the meantime there is, for him, another history to write; for me, another comedy to stage. Perhaps, after all, that is what wars are for, and what historians and playwrights are for. If men will not learn until their lessons are written in blood, why, blood they must have, their own for preference.

THE EPHEMERAL THRONES
AND THE ETERNAL THEATRE

To the theatre it will not matter. Whatever Bastilles fall, the theatre will stand. Apostolic Hapsburg has collapsed; All Highest Hohenzollern languishes in Holland, threatened with trial on a capital charge of fighting for his country against England; Imperial Romanoff, said to have perished miserably by a more summary method of murder, is perhaps

alive or perhaps dead: nobody cares more than if he had been a peasant; the lord of Hellas is level with his lackeys in republican Switzerland; Prime Ministers and Commanders-in-Chief have passed from a brief glory as Solons and Caesars into failure and obscurity as closely on one another's heels as the descendants of Banquo; but Euripides and Aristophanes, Shakespear and Molière, Goethe and Ibsen remain fixed in their everlasting seats.

HOW WAR MUZZLES
THE DRAMATIC POET

As for myself, why, it may be asked, did I not write two plays about the war instead of two pamphlets on it? The answer is significant. You cannot make war on war and on your neighbor at the same time. War cannot bear the terrible castigation of comedy, the ruthless light of laughter that glares on the stage. When men are heroically dying for their country, it is not the time to shew their lovers and wives and fathers and mothers how they are being sacrificed to the blunders of boobies, the cupidity of capitalists, the ambition of conquerors, the electioneering of demagogues, the Pharisaism of patriots, the lusts and lies and rancors and bloodthirsts that love war because it opens their prison doors, and sets them in the thrones of power and popularity. For unless these things are mercilessly exposed they will hide under the mantle of the ideals on the stage just as they do in real life.

And though there may be better things to reveal, it may not, and indeed cannot, be militarily expedient to reveal them whilst the issue is still in the balance. Truth telling is not compatible with the defence of the realm. We are just now reading the revelations of our generals and admirals, unmuzzled at last by the armistice. During the war, General A, in his moving despatches from the field, told how General B had covered himself with deathless glory in such and such a battle. He now tells us that General B came within an ace of losing us the war by disobeying his orders on that occasion, and fighting instead of running away as he ought to have done. An excellent subject for comedy now that the war is over, no doubt; but if General A had let this out at the time, what would have been the effect on General B's soldiers? And had the stage made known what the Prime Minister and the Secretary of State for War who overruled General A thought of him, and what he thought of them, as now revealed in raging controversy, what would have been the effect on the nation? That is why comedy, though sorely tempted, had to be loyally silent; for the art of the dramatic poet knows no patriotism; recognizes no obligation but truth to natural history; cares not whether Germany or England perish; is ready to cry with Brynhild, 'Lass' uns verderben, lachend zu Grunde geh'n' sooner than deceive or be deceived; and thus becomes in time of war a greater military danger than poison, steel, or trinitrotoluene. That is why I had to withhold *Heartbreak House* from the footlights during the war; for the Germans might on any night have turned the last act from play into earnest, and even then might not have waited for their cues.

June 1919

John Millington Synge 1871–1909

The poet and dramatist John Millington Synge was born in a Dublin suburb to a well-established Irish Protestant family of English descent. His father died shortly after the child's birth, but despite the family's straitened circumstances Synge received a good education and took a B.A. at Trinity College, Dublin in 1892. His chief interest at the time was music, and he went to Germany to pursue further study. Gradually Synge turned from music to literature and set up in Paris to study the new trends in French letters. While there he met William Butler Yeats and briefly joined the Paris branch of the Young Ireland Society, a nationalist movement for Irish independence and cultural revival. But the revolutionary goals of Young Ireland were not for the quiet and withdrawn Synge. Upon Yeats's advice Synge returned to Ireland and spent six weeks among the peasants of the primitive Aran Islands. During the next few years, he drifted between France and Ireland, becoming more and more absorbed in the study of Irish speech, legend, and folkways. In 1902 Synge wrote two one-act plays, the ironic comedy *In the Shadow of the Glen* and the powerful symbolist tragedy *Riders to the Sea*. The first was produced in 1903 by the Irish National Theatre Society (later the famous Abbey Theatre), founded by Yeats, Lady Gregory, and Edward Martyn. It was poorly received by the nationalist press that found the play's theme of loveless marriage a libel on Irish womanhood. *Riders to the Sea* (1904) fared somewhat better, and Synge's next play, *The Well of the Saints* (1905), was ignored. But with the production of *The Playboy of the Western World* (1907) nationalist fury broke forth. For two acts the audience sat tensely quiet, but when in the third act Christy used the word *shifts* (female underclothes) violent hissing erupted countered by applause. Hypersensitive to any criticism of Irish life and morals, the nationalists denounced the comedy as a slander of the Irish peasant, a "squalid, offensive production," and for the remaining week police were required to control the audience. Synge, by then seriously ill with cancer, had but two years to live. Rejecting the "joyless and pallid words" of naturalistic drama, he had drawn on the eloquent dialects of Irish speech to fashion a drama rooted in Irish folk life and tinged with fancy, romance, and irony. Synge died at thirty-eight without having completed his last tragic play, *Deirdre of the Sorrows*, a lyrical work based on Irish myth and expressing in the sad but noble fate of Deirdre the dying author's reflections on the fragility of beauty and love in the grip of destructive time.

RIDERS TO THE SEA

JOHN MILLINGTON SYNGE

CHARACTERS

MAURYA, *an old woman*
BARTLEY, *her son*
CATHLEEN, *her daughter*

NORA, *a younger daughter*
MEN *and* WOMEN

[SCENE: *An island off the West of Ireland. Cottage kitchen, with nets, oilskins, spinning-wheel, some new boards standing by the wall, etc.* CATHLEEN, *a girl of about twenty, finishes kneading cake, and puts it down in the pot-oven by the fire; then wipes her hands, and begins to spin at the wheel.* NORA, *a young girl, puts her head in at the door.*]

NORA [*in a low voice*]. Where is she?

CATHLEEN. She's lying down, God help her, and may be sleeping, if she's able.

[NORA *comes in softly, and takes a bundle from under her shawl.*]

CATHLEEN [*spinning the wheel rapidly*]. What is it you have?

NORA. The young priest is after bringing them. It's a shirt and a plain stocking were got off a drowned man in Donegal.

[CATHLEEN *stops her wheel with a sudden movement, and leans out to listen.*]

NORA. We're to find out if it's Michael's they are, some time herself will be down looking by the sea.

CATHLEEN. How would they be Michael's, Nora? How would he go the length of that way to the far north?

NORA. The young priest says he's known the like of it. "If it's Michael's they are," says he, "you can tell herself he's got a clean burial by the grace of God, and if they're not his, let no one

say a word about them, for she'll be getting her death," says he, "with crying and lamenting."

[*The door which* NORA *half closed is blown open by a gust of wind.*]

CATHLEEN [*looking out anxiously*]. Did you ask him would he stop Bartley going this day with the horses to the Galway fair?

NORA. "I won't stop him," says he, "but let you not be afraid. Herself does be saying prayers half through the night, and the Almighty God won't leave her destitute," says he, "with no son living."

CATHLEEN. Is the sea bad by the white rocks, Nora?

NORA. Middling bad, God help us. There's a great roaring in the west, and it's worse it'll be getting when the tide's turned to the wind. [*She goes over to the table with the bundle.*] Shall I open it now?

CATHLEEN. Maybe she'd wake up on us, and come in before we'd done. [*Coming to the table.*] It's a long time we'll be, and the two of us crying.

NORA [*goes to the inner door and listens*]. She's moving about on the bed. She'll be coming in a minute.

CATHLEEN. Give me the ladder, and I'll put them up in the turf-loft, the way she won't know of them at all, and maybe when the tide turns she'll be going down to see would he be floating from the east.

SOURCE: *Riders to the Sea* by John M. Synge. From *The Complete Works of John M. Synge.* Copyright 1935 by the Modern Library, Inc. Reprinted by permission of Random House, Inc. and George Allen and Unwin, Ltd.

[*They put the ladder against the gable of the chimney;* CATHLEEN *goes up a few steps and hides the bundle in the turf-loft.* MAURYA *comes in from the inner room.*]

MAURYA [*looking up at* CATHLEEN *and speaking querulously*]. Isn't it turf enough you have for this day and evening?

CATHLEEN. There's a cake baking at the fire for a short space [*throwing down the turf*] and Bartley will want it when the tide turns if he goes to Connemara.

[NORA *picks up the turf and puts it round the pot-oven.*]

MAURYA [*sitting down on a stool at the fire*]. He won't go this day with the wind rising from the south and west. He won't go this day, for the young priest will stop him surely.

NORA. He'll not stop him, Mother, and I heard Eamon Simon and Stephen Pheety and Colum Shawn saying he would go.

MAURYA. Where is he itself?

NORA. He went down to see would there be another boat sailing in the week, and I'm thinking it won't be long till he's here now, for the tide's turning at the green head, and the hooker's tacking from the east.

CATHLEEN. I hear some one passing the big stones.

NORA [*looking out*]. He's coming now, and he in a hurry.

BARTLEY [*comes in and looks round the room. Speaking sadly and quietly*]. Where is the bit of new rope, Cathleen, was bought in Connemara?

CATHLEEN [*coming down*]. Give it to him, Nora; it's on a nail by the white boards. I hung it up this morning, for the pig with the black feet was eating it.

NORA [*giving him a rope*]. Is that it, Bartley?

MAURYA. You'd do right to leave that rope, Bartley, hanging by the boards. [BARTLEY *takes the rope.*] It will be wanting in this place, I'm telling you, if Michael is washed up tomorrow morning, or the next morning, or any morning in the week, for it's a deep grave we'll make him by the grace of God.

BARTLEY [*beginning to work with the rope*]. I've no halter the way I can ride down on the mare, and I must go now

quickly. This is the one boat going for two weeks or beyond it, and the fair will be a good fair for horses. I heard them saying below.

MAURYA. It's a hard thing they'll be saying below if the body is washed up and there's no man in it to make the coffin, and I after giving a big price for the finest white boards you'd find in Connemara.

[*She looks around at the boards.*]

BARTLEY. How would it be washed up, and we after looking each day for nine days, and a strong wind blowing a while back from the west and south?

MAURYA. If it wasn't found itself, that wind is raising the sea, and there was a star up against the moon, and it rising in the night. If it was a hundred horses, or a thousand horses you had itself, what is the price of a thousand horses against a son where there is one son only?

BARTLEY [*working at the halter, to* CATHLEEN]. Let you go down each day, and see the sheep aren't jumping in on the rye, and if the jobber comes you can sell the pig with the black feet if there is a good price going.

MAURYA. How would the like of her get a good price for a pig?

BARTLEY [*to* CATHLEEN]. If the west wind holds with the last bit of the moon let you and Nora get up weed enough for another cock for the kelp. It's hard set we'll be from this day with no one in it but one man to work.

MAURYA. It's hard set we'll be surely the day you're drownd'd with the rest. What way will I live and the girls with me, and I an old woman looking for the grave?

[BARTLEY *lays down the halter, takes off his old coat, and puts on a newer one of the same flannel.*]

BARTLEY [*to* NORA]. Is she coming to the pier?

NORA [*looking out*]. She's passing the green head and letting fall her sails.

BARTLEY [*getting his purse and tobacco*]. I'll have half an hour to go down, and you'll see me coming again in two days, or in three days, or maybe in four days if the wind is bad.

MAURYA [*turning around to the fire, and putting her shawl over her head*]. Isn't it a hard and cruel man won't hear a word from an old woman, and she holding him from the sea?

CATHLEEN. It's the life of a young man to be going on the sea, and who would listen to an old woman with one thing and she saying it over?

BARTLEY [taking the halter]. I must go now quickly. I'll ride down on the red mare, and the gray pony'll run behind me. . . . The blessing of God on you.

[He goes out.]

MAURYA [crying out as he is in the door]. He's gone now, God spare us, and we'll not see him again. He's gone now, and when the black night is falling I'll have no son left me in the world.

CATHLEEN. Why wouldn't you give him your blessing and he looking round in the door? Isn't it sorrow enough is on every one in this house without your sending him out with an unlucky word behind him, and a hard word in his ear?

[MAURYA takes up the tongs and begins raking the fire aimlessly without looking around.]

NORA [turning toward her]. You're taking away the turf from the cake.

CATHLEEN [crying out]. The Son of God forgive us, Nora, we're after forgetting his bit of bread. [She comes over to the fire.]

NORA. And it's destroyed he'll be going till dark night, and he after eating nothing since the sun went up.

CATHLEEN [turning the cake out of the oven]. It's destroyed he'll be, surely. There's no sense left in any person in a house where an old woman will be talking forever.

[MAURYA sways herself on her stool.]

CATHLEEN [cutting off some of the bread and rolling it in a cloth; to MAURYA]. Let you go down now to the spring well and give him this and he passing. You'll see him then and the dark word will be broken, and you can say "God speed you," the way he'll be easy in his mind.

MAURYA [taking the bread]. Will I be in it as soon as himself?

CATHLEEN. If you go now quickly.

MAURYA [standing up unsteadily]. It's hard set I am to walk.

CATHLEEN [looking at her anxiously]. Give her the stick, Nora, or maybe she'll slip on the big stones.

NORA. What stick?

CATHLEEN. The stick Michael brought from Connemara.

MAURYA [taking a stick NORA gives her]. In the big world the old people do be leaving things after them for their sons and children, but in this place it is the young men do be leaving things behind for them that do be old.

[She goes out slowly. NORA goes over to the ladder.]

CATHLEEN. Wait, Nora, maybe she'd turn back quickly. She's that sorry, God help her, you wouldn't know the thing she'd do.

NORA. Is she gone round by the bush?

CATHLEEN [looking out]. She's gone now. Throw it down quickly, for the Lord knows when she'll be out of it again.

NORA [getting the bundle from the left]. The young priest said he'd be passing tomorrow, and we might go down and speak to him below if it's Michael's they are surely.

CATHLEEN [taking the bundle]. Did he say what way they were found?

NORA [coming down]. "There were two men," says he, "and they rowing round with poteen before the cocks crowed, and the oar of one of them caught the body, and they passing the black cliffs of the north."

CATHLEEN [trying to open the bundle]. Give me a knife, Nora, the string's perished with the salt water, and here's a black knot on it you wouldn't loosen in a week.

NORA [giving her a knife]. I've heard tell it was a long way to Donegal.

CATHLEEN [cutting the string]. It is surely. There was a man in here a while ago—the man sold us that knife—and he said if you set off walking from the rocks beyond, it would be seven days you'd be in Donegal.

NORA. And what time would a man take, and he floating?

[CATHLEEN opens the bundle and takes out a bit of stocking. They look at them eagerly.]

CATHLEEN [in a low voice]. The Lord spare us, Nora! Isn't it a queer hard thing to say if it's his they are surely?

NORA. I'll get his shirt off the hook the way we can put the one flannel on the other. [*She looks through some clothes hanging in the corner.*] It's not with them, Cathleen, and where will it be?

CATHLEEN. I'm thinking Bartley put it on him in the morning, for his own shirt was heavy with the salt in it. [*Pointing to the corner.*] There's a bit of a sleeve was of the same stuff. Give me that and it will do.

[NORA *brings it to her and they compare the flannel.*]

CATHLEEN. It's the same stuff, Nora; but if it is itself aren't there great rolls of it in the shops of Galway, and isn't it many another man may have a shirt of it as well as Michael himself?

NORA [*who has taken up the stocking and counted the stitches, crying out*]. It's Michael, Cathleen, it's Michael; God spare his soul, and what will herself say when she hears this story, and Bartley on the sea?

CATHLEEN [*taking the stocking*]. It's a plain stocking.

NORA. It's the second one of the third pair I knitted, and I put up three score stitches, and I dropped four of them.

CATHLEEN [*counts the stitches*]. It's that number is in it. [*Crying out.*] Ah, Nora, isn't it a bitter thing to think of him floating that way to the far north, and no one to keen him but the black hags that do be flying on the sea?

NORA [*swinging herself around, and throwing out her arms on the clothes*]. And isn't it a pitiful thing when there is nothing left of a man who was a great rower and fisher, but a bit of an old shirt and a plain stocking?

CATHLEEN [*after an instant*]. Tell me, is herself coming, Nora? I hear a little sound on the path.

NORA [*looking out*]. She is, Cathleen. She's coming up to the door.

CATHLEEN. Put these things away before she'll come in. Maybe it's easier she'll be after giving her blessing to Bartley, and we won't let on we've heard anything the time he's on the sea.

NORA [*helping* CATHLEEN *to close the bundle*]. We'll put them here in the corner.

[*They put them into a hole in the chimney corner.* CATHLEEN *goes back to the spinning-wheel.*]

NORA. Will she see it was crying I was?

CATHLEEN. Keep your back to the door the way the light'll not be on you.

[NORA *sits down at the chimney corner, with her back to the door.* MAURYA *comes in very slowly, without looking at the girls, and goes over to her stool at the other side of the fire. The cloth with the bread is still in her hand. The girls look at each other, and* NORA *points to the bundle of bread.*]

CATHLEEN [*after spinning for a moment*]. You didn't give him his bit of bread?

[MAURYA *begins to keen softly, without turning around.*]

CATHLEEN. Did you see him riding down?

[MAURYA *goes on keening.*]

CATHLEEN [*a little impatiently*]. God forgive you; isn't it a better thing to raise your voice and tell what you seen, than to be making lamentation for a thing that's done? Did you see Bartley, I'm saying to you.

MAURYA [*with a weak voice*]. My heart's broken from this day.

CATHLEEN [*as before*]. Did you see Bartley?

MAURYA. I seen the fearfulest thing.

CATHLEEN [*leaves her wheel and looks out*]. God forgive you; he's riding the mare now over the green head, and the gray pony behind him.

MAURYA [*starts, so that her shawl falls back from her head and shows her white tossed hair. With a frightened voice*]. The gray pony behind him.

CATHLEEN [*coming to the fire*]. What is it ails you, at all?

MAURYA [*speaking very slowly*]. I've seen the fearfulest thing any person has seen, since the day Bride Dara seen the dead man with the child in his arms.

CATHLEEN and NORA. Uah.

[*They crouch down in front of the old woman at the fire.*]

NORA. Tell us what it is you seen.

MAURYA. I went down to the spring well, and I stood there saying a prayer to myself. Then Bartley came along, and he riding on the red mare with the gray pony behind him. [*She puts up her hands, as if to hide something from her eyes.*] The Son of God spare us, Nora!

CATHLEEN. What is it you seen?

MAURYA. I seen Michael himself.

CATHLEEN [speaking softly]. You did not, Mother. It wasn't Michael you seen, for his body is after being found in the far north, and he's got a clean burial by the grace of God.

MAURYA [a little defiantly]. I'm after seeing him this day, and he riding and galloping. Bartley came first on the red mare; and I tried to say "God speed you," but something choked the words in my throat. He went by quickly; and "the blessing of God on you," says he, and I could say nothing. I looked up then, and I crying, at the gray pony, and there was Michael upon it—with fine clothes on him, and new shoes on his feet.

CATHLEEN [begins to keen]. It's destroyed we are from this day. It's destroyed, surely.

NORA. Didn't the young priest say the Almighty God wouldn't leave her destitute with no son living?

MAURYA [in a low voice, but clearly]. It's little the like of him knows of the sea. . . . Bartley will be lost now, and let you call in Eamon and make me a good coffin out of the white boards, for I won't live after them. I've had a husband, and a husband's father, and six sons in this house—six fine men, though it was a hard birth I had with every one of them and they coming to the world—and some of them were found and some of them were not found, but they're gone now, the lot of them. . . . There were Stephen, and Shawn, were lost in the great wind, and found after in the Bay of Gregory of the Golden Mouth, and carried up the two of them on the one plank, and in by that door.

[She pauses for a moment. The GIRLS start as if they heard something through the door that is half open behind them.]

NORA [in a whisper]. Did you hear that, Cathleen? Did you hear a noise in the northeast?

CATHLEEN [in a whisper]. There's some one after crying out by the seashore.

MAURYA [continues without hearing anything]. There was Sheamus and his father, and his own father again, were lost in a dark night, and not a stick or sign was seen of them when the sun went up. There was Patch after was drowned out of a curagh that turned over. I was sitting here with Bartley, and he a baby, lying on my two knees, and I seen two women, and three women, and four women coming in, and they crossing themselves, and not saying a word. I looked out then, and there were men coming after them, and they holding a thing in the half of a red sail, and water dripping out of it—it was a dry day, Nora—and leaving a track to the door.

[She pauses again with her hand stretched out toward the door. It opens softly and OLD WOMEN begin to come in, crossing themselves on the threshold, and kneeling down in front of the stage with red petticoats over their heads.]

MAURYA [half in a dream, to CATHLEEN]. Is it Patch, or Michael, or what is it at all?

CATHLEEN. Michael is after being found in the far north, and when he is found there how could he be here in this place?

MAURYA. There does be a power of young men floating round in the sea, and what way would they know if it was Michael they had, or another man like him, for when a man is nine days in the sea, and the wind blowing, it's hard set his own mother would be to say what man was it.

CATHLEEN. It's Michael, God spare him, for they're after sending us a bit of clothes from the far north.

[She reaches out and hands MAURYA the clothes that belong to MICHAEL. MAURYA stands up slowly, and takes them in her hands. NORA looks out.]

NORA. They're carrying a thing among them and there's water dripping out of it and leaving a track by the big stones.

CATHLEEN [in a whisper to the WOMEN who have come in]. Is it Bartley it is?

ONE OF THE WOMEN. It is surely, God rest his soul.

[Two YOUNGER WOMEN come in and pull out the table. Then MEN carry in the body of BARTLEY, laid on a plank, with a bit of a sail over it, and lay it on the table.]

CATHLEEN [to the WOMEN, as they are doing so]. What way was he drowned?

ONE OF THE WOMEN. The gray pony knocked him into the sea, and he was washed out where there is a great surf on the white rocks.

[MAURYA *has gone over and knelt down at the head of the table. The* WOMEN *are keening softly and swaying themselves with a slow movement.* CATHLEEN *and* NORA *kneel at the other end of the table. The* MEN *kneel near the door.*]

MAURYA [*raising her head and speaking as if she did not see the people around her*]. They're all gone now, and there isn't anything more the sea can do to me.... I'll have no call now to be up crying and praying when the wind breaks from the south, and you can hear the surf is in the east, and the surf is in the west, making a great stir with the two noises, and they hitting one on the other. I'll have no call now to be going down and getting Holy Water in the dark nights after Samhain, and I won't care what way the sea is when the other women will be keening. [*To* NORA.] Give me the Holy Water, Nora, there's a small sup still on the dresser.

[NORA *gives it to her.*]

MAURYA [*drops* MICHAEL'S *clothes across* BARTLEY'S *feet, and sprinkles the Holy Water over him*]. It isn't that I haven't prayed for you, Bartley, to the Almighty God. It isn't that I haven't said prayers in the dark night till you wouldn't know what I'd be saying; but it's a great rest I'll have now, and it's time surely. It's a great rest I'll have now, and great sleeping in the long nights after Samhain, if it's only a bit of wet flour we do have to eat, and maybe a fish that would be stinking.

[*She kneels down again, crossing herself, and saying prayers under her breath.*]

CATHLEEN [*to an* OLD MAN]. Maybe yourself and Eamon would make a coffin when the sun rises. We have fine white boards herself bought, God help her, thinking Michael would be found, and I

have a new cake you can eat while you'll be working.

THE OLD MAN [*looking at the boards*]. Are there nails with them?

CATHLEEN. There are not, Colum; we didn't think of the nails.

ANOTHER MAN. It's a great wonder she wouldn't think of the nails, and all the coffins she's seen made already.

CATHLEEN. It's getting old she is, and broken.

[MAURYA *stands up again very slowly and spreads out the pieces of* MI-CHAEL'S *clothes beside the body, sprinkling them with the last of the Holy Water.*]

NORA [*in a whisper to* CATHLEEN]. She's quiet now, and easy; but the day Michael was drowned you could hear her crying out from this to the spring well. It's fonder she was of Michael, and would any one have thought that?

CATHLEEN [*slowly and clearly*]. An old woman will be soon tired with anything she will do, and isn't it nine days herself is after crying and keening, and making great sorrow in the house?

MAURYA [*puts the empty cup mouth downwards on the table, and lays her hands together on* BARTLEY'S *feet*]. They're all together this time, and the end is come. May the Almighty God have mercy on Bartley's soul, and on Michael's soul, and on the souls of Shea-mus and Patch, and Stephen and Shawn. [*Bending her head.*] And may He have mercy on my soul, Nora, and on the soul of every one is left living in the world.

[*She pauses, and the keen rises a little more loudly from the* WOMEN, *then sinks away.*]

MAURYA [*continuing*]. Michael has a clean burial in the far north, by the grace of the Almighty God. Bartley will have a fine coffin out of the white boards, and a deep grave surely. What more can we want than that? No man at all can be living forever, and we must be satisfied.

[*She kneels down again and the* CUR-TAIN *falls slowly.*]

John Millington Synge

PREFACE TO
THE PLAYBOY OF THE WESTERN WORLD

January 21, 1907

In writing *The Playboy of the Western World*, as in my other plays, I have used one or two words only that I have not heard among the country people of Ireland, or spoken in my own nursery before I could read the newspapers. A certain number of the phrases I employ I have heard also from herds and fishermen along the coast from Kerry to Mayo or from beggar-women and ballad-singers nearer Dublin; and I am glad to acknowledge how much I owe to the folk-imagination of these fine people. Anyone who has lived in real intimacy with the Irish peasantry will know that the wildest sayings and ideas in this play are tame indeed, compared with the fancies one may hear in any little hillside cabin in Geesala, or Carraroe, or Dingle Bay. All art is a collaboration; and there is little doubt that in the happy ages of literature, striking and beautiful phrases were as ready to the story-teller's or the play-wright's hand, as the rich cloaks and dresses of his time. It is probable that when the Elizabethan dramatist took his ink-horn and sat down to his work he used many phrases that he had just heard, as he sat at dinner, from his mother or his children. In Ireland, those of us who know the people have the same privilege. When I was writing *The Shadow of the Glen*, some years ago, I got more aid than any learning could have given me from a chink in the floor of the old Wicklow house where I was staying, that let me hear what was being said by the servant girls in the kitchen. This matter, I think, is of importance, for in countries where the imagination of the people, and the language they use, is rich and living, it is possible for a writer to be rich and copious in his words, and at the same time to give the reality, which is the root of all poetry, in a comprehensive and natural form. In the modern literature of towns, however, richness is found only in sonnets, or prose poems, or in one or two elaborate books that are far away from the profound and common interests of life. One has, on one side, Mallarmé and Huysmans producing this literature; and on the other, Ibsen and Zola dealing with the reality of life in joyless and pallid words. On the stage one must have reality, and one must have joy; and that is why the intellectual modern drama has failed, and people have grown sick of the false joy of the musical comedy, that has been given them in place of the rich joy found only in what is superb and wild in reality. In a good play every speech should be as fully flavoured as a nut or apple, and such speeches cannot be written by anyone who works among people who have shut their lips on poetry. In Ireland, for a few years more, we have a popular imagination that is fiery, and magnificent, and tender; so that those of us who wish to write start with a chance that is not given to writers in places where the spring-time of the local life has been forgotten, and the harvest is a memory only, and the straw has been turned into bricks.

SOURCE: From *The Complete Works of John M. Synge*. Copyright 1935 by the Modern Library, Inc. Reprinted by permission of Random House, Inc.

EXTRACTS FROM NOTE BOOKS OF J. M. SYNGE

(1907)

The artistic value of any work of art is measured by its *uniqueness*. Its human value is given largely by its intensity and its richness, for if it is rich it is many-sided or universal, and, for this reason, sane—another word for wholesome, since all insanities are due to a one-sided excitement.

No personal originality is enough to make a rich work unique, unless it has also the characteristic of a particular time and locality and the life that is in it. For this reason all historical plays and novels and poems—except a very few that continue the tradition of a country—or like *Faust* and *Don Juan* renew some stock type—are relatively worthless. Every healthy mind is more interested in *Tit-Bits* than in *Idylls of the King*, or any of the other more or less artificial retellings of classical or saga stories. The most that one can claim for work of this kind—such as Keats's *Isabella*—when it is beautiful, is that it is made for a Utopia of art.

All Utopian work is unsatisfying, first because it is weak and therefore vague and therefore wanting in uniqueness, and also because it is only the catastrophes of life that give substance and power to the tragedy and humour which are the true poles of art. The religious art is a thing of the past only—a vain and foolish regret—and its place has been taken by our quite modern feeling for the beauty and mystery of nature, an emotion that has gradually risen up as religion in the dogmatic sense has gradually died. Our pilgrimages are not to Canterbury or Jerusalem, but to Killarney, Cumberland and the Alps.

In my plays and topographical books I have tried to give humanity and this mysterious external world.

Man has gradually grown up in this world that is about us, and I think that while Tolstoy is wrong in claiming that art should be intelligible to the peasant, he is right in seeking a criterion for the arts, and I think this is to be found in testing art by its compatibility with the outside world and the peasants or people who live near it. A book, I mean, that one feels ashamed to read in a cottage of Dingle Bay one may fairly call a book that is not healthy—or universal.

All theorizing is bad for the artist, because it makes him live in the intelligence instead of in the half-subconscious faculties by which all real creation is performed. This is one reason why hostile criticism is harmful to an artist, because it forces him to construct systems and defend and explain his own work.

Young and therefore living truths, views, what you will, have a certain diffidence or tenderness that makes it impossible to state them without the accompanying emotional or imaginative life in which they naturally arise. That is, they are stated in the arts when they are dead, only the flesh is cleared away and the naked skeletons are shown by essayists and metaphysicians.

Humour is the test of morals, as no vice is humorous. Bestial is, in its very essence, opposed to the idea of humour. All decadence is opposed to true humour. The heartiness of real and frank laughter is a sign that cannot be mistaken that what we laugh at is not out of harmony with that instinct of sanity that we call by so many names.

The shopman says that a work of art is not artistic if it is unwholesome, which is foolish; the fashionable critic says that it is absurd to say a work of art is unwholesome if it is good art, which is

SOURCE: From *Plays*, by John M. Synge. London, George Allen & Unwin, n.d.

foolish also. There are beautiful and interesting plants which are deadly, and others that are kindly. It is absurd to say a flower is not beautiful nor admire its beauty because it is deadly, but it is absurd also to deny its deadliness.

(1908)

No one is less fond of theories and divisions in the arts than I am, and yet they cannot altogether be gone without. In these matters we need not expect to say anything very new, but in applying, for ourselves, to our own life, what is thought in different ways by many, we are likely to hit on matters of some value. For a long time I have felt that Poetry roughly is of two kinds, the poetry of real life—the poetry of Burns and Shakespeare and Villon, and the poetry of a land of fancy—the poetry of Spenser and Keats and Ronsard. That is obvious enough, but what is highest in poetry is always reached where the dreamer is leaning out to reality, or where the man of real life is lifted out of it, and in all the poets the greatest have both these elements, that is, they are supremely engrossed with life, and yet with the wildness of their fancy they are always passing out of what is simple and plain. Such is the case with Dante and Chaucer and Goethe and Shakespeare. In Ireland Mr. Yeats, one of the poets of the fancy land, has interests in the world and, for this reason, his poetry has had a lifetime in itself, but A. E., on the other hand, who is of the fancy land only, ended his career of poetry in his first volume.

It would be easy to carry this division a long way, to compare the romances of the Arthurian style with the modern realistic novel. Gottfried of Strassburg and Malory become real here and there—suddenly a real voice seems to speak out of their golden and burning words—and they are then extraordinarily powerful. So, on the other hand, it is only with Huysmans that the realistic becomes of interest.

Eugene
O'Neill
1888–1953

O'Neill was aloof, shy, and brooding; his life was full of pain and frustration. His father, a rich and successful actor, was pathologically tight-fisted; his mother was the victim of drugs; an older brother was alcoholic; O'Neill himself was twice divorced; his eldest child committed suicide in 1950. His early years were divided between traveling with his family on theatrical tours and boarding in various Catholic schools. After an unsuccessful year at Princeton, O'Neill turned briefly to business, but soon left to prospect for gold in Honduras. He failed to find it, returned to business, failed at that, and in 1910 shipped as a merchant seaman. After a rough, heavy-drinking, vagabond life, O'Neill joined his father's acting company for a time; presently, however, he took a job on a newspaper in New London, Connecticut. Then his strained health broke, and O'Neill found himself hospitalized with tuberculosis. During his convalescence he thought seriously about drama and apparently began to write. In 1914, he was enrolled in George Pierce Baker's playwriting course at Harvard, and the following year he was living in New York among the artists of Greenwich Village. O'Neill's first play was produced in 1916 in the summer art colony at Provincetown, Massachusetts, and when the Provincetown Players moved to New York, O'Neill provided them with other one-act dramas of the sea. His full-length play *Beyond the Horizon* was produced in 1920, and from then on O'Neill's reputation was secured as play followed play during the nineteen-twenties and established him as America's leading dramatist. From realistic drama O'Neill turned restlessly to more experimental forms in plays such as *The Hairy Ape* (1921) and *The Great God Brown* (1925). An increasing interest in metaphysical and psychoanalytical themes now directed his work—notably in *Desire Under the Elms* (1924)—as O'Neill, grappling with man's tragic relation to the universe, broke through conventional dramaturgy in the massive forms of *Strange Interlude* (1927) and *Mourning Becomes Electra* (1931), his transformation of the Oresteian trilogy of Aeschylus. In the mid-thirties O'Neill withdrew from the stage to work on a cycle of nine plays encompassing the history of an American family, but the project never materialized. His absence from the theater was broken in 1946 with the appearance of *The Iceman Cometh* (written in 1939), a naturalistic play that echoed O'Neill's past. His powerful autobiographical play, *Long Day's Journey into Night* (1956) was composed from 1939 to 1941, but in accordance with the playwright's wishes it was not produced until after his death in 1953.

THE HAIRY APE

A comedy of ancient and modern life

EUGENE O'NEILL

CHARACTERS

ROBERT SMITH, "YANK"
PADDY
LONG
MILDRED DOUGLAS
HER AUNT

SECOND ENGINEER
A GUARD
A SECRETARY OF AN ORGANIZATION
STOKERS, LADIES, GENTLEMEN, ETC.

SCENES

SCENE ONE. The fireman's forecastle of an ocean liner—an hour after sailing from New York

SCENE TWO. Section of promenade deck, two days out—morning

SCENE THREE. The stokehole. A few minutes later

SCENE FOUR. Same as Scene One. Half an hour later

SCENE FIVE. Fifth Avenue, New York. Three weeks later

SCENE SIX. An island near the city. The next night

SCENE SEVEN. In the city. About a month later

SCENE EIGHT. In the city. Twilight of the next day

SCENE ONE

[Scene: The fireman's forecastle of a transatlantic liner an hour after sailing from New York for the voyage across. Tiers of narrow, steel bunks, three deep, on all sides. An entrance in rear. Benches on the floor before the bunks. The room is crowded with men, shouting, cursing, laughing, singing—a confused, inchoate uproar swelling into a sort of unity, a meaning—the bewildered, furious, baffled defiance of a beast in a cage. Nearly all the men are drunk. Many bottles are passed from hand to hand. All are dressed in dungaree pants, heavy ugly shoes. Some wear singlets, but the majority are stripped to the waist.

The treatment of this scene, or of any other scene in the play, should by no means be naturalistic. The effect sought after is a cramped space in the bowels of a ship, imprisoned by white steel. The lines of bunks, the uprights supporting them, cross each other like the steel framework of a cage. The ceiling crushes down upon the men's heads. They cannot stand upright. This accentuates the natural stooping posture which shoveling coal and the resultant over-development of back and shoulder muscles have given them. The men themselves should resemble those pictures in which the appearance of Neanderthal Man is guessed at. All are hairy-chested, with long arms of tremendous power, and low, receding brows above their small, fierce, resentful eyes. All the civilized white races are represented, but except for the slight differentiation in color of hair, skin, eyes, all these men are alike.

The curtain rises on a tumult of sound. YANK is seated in the foreground. He

SOURCE: From *Selected Plays of Eugene O'Neill.* Copyright 1922 and renewed 1950 by Eugene O'Neill. Reprinted by permission of Random House, Inc.

seems broader, fiercer, more truculent, more powerful, more sure of himself than the rest. They respect his superior strength—the grudging respect of fear. Then, too, he represents to them a self-expression, the very last word in what they are, their most highly developed individual.]

VOICES. Gif me trink dere, you!
'Ave a wet!
Salute!
Gesundheit!
Skoal!
Drunk as a lord, God stiffen you!
Here's how!
Luck!
Pass back that bottle, damn you!
Pourin' it down his neck!
Ho, Froggy! Where the devil have you been?
La Touraine.
I hit him smash in yaw, py Gott!
Jenkins—the First—he's a rotten swine——
And the coppers nabbed him—and I run——
I like peer better. It don't pig head gif you.
A slut, I'm sayin'! She robbed me aslape——
To hell with 'em all!
You're a bloody liar!
Say dot again! [Commotion. Two men about to fight are pulled apart.]
No scrappin' now!
Tonight——
See who's the best man!
Bloody Dutchman!
Tonight on the for'ard square.
I'll bet on Dutchy.
He packa da wallop, I tella you!
Shut up, Wop!
No fightin', maties. We're all chums ain't we?
[A voice starts bawling a song.]

Beer, beer, glorious beer!
Fill yourselves right up to here.

YANK [for the first time seeming to take notice of the uproar about him, turns around threateningly—in a tone of contemptuous authority]. Choke off dat noise! Where d'yuh get dat beer stuff? Beer, hell! Beer's for goils—and Dutchmen. Me for somep'n wit a kick to it!

Gimme a drink, one of youse guys. [Several bottles are eagerly offered. He takes a tremendous gulp at one of them; then, keeping the bottle in his hand, glares belligerently at the owner, who hastens to acquiesce in this robbery by saying] All righto, Yank. Keep it and have another. [YANK contemptuously turns his back on the crowd again. For a second there is an embarrassed silence. Then——]

VOICES. We must be passing the Hook.
She's beginning to roll to it.
Six days in hell—and then Southampton.
Pi Yesus, I vish somepody take my first vatch for me!
Gittin' seasick, Square-head?
Drink up and forget it!
What's in your bottle?
Gin.
Dot's nigger trink.
Absinthe? It's doped. You'll go off your chump, Froggy!
Cochon!
Whisky, that's the ticket!
Where's Paddy?
Going asleep.
Sing us that whisky song, Paddy.
[They all turn to an old, wizened Irishman who is dozing, very drunk, on the benches forward. His face is extremely monkey-like with all the sad, patient pathos of that animal in his small eyes.]
Singa da song, Caruso Pat!
He's gettin' old. The drink is too much for him.
He's too drunk.

PADDY [blinking about him, starts to his feet resentfully, swaying, holding on to the edge of a bunk]. I'm never too drunk to sing. 'Tis only when I'm dead to the world I'd be wishful to sing at all. [With a sort of sad contempt.] "Whisky Johnny," ye want? A chanty, ye want? Now that's a queer wish from the ugly like of you, God help you. But no mather. [He starts to sing in a thin, nasal, doleful tone.]

Oh, whisky is the life of man!
Whisky! O Johnny! [They all join in on this.]
Oh, whisky is the life of man!
Whisky for my Johnny! [Again chorus.]

Oh, whisky drove my old man mad!
  Whisky! O Johnny!
Oh, whisky drove my old man mad!
  Whisky for my Johnny!

YANK [*again turning around scornfully*]. Aw hell! Nix on dat old sailing ship stuff? All dat bull's dead, see? And you're dead, too, yuh damned old Harp, on'y yuh don't know it. Take it easy, see. Give us a rest. Nix on de loud noise. [*With a cynical grin.*] Can't youse see I'm tryin' to t'ink?

ALL [*repeating the word after him as one with the same cynical amused mockery*]. Think! [*The chorused word has a brazen metallic quality as if their throats were phonograph horns. It is followed by a general uproar of hard, barking laughter.*]

VOICES. Don't be cracking your head with ut, Yank.
You gat headache, py yingo!
One thing about it—it rhymes with
    drink!
Ha, ha, ha!
Drink, don't think!
Drink, don't think!
    Drink, don't think! [*A whole chorus of voices has taken up this refrain, stamping on the floor, pounding on the benches with fists.*]

YANK [*taking a gulp from his bottle—good-naturedly*]. Aw right. Can de noise. I got yuh de foist time. [*The uproar subsides. A very drunken sentimental tenor begins to sing.*]

      Far away in Canada,
        Far across the sea,
      There's a lass who fondly waits
        Making a home for me——

YANK [*fiercely contemptuous*]. Shut up, yuh lousy boob! Where d'yuh get dat tripe? Home? Home, hell! I'll make a home for yuh! I'll knock yuh dead. Home! T'hell wit home! Where d'yuh get dat tripe? Dis is home, see? What d'yuh want wit home? [*Proudly.*] I runned away from mine when I was a kid. On'y too glad to beat it, dat was me. Home was lickings for me, dat's all. But yuh can bet your shoit no one ain't never licked me since! Wanter try it, any of youse? Huh! I guess not. [*In a more placated but still contemptuous tone.*]

Goils waitin' for yuh, huh? Aw, hell! Dat's all tripe. Dey don't wait for no one. Dey'd double-cross yuh for a nickel. Dey're all tarts, get me? Treat 'em rough, dat's me. To hell wit 'em. Tarts, dat's what, de whole bunch of 'em.

LONG [*very drunk, jumps on a bench excitedly, gesticulating with a bottle in his hand*]. Listen 'ere, Comrades. Yank 'ere is right. 'E says this 'ere stinkin' ship is our 'ome. And 'e says as 'ome is 'ell. And 'e's right! This is 'ell. We lives in 'ell, Comrades—and right enough we'll die in it. [*Raging.*] And who's ter blame, I arsks yer? We ain't. We wasn't born this rotten way. All men is born free and ekal. That's in the bleedin' Bible, maties. But what d'they care for the Bible—them lazy, bloated swine what travels first cabin? Them's the ones. They dragged us down 'til we're on'y wage slaves in the bowels of a bloody ship, sweatin', burnin' up, eatin' coal dust! Hit's them's ter blame—the damned Capitalist clarss! [*There had been a gradual murmur of contemptuous resentment rising among the men until now he is interrupted by a storm of catcalls, hisses, boos, hard laughter.*]

VOICES. Turn it off!
Shut up!
Sit down!
Closa da face!
Tamn fool! [*Etc.*]

YANK [*standing up and glaring at* LONG]. Sit down before I knock yuh down! [LONG *makes haste to efface himself.* YANK *goes on contemptuously.*] De Bible, huh? De Cap'tlist class, huh? Aw nix on dat Salvation Army-Socialist bull. Git a soapbox! Hire a hall! Come and be saved, huh? Jerk us to Jesus, huh? Aw g'wan! I've listened to lots of guys like you, see. Yuh're all wrong. Wanter know what I t'ink? Yuh ain't no good for no one. Yuh're de bunk. Yuh ain't got no noive, get me? Yuh're yellow, dat's what. Yellow, dat's you. Say! What's dem slobs in de foist cabin got to do wit us? We're better men dan dey are, ain't we? Sure? One of us guys could clean up de whole mob wit one mit. Put one of 'em down here for one watch in de stokehole, what'd happen? Dey'd carry him off on a stretcher. Dem boids don't amount to nothin'. Dey're just baggage. Who makes dis old tub run? Ain't it us guys? Well den, we belong, don't we? We belong and dey don't. Dat's all. [*A loud chorus of approval.* YANK *goes on.*] As for dis bein' hell—aw, nuts! Yuh lost your noive, dat's what. Dis is a man's job, get me? It belongs. It runs dis tub. No stiffs need apply. But yuh're a stiff, see? Yuh're yellow, dat's you.

VOICES [*with a great hard pride in them*].
Righto!
A man's job!
Talk is cheap, Long.
He never could hold up his end.
Divil take him!
Yank's right. We make it go.
Py Gott, Yank say right ting!
We don't need no one cryin' over us.
Makin' speeches.
Throw him out!
Yellow!
Chuck him overboard!
I'll break his jaw for him!

[*They crowd around* LONG *threateningly.*]

YANK [*half good-natured again—contemptuously*]. Aw, take it easy. Leave him alone. He ain't woith a punch. Drink up. Here's how, whoever owns dis. [*He takes a long swallow from his bottle. All drink with him. In a flash all is hilarious amiability again, back-slapping, loud talk, etc.*]

PADDY [*who has been sitting in a blinking, melancholy daze—suddenly cries out in a voice full of old sorrow*]. We belong to this, you're saying? We make the ship to go, you're saying? Yerra then, that Almighty God have pity on us! [*His voice runs into the wail of a keen, he rocks back and forth on his bench. The men stare at him, startled and impressed in spite of themselves.*] Oh, to be back in the fine days of my youth, ochone! Oh, there was fine beautiful ships them days—clippers wid tall masts touching the sky—fine strong men in them—men that was sons of the sea as if 'twas the mother that bore them. Oh, the clean skins of them, and the clear eyes, the straight backs and full chests of them! Brave men they was, and bold men surely! We'd be sailing out, bound down round the Horn maybe. We'd be making sail in the dawn, with a fair breeze, singing a chanty song wid

no care to it. And astern the land would be sinking low and dying out, but we'd give it no heed but a laugh, and never a look behind. For the day that was, was enough, for we was free men—and I'm thinking 'tis only slaves do be giving heed to the day that's gone or the day to come—until they're old like me. [*With a sort of religious exaltation.*] Oh, to be scudding south again wid the power of the Trade Wind driving her on steady through the nights and the days! Full sail on her! Nights and days! Nights when the foam of the wake would be flaming wid fire, when the sky'd be blazing and winking wid stars. Or the full of the moon maybe. Then you'd see her driving through the gray night, her sails stretching aloft all silver and white, not a sound on the deck, the lot of us dreaming dreams, till you'd believe 'twas no real ship at all you was on but a ghost ship like the *Flying Dutchman* they say does be roaming the seas forevermore widout touching a port. And there was the days, too. A warm sun on the clean decks. Sun warming the blood of you, and wind over the miles of shiny green ocean like strong drink to your lungs. Work—aye, hard work—but who'd mind that at all? Sure, you worked under the sky and 'twas work wid skill and daring to it. And wid the day done, in the dog watch, smoking me pipe at ease, the lookout would be raising land maybe, and we'd see the mountains of South Americy wid the red fire of the setting sun painting their white tops and the clouds floating by them! [*His tone of exaltation ceases. He goes on mournfully.*] Yerra, what's the use of talking? 'Tis a dead man's whisper. [*To* YANK *resentfully.*] 'Twas them days men belonged to ships, not now. 'Twas them days a ship was part of the sea, and a man was part of a ship, and the sea joined all together and made it one. [*Scornfully.*] Is it one wid this you'd be, Yank—black smoke from the funnels smudging the sea, smudging the decks—the bloody engines pounding and throbbing and shaking—wid divil a sight of sun or a breath of clean air—choking our lungs wid coal dust—breaking our backs and hearts in the hell of the stokehole—feeding the bloody furnace—feeding our

lives along wid the coal, I'm thinking—
caged in by steel from a sight of the sky
like bloody apes in the Zoo! [*With a
harsh laugh.*] Ho-ho, divil mend you! Is
it to belong to that you're wishing? Is
it a flesh and blood wheel of the engines
you'd be?

YANK [*who has been listening with a
contemptuous sneer, barks out the answer*]. Sure ting! Dat's me. What about
it?

PADDY [*as if to himself—with great
sorrow*]. Me time is past due. That a
great wave wid sun in the heart of it may
sweep me over the side sometime I'd be
dreaming of the days that's gone!

YANK. Aw, yuh crazy Mick! [*He
springs to his feet and advances on
Paddy threateningly—then stops, fighting some queer struggle within himself
—lets his hands fall to his sides—contemptuously.*] Aw, take it easy. Yuh're
aw right, at dat. Yuh're bugs, dat's all—
nutty as a cuckoo. All dat tripe yuh been
pullin'— Aw, dat's all right. On'y it's
dead, get me? Yuh don't belong no more,
see. Yuh don't get de stuff. Yuh're too
old. [*Disgustedly.*] But aw say, come up
for air onct in a while, can't yuh? See
what's happened since yuh croaked. [*He
suddenly bursts forth vehemently, growing more and more excited.*] Say! Sure!
Sure I meant it! What de hell— Say,
lemme talk! Hey! Hey, you old Harp!
Hey, youse guys! Say, listen to me—
wait a moment—I gotta talk, see. I belong and he don't. He's dead but I'm
livin'. Listen to me! Sure I'm part of de
engines! Why de hell not? Dey move,
don't dey? Dey're speed, ain't dey? Dey
smash trou, don't dey? Twenty-five knots
a hour! Dat's goin' some! Dat's new
stuff! Dat belongs! But him, he's too old.
He gets dizzy. Say, listen. All dat crazy
tripe about nights and days; all dat crazy
tripe about stars and moons; all dat crazy
tripe about suns and winds, fresh air
and de rest of it— Aw, hell, dat's all a
dope dream! Hittin' de pipe of de past,
dat's what he's doin'. He's old and don't
belong no more. But me, I'm young! I'm
in de pink! I move wit it! It, get me! I
mean de ting dat's de guts of all dis. It
ploughs trou all de tripe he's been sayin'.
It blows dat up! It knocks dat dead! It
slams dat offen de face of de oith! It,

get me! De engines and de coal and de
smoke and all de rest of it! He can't
breathe and swallow coal dust, but I
kin, see? Dat's fresh air for me! Dat's
food for me! I'm new, get me? Hell in
de stokehole? Sure! It takes a man to
work in hell. Hell, sure, dat's my fav'rite
climate. I eat it up! I git fat on it! It's
me makes it hot! It's me makes it roar!
It's me makes it move! Sure, on'y for me
everyting stops. It all goes dead, get
me? De noise and smoke and all de
engines movin' de woild, dey stop. Dere
ain't nothin' no more! Dat's what I'm
sayin'. Everyting else dat makes de woild
move, somep'n makes it move. It can't
move witout somep'n else, see? Den yuh
get down to me. I'm at de bottom, get
me! Dere ain't nothin' foither. I'm de
end! I'm de start! I start somep'n and de
woild moves! It—dat's me!—de new
dat's moiderin' de old! I'm de ting in
coal dat makes it boin; I'm steam and
oil for de engines; I'm de ting in noise
dat makes yuh hear it; I'm smoke and
express trains and steamers and factory
whistles; I'm de ting in gold dat makes
money! And I'm what makes iron into
steel! Steel, dat stands for de whole ting!
And I'm steel—steel—steel! I'm de
muscles in steel, de punch behind it! [*As
he says this he pounds with his fist
against the steel bunks. All the men,
roused to a pitch of frenzied self-glori-
fication by his speech, do likewise. There
is a deafening metallic roar, through
which* YANK's *voice can be heard bellow-
ing.*] Slaves, hell! We run de whole
woiks. All de rich guys dat tink dey're
somep'n, dey ain't nothin'! Dey don't
belong. But us guys, we're in de move,
we're at de bottom, de whole ting is us!
[PADDY *from the start of* YANK's *speech
has been taking one gulp after another
from his bottle, at first frightenedly, as if
he were afraid to listen, then desperately,
as if to drown his senses, but finally
has achieved complete indifferent, even
amused, drunkenness.* YANK *sees his lips
moving. He quells the uproar with a
shout.*] Hey, youse guys, take it easy!
Wait a moment! De nutty Harp is sayin'
somep'n.

PADDY [*is heard now—throws his head
back with a mocking burst of laughter*].
Ho-ho-ho-ho-ho——

YANK [*drawing back his fist, with a snarl*]. Aw! Look out who yuh're givin' the bark!

PADDY [*begins to sing the "Miller of Dee" with enormous good nature*].

I care for nobody, no, not I,
And nobody cares for me.

YANK [*good-natured himself in a flash, interrupts* PADDY *with a slap on the bare back like a report*]. Dat's de stuff! Now yuh're gettin' wise to somep'n. Care for nobody, dat's de dope! To hell wit 'em all! And nix on nobody else carin'. I kin care for myself, get me! [*Eight bells sound, muffled, vibrating through the steel walls as if some enormous brazen gong were imbedded in the heart of the ship. All the men jump up mechanically, file through the door silently close upon each other's heels in what is very like a prisoners' lockstep.* YANK *slaps* PADDY *on the back.*] Our watch, yuh old Harp! [*Mockingly.*] Come on down in hell. Eat up de coal dust. Drink in de heat. It's it, see! Act like yuh liked it, yuh better —or croak yuhself.

PADDY [*with jovial defiance*]. To the divil wid it! I'll not report this watch. Let thim log me and be damned. I'm no slave the like of you. I'll be sittin' here at me ease, and drinking, and thinking, and dreaming dreams.

YANK [*contemptuously*]. Tinkin' and dreamin', what'll that get yuh? What's tinkin' got to do wit it? We move, don't we? Speed, ain't it? Fog, dat's all you stand for. But we drive trou dat, don't we? We split dat up and smash trou— twenty-five knots a hour! [*Turns his back on* PADDY *scornfully.*] Aw, yuh make me sick! Yuh don't belong! [*He strides out the door in rear. Paddy hums to himself, blinking drowsily.*]

CURTAIN

SCENE TWO

[*Scene: Two days out. A section of the promenade deck.* MILDRED DOUGLAS *and her* AUNT *are discovered reclining in deck chairs. The former is a girl of twenty, slender, delicate, with a pale, pretty face marred by a self-conscious expres-* sion of disdainful superiority. She looks fretful, nervous, and discontented, bored by her own anemia. Her AUNT is a pompous and proud—and fat—old lady. She is a type even to the point of a double chin and lorgnettes. She is dressed pretentiously, as if afraid her face alone would never indicate her position in life. MILDRED *is dressed all in white.*

The impression to be conveyed by this scene is one of the beautiful, vivid life of the sea all about—sunshine on the deck in a great flood, the fresh sea wind blowing across it. In the midst of this, these two incongruous, artificial figures, inert and disharmonious, the elder like a gray lump of dough touched up with rouge, the younger looking as if the vitality of her stock had been sapped before she was conceived, so that she is the expression not of its life energy but merely of the artificialities that energy had won for itself in the spending.]

MILDRED [*looking up with affected dreaminess*]. How the black smoke swirls back against the sky! Is it not beautiful?

AUNT [*without looking up*]. I dislike smoke of any kind.

MILDRED. My great-grandmother smoked a pipe—a clay pipe.

AUNT [*ruffling*]. Vulgar!

MILDRED. She was too distant a relative to be vulgar. Time mellows pipes.

AUNT [*pretending boredom but irritated*]. Did the sociology you took up at college teach you that—to play the ghoul on every possible occasion, excavating old bones? Why not let your great-grandmother rest in her grave?

MILDRED [*dreamily*]. With her pipe beside her—puffing in Paradise.

AUNT [*with spite*]. Yes, you are a natural born ghoul. You are even getting to look like one, my dear.

MILDRED [*in a passionless tone*]. I detest you, Aunt. [*Looking at her critically.*] Do you know what you remind me of? Of a cold pork pudding against a background of linoleum tablecloth in the kitchen of a—but the possibilities are wearisome. [*She closes her eyes.*]

AUNT [*with a bitter laugh*]. Merci for your candor. But since I am and must be your chaperon—in appearance—at least—let us patch up some sort of armed truce. For my part you are quite free to indulge any pose of eccentricity that beguiles you—as long as you observe the amenities——

MILDRED [drawling]. The inanities?

AUNT [going on as if she hadn't heard]. After exhausting the morbid thrills of social service work on New York's East Side—how they must have hated you, by the way, the poor that you made so much poorer in their own eyes! —you are now bent on making your slumming international. Well, I hope Whitechapel will provide the needed nerve tonic. Do not ask me to chaperon you there, however. I told your father I would not. I loathe deformity. We will hire an army of detectives and you may investigate everything—they allow you to see.

MILDRED [protesting with a trace of genuine earnestness]. Please do not mock at my attempts to discover how the other half lives. Give me credit for some sort of groping sincerity in that at least. I would like to help them. I would like to be of some use in the world. Is it my fault I don't know how? I would like to be sincere, to touch life somewhere. [With weary bitterness.] But I'm afraid I have neither the vitality nor integrity. All that was burned out in our stock before I was born. Grandfather's blast furnaces, flaming to the sky, melting steel, making millions—then Father keeping those home fires burning, making more millions—and little me at the tail-end of it all. I'm a waste product in the Bessemer process—like the millions. Or, rather, I inherit the acquired trait of the by-product, wealth, but none of the energy, none of the strength of the steel that made it. I am sired by gold and damned by it, as they say at the race track—damned in more ways than one. [She laughs mirthlessly.]

AUNT [unimpressed—superciliously]. You seem to be going in for sincerity today. It isn't becoming to you, really— except as an obvious pose. Be as artificial as you are, I advise. There's a sort of sincerity in that, you know. And, after all, you must confess you like that better.

MILDRED [again affected and bored]. Yes, I suppose I do. Pardon me for my outburst. When a leopard complains of its spots, it must sound rather grotesque. [In a mocking tone.] Purr, little leopard. Purr, scratch, tear, kill, gorge yourself and be happy—only stay in the jungle where your spots are camouflage. In a cage they make you conspicuous.

AUNT. I don't know what you are talking about.

MILDRED. It would be rude to talk about anything to you. Let's just talk. [She looks at her wrist watch.] Well, thank goodness, it's about time for them to come for me. That ought to give me a new thrill, Aunt.

AUNT [affectedly troubled]. You don't mean to say you're really going? The dirt—the heat must be frightful——

MILDRED. Grandfather started as a puddler. I should have inherited an immunity to heat that would make a salamander shiver. It will be fun to put it to the test.

AUNT. But don't you have to have the captain's—or someone's—permission to visit the stokehole?

MILDRED [with a triumphant smile]. I have it—both his and the chief engineer's. Oh, they didn't want to at first, in spite of my social service credentials. They didn't seem a bit anxious that I should investigate how the other half lives and works on a ship. So I had to tell them that my father, the president of Nazareth Steel, chairman of the board of directors of this line, had told me it would be all right.

AUNT. He didn't.

MILDRED. How naïve age makes one! But I said he did, Aunt. I even said he had given me a letter to them—which I had lost. And they were afraid to take the chance that I might be lying. [Excitedly.] So it's ho! for the stokehole. The second engineer is to escort me. [Looking at her watch again.] It's time. And here he comes, I think. [The SECOND ENGINEER enters. He is a husky, fine-looking man of thirty-five or so. He stops before the two and tips his cap, visibly embarrassed and ill-at-ease.]

SECOND ENGINEER. Miss Douglas?

MILDRED. Yes. [Throwing off her rugs and getting to her feet.] Are we all ready to start?

SECOND ENGINEER. In just a second, ma'am. I'm waiting for the Fourth. He's coming along.

MILDRED [with a scornful smile]. You don't care to shoulder this responsibility alone, is that it?

SECOND ENGINEER [forcing a smile]. Two are better than one. [Disturbed by her eyes, glances out to sea—blurts out.] A fine day we're having.

MILDRED. Is it?

SECOND ENGINEER. A nice warm breeze——

MILDRED. It feels cold to me.

SECOND ENGINEER. But it's hot enough in the sun——

MILDRED. Not hot enough for me. I don't like Nature. I was never athletic.

SECOND ENGINEER [forcing a smile]. Well, you'll find it hot enough where you're going.

MILDRED. Do you mean hell?

SECOND ENGINEER [flabbergasted, decides to laugh]. Ho-ho! No, I mean the stokehole.

MILDRED. My grandfather was a puddler. He played with boiling steel.

SECOND ENGINEER [all at sea—uneasily]. Is that so? Hum, you'll excuse me, ma'am, but are you intending to wear that dress?

MILDRED. Why not?

SECOND ENGINEER. You'll likely rub against oil and dirt. It can't be helped.

MILDRED. It doesn't matter. I have lots of white dresses.

SECOND ENGINEER. I have an old coat you might throw over——

MILDRED. I have fifty dresses like this. I will throw this one into the sea when I come back. That ought to wash it clean, don't you think?

SECOND ENGINEER [doggedly]. There's ladders to climb down that are none too clean—and dark alleyways——

MILDRED. I will wear this very dress and none other.

SECOND ENGINEER. No offense meant. It's none of my business. I was only warning you——

MILDRED. Warning? That sounds thrilling.

SECOND ENGINEER [looking down the deck—with a sigh of relief]. There's the Fourth now. He's waiting for us. If you'll come——

MILDRED. Go on. I'll follow you. [He goes. MILDRED turns a mocking smile on her aunt.] An oaf—but a handsome, virile oaf.

AUNT [scornfully]. Poser!

MILDRED. Take care. He said there were dark alleyways——

AUNT [in the same tone]. Poser!

MILDRED [biting her lips angrily]. You are right. But would that my millions were not so anemically chaste!

AUNT. Yes, for a fresh pose I have no doubt you would drag the name of Douglas in the gutter!

MILDRED. From which it sprang. Good-by, Aunt. Don't pray too hard that I may fall into the fiery furnace.

AUNT. Poser!

MILDRED [viciously]. Old hag! [She slaps her aunt insultingly across the face and walks off, laughing gaily.]

AUNT [screams after her]. I said poser!

CURTAIN

SCENE THREE

[Scene: The stokehole. In the rear, the dimly outlined bulks of the furnaces and boilers. High overhead one hanging electric bulb sheds just enough light through the murky air laden with coal dust to pile up masses of shadows everywhere. A line of men, stripped to the waist, is before the furnace doors. They bend over, looking neither to right nor left, handling their shovels as if they were part of their bodies, with a strange, awkward, swinging rhythm. They use the shovels to throw open the furnace doors. Then from these fiery round holes in the black a flood of terrific light and heat pours full upon the men, who are outlined in silhouette in the crouching, inhuman attitudes of chained gorillas. The men shovel with a rhythmic motion, swinging as on a pivot from the coal which lies in heaps on the floor behind to hurl it into the flaming mouths before them. There is a tumult of noise—the brazen clang of the furnace doors as they are flung open or slammed shut, the grating, teeth-gritting grind of steel against steel, of crunching coal. This clash of sounds stuns one's ears with its rending dissonance. But there is order in it, rhythm, a mechanical regulated recurrence, a tempo. And rising above all, making the air hum with the quiver of liberated energy, the roar of leaping flames in the furnaces, the monotonous throbbing beat of the engines.

As the curtain rises, the furnace doors are shut. The men are taking a breathing spell. One or two are arranging the coal behind them, pulling it into more accessible heaps. The others can be dimly made out leaning on their shovels in relaxed attitudes of exhaustion.]

PADDY [from somewhere in the line—plaintively]. Yerra, will this divil's own watch nivir end? Me back is broke. I'm destroyed entirely.

YANK [from the center of the line—with exuberant scorn]. Aw, yuh make me sick! Lie down and croak, why don't yuh? Always beefin', dat's you? Say, dis is a cinch! Dis was made for me! It's my meat, get me! [A whistle is blown—a thin, shrill note from somewhere overhead in the darkness. YANK curses without resentment.] Dere's de damn engineer crackin' de whip. He tinks we're loafin'.

PADDY [vindictively]. God stiffen him!

YANK [in an exultant tone of command]. Come on, youse guys! Git into de game! She's gittin' hungry! Pile some grub in her. Trow it into her belly. Come on now, all of youse! Open her up! [At this last all the men, who have followed his movements of getting into position, throw open their furnace doors with a deafening clang. The fiery light floods over their shoulders as they bend round for the coal. Rivulets of sooty sweat have traced maps on their backs. The enlarged muscles form bunches of high light and shadow.]

YANK [chanting a count as he shovels without seeming effort]. One—two—tree—— [His voice rising exultantly in the joy of battle.] Dat's de stuff! Let her have it! All togedder now! Sling it into her! Let her ride! Shoot de piece now! Call de toin on her! Drive her into it! Feel her move! Watch her smoke! Speed, dat's her middle name! Give her coal, youse guys! Coal, dat's her booze! Drink it up, baby! Let's see yuh sprint! Dig in and gain a lap. Dere she go-o-es [This last in the chanting formula of the gallery gods at the six-day bike race. He slams his furnace door shut. The others do likewise with as much unison as their wearied bodies will permit. The effect is

of one fiery eye after another being blotted out with a series of accompanying bangs.]

PADDY [groaning]. Me back is broke. I'm bate out—bate—— [There is a pause. Then the inexorable whistle sounds again from the dim regions above the electric light. There is a growl of cursing rage from all sides.]

YANK [shaking his fist upward—contemptuously]. Take it easy dere, you! Who d'yuh tinks runnin' dis game, me or you? When I git ready, we move. Not before! When I git ready, get me!

VOICES [approvingly]. That's the stuff!
Yank tal him, py golly;
Yank ain't afeerd.
Goot poy, Yank!
Give him hell!
Tell 'im 'e's a bloody swine!
Bloody slave-driver!

YANK [contemptuously]. He ain't got no noive. He's yellow, get me? All de engineers is yellow. Dey got streaks a mile wide. Aw, to hell with him! Let's move, youse guys. We had a rest. Come on, she needs it! Give her pep! It ain't for him. Him and his whistle, dey don't belong. But we belong, see! We gotter feed de baby! Come on! [He turns and flings his furnace door open. They all follow his lead. At this instant the SECOND and FOURTH ENGINEERS enter from the darkness on the left with MILDRED between them. She starts, turns paler, her pose is crumbling, she shivers with fright in spite of the blazing heat, but forces herself to leave the ENGINEERS and take a few steps near the men. She is right behind YANK. All this happens quickly while the men have their backs turned.]

YANK. Come on, youse guys! [He is turning to get coal when the whistle sounds again in a peremptory, irritating note. This drives YANK into a sudden fury. While the other men have turned full around and stopped dumbfounded by the spectacle of MILDRED standing there in her white dress, YANK does not turn far enough to see her. Besides, his head is thrown back, he blinks upward through the murk trying to find the owner of the whistle, he brandishes his shovel murderously over his head in one hand, pounding on his chest, gorilla-like, with the other, shouting.] Toin off dat whistle!

Come down outa dere, yuh yellow, brass-buttoned, Belfast bum, yuh! Come down and I'll knock yer brains out! Yuh lousy, stinkin', yellow mut of a Catholic-moiderin' bastard! Come down and I'll moider yuh! Pullin' dat whistle on me, huh? I'll show yuh! I'll crash yer skull in! I'll drive yer teet' down yer troat! I'll slam yer nose trou de back of yer head! I'll cut yer guts out for a nickel, yuh lousy boob, yuh dirty, crummy, muck-eatin' son of a—— [*Suddenly he becomes conscious of all the other men staring at something directly behind his back. He whirls defensively with a snarling, murderous growl, crouching to spring, his lips drawn back over his teeth, his small eyes gleaming ferociously. He sees* MILDRED, *like a white apparition in the full light from the open furnace doors. He glares into her eyes, turned to stone. As for her, during his speech she has listened, paralyzed with horror, terror, her whole personality crushed, beaten in, collapsed, by the terrific impact of this unknown, abysmal brutality, naked and shameless. As she looks at his gorilla face, as his eyes bore into hers, she utters a low, choking cry and shrinks away from him, putting both hands up before her eyes to shut out the sight of his face, to protect her own. This startles* YANK *to a reaction. His mouth falls open, his eyes grow bewildered.*]

MILDRED [*about to faint—to the* ENGINEERS, *who now have her one by each arm—whimperingly*]. Take me away! Oh, the filthy beast! [*She faints. They carry her quickly back, disappearing in the darkness at the left, rear. An iron door clangs shut. Rage and bewildered fury rush back on* YANK. *He feels himself insulted in some unknown fashion in the very heart of his pride. He roars.*] God damn yuh! [*And hurls his shovel after them at the door which has just closed. It hits the steel bulkhead with a clang and falls clattering on the steel floor. From overhead the whistle sounds again in a long, angry, insistent command.*]

CURTAIN

SCENE FOUR

[*Scene: The firemen's forecastle.* YANK'S *watch has just come off duty and had din-*

ner. *Their faces and bodies shine from a soap and water scrubbing but around their eyes, where a hasty dousing does not touch, the coal dust sticks like black make-up, giving them a queer, sinister expression.* YANK *has not washed either face or body. He stands out in contrast to them, a blackened, brooding figure. He is seated forward on a bench in the exact attitude of Rodin's "The Thinker." The others, most of them smoking pipes, are staring at* YANK *half-apprehensively, as if fearing an outburst; half-amusedly, as if they saw a joke somewhere that tickled them.*]

VOICES. He ain't ate nothin'.
Py golly, a fallar gat to gat grub in him.
Divil a lie.
Yank feeda da fire, no feeda da face.
Ha-ha.
He ain't even washed hisself.
He's forgot.
Hey, Yank, you forgot to wash.
YANK [*sullenly*]. Forgot nothin'! To hell wit washin'.
VOICES. It'll stick to you.
It'll get under your skin.
Give yer the bleedin' itch, that's wot.
It makes spots on you—like a leopard.
Like a piebald nigger, you mean.
Better wash up, Yank.
You sleep better.
Wash up, Yank.
Wash up! Wash up!
YANK [*resentfully*]. Aw say, youse guys. Lemme alone. Can't youse see I'm tryin' to tink?
ALL [*repeating the word after him as one with cynical mockery*]. Think! [*The word has a brazen, metallic quality as if their throats were phonograph horns. It is followed by a chorus of hard, barking laughter.*]
YANK [*springing to his feet and glaring at them belligerently*]. Yes, tink! Tink, dat's what I said! What about it? [*They are silent, puzzled by his sudden resentment at what used to be one of his jokes.* YANK *sits down again in the same attitude of "The Thinker."*]
VOICES. Leave him alone.
He's got a grouch on.
Why wouldn't he?
PADDY [*with a wink at the others*]. Sure I know what's the matther. 'Tis aisy to see. He's fallen in love, I'm telling you.

ALL [repeating the word after him as one with cynical mockery]. Love! [The word has a brazen, metallic quality as if their throats were phonograph horns. It is followed by a chorus of hard, barking laughter.]

YANK [with a contemptuous snort]. Love, hell! Hate, dat's what. I've fallen in hate, get me?

PADDY [philosophically]. 'Twould take a wise man to tell one from the other. [With a bitter, ironical scorn, increasing as he goes on.] But I'm telling you it's love that's in it. Sure what else but love for us poor bastes in the stokehole would be bringing a fine lady, dressed like a white quane, down a mile of ladders and steps to be havin' a look at us? [A growl of anger goes up from all sides.]

LONG [jumping on a bench—hectically]. Hinsultin' us! Hinsultin' us, the bloody cow! And them bloody engineers! What right 'as they got to be exhibitin' us 's if we was bleedin' monkeys in a menagerie? Did we sign for hinsults to our dignity as 'onest workers? Is that in the ship's articles? You kin bloody well bet it ain't! But I knows why they done it. I arsked a deck steward 'o she was and 'e told me. 'Er old man's a bleedin' millionaire, a bloody Capitalist! 'E's got enuf bloody gold to sink this bleedin' ship! 'E makes arf the bloody steel in the world! 'E owns this bloody boat! And you and me, Comrades, we're 'is slaves! And the skipper and mates and engineers, they're 'is slaves! And she's 'is bloody daughter and we're all 'er slaves, too! And she gives 'er orders as 'ow she wants to see the bloody animals below decks and down they takes 'er! [There is a roar of rage from all sides.]

YANK [blinking at him bewilderingly]. Say! Wait a moment! Is all dat straight goods?

LONG. Straight as string! The bleedin' steward as waits on 'em, 'e told me about 'er. And what're we goin' ter do, I arsks yer? 'Ave we got ter swaller 'er hinsults like dogs? It ain't in the ship's article. I tell yer we got a case. We kin go to law——

YANK [with abysmal contempt]. Hell! Law!

ALL [repeating the word after him as one with cynical mockery]. Law! [The word has a brazen metallic quality as if their throats were phonograph horns. It is followed by a chorus of hard, barking laughter.]

LONG [feeling the ground slipping from under his feet—desperately]. As voters and citizens we kin force the bloody governments——

YANK [with abysmal contempt]. Hell! Governments!

ALL [repeating the word after him as one with cynical mockery]. Governments! [The word has a brazen metallic quality as if their throats were phonograph horns. It is followed by a chorus of hard, barking laughter.]

LONG [hysterically]. We're free and equal in the sight of God——

YANK [with abysmal contempt]. Hell! God!

ALL [repeating the word after him as one with cynical mockery]. God! [The word has a brazen metallic quality as if their throats were phonograph horns. It is followed by a chorus of hard, barking laughter.]

YANK [witheringly]. Aw, join de Salvation Army!

ALL. Sit down! Shut up! Damn fool! Sea-lawyer! [LONG slinks back out of sight.]

PADDY [continuing the trend of his thoughts as if he had never been interrupted—bitterly]. And there she was standing behind us, and the Second pointing at us like a man you'd hear in a circus would be saying: In this cage is a queerer kind of baboon than ever you'd find in darkest Africy. We roast them in their own sweat—and be damned if you won't hear some of thim saying they like it! [He glances scornfully at YANK.]

YANK [with a bewildered uncertain growl]. Aw!

PADDY. And there was Yank roarin' curses and turning round wid his shovel to brain her—and she looked at him, and him at her——

YANK [slowly]. She was all white. I tought she was a ghost. Sure.

PADDY [with heavy, biting sarcasm]. 'Twas love at first sight, divil a doubt of it! If you'd seen the endearin' look on her pale mug when she shriveled away with her hands over her eyes to shut out the sight of him! Sure, 'twas as if she'd seen a great hairy ape escaped from the Zoo!

YANK [*stung—with a growl of rage*]. Aw!

PADDY. And the loving way Yank heaved his shovel at the skull of her, only she was out the door! [*A grin breaking over his face.*] 'Twas touching, I'm telling you! It put the touch of home, swate home in the stokehole. [*There is a roar of laughter from all.*]

YANK [*glaring at* PADDY *menacingly*]. Aw, choke dat off, see!

PADDY [*not heeding him—to the others*]. And her grabbin' at the Second's arm for protection. [*With a grotesque imitation of a woman's voice.*] Kiss me, Engineer dear, for it's dark down here and me old man's in Wall Street making money! Hug me tight, darlin', for I'm afeerd in the dark and me mother's on deck makin' eyes at the skipper! [*Another roar of laughter.*]

YANK [*threateningly*]. Say! What yuh tryin' to do, kid me, yuh old Harp?

PADDY. Divil a bit! Ain't I wishin' myself you'd brained her?

YANK [*fiercely*]. I'll brain her! I'll brain her yet, wait 'n' see! [*Coming over to* PADDY *slowly.*] Say, is dat what she called me—a hairy ape?

PADDY. She looked it at you if she didn't say the word itself.

YANK [*grinning horribly*]. Hairy ape, huh? Sure! Dat's de way she looked at me, aw right. Hairy ape! So dat's me, huh? [*Bursting into rage—as if she were still in front of him.*] Yuh skinny tart! Yuh white-faced bum, yuh! I'll show yuh who's a ape! [*Turning to the others, bewilderment seizing him again.*] Say, youse guys. I was bawlin' him out for pullin' de whistle on us. You heard me. And den I seen youse lookin' at somep'n and I tought he'd sneaked down to come up in back of me, and I hopped round to knock him dead wit de shovel. And dere she was wit de light on her! Christ, yuh coulda pushed me over with a finger! I was scared, get me? Sure! I tought she was a ghost, see? She was all in white like dey wrap around stiffs. You seen her. Kin yuh blame me? She didn't belong, dat's what. And den when I come to and seen it was a real skoit and seen de way she was lookin' at me—like Paddy said— Christ, I was sore, get me? I don't stand for dat stuff from nobody. And I flung de

shovel—on'y she'd beat it. [*Furiously.*] I wished it'd banged her! I wished it'd knocked her block off!

LONG. And be 'anged for murder or 'lectrocuted? She ain't bleedin' well worth it.

YANK. I don't give a damn what! I'd be square wit her, wouldn't I? Tink I wanter let her put somep'n over on me? Tink I'm goin' to let her git away wit dat stuff? Yuh don't know me! No one ain't never put nothin' over on me and got away wit it, see!—not dat kind of stuff— no guy and no skoit neither! I'll fix her! Maybe she'll come down again——

VOICE. No chance, Yank. You scared her out of a year's growth.

YANK. I scared her? Why de hell should I scare her? Who de hell is she? Ain't she de same as me? Hairy ape, huh? [*With his old confident bravado.*] I'll show her I'm better'n her, if she on'y knew it. I belong and she don't, see! I move and she's dead! Twenty-five knots a hour, dat's me! Dat carries her but I make dat. She's only baggage. Sure! [*Again bewilderedly.*] But, Christ, she was funny lookin'! Did yuh pipe her hands? White and skinny. Yuh could see de bones through 'em. And her mush, dat was dead white, too. And her eyes, dey was like dey'd seen a ghost. Me, dat was! Sure! Hairy ape! Ghost, huh? Look at dat arm! [*He extends his right arm, swelling out the great muscles.*] I coulda took her wit dat, wit' just my little finger even, and broke her in two. [*Again bewilderedly.*] Say, who is dat skoit, huh? What is she? What's she come from? Who made her? Who give her de noive to look at me like dat? Dis ting's got my goat right. I don't get her. She's new to me. What does a skoit like her mean, huh? She don't belong, get me! I can't see her. [*With growing anger.*] But one ting I'm wise to, aw right, aw right! Youse all kin bet your shoits I'll git even wit her. I'll show her if she tinks she— She grinds de organ and I'm on de string, huh? I'll fix her! Let her come down again and I'll fling her in de furnace! She'll move den! She won't shiver at nothin', den! Speed, dat'll be her! She'll belong den! [*He grins horribly.*]

PADDY. She'll never come. She's had her belly-full, I'm telling you. She'll be in bed now, I'm thinking, wid ten doctors and nurses feedin' her salts to clean the fear out of her.

YANK [enraged]. Yuh tink I made her sick, too, do yuh? Just lookin' at me, huh? Hairy ape, huh? [In a frenzy of rage.] I'll fix her! I'll tell her where to git off! She'll git down on her knees and take it back or I'll bust de face offen her! [Shaking one fist upward and beating on his chest with the other.] I'll find yuh! I'm comin', d'yuh hear? I'll fix yuh, God damn yuh! [He makes a rush for the door.]

VOICES. Stop him!
He'll get shot!
He'll murder her!
Trip him up!
Hold him!
He's gone crazy!
Gott, he's strong!
Hold him down!
Look out for a kick!
Pin his arms!

[They have all piled on him and, after a fierce struggle, by sheer weight of numbers have borne him to the floor just inside the door.]

PADDY [who has remained detached]. Kape him down till he's cooled off. [Scornfully.] Yerra, Yank, you're a great fool. Is it payin' attention at all you are to the like of that skinny sow without one drop of rale blood in her?

YANK [frenziedly, from the bottom of the heap]. She done me doit! She done me doit, didn't she? I'll git square wit her! I'll get her some way! Git offen me, youse guys! Lemme up! I'll show her who's a ape!

CURTAIN

SCENE FIVE

[Scene: Three weeks later. A corner of Fifth Avenue in the Fifties on a fine Sunday morning. A general atmosphere of clean well-tidied, wide street; a flood of mellow, tempered sunshine; gentle, genteel breezes. In the rear, the show windows of two shops, a jewelry establishment on the corner, a furrier's next to it. Here the adornments of extreme wealth are tantalizingly displayed. The jeweler's window is gaudy with glittering diamonds, emeralds, rubies, pearls, etc., fashioned in ornate tiaras, crowns, necklaces, collars, etc. From each piece hangs an enormous tag from which a dollar sign and numerals in intermittent electric lights wink out the incredible prices. The same in the furrier's. Rich furs of all varieties hang there bathed in a downpour of artificial light. The general effect is of a background of magnificence cheapened and made grotesque by commercialism, a background in tawdry disharmony with the clear light and sunshine on the street itself.

Up the side street YANK and LONG come swaggering. LONG is dressed in shore clothes, wears a black Windsor tie, cloth cap. YANK is in his dirty dungarees. A fireman's cap with black peak is cocked defiantly on the side of his head. He has not shaved for days and around his fierce, resentful eyes—as around those of LONG to a lesser degree—the black smudge of coal dust still sticks like make-up. They hesitate and stand together at the corner, swaggering, looking about them with a forced, defiant contempt.]

LONG [indicating it all with an oratorical gesture]. Well, 'ere we are. Fif' Avenoo. This 'ere's their bleedin' private lane, as yer might say. [Bitterly.] We're trespassers 'ere. Proletarians keep orf the grass!

YANK [dully]. I don't see no grass, yuh boob. [Staring at the sidewalk.] Clean, ain't it? Yuh could eat a fried egg offen it. The white wings got some job sweepin' dis up. [Looking up and down the avenue—surlily.] Where's all de white-collar stiffs yuh said was here—and de skoits—her kind?

LONG. In church, blarst 'em! Arskin' Jesus to give 'em more money.

YANK. Choich, huh? I useter go to choich onct—sure—when I was a kid. Me old man and woman, dey made me. Dey never went demselves, dough. Always got too big a head on Sunday mornin', dat was dem. [With a grin.] Dey was scrappers for fair, bot' of dem. On Satiday nights when dey bot' got a skinful dey could put up a bout oughter been staged at de Garden. When dey got trough dere wasn't a chair or table wit a leg under it. Or else dey bot' jumped on me for somep'n. Dat was where I loined to take punishment. [With a grin and a swagger.] I'm a chip offen de old block, get me?

LONG. Did yer old man follow the sea?

YANK. Naw. Worked along shore. I runned away when me old lady croaked wit de tremens. I helped at truckin' and in de market. Den I shipped in de stokehole. Sure. Dat belongs. De rest was nothin'. [Looking around him.] I ain't never seen dis before. De Brooklyn waterfront, dat was where I was dragged up. [Taking a deep breath.] Dis ain't so bad at dat, huh?

LONG. Not bad? Well, we pays for it wiv our bloody sweat, if yer wants to know!

YANK [with sudden angry disgust]. Aw, hell! I don't see no one, see—like her. All dis gives me a pain. It don't belong. Say, ain't dere a back room around dis dump? Let's go shoot a ball. All dis is too clean and quiet and dolled-up, get me? It gives me a pain.

LONG. Wait and yer'll bloody well see——

YANK. I don't wait for no one. I keep on de move. Say, what yuh drag me up here for, anyway? Tryin' to kid me, yuh simp, yuh?

LONG. Yer wants to get back at 'er, don't yer? That's what yer been sayin' every bloomin' hour since she hinsulted yer.

YANK [vehemently]. Sure ting I do! Didn't I try to get even wit her in Southampton? Didn't I sneak on de dock and wait for her by de gangplank? I was goin' to spit in her pale mug, see! Sure, right in her pop-eyes! Dat woulda made me even, see? But no chanct. Dere was a whole army of plainclothes bulls around. Dey spotted me and gimme de bum's rush. I never seen her. But I'll git square wit her yet, you watch! [Furiously.] De lousy tart! She tinks she kin get away with moider—but not wit me! I'll fix her! I'll tink of a way!

LONG [as disgusted as he dares to be]. Ain't that why I brought yer up 'ere—to show yer? Yer been lookin, at this 'ere 'ole affair wrong. Yer been actin' an' talkin' 's if it was all a bleedin' personal matter between yer and that bloody cow. I wants to convince yer she was on'y a representative of 'er clarss. I wants to awaken yer bloody clarss consciousness. Then yer'll see it's 'er clarss you've got to fight, not 'er alone. There's a 'ole mob of 'em like 'er, Gawd blind 'em!

YANK [spitting on his hands—belligerently]. De more de merrier when I gits started. Bring on de gang!

LONG. Yer'll see 'em in arf a mo', when that church lets out. [He turns and sees the window display in the two stores for the first time.] Blimey! Look at that, will yer? [They both walk back and stand looking in the jeweler's. LONG flies into a fury.] Just look at this 'ere bloomin' mess! Just look at it! Look at the bleedin' prices on 'em—more'n our 'ole bloody stokehole makes in ten voyages sweatin' in 'ell! And they—'er and 'er bloody clarss—buys 'em for toys to dangle on 'em! One of these 'ere would buy scoff for a starvin' family for a year!

YANK. Aw, cut de sob stuff! T' hell wit de starvin' family! Yuh'll be passin' de hat to me next. [With naïve admiration.] Say, dem tings is pretty, huh? Bet yuh dey'd hock for a piece of change aw right. [Then turning away, bored.] But, aw hell, what good are dey? Let 'er have 'em. Dey don't belong no more'n she does. [With a gesture of sweeping the jeweler's into oblivion.] All dat don't count, get me?

LONG [who has moved to the furrier's—indignantly]. And I s'pose this 'ere don't count neither—skins of poor, 'armless animals slaughtered so as 'er and 'ers can keep their bleedin' noses warm!

YANK [who has been staring at something inside—with queer excitement]. Take a slant at dat! Give it de once-over! Monkey fur—two t'ousand bucks! [Bewilderedly.] Is dat straight goods—monkey fur? What de hell——?

LONG [bitterly]. It's straight enuf. [With grim humor.] They wouldn't bloody well pay that for a 'airy ape's skin —no, nor for the 'ole livin' ape with all 'is 'ead, and body, and soul thrown in!

YANK [clenching his fists, his face growing pale with rage as if the skin in the window were a personal insult]. Trowin' it up in my face! Christ! I'll fix her!

LONG [excitedly]. Church is out. 'Ere they come, the bleedin' swine. [After a glance at YANK's lowering face—uneasily.] Easy goes, Comrade. Keep yer bloomin' temper. Remember force defeats itself. It ain't our weapon. We must impress our demands through peaceful means—the votes of the on-marching proletarians of the bloody world!

YANK [with abysmal contempt]. Votes hell! Votes is a joke, see. Votes for women! Let dem do it!

LONG [still more uneasily]. Calm, now. Treat 'em wiv the proper contempt. Observe the bleedin' parasites but 'old yer 'orses.

YANK [angrily]. Git away from me! Yuh're yellow, dat's what. Force, dat's me! De punch, dat's me every time, see! [The crowd from church enter from the right, sauntering slowly and affectedly, their heads held stiffly up, looking neither to right nor left, talking in toneless simpering voices. The women are rouged, calcimined, dyed, overdressed to the nth degree. The men are in Prince Alberts, high hats, spats, canes, etc. A procession of gaudy marionettes, yet with something of the relentless horror of Frankenstein monsters in their detached, mechanical unawareness.]

VOICES. Dear Doctor Caiaphas! He is so sincere!

What was the sermon? I dozed off.

About the radicals, my dear—and the false doctrines that are being preached.

We must organize a hundred per cent American bazaar.

And let everyone contribute one one-hundredth per cent of their income tax.

What an original idea!

We can devote the proceeds to rehabilitating the veil of the temple.

But that has been done so many times.

YANK [glaring from one to the other of them—with an insulting snort of scorn]. Huh! Huh! [Without seeming to see him, they make wide detours to avoid the spot where he stands in the middle of the sidewalk.]

LONG [frightenedly]. Keep yer bloomin' mouth shut, I tells yer.

YANK [viciously]. G'wan! Tell it to Sweeney! [He swaggers away and deliberately lurches into a top-hatted gentleman, then glares at him pugnaciously.] Say, who d'yuh tink you're bumpin'? Tink yuh own de oith?

GENTLEMAN [coldly and affectedly]. I beg your pardon. [He has not looked at YANK and passes on without a glance, leaving him bewildered.]

LONG [rushing up and grabbing YANK's arm]. 'Ere! Come away! This wasn't what I meant. Yer'll 'ave the bloody coppers down on us.

YANK [savagely—giving him a push that sends him sprawling]. G'wan!

LONG [picks himself up—hysterically]. I'll pop orf then. This ain't what I meant. And whatever 'appens, yer can't blame me. [He slinks off left.]

YANK. T' hell wit youse! [He approaches a lady—with a vicious grin and a smirking wink.] Hello, Kiddo. How's every little ting? Got anyting on for tonight? I know an old boiler down to de docks we kin crawl into. [The lady stalks by without a look, without a change of pace. YANK turns to others—insultingly.] Holy smokes, what a mug! Go hide yuhself before de horses shy at yuh. Gee, pipe de heine on dat one! Say, youse, yuh look like de stoin of a ferryboat. Paint and powder! All dolled up to kill! Yuh look like stiffs laid out for de boneyard! Aw, g'wan, de lot of youse! Yuh give me de eye-ache. Yuh don't belong, get me! Look at me, why don't youse dare? I belong, dat's me! [Pointing to a skyscraper across the street which is in process of construction—with bravado.] See dat building goin' up dere? See de steel work? Steel, dat's me! Youse guys live on it and tink yuh're somep'n. But I'm in it, see! I'm de hoistin' engine dat makes it go up! I'm it—de inside and bottom of it! Sure! I'm steel and steam and smoke and de rest of it! It moves—speed—twenty-five stories up—and me at de top and bottom—movin'! Youse simps don't move. Yuh're on'y dolls I winds up to see 'm spin. Yuh're de garbage, get me—de leavins—de ashes we dump over de side! Now, what 'a' yuh gotta say? [But as they seem neither to see nor hear him, he flies into a fury.] Bums! Pigs! Tarts! Bitches! [He turns in a rage on the men, bumping viciously into them but not jarring them the least bit. Rather it is he who recoils after each collision. He keeps growling.] Git off de oith! G'wan, yuh bum! Look where yuh're goin', can't yuh? Git outa here! Fight, why don't yuh? Put up yer mits! Don't be a dog! Fight or I'll knock yuh dead! [But, without seeming to see him, they all answer with mechanical affected politeness.] I beg your pardon. [Then at a cry from one of the women, they all scurry to the furrier's window.]

THE WOMAN [ecstatically, with a gasp of delight]. Monkey fur! [The whole crowd of men and women chorus after her in the same tone of affected delight.] Monkey fur!

YANK [with a jerk of his head back on his shoulders, as if he had received a punch full in the face—raging]. I see yuh, all in white! I see yuh, yuh white-faced tart, yuh! Hairy ape, huh? I'll hairy ape yuh! [He bends down and grips at the street curbing as if to pluck it out and hurl it. Foiled in this, snarling with passion, he leaps to the lamp-post on the corner and tries to pull it up for a club. Just at that moment a bus is heard rumbling up. A fat, high-hatted, spatted gentleman runs out from the side street. He calls out plaintively.] Bus! Bus! Stop there! [And runs full tilt into the bending, straining YANK, who is bowled off his balance.]

YANK [seeing a fight—with a roar of joy as he springs to his feet.] At last! Bus, huh! I'll bust yuh! [He lets drive a terrific swing, his fist landing full on the fat gentleman's face. But the gentleman stands unmoved as if nothing had happened.]

GENTLEMAN. I beg your pardon. [Then irritably.] You have made me lose my bus. [He claps his hands and begins to scream.] Officer! Officer! [Many police whistles shrill out on the instant and a whole platoon of policemen rush in on YANK from all sides. He tries to fight but is clubbed to the pavement and fallen upon. The crowd at the window have not moved or noticed this disturbance. The clanging gong of the patrol wagon approaches with a clamoring din.]

CURTAIN

SCENE SIX

[Scene: Night of the following day. A row of cells in the prison on Blackwell's Island. The cells extend back diagonally from right front to left rear. They do not stop, but disappear in the dark background as if they ran on, numberless, into infinity. One electric bulb from the low ceiling of the narrow corridor sheds its light through the heavy steel bars of the cell at the extreme front and reveals part of the interior. YANK can be seen within, crouched on the edge of his cot in the attitude of Rodin's "The Thinker." His face is spotted with black and blue bruises. A blood-stained bandage is wrapped around his head.]

YANK [suddenly starting as if awakening from a dream, reaches out and shakes the bars—aloud to himself, wonderingly]. Steel. Dis is de Zoo, huh? [A burst of hard, barking laughing comes from the unseen occupants of the cells, runs back down the tier, and abruptly ceases.]

VOICES [mockingly]. The Zoo? That's a new name for this coop—a damn good name!

Steel, eh? You said a mouthful. This is the old iron house.

Who is that boob talkin'?

He's the bloke they brung in out of his head. The bulls had beat him up fierce.

YANK [dully]. I musta been dreamin'. I tought I was in a cage at de Zoo—but de apes don't talk, do dey?

VOICES [with mocking laughter]. You're in a cage aw right.

A coop!

A pen!

A sty!

A kennel! [Hard laughter—a pause.]

Say, guy! Who are you? No, never mind lying. What are you?

Yes, tell us your sad story. What's your game?

What did they jug yuh for?

YANK [dully]. I was a fireman—stokin' on de liners. [Then with sudden rage, rattling his cell bars.] I'm a hairy ape, get me? And I'll bust youse all in de jaw if yuh don't lay off kiddin' me.

VOICES. Huh! You're a hard boiled duck, ain't you!

When you spit, it bounces! [Laughter.]

Aw, can it. He's a regular guy. Ain't you?

What did he say he was—a ape?

YANK [defiantly]. Sure ting! Ain't dat what youse all are—apes? [A silence.

Then a furious rattling of bars from down the corridor.]

A VOICE [*thick with rage*]. I'll show yuh who's a ape, yuh bum!

VOICES. Ssshh! Nix!

Can de noise!

Piano!

You'll have the guard down on us!

YANK [*scornfully*]. De guard? Yuh mean de keeper, don't yuh? [*Angry exclamations from all the cells.*]

VOICE [*placatingly*]. Aw, don't pay no attention to him. He's off his nut from the beatin'-up he got. Say, you guy! We're waitin' to hear what they landed you for—or ain't yuh tellin'?

YANK. Sure, I'll tell youse. Sure! Why de hell not? On'y—youse won't get me. Nobody gets me but me, see? I started to tell de Judge and all he says was: "Toity days to tink it over." Tink it over! Christ, dat's all I been doin' for weeks! [*After a pause.*] I was tryin' to git even wit someone, see?—someone dat done me doit.

VOICES [*cynically*]. De old stuff, I bet. Your goil, huh?

Give yuh the double-cross, huh?

That's them every time!

Did yuh beat up de odder guy?

YANK [*disgustedly*]. Aw, yuh're all wrong! Sure dere was a skoit in it—but not what youse mean, not dat old tripe. Dis was a new kind of skoit. She was dolled up all in white—in de stokehole. I tought she was a ghost. Sure. [*A pause.*]

VOICES [*whispering*]. Gee, he's still nutty.

Let him rave. It's fun listenin'.

YANK [*unheeding—groping in his thoughts*]. Her hands—dey was skinny and white like dey wasn't real but painted on somep'n. Dere was a million miles from me to her—twenty-five knots a hour. She was like some dead ting de cat brung in. Sure, dat's what. She didn't belong. She belonged in de window of a toy store, or on de top of a garbage can, see! Sure! [*He breaks out angrily.*] But would yuh believe it, she had de noive to do me doit. She lamped me like she was seein' somep'n broke loose from de menagerie. Christ, yuh'd oughter seen her eyes! [*He rattles the bars of his cell furiously.*] But I'll get back at her yet, you watch! And if I can't find her I'll take it out on de gang she runs wit. I'm wise to

where dey hangs out now. I'll show her who belongs! I'll show her who's in de move and who ain't. You watch my smoke!

VOICES [*serious and joking*]. Dat's de talkin'!

Take her for all she's got!

What was this dame, anyway? Who was she, eh?

YANK. I dunno. First cabin stiff. Her old man's a millionaire, dey says—name of Douglas.

VOICES. Douglas? That's the president of the Steel Trust, I bet.

Sure. I seen his mug in de papers.

He's filthy with dough.

VOICE. Hey, feller, take a tip from me. If you want to get back at that dame, you better join the Wobblies. You'll get some action then.

YANK. Wobblies? What de hell's dat?

VOICE. Ain't you ever heard of the I.W.W.?

YANK. Naw. What is it?

VOICE. A gang of blokes—a tough gang. I been readin' about 'em today in the paper. The guard give me the *Sunday Times*. There's a long spiel about 'em. It's from a speech made in the Senate by a guy named Senator Queen. [*He is in the cell next to YANK's. There is a rustling of paper.*] Wait'll I see if I got light enough and I'll read you. Listen. [*He reads.*] "There is a menace existing in this country today which threatens the vitals of our fair Republic—as foul a menace against the very life-blood of the American Eagle as was the foul conspiracy of Cataline against the eagles of ancient Rome!"

VOICE [*disgustedly*]. Aw, hell! Tell him to salt de tail of dat eagle!

VOICE [*reading*]. "I refer to that devil's brew of rascals, jailbirds, murderers and cutthroats who libel all honest working men by calling themselves the Industrial Workers of the World; but in the light of their nefarious plots, I call them the Industrious Wreckers of the World!"

YANK [*with vengeful satisfaction*]. Wreckers, dat's de right dope! Dat belongs! Me for dem!

VOICE. Ssshh! [*Reading.*] "This fiendish organization is a foul ulcer on the fair body of our Democracy——"

VOICE. Democracy, hell! Give him the boid, fellers—the raspberry! [*They do.*]

VOICE. Ssshh! [*Reading.*] "Like Cato I say to this Senate, the I.W.W. must be destroyed! For they represent an ever-present dagger pointed at the heart of the greatest nation the world has ever known, where all men are born free and equal, with equal opportunities to all, where the Founding Fathers have guaranteed to each one happiness, where Truth, Honor, Liberty, Justice, and the Brotherhood of Man are a religion absorbed with one's mother's milk, taught at our father's knee, sealed, signed, and stamped upon in the glorious Constitution of these United States!" [*A perfect storm of hisses, catcalls, boos, and hard laughter.*]

VOICES [*scornfully*]. Hurrah for de Fort' of July!
Pass de hat!
Liberty!
Justice!
Honor!
Opportunity!
Brotherhood!

ALL [*with abysmal scorn*]. Aw, hell!

VOICE. Give that Queen Senator guy the bark! All togedder now—one—two—tree—— [*A terrific chorus of barking and yapping.*]

GUARD [*from a distance*]. Quiet there, youse—or I'll git the hose. [*The noise subsides.*]

YANK [*with growling rage*]. I'd like to catch dat senator guy alone for a second. I'd loin him some trute!

VOICE. Ssshh! Here's where he gits down to cases on the Wobblies. [*Reads.*] "They plot with fire in one hand and dynamite in the other. They stop not before murder to gain their ends, nor at the outraging of defenseless womanhood. They would tear down society, put the lowest scum in the seats of the mighty, turn Almighty God's revealed plan for the world topsy-turvy, and make of our sweet and lovely civilization a shambles, a desolation where man, God's masterpiece, would soon degenerate back to the ape!"

VOICE [*to* YANK]. Hey, you guy. There's your ape stuff again.

YANK [*with a growl of fury*]. I got him. So dey blow up tings, do dey? Dey turn tings round, do dey? Hey, lend me dat paper, will yuh?

VOICE. Sure. Give it to him. On'y keep it to yourself, see. We don't wanter listen to no more of that slop.

VOICE. Here you are. Hide it under your mattress.

YANK [*reaching out*]. Tanks. I can't read much but I kin manage. [*He sits, the paper in the hand at his side, in the attitude of Rodin's "The Thinker." A pause. Several snores from down the corridor. Suddenly* YANK *jumps to his feet with a furious groan as if some appalling thought had crashed on him—bewilderedly.*] Sure—her old man—president of de Steel Trust—makes half de steel in de world—steel—where I tought I belonged—drivin' trou—movin'—in dat—to make her—and cage me in for her to spit on! Christ— [*He shakes the bars of his cell door till the whole tier trembles. Irritated, protesting exclamations from those awakened or trying to get to sleep.*] He made dis—dis cage! Steel! It don't belong, dat's what! Cages, cells, locks, bolts, bars—dat's what it means!—holdin' me down wit him at de top! But I'll drive trou! Fire, dat melts it! I'll be fire—under de heap—fire dat never goes out—hot as hell—breakin' out in de night—— [*While he has been saying this last he has shaken his cell door to a clanging accompaniment. As he comes to the "breakin' out" he seizes one bar with both hands and, putting his two feet up against the others so that his position is parallel to the floor like a monkey's, he gives a great wrench backward. The bar bends like a licorice stick under his tremendous strength. Just at this moment the* PRISON GUARD *rushes in, dragging a hose behind him.*]

GUARD [*angrily*]. I'll loin youse bums to wake me up! [*Sees* YANK.] Hello, it's you, huh? Got the D.Ts, hey? Well, I'll cure 'em. I'll drown your snakes for yuh! [*Noticing the bar.*] Hell, look at dat bar bended! On'y a bug is strong enough for dat!

YANK [*glaring at him*]. Or a hairy ape, yuh big yellow bum! Look out! Here I come! [*He grabs another bar.*]

GUARD [*scared now—yelling off left*]. Toin de hose on, Ben!—full pressure! And call de others—and a straitjacket! [*The curtain is falling. As it hides* YANK *from view, there is a splattering smash as the stream of water hits the steel of* YANK's *cell.*]

CURTAIN

SCENE SEVEN

[Scene: Nearly a month later. An I.W.W. local near the waterfront, showing the interior of a front room on the ground floor, and the street outside. Moonlight on the narrow street, buildings massed in black shadows. The interior of the room, which is general assembly room, office, and reading room, resembles some dingy settlement boys' club. A desk and high stool are in one corner. A table with papers, stacks of pamphlets, chairs about it, is at center. The whole is decidedly cheap, banal, commonplace and unmysterious as a room could well be. The SECRETARY is perched on the stool making entries in a large ledger. An eye shade casts his face into shadows. Eight or ten men, longshoremen, iron workers, and the like are grouped about the table. Two are playing checkers. One is writing a letter. Most of them are smoking pipes. A big signboard is on the wall at the rear, "Industrial Workers of the World—Local No. 57."]

[YANK comes down the street outside. He is dressed as in Scene 5. He moves cautiously, mysteriously. He comes to a point opposite the door, tiptoes softly up to it, listens, is impressed by the silence within, knocks carefully, as if he were guessing at the password to some secret rite. Listens. No answer. Knocks again a bit louder. No answer. Knocks impatiently, much louder.]

SECRETARY [turning around on his stool]. What the hell is that—someone knocking? [Shouts.] Come in, why don't you? [All the men in the room look up. YANK opens the door slowly, gingerly, as if afraid of an ambush. He looks around for secret doors, mystery, is taken aback by the commonplaceness of the room and the men in it, thinks he may have gotten in the wrong place, then sees the signboard on the wall and is reassured.]

YANK [blurts out]. Hello.

MEN [reservedly]. Hello.

YANK [more easily]. I tought I'd bumped into de wrong dump.

SECRETARY [scrutinizing him carefully]. Maybe you have. Are you a member?

YANK. Naw, not yet. Dat's what I come for—to join.

SECRETARY. That's easy. What's your job—longshore?

YANK. Naw. Fireman—stoker on de liners.

SECRETARY [with satisfaction]. Welcome to our city. Glad to know you people are waking up at last. We haven't got many members in your line.

YANK. Naw. Dey're all dead to de woild.

SECRETARY. Well, you can help to wake 'em. What's your name? I'll make out your card.

YANK [confused]. Name? Lemme tink.

SECRETARY [sharply]. Don't you know your own name?

YANK. Sure; but I been just Yank for so long—Bob, dat's it—Bob Smith.

SECRETARY [writing]. Robert Smith. [Fills out the rest of card.] Here you are. Cost you half a dollar.

YANK. Is dat all—four bits? Dat's easy. [Gives the SECRETARY the money.]

SECRETARY [throwing it in drawer]. Thanks. Well, make yourself at home. No introductions needed. There's literature on the table. Take some of those pamphlets with you to distribute aboard ship. They may bring results. Sow the seed, only go about it right. Don't get caught and fired. We got plenty out of work. What we need is men who can hold their jobs—and work for us at the same time.

YANK. Sure. [But he still stands, embarrassed and uneasy.]

SECRETARY [looking at him—curiously]. What did you knock for? Think we had a coon in uniform to open doors?

YANK. Naw. I thought it was locked—and dat yuh'd wanter give me the once-over trou a peep-hole or somep'n to see if I was right.

SECRETARY [alert and suspicious but with an easy laugh]. Think we were running a crap game? That door is never locked. What put that in your nut?

YANK [with a knowing grin, convinced that this is all camouflage, a part of the secrecy]. Dis burg is full of bulls, ain't it?

SECRETARY [sharply]. What have the cops got to do with us? We're breaking no laws.

YANK [with a knowing wink]. Sure. Youse wouldn't for woilds. Sure. I'm wise to dat.

SECRETARY. You seem to be wise to a lot of stuff none of us knows about.

YANK [with another wink]. Aw, dat's aw right, see. [Then made a bit resentful by the suspicious glances from all sides.] Aw, can it! Youse needn't put me trou de toid degree. Can't youse see I belong? Sure! I'm reg'lar. I'll stick, get me? I'll shoot de woiks for youse. Dat's why I wanted to join in.

SECRETARY [breezily, feeling him out]. That's the right spirit. Only are you sure you understand what you've joined? It's all plain and aboveboard; still, some guys get a wrong slant on us. [Sharply.] What's your notion of the purpose of the I.W.W.?

YANK. Aw, I know all about it.

SECRETARY [sarcastically]. Well, give us some of your valuable information.

YANK [cunningly]. I know enough not to speak outa my toin. [Then resentfully again.] Aw, say? I'm reg'lar. I'm wise to de game. I know yuh got to watch your step wit a stranger. For all youse know, I might be a plain-clothes dick, or somep'n, dat's what yuh're tinkin', huh? Aw, forget it! I belong, see? Ask any guy down to de docks if I don't.

SECRETARY. Who said you didn't?

YANK. After I'm 'nitiated, I'll show yuh.

SECRETARY [astounded]. Initiated? There's no initiation.

YANK [disappointed]. Ain't there no password—no grip nor nothin'?

SECRETARY. What'd you think this is —the Elks—or the Black Hand?

YANK. De Elks, hell! De Black Hand, dey're a lot of yellow backstickin' Ginces. Naw. Dis is a man's gang, ain't it?

SECRETARY. You said it! That's why we stand on our two feet in the open. We got no secrets.

YANK [surprised but admiringly]. Yuh mean to say yuh always run wide open —like dis?

SECRETARY. Exactly.

YANK. Den yuh sure got your noive wit youse!

SECRETARY [sharply]. Just what was it made you want to join us? Come out with that straight.

YANK. Yuh call me? Well, I got noive, too! Here's my hand. Yuh wanter blow tings up, don't yuh? Well, dat's me! I belong!

SECRETARY [with pretended carelessness]. You mean change the unequal conditions of society by legitimate direct action—or with dynamite?

YANK. Dynamite! Blow it offen de oith—steel—all de cages—all de factories, steamers, buildings, jails—de Steel Trust and all dat makes it go.

SECRETARY. So—that's your idea, eh? And did you have any special job in that line you wanted to propose to us? [He makes a sign to the men, who get up cautiously one by one and group behind YANK.]

YANK [boldly]. Sure, I'll come out wit it. I'll show youse I'm one of de gang. Dere's dat millionaire guy, Douglas——

SECRETARY. President of the Steel Trust, you mean? Do you want to assassinate him?

YANK. Naw, dat don't get yuh nothin', I mean blow up de factory, de woiks, where he makes de steel. Dat's what I'm after—to blow up de steel, knock all de steel in de woild up to de moon. Dat'll fix things! [Eagerly, with a touch of bravado.] I'll do it by me lonesome! I'll show yuh! Tell me where his woiks is, how to git there, all de dope. Gimme de stuff, de old butter—and watch me do de rest! Watch de smoke and see it move! I don't give a damn if dey nab me—long as it's done! I'll soive life for it—and give 'em de laugh! [Half to himself.] And I'll write her a letter and tell her de hairy ape done it. Dat'll square tings.

SECRETARY [stepping away from YANK]. Very interesting. [He gives a signal. The men, huskies all, throw themselves on YANK and before he knows it they have his legs and arms pinioned. But he is too flabbergasted to make a struggle, anyway. They feel him over for weapons.]

MAN. No gat, no knife. Shall we give him what's what and put the boots to him?

SECRETARY. No. He isn't worth the trouble we'd get into. He's too stupid. [He comes closer and laughs mockingly in YANK's face.] Ho-ho! By God, this is the biggest joke they've put up on us yet. Hey, you Joke! Who sent you—Burns or Pinkerton? No, by God, you're such a bonehead I'll bet you're in the Secret Service! Well, you dirty spy, you rotten agent provocator, you can go back and tell whatever skunk is paying you blood-money for betraying your brothers that he's wasting his coin. You couldn't catch a cold. And tell him that all he'll ever get on us, or ever has got, is just his own sneaking plots that he's framed up to put us in jail. We are what our manifesto says we are, neither more nor less—and we'll give him a copy of that any time he calls. And as for you—— [He glares scornfully at YANK, who is sunk in an oblivious stupor.] Oh, hell, what's the use of talking? You're a brainless ape.

YANK [aroused by the word to fierce but futile struggles.] What's dat, yuh Sheeny bum, yuh!

SECRETARY. Throw him out, boys. [In spite of his struggles, this is done with gusto and éclat. Propelled by several parting kicks, YANK lands sprawling in the middle of the narrow cobbled street. With a growl he starts to get up and storm the closed door, but stops bewildered by the confusion in his brain, pathetically impotent. He sits there, brooding, in as near to the attitude of Rodin's "Thinker" as he can get in his position.]

YANK [bitterly]. So dem boids don't tink I belong, neider. Aw, to hell wit 'em! Dey're in de wrong pew—de same old bull—soapboxes and Salvation Army —no guts! Cut out an hour offen de job a day and make me happy! Gimme a dollar more a day and make me happy! Tree square a day, and cauliflowers in de front yard—ekal rights—a woman and kids—a lousy vote—and I'm all fixed for Jesus, huh? Aw, hell! What does dat get yuh? Dis ting's in your inside, but it ain't your belly. Feedin' your face— sinkers and coffee—dat don't touch it. It's way down—at de bottom. Yuh can't grab it, and yuh can't stop it. It moves, and everything moves. It stops and de whole woild stops. Dat's me now—I don't tick, see?—I'm a busted Ingersoll,[1] dat's what. Steel was me, and I owned de woild. Now I ain't steel, and de woild owns me. Aw, hell! I can't see—it's all dark, get me? It's all wrong! [He turns a bitter mocking face up like an ape gibbering at the moon.] Say, youse up dere, Man in de Moon, yuh look so wise,

gimme de answer, huh? Slip me de in-side dope, de information right from de stable—where do I get off at, huh?

A POLICEMAN [who has come up the street in time to hear this last—with grim humor]. You'll get off at the station, you boob, if you don't get up out of that and keep movin'.

YANK [looking up at him—with a hard, bitter laugh]. Sure! Lock me up! Put me in a cage! Dat's de on'y answer yuh know. G'wan, lock me up!

POLICEMAN. What you been doin'?

YANK. Enuf to·gimme life for! I was born, see? Sure, dat's de charge. Write it in de blotter. I was born, get me!

POLICEMAN [jocosely]. God pity your old woman! [Then matter-of-fact.] But I've no time for kidding. You're soused. I'd run you in but it's too long a walk to the station. Come on now, get up, or I'll fan your ears with this club. Beat it now! [He hauls YANK to his feet.]

YANK [in a vague mocking tone]. Say, where do I go from here?

POLICEMAN [giving him a push—with a grin, indifferently]. Go to hell.

CURTAIN

SCENE EIGHT

[Scene: Twilight of the next day. The monkey house at the Zoo. One spot of clear gray light falls on the front of one cage so that the interior can be seen. The other cages are vague, shrouded in shadow from which chatterings pitched in a conversational tone can be heard. On the one cage a sign from which the word "gorilla" stands out. The gigantic animal himself is seen squatting on his haunches on a bench in much the same attitude as Rodin's "Thinker." YANK enters from the left. Immediately a chorus of angry chattering and screeching breaks out. The gorilla turns his eyes but makes no sound or move.]

YANK [with a hard, bitter laugh]. Welcome to your city, huh? Hail, hail, de gang's all here! [At the sound of his voice the chattering dies away into an

---

[1] A "dollar watch."

attentive silence. YANK walks up to the gorilla's cage and, leaning over the railing, stares in at its occupant, who stares back at him, silent and motionless. There is a pause of dead stillness. Then YANK begins to talk in a friendly confidential tone, half-mockingly, but with a deep undercurrent of sympathy.] Say, yuh're some hard-lookin' guy, ain't yuh? I seen lots of tough nuts dat de gang called gorillas, but yuh're de foist real one I ever seen. Some chest yuh got, and shoulders, and dem arms and mits! I bet yuh got a punch in eider fist dat'd knock 'em all silly! [This with genuine admiration. The gorilla, as if he understood, stands upright, swelling out his chest and pounding on it with his fist. YANK grins sympathetically.] Sure, I get yuh. Yuh challenge de whole woild, huh? Yuh got what I was sayin' even if yuh muffed de woids. [Then bitterness creeping in.] And why wouldn't yuh get me? Ain't we both members of de same club—de Hairy Apes? [They stare at each other— a pause—then YANK goes on slowly and bitterly.] So yuh're what she seen when she looked at me, de white-faced tart! I was you to her, get me? On'y outa de cage—broke out—free to moider her, see? Sure! Dat's what she tought. She wasn't wise dat I was in a cage, too— worser'n yours—sure—a damn sight— 'cause you got some chanct to bust loose —but me—— [He grows confused.] Aw, hell! It's all wrong, ain't it? [A pause.] I s'pose yuh wanter know what I'm doin' here, huh? I been warmin' a bench down to de Battery—ever since last night. Sure. I seen de sun come up. Dat was pretty, too—all red and pink and green. I was lookin' at de skyscrapers—steel—and all de ships comin' in, sailin' out, all over de oith—and dey was steel, too. De sun was warm, dey wasn't no clouds, and dere was a breeze blowin'. Sure, it was great stuff. I got it aw right—what Paddy said about dat bein' de right dope—on'y I couldn't get in it, see? I couldn't belong in dat. It was over my head. And I kept tinkin'—and den I beat it up here to see what youse was like. And I waited till dey was all gone to git yuh alone. Say, how d'yuh feel sittin' in dat pen all de time, havin' to stand for 'em comin' and starin' at yuh—de white-faced, skinny tarts and de boobs what marry 'em—

makin' fun of yuh, laughin' at yuh, gittin' scared of yuh—damn 'em! [He pounds on the rail with his fist. The gorilla rattles the bars of his cage and snarls. All the other monkeys set up an angry chattering in the darkness. YANK goes on excitedly.] Sure! Dat's de way it hits me, too. On'y yuh're lucky, see? Yuh don't belong wit 'em and yuh know it. But me, I belong wit 'em—but I don't, see? Dey don't belong wit me, dat's what. Get me? Tinkin' is hard—— [He passes one hand across his forehead with a painful gesture. The gorilla growls impatiently. YANK goes on gropingly.] It's dis way, what I'm drivin' at. Youse can sit and dope dream in de past, green woods, de jungle and de rest of it. Den yuh belong and dey don't. Den yuh kin laugh at 'em, see? Yuh're de champ of de woild. But me—I ain't got no past to tink in, nor nothin' dat's comin', on'y what's now— and dat don't belong. Sure, you're de best off! Yuh cant tink, can yuh? Yuh can't talk neider. But I kin make a bluff at talkin' and tinkin'—a'most git away wit it—a'most!—and dat's where de joker comes in. [He laughs.] I ain't on oith and I ain't in heaven, get me? I'm in de middle tryin' to separate 'em, takin' all de woist punches from bot' of 'em. Maybe dat's what dey call hell, huh? But you, yuh're at de bottom. You belong! Sure! Yuh're de on'y one in de woild dat does, yuh lucky stiff! [The gorilla growls proudly.] And dat's why dey gotter put yuh in a cage, see? [The gorilla roars angrily.] Sure! Yuh get me. It beats it when you try to tink it or talk it—it's way down—deep—behind—you 'n' me we feel it. Sure! Bot' members of dis club! [He laughs—then in a savage tone.] What de hell! T' hell wit it! A little action, dat's our meat! Dat belongs! Knock 'em down and keep bustin' 'em till dey croaks yuh wit a gat—wit steel! Sure! Are yuh game? Dey've looked at youse, ain't dey—in a cage? Wanter get even? Wanter wind up like a sport 'stead of croakin' slow in dere? [The gorilla roars an emphatic affirmative. YANK goes on with a sort of furious exaltation.] Sure! Yuh're reg'lar! Yuh'll stick to de finish! Me 'n' you, huh?—bot' members of this club! We'll put up one last star bout dat'll knock 'em offen deir seats! Dey'll have to make de cages stronger after we're trou! [*The gorilla is straining at his bars, growling, hopping from one foot to the other.* YANK *takes a jimmy from under his coat and forces the lock on the cage door. He throws this open.*] Pardon from de governor! Step out and shake hands! I'll take yuh for a walk down Fif' Avenoo. We'll knock 'em offen de oith and croak wit de band playin'. Come on, Brother. [*The gorilla scrambles gingerly out of his cage. Goes to* YANK *and stands looking at him.* YANK *keeps his mocking tone—holds out his hand.*] Shake—de secret grip of our order. [*Something, the tone of mockery, perhaps, suddenly enrages the animal. With a spring he wraps his huge arms around* YANK *in a murderous hug. There is a crackling snap of crushed ribs—a gasping cry, still mocking, from* YANK.] Hey, I didn't say kiss me! [*The gorilla lets the crushed body slip to the floor; stands over it uncertainly, considering; then picks it up, throws it in the cage, shuts the door, and shuffles off menacingly into the darkness at left. A great uproar of*

---

2 Stanislaus Zybszko, wrestling champion.

frightened chattering and whimpering comes from the other cages. Then YANK *moves, groaning, opening his eyes, and there is silence. He mutters painfully.*] Say—dey oughter match him—wit Zybszko.[2] He got me, aw right. I'm trou. Even him didn't tink I belonged. [*Then, with sudden passionate despair.*] Christ, where do I get off at? Where do I fit in? [*Checking himself as suddenly.*] Aw, what de hell! No squawkin', see! No quittin', get me! Croak with your boots on! [*He grabs hold of the bars of the cage and hauls himself painfully to his feet—looks around him bewilderedly—forces a mocking laugh.*] In de cage, huh? [*In the strident tones of a circus barker.*] Ladies and gents, step forward and take a slant at de one and only—[*His voice weakened.*]—one and original—Hairy Ape from de wilds of—— [*He slips in a heap on the floor and dies. The monkeys set up a chattering, whimpering wail. And, perhaps, the Hairy Ape at last belongs.*]

CURTAIN

Eugene O'Neill

A LETTER TO ARTHUR HOBSON QUINN

It's not in me to pose much as a "misunderstood one," but it does seem discouragingly (that is, if one lacked a sense of ironic humor!) evident to me that most of my critics don't want to see what I'm trying to do or how I'm trying to do it, although I flatter myself that end and means are characteristic, individual and positive enough not to be mistaken for anyone's else, or for those of any "modern" or "pre-modern" school. To be called a "sordid realist" one day, a "grim, pessimistic Naturalist" the next, a "lying Moral Romanticist" the next, etc. is quite perplexing—not to add the *Times* editorial that settled *Desire* once and for all by calling it a "Neo-Primitive," a Matisse of the drama, as it were! So I'm really longing to explain and try and convince some sympathetic ear that I've tried to make myself a melting pot for all these methods, seeing some virtues for my ends in each of them, and thereby, if there is enough real fire in me, boil down to my own technique. But where I feel myself most neglected is just where I set most store by myself— as a bit of a poet, who has labored with the spoken word to evolve original rhythms of beauty, where beauty appar-

ently isn't—*Jones, Ape, God's Chillun, Desire,* etc.—and to see the transfiguring nobility of tragedy, in as near the Greek sense as one can grasp it, in seemingly the most ignoble, debased lives. And just here is where I am a most confirmed mystic, too, for I'm always, always trying to interpret Life in terms of lives, never just lives in terms of character. I'm always acutely conscious of the Force behind— Fate, God, our biological past creating our present, whatever one calls it—Mystery certainly—and of the one eternal tragedy of Man in his glorious, self-destructive struggle to make the Force express him instead of being, as an animal is, an infinitesimal incident in its expression. And my profound conviction is that this is the only subject worth writing about and that it is possible—or can be—to develop a tragic expression in terms of transfigured modern values and symbols in the theatre which may to some degree bring home to members of a modern audience their ennobling identity with the tragic figures on the stage. Of course, this is very much of a dream, but where the theatre is concerned, one must have a dream, and the Greek dream in tragedy is the noblest ever!

SOURCE: From a letter to Arthur Hobson Quinn published in Quinn's *A History of the American Drama*, vol. 2, F. S. Crofts & Co., 1945. Reprinted by permission of Yale University.

Mary B. Mullett

THE EXTRAORDINARY STORY OF EUGENE O'NEILL

Three years ago,[1] Eugene O'Neill was practically unknown, except to a small group of people in New York. A few of his one-act plays had been produced by the Provincetown Players in a makeshift theatre down in the Greenwich Village part of the city; but to up-town Broadway, and to the great world outside, he was not even a name. Yet to-day he is the most talked-of playwright in America.

It is less than three years since *Beyond the Horizon*—which was the first of O'Neill's long plays to get a production—made the general public realize that here was a man who not only had something interesting to say but could say it in a new way. All New York began to talk about Eugene O'Neill.

Then, two years ago, the Provincetown Players put on *The Emperor Jones* in their little theatre made out of an old stable. It crowded the wooden benches; turned people away; was taken to an up-town theatre and became the sensation of the dramatic season. It was on tour last year and will be taken to London.

Twice O'Neill had scored and he had done it with plays which the average theatrical manager would have sworn the public would not accept.

Then came last season, with another brace of O'Neill plays: *Anna Christie* and *The Hairy Ape*. Grim pictures of grim life, a rough slap in the face to people accustomed to the conventions of society and the traditions of the theatre. Yet crowds of these people went to see both plays—and applauded enthusiastically when their faces were metaphorically slapped.

It wasn't the slap itself that got this reaction. It was the thing, the force itself, the meaning behind the blow. As O'Neill said to me:

"The audiences sat there and listened to ideas absolutely opposed to their ordinary habits of thought—and applauded these ideas."

"Why?" I asked.

"Because they had been appealed to through their emotions," he said, "and our emotions are a better guide than our thoughts. Our emotions are instinctive. They are the result not only of our individual experiences but of the experiences of the whole human race, back through all the ages. They are the deep undercurrent, whereas our thoughts are often only the small individual surface reactions. Truth usually goes deep. So it reaches you through your emotions."

The inference is that O'Neill thinks he gives us the truth in his plays. Certainly he tries to give us the truth as he sees it. He has courage and sincerity. But he does not use it to preach a hidebound creed. He does not tell us flatly what we "ought" to do. He shows us human beings, living in an environment that is "absolutely strange to the average person: a negro, crazed by superstitious terror; a girl, drinking in a waterfront dive; a stoker, shoveling coal in the furnace-room of an ocean steamer—"queer" people with whom we might think we could have nothing in common.

O'Neill puts these "queer" people before us, and shows them groping their way through the very same spiritual problems we know to be our own. He wants to accomplish two things: He wants to give us a better understanding of ourselves and a better understanding of one another. . . .

SOURCE: From *The American Magazine*, 94, no. 5 (November 1922). Reprinted by permission of Yale University.
[1] O'Neill was thirty-four when this article appeared in 1922.—Ed.

Let me describe the man as he is to-day. It will help you to appreciate the strangeness of the life he led during his early twenties. He is tall and dark and thin. Everything about him (except his hair and eyes!) seems to be long and thin. I believe his hands, for instance, are the longest and the most slender I ever have seen. They are the type of hands that go with the dreamer temperament.

His eyes are very dark, very intense. His hair is dark; but, young as he is, it is already showing a little gray at the temples. He is quiet and slow of speech with strangers. When it comes to ordinary "small talk" he is a good imitation of a sphinx. Even when he is interested, there are long pauses, when, unless you know his ways, you think he isn't going to say anything more. Then, unexpectedly, he begins again; and he is likely to say something so interesting that you soon learn not to break in on these pauses.

I went to see him recently at his summer home, though he sometimes stays there as late as November. The house, until a few years ago, was the Peakèd Hill Bars Coast Guard station, on the dunes a few miles from Provincetown, Massachusetts. From it, not another house is to be seen. The only human habitations are the new station, a quarter of a mile away, and a small shack. But these are hidden by the hills of sand.

It is a desolation of sand and sea; but very beautiful—also very remote! Few persons could plow through the soft sand to reach it, fewer still would do so. An automobile would be "mired" in sand within a few feet. Only a horse can make the trip.

From June until late in the autumn, O'Neill lives and works there. The household consists of himself, his wife, their three-year-old son, a housekeeper, and the child's nurse.

And here is an interesting fact: O'Neill has a regular habit of work. The craving for freedom, for the indulgence of his own desires, which controlled him in his early manhood, is subordinated now to the good of his work. He, who used to be a rebel against routine, voluntarily follows a routine now, in this one direction. Like the rest of us, he has found that he must follow a regular habit of work if he is to accomplish anything.

Well, this is the man who, at twenty, shipped as a common sailor on a voyage that lasted sixty-five days, all of the time out of sight of land. The food was chiefly dried codfish, sea biscuit, sweet soup, and "something they called coffee, and something they called tea."

His quarters below deck were in the forecastle—the "fo'c'sle"—shared by all the seamen of the crew. Practically without ventilation, it recked of tobacco smoke, wet clothing, and unkempt human beings.

The voyage ended at Buenos Aires; and here again the young man tried his hand at the sort of work which would appeal to most men of his breeding and education. One after another, he got jobs with the Westinghouse Company, the Swift Packing Company, and the Singer Sewing Machine Company. But in each case he either was fired, or else gave it up in disgust.

"The Singer people," he explained, "made about five hundred and seventy-five different types of sewing machines at that time, and I was supposed to learn every detail of every one of them. I got about as far as Number Ten, I guess, before they gave me up as hopeless.

"I had spent a good deal of my time down on the waterfront when I should have been studying bobbins and needles. Now I went there again, like a boy let out of school; and when my money was gone I shipped on a British vessel bound for Portuguese South Africa. I made the voyage over there and back, then shipped on another British vessel for New York.

"In New York, I lived at 'Jimmy the Priest's'; a waterfront dive, with a back room where you could sleep with your head on the table if you bought a schooner of beer. 'Jimmy the Priest's' place is the original of the saloon in Anna Christie.[2] And an old sailor whom I knew there is the original of 'Chris,' the father in the play.

"Again I hung around the waterfront for a while. There, as at Buenos Aires, I picked up an occasional job aboard a ves-

[2] Also that of O'Neill's later play The Iceman Cometh.—Ed.

sel that was loading or unloading. The work was mostly cleaning ship; painting, washing the decks, and so on.

"After a few weeks, or months, I shipped on the American Liner *New York*, as an able seaman. I made the voyage to Southampton; and as the *New York* was disabled, I came back on the *Philadelphia*. But there was about as much 'sea glamour' in working aboard a passenger steamship as there would have been in working in a summer hotel! I washed enough deck area to cover a good-sized town.

"It was on these two voyages that I got to know the stokers, although it did not really begin aboard ship. There is class distinction even among the groups that make up the crew of an ocean liner. But in this case, one group does not regard another as superior to it. Each has a healthy contempt for the others.

"I shouldn't have known the stokers if I hadn't happened to scrape an acquaintance with one of our own furnace-room gang at Jimmy the Priest's. His name was Driscoll, and he was a Liverpool Irishman. It seems that years ago some Irish families settled in Liverpool. Most of them followed the sea, and they were a hard lot. To sailors all over the world, a 'Liverpool Irishman' is the synonym for a tough customer. It was through Driscoll that I got to know other stokers. Driscoll himself came to a strange end. He committed suicide by jumping overboard in mid-ocean."

"Why?" I asked.

"That's it," said O'Neill thoughtfully. "That's what I asked *myself*. 'Why?' It was the *why* of Driscoll's suicide that gave me the germ of the idea for my play, *The Hairy Ape*."

... Once, when he was talking about the men who were his friends along the waterfront and in the fo'c'sle, I said to him, "Why did you do it? Why did you want to be with men of that type?"

"I guess," he said in his slow way, "it was because I liked them better than I did men of my own kind. They were sincere, loyal, generous. You have heard people use the expression: 'He would give away his shirt.' I've known men who actually did give away their shirts. I've seen them give their own clothes to stowaways.

"I hated a life ruled by the conventions and traditions of society. Sailors' lives, too, were ruled by conventions and traditions; but they were of a sort I liked and that had a meaning which appealed to me.

"You might think, for instance, that I would have rebelled at the discipline aboard ship. But 'discipline' on a sailing vessel was not a thing that was imposed on the crew by superior authority. It was essentially voluntary. The motive behind it was loyalty to the ship! Among seamen, at that time, this love of the ship was what really controlled them.

"Suppose, just as an example, that one of the yards was loose, hanging by a thread, so to speak. Suppose a gale was blowing and the captain or the mate ordered two men to go aloft to secure this loose spar. This might be a dangerous proceeding. The men could refuse to do it. And they would be entirely within their rights, because if any complaint was made of them, or any punishment imposed, they could go before their consul at the next port and justify their refusal to obey.

"Now the motive of the captain, or of the mate, in giving the order, might be simply a wish to save a spar which, if lost, would add an item of expense to the owners of the vessel. But the men who risked injury, or even death, by carrying out the order, would be impelled solely by their love of the ship. They wouldn't care about saving the owners a few dollars, nor about saving the captain's face. They would go simply because of their feeling that they owed the service to the ship itself.

"This feeling, by the way, does not exist so strongly now. Labor leaders have organized the seamen and have got them to thinking more about what is due *them* than what is due *from* them to the vessel. The new type of sailor wants his contract, all down in black and white; such and such work, so many hours, for so many dollars.

"Probably some abuses have been corrected by this new order of things. But under it there has been lost the old spirit. It was more like the spirit of medieval guilds than anything that survives in this mechanistic age—the spirit of craftsmanship, of giving one's heart as well as one's hands to one's work, of doing it for the inner satisfaction of carrying out one's own ideals, not merely as obedience of orders. So far as I can see, the gain is overbalanced by the loss.

"That probably will surprise a good many people who know your plays about life at sea," I said. "They undoubtedly think you are trying to arouse pity for the sailor."

"Yes, I know," said O'Neill. "Take the fo'c'sle scenes in *The Hairy Ape*, for instance. People think I am giving an exact picture of the reality. They don't understand that the whole play is expressionistic.

"Yank is really yourself, and myself. He is every human being. But, apparently, very few people seem to get this. They have written, picking out one thing or another in the plays and saying 'how true' it is. But no one has said: 'I am Yank! Yank is my own self!'

"Yet that was what I meant him to be. His struggle to 'belong,' to find the thread that will make him a part of the fabric of Life—we are all struggling to do just that. One idea I had in writing the play was to show that the missing thread, literally 'the tie that binds,' is understanding of one another.

"In the scene where the bell rings for the stokers to go on duty, you remember that they all stand up, come to attention, then go out in a lockstep file. Some people think even that is an actual custom aboard ship! But it is only symbolic of the regimentation of men who are the slaves of machinery. In a larger sense, it applies to all of us, because we all are more or less the slaves of convention, or of discipline, or of a rigid formula of some sort.

"The whole play is expressionistic. The coal shoveling in the furnace-room, for instance. Stokers do not really shovel coal that way. But it is done in the play in order to contribute to the rhythm. For rhythm is a powerful factor in making anything expressive. People do not know how sensitive they are to rhythm. You can actually produce and control emotions by that means alone.

"In *Beyond the Horizon*, there are three acts of two scenes each. One scene is out of doors, showing the horizon, sug-gesting the man's desire and dream. The other is indoors, the horizon gone, suggesting what has come between him and his dream. In that way I tried to get rhythm, the alternation of longing and of loss.

"Probably very few people who saw the play knew that this was definitely planned to produce the effect. But I am sure they all unconsciously *get* the effect. It is often easier to express an idea through such means than through words or mere copies of real actions. Sometimes I try to do it in the one way, sometimes in the other. If I thought there was *only* one way," he said with a smile, "I should be following the mechanistic creed, which is the very thing I condemn."

"Just how do you get, and work out, an idea for a play?" I asked.

"Oh, the idea usually begins in a small way," he said, "I may have it sort of hanging around in my mind for a long time before it grows into anything definite enough to work on. The idea for *The Emperor Jones* was in my mind for two years before I wrote the play. I never try to force an idea. I think about it, off and on. If nothing seems to come of it, I put it away and forget it. But apparently my subconscious mind keeps working on it; for, all of a sudden, some day, it comes back to my conscious mind as a pretty well-formed scheme.

"When I finally get to work I write the whole play out in long hand. Then I go over it, and rewrite it in long hand. Then I type it, making a good many changes as I go along. After that, I like to put it away for a few months, if possible; then take it out and go over it again. There wasn't any difficulty in doing this until recently," he said with a laugh. "When I began writing, I would have put my plays away for a few years, without anyone knowing or caring. It is getting to be different now."

"Is that one of the dangers of success?" I asked.

"I hardly think I am in much danger," he said. "A man's work is in danger of deteriorating when he thinks he has found the *one best formula* for doing it. If he thinks that, he is likely to feel that all he needs is merely to go on repeating himself. I certainly haven't any such delusion.

And so long as a person is searching for better ways of doing his work he is fairly safe."

It seems a strange transformation—this change from the Eugene O'Neill, who used to hang around dives like Jimmy the Priest's, to this man who is already placed in the front rank of American dramatists. "The most significant playwright in America," as one English critic called him. No one can do the kind of work he is doing without having some sort of a fundamental scheme of life: a creed, a philosophy—call it whatever you want to. I asked him once what it was.

"Well," he said, "I suppose it is the idea I try to put into all of my plays. People talk of the 'tragedy' in them, and call it 'sordid,' 'depressing,' 'pessimistic' —the words usually applied to anything of a tragic nature. But tragedy, I think, has the meaning the Greeks gave it. To them it brought exaltation, an urge toward life and ever more life. It roused them to deeper spiritual understandings and released them from the petty greeds of everyday existence. When they saw a tragedy on the stage they felt their own hopeless hopes ennobled in art."

"Hopeless hopes?" I echoed.

"Yes," said O'Neill, "because any victory we may win is never the one we dreamed of winning. The point is that life in itself is nothing. It is the *dream* that keeps us fighting, willing—living! Achievement, in the narrow sense of possession, is a stale finale. The dreams that can be completely realized are not worth dreaming. The higher the dream, the more impossible it is to realize it fully. But you would not say, since this is true, that we should dream only of easily attained ideals. A man wills his own defeat when he pursues the unattainable. But his *struggle* is his success! He is an example of the spiritual significance which life attains when it aims high enough, when the individual fights all the hostile forces within and without himself to achieve a future of nobler values.

"Such a figure is necessarily tragic. But to me he is not depressing; he is exhilarating! He may be a failure in our materialistic sense. His treasures are in other kingdoms. Yet isn't he the most inspiring of all successes?

"If a person is to get the meaning of life he must 'learn to like' the facts about himself—ugly as they may seem to his sentimental vanity—before he can lay hold on the truth *behind* the facts; and that truth is never ugly!"

Luigi Pirandello
1867–1936

Pirandello was born in Sicily, the son of a rich mine-owner, a powerful man able to use his fists, and a gentle mother. At the University of Rome, to which he went after his early schooling, Pirandello fought outmoded methods of teaching and was attracted to the study of philology, a subject he further pursued at the University of Bonn. After receiving his doctor's degree, Pirandello published several volumes of verse, and in 1893 he settled into an abandoned convent near Rome and joined the literary life of the capital. The following year he entered into a marriage—arranged by his father—with a girl whom he had never seen before. For ten years the couple lived in Rome on allowances contributed by their parents, but in 1904 the family fortunes suddenly declined and Pirandello was forced to take up teaching. At about the same time his wife's mind gave way, and for fourteen years Pirandello underwent the agony of coping with an insane woman. The focus of his writing now shifted from the local color of Sicilian life to probing into states of mind and preoccupation with old age, death, and insanity. His work took on the marks of a morbidly obsessed intellect, of a grim humor tragically oriented, and of an attraction for the grotesque. In 1916 he won European acclaim with his play *Right You Are If You Think You Are*. His recurrent theme was of illusion and reality, of the true self behind the social mask, a theme which he explored in such plays as *Six Characters in Search of an Author* (1921) and *Henry IV* (1922). Pirandello's earlier liberalism had been replaced by a cynical evaluation of society's sham respectability. Though his writings indicate that he was basically anarchistic, he nevertheless defended Italy's attack on Ethiopia in 1935 and accepted a decoration from Italy's Fascist dictator, Mussolini. Late in life Pirandello attempted to establish a national theatre, but failed. In 1934, two years before his death, he received the Nobel Prize.

HENRY IV

LUIGI PIRANDELLO

Translated by Edward Storer

HENRY IV	HAROLD	⎫
THE MARCHIONESS MATILDA SPINA	[FRANK]	
FRIDA, *her daughter*	LANDOLPH	*The four private counsel-*
CHARLES DI NOLLI, *the young Marquis*	[LOLO]	*lors [The names in paren-*
BARON TITO BELCREDI	ORDULPH	*theses are nicknames]*
DOCTOR DIONYSIUS GENONI	[MOMO]	
JOHN, *the old waiter*	BERTHOLD	
THE TWO VALETS IN COSTUME	[FINO]	⎭

[A solitary villa in Italy in our own time]

ACT I

[Salon in the villa, furnished and decorated so as to look exactly like the throne room of Henry IV in the royal residence at Goslar. Among the antique decorations there are two modern life-size portraits in oil painting. They are placed against the back wall, and mounted in a wooden stand that runs the whole length of the wall. (It is wide and protrudes, so that it is like a large bench.) One of the paintings is on the right; the other on the left of the throne, which is in the middle of the wall and divides the stand.

The Imperial chair and Baldachin.

The two portraits represent a lady and gentleman, both young, dressed up in carnival costumes: one as "Henry IV," the other as the "Marchioness Matilda of Tuscany." Exits to right and left.

When the curtain goes up, the two valets jump down, as if surprised, from the stand on which they have been lying, and go and take their positions, as rigid as statues, on either side below the throne with their halberds in their hands. Soon after, from the second exit, right,

enter HAROLD, LANDOLPH, ORDULPH and BERTHOLD, *young men employed by the* MARQUIS CHARLES DI NOLLI *to play the part of "Secret Counsellors" at the court of "Henry IV." They are, therefore, dressed like German knights of the eleventh century.* BERTHOLD, *nicknamed Fino, is just entering on his duties for the first time. His companions are telling him what he has to do and amusing themselves at his expense. The scene is to be played rapidly and vivaciously.]*

LANDOLPH *[to* BERTHOLD *as if explaining]*. And this is the throne room.

HAROLD. At Goslar.

ORDULPH. Or at the castle in the Hartz, if you prefer.

HAROLD. Or at Worms.

LANDOLPH. According as to what's doing, it jumps about with us, now here, now there.

ORDULPH. In Saxony.

HAROLD. In Lombardy.

LANDOLPH. On the Rhine.

ONE OF THE VALETS *[without moving, just opening his lips]*. I say . . .

HAROLD *[turning round]*. What is it?

SOURCE: From the book *Naked Masks: Five Plays* by Luigi Pirandello. Edited by Eric Bentley. Copyright, 1922, by E. P. Dutton & Co., Inc. Renewal, 1950, in the names of Stefano, Fausto, and Lietta Pirandello. Published by E. P. Dutton & Co., Inc. and used with their permission.

FIRST VALET [like a statue]. Is he coming in or not? [He alludes to HENRY IV.]

ORDULPH. No, no, he's asleep. You needn't worry.

SECOND VALET [releasing his pose, taking a long breath and going to lie down again on the stand]. You might have told us at once.

FIRST VALET [going over to HAROLD]. Have you got a match, please?

LANDOLPH. What? You can't smoke a pipe here, you know.

FIRST VALET [while HAROLD offers him a light]. No; a cigarette. [Lights his cigarette and lies down again on the stand.]

BERTHOLD [who has been looking on in amazement, walking round the room, regarding the costumes of the others]. I say . . . this room . . . these costumes . . . Which Henry IV is it? I don't quite get it. Is he Henry IV of France or not? [At this LANDOLPH, HAROLD, and ORDULPH, burst out laughing.]

LANDOLPH [still laughing; and pointing to BERTHOLD as if inviting the others to make fun of him]. Henry of France he says: ha! ha!

ORDULPH. He thought it was the king of France!

HAROLD. Henry IV of Germany, my boy: the Salian dynasty!

ORDULPH. The great and tragic Emperor!

LANDOLPH. He of Canossa. Every day we carry on here the terrible war between Church and State, by Jove.

ORDULPH. The Empire against the Papacy!

HAROLD. Antipopes against the Pope!

LANDOLPH. Kings against anti-kings!

ORDULPH. War on the Saxons!

HAROLD. And all the rebels Princes!

LANDOLPH. Against the Emperor's own sons!

BERTHOLD [covering his head with his hands to protect himself against this avalanche of information]. I understand! I understand! Naturally, I didn't get the idea at first. I'm right then: these aren't costumes of the sixteenth century?

HAROLD. Sixteenth century be hanged!

ORDULPH. We're somewhere between a thousand and eleven hundred.

LANDOLPH. Work it out for yourself: if we are before Canossa on the 25th January, 1071 . . .

BERTHOLD [more confused than ever]. Oh my God! What a mess I've made of it!

ORDULPH. Well, just slightly, if you supposed you were at the French court.

BERTHOLD. All that historical stuff I've worked up!

LANDOLPH. My dear boy, it's four hundred years earlier.

BERTHOLD [getting angry]. Good Heavens! You ought to have told me it was Germany and not France. I can't tell you how many books I've read in the last fifteen days.

HAROLD. But I say, surely you knew that poor Tito was Adalbert of Bremen, here?

BERTHOLD. Not a damned bit!

LANDOLPH. Well, don't you see how it is? When Tito died, the Marquis Di Nolli . . .

BERTHOLD. Oh, it was he, was it? He might have told me.

HAROLD. Perhaps he thought you knew.

LANDOLPH. He didn't want to engage anyone else in substitution. He thought the remaining three of us would do. But he began to cry out: "With Adalbert driven away . . ." because, you see, he didn't imagine poor Tito was dead; but that, as Bishop Adalbert, the rival bishops of Cologne and Mayence had driven him off . . .

BERTHOLD [taking his head in his hand]. But I don't know a word of what you're talking about.

ORDULPH. So much the worse for you, my boy!

HAROLD. But the trouble is that not even we know who you are.

BERTHOLD. What? Not even you? You don't know who I'm supposed to be?

ORDULPH. Hum! "Berthold."

BERTHOLD. But which Berthold? And why Berthold?

LANDOLPH [solemnly imitating HENRY IV]. "They've driven Adalbert away from me. Well then, I want Berthold! I want Berthold!" That's what he said.

HAROLD. We three looked one another in the eyes: who's got to be Berthold?

ORDULPH. And so here you are, "Berthold," my dear fellow!

LANDOLPH. I'm afraid you will make a bit of a mess of it.

BERTHOLD [indignant, getting ready to

go]. Ah, no! Thanks very much, but I'm off! I'm out of this!

HAROLD [restraining him with the other two, amid laughter]. Steady now! Don't get excited!

LANDOLPH. Cheer up, my dear fellow! We don't any of us know who we are really. He's Harold; he's Ordulph; I'm Landolph! That's the way he calls us. We've got used to it. But who are we? Names of the period! Yours, too, is a name of the period: Berthold! Only one of us, poor Tito, had got a really decent part, as you can read in history: that of the Bishop of Bremen. He was just like a real bishop. Tito did it awfully well, poor chap!

HAROLD. Look at the study he put into it!

LANDOLPH. Why, he even ordered his Majesty about, opposed his views, guided and counselled him. We're "secret counsellors"—in a manner of speaking only; because it is written in history that Henry IV was hated by the upper aristocracy for surrounding himself at court with young men of the lower classes.

ORDULPH. Us, that is.

LANDOLPH. Yes, small devoted vassals, a bit dissolute and very gay . . .

BERTHOLD. So I've got to be gay as well?

HAROLD. I should say so! Same as we are!

ORDULPH. And it isn't too easy, you know.

LANDOLPH. It's a pity; because the way we're got up, we could do a fine historical reconstruction. There's any amount of material in the story of Henry IV. But, as a matter of fact, we do nothing. We have the form without the content. We're worse than the real secret counsellors of Henry IV; because certainly no one had given them a part to play—at any rate, they didn't feel they had a part to play. It was their life. They looked after their own interests at the expense of others, sold investitures and—what not! We stop here in this magnificent court—for what?—Just doing nothing. We're like so many puppets hung on the wall, waiting for someone to come and move us or make us talk.

HAROLD. Ah, no, old sport, not quite that! We've got to give the proper an-

swer, you know. There's trouble if he asks you something and you don't chip in with the cue.

LANDOLPH. Yes, that's true.

BERTHOLD. Don't rub it in too hard! How the devil am I to give him the proper answer, if I've worked up Henry IV of France, and now he turns out to be Henry IV of Germany? [The other three laugh.]

HAROLD. You'd better start and prepare yourself at once.

ORDULPH. We'll help you out.

HAROLD. We've got any amount of books on the subject. A brief run through the main points will do to begin with.

ORDULPH. At any rate, you must have got some sort of general idea.

HAROLD. Look here! [Turns him around and shows him the portrait of the Marchioness Matilda on the wall.] Who's that?

BERTHOLD [looking at it]. That? Well, the thing seems to me somewhat out of place, anyway: two modern paintings in the midst of all this respectable antiquity!

HAROLD. You're right! They weren't there in the beginning. There are two niches there behind the pictures. They were going to put up two statues in the style of the period. Then the places were covered with those canvases there.

LANDOLPH [interrupting and continuing]. They would certainly be out of place if they really were paintings!

BERTHOLD. What are they, if they aren't paintings?

LANDOLPH. Go and touch them! Pictures all right . . . but for him! [Makes a mysterious gesture to the right, alluding to HENRY IV.] . . . who never touches them! . . .

BERTHOLD. No? What are they for him?

LANDOLPH. Well, I'm only supposing, you know; but I imagine I'm about right. They're images such as . . . well—such as a mirror might throw back. Do you understand? That one there represents himself, as he is in this throne room, which is all in the style of the period. What's there to marvel at? If we put you before a mirror, won't you see yourself, alive, but dressed up in ancient costume? Well, it's as if there were two mirrors there, which cast back living images in the midst of a world which, as you will see, when you have lived with us, comes to life too.

BERTHOLD. I say, look here . . . I've no particular desire to go mad here.

HAROLD. Go mad, be hanged! You'll have a fine time!

BERTHOLD. Tell me this: how have you all managed to become so learned?

LANDOLPH. My dear fellow, you can't go back over eight hundred years of history without picking up a bit of experience.

HAROLD. Come on! Come on! You'll see how quickly you get into it!

ORDULPH. You'll learn wisdom, too, at this school.

BERTHOLD. Well, for Heaven's sake, help me a bit! Give me the main lines, anyway.

HAROLD. Leave it to us. We'll do it all between us.

LANDOLPH. We'll put your wires on you and fix you up like a first-class marionette. Come along! [They take him by the arm to lead him away.]

BERTHOLD [stopping and looking at the portrait on the wall]. Wait a minute! You haven't told me who that is. The Emperor's wife?

HAROLD. No! The Emperor's wife is Bertha of Susa, the sister of Amadeus II of Savoy.

ORDULPH. And the Emperor, who wants to be young with us, can't stand her, and wants to put her away.

LANDOLPH. That is his most ferocious enemy: Matilda, Marchioness of Tuscany.

BERTHOLD. Ah, I've got it: the one who gave hospitality to the Pope!

LANDOLPH. Exactly: at Canossa!

ORDULPH. Pope Gregory VII!

HAROLD. Our bête noir! Come on! come on!

[All four move toward the right to go out, when, from the left, the old servant JOHN enters in evening dress.]

JOHN [quickly, anxiously]. Hss! Hss! Frank! Lolo!

HAROLD [turning round]. What is it?

BERTHOLD [marveling at seeing a man in modern clothes enter the throne room]. Oh! I say, this is a bit too much, this chap here!

LANDOLPH. A man of the twentieth century, here! Oh, go away! [They run over to him, pretending to menace him and throw him out.]

ORDULPH [heroically]. Messenger of Gregory VII, away!

HAROLD. Away! Away!

JOHN [annoyed, defending himself]. Oh, stop it! Stop it, I tell you!

ORDULPH. No, you can't set foot here!

HAROLD. Out with him!

LANDOLPH [to BERTHOLD]. Magic, you know! He's a demon conjured up by the Wizard of Rome! Out with your swords! [Makes as if to draw a sword.]

JOHN [shouting]. Stop it, will you? Don't play the fool with me! The Marquis has arrived with some friends . . .

LANDOLPH. Good! Good! Are there ladies too?

ORDULPH. Old or young?

JOHN. There are two gentlemen.

HAROLD. But the ladies, the ladies, who are they?

JOHN. The Marchioness and her daughter.

LANDOLPH [surprised]. What do you say?

ORDULPH. The Marchioness?

JOHN. The Marchioness! The Marchioness!

HAROLD. Who are the gentlemen?

JOHN. I don't know.

HAROLD [to BERTHOLD]. They're coming to bring us a message from the Pope, do you see?

ORDULPH. All messengers of Gregory VII! What fun!

JOHN. Will you let me speak, or not?

HAROLD. Go on, then!

JOHN. One of the two gentlemen is a doctor, I fancy.

LANDOLPH. Oh, I see, one of the usual doctors.

HAROLD. Bravo Berthold, you'll bring us luck!

LANDOLPH. You wait and see how we'll manage this doctor!

BERTHOLD. It looks as if I were going to get into a nice mess right away.

JOHN. If the gentlemen would allow me to speak . . . they want to come here into the throne room.

LANDOLPH [surprised]. What? She? The Marchioness here?

HAROLD. Then this is something quite different! No play-acting this time!

LANDOLPH. We'll have a real tragedy: that's what!

BERTHOLD [curious]. Why? Why?

ORDULPH [pointing to the portrait]. She is that person there, don't you understand?

LANDOLPH. The daughter is the fiancée ot the Marquis. But what have they come for, I should like to know?

ORDULPH. If he sees her, there'll be trouble.

LANDOLPH. Perhaps he won't recognize her any more.

JOHN. You must keep him there, if he should wake up . . .

ORDULPH. Easier said than done, by Jove!

HAROLD. You know what he's like!

JOHN. —even by force, if necessary! Those are my orders. Go on! Go on!

HAROLD. Yes, because who knows if he hasn't already wakened up?

ORDULPH. Come on then!

LANDOLPH [going toward JOHN with the others]. You'll tell us later what it all means.

JOHN [shouting after them]. Close the door there, and hide the key! That other door too. [Pointing to the other door on right.]

JOHN [to the TWO VALETS]. Be off, you two! There! [Pointing to exit right.] Close the door after you, and hide the key!

[The TWO VALETS go out by the first door on right. JOHN moves over to the left to show in: DONNA MATILDA SPINA, the young MARCHIONESS FRIDA, DR. DIONYSIUS GENONI, the BARON TITO BELCREDI and the young MARQUIS CHARLES DI NOLLI, who, as master of the house, enters last.]

DONNA MATILDA SPINA is about forty-five, still handsome, although there are too patent signs of her attempts to remedy the ravages of time with make-up. Her head is thus rather like a Valkyrie. This facial make-up contrasts with her beautiful sad mouth. A widow for many years, she now has as her friend the BARON TITO BELCREDI, whom neither she nor anyone else takes seriously—at least so it would appear.

What TITO BELCREDI really is for her at bottom he alone knows; and he is, therefore, entitled to laugh, if his friend feels the need of pretending not to know. He can always laugh at the jests which the beautiful Marchioness makes with the others at his expense. He is slim, prematurely gray, and younger than she is. His head is bird-like in shape. He would be a very vivacious person, if his ductile agility (which among other things makes him a redoubtable swordsman) were not enclosed in a sheath of Arab-like laziness, which is revealed in his strange, nasal drawn-out voice.

FRIDA, the daughter of the Marchioness is nineteen. She is sad; because her imperious and too beautiful mother puts her in the shade, and provokes facile gossip against her daughter as well as against herself. Fortunately for her, she is engaged to the MARQUIS CHARLES DI NOLLI.

CHARLES DI NOLLI is a stiff young man, very indulgent toward others, but sure of himself for what he amounts to in the world. He is worried about all the responsibilities which he believes weigh on him. He is dressed in deep mourning for the recent death of his mother.

DR. DIONYSIUS GENONI has a bold rubicund Satyr-like face, prominent eyes, a pointed beard (which is silvery and shiny) and elegant manners. He is nearly bald. All enter in a state of perturbation, almost as if afraid, and all (except DI NOLLI) looking curiously about the room. At first, they speak sotto voce.

DI NOLLI [to JOHN]. Have you given the orders properly?

JOHN. Yes, my Lord; don't be anxious about that.

BELCREDI. Ah, magnificent! magnificent!

DOCTOR. How extremely interesting! Even in the surroundings his raving madness—is perfectly taken into account!

DONNA MATILDA [glancing round for her portrait, discovers it, and goes up close to it]. Ah! Here it is! [Going back to admire it, while mixed emotions stir within her.] Yes . . . Yes . . . [Calls her daughter FRIDA.]

FRIDA. Ah, your portrait!

DONNA MATILDA. No, no . . . look again; it's you, not I, there!

DI NOLLI. Yes, it's quite true. I told you so, I . . .

DONNA MATILDA. But I would never have believed it! [*Shaking as if with a chill.*] What a strange feeling it gives one! [*Then looking at her daughter.*] Frida, what's the matter? [*She pulls her to her side, and slips an arm round her waist.*] Come: don't you see yourself in me there?

FRIDA. Well, I really . . .

DONNA MATILDA. Don't you think so? Don't you, really? [*Turning to BELCREDI.*] Look at it, Tito! Speak up, man!

BELCREDI [*without looking*]. Ah, no! I shan't look at it. For me, *a priori*, certainly not!

DONNA MATILDA. Stupid! You think you are paying me a compliment! [*Turning to DOCTOR GENONI.*] What do you say, Doctor? Do say something, please!

[DOCTOR *makes a movement to go near to the picture.*]

BELCREDI [*with his back turned, pretending to attract his attention secretly*]. —Hss! No, Doctor! For the love of Heaven, have nothing to do with it!

DOCTOR [*getting bewildered and smiling*]. And why shouldn't I?

DONNA MATILDA. Don't listen to him! Come here! He's insufferable!

FRIDA. He acts the fool by profession, didn't you know that?

BELCREDI [*to the DOCTOR, seeing him go over*]. Look at your feet, Doctor! Mind where you're going!

DOCTOR. Why?

BELCREDI. Be careful you don't put your foot in it!

DOCTOR [*laughing feebly*]. No, no. After all, it seems to me there's no reason to be astonished at the fact that a daughter should resemble her mother!

BELCREDI. Oh oh! He's done it now; he's said it.

DONNA MATILDA [*with exaggerated anger, advancing toward BELCREDI*]. What's the matter? What has he said? What has he done?

DOCTOR [*candidly*]. Well, isn't it so?

BELCREDI [*answering the MARCHIONESS*]. I said there was nothing to be astounded at—and you are astounded! And why so, then, if the thing is so simple and natural for you now?

DONNA MATILDA [*still more angry*]. Fool! fool! It's just because it is so natural! Just because it isn't my daughter who is there. [*Pointing to the canvas.*] That is my portrait; and to find my daughter there instead of me fills me with astonishment, an astonishment which, I beg you to believe, is sincere. I forbid you to cast doubts on it.

FRIDA [*slowly and wearily*]. My God! It's always like this . . . quarrels over nothing . . .

BELCREDI [*also slowly, looking dejected, in accents of apology*]. I cast no doubt on anything! I noticed from the beginning that you haven't shared your mother's astonishment; or, if something did astonish you, it was because the likeness between you and the portrait seemed so strong.

DONNA MATILDA. Naturally! She cannot recognize herself in me as I was at her age; while I, there, can very well recognize myself in her as she is now!

DOCTOR. Quite right! Because a portrait is always there, fixed in the twinkling of an eye: for the young lady something far away and without memories, while, for the Marchioness, it can bring back everything: movements, gestures, looks, smiles, so many things . . .

DONNA MATILDA. Exactly!

DOCTOR [*continuing, turning toward her*]. Naturally enough, you can live all these old sensations again in your daughter.

DONNA MATILDA. He always spoils every innocent pleasure for me, every touch I have of spontaneous sentiment! He does it merely to annoy me.

DOCTOR [*frightened at the disturbance he has caused, adopts a professional tone*]. Likeness, dear Baron, is often the result of imponderable things. So one explains that . . .

BELCREDI [*interrupting the discourse*]. Somebody will soon be finding a likeness between you and me, my dear Professor!

DI NOLLI. Oh! let's finish with this, please! [*Points to the two doors on the right, as a warning that there is someone there who may be listening.*] We've wasted too much time as it is!

FRIDA. As one might expect when *he's* present. [*Alludes to BELCREDI.*]

DI NOLLI. Enough! The Doctor is here; and we have come for a very serious purpose which you all know is important for me.

DOCTOR. Yes, that is so! But now, first of all, let's try to get some points down exactly. Excuse me, Marchioness, will you tell me why your portrait is here? Did you present it to him then?

DONNA MATILDA. No, not at all. How could I have given it to him? I was just like Frida then—and not even engaged. I gave it to him three or four years after the accident. I gave it to him because his mother wished it so much . . . [*Points to* DI NOLLI.]

DOCTOR. She, was his sister? [*Alludes to* HENRY IV.]

DI NOLLI. Yes, Doctor; and our coming here is a debt we pay to my mother who has been dead for more than a month. Instead of being here, she and I [*Indicating* FRIDA] ought to be traveling together . . .

DOCTOR. . . . taking a cure of quite a different kind!

DI NOLLI. —Hum! Mother died in the firm conviction that her adored brother was just about to be cured.

DOCTOR. And can't you tell me, if you please, how she inferred this?

DI NOLLI. The conviction would appear to have derived from certain strange remarks which he made, a little before mother died.

DOCTOR. Oh, remarks! . . . Ah! . . . It would be extremely useful for me to have those remarks, word for word, if possible.

DI NOLLI. I can't remember them. I know that mother returned awfully upset from her last visit with him. On her death-bed, she made me promise that I would never neglect him, that I would have doctors see him, and examine him.

DOCTOR. Um! Um! Let me see! let me see! Sometimes very small reasons determine . . . and this portrait here then? . . .

DONNA MATILDA. For Heaven's sake, Doctor, don't attach excessive importance to this. It made an impression on me because I had not seen it for so many years!

DOCTOR. If you please, quietly, quietly . . .

DI NOLLI. —Well, yes, it must be about fifteen years ago.

DONNA MATILDA. More, more: eighteen!

DOCTOR. Forgive me, but you don't quite know what I'm trying to get at. I attach a very great importance to these two portraits. . . . They were painted, naturally, prior to the famous—and most regrettable pageant, weren't they?

DONNA MATILDA. Of course!

DOCTOR. That is . . . when he was quite in his right mind—that's what I've been trying to say. Was it his suggestion that they should be painted?

DONNA MATILDA. Lots of the people who took part in the pageant had theirs done as a souvenir . . .

BELCREDI. I had mine done—as "Charles of Anjou!"

DONNA MATILDA. . . . . as soon as the costumes were ready.

BELCREDI. As a matter of fact, it was proposed that the whole lot of us should be hung together in a gallery of the villa where the pageant took place. But in the end, everybody wanted to keep his own portrait.

DONNA MATILDA. And I gave him this portrait of me without very much regret . . . since his mother . . . [*Indicates* DI NOLLI.]

DOCTOR. You don't remember if it was he who asked for it?

DONNA MATILDA. Ah, that I don't remember. . . . Maybe it was his sister, wanting to help out. . . .

DOCTOR. One other thing: was it his idea, this pageant?

BELCREDI [*at once*]. No, no, it was mine!

DOCTOR. If you please . . .

DONNA MATILDA. Don't listen to him! It was poor Belassi's idea.

BELCREDI. Belassi! What had he got to do with it?

DONNA MATILDA. Count Belassi, who died, poor fellow, two or three months after . . .

BELCREDI. But if Belassi wasn't there when . . .

DI NOLLI. Excuse me, Doctor; but is it really necessary to establish whose the original idea was?

DOCTOR. It would help me, certainly!

BELCREDI. I tell you the idea was mine! There's nothing to be proud of in it, seeing what the result's been. Look here, Doctor, it was like this. One evening, in the first days of November, I was looking at an illustrated German review in the club. I was merely glancing at the pictures, because I can't read German.

There was a picture of the Kaiser, at some University town where he had been a student . . . I don't remember which.

DOCTOR. Bonn, Bonn!

BELCREDI. —You are right: Bonn! He was on horseback, dressed up in one of those ancient German student guild-costumes, followed by a procession of noble students, also in costume. The picture gave me the idea. Already someone at the club had spoken of a pageant for the forthcoming carnival. So I had the notion that each of us should choose for this Tower of Babel pageant to represent some character: a king, an emperor, a prince, with his queen, empress, or lady, alongside of him—and all on horseback. The suggestion was at once accepted.

DONNA MATILDA. I had my invitation from Belassi.

BELCREDI. Well, he wasn't speaking the truth! That's all I can say, if he told you the idea was his. He wasn't even at the club the evening I made the suggestion, just as he [Meaning HENRY IV] wasn't there either.

DOCTOR. So he chose the character of Henry IV?

DONNA MATILDA. Because I . . . thinking of my name, and not giving the choice any importance, said I would be the Marchioness Matilda of Tuscany.

DOCTOR I . . . don't understand the relation between the two.

DONNA MATILDA. —Neither did I, to begin with, when he said that in that case he would be at my feet like Henry IV at Canossa. I had heard of Canossa of course; but to tell the truth, I'd forgotten most of the story; and I remember I received a curious impression when I had to get up my part, and found that I was the faithful and zealous friend of Pope Gregory VII in deadly enmity with the Emperor of Germany. Then I understood why, since I had chosen to repre-sent his implacable enemy, he wanted to be near me in the pageant as Henry IV.

DOCTOR. Ah, perhaps because . . .

BELCREDI. —Good Heavens, Doctor, because he was then paying furious court to her! [Indicates the MARCHIONESS.] And she, naturally . . .

DONNA MATILDA. Naturally? Not naturally at all . . .

BELCREDI [pointing to her]. She couldn't stand him . . .

DONNA MATILDA. —No, that isn't true! I didn't dislike him. Not at all! But for me, when a man begins to want to be taken seriously, well . . .

BELCREDI [continuing for her]. He gives you the clearest proof of his stupidity.

DONNA MATILDA. No, dear; not in this case; because he was never a fool like you.

BELCREDI. Anyway, I've never asked you to take me seriously.

DONNA MATLDA. Yes, I know. But with him one couldn't joke. [Changing her tone and speaking to the DOCTOR.] One of the many misfortunes which happen to us women, Doctor, is to see before us every now and again a pair of eyes glaring at us with a contained intense promise of eternal devotion. [Bursts out laughing.] There is nothing quite so funny. If men could only see themselves with that eternal look of fidelity in their faces! I've always thought it comic; then more even than now. But I want to make a confession—I can do so after twenty years or more. When I laughed at him then, it was partly out of fear. One might have almost believed a promise from those eyes of his. But it would have been very dangerous.

DOCTOR [with lively interest]. Ah! ah! This is most interesting! Very dangerous, you say?

DONNA MATILDA. Yes, because he was very different from the others. And then, I am . . . well . . . what shall I say? . . . a little impatient of all that is pondered, or tedious. But I was too young then, and a woman. I had the bit between my teeth. It would have required more courage than I felt I possessed. So I laughed at him too—with remorse, to spite myself, indeed; since I saw that my own laugh mingled with those of all the others—the other fools—who made fun of him.

BELCREDI. My own case, more or less!

DONNA MATILDA. You make people laugh at you, my dear, with your trick of always humiliating yourself. It was quite a different affair with him. There's a vast difference. And you—you know—people laugh in your face!

BELCREDI. Well, that's better than behind one's back!

DOCTOR. Let's get to the facts. He was

then already somewhat exalted, if I understand rightly.

BELCREDI. Yes, but in a curious fashion, Doctor.

DOCTOR. How?

BELCREDI. Well, cold-bloodedly so to speak.

DONNA MATILDA. Not at all! It was like this, Doctor! He was a bit strange, certainly; but only because he was fond of life: eccentric, there!

BELCREDI. I don't say he simulated exaltation. On the contrary, he was often genuinely exalted. But I could swear, Doctor, that he saw himself at once in his own exaltation. Moreover, I'm certain it made him suffer. Sometimes he had the most comical fits of rage against himself.

DOCTOR. Yes?

DONNA MATILDA. That is true.

BELCREDI [to DONNA MATILDA]. And why? [To the DOCTOR.] Evidently, because that immediate lucidity that comes from acting, assuming a part, at once put him out of key with his own feelings, which seemed to him not exactly false, but like something he was obliged to give the value there and then of—what shall I say—of an act of intelligence, to make up for that sincere cordial warmth he felt lacking. So he improvised, exaggerated, let himself go, so as to distract and forget himself. He appeared inconstant, fatuous, and—yes—even ridiculous, sometimes.

DOCTOR. And may we say unsociable?

BELCREDI. No, not at all. He was famous for getting up things: tableaux vivants, dances, theatrical performances for charity: all for the fun of the thing, of course. He was a jolly good actor, you know!

DI NOLLI. Madness has made a superb actor of him.

BELCREDI. —Why, so he was even in the old days. When the accident happened, after the horse fell . . .

DOCTOR. Hit the back of his head, didn't he?

DONNA MATILDA. Oh, it was horrible! He was beside me! I saw him between the horse's hoofs! It was rearing!

BELCREDI. None of us thought it was anything serious at first. There was a stop in the pageant, a bit of disorder. People wanted to know what had happened. But they'd already taken him off to the villa.

DONNA MATILDA. There wasn't the least sign of a wound, not a drop of blood.

BELCREDI. We thought he had merely fainted.

DONNA MATILDA. But two hours afterward . . .

BELCREDI. He reappeared in the drawing-room of the villa . . . that is what I wanted to say . . .

DONNA MATILDA. My God! What a face he had. I saw the whole thing at once!

BELCREDI. No, no! that isn't true. Nobody saw it, Doctor, believe me!

DONNA MATILDA. Doubtless, because you were all like mad men.

BELCREDI. Everybody was pretending to act his part for a joke. It was a regular Babel.

DONNA MATILDA. And you can imagine, Doctor, what terror struck into us when we understood that he, on the contrary, was playing his part in deadly earnest . . .

DOCTOR. Oh, he was there too, was he?

BELCREDI. Of course! He came straight into the midst of us. We thought he'd quite recovered, and was pretending, fooling, like all the rest of us . . . only doing it rather better; because, as I say, he knew how to act.

DONNA MATILDA. Some of them began to hit him with their whips and fans and sticks.

BELCREDI. And then—as a king, he was armed, of course—he drew out his sword and menaced two or three of us. . . . It was a terrible moment, I can assure you!

DONNA MATILDA. I shall never forget that scene—all our masked faces hideous and terrified gazing at him, at that terrible mask of his face, which was no longer a mask, but madness personified.

BELCREDI. He was Henry IV, Henry IV in person, in a moment of fury.

DONNA MATILDA. He'd got into it all the detail and minute preparation of a month's careful study. And it all burned and blazed there in the terrible obsession which lit his face.

DOCTOR. Yes, that is quite natural, of course. The momentary obsession of a dilettante became fixed, owing to the fall and the damage to the brain.

BELCREDI [to FRIDA and DI NOLLI]. You see the kind of jokes life can play on us. [To DI NOLLI.] You were four or five years old. [To FRIDA.] Your mother imagines you've taken her place there in that portrait; when, at the time, she had not the remotest idea that she would bring you into the world. My hair is already gray; and he—look at him—[*Points to portrait.*]—ha! A smack on the head, and he never moves again: Henry IV forever!

DOCTOR [*seeking to draw the attention of the others, looking learned and imposing*].—Well, well, then it comes, we may say, to this. . . .

[*Suddenly the first exit to right, the one nearest footlights, opens, and* BERTHOLD *enters all excited.*]

BERTHOLD [*rushing in*]. I say! I say! [*Stops for a moment, arrested by the astonishment which his appearance has caused in the others.*]

FRIDA [*running away terrified*]. Oh dear! oh dear! it's he, it's . . .

DONNA MATILDA [*covering her face with her hands so as not to see*]. Is it, is it he?

DI NOLLI. No, no, what are you talking about? Be calm!

DOCTOR. Who is it then?

BELCREDI. One of our masqueraders.

DI NOLLI. He is one of the four youths we keep here to help him out in his madness. . . .

BERTHOLD. I beg your pardon, Marquis. . . .

DI NOLLI. Pardon be damned! I gave orders that the doors were to be closed, and that nobody should be allowed to enter.

BERTHOLD. Yes, sir, but I can't stand it any longer, and I ask you to let me go away this very minute.

DI NOLLI. Oh, you're the new valet, are you? You were supposed to begin this morning, weren't you?

BERTHOLD. Yes, sir, and I can't stand it, I can't bear it.

DONNA MATILDA [*to* DI NOLLI *excitedly*]. What? Then he's not so calm as you said?

BERTHOLD [*quickly*].—No, no, my lady, it isn't he; it's my companions. You say "help him out with his madness," Marquis; but they don't do anything of the kind. They're the real madmen. I come here for the first time, and instead of helping me . . .

[LANDOLPH *and* HAROLD *come in from the same door, but hesitate on the threshold.*]

LANDOLPH. Excuse me?

HAROLD. May I come in, my Lord?

DI NOLLI. Come in! What's the matter? What are you all doing?

FRIDA. Oh God! I'm frightened! I'm going to run away. [*Makes toward exit at left.*]

DI NOLLI [*restraining her at once*]. No, no, Frida!

LANDOLPH. My lord, this fool here . . . [*Indicates* BERTHOLD.]

BERTHOLD [*protesting*]. Ah, no thanks, my friends, no thanks! I'm not stopping here! I'm off!

LANDOLPH. What do you mean—you're not stopping here?

HAROLD. He's ruined everything, my Lord, running away in here!

LANDOLPH. He's made him quite mad. We can't keep him in there any longer. He's given orders that he's to be arrested; and he wants to "judge" him at once from the throne: What is to be done?

DI NOLLI. Shut the door, man! Shut the door! Go and close that door! [LANDOLPH *goes over to close it.*]

HAROLD. Ordulph, alone, won't be able to keep him there.

LANDOLPH. —My Lord, perhaps if we could announce the visitors at once, it would turn his thoughts. Have the gentlemen thought under what pretext they will present themselves to him?

DI NOLLI. —It's all been arranged! [*To the* DOCTOR.] If you, Doctor, think it well to see him at once. . . .

FRIDA. I'm not coming! I'm not coming! I'll keep out of this. You too, Mother, for Heaven's sake, come away with me!

DOCTOR. —I say . . . I suppose he's not armed, is he?

DI NOLLI. —Nonsense! Of course not. [*To* FRIDA.] Frida, you know this is childish of you. You wanted to come!

FRIDA. I didn't at all. It was mother's idea.

DONNA MATILDA. And I'm quite ready to see him. What are we going to do?

BELCREDI. Must we absolutely dress up in some fashion or other?

LANDOLPH. —Absolutely essential, indispensable, sir. Alas! as you see . . . [*shows his costume*], there'd be awful trouble if he saw you gentlemen in modern dress.

HAROLD. He would think it was some diabolical masquerade.

DI NOLLI. As these men seem to be in costume to you, so we appear to be in costume to him, in these modern clothes of ours.

LANDOLPH. It wouldn't matter so much if he wouldn't suppose it to be the work of his mortal enemy.

BELCREDI. Pope Gregory VII?

LANDOLPH. Precisely. He calls him "a pagan."

BELCREDI. The Pope a pagan? That's not bad!

LANDOLPH. —Yes, sir . . . and a man who calls up the dead! He accuses him of all the diabolical arts. He's terribly afraid of him.

DOCTOR. Persecution mania!

HAROLD. He'd be simply furious.

DI NOLLI [to BELCREDI]. But there's no need for you to be there, you know. It's sufficient for the Doctor to see him.

DOCTOR. —What do you mean? . . . I? Alone?

DI NOLLI. —But they are there. [Indicates the three young men.]

DOCTOR. I don't mean that. . . . I mean if the Marchioness . . .

DONNA MATILDA. Of course. I mean to see him too, naturally. I want to see him again.

FRIDA. Oh, why, Mother, why? Do come away with me, I implore you!

DONNA MATILDA [imperiously]. Let me do as I wish! I came here for this purpose! [To LANDOLPH.] I shall be "Adelaide," the mother.

LANDOLPH. Excellent! The mother of the Empress Bertha. Good! It will be enough if her Ladyship wears the ducal crown and puts on a mantle that will hide her other clothes entirely. [To HAROLD.] Off you go, Harold!

HAROLD. Wait a moment! And this gentleman here? . . . [Alludes to the DOCTOR.]

DOCTOR. —Ah yes . . . we decided I was to be . . . the Bishop of Cluny, Hugh of Cluny!

HAROLD. The gentleman means the Abbot. Very good! Hugh of Cluny.

LANDOLPH. —He's often been here before!

DOCTOR [amazed]. —What? Been here before?

LANDOLPH. —Don't be alarmed! I mean that it's an easily prepared disguise. . . .

HAROLD. We've made use of it on other occasions, you see!

DOCTOR. But . . .

LANDOLPH. Oh, no, there's no risk of his remembering. He pays more attention to the dress than to the person.

DONNA MATILDA. That's fortunate for me too then.

DI NOLLI. Frida, you and I'll get along. Come on, Tito!

BELCREDI. Ah no. If she [indicates the MARCHIONESS] stops here, so do I!

DONNA MATILDA. But I don't need you at all.

BELCREDI. You may not need me, but I should like to see him again myself. Mayn't I?

LANDOLPH. Well, perhaps it would be better if there were three.

HAROLD. How is the gentleman to be dressed then?

BELCREDI. Oh, try and find some easy costume for me.

LANDOLPH [to HAROLD]. Hum! Yes . . . he'd better be from Cluny too.

BELCREDI. What do you mean—from Cluny?

LANDOLPH. A Benedictine's habit of the Abbey of Cluny. He can be in attendance on Monsignor. [To HAROLD.] Off you go! [To BERTHOLD.] And you too get away and keep out of sight all today. No, wait a moment. [To BERTHOLD.] You bring here the costumes he will give you. [To HAROLD.] You go at once and announce the visit of the "Duchess Adelaide" and "Monsignor Hugh of Cluny." Do you understand? [HAROLD and BERTHOLD go off by the first door on the right.]

DI NOLLI. We'll retire now. [Goes off with FRIDA, left.]

DOCTOR. Shall I be a persona grata to him, as Hugh of Cluny?

LANDOLPH. Oh, rather! Don't worry about that! Monsignor has always been received here with great respect. You too, my Lady, he will be glad to see. He never forgets that it was owing to the intercession of you two that he was admitted to the Castle of Canossa and the presence of Gregory VII, who didn't want to receive him.

BELCREDI. And what do I do?

LANDOLPH. You stand a little apart, respectfully: that's all.

DONNA MATILDA [*irritated, nervous*]. You would do well to go away, you know.

BELCREDI [*slowly, spitefully*]. How upset you seem! . . .

DONNA MATILDA [*proudly*]. I am as I am. Leave me alone!

[BERTHOLD *comes in with the costumes.*]

LANDOLPH [*seeing him enter*]. Ah, the costumes: here they are. This mantle is for the Marchioness . . .

DONNA MATILDA. Wait a minute! I'll taffe off my hat. [*Does so and gives it to* BERTHOLD.]

LANDOLPH. Put it down there! [*Then to the* MARCHIONESS, *while he offers to put the ducal crown on her head.*] Allow me!

DONNA MATILDA. Dear, dear! Isn't there a mirror here?

LANDOLPH. Yes, there's one there. [*Points to the door on the left.*] If the Marchioness would rather put it on herself . . .

DONNA MATILDA. Yes, yes, that will be better. Give it to me! [*Takes up her hat and goes off with* BERTHOLD, *who carries the cloak and the crown.*]

BELCREDI. Well, I must say, I never thought I should be a Benedictine monk! By the way, this business must cost an awful lot of money.

DOCTOR. Like any other fantasy, naturally!

BELCREDI. Well, there's a fortune to go upon.

LANDOLPH. We have got there a whole wardrobe of costumes of the period, copied to perfection from old models. This is my special job. I get them from the best theatrical costumers. They cost losts of money. [DONNA MATILDA *re-enters, wearing mantle and crown.*]

BELCREDI [*at once, in admiration*]. Oh magnificent! Truly regal!

DONNA MATILDA [*looking at* BELCREDI *and bursting out into laughter*]. Oh no, no! Take it off! You're impossible. You look like an ostrich dressed up as a monk.

BELCREDI. Well, how about the Doctor?

DOCTOR. I don't think I look so bad, do I?

DONNA MATILDA. No; the Doctor's all right, . . . but you are too funny for words.

DOCTOR. Do you have many receptions here then?

LANDOLPH. It depends. He often gives orders that such and such a person appear before him. Then we have to find someone who will take the part. Women too. . . .

DONNA MATILDA [*hurt, but trying to hide the fact*]. Ah, women too?

LANDOLPH. Oh, yes; many at first.

BELCREDI [*laughing*]. Oh, that's great! In costume, like the Marchioness?

LANDOLPH. Oh well, you know, women of the kind that lend themselves to . . .

BELCREDI. Ah, I see! [*Perfidiously to the* MARCHIONESS.] Look out, you know he's becoming dangerous for you.

[*The second door on the right opens, and* HAROLD *appears making first of all a discreet sign that all conversation should cease.*]

HAROLD. His Majesty, the Emperor!

[*The* TWO VALETS *enter first, and go and stand on either side of the throne. Then* HENRY IV *comes in between* ORDULPH *and* HAROLD, *who keep a little in the rear respectfully.*]

HENRY IV *is about fifty and very pale. The hair on the back of his head is already gray; over the temples and forehead it appears blond, owing to its having been tinted in an evident and puerile fashion. On his cheek-bones he has two small, doll-like dabs of color, that stand out prominently against the rest of his tragic pallor. He is wearing a penitent's sack over his regal habit, as at Canossa. His eyes have a fixed look which is dreadful to see, and this expression is in strained contrast with the sackcloth.* ORDULPH *carries the Imperial crown;* HAROLD, *the sceptre with eagle, and the globe with the cross.*

HENRY IV [*bowing first to* DONNA MATILDA *and afterward to the* DOCTOR]. My Lady . . . Monsignor . . . [*Then he looks at* BELCREDI *and seems about to greet him too; when, suddenly, he turns to* LANDOLPH, *who has approached him, and asks him sotto voce and with diffidence.*] Is that Peter Damiani?

LANDOLPH. No, Sire. He is a monk from Cluny who is accompanying the Abbot.

HENRY IV [*looks again at* BELCREDI *with increasing mistrust, and then noticing that he appears embarrassed and keeps glancing at* DONNA MATILDA *and the* DOCTOR, *stands upright and cries out*]. No, it's Peter Damiani! It's no use, Father, your looking at the Duchess. [*Then turning quickly to* DONNA MATILDA *and the* DOCTOR *as though to ward off a danger.*] I swear it! I swear that my heart is changed toward your daughter. I confess that if he [*indicates* BELCREDI] hadn't come to forbid it in the name of Pope Alexander, I'd have repudiated her. Yes, yes, there were people ready to favor the repudiation: the Bishop of Mayence would have done it for a matter of one hundred and twenty farms. [*Looks at* LANDOLPH *a little perplexed and adds.*] But I mustn't speak ill of the bishops at this moment! [*More humbly to* BELCREDI.] I am grateful to you, believe me, I am grateful to you for the hindrance you put in my way!—God knows, my life's been all made of humiliations: my mother, Adalbert, Tribur, Goslar! And now this sackcloth you see me wearing! [*Changes tone suddenly and speaks like one who goes over his part in a parenthesis of astuteness.*] It doesn't matter: clarity of ideas, perspicacity, firmness, and patience under adversity, that's the thing. [*Then turning to all and speaking solemnly.*] I know how to make amends for the mistakes I have made; and I can humiliate myself even before you, Peter Damiani. [*Bows profoundly to him and remains curved. Then a suspicion is born in him which he is obliged to utter in menacing tones, almost against his will.*] Was it not perhaps you who started that obscene rumor that my holy mother had illicit relations with the Bishop of Augusta?

BELCREDI [*since* HENRY IV *has his finger pointed at him*]. No, no, it wasn't I. . . .

HENRY IV [*straightening up*]. Not true, not true? Infamy! [*Looks at him and then adds.*] I didn't think you capable of it! [*Goes to the* DOCTOR *and plucks his sleeve, while winking at him knowingly.*] Always the same, Monsignor, those bishops, always the same!

HAROLD [*softly, whispering as if to help out the* DOCTOR]. Yes, yes, the rapacious bishops!

DOCTOR [*to* HAROLD, *trying to keep it up*]. Ah, yes, those fellows . . . ah yes . . .

HENRY IV. Nothing satisfies them! I was a little boy, Monsignor . . . One passes the time, playing even, when, without knowing it, one is a king. I was six years old; and they tore me away from my mother, and made use of me against her without my knowing anything about it . . . always profaning, always stealing, stealing! . . . One greedier than the other. . . . Hanno worse than Stephen! Stephen worse than Hanno!

LANDOLPH [*sotto voce, persuasively, to call his attention*]. Majesty!

HENRY IV [*turning round quickly*]. Ah yes . . . this isn't the moment to speak ill of the bishops. But this infamy against my mother, Monsignor, is too much. [*Looks at the* MARCHIONESS *and grows tender.*] And I can't even weep for her, Lady. . . . I appeal to you who have a mother's heart! She came here to see me from her convent a month ago. . . . They had told me she was dead! [*Sustained pause full of feeling. Then smiling sadly.*] I can't weep for her; because if you are here now, and I am like this [*shows the sackcloth he is wearing*] it means I am twenty-six years old!

HAROLD. And that she is therefore alive, Majesty! . . .

ORDULPH. Still in her convent!

HENRY IV [*looking at them*]. Ah yes! And I can postpone my grief to another time. [*Shows the* MARCHIONESS *almost with coquetry the tint he has given to his hair.*] Look! I am still fair. . . . [*Then slowly as if in confidence.*] For you . . . there's no need! But little exterior details do help! A matter of time, Monsignor, do you understand me? [*Turns to the* MARCHIONESS *and notices her hair.*] Ah, but I see that you too, Duchess . . . Italian, eh? [*As much as to say "false"; but without any indignation indeed rather with malicious admiration.*] Heaven forbid that I should show disgust or surprise! Nobody cares to recognize that obscure and fatal power which sets limits to our will. But I say, if one is born and one dies . . . Did you want to be born, Monsignor? I didn't! And in both cases, independently of our wills, so many things happen we would wish didn't happen, and to which we resign ourselves as best we can! . . .

DOCTOR [*merely to make a remark, while studying* HENRY IV *carefully*]. Alas! Yes, alas!

HENRY IV. It's like this: When we are

not resigned, out come our desires. A woman wants to be a man . . . an old man would be young again. Desires, ridiculous fixed ideas of course— But reflect! Monsignor, those other desires are not less ridiculous: I mean, those desires where the will is kept within the limits of the possible. Not one of us can lie or pretend. We're all fixed in good faith in a certain concept of ourselves. However, Monsignor, while you keep yourself in order, holding on with both your hands to your holy habit, there slips down from your sleeves, there peels off from you like . . . like a serpent . . . something you don't notice: life, Monsignor! [*Turns to the* MARCHIONESS.] Has it never happened to you, my Lady, to find a different self in yourself? Have you always been the same? My God! One day . . . how was it, how was it you were able to commit this or that action? [*Fixes her so intently in the eyes as almost to make her blanch.*] Yes, that particular action, that very one: we understand each other! But don't be afraid: I shall reveal it to none. And you, Peter Damiani, how could you be a friend of that man? . . .

LANDOLPH. Majesty!

HENRY IV [*at once*]. No, I won't name him! [*Turning to* BELCREDI.] What did you think of him? But we all of us cling tight to our conceptions of ourselves, just as he who is growing old dyes his hair. What does it matter that this dyed hair of mine isn't a reality for you, if it *is*, to some extent, for me?—you, you, my Lady, certainly don't dye your hair to deceive the others, nor even yourself; but only to cheat your own image a little before the looking-glass. I do it for a joke! You do it seriously! But I assure you that you too, Madam, are in masquerade, though it be in all seriousness; and I am not speaking of the venerable crown on your brows or the ducal mantle. I am speaking only of the memory you wish to fix in yourself of your fair complexion one day when it pleased you— or of your dark complexion, if you were dark: the fading image of your youth! For you, Peter Damiani, on the contrary, the memory of what you have been, of what you have done, seems to you a recognition of past realities that remain within you like a dream. I'm in the same case too: with so many inexplicable

memories—like dreams! Ah! . . . There's nothing to marvel at in it, Peter Damiani! Tomorrow it will be the same thing with our life of today! [*Suddenly getting excited and taking hold of his sackcloth.*] This sackcloth here . . . [*Beginning to take it off with a gesture of almost ferocious joy while the* THREE VALETS *run over to him, frightened, as if to prevent his doing so.*] Ah, my God! [*Draws back and throws off sackcloth.*] Tomorrow, at Bressanone, twenty-seven German and Lombard bishops will sign with me the act of deposition of Gregory VII! No Pope at all! Just a false monk!

ORDULPH [*with the other three*]. Majesty! Majesty! In God's name! . . .

HAROLD [*inviting him to put on the sackcloth again*]. Listen to what he says, Majesty!

LANDOLPH. Monsignor is here with the Duchess to intercede in your favor. [*Makes secret signs to the* DOCTOR *to say something at once.*]

DOCTOR [*foolishly*]. Ah yes . . . yes . . . we are here to intercede . . .

HENRY IV [*repenting at once, almost terrified, allowing the three to put on the sackcloth again, and pulling it down over him with his own hands*]. Pardon . . . yes . . . yes . . . pardon, Monsignor: forgive me, my Lady. . . . I swear to you I feel the whole weight of the anathema. [*Bends himself, takes his face between his hands, as though waiting for something to crush him. Then changing tone, but without moving, says softly to* LANDOLPH, HAROLD, *and* ORDULPH.] But I don't know why I cannot be humble before that man there! [*Indicates* BELCREDI.]

LANDOLPH [*sotto voce*]. But why, Majesty, do you insist on believing he is Peter Damiani, when he isn't, at all?

HENRY IV [*looking at him timorously*]. He isn't Peter Damiani?

HAROLD. No, no, he is a poor monk, Majesty.

HENRY IV [*sadly with a touch of exasperation*]. Ah! None of us can estimate what we do when we do it from instinct. . . . You perhaps, Madam, can understand me better than the others, since you are a woman and a Duchess. This is a solemn and decisive moment. I could, you know, accept the assistance of the Lombard bishops, arrest the Pope, lock him up here in the castle, run to Rome and elect an anti-Pope; offer alliance to Robert Guiscard—and Gregory VII would be lost! I resist the temptation; and, believe me, I am wise in doing so. I feel the atmosphere of our times and the majesty of one who knows how to be what he ought to be! a Pope! Do you feel inclined to laugh at me, seeing me like this? You would be foolish to do so; for you don't understand the political wisdom which makes this penitent's sack advisable. The parts may be changed tomorrow. What would you do then? Would you laugh to see the Pope a prisoner? No! It would come to the same thing: I dressed as a penitent, today; he, as prisoner tomorrow! But woe to him who doesn't know how to wear his mask, be he king or Pope!—Perhaps he is a bit too cruel! No! Yes, yes, maybe!—You remember, my Lady, how your daughter Bertha, for whom, I repeat, my feelings have changed [turns to BELCREDI and shouts to his face as if he were being contradicted by him]—yes, changed on account of the affection and devotion she showed me in that terrible moment . . . [Then once again to the MARCHIONESS.] . . . you remember how she came with me, my Lady, followed me like a beggar and passed two nights out in the open, in the snow? You are her mother! Doesn't this touch your mother's heart? Doesn't this urge you to pity, so that you will beg His Holiness for pardon, beg him to receive us?

DONNA MATILDA [trembling, with feeble voice]. Yes, yes, at once. . . .

DOCTOR. It shall be done!

HENRY IV. And one thing more! [Draws them in to listen to him.] It isn't enough that he should receive me! You know he can do everything—everything I tell you! He can even call up the dead. [Touches his chest.] Behold me! Do you see me? There is no magic art unknown to him. Well, Monsignor, my Lady, my torment is really this: that whether here or there [pointing to his portrait almost in fear] I can't free myself from this magic. I am a penitent now, you see; and I swear to you I shall remain so until he receives me. But you two, when the excommunication is taken off, must ask the Pope to do this thing he can so easily do: to take me away from that; [indicating the portrait again] and let me live wholly and freely my miser-able life. A man can't always be twenty-six, my Lady. I ask this of you for your daughter's sake too; that I may love her as she deserves to be loved, well disposed as I am now, all tender toward her for her pity. There: it's all there! I am in your hands! [Bows.] My Lady! Monsignor!

[He goes off, bowing grandly, through the door by which he entered, leaving everyone stupefied, and the MARCHIONESS so profoundly touched, that no sooner has he gone than she breaks out into sobs and sits down almost fainting.]

ACT II

[Another room of the villa, adjoining the throne room. Its furniture is antique and severe. Principal exit at rear in the background. To the left, two windows looking on the garden. To the right, a door opening into the throne room.

Late afternoon of the same day.

DONNA MATILDA, the DOCTOR and BELCREDI are on the stage engaged in conversation; but DONNA MATILDA stands to one side, evidently annoyed at what the other two are saying; although she cannot help listening, because, in her agitated state, everything interests her in spite of herself. The talk of the other two attracts her attention, because she instinctively feels the need for calm at the moment.]

BELCREDI. It may be as you say, Doctor, but that was my impression.

DOCTOR. I won't contradict you; but, believe me, it is only . . . an impression.

BELCREDI. Pardon me, but he even said so, and quite clearly. [Turning to the MARCHIONESS.] Didn't he, Marchioness?

DONNA MATILDA [turning round]. What did he say? . . . [Then not agreeing.] Oh yes . . . but not for the reason you think!

DOCTOR. He was alluding to the costumes we had slipped on. . . . Your cloak [indicating the MARCHIONESS] our Benedictine habits. . . . But all this is childish!

DONNA MATILDA [turning quickly, indignant]. Childish? What do you mean, Doctor?

DOCTOR. From one point of view, it is —I beg you to let me say so, Marchioness! Yet, on the other hand, it is much more complicated than you can imagine.

DONNA MATILDA. To me, on the contrary, it is perfectly clear!

DOCTOR [*with a smile of pity of the competent person toward those who do not understand*]. We must take into account the peculiar psychology of madmen; which, you must know, enables us to be certain that they observe things and can, for instance, easily detect people who are disguised; can in fact recognize the disguise and yet believe in it; just as children do, for whom disguise is both play and reality. That is why I used the word childish. But the thing is extremely complicated, inasmuch as he must be perfectly aware of being an image to himself and for himself—that image there, in fact! [*Alluding to the portrait in the throne room, and pointing to the left.*]

BELCREDI. That's what he said!

DOCTOR. Very well then— An image before which other images, ours, have appeared: understand? Now he, in his acute and perfectly lucid delirium, was able to detect at once a difference between his image and ours: that is, he saw that ours were make-believes. So he suspected us; because all madmen are armed with a special diffidence. But that's all there is to it! Our make-believe, built up all round his, did not seem pitiful to him. While his seemed all the more tragic to us, in that he, as if in defiance—understand?—and induced by his suspicion, wanted to show us up merely as a joke. That was also partly the case with him, in coming before us with painted cheeks and hair, and saying he had done it on purpose for a jest.

DONNA MATILDA [*impatiently*]. No, it's not that, Doctor. It's not like that! It's not like that!

DOCTOR. Why isn't it, may I ask?

DONNA MATILDA [*with decision but trembling*]. I am perfectly certain he recognized me!

DOCTOR. It's not possible . . . it's not possible!

BELCREDI [*at the same time*]. Of course not!

DONNA MATILDA [*more than ever determined, almost convulsively*]. I tell you,

he recognized me! When he came close up to speak to me—looking in my eyes, right into my eyes—he recognized me!

BELCREDI. But he was talking of your daughter!

DONNA MATILDA. That's not true! He was talking of me! Of me!

BELCREDI. Yes, perhaps, when he said . . .

DONNA MATILDA [*letting herself go*]. About my dyed hair! But didn't you notice that he added at once: "or the memory of your dark hair, if you were dark"? He remembered perfectly well that I was dark—then!

BELCREDI. Nonsense! nonsense!

DONNA MATILDA [*not listening to him, turning to the DOCTOR*]. My hair, Doctor, is really dark—like my daughter's! That's why he spoke of her.

BELCREDI. But he doesn't even know your daughter! He's never seen her!

DONNA MATILDA. Exactly! Oh, you never understand anything! By my daughter, stupid, he meant me—as I was then!

BELCREDI. Oh, this is catching! This is catching, this madness!

DONNA MATILDA [*softly, with contempt*]. Fool!

BELCREDI. Excuse me, were you ever his wife? Your daughter is his wife—in his delirium: Bertha of Susa.

DONNA MATILDA. Exactly! Because I, no longer dark—as he remembered me—but fair, introduced myself as "Adelaide," the mother. My daughter doesn't exist for him: he's never seen her—you said so yourself! So how can he know whether she's fair or dark?

BELCREDI. But he said dark, speaking generally, just as anyone who wants to recall, whether fair or dark, a memory of youth in the color of the hair! And you, as usual, begin to imagine things! Doctor, you said I ought not to have come! It's she who ought not to have come!

DONNA MATILDA [*upset for a moment by BELCREDI's remark, recovers herself. Then with a touch of anger, because doubtful*]. No, no . . . he spoke of me. . . . He spoke all the time to me, with me, of me. . . .

BELCREDI. That's not bad! He didn't leave me a moment's breathing space; and you say he was talking all the time to you? Unless you think he was alluding to you too, when he was talking to Peter Damiani!

DONNA MATILDA [*defiantly, almost exceeding the limits of courteous discussion*]. Who knows? Can you tell me why, from the outset, he showed a strong dislike for you, for you alone? [*From the tone of the question, the expected answer must almost explicitly be: "because he understands you are my lover." BELCREDI feels this so well that he remains silent and can say nothing.*]

DOCTOR. The reason may also be found in the fact that only the visit of the Duchess Adelaide and the Abbot of Cluny was announced to him. Finding a third person present, who had not been announced, at once his suspicions . . .

BELCREDI. Yes, exactly! His suspicion made him see an enemy in me: Peter Damiani! But she's got it into her head, that he recognized her . . .

DONNA MATILDA. There's no doubt about it! I could see it from his eyes, Doctor. You know, there's a way of looking that leaves no doubt whatever. . . . Perhaps it was only for an instant, but I am sure!

DOCTOR. It is not impossible: a lucid moment . . .

DONNA MATILDA. Yes, perhaps. . . . And then his speech seemed to me full of regret for his and my youth—for the horrible thing that happened to him, that has held him in that disguise from which he has never been able to free himself, and from which he longs to be free—he said so himself!

BELCREDI. Yes, so as to be able to make love to your daughter, or you, as you believe—having been touched by your pity.

DONNA MATILDA. Which is very great, I would ask you to believe.

BELCREDI. As one can see, Marchioness; so much so that a miracle-worker might expect a miracle from it!

DOCTOR. Will you let me speak? I don't work miracles, because I am a doctor and not a miracle-worker. I listened very intently to all he said; and I repeat that a certain analogical elasticity, common in all systematized delirium, is evidently with him much—what shall I say? —much relaxed! The elements, that is, of his delirium no longer hold together. It

seems to me he has lost the equilibrium of his second personality and sudden recollections drag him—and this is very comforting—not from a state of incipient apathy, but rather from a morbid inclination to reflective melancholy, which shows a . . . a very considerable cerebral activity. Very comforting, I repeat! Now if, by this violent trick we've planned . . .

DONNA MATILDA [*turning to the window, in the tone of a sick person complaining*]. But how is it that the car has not returned? It's three hours and a half since . . .

DOCTOR. What do you say?

DONNA MATILDA. The car, Doctor! It's more than three hours and a half . . .

DOCTOR [*taking out his watch and looking at it*]. Yes, more than four hours, by this!

DONNA MATILDA. It could have reached here an hour ago at least! But, as usual . . .

BELCREDI. Perhaps they can't find the dress . . .

DONNA MATILDA. But I explained exactly where it was! [*Impatiently.*] And Frida . . . where is Frida?

BELCREDI [*looking out of the window*]. Perhaps she is in the garden with Charles . . .

DOCTOR. He'll talk her out of her fright.

BELCREDI. She's not afraid, Doctor; don't you believe it: the thing bores her rather . . .

DONNA MATILDA. Just don't ask anything of her! I know what she's like.

DOCTOR. Let's wait patiently. Anyhow, it will soon be over, and it has to be in the evening . . . It will only be the matter of a moment! If we can succeed in rousing him, as I was saying, and in breaking at one go the threads—already slack—which still bind him to this fiction of his, giving him back what he himself asks for—you remember, he said: "one cannot always be twenty-six years old, madam!"—if we can give him freedom from this torment, which even *he* feels is a torment, then if he is able to recover at one bound the sensation of the distance of time . . .

BELCREDI [*quickly*]. He'll be cured! [*Then emphatically with irony.*] We'll pull him out of it all!

DOCTOR. Yes, we may hope to set him going again, like a watch which has stopped at a certain hour ... just as if we had our watches in our hands and were waiting for that other watch to go again. A shake—so—and let's hope it'll tell the time again after its long stop. [*At this point the* MARQUIS CHARLES DI NOLLI *enters from the principal entrance.*]

DONNA MATILDA. Oh, Charles! ... And Frida? Where is she?

DI NOLLI. She'll be here in a moment.

DOCTOR. Has the car arrived?

DI NOLLI. Yes.

DONNA MATILDA. Yes? Has the dress come?

DI NOLLI. It's been here some time.

DOCTOR. Good! Good!

DONNA MATILDA [*trembling*]. Where is she? Where's Frida?

DI NOLLI [*shrugging his shoulders and smiling sadly, like one lending himself unwillingly to an untimely joke*]. You'll see, you'll see! ... [*Pointing toward the hall.*] Here she is! ... [BERTHOLD *appears at the threshold of the hall, and announces with solemnity.*]

BERTHOLD. Her Highness the Countess Matilda of Canossa! [FRIDA *enters, magnificent and beautiful, arrayed in the robes of her mother as "Countess Matilda of Tuscany," so that she is a living copy of the portrait in the throne room.*]

FRIDA [*passing* BERTHOLD, *who is bowing, says to him with disdain*]. Of Tuscany, of Tuscany! Canossa is just one of my castles!

BELCREDI [*in admiration*]. Look! Look! She seems another person. ...

DONNA MATILDA. One would say it were I! Look! Why, Frida, look! She's exactly my portrait, alive!

DOCTOR. Yes, yes ... Perfect! Perfect! The portrait, to the life.

BELCREDI. Yes, there's no question about it. She *is* the portrait! Magnificent!

FRIDA. Don't make me laugh, or I shall burst! I say, Mother, what a tiny waist you had! I had to squeeze so to get into this!

DONNA MATILDA [*arranging her dress a little*]. Wait! ... Keep still! ... These pleats ... is it really so tight?

FRIDA. I'm suffocating! I implore you, be quick! ...

DOCTOR. But we must wait till it's evening!

FRIDA. No, no, I can't hold out till evening!

DONNA MATILDA. Why did you put it on so soon?

FRIDA. The moment I saw it, the temptation was irresistible. ...

DONNA MATILDA. At least you could have called me, or have had someone help you! It's still all crumpled.

FRIDA. So I saw, Mother; but they are old creases; they won't come out.

DOCTOR. It doesn't matter, Marchioness! The illusion is perfect. [*Then coming nearer and asking her to come in front of her daughter, without hiding her.*] If you please, stay there ... at a certain distance ... now a little more forward. ...

BELCREDI. For the feeling of the distance of time. ...

DONNA MATILDA [*slightly turning to him*]. Twenty years after! A disaster! A tragedy!

BELCREDI. Now don't let's exaggerate!

DOCTOR [*embarrassed, trying to save the situation*]. No, no! I meant the dress ... so as to see ... You know ...

[*Pointing first to* FRIDA *and then to the* MARCHIONESS.]

BELCREDI [*laughing*]. Oh, as for the dress, Doctor, it isn't a matter of twenty years! It's eight hundred! An abyss! Do you really want to shove him across it from there to here? But you'll have to pick him up in pieces with a basket! Just think now: for us it is a matter of twenty years, a couple of dresses, and a masquerade. But, if, as you say, Doctor, time has stopped for and around him: if he lives there [*pointing to* FRIDA] with her, eight hundred years ago ... I repeat: the giddiness of the jump will be such, that finding himself suddenly among us ... [*The* DOCTOR *shakes his head in dissent.*] You don't think so?

DOCTOR. No, because life, my dear baron, can take up its rhythms. This— our life—will at once become real also to him; and will pull him up directly, wresting from him suddenly the illusion, and showing him that the eight hundred years, as you say, are only twenty! It will be like one of those tricks, such as the leap into space, for instance, of the Masonic rite, which appears to be heaven knows how far, and is only a step down the stairs.

BELCREDI. Ah! An idea! Yes! Look at Frida and the Marchioness, Doctor! Which is more advanced in time? We old people, Doctor! The young ones think they are more ahead; but it isn't true: we are more ahead, because time belongs to us more than to them.

DOCTOR. If the past didn't alienate us. . . .

BELCREDI. It doesn't matter at all! How does it alienate us? They [pointing to FRIDA and DI NOLLI] have still to do what we have accomplished, Doctor: to grow old, doing the same foolish things, more or less, as we did. . . . This is the illusion: that one comes forward through a door to life. It isn't so! As soon as one is born, one starts dying; therefore, he who started first is the most advanced of all. The youngest of us is father Adam! Look there: [pointing to FRIDA] eight hundred years younger than all of us—the Countess Matilda of Tuscany. [He makes her a deep bow.]

DI NOLLI. I say, Tito, don't start joking.

BELCREDI. Oh, you think I am joking? . . .

DI NOLLI. Of course, of course . . . all the time.

BELCREDI. Impossible! I've even dressed up as a Benedictine. . . .

DI NOLLI. Yes, but for a serious purpose.

BELCREDI. Well, exactly. If it has been serious for the others . . . for Frida, now, for instance. [Then turning to the DOCTOR]. I swear, Doctor, I don't yet understand what you want to do.

DOCTOR [annoyed]. You'll see! Let me do as I wish. . . . At present you see the Marchioness still dressed as. . . .

BELCREDI. Oh, she also . . . has to masquerade?

DOCTOR. Of course! of course! In another dress that's in there ready to be used when it comes into his head he sees the Countess Matilda of Canossa before him.

FRIDA [while talking quietly to DI NOLLI notices the DOCTOR's mistake]. Of Tuscany, of Tuscany!

DOCTOR. It's all the same!

BELCREDI. Oh, I see; He'll be faced by two of them. . . .

DOCTOR. Two, precisely! And then . . .

FRIDA [calling him aside]. Come here, Doctor! Listen!

DOCTOR. Here I am! [Goes near the two young people and pretends to give some explanations to them.]

BELCREDI [softly to DONNA MATILDA]. I say, this is getting rather strong, you know!

DONNA MATILDA [looking him firmly in the face]. What?

BELCREDI. Does it really interest you as much as all that—to make you willing to take part in . . . ? For a woman this is simply enormous! . . .

DONNA MATILDA. Yes, for an ordinary woman.

BELCREDI. Oh, no, my dear, for all women—in a question like this! It's an abnegation.

DONNA MATILDA. I owe it to him.

BELCREDI. Don't lie! You know well enough it's not hurting you!

DONNA MATILDA. Well, then where does the abnegation come in?

BELCREDI. Just enough to prevent you losing caste in other people's eyes—and just enough to offend me! . . .

DONNA MATILDA. But who is worrying about you now?

DI NOLLI [coming forward]. It's all right. It's all right. That's what we'll do! [Turning toward BERTHOLD.] Here you, go and call one of those fellows!

BERTHOLD. At once! [Exit.]

DONNA MATILDA. But first of all we've got to pretend that we are going away.

DI NOLLI. Exactly! I'll see to that. . . . [To BELCREDI.] You don't mind staying here?

BELCREDI [ironically]. Oh, no, I don't mind, I don't mind! . . .

DI NOLLI. We must look out not to make him suspicious again, you know.

BELCREDI. Oh, Lord! He doesn't amount to anything!

DOCTOR. He must believe absolutely that we've gone away. [LANDOLPH followed by BERTHOLD enters from the right.]

LANDOLPH. May I come in?

DI NOLLI. Come in! Come in! I say— your name's Lolo, isn't it?

LANDOLPH. Lolo, or Landolph, just as you like!

DI NOLLI. Well, look here: the Doctor and the Marchioness are leaving, at once.

LANDOLPH. Very well. All we've got to say is that they have been able to obtain the permission for the reception from His Holiness. He's in there in his own apartments repenting of all he said —and in an awful state to have the pardon! Would you mind coming a minute? ... If you would, just for a minute ... put on the dress again. ...

DOCTOR. Why, of course, with pleasure. ...

LANDOLPH. Might I be allowed to make a suggestion? Why not add that the Marchioness of Tuscany has interceded with the Pope that he should be received?

DONNA MATILDA. You see, he has recognized me!

LANDOLPH. Forgive me ... I don't know my history very well. I am sure you gentlemen know it much better! But I thought it was believed that Henry IV had a secret passion for the Marchioness of Tuscany.

DONNA MATILDA [at once]. Nothing of the kind! Nothing of the kind!

LANDOLPH. That's what I thought! But he says he's loved her ... he's always saying it. ... And now he fears that her indignation for this secret love of his will work him harm with the Pope.

BELCREDI. We must let him understand that this aversion no longer exists.

LANDOLPH. Exactly! Of course!

DONNA MATILDA [To BELCREDI]. History says—I don't know whether you know it or not—that the Pope gave way to the supplications of the Marchioness Matilda and the Abbot of Cluny. And I may say, my dear Belcredi, that I intended to take advantage of this fact— at the time of the pageant—to show him my feelings were not so hostile to him as he supposed.

BELCREDI. You are most faithful to history, Marchioness. ...

LANDOLPH. Well then, the Marchioness could spare herself a double disguise and present herself with Monsignor [indicating the DOCTOR] as the Marchioness of Tuscany.

DOCTOR [quickly, energetically]. No, no! That won't do at all. It would ruin everything. The impression from the confrontation must be a sudden one, give a shock! No, no, Marchioness, you will appear again as the Duchess Adelaide, the mother of the Empress. And then we'll go away. This is most necessary:

that he should know we've gone away. Come on! Don't let's waste any more time! There's a lot to prepare.

[Exeunt the DOCTOR, DONNA MATILDA, and LANDOLPH, right.]

FRIDA. I am beginning to feel afraid again.

DI NOLLI. Again, Frida?

FRIDA. It would have been better if I had seen him before.

DI NOLLI. There's nothing to be frightened of, really.

FRIDA. He isn't furious, is he?

DI NOLLI. Of course not! he's quite calm.

BELCREDI [with ironic sentimental affectation]. Melancholy! Didn't you hear that he loves you?

FRIDA. Thanks! That's just why I am afraid.

BELCREDI. He won't do you any harm.

DI NOLLI. It'll only last a minute. ...

FRIDA. Yes, but there in the dark with him. ...

DI NOLLI. Only for a moment; and I will be near you, and all the others behind the door ready to run in. As soon as you see your mother, your part will be finished.

BELCREDI. I'm afraid of a different thing: that we're wasting our time. ...

DI NOLLI. Don't begin again! The remedy seems a sound one to me.

FRIDA. I think so too! I feel it! I'm all trembling!

BELCREDI. But, mad people, my dear friends—though they don't know it, alas —have this felicity which we don't take into account. ...

DI NOLLI [interrupting, annoyed]. What felicity? Nonsense!

BELCREDI [forcefully]. They don't reason!

DI NOLLI. What's reasoning got to do with it, anyway?

BELCREDI. Don't you call it reasoning that he will have to do—according to us —when he sees her [indicates FRIDA] and her mother? We've reasoned it all out, surely!

DI NOLLI. Nothing of the kind: no reasoning at all! We put before him a double image of his own fantasy, or fiction, as the doctor says.

BELCREDI [suddenly]. I say, I've never understood why they take degrees in medicine.

DI NOLLI [amazed]. Who?

BELCREDI. The psychiatrists.

DI NOLLI. What ought they to take degrees in, then?

FRIDA. If they are psychiatrists, in what else should they take degrees?

BELCREDI. In law, of course! All a matter of talk! The more they talk, the more highly they are considered. "Analogous elasticity," "the sensation of distance in time!" And the first thing they tell you is that they don't work miracles —when a miracle's just what is wanted! But they know that the more they say they are not miracle-workers, the more people believe in their seriousness!

BERTHOLD [who has been looking through the keyhole of the door on right]. There they are! There they are! They're coming in here.

DI NOLLI. Are they?

BERTHOLD. He wants to come with them. . . . Yes! . . . He's coming too!

DI NOLLI. Let's get away, then! Let's get away, at once! [To BERTHOLD.] You stop here!

BERTHOLD. Must I?

[Without answering him, DI NOLLI, FRIDA, and BELCREDI go out by the main exit, leaving BERTHOLD surprised. The door on the right opens, and LANDOLPH enters first, bowing. Then DONNA MATILDA comes in, with mantle and ducal crown as in the first act; also the DOCTOR as the ABBOT OF CLUNY. HENRY IV is among them in royal dress. ORDULPH and HAROLD enter last of all.]

HENRY IV [following up what he has been saying in the other room]. And now I will ask you a question: how can I be astute, if you think me obstinate?

DOCTOR. No, no, not obstinate!

HENRY IV [smiling, pleased]. Then you think me really astute?

DOCTOR. No, no, neither obstinate, nor astute.

HENRY IV [with benevolent irony]. Monsignor, if obstinacy is not a vice which can go with astuteness, I hoped that in denying me the former, you would at least allow me a little of the latter. I can assure you I have great need of it. But if you want to keep it all for yourself . . .

DOCTOR. I? I? Do I seem astute to you?

HENRY IV. No. Monsignor! What do you say? Not in the least! Perhaps in this case, I may seem a little obstinate to you. . . . [Cutting short to speak to DONNA MATILDA.] With your permission: a word in confidence to the Duchess. [Leads her aside and asks her very earnestly.] Is your daughter really dear to you?

DONNA MATILDA [dismayed]. Why, yes, certainly. . . .

HENRY IV. Do you wish me to compensate her with all my love, with all my devotion, for the grave wrongs I have done her—though you must not believe all the stories my enemies tell about my dissoluteness!

DONNA MATILDA. No, no, I don't believe them. I never have believed such stories.

HENRY IV. Well, then are you willing?

DONNA MATILDA [confused]. What?

HENRY IV. That I return to love your daughter again? [Looks at her and adds, in a mysterious tone of warning.] You mustn't be a friend of the Marchioness of Tuscany!

DONNA MATILDA. I tell you again that she has begged and tried not less than ourselves to obtain your pardon. . . .

HENRY IV [softly, but excitedly]. Don't tell me that! Don't say that to me! Don't you see the effect it has on me, my Lady?

DONNA MATILDA [looks at him; then very softly as if in confidence]. You love her still?

HENRY IV [puzzled]. Still? Still, you say? You know, then? But nobody knows! Nobody must know!

DONNA MATILDA. But perhaps she knows, if she has begged so hard for you!

HENRY IV [looks at her and says]. And you love your daughter? [Brief pause. He turns to the DOCTOR with laughing accents.] Ah, Monsignor, it's strange how little I think of my wife! It may be a sin, but I swear to you that I hardly feel her at all in my heart. What is stranger is that her own mother scarcely feels her in her heart. Confess, my Lady, that she amounts to very little for you. [Turning to DOCTOR.] She talks to me of that other woman, insistently, insistently, I don't know why! . . .

LANDOLPH [humbly]. Maybe, Majesty, it is to disabuse you of some ideas you have had about the Marchioness of Tuscany. [*Then, dismayed at having allowed himself this observation, adds.*] I mean just now, of course. . . .

HENRY IV. You too maintain that she has been friendly to me?

LANDOLPH. Yes, at the moment, Majesty.

DONNA MATILDA. Exactly! Exactly! . . .

HENRY IV. I understand. That is to say, you don't believe I love her. I see! I see! Nobody's every believed it, nobody's ever thought it. Better so, then! But enough, enough! [*Turns to the* DOCTOR *with changed expression.*] Monsignor, you see? The reasons the Pope has had for revoking the excommunication have nothing at all to do with the reasons for which he excommunicated me originally. Tell Pope Gregory we shall meet again at Bressanone. And you, Madame, should you chance to meet your daughter in the courtyard of the castle of your friend the Marchioness, ask her to visit me. We shall see if I succeed in keeping her close beside me as wife and Empress. Many women have presented themselves here already assuring me that they were she. And I thought to have her—yes, I tried sometimes—there's no shame in it, with one's wife!—But when they said they were Bertha, and they were from Susa, all of them—I can't think why—started laughing! [*Confidentially.*] Understand? —In bed—I undressed—so did she—yes, by God, undressed—a man and a woman —it's natural after all! Like that, we don't bother much about who we are. And one's dress is like a phantom that hovers always near one. Oh, Monsignor, phantoms in general are nothing more than trifling disorders of the spirit: images we cannot contain within the bounds of sleep. They reveal themselves even when we are awake, and they frighten us. I . . . ah . . . I am always afraid when, at night-time, I see disordered images before me. Sometimes I am even afraid of my own blood pulsing loudly in my arteries in the silence of night, like the sound of a distant step in a lonely corridor! . . . But, forgive me! I have kept you standing too long already. I thank you, my Lady, I thank you, Monsignor. [DONNA MATILDA *and the* DOCTOR *go off bowing. As soon as they have gone,* HENRY IV *suddenly changes his tone.*] Buffoons, buffoons! One can play any tune on them! And

that other fellow . . . Pietro Damiani! . . . Caught him out perfectly! He's afraid to appear before me again. [*Moves up and down excitedly while saying this; then sees* BERTHOLD, *and points him out to the other* THREE VALETS.] Oh, look at this imbecile watching me with his mouth wide open! [*Shakes him.*] Don't you understand? Don't you see, idiot, how I treat them, how I play the fool with them, make them appear before me just as I wish? Miserable, frightened clowns that they are! And you [*addressing the* VALETS] are amazed that I tear off their ridiculous masks now, just as if it wasn't I who had made them mask themselves to satisfy this taste of mine for playing the madman!

LANDOLPH—HAROLD—ORDULPH [*bewildered, looking at one another*]. What? What does he say? What?

HENRY IV [*answers them imperiously*]. Enough! enough! Let's stop it. I'm tired of it. [*Then as if the thought left him no peace.*] By God! The impudence! To come here along with her lover! . . . And pretending to do it out of pity! So as not to infuriate a poor devil already out of the world, out of time, out of life! If it weren't supposed to be done out of pity, one can well imagine that fellow wouldn't have allowed it. Those people expect others to behave as they wish all the time. And, of course, there's nothing arrogant in that! Oh, no! Oh, no! It's merely their way of thinking, of feeling, of seeing. Everybody has his own way of thinking; you fellows, too. Yours is that of a flock of sheep—miserable, feeble, uncertain. . . . But those others take advantage of this and make you accept their way of thinking; or, at least, they suppose they do; because, after all, what do they succeed in imposing on you? Words, words which anyone can interpret in his own manner! That's the way public opinion is formed! And it's a bad outlook for a man who finds himself labeled one day with one of these words which everyone repeats; for example "madman," or "imbecile." Don't you think it is rather hard for a man to keep quiet, when he knows that there is a fellow going about trying to persuade everybody that he is as he sees him, trying to fix him in other people's opinion as a "madman"—according to him? Now I am talking seriously!

Before I hurt my head, falling from my horse... [Stops suddenly, noticing the dismay of the four young men.] What's the matter with you? [Imitates their amazed looks.] What? Am I, or am I not, mad? Oh, yes! I'm mad all right! [He becomes terrible.] Well, then, by God, down on your knees, down on your knees! [Makes them go down on their knees one by one.] I order you to go down on your knees before me! And touch the ground three times with your foreheads! Down, down! That's the way you've got to be before madmen! [Then annoyed with their facile humiliation.] Get up, sheep! You obeyed me, didn't you? You might have put the strait jacket on me!... Crush a man with the weight of a word—it's nothing—a fly! All our life is crushed by the weight of words: the weight of the dead. Look at me here: can you really suppose that Henry IV is still alive? All the same, I speak, and order you live men about! Do you think it's a joke that the dead continue to live?—Yes, here it's a joke! But get out into the live world!—Ah, you say: what a beautiful sunrise—for us! All time is before us!—Dawn! We will do what we like with this day.... Ah, yes! To Hell with tradition, the old conventions! Well, go on! You will do nothing but repeat the old, old words, while you imagine you are living! [Goes up to BERTHOLD who has now become quite stupid.] You don't understand a word of this, do you? What's your name?

BERTHOLD. I?... What?... Berthold...

HENRY IV. Poor Berthold! What's your name here?

BERTHOLD. I... I... my name is Fino.

HENRY IV [feeling the warning and critical glances of the others, turns to them to reduce them to silence]. Fino?

BERTHOLD. Fino Pagliuca, Sire.

HENRY IV [turning to LANDOLPH]. I've heard you call each other by your nicknames often enough! Your name is Lolo, isn't it?

LANDOLPH. Yes, Sire... [Then with a sense of immense joy.] Oh Lord! Oh Lord! Then he is not mad....

HENRY IV [brusquely]. What?

LANDOLPH [hesitating]. No... I said...

HENRY IV. Not mad, any more. No.

Don't you see? We're having a joke on those that think I am mad! [To HAROLD.] I say, boy, your name's Franco.... [To ORDULPH.] And yours...

ORDULPH. Momo.

HENRY IV. Momo, Momo... A nice name that!

LANDOLPH. So he isn't...

HENRY IV. What are you talking about? Of course not! Let's have a jolly, good laugh!... [Laughs.] Ah!... Ah!... Ah!...

LANDOLPH—HAROLD—ORDULPH [looking at each other half happy and half dismayed]. Then he's cured!... he's all right!...

HENRY IV. Silence! Silence!... [To BERTHOLD.] Why don't you laugh? Are you offended? I didn't mean it especially for you. It's convenient for everybody to insist that certain people are mad, so they can be shut up. Do you know why? Because it's impossible to hear them speak! What shall I say of these people who've just gone away? That one is a whore, another a libertine, another a swindler.... Don't you think so? You can't believe a word he says.... Don't you think so? By the way, they all listen to me terrified. And why are they terrified, if what I say isn't true? Of course, you can't believe what madmen say—yet, at the same time, they stand there with their eyes wide open with terror!—Why? Tell me, tell me, why?—You see I'm quite calm now!

BERTHOLD. But, perhaps, they think that...

HENRY IV. No, no, my dear fellow! Look me well in the eyes!... I don't say that it's true—nothing is true, Berthold! But... look me in the eyes!

BERTHOLD. Well...

HENRY IV. You see? You see?... You have terror in your own eyes now because I seem mad to you! There's the proof of it! [Laughs.]

LANDOLPH [coming forward in the name of the others, exasperated]. What proof?

HENRY IV. Your being so dismayed because now I seem again mad to you. You have thought me mad up to now, haven't you? You feel that this dismay of yours can become terror too—something to dash away the ground from under your feet and deprive you of the air you breathe! Do you know what it means to find yourselves face to face with a mad-man—with one who shakes the foundations of all you have built up in yourselves, your logic, the logic of all your constructions? Madmen, lucky folk, construct without logic, or rather with a logic that flies like a feather. Voluble! Voluble! Today like this and tomorrow—who knows? You say: "This cannot be"; but for them everything can be. You say: "This isn't true!" And why? Because it doesn't seem true to you, or you, or you. ... [*Indicates the three of them in succession.*] ... and to a hundred thousand others! One must see what seems true to these hundred thousand others who are not supposed to be mad! What a magnificent spectacle they afford, when they reason! What flowers of logic they scatter! I know that when I was a child, I thought the moon in the pond was real. How many things I thought real! I believed everything I was told—and I was happy! Because it's a terrible thing if you don't hold on to that which seems true to you today—to that which will seem true to you tomorrow, even if it is the opposite of that which seemed true to you yesterday. I would never wish you to think, as I have done, on this horrible thing which really drives one mad: that if you were beside another and looking into his eyes —as I one day looked into somebody's eyes—you might as well be a beggar before a door never to be opened to you; for he who does enter there will never be you, but someone unknown to you with his own different and impenetrable world. ... [*Long pause. Darkness gathers in the room, increasing the sense of strangeness and consternation in which the four young men are involved.* HENRY IV *remains aloof, pondering on the misery which is not only his, but everybody's. Then he pulls himself up, and says in an ordinary tone.*] It's getting dark here. ...

ORDULPH. Shall I go for a lamp?

HENRY IV [*ironically*]. The lamp, yes the lamp! ... Do you suppose I don't know that as soon as I turn my back with my oil lamp to go to bed, you turn on the electric light for yourselves, here, and even there, in the throne room? I pretend not to see it!

ORDULPH. Well, then, shall I turn it on now?

HENRY IV. No, it would blind me! I want my lamp!

ORDULPH. It's ready here behind the door. [*Goes to the main exit, opens the door, goes out for a moment, and returns with an ancient lamp which is held by a ring at the top.*]

HENRY IV. Ah, a little light! Sit there around the table, no, not like that; in an elegant, easy, manner! ... [*To* HAROLD.] Yes, you, like that! [*Poses him. Then to* BERTHOLD.] You so! ... and I, here! [*Sits opposite them.*] We could do with a little decorative moonlight. It's very useful for us, the moonlight. I feel a real necessity for it, and pass a lot of time looking up at the moon from my window. Who would think, to look at her that she knows that eight hundred years have passed, and that I, seated at the window, cannot really be Henry IV gazing at the moon like any poor devil? But, look, look! See what a magnificent night scene we have here: the Emperor surrounded by his faithful counselors! ... How do you like it?

LANDOLPH [*softly to* HAROLD, *so as not to break the enchantment*]. And to think it wasn't true! ...

HENRY IV. True? What wasn't true?

LANDOLPH [*timidly as if to excuse himself*]. No ... I mean ... I was saying this morning to him [*Indicates* BERTHOLD.]— he has just started working here—I was saying: what a pity that dressed like this and with so many beautiful costumes in the wardrobe ... and with a room like that ... [*Indicates the throne room.*]

HENRY IV. Well? what's the pity?

LANDOLPH. Well ... that we didn't know ...

HENRY IV. That it was all done in jest, this comedy?

LANDOLPH. Because we thought that ...

HAROLD [*coming to his assistance*]. Yes ... that it was done seriously!

HENRY IV. What do you say? Doesn't it seem serious to you?

LANDOLPH. But if you say that ...

HENRY IV. I say that—you are fools! You ought to have known how to create a fantasy for yourselves, not to act it for me, or anyone coming to see me; but naturally, simply, day by day, before nobody, feeling yourselves alive in the history of the eleventh century, here at the court of your emperor, Henry IV! You, Ordulph [taking him by the arm], alive in the castle of Goslar, waking up in the morning, getting out of bed, and entering straight into the dream, clothing yourself in the dream that would be no more a dream, because you would have lived it, felt it all alive in you. You would have drunk it in with the air you breathed; yet knowing all the time that it was a dream, so you could better enjoy the privilege afforded you of having to do nothing else but live this dream, this far off and yet actual dream! And to think that at a distance of eight centuries from this remote age of ours, so colored and so sepulchral, the men of the twentieth century are torturing themselves in ceaseless anxiety to know how their fates and fortunes will work out! Whereas you are already in history with me. . . .

LANDOLPH. Yes, yes, very good!

HENRY IV. . . . Everything determined, everything settled!

ORDULPH. Yes, yes!

HENRY IV. And sad as is my lot, hideous as some of the events are, bitter the struggles, and troubled the time—still all history! All history that cannot change, understand? All fixed for ever! And you could have admired at your ease how every effect followed obediently its cause with perfect logic, how every event took place precisely and coherently in each minute particular! The pleasure, the pleasure of history, in fact, which is so great, was yours.

LANDOLPH. Beautiful, beautiful!

HENRY IV. Beautiful, but it's finished! Now that you know, I could not do it any more! [Takes his lamp to go to bed.] Neither could you, if up to now you haven't understood the reason of it! I am sick of it now. [Almost to himself with violent contained rage.] By God, I'll make her sorry she came here! Dressed herself up as a mother-in-law for me! . . . And he as an abbot! . . . And they bring a doctor with them to study me! . . . Who knows if they don't hope to cure me? . . . Clowns! . . . I'd like to smack one of them at least in the face: yes, that one—a famous swordsman, they say! . . . He'll kill me . . . Well, we'll see, we'll see! . . . [A knock at the door.] Who is it?

THE VOICE OF JOHN. Deo Gratias!

HAROLD [very pleased at the chance for another joke]. Oh, it's John, it's old John, who comes every night to play the monk.

ORDULPH [rubbing his hands]. Yes, yes! Let's make him do it!

HENRY IV [at once, severely]. Fool, why? Just to play a joke on a poor old man who does it for love of me?

LANDOLPH [to ORDULPH]. It has to be as if it were true.

HENRY IV. Exactly, as if true! Because, only so, truth is not a jest. [Opens the door and admits JOHN dressed as a humble friar with a roll of parchment under his arm.] Come in, come in, Father! [Then assuming a tone of tragic gravity and deep resentment.] All the documents of my life and reign favorable to me were destroyed deliberately by my enemies. One only has escaped destruction, this, my life, written by a humble monk who is devoted to me. And you would laugh at him! [Turns affectionately to JOHN, and invites him to sit down at the table.] Sit down, Father, sit down! Have the lamp near you! [Puts the lamp near him.] Write! Write!

JOHN [opens the parchment and prepares to write from dictation]. I am ready, your Majesty!

HENRY IV [dictating]. "The decree of peace proclaimed at Mayence helped the poor and the good, while it damaged the powerful and the bad. [Curtain begins to fall.] It brought wealth to the former, hunger and misery to the latter. . . ."

CURTAIN

ACT III

[The throne room is so dark that the wall at the bottom is hardly seen. The canvases of the two portraits have been taken away; and, within their frames, FRIDA, dressed as the "Marchioness of Tuscany," and CHARLES DI NOLLI, as "Henry IV," have taken the exact positions of the portraits.

For a moment, after the raising of the curtain, the stage is empty. Then the door on the left opens; and HENRY IV, holding the lamp by the ring on top of it, enters. He looks back to speak to the four young men, who, with JOHN, are presumedly in the adjoining hall, as at the end of the second act.]

HENRY IV. No, stay where you are, stay where you are. I shall manage all right by myself. Good night! [Closes the door and walks, very sad and tired, across the hall toward the second door on the right, which leads into his apartments.]

FRIDA [as soon as she sees that he has just passed the throne, whispers from the niche like one who is on the point of fainting away with fright]. Henry . . .

HENRY IV [stopping at the voice, as if someone had stabbed him traitorously in the back, turns a terrorstricken face toward the wall at the bottom of the room; raising an arm instinctively, as if to defend himself and ward off a blow]. Who is calling me? [It is not a question, but an exclamation vibrating with terror, which does not expect a reply from the darkness and the terrible silence of the hall, which suddenly fills him with the suspicion that he is really mad.]

FRIDA [at his shudder of terror, is herself not less frightened at the part she is playing, and repeats a little more loudly]. Henry! . . . [But, although she wishes to act the part as they have given it to her, she stretches her head a little out of the frame toward the other frame.]

HENRY IV [gives a dreadful cry; lets the lamp fall from his hands to cover his head with his arms, and makes a movement as if to run away].

FRIDA [jumping from frame on to the stand and shouting like a mad woman]. Henry! . . . Henry! . . . I'm afraid! . . . I'm terrified! . . .

[And while DI NOLLI jumps in turn on to the stand and thence to the floor and runs to FRIDA who, on the verge of fainting, continues to cry out, the DOCTOR, DONNA MATILDA, also dressed as "Matilda of Tuscany," TITO BELCREDI, LANDOLPH, BERTHOLD and JOHN enter the hall from the doors on the right and on the left. One of them turns on the light: a strange light coming from lamps hidden in the ceiling so that only the upper part of the stage is well lighted. The others without taking notice of HENRY IV, who looks on astonished by the unex-pected inrush, after the moment of terror which still causes him to tremble, run anxiously to support and comfort the still shaking FRIDA, who is moaning in the arms of her fiancé. All are speaking at the same time.]

DI NOLLI. No, no, Frida . . . Here I am . . . I am beside you!

DOCTOR [coming with the others]. Enough! Enough! There's nothing more to be done! . . .

DONNA MATILDA. He is cured, Frida. Look! He is cured! Don't you see?

DI NOLLI [astonished]. Cured?

BELCREDI. It was only for fun! Be calm!

FRIDA. No! I am afraid! I am afraid!

DONNA MATILDA. Afraid of what? Look at him! He was never mad at all! . . .

DI NOLLI. That isn't true! What are you saying? Cured?

DOCTOR. It appears so. I should say so . . .

BELCREDI. Yes, yes! They have told us so. [Pointing to the four young men.]

DONNA MATILDA. Yes, for a long time! He has confided in them, told them the truth!

DI NOLLI [now more indignant than astonished]. But what does it mean? If, up to a short time ago . . . ?

BELCREDI. Hum! He was acting, to take you in and also us, who in good faith . . .

DI NOLLI. Is it possible? To deceive his sister too, right up to the time of her death?

HENRY IV [remains apart, peering at one and now at the other under the accusation and the mockery of what all believe to be a cruel joke of his, which is now revealed. He has shown by the flashing of his eyes that he is meditating a revenge, which his violent contempt prevents him from defining clearly, as yet. Stung to the quick and with a clear idea of accepting the fiction they have insidiously worked up as true, he bursts forth at this point]. Go on, I say! Go on!

DI NOLLI [astonished at the cry]. Go on! What do you mean?

HENRY IV. It isn't your sister only that is dead!

DI NOLLI. My sister? Yours, I say, whom you compelled up to the last moment, to present herself here as your mother, Agnes!

HENRY IV. And was she not your mother?

DI NOLLI. My mother? Certainly my mother!

HENRY IV. But your mother is dead for me, *old and far away!* You have just got down now from there. [*Pointing to the frame from which he jumped down.*] And how do you know whether I have not wept her long in secret, dressed even as I am?

DONNA MATILDA [*dismayed, looking at the others*]. What does he say?

DOCTOR [*much impressed, observing him*]. Quietly! quietly, for Heaven's sake!

HENRY IV. What do I say? I ask all of you if Agnes was not the mother of Henry IV? [*Turns to FRIDA as if she were really the "Marchioness of Tuscany."*] You, Marchioness, it seems to me, ought to know.

FRIDA [*still frightened, draws closer to DI NOLLI*]. No, no, I don't know. Not I!

DOCTOR. It's the madness returning. . . . Quiet now, everybody!

BELCREDI [*indignant*]. Madness indeed, Doctor! He's acting again! . . .

HENRY IV [*suddenly*]. I? You have emptied those two frames over there, and he stands before my eyes as Henry IV. . . .

BELCREDI. We've had enough of this joke now.

HENRY IV. Who said joke?

DOCTOR [*loudly to BELCREDI*]. Don't excite him, for the love of God!

BELCREDI [*without lending an ear to him, but speaking louder*]. But they have said so [*pointing again to the four young men*], they, they!

HENRY IV [*turning round and looking at them*]. You? Did you say it was all a joke?

LANDOLPH [*timid and embarrassed*]. No . . . really we said that you were cured.

BELCREDI. Look here! Enough of this! [*To DONNA MATILDA.*] Doesn't it seem to you that the sight of him [*pointing to DI NOLLI*], Marchioness, and that of your daughter dressed so, is becoming intolerably childish?

DONNA MATILDA. Oh, be quiet! What does the dress matter, if he is cured?

HENRY IV. Cured, yes! I am cured! [*To BELCREDI.*] Ah, but not to let it end this way all at once, as you suppose! [*Attacks*

him.*] Do you know that for twenty years nobody has ever dared to appear before me here like you and that gentleman? [*Pointing to the DOCTOR.*]

BELCREDI. Of course I know it. As a matter of fact, I too appeared before you this morning dressed . . .

HENRY IV. As a monk, yes!

BELCREDI. And you took me for Peter Damiani! And I didn't even laugh, believing, in fact, that . . .

HENRY IV. That I was mad! Does it make you laugh seeing her like that, now that I am cured? And yet you might have remembered that in my eyes her appearance now . . . [*Interrupts himself with a gesture of contempt.*] Ah! [*Suddenly turns to the DOCTOR.*] You are a doctor, aren't you?

DOCTOR. Yes.

HENRY IV. And you also took part in dressing her up as the Marchioness of Tuscany? To prepare a counter-joke for me here, eh?

DONNA MATILDA [*impetuously*]. No, no! What do you say? It was done for you! I did it for your sake.

DOCTOR [*quickly*]. To attempt, to try, not knowing . . .

HENRY IV [*cutting him short*]. I understand. I say counter-joke, in his case [*indicates BELCREDI*] because he believes that I have been carrying on a jest. . . .

BELCREDI. But excuse me, what do you mean? You say yourself you are cured.

HENRY IV. Let me speak! [*To the DOCTOR.*] Do you know, Doctor, that for a moment you ran the risk of making me mad again? By God, to make the portraits speak; to make them jump alive out of their frames . . .

DOCTOR. But you saw that all of us ran in at once, as soon as they told us . . .

HENRY IV. Certainly! [*Contemplates FRIDA and DI NOLLI, and then looks at the MARCHIONESS, and finally at his own costume.*] The combination is very beautiful. . . . Two couples. . . . Very good, very good, Doctor! For a madman, not bad! . . . [*With a slight wave of his hand to BELCREDI.*] It seems to him now to be a carnival out of season, eh? [*Turns to look at him.*] We'll get rid now of this masquerade costume of mine, so that I may come away with you. What do you say?

BELCREDI. With me? With us!

HENRY IV. Where shall we go? To the Club? In dress coats and with white ties? Or shall both of us go to the Marchioness' house?

BELCREDI. Wherever you like! Do you want to remain here still, to continue— alone—what was nothing but the unfortunate joke of a day of carnival? It is really incredible, incredible how you have been able to do all this, freed from the disaster that befell you!

HENRY IV. Yes, you see how it was! The fact is that falling from my horse and striking my head as I did, I was really mad for I know not how long. . . .

DOCTOR. Ah! Did it last long?

HENRY IV [very quickly to the DOCTOR]. Yes, Doctor, a long time! I think it must have been about twelve years. [Then suddenly turning to speak to BELCREDI.] Thus I saw nothing, my dear fellow, of all that, after that day of carnival, happened for you but not for me: how things changed, how my friends deceived me, how my place was taken by another, and all the rest of it! And suppose my place had been taken in the heart of the woman I loved? . . . And how should I know who was dead or who had disappeared? . . . All this, you know, wasn't exactly a joke for me, as it seems to you. . . .

BELCREDI. No, no! I don't mean that! I mean after . . .

HENRY IV. Ah, yes? After? One day— [Stops and addresses the DOCTOR.] A most interesting case, Doctor! Study me well! Study me carefully! [Trembles while speaking.]—All by itself, who knows how, one day the trouble here [touches his forehead] mended. Little by little, I open my eyes, and at first I don't know whether I am asleep or awake. Then I know I am awake. I touch this thing and that; I see clearly again. . . . Ah!—then, as he says [alludes to BELCREDI] away, away with this masquerade, this incubus! Let's open the windows, breathe life once again! Away! Away! Let's run out! [Suddenly pulling himself up.] But where? And to do what? To show myself to all, secretly, as Henry IV, not like this, but arm in arm with you, among my dear friends?

BELCREDI. What are you saying?

DONNA MATILDA. Who could think it?

It's not to be imagined. It was an accident.

HENRY IV. They all said I was mad before. [To BELCREDI.] And you know it! You were more ferocious than anyone against those who tried to defend me.

BELCREDI. Oh, that was only a joke!

HENRY IV. Look at my hair! [Shows him the hair on the nape of his neck.]

BELCREDI. But mine is gray too!

HENRY IV. Yes, with this difference: that mine went gray here, as Henry IV, do you understand? And I never knew it! I perceived it all of a sudden, one day, when I opened my eyes; and I was terrified because I understood at once that not only had my hair gone gray, but that I was all gray, inside; that everything had fallen to pieces, that everything was finished; and I was going to arrive, hungry as a wolf, at a banquet which had already been cleared away. . . .

BELCREDI. Yes, but, what about the others? . . .

HENRY IV [quickly]. Ah, yes, I know! They couldn't wait until I was cured, not even those, who, behind my back, pricked my saddled horse till it bled. . . .

DI NOLLI [agitated]. What, what?

HENRY IV. Yes, treacherously, to make it rear and cause me to fall.

DONNA MATILDA [quickly, in horror]. This is the first time I knew that.

HENRY IV. That was also a joke, probably!

DONNA MATILDA. But who did it? Who was behind us, then?

HENRY IV. It doesn't matter who it was. All those that went on feasting and were ready to leave me their scrapings, Marchioness, of miserable pity, or some dirty remnant of remorse in the filthy plate! Thanks! [Turning quickly to the DOCTOR.] Now, Doctor, the case must be absolutely new in the history of madness; I preferred to remain mad—since I found everything ready and at my disposal for this new exquisite fantasy. I would live it —this madness of mine—with the most lucid consciousnsess; and thus revenge myself on the brutality of a stone which had dented my head. The solitude—this solitude—squalid and empty as it appeared to me when I opened my eyes again—I determined to deck it out with all the colors and splendors of that far off day of carnival, when you [*looks at* DONNA MATILDA *and points* FRIDA *out to her*]— when you, Marchioness, triumphed. So I would oblige all those who were around me to follow, by God, at my orders that famous pageant which had been—for you and not for me—the jest of a day. I would make it become—forever—no more a joke but a reality, the reality of a real madness: here, all in masquerade, with throne room, and these my four secret counselors: secret and, of course, traitors. [*He turns quickly toward them.*] I should like to know what you have gained by revealing the fact that I was cured! If I am cured, there's no longer any need of you, and you will be discharged! To give anyone one's confidence ... that is really the act of a madman. But now I accuse you in my turn. [*Turning to the others.*] Do you know? They thought [*Alludes to the others.*] Do you know? They thought [*alludes to the* VALETS] they could make fun of me too with you. [*Bursts out laughing. The others laugh, but shamefacedly, except* DONNA MATILDA.]

BELCREDI [*to* DI NOLLI]. Well, imagine that.... That's not bad....

DI NOLLI [*to the four young men*]. You?

HENRY IV. We must pardon them. This dress [*plucking his dress*] which is for me the evident, voluntary caricature of that other continuous, everlasting masquerade, of which we are the involuntary puppets [*indicates* BELCREDI], when without knowing it, we mask ourselves with that which we appear to be ... ah, that dress of theirs, this masquerade of theirs, of course, we must forgive it them, since they do not yet see it is identical with themselves.... [*Turning again to* BELCREDI.] You know, it is quite easy to get accustomed to it. One walks about as a tragic character, just as if it were nothing ... [*imitates the tragic manner*] in a room like this.... Look here, Doctor! I remember a priest, certainly Irish, a nice-looking priest, who was sleeping in the sun one November day, with his arm on the corner of the bench of a public garden. He was lost in the golden delight of the mild sunny air which must have seemed for him almost summery. One may be sure that in that moment he did

not know any more that he was a priest, or even where he was. He was dreaming. ... A little boy passed with a flower in his hand. He touched the priest with it here on the neck. I saw him open his laughing eyes, while all his mouth smiled with the beauty of his dream. He was forgetful of everything.... But all at once, he pulled himself together, and stretched out his priest's cassock; and there came back to his eyes the same seriousness which you have seen in mine; because the Irish priests defend the seriousness of their Catholic faith with the same zeal with which I defend the sacred rights of hereditary monarchy! I am cured, gentlemen: because I can act the madman to perfection, here; and I do it very quietly. I'm only sorry for you that have to live your madness so agitatedly, without knowing it or seeing it.

BELCREDI. It comes to this, then, that it is we who are mad. That's what it is!

HENRY IV [*containing his irritation*]. But if you weren't mad, both you and she [*indicating the* MARCHIONESS], would you have come here to see me?

BELCREDI. To tell the truth, I came here believing that you were the madman.

HENRY IV [*suddenly indicating the* MARCHIONESS]. And she?

BELCREDI. Ah, as for her ... I can't say. I see she is fascinated by your words, by this *conscious* madness of yours. [*Turns to her.*] Dressed as you are [*speaking to her*], you could even remain here to live it out, Marchioness.

DONNA MATILDA. You are insolent!

HENRY IV [*conciliatingly*]. No, Marchioness, what he means to say is that the miracle would be complete, according to him, with you here, who—as the Marchioness of Tuscany, you well know —could not be my friend, save, as at Canossa, to give me a little pity....

BELCREDI. Or even more than a little! She said so herself!

HENRY IV [*to the* MARCHIONESS, *continuing*]. And even, shall we say, a little remorse! ...

BELCREDI. Yes, that too she has admitted.

DONNA MATILDA [*angry*]. Now look here ...

HENRY IV [*quickly, to placate her*].

Don't bother about him! Don't mind him! Let him go on infuriating me— though the Doctor's told him not to. [*Turns to* BELCREDI.] But do you suppose I am going to trouble myself any more about what happened between us —the share you had in my misfortune with her [*indicates the* MARCHIONESS *to him and pointing* BELCREDI *out to her*], the part he has now in your life? This is my life! Quite a different thing from your life! Your life, the life in which you have grown old—I have not lived that life. [*To* DONNA MATILDA.] Was this what you wanted to show me with this sacrifice of yours, dressing yourself up like this, according to the Doctor's idea? Excellently done, Doctor! Oh, an excellent idea: "As we were then, eh? and as we are now?" But I am not a madman according to your way of thinking, Doctor. I know very well that that man there [*indicates* DI NOLLI] cannot be me; because I am Henry IV, and have been, these twenty years, cast in this eternal masquerade. She has lived these years! [*Indicates the* MARCHIONESS.] She has enjoyed them and has become—look at her!—a woman I can no longer recognize. It is so that I knew her! [*Points to* FRIDA *and draws near her.*] This is the Marchioness I know, always this one! ... You seem a lot of children to be so easily frightened by me.... [*To* FRIDA.] And you're frightened too, little girl, aren't you, by the jest that they made you take part in—though they didn't understand it wouldn't be the jest they meant it to be, for me? Oh miracle of miracles! Prodigy of prodigies! The dream alive in you! More than ever, alive in you! It was an image that wavered there and they've made you come to life! Oh, mine! You're mine, mine, mine in my own right! [*He holds her in his arms, laugh-*

ing like a madman, while all stand still terrified. Then as they advance to tear FRIDA *from his arms, he becomes furious, terrible, and cries imperiously to his* VALETS.] Hold them! Hold them! I order you to hold them!

[*The four young men amazed, yet fascinated, move to execute his orders, automatically, and seize* DI NOLLI, *the* DOCTOR, *and* BELCREDI.]

BELCREDI [*freeing himself*]. Leave her alone! Leave her alone! You're no madman!

HENRY IV [*in a flash, draws the sword from the side of* LANDOLPH, *who is close to him*]. I'm not mad, eh! Take that, you! ... [*Drives sword into him. A cry of horror follows. All rush over to assist* BELCREDI, *crying out together.*]

DI NOLLI. Has he wounded you?

BERTHOLD. Yes, yes, seriously!

DOCTOR. I told you so!

FRIDA. Oh God, oh God!

DI NOLLI. Frida, come here!

DONNA MATILDA. He's mad, mad!

DI NOLLI. Hold him!

BELCREDI [*while they take him away by the left exit, he protests as he is borne out*]. No, no, you're not mad! You're not mad. He's not mad!

[*They go out by the left amid cries and excitement. After a moment, one hears a still sharper, more piercing cry from* DONNA MATILDA, *and then, silence.*]

HENRY IV [*who has remained on the stage between* LANDOLPH, HAROLD, *and* ORDULPH, *with his eyes almost starting out of his head, terrified by the life of his own masquerade which has driven him to crime*]. Now, yes ... we'll have to ... [*Calls his* VALETS *around him as if to protect him.*] Here we are ... together ... forever!

CURTAIN

Robert Brustein

LUIGI PIRANDELLO

... The basic Pirandellian concept is borrowed from Bergson, and, briefly stated, it is this. Life (or reality or time) is fluid, mobile, evanescent, and indeterminate. It lies beyond the reach of reason, and is reflected only through spontaneous action, or instinct. Yet man, endowed with reason, cannot live instinctually like the beasts, nor can he accept an existence which constantly changes. In consequence, he uses reason to fix life through ordering definitions. Since life is indefinable, such concepts are illusions. Man is occasionally aware of the illusionary nature of his concepts; but to be human is to desire form; anything formless fills man with dread and uncertainty. "Humankind cannot bear very much reality"—T. S. Eliot's perception in *Burnt Norton* (and *Murder in the Cathedral*) is the spine of Pirandello's philosophy.

The way humankind evades reality is by stopping time, for, as Eliot goes on to say, "To be conscious is not to be in time." Through the exercise of consciousness, or reason, man temporarily achieves the timeless. Existence is chaotic, irrational, in flux; man essentializes for the sake of order and form. To quote Eliot once more, "Except for the point, the still point, there would be no dance, and there is only the dance." For Pirandello's characters, too, there is only the dance, and so each one labors to find his still point in the turning world.

The drama Pirandello distills from this concept is usually described through reference to the face and the mask—a conflict he borrowed from the *teatro del grottesco*. The authors who constitute the grotesque movement—Chiarelli, Martini, Antonelli—use this conflict as the basis for bizarre situations, presented in a ludicrous way. The face represents the suffering individual in all his complexity; the mask reflects external forms and social laws. The individual yields to instinct, but he is also ruled by the demands of a rigid code, and the conflict pulls him in opposite directions. This seems like a modern version of the Heroic conflict of love and honor, except that, in the *teatro del grottesco*, the central character tries to accommodate both demands at the same time. He is, as a result, not heroic but absurd—and the effect of the play is neither tragic nor comic but grotesque. In Luigi Chiarelli's *The Mask and the Face* (*La maschera ed il volto*, 1916), for example, a passionate Italian announces in public that he will kill his wife if she is unfaithful to him. When he finds her in the arms of another, he is reluctant to exact vengeance, so he exiles her, pretends she has been killed, and goes to trial for her murder. The mask of honor and the face of love have both been preserved. But in order to achieve this, the Italian has had to turn actor, playing his role to the limits of his endurance.

Pirandello takes over this antinomy intact, and proceeds to work manifold variations on it, both social and existential. For in his work, the mask of appearances is shaped both by the self and others. The others constitute the social world, a world which owes its existence to the false assumption that its members adhere to narrow definitions. Man, like life, may be unknowable, and the human soul, like time, may be in constant flight, but society demands certainty, and tries to imprison man in its fictitious concepts. To Pirandello, all social institutions and systems of thought—religion, law, government, science, morality, philosophy, so-

SOURCE: From *The Theatre of Revolt* by Robert Brustein, by permission of Atlantic-Little, Brown and Co. Copyright © 1962, 1963, 1964 by Robert Brustein.

ciology, even language itself—are means by which society creates masks, trying to catch the elusive face of man and fix it with a classification. "Basically," writes Pirandello, "I have constantly attempted to show that nothing offends life so much as reducing it to a hollow concept." Concepts are the death of spontaneity, he explains in his essay, *L'Umorismo* (1908), and reason is inadequate before the mysterious quality of existence. The human mystery remains beyond human comprehension; and those who would pluck it out will come away baffled and in tears.

On the other hand, the mind of man, being stuffed with concepts, has no defense against these social definitions. Because he is uncertain of his identity, he accepts the identity given him by others —sometimes willingly, like the heroine of *As You Desire Me*, sometimes reluctantly, like the hero of *When One Is Somebody*. Looking for the elusive self, he sees it reflected in the eyes of others, and takes the reflection for the original. This acceptance of a superimposed identity is one side of Pirandello's *teatro dello specchio* (theatre of the looking glass)— aptly named, since the image of the mirror occurs in almost every one of his plays. Laudisi, for example, examining his image in a glass, asks: "What are you for other people? What are you in their eyes? An image, dear sir, just an image in the glass! They're all carrying just such a phantom around inside themselves, and here they are racking their brains about the phantoms in other people...." Knowledge, facts, opinions, all are phantasms, and even conscience is "nothing but other people inside you." As Diego Cinci puts it, in *Each in His Own Way*: "We have of each other reciprocally, and each has of himself, knowledge of some small, insignificant certainty of today, which is not the certainty it was yesterday, and will not be the certainty of tomorrow." In this sliding world, the human personality dissolves and changes, and like the hero of Pirandello's novel, *The Late Mattia Pascal*, who awoke one morning holding on to this one positive fact, the only thing you can be certain of is your name.

These are the social implications of Pirandello's treatment of masks. The au-thor—always identifying with the suffering individual in opposition to the collective mind—is in revolt against the social world, and all its theoretical, conceptual, institutional extensions. As he said in an interview with Domenico Vittorini: "Society is necessarily formal, and in this sense I am antisocial, but only in the sense that I am opposed to social hypocrisies and conventions. My art teaches each individual to accept his lot with candor and humility, and with full consciousness of the imperfections that are inherent in it." The stoical sound of this qualification, however, suggests that Pirandello's social revolt has existential roots. Indeed it has because, in Pirandello's view, the adoption of the mask is the inevitable consequence of being human. If the mask is sometimes imposed on the face by the external world, it is more often the construct of internal demands. Hamlet says, "I know not seems" —but Pirandello's characters know almost nothing else.

For whether they know it or not, they are all devoted to appearances, as a defense against the agony of the changing personality. "Continually I hide my face from myself," says a character in *Each in His Own Way*, "so ashamed am I at seeing myself change." The shame is increased by time, for old age etches change, irremediably, on the human features. "Age," observes a character in *Diana and Tuda*, "which is time reduced to human dimensions—time when it is painful—and we are made of flesh." Or, as the aging writer in *When One Is Somebody* complains, "You don't know what an atrocious thing happens to an old man, to see himself all of a sudden in a mirror, when the sorrow of seeing himself is greater than the astonishment of no longer remembering. You don't know the obscene shame of feeling a young and hotblooded heart within an old body." The body is form, but form which changes under the hungry eye of the cormorant, time. To stop time, to achieve stasis, to locate the still point, Pirandello's characters put on their masks, hoping to hide their shameful faces by playing a role.

This is what Pirandello means by *costruirsi*, building yourself up. Man begins as nothing definite, and becomes a costruzione, creating himself according to predetermined patterns or roles. Thus, he plays family roles (husband, wife, father, mother), religious roles (saint, blasphemer, priest, atheist), psychological roles (madman, neurotic, normal man), and social roles (mayor, citizen, socialist, revolutionary). No matter how well these roles are played, however, none of them reveals the face of the actor. They are disguises, designed to give purpose and form to a meaningless existence—masks in an infinite comedy of illusion. The true self is revealed only in a moment of blind instinct, which has the power to break down all codes and concepts.[1] But even then, the self is on the point of changing. Thus, Pirandello refuses to idealize the personality in the manner of the messianic rebels; for him, personality remains a fictional construct. Instead, he concentrates on the disintegration of personality in a scene of bondage and frustration—existential revolt in the ironic mode. Pirandellian man has freedom, but his freedom is unbearable; it beckons him toward the waste and void. Though he sometimes plunges into reality through spontaneous, instinctual action, he more often takes refuge from reality in a beneficial illusion. "The greater the struggle for life," as Pirandello phrases it in *L'Umorismo*, "the greater the need for mutual deceit."

The histrionic implications of this are tremendous—the Pirandellian hero is an actor, a character in disguise. But Pirandello broadens these implications even further. For if his hero is an actor, he is also a critic who cruelly judges his own performance. "Yes I laugh sometimes," says Leone Gala in *The Rules of the Game*, "as I watch myself playing this self-imposed role. . . ." In Elizabethan drama, the disguised character is anxious to protect his disguise from others; in Pirandello, he is also anxious to protect it from himself. Yet, reason, which created the mask, exposes its illusionary nature. In the *teatro dello specchio*, the

reflecting mirror is not only the eye of the world but the inner eye as well:

> When a man lives [writes Pirandello], he lives and does not see himself. Well, put a mirror before him and make him see himself in the act of living. Either he is astonished at his own appearance, or else he turns away his eyes so as not to see himself, or else in disgust he spits at his image, or, again, clenches his fist to break it. In a word, there arises a crisis, and that crisis is my theatre.

In another place, he adds: "If we present ourselves to others as artificial constructions in relation to what we really are, it is logical that upon looking at ourselves in a mirror we see our falseness reflected there, made galling and unbearable by its fixity." It is for this reason that a character like Baldovino, in *The Pleasures of Honesty*, experiences "an unspeakable nausea for the self that I am compelled to build up and display in the relations I must assume with my fellow men." If Pirandello's characters want to be fixed, they also want to move.

The conflict between appearance and reality, or Art and Nature, has been a traditional subject of Western literature since its beginnings, with Anglo-Saxon writers generally supporting reality and Latin writers generally supporting appearances. The blunt, plain-spoken man, who will not hide his true feelings, is a crucial figure in a certain strain of English drama and satire, while French, Spanish, and Italian literature is often more tolerant of the courteous man, who knows how to moderate his temper and disguise his desires. When the Italian Iago goes into disguise, he assumes the appearance of a gruff, honest soldier; when Molière's "misanthrope" enters English drama, he becomes Wycherly's "plaindealer." In Pirandello's drama, on the other hand, the conflict between Art and Nature is translated into a conflict between life and form, while appearances become illusions; but with him, the conflict becomes a real dialectic. Pirandello evokes sym-

[1] Since Pirandello believed so firmly in the power of the sexual instinct, he was compared—by an adoring disciple, Domenico Vittorini—to his rival D'Annunzio. Pirandello's reply is instructive: "No, no. D'Annunzio is immoral in order to proclaim the glory of instinct. I present this individual case to add another proof of the tragedy of being human. D'Annunzio is exultant over evil; I grieve over it." Or, in the terminology of revolt, D'Annunzio is messianic, Pirandello is existential.

pathy for the man who tries to hide from reality and sympathy for the man who tries to plunge back into it. Life and form—reality and illusion—are opposed, but they are the twin poles of human existence.

Pirandello is similarly ambivalent about the faculty of reason. His philosophy, founded as it is on the belief that real knowledge is unattainable, is profoundly anti-intellectual; yet, it is through the intellect that he reaches his conclusions. Such paradoxes proliferate in Pirandello's drama. Reason is both man's consolation and his curse; it creates a false identity which it can also destroy; it applies the masks to the face, and then rips them off. Under the cold eye of reason, the human ego expands and contracts; the costruzione is erected, and then demolished. The disguised character in Pirandello is a creature of appearances, whose intellect has created his illusion, but he also has the capacity, through the agency of intellect, to penetrate to a deeper reality. He escapes from life into form, and from form into life. Or, put into the metaphor of the theatre, the improvising actor struts and frets his hour on the stage before the ruthless critic sends him back to his dressing-room mirror, weeping over the inauthenticity of his performance.

This probably sounds impossibly abstruse, an exercise in epistemology rather than drama, but the wonder is the number of effective situations Pirandello is able to create out of such reflections. For Pirandello's concept always takes the form of conflict, and conflict remains the heart of his drama. These conflicts take an internal and external form, depending on which aspect of Pirandello's revolt is in the ascendant. As an existential rebel, Pirandello explores the roles men play in order to escape from life—revolt turns inward against the elusiveness of human existence. As a social rebel, he attacks the busybodies, gossips, and scandalmongers who think they can understand the unknowable mystery of man—revolt turns outwards against the intruding social

world. The two levels of Pirandello's revolt generally run parallel in each of his plays; and, as a result, his drama has a "spatial design," in Eric Bentley's words, which consists of "a center of suffering within a periphery of busybodies—the pattern of the Sicilian village."

Extending this description a little further, let us call those in the outer circle alazōnes (impostors or buffoons) and those in the center eirones (self-deprecators)—terms by which I mean to suggest the affinities of Pirandello's characters with the stock masks of Aristophanic comedy and the commedia dell'arte.[2] In traditional comedy, as Northrop Frye tells us, the alazōn is typified as "the miles gloriosus and the learned crank or obsessed philosopher." In Pirandello's drama, the alazōn is an agent of organized society, and is usually identified with one of its institutions—science, bureaucracy, or the state. He is sometimes a doctor, sometimes a petty official, sometimes a magistrate, sometimes a policeman—always a pretender, whose pretense lies in thinking himself a wise man when he is really a fool. The eiron, on the other hand, is a suffering individual who has hidden some private secret under a mask of appearances. Sometimes, he is unaware he is wearing a mask, in which case he is merely a pathetic sufferer—a pharmakos, or scapegoat. More often, he is a man of superior wisdom, because, like Socrates (the original eiron), he knows he knows nothing. Hounded and tormented by his persecutors, the buffoonish alazōnes, he replies with the dry mock: ironic laughter is his only weapon. As Diego Cinci puts it, in Each in His Own Way: "I laugh because I have reasoned my heart dry.... I laugh in my own way, and my ridicule falls upon myself sooner than on anyone else!" He is thus ironic in the original Greek sense of dissimulation—of ignorance purposely affected.

The clash between the two groups occurs when the alazōnes try to peel off the masks of the eirones—an action which

---

[2] F. L. Cornford was the first to apply these terms to Aristophanes in his book The Origins of Attic Comedy; Northrop Frye, in The Anatomy of Criticism, applies them to literature as a whole. Pirandello, who was familiar with the stock masks of traditional comedy, uses them, I think, in a much more conscious way than other Western writers.

has both tragic and comic consequences. On the one hand, this impertinent invasion of another's privacy may be dangerous, since the *eiron*'s illusion is necessary to his life; on the other, the attempt to discover another's secret self is ludicrously impossible, since the face beneath the mask cannot be known. The comic action, then, proceeds along the social level of the play where the *alazōnes* are frustrated in their curiosity, their state changing from knowledge to ignorance, from smug complacency to stupefied bafflement. The tragic action proceeds along the existential level of the play where the *eirones* are dragged under a painfully blinding spotlight which causes them terrible discomfort and suffering. As for the author, his literary endeavors identify him as an *alazōn*, since by writing about the *eirones*, he is meddling in their private affairs.[3] But his tone is that of an *eiron*, since, in his sympathetic identification with the sufferers, he expresses ironic contempt for the social busybodies. . . .

. . . In *Henry IV* (*Enrico IV*, 1922), . . . Pirandello dispenses with the *raisonneur* entirely, embodying his ideas in a brilliant theatrical metaphor, and concentrating not so much on the social world of the dumbfounded buffoons as on the existential world of the chief sufferer. And now this world is wonderfully rich and varied. The central character of the play is both *pharmakos* and *eiron*, both a living person and an articulate personification, both the mechanism of the action and the source of the ideas. In Henry's character, Pirandello's reflections on the conflict between life and form, on the elusiveness of identity, and on man's revolt against time, achieve their consummation in a powerfully eerie manner. Henry is the culmination of Pirandello's concept of the mask and the face, as well as embodying Pirandello's notions (developed more elaborately in his theatre plays) about the timeless

world of art. In trying to fix his changing life in significant form, Henry emerges as Actor, Artist, and Madman, and, besides this, possesses an extraordinary intellect, reflecting on all three. . . .

Henry IV is unquestionably Pirandello's masterpiece, a complex artwork in which the themes arise naturally from the action—neither discursive nor superfluous, yet, at the same time, eloquently and coherently stated. In the figure of Henry, moreover, Pirandello has found his perfect *eiron-pharmakos*, one who acts and suffers, murders and creates, and one who can enunciate the author's ideas about the need for privacy from interfering busybodies, the vanity of learning, and the way man takes refuge from a harsh reality in beneficial illusions. In Henry, too, Pirandello has dramatized the dreadful loneliness of human beings, encased in shells of steel, never able to know or communicate with another. Pirandello's Henry, like Brecht's Shlink in *In the Jungle of Cities*, watches the hungry generations stare coldly into each other's eyes:

> I would never wish you to think, as I have done [he tells his retainers], on this horrible thing which really drives one mad; that if you were beside another and looking into his eyes—as I one day looked into somebody's eyes —you might as well be a beggar before a door never to be opened to you; for he who does enter there will never be you, but someone unknown to you, within his different and impenetrable world. . . .

This "misery which is not only his, but everybody's," as the author describes it in a stage direction, is Pirandello's finest expression of his rage against existence, the source both of his philosophy and his drama. And in *Henry IV*, Pirandello has finally converted intellect into genuine passion, making his existential rebellion the occasion for a rewarding and absorbing play.

---

[3] Pirandello suggests this role for himself in *Each in His Own Way*—a *commedia a chiave*, or comedy with a key. This play, which is based on living personages, is interrupted in the middle by some of the figures being represented on the stage; and it is rumored that they have slapped Pirandello's face in the lobby. "It's a disgrace," one of them cries. "Two people pilloried in public! The private affairs of two people exposed to public ridicule!" In this *roman à clef*, therefore, Pirandello clearly assigns himself the function of the meddling *alazōn*.

Federico
García
Lorca
1889–1936

Lorca, born in the Spanish province of Granada to prosperous, cultivated parents, was a sickly child. The resulting close contact with the women of the household may explain Lorca's extraordinary ability to identify with the feminine sex. From a peasant servant he learned the folk legends and songs of his people, and even in early life he showed his inclination towards drama by staging plays for his friends. Some years later his family moved into the city of Granada, where Lorca began his university studies in law. At the same time he was writing poetry, studying folk music, and participating in the intellectual life of Granada. On the advice of a friend, Lorca abandoned his studies in Granada and moved into the cosmopolitan intellectual circle in Madrid. In 1928 he published, to great critical acclaim, *Romancero Gitano*, a collection of poems based on gypsy chants and ballads. Lorca then became interested in surrealism. In 1929 he left Spain, passed through Paris and London, and went on to New York, where he stayed at Columbia University and spent some time in the Catskill Mountains, writing poems which were published posthumously as *Poeta in Neuva York*. The following year he returned to Spain; his experiments with folk forms and surrealism were now succeeded by poems and plays which fused popular and cultivated styles. In 1932 he formed a theatrical troupe, La Barraca, which traveled throughout Spain and presented the Spanish classics as well as Lorca's own plays, which gave passionate and somber voice to the sufferings of his people and to the themes of love and death. Still, he could display a lighter side in his puppet play, *The Shoemaker's Marvelous Wife*, for example. *Blood Wedding*, the first of his rural tragedies, was produced in 1933; *Yerma* followed in 1934. Two years later he completed *The House of Bernarda Alba*. But on July 18, 1936, the Spanish Civil War broke out. Lorca tended to be apolitical, but he was associated with left-wing intellectuals, and though a Falangist friend offered to hide him he was arrested by a group of ultra-Catholic fanatics. Along with other Republican prisoners, he was shot.

BLOOD WEDDING

FEDERICO GARCÍA LORCA

Translated by James Graham-Lujan and Richard L. O'Connell

CHARACTERS

THE MOTHER	LEONARDO
THE BRIDE	THE BRIDEGROOM
THE MOTHER-IN-LAW	THE BRIDE'S FATHER
LEONARDO'S WIFE	THE MOON
THE SERVANT WOMAN	DEATH [AS A BEGGAR WOMAN]
THE NEIGHBOR WOMAN	WOODCUTTERS
YOUNG GIRLS	YOUNG MEN

ACT I

Scene One

[A room painted yellow.]

BRIDEGROOM [entering]. Mother.
MOTHER. What?
BRIDEGROOM. I'm going.
MOTHER. Where?
BRIDEGROOM. To the vineyard.
[He starts to go.]

MOTHER. Wait.
BRIDEGROOM. You want something?
MOTHER. Your breakfast, son.
BRIDEGROOM. Forget it. I'll eat grapes. Give me the knife.
MOTHER. What for?
BRIDEGROOM [laughing]. To cut the grapes with.
MOTHER [muttering as she looks for the knife]. Knives, knives. Cursed be all knives, and the scoundrel who invented them.
BRIDEGROOM. Let's talk about something else.

SOURCE: From Federico García Lorca, *Three Tragedies*, translated by James Graham-Lujan and Richard O'Connell. Copyright 1947, 1955 by New Directions Publishing Corporation. All Rights Reserved. Reprinted by permission of New Directions Publishing Corporation.

MOTHER. And guns and pistols and the smallest little knife—and even hoes and pitchforks.

BRIDEGROOM. All right.

MOTHER. Everything that can slice a man's body. A handsome man, full of young life, who goes out to the vineyards or to his own olive groves—his own because he's inherited them . . .

BRIDEGROOM [*lowering his head*]. Be quiet.

MOTHER. . . . and then that man doesn't come back. Or if he does come back it's only for someone to cover him over with a palm leaf or a plate of rock salt so he won't bloat. I don't know how you dare carry a knife on your body—or how I let this serpent [*she takes a knife from a kitchen chest*] stay in the chest.

BRIDEGROOM. Have you had your say?

MOTHER. If I lived to be a hundred I'd talk of nothing else. First your father; to me he smelled like a carnation and I had him for barely three years. Then your brother. Oh, is it right—how can it be—that a small thing like a knife or a pistol can finish off a man—a bull of a man? No, I'll never be quiet. The months pass and the hopelessness of it stings in my eyes and even to the roots of my hair.

BRIDEGROOM [*forcefully*]. Let's quit this talk!

MOTHER. No. No. Let's not quit this talk. Can anyone bring me your father back? Or your brother? Then there's the jail. What do they mean, jail? They eat there, smoke there, play music there! My dead men choking with weeds, silent, turning to dust. Two men like two beautiful flowers. The killers in jail, carefree, looking at the mountains.

BRIDEGROOM. Do you want me to go kill them?

MOTHER. No . . . If I talk about it it's because . . . Oh, how can I help talking about it, seeing you go out that door? It's . . . I don't like you to carry a knife. It's just that . . . that I wish you wouldn't go out to the fields.

BRIDEGROOM [*laughing*]. Oh, come now!

MOTHER. I'd like it if you were a woman. Then you wouldn't be going out to the arroyo now and we'd both of us embroider flounces and little woolly dogs.

BRIDEGROOM [*he puts his arm around his* MOTHER *and laughs*]. Mother, what if I should take you with me to the vineyards?

MOTHER. What would an old lady do in the vineyards? Were you going to put me down under the young vines?

BRIDEGROOM [*lifting her in his arms*]. Old lady, old lady—you little old, little old lady!

MOTHER. Your father, he used to take me. That's the way with men of good stock; good blood. Your grandfather left a son on every corner. That's what I like. Men, men; wheat, wheat.

BRIDEGROOM. And I, Mother?

MOTHER. You, what?

BRIDEGROOM. Do I need to tell you again?

MOTHER [*seriously*]. Oh!

BRIDEGROOM. Do you think it's bad?

MOTHER. No.

BRIDEGROOM. Well, then?

MOTHER. I don't really know. Like this, suddenly, it always surprises me. I know the girl is good. Isn't she? Well behaved. Hard working. Kneads her bread, sews her skirts, but even so when I say her name I feel as though someone had hit me on the forehead with a rock.

BRIDEGROOM. Foolishness.

MOTHER. More than foolishness. I'll be left alone. Now only you are left me —I hate to see you go.

BRIDEGROOM. But you'll come with us.

MOTHER. No. I can't leave your father and brother here alone. I have to go to them every morning and if I go away it's possible one of the Félix family, one of the killers, might die—and they'd bury him next to ours. And that'll never happen! Oh, no! That'll never happen! Because I'd dig them out with my nails and, all by myself, crush them against the wall.

BRIDEGROOM [*sternly*]. There you go again.

MOTHER. Forgive me. [*Pause.*] How long have you known her?

BRIDEGROOM. Three years. I've been able to buy the vineyard.

MOTHER. Three years. She used to have another sweetheart, didn't she?

BRIDEGROOM. I don't know. I don't think so. Girls have to look at what they'll marry.

MOTHER. Yes. I looked at nobody. I looked at your father, and when they killed him I looked at the wall in front

of me. One woman with one man, and
that's all.

BRIDEGROOM. You know my girl's good.

MOTHER. I don't doubt it. All the
same, I'm sorry not to have known what
her mother was like.

BRIDEGROOM. What difference does it
make now?

MOTHER [looking at him]. Son.

BRIDEGROOM. What is it?

MOTHER. That's true! You're right!
When do you want me to ask for her?

BRIDEGROOM. [happily]. Does Sunday
seem all right to you?

MOTHER [seriously]. I'll take her the
bronze earrings, they're very old—and
you buy her . . .

BRIDEGROOM. You know more about
that . . .

MOTHER. . . . you buy her some openwork stockings—and for you, two suits—
three! I have no one but you now!

BRIDEGROOM. I'm going. Tomorrow
I'll go see her.

MOTHER. Yes, yes—and see if you can
make me happy with six grandchildren—
or as many as you want, since your father
didn't live to give them to me.

BRIDEGROOM. The first-born for you!

MOTHER. Yes, but have some girls. I
want to embroider and make lace, and be
at peace.

BRIDEGROOM. I'm sure you'll love my
wife.

MOTHER. I'll love her. [She starts to
kiss him but changes her mind.] Go on.
You're too big now for kisses. Give them
to your wife. [Pause. To herself.] When
she is your wife.

BRIDEGROOM. I'm going.

MOTHER. And that land around the
little mill—work it over. You've not
taken good care of it.

BRIDEGROOM. You're right. I will.

MOTHER. God keep you. [THE SON
goes out. THE MOTHER remains seated—
her back to the door. A NEIGHBOR
WOMAN with a 'kerchief on her head
appears in the door.] Come in.

NEIGHBOR. How are you?

MOTHER. Just as you see me.

NEIGHBOR. I came down to the store
and stopped in to see you. We live so
far away!

MOTHER. It's twenty years since I've
been up to the top of the street.

NEIGHBOR. You're looking well.

MOTHER. You think so?

NEIGHBOR. Things happen. Two days
ago they brought in my neighbor's son
with both arms sliced off by the machine.
[She sits down.]

MOTHER. Rafael?

NEIGHBOR. Yes. And there you have
him. Many times I've thought your son
and mine are better off where they are—
sleeping, resting—not running the risk of
being left helpless.

MOTHER. Hush. That's all just something thought up—but no consolation.

NEIGHBOR [sighing]. Ay!

MOTHER [sighing]. Ay!

[Pause.]

NEIGHBOR [sadly]. Where's your son?

MOTHER. He went out.

NEIGHBOR. He finally bought the vineyard!

MOTHER. He was lucky.

NEIGHBOR. Now he'll get married.

MOTHER [as though reminded of
something, she draws her chair near THE
NEIGHBOR]. Listen.

NEIGHBOR [in a confidential manner].
Yes. What is it?

MOTHER. You know my son's sweetheart?

NEIGHBOR. A good girl!

MOTHER. Yes, but . . .

NEIGHBOR. But who knows her really
well? There's nobody. She lives out there
alone with her father—so far away—fifteen miles from the nearest house. But
she's a good girl. Used to being alone.

MOTHER. And her mother?

NEIGHBOR. Her mother I did know.
Beautiful. Her face glowed like a saint's
—but I never liked her. She didn't love
her husband.

MOTHER [sternly]. Well, what a lot of
things certain people know!

NEIGHBOR. I'm sorry. I didn't mean to
offend—but it's true. Now, whether she
was decent or not nobody said. That
wasn't discussed. She was haughty.

MOTHER. There you go again!

NEIGHBOR. You asked me.

MOTHER. I wish no one knew anything about them—either the live one
or the dead one—that they were like two
thistles no one even names but cuts off
at the right moment.

NEIGHBOR. You're right. Your son is
worth a lot.

MOTHER. Yes—a lot. That's why I look

after him. They told me the girl had a sweetheart some time ago.

NEIGHBOR. She was about fifteen. He's been married two years now—to a cousin of hers, as a matter of fact. But nobody remembers about their engagement.

MOTHER. How do you remember it?

NEIGHBOR. Oh, what questions you ask!

MOTHER. We like to know all about the things that hurt us. Who was the boy?

NEIGHBOR. Leonardo.

MOTHER. What Leonardo?

NEIGHBOR. Leonardo Félix.

MOTHER. Félix!

NEIGHBOR. Yes, but—how is Leonardo to blame for anything? He was eight years old when those things happened.

MOTHER. That's true. But I hear that name—Félix—and it's all the same. [Muttering.] Félix, a slimy mouthful. [She spits.] It makes me spit—spit so I won't kill!

NEIGHBOR. Control yourself. What good will it do?

MOTHER. No good. But you see how it is.

NEIGHBOR. Don't get in the way of your son's happiness. Don't say anything to him. You're old. So am I. It's time for you and me to keep quiet.

MOTHER. I'll say nothing to him.

NEIGHBOR [kissing her]. Nothing.

MOTHER [calmly]. Such things . . . !

NEIGHBOR. I'm going. My men will soon be coming in from the fields.

MOTHER. Have you ever known such a hot sun?

NEIGHBOR. The children carrying water out to the reapers are black with it. Goodbye, woman.

MOTHER. Goodbye.

[THE MOTHER starts toward the door at the left. Halfway there she stops and slowly crosses herself.]

CURTAIN

Scene Two

[A room painted rose with copperware and wreaths of common flowers. In the center of the room is a table with a tablecloth. It is morning.]

[LEONARDO'S MOTHER-IN-LAW sits in one corner holding a child in her arms and rocking it. His WIFE is in the other corner mending stockings.]

MOTHER-IN-LAW.
Lullaby, my baby
once there was a big horse
who didn't like water.
The water was black there
under the branches.
When it reached the bridge
it stopped and it sang.
Who can say, my baby,
what the stream holds
with its long tail
in its green parlor?

WIFE [softly].
Carnation, sleep and dream,
the horse won't drink from the stream.

MOTHER-IN-LAW.
My rose, asleep now lie,
the horse is starting to cry.
His poor hooves were bleeding,
his long mane was frozen,
and deep in his eyes
stuck a silvery dagger.
Down he went to the river,
Oh, down he went down!
And his blood was running,
Oh, more than the water.

WIFE.
Carnation, sleep and dream,
the horse won't drink from the stream.

MOTHER-IN-LAW.
My rose, asleep now lie,
the horse is starting to cry.

WIFE.
He never did touch
the dank river shore
though his muzzle was warm
and with silvery flies.
So, to the hard mountains
he could only whinny
just when the dead stream
covered his throat.
Ay-y-y, for the big horse
who didn't like water!
Ay-y-y, for the snow-wound,
big horse of the dawn!

MOTHER-IN-LAW.
Don't come in! Stop him
and close up the window
with branches of dreams

and a dream of branches.

WIFE.
My baby is sleeping.

MOTHER-IN-LAW.
My baby is quiet.

WIFE.
Look, horse, my baby
has him a pillow.

MOTHER-IN-LAW.
His cradle is metal.

WIFE.
His quilt a fine fabric.

MOTHER-IN-LAW.
Lullaby, my baby.

WIFE.
Ay-y-y, for the big horse
who didn't like water!

MOTHER-IN-LAW.
Don't come near, don't come in!
Go away to the mountains
and through the grey valleys,
that's where your mare is.

WIFE [looking at the baby].
My baby is sleeping.

MOTHER-IN-LAW.
My baby is resting.

WIFE [softly].
Carnation, sleep and dream,
The horse won't drink from the stream.

MOTHER-IN-LAW [getting up, very softly].
My rose, asleep now lie
for the horse is starting to cry.

[She carries the child out. LEONARDO enters.]

LEONARDO. Where's the baby?

WIFE. He's sleeping.

LEONARDO. Yesterday he wasn't well. He cried during the night.

WIFE. Today he's like a dahlia. And you? Were you at the blacksmith's?

LEONARDO. I've just come from there. Would you believe it? For more than two months he's been putting new shoes on the horse and they're always coming off. As far as I can see he pulls them off on the stones.

WIFE. Couldn't it just be that you use him so much?

LEONARDO. No. I almost never use him.

WIFE. Yesterday the neighbors told me they'd seen you on the far side of the plains.

LEONARDO. Who said that?

WIFE. The women who gather capers.

It certainly surprised me. Was it you?

LEONARDO. No. What would I be doing there, in that wasteland?

WIFE. That's what I said. But the horse was streaming sweat.

LEONARDO. Did you see him?

WIFE. No. Mother did.

LEONARDO. Is she with the baby?

WIFE. Yes. Do you want some lemonade?

LEONARDO. With good cold water.

WIFE. And then you didn't come to eat!

LEONARDO. I was with the wheat weighers. They always hold me up.

WIFE [very tenderly, while she makes the lemonade]. Did they pay you a good price?

LEONARDO. Fair.

WIFE. I need a new dress and the baby a bonnet with ribbons.

LEONARDO [getting up]. I'm going to take a look at him.

WIFE. Be careful. He's asleep.

MOTHER-IN-LAW [coming in]. Well! Who's been racing the horse that way? He's down there, worn out, his eyes popping from their sockets as though he'd come from the ends of the earth.

LEONARDO [acidly]. I have.

MOTHER-IN-LAW. Oh, excuse me! He's your horse.

WIFE [timidly]. He was at the wheat buyers.

MOTHER-IN-LAW. He can burst for all of me!

[She sits down. Pause.]

WIFE. Your drink. Is it cold?

LEONARDO. Yes.

WIFE. Did you hear they're going to ask for my cousin?

LEONARDO. When?

WIFE. Tomorrow. The wedding will be within a month. I hope they're going to invite us.

LEONARDO [gravely]. I don't know.

MOTHER-IN-LAW. His mother, I think, wasn't very happy about the match.

LEONARDO. Well, she may be right. She's a girl to be careful with.

WIFE. I don't like to have you thinking bad things about a good girl.

MOTHER-IN-LAW [meaningfully]. If he does, it's because he knows her. Didn't you know he courted her for three years?

LEONARDO. But I left her. [To his

WIFE.] Are you going to cry now? Quit that! [He brusquely pulls her hands away from her face.] Let's go see the baby.

[They go in with their arms around each other. A GIRL appears. She is happy. She enters running.]

GIRL. Señora.

MOTHER-IN-LAW. What is it?

GIRL. The groom came to the store and he's bought the best of everything they had.

MOTHER-IN-LAW. Was he alone?

GIRL. No. With his mother. Stern, tall. [She imitates her.] And such extravagance!

MOTHER-IN-LAW. They have money.

GIRL. And they bought some openwork stockings! Oh, such stockings! A woman's dream of stockings! Look: a swallow here, [She points to her ankle.] a ship here, [She points to her calf.] and here, [She points to her thigh.] a rose!

MOTHER-IN-LAW. Child!

GIRL. A rose with the seeds and the stem! Oh! All in silk.

MOTHER-IN-LAW. Two rich families are being brought together.

[LEONARDO and his WIFE appear.]

GIRL. I came to tell you what they're buying.

LEONARDO [loudly]. We don't care.

WIFE. Leave her alone.

MOTHER-IN-LAW. Leonardo, it's not that important.

GIRL. Please excuse me.

[She leaves, weeping.]

MOTHER-IN-LAW. Why do you always have to make trouble with people?

LEONARDO. I didn't ask for your opinion.

[He sits down.]

MOTHER-IN-LAW. Very well.

[Pause.]

WIFE [to LEONARDO]. What's the matter with you? What idea've you got boiling there inside your head? Don't leave me like this, not knowing anything.

LEONARDO. Stop that.

WIFE. No. I want you to look at me and tell me.

LEONARDO. Let me alone.

[He rises.]

WIFE. Where are you going, love?

LEONARDO [sharply]. Can't you shut up?

MOTHER-IN-LAW [energetically, to her daughter]. Be quiet! [LEONARDO goes out.] The baby!

[She goes into the bedroom and comes out again with the baby in her arms. THE WIFE has remained standing, unmoving.]

MOTHER-IN-LAW.
His poor hooves were bleeding,
his long mane was frozen,
and deep in his eyes
stuck a silvery dagger.
Down he went to the river,
Oh, down he went down!
And his blood was running,
Oh, more than the water.

WIFE [turning slowly, as though dreaming].
Carnation, sleep and dream,
the horse is drinking from the stream.

MOTHER-IN-LAW.
My rose, asleep now lie
the horse is starting to cry.

WIFE.
Lullaby, my baby.

MOTHER-IN-LAW.
Ay-y-y, for the big horse
who didn't like water!

WIFE [dramatically].
Don't come near, don't come in!
Go away to the mountains!
Ay-y-y, for the snow-wound,
big horse of the dawn!

MOTHER-IN-LAW [weeping].
My baby is sleeping . . .

WIFE [weeping, as she slowly moves closer].
My baby is resting . . .

MOTHER-IN-LAW.
Carnation, sleep and dream,
the horse won't drink from the stream.

WIFE [weeping, and leaning on the table].
My rose, asleep now lie,
the horse is starting to cry.

CURTAIN

Scene Three

[Interior of the cave where THE BRIDE lives. At the back is a cross of large rose-colored flowers. The rounded doors have lace curtains with rose-colored ties.

Around the walls, which are of a white and hard material, are round fans, blue jars, and little mirrors.]

SERVANT. Come right in . . . [*She is very affable, full of humble hypocrisy.* THE BRIDEGROOM *and his* MOTHER *enter.* THE MOTHER *is dressed in black satin and wears a lace mantilla;* THE BRIDEGROOM *in black corduroy with a great golden chain.*] Won't you sit down? They'll be right here.

[*She leaves.* THE MOTHER *and* SON *are left sitting motionless as statues. Long pause.*]

MOTHER. Did you wear the watch?

BRIDEGROOM. Yes.

[*He takes it out and looks at it.*]

MOTHER. We have to be back on time. How far away these people live!

BRIDEGROOM. But this is good land.

MOTHER. Good; but much too lonesome. A four-hour trip and not one house, not one tree.

BRIDEGROOM. This is the wasteland.

MOTHER. Your father would have covered it with trees.

BRIDEGROOM. Without water?

MOTHER. He would have found some. In the three years we were married he planted ten cherry trees, [*remembering*] those three walnut trees by the mill, a whole vineyard and a plant called Jupiter which had scarlet flowers—but it dried up.

[*Pause.*]

BRIDEGROOM [*referring to* THE BRIDE]. She must be dressing.

[THE BRIDE'S FATHER *enters. He is very old, with shining white hair. His head is bowed.* THE MOTHER *and* THE BRIDEGROOM *rise. They shake hands in silence.*]

FATHER. Was it a long trip?

MOTHER. Four hours.

[*They sit down.*]

FATHER. You must have come the longest way.

MOTHER. I'm too old to come along the cliffs by the river.

BRIDEGROOM. She gets dizzy.

[*Pause.*]

FATHER. A good hemp harvest.

BRIDEGROOM. A really good one.

FATHER. When I was young this land didn't even grow hemp. We've had to punish it, even weep over it, to make it give us anything useful.

MOTHER. But now it does. Don't complain. I'm not here to ask you for anything.

FATHER [*smiling*]. You're richer than I. Your vineyards are worth a fortune. Each young vine a silver coin. But—do you know?—what bothers me is that our lands are separated. I like to have everything together. One thorn I have in my heart, and that's the little orchard there, stuck in between my fields—and they won't sell it to me for all the gold in the world.

BRIDEGROOM. That's the way it always is.

FATHER. If we could just take twenty teams of oxen and move your vineyards over here, and put them down on that hillside, how happy I'd be!

MOTHER. But why?

FATHER. What's mine is hers and what's yours is his. That's why. Just to see it all together. How beautiful it is to bring things together!

BRIDEGROOM. And it would be less work.

MOTHER. When I die, you could sell ours and buy here, right alongside.

FATHER. Sell, sell? Bah! Buy, my friend, buy everything. If I had had sons I would have bought all this mountainside right up to the part with the stream. It's not good land, but strong arms can make it good, and since no people pass by, they don't steal your fruit and you can sleep in peace.

[*Pause.*]

MOTHER. You know what I'm here for.

FATHER. Yes.

MOTHER. And?

FATHER. It seems all right to me. They have talked it over.

MOTHER. My son has money and knows how to manage it.

FATHER. My daughter too.

MOTHER. My son is handsome. He's never known a woman. His good name cleaner than a sheet spread out in the sun.

FATHER. No need to tell you about my daughter. At three, when the morning star shines, she prepares the bread. She never talks: soft as wool, she embroiders all kinds of fancy work and she can cut a strong cord with her teeth.

MOTHER. God bless her house.

FATHER. May God bless it.

[THE SERVANT *appears with two trays. One with drinks and the other with sweets.*]

MOTHER [*to the* SON]. When would you like the wedding?

BRIDEGROOM. Next Thursday.

FATHER. The day on which she'll be exactly twenty-two years old.

MOTHER. Twenty-two! My oldest son would be that age if he were alive. Warm and manly as he was, he'd be living now if men hadn't invented knives.

FATHER. One mustn't think about that.

MOTHER. Every minute. Always a hand on your breast.

FATHER. Thursday, then? Is that right?

BRIDEGROOM. That's right.

FATHER. You and I and the bridal couple will go in a carriage to the church which is very far from here; the wedding party on the carts and horses they'll bring with them.

MOTHER. Agreed.

[THE SERVANT *passes through.*]

FATHER. Tell her she may come in now. [*To the* MOTHER.] I shall be much pleased if you like her.

[THE BRIDE *appears. Her hands fall in a modest pose and her head is bowed.*]

MOTHER. Come here. Are you happy?

BRIDE. Yes, señora.

FATHER. You shouldn't be so solemn. After all, she's going to be your mother.

BRIDE. I'm happy. I've said "yes" because I wanted to.

MOTHER. Naturally. [*She takes her by the chin.*] Look at me.

FATHER. She resembles my wife in every way.

MOTHER. Yes? What a beautiful glance! Do you know what it is to be married, child?

BRIDE [*seriously*]. I do.

MOTHER. A man, some children and a wall two yards thick for everything else.

BRIDEGROOM. Is anything else needed?

MOTHER. No. Just that you all live— that's it! Live long!

BRIDE. I'll know how to keep my word.

MOTHER. Here are some gifts for you.

BRIDE. Thank you.

FATHER. Shall we have something?

MOTHER. Nothing for me. [*To the* SON.] But you?

BRIDEGROOM. Yes, thank you.

[*He takes one sweet,* THE BRIDE *another.*]

FATHER [*to the* BRIDEGROOM]. Wine?

MOTHER. He doesn't touch it.

FATHER. All the better.

[*Pause. All are standing.*]

BRIDEGROOM [*to the* BRIDE]. I'll come tomorrow.

BRIDE. What time?

BRIDEGROOM. Five.

BRIDE. I'll be waiting for you.

BRIDEGROOM. When I leave your side I feel a great emptiness, and something like a knot in my throat.

BRIDE. When you are my husband you won't have it any more.

BRIDEGROOM. That's what I tell myself.

MOTHER. Come. The sun doesn't wait. [*To the* FATHER.] Are we agreed on everything?

FATHER. Agreed.

MOTHER [*to the* SERVANT]. Goodbye, woman.

SERVANT. God go with you!

[THE MOTHER *kisses* THE BRIDE *and they begin to leave in silence.*]

MOTHER [*at the door*]. Goodbye, daughter.

[THE BRIDE *answers with her hand.*]

FATHER. I'll go out with you.

[*They leave.*]

SERVANT. I'm bursting to see the presents.

BRIDE [*sharply*]. Stop that!

SERVANT. Oh, child, show them to me.

BRIDE. I don't want to.

SERVANT. At least the stockings. They say they're all open work. Please!

BRIDE. I said no.

SERVANT. Well, my Lord. All right then. It looks as if you didn't want to get married.

BRIDE [*biting her hand in anger*]. Ay-y-y!

SERVANT. Child, child! What's the matter with you? Are you sorry to give up your queen's life? Don't think of bitter things. Have you any reason to? None. Let's look at the presents.

[*She takes the box.*]

BRIDE [*holding her by the wrists*]. Let go.

SERVANT. Ay-y-y, girl!

BRIDE. Let go, I said.

SERVANT. You're stronger than a man.

BRIDE. Haven't I done a man's work? I wish I were.

SERVANT. Don't talk like that.

BRIDE. Quiet, I said. Let's talk about something else.

[*The light is fading from the stage. Long pause.*]

SERVANT. Did you hear a horse last night?

BRIDE. What time?

SERVANT. Three.

BRIDE. It might have been a stray horse —from the herd.

SERVANT. No. It carried a rider.

BRIDE. How do you know?

SERVANT. Because I saw him. He was standing by your window. It shocked me greatly.

BRIDE. Maybe it was my fiancé. Sometimes he comes by at that time.

SERVANT. No.

BRIDE. You saw him?

SERVANT. Yes.

BRIDE. Who was it?

SERVANT. It was Leonardo.

BRIDE [*strongly*]. Liar! You liar! Why should he come here?

SERVANT. He came.

BRIDE. Shut up! Shut your cursed mouth.

[*The sound of a horse is heard.*]

SERVANT [*at the window*]. Look. Lean out. Was it Leonardo?

BRIDE. It was!

QUICK CURTAIN

ACT II

Scene One

[*The entrance hall of* THE BRIDE's *house. A large door in the back. It is night.*]

[THE BRIDE *enters wearing ruffled white petticoats full of laces and embroidered bands, and a sleeveless white bodice.* THE SERVANT *is dressed the same way.*]

SERVANT. I'll finish combing your hair out here.

BRIDE. It's too warm to stay in there.

SERVANT. In this country it doesn't even cool off at dawn.

[THE BRIDE *sits on a low chair and looks into a little hand mirror.* THE SERVANT *combs her hair.*]

BRIDE. My mother came from a place with lots of trees—from a fertile country.

SERVANT. And she was so happy!

BRIDE. But she wasted away here.

SERVANT. Fate.

BRIDE. As we're all wasting away here. The very walls give off heat. Ay-y-y! Don't pull so hard.

SERVANT. I'm only trying to fix this wave better. I want it to fall over your forehead. [THE BRIDE *looks at herself in the mirror.*] How beautiful you are! Ay-y-y!

[*She kisses her passionately.*]

BRIDE [*seriously*]. Keep right on combing.

SERVANT [*combing*]. Oh, lucky you— going to put your arms around a man; and kiss him; and feel his weight.

BRIDE. Hush.

SERVANT. And the best part will be when you'll wake up and you'll feel him at your side and when he caresses your shoulders with his breath, like a little nightingale's feather.

BRIDE [*sternly*]. Will you be quiet?

SERVANT. But, child! What *is* a wedding? A wedding is just that and nothing more. Is it the sweets—or the bouquets of flowers? No. It's a shining bed and a man and a woman.

BRIDE. But you shouldn't talk about it.

SERVANT. Oh, *that's* something else again. But fun enough too.

BRIDE. Or bitter enough.

SERVANT. I'm going to put the orange blossoms on from here to here, so the wreath will shine out on top of your hair.

[*She tries on the sprigs of orange blossom.*]

BRIDE [*looking at herself in the mirror*]. Give it to me.

[*She takes the wreath, looks at it and lets her head fall in discouragement.*]

SERVANT. Now what's the matter?

BRIDE. Leave me alone.

SERVANT. This is no time for you to

start feeling sad. [*Encouragingly.*] Give me the wreath. [THE BRIDE *takes the wreath and hurls it away.*] Child! You're just asking God to punish you, throwing the wreath on the floor like that. Raise your head! Don't you want to get married? Say it. You can still withdraw.

[THE BRIDE *rises.*]

BRIDE. Storm clouds. A chill wind that cuts through my heart. Who hasn't felt it?

SERVANT. You love your sweetheart, don't you?

BRIDE. I love him.

SERVANT. Yes, yes. I'm sure you do.

BRIDE. But this is a very serious step.

SERVANT. You've got to take it.

BRIDE. I've already given my word.

SERVANT. I'll put on the wreath.

BRIDE [*she sits down*]. Hurry. They should be arriving by now.

SERVANT. They've already been at least two hours on the way.

BRIDE. How far is it from here to the church?

SERVANT. Five leagues by the stream, but twice that by the road.

[THE BRIDE *rises and* THE SERVANT *grows excited as she looks at her.*]

SERVANT.
Awake, O Bride, awaken,
On your wedding morning waken!
The world's rivers may all
Bear along your bridal Crown!

BRIDE [*smiling*]. Come now.

SERVANT [*enthusiastically kissing her and dancing around her*].
Awake,
with the fresh bouquet
of flowering laurel.
Awake,
by the trunk and branch
of the laurels!

[*The banging of the front door latch is heard.*]

BRIDE. Open the door! That must be the first guests.

[*She leaves.* THE SERVANT *opens the door.*]

SERVANT [*in astonishment*]. You!

LEONARDO. Yes, me. Good morning.

SERVANT. The first one!

LEONARDO. Wasn't I invited?

SERVANT. Yes.

LEONARDO. That's why I'm here.

SERVANT. Where's your wife?

LEONARDO. I came on my horse. She's coming by the road.

SERVANT. Didn't you meet anyone?

LEONARDO. I passed them on my horse.

SERVANT. You're going to kill that horse with so much racing.

LEONARDO. When he dies, he's dead! [*Pause.*]

SERVANT. Sit down. Nobody's up yet.

LEONARDO. Where's the bride?

SERVANT. I'm just on my way to dress her.

LEONARDO. The bride! She ought to be happy!

SERVANT [*changing the subject*]. How's the baby?

LEONARDO. What baby?

SERVANT. Your son.

LEONARDO [*remembering, as though in a dream*]. Ah!

SERVANT. Are they bringing him?

LEONARDO. No.

[*Pause. Voices sing distantly.*]

VOICES.
Awake, O Bride, awaken,
On your wedding morning waken!

LEONARDO.
Awake, O Bride, awaken,
On your wedding morning waken!

SERVANT. It's the guests. They're still quite a way off.

LEONARDO. The bride's going to wear a big wreath, isn't she? But it ought not to be so large. One a little smaller would look better on her. Has the groom already brought her the orange blossom that must be worn on the breast?

BRIDE [*appearing, still in petticoats and wearing the wreath*]. He brought it.

SERVANT [*sternly*]. Don't come out like that.

BRIDE. What does it matter? [*Seriously.*] Why do ask if they brought the orange blossom? Do you have something in mind?

LEONARDO. Nothing. What would I have in mind? [*Drawing near her.*] You, you know me; you know I don't. Tell me so. What have I ever meant to you? Open your memory, refresh it. But two oxen and an ugly little hut are almost nothing. That's the thorn.

BRIDE. What have you come here to do?

LEONARDO. To see your wedding.

BRIDE. Just as I saw yours!

LEONARDO. Tied up by you, done with your two hands. Oh, they can kill me but they can't spit on me. But even money, which shines so much, spits sometimes.

BRIDE. Liar!

LEONARDO. I don't want to talk. I'm hot-blooded and I don't want to shout so all these hills will hear me.

BRIDE. My shouts would be louder.

SERVANT. You'll have to stop talking like this. [To THE BRIDE.] You don't have to talk about what's past.

[THE SERVANT looks around uneasily at the doors.]

BRIDE. She's right. I shouldn't even talk to you. But it offends me to the soul that you come here to watch me, and spy on my wedding, and ask about the orange blossom with something on your mind. Go and wait for your wife at the door.

LEONARDO. But can't you and I even talk?

SERVANT [with rage]. No! No, you can't talk.

LEONARDO. Ever since I got married I've been thinking night and day about whose fault it was, and every time I think about it, out comes a new fault to eat up the old one; but always there's a fault left!

BRIDE. A man with a horse knows a lot of things and can do a lot to ride rough-shod over a girl stuck out in the desert. But I have my pride. And that's why I'm getting married. I'll lock myself in with my husband and then I'll have to love him above everyone else.

LEONARDO. Pride won't help you a bit. [He draws near to her.]

BRIDE. Don't come near me!

LEONARDO. To burn with desire and keep quiet about it is the greatest punishment we can bring on ourselves. What good was pride to me—and not seeing you, and letting you lie awake night after night? No good! It only served to bring the fire down on me! You think that time heals and walls hide things, but it isn't true, it isn't true! When things get that deep inside you there isn't anybody can change them.

BRIDE [trembling]. I can't listen to you. I can't listen to your voice. It's as though I'd drunk a bottle of anise and fallen asleep wrapped in a quilt of roses. It pulls me along, and I know I'm drowning—but I go on down.

SERVANT [seizing LEONARDO by the lapels]. You've got to go right now!

LEONARDO. This is the last time I'll ever talk to her. Don't you be afraid of anything.

BRIDE. And I know I'm crazy and I know my breast rots with longing; but here I am—calmed by hearing him, by just seeing him move his arms.

LEONARDO. I'd never be at peace if I didn't tell you these things. I got married. Now you get married.

SERVANT. But she is getting married!

[Voices are heard singing, nearer.]

VOICES.
Awake, O Bride, awaken,
On your wedding morning waken!

BRIDE.
Awake, O Bride, awaken!

[She goes out, running toward her room.]

SERVANT. The people are here now. [To LEONARDO.] Don't you come near her again.

LEONARDO. Don't worry.

[He goes out to the left. Day begins to break.]

FIRST GIRL [entering].
Awake, O Bride, awaken,
the morning you're to marry;
sing round and dance round;
balconies a wreath must carry.

VOICES.
Bride, awaken!

SERVANT [creating enthusiasm].
Awake,
with the green bouquet
of love in flower.
Awake,
by the trunk and the branch
of the laurels!

SECOND GIRL [entering].
Awake,
with her long hair,
snowy sleeping gown,
patent leather boots with silver—
her forehead jasmines crown.

SERVANT.
Oh, shepherdess,
the moon begins to shine!

FIRST GIRL.
Oh, gallant,
leave your hat beneath the vine!

FIRST YOUNG MAN [*entering, holding his hat on high*].
Bride, awaken,
for over the fields
the wedding draws nigh
with trays heaped with dahlias
and cakes piled high.
    VOICES.
Bride, awaken!
    SECOND GIRL.
The bride
has set her white wreath in place
and the groom
ties it on with a golden lace.
    SERVANT.
By the orange tree,
sleepless the bride will be.
    THIRD GIRL [*entering*].
By the citron vine,
gifts from the groom will shine.
    [*Three* GUESTS *come in.*]
    FIRST YOUTH.
Dove, awaken!
In the dawn
shadowy bells are shaken.
    GUEST.
The bride, the white bride
today a maiden,
tomorrow a wife.
    FIRST GIRL.
Dark one, come down
trailing the train of your silken gown.
    GUEST.
Little dark one, come down,
cold morning wears a dewy crown.
    FIRST YOUTH.
Awaken, wife, awake,
orange blossoms the breezes shake.
    SERVANT.
A tree I would embroider her
with garnet sashes wound,
And on each sash a cupid,
with "Long Live" all around.
    VOICES.
Bride, awaken.
    FIRST YOUTH.
The morning you're to marry!
    GUEST.
The morning you're to marry
how elegant you'll seem;
worthy, mountain flower,
of a captain's dream.
    FATHER [*entering*].
A captain's wife
the groom will marry.
He comes with his oxen the treasure to
    carry!

    THIRD GIRL.
The groom
is like a flower of gold.
When he walks,
blossoms at his feet unfold.
    SERVANT.
Oh, my lucky girl!
    SECOND YOUTH.
Bride, awaken.
    SERVANT.
Oh, my elegant girl!
    FIRST GIRL.
Through the windows
hear the wedding shout.
    SECOND GIRL.
Let the bride come out.
    FIRST GIRL.
Come out, come out!
    SERVANT.
Let the bells
ring and ring out clear!
    FIRST YOUTH.
For here she comes!
For now she's near!
    SERVANT.
Like a bull, the wedding
is arising here!
    [THE BRIDE *appears. She wears a black dress in the style of 1900, with a bustle and large train covered with pleated gauzes and heavy laces. Upon her hair, brushed in a wave over her forehead, she wears an orange blossom wreath. Guitars sound. The* GIRLS *kiss* THE BRIDE.]
    THIRD GIRL. What scent did you put on your hair?
    BRIDE [*laughing*]. None at all.
    SECOND GIRL [*looking at her dress*]. This cloth is what you can't get.
    FIRST YOUTH. Here's the groom!
    BRIDEGROOM. Salud!
    FIRST GIRL [*putting a flower behind his ear*].
The groom
is like a flower of gold.
    SECOND GIRL.
Quiet breezes
from his eyes unfold.
    [THE GROOM *goes to* THE BRIDE.]
    BRIDE. Why did you put on those shoes?
    BRIDEGROOM. They're gayer than the black ones.
    LEONARDO'S WIFE [*entering and kissing* THE BRIDE]. Salud!
    [*They all speak excitedly.*]

LEONARDO [*entering as one who performs a duty*].
The morning you're to marry
We give you a wreath to wear.

LEONARDO'S WIFE.
So the fields may be made happy
with the dew dropped from your hair!

MOTHER [*to the father*]. Are those people here, too?

FATHER. They're part of the family. Today is a day of forgiveness!

MOTHER. I'll put up with it, but I don't forgive.

BRIDEGROOM. With your wreath, it's a joy to look at you!

BRIDE. Let's go to the church quickly.

BRIDEGROOM. Are you in a hurry?

BRIDE. Yes. I want to be your wife right now so that I can be with you alone, not hearing any voice but yours.

BRIDEGROOM. That's what I want!

BRIDE. And not seeing any eyes but yours. And for you to hug me so hard that even though my dead mother should call me I wouldn't be able to draw away from you.

BRIDEGROOM. My arms are strong. I'll hug you for forty years without stopping.

BRIDE. [*Taking his arm, dramatically.*] Forever!

FATHER. Quick now! Round up the teams and carts! The sun's already out.

MOTHER. And go along carefully! Let's hope nothing goes wrong.
[*The great door in the background opens.*]

SERVANT [*weeping*].
As you set out from your house,
oh, maiden white,
remember you leave shining
with a star's light.

FIRST GIRL.
Clean of body, clean of clothes
from her home to church she goes.
[*They start leaving.*]

SECOND GIRL.
Now you leave your home
for the church!

SERVANT.
The wind sets flowers
on the sands.

THIRD GIRL.
Ah, the white maid!

SERVANT.
Dark winds are the lace
of her mantilla.
[*They leave. Guitars, castanets and*

tambourines *are heard.* LEONARDO *and his* WIFE *are left alone.*]

WIFE. Let's go.

LEONARDO. Where?

WIFE. To the church. But not on your horse. You're coming with me.

LEONARDO. In the cart?

WIFE. Is there anything else?

LEONARDO. I'm not the kind of man to ride in a cart.

WIFE. Nor I the wife to go to a wedding without her husband. I can't stand any more of this!

LEONARDO. Neither can I!

WIFE. And why do you look at me that way? With a thorn in each eye.

LEONARDO. Let's go!

WIFE. I don't know what's happening. But I think, and I don't want to think. One thing I do know. I'm already cast off by you. But I have a son. And another coming. And so it goes. My mother's fate was the same. Well, I'm not moving from here.

VOICES [*outside*].
As you set out from your home
and to the church go
remember you leave shining
with a star's glow.

WIFE [*weeping*].
Remember you leave shining
with a star's glow!
I left my house like that too. They could have stuffed the whole countryside in my mouth. I was that trusting.

LEONARDO [*rising*]. Let's go!

WIFE. But you with me!

LEONARDO. Yes. [*Pause.*] Start moving!
[*They leave.*]

VOICES.
As you set out from your home
and to the church go,
remember you leave shining
with a star's glow.

SLOW CURTAIN

Scene Two

[*The exterior of* THE BRIDE's *Cave Home, in white gray and cold blue tones. Large cactus trees. Shadowy and silver tones. Panoramas of light tan tablelands, everything hard like a landscape in popular ceramics.*]

SERVANT [arranging glasses and trays on a table].

A-turning,
the wheel was a-turning
and the water was flowing,
for the wedding night comes.
May the branches part
and the moon be arrayed
at her white balcony rail.
[In a loud voice.] Set out the tablecloths!
   [In a pathetic voice.]
A-singing,
bride and groom were singing
and the water was flowing
for their wedding night comes.
Oh, rime-frost, flash!—
and almonds bitter
fill with honey!
   [In a loud voice.] Get the wine ready!
   [In a poetic tone.]
Elegant girl,
most elegant in the world,
see the way the water is flowing,
for your wedding night comes.
Hold your skirts close in
under the bridegroom's wing
and never leave your house,
for the Bridegroom is a dove
with his breast a firebrand
and the fields wait for the whisper
of spurting blood.
A-turning
the wheel was a-turning
and the water was flowing
and your wedding night comes.
Oh, water, sparkle!

MOTHER [entering]. At last!

FATHER. Are we the first ones?

SERVANT. No. Leonardo and his wife arrived a while ago. They drove like demons. His wife got here dead with fright. They made the trip as though they'd come on horseback.

FATHER. That one's looking for trouble. He's not of good blood.

MOTHER. What blood would you expect him to have? His whole family's blood. It comes down from his great-grandfather, who started in killing, and it goes on down through the whole evil breed of knife-wielding and false-smiling men.

FATHER. Let's leave it at that!

SERVANT. But how can she leave it at that?

MOTHER. It hurts me to the tips of my veins. On the forehead of all of them I see only the hand with which they killed what was mine. Can you really see me? Don't I seem mad to you? Well, it's the madness of not having shrieked out all my breast needs to. Always in my breast there's a shriek standing tiptoe that I have to beat down and hold in under my shawls. But the dead are carried off and one has to keep still. And then, people find fault.
[She removes her shawl.]

FATHER. Today's not the day for you to be remembering these things.

MOTHER. When the talk turns on it, I have to speak. And more so today. Because today I'm left alone in my house.

FATHER. But with the expectation of having someone with you.

MOTHER. That's my hope: grandchildren.
[They sit down.]

FATHER. I want them to have a lot of them. This land needs hands that aren't hired. There's a battle to be waged against weeds, the thistles, the big rocks that come from one doesn't know where. And those hands have to be the owner's, who chastises and dominates, who makes the seeds grow. Lots of sons are needed.

MOTHER. And some daughters! Men are like the wind! They're forced to handle weapons. Girls never go out into the street.

FATHER [happily]. I think they'll have both.

MOTHER. My son will cover her well. He's of good seed. His father could have had many sons with me.

FATHER. What I'd like is to have all this happen in a day. So that right away they'd have two or three boys.

MOTHER. But it's not like that. It takes a long time. That's why it's so terrible to see one's own blood spilled out on the ground. A fountain that spurts for a minute, but costs us years. When I got to my son, he lay fallen in the middle of the street. I wet my hands with his blood and licked them with my tongue—because it was my blood. You don't know what that's like. In a glass and topaz shrine I'd put the earth moistened by his blood.

FATHER. Now you must hope. My daughter is wide-hipped and your son is strong.

MOTHER. That's why I'm hoping.
[*They rise.*]

FATHER. Get the wheat trays ready!

SERVANT. They're all ready.

LEONARDO'S WIFE [*entering*]. May it be for the best!

MOTHER. Thank you.

LEONARDO. Is there going to be a celebration?

FATHER. A small one. People can't stay long.

SERVANT. Here they are!

[GUESTS *begin entering in gay groups.*
THE BRIDE *and* GROOM *come in arm-in-arm.* LEONARDO *leaves.*]

BRIDEGROOM. There's never been a wedding with so many people!

BRIDE [*sullen*]. Never.

FATHER. It was brilliant.

MOTHER. Whole branches of families came.

BRIDEGROOM. People who never went out of the house.

MOTHER. Your father sowed well, and now you're reaping it.

BRIDEGROOM. There were cousins of mine whom I no longer knew.

MOTHER. All the people from the seacoast.

BRIDEGROOM [*happily*]. They were frightened of the horses.

[*They talk.*]

MOTHER [*to* THE BRIDE]. What are you thinking about?

BRIDE. I'm not thinking about anything.

MOTHER. Your blessings weigh heavily.
[*Guitars are heard.*]

BRIDE. Like lead.

MOTHER [*stern*]. But they shouldn't weigh so. Happy as a dove you ought to be.

BRIDE. Are you staying here tonight?

MOTHER. No. My house is empty.

BRIDE. You ought to stay!

FATHER [*to* THE MOTHER]. Look at the dance they're forming. Dances of the far away seashore.

[LEONARDO *enters and sits down. His*
WIFE *stands rigidly behind him.*]

MOTHER. They're my husband's cousins. Stiff as stones at dancing.

FATHER. It makes me happy to watch them. What a change for this house!
[*He leaves.*]

BRIDEGROOM [*to* THE BRIDE]. Did you like the orange blossom?

BRIDE [*looking at him fixedly*]. Yes.

BRIDEGROOM. It's all of wax. It will last forever. I'd like you to have had them all over your dress.

BRIDE. No need of that.

[LEONARDO *goes off to the right.*]

FIRST GIRL. Let's go and take out your pins.

BRIDE [*to* THE GROOM]. I'll be right back.

LEONARDO'S WIFE. I hope you'll be happy with my cousin!

BRIDEGROOM. I'm sure I will.

LEONARDO'S WIFE. The two of you here; never going out; building a home. I wish I could live far away like this, too!

BRIDEGROOM. Why don't you buy land? The mountainside is cheap and children grow up better.

LEONARDO'S WIFE. We don't have any money. And at the rate we're going . . . !

BRIDEGROOM. Your husband is a good worker.

LEONARDO'S WIFE. Yes, but he likes to fly around too much; from one thing to another. He's not a patient man.

SERVANT. Aren't you having anything? I'm going to wrap up some wine cakes for your mother. She likes them so much.

BRIDEGROOM. Put up three dozen for her.

LEONARDO'S WIFE. No, no. A half-dozen's enough for her!

BRIDEGROOM. But today's a day!

LEONARDO'S WIFE [*to* THE SERVANT]. Where's Leonardo?

BRIDEGROOM. He must be with the guests.

LEONARDO'S WIFE. I'm going to go see.
[*She leaves.*]

SERVANT [*looking off at the dance*]. That's beautiful there.

BRIDEGROOM. Aren't you dancing?

SERVANT. No one will ask me.

[TWO GIRLS *pass across the back of the stage; during this whole scene the background should be an animated crossing of figures.*]

BRIDEGROOM [*happily*]. They just don't know anything. Lively old girls like you dance better than the young ones.

SERVANT. Well! Are you tossing me a compliment, boy? What a family yours is! Men among men! As a little girl I saw your grandfather's wedding. What a figure! It seemed as if a mountain were getting married.

BRIDEGROOM. I'm not as tall.

SERVANT. But there's the same twinkle in your eye. Where's the girl?

BRIDEGROOM. Taking off her wreath.

SERVANT. Ah! Look. For midnight, since you won't be sleeping, I have prepared ham for you, and some large glasses of old wine. On the lower shelf of the cupboard. In case you need it.

BRIDEGROOM [smiling]. I won't be eating at midnight.

SERVANT [slyly]. If not you, maybe the bride.

[She leaves.]

FIRST YOUTH [entering]. You've got to come have a drink with us!

BRIDEGROOM. I'm waiting for the bride.

SECOND YOUTH. You'll have her at dawn!

FIRST YOUTH. That's when it's best!

SECOND YOUTH. Just for a minute.

BRIDEGROOM. Let's go.

[They leave. Great excitement is heard. THE BRIDE enters. From the opposite side TWO GIRLS come running to meet her.]

FIRST GIRL. To whom did you give the first pin; me or this one?

BRIDE. I don't remember.

FIRST GIRL. To me, you gave it to me here.

SECOND GIRL. To me, in front of the altar.

BRIDE [uneasily, with a great inner struggle]. I don't know anything about it.

FIRST GIRL. It's just that I wish you'd . . .

BRIDE [interrupting]. Nor do I care. I have a lot to think about.

SECOND GIRL. Your pardon.

[LEONARDO crosses at the rear of the stage.]

BRIDE [She sees LEONARDO]. And this is an upsetting time.

FIRST GIRL. We wouldn't know anything about that!

BRIDE. You'll know about it when your time comes. This step is a very hard one to take.

FIRST GIRL. Has she offended you?

BRIDE. No. You must pardon me.

SECOND GIRL. What for? But both the pins are good for getting married, aren't they?

BRIDE. Both of them.

FIRST GIRL. Maybe now one will get married before the other.

BRIDE. Are you so eager?

SECOND GIRL [shyly]. Yes.

BRIDE. Why?

FIRST GIRL. Well . . .

[She embraces THE SECOND GIRL. Both go running off. THE GROOM comes in very slowly and embraces THE BRIDE from behind.]

BRIDE [in sudden fright]. Let go of me!

BRIDEGROOM. Are you frightened of me?

BRIDE. Ay-y-y! It's you?

BRIDEGROOM. Who else would it be? [Pause.] Your father or me.

BRIDE. That's true!

BRIDEGROOM. Of course, your father would have hugged you more gently.

BRIDE [darkly]. Of course!

BRIDEGROOM [embracing her strongly and a little bit brusquely]. Because he's old.

BRIDE [curtly]. Let me go!

BRIDEGROOM. Why?

[He lets her go.]

BRIDE. Well . . . the people. They can see us.

[THE SERVANT crosses at the back of the stage again without looking at THE BRIDE and BRIDEGROOM.]

BRIDEGROOM. What of it? It's consecrated now.

BRIDE. Yes, but let me be . . . Later.

BRIDEGROOM. What's the matter with you? You look frightened!

BRIDE. I'm all right. Don't go.

LEONARDO'S WIFE [enters]. I don't mean to intrude . . .

BRIDEGROOM. What is it?

LEONARDO'S WIFE. Did my husband come through here?

BRIDEGROOM. No.

LEONARDO'S WIFE. Because I can't find him, and his horse isn't in the stable either.

BRIDEGROOM [happily]. He must be out racing it.

[THE WIFE leaves, troubled. THE SERVANT enters.]

SERVANT. Aren't you two proud and happy with so many good wishes?

BRIDEGROOM. I wish it were over with. The bride is a little tired.

SERVANT. That's no way to act, child.

BRIDE. It's as though I'd been struck on the head.

SERVANT. A bride from these mountains must be strong. [*To* THE GROOM.] You're the only one who can cure her, because she's yours.

[*She goes running off.*]

BRIDEGROOM [*embracing* THE BRIDE]. Let's go dance a little.

[*He kisses her.*]

BRIDE [*worried*]. No. I'd like to stretch out on my bed a little.

BRIDEGROOM. I'll keep you company.

BRIDE. Never! With all these people here? What would they say? Let me be quiet for a moment.

BRIDEGROOM. Whatever you say! But don't be like that tonight!

BRIDE [*at the door*]. I'll be better tonight.

BRIDEGROOM. That's what I want.

[THE MOTHER *appears.*]

MOTHER. Son.

BRIDEGROOM. Where've you been?

MOTHER. Out there—in all that noise. Are you happy?

BRIDEGROOM. Yes.

MOTHER. Where's your wife?

BRIDEGROOM. Resting a little. It's a bad day for brides!

MOTHER. A bad day? The only good one. To me it was like coming into my own. [THE SERVANT *enters and goes toward* THE BRIDE's *room.*] Like the breaking of new ground; the planting of new trees.

BRIDEGROOM. Are you going to leave?

MOTHER. Yes. I ought to be at home.

BRIDEGROOM. Alone.

MOTHER. Not alone. For my head is full of things: of men, and fights.

BRIDEGROOM. But now the fights are no longer fights.

[THE SERVANT *enters quickly; she disappears at the rear of the stage, running.*]

MOTHER. While you live, you have to fight.

BRIDEGROOM. I'll always obey you!

MOTHER. Try to be loving with your wife, and if you see she's acting foolish or touchy, caress her in a way that will hurt her a little: a strong hug, a bite and then a soft kiss. Not so she'll be angry, but just so she'll feel you're the man, the boss, the one who gives orders. I learned that from your father. And since you don't have him, I have to be the one to tell you about these strong defenses.

BRIDEGROOM. I'll always do as you say.

FATHER [*entering*]. Where's my daughter?

BRIDEGROOM. She's inside.

[THE FATHER *goes to look for her.*]

FIRST GIRL. Get the bride and groom! We're going to dance a round!

FIRST YOUTH [*To* THE BRIDEGROOM]. You're going to lead it.

FATHER [*entering*]. She's not there.

BRIDEGROOM. No?

FATHER. She must have gone up to the railing.

BRIDEGROOM. I'll go see!

[*He leaves. A hubbub of excitement and guitars is heard.*]

FIRST GIRL. They've started it already! [*She leaves.*]

BRIDEGROOM [*entering*]. She isn't there.

MOTHER [*uneasily*]. Isn't she?

FATHER. But where could she have gone?

SERVANT [*entering*]. But where's the girl, where is she?

MOTHER [*seriously*]. That we don't know.

[THE BRIDEGROOM *leaves. Three* GUESTS *enter.*]

FATHER [*dramatically*]. But, isn't she in the dance?

SERVANT. She's not in the dance.

FATHER [*with a start*]. There are a lot of people. Go look!

SERVANT. I've already looked.

FATHER [*tragically*]. Then where is she?

BRIDEGROOM [*entering*]. Nowhere. Not anywhere.

MOTHER [*to* THE FATHER]. What does this mean? Where is your daughter?

[LEONARDO'S WIFE *enters.*]

LEONARDO'S WIFE. They've run away! They've run away! She and Leonardo. On the horse. With their arms around each other, they rode off like a shooting star!

FATHER. That's not true! Not my daughter!

MOTHER. Yes, your daughter! Spawn of a wicked mother, and he, he too. But now she's my son's wife!

BRIDEGROOM. Let's go after them! Who has a horse?

MOTHER. Who has a horse? Right away! Who has a horse? I'll give him all I have—my eyes, my tongue even. . . .

VOICE. Here's one.

MOTHER [to THE SON]. Go! After them! [He leaves with two YOUNG MEN.] No. Don't go. Those people kill quickly and well . . . but yes, run, and I'll follow!

FATHER. It couldn't be my daughter. Perhaps she's thrown herself in the well.

MOTHER. Decent women throw themselves in water; not that one! But now she's my son's wife. Two groups. There are two groups here. [They all enter.] My family and yours. Everyone set out from here. Shake the dust from your heels! We'll go help my son. [The PEOPLE separate into two groups.] For he has his family: his cousins from the sea, and all who came from inland. Out of here! On all roads. The hour of blood has come again. Two groups! You with yours and I with mine. After them! After them!

CURTAIN

ACT III

Scene One

[A forest. It is nighttime. Great moist tree trunks. A dark atmosphere. Two violins are heard. THREE WOODCUTTERS enter.]

FIRST WOODCUTTER. And have they found them?

SECOND WOODCUTTER. No. But they're looking for them everywhere.

THIRD WOODCUTTER. They'll find them.

SECOND WOODCUTTER. Sh-h-h!

THIRD WOODCUTTER. What?

SECOND WOODCUTTER. They seem to be coming closer on all the roads at once.

FIRST WOODCUTTER. When the moon comes out they'll see them.

SECOND WOODCUTTER. They ought to let them go.

FIRST WOODCUTTER. The world is wide. Everybody can live in it.

THIRD WOODCUTTER. But they'll kill them.

SECOND WOODCUTTER. You have to follow your passion. They did right to run away.

FIRST WOODCUTTER. They were deceiving themselves but at the last blood was stronger.

THIRD WOODCUTTER. Blood!

FIRST WOODCUTTER. You have to follow the path of your blood.

SECOND WOODCUTTER. But blood that sees the light of day is drunk up by the earth.

FIRST WOODCUTTER. What of it? Better dead with the blood drained away than alive with it rotting.

THIRD WOODCUTTER. Hush!

FIRST WOODCUTTER. What? Do you hear something?

THIRD WOODCUTTER. I hear the crickets, the frogs, the night's ambush.

FIRST WOODCUTTER. But not the horse.

THIRD WOODCUTTER. No.

FIRST WOODCUTTER. By now he must be loving her.

SECOND WOODCUTTER. Her body for him; his body for her.

THIRD WOODCUTTER. They'll find them and they'll kill them.

FIRST WOODCUTTER. But by then they'll have mingled their bloods. They'll be like two empty jars, like two dry arroyos.

SECOND WOODCUTTER. There are many clouds and it would be easy for the moon not to come out.

THIRD WOODCUTTER. The bridegroom will find them with or without the moon. I saw him set out. Like a raging star. His face the color of ashes. He looked the fate of all his clan.

FIRST WOODCUTTER. His clan of dead men lying in the middle of the street.

SECOND WOODCUTTER. There you have it!

THIRD WOODCUTTER. You think they'll be able to break through the circle?

SECOND WOODCUTTER. It's hard to. There are knives and guns for ten leagues 'round.

THIRD WOODCUTTER. He's riding a good horse.

SECOND WOODCUTTER. But he's carrying a woman.

FIRST WOODCUTTER. We're close by now.

SECOND WOODCUTTER. A tree with forty branches. We'll soon cut it down.

THIRD WOODCUTTER. The moon's coming out now. Let's hurry.

[*From the left shines a brightness.*]
FIRST WOODCUTTER.
O rising moon!
Moon among the great leaves.
SECOND WOODCUTTER.
Cover the blood with jasmines!
FIRST WOODCUTTER.
O lonely moon!
Moon among the great leaves.
SECOND WOODCUTTER.
Silver on the bride's face.
THIRD WOODCUTTER.
O evil moon!
Leave for their love a branch in shadow.
FIRST WOODCUTTER.
O sorrowing moon!
Leave for their love a branch in shadow.
[*They go out.* THE MOON *appears
through the shining brightness at
the left.* THE MOON *is a young wood-
cutter with a white face. The stage
takes on an intense blue radiance.*]
MOON.
Round swan in the river
and a cathedral's eye,
false dawn on the leaves,
they'll not escape; these things am I!
Who is hiding? And who sobs
in the thornbrakes of the valley?
The moon sets a knife
abandoned in the air
which being a leaden threat
yearns to be blood's pain.
Let me in! I come freezing
down to walls and windows!
Open roofs, open breasts
where I may warm myself!
I'm cold! My ashes
of somnolent metals
seek the fire's crest
on mountains and streets.
But the snow carries me
upon its mottled back
and pools soak me
in their water, hard and cold.
But this night there will be
red blood for my cheeks,
and for the reeds that cluster
at the wide feet of the wind.
Let there be neither shadow nor bower,
and then they can't get away!
O let me enter a breast
where I may get warm!
A heart for me!
Warm! That will spurt
over the mountains of my chest;

let me come in, oh let me!
[*To the branches.*]
I want no shadows. My rays
must get in everywhere,
even among the dark trunks I want
the whisper of gleaming lights,
so that this night there will be
sweet blood for my cheeks,
and for the reeds that cluster
at the wide feet of the wind.
Who is hiding? Out, I say!
No! They will not get away!
I will light up the horse
with a fever bright as diamonds.
[*He disappears among the trunks, and
the stage goes back to its dark lighting. An* OLD WOMAN *comes out completely covered by thin green cloth.
She is barefooted. Her face can
barely be seen among the folds.*]
BEGGAR WOMAN.
That moon's going away, just when
they're near.
They won't get past here. The river's
whisper
and the whispering tree trunks will
muffle
the torn flight of their shrieks.
It has to be here, and soon. I'm worn
out.
The coffins are ready, and white sheets
wait on the floor of the bedroom
for heavy bodies with torn throats.
Let not one bird awake, let the breeze,
gathering their moans in her skirt,
fly with them over black tree tops
or bury them in soft mud.
[*Impatiently.*]
Oh, that moon! That moon!
[THE MOON *appears. The intense blue
light returns.*]
MOON. They're coming. One band
through the ravine and the other along
the river. I'm going to light up the boulders. What do you need?
BEGGAR WOMAN. Nothing.
MOON. The wind blows hard now, with
a double edge.
BEGGAR WOMAN. Light up the waistcoat and open the buttons; the knives
will know the path after that.
MOON.
But let them be a long time a-dying. So
the blood
will slide its delicate hissing between my
fingers.

Look how my ashen valleys already are
  waking
in longing for this fountain of shuddering
  gushes!
BEGGAR WOMAN. Let's not let them
past the arroyo. Silence!
MOON. There they come!
[*He goes. The stage is left dark.*]
BEGGAR WOMAN. Quick! Lots of light!
Do you hear me? They can't get away!
  [THE BRIDEGROOM *and* THE FIRST
    YOUTH *enter.* THE BEGGAR WOMAN
    *sits down and covers herself with
    her cloak.*]
BRIDEGROOM. This way.
FIRST YOUTH. You won't find them.
BRIDEGROOM [*angrily*]. Yes, I'll find
them.
FIRST YOUTH. I think they've taken an-
other path.
BRIDEGROOM. No. Just a moment ago
I felt the galloping.
FIRST YOUTH. It could have been an-
other horse.
BRIDEGROOM [*intensely*]. Listen to me.
There's only one horse in the whole
world, and this one's it. Can't you understand that? If you're going to follow
me, follow me without talking.
FIRST YOUTH. It's only that I want
to . . .
BRIDEGROOM. Be quiet. I'm sure of
meeting them there. Do you see this
arm? Well, it's not my arm. It's my
brother's arm, and my father's, and that
of all the dead ones in my family. And
it has so much strength that it can
pull this tree up by the roots, if it
wants to. And let's move on, because
here I feel the clenched teeth of all
my people in me so that I can't breathe
easily.
BEGGAR WOMAN [*whining*]. Ay-y-y!
FIRST YOUTH. Did you hear that?
BRIDEGROOM. You go that way and
then circle back.
FIRST YOUTH. This is a hunt.
BRIDEGROOM. A hunt. The greatest
hunt there is.
  [THE YOUTH *goes off.* THE BRIDEGROOM
    *goes rapidly to the left and stumbles
    over* THE BEGGAR WOMAN, DEATH.]
BEGGAR WOMAN. Ay-y-y!
BRIDEGROOM. What do you want?
BEGGAR WOMAN. I'm cold.
BRIDEGROOM. Which way are you go-
ing?

BEGGAR WOMAN [*always whining like
a beggar*]. Over there, far away . . .
BRIDEGROOM. Where are you from?
BEGGAR WOMAN. Over there . . . very
far away.
BRIDEGROOM. Have you seen a man
and a woman running away on a horse?
BEGGAR WOMAN [*awakening*]. Wait a
minute . . . [*She looks at him.*] Handsome young man. [*She rises.*] But you'd
be much handsomer sleeping.
BRIDEGROOM. Tell me; answer me. Did
you see them?
BEGGAR WOMAN. Wait a minute . . .
What broad shoulders! How would you
like to be laid out on them and not have
to walk on the soles of your feet which
are so small?
BRIDEGROOM [*shaking her*]. I asked
you if you saw them! Have they passed
through here?
BEGGAR WOMAN [*energetically*]. No.
They haven't passed; but they're coming
from the hill. Don't you hear them?
BRIDEGROOM. No.
BEGGAR WOMAN. Do you know the
road?
BRIDEGROOM. I'll go, whatever it's like!
BEGGAR WOMAN. I'll go along with you.
I know this country.
BRIDEGROOM [*impatiently*]. Well, let's
go! Which way?
BEGGAR WOMAN [*dramatically*]. This
way!
  [*They go rapidly out. Two violins,
    which represent the forest, are heard
    distantly.* THE WOODCUTTERS *return.
    They have their axes on their shoul-
    ders. They move slowly among the
    tree trunks.*]
FIRST WOODCUTTER.
O rising death!
Death among the great leaves.
SECOND WOODCUTTER.
Don't open the gush of blood!
FIRST WOODCUTTER.
O lonely death!
Death among the dried leaves.
THIRD WOODCUTTER.
Don't lay flowers over the wedding!
SECOND WOODCUTTER.
O sad death!
Leave for their love a green branch.
FIRST WOODCUTTER.
O evil death!
Leave for their love a branch of green!
  [*They go out while they are talking.*

LEONARDO *and* THE BRIDE *appear*.]

LEONARDO.

Hush!

BRIDE.

From here I'll go on alone.
You go now! I want you to turn back.

LEONARDO.

Hush, I said!

BRIDE.

With your teeth, with your hands, anyway you can,
take from my clean throat
the metal of this chain,
and let me live forgotten
back there in my house in the ground.
And if you don't want to kill me
as you would kill a tiny snake,
set in my hands, a bride's hands,
the barrel of your shotgun.
Oh, what lamenting, what fire,
sweeps upward through my head!
What glass splinters are stuck in my
tongue!

LEONARDO.

We've taken the step now; hush!
because they're close behind us,
and I must take you with me.

BRIDE.

Then it must be by force!

LEONARDO.

By force? Who was it first
went down the stairway?

BRIDE.

I went down it.

LEONARDO.

And who was it put
a new bridle on the horse?

BRIDE.

I myself did it. It's true.

LEONARDO.

And whose were the hands
strapped spurs to my boots?

BRIDE.

The same hands, these that are yours,
but which when they see you would like
to break the blue branches
and sunder the purl of your veins.
I love you! I love you! But leave me!
For if I were able to kill you
I'd wrap you 'round in a shroud
with the edges bordered in violets.
Oh, what lamenting, what fire,
sweeps upward through my head!

LEONARDO.

What glass splinters are stuck in my
tongue!
Because I tried to forget you
and put a wall of stone
between your house and mine.
It's true. You remember?
And when I saw you in the distance
I threw sand in my eyes.
But I was riding a horse
and the horse went straight to your door.
And the silver pins of your wedding
turned my red blood black.
And in me our dream was choking
my flesh with its poisoned weeds.
Oh, it isn't my fault—
the fault is the earth's—
and this fragrance that you exhale
from your breasts and your braids.

BRIDE.

Oh, how untrue! I want
from you neither bed nor food,
yet there's not a minute each day
that I don't want to be with you,
because you drag me, and I come,
then you tell me to go back
and I follow you,
like chaff blown on the breeze.
I have left a good, honest man,
and all his people,
with the wedding feast half over
and wearing my bridal wreath.
But you are the one will be punished
and that I don't want to happen.
Leave me alone now! You run away!
There is no one who will defend you.

LEONARDO.

The birds of early morning
are calling among the trees.
The night is dying
on the stone's ridge.
Let's go to a hidden corner
where I may love you forever,
for to me the people don't matter,
nor the venom they throw on us.

[*He embraces her strongly.*]

BRIDE.

And I'll sleep at your feet,
to watch over your dreams.
Naked, looking over the fields,
as though I were a bitch.
Because that's what I am! Oh, I look at
you
and your beauty sears me.

LEONARDO.

Fire is stirred by fire.
The same tiny flame
will kill two wheat heads together.
Let's go!

BRIDE.

Where are you taking me?

LEONARDO.
Where they cannot come,
these men who surround us.
Where I can look at you!
BRIDE [sarcastically].
Carry me with you from fair to fair,
a shame to clean women,
so that people will see me
with my wedding sheets
on the breeze like banners.
LEONARDO.
I, too, would want to leave you
if I thought as men should.
But wherever you go, I go.
You're the same. Take a step. Try.
Nails of moonlight have fused
my waist and your chains.
[This whole scene is violent, full of
great sensuality.]
BRIDE.
Listen!
LEONARDO.
They're coming.
BRIDE.
Run!
It's fitting that I should die here,
with water over my feet,
with thorns upon my head.
And fitting the leaves should mourn me,
a woman lost and virgin.
LEONARDO.
Be quiet. Now they're appearing.
BRIDE.
Go now!
LEONARDO.
Quiet. Don't let them hear us.
[THE BRIDE hesitates.]
BRIDE.
Both of us!
LEONARDO [embracing her].
Any way you want!
If they separate us, it will be
because I am dead.
BRIDE.
And I dead too.

[They go out in each other's arms. THE
MOON appears very slowly. The stage
takes on a strong blue light. The two
violins are heard. Suddenly two long,
ear-splitting shrieks are heard, and
the music of the two violins is cut
short. At the second shriek THE BEG-
GAR WOMAN appears and stands with
her back to the audience. She opens
her cape and stands in the center of
the stage like a great bird with immense wings. THE MOON halts. The
curtain comes down in absolute
silence.]

CURTAIN

Scene Two

The Final Scene

[A white dwelling with arches and
thick walls. To the right and left, are
white stairs. At the back, a great arch and
a wall of the same color. The floor also
should be shining white. This simple
dwelling should have the monumental
feeling of a church. There should not
be a single gray nor any shadow, not
even what is necessary for perspective.]
[TWO GIRLS dressed in dark blue are
winding a red skein.]

FIRST GIRL.
Wool, red wool,
what would you make?
SECOND GIRL.
Oh, jasmine for dresses,
fine wool like glass.
At four o'clock born,
at ten o'clock dead.
A thread from this wool yarn,
a chain 'round your feet
a knot that will tighten
the bitter white wreath.
LITTLE GIRL [singing].
Were you at the wedding?
FIRST GIRL.
No.
LITTLE GIRL.
Well, neither was I!
What could have happened
'midst the shoots of the vineyards?
What could have happened
'neath the branch of the olive?
What really happened
that no one came back?
Were you at the wedding?
SECOND GIRL.
We told you once, no.
LITTLE GIRL [leaving].
Well, neither was I!
SECOND GIRL.
Wool, red wool,
what would you sing?

FIRST GIRL.
Their wounds turning waxen
balm-myrtle for pain.
Asleep in the morning,
and watching at night.
LITTLE GIRL [*in the doorway*].
And then, the thread stumbled
on the flinty stones,
but mountains, blue mountains,
are letting it pass.
Running, running, running,
and finally to come
to stick in a knife blade,
to take back the bread.
[*She goes out.*]
SECOND GIRL.
Wool, red wool,
what would you tell?
FIRST GIRL.
The lover is silent,
crimson the groom,
at the still shoreline
I saw them laid out.
[*She stops and looks at the skein.*]
LITTLE GIRL [*appearing in the door-
way*].
Running, running, running,
the thread runs to here.
All covered with clay
I feel them draw near.
Bodies stretched stiffly
in ivory sheets!
[THE WIFE *and* MOTHER-IN-LAW *of*
LEONARDO *appear. They are an-
guished.*]
FIRST GIRL. Are they coming yet?
MOTHER-IN-LAW [*harshly*]. We don't
know.
SECOND GIRL. What can you tell us
about the wedding?
FIRST GIRL. Yes, tell me.
MOTHER-IN-LAW [*curtly*]. Nothing.
LEONARDO'S WIFE. I want to go back
and find out all about it.
MOTHER-IN-LAW [*sternly*].
You, back to your house.
Brave and alone in your house.
To grow old and to weep.
But behind closed doors.
Never again. Neither dead nor alive.
We'll nail up our windows
and let rains and nights
fall on the bitter weeds.
LEONARDO'S WIFE. What could have
happened?
MOTHER-IN-LAW.
It doesn't matter what.

Put a veil over your face.
Your children are yours,
that's all. On the bed
put a cross of ashes
where his pillow was.
[*They go out.*]
BEGGAR WOMAN [*at the door*]. A crust
of bread, little girls.
LITTLE GIRL. Go away!
[THE GIRLS *huddle close together.*]
BEGGAR WOMAN. Why?
LITTLE GIRL. Because you whine; go
away!
FIRST GIRL. Child!
BEGGAR WOMAN.
I might have asked for your eyes! A cloud
of birds is following me. Will you have
   one?
LITTLE GIRL. I want to get away from
here!
SECOND GIRL [*to* THE BEGGAR WOMAN].
Don't mind her!
FIRST GIRL. Did you come by the road
through the arroyo?
BEGGAR WOMAN. I came that way!
FIRST GIRL [*timidly*]. Can I ask you
something?
BEGGAR WOMAN.
I saw them: they'll be here soon; two
   torrents
still at last, among the great boulders,
two men at the horse's feet.
Two dead men in the night's splendor.
[*With pleasure.*]
Dead, yes, dead.
FIRST GIRL. Hush, old woman, hush!
BEGGAR WOMAN.
Crushed flowers for eyes, and their teeth
two fistfuls of hard-frozen snow.
Both of them fell, and the Bride returns
with bloodstains on her skirt and hair.
And they come covered with two sheets
carried on the shoulders of two tall
   boys.
That's how it was; nothing more. What
   was fitting.
Over the golden flower, dirty sand.
[*She goes.* THE GIRLS *bow their heads
   and start going out rhythmically.*]
FIRST GIRL.
Dirty sand.
SECOND GIRL.
Over the golden flower.
LITTLE GIRL.
Over the golden flower
they're bringing the dead from the ar-
royo.

Dark the one,
dark the other.
What shadowy nightingale flies and
     weeps over the golden flower!
[*She goes. The stage is left empty.*
     THE MOTHER *and a* NEIGHBOR
     WOMAN *appear.* THE NEIGHBOR *is*
     weeping.]
MOTHER. Hush.
NEIGHBOR. I can't.
MOTHER. Hush, I said. [*At the door.*]
Is there nobody here? [*She puts her*
hands to her forehead.] My son ought
to answer me. But now my son is an
armful of shrivelled flowers. My son is a
fading voice beyond the mountains now.
[*With rage, to* THE NEIGHBOR.] Will you
shut up? I want no wailing in this house.
Your tears are only tears from your eyes,
but when I'm alone mine will come—
from the soles of my feet, from my roots
—burning more than blood.
NEIGHBOR. You come to my house;
don't you stay here.
MOTHER. I want to be here. Here. In
peace. They're all dead now: and at midnight I'll sleep, sleep without terror of
guns or knives. Other mothers will go to
their windows, lashed by rain, to watch
for their sons' faces. But not I. And of
my dreams I'll make a cold ivory dove
that will carry camellias of white frost to
the graveyard. But no; not graveyard, not
graveyard: the couch of earth, the bed
that shelters them and rocks them in the
sky. [A WOMAN *dressed in black enters,*
goes toward the right, and there kneels.
To THE NEIGHBOR.] Take your hands
from your face. We have terrible days
ahead. I want to see no one. The earth
and I. My grief and I. And these four
walls. Ay-y-y! Ay-y-y!
[*She sits down, overcome.*]
NEIGHBOR. Take pity on yourself!
MOTHER [*pushing back her hair*].
I must be calm. [*She sits down.*] Because
the neighbor women will come and I
don't want them to see me so poor. So
poor! A woman without even one son
to hold to her lips.
[THE BRIDE *appears. She is without*
     her wreath and wears a black shawl.]
NEIGHBOR [*with rage, seeing* THE
BRIDE]. Where are you going?
BRIDE. I'm coming here.
MOTHER [*to* THE NEIGHBOR]. Who is it?
NEIGHBOR. Don't you recognize her?

MOTHER. That's why I asked who it
was. Because I don't want to recognize
her, so I won't sink my teeth in her
throat. You snake! [*She moves wrathfully*
on THE BRIDE, *then stops. To* THE NEIGH-
BOR.] Look at her! There she is, and
she's crying, while I stand here calmly
and don't tear her eyes out. I don't
understand myself. Can it be I didn't
love my son? But where's his good name?
Where is it now? Where is it?
[*She beats* THE BRIDE *who drops to the*
     floor.]
NEIGHBOR. For God's sake!
[*She tries to separate them.*]
BRIDE [*to* THE NEIGHBOR]. Let her; I
came here so she'd kill me and they'd
take me away with them. [*To* THE
MOTHER.] But not with her hands; with
grappling hooks, with a sickle—and with
force—until they break on my bones.
Let her! I want her to know I'm clean,
that I may be crazy, but that they can
bury me without a single man ever having seen himself in the whiteness of my
breasts.
MOTHER. Shut up, shut up; what do I
care about that?
BRIDE. Because I ran away with the
other one; I ran away. [*With anguish.*]
You would have gone, too. I was a
woman burning with desire, full of sores
inside and out, and your son was a little
bit of water from which I hoped for
children, land, health; but the other one
was a dark river, choked with brush, that
brought near me the undertone of its
rushes and its whispered song. And I
went along with your son who was like
a little boy of cold water—and the
other sent against me hundreds of birds
who got in my way and left white frost
on my wounds, my wounds of a poor
withered woman, of a girl caressed by
fire. I didn't want to; remember that!
I didn't want to. Your son was my destiny and I have not betrayed him, but
the other one's arm dragged me along
like the pull of the sea, like the head toss
of a mule, and he would have dragged
me always, always, always—even if I
were an old woman and all your son's
sons held me by the hair!
[A NEIGHBOR *enters.*]
MOTHER. She is not to blame; nor
am I! [*Sarcastically.*] Who is, then? It's
a delicate, lazy, sleepless woman who

throws away an orange blossom wreath and goes looking for a piece of bed warmed by another woman!

BRIDE. Be still! Be still! Take your revenge on me; here I am! See how soft my throat is; it would be less work for you than cutting a dahlia in your garden. But never that! Clean, clean as a new-born little girl. And strong enough to prove it to you. Light the fire. Let's stick our hands in; you, for your son, I, for my body. *You'll* draw yours out first.

[ANOTHER NEIGHBOR *enters.*]

MOTHER. But what does your good name matter to me? What does your death matter to me? What does anything about anything matter to me? Blesséd be the wheat stalks, because my sons are under them; blesséd be the rain, because it wets the face of the dead. Blesséd be God, who stretches us out together to rest.

[ANOTHER NEIGHBOR *enters.*]

BRIDE. Let me weep with you.

MOTHER. Weep. But at the door.

[*The* LITTLE GIRL *enters.* THE BRIDE *stays at the door.* THE MOTHER *is at the center of the stage.*]

LEONARDO'S WIFE [*entering and going to the left*].
He was a beautiful horseman,
now he's a heap of snow.
He rode to fairs and mountains
and women's arms.
Now, the night's dark moss
crowns his forehead.

MOTHER.
A sunflower to your mother,
a mirror of the earth.
Let them put on your breast
the cross of bitter rosebay;
and over you a sheet
of shining silk;
between your quiet hands
let water form its lament.

WIFE.
Ay-y-y, four gallant boys
come with tired shoulders!

BRIDE.
Ay-y-y, four gallant boys

carry death on high!

MOTHER.
Neighbors.

LITTLE GIRL [*at the door*].
They're bringing them now.

MOTHER.
It's the same thing.
Always the cross, the cross.

WOMEN.
Sweet nails,
cross adored,
sweet name
of Christ our Lord.

BRIDE. May the cross protect both the quick and the dead.

MOTHER.
Neighbors: with a knife,
with a little knife,
on their appointed day, between two and three,
these two men killed each other for love.
With a knife,
with a tiny knife
that barely fits the hand,
but that slides in clean
through the astonished flesh
and stops at the place
where trembles, enmeshed,
the dark root of a scream.

BRIDE.
And this is a knife,
a tiny knife
that barely fits the hand;
fish without scales, without river,
so that on their appointed day, between two and three,
with this knife,
two men are left stiff,
with their lips turning yellow.

MOTHER.
And it barely fits the hand
but it slides in clean
through the astonished flesh
and stops there, at the place
where trembles enmeshed
the dark root of a scream.

[THE NEIGHBORS, *kneeling on the floor, sob.*]

CURTAIN

Arturo Barea

THE POET AND SEX

Federico García Lorca, who never wanted to face politics, did face the problems of sex with the greatest clarity. Now, sexual life has in every nation its definite characteristics, traditions, and rites, even though the sexual problems are universal and non-national. In every nation there exists a cultured, sophisticated minority which shares its rules of behavior and its conscious ideals with similar minorities of all other nations within the same sphere of civilization; and there exists the great mass of people following their national sexual code, their peculiar unwritten but unviolable sexual laws. Lorca felt and expressed the problems of sex such as they had been shaped and transformed by the complex conventions of his people. He felt the emotions at the root of the Spanish sexual code so deeply that in his art he magnified them until traditional values stood out with a perturbing significance.

His three rural tragedies, *Bodas de Sangre, Yerma,* and *La Casa de Bernarda Alba,* show these traditions and the problems behind them with the greatest force. *Bodas de Sangre,* "Blood Wedding," has a simple pattern of love, honor, and vengeance. The only son of a widow, whose husband and first-born son were killed by the men of a neighboring family, is in love with the daughter of a widower, a rich farmer like himself. A marriage is arranged in which the father's greed for more land and the mother's wish to bury the memory of bloodshed and see new life created have as much part as the son's love. The girl, however, has long been in love with the son of the man who had killed her betrothed's father and brother. Neither of the young men wants to carry on the feud which is ever present in the mind of the mother.

The girl has been fighting against her passion for years and intends to fulfill her contract. The man she loves has even married to escape from his forbidden desire for her. But neither he nor the girl can bear the idea that she should deliver herself to another; they elope on her wedding day. There is only one thing to be done. "The hour of blood has struck again." The mother knows that she now has lost her hope of grandchildren and will lose her only remaining son, but she sends him in pursuit of the couple, because the murderer of her hope must be killed—the blood of the son of her husband's murderer must be shed. The two men meet, fight, and kill each other.

The outline of this triangle-and-vendetta story is familiar. But Lorca has filled it with an essentially Spanish tragedy.

The mother is the incarnation of this tragedy. A strong woman who enjoyed life with her husband, she has become dominated by the fear of the extinction of her blood—fear of death, not for herself but for the seed—and by an anxiety to see her physical existence continued, perpetuated by her son's children. This constant fear fills her with a sense of doom. Vengeance of her "blood" follows from her possessive, death-haunted love: to let the enemy's seed survive one's own would mean final death.

Centuries of Moorish and medieval-Catholic breeding, centuries of a social order in which women were valued only for the sons they produced, created this attitude. The code which sprang from it is still valid in Spain. Lorca's "mother," who likes men to be lusty and wild because it means more sons, is deeply convinced that procreation and fecundity are

SOURCE: From *Lorca: The Poet and His People* by Arturo Barea. Copyright 1949, by Harcourt, Brace & World, Inc. and reprinted with the permission of the Barea Estate.

the object, not the correlate, of married sexual love. Her son must marry to give her, the mother, grandchildren: "... and see to it that you make me happy by giving me six grandchildren, or as many as you like, since your father did not have the time to make me more sons."

She glories in man's procreative strength: "Your grandfather left a son at every corner," she says proudly to her son. But she believes that a man must not only beget children but also engender life around him, be fecund in every sense.

Mother and son talk about this while they are walking over the land of his betrothed:

SON. These are dry lands.
MOTHER. Your father would have covered them with trees.
SON. Without water—?
MOTHER. He would have found it. In the three years he lived with me, he planted ten cherry trees, the three walnut trees by the mill, a whole vineyard, and the plant called Jupiter which had scarlet flowers and withered.

This moral conviction that men and women must be fecund and that the man and husband is the master because he is the instrument of fecundation has the deepest possible psychological and social roots. In peasant communities it is kept alive in its ancient form by a powerful economic fact: there must be sons to work the land and to defend the property. In Spain this law was reinforced by the rules of the Moorish harem, rules which influenced the non-Moorish society of the country and survived the expulsion of the Moors. It was adjusted, exalted, and perpetuated in the stern teachings of the Church, which made it sinful for husband and wife to enjoy each other, but righteous to multiply. The code of honor which demands the taking of life and the preservation of virginity, not for the sake of "virtue" or love but for the sake of the purity of the "blood," is part of this tradition; it provides the sanctions against sexual offenses and protects the property of the family.

This code and the elements that went into its making were by no means confined to Spain. But the interesting point is that the code is still real to Spaniards, including those who have rationally repudiated it. Even in the towns, the same men and women who will look unmoved at the display of an exaggerated "point of honor" in some of the plays of Calderón and Lope de Vega are stirred by the sterner, simpler justice of the *Alcalde de Zalamea*, the village mayor who kills the violator of his daughter and earns the approval of the King for his act. And they are moved in the recesses of their consciousness by the ancient popular emotions crystallized in Lorca's images.

In fact, blood feud and its code of honor are things of this age, not merely of the past, to Spaniards. The modern laws have prosecuted and suppressed vendettas, but they were powerless against family feuds which lasted through generations and destroyed generations. The same fierce possessive love and haunting fear of extinction which drive the mother in Lorca's tragedy, drove many women during the Spanish Civil War and, through children steeped in hatred against the murderers of their "blood," threaten to breed relentless feuds for generations to come.

On this hard soil, the code of the blood is stronger than love. The mother in *Bodas de Sangre* admits no justification for the betrayal of the law of purity. A woman must have no lover. Contemptuously she says of the girl who followed her beloved: "Honest women, clean women, go into the water. But not she." This rule is accepted by the girl herself. She knows that she did wrong in following the other man, whom she could never marry, and in wanting to live with him. She accepts the law that the honor of the family and her own honor are safe only if her virginity is left intact for her husband to convert it into maternity.

When the two dead bodies have been carried back to the village the unfaithful bride goes to the house of her dead bridegroom's mother and faces her curses. The mother cries out: "But his honor—what about his honor?" The bride then justifies her "crime," not by her love but by the other man's fatal erotic attraction. Fiercely she defends her "intact" honor, ready to pass through an ordeal by fire to prove it:

I want her to know that I am pure.
That I may be mad, but that if they

were to bury me now, no man would have seen himself in the whiteness of my breasts. . . . For I went away with the other one. I went. You would have done the same. I was a seared woman, covered with sores within and without, and your son was a trickle of water from which I hoped to get children, land, and health. But the other was a dark leaf-grown river, he overcame me with the sounds of reeds, singing through his teeth. And I went along with your son who was like a little child of cold water, and the other sent me hundreds of birds which would not let me walk and which left white frost on my wounds, the wounds of a poor blighted woman, of a girl kissed by fire. . . . But what you say—no. I am clean and honest as a newborn girl child, and I am strong enough to prove it to you. Light the fire. We shall put our hands in the flame. You for your son, I for my body. And you will be the first to drop your hands.

The lyrical language is the poet's, but the images come from the speech people of the Andalusian countryside use in emotional moments, describing their passions and half-comprehended thoughts in ageless, occult metaphors, as though in magic formulas. . . .

In reshaping the old, familiar, half-forgotten tale Lorca thus made visible not merely the behavior of people possessed by their blood code, but the "dark root of the cry" in a ritual in which sex is possession of life and salvation from death, but death the final, ordained frustration. To this ritual all Spaniards respond. . . .

The exceptional sensitiveness to feminine reactions which fills Lorca's plays runs through the whole of his poetry, wherever it touches themes of love, and even when the man appears as the actor and conqueror. Perhaps it was this power to identify himself with both men and women which made it possible for Lorca to capture and express all the main elements in Spanish sexual consciousness, including those subtly entangled with the religious life of the people.

Spanish children first learn about the supreme value of chastity in men and virginity in women through the stories of saints and martyrs on which religious tuition centers during the early years of childhood. Except for St. Anna, the mother of the Virgin—of the "Immaculate Conception"—most of the female saints in Spanish hagiology and martyrology are virgins. In popular language "virgin" and "martyr" are always coupled. Through their religious instruction and their studies of classical literature Spanish boys are forced to visualize the female body as a "sack of uncleanliness" and to imagine its putrefaction in slow, loathsome stages. They are shown the virginal martyrs in the clean loveliness of their young flesh and in the horror of their mutilated bodies. Perversely, a deeper exaltation and a deeper compassion are produced when the breasts hacked off by the executioner are described as young and virginal than when they are the good tired breasts of a mother of many children. Young boys and girls are taught to long for a martyr's death which, in the midst of unbearable pain, contains the searing joy of union with the Savior, the felicity of a transition to a better life. This educational process breeds, particularly in the girls, the ideas and ideals of Lust through Pain, Holiness through Horror, and Virginity triumphant over Violence and crowned by the Heavenly Bridegroom. Juvenile sadomasochism is cultivated by those unimpeachable legends and developed by the terrifying, grimly naturalistic paintings of martyred saints in Spanish churches, where the air is thick with sensuous exaltation, cruel and cloying. . . .

There is another important side to religious eroticism as it exists in Spain today. The terrible realism of the old, stern images of Christ on the Cross and of tortured saints was followed in Renaissance and Baroque art by the sensuous idealization of beauty in the paintings or sculptures of beings "in the Glory," the Virgin, the beatified saints, the archangels—including the fallen Lucifer—and the hosts of the angels. The sinless, disembodied subjects gave the artists liberty to create stainless, "immaculate" bodies, and justified, indeed demanded, adoring contemplation. It is impossible not to feel the bodily warmth of Murillo's glowing, oversweet Virgins and female saints. Less obvious, but of greater psychological importance, is the physical fascination of the images of juvenile male martyrs—such as St. Sebastian—and above all of the angels. In them women who had been taught to renounce all sensual thoughts of the masculine body found "innocent," concrete shapes on which their imagination was allowed to dwell. The traditional images of the archangels are androgynous, and the Baroque artists particularly created ideal forms of an ambiguous beauty which is not sexless, but belongs to neither sex, and to both. In Murcia there is a polychrome wood sculpture of the archangel Gabriel, by the eighteenth-century monk Salzillo, in which feminine and masculine elements are inextricably fused to a gentle, perfect, and seductive shape of great purity. . . .

Yet there runs a pagan streak through Spanish eroticism even if, in the traditional moral code guarded by the Church, it is banned from married life and altogether from the life of the women. It emerges in the man's delight in the body of a woman or another man. It breaks loose, unexpectedly, in the almost orgiastic mass festivals which transform ecclesiastic holidays or pilgrimages, such as that which Lorca brought into his story of Yerma. It is strong and joyful in some of the folk songs and folk sayings, diluted in sensuous romantic poetry, and perverted to "adulterous" passion in conventional drama. But it exists, a dark and powerful undertow, and Lorca had to give it form, just as he uncovered the other currents in the sex life of his people. And what he shows is not so much the joyous freedom or the physical delight, but rather the frightening, ruthless force of lust.

Bertolt
Brecht
1898–1956

Brecht was born in Augsburg, Germany, the son of a factory manager. Early in adult life he developed an antipathy toward militarism; he joined radical groups, and his writings and political activities earned him the enmity of the military and Fascist elements in Germany. As a student in Berlin and Munich he studied natural sciences and medicine, but Brecht's true interest lay in literature and particularly in drama. At one time he supported himself by singing in cabarets, but soon he scored a success with his play *Drums in the Night* (1922). Brecht joined the Deutsches Theater, where he produced Elizabethan, Spanish, and Chinese dramas along with his own works. He next accepted direction of the Schiffbauerdam Theater in Berlin, where he based his productions on his famous theory of "epic theatre" and gathered about him one of the outstanding acting troupes in Europe. Rather than lure the spectator into the play and give him an illusion of reality, Brecht attempted to place the audience at a distance from the play (the "alienation" principle) and to keep them from identifying emotionally with his characters. His use of naked staging, a commenting narrator, pantomime, songs, film projections, captions, and similar devices was intended to keep the audience aware that they were in a theatre, not participating in real life, and thus to compel them to a critical rather than a blindly emotional response. In 1928 Brecht triumphed with his *Three Penny Opera*, a bitingly satirical play with music by Kurt Weill. Other plays followed, in a variety of forms but all with a radical Marxist orientation. With Hitler's rise to power, Brecht was forced to leave Germany; he lived in France, Norway, the Soviet Union, and the United States. It was during this period of exile that Brecht wrote several of his most significant plays: *Mother Courage* (1939), *Galileo* (1939), *The Good Woman of Setzuan* (1940), and *Herr Puntila and His Servant Matti* (1941). Brecht was iconoclastic and bohemian, antibourgeois and revolutionary to the end. After the war he returned to Germany and settled in East Berlin, where until his death he directed the famous Berliner Ensemble. His last major play was *The Caucasian Chalk Circle* (1945).

MOTHER COURAGE AND HER CHILDREN

A chronicle of the thirty years' war

BERTOLT BRECHT

Translated by Ralph Manheim

CHARACTERS

MOTHER COURAGE
KATTRIN, *her mute daughter*
EILIF, *her elder son*
SWISS CHEESE, *her younger son*
THE RECRUITER
THE SERGEANT
THE COOK
THE GENERAL
THE CHAPLAIN
THE ORDNANCE OFFICER
YVETTE POTTIER
THE MAN WITH THE PATCH
    OVER HIS EYE
THE OTHER SERGEANT

THE OLD COLONEL
A CLERK
A YOUNG SOLDIER
AN OLDER SOLDIER
A PEASANT
THE PEASANT'S WIFE
THE YOUNG MAN
THE OLD WOMAN
ANOTHER PEASANT
THE PEASANT WOMAN
A YOUNG PEASANT
THE LIEUTENANT
SOLDIERS
A VOICE

Scene One

[*Spring, 1624. General Oxenstjerna recruits troops in Dalarna for the Polish campaign. The canteen woman, Anna Fierling, known as Mother Courage, loses a son.*

Highway near a city.

A SERGEANT *and a* RECRUITER *stand shivering.*]

THE RECRUITER. How can anybody get a company together in a place like this? Sergeant, sometimes I feel like committing suicide. The general wants me to recruit four platoons by the twelfth, and the people around here are so depraved I can't sleep at night. I finally get hold of a man, I close my eyes and pretend not to see that he's chicken-breasted and he's got varicose veins, I get him good and drunk and he signs up. While I'm paying for the drinks, he steps out, I follow him to the door because I smell a rat: Sure enough, he's gone, like a fart out of a goose. A man's word doesn't mean a thing, there's no honor, no loyalty. This place has undermined my faith in humanity, sergeant.

THE SERGEANT. It's easy to see these people have gone too long without a war. How can you have morality without a

SOURCE: *Mother Courage and Her Children* by Bertolt Brecht, translated by Ralph Manheim. From *Collected Plays*, vol. 5, by Bertolt Brecht, edited by Ralph Manheim and John Willett. Copyright © 1960, 1970 by Stefan S. Brecht. Reprinted by permission of Pantheon Books, a Division of Random House, Inc. and of Methuen & Co., Ltd.

war, I ask you? Peace is a mess, it takes
a war to put things in order. In peacetime the human race goes to the dogs.
Man and beast are treated like so much
dirt. Everybody eats what they like, a big
piece of cheese on white bread, with a
slice of meat on top of the cheese. Nobody knows how many young men or
good horses there are in that town up
ahead, they've never been counted. I've
been in places where they hadn't had a
war in as much as seventy years, the
people had no names, they didn't even
know who they were. It takes a war before you get decent lists and records;
then your boots are done up in bales and
your grain in sacks, man and beast are
properly counted and marched away, because people realize that without order
they can't have a war.

THE RECRUITER. How right you are!

THE SERGEANT. Like all good things, a
war is hard to get started. But once it
takes root, it's vigorous; then people are
as scared of peace as dice players are of
laying off, because they'll have to reckon
up their losses. But at first they're scared
of war. It's the novelty.

THE RECRUITER. Say, there comes a
wagon. Two women and two young fellows. Keep the old woman busy, sergeant. If this is another flop, you won't
catch me standing out in this April wind
any more.

[A Jew's harp is heard. Drawn by two
young men, a covered wagon approaches. In the wagon sit MOTHER
COURAGE and her mute daughter
KATTRIN.]

MOTHER COURAGE. Good morning, sergeant.

SERGEANT [barring the way]. Good
morning, friends. Who are you?

MOTHER COURAGE. Business people.
[Sings.]

Hey, Captains, make the drum stop
    drumming
And let your soldiers take a seat.
Here's Mother Courage, with boots she's
    coming
To help along their aching feet.
How can they march off to the slaughter
With baggage, cannon, lice and fleas
Across the rocks and through the water
Unless their boots are in one piece?

The spring is come. Christian, revive!
The snowdrifts melt. The dead lie
    dead.
And if by chance you're still alive
It's time to rise and shake a leg.

O Captains, don't expect to send them
To death with nothing in their crops.
First you must let Mother Courage mend
    them
In mind and body with her schnapps.
On empty bellies it's distressing
To stand up under shot and shell.
But once they're full, you have my bless-
    ing
To lead them to the jaws of hell.
    The spring is come. Christian, revive!
    The snowdrifts melt, the dead lie
        dead.
    And if by chance you're still alive
    It's time to rise and shake a leg.

THE SERGEANT. Halt, you scum. Where
do you belong?

THE ELDER SON. Second Finnish Regiment.

THE SERGEANT. Where are your papers?

MOTHER COURAGE. Papers?

THE YOUNGER SON. But she's Mother
Courage!

THE SERGEANT. Never heard of her.
Why Courage?

MOTHER COURAGE. They call me Courage, sergeant, because when I saw ruin
staring me in the face I drove out of
Riga through cannon fire with fifty loaves
of bread in my wagon. They were getting
moldy, it was high time, I had no choice.

THE SERGEANT. No wisecracks. Where
are your papers?

MOTHER COURAGE [fishing a pile of
papers out of a tin box and climbing
down]. Here are my papers, sergeant.
There's a whole missal, picked it up in
Alt-Ötting to wrap cucumbers in, and a
map of Moravia, God knows if I'll ever
get there, if I don't it's a total loss. And
this here certifies that my horse hasn't
got foot-and-mouth disease, too bad, he
croaked on us, he cost fifteen guilders,
but not out of my pocket, glory be. Is
that enough paper?

THE SERGEANT. Are you trying to pull
my leg? I'll teach you to get smart. You
know you need a license.

MOTHER COURAGE. You mind your

manners and don't go telling my innocent children that I'd go anywhere near your leg, it's indecent. I want no truck with you. My license in the Second Regiment is my honest face, and if you can't read it, that's not my fault. I'm not letting anybody put his seal on it.

THE RECRUITER. Sergeant, I detect a spirit of insubordination in this woman. In our camp we need respect for authority.

MOTHER COURAGE. Wouldn't sausage be better?

THE SERGEANT. Name.

MOTHER COURAGE. Anna Fierling.

THE SERGEANT. Then you're all Fierlings?

MOTHER COURAGE. What do you mean? Fierling is my name. Not theirs.

THE SERGEANT. Aren't they all your children?

MOTHER COURAGE. That they are, but why should they all have the same name? [Pointing at the elder son.] This one, for instance. His name is Eilif Nojocki. How come? Because his father always claimed to be called Kojocki or Mojocki. The boy remembers him well, except the one he remembers was somebody else, a Frenchman with a goatee. But aside from that, he inherited his father's intelligence; that man could strip the pants off a peasant's ass without his knowing it. So, you see, we've each got our own name.

THE SERGEANT. Each different, you mean?

MOTHER COURAGE. Don't act so innocent.

THE SERGEANT. I suppose that one's a Chinaman? [Indicating the younger son.]

MOTHER COURAGE. Wrong. He's Swiss.

THE SERGEANT. After the Frenchman?

MOTHER COURAGE. What Frenchman? I never heard of any Frenchman. Don't get everything balled up or we'll be here all day. He's Swiss, but his name is Fejos, the name has nothing to do with his father. He had an entirely different name, he was an engineer, built fortifications, but he drank.

[SWISS CHEESE nods, beaming; the mute KATTRIN is also tickled.]

THE SERGEANT. Then how can his name be Fejos?

MOTHER COURAGE. I wouldn't want to offend you, but you haven't got much imagination. Naturally his name is Fejos because when he came I was with a Hungarian, it was all the same to him, he was dying of kidney trouble though he never touched a drop, a very decent man. The boy takes after him.

THE SERGEANT. But you said he wasn't his father?

MOTHER COURAGE. He takes after him all the same. I call him Swiss Cheese, how come, because he's good at pulling the wagon. [Pointing at her daughter.] Her name is Kattrin Haupt, she's half German.

THE SERGEANT. A fine family, I must say.

MOTHER COURAGE. Yes, I've been all over the world with my wagon.

THE SERGEANT. It's all being taken down. [He takes it down.] You're from Bamberg, Bavaria. What brings you here?

MOTHER COURAGE. I couldn't wait for the war to kindly come to Bamberg.

THE RECRUITER. You wagon pullers ought to be called Jacob Ox and Esau Ox. Do you ever get out of harness?

EILIF. Mother, can I clout him one on the kisser? I'd like to.

MOTHER COURAGE. And I forbid you. You stay put. And now, gentlemen, wouldn't you need a nice pistol, or a belt buckle, yours is all worn out, sergeant.

THE SERGEANT. I need something else. I'm not blind. Those young fellows are built like tree trunks, big broad chests, sturdy legs. Why aren't they in the army? That's what I'd like to know.

MOTHER COURAGE [quickly]. Nothing doing, sergeant. My children aren't cut out for soldiers.

THE RECRUITER. Why not? There's profit in it, and glory. Peddling shoes is woman's work. [To EILIF.] Step up; let's feel if you've got muscles or if you're a sissy.

MOTHER COURAGE. He's a sissy. Give him a mean look and he'll fall flat on his face.

THE RECRUITER. And kill a calf if it happens to be standing in the way. [Tries to lead him away.]

MOTHER COURAGE. Leave him alone. He's not for you.

THE RECRUITER. He insulted me. He referred to my face as a kisser. Him and me will now step out in the field and discuss this thing as man to man.

EILIF. Don't worry, mother. I'll take care of him.

MOTHER COURAGE. You stay put. You no-good! I know you, always fighting. He's got a knife in his boot, he's a knifer.

THE RECRUITER. I'll pull it out of him like a milk tooth. Come on, boy.

MOTHER COURAGE. Sergeant, I'll report you to the colonel. He'll throw you in the lock-up. The lieutenant is courting my daughter.

THE SERGEANT. No rough stuff, brother. [To MOTHER COURAGE.] What have you got against the army? Wasn't his father a soldier? Didn't he die fair and square? You said so yourself.

MOTHER COURAGE. He's only a child. You want to lead him off to slaughter, I know you. You'll get five guilders for him.

THE RECRUITER. He'll get a beautiful cap and top boots.

EILIF. Not from you.

MOTHER COURAGE. Oh, won't you come fishing with me? said the fisherman to the worm. [To SWISS CHEESE.] Run and yell that they're trying to steal your brother. [She pulls a knife.] Just try and steal him. I'll cut you down, you dogs. I'll teach you to put him in your war! We do an honest business in ham and shirts, we're peaceful folk.

THE SERGEANT. I can see by the knife how peaceful you are. You ought to be ashamed of yourself, put that knife away, you bitch. A minute ago you admitted you lived off war, how else would you live, on what? How can you have a war without soldiers?

MOTHER COURAGE. It doesn't have to be my children.

THE SERGEANT. I see. You'd like the war to eat the core and spit out the apple. You want your brood to batten on war, taxfree. The war can look out for itself, is that it? You call yourself Courage, eh? And you're afraid of the war that feeds you. Your sons aren't afraid of it, I can see that.

EILIF. I'm not afraid of any war.

THE SERGEANT. Why should you be? Look at me: Has the soldier's life disagreed with me? I was seventeen when I joined up.

MOTHER COURAGE. You're not seventy yet.

THE SERGEANT. I can wait.

MOTHER COURAGE. Sure. Under ground.

THE SERGEANT. Are you trying to insult me? Telling me I'm going to die?

MOTHER COURAGE. But suppose it's the truth? I can see the mark on you. You look like a corpse on leave.

SWISS CHEESE. She's got second sight. Everybody says so. She can tell the future.

THE RECRUITER. Then tell the sergeant his future. It might amuse him.

THE SERGEANT. I don't believe in that stuff.

MOTHER COURAGE. Give me your helmet. [He gives it to her.]

THE SERGEANT. It doesn't mean any more than taking a shit in the grass. But go ahead for the laugh.

MOTHER COURAGE [takes a sheet of parchment and tears it in two]. Eilif, Swiss Cheese, Kattrin: That's how we'd all be torn apart if we got mixed up too deep in the war. [To the SERGEANT.] Seeing it's you, I'll do it for nothing. I make a black cross on this piece. Black is death.

SWISS CHEESE. She leaves the other one blank. Get it?

MOTHER COURAGE. Now I fold them, and now I shake them up together. Same as we're all mixed up together from the cradle to the grave. And now you draw, and you'll know the answer. [The SERGEANT hesitates.]

THE RECRUITER [to EILIF]. I don't take everybody, I'm known to be picky and choosy, but you've got spirit, I like that.

THE SERGEANT [fishing in the helmet]. Damn foolishness! Hocus-pocus!

SWISS CHEESE. He's pulled a black cross. He's through.

THE RECRUITER. Don't let them scare you, there's not enough bullets for everybody.

THE SERGEANT [hoarsely]. You've fouled me up.

MOTHER COURAGE. You fouled yourself up the day you joined the army. And now we'll be going, there isn't a war every day, I've got to take advantage.

THE SERGEANT. Hell and damnation! Don't try to hornswoggle me. We're taking your bastard to be a soldier.

EILIF. I'd like to be a soldier, mother.

MOTHER COURAGE. You shut your trap, you Finnish devil.

EILIF. Swiss Cheese wants to be a soldier too.

MOTHER COURAGE. That's news to me. I'd better let you draw too, all three of you. [She goes to the rear to mark crosses on slips of parchment.]

THE RECRUITER [to EILIF]. It's been said to our discredit that a lot of religion goes on in the Swedish camp, but that's slander to blacken our reputation. Hymn singing only on Sunday, one verse! And only if you've got a voice.

MOTHER COURAGE [comes back with the slips in the SERGEANT's helmet]. Want to sneak away from their mother, the devils, and run off to war like calves to a salt lick. But we'll draw lots on it, then they'll see that the world is no vale of smiles with a "Come along, son, we're short on generals." Sergeant, I'm very much afraid they won't come through the war. They've got terrible characters, all three of them. [She holds out the helmet to EILIF.] There. Pick a slip. [He picks one and unfolds it. She snatches it away from him.] There you have it. A cross! Oh, unhappy mother that I am, oh, mother of sorrows. Has he got to die? Doomed to perish in the springtime of his life? If he joins the army, he'll bite the dust, that's sure. He's too brave, just like his father. If he's not smart, he'll go the way of all flesh, the slip proves it. [She roars at him.] Are you going to be smart?

EILIF. Why not?

MOTHER COURAGE. The smart thing to do is to stay with your mother, and if they make fun of you and call you a sissy, just laugh.

THE RECRUITER. If you're shitting in your pants, we'll take your brother.

MOTHER COURAGE. I told you to laugh. Laugh! And now you pick, Swiss Cheese. I'm not so worried about you, you're honest. [He picks a slip.] Oh! Why, have you got that strange look? It's got to be blank. There can't be a cross on it. No, I can't lose you. [She takes a slip.] A cross? Him too? Maybe it's because he's so stupid. Oh, Swiss Cheese, you'll die too, unless you're very honest the whole time, the way I've taught you since you

were a baby, always bringing back the change when I sent you to buy bread. That's the only way you can save yourself. Look, sergeant, isn't that a black cross?

THE SERGEANT. It's a cross all right. I don't see how I could have pulled one. I always stay in the rear. [To the RECRUITER.] It's on the up and up. Her own get it too.

SWISS CHEESE. I get it too. But I can take a hint.

MOTHER COURAGE [to KATTRIN]. Now you're the only one I'm sure of, you're a cross yourself because you've got a good heart. [She holds up the helmet to KATTRIN in the wagon, but she herself takes out the slip.] It's driving me to despair. It can't be right, maybe I mixed them wrong. Don't be too good-natured, Kattrin, don't, there's a cross on your path too. Always keep very quiet, that ought to be easy seeing you're dumb. Well, now you know. Be careful, all of you, you'll need to be. And now we'll climb up and drive on. [She returns the SERGEANT's helmet and climbs up into the wagon.]

THE RECRUITER [to the SERGEANT]. Do something!

THE SERGEANT. I'm not feeling so good.

THE RECRUITER. Maybe you caught cold when you took your helmet off in the wind. Tell her you want to buy something. Keep her busy. [Aloud.] You could at least take a look at that buckle, sergeant. After all, selling things is these good people's living. Hey, you, the sergeant wants to buy that belt buckle.

MOTHER COURAGE. Half a guilder. A buckle like that is worth two guilders. [She climbs down.]

THE SERGEANT. It's not new. This wind! I can't examine it here. Let's go where it's quiet. [He goes behind the wagon with the buckle.]

MOTHER COURAGE. I haven't noticed any wind.

THE SERGEANT. Maybe it is worth half a guilder. It's silver.

MOTHER COURAGE [joins him behind the wagon]. Six solid ounces.

THE RECRUITER [to EILIF]. And then we'll have a drink, just you and me. I've got your enlistment bonus right here. Come on. [EILIF stands undecided.]

MOTHER COURAGE. All right. Half a guilder.

THE SERGEANT. I don't get it. I always stay in the rear. There's no safer place for a sergeant. You can send the men up forward to win glory. You've spoiled my dinner. It won't go down, I know it, not a bite.

MOTHER COURAGE. Don't take it to heart. Don't let it spoil your appetite. Just keep behind the lines. Here, take a drink of schnapps, man. [She hands him the bottle.]

THE RECRUITER [has taken EILIF's arm and is pulling him away toward the rear]. A bonus of ten guilders, and you'll be a brave man and you'll fight for the king, and the women will tear each other's hair out over you. And you can clout me one on the kisser for insulting you. [Both go out.]

[Mute KATTRIN jumps down from the wagon and emits raucous sounds.]

MOTHER COURAGE. Just a minute, Kattrin, just a minute. The sergeant's paying up. [Bites the half guilder.] I'm always suspicious of money. I'm a burnt child, sergeant. But your coin is good. And now we'll be going. Where's Eilif?

SWISS CHEESE. He's gone with the recruiter.

MOTHER COURAGE [stands motionless, then]. You simple soul. [To KATTRIN.] I know. You can't talk, you couldn't help it.

THE SERGEANT. You could do with a drink yourself, mother. That's the way it goes. Soldiering isn't the worst thing in the world. You want to live off the war, but you want to keep you and yours out of it. Is that it?

MOTHER COURAGE. Now you'll have to pull with your brother, Kattrin.

[Brother and sister harness themselves to the wagon and start pulling. MOTHER COURAGE walks beside them. The wagon rolls off.]

THE SERGEANT [looking after them].

If you want the war to work for you
You've got to give the war its due.

Scene Two

[In 1625 and 1626 MOTHER COURAGE crosses Poland in the train of the Swedish armies. Outside the fortress of Wallhof she meets her son again.—A capon is successfully sold, the brave son's fortunes are at their zenith.

The GENERAL's tent.

Beside it the kitchen. The thunder of cannon. The cook is arguing with MOTHER COURAGE, who is trying to sell him a capon.]

THE COOK. Sixty hellers for that pathetic bird?

MOTHER COURAGE. Pathetic bird? You mean this plump beauty? Are you trying to tell me that a general who's the biggest eater for miles around—God help you if you haven't got anything for his dinner—can't afford a measly sixty hellers?

THE COOK. I can get a dozen like it for ten hellers right around the corner.

MOTHER COURAGE. What, you'll find a capon like this right around the corner? With a siege on and everybody so starved you can see right through them. Maybe you'll scare up a rat, maybe, I say, 'cause they've all been eaten, I've seen five men chasing a starved rat for hours. Fifty hellers for a giant capon in the middle of a siege.

THE COOK. We're not besieged; they are. We're the besiegers, can't you get that through your head?

MOTHER COURAGE. But we haven't got anything to eat either, in fact we've got less than the people in the city. They've hauled it all inside. I hear their life is one big orgy. And look at us. I've been around to the peasants, they haven't got a thing.

THE COOK. They've got plenty. They hide it.

MOTHER COURAGE [triumphantly]. Oh, no! They're ruined, that's what they are. They're starving. I've seen them. They're so hungry they're digging up roots. They lick their fingers when they've eaten a boiled strap. That's the situation. And here I've got a capon and I'm supposed to let it go for forty hellers.

THE COOK. Thirty, not forty. Thirty, I said.

MOTHER COURAGE. It's no common capon. They tell me this bird was so talented that he wouldn't eat unless they played music, he had his own favorite march. He could add and subtract, that's how intelligent he was. And you're trying to tell me forty hellers is too much. The general will bite your head off if there's nothing to eat.

THE COOK. You know what I'm going to do? [*He takes a piece of beef and sets his knife to it.*] Here I've got a piece of beef. I'll roast it. Think it over. This is your last chance.

MOTHER COURAGE. Roast and be damned. It's a year old.

THE COOK. A day old. That ox was running around only yesterday afternoon, I saw him with my own eyes.

MOTHER COURAGE. Then he must have stunk on the hoof.

THE COOK. I'll cook it five hours if I have to. We'll see if it's still tough. [*He cuts into it.*]

MOTHER COURAGE. Use plenty of pepper, maybe the general won't notice the stink.

[*The* GENERAL, *a* CHAPLAIN *and* EILIF *enter the tent.*]

THE GENERAL [*slapping* EILIF *on the back*]. All right, son, into your general's tent you go, you'll sit at my right hand. You've done a heroic deed and you're a pious trooper, because this is a war of religion and what you did was done for God, that's what counts with me. I'll reward you with a gold bracelet when I take the city. We come here to save their souls and what do those filthy, shameless peasants do? They drive their cattle away. And they stuff their priests with meat, front and back. But you taught them a lesson. Here's a tankard of red wine for you. [*He pours.*] We'll down it in one gulp. [*They do so.*] None for the chaplain, he's got his religion. What would you like for dinner, sweetheart?

EILIF. A scrap of meat. Why not?

THE GENERAL. Cook! Meat!

THE COOK. And now he brings company when there's nothing to eat.

[*Wanting to listen,* MOTHER COURAGE *makes him stop talking.*]

EILIF. Cutting down peasants whets the appetite.

MOTHER COURAGE. God, it's my Eilif.

THE COOK. Who?

MOTHER COURAGE. My eldest. I haven't seen hide nor hair of him in two years, he was stolen from me on the highway. He must be in good if the general invites him to dinner, and what have you

got to offer? Nothing. Did you hear what the general's guest wants for dinner? Meat! Take my advice, snap up this capon. The price is one guilder.

THE GENERAL [*has sat down with* EILIF. *Bellows*]. Food, Lamb, you lousy, no-good cook, or I'll kill you.

THE COOK. All right, hand it over. This is extortion.

MOTHER COURAGE. I thought it was a pathetic bird.

THE COOK. Pathetic is the word. Hand it over. Fifty hellers! It's highway robbery.

MOTHER COURAGE. One guilder, I say. For my eldest son, the general's honored guest, I spare no expense.

THE COOK [*gives her the money*]. Then pluck it at least while I make the fire.

MOTHER COURAGE [*sits down to pluck the capon*]. Won't he be glad to see me! He's my brave, intelligent son. I've got a stupid one too, but he's honest. The girl's a total loss. But at least she doesn't talk, that's something.

THE GENERAL. Take another drink, son, it's my best Falerno, I've only got another barrel or two at the most, but it's worth it to see that there's still some true faith in my army. The good shepherd here just looks on, all he knows how to do is preach. Can he do anything? No. And now, Eilif my son, tell us all about it, how cleverly you hoodwinked those peasants and captured those twenty head of cattle. I hope they'll be here soon.

EILIF. Tomorrow. Maybe the day after.

MOTHER COURAGE. Isn't my Eilif considerate, not bringing those oxen in until tomorrow, or you wouldn't have even said hello to my capon.

EILIF. Well, it was like this: I heard the peasants were secretly—mostly at night—rounding up the oxen they'd hidden in a certain forest. The city people had arranged to come and get them. I let them round the oxen up, I figured they'd find them easier than I would. I made my men ravenous for meat, put them on short rations for two days until their mouths watered if they even heard a word beginning with me ... like measles.

THE GENERAL. That was clever of you.

EILIF. Maybe. The rest was a pushover. Except the peasants had clubs and there were three times more of them and they fell on us like bloody murder. Four of them drove me into a clump of bushes, they knocked my sword out of my hand and yelled: Surrender! Now what'll I do, I says to myself, they'll make hash out of me.

THE GENERAL. What did you do?

EILIF. I laughed.

THE GENERAL. You laughed?

EILIF. I laughed. Which led to a conversation. The first thing you know, I'm bargaining. Twenty guilders is too much for that ox, I say, how about fifteen? Like I'm meaning to pay. They're flummoxed, they scratch their heads. Quick, I reach for my sword and mow them down. Necessity knows no law. See what I mean?

THE GENERAL. What do you say to that, shepherd?

CHAPLAIN. Strictly speaking, that maxim is not in the Bible. But our Lord was able to turn five loaves into five hundred. So there was no question of poverty; he could tell people to love their neighbors because their bellies were full. Nowadays it's different.

THE GENERAL [laughs]. Very different. All right, you Pharisee, take a swig. [To EILIF.] You mowed them down, splendid, so my fine troops could have a decent bite to eat. Doesn't the Good Book say: "Whatsoever thou doest for the least of my brethren, thou doest for me"? And what have you done for them? You've got them a good chunk of beef for their dinner. They're not used to moldy crusts; in the old days they had a helmetful of white bread and wine before they went out to fight for God.

EILIF. Yes, I reached for my sword and I mowed them down.

THE GENERAL. You're a young Caesar. You deserve to see the king.

EILIF. I have, in the distance. He shines like a light. He's my ideal.

THE GENERAL. You're something like him already, Eilif. I know the worth of a brave soldier like you. When I find one, I treat him like my own son. [He leads him to the map.] Take a look at the situation, Eilif; we've still got a long way to go.

MOTHER COURAGE [who has been listening starts plucking her capon furiously]. He must be a rotten general.

THE COOK. Eats like a pig, but why rotten?

MOTHER COURAGE. Because he needs brave soldiers, that's why. If he planned his campaigns right, what would he need brave soldiers for? The run-of-the-mill would do. Take it from me, whenever you find a lot of virtues, it shows that something's wrong.

THE COOK. I'd say it proves that something is all right.

MOTHER COURAGE. No, that something's wrong. See, when a general or a king is real stupid and leads his men up shit creek, his troops need courage, that's a virtue. If he's stingy and doesn't hire enough soldiers, they've all got to be Herculeses. And if he's a slob and lets everything go to pot, they've got to be as sly as serpents or they're done for. And if he's always expecting too much of them, they need an extra dose of loyalty. A country that's run right, or a good king or a good general, doesn't need any of these virtues. You don't need virtues in a decent country, the people can all be perfectly ordinary, medium-bright, and cowards too for my money.

THE GENERAL. I bet your father was a soldier.

EILIF. A great soldier, I'm told. My mother warned me about it. Makes me think of a song.

THE GENERAL. Sing it! [Bellowing.] Where's that food!

EILIF. It's called: The Song of the Old Wife and the Soldier.

[He sings, doing a war dance with his saber.]

A gun or a pike, they can kill who they
    like
And the torrent will swallow a wader
You had better think twice before bat-
    tling with ice
Said the old wife to the soldier.
Cocking his rifle he leapt to his feet
Laughing for joy as he heard the drum
    beat
The wars cannot hurt me, he told her.
He shouldered his gun and he picked up
    his knife
To see the wide world. That's the sol-
    dier's life.
Those were the words of the soldier.

Ah, deep will they lie who wise counsel
    defy

Learn wisdom from those that are older
Oh, don't venture too high or you'll fall
    from the sky
Said the old wife to the soldier.
But the young soldier with knife and
    with gun
Only laughed a cold laugh and stepped
    into the run.
The water can't hurt me, he told her.
And when the moon on the rooftop
    shines white
We'll be coming back. You can pray for
    that night.
Those were the words of the soldier.

MOTHER COURAGE [in the kitchen, continues the song, beating a pot with a spoon].

Like the smoke you'll be gone and no
    warmth linger on
And your deeds only leave me the colder!
Oh, see the smoke race. Oh, dear God
    keep him safe!
That's what she said of the soldier.

EILIF. What's that?
MOTHER COURAGE [goes on singing].

And the young soldier with knife and
    with gun
Was swept from his feet till he sank in
    the run
And the torrent swallowed the waders.
Cold shone the moon on the rooftop
    white
But the soldier was carried away with the
    ice
And what was it she heard from the
    soldiers?

Like the smoke he was gone and no
    warmth lingered on
And his deeds only left her the colder.
Ah, deep will they lie who wise counsel
    defy!
That's what she said to the soldiers.

THE GENERAL. What do they think they're doing in my kitchen?

EILIF [has gone into the kitchen. He embraces his mother]. Mother! It's you! Where are the others?

MOTHER COURAGE [in his arms]. Snug as a bug in a rug. Swiss Cheese is paymaster of the Second Regiment; at least he won't be fighting, I couldn't keep him out altogether.

EILIF. And how about your feet?

MOTHER COURAGE. Well, it's hard getting my shoes on in the morning.

THE GENERAL [has joined them]. Ah, so you're his mother. I hope you've got more sons for me like this fellow here.

EILIF. Am I lucky! There you're sitting in the kitchen hearing your son being praised.

MOTHER COURAGE. I heard it all right! [She gives him a slap in the face.]

EILIF [holding his cheek]. For capturing the oxen?

MOTHER COURAGE. No. For not surrendering when the four of them were threatening to make hash out of you! Didn't I teach you to take care of yourself? You Finnish devil! [The GENERAL and the CHAPLAIN laugh.]

Scene Three

[Three years later MOTHER COURAGE and parts of a Finnish regiment are taken prisoner. She is able to save her daughter and her wagon, but her honest son dies. Army camp.

Afternoon. On a pole the regimental flag. MOTHER COURAGE has stretched a clothesline between her wagon, on which all sorts of merchandise is hung in display, and a large cannon. She and KATTRIN are folding washing and piling it on the cannon. At the same time she is negotiating with an ordnance officer over a sack of bullets. SWISS CHEESE, now in the uniform of a paymaster, is looking on. A pretty woman, YVETTE POTTIER, is sitting with a glass of brandy in front of her, sewing a gaudy-colored hat. She is in her stocking feet, her red high-heeled shoes are on the ground beside her.]

THE ORDNANCE OFFICER. I'll let you have these bullets for two guilders. It's cheap, I need the money, because the colonel's been drinking with the officers for two days and we're out of liquor.

MOTHER COURAGE. That's ammunition for the troops. If it's found here, I'll be court-martialed. You punks sell their bullets and the men have nothing to shoot at the enemy.

THE ORDNANCE OFFICER. Don't be

hard-hearted, you scratch my back, I'll scratch yours.

MOTHER COURAGE. I'm not taking any army property. Not at that price.

THE ORDNANCE OFFICER. You can sell it for five guilders, maybe eight, to the ordnance officer of the Fourth before the day is out, if you're quiet about it and give him a receipt for twelve. He hasn't an ounce of ammunition left.

MOTHER COURAGE. Why don't you do it yourself?

THE ORDNANCE OFFICER. Because I don't trust him, he's a friend of mine.

MOTHER COURAGE [takes the sack]. Hand it over. [To KATTRIN.] Take it back there and pay him one and a half guilders. [In response to the ORDNANCE OFFICER's protest.] One and a half guilders, I say. [KATTRIN drags the sack behind the wagon, the ORDNANCE OFFICER follows her. MOTHER COURAGE to SWISS CHEESE.] Here's your underdrawers, take good care of them, this is October, might be coming on fall, I don't say it will be, because I've learned that nothing is sure to happen the way we think, not even the seasons. But whatever happens, your regimental funds have to be in order. Are your funds in order?

SWISS CHEESE. Yes, mother.

MOTHER COURAGE. Never forget that they made you paymaster because you're honest and not brave like your brother, and especially because you're too simple-minded to get the idea of making off with the money. That's a comfort to me. And don't go mislaying your drawers.

SWISS CHEESE. No, mother. I'll put them under my mattress. [Starts to go.]

ORDNANCE OFFICER. I'll go with you, paymaster.

MOTHER COURAGE. Just don't teach him any of your tricks. [Without saying good-bye the ORDNANCE OFFICER goes out with SWISS CHEESE.]

YVETTE [waves her hand after the ORDNANCE OFFICER]. You might say good-bye, officer.

MOTHER COURAGE [to YVETTE]. I don't like to see those two together. He's not the right kind of company for my Swiss Cheese. But the war's getting along pretty well. More countries are joining in all the time, it can go on for another four, five years, easy. With a little planning ahead, I can do good business if I'm careful. Don't you know you shouldn't drink in the morning with your sickness?

YVETTE. Who says I'm sick, it's slander.

MOTHER COURAGE. Everybody says so.

YVETTE. Because they're all liars. Mother Courage, I'm desperate. They all keep out of my way like I'm a rotten fish on account of those lies. What's the good of fixing my hat? [She throws it down.] That's why I drink in the morning, I never used to, I'm getting crow's-feet, but it doesn't matter now. In the Second Finnish Regiment they all know me. I should have stayed home when my first love walked out on me. Pride isn't for the likes of us. If we can't put up with shit, we're through.

MOTHER COURAGE. Just don't start in on your Pieter and how it all happened in front of my innocent daughter.

YVETTE. She's just the one to hear it, it'll harden her against love.

MOTHER COURAGE. Nothing can harden them.

YVETTE. Then I'll talk about it because it makes me feel better. It begins with my growing up in fair Flanders, because if I hadn't I'd never have laid eyes on him and I wouldn't be here in Poland now, because he was an army cook, blond, a Dutchman, but skinny. Kattrin, watch out for the skinny ones, but I didn't know that then, and another thing I didn't know is that he had another girl even then, and they all called him Pete the Pipe, because he didn't even take his pipe out of his mouth when he was doing it, that's all it meant to him. [She sings the Song of Fraternization.]

When I was only sixteen
The foe came into our land.
He laid aside his sabre
And with a smile he took my hand.
   After the May parade
   The May light starts to fade.
   The regiment dressed by the right
   Then drums were beaten, that's the drill.
   The foe took us behind the hill
   And fraternized all night.

There were so many foes came
And mine worked in the mess.

I loathed him in the daytime.
At night I loved him none the less.
   After the May parade
   The May light starts to fade.
   The regiment dressed by the right
   Then drums were beaten, that's the
      drill.
   The foe took us behind the hill
   And fraternized all night.

The love which came upon me
Was wished on me by fate.
My friends could never grasp why
I found it hard to share their hate.
   The fields were wet with dew
   When sorrow first I knew.
   The regiment dressed by the right
   Then drums were beaten, that's the
      drill.
   And then the foe, my lover still
   Went marching from our sight.

Well, I followed him, but I never found him. That was five years ago. [*She goes behind the wagon with an unsteady gait.*]

MOTHER COURAGE. You've left your hat.

YVETTE. Anybody that wants it can have it.

MOTHER COURAGE. Let that be a lesson to you, Kattrin. Have no truck with soldiers. It's love that makes the world go round, so you'd better watch out. Even with a civilian it's no picnic. He says he'd kiss the ground you put your little feet on, talking of feet, did you wash yours yesterday, and then you're his slave. Be glad you're dumb, that way you'll never contradict yourself or want to bite your tongue off because you've told the truth, it's a gift of God to be dumb. Here comes the general's cook, I wonder what he wants.

[*The* COOK *and the* CHAPLAIN *enter.*]

THE CHAPLAIN. I've got a message for you from your son Eilif. The cook here thought he'd come along, he's taken a shine to you.

THE COOK. I only came to get a breath of air.

MOTHER COURAGE. You can always do that here if you behave, and if you don't, I can handle you. Well, what does he want? I've got no money to spare.

THE CHAPLAIN. Actually he wanted me to see his brother, the paymaster.

MOTHER COURAGE. He's not here any more, or anywhere else either. He's not his brother's paymaster. I don't want him leading him into temptation and being smart at his expense. [*Gives him money from the bag slung around her waist.*] Give him this, it's a sin, he's speculating on mother love and he ought to be ashamed.

THE COOK. He won't do it much longer, then he'll be marching off with his regiment, maybe to his death, you never can tell. Better make it a little more, you'll be sorry later. You women are hard-hearted, but afterwards you're sorry. A drop of brandy wouldn't have cost much when it was wanted, but it wasn't given, and later, for all you know, he'll be lying in the cold ground and you can't dig him up again.

THE CHAPLAIN. Don't be sentimental, cook. There's nothing wrong with dying in battle, it's a blessing, and I'll tell you why. This is a war of religion. Not a common war, but a war for the faith, and therefore pleasing to God.

THE COOK. That's a fact. In a way you could call it a war, because of the extortion and killing and looting, not to mention a bit of rape, but it's a war of religion, which makes it different from all other wars, that's obvious. But it makes a man thirsty all the same, you've got to admit that.

THE CHAPLAIN [*to* MOTHER COURAGE, *pointing at the cook*]. I tried to discourage him, but he says you've turned his head, he sees you in his dreams.

THE COOK [*lights a short-stemmed pipe*]. All I want is a glass of brandy from your fair hand, nothing more sinful. I'm already so shocked by the jokes the chaplain's been telling me, I bet I'm still red in the face.

MOTHER COURAGE. And him a clergyman! I'd better give you fellows something to drink or you'll be making me immoral propositions just to pass the time.

THE CHAPLAIN. This is temptation, said the deacon, and succumbed to it. [*Turning toward* KATTRIN *as he leaves.*] And who is this delightful young lady?

MOTHER COURAGE. She's not delightful, she's a respectable young lady.

[*The* CHAPLAIN *and the* COOK *go behind the wagon with* MOTHER COUR-

AGE. KATTRIN *looks after them, then she walks away from the washing and approaches the hat. She picks it up, sits down and puts on the red shoes. From the rear* MOTHER COURAGE *is heard talking politics with the* CHAPLAIN *and the* COOK.]

MOTHER COURAGE. The Poles here in Poland shouldn't have butted in. All right, our king marched his army into their country. But instead of keeping the peace, the Poles start butting into their own affairs and attack the king while he's marching quietly through the landscape. That was a breach of the peace and the blood is on their head.

THE CHAPLAIN. Our king had only one thing in mind: freedom. The emperor had everybody under his yoke, the Poles as much as the Germans; the king had to set them free.

THE COOK. I see it this way, your brandy's first-rate, I can see why I liked your face, but we were talking about the king. This freedom he was trying to introduce into Germany cost him a fortune, he had to levy a salt tax in Sweden, which, as I said, cost the poor people a fortune. Then he had to put the Germans in jail and break them on the rack because they liked being the emperor's slaves. Oh yes, the king made short shrift of anybody that didn't want to be free. In the beginning he only wanted to protect Poland against wicked people, especially the emperor, but the more he ate the more he wanted, and pretty soon he was protecting all of Germany. But the Germans didn't take it lying down and the king got nothing but trouble for all his kindness and expense, which naturally had to defray from taxes, which made for bad blood, but that didn't discourage him. He had one thing in his favor, the word of God, which was lucky, because otherwise people would have said he was doing it all for himself and what he hoped to get out of it. As it was, he always had a clear conscience and that was all he really cared about.

MOTHER COURAGE. It's easy to see you're not a Swede, or you wouldn't talk like that about the Hero-King.

THE CHAPLAIN. You're eating his bread, aren't you?

THE COOK. I don't eat his bread, I bake it.

MOTHER COURAGE. He can't be defeated because his men believe in him. [*Earnestly.*] When you listen to the big wheels talk, they're making war for reasons of piety, in the name of everything that's fine and noble. But when you take another look, you see that they're not so dumb; they're making war for profit. If they weren't, the small fry like me wouldn't have anything to do with it.

THE COOK. That's a fact.

THE CHAPLAIN. And it wouldn't hurt you as a Dutchman to take a look at that flag up there before you express opinions in Poland.

MOTHER COURAGE. We're all good Protestants here! Prosit!

[KATTRIN *has started strutting about with* YVETTE'S *hat on, imitating* YVETTE'S *gait.*]

[*Suddenly cannon fire and shots are heard. Drums.* MOTHER COURAGE, *the* COOK *and the* CHAPLAIN *run out from behind the wagon, the two men still with glasses in hand. The* ORDNANCE OFFICER *and a* SOLDIER *rush up to the cannon and try to push it away.*]

MOTHER COURAGE. What's going on? Let me get my washing first, you lugs. [*She tries to rescue her washing.*]

THE ORDNANCE OFFICER. The Catholics. They're attacking. I don't know as we'll get away. [*To the* SOLDIER.] Get rid of the gun! [*Runs off.*]

THE COOK. Christ, I've got to find the general. Courage, I'll be back for a little chat in a day or two. [*Rushes out.*]

MOTHER COURAGE. Stop, you've forgotten your pipe.

THE COOK [*from the distance*]. Keep it for me! I'll need it.

MOTHER COURAGE. Just when we were making a little money!

THE CHAPLAIN. Well, I guess I'll be going too. It might be dangerous though, with the enemy so close. Blessed are the peaceful is the best motto in wartime. If only I had a cloak to cover up with.

MOTHER COURAGE. I'm not lending any cloaks, not on your life. I've had bitter experience in that line.

THE CHAPLAIN. But my religion puts me in special danger.

MOTHER COURAGE [*bringing him a*

cloak]. It's against my better conscience.
And now run along.

THE CHAPLAIN. Thank you kindly,
you've got a good heart. But maybe I'd
better sit here a while. The enemy might
get suspicious if they see me running.

MOTHER COURAGE [to the soldier].
Leave it lay, you fool, you won't get paid
extra. I'll take care of it for you, you'd
only get killed.

THE SOLDIER [running away]. I tried.
You're my witness.

MOTHER COURAGE. I'll swear it on the
Bible. [Sees her daughter with the hat.]
What are you doing with that floozy hat?
Take it off, have you gone out of your
mind? Now of all times, with the enemy
on top of us? [She tears the hat off KAT-
TRIN's head.] You want them to find you
and make a whore out of you? And those
shoes! Take them off, you woman of
Babylon! [She tries to pull them off.]
Jesus Christ, chaplain, make her take
those shoes off! I'll be right back. [She
runs to the wagon.]

YVETTE [enters, powdering her face].
What's this I hear? The Catholics are
coming? Where's my hat? Who's been
stamping on it? I can't be seen like this
if the Catholics are coming. What'll they
think of me? I haven't even got a mirror.
[To the CHAPLAIN.] How do I look? Too
much powder?

THE CHAPLAIN. Just right.

YVETTE. And where are my red shoes?
[She doesn't see them because KATTRIN
hides her feet under her skirt.] I left
them here. I've got to get back to my
tent. In my bare feet. It's disgraceful!
[Goes out.]

[SWISS CHEESE runs in carrying a small
box.]

MOTHER COURAGE [comes out with her
hands full of ashes. To KATTRIN]. Ashes.
[To SWISS CHEESE.] What you got there?

SWISS CHEESE. The regimental funds.

MOTHER COURAGE. Throw it away! No
more paymastering for you.

SWISS CHEESE. I'm responsible for it.
[He goes rear.]

MOTHER COURAGE [to the CHAPLAIN].
Take your clergyman's coat off, chaplain,
or they'll recognize you, cloak or no cloak.
[She rubs KATTRIN's face with ashes.]
Hold still! There. With a little dirt you'll
be safe. What a mess! The sentries were
drunk. Hide your light under a bushel, as

the Good Book says. When a soldier, especially a Catholic, sees a clean face, she's
a whore before she knows it. Nobody
feeds them for weeks. When they finally
loot some provisions, the next thing they
want is women. That'll do it. Let me
look at you. Not bad. Like you'd been
wallowing in a pigsty. Stop shaking.
You're safe now. [To SWISS CHEESE.]
What did you do with the cashbox?

SWISS CHEESE. I thought I'd put it in
the wagon.

MOTHER COURAGE [horrified]. What!
In my wagon? Of all the sinful stupidity!
If my back is turned for half a second!
They'll hang us all!

SWISS CHEESE. Then I'll put it somewhere else, or I'll run away with it.

MOTHER COURAGE. You'll stay right
here. It's too late.

THE CHAPLAIN [still changing, comes
forward]. Heavens, the flag!

MOTHER COURAGE [takes down the regimental flag]. Bozhe moi! I'm so used to
it I don't see it. Twenty-five years I've
had it.

[The cannon fire grows louder.]

[Morning, three days later. The cannon
    is gone. MOTHER COURAGE, KATTRIN,
    the CHAPLAIN and SWISS CHEESE are
    sitting dejectedly over a meal.]

SWISS CHEESE. This is the third day I've
been sitting here doing nothing; the sergeant has always been easy on me, but
now he must be starting to wonder:
where can Swiss Cheese be with the cashbox?

MOTHER COURAGE. Be glad they haven't
tracked you down.

THE CHAPLAIN. What about me? I
can't hold a service here either. The
Good Book says: "Whosoever hath a full
heart, his tongue runneth over." Heaven
help me if mine runneth over.

MOTHER COURAGE. That's the way it is.
Look what I've got on my hands: one
with a religion and one with a cashbox. I
don't know which is worse.

THE CHAPLAIN. Tell yourself that we're
in the hands of God.

MOTHER COURAGE. I don't think we're
that bad off, but all the same I can't sleep
at night. If it weren't for you, Swiss
Cheese, it'd be easier. I think I've put
myself in the clear. I told them I was

against the antichrist; he's a Swede with horns, I told them, and I'd noticed the left horn was kind of worn down. I interrupted the questioning to ask where I could buy holy candles cheap. I knew what to say because Swiss Cheese's father was a Catholic and he used to make jokes about it. They didn't really believe me, but their regiment had no provisioner, so they looked the other way. Maybe we stand to gain. We're prisoners, but so are lice on a dog.

THE CHAPLAIN. This milk is good. Though there's not very much of it or of anything else. Maybe we'll have to cut down on our Swedish appetites. But such is the lot of the vanquished.

MOTHER COURAGE. Who's vanquished? Victory and defeat don't always mean the same thing to the big wheels up top and the small fry underneath. Not by a long shot. In some cases defeat is a blessing to the small fry. Honor's lost, but nothing else. One time in Livonia our general got such a shellacking from the enemy that in the confusion I laid hands on a beautiful white horse from the baggage train. That horse pulled my wagon for seven months, until we had a victory and they checked up. On the whole, you can say that victory and defeat cost us plain people plenty. The best thing for us is when politics gets bogged down. [To SWISS CHEESE.] Eat!

SWISS CHEESE. I've lost my appetite. How's the sergeant going to pay the men?

MOTHER COURAGE. Troops never get paid when they're running away.

SWISS CHEESE. But they've got it coming to them. If they're not paid, they don't need to run. Not a step.

MOTHER COURAGE. Swiss Cheese, you're too conscientious, it almost frightens me. I brought you up to be honest, because you're not bright, but somewhere it's got to stop. And now me and the chaplain are going to buy a Catholic flag and some meat. Nobody can buy meat like the chaplain, he goes into a trance and heads straight for the best piece, I guess it makes his mouth water and that shows him the way. At least they let me carry on my business. Nobody cares about a shopkeeper's religion, all they want to know is the price. Protestant pants are as warm as any other kind.

THE CHAPLAIN. Like the friar said when somebody told him the Lutherans were going to stand the whole country on its head. They'll always need beggars, he says. [MOTHER COURAGE disappears into the wagon.] But she's worried about that cashbox. They've taken no notice of us so far, they think we're all part of the wagon, but how long can that go on?

SWISS CHEESE. I can take it away.

THE CHAPLAIN. That would be almost more dangerous. What if somebody sees you? They've got spies. Yesterday morning, just as I'm relieving myself, one of them jumps out of the ditch. I was so scared I almost let out a prayer. That would have given me away. I suppose they think they can tell a Protestant by the smell of his shit. He was a little runt with a patch over one eye.

MOTHER COURAGE [climbing down from the wagon with a basket]. Look what I've found. You shameless slut! [She holds up the red shoes triumphantly.] Yvette's red shoes! She's swiped them in cold blood. It's your fault. Who told her she was a delightful young lady? [She puts them into the basket.] I'm giving them back. Stealing Yvette's shoes! She ruins herself for money, that I can understand. But you'd like to do it free of charge, for pleasure. I've told you, you'll have to wait for peace. No soldiers! Just wait for peace with your worldly ways.

THE CHAPLAIN. She doesn't seem very worldly to me.

MOTHER COURAGE. Too worldly for me. In Dalarna she was like a stone, which is all they've got around there. The people used to say: We don't see the cripple. That's the way I like it. That way she's safe. [To SWISS CHEESE.] You leave that box where it is, hear? And keep an eye on your sister, she needs it. The two of you will be the death of me. I'd sooner take care of a bag of fleas. [She goes off with the CHAPLAIN. KATTRIN starts clearing away the dishes.]

SWISS CHEESE. Won't be many more days when I can sit in the sun in my shirtsleeves. [KATTRIN points to a tree.] Yes, the leaves are all yellow. [KATTRIN asks him, by means of gestures, whether he wants a drink.] Not now. I'm thinking. [Pause.] She says she can't sleep. I'd better get the cashbox out of here, I've found a hiding place. All right, get me a drink. [KATTRIN goes behind the wagon.] I'll hide it in the rabbit hole down by the river until I can take it away. Maybe late tonight. I'll go get it and take it to the regiment. I wonder how far they've run in three days? Won't the sergeant be surprised! Well, Swiss Cheese, this is a pleasant disappointment, that's what he'll say. I trust you with the regimental cashbox and you bring it back.

[As KATTRIN comes out from behind the wagon with a glass of brandy, she comes face to face with two men. One is a SERGEANT. The other removes his hat and swings it through the air in a ceremonious greeting. He has a patch over one eye.]

THE MAN WITH THE PATCH. Good morning, my dear. Have you by any chance seen a man from the headquarters of the Second Finnish Regiment?

[Scared out of her wits, KATTRIN runs front, spilling the brandy. The two exchange looks and withdraw after seeing SWISS CHEESE sitting there.]

SWISS CHEESE [starting up from his thoughts]. You've spilled half of it. What's the fuss about? Poke yourself in the eye? I don't understand you. I'm getting out of here, I've made up my mind, it's best. [He stands up. She does everything she can think of to call his attention to the danger. He only evades her.] I wish I could understand you. Poor thing, I know you're trying to tell me something, you just can't say it. Don't worry about spilling the brandy, I'll be drinking plenty more. What's one glass? [He takes the cashbox out of the wagon and hides it under his jacket.] I'll be right back. Let me go, you're making me angry. I know you mean well. If only you could talk.

[When she tries to hold him back, he kisses her and tears himself away. He goes out. She is desperate, she races back and forth, uttering short inarticulate sounds. The CHAPLAIN and MOTHER COURAGE come back. KATTRIN gesticulates wildly at her mother.]

MOTHER COURAGE. What's the matter? You're all upset. Has somebody hurt you? Where's Swiss Cheese? Tell it to me in order, Kattrin. Your mother understands you. What, the no-good's taken the cashbox? I'll hit him over the head with it, the sneak. Take your time, don't talk nonsense, use your hands, I don't like it when you howl like a dog, what will the chaplain think? It gives him the creeps. A one-eyed man?

THE CHAPLAIN. The one-eyed man is a spy. Did they arrest Swiss Cheese? [KATTRIN shakes her head and shrugs her shoulders.] We're done for.

MOTHER COURAGE [takes a Catholic flag out of her basket. The CHAPLAIN fastens it to the flagpole]. Hoist the new flag!

THE CHAPLAIN [bitterly]. All good Catholics here.

[Voices are heard from the rear. The two men bring in SWISS CHEESE.]

SWISS CHEESE. Let me go, I haven't got anything. Stop twisting my shoulder, I'm innocent.

THE SERGEANT. He belongs here. You know each other.

MOTHER COURAGE. What makes you think that?

SWISS CHEESE. I don't know them. I don't even know who they are. I had a meal here, it cost me ten hellers. Maybe you saw me sitting here, it was too salty.

THE SERGEANT. Who are you anyway?

MOTHER COURAGE. We're respectable people. And it's true. He had a meal here. He said it was too salty.

THE SERGEANT. Are you trying to tell me you don't know each other?

MOTHER COURAGE. Why should I know him? I don't know everybody. I don't ask people what their name is or if they're heathens; if they pay, they're not heathens. Are you a heathen?

SWISS CHEESE. Of course not.

THE CHAPLAIN. He ate his meal and he behaved himself. He didn't open his mouth except when he was eating. Then you have to.

THE SERGEANT. And who are you?

MOTHER COURAGE. He's only my bartender. You gentlemen must be thirsty, I'll get you a drink of brandy, you must be hot and tired.

THE SERGEANT. We don't drink on duty. [To SWISS CHEESE.] You were carrying something. You must have hidden it by the river. You had something under your jacket when you left here.

MOTHER COURAGE. Was it really him?

SWISS CHEESE. I think you must have seen somebody else. I saw a man running with something under his jacket. You've got the wrong man.

MOTHER COURAGE. That's what I think too, it's a misunderstanding. These things happen. I'm a good judge of people, I'm Mother Courage, you've heard of me, everybody knows me. Take it from me, this man has an honest face.

THE SERGEANT. We're looking for the cashbox of the Second Finnish Regiment. We know what the man in charge of it looks like. We've been after him for two days. You're him.

SWISS CHEESE. I'm not.

THE SERGEANT. Hand it over. If you don't you're a goner, you know that. Where is it?

MOTHER COURAGE [with urgency]. He'd hand it over, wouldn't he, knowing he was a goner if he didn't? I've got it, he'd say, take it, you're stronger. He's not that stupid. Speak up, you stupid idiot, the sergeant's giving you a chance.

SWISS CHEESE. But I haven't got it.

THE SERGEANT. In that case come along. We'll get it out of you. [They lead him away.]

MOTHER COURAGE [shouts after them]. He'd tell you. He's not that stupid. And don't twist his shoulder off! [Runs after them.]

[The same evening. The CHAPLAIN and mute KATTRIN are washing dishes and scouring knives.]

THE CHAPLAIN. That boy's in trouble. There are cases like that in the Bible. Take the Passion of our Lord and Saviour. There's an old song about it. [He sings the Song of the Hours.]

In the first hour Jesus mild
Who had prayed since even
Was betrayed and led before
Pontius the heathen.

Pilate found him innocent
Free from fault and error.
Therefore, having washed his hands
Sent him to King Herod.

In the third hour he was scourged
Stripped and clad in scarlet

And a plaited crown of thorns
Set upon his forehead.

On the Son of Man they spat
Mocked him and made merry.
Then the cross of death was brought
Given him to carry.

At the sixth hour with two thieves
To the cross they nailed him
And the people and the thieves
Mocked him and reviled him.

This is Jesus King of Jews
Cried they in derision
Till the sun withdrew its light
From that awful vision.

At the ninth hour Jesus wailed
Why hast thou me forsaken?
Soldiers brought him vinegar
Which he left untaken.

Then he yielded up the ghost
And the earth was shaken.
Rended was the temple's veil
And the saints were wakened.

Soldiers broke the two thieves' legs
As the night descended
Thrust a spear in Jesus' side
When his life had ended.

Still they mocked, as from his wound
Flowed the blood and water
Thus blasphemed the Son of Man
With their cruel laughter.

MOTHER COURAGE [enters in a state of agitation]. His life's at stake. But they say the sergeant will listen to reason. Only it mustn't come out that he's our Swiss Cheese, or they'll say we've been giving him aid and comfort. All they want is money. But where will we get the money? Hasn't Yvette been here? I met her just now, she's latched onto a colonel, he's thinking of buying her a provisioner's business.

THE CHAPLAIN. Are you really thinking of selling?

MOTHER COURAGE. How else can I get the money for the sergeant?

THE CHAPLAIN. But what will you live on?

MOTHER COURAGE. That's the hitch.

[YVETTE POTTIER comes in with a doddering COLONEL.]

YVETTE [embracing MOTHER COURAGE]. My dear Mother Courage. Here we are again! [*Whispering.*] He's willing. [*Aloud.*] This is my dear friend who advises me on business matters. I just chanced to hear that you wish to sell your wagon, due to circumstances. I might be interested.

MOTHER COURAGE. Mortgage it, not sell it, let's not be hasty. It's not so easy to buy a wagon like this in wartime.

YVETTE [*disappointed*]. Only mortgage it? I thought you wanted to sell it. In that case, I don't know if I'm interested. [*To the* COLONEL.] What do you think?

THE COLONEL. Just as you say, my dear.

MOTHER COURAGE. It's only being mortgaged.

YVETTE. I thought you needed money.

MOTHER COURAGE [*firmly*]. I need the money, but I'd rather run myself ragged looking for an offer than sell now. The wagon is our livelihood. It's an opportunity for you, Yvette, God knows when you'll find another like it and have such a good friend to advise you. See what I mean?

YVETTE. My friend thinks I should snap it up, but I don't know. If it's only being mortgaged . . . Don't you agree that we ought to buy?

THE COLONEL. Yes, my dear.

MOTHER COURAGE. Then you'll have to look for something that's for sale, maybe you'll find something if you take your time and your friend goes around with you. Maybe in a week or two you'll find the right thing.

YVETTE. Then we'll go looking, I love to go looking for things, and I love to go around with you, Poldi, it's a real pleasure. Even if it takes two weeks. When would you pay the money back if you get it?

MOTHER COURAGE. I can pay it back in two weeks, maybe one.

YVETTE. I can't make up my mind, Poldi, chéri, tell me what to do. [*She takes the* COLONEL *aside.*] I know she's got to sell, that's definite. The lieutenant, you know who I mean, the blond one, he'd be glad to lend me the money. He's mad about me, he says I remind him of somebody. What do you think?

THE COLONEL. Keep away from that lieutenant. He's no good. He'll take advantage. Haven't I told you I'd buy you something, pussykins?

YVETTE. I can't accept it from you. But then if you think the lieutenant might take advantage . . . Poldi, I'll accept it from you.

THE COLONEL. I hope so.

YVETTE. Your advice is to take it?

THE COLONEL. That's my advice.

YVETTE [*goes back to* MOTHER COURAGE]. My friend advises me to do it. Write me out a receipt, say the wagon belongs to me complete with stock and furnishings when the two weeks are up. We'll take inventory right now, then I'll bring you the two hundred guilders. [*To the* COLONEL.] You go back to camp, I'll join you in a little while, I've got to take inventory, I don't want anything missing from my wagon. [*She kisses him. He leaves. She climbs up in the wagon.*] I don't see very many boots.

MOTHER COURAGE. Yvette. This is no time to inspect your wagon if it is yours. You promised to see the sergeant about my Swiss Cheese, you've got to hurry. They say he's to be court-martialed in an hour.

YVETTE. Just let me count the shirts.

MOTHER COURAGE [*pulls her down by the skirt*]. You hyena, it's Swiss Cheese, his life's at stake. And don't tell anybody where the offer comes from, in heaven's name say it's your gentleman friend, or we'll all get it, they'll say we helped him.

YVETTE. I've arranged to meet One-Eye in the woods, he must be there already.

THE CHAPLAIN. And there's no need to start out with the whole two hundred, offer a hundred and fifty, that's plenty.

MOTHER COURAGE. Is it your money? You just keep out of this. Don't worry, you'll get your bread and soup. Go on now and don't haggle. It's his life. [*She gives* YVETTE *a push to start her on her way.*]

THE CHAPLAIN. I didn't mean to butt in, but what are we going to live on? You've got an unemployable daughter on your hands.

MOTHER COURAGE. You muddlehead, I'm counting on the regimental cashbox. They'll allow for his expenses, won't they?

THE CHAPLAIN. But will she handle it right?

MOTHER COURAGE. It's in her own interest. If I spend her two hundred, she gets the wagon. She's mighty keen on it, how long can she expect to hold on to her colonel? Kattrin, you scour the knives, use pumice. And you, don't stand around like Jesus on the Mount of Olives, bestir yourself, wash those glasses, we're expecting at least fifty for dinner, and then it'll be the same old story: "Oh my feet, I'm not used to running around, I don't run around in the pulpit." I think they'll set him free. Thank God they're open to bribery. They're not wolves, they're human and out for money. Bribe-taking in humans is the same as mercy in God. It's our only hope. As long as people take bribes, you'll have mild sentences and even the innocent will get off once in a while.

YVETTE [comes in panting]. They want two hundred. And we've got to be quick. Or it'll be out of their hands. I'd better take One-Eye to see my colonel right away. He confessed that he'd had the cashbox, they put the thumb screws on him. But he threw it in the river when he saw they were after him. The box is gone. Should I run and get the money from my colonel?

MOTHER COURAGE. The box is gone? How will I get my two hundred back?

YVETTE. Ah, so you thought you could take it out of the cashbox? You thought you'd put one over on me. Forget it. If you want to save Swiss Cheese, you'll just have to pay, or maybe you'd like me to drop the whole thing and let you keep your wagon?

MOTHER COURAGE. This is something I hadn't reckoned with. But don't rush me, you'll get the wagon, I know it's down the drain, I've had it for seventeen years. Just let me think a second, it's all so sudden. What'll I do, I can't give them two hundred, I guess you should have bargained. If I haven't got a few guilders to fall back on, I'll be at the mercy of the first Tom, Dick, or Harry. Say I'll give them a hundred and twenty, I'll lose my wagon anyway.

YVETTE. They won't go along. One-Eye's in a hurry, he's so keyed-up he keeps looking behind him. Hadn't I better give them the whole two hundred?

MOTHER COURAGE [in despair]. I can't do it. Thirty years I've worked. She's twenty-five and no husband. I've got her

to keep too. Don't needle me, I know what I'm doing. Say a hundred and twenty or nothing doing.

YVETTE. It's up to you. [Goes out quickly.]

[MOTHER COURAGE looks neither at the CHAPLAIN nor at her daughter. She sits down to help KATTRIN scour the knives.]

MOTHER COURAGE. Don't break the glasses. They're not ours any more. Watch what you're doing, you'll cut yourself. Swiss Cheese will be back, I'll pay two hundred if I have to. You'll have your brother. With eighty guilders we can buy a peddler's pack and start all over. Worse things have happened.

THE CHAPLAIN. The Lord will provide.

MOTHER COURAGE. Rub them dry. [They scour the knives in silence. Suddenly KATTRIN runs sobbing behind the wagon.]

YVETTE [comes running]. They won't go along. I warned you. One-Eye wanted to run out on me, he said it was no use. He said we'd hear the drums any minute, meaning he'd been sentenced. I offered a hundred and fifty. He didn't even bother to shrug his shoulders. When I begged and pleaded, he promised to wait till I'd spoken to you again.

MOTHER COURAGE. Say I'll give him the two hundred. Run. [YVETTE runs off. They sit in silence. The CHAPLAIN has stopped washing the glasses.] Maybe I bargained too long. [Drums are heard in the distance. The CHAPLAIN stands up and goes to the rear. MOTHER COURAGE remains seated. It grows dark. The drums stop. It grows light again. MOTHER COURAGE has not moved.]

YVETTE [enters, very pale]. Now you've done it with your haggling and wanting to keep your wagon. Eleven bullets he got, that's all. I don't know why I bother with you any more, you don't deserve it. But I've picked up a little information. They don't believe the cashbox is really in the river. They suspect it's here and they think you were connected with him. They're going to bring him here, they think maybe you'll give yourself away when you see him. I'm warning you: You don't know him, or you're all dead ducks. I may as well tell you, they're right behind me. Should I keep Kattrin out of the way? [MOTHER COURAGE shakes her head.] Does she know? Maybe she didn't hear the drums or maybe she didn't understand.

MOTHER COURAGE. She knows. Get her.

[YVETTE brings KATTRIN, who goes to her mother and stands beside her. MOTHER COURAGE takes her by the hand. Two soldiers come in with a stretcher on which something is lying under a sheet. The SERGEANT walks beside them. They set the stretcher down.]

THE SERGEANT. We've got a man here and we don't know his name. We need it for the records. He had a meal with you. Take a look, see if you know him. [He removes the sheet.] Do you know him? [MOTHER COURAGE shakes her head.] What? You'd never seen him before he came here for a meal? [MOTHER COURAGE shakes her head.] Pick him up. Throw him on the dump. Nobody knows him. [They carry him away.]

Scene Four

[MOTHER COURAGE sings the Song of the Great Capitulation.

Outside an officer's tent.

MOTHER COURAGE is waiting. A CLERK looks out of the tent.]

THE CLERK. I know you. You had a Protestant paymaster at your place, he was hiding. I wouldn't put in any complaints if I were you.

MOTHER COURAGE. I'm putting in a complaint. I'm innocent. If I take this lying down, it'll look as if I had a guilty conscience. First they ripped up my whole wagon with their sabers, then they wanted me to pay a fine of five talers for no reason at all.

THE CLERK. I'm advising you for your own good: Keep your trap shut. We haven't got many provisioners and we'll let you keep on with your business, especially if you've got a guilty conscience and pay a fine now and then.

MOTHER COURAGE. I'm putting in a complaint.

THE CLERK. Have it your way. But you'll have to wait till the captain can see you. [Disappears into the tent.]

A YOUNG SOLDIER [enters in a rage].

Bouque la Madonne! Where's that stinking captain? He embezzled my reward and now he's drinking it up with his whores. I'm going to get him!

AN OLDER SOLDIER [comes running after him]. Shut up. They'll put you in the stocks!

THE YOUNG SOLDIER. Come on out, you crook! I'll make chops out of you. Embezzling my reward! Who jumps in the river? Not another man in the whole squad, only me. And I can't even buy myself a beer. I won't stand for it. Come on out and let me cut you to pieces!

THE OLDER SOLDIER. Holy Mary! He'll ruin himself.

MOTHER COURAGE. They didn't give him a reward?

THE YOUNG SOLDIER. Let me go. I'll run you through too, the more the merrier.

THE OLDER SOLDIER. He saved the colonel's horse and they didn't give him a reward. He's young, he hasn't been around long.

MOTHER COURAGE. Let him go, he's not a dog, you don't have to tie him up. Wanting a reward is perfectly reasonable. Why else would he distinguish himself?

THE YOUNG SOLDIER. And him drinking in there! You're all a lot of yellowbellies. I distinguished myself and I want my reward.

MOTHER COURAGE. Young man, don't shout at me. I've got my own worries and besides, go easy on your voice, you may need it. You'll be hoarse when the captain comes out, you won't be able to say boo and he won't be able to put you in the stocks till you're blue in the face. People that yell like that don't last long, maybe half an hour, then they're so exhausted you have to sing them to sleep.

THE YOUNG SOLDIER. I'm not exhausted and who wants to sleep? I'm hungry. They make our bread out of acorns and hemp seed, and they skimp on that. He's whoring away my reward and I'm hungry. I'll murder him.

MOTHER COURAGE. I see. You're hungry. Last year your general made you cut across the fields to trample down the grain. I could have sold a pair of boots for ten guilders if anybody'd had ten guilders and if I'd had any boots. He thought he'd be someplace else this year, but now he's still here and everybody's starving. I can see that you might be good and mad.

THE YOUNG SOLDIER. He can't do this to me, save your breath, I won't put up with injustice.

MOTHER COURAGE. You're right, but for how long? How long won't you put up with injustice? An hour? Two hours? You see, you never thought of that, though it's very important, because it's miserable in the stocks when it suddenly dawns on you that you *can* put up with injustice.

THE YOUNG SOLDIER. I don't know why I listen to you. Bouque la Madonne! Where's the captain?

MOTHER COURAGE. You listen to me because I'm not telling you anything new. You know your temper has gone up in smoke, it was a short temper and you need a long one, but that's a hard thing to come by.

THE YOUNG SOLDIER. Are you trying to say I've no right to claim my reward?

MOTHER COURAGE. Not at all. I'm only saying your temper isn't long enough, it won't get you anywhere. Too bad. If you had a long temper, I'd even egg you on. Chop the bastard up, that's what I'd say, but suppose you don't chop him up, because your tail's drooping and you know it. I'm left standing there like a fool and the captain takes it out on me.

THE OLDER SOLDIER. You're right. He's only blowing off steam.

THE YOUNG SOLDIER. We'll see about that. I'll cut him to pieces. [*He draws his sword.*] When he comes out, I'll cut him to pieces.

THE CLERK [*looks out*]. The captain will be here in a moment. Sit down.

[*The* YOUNG SOLDIER *sits down.*]

MOTHER COURAGE. There he sits. What did I tell you? Sitting, aren't you? Oh, they know us like a book, they know how to handle us. Sit down! And down we sit. You can't start a riot sitting down. Better not stand up again, you won't be able to stand the way you were standing before. Don't be embarrassed on my account, I'm no better, not a bit of it. We were full of piss and vinegar, but they've bought it off. Look at me. No back talk, it's bad for business. Let me tell you about the great capitulation. [*She sings the Song of the Great Capitulation.*]

When I was young, no more than a spring chicken
I too thought that I was really quite the cheese
(No common peddler's daughter, not I with my looks and my talent and striving for higher things!)
One little hair in the soup would make me sicken
And at me no man would dare to sneeze.
(It's all or nothing, no second best for me. I've got what it takes, the rules are for somebody else!)
But a chickadee
Sang wait and see!
    And you go marching with the show
    In step, however fast or slow
    And rattle off your little song:
    It won't be long.
    And then the whole thing slides.
    You think God provides—
    But you've got it wrong.

And before one single year had wasted
I had learned to swallow down the bitter brew
(Two kids on my hands and the price of bread and who do they take me for anyway!)
Man, the double-edged shellacking that I tasted
On my ass and knees I was when they were through.
(You've got to get along with people, one good turn deserves another, no use trying to ram your head through the wall!)
And the chickadee
Sang wait and see!
    And she goes marching with the show
    In step, however fast or slow
    And rattles off her little song:
    It won't be long.
    And then the whole thing slides
    You think God provides—
    But you've got it wrong.

I've seen many fired by high ambition
No star's big or high enough to reach out for.
(It's ability that counts, where there's a will there's a way, one way or another we'll swing it!)
Then while moving mountains they get a suspicion

That to wear a straw hat is too big a
    chore.
(No use being too big for your britches!)
And the chickadee
Sings wait and see!
    And they go marching with the show
    In step, however fast or slow
    And rattle off their little song:
    It won't be long.
    And then the whole thing slides!
    You think God provides—
    But you've got it wrong!

MOTHER COURAGE [to the YOUNG SOL-
DIER]. So here's what I think: Stay here
with your sword if your anger's big
enough, I know you have good reason,
but if it's a short quick anger, better make
tracks!

THE YOUNG SOLDIER. Kiss my ass! [He
staggers off, the OLDER SOLDIER after
him.]

THE CLERK [sticking his head out]. The
captain is here. You can put in your complaint now.

MOTHER COURAGE. I've changed my
mind. No complaint. [She goes out.]

Scene Five

[Two years have passed. The war has
spread far and wide. With scarcely a
pause Mother Courage's little wagon rolls
through Poland, Moravia, Bavaria, Italy,
and back again to Bavaria. 1631. Tilly's
victory at Magdeburg costs MOTHER
COURAGE four officers' shirts.

MOTHER COURAGE's wagon has stopped
in a devastated village.

Thin military music is heard from the
distance. Two soldiers at the bar are being waited on by KATTRIN and MOTHER
COURAGE. One of them is wearing a lady's
fur coat over his shoulders.]

MOTHER COURAGE. What's that? You
can't pay? No money, no schnapps.
Plenty of victory marches for the Lord but
no pay for the men.

THE SOLDIER. I want my schnapps. I
came too late for the looting. The general
skunked us: permission to loot the city
for exactly one hour. Says he's not a monster; the mayor must have paid him.

THE CHAPLAIN [staggers in]. There's
still some wounded in the house. The
peasant and his family. Help me, somebody, I need linen.

[The SECOND SOLDIER goes out with
him. KATTRIN gets very excited and
tries to persuade her mother to hand
out linen.]

MOTHER COURAGE. I haven't got any.
The regiment's bought up all my bandages. You think I'm going to rip up my
officers' shirts for the likes of them?

THE CHAPLAIN [calling back]. I need
linen, I tell you.

MOTHER COURAGE [sitting down on the
wagon steps to keep KATTRIN out]. Nothing doing. They don't pay, they got nothing to pay with.

THE CHAPLAIN [bending over a WOMAN
whom he has carried out]. Why did you
stay here in all that gunfire?

THE PEASANT WOMAN [feebly]. Farm.

MOTHER COURAGE. You won't catch
them leaving their property. And I'm expected to foot the bill. I won't do it.

THE FIRST SOLDIER. They're Protestants. Why do they have to be Protestants?

MOTHER COURAGE. Religion is the least
of their worries. They've lost their farm.

THE SECOND SOLDIER. They're no Protestants. They're Catholics like us.

THE FIRST SOLDIER. How do we know
who we're shooting at?

A PEASANT [whom the CHAPLAIN brings
in]. They got my arm.

THE CHAPLAIN. Where's the linen?

[All look at MOTHER COURAGE, who
does not move.]

MOTHER COURAGE. I can't give you a
thing. What with all my taxes, duties,
fees and bribes! [Making guttural sounds,
KATTRIN picks up a board and threatens
her mother with it.] Are you crazy? Put
that board down, you slut, or I'll smack
you. I'm not giving anything, you can't
make me, I've got to think of myself.
[The CHAPLAIN picks her up from the
step and puts her down on the ground.
Then he fishes out some shirts and tears
them into strips.]

My shirts! Half a guilder apiece! I'm
ruined!

[The anguished cry of a baby is heard
from the house.]

THE PEASANT. The baby's still in there!

[KATTRIN runs in.]

THE CHAPLAIN [to the WOMAN]. Don't move. They're bringing him out.

MOTHER COURAGE. Get her out of there. The roof'll cave in.

THE CHAPLAIN. I'm not going in there again.

MOTHER COURAGE [torn]. Don't run hog-wild with my expensive linen.

[KATTRIN emerges from the ruins carrying an infant.]

MOTHER COURAGE. Oh, so you've found another baby to carry around with you? Give that baby back to its mother this minute, or it'll take me all day to get it away from you. Do you hear me? [To the SECOND SOLDIER.] Don't stand there gaping, go back and tell them to stop that music, I can see right here that they've won a victory. Your victory's costing me a pretty penny.

[KATTRIN rocks the baby in her arms, humming a lullaby.]

MOTHER COURAGE. There she sits, happy in all this misery; give it back this minute, the mother's coming to. [She pounces on the FIRST SOLDIER who has been helping himself to the drinks and is now making off with the bottle.] Psha-greff! Beast! Haven't you had enough victories for today? Pay up.

FIRST SOLDIER. I'm broke.

MOTHER COURAGE [tears the fur coat off him]. Then leave the coat here, it's stolen anyway.

THE CHAPLAIN. There's still somebody in there.

Scene Six

[Outside Ingolstadt in Bavaria MOTHER COURAGE attends the funeral of Tilly, the imperial field marshal. Conversations about heroes and the longevity of the war. The CHAPLAIN deplores the waste of his talents. Mute KATTRIN gets the red shoes. 1632.

Inside MOTHER COURAGE's tent.

A bar open to the rear. Rain. In the distance drum rolls and funeral music. The CHAPLAIN and the REGIMENTAL CLERK are playing a board game. MOTHER COURAGE and her daughter are taking inventory.]

THE CHAPLAIN. The procession's starting.

MOTHER COURAGE. It's a shame about the general—socks: twenty-two pairs—I hear he was killed by accident. On account of the fog in the fields. He's up front encouraging the troops. "Fight to the death, boys," he sings out. Then he rides back, but he gets lost in the fog and rides back forward. Before you know it he's in the middle of the battle and stops a bullet—lanterns: we're down to four. [A whistle from the rear. She goes to the bar.] You men ought to be ashamed, running out on your late general's funeral! [She pours drinks.]

THE CLERK. They shouldn't have been paid before the funeral. Now they're getting drunk instead.

THE CHAPLAIN [to the CLERK]. Shouldn't you be at the funeral?

THE CLERK. In this rain?

MOTHER COURAGE. With you it's different, the rain might spoil your uniform. It seems they wanted to ring the bells, naturally, but it turned out the churches had all been shot to pieces by his orders, so the poor general won't hear any bells when they lower him into his grave. They're going to fire a three-gun salute instead, so it won't be too dull—seventeen sword belts.

CRIES [from the bar]. Hey! Brandy!

MOTHER COURAGE. Money first! No, you can't come into my tent with your muddy boots! You can drink outside, rain or no rain. [To the CLERK.] I'm only letting officers in. It seems the general had been having his troubles. Mutiny in the Second Regiment because he hadn't paid them. It's a war of religion, he says, should they profit by their faith?

[Funeral march. All look to the rear.]

THE CHAPLAIN. Now they're marching past the body.

MOTHER COURAGE. I feel sorry when a general or an emperor passes away like this, maybe he thought he'd do something big, that posterity would still be talking about and maybe put up a statue in his honor, conquer the world, for instance, that's a nice ambition for a general, he doesn't know any better. So he knocks himself out, and then the common people come and spoil it all, because what do they care about greatness, all they care about is a mug of beer and maybe a little company. The most beautiful plans have been wrecked by the smallness of the people that are supposed to carry them out. Even an emperor can't do anything by himself, he needs the support of his soldiers and his people. Am I right?

THE CHAPLAIN [laughing]. Courage, you're right, except about the soldiers. They do their best. With those fellows out there, for instance, drinking their brandy in the rain, I'll undertake to carry on one war after another for a hundred years, two at once if I have to, and I'm not a general by trade.

MOTHER COURAGE. Then you don't think the war might stop?

THE CHAPLAIN. Because the general's dead? Don't be childish. They grow by the dozen, there'll always be plenty of heroes.

MOTHER COURAGE. Look here, I'm not asking you for the hell of it. I've been wondering whether to lay in supplies while they're cheap, but if the war stops, I can throw them out the window.

THE CHAPLAIN. I understand. You want a serious answer. There have always been people who say: "The war will be over some day." I say there's no guarantee the war will ever be over. Naturally a brief intermission is conceivable. Maybe the war needs a breather, a war can even break its neck, so to speak. There's always a chance of that, nothing is perfect here below. Maybe there never will be a perfect war, one that lives up to all our expectations. Suddenly, for some unforeseen reason, a war can bog down, you can't think of everything. Some little oversight and your war's in trouble. And then you've got to pull it out of the mud. But the kings and emperors, not to mention the pope, will always come to its help in adversity. On the whole, I'd say this war has very little to worry about, it'll live to a ripe old age.

A SOLDIER [sings at the bar].

A drink, and don't be slow!
A soldier's got to go
And fight for his religion.

Make it double, this is a holiday.

MOTHER COURAGE. If I could only be sure . . .

THE CHAPLAIN. Figure it out for yourself. What's to stop the war?

THE SOLDIER [sings].

Your breasts, girl, don't be slow!
A soldier's got to go
And ride away to Pilsen.

THE CLERK [suddenly]. But why can't we have peace? I'm from Bohemia, I'd like to go home when the time comes.

THE CHAPLAIN. Oh, you'd like to go home? Ah, peace! What becomes of the hole when the cheese has been eaten?

THE SOLDIER [sings].

Play cards, friends, don't be slow!
A soldier's got to go
No matter if it's Sunday.

A prayer, priest, don't be slow!
A soldier's got to go
And die for king and country.

THE CLERK. In the long run nobody can live without peace.

THE CHAPLAIN. The way I see it, war gives you plenty of peace. It has its peaceful moments. War meets every need, including the peaceful ones, everything's taken care of, or your war couldn't hold its own. In a war you can shit the same as in the dead of peace, you can stop for a beer between battles, and even on the march you can always lie down on your elbows and take a little nap by the roadside. You can't play cards when you're fighting; but then you can't when you're plowing in the dead of peace either, but after a victory the sky's the limit. Maybe you've had a leg shot off, at first you raise a howl, you make a big thing of it. But then you calm down or they give you schnapps, and in the end you're hopping around again and the war's no worse off than before. And what's to prevent you from multiplying in the thick of the slaughter, behind a barn or someplace, in the long run how can they stop you, and then the war has your progeny to help it along. Take it from me, the war will always find an answer. Why would it have to stop?

[KATTRIN has stopped working and is staring at the CHAPLAIN.]

MOTHER COURAGE. Then I'll buy the merchandise. You've convinced me. [KATTRIN suddenly throws down a basket full of bottles and runs out.] Kattrin!

[*Laughs.*] My goodness, the poor thing's been hoping for peace. I promised her she'd get a husband when peace comes. [*She runs after her.*]

THE CLERK [*getting up*]. I win, you've been too busy talking. Pay up.

MOTHER COURAGE [*comes back with* KATTRIN]. Be reasonable, the war'll go on a little longer and we'll make a little more money, then peace will be even better. Run along to town now, it won't take you ten minutes, and get the stuff from the Golden Lion, only the expensive things, we'll pick up the rest in the wagon later, it's all arranged, the regimental clerk here will go with you. They've almost all gone to the general's funeral, nothing can happen to you. Look sharp, don't let them take anything away from you, think of your dowry.

[KATTRIN *puts a kerchief over her head and goes with the* CLERK.]

THE CHAPLAIN. Is it all right letting her go with the clerk?

MOTHER COURAGE. Who'd want to ruin her? She's not pretty enough.

THE CHAPLAIN. I've come to admire the way you handle your business and pull through every time. I can see why they call you Mother Courage.

MOTHER COURAGE. Poor people need courage. Why? Because they're sunk. In their situation it takes gumption just to get up in the morning. Or to plow a field in the middle of a war. They even show courage by bringing children into the world, because look at the prospects. The way they butcher and execute each other, think of the courage they need to look each other in the face. And putting up with an emperor and a pope takes a whale of a lot of courage, because those two are the death of the poor. [*She sits down, takes a small pipe from her pocket and smokes.*] You could be making some kindling.

THE CHAPLAIN [*reluctantly takes his jacket off and prepares to chop*]. Chopping wood isn't really my trade, you know, I'm a shepherd of souls.

MOTHER COURAGE. Sure. But I have no soul and I need firewood.

THE CHAPLAIN. What's that pipe?

MOTHER COURAGE. Just a pipe.

THE CHAPLAIN. No, it's not "just a pipe," it's a very particular pipe.

MOTHER COURAGE. Really?

THE CHAPLAIN. It's the cook's pipe from the Oxenstjerna regiment.

MOTHER COURAGE. If you know it all, why the mealy-mouthed questions?

THE CHAPLAIN. I didn't know if you knew. You could have been rummaging through your belongings and laid hands on some pipe and picked it up without thinking.

MOTHER COURAGE. Yes. Maybe that's how it was.

THE CHAPLAIN. Except it wasn't. You knew who that pipe belongs to.

MOTHER COURAGE. What of it?

THE CHAPLAIN. Courage, I'm warning you. It's my duty. I doubt if you ever lay eyes on the man again, but that's no calamity, in fact you're lucky. If you ask me, he wasn't steady. Not at all.

MOTHER COURAGE. What makes you say that? He was a nice man.

THE CHAPLAIN. Oh, you think he was nice? I differ. Far be it from me to wish him any harm, but I can't say he was nice. I'd say he was a scheming Don Juan. If you don't believe me, take a look at his pipe. You'll have to admit that it shows up his character.

MOTHER COURAGE. I don't see anything. It's beat up.

THE CHAPLAIN. It's half bitten through. A violent man. That is the pipe of a ruthless, violent man, you must see that if you've still got an ounce of good sense.

MOTHER COURAGE. Don't wreck my chopping block.

THE CHAPLAIN. I've told you I wasn't trained to chop wood. I studied theology. My gifts and abilities are being wasted on muscular effort. The talents that God gave me are lying fallow. That's a sin. You've never heard me preach. With one sermon I can whip a regiment into such a state that they take the enemy for a flock of sheep. Then men care no more about their lives than they would about a smelly old sock that they're ready to throw away in hopes of final victory. God has made me eloquent. You'll swoon when you hear me preach.

MOTHER COURAGE. I don't want to swoon. What good would that do me?

THE CHAPLAIN. Courage, I've often wondered if maybe you didn't conceal a warm heart under that hard-bitten talk of yours. You too are human, you need warmth.

MOTHER COURAGE. The best way to keep this tent warm is with plenty of firewood.

THE CHAPLAIN. Don't try to put me off. Seriously, Courage, I sometimes wonder if we couldn't make our relationship a little closer. I mean, seeing that the whirlwind of war has whirled us so strangely together.

MOTHER COURAGE. Seems to me it's close enough. I cook your meals and you do chores, such as chopping wood, for instance.

THE CHAPLAIN [goes toward her]. You know what I mean by "closer"; it has nothing to do with meals and chopping wood and such mundane needs. Don't harden your heart, let it speak.

MOTHER COURAGE. Don't come at me with that ax. That's too close a relationship.

THE CHAPLAIN. Don't turn it to ridicule. I'm serious, I've given it careful thought.

MOTHER COURAGE. Chaplain, don't be silly. I like you, I don't want to have to scold you. My aim in life is to get through, me and my children and my wagon. I don't think of it as mine and besides I'm not in the mood for private affairs. Right now I'm taking a big risk, buying up merchandise with the general dead and everybody talking peace. What'll you do if I'm ruined? See? You don't know. Chop that wood, then we'll be warm in the evening, which is a good thing in times like these. Now what? [She stands up.]

[Enter KATTRIN out of breath, with a wound across her forehead and over one eye. She is carrying all sorts of things, packages, leather goods, a drum, etc.]

MOTHER COURAGE. What's that? Assaulted? On the way back? She was assaulted on the way back. Must have been that soldier that got drunk here! I shouldn't have let you go! Throw the stuff down! It's not bad, only a flesh wound. I'll bandage it, it'll heal in a week. They're worse than wild beasts. [She bandages the wound.]

THE CHAPLAIN. I can't find fault with them. At home they never raped anybody. I blame the people that start wars, they're the ones that dredge up man's lowest instincts.

MOTHER COURAGE. Didn't the clerk bring you back? That's because you're respectable, they don't give a damn. It's not a deep wound, it won't leave a mark. There, all bandaged. Don't fret, I've got something for you. I've been keeping it for you on the sly, it'll be a surprise. [She fishes YVETTE's red shoes out of a sack.] See? You've always wanted them. Now you've got them. Put them on quick before I regret it. It won't leave a mark, though I wouldn't mind if it did. The girls that attract them get the worst of it. They drag them around till there's nothing left of them. If you don't appeal to them, they won't harm you. I've seen girls with pretty faces, a few years later they'd have given a wolf the creeps. They can't step behind a bush without fearing the worst. It's like trees. The straight tall ones get chopped down for ridgepoles, the crooked ones enjoy life. In other words, it's a lucky break. The shoes are still in good condition, I've kept them nicely polished.

[KATTRIN leaves the shoes where they are and crawls into the wagon.]

THE CHAPLAIN. I hope she won't be disfigured.

MOTHER COURAGE. There'll be a scar. She can stop waiting for peace.

THE CHAPLAIN. She didn't let them take anything.

MOTHER COURAGE. Maybe I shouldn't have drummed it into her. If I only knew what went on in her head. One night she stayed out, the only time in all these years. Afterwards she traipsed around as usual, except she worked harder. I never could find out what happened. I racked my brains for quite some time. [She picks up the articles brought by KATTRIN and sorts them angrily.] That's war for you. A fine way to make a living!

[Cannon salutes are heard.]

THE CHAPLAIN. Now they're burying the general. This is a historic moment.

MOTHER COURAGE. To me it's a historic moment when they hit my daughter over the eye. She's a wreck, she'll never get a husband now, and she's so crazy about children. It's the war that made her dumb too, a soldier stuffed something in her mouth when she was little. I'll never see Swiss Cheese again and where Eilif is, God knows. God damn the war.

Scene Seven

[MOTHER COURAGE *at the height of her business career.*
Highway.
The CHAPLAIN, MOTHER COURAGE *and her daughter* KATTRIN *are pulling the wagon. New wares are hanging on it.* MOTHER COURAGE *is wearing a necklace of silver talers.*]

MOTHER COURAGE. Stop running down the war. I won't have it. I know it destroys the weak, but the weak haven't a chance in peacetime either. And war is a better provider. [*Sings.*]

If you're not strong enough to take it
The victory will find you dead.
A war is only what you make it.
It's business, not with cheese but lead.

And what good is it staying in one place? The stay-at-homes are the first to get it. [*Sings.*]

Some people think they'd like to ride out
The war, leave danger to the brave
And dig themselves a cozy hideout—
They'll dig themselves an early grave.
I've seen them running from the thunder
To find a refuge from the war
But once they're resting six feet under
They wonder what they hurried for.

[*They plod on.*]

Scene Eight

[*In the same year Gustavus Adolphus, King of Sweden, is killed at the battle of Lützen. Peace threatens to ruin* MOTHER COURAGE'S *business. Her brave son performs one heroic deed too many and dies an ignominious death.*
A camp.
A summer morning. An OLD WOMAN *and her son are standing by the wagon. The son is carrying a large sack of bedding.*]

MOTHER COURAGE'S VOICE [*from the wagon*]. Does it have to be at this unearthly hour?
THE YOUNG MAN. We've walked all night, twenty miles, and we've got to go back today.
MOTHER COURAGE'S VOICE. What can I do with bedding? The people haven't any houses.
THE YOUNG MAN. Wait till you've seen it.
THE OLD WOMAN. She won't take it either. Come on.
THE YOUNG MAN. They'll sell the roof from over our heads for taxes. Maybe she'll give us three guilders if you throw in the cross. [*Bells start ringing.*] Listen, mother!
VOICES [*from the rear*]. Peace! The king of Sweden is dead!
MOTHER COURAGE [*sticks her head out of the wagon. She has not yet done her hair*]. Why are the bells ringing in the middle of the week?
THE CHAPLAIN [*crawls out from under the wagon*]. What are they shouting?
MOTHER COURAGE. Don't tell me peace has broken out when I've just taken in more supplies.
THE CHAPLAIN [*shouting toward the rear*]. Is it true? Peace?
VOICE. Three weeks ago, they say. But we just found out.
THE CHAPLAIN [*to* MOTHER COURAGE]. What else would they ring the bells for?
VOICE. There's a whole crowd of Lutherans, they've driven their carts into town. They brought the news.
THE YOUNG MAN. Mother, it's peace. What's the matter?
[*The* OLD WOMAN *has collapsed.*]
MOTHER COURAGE [*going back into the wagon*]. Heavenly saints! Kattrin, peace! Put your black dress on! We're going to church. We owe it to Swiss Cheese. Can it be true?
THE YOUNG MAN. The people here say the same thing. They've made peace. Can you get up? [*The* OLD WOMAN *stands up, still stunned.*] I'll get the saddle shop started again. I promise. Everything will be all right. Father will get his bed back. Can you walk? [*To the* CHAPLAIN.] She fainted. It was the news. She thought peace would never come again. Father said it would. We'll go straight home. [*Both go out.*]
MOTHER COURAGE'S VOICE. Give her some brandy.
THE CHAPLAIN. They're gone.

MOTHER COURAGE'S VOICE. What's going on in camp?

THE CHAPLAIN. A big crowd. I'll go see. Shouldn't I put on my clericals?

MOTHER COURAGE'S VOICE. Better make sure before you step out in your antichrist costume. I'm glad to see peace, even if I'm ruined. At least I've brought two of my children through the war. Now I'll see my Eilif again.

THE CHAPLAIN. Look who's coming down the road. If it isn't the general's cook!

THE COOK [rather bedraggled, carrying a bundle]. Can I believe my eyes? The chaplain!

THE CHAPLAIN. Courage! A visitor!

[MOTHER COURAGE climbs down.]

THE COOK. Didn't I promise to come over for a little chat as soon as I had time? I've never forgotten your brandy, Mrs. Fierling.

MOTHER COURAGE. Mercy, the general's cook! After all these years! Where's Eilif, my eldest?

THE COOK. Isn't he here yet? He left ahead of me, he was coming to see you too.

THE CHAPLAIN. I'll put on my clericals, wait for me. [Goes out behind the wagon.]

MOTHER COURAGE. Then he'll be here any minute. [Calls into the wagon.] Kattrin, Eilif's coming! Bring the cook a glass of brandy! [KATTRIN does not appear.] Put a lock of hair over it, and forget it! Mr. Lamb is no stranger. [Gets the brandy herself.] She won't come out. Peace doesn't mean a thing to her, it's come too late. They hit her over the eye, there's hardly any mark, but she thinks people are staring at her.

THE COOK. Ech, war! [He and MOTHER COURAGE sit down.]

MOTHER COURAGE. Cook, you find me in trouble. I'm ruined.

THE COOK. What? Say, that's a shame.

MOTHER COURAGE. Peace has done me in. Only the other day I stocked up. The chaplain's advice. And now they'll all demobilize and leave me sitting on my merchandise.

THE COOK. How could you listen to the chaplain? If I'd had time, I'd have warned you against him, but the Catholics came too soon. He's a fly-by-night. So now he's the boss here?

MOTHER COURAGE. He washed my dishes and helped me pull the wagon.

THE COOK. Him? Pulling? I guess he's told you a few of his jokes too, I wouldn't put it past him, he has an unsavory attitude toward women, I tried to reform him, it was hopeless. He's not steady.

MOTHER COURAGE. Are you steady?

THE COOK. If nothing else, I'm steady. Prosit!

MOTHER COURAGE. Steady is no good. I've only lived with one steady man, thank the Lord. I never had to work so hard, he sold the children's blankets when spring came, and he thought my harmonica was unchristian. In my opinion you're not doing yourself any good by admitting you're steady.

THE COOK. You've still got your old bite, but I respect you for it.

MOTHER COURAGE. Don't tell me you've been dreaming about my old bite.

THE COOK. Well, here we sit, with the bells of peace and your world-famous brandy, that hasn't its equal.

MOTHER COURAGE. The bells of peace don't strike my fancy right now. I don't see them paying the men, they're behind-hand already. Where does that leave me with my famous brandy? Have you been paid?

THE COOK [hesitantly]. Not really. That's why we demobilized ourselves. Under the circumstances, I says to myself, why should I stay on? I'll go see my friends in the meantime. So here we are.

MOTHER COURAGE. You mean you're out of funds?

THE COOK. If only they'd stop those damn bells! I'd be glad to go into some kind of business. I'm sick of being a cook. They give me roots and shoe leather to work with, and then they throw the hot soup in my face. A cook's got a dog's life these days. I'd rather be in combat, but now we've got peace. [The CHAPLAIN appears in his original dress.] We'll discuss it later.

THE CHAPLAIN. It's still in good condition. There were only a few moths in it.

THE COOK. I don't see why you bother. They won't take you back. Who are you going to inspire now to be an honest soldier and earn his pay at the risk of his life? Besides, I've got a bone to pick with you. Advising this lady to buy useless merchandise on the ground that the war would last forever.

THE CHAPLAIN [*heatedly*]. And why, I'd like to know, is it any of your business?

THE COOK. Because it's unscrupulous. How can you meddle in other people's business and give unsolicited advice?

THE CHAPLAIN. Who's meddling? [*To* MOTHER COURAGE.] I didn't know you were accountable to this gentleman, I didn't know you were so intimate with him.

MOTHER COURAGE. Don't get excited, the cook is only giving his private opinion. And you can't deny that your war was a dud.

THE CHAPLAIN. Courage, don't blaspheme against peace. You're a battlefield hyena.

MOTHER COURAGE. What am I?

THE COOK. If you insult this lady, you'll hear from me.

THE CHAPLAIN. I'm not talking to you. Your intentions are too obvious. [*To* MOTHER COURAGE.] But when I see you picking up peace with thumb and forefinger like a snotty handkerchief, it revolts my humanity; you don't want peace, you want war, because you profit by it, but don't forget the old saying: "He hath need of a long spoon that eateth with the devil."

MOTHER COURAGE. I've no use for war and war hasn't much use for me. Anyway, I'm not letting anybody call me a hyena, you and me are through.

THE CHAPLAIN. How can you complain about peace when it's such a relief to everybody else? On account of the old rags in your wagon?

MOTHER COURAGE. My merchandise isn't old rags, it's what I live off, and so did you.

THE CHAPLAIN. Off war, you mean. Aha!

THE COOK [*to the* CHAPLAIN]. You're a grown man, you ought to know there's no sense in giving advice. [*To* MOTHER COURAGE.] The best thing you can do now is to sell off certain articles quick, before the prices hit the floor. Dress yourself and get started, there's no time to lose.

MOTHER COURAGE. That's very sensible advice. I think I'll do it.

THE CHAPLAIN. Because the cook says so!

MOTHER COURAGE. Why didn't you say so? He's right, I'd better run over to the market. [*She goes into the wagon.*]

THE COOK. My round, chaplain. No presence of mind. Here's what you should have said: me give you advice? All I ever did was talk politics! Don't try to take me on. Cockfighting is undignified in a clergyman.

THE CHAPLAIN. If you don't shut up, I'll murder you, undignified or not.

THE COOK [*taking off his shoe and unwinding the wrappings from his feet*]. If the war hadn't made a godless bum out of you, you could easily come by a parsonage now that peace is here. They won't need cooks, there's nothing to cook, but people still do a lot of believing, that hasn't changed.

THE CHAPLAIN. See here, Mr. Lamb. Don't try to squeeze me out. Being a bum has made me a better man. I couldn't preach to them any more.

[YVETTE POTTIER *enters, elaborately dressed in black, with a cane. She is much older and fatter and heavily powdered. Behind her a servant.*]

YVETTE. Hello there! Is this the residence of Mother Courage?

CHAPLAIN. Right you are. With whom have we the pleasure?

YVETTE. The Countess Starhemberg, my good people. Where is Mother Courage?

THE CHAPLAIN [*calls into the wagon*]. Countess Starhemberg wishes to speak to you!

MOTHER COURAGE. I'm coming.

YVETTE. It's Yvette!

MOTHER COURAGE'S VOICE. My goodness! It's Yvette!

YVETTE. Just dropped in to see how you're doing. [*The* COOK *has turned around in horror.*] Pieter!

THE COOK. Yvette!

YVETTE. Blow me down! How did you get here?

THE COOK. In a cart.

THE CHAPLAIN. Oh, you know each other? Intimately?

YVETTE. I should think so. [*She looks the* COOK *over.*] Fat!

THE COOK. You're not exactly willowy yourself.

YVETTE. All the same I'm glad I ran into you, you bum. Now I can tell you what I think of you.

THE CHAPLAIN. Go right ahead, spare no details, but wait until Courage comes out.

MOTHER COURAGE [comes out with all sorts of merchandise]. Yvette! [They embrace.] But what are you in mourning for?

YVETTE. Isn't it becoming? My husband the colonel died a few years ago.

MOTHER COURAGE. The old geezer that almost bought my wagon?

YVETTE. His elder brother.

MOTHER COURAGE. You must be pretty well fixed. It's nice to find somebody that's made a good thing out of the war.

YVETTE. Oh well, it's been up and down and back up again.

MOTHER COURAGE. Let's not say anything bad about colonels. They make money by the bushel.

THE CHAPLAIN. If I were you, I'd put my shoes back on again. [To YVETTE.] Countess Starhemberg, you promised to tell us what you think of this gentleman.

THE COOK. Don't make a scene here.

MOTHER COURAGE. He's a friend of mine, Yvette.

YVETTE. He's Pete the Pipe, that's who he is.

THE COOK. Forget the nicknames, my name is Lamb.

MOTHER COURAGE [laughs]. Pete the Pipe! That drove the women crazy! Say, I've saved your pipe.

THE CHAPLAIN. And smoked it.

YVETTE. It's lucky I'm here to warn you. He's the worst rotter that ever infested the coast of Flanders. He ruined more girls than he's got fingers.

THE COOK. That was a long time ago. I've changed.

YVETTE. Stand up when a lady draws you into a conversation! How I loved this man! And all the while he was seeing a little bandylegged brunette, ruined her too, naturally.

THE COOK. Seems to me I started you off on a prosperous career.

YVETTE. Shut up, you depressing wreck! Watch your step with him, his kind are dangerous even when they've gone to seed.

MOTHER COURAGE [to YVETTE]. Come along, I've got to sell my stuff before the prices drop. Maybe you can help me, with your army connections. [Calls into the wagon.] Kattrin, forget about church, I'm running over to the market. When Eilif comes, give him a drink. [Goes out with YVETTE.]

YVETTE [in leaving]. To think that such a man could lead me astray! I can thank my lucky stars that I was able to rise in the world after that. I've put a spoke in your wheel, Pete the Pipe, and they'll give me credit for it in heaven when my time comes.

THE CHAPLAIN. Our conversation seems to illustrate the old adage: The mills of God grind slowly. What do you think of my jokes now?

THE COOK. I'm just unlucky. I'll come clean: I was hoping for a hot meal. I'm starving. And now they're talking about me, and she'll get the wrong idea. I think I'll beat it before she comes back.

THE CHAPLAIN. I think so too.

THE COOK. Chaplain, I'm fed up on peace already. Men are sinners from the cradle, fire and sword are their natural lot. I wish I were cooking for the general again, God knows where he is, I'd roast a fine fat capon, with mustard sauce and a few carrots.

THE CHAPLAIN. Red cabbage. Red cabbage with capon.

THE COOK. That's right, but he wanted carrots.

THE CHAPLAIN. He was ignorant.

THE COOK. That didn't prevent you from gorging yourself.

THE CHAPLAIN. With repugnance.

THE COOK. Anyway you'll have to admit those were good times.

THE CHAPLAIN. I might admit that.

THE COOK. Now you've called her a hyena, your good times here are over. What are you staring at?

THE CHAPLAIN. Eilif! [EILIF enters, followed by soldiers with pikes. His hands are fettered. He is deathly pale.] What's wrong?

EILIF. Where's mother?

THE CHAPLAIN. Gone to town.

EILIF. I heard she was here. They let me come and see her.

THE COOK [to the SOLDIERS]. Where are you taking him?

A SOLDIER. No good place.

THE CHAPLAIN. What has he done?

THE SOLDIER. Broke into a farm. The peasant's wife is dead.

THE CHAPLAIN. How could you do such a thing?

EILIF. It's what I've been doing all along.

THE COOK. But in peacetime!

EILIF. Shut your trap. Can I sit down till she comes?

THE SOLDIER. We haven't time.

THE CHAPLAIN. During the war they honored him for it, he sat at the general's right hand. Then it was bravery. Couldn't we speak to the officer?

THE SOLDIER. No use. What's brave about taking a peasant's cattle?

THE COOK. It was stupid.

EILIF. If I'd been stupid, I'd have starved, wise guy.

THE COOK. And for being smart your head comes off.

THE CHAPLAIN. Let's get Kattrin at least.

EILIF. Leave her be. Get me a drink of schnapps.

THE SOLDIER. No time. Let's go!

THE CHAPLAIN. And what should we tell your mother?

EILIF. Tell her it wasn't any different, tell her it was the same. Or don't tell her anything.

[The SOLDIERS drive him away.]

THE CHAPLAIN. I'll go with you on your hard journey.

EILIF. I don't need any sky pilot.

THE CHAPLAIN. You don't know yet. [He follows him.]

THE COOK [calls after them]. I'll have to tell her, she'll want to see him.

THE CHAPLAIN. Better not tell her anything. Or say he was here and he'll come again, maybe tomorrow. I'll break it to her when I get back. [Hurries out.]

[The COOK looks after them, shaking his head, then he walks anxiously about. Finally he approaches the wagon.]

THE COOK. Hey! Come on out! I can see why you'd hide from peace. I wish I could do it myself. I'm the general's cook, remember? Wouldn't you have a bite to eat, to do me till your mother gets back? A slice of ham or just a piece of bread while I'm waiting. [He looks in.]

She's buried her head in a blanket. [The sound of gunfire in the rear.]

MOTHER COURAGE [runs in. She is out of breath and still has her merchandise]. Cook, the peace is over, the war started up again three days ago. I hadn't sold my stuff yet when I found out. Heaven be praised! They're shooting each other up in town, the Catholics and Lutherans. We've got to get out of here. Kattrin, start packing. What have you got such a long face about? What's wrong?

THE COOK. Nothing.

MOTHER COURAGE. Something's wrong, I can tell by your expression.

THE COOK. Maybe it's the war starting up again. Now I probably won't get anything hot to eat before tomorrow night.

MOTHER COURAGE. That's a lie, cook.

THE COOK. Eilif was here. He couldn't stay.

MOTHER COURAGE. He was here? Then we'll see him on the march. I'm going with our troops this time. How does he look?

THE COOK. The same.

MOTHER COURAGE. He'll never change. The war couldn't take him away from me. He's smart. Could you help me pack? [She starts packing.] Did he tell you anything? Is he in good with the general? Did he say anything about his heroic deeds?

THE COOK [gloomily]. They say he's been at one of them again.

MOTHER COURAGE. Tell me later, we've got to be going. [KATTRIN emerges.] Kattrin, peace is over. We're moving. [To the COOK.] What's the matter with you?

THE COOK. I'm going to enlist.

MOTHER COURAGE. I've got a suggestion. Why don't . . . ? Where's the chaplain?

THE COOK. Gone to town with Eilif.

MOTHER COURAGE. Then come a little way with me, Lamb. I need help.

THE COOK. That incident with Yvette . . .

MOTHER COURAGE. It hasn't lowered you in my estimation. Far from it. Where there's smoke there's fire. Coming?

THE COOK. I won't say no.

MOTHER COURAGE. The Twelfth Regiment has shoved off. Take the shaft. Here's a chunk of bread. We'll have to circle around to meet the Lutherans.

Maybe I'll see Eilif tonight. He's my favorite. It's been a short peace. And we're on the move again. [*She sings, while the* COOK *and* KATTRIN *harness themselves to the wagon.*]

From Ulm to Metz, from Metz to Pilsen
Courage is right there in the van.
The war both in and out of season
With shot and shell will feed its man.
But lead alone is not sufficient
The war needs soldiers to subsist!
Its diet elseways is deficient.
The war is hungry! So enlist!

Scene Nine

[*The great war of religion has been going on for sixteen years. Germany has lost more than half its population. Those whom the slaughter has spared have been laid low by epidemics. Once-flourishing countrysides are ravaged by famine. Wolves prowl through the charred ruins of the cities. In the fall of 1634 we find* MOTHER COURAGE *in Germany, in the Fichtelgebirge, at some distance from the road followed by the Swedish armies. Winter comes early and is exceptionally severe. Business is bad, begging is the only resort. The cook receives a letter from Utrecht and is dismissed.*

Outside a half-demolished presbytery. Gray morning in early winter. Gusts of wind. MOTHER COURAGE *and the* COOK *in shabby sheepskins by the wagon.*]

THE COOK. No light. Nobody's up yet.

MOTHER COURAGE. But it's a priest. He'll have to crawl out of bed to ring the bells. Then he'll get himself a nice bowl of hot soup.

THE COOK. Go on, you saw the village, everything's been burned to a crisp.

MOTHER COURAGE. But somebody's here, I heard a dog bark.

THE COOK. If the priest's got anything, he won't give it away.

MOTHER COURAGE. Maybe if we sing . . .

THE COOK. I've had it up to here. [*Suddenly.*] I got a letter from Utrecht. My mother's died of cholera and the tavern belongs to me. Here's the letter if you don't believe me. It's no business

of yours what my aunt says about my evil ways, but never mind, read it.

MOTHER COURAGE [*reads the letter*]. Lamb, I'm sick of roaming around, myself. I feel like a butcher's dog that pulls the meat cart but doesn't get any for himself. I've nothing left to sell and the people have no money to pay for it. In Saxony a man in rags tried to foist a cord of books on me for two eggs, and in Württemberg they'd have let their plow go for a little bag of salt. What's the good of plowing? Nothing grows but brambles. In Pomerania they say the villagers have eaten up all the babies, and that nuns have been caught at highway robbery.

THE COOK. It's the end of the world.

MOTHER COURAGE. Sometimes I have visions of myself driving through hell, selling sulphur and brimstone, or through heaven peddling refreshments to the roaming souls. If me and the children I've got left could find a place where there's no shooting, I wouldn't mind a few years of peace and quiet.

THE COOK. We could open up the tavern again. Think it over, Anna. I made up my mind last night; with or without you, I'm going back to Utrecht. In fact I'm leaving today.

MOTHER COURAGE. I'll have to talk to Kattrin. It's kind of sudden, and I don't like to make decisions in the cold with nothing in my stomach. Kattrin! [KATTRIN *climbs out of the wagon.*] Kattrin, I've got something to tell you. The cook and me are thinking of going to Utrecht. They've left him a tavern there. You'd be living in one place, you'd meet people. A lot of men would be glad to get a nice, well-behaved girl, looks aren't everything. I'm all for it. I get along fine with the cook. I've got to hand it to him: He's got a head for business. We'd eat regular meals, wouldn't that be nice? And you'd have your own bed, wouldn't you like that? It's no life on the road, year in year out. You'll go to rack and ruin. You're crawling with lice already. We've got to decide, you see, we could go north with the Swedes, they must be over there. [*She points to the left.*] I think we'll do it, Kattrin.

THE COOK. Anna, could I have a word with you alone?

MOTHER COURAGE. Get back in the wagon, Kattrin.

[KATTRIN *climbs back in.*]

THE COOK. I interrupted you because I see there's been a misunderstanding. I thought it was too obvious to need saying. But if it isn't, I'll just have to say it. You can't take her, it's out of the question. Is that plain enough for you?

[KATTRIN *sticks her head out of the wagon and listens.*]

MOTHER COURAGE. You want me to leave Kattrin?

THE COOK. Look at it this way. There's no room in the tavern. It's not one of those places with three taprooms. If the two of us put our shoulder to the wheel, we can make a living, but not three, it can't be done. Kattrin can keep the wagon.

MOTHER COURAGE. I'd been thinking she could find a husband in Utrecht.

THE COOK. Don't make me laugh! How's she going to find a husband? At her age? And dumb! And with that scar!

MOTHER COURAGE. Not so loud.

THE COOK. Shout or whisper, the truth's the truth. And that's another reason why I can't have her in the tavern. The customers won't want a sight like that staring them in the face. Can you blame them?

MOTHER COURAGE. Shut up. Not so loud, I say.

THE COOK. There's a light in the presbytery. Let's sing.

MOTHER COURAGE. How could she pull the wagon by herself? She's afraid of the war. She couldn't stand it. The dreams she must have! I hear her groaning at night. Especially after battles. What she sees in her dreams, God knows. It's pity that makes her suffer so. The other day the wagon hit a hedgehog, I found it hidden in her blanket.

THE COOK. The tavern's too small. [*He calls.*] Worthy gentleman and members of the household! We shall now sing the Song of Solomon, Julius Caesar, and other great men, whose greatness didn't help them any. Just to show you that we're God-fearing people ourselves, which makes it hard for us, especially in the winter. [*They sing.*]

You saw the wise King Solomon
You know what came of him.
To him all hidden things were plain.
He cursed the hour gave birth to him
And saw that everything was vain.
How great and wise was Solomon!
Now think about his case. Alas
A useful lesson can be won.
It's wisdom that had brought him to that
    pass!
How happy is the man with none!

Our beautiful song proves that virtues are dangerous things, better steer clear of them, enjoy life, eat a good breakfast, a bowl of hot soup, for instance. Take me, I haven't got any soup and wish I had. I'm a soldier, but what has my bravery in all those battles got me, nothing, I'm starving, I'd be better off if I'd stayed home like a yellowbelly. And I'll tell you why.

You saw the daring Caesar next
You know what he became.
They deified him in his life
But then they killed him just the same.
And as they raised the fatal knife
How loud he cried: "You too, my son!"
Now think about his case. Alas
A useful lesson can be won.
It's daring that had brought him to that
    pass!
How happy is the man with none!

[*In an undertone.*] They're not even looking out. Worthy gentleman and members of the household! Maybe you'll say, all right, if bravery won't keep body and soul together, try honesty. That may fill your belly or at least get you a drop to drink. Let's look into it.

You've heard of honest Socrates
Who never told a lie.
They weren't so grateful as you'd think
Instead they sentenced him to die
And handed him the poisoned drink.
How honest was the people's noble son!
Now think about his case. Alas
A useful lesson can be won.
His honesty had brought him to that
    pass.
How happy is the man with none!

Yes, they tell us to be charitable and to share what we have, but what if we haven't got anything? Maybe philanthropists have a rough time of it too, it stands to reason, they need a little something for themselves. Yes, charity is a rare virtue, because it doesn't pay.

St. Martin couldn't bear to see
His fellows in distress.
He saw a poor man in the snow.
"Take half my cloak!" He did, and lo!
They both of them froze none the less.
He thought his heavenly reward was won.
Now think about his case. Alas
A useful lesson can be won.
Unselfishness had brought him to that
    pass.
How happy is the man with none!

That's our situation. We're God-fearing folk, we stick together, we don't steal, we don't murder, we don't set fire to anything! You could say that we set an example which bears out the song, we sink lower and lower, we seldom see any soup, but if we were different, if we were thieves and murderers, maybe our bellies would be full. Because virtue isn't rewarded, only wickedness, the world needn't be like this, but it is.

And here you see God-fearing folk
Observing God's ten laws.
So far He hasn't taken heed.
You people sitting warm indoors
Help to relieve our bitter need!
Our virtue can be counted on.
Now think about our case. Alas
A useful lesson can be won.
The fear of God has brought us to this
    pass.
How happy is the man with none!

VOICE [from above]. Hey, down there! Come on up! We've got some good thick soup.

MOTHER COURAGE. Lamb, I couldn't get anything down. I know what you say makes sense, but is it your last word? We've always been good friends.

THE COOK. My last word. Think it over.

MOTHER COURAGE. I don't need to think it over. I won't leave her.

THE COOK. It wouldn't be wise, but there's nothing I can do. I'm not inhuman, but it's a small tavern. We'd better go in now, or there won't be anything left, we'll have been singing in the cold for nothing.

MOTHER COURAGE. I'll get Kattrin.

THE COOK. Better bring it down for her. They'll get a fright if the three of us barge in. [They go out.]

[KATTRIN climbs out of the wagon. She is carrying a bundle. She looks around to make sure the others are gone. Then she spreads out an old pair of the COOK's trousers and a skirt belonging to her mother side by side on a wheel of the wagon so they can easily be seen. She is about to leave with her bundle when MOTHER COURAGE comes out of the house.]

MOTHER COURAGE [with a dish of soup]. Kattrin! Stop! Kattrin! Where do you think you're going with that bundle? Have you taken leave of your wits? [She examines the bundle.] She's packed her things. Were you listening? I've told him it's no go with Utrecht and his lousy tavern, what would we do there? A tavern's no place for you and me. The war still has a thing or two up its sleeve for us. [She sees the trousers and skirt.] You're stupid. Suppose I'd seen that and you'd been gone? [KATTRIN tries to leave, MOTHER COURAGE holds her back.] And don't go thinking I've given him the gate on your account. It's the wagon. I won't part with the wagon, I'm used to it, it's not you, it's the wagon. We'll go in the other direction, we'll put the cook's stuff out here where he'll find it, the fool. [She climbs up and throws down a few odds and ends to join the trousers.] There. Now we're shut of him, you won't see me taking anyone else into the business. From now on it's you and me. This winter will go by like all the rest. Harness up, it looks like snow. [They harness themselves to the wagon, turn it around and pull it away. When the COOK comes out he sees his things and stands dumbfounded.]

Scene Ten

[Throughout 1635 MOTHER COURAGE and her daughter KATTRIN pull the wagon over the roads of central Germany in the wake of the increasingly bedraggled armies.

Highway.

MOTHER COURAGE and KATTRIN are

pulling the wagon. They come to a peasant's house. A voice is heard singing from within.]

THE VOICE.
The rose bush in our garden
Rejoiced our hearts in spring
It bore such lovely flowers.
We planted it last season
Before the April showers.
A garden is a blessèd thing
It bore such lovely flowers.

When winter comes a-stalking
And gales great snow storms bring
They trouble us but little.
We've lately finished caulking
The roof with moss and wattle.
A sheltering roof's a blessèd thing
When winter comes a-stalking.

[MOTHER COURAGE *and* KATTRIN *have stopped to listen. Then they move on.]*

Scene Eleven

[January 1636. The imperial troops threaten the Protestant city of Halle. The stone speaks. MOTHER COURAGE *loses her daughter and goes on alone. The end of the war is not in sight.*

The wagon, much the worse for wear, is standing beside a peasant house with an enormous thatch roof. The house is built against the side of a stony hill. Night.

A LIEUTENANT *and three* SOLDIERS *in heavy armor step out of the woods.]*

THE LIEUTENANT. I don't want any noise. If anybody yells, run him through with your pikes.

FIRST SOLDIER. But we need a guide. We'll have to knock if we want them to come out.

THE LIEUTENANT. Knocking sounds natural. It could be a cow bumping against the barn wall.

[The SOLDIERS *knock on the door. A* PEASANT WOMAN *opens. They hold their hands over her mouth. Two* SOLDIERS *go in.]*

A MAN'S VOICE *[inside].* Who's there?

[The SOLDIERS *bring out a* PEASANT *and his son.]*

THE LIEUTENANT *[points to the wagon, in which* KATTRIN *has appeared].* There's another one. *[A* SOLDIER *pulls her out.]* Anybody else live here?

THE PEASANT COUPLE. This is our son. —That's a dumb girl.—Her mother's gone into the town on business.—Buying up people's belongings, they're selling cheap because they're getting out.— They're provisioners.

THE LIEUTENANT. I'm warning you to keep quiet, one squawk and you'll get a pike over the head. All right. I need somebody who can show us the path into the city. *[Points to the* YOUNG PEASANT.] You. Come here!

THE YOUNG PEASANT. I don't know no path.

THE SECOND SOLDIER *[grinning].* He don't know no path.

THE YOUNG PEASANT. I'm not helping the Catholics.

THE LIEUTENANT *[to the* SECOND SOLDIER]. Give him a feel of your pike!

THE YOUNG PEASANT *[forced down on his knees and threatened with the pike].* You can kill me. I won't do it.

THE FIRST SOLDIER. I know what'll make him think twice. *[He goes over to the barn.]* Two cows and an ox. Get this: If you don't help us, I'll cut them down.

THE YOUNG PEASANT. Not the animals!

THE PEASANT WOMAN *[in tears].* Captain, spare our animals or we'll starve.

THE LIEUTENANT. If he insists on being stubborn, they're done for.

THE FIRST SOLDIER. I'll start with the ox.

THE YOUNG PEASANT *[to the old man].* Do I have to? *[The old woman nods.]* I'll do it.

THE PEASANT WOMAN. And thank you kindly for your forbearance, Captain, for ever and ever, amen.

[The PEASANT *stops her from giving further thanks.]*

THE FIRST SOLDIER. Didn't I tell you? With them it's the animals that come first.

[Led by the YOUNG PEASANT, *the* LIEUTENANT *and the* SOLDIERS *continue on their way.]*

THE PEASANT. I wish I knew what they're up to. Nothing good.

THE PEASANT WOMAN. Maybe they're only scouts.—What are you doing?

THE PEASANT *[putting a ladder against the roof and climbing up].* See if they're alone. [*On the roof.*] Men moving in the woods. All the way to the quarry. Armor in the clearing. And a cannon. It's more than a regiment. God have mercy on the city and everybody in it.

THE PEASANT WOMAN. See any light in the city?

THE PEASANT. No. They're all asleep. [*He climbs down.*] If they get in, they'll kill everybody.

THE PEASANT WOMAN. The sentry will see them in time.

THE PEASANT. They must have killed the sentry in the tower on the hill, or he'd have blown his horn.

THE PEASANT WOMAN. If there were more of us . . .

THE PEASANT. All by ourselves up here with a cripple . . .

THE PEASANT WOMAN. We can't do a thing. Do you think . . .

THE PEASANT. Not a thing.

THE PEASANT WOMAN. We couldn't get down there in the dark.

THE PEASANT. The whole hillside is full of them. We can't even give a signal.

THE PEASANT WOMAN. They'd kill us.

THE PEASANT. No, we can't do a thing.

THE PEASANT WOMAN [*to* KATTRIN]. Pray, poor thing, pray! We can't stop the bloodshed. If you can't talk, at least you can pray. He'll hear you if nobody else does. I'll help you. [*All kneel,* KATTRIN *behind the peasants.*] Our Father which art in heaven, hear our prayer. Don't let the town perish with everybody in it, all asleep and unsuspecting. Wake them, make them get up and climb the walls and see the enemy coming through the night with cannon and pikes, through the fields and down the hillside. [*Back to* KATTRIN.] Protect our mother and don't let the watchman sleep, wake him before it's too late. And succor our brother-in-law, he's in there with his four children, let them not perish, they're innocent and don't know a thing. [*To* KATTRIN, *who groans.*] The littlest is less than two, the oldest is seven. [*Horrified,* KATTRIN *stands up.*] Our Father, hear us, for Thou alone canst help, we'll all be killed, we're weak, we haven't any pikes or anything, we are powerless and in Thine hands, we and our animals and the whole farm, and the city too, it's in Thine hands, and the enemy is under the walls with great might.

[KATTRIN *has crept unnoticed to the wagon, taken something out of it, put it under her apron and climbed up the ladder to the roof of the barn.*]

THE PEASANT WOMAN. Think upon the children in peril, especially the babes in arms and the old people that can't help themselves and all God's creatures.

THE PEASANT. And forgive us our trespasses as we forgive them that trespass against us. Amen.

[KATTRIN, *sitting on the roof, starts beating the drum that she has taken out from under her apron.*]

THE PEASANT WOMAN. Jesus! What's she doing?

THE PEASANT. She's gone crazy.

THE PEASANT WOMAN. Get her down, quick!

[*The* PEASANT *runs toward the ladder, but* KATTRIN *pulls it up on the roof.*]

THE PEASANT WOMAN. She'll be the death of us all.

THE PEASANT. Stop that, you cripple!

THE PEASANT WOMAN. She'll have the Catholics down on us.

THE PEASANT [*looking around for stones*]. I'll throw rocks at you.

THE PEASANT WOMAN. Have you no pity? Have you no heart? We're dead if they find out it's us! They'll run us through! [KATTRIN *stares in the direction of the city, and goes on drumming.*]

THE PEASANT WOMAN [*to the* PEASANT]. I told you not to let those tramps stop here. What do they care if the soldiers drive our last animals away?

THE LIEUTENANT [*rushes in with his* SOLDIERS *and the* YOUNG PEASANT]. I'll cut you to pieces!

THE PEASANT WOMAN. We're innocent, captain. We couldn't help it. She sneaked up there. We don't know her.

THE LIEUTENANT. Where's the ladder?

THE PEASANT. Up top.

THE LIEUTENANT [*to* KATTRIN]. Throw down that drum. It's an order!

[KATTRIN *goes on drumming.*]

THE LIEUTENANT. You're all in this together! This'll be the end of you!

THE PEASANT. They've felled some pine trees in the woods over there. We could get one and knock her down . . .

THE FIRST SOLDIER [*to the* LIEUTENANT]. Request permission to make a suggestion. [*He whispers something in the*

LIEUTENANT's *ear. He nods.*] Listen. We've got a friendly proposition. Come down, we'll take you into town with us. Show us your mother and we won't touch a hair of her head.

[KATTRIN *goes on drumming.*]

THE LIEUTENANT [*pushes him roughly aside*]. She doesn't trust you. No wonder with your mug. [*He calls up.*] If I give you my word? I'm an officer, you can trust my word of honor.

[*She drums still louder.*]

THE LIEUTENANT. Nothing is sacred to her.

THE YOUNG PEASANT. It's not just her mother, lieutenant!

THE FIRST SOLDIER. We can't let this go on. They'll hear it in the city.

THE LIEUTENANT. We'll have to make some kind of noise that's louder than the drums. What could we make noise with?

THE FIRST SOLDIER. But we're not supposed to make noise.

THE LIEUTENANT. An innocent noise, stupid. A peaceable noise.

THE PEASANT. I could chop wood.

THE LIEUTENANT. That's it, chop! [*The* PEASANT *gets an ax and chops at a log.*] Harder! Harder! You're chopping for your life.

[*Listening,* KATTRIN *has been drumming more softly. Now she looks anxiously around and goes on drumming as before.*]

THE LIEUTENANT [*to the* PEASANT]. Not loud enough. [*To the* FIRST SOLDIER.] You chop too.

THE PEASANT. There's only one ax. [*Stops chopping.*]

THE LIEUTENANT. We'll have to set the house on fire. Smoke her out.

THE PEASANT. That won't do any good, captain. If the city people see fire up here, they'll know what's afoot.

[*Still drumming,* KATTRIN *has been listening again. Now she laughs.*]

THE LIEUTENANT. Look, she's laughing at us. I'll shoot her down, regardless. Get the musket!

[*Two* SOLDIERS *run out.* KATTRIN *goes on drumming.*]

THE PEASANT WOMAN. I've got it, captain. That's their wagon over there. If we start smashing it up, she'll stop. The wagon's all they've got.

THE LIEUTENANT [*to the* YOUNG

PEASANT]. Smash away. [*To* KATTRIN.] We'll smash your wagon if you don't stop.

[*The* YOUNG PEASANT *strikes a few feeble blows at the wagon.*]

THE PEASANT WOMAN. Stop it, you beast!

[KATTRIN *stares despairingly at the wagon and emits pitiful sounds. But she goes on drumming.*]

THE LIEUTENANT. Where are those stinkers with the musket?

THE FIRST SOLDIER. They haven't heard anything in the city yet, or we'd hear their guns.

THE LIEUTENANT [*to* KATTRIN]. They don't hear you. And now we're going to shoot you down. For the last time: Drop that drum!

THE YOUNG PEASANT [*suddenly throws the plank away*]. Keep on drumming! Or they'll all be killed! Keep on drumming, keep on drumming . . .

[*The* SOLDIER *throws him down and hits him with his pike.* KATTRIN *starts crying, but goes on drumming.*]

THE PEASANT WOMAN. Don't hit him in the back! My God, you're killing him.

[*The* SOLDIERS *run in with the musket.*]

THE SECOND SOLDIER. The colonel's foaming at the mouth. We'll be court-martialed.

THE LIEUTENANT. Set it up! Set it up! [*To* KATTRIN, *while the musket is being set up on its stand.*] For the last time: Stop that drumming! [KATTRIN *in tears drums as loud as she can.*] Fire!

[*The* SOLDIERS *fire.* KATTRIN *is hit. She beats the drum a few times more and then slowly collapses.*]

THE LIEUTENANT. Now we'll have some quiet.

[*But* KATTRIN's *last drumbeats are answered by the city's cannon. A confused hubbub of alarm bells and cannon is heard in the distance.*]

FIRST SOLDIER. She's done it.

Scene Twelve

[*Night, toward morning. The fifes and drums of troops marching away.*

Outside the wagon MOTHER COURAGE *sits huddled over her daughter. The* PEASANT COUPLE *are standing beside them.*]

THE PEASANT [hostile]. You'll have to be going, woman. There's only one more regiment to come. You can't go alone.

MOTHER COURAGE. Maybe I can get her to sleep. [She sings.]

Lullaby baby
What stirs in the hay?
The neighbor brats whimper
Mine are happy and gay.
They go in tatters
And you in silk down
Cut from an angel's
Best party gown.

They've nothing to munch on
And you will have pie
Just tell your mother
In case it's too dry.
Lullaby baby
What stirs in the hay?
The one lies in Poland
The other—who can say?

Now she's asleep. You shouldn't have told her about your brother-in-law's children.

THE PEASANT. Maybe it wouldn't have happened if you hadn't gone to town to swindle people.

MOTHER COURAGE. I'm glad she's sleeping now.

THE PEASANT WOMAN. She's not sleeping, you'll have to face it, she's dead.

THE PEASANT. And it's time you got started. There are wolves around here, and what's worse, marauders.

MOTHER COURAGE. Yes. [She goes to the wagon and takes out a sheet of canvas to cover the body with.]

THE PEASANT WOMAN. Haven't you anybody else? Somebody you can go to?

MOTHER COURAGE. Yes, there's one of them left. Eilif.

THE PEASANT [while MOTHER COURAGE covers the body]. Go find him. We'll attend to this one, give her a decent burial. Set your mind at rest.

MOTHER COURAGE. Here's money for your expenses. [She gives the PEASANT money.]

[The PEASANT and his son shake hands with her and carry KATTRIN away.]

THE PEASANT WOMAN [on the way out]. Hurry up!

MOTHER COURAGE [harnesses herself to the wagon]. I hope I can pull the wagon alone. I'll manage, there isn't much in it. I've got to get back in business.

[Another regiment marches by with fifes and drums in the rear.]

MOTHER COURAGE. Hey, take me with you! [She starts to pull.]

[Singing is heard in the rear:]
With all the killing and recruiting
The war will worry on a while.
In ninety years they'll still be shooting.
It's hardest on the rank-and-file.
Our food is swill, our pants all patches
The higher-ups steal half our pay
And still we dream of God-sent riches.
Tomorrow is another day!

The spring is come! Christian, revive!
The snowdrifts melt, the dead lie dead!
And if by chance you're still alive
It's time to rise and shake a leg.

Bertolt Brecht

THEATRE FOR LEARNING

Translated by Edith Anderson

When anyone spoke of modern theatre a few years ago, he mentioned the Moscow, the New York or the Berlin theatre. He may also have spoken of a particular production of Jouvet's in Paris, of Cochran's in London, or the Habima performance of *The Dybbuk*, which, in fact, belonged to Russian theatre since it was directed by Vakhtangov; but by and large, there were only three capitals so far as modern theatre was concerned.

The Russian, the American and the German theatres were very different from one another, but they were alike in being modern, i.e., in introducing technical and artistic innovations. In a certain sense they even developed stylistic similarities, probably because technique is international (not only the technique directly required for the stage, but also that which exerts an influence on it, the film, for example) and because the cities in question were great progressive cities in great industrial countries. Most recently, the Berlin theatre seemed to have taken the lead among the most advanced capitalist countries. What was common to modern theatre found there its strongest and, for the moment, most mature expression.

The last phase of the Berlin theatre, which as I said only revealed in its purest form the direction in which modern theatre was developing, was the so-called epic theatre. What was known as the Zeitstueck[1] or Piscator theatre or the didactic play all belonged to epic theatre.

EPIC THEATRE

The expression "epic theatre" seemed self-contradictory to many people, since according to the teachings of Aristotle the epic and the dramatic forms of presenting a story were considered basically different from one another. The difference between the two forms was by no means merely seen in the fact that one was performed by living people while the other made use of a book—epic works like those of Homer and the minnesingers of the Middle Ages were likewise theatrical performances, and dramas like Goethe's *Faust* or Byron's *Manfred* admittedly achieved their greatest effect as books. Aristotle's teachings themselves distinguished the dramatic from the epic form as a difference in construction, whose laws were dealt with under two different branches of aesthetics. This construction depended on the different way in which the works were presented to the public, either on the stage or through a book, but nevertheless, apart from that, "the dramatic" could also be found in epic works and "the epic" in dramatic works. The bourgeois novel in the last century considerably developed "the dramatic," which meant the strong centralization of plot and an organic interdependence of the separate parts. The dramatic is characterized by a certain passion in the tone of the exposition and a working out of the collision of forces. The epic writer, Döblin,[2] gave an excellent description when he said that the epic, in contrast to the dramatic, could practically be cut up with a scissors into single pieces, each of which could stand alone.

I do not wish to discuss here in what way the contrasts between epic and dramatic, long regarded as irreconcilable, lost their rigidity, but simply to point out that (other causes aside) technical achieve-

First published in *The [Tulane] Drama Review*, Vol. 6, no. 1, Fall 1961. Copyright © 1961 by *The [Tulane] Drama Review*. Reprinted by permission. All rights reserved.
1 Play dealing with current problems.
2 Alfred Döblin (1878–1957), German novelist and essayist, author of *Berlin Alexanderplatz*, etc.

ments enabled the stage to include narrative elements in dramatic presentations. The potentialities of projection, the film, the greater facility in changing sets through machinery, completed the equipment of the stage and did so at a moment when the most important human events could no longer be so simply portrayed as through personification of the driving forces or through subordinating the characters to invisible, metaphysical powers.

To make the events understandable, it had become necessary to play up the "bearing" of the *environment* upon the people living in it.

Of course this environment had been shown in plays before, not, however, as an independent element but only from the viewpoint of the main figure of the drama. It rose out of the hero's reaction to it. It was seen as a storm may be "seen" if you observe on the sea a ship

---

TWO OUTLINES

The following little outlines may indicate in what respect the function of the epic is distinguished from that of the dramatic theatre:

1

Dramatic Form	*Epic Form*
The stage "incarnates" an event.	It relates it.
Involves the audience in an action, uses up its activity.	Makes the audience an observer, but arouses its activity.
Helps it to feel.	Compels it to make decisions.
Communicates experiences.	Communicates insights.
The audience is projected into an event.	Is confronted with it.
Suggestion is used.	Arguments are used.
Sensations are preserved.	Impelled to the level of perceptions.
The character is a known quantity.	The character is subjected to investigation.
Man unchangeable.	Man who can change and make changes.
His drives.	His motives.
Events move in a straight line.	In "irregular" curves.
Natura non facit saltus.	Facit saltus.
The world as it is.	The world as it is becoming.

2

The audience in the dramatic theatre says:

Yes, I have felt that too.—That's how I am.—That is only natural.—That will always be so.—This person's suffering shocks me because he has no way out.—This is great art: everything in it is self-evident.—I weep with the weeping, I laugh with the laughing.

The audience in the epic theatre says:

I wouldn't have thought that.—People shouldn't do things like that.—That's extremely odd, almost unbelievable.—This has to stop.—This person's suffering shocks me, because there might be a way out for him.—This is great art: nothing in it is self-evident.—I laugh over the weeping, I weep over the laughing.

spreading its sails and the sails bellying. But in the epic theatre it was now to appear as an independent element.

The stage began to narrate. The narrator no longer vanished with the fourth wall. Not only did the background make its own comment on stage happenings through large screens which evoked other events occurring at the same time in other places, documenting or contradicting statements by characters through quotations projected onto a screen, lending tangible, concrete statistics to abstract discussions, providing facts and figures for happenings which were plastic but unclear in their meaning; the actors no longer threw themselves completely into their roles but maintained a certain distance from the character performed by them, even distinctly inviting criticism.

Nothing permitted the audience any more to lose itself through simple empathy, uncritically (and practically without any consequences) in the experiences of the characters on the stage. The presentation exposed the subject matter and the happenings to a process of de-familiarization.[3] De-familiarization was required to make things understood. When things are "self-evident," understanding is simply dispensed with. The "natural" had to be given an element of the conspicuous. Only in this way could the laws of cause and effect become plain. Characters had to behave as they did behave, and at the same time be capable of behaving otherwise.

These were great changes.

DIDACTIC THEATRE

The stage began to instruct.

Oil, inflation, war, social struggles, the family, religion, wheat, the meat-packing industry became subjects for theatrical portrayal. Choruses informed the audience about facts it did not know. In montage form, films showed events all over the world. Projections provided statistical data. As the "background" came to the fore, the actions of the characters became exposed to criticism. Wrong and right actions were exhibited. People were shown who knew what they were doing, and other people were shown who did not know. The theatre entered the province of the philosophers—at any rate, the sort of philosophers who wanted not only to explain the world but also to change it. Hence the theatre philosophized; hence it instructed. And what became of entertainment? Were the audience put back in school, treated as illiterates? Were they to take examinations and be given marks?

It is the general opinion that a very decided difference exists between learning and being entertained. The former may be useful, but only the latter is pleasant. Thus we have to defend the epic theatre against a suspicion that it must be an extremely unpleasant, a joyless, indeed a wearying business.

Well, we can only say that the contrast between learning and being entertained does not necessarily exist in nature; it has not always existed and it need not always exist.

Undoubtedly, the kind of learning we experienced in school, in training for a profession, etc., is a laborious business. But consider under what circumstances and for what purpose it is done. It is, in fact, a purchase. Knowledge is simply a commodity. It is acquired for the purpose of being resold. All those who have grown too old for school have to pursue knowledge on the Q.T., so to speak, because anybody who admits he still has to study depreciates himself as one who knows too little. Apart from that, the utility of learning is very much limited by factors over which the student has no control. There is unemployment, against which no knowledge protects. There is the division of labor, which makes comprehensive knowledge unnecessary and impossible. Often, those who study do it only when they see no other possibility of getting ahead. There is not much knowledge that procures power, but much knowledge is only procured through power.

Learning means something very different to people in different strata of society. There are people who cannot conceive of any improvement in conditions; conditions seem good enough to them. Whatever may happen to petroleum, they make a profit out of it. And they

---

[3] *Entfremdung*—alienation.

feel, after all, that they are getting rather old. They can scarcely expect many more years of life. So why continue to learn? They have already spoken their "Ugh!" [4] But there are also people who have not yet "had their turn," who are discontented with the way things are, who have an immense practical interest in learning, who want orientation badly, who know they are lost without learning—these are the best and most ambitious learners. Such differences also exist among nations and peoples. Thus the lust for learning is dependent on various things; in short, there is thrilling learning, joyous and militant learning.

If learning could not be delightful, then the theatre, by its very nature, would not be in a position to instruct.

Theatre remains theatre, even when it is didactic theatre; and if it is good theatre it will entertain.

THEATRE AND SCIENCE

"But what has science to do with art? We know very well that science can be diverting, but not everything that diverts belongs in the theatre."

I have often been told when I pointed out the inestimable services that modern science, properly utilized, could render to art (especially to the theatre), that art and science were two admirable but completely different fields of human activity. This is a dreadful platitude, of course, and the best thing to do is admit at once that it is quite right, like most platitudes. Art and science operate in very different ways—agreed. Still, I must admit—bad as this may sound—that I cannot manage as an artist without making use of certain sciences. This may make many people seriously doubt my artistic ability. They are accustomed to regarding poets as unique, almost unnatural beings who unerringly, almost like gods, perceive things that others can only perceive through the greatest efforts and hard work. Naturally, it is unpleasant to have to admit not being one of those so endowed. But it must be admitted. It must also be denied that this application to science has any-

thing to do with some pardonable avocation indulged in the evening after work is done. Everyone knows that Goethe also went in for natural science, Schiller for history, presumably—this is the charitable assumption—as a sort of hobby. I would not simply accuse these two of having needed the science for their poetic labors, nor would I use them to excuse myself, but I must say I need the sciences. And I must even admit that I regard suspiciously all sorts of people who I know do not keep abreast of science, who, in other words, sing as the birds sing, or as they imagine the birds sing. This does not mean that I would reject a nice poem about the taste of a flounder or the pleasure of a boating party just because the author had not studied gastronomy or navigation. But I think that unless every resource is employed towards understanding the great, complicated events in the world of man, they cannot be seen adequately for what they are.

Let us assume that we want to portray great passions or events which influence the fates of peoples. Such a passion today might be the drive for power. Supposing that a poet "felt" this drive and wanted to show someone striving for power—how could he absorb into his own experience the extremely complicated mechanism within which the struggle for power today takes place? If his hero is a political man, what are the workings of politics? If he is a business man, what are the workings of business? And then there are poets who are much less passionately interested in any individual's drive for power than in business affairs and politics as such! How are they to acquire the necessary knowledge? They will scarcely find out enough by going around and keeping their eyes open, although that is at least better than rolling their eyes in a fine frenzy. The establishment of a newspaper like the *Völkische Beobachter* or a business like Standard Oil is a rather complicated matter, and these things are not simply absorbed through the pores. Psychology is an important field for the dramatist. It is supposed that while an ordinary person may not be in a position to dis-

---

[4] Reference to popular German literature about Red Indians, by the author Karl May, in which, after a chieftain had given his opinion at a pow-wow he would conclude, "I have spoken. Ugh!"

cover, without special instruction, what makes a man commit murder, certainly a writer ought to have the "inner resources" to be able to give a picture of a murderer's mental state. The assumption is that you only need look into yourself in such a case; after all, there is such a thing as imagination. . . . For a number of reasons I can no longer abandon myself to this amiable hope of managing so comfortably. I cannot find in myself alone all the motives which, as we learn from newspapers and scientific reports, are discovered in human beings. No more than any judge passing sentence am I able to imagine adequately, unaided, the mental state of a murderer. Modern psychology, from psychoanalysis to behaviorism, provides me with insights which help me to form a quite different judgment of the case, especially when I take into consideration the findings of sociology, and do not ignore economics or history. You may say: This is getting complicated. I must answer, it is complicated. Perhaps I can talk you into agreeing with me that a lot of literature is extremely primitive; yet you will ask in grave concern: Wouldn't such an evening in the theatre be a pretty alarming business? The answer to that is: No.

Whatever knowledge may be contained in a poetic work, it must be completely converted into poetry. In its transmuted form, it gives the same type of satisfaction as any poetic work. And although it does not provide that satisfaction found in science as such, a certain inclination to penetrate more deeply into the nature of things, a desire to make the world controllable, are necessary to ensure enjoyment of poetic works generated by this era of great discoveries and inventions.

IS THE EPIC THEATRE A SORT OF "MORAL INSTITUTION"?

According to Friedrich Schiller the theatre should be a moral institution. When Schiller posed this demand it scarcely occurred to him that by moralizing from the stage he might drive the audience out of the theatre. In his day the audience had no objection to moralizing. Only later on did Friedrich Nietzsche abuse him as the moral trumpeter of Säckingen.[5] To Nietzsche a concern with morality seemed a dismal affair; to Schiller it seemed completely gratifying. He knew of nothing more entertaining and satisfying than to propagate ideals. The bourgeoisie was just establishing the concept of the nation. To furnish your house, show off your new hat, present your bills for payment is highly gratifying. But to speak of the decay of your house, to have to sell your old hat and pay the bills yourself is a truly dismal affair, and that was how Nietzsche saw it a century later. It was no use talking to him about morality or, in consequence, about the other Friedrich. Many people also attacked the epic theatre, claiming it was too moralistic. Yet moral utterances were secondary in the epic theatre. Its intention was less to moralize than to study. And it did study; but then came the rub: the moral of the story. Naturally, we cannot claim that we began making studies just because studying was so much fun and not for any concrete reason, or that the results of our studies then took us completely by surprise. Undoubtedly there were painful discrepancies in the world around us, conditions that were hard to bear, conditions of a kind not only hard to bear for moral reasons. Hunger, cold and hardship are not only burdensome for moral reasons. And the purpose of our investigation was not merely to arouse moral misgivings about certain conditions (although such misgivings might easily be felt, if not by every member of the audience; such misgivings, for example, were seldom felt by those who profited by the conditions in question). The purpose of our investigation was to make visible the means by which those onerous conditions could be done away with. We were not speaking on behalf of morality but on behalf of the wronged. These are really two different things, for moral allusions are often used in telling the wronged that they must put up with their situation. For such moral-

[5] Nietzsche's quip referred to a banal verse tale by Viktor Scheffel, *Der Trompeter von Sâckingen,* a standard favorite in Germany's "plush sofa kultur"—a parallel of Victorianism—in the second half of the nineteenth century.

ists, people exist for morality, not morality for people.

Nevertheless it can be deduced from these remarks to what extent and in what sense the epic theatre is a moral institution.

CAN EPIC THEATRE BE PERFORMED ANYWHERE?

From the standpoint of style, the epic theatre is nothing especially new. In its character of show, of demonstration, and its emphasis on the artistic, it is related to the ancient Asian theatre. The medieval mystery play, and also the classical Spanish and Jesuit theatres, showed an instructive tendency.

Those theatre forms corresponded to certain tendencies of their time and disappeared with them. The modern epic theatre is also linked with definite ten-dencies. It can by no means be performed anywhere. Few of the great nations today are inclined to discuss their problems in the theatre. London, Paris, Tokyo and Rome maintain their theatres for quite different purposes. Only in a few places, and not for long, have circumstances been favorable to an epic, instructive theatre. In Berlin, fascism put a violent end to the development of such a theatre.[6]

Besides a certain technical standard, it presupposes a powerful social movement which has an interest in the free discussion of vital problems, the better to solve them, and can defend this interest against all opposing tendencies.

The epic theatre is the broadest and most far-reaching experiment in great modern theatre, and it has to overcome all the enormous difficulties that all vital forces in the area of politics, philosophy, science and art have to overcome.

---

[6] After the defeat of the Nazis in 1945, the German administrators of the then Soviet-occupied zone—now the German Democratic Republic—invited Brecht to establish his own theatre in East Berlin. This theatre, the "Berliner Ensemble," is recognized today all over the world as a classical type of epic theatre.

Eugène
Ionesco
1912 –

Eugène Ionesco, French playwright and controversialist, did not begin writing plays until he was thirty-six. A failure at first, he finally achieved success in the late 1950's as an avant-garde dramatist and exemplar of the "theatre of the absurd." Ionesco was born in Romania; his family moved to France while he was a child, but later returned to Romania where Ionesco became a teacher of French. During the late 1930's, the rise of native Fascism in Romania led Ionesco to return to France, where he worked obscurely for a publishing firm and assumed French citizenship. A turning point in his career came in 1948, when Ionesco, studying a primer of conversational English, was struck by the absurdity of the sentences he was memorizing and proceeded to write his first play, *The Bald Soprano*. When produced in 1950 the play was quietly ignored. But Ionesco continued to mine his original vein of surrealist fantasy in plays such as *The Lesson* (1950), *Jack* (1950), *The Chairs* (1951), *Amédée* (1953), *The New Tenant* (1955), *The Killer* (1957), *Rhinoceros* (1958), and *Exit the King* (1962). Based on ingenious theatrical metaphors, Ionesco's "anti-plays" break completely with naturalistic theatre and present tragi-farcical parodies of what, to Ionesco, is the human condition: the general absurdity of life, the sterility of bourgeois culture, the terrifying emptiness of technological society, the animal stupidity of conformist man, and the failure of human feeling, thought, and language. In Ionesco we find the "sadness and weariness of a clown" who cloaks serious purpose beneath a mask of comedy. And his unique serio-comic imagination is most effectively projected in the short forms of his early plays with their startling images, varied rhythms, surreal dialogue, and wild farce moving over undercurrents of violence and sex. In addition, Ionesco possesses acute debating skill and aggressive esthetic principles which he argued at length in his *Notes and Counternotes* (1962). Opposed to Brecht and all ideological theatre, he nevertheless shares with Brecht an antibourgeois direction, but one that is antipolitical and militantly individualistic.

JACK OR THE SUBMISSION

A naturalistic comedy

EUGÈNE IONESCO

THE CHARACTERS

JACK	GRANDMOTHER JACK
JACQUELINE, *his sister*	ROBERTA I ⎫ *These two roles must be*
FATHER JACK	ROBERTA II ⎭ *played by the same actress*
MOTHER JACK	FATHER ROBERT
GRANDFATHER JACK	MOTHER ROBERT

[SCENE: *Somber decor, in gray mono-chrome. A messy room. There is a narrow door, not very high, upstage right. Up-stage center, a window with soiled cur-tains, through which comes a pale, color-less light. On the wall hangs a picture that doesn't represent anything; a dirty, old, worn armchair is at stage center with a bedside table; and there are some in-definite objects, strange yet banal, such as old slippers; in a corner perhaps there is a collapsed sofa; and there are some rickety chairs.*

When the curtain rises we see Jack sprawled on the equally sprawled arm-chair, wearing a cap, and clothes that are too small for him; he wears a sullen, ill-natured expression. Around him his par-ents are standing, or perhaps they are seated too. Their clothes are shabby.

The somber decor of the beginning becomes transformed by the lighting dur-ing the seduction scene, when it grows greenish, aquatic, towards the end of that scene; then it darkens again at the end of the play.

All of the characters, except Jack, could wear masks.]

MOTHER JACK [*weeping*]. My son, my child, after all that we have done for you. After all our sacrifices! Never would I

have believed you capable of this. You were my greatest hope ... You still are, for I cannot believe, no I cannot believe, by Jove, that you will go on being so stubborn! Then, you don't love your parents any more, you don't love your clothes, your sister, your grandparents!!! But remember, my son, remember that I gave you suck at the bottle, I let your diapers dry on you, like your sister too ... [*To* JACQUELINE.] Isn't that right, my daughter?

JACQUELINE. Yes, mom, that's true. Oh, after so many sacrifices, and so much finagling!

MOTHER JACK. You see ... you see? It was I, my son, who gave you your first spankings, not your father, standing here, who could have done it better than I, for he is stronger, no, it was I, for I loved you too much. And it was I, too, who sent you from table without dessert, who kissed you, cared for you, housebroke you, taught you to progress, to transgress, to roll your r's, who left goodies for you in your socks. I taught you to climb stairs, when there were any, to rub your knees with nettles, when you wanted to be stung. I have been more than a mother to you, I've been a true sweetheart, a husband, a sailor, a buddy, a goose. I've never been deterred by any obstacle, any

SOURCE: From *Four Plays* by Eugène Ionesco. Copyright © 1958 by Grove Press, Inc. Reprinted by permission of Grove Press, Inc.

barricade, from satisfying all your childish whims. Oh, ungrateful son, you do not even remember how I held you on my knees and pulled out your cute little baby teeth, and tore off your toe nails so as to make you bawl like an adorable little calf.

JACQUELINE. Oh! Calves are so sweet! Moo! Moo! Moo!

MOTHER JACK. And to think you won't say a word, stubborn boy! You refuse to listen to a word I say.

JACQUELINE. He's plugged up his ears, he's wearing a disgusting look.

MOTHER JACK. I am a wretched mother. I've brought a mononster into the world; a mononster, that's what you are! Here is your grandmother, who wants to speak to you. She's tottering. She is octogeneric. Perhaps you'll be swayed by her, by her age, her past, her future.

GRANDMOTHER JACK [octogeneric voice]. Listen, listen well to me, I've had experience, there's a lot of it behind me. I, too, like you, had a great-uncle who had three addresses: he gave out the address and telephone number of two of them but never that of the third where he sometimes hid out, for he was in the secret service. [Jack obstinately remains silent.] No, I've not been able to convince him. Oh! poor us!

JACQUELINE. And here is your grandfather who would like to speak to you. Alas, he cannot. He is much too old. He is centagenet!

MOTHER JACK [weeping]. Like the Plantagenets!

FATHER JACK. He's deaf and dumb. He is tottering.

JACQUELINE. He can only toot.

GRANDFATHER JACK [in the voice of a centagenet]. Hum! Hum! Heu! Heu! Hum! [Hoarse but loud.]

A char-ar-ming tipster
Sang plain-ain-tive-ly-ie . . .
I'm only eigh-eigh-tee-een
And mor-ore's the pi-i-ty-y.

[Jack remains obstinately silent.]

FATHER JACK. It's all useless, he won't budge.

JACQUELINE. My dear brother . . . you're a naughty boyble. In spite of all the immense love I have for you, which swells my heart to the breaking point, I detest you, I exceecrate you. You're making our mamma weep, you're unstringing our father with his big ugly police inspector's mustaches, and his sweet big hairy foot full of horns. As for your grandparents, look at what you've done to them. You've not been well brought up. I'm going to punish you. Never again will I bring over my little playmates so that you can watch them make peepee. I thought you had better manners than that. Comes on, don't make our mamma weep, don't make our papa angry. Don't make grandmother and grandfather blush with shame.

FATHER JACK. You are no son of mine. I disown you. You're not worthy of my ancestors. You resemble your mother and the idiots and imbeciles in her family. This doesn't matter to her for she's only a woman, and what a woman! In short, I needn't elegize her here. I have only this to say to you: impeccably brought up, like an aristocrant, in a family of veritable leeches, of authentic torpedoes, with all the regard due to your rank, to your sex, to the talent that you possess, to the hot blood that can express—if you only wanted it to, all this that your blood itself could but suggest with imperfect words—you, in spite of all this, you show yourself unworthy, at one and the same time of your ancestors, of my ancestors, who disown you for the same reason that I do, and of your descendants who certainly will never see the light of day for they'll prefer to let themselves be killed before they ever come into being. Murderer! Patricide! You have nothing more to envy me for. When I think that I had the unfortunate idea of wishing for a son and not a red poppy! [To MOTHER JACK.] This is all your fault!

MOTHER JACK. Alas! My husband! I believed I was doing the right thing! I'm completely half desperate.

JACQUELINE. Ploor mamma!

FATHER JACK. This boy or this toy that you see there, who has come into the world in order to be our shame, this son or this hun, is another one of your stupid female tricks.

MOTHER JACK. Alack and alas! [To her son.] You see, because of you I suffer all this from your father who no longer minces his feelings and now abuses me.

JACQUELINE [to her brother]. Go on, tell it to the turkies.

FATHER JACK. Useless to linger longer crying over a destiny irrevocably spilt. I'll remain here no more. I want to remain worthy of my bearfors. The whole tradition, all of it, remains with me. I'm blowing this joint. Frew it!

MOTHER JACK. Oh! Oh! Oh! don't go away. [To her son.] You see, because of you, your father is leaving us.

JACQUELINE [sighing]. Kangareen!

GRANDFATHER JACK [singing]. A ... charm ... ing ... tip ... ster ... sang ... mur-mur ... ing.

GRANDMOTHER JACK [to the old man]. Be quiet. Be quiet or I'll smack you.

[She hits him on the head with her fist, and smashes in his cap.]

FATHER JACK. Once and for all, I'm leaving this room to its own destiny. There's nothing else to do, anyway. I'm going to my bedroom next door. I'll pack my bags and you'll never see me again except at mealtimes and sometimes during the day and in the night to get a bite to eat. [To JACK.] And you'll pay me back for your nastiness. And to think it was all to make Jupiter jubilate!

JACQUELINE. Oh, Father, this is the obnubilation of puberty.

FATHER JACK. That's enough! Useless. [He goes to the door.] Farewell, Son of a pig in a poke, farewell, Wife, farewell, Brother, farewell, Sister of your brother.

[He exits with a violently resolute step.]

JACQUELINE [bitterly]. Of a pig in a poke! [To her brother.] How can you tolerate that? He's insulting her and insulting himself. And vice versa.

MOTHER JACK [to her son]. You see, you see, you are disowned, wretch. He'll will you the whole inheritance, but he can't, thank heaven!

JACQUELINE [to her brother]. It's the first time, if not the last, that he has made such a scene with mamma, and I have no idea how we're going to get out of it.

MOTHER JACK. Son! Son! Listen to me. I beg you, do not reply to my brave mother's heart, but speak to me, without reflecting on what you say. It is the best way to think correctly, as an intellectual and as a good son. [She waits in vain for a reply; JACK obstinately remains silent.]

But you are not a good son. Come, Jacqueline, you alone have sense enough to come in out of the rain.

JACQUELINE. Oh! Mother, all roads lead to Rome.

MOTHER JACK. Let's leave your brother to his slow consumption.

JACQUELINE. Or rather to his consumbrition!

MOTHER JACK [she starts to go, weeping, pulling her daughter by the hand, who goes unwillingly, turning her head back towards her brother. At the door MOTHER JACK pronounces this henceforth historic sentence]. We'll hear about you in the newspapers, actograph!

JACQUELINE. Pawnbroker!

[They exit together, followed by the GRANDFATHER and the GRANDMOTHER, but they go no farther than the embrasure of the door where they remain to spy, visible to the audience.]

GRANDMOTHER JACK. Keep a watch ... on his telephone, that's all I can tell you.

GRANDFATHER JACK [singing waveringly].

Fi-i-il-thy but honest ...
The tip-ip-ster sang ... [He exits.]

JACK [alone, he remains silent a long moment, absorbed in his thoughts, then gravely]. Let's pretend that I've said nothing, and anyway, what do they want of me?

[Silence. At the end of a long moment, JACQUELINE re-enters. She goes towards her brother with an air of profound conviction; she goes up to him, stares him straight in the eye, and says.]

JACQUELINE. Listen to me, my dear brother, dear colleague, and dear compatriot, I am going to speak to you as between the two candid eyes of brother and sister. I come to you one last time, which will certainly not be the last, but what'll you have, so much the worse. You do not understand that I have been sent to you, like a letter through the mails, stamped, stamped, by my aerial voices, bloody bad.

[JACK remains somber.]

JACK. Alas, blood will tell!

JACQUELINE [she's got it]. Ah, at last! There you've blurted out the key word!

JACK [desperate, with a most woebe-gone expression]. Show me that you are a sister worthy of a brother such as I.

JACQUELINE. Far be it from me to be guilty of such a fault. I'm going to teach you one thing. I'm not an abracante, he's not an abracante, she is not an abra-cante, nor are you an abracante.

JACK. So?

JACQUELINE. You don't understand me because you don't follow me. It's very simple.

JACK. That's what you think! For sis-ters like you hours don't count, but what a waste of time!

JACQUELINE. That's not the point. None of that has anything to do with me. But History has her eyes on us.

JACK. Oh words, what crimes are com-mitted in your name!

JACQUELINE. I'm going to tell you the whole thing in twenty-seven words. Here it is, and try to remember it: You are chronometrable.

JACK. And the rest?

JACQUELINE. That's all. The twenty-seven words are contained in those three words, according to their gender.

JACK. Chro-no-me-trable! [Frightened, an anguished cry.] But, it's not possible! It's not possible!

[He gets up, walks feverishly from one end of the stage to the other.]

JACQUELINE. Oh yes, it is. You've got to figure it out.

JACK. Chronometrable! Chronome-trable! Me? [He calms down little by little, sits down, reflects at length, sprawled out in the armchair.] This is not possible and if it is possible, it's frightful. But, then, I must. Cruel inde-cision! There's no legal protection. Hide-ous, frightful! All law becomes self-de-stroying when it's not defended.

[JACQUELINE, smiling with a trium-phant air, leaves him to his agita-tion; she exits on tiptoe.]

MOTHER JACK [at the door, in a low voice]. Did the system work?

JACQUELINE [a finger to her lips]. Shh! My dear mamma! We must wait, wait for the result of the operation.

[They exit. JACK is agitated, he is about to make a decision.]

JACK. Let's abide by the circumstances, the conclusions oblige me. It's tough, but it's the game of the rule. It applies in such cases. [Mute debate with his con-science. Occasionally, from time to time, he mutters: "Chro-nome-trable, chr-no-me-trable?" Then, finally, worn out, in a loud voice.] Oh well, yes, yes, na, I adore hashed brown potatoes!

[MOTHER JACK and JACQUELINE, who have been spying on him and only waiting for this, enter quickly, ex-ultantly, followed by the GRAND-PARENTS.]

MOTHER JACK. Oh, my son, you are truly my son!

JACQUELINE [to her mother]. I told you that my idea would get him on his feet again.

GRANDMOTHER JACK. I certainly told you that to make carrots boil you have to . . .

MOTHER JACK [to her daughter]. Go on, little vixen. [She embraces her son, who lets her do so without showing any sign of pleasure.] My boy! It's really true, you really love hashed brown potatoes? You make me so happy.

JACK [without conviction]. Yes, I like them, I adore them!

MOTHER JACK. I'm happy, I'm proud of you! Say it again, my little Jack, say it again, let me hear it.

JACK [like an automaton]. I adore hashed brown potatoes! I adore hashed brown potatoes! I adore hashed brown potatoes!

JACQUELINE [to her mother]. Oh, you're the clever one! Don't abuse your child if you'd be a truly motherly mother. Oh, that's making Grandfather sing.

GRANDFATHER JACK [singing].

A char-mar-mink tip-ip-ster
was singing a song
melan-cho-li-ly and so-o-omber
full of joy and li-i-ight . . .
Let . . . the . . . little . . . children
amu-mu-se themselves without gi-i-iggling
They'll . . . have plenty of time
to ru . . . ru . . . run
after the girls-girls-irls!

MOTHER JACK [towards the door]. Gaston, come here! Your son, your son adores hashed brown potatoes!

JACQUELINE [same]. Come, Papa, he's just said that he adores hashed brown potatoes!

FATHER JACK [entering, severe]. Is this really true?

MOTHER JACK [to her son]. Tell your father, my little Jackie, what you just told your sister, and what you told your darling mother all overcome with motherly feelings that shake her with delight.

JACK. I love hashed brown potatoes!

JACQUELINE. You adore them!

FATHER JACK. What?

MOTHER JACK. Speak, my darling.

JACK. Hashed brown potatoes. I adore hashed brown potatoes.

FATHER JACK [aside]. Can it be that all is not lost? That would be too wonderful, but not a moment too soon. [To his wife and daughter.] The whole shebang?

JACQUELINE. Oh, yes, Papa, didn't you hear?

MOTHER JACK. Have confidence in your son . . . your son of sons.

GRANDMOTHER JACK. The son of my son is my son . . . and my son is your son. There is no other son.

FATHER JACK [to his son]. My son, solemnly, come to my arms. [He does not embrace him.] That's enough. I take back my renunciation. I am happy that you adore hashed brown potatoes. I reintegrate you with your ancestors. With tradition. With hashing. With everything. [To JACQUELINE.] But he must still believe in regional aspirations.

GRANDMOTHER JACK. That's important too!

JACQUELINE. That will come, Papa, have patience, don't worry, Papa!

GRANDFATHER JACK. The char-ar-arming tip-ip-ster!

GRANDMOTHER JACK [hitting the old man on the head]. Crap!!!

FATHER JACK. I pardon you then. I overlook, and involuntarily moreover, all your youthful faults as well as mine, and naturally I am going to let you in on the profits of our familial and national endeavors.

MOTHER JACK. How good you are.

JACQUELINE. Oh, indigent Father!

FATHER JACK. Listen. I'm thinking it over. [To his son.] You will percuss. So keep at it.

JACK [in a smothered voice]. I adore potatoes!

JACQUELINE. Let's not waste time.

MOTHER JACK [to her husband]. Gaston, if that's the case, if things are that way, we could marry him off. We were only waiting for him to make honorable amends, and two would have been better than one, and he has done it. Jack, all is under control, the plan foreseen at the beginning is already realized, the engagement is completely prepared, your fiancée is here. And her parents, too. Jack, you may remain seated. Your resigned air satisfies me. But be polished to your fingernails . . .

JACK. Ouf! Yes.

FATHER JACK [striking his hands together]. Let the fiancée enter then!

JACK. Oh! That's the agreed-on signal!

[Enter ROBERTA, the fiancée, FATHER ROBERT, and MOTHER ROBERT. FATHER ROBERT enters first, big, fat, majestic, then MOTHER ROBERT, a round ball, very heavy; then the parents separate in order to let ROBERTA herself enter, advancing between her father and mother. She is wearing a wedding gown; her white veil conceals her face; her entrance must make a sensation. MOTHER JACK joyously crosses her hands on her breast; in ecstasy, she lifts her hands to heaven, then goes up to ROBERTA, looks at her up close, touches her, at first timidly, then paws her vigorously and finally sniffs her. ROBERTA's parents encourage her with friendly and eager gestures; the GRANDMOTHER also must smell the fiancée, and the GRANDFATHER should too, while singing "Too-oo old! . . . Char-ar-mi-ing tip-ip-ipster." FATHER JACK does the same. JACQUELINE, at the entrance of ROBERTA, gaily claps her hands and shouts out.]

JACQUELINE. The future is ours!

[Then, approaching ROBERTA, she lifts up her dress, screams in her ear, and, finally, smells her. The behavior of FATHER JACK is more dignified and restrained; he continues to exchange naughty glances and gestures with FATHER ROBERT. As for MOTHER ROBERT, at the end of the scene she finds herself immobile downstage to the left, a large smug smile on her face. The old GRANDFATHER makes ribald, indecent gestures, wanting to do more but prevented by the old GRANDMOTHER, who says.]

GRANDMOTHER JACK. Come . . . on . . .
no . . . but . . . come . . . on . . . you're
making me . . . jea . . . lous!

[*While the others are sniffing* RO-
BERTA, JACK *alone seems to be un-
impressed; he remains seated, im-
passive; he snaps out a single word
of scorn, aside.*]

JACK. Hill billy!

[MOTHER ROBERT, *during this appreciation, appears to be slightly in-
trigued, but this is only a very fugi-
tive restlessness, and she goes back
to smiling again. She makes a sign
to* ROBERTA *that she should approach* JACK, *but* ROBERTA *is timid,
and advances downstage only when
led, almost dragged, by* FATHER
ROBERT *and pushed by* MOTHER
JACK *and* JACQUELINE. JACK *makes
no movement, his face remains
blank.*]

FATHER JACK [*noticing that something
isn't right, he remains in the background
for a moment, hands on hips, murmuring*]. At least I won't be caught with my
pants down.

[*Near to* JACK, FATHER ROBERT *cata-
logs his daughter, assisted by* JAC-
QUELINE, MOTHER JACK, MOTHER
ROBERT, *and the* GRANDPARENTS.]

FATHER ROBERT. She's got feet. They're
truffled.

[JACQUELINE *lifts up the fiancée's
dress to convince* JACK.]

JACK [*lightly raising his shoulder*].
That's natural!

JACQUELINE. And they're for walking.

MOTHER JACK. For walking!

GRANDMOTHER JACK. Why yes, the
better to twickle you.

MOTHER ROBERT [*to her daughter*].
Let's see, prove it.

[ROBERTA *walks with her feet.*]

FATHER ROBERT. And she's got a hand!

MOTHER ROBERT. Show it.

[ROBERTA *shows a hand to* JACK, *almost sticking her fingers into his
eyes.*]

GRANDMOTHER JACK [*nobody listens
to her*]. Do you want a piece of advice?

JACQUELINE. For scouring pots and
pans . . .

JACK. Sure enough! Sure enough! But
I suspected as much.

FATHER ROBERT. And toes.

JACQUELINE. To stub! . . .

MOTHER JACK. But yes, my child!

FATHER ROBERT. And she's got arm-
pits!

JACQUELINE. For turnspits.

GRANDMOTHER JACK [*nobody listens to
her*]. Do you want a piece of advice?

MOTHER ROBERT. And what calves!
true calves!

GRANDMOTHER JACK. Ah yes, like in
my time!

JACK [*uninterested*]. Melanchton did
better!

GRANDFATHER JACK [*singing*]. A char
. . . ar . . . ming tip-ip . . . ip . . . ster . . .

GRANDMOTHER JACK [*to the old man*].
Come on, make love to me, you're my
husband!

FATHER JACK. Listen carefully to me,
my son. I hope that you have understood.

JACK [*resigned, acquiescent*]. Oh yes,
of course . . . I was forgetting . . .

FATHER ROBERT. She's got hips . . .

MOTHER JACK. All the better to eat
you, my child!

FATHER ROBERT. And then she's got
green pimples on her beige skin, red
breasts on a mauve background, an illuminated navel, a tongue the color of
tomato sauce, pan-browned square shoulders, and all the meat needed to merit the
highest commendation. What more do
you need?

GRANDFATHER JACK [*singing*]. A char
. . . ar . . . ming tip . . . ip . . . ster!

JACQUELINE [*shaking her head, lifting
her arms, and letting them fall*]. Ah, what
a brother I'm stuck with!

MOTHER JACK. He's always been difficult. I had a hard time bringing him up.
All he liked was hahaha.

MOTHER ROBERT. But my dear, that's
incomprehensible, it's incredible! I'd
never have thought that! If I'd known
this in time, I'd have taken precau-
tions . . .

FATHER ROBERT [*proud, a little
wounded*]. She's our only daughter.

GRANDFATHER JACK [*singing*]. A char
. . . ar . . . ming . . . tip . . . ip . . . ster!

MOTHER JACK. This distresses me!

FATHER JACK. Jack, this is my last
warning!

GRANDMOTHER JACK. Do you want a
piece of advice?

JACK. Good. Then we agree! That'll go with the potatoes.

[*General relief, effervescence, congratulations.*]

JACQUELINE. His honorable sentiments always end up by getting the upper hand. [*She smiles at* JACK.]

FATHER JACK. Now it's my turn to ask a simple question. Don't take it badly.

FATHER ROBERT. Oh no, it's different. Go ahead.

FATHER JACK. One single uncertainty: are there trunks?

GRANDFATHER JACK [*ribaldly*]. Hi . . . hii . . .

MOTHER ROBERT. Ah that . . .

MOTHER JACK. Perhaps that's asking too much.

FATHER ROBERT. I believe . . . heu . . . yes . . . they must be there . . . but I wouldn't know how to tell you . . .

FATHER JACK. And where then?

JACQUELINE. But Papa, don't you see, in the trunks, Papa, really!

FATHER JACK. Perfect. That's perfect. Completely satisfied. Agreed.

GRANDMOTHER JACK. Would you like a piece of advice?

MOTHER ROBERT. Ah . . . happily!

FATHER ROBERT. I knew that everything would be all right!

GRANDFATHER JACK [*singing*].

A . . . char . . . arming . . . tipster . . .
In the streets of Paris . . . [*He waltzes.*]

MOTHER JACK. In short, you'll have nothing to fear, the fit's in the fire.

FATHER JACK [*to his son*]. Good! It's a bargain. Your heart has chosen in spite of yourself!

MOTHER JACK. The word "heart" always makes me weep.

MOTHER ROBERT. Me too, it melts me.

FATHER ROBERT. It melts me in one eye, it makes me cry in the other two.

FATHER JACK. That's the truth!

JACQUELINE. Oh, there's no need to be astonished. All parents feel that way. It's a sort of sensitivity, in the true sense of the word.

FATHER JACK. That's our business!

JACQUELINE. Don't be angry, Papa. I said it without thinking. But knowingly.

GRANDMOTHER JACK. Do you want a piece of advice?

FATHER JACK. Oh, my daughter always knows how to arrange things! Besides, that's her specialty.

MOTHER ROBERT. What is her specialty?

MOTHER JACK. She doesn't have one, dear!

FATHER ROBERT. That's very natural.

FATHER JACK. Oh, it's not so natural as all that. But she's passing through a phase. [*Changing his tone.*] Finally, in short. Let's place the fiancés face to face. And let's see the face of the young bride. [*To* FATHER *and* MOTHER ROBERT.] This is only a simple formality.

FATHER ROBERT. Of course, it's normal, go ahead.

MOTHER ROBERT. We were going to suggest it to you.

GRANDMOTHER JACK [*annoyed*]. Do you want a piece of advice! . . . Well, crap!

JACQUELINE. Come on, then, the face of the bride!

[FATHER ROBERT *lifts up the white veil which hides* ROBERTA'S *face. She is revealed all smiles and with two noses; murmurs of admiration, except from* JACK.]

JACQUELINE. Oh! Ravishing!

MOTHER ROBERT. What do you have to say?

FATHER JACK. Ah, if I were twenty years younger!

GRANDFATHER JACK. And me . . . ah . . . euh . . . and me!

FATHER ROBERT. Ha, ah, twenty years to the day! . . . To the window fastener!

FATHER JACK. As much as possible!

MOTHER JACK. You must be proud of her. You really are lucky! My daughter has only one!

JACQUELINE. Don't get upset, Mamma.

FATHER JACK [*to* JACQUELINE]. It's your mother's fault.

MOTHER JACK. Oh, Gaston, you're always nagging.

JACQUELINE. This is not the time, Papa, on such a red-letter day!

FATHER ROBERT [*to* JACK]. You've got nothing to say? Kiss her!

GRANDMOTHER JACK. Ah, my little children . . . Would you like a piece of advice? . . . oh . . . crap!

MOTHER ROBERT. This is going to be charming! Oh, my children!

MOTHER JACK [to JACK]. You are happy, aren't you?

FATHER JACK [to JACK]. Well, then, you are a man. My expenses will be reimbursed.

MOTHER ROBERT. Come on, my son-in-law.

JACQUELINE. Come on, my brother, my sister.

FATHER ROBERT. You will get along well together, the two of you.

MOTHER JACK [to GASTON]. Oh, they are truly made for each other, and all the rest that people say on such occasions!

FATHER ROBERT, MOTHER ROBERT, FATHER and MOTHER JACK, and JACQUELINE. Oh! My children!

[They applaud enthusiastically.]

GRANDFATHER JACK. A char ... ar ... ming ... tip-ipster!

JACK. No! no! She hasn't got enough! What I want is one with three noses. I tell you: three noses, at least!

[General stupefaction, consternation.]

MOTHER JACK. Oh! Isn't he naughty!

JACQUELINE [she consoles her mother, all the time speaking to her brother]. Aren't you forgetting all the handkerchiefs she'd need in the winter?

JACK. That's the least of my worries. Moreover, they would be included in the dowry.

[During this scene, ROBERTA doesn't understand what's going on. The GRANDPARENTS remain outside the action. From time to time, the old man wants to sing; the old lady wants to give her advice. Between times, they dance, vaguely miming the action.]

FATHER JACK. I'm going to pack my bag! I'm going to pack my bag! [To his son.] Your finer feelings are not getting the upper hand! Insensate! Listen carefully to me: truth has only two sides, but it's the third side that's best! You can take my word for it! On the other hand, I expected this.

MOTHER ROBERT. It's annoying ... it's annoying ... but not terribly ... if it's only that, everything can still be arranged!

FATHER ROBERT [jovial]. This is nothing, there's nothing wrong, ladies and gentlemen. [He slaps JACK on the shoulder; JACK still sits stiffly.] We've foreseen this incident. We have at your disposal a second only daughter. And she, she's completely equipped with three noses.

MOTHER ROBERT. She's trinary. In everything, moreover. And for everything.

MOTHER JACK. Oh! What a relief! ... The important thing is the children's future ... Hurrah, do you hear, Jack?

JACQUELINE. Do you hear, sweetheart?

FATHER JACK. Let's try again. But I don't have much faith in it anymore. However, if you insist on it ...

[He throws angry looks at his son.]

MOTHER JACK. Oh, Gaston, don't say that. I'm full of hope. Everything will work out.

FATHER ROBERT. Don't be afraid. You'll see. [He takes ROBERTA by the hand, turns her head, and leads her to the door.] You'll see.

ROBERTA I. Goodbye, everybody. [She curtsies.]

[FATHER JACK is dissatisfied; MOTHER JACK is disturbed but hopeful, she looks towards her son; JACQUELINE is severe and looks at her brother with a disapproving air. MOTHER ROBERT is smiling.]

MOTHER JACK. How sweet she is, nevertheless!

MOTHER ROBERT. That doesn't matter, I tell you. You're going to see the other one now, and you won't have anything to complain about either.

JACK. One with three noses! At least one with three noses! Anyway, it's not so hard as all that.

JACQUELINE. A lily is not a tiger ... that says it all.

[FATHER ROBERT re-enters, holding by the hand ROBERTA II, who is dressed the same—after all the role is being played by the same actress; her face with three noses is revealed.]

JACQUELINE. Thrilling! Oh, Brother, this time you can't hold out for any more.

MOTHER JACK. Oh, my child! my children! [To MOTHER ROBERT.] You must be darned proud of her!

MOTHER ROBERT. Somewhat, a lot, quite a bit ... you bet!

FATHER ROBERT [approaching JACK, holding his daughter by the hand]. Now, my friend, you're in luck. To the bottle! Your desire has been specifically gratified. Here she is, here she is, your three-nosed fiancée!

MOTHER ROBERT. Here she is, your three-nosed fiancée.

JACQUELINE. So here she is, here she is then . . .

MOTHER JACK. My darling, you see her, she is yours, your little three-nosed bride, just as you wanted her!

FATHER JACK. What's that? You don't speak? You don't see her then? Here she is, here's the three-nosed girl for your special tastes.

JACK. No, I don't want her. She's not homely enough! She's even passable. There are others that are homelier. I want a much homelier one.

JACQUELINE. Well, now, what do you want!

FATHER ROBERT. This is too much. This is intolerable. It's inadmissible.

MOTHER ROBERT [to FATHER ROBERT]. You're not going to let people ridicule your daughter, your wife and yourself. Yes, we've been lured into this trap only to be ridiculed!

MOTHER JACK [sobbing]. Ah! ah! my God! Jack, Gaston, Jack, wicked son! If I had known I'd have strangled you in your last cradle, yes, with my maternal hands. Or I'd have aborted you! Or not have conceived you! I, I, who was so happy when I was pregnant with you . . . with a boy . . . I showed your photo to everybody, to the neighbors, to the cops! . . . Ah! ah! I am an unfortunate mother . . .

JACQUELINE. Mamma! Mamma!

[The GRANDMOTHER gives her a bit of advice, the GRANDFATHER begins a song.]

FATHER ROBERT. You can't get out of it that way. Ah, this can't go on like this!

MOTHER ROBERT. Don't do anything rash!

FATHER ROBERT. I demand reparations, excuses, explanations, and a total cleansing of this stain on our honor which, however, will never be completely erased! . . . at least concurrently . . .

MOTHER JACK. Ah! ah! ah! That word "concurrently" has always made me groan for it evokes concurrence!

JACQUELINE. Mamma, Mamma, don't task your brain! It isn't worth the bubble!

FATHER JACK. What do you expect me to do! Destiny has willed it. [To his son.] There's no word for your attitude; henceforth, you will have no need for respect. Don't count on it anymore!

MOTHER JACK. Ah! ah! ah!

JACQUELINE. Mamma, Mamma, my sweet potato Mamma!

JACK. She's not homely enough!

MOTHER ROBERT. What an insolent boy! [To MOTHER JACK.] It's shameful, madam.

JACQUELINE [to MOTHER ROBERT]. Leave her be! She's going to be sick.

FATHER ROBERT [to JACK]. Well then, my dear fellow, what do you want! My daughter, my daughter's not homely enough?

MOTHER ROBERT [to JACQUELINE]. I don't give a damn if she is sick, your mammery! So much the butter.

FATHER ROBERT [to JACK]. Not homely enough! Not ugly enough! Have you really looked at her, have you eyes?

JACK. But I tell you that I don't find her ugly enough.

FATHER JACK [to his son]. You don't even know what you're saying!

MOTHER JACK. Ah! ah! ah!

FATHER ROBERT. Not homely enough. My daughter, my daughter to whom I have given so complicated an education? I can't get over it! It's too much!

JACQUELINE [to her mother]. Don't faint just yet! Wait for the end of the scene!

MOTHER ROBERT. We must assert our rights! You must demand reparations!

MOTHER JACK [to JACQUELINE]. The end of the scream?

JACQUELINE [to MOTHER JACK]. No . . . the scene, of this scene . . .

FATHER JACK. That's all right! It's no one's fault! Nobody's to blame.

MOTHER ROBERT. It's the fault of all of you! You pack of hounds! Low scoundrels! Devils! Huns!

MOTHER JACK. Oh! Oh! Is this going to last much longer?

JACQUELINE. I don't think so.

MOTHER JACK. Oh! Oh! Oh!

JACK. But what do you want me to do, she's not homely enough. That's the way it is and that's all there is to it.

MOTHER ROBERT. He goes on insulting us, this puppy!

FATHER JACK. He doesn't know a thing about women!

FATHER ROBERT [to JACK]. There's no point in putting on that photogenic little pose. You're not any smarter than we are.

JACK. She's not ugly! She's not ugly! She wouldn't even sour milk . . . she's almost pretty . . .

MOTHER ROBERT. Have you any milk here so that we can see?

FATHER ROBERT. He doesn't want to, he's bluffing. He knows that milk would sour. This just doesn't suit his convenience, the little prick! It's not going to work that way. I'm going to . . .

[Intervention of the GRANDPARENTS: advice, song.]

MOTHER ROBERT [to her husband]. No, I beg of you, Robert-Cornelius, none of that here, no blood between your hands, don't be so assassinous, we'll appeal directly to the law . . . in the palace of justice! . . . with all our plates.

FATHER JACK [in a terrifying voice]. I wash my hands of this! [To JACK.] I dishonor you forever, just like when you were two years old! [To everyone.] And you too, I dishonor you all!

JACK. Good. So much the better. This will be over all the faster.

[FATHER JACK moves towards his son. A very charged moment of silence, interrupted by.]

MOTHER JACK. Oh! Oh! Oh! . . . Poo-poo-poo-poo! [She faints.]

JACQUELINE. Mamma! Mamma! [Again a tense silence.]

FATHER JACK [to his son]. Then you've lied to us. I suspected it. I'm nobody's fool. Do you want me to tell you the truth?

JACK. Yes, for it comes from the mouths of little children.

FATHER JACK [to his son]. You've lied to us just now . . .

JACQUELINE [near her mother]. Mamma . . . Ma . . .

[She stops and turns her head, like all the other actors, towards the two JACKS. MOTHER JACK returns to consciousness in order to hear the grave words which FATHER JACK utters.]

FATHER JACK [to his son]. . . . . When you declared to us, on your honor, that you adored hashed brown potatoes. Yes, you ignobly lied, lied, lied! Like alkali! This was nothing but a mean trick unworthy of the respect that we all have borne you in this house with its noble traditions, since your infancy. The reality is really this: You don't love hashed brown potatoes, you've never loved them. You will never love them!!!

[Stupefaction, awed horror, silent contemplation. Advice from the GRANDMOTHER, song from the GRANDFATHER.]

JACK. I exceecrate them.

FATHER ROBERT. What cynicism!

JACQUELINE. Alas! So far gone. My big brother!

MOTHER ROBERT. The unnatural son of an unfortunate mother and father!

MOTHER JACK. Ooooooh!

FATHER JACK. Let this serve as a revelation to us.

JACK. Whether this serves you as a revelation or not . . . and if it could serve you as a revelation: so much the better for you. There's nothing I can do about it, I was born like this . . . I've done all that was in my power! [Pause.] I am what I am.

MOTHER ROBERT [whispering]. What an unfeeling heart! Not a nerve twitches in his face . . .

FATHER ROBERT [whispering]. He's an intransigent stranger. Worse than that.

[The characters, except JACK, look at each other. They also look at JACK, who sits mute in his armchair, then they look again at each other in silence. JACK's last speech has created an atmosphere of restrained horror. JACK is truly a monster. They all move away on tiptoe. ROBERTA II has not uttered a word during this last scene, but by rather distressed gestures and a discouraged attitude of dejection has shown that she was responding to the development of the action, and now she seems lost. She appears to want to follow her parents. She takes a step towards the exit, but a gesture of her father stops her where she is.]

FATHER ROBERT [to his daughter]. You . . . chin up and do your duty!

MOTHER ROBERT [melodramatically]. Remain, unhappy girl, with your lover, since you are his presumed spouse.

[ROBERTA II makes a gesture of despair, but she obeys. FATHER JACK, MOTHER JACK, JACQUELINE, FATHER

ROBERT, MOTHER ROBERT *exit on tiptoe, horrified, throwing back occasional glances, stopping often and murmuring.*]

"He doesn't like hashed brown potatoes!"

"No! He doesn't like them!"

"He exceecrates them!"

"Oh, they're two of a kind."

"They're well matched."

"The young people nowadays . . ."

"Better not count on their gratitude."

"They don't like hashed brown potatoes."

[*They exit. The* GRANDPARENTS *exit too, more smiling than ever, strangers to the action. They all stay to spy from behind the door, frequently showing one, two, or three heads at a time. We don't see more than their grotesque heads.* ROBERTA II, *timidly, humbly, with some difficulty, decides to go sit down facing* JACK, *who still wears his cap on his head and remains scowling. Silence.*]

ROBERTA II [*attempting to win his interest, then, little by little, to seduce him*]. I am by nature very gay. [*She has a macabre voice.*] You could see it if you wanted to . . . I am eccentric . . . I am the gaiety in sorrow . . . in travail . . . in ruin . . . in desolation . . . Ah! Ah! Ah! . . . bread, peace, liberty, mourning and gaiety . . . [*Sobbing.*] They used to call me the gaiety ready to hand . . . the gay distress . . . [*He remains silent.*] Are you reflecting? Me too, at times. But in a mirror. [*At a given moment, she dares to rise, walk, approach* JACK, *to touch him, more and more sure of herself.*] I am the gaiety of death in life . . . the joy of living, of dying. [JACK *remains obstinately silent.*] They used to call me also gaiety the elder . . .

JACK. Because of your noses?

ROBERTA II. Oh no. It's because I'm taller than my sister . . . sir,

In all the world there's not another like me.
I'm light, frivolous, I'm very serious.
I'm not so serious, nor very frivolous,
I know all about making hay,
And there are other kinds of work I can do
Less well, as well, or even better
I'm just the tonic for you.
I'm honest, but don't trust me,

With me your life will be a ball.
I can play the piano,
I can arch my back,
I've been properly housebroke.
I've had a solid bringing up . . .

JACK. Let's talk about something else!

ROBERTA II. Ah! I understand you, you're not like the others. You're a superior being. Everything I told you was false, yes. Here is something that will interest you.

JACK. It will interest me if it is the truth.

ROBERTA II. Once, I felt like taking a bath. In the bathtub, which was full almost to the brim, I saw a white guinea-pig who had made himself at home there. He was breathing under water. I leaned over in order to see him close up: I saw his snout quiver a little. He was very still. I wanted to plunge my arm into the water in order to seize him, but I was too afraid that he would bite me. They say that these little animals don't bite, but one can never be sure! He clearly saw me, he was watching me, he was on the alert. He had half-opened a tiny eye, and was looking at me, motionless. He didn't appear to be living, but he was though. I saw him in profile. I wanted to see him full face. He lifted his little head with his very tiny eyes toward me, without moving his body. Since the water was very clear, I was able to see on his forehead two dark spots, chestnut colored, perhaps. When I had a good look at them, I saw that they were swelling gently, two excrescences . . . two very tiny guinea pigs, wet and soft, his little ones that were coming out there . . .

JACK [*coldly*]. This little animal in the water, why it's cancer! Actually it was cancer that you saw in your dream. Exactly that.

ROBERTA II. I know it.

JACK. Oh! listen, I feel I can trust you.

ROBERTA II. Speak then.

JACK. When I was born, I was almost fourteen years old. That's why I was able to understand more easily than most what it was all about. Yes, I understood it quickly. I hadn't wanted to accept the situation. I said as much without mincing words. I refused to accept it. But it wasn't to these people you know, who were here a little while ago, that I said this. It was to the others. Those people you know, they don't understand very well . . . no . . . no . . . but they felt it . . . they assured me that someone would devise a remedy. They promised me some decorations, some derogations, some decors, some new flowers, some new wallpaper, new profundities. What else? I insisted. They swore that they would give me satisfaction. They swore it, reswore it, promised formally, officially, presidentially. Registered . . . I made other criticisms in order finally to declare to them that I preferred to withdraw, do you understand? They replied that they would find it hard to do without me. In short, I stipulated my absolute conditions! The situation would surely change, they said. They would take useful measures. They implored me to hope, they appealed to my understanding, to all my feelings, to my love, to my pity. This couldn't go on for long, not for too long a time, they assured me. As for me personally, I would enjoy the highest regard! . . . In order to coax me, they showed me assorted prairies, assorted mountains, assorted oceans . . . maritime, naturally . . . one star, two cathedrals chosen from among the most successful. The prairies were not at all bad . . . I fell for it! But everything was fake . . . Ah, they had lied to me. Centuries and centuries have passed! People . . . they all had the word goodness in their mouths, a bloody knife between their teeth . . . Do you understand me? I was patient, patient, patient. Someone would surely come to look for me. I had wanted to protest: there was no longer anyone . . . except those people there that you know, who do not count. They deceived me . . . And how to escape? They've boarded up the doors, the windows with nothing, they've taken away the stairs . . . One can't get out through the attic anymore, there's no way out up there . . . nevertheless, according to what I was told, they've left a few trapdoors all over the place . . . If I should find them . . . I absolutely want to go away. If one can't exit through the attic, there's always the cellar, yes, the cellar. It would be better to go out down there than to be here. Anything is preferable

to my present situation. Even a new one.

ROBERTA II. Oh yes, the cellar . . . I know all the trapdoors.

JACK. We can understand each other.

ROBERTA II. Listen, I have some horses, some stallions, some brood mares, I have only those, would you like them?

JACK. Yes, tell me about your horses.

ROBERTA II. In my place, I have a neighbor who's a miller. He had a mare who dropped two sweet little foals. Very sweet, very cute. The bitch also dropped two little puppies, in the stable. The miller is old, his eyesight isn't very good. The miller took the foals to drown them in the pond, in place of the little puppies . . .

JACK. Ah! Ah!

ROBERTA II. When he realized his error, it was too late. He wasn't able to save them.

JACK [a little amused, he smiles]. Yes? Hm.

[As ROBERTA tells her story, JACK'S smile becomes a full laugh, but he's still calm. During the following scene both ROBERTA and JACK develop—very slowly at first—a declamatory style; the rhythm intensifies progressively, then slows down toward the end.]

ROBERTA II. No, he wasn't able to save them. But it wasn't really the foals either that he drowned. In fact, when he returned to the stable, the miller saw that the foals were there with their mamma; the little puppies were there too with their mamma, who was barking. But his own child, his baby who had just been born, was no longer beside his mother, the milleress. It was really the baby that he'd thrown into the water. He ran quickly to the pond. The child held out his arms and cried: "Papa, Papa" . . . It was heart-rending. Only his tiny arm could be seen which said: "Papa, Papa! Mamma, Mamma." And then he sank, and that was all. And that was all. He didn't see him again. The miller went mad. Killed his wife. Destroyed everything. Set fire to it. Hung himself.

JACK [very satisfied with this story]. What a tragic error. A sublime error!

ROBERTA II. But the foals frolic in the meadow. The little puppies have grown big.

JACK. I love your horses. They're intoxicating. Tell me another about a dog, or a horse.

ROBERTA II. The one who was engulfed in the marsh, buried alive, so that you could hear him leaping, howling, and rolling in his grave before he died?

JACK. That one or another.

ROBERTA II. Would you like the one about a horse of the desert, of a city in the Sahara?

JACK [interested, as though in spite of himself, and louder and louder]. The metropolis of the desert! . . .

ROBERTA II. All of bricks, all the houses there are made of bricks, the streets are burning . . . the fire runs through underneath . . . the dry air, the very red dust.

JACK. And the fiery dust.

ROBERTA II. The natives there have been dead for a long time, their cadavers are desiccating in the houses.

JACK. Behind the closed shutters. Behind the red iron grills.

ROBERTA II. Not a man in the empty streets. Not a beast. Not a bird. Not a blade of grass, not even a withered one. Not a rat, not a fly . . .

JACK. Metropolis of my future!

ROBERTA II. Suddenly, in the distance, a horse whinnies . . . han! han! Approaches, han! han! han! han!

JACK [suddenly happy]. Oh yes, that's it, han! han! han!

ROBERTA II. Galloping at full speed, galloping at full speed . . .

JACK. Haan! haan! haan!

ROBERTA II. There he is on the great empty square, there he is . . . He whinnies, runs around, galloping, runs around, galloping . . . runs around, galloping, runs around, galloping.

JACK. Han! han! haan! at full speed, galloping, at full speed, galloping . . . Oh yes, han! han! han! galloping, galloping, galloping as hard as he can.

ROBERTA II. His hooves: click clack click clack, galloping, striking sparks. Click . . . clack . . . clack . . . clack . . . vrr . . .

JACK [laughing]. Oh yes, yes, bravo, I know, I know what's going to happen. But quickly . . . quickly . . . go on . . . hurrah . . .

ROBERTA II. He trembles, he's afraid . . . the stallion . . .

JACK. Yes, hurrah . . . He whinnies, he cries with fear, han! . . . Han! . . . He cries out his fear, han! han! let's hurry . . . let's hurry . . .

[A blazing horse's mane crosses from one end of the stage to the other.]

ROBERTA II. Oh! he won't escape . . . never fear . . . He turns around and around, gallops in a circle . . .

JACK. Bravo, that's it! I see . . . I see . . . a spark in his mane . . . He shakes his head . . . Ah! ah! ah! it burns him! it hurts him!

ROBERTA II. He's afraid! he gallops. In a circle. He rears! . . .

JACK. His mane is blazing! His beautiful mane . . . He cries, he whinnies. Han! han! The flame flashes up . . . His mane is blazing. His mane is burning. Han! han! burn! burn! han! han!

ROBERTA II. The more he gallops, the more the flame spreads. He is mad, he's terrified, he's in pain, he's sick, he's afraid, he's in pain . . . it flames up, it spreads all over his body! . . .

JACK. Han! han! he leaps. Oh, what flaming leaps, flaming flaming! He cries, he rears up. Stop, stop, Roberta. It's too fast . . . not so fast . . .

ROBERTA II [aside]. Oh . . . he called me by my given name . . . He's going to love me!

JACK. He's burning too fast . . . It's going to end! Make the fire last . . .

ROBERTA II. It's the fire that goes so fast—the flames are coming out of his ears and his nostrils, and thick smoke . . .

JACK. He screams with fear, he screams with pain. He leaps so high. He has wings of flame!

ROBERTA II. How beautiful he is, he's turning all pink, like an enormous lampshade. He wants to fly. He stops, he doesn't know what to do . . . His horseshoes smoke and redden. Haan! Through his transparent hide, we see the fire burning inside him. Han! he flames! He's a living torch . . . He's only a handful of cinders . . . He's no more, but we hear still in the distance the echo of his cries reverberating, and weakening . . . like the whinnyings of another horse in the empty streets.

JACK. My throat is parched, this has

made me thirsty . . . Water, water. Ah!
how he flamed, the stallion . . . how beautiful it was . . . what a flame . . . ah! [*Exhausted.*] I'm thirsty . . .

ROBERTA II. Come on . . . don't be
afraid . . . I'm moist . . . My necklace is
made of mud, my breasts are dissolving,
my pelvis is wet, I've got water in my
crevasses, I'm sinking down. My true
name is Liza. In my belly, there are
pools, swamps . . . I've got a house of
clay. I'm always cool . . . There's moss
. . . big flies, cockroaches, sowbugs, toads.
Under the wet covers they make love . . .
they're swollen with happiness! I wrap
my arms around you like snakes; with my
soft thighs . . . you plunge down and you
dissolve . . . in my locks which drizzle,
drizzle, rain, rain. My mouth trickles
down, my legs trickle, my naked shoulders trickle, my hair trickles, everything
trickles down, runs, everything trickles,
the sky trickles down, the stars run,
trickle down, trickle . . .

JACK [*in ecstasy*]. Cha-a-arming!

ROBERTA II. Make yourself comfortable.
Why don't you take off this thing that
you're wearing? What is it? Or who is it?

JACK [*still in ecstasy*]. Cha-a-arming!

ROBERTA II. What is this, on your
head?

JACK. Guess! It's a kind of cat. I put
it on at dawn.

ROBERTA II. Is it a castle?

JACK. I keep it on my head all day. At
table, in the parlor, I never take it off. I
don't tip it to people.

ROBERTA II. Is it a camel? A capricorn?

JACK. It'll strike with its paws, but it
can till the soil.

ROBERTA II. Is it a catapult?

JACK. It weeps sometimes.

ROBERTA II. Is it a catarrh?

JACK. It can live under water.

ROBERTA II. Is it a catfish?

JACK. It can also float on the waves.

ROBERTA II. Is it a catamaran?

JACK. You're warm.

ROBERTA II. Is it a caterpillar?

JACK. Sometimes it likes to hide in the
mountain. It's not pretty.

ROBERTA II. Is it a catamount?

JACK. It makes me laugh.

ROBERTA II. Is it a cataclysm, or a
catalog?

JACK. It screams, it splits my ears.

ROBERTA II. Is it a caterwaul?

JACK. It loves ornaments.

ROBERTA II. Is it a catacomb?

JACK. No!

ROBERTA II. The cat's got my tongue.

JACK. It's a cap.

ROBERTA II. Oh, take it off. Take it off,
Jack. My Jack. With me, you'll be in
your element. I have some, I have as
many as you want, quantities!

JACK. . . . Of caps?

ROBERTA II. No . . . of cats . . . skinless
ones!

JACK. Oh, my cat . . .

[*He takes off his cap, he has green
hair.*]

ROBERTA II. Oh, my cat . . .

JACK. My cat, my catawampous.

ROBERTA II. In the cellar of my castle,
everything is cat . . .

JACK. Everything is cat.

ROBERTA II. All we need to designate
things is one single word: cat. Cats are
called cat, food: cat, insects: cat, chairs:
cat, you: cat, me: cat, the roof: cat, the
number one: cat, number two: cat, three:
cat, twenty: cat, thirty: cat, all the adverbs: cat, all the prepositions: cat. It's
easier to talk that way . . .

JACK. In order to say: I'm terribly
sleepy, let's go to sleep, let's go to
sleep . . .

ROBERTA II. Cat, cat, cat, cat.

JACK. In order to say, bring me some
cold noodles, some warm lemonade, and
no coffee . . .

ROBERTA II. Cat, cat, cat, cat, cat, cat,
cat, cat.

JACK. And Jack, and Roberta?

ROBERTA II. Cat, cat.

[*She takes out her hand with nine
fingers that she has kept hidden
under her gown.*]

JACK. Oh yes! It's easy to talk now . . .
In fact it's scarcely worth the bother . . .
[*He sees her hand with nine fingers.*] Oh!
You've got nine fingers on your left
hand? You're rich, I'll marry you . . .

[*They put their arms around each
other very awkwardly.* JACK *kisses
the noses of* ROBERTA II, *one after
the other, while* FATHER JACK,
MOTHER JACK, JACQUELINE, *the*
GRANDPARENTS, FATHER ROBERT, *and*
MOTHER ROBERT *enter without saying a word, one after the other, waddling along, in a sort of ridiculous
dance, embarrassing, in a vague cir-*

cle, around JACK and ROBERTA II who remain at stage center, awkwardly enlaced. FATHER ROBERT silently and slowly strikes his hands together. MOTHER ROBERT, her arms clasped behind her neck, makes pirouettes, smiling stupidly. MOTHER JACK, with an expressionless face, shakes her shoulders in a grotesque fashion. FATHER JACK pulls up his pants and walks on his heels. JACQUELINE nods her head, then they continue to dance, squatting down, while JACK and ROBERTA II squat down too, and remain motionless. The GRANDPARENTS turn around, idiotically, looking at each other, and smiling; then they squat down in their turn. All this must produce in the audience a feeling of embarrassment, awkwardness, and shame. The darkness increases. On stage, the actors utter vague miaows while turning around, bizarre moans, croakings. The darkness increases. We can still see the JACKS and ROBERTS crawling on the stage. We hear their animal noises, then we don't see them any more. We hear only their moans, their sighs, then all fades away, all is extinguished. Again, a gray light comes on. All the characters have disappeared, except ROBERTA, who is lying down, or rather squatting down, buried beneath her gown. We see only her pale face, with its three noses quivering, and her nine fingers moving like snakes.]

Summer, 1950

Kenneth Tynan

IONESCO: MAN OF DESTINY

...Ever since the Fry-Eliot "poetic revival" caved in on them, the ostriches of our theatrical intelligentsia have been seeking another faith. Anything would do as long as it shook off what are known as "the fetters of realism." Now the broad definition of a realistic play is that its characters and events have traceable roots in life. Gorki and Chekhov, Arthur Miller and Tennessee Williams, Brecht and O'Casey, Osborne and Sartre have all written such plays. They express one man's view of the world in terms of people we can all recognize. Like all hard disciplines, realism can easily be corrupted. It can sink into sentimentality ..., half truth ..., or mere photographic reproduction of the trivia of human behavior. Even so, those who have mastered it have created the lasting body of twentieth century drama; and I have been careful not to except Brecht, who employed stylized production techniques to set off eventually realistic characters.

That, for the ostriches, was what ruled him out of court. He was too real. Similarly, they preferred Beckett's *Endgame*, in which the human element was minimal, to *Waiting for Godot*, which not only contained two tramps of mephitic reality but even seemed to regard them, as human beings, with love. Veiling their disapproval, the ostriches seized on Beckett's more blatant verbal caprices and called them "authentic images of a disintegrated society." But it was only when M. Ionesco arrived that they hailed a messiah. Here at last was a self-proclaimed advocate of *anti-theatre*: explicitly anti-realist, and by implication anti-reality as well. Here was a writer ready to declare that words were meaningless and that all communication between human beings was impossible. The aged (as in *The Chairs*) are wrapped in an impenetrable cocoon of hallucinatory memories; they can speak intelligibly neither to each other nor to the world. The teacher in *The Lesson* can "get through" to his pupil only by means of sexual assault, followed by murder. Words, the magic innovation of our species, are dismissed as useless and fraudulent.

Ionesco's is a world of isolated robots, conversing in cartoon-strip balloons of dialogue that are sometimes hilarious, sometimes evocative, and quite often neither, on which occasions they become profoundly tiresome.... This world is not mine, but I recognize it to be a valid personal vision, presented with great imaginative aplomb and verbal audacity. The peril arises when it is held up for general emulation as the gateway to the theatre of the future, that bleak new world from which the humanist heresies of faith in logic and belief in man will forever be banished.

M. Ionesco certainly offers an "escape from realism"; but an escape into what? A blind alley, perhaps, adorned with *tachiste* murals. Or a self-imposed vacuum, wherein the author ominously bids us observe the absence of air. Or, best of all, a funfair ride on a ghost train, all skulls and hooting waxworks, from which we emerge into the far more intimidating clamor of diurnal reality. M. Ionesco's theatre is pungent and exciting, but it remains a diversion. It is not on the main road; and we do him no good, nor the drama at large, to pretend that it is....

SOURCE: From *The Observer*, June 22, 1958. Copyright 1958 by *The Observer*. Reprinted by permission of publisher and author.

Eugène Ionesco

A REPLY TO KENNETH TYNAN: THE PLAYWRIGHT'S ROLE

I was of course honored by the article Mr. Tynan devoted to my two plays, *The Chairs* and *The Lesson*, in spite of the strictures it contained, which a critic has a perfect right to make. However, since some of his objections seem to me to be based on premises that are not only false but, strictly speaking, outside the domain of the theatre, I think I have the right to make certain comments.

In effect, Mr. Tynan says that it has been claimed, and that I myself have approved or supported this claim, that I was a sort of "messiah" of the theatre. This is doubly untrue because I do not like messiahs and I certainly do not consider the vocation of the artist or the playwright to lie in that direction. I have a distinct impression that it is Mr. Tynan who is in search of messiahs. But to deliver a message to the world, to wish to direct its course, to save it, is the business of the founders of religions, of the moralists or the politicians who, incidentally, as we know only too well, make a pretty poor job of it. A playwright simply writes plays, in which he can offer only a testimony, not a didactic message, a personal, affective testimony of his anguish and the anguish of others or, which is rare, of his happiness—or he can express his feelings, comic or tragic, about life.

A work of art has nothing to do with doctrine. I have already written elsewhere that any work of art which was ideological and nothing else would be pointless, tautological, inferior to the doctrine it claimed to illustrate, which would already have been expressed in its proper language, that of discursive demonstration. An ideological play can be no more than the vulgarization of an ideology. In my view, a work of art has its own unique system of expression, its own means of directly apprehending the real.

Mr. Tynan seems to accuse me of being deliberately, explicitly, anti-realist; of having declared that words have no meaning and that all language is incommunicable. That is only partly true, for the very fact of writing and presenting plays is surely incompatible with such a view. I simply hold that it is difficult to make oneself understood, not absolutely impossible, and my play *The Chairs* is a plea, pathetic perhaps, for mutual understanding. As for the idea of reality, Mr. Tynan seems . . . to acknowledge only one plane of reality: what is called the "social" plane, which seems to me to be the most external, in other words, the most superficial. That is why I think that writers like Sartre . . . , Osborne, Miller, Brecht, etc., are simply the new *auteurs du boulevard*, representatives of a left-wing conformism which is just as lamentable as the right-wing sort. These writers offer nothing that one does not know already, through books and political speeches.

But that is not all; it is not enough to be a social realist writer, one must also, apparently, be a militant believer in what is known as progress. The only worthwhile authors, those who are on the "main road" of the theatre, would be those who thought in a certain clearly defined way, obeying certain pre-established principles or directives. This would be to make the "main road" a very narrow one; it would considerably restrict the planes of reality (which are innumerable) and limit the field open to the investigation of artistic research and creation.

I believe that what separates us all from one another is simply society itself, or, if you like, politics. This is what raises

SOURCE: From *The Observer*, June 29, 1958. Copyright 1958 by *The Observer*. Reprinted by permission of publisher and author.

barriers between men, this is what creates misunderstanding.

If I may be allowed to express myself paradoxically, I should say that the true society, the authentic human community, is extra-social—a wider, deeper society, that which is revealed by our common anxieties, our desires, our secret nostalgias. The whole history of the world has been governed by these nostalgias and anxieties, which political action does no more than reflect and interpret, very imperfectly. No society has been able to abolish human sadness, no political system can deliver us from the pain of living, from our fear of death, our thirst for the absolute; it is the human condition that directs the social condition, not vice versa.

This "reality" seems to me much vaster and more complex than the one to which Mr. Tynan and many others want to limit themselves. The problem is to get to the source of our malady, to find the non-conventional language of this anguish, perhaps by breaking down this "social" language which is nothing but clichés, empty formulas, and slogans. The "robot" characters Mr. Tynan disapproves of seem to me to be precisely those who belong *solely* to this or that *milieu* or social "reality," who are prisoners of it, and who—being no more than social, seeking a solution to their problems only by so-called social means—have become impoverished, alienated, empty. It is precisely the conformist, the *petit-bourgeois*, the ideologist of *every* society who is lost and dehumanized. If anything needs demystifying it is our ideologies, which offer ready-made solutions . . . in a language that congeals *as soon as it is formulated*. It is these ideologies which must be continually re-examined in the light of our anxieties and dreams, and their congealed language must be relentlessly split apart in order to find the living sap beneath.

To discover the fundamental problem common to all mankind, I must ask myself what *my* fundamental problem is, what *my* most ineradicable fear is. I am certain, then, to find the problems and fears of literally everyone. That is the true road, into my own darkness, our darkness, which I try to bring to the light of day.

It would be amusing to try an experiment, which I have no room for here but which I hope to carry out some day. I could take almost any work of art, any play, and guarantee to give it in turn a Marxist, a Buddhist, a Christian, an Existentialist, psycho-analytical interpretation and "prove" that the work subjected to each interpretation is a perfect and exclusive illustration of each creed, that it confirms this or that ideology beyond all doubt. For me this proves another thing: that every work of art (unless it is a pseudo-intellectualist work, a work already comprised in some ideology that it merely illustrates, as with Brecht) is outside ideology, is not reducible to ideology. Ideology circumscribes without penetrating it. The absence of ideology in a work does not mean an absence of ideas; on the contrary it fertilizes them. In other words, it was not Sophocles who was inspired by Freud but, obviously, the other way round. Ideology is not the source of art. A work of art is the source and the raw material of ideologies to come.

What, then, should the critic do? Where should he look for his criteria? Inside the work itself, its universe and its mythology. He must look at it, listen to it, and simply say whether it is true to its own nature. The best judgment is a careful exposition of the work itself. For that, the work must be allowed to speak, uncolored by preconceptions or prejudices.

Whether or not it is on the "main road"; whether or not it is what you would like it to be—to consider this is already to pass judgment, a judgment that is external, pointless and false. A work of art is the expression of an incommunicable reality that one tries to communicate—and which sometimes can be communicated. That is its paradox, and its truth.

Kenneth Tynan

IONESCO AND THE PHANTOM

M. Ionesco's article on "The Playwright's Role" is discussed elsewhere in these pages. . . . I want to add what I hope will not be a postscript, for this is a debate that should continue.

As I read the piece I felt first bewilderment, next admiration, and finally regret. Bewilderment at his assumption that I wanted drama to be forced to echo a particular political creed, when all I want is for drama to realize that it is a *part* of politics, in the sense that every human activity, even buying a packet of cigarettes, has social and political repercussions. Then admiration; no one could help admiring the sincerity and skill with which . . . M. Ionesco marshalled prose for his purposes. And ultimately, regret: regret that a man so capable of stating a positive attitude towards art should deny that there was any positive attitude worth taking towards life. Or even (which is essential) that there was an umbilical connection between the two.

The position towards which M. Ionesco is moving is that which regards art as if it were something different from and independent of everything else in the world; as if it not only did not but should not correspond to anything outside the mind of the artist. This position, as it happens, was reached some years ago by a French painter who declared that, since nothing in nature exactly resembled anything else, he proposed to burn all of his paintings which in any way resembled anything that already existed. The end of that line, of course, is Action Painting.

Mr. Ionesco has not yet gone so far. He is stuck, to pursue the analogy, in an earlier groove, the groove of cubism, which has fascinated him so much that he has begun to confuse ends and means. The Cubists employed distortion to make

discoveries about the nature of objective reality. M. Ionesco, I fear, is on the brink of believing that his distortions are more valid and important than the external world it is their proper function to interpert. To adapt Johnson, I am not yet so lost in drama criticism as to forget that plays are the daughters of the earth, and that things are the sons of heaven. But M. Ionesco is in danger of forgetting; of locking himself up in that hall of mirrors which in philosophy is known as solipsism.

Art is parasitic on life, just as criticism is parasitic on art. M. Ionesco and his followers are breaking the chain, applying the tourniquet, aspiring as writers to a condition of stasis. At their best, of course, they don't succeed; the alarming thing is that they try. As in physiology, note how quickly the brain, starved of blood, produces hallucinations and delusions of grandeur. "A work of art," says M. Ionesco, "is the source and the raw material of ideologies to come." O hubris! Art and ideology often interact on each other; but the plain fact is that they both spring from a common source. Both draw on human experience to explain mankind to itself; both attempt, in very different ways, to assemble coherence from seemingly unrelated phenomena; both stand guard for us against chaos. They are brothers, not child and parent. To say, as M. Ionesco does, that Freud was inspired by Sophocles is the direst nonsense. Freud merely found in Sophocles confirmation of a theory he had formed on a basis of empirical evidence. This does not make Sophocles a Freudian, or vice versa; it is simply a pleasing instance of fraternal corroboration.

You may wonder why M. Ionesco is so keen on this phantom notion of art as a

SOURCE: From *The Observer*, July 6, 1958. Copyright 1958 by *The Observer*. Reprinted by permission of publisher and author.

world of its own, answerable to none but its own laws. Wonder no more: he is merely seeking to exempt himself from any kind of value judgment. His aim is to blind us to the fact that we are all in some sense critics, who bring to the theatre not only those "nostalgias and anxieties" by which, as he rightly says, world history has largely been governed, but also a whole series of new ideas—moral, social, psychological, political—through which we hope some day to free ourselves from the rusty hegemony of *Angst*. These fond ideas, M. Ionesco quickly assures us, do not belong in the theatre. Our job, as critics, is just to hear the play and "simply say whether it is true to its own nature." Not, you notice, whether it is true to ours; or even relevant; for we, as an audience, have forfeited our right to a hearing as conscious, sentient beings. "Clear evidence of cancer here, sir." "Very well, leave it alone; it's being true to its own nature."

Whether M. Ionesco admits it or not, every play worth serious consideration is a statement. It is a statement addressed in the first person singular to the first person plural; and the latter must retain the right to dissent. I am rebuked in the current *Encounter* for having disagreed with the nihilistic philosophy expressed in Strindberg's *Dream Play*: "The important thing," says my interviewer, "seems to me to be not the rightness of Strindberg's belief, but rather how he has expressed it. . . ." Strindberg expressed it very vividly, but there are things more important than that. If a man tells me something I believe to be an untruth, am I forbidden to do more than congratulate him on the brilliance of his lying?

Cyril Connolly once said, once and wanly, that it was closing time in the gardens of the West; but I deny the rest of that suavely cadenced sentence, which asserts that "from now on an artist will be judged only by the resonance of his solitude or the quality of his despair." Not by me he won't. I shall, I hope, respond to the honesty of such testimonies; but I shall be looking for something more, something harder: for evidence of the artist who is not content with the passive role of a symptom, but concerns himself, from time to time, with such things as healing. M. Ionesco correctly says that no ideology has as yet abolished fear, pain or sadness. Nor has any work of art. But both are in the business of trying. What other business is there?

Samuel
Beckett
1906–

Like Ionesco, Samuel Beckett came to the theatre relatively late—he was forty-seven when his first play was produced. One of the most discussed of contemporary writers, Beckett is Irish by birth, French by choice, a master of English who prefers to write in French and then translate into his native tongue, a commanding figure in the "theatre of the absurd." His well-to-do parents in Dublin gave him an excellent education, and he went on to distinguish himself as a student of French and Italian at Trinity College, Dublin. Upon graduation he received an appointment to teach English in Paris. While in Paris, Beckett moved in the literary circle that gathered about his compatriot James Joyce; he wrote an essay on Joyce, another on Proust, and published a long poem *Whoroscope* (1930). He then returned to Trinity College to lecture on French and to take his master's degree, but he soon abandoned an academic career and went abroad, where for several years he wandered about Germany and France, doing odd jobs and writing short stories and poems. In 1937 he took up permanent residence in Paris. For years he wrote little and lived in relative obscurity. But after World War II, in a burst of creativity, he produced a trilogy of novels (*Molloy*, 1951; *Malone Dies*, 1951; *The Unnamable*, 1953) and two major plays, *Waiting for Godot* (1952) and *Endgame* (1957). The decisive turn in Beckett's fortunes came with *Waiting for Godot*, a complex tragi-comedy that defies conventional dramaturgy and expresses Beckett's dark view of man's condition. In 1956, at the invitation of the British Broadcasting Corporation, Beckett wrote—in English—a radio drama, *All That Fall*, perhaps his most accessible work. Other plays followed: *Krapp's Last Tape* (1958), *Happy Days* (1961), *Play* (1963); several radio dramas: *Embers* (1959), *Words and Music* (1962), *Cascando* (1963); a television play, *Eh Joe* (1966), and a brief movie, *Film* (1964). In his two wordless mimes, *Act Without Words I* and *Act Without Words II*, Beckett carried to their logical extremes his tendencies to constrict the theatre to its ascetic essentials and to view man's lot as one of grim futility and impotence in a senseless universe. In 1969, Beckett was awarded the Nobel Prize in Literature for having produced new forms of the novel and drama in which "the destitution of man acquires its elevation." Whether it in fact acquires elevation or remains a grim joke is debatable. A product of our times of crisis, Beckett, in a variety of images, posits a tantalizing world of cruelty, isolation, and anxiety in which man, grotesque and crippled, is trapped yet doggedly goes on enduring. All around is "the mess," and the best answer one can hope for is "Perhaps."

ALL THAT FALL

A play for radio

SAMUEL BECKETT

CHARACTERS

MRS. ROONEY [MADDY], *a lady in her sev-
enties*
CHRISTY, *a carter*
MR. TYLER, *a retired bill-broker*
MR. SLOCUM, *Clerk of the Racecourse*
TOMMY, *a porter*
MR. BARRELL, *a station-master*

MISS FITT, *a lady in her thirties*
A FEMALE VOICE
DOLLY, *a small girl*
MR. ROONEY [DAN], *husband of Mrs.
Rooney, blind*
JERRY, *a small boy*

[*Rural sounds. Sheep, bird, cow, cock,
severally, then together.*
Silence.
MRS. ROONEY *advances along country
road towards railway-station. Sound of
her dragging feet.*
*Music, faint from house by way.
"Death and the Maiden." The steps slow
down, stop.*]

MRS. ROONEY. Poor woman. All alone
in that ruinous old house.
[*Music louder. Silence but for music
playing.*
The steps resume. Music dies. MRS.
ROONEY *murmurs melody. Her mur-
mur dies.*
*Sound of approaching cartwheels. The
cart stops. The steps slow down,
stop.*]
MRS. ROONEY. Is that you, Christy?
CHRISTY. It is, Ma'am.
MRS. ROONEY. I thought the hinny was
familiar. How is your poor wife?
CHRISTY. No better, Ma'am.
MRS. ROONEY. Your daughter then?
CHRISTY. No worse, Ma'am.
[*Silence.*]

MRS. ROONEY. Why do you halt?
[*Pause.*] But why do I halt?
[*Silence.*]
CHRISTY. Nice day for the races,
Ma'am.
MRS. ROONEY. No doubt it is. [*Pause.*]
But will it hold up? [*Pause. With emo-
tion.*] Will it hold up?
[*Silence.*]
CHRISTY. I suppose you wouldn't—
MRS. ROONEY. Hist! [*Pause.*] Surely to
goodness that cannot be the up mail I
hear already?
[*Silence. The hinny neighs. Silence.*]
CHRISTY. Damn the mail.
MRS. ROONEY. Oh thank God for that!
I could have sworn I heard it, thunder-
ing up the track in the far distance.
[*Pause.*] So hinnies whinny. Well, it is
not surprising.
CHRISTY. I suppose you wouldn't be in
need of a small load of dung?
MRS. ROONEY. Dung? What class of
dung?
CHRISTY. Stydung.
MRS. ROONEY. Stydung . . . I like your
frankness, Christy. [*Pause.*] I'll ask the
master [*Pause.*] Christy.

CHRISTY. Yes, Ma'am.

MRS. ROONEY. Do you find anything
. . . bizarre about my way of speaking?
[Pause.] I do not mean the voice. [Pause.]
No, I mean the words. [Pause. More to
herself.] I use none but the simplest
words, I hope, and yet I sometimes find
my way of speaking very . . . bizarre.
[Pause.] Mercy! What was that?

CHRISTY. Never mind her, Ma'am,
she's very fresh in herself to-day.

[Silence.]

MRS. ROONEY. Dung? What would we
want with dung, at our time of life?
[Pause.] Why are you on your feet down
on the road? Why do you not climb up
on the crest of your manure and let yourself be carried along? Is it that you have
no head for heights?

[Silence.]

CHRISTY [to the hinny]. Yep! [Pause.
Louder.] Yep wiyya to hell owwa that!

[Silence.]

MRS. ROONEY. She does not move a
muscle. [Pause.] I too should be getting
along, if I do not wish to arrive late at
the station. [Pause.] But a moment ago
she neighed and pawed the ground. And
now she refuses to advance. Give her a
good welt on the rump. [Sound of welt.
Pause.] Harder [Sound of welt. Pause.]
Well! If someone were to do that for
me I should not dally. [Pause.] How she
gazes at me to be sure, with her great
moist cleg-tormented eyes? Perhaps if I
were to move on, down the road, out of
her field of vision . . . [Sound of welt.]
No, no, enough! Take her by the snaffle
and pull her eyes away from me. Oh this
is awful! [She moves on. Sound of her
dragging feet.] What have I done to deserve all this, what, what? [Dragging
feet.] So long ago . . . No! No! [Drag-
ging feet. Quotes.] "Sigh out a something something tale of things, Done
long ago and ill done." [She halts.] How
can I go on, I cannot. Oh let me just flop
down flat on the road like a big fat jelly
out of a bowl and never move again! A
great big slop thick with grit and dust
and flies, they would have to scoop me up
with a shovel. [Pause.] Heavens, there is
that up mail again, what will become of
me! [The dragging steps resume.] Oh I
am just a hysterical old hag, I know, destroyed with sorrow and pining and gentility and church-going and fat and rheu-

matism and childlessness. [Pause. Brokenly.] Minnie! Little Minnie! [Pause.]
Love, that is all I asked, a little love,
daily, twice daily, fifty years of twice daily
love like a Paris horse-butcher's regular,
what normal woman wants affection? A
peck on the jaw at morning, near the ear,
and another at evening, peck, peck, till
you grow whiskers on you. There is that
lovely laburnum again.

[Dragging feet. Sound of bicycle-bell.
It is old MR. TYLER coming up behind her on his bicycle, on his way
to the station. Squeak of brakes. He
slows down and rides abreast of her.]

MR. TYLER. Mrs. Rooney! Pardon me
if I do not doff my cap, I'd fall off. Divine day for the meeting.

MRS. ROONEY. Oh, Mr. Tyler, you
startled the life out of me stealing up behind me like that like a deer-stalker! Oh!

MR. TYLER [playfully]. I rang my bell,
Mrs. Rooney, the moment I sighted you
I started tinkling my bell, now don't you
deny it.

MRS. ROONEY. Your bell is one thing,
Mr. Tyler, and you are another. What
news of your daughter?

MR. TYLER. Fair, fair. They removed
everything, you know, the whole . . . er
. . . bag of tricks. Now I am grandchild-
less.

[Dragging feet.]

MRS. ROONEY. Gracious how you wob-
ble! Dismount, for mercy's sake, or ride
on.

MR. TYLER. Perhaps if I were to lay
my hand lightly on your shoulder, Mrs.
Rooney, how would that be? [Pause.]
Would you permit that?

MRS. ROONEY. No, Mr. Rooney, Mr.
Tyler I mean, I am tired of light old
hands on my shoulders and other senseless places, sick and tired of them.
Heavens, here comes Connolly's van!
[She halts. Sound of motor-van. It approaches, passes with thunderous rattle,
recedes.] Are you all right, Mr. Tyler?
[Pause.] Where is he? [Pause.] Ah there
you are! [The dragging steps resume.]
That was a narrow squeak.

MR. TYLER. I alit in the nick of time.

MRS. ROONEY. It is suicide to be abroad.
But what is it to be at home, Mr. Tyler,
what is it to be at home? A lingering dis-
solution. Now we are white with dust
from head to foot. I beg your pardon?

MR. TYLER. Nothing, Mrs. Rooney, nothing, I was merely cursing, under my breath, God and man, under my breath, and the wet Saturday afternoon of my conception. My back tire has gone down again. I pumped it hard as iron before I set out. And now I am on the rim.

MRS. ROONEY. Oh what a shame!

MR. TYLER. Now if it were the front I should not so much mind. But the back. The back! The chain! The oil! The grease! The hub! The brakes! The gear! No! It is too much!

[Dragging feet.]

MRS. ROONEY. Are we very late, Mr. Tyler, I have not the courage to look at my watch.

MR. TYLER [bitterly]. Late! I on my bicycle as I bowled along was already late. Now therefore we are doubly late, trebly, quadrupedly late. Would I had shot by you, without a word.

[Dragging feet.]

MRS. ROONEY. Whom are you meeting, Mr. Tyler?

MR. TYLER. Hardy. [Pause.] We used to climb together. [Pause.] I saved his life once. [Pause.] I have not forgotten it.

[Dragging feet. They stop.]

MRS. ROONEY. Let us a halt a moment and this vile dust fall back upon the viler worms.

[Silence. Rural sounds.]

MR. TYLER. What sky! What light! Ah in spite of all it is a blessed thing to be alive in such weather, and out of hospital.

MRS. ROONEY. Alive?

MR. TYLER. Well half alive, shall we say?

MRS. ROONEY. Speak for yourself, Mr. Tyler. I am not half alive nor anything approaching it. [Pause.] What are we standing here for? This dust will not settle in our time. And when it does some great roaring machine will come and whirl it all skyhigh again.

MR. TYLER. Well, shall we be getting along in that case?

MRS. ROONEY. No.

MR. TYLER. Come, Mrs. Rooney—

MRS. ROONEY. Go, Mr. Tyler, go on and leave me, listening to the cooing of the ringdoves. [Cooing.] If you see my poor blind Dan tell him I was on my way to meet him when it all came over me again, like a flood. Say to him, Your poor wife, she told me to tell you it all came flooding over her again and . . . [the voice breaks] . . . she simply went back home . . . straight back home . . .

MR. TYLER. Come, Mrs. Rooney, come, the mail has not yet gone up, just take my free arm and we'll be there with time and to spare.

MRS. ROONEY [sobbing]. What? What's all this now? [Calmer.] Can't you see I'm in trouble? [With anger.] Have you no respect for misery? [Sobbing.] Minnie! Little Minnie!

MR. TYLER. Come, Mrs. Rooney, come, the mail has not yet gone up, just take my free arm and we'll be there with time and to spare.

MRS. ROONEY [brokenly]. In her forties now she'd be, I don't know, fifty, girding up her lovely little loins, getting ready for the change . . .

MR. TYLER. Come, Mrs. Rooney, come, the mail—

MRS. ROONEY [exploding]. Will you get along with you, Mr. Rooney, Mr. Tyler I mean, will you get along with you now and cease molesting me? What kind of a country is this where a woman can't weep her heart out on the highways and by-ways without being tormented by retired bill-brokers! [MR. TYLER prepares to mount his bicycle.] Heavens, you're not going to ride her flat! [MR. TYLER mounts.] You'll tear your tube to ribbons! [MR. TYLER rides off. Receding sound of bumping bicycle. Silence. Cooing.] Venus birds! Billing in the woods all the long summer long. [Pause.] Oh cursed corset! If I could let it out, without indecent exposure. Mr. Tyler! Mr. Tyler! Come back and unlace me behind the hedge! [She laughs wildly, ceases.] What's wrong with me, what's wrong with me, never tranquil, seething out of my dirty old pelt, out of my skull, oh to be in atoms, in atoms! [Frenziedly.] ATOMS! [Silence. Cooing. Faintly.] Jesus! [Pause.] Jesus!

[Sound of car coming up behind her. It slows down and draws up beside her, engine running. It is MR. SLOCUM, the Clerk of the Racecourse.]

MR. SLOCUM. Is anything wrong, Mrs. Rooney? You are bent all double. Have you a pain in the stomach?

[Silence. MRS. ROONEY laughs wildly. Finally.]

MRS. ROONEY. Well, if it isn't my old admirer, the Clerk of the Course, in his limousine.

MR. SLOCUM. May I offer you a lift, Mrs. Rooney? Are you going in my direction?

MRS. ROONEY. I am, Mr. Slocum, we all are. [Pause.] How is your poor mother?

MR. SLOCUM. Thank you, she is fairly comfortable. We manage to keep her out of pain. That is the great thing, Mrs. Rooney, is it not?

MRS. ROONEY. Yes, indeed, Mr. Slocum, that is the great thing, I don't know how you do it. [Pause. She slaps her cheek violently.] Ah these wasps!

MR. SLOCUM [coolly]. May I then offer you a seat, Madam?

MRS. ROONEY [with exaggerated enthusiasm]. Oh that would be heavenly, Mr. Slocum, just simply heavenly. [Dubiously.] But would I ever get in, you look very high off the ground to-day, these new balloon tires, I presume. [Sound of door opening and MRS. ROONEY trying to get in.] Does this roof never come off? No? [Efforts of MRS. ROONEY.] No . . . I'll never do it . . . you'll have to get down, Mr. Slocum, and help me from the rear. [Pause.] What was that? [Pause. Aggrieved.] This is all your suggestion, Mr. Slocum, not mine. Drive on, Sir, drive on.

MR. SLOCUM [switching off the engine]. I'm coming, Mrs. Rooney, I'm coming, give me time, I'm as stiff as yourself.

[Sound of MR. SLOCUM extracting himself from driver's seat.]

MRS. ROONEY. Stiff! Well I like that! And me heaving all over back and front. [To herself.] The dry old reprobate!

MR. SLOCUM [in position behind her]. Now, Mrs. Rooney, how shall we do this?

MRS. ROONEY. As if I were a bale, Mr. Slocum, don't be afraid. [Pause. Sounds of effort.] That's the way! [Effort.] Lower! [Effort.] Wait! [Pause.] No, don't let go! [Pause.] Suppose I do get up, will I ever get down?

MR. SLOCUM [breathing hard]. You'll get down, Mrs. Rooney, you'll get down. We may not get you up, but I warrant you we'll get you down.

[He resumes his efforts. Sound of these.]

MRS. ROONEY. Oh! . . Lower! . . Don't be afraid! . . We're past the age when . . . There! . . Now! . . Get your shoulder under it . . . Oh! . . [Giggles.] Oh glory! . . Up! Up! . . Ah! . . I'm in! [Panting of MR. SLOCUM. He slams the door. In a scream.] My frock! You've nipped my frock! [MR. SLOCUM opens the door. MRS. ROONEY frees her frock. MR. SLOCUM slams the door. His violent unintelligible muttering as he walks round to the other door. Tearfully.] My nice frock! Look what you've done to my nice frock! [MR. SLOCUM gets into his seat, slams driver's door, presses starter. The engine does not start. He releases starter.] What will Dan say when he sees me?

MR. SLOCUM. Has he then recovered his sight?

MRS. ROONEY. No, I mean when he knows, what will he say when he feels the hole? [MR. SLOCUM presses starter. As before. Silence.] What are you doing, Mr. Slocum?

MR. SLOCUM. Gazing straight before me, Mrs. Rooney, through the windscreen, into the void.

MRS. ROONEY. Start her up, I beseech you, and let us be off. This is awful!

MR. SLOCUM [dreamily]. All morning she went like a dream and now she is dead. That is what you get for a good deed. [Pause. Hopefully.] Perhaps if I were to choke her. [He does so, presses the starter. The engine roars. Roaring to make himself heard.] She was getting too much air!

[He throttles down, grinds in his first gear, moves off, changes up in a grinding of gears.]

MRS. ROONEY [in anguish]. Mind the hen! [Scream of brakes. Squawk of hen.] Oh mother, you have squashed her, drive on, drive on! [The car accelerates. Pause.] What a death! One minute picking happy at the dung, on the road, in the sun, with now and then a dust bath, and then— bang!—all her troubles over. [Pause.] All the laying and the hatching. [Pause.] Just one great squawk and then . . . peace. [Pause.] They would have slit her weasand in any case. [Pause.] Here we are, let me down. [The car slows down, stops, engine running. MR. SLOCUM blows his horn. Pause. Louder. Pause.] What are you up to now, Mr. Slocum? We are at a standstill, all danger is past and you blow your horn. Now if instead of blowing it now you had blown it at that unfortunate—

[*Horn violently.* TOMMY *the porter appears at top of station steps.*]

MR. SLOCUM [*calling*]. Will you come down, Tommy, and help this lady out, she's stuck. [TOMMY *descends the steps.*] Open the door, Tommy, and ease her out.

[TOMMY *opens the door.*]

TOMMY. Certainly, Sir. Nice day for the races, Sir. What would you fancy for—

MRS. ROONEY. Don't mind me. Don't take any notice of me. I do not exist. The fact is well known.

MR. SLOCUM. Do as you're asked, Tommy, for the love of God.

TOMMY. Yessir. Now, Mrs. Rooney.

[*He starts pulling her out.*]

MRS. ROONEY. Wait, Tommy, wait now, don't bustle me, just let me wheel round and get my feet to the ground. [*Her efforts to achieve this.*] Now.

TOMMY. [*pulling her out*]. Mind your feather, Ma'am. [*Sounds of effort.*] Easy now, easy.

MRS. ROONEY. Wait, for God's sake, you'll have me beheaded.

TOMMY. Crouch down, Mrs. Rooney, crouch down, and get your head in the open.

MRS. ROONEY. Crouch down! At my time of life! This is lunacy!

TOMMY. Press her down, Sir.

[*Sounds of combined efforts.*]

MRS. ROONEY. Merde!

TOMMY. Now! She's coming! Straighten up, Ma'am! There!

[MR. SLOCUM *slams the door.*]

MRS. ROONEY. Am I out?

[*The voice of* MR. BARRELL, *the station-master, raised in anger.*]

MR. BARRELL. Tommy! Tommy! Where the hell is he?

[MR. SLOCUM *grinds in his gear.*]

TOMMY [*hurriedly*]. You wouldn't have something for the Ladies Plate, Sir, I was given Flash Harry.

MR. SLOCUM [*scornfully*]. Flash Harry! That carthorse!

MR. BARRELL [*at top of steps, roaring*]. Tommy! Blast your bleeding bloody— [*He sees* MRS. ROONEY.] Oh, Mrs. Rooney ... [MR. SLOCUM *drives away in a grinding of gears.*] Who's that crucifying his gearbox, Tommy?

TOMMY. Old Cissy Slocum.

MRS. ROONEY. Cissy Slocum! That's a nice way to refer to your betters. Cissy Slocum! And you an orphan!

MR. BARRELL [*angrily to* TOMMY]. What are you doing stravaging down here on the public road? This is no place for you at all! Nip up there on the platform now and whip out the truck! Won't the twelve thirty be on top of us before we can turn round?

TOMMY [*bitterly*]. And that's the thanks you get for a Christian act.

MR. BARRELL [*violently*]. Get on with you now before I report you! [*Slow feet of* TOMMY *climbing steps.*] Do you want me to come down to you with the shovel? [*The feet quicken, recede, cease.*] Ah, God forgive me, it's a hard life. [*Pause.*] Well, Mrs. Rooney, it's nice to see you up and about again. You were laid up there a long time.

MRS. ROONEY. Not long enough, Mr. Barrell. [*Pause.*] Would I were still in bed, Mr. Barrell. [*Pause.*] Would I were lying stretched out in my comfortable bed, Mr. Barrell, just wasting slowly, painlessly away, keeping up my strength with arrowroot and calves-foot jelly, till in the end you wouldn't see me under the blankets any more than a board. [*Pause.*] Oh no coughing or spitting or bleeding or vomiting, just drifting gently down into the higher life, and remembering, remembering ... [*the voice breaks*] ... all the silly unhappiness ... as though ... it had never happened ... what did I do with that handkerchief? [*Sound of handkerchief loudly applied.*] How long have you been master of this station now, Mr. Barrell?

MR. BARRELL. Don't ask me, Mrs. Rooney, don't ask me.

MRS. ROONEY. You stepped into your father's shoes, I believe, when he took them off.

MR. BARRELL. Poor Pappy! [*Reverent pause.*] He didn't live long to enjoy his ease.

MRS. ROONEY. I remember him clearly. A small ferrety purple-faced widower, deaf as a doornail, very testy and snappy. [*Pause.*] I suppose you'll be retiring soon yourself, Mr. Barrell, and growing your roses. [*Pause.*] Did I understand you to say the twelve thirty would soon be upon us?

MR. BARRELL. Those were my words.

MRS. ROONEY. But according to my watch, which is more or less right—or was—by the eight o'clock ñews, the time is now coming up to twelve ... [*pause as she consults her watch*] ... thirty-six. [*Pause.*] And yet upon the other hand the up mail has not yet gone through. [*Pause.*] Or has it sped by unbeknown to me? [*Pause.*] For there was a moment there, I remember now, I was so plunged in sorrow I wouldn't have heard a steam roller go over me. [*Pause.* MR. BARRELL *turns to go.*] Don't go, Mr. Barrell! [MR. BARRELL *goes. Loud.*] Mr. Barrell! [*Pause. Louder.*] Mr. Barrell!

[MR. BARRELL *comes back.*]

MR. BARRELL [*testily*]. What is it, Mrs. Rooney, I have my work to do.

[*Silence. Sound of wind.*]

MRS. ROONEY. The wind is getting up. [*Pause. Wind.*] The best of the day is over. [*Pause. Wind. Dreamily.*] Soon the rain will begin to fall and go on falling, all afternoon. [MR. BARRELL *goes.*] Then at evening the clouds will part, the setting sun will shine an instant, then sink, behind the hills. [*She realizes* MR. BARRELL *has gone.*] Mr. Barrell! Mr. Barrell! [*Silence.*] I estrange them all. They come towards me, uninvited, bygones bygones, full of kindness, anxious to help ... [*the voice breaks*] ... genuinely pleased ... to see me again ... looking so well ... [*Handkerchief.*] A few simple words ... from my heart ... and I am all alone ... once more ... [*Handkerchief. Vehemently.*] I should not be out at all! I should never leave the grounds! [*Pause.*] Oh there is that Fitt woman, I wonder will she bow to me. [*Sound of* MISS FITT *approaching, humming a hymn. She starts climbing the steps.*] Miss Fitt! [MISS FITT *halts, stops humming.*] Am I then invisible, Miss Fitt? Is this cretonne so becoming to me that I merge into the masonry? [MISS FITT *descends a step.*] That is right, Miss Fitt, look closely and you will finally distinguish a once female shape.

MISS FITT. Mrs. Rooney! I saw you, but I did not know you.

MRS. ROONEY. Last Sunday we wor-

shipped together. We knelt side by side at the same altar. We drank from the same chalice. Have I so changed since then?

MISS FITT [*shocked*]. Oh but in church, Mrs. Rooney, in church I am alone with my Maker. Are not you? [*Pause.*] Why, even the sexton himself, you know, when he takes up the collection, knows it is useless to pause before me. I simply do not see the plate, or bag, whatever it is they use, how could I? [*Pause.*] Why even when all is over and I go out into the sweet fresh air, why even then for the first furlong or so I stumble in a kind of daze as you might say, oblivious to my coreligionists. And they are very kind, I must admit—the vast majority—very kind and understanding. They know me now and take no umbrage. There she goes, they say, there goes the dark Miss Fitt, alone with her Maker, take no notice of her. And they step down off the path to avoid my running into them. [*Pause.*] Ah yes, I am distray, very distray, even on week-days. Ask Mother, if you do not believe me. Hetty, she says, when I start eating my doily instead of the thin bread and butter, Hetty, how can you be so distray? [*Sighs.*] I suppose the truth is I am not there, Mrs. Rooney, just not really there at all. I see, hear, smell, and so on, I go through the usual motions, but my heart is not in it, Mrs. Rooney, but heart is in none of it. Left to myself, with no one to check me, I would soon be flown ... home. [*Pause.*] So if you think I cut you just now, Mrs. Rooney, you do me an injustice. All I saw was a big pale blur, just another big pale blur. [*Pause.*] Is anything amiss, Mrs. Rooney, you do not look normal somehow. So bowed and bent.

MRS. ROONEY [*ruefully*]. Maddy Rooney, née Dunne, the big pale blur. [*Pause.*] You have piercing sight, Miss Fitt, if you only knew it, literally piercing.

[*Pause.*]

MISS FITT. Well ... is there anything I can do, now that I am here?

MRS. ROONEY. If you would help me up the face of this cliff, Miss Fitt, I have little doubt your Maker would requite you, if no one else.

MISS FITT. Now now, Mrs. Rooney, don't put your teeth in me. Requite! I make these sacrifices for nothing—or not at all. [*Pause. Sound of her descending steps.*] I take it you want to lean on me, Mrs. Rooney.

MRS. ROONEY. I asked Mr. Barrell to give me his arm, just give me his arm. [*Pause.*] He turned on his heel and strode away.

MISS FITT. Is it my arm you want then? [*Pause. Impatiently.*] Is it my arm you want, Mrs. Rooney, or what is it?

MRS. ROONEY [*exploding*]. Your arm! Any arm! A helping hand! For five seconds! Christ, what a planet!

MISS FITT. Really . . . Do you know what it is, Mrs. Rooney, I do not think it is wise of you to be going about at all.

MRS. ROONEY [*violently*]. Come down here, Miss Fitt, and give me your arm, before I scream down the parish!

[*Pause. Wind. Sound of* MISS FITT *descending last steps.*]

MISS FITT [*resignedly*]. Well, I suppose it is the Protestant thing to do.

MRS. ROONEY. Pismires do it for one another. [*Pause.*] I have seen slugs do it. [MISS FITT *proffers her arm.*] No, the other side, my dear, if it's all the same to you, I'm left-handed on top of everything else. [*She takes* MISS FITT's *right arm.*] Heavens, child, you're just a bag of bones, you need building up. [*Sound of her toiling up steps on* MISS FITT's *arm.*] This is worse than the Matterhorn, were you ever up the Matterhorn, Miss Fitt, great honeymoon resort. [*Sound of toiling.*] Why don't they have a handrail? [*Panting.*] Wait till I get some air. [*Pause.*] Don't let me go! [MISS FITT *hums her hymn. After a moment* MRS. ROONEY *joins in with the words.*] . . . the encircling gloo-oom [MISS FITT *stops humming*] . . . tum tum me on. [*Forte.*] The night is dark and I am far from ho-ome, tum tum—

MISS FITT [*hysterically*]. Stop it, Mrs. Rooney, stop it, or I'll drop you!

MRS. ROONEY. Wasn't it that they sung on the Lusitania? Or Rock of Ages? Most touching it must have been. Or was it the Titanic?

[*Attracted by the noise a group, including* MR. TYLER, MR. BARRELL *and* TOMMY, *gathers at top of steps.*]

MR. BARRELL. What the—

[*Silence.*]

MR. TYLER. Lovely day for the fixture. [*Loud titter from* TOMMY *cut short by* MR. BARRELL *with backhanded blow in the stomach. Appropriate noise from* TOMMY.]

FEMALE VOICE [*shrill*]. Oh look, Dolly, look!

DOLLY. What, Mamma?

FEMALE VOICE. They are stuck! [*Cackling laugh.*] They are stuck!

MRS. ROONEY. Now we are the laughing-stock of the twenty-six counties. Or is it thirty-six?

MR. TYLER. That is a nice way to treat your defenceless subordinates, Mr. Barrell, hitting them without warning in the pit of the stomach.

MISS FITT. Has anybody seen my mother?

MR. BARRELL. Who is that?

TOMMY. The dark Miss Fitt.

MR. BARRELL. Where is her face?

MRS. ROONEY. Now, deary, I am ready if you are. [*They toil up remaining steps.*] Stand back, you cads!

[*Shuffle of feet.*]

FEMALE VOICE. Mind yourself, Dolly!

MRS. ROONEY. Thank you, Miss Fitt, thank you, that will do, just prop me up against the wall like a roll of tarpaulin and that will be all, for the moment. [*Pause.*] I am sorry for all this ramdam, Miss Fitt, had I known you were looking for your mother I should not have importuned you, I know what it is.

MR. TYLER [*in marvelling aside*]. Ramdam!

FEMALE VOICE. Come, Dolly darling, let us take up our stand before the first-class smokers. Give me your hand and hold me tight, one can be sucked under.

MR. TYLER. You have lost your mother, Miss Fitt?

MISS FITT. Good-morning, Mr. Tyler.

MR. TYLER. Good-morning, Miss Fitt.

MR. BARRELL. Good-morning, Miss Fitt.

MISS FITT. Good-morning, Mr. Barrell.

MR. TYLER. You have lost your mother, Miss Fitt?

MISS FITT. She said she would be on the last train.

MRS. ROONEY. Do not imagine, because I am silent, that I am not present, and alive, to all that is going on.

MR. TYLER [*to* MISS FITT]. When you say the last train—

MRS. ROONEY. Do not flatter yourselves for one moment, because I hold aloof, that my sufferings have ceased. No. The entire scene, the hills, the plain, the racecourse with its miles and miles of white rails and three red stands, the pretty little wayside station, even you yourselves, yes, I mean it, and over all the clouding blue, I see it all, I stand here and see it all with eyes . . . [*the voice breaks*] . . . through eyes . . . oh, if you had my eyes . . . you would understand. . . the things they have seen . . . and not looked away . . . this is nothing . . . nothing . . . what did I do with that handkerchief?

[*Pause.*]

MR. TYLER [*to* MISS FITT]. When you say the last train—[MRS. ROONEY *blows her nose violently and long*]—when you say the last train, Miss Fitt, I take it you mean the twelve thirty.

MISS FITT. What else could I mean, Mr. Tyler, what else could I *conceivably* mean?

MR. TYLER. Then you have no cause for anxiety, Miss Fitt, for the twelve thirty has not yet arrived. Look. [MISS FITT *looks.*] No, up the line. [MISS FITT *looks. Patiently.*] No, Miss Fitt, follow the direction of my index. [MISS FITT *looks.*] There. You see now. The signal. At the bawdy hour of nine. [*In rueful afterthought.*] Or three alas! [MR. BARRELL *stifles a guffaw.*] Thank you, Mr. Barrell.

MISS FITT. But the time is now getting on for—

MR. TYLER [*patiently*]. We all know, Miss Fitt, we all know only too well what the time is now getting on for, and yet the cruel fact remains that the twelve thirty has not yet arrived.

MISS FITT. Not an accident, I trust! [*Pause.*] Do not tell me she has left the track! [*Pause.*] Oh darling mother! With the fresh sole for lunch!

[*Loud titter from* TOMMY, *checked as before by* MR. BARRELL.]

MR. BARRELL. That's enough old guff out of you. Nip up to the box now and see has Mr. Case anything for me.

[TOMMY *goes.*]

MRS. ROONEY [*sadly*]. Poor Dan!

MISS FITT [*in anguish*]. What terrible thing has happened?

MR. TYLER. Now now, Miss Fitt, do not—

MRS. ROONEY [*with vehement sadness*]. Poor Dan!

MR. TYLER. Now now, Miss Fitt, do not give way . . . to despair, all will come right . . . in the end. [*Aside to* MR. BARRELL.] What *is* the situation, Mr. Barrell? Not a collision, surely?

MRS. ROONEY [*enthusiastically*]. A collision! Oh that would be wonderful!

MISS FITT [*horrified*]. A collision! I knew it!

MR. TYLER. Come, Miss Fitt, let us move a little up the platform.

MRS. ROONEY. Yes, let us all do that. [*Pause.*] No? [*Pause.*] You have changed your mind? [*Pause.*] I quite agree, we are better here, in the shadow of the waiting-room.

MR. BARRELL. Excuse me a moment.

MRS. ROONEY. Before you slink away, Mr. Barrell, please, a statement of some kind, I insist. Even the slowest train on this brief line is not ten minutes and more behind its scheduled time without good cause, one imagines. [*Pause.*] We all know your station is the best kept of the entire network, but there are times when that is not enough, just not enough. [*Pause.*] Now, Mr. Barrell, leave off chewing your whiskers, we are waiting to hear from you—we, the unfortunate ticket-holders' nearest if not dearest.

[*Pause.*]

MR. TYLER [*reasonably*]. I do think we are owed some kind of explanation, Mr. Barrell, if only to set our minds at rest.

MR. BARRELL. I know nothing. All I know is there has been a hitch. All traffic is retarded.

MRS. ROONEY [*derisively*]. Retarded! A hitch! Ah these celibates! Here we are eating our hearts out with anxiety for our loved ones and he calls that a hitch! Those of us like myself with heart and kidney trouble may collapse at any moment and he calls that a hitch! In our ovens the Saturday roast is burning to a shrivel and he calls that—

MR. TYLER. Here comes Tommy, running! I am glad I have been spared to see this.

TOMMY [*excitedly, in the distance*]. She's coming. [*Pause. Nearer.*] She's at the level-crossing!

[*Immediately exaggerated station sounds. Falling signals. Bells. Whistles. Crescendo of train whistle approaching. Sound of train rushing through station.*]

MRS. ROONEY [*above rush of train*]. The up mail! The up mail! [*The up mail recedes, the down train approaches, enters the station, pulls up with great hissing of steam and clashing of couplings. Noise of passengers descending, doors banging,* MR. BARRELL *shouting "Boghill! Boghill!", etc. Piercingly.*] Dan! . . Are you all right? . . Where is he? . . Dan! . . Did you see my husband? . . Dan! . . [*Noise of station emptying. Guard's whistle. Train departing, receding. Silence.*] He isn't on it! The misery I have endured, to get here, and he isn't on it! . . Mr. Barrell! . . Was he not on it? [*Pause.*] Is anything the matter, you look as if you had seen a ghost. [*Pause.*] Tommy! . . Did you see the master?

TOMMY. He'll be along, Ma'am, Jerry is minding him.

[MR. ROONEY *suddenly appears on platform, advancing on small boy* JERRY's *arm. He is blind, thumps the ground with his stick and pants incessantly.*]

MRS. ROONEY. Oh, Dan! There you are! [*Her dragging feet as she hastens towards him. She reaches him. They halt.*] Where in the world were you?

MR. ROONEY [*coolly*]. Maddy.

MRS. ROONEY. Where were you all this time?

MR. ROONEY. In the men's.

MRS. ROONEY. Kiss me!

MR. ROONEY. Kiss you? In public? On the platform? Before the boy? Have you taken leave of your senses?

MRS. ROONEY. Jerry wouldn't mind. Would you, Jerry?

JERRY. No, Ma'am.

MRS. ROONEY. How is your poor father?

JERRY. They took him away, Ma'am.

MRS. ROONEY. Then you are all alone?

JERRY. Yes, Ma'am.

MR. ROONEY. Why are you here? You did not notify me.

MRS. ROONEY. I wanted to give you a surprise. For your birthday.

MR. ROONEY. My birthday?

MRS. ROONEY. Don't you remember? I wished you your happy returns in the bathroom.

MR. ROONEY. I did not hear you.

MRS. ROONEY. But I gave you a tie! You have it on!

[*Pause.*]

MR. ROONEY. How old am I now?

MRS. ROONEY. Now never mind about that. Come.

MR. ROONEY. Why did you not cancel the boy? Now we shall have to give him a penny.

MRS. ROONEY [*miserably*]. I forgot! I had such a time getting here! Such horrid nasty people! [*Pause. Pleading.*] Be nice to me, Dan, be nice to me to-day!

MR. ROONEY. Give the boy a penny.

MRS. ROONEY. Here are two halfpennies, Jerry. Run along now and buy yourself a nice gobstopper.

JERRY. Yes, Ma'am.

MR. ROONEY. Come for me on Monday, if I am still alive.

JERRY. Yessir.

[*He runs off.*]

MR. ROONEY. We could have saved sixpence. We have saved fivepence. [*Pause.*] But at what cost?

[*They move off along platform arm in arm. Dragging feet, panting, thudding stick.*]

MRS. ROONEY. Are you not well?

[*They halt, on* MR. ROONEY's *initiative.*]

MR. ROONEY. Once and for all, do not ask me to speak and move at the same time. I shall not say this in this life again.

[*They move off. Dragging feet, etc. They halt at top of steps.*]

MRS. ROONEY. Are you not—

MR. ROONEY. Let us get this precipice over.

MRS. ROONEY. Put your arm round me.

MR. ROONEY. Have you been drinking again? [*Pause.*] You are quivering like a blanc-mange. [*Pause.*] Are you in a condition to lead me? [*Pause.*] We shall fall into the ditch.

MRS. ROONEY. Oh, Dan! It will be like old times!

MR. ROONEY. Pull yourself together or I shall send Tommy for the cab. Then, instead of having saved sixpence, no, fivepence, we shall have lost . . . [*calculating mumble*] . . . two and three less six one and no plus one one and no plus three one and nine and one ten and three two and one . . . [*normal voice*] two and one, we shall be the poorer to the tune of two and one. [*Pause.*] Curse that sun, it has gone in. What is the day doing?

[*Wind.*]

MRS. ROONEY. Shrouding, shrouding,

the best of it is past. [*Pause.*] Soon the first great drops will fall splashing in the dust.

MR. ROONEY. And yet the glass was firm. [*Pause.*] Let us hasten home and sit before the fire. We shall draw the blinds. You will read to me. I think Effie is going to commit adultery with the Major. [*Brief drag of feet.*] Wait! [*Feet cease. Stick tapping at steps.*] I have been up and down these steps five thousand times and still I do not know how many there are. When I think there are six there are four or five or seven or eight and when I remember there are five there are three or four or six or seven and when finally I realize there are seven there are five or six or eight or nine. Sometimes I wonder if they do not change them in the night. [*Pause. Irritably.*] Well? How many do you make them to-day?

MRS. ROONEY. Do not ask me to count, Dan, not now.

MR. ROONEY. Not count! One of the few satisfactions in life?

MRS. ROONEY. Not steps, Dan, please, I always get them wrong. Then you might fall on your wound and I would have that on my manure-heap on top of everything else. No, just cling to me and all will be well.

[*Confused noise of their descent. Panting, stumbling, ejaculations, curses. Silence.*]

MR. ROONEY. Well! That is what you call well!

MRS. ROONEY. We are down. And little the worse. [*Silence. A donkey brays. Silence.*] That was a true donkey. Its father and mother were donkeys.

[*Silence.*]

MR. ROONEY. Do you know what, I think I shall retire.

MRS. ROONEY [*appalled*]. Retire! And live at home? On your grant?

MR. ROONEY. Never tread these cursed steps again. Trudge this hellish road for the last time. Sit at home on the remnants of my bottom counting the hours —till the next meal. [*Pause.*] The very thought puts life in me! Forward, before it dies!

[*They move on. Dragging feet, panting, thudding stick.*]

MRS. ROONEY. Now mind, here is the path . . . Up! . . Well done! Now we are in safety and a straight run home.

MR. ROONEY [*without halting, between gasps*]. A straight . . . run! . . She calls that . . . a straight . . . run! . .

MRS. ROONEY. Hush! do not speak as you go along, you know it is not good for your coronary. [*Dragging steps, etc.*] Just concentrate on putting one foot before the next or whatever the expression is. [*Dragging feet, etc.*] That is the way, now we are doing nicely. [*Dragging feet, etc. They suddenly halt, on* MRS. ROONEY's *initiative.*] Heavens! I knew there was something! With all the excitement! I forgot!

MR. ROONEY [*quietly*]. Good God.

MRS. ROONEY. But you must know, Dan, of course, you were on it. What ever happened? Tell me!

MR. ROONEY. I have never known anything to happen.

MRS. ROONEY. But you must—

MR. ROONEY [*violently*]. All this stopping and starting again is devilish, devilish! I get a little way on me and begin to be carried along when suddenly you stop dead! Two hundred pounds of unhealthy fat! What possessed you to come out at all? Let go of me!

MRS. ROONEY [*in great agitation*]. No, I must know, we won't stir from here till you tell me. Fifteen minutes late! On a thirty minute run! It's unheard of!

MR. ROONEY. I know nothing. Let go of me before I shake you off.

MRS. ROONEY. But you must know! You were on it! Was it at the terminus? Did you leave on time? Or was it on the line? [*Pause.*] Did something happen on the line? [*Pause.*] Dan! [*Brokenly.*] Why won't you tell me!

[*Silence. They move off. Dragging feet, etc. They halt. Pause.*]

MR. ROONEY. Poor Maddy! [*Pause. Children's cries.*] What was that?

[*Pause for* MRS. ROONEY *to ascertain.*]

MRS. ROONEY. The Lynch twins jeering at us.

[*Cries.*]

MR. ROONEY. Will they pelt us with mud to-day, do you suppose?

[*Cries.*]

MRS. ROONEY. Let us turn and face them. [*Cries. They turn. Silence.*] Threaten them with your stick. [*Silence.*] They have run away.

[*Pause.*]

MR. ROONEY. Did you ever wish to kill

a child? [*Pause.*] Nip some young doom in the bud. [*Pause.*] Many a time at night, in winter, on the black road home, I nearly attacked the boy. [*Pause.*] Poor Jerry! [*Pause.*] What restrained me then? [*Pause.*] Not fear of man. [*Pause.*] Shall we go on backwards now a little?

MRS. ROONEY. Backwards?

MR. ROONEY. Yes. Or you forwards and I backwards. The perfect pair. Like Dante's damned, with their faces arsyversy. Our tears will water our bottoms.

MRS. ROONEY. What is the matter, Dan? Are you not well?

MR. ROONEY. Well! Did you ever know me to be well? The day you met me I should have been in bed. The day you proposed to me the doctors gave me up. You knew that, did you not? The night you married me they came for me with an ambulance. You have not forgotten that, I suppose? [*Pause.*] No, I cannot be said to be well. But I am no worse. Indeed I am better than I was. The loss of my sight was a great fillip. If I could go deaf and dumb I think I might pant on to be a hundred. Or have I done so? [*Pause.*] Was I a hundred to-day? [*Pause.*] Am I a hundred, Maddy?

[*Silence.*]

MRS. ROONEY. All is still. No living soul in sight. There is no one to ask. The world is feeding. The wind—[*brief wind*]—scarcely stirs the leaves and the birds—[*brief chirp*]—are tired singing. The cows—[*brief moo*]—and sheep—[*brief baa*]—ruminate in silence. The dogs—[*brief bark*]—are hushed and the hens—[*brief cackle*]—sprawl torpid in the dust. We are alone. There is no one to ask.

[*Silence.*]

MR. ROONEY [*clearing his throat, narrative tone*]. We drew out on the tick of time, I can vouch for that. I was—

MRS. ROONEY. How can you vouch for it?

MR. ROONEY [*normal tone, angrily*]. I can vouch for it, I tell you! Do you want my relation or don't you? [*Pause. Narrative tone.*] On the tick of time. I had the compartment to myself, as usual. At least I hope so, for I made no attempt to restrain myself. My mind—[*Normal tone.*] But why do we not sit down somewhere? Are we afraid we should never rise again?

MRS. ROONEY. Sit down on what?

MR. ROONEY. On a bench, for example.

MRS. ROONEY. There is no bench.

MR. ROONEY. Then on a bank, let us sink down upon a bank.

MRS. ROONEY. There is no bank.

MR. ROONEY. Then we cannot. [*Pause.*] I dream of other roads, in other lands. Of another home, another—[*he hesitates*]—another home. [*Pause.*] What was I trying to say?

MRS. ROONEY. Something about your mind.

MR. ROONEY [*startled*]. My mind? Are you sure? [*Pause. Incredulous.*] My mind?.. [*Pause.*] Ah yes. [*Narrative tone.*] Alone in the compartment my mind began to work, as so often after office hours, on the way home, in the train, to the lilt of the bogeys. Your season-ticket, I said, costs you twelve pounds a year and you earn, on an average, seven and six a day, that is to say barely enough to keep you alive and twitching with the help of food, drink, tobacco and periodicals until you finally reach home and fall into bed. Add to this—or subtract from it—rent, stationery, various subscriptions, tramfares to and fro, light and heat, permits and licenses, hairtrims and shaves, tips to escorts, upkeep of premises and appearances, and a thousand unspecifiable sundries, and it is clear that by lying at home in bed, day and night, winter and summer, with a change of pyjamas once a fortnight, you would add very considerably to your income. Business, I said—[*A cry. Pause. Again. Normal tone.*] Did I hear a cry?

MRS. ROONEY. Mrs. Tully, I fancy. Her poor husband is in constant pain and beats her unmercifully.

[*Silence.*]

MR. ROONEY. That was a short knock. [*Pause.*] What was I trying to get at?

MRS. ROONEY. Business.

MR. ROONEY. Ah yes, business. [*Narrative tone.*] Business, old man, I said, retire from business, it has retired from you. [*Normal tone.*] One has these moments of lucidity.

MRS. ROONEY. I feel very cold and weak.

MR. ROONEY [*narrative tone*]. On the other hand, I said, there are the horrors of home life, the dusting, sweeping, airing, scrubbing, waxing, waning, washing, mangling, drying, mowing, clipping, raking, rolling, scuffling, shoveling, grinding, tearing, pounding, banging and slamming. And the brats, the happy little hearty little howling neighbours' brats. Of all this and much more the week-end, the Saturday intermission and then the day of rest, have given you some idea. But what must it be like on a working-day? A Wednesday? A Friday! What must it be like on a Friday! And I fell to thinking of my silent, back-street, basement office, with its obliterated plate, rest-couch and velvet hangings, and what it means to be buried there alive, if only from ten to five, with convenient to the one hand a bottle of light pale ale and to the other a long ice-cold fillet of hake. Nothing, I said, not even fully certified death, can ever take the place of that. It was then I noticed we were at a standstill. [*Pause. Normal tone. Irritably.*] Why are you hanging out of me like that? Have you swooned away?

MRS. ROONEY. I feel very cold and faint. The wind—[*whistling wind*]—is whistling through my summer frock as if I had nothing on over my bloomers. I have had no solid food since my elevenses.

MR. ROONEY. You have ceased to care. I speak—and you listen to the wind.

MRS. ROONEY. No no, I am agog, tell me all, then we shall press on and never pause, never pause, till we come safe to haven.

[*Pause.*]

MR. ROONEY. Never pause . . . safe to haven . . . Do you know, Maddy, sometimes one would think you were struggling with a dead language.

MRS. ROONEY. Yes indeed, Dan, I know full well what you mean, I often have that feeling, it is unspeakably excruciating.

MR. ROONEY. I confess I have it sometimes myself, when I happen to overhear what I am saying.

MRS. ROONEY. Well, you know, it will be dead in time, just like our own poor dear Gaelic, there is that to be said.

[*Urgent baa.*]

MR. ROONEY [*startled*]. Good God!

MRS. ROONEY. Oh, the pretty little woolly lamb, crying to suck its mother! Theirs has not changed, since Arcady.

[*Pause.*]

MR. ROONEY. Where was I in my composition?

MRS. ROONEY. At a standstill.

MR. ROONEY. Ah yes. [*Clears his throat. Narrative tone.*] I concluded naturally that we had entered a station and would soon be on our way again, and I sat on, without misgiving. Not a sound. Things are very dull to-day, I said, nobody getting down, nobody getting on. Then as time flew by and nothing happened I realized my error. We had not entered a station.

MRS. ROONEY. Did you not spring up and poke your head out of the window?

MR. ROONEY. What good would that have done me?

MRS. ROONEY. Why to call out to be told what was amiss.

MR. ROONEY. I did not care what was amiss. No, I just sat on, saying, If this train were never to move again I should not greatly mind. Then gradually a—how shall I say—a growing desire to—er—you know—welled up within me. Nervous, probably. In fact now I am sure. You know, the feeling of being confined.

MRS. ROONEY. Yes yes, I have been through that.

MR. ROONEY. If we sit here much longer, I said, I really do not know what I shall do. I got up and paced to and fro between the seats, like a caged beast.

MRS. ROONEY. That is a help sometimes.

MR. ROONEY. After what seemed an eternity we simply moved off. And the next thing was Barrell bawling the abhorred name. I got down and Jerry led me to the men's, or Fir as they call it now, from Vir Viris I suppose, the V becoming *F*, in accordance with Grimm's Law. [*Pause.*] The rest you know. [*Pause.*] You say nothing? [*Pause.*] Say something, Maddy. Say you believe me.

MRS. ROONEY. I remember once attending a lecture by one of these new mind doctors, I forget what you call them. He spoke—

MR. ROONEY. A lunatic specialist?

MRS. ROONEY. No no, just the troubled mind, I was hoping he might shed a little light on my lifelong preoccupation with horses' buttocks.

MR. ROONEY. A neurologist.

MRS. ROONEY. No no, just mental distress, the name will come back to me in the night. I remember his telling us the

story of a little girl, very strange and unhappy in her ways, and how he treated
her unsuccessfully over a period of years
and was finally obliged to give up the
case. He could find nothing wrong with
her, he said. The only thing wrong with
her as far as he could see was that she
was dying. And she did in fact die,
shortly after he washed his hands of her.

MR. ROONEY. Well? What is there so
wonderful about that?

MRS. ROONEY. No, it was just something he said, and the way he said it, that
have haunted me ever since.

MR. ROONEY. You lie awake at night,
tossing to and fro and brooding on it.

MRS. ROONEY. On it and other . . .
wretchedness. [Pause.] When he had
done with the little girl he stood there
motionless for some time, quite two minutes I should say, looking down at his
table. Then he suddenly raised his head
and exclaimed, as if he had had a revelation, The trouble with her was she had
never been really born! [Pause.] He spoke
throughout without notes. [Pause.] I left
before the end.

MR. ROONEY. Nothing about your buttocks? [MRS. ROONEY weeps. In affectionate remonstrance.] Maddy!

MRS. ROONEY. There is nothing to be
done for those people.

MR. ROONEY. For which is there?
[Pause.] That does not sound right somehow. [Pause.] What way am I facing?

MRS. ROONEY. What?

MR. ROONEY. I have forgotten what
way I am facing.

MRS. ROONEY. You have turned aside
and are bowed down over the ditch.

MR. ROONEY. There is a dead dog down
there.

MRS. ROONEY. No no, just the rotting
leaves.

MR. ROONEY. In June? Rotting leaves
in June?

MRS. ROONEY. Yes dear, from last year,
and from the year before last, and from
the year before that again. [Silence. Rainy
wind. They move on. Dragging steps,
etc.] There is that lovely laburnum again.
Poor thing, it is losing all its tassels.
[Dragging steps, etc.] There are the first
drops. [Rain. Dragging feet, etc.] Golden
drizzle. [Dragging steps, etc.] Do not
mind me, dear, I am just talking to my-

self. [Rain heavier. Dragging steps, etc.]
Can hinnies procreate, I wonder.

[They halt, on MR. ROONEY's initiative.]

MR. ROONEY. Say that again.

MRS. ROONEY. Come on, dear, don't
mind me, we are getting drenched.

MR. ROONEY [forcibly]. Can what
what?

MRS. ROONEY. Hinnies procreate. [Si-
lence.] You know, hinnies, or is it jinnies,
aren't they barren, or sterile, or whatever
it is? [Pause.] It wasn't an ass's colt
at all, you know, I asked the Regius
Professor.

[Pause.]

MR. ROONEY. He should know.

MRS. ROONEY. Yes, it was a hinny, he
rode into Jerusalem, or wherever it was,
on a hinny. [Pause.] That must mean
something. [Pause.] It's like the sparrows,
than many of which we are of more value,
they weren't sparrows at all.

MR. ROONEY. Than many of which . . .
You exaggerate, Maddy.

MRS. ROONEY [with emotion]. They
weren't sparrows at all!

MR. ROONEY. Does that put our price
up?

[Silence. They move on. Wind and
rain. Dragging feet, etc. They halt.]

MRS. ROONEY. Do you want some
dung? [Silence. They move on. Wind
and rain, etc. They halt.] Why do you
stop? Do you want to say something?

MR. ROONEY. No.

MRS. ROONEY. Then why do you stop?

MR. ROONEY. It is easier.

MRS. ROONEY. Are you very wet?

MR. ROONEY. To the buff.

MRS. ROONEY. The buff?

MR. ROONEY. The buff. From buffalo.

MRS. ROONEY. We shall hang up all
our things in the hot-cupboard and get
into our dressing-gowns. [Pause.] Put
your arm round me. [Pause.] Be nice to
me! [Pause. Gratefully.] Ah Dan! [They
move on. Wind and rain. Dragging feet,
etc. Faintly same music as before. They
halt. Music clearer. Silence but for music
playing. Music dies.] All day the same
old record. All alone in that great empty
house. She must be a very old woman
now.

MR. ROONEY [indistinctly]. Death and
the Maiden.

[*Silence.*]

MRS. ROONEY. You are crying. [*Pause.*] Are you crying?

MR. ROONEY [*violently*]. Yes! [*They move on. Wind and rain. Dragging feet, etc. They halt. They move on. Wind and rain. Dragging feet, etc. They halt.*] Who is the preacher to-morrow? The incumbent?

MRS. ROONEY. No.

MR. ROONEY. Thank God for that. Who?

MRS. ROONEY. Hardy.

MR. ROONEY. "How to be Happy though Married"?

MRS. ROONEY. No no, he died, you remember. No connexion.

MR. ROONEY. Has he announced the text?

MRS. ROONEY. "The Lord upholdeth all that fall and raiseth up all those that be bowed down." [*Silence. They join in wild laughter. They move on. Wind and rain. Dragging feet, etc.*] Hold me tighter, Dan! [*Pause.*] Oh yes!

[*They halt.*]

MR. ROONEY. I hear something behind us.

[*Pause.*]

MRS. ROONEY. It looks like Jerry. [*Pause.*] It is Jerry.

[*Sound of* JERRY'S *running steps approaching. He halts beside them, panting.*]

JERRY [*panting*]. You dropped—

MRS. ROONEY. Take your time, my little man, you will burst a bloodvessel.

JERRY [*panting*]. You dropped something, Sir, Mr. Barrell told me to run after you.

MRS. ROONEY. Show. [*She takes the object.*] What is it? [*She examines it.*] What is this thing, Dan?

MR. ROONEY. Perhaps it is not mine at all.

JERRY. Mr. Barrell said it was, Sir.

MRS. ROONEY. It looks like a kind of ball. And yet it is not a ball.

MR. ROONEY. Give it to me.

MRS. ROONEY [*giving it*]. What *is* it, Dan?

MR. ROONEY. It is a thing I carry about with me.

MRS. ROONEY. Yes, but what—

MR. ROONEY [*violently*]. It is a thing I carry about with me!

[*Silence.* MRS. ROONEY *looks for a penny.*]

MRS. ROONEY. I have no small money. Have you?

MR. ROONEY. I have none of any kind.

MRS. ROONEY. We are out of change, Jerry. Remind Mr. Rooney on Monday and he will give you a penny for your pains.

JERRY. Yes, Ma'am.

MR. ROONEY. If I am alive.

JERRY. Yessir.

[JERRY *starts running back towards the station.*]

MRS. ROONEY. Jerry! [JERRY *halts.*] Did you hear what the hitch was? [*Pause.*] Did you hear what kept the train so late?

MR. ROONEY. How would he have heard? Come on.

MRS. ROONEY. What was it, Jerry?

JERRY. It was a—

MR. ROONEY. Leave the boy alone, he knows nothing! Come on!

MRS. ROONEY. What was it, Jerry?

JERRY. It was a little child, Ma'am.

[MR. ROONEY *groans.*]

MRS. ROONEY. What do you mean, it was a little child?

JERRY. It was a little child fell out of the carriage. On to the line, Ma'am. [*Pause.*] Under the wheels, Ma'am.

[*Silence.* JERRY *runs off. His steps die away. Tempest of wind and rain. It abates. They move on. Dragging steps, etc. They halt. Tempest of wind and rain.*]

Tom F. Driver

BECKETT BY THE MADELEINE

Nothing like Godot, he arrived before the hour. His letter had suggested we meet at my hotel at noon on Sunday, and I came into the lobby as the clock struck twelve. He was waiting.

My wish to meet Samuel Beckett had been prompted by simple curiosity and interest in his work. American newspaper reviewers like to call his plays nihilistic. They find deep pessimism in them. Even so astute a commentator as Harold Clurman of *The Nation* has said that *Waiting for Godot* is "the concentrate . . . of the contemporary European . . . mood of despair." But to me Beckett's writing had seemed permeated with love for human beings and with a kind of humor that I could reconcile neither with despair nor with nihilism. Could it be that my own eyes and ears had deceived me? Is his a literature of defeat, irrelevant to the social crises we face? Or is it relevant because it teaches us something useful to know about ourselves?

I knew that a conversation with the author would not settle such questions, because a man is not the same as his writing: in the last analysis, the questions had to be settled by the work itself. Nevertheless I was curious.

My curiosity was sharpened a day or two before the interview by a conversation I had with a well-informed teacher of literature, a Jesuit father, at a conference on religious drama near Paris. When Beckett's name came into the discussion, the priest grew loud and told me that Beckett "hates life." That, I thought, is at least one thing I can find out when we meet.

Beckett's appearance is rough-hewn Irish. The features of his face are distinct, but not fine. They look as if they had been sculptured with an unsharpened chisel. Unruly hair goes straight up from his forehead, standing so high that the top falls gently over, as if to show that it really is hair and not bristle. One might say it combines the man's own pride and humility. For he has the pride that comes of self-acceptance and the humility, perhaps of the same genesis, not to impose himself upon another. His light blue eyes, set deep within the face, are actively and continually looking. He seems, by some unconscious division of labor, to have given them that one function and no other, leaving communication to the rest of the face. The mouth frequently breaks into a disarming smile. The voice is light in timbre, with a rough edge that corresponds to his visage. The Irish accent is, as one would expect, combined with slight inflections from the French. His tweed suit was a baggy gray and green. He wore a brown knit sports shirt with no tie.

We walked down the Rue de L'Arcade, thence along beside the Madeleine and across to a sidewalk cafe opposite that church. The conversation that ensued may have been engrossing but it could hardly be called world-shattering. For one thing, the world that Beckett sees is already shattered. His talk turns to what he calls "the mess," or sometimes "this buzzing confusion." I reconstruct his sentences from notes made immediately after our conversation. What appears here is shorter than what he actually said but very close to his own words.

"The confusion is not my invention. We cannot listen to a conversation for five minutes without being acutely aware of the confusion. It is all around us and our only chance now is to let it in. The

SOURCE: From *Columbia University Forum*, 4 (Summer 1961). Copyright © 1961 by Tom F. Driver. Reprinted by permission of the Author and his Agents, James Brown Associates, Inc.

only chance of renovation is to open our eyes and see the mess. It is not a mess you can make sense of."

I suggested that one must let it in because it is the truth, but Beckett did not take to the word truth.

"What is more true than anything else? To swim is true, and to sink is true. One is not more true than the other. One cannot speak anymore of being, one must speak only of the mess. When Heidegger and Sartre speak of a contrast between being and existence, they may be right, I don't know, but their language is too philosophical for me. I am not a philosopher. One can only speak of what is in front of him, and that now is simply the mess."

Then he began to speak about the tension in art between the mess and form. Until recently, art has withstood the pressure of chaotic things. It has held them at bay. It realized that to admit them was to jeopardize form. "How could the mess be admitted, because it appears to be the very opposite of form and therefore destructive of the very thing that art holds itself to be?" But now we can keep it out no longer, because we have come into a time when "it invades our experience at every moment. It is there and it must be allowed in."

I granted this might be so, but found the result to be even more attention to form than was the case previously. And why not? How, I asked, could chaos be admitted to chaos? Would not that be the end of thinking and the end of art? If we look at recent art we find it preoccupied with form. Beckett's own work is an example. Plays more highly formalized than Waiting for Godot, Endgame, and Krapp's Last Tape would be hard to find.

"What I am saying does not mean that there will henceforth be no form in art. It only means that there will be new form, and that this form will be of such a type that it admits the chaos and does not try to say that the chaos is really something else. The form and the chaos remain separate. The latter is not reduced to the former. That is why the form itself becomes a preoccupation, because it exists as a problem separate from the material it accommodates. To find a form that accommodates the mess, that is the task of the artist now."

Yet, I responded, could not similar things be said about the art of the past? Is it not characteristic of the greatest art that it confronts us with something we cannot clarify, demanding that the viewer respond to it in his own never-predictable way? What is the history of criticism but the history of men attempting to make sense of the manifold elements in art that will not allow themselves to be reduced to a single philosophy or a single aesthetic theory? Isn't all art ambiguous?

"Not this," he said, and gestured toward the Madeleine. The classical lines of the church, which Napoleon thought of as a Temple of Glory, dominated all the scene where we sat. The Boulevard de la Madeleine, the Boulevard Malesherbes, and the Rue Royale ran to it with graceful flattery, bearing tidings of the Age of Reason. "Not this. This is clear. This does not allow the mystery to invade us. With classical art, all is settled. But it is different at Chartres. There is the unexplainable, and there art raises questions that it does not attempt to answer."

I asked about the battle between life and death in his plays. Didi and Gogo hover on the edge of suicide; Hamm's world is death and Clov may or may not get out of it to join the living child outside. Is this life-death question a part of the chaos?

"Yes. If life and death did not both present themselves to us, there would be no inscrutability. If there were only darkness, all would be clear. It is because there is not only darkness but also light that our situation becomes inexplicable. Take Augustine's doctrine of grace given and grace withheld: have you pondered the dramatic qualities in this theology? Two thieves are crucified with Christ, one saved and the other damned. How can we make sense of this division? In classical drama, such problems do not arise. The destiny of Racine's Phèdre is sealed from the beginning: she will proceed into the dark. As she goes, she herself will be illuminated. At the beginning of the play she has partial illumination and at the end she has complete illumination, but there has been no question but that she moves toward the dark. That is the play. Within this notion clarity is possible, but for us who are neither Greek nor Jansenist there is not such clarity. The question would also be removed if we believed in the contrary—total salvation. But where we have both dark and light we have also the inexplicable. The key word in my plays is 'perhaps.'"

Given a theological lead, I asked what he thinks about those who find a religious significance to his plays.

"Well, really there is none at all. I have no religious feeling. Once I had a religious emotion. It was at my first Communion. No more. My mother was deeply religious. So was my brother. He knelt down at his bed as long as he could kneel. My father had none. The family was Protestant, but for me it was only irksome and I let it go. My brother and mother got no value from their religion when they died. At the moment of crisis it had no more depth than an old-school tie. Irish Catholicism is not attractive, but it is deeper. When you pass a church on an Irish bus, all the hands flurry in the sign of the cross. One day the dogs of Ireland will do that too and perhaps also the pigs."

But do the plays deal with the same facets of experience religion must also deal with?

"Yes, for they deal with distress. Some people object to this in my writing. At a party an English intellectual—so-called— asked me why I write always about distress. As if it were perverse to do so! He wanted to know if my father had beaten me or my mother had run away from home to give me an unhappy childhood. I told him no, that I had had a very happy childhood. Then he thought me more perverse than ever. I left the party as soon as possible and got into a taxi. On the glass partition between me and the driver were three signs: one asked for help for the blind, another, help for orphans, and the third for relief for the war refugees. One does not have to look for distress. It is screaming at you even in the taxis of London."

Lunch was over, and we walked back to the hotel with the light and dark of Paris screaming at us.

The personal quality of Samuel Beckett is similar to qualities I had found in the plays. He says nothing that compresses experience within a closed pattern. "Perhaps" stands in place of commitment. At the same time, he is plainly sympathetic, clearly friendly. If there were only the mess, all would be clear; but there is also compassion.

As a Christian, I know I do not stand where Beckett stands, but I do see much of what he sees. As a writer on the theater, I have paid close attention to the plays. Harold Clurman is right to say that *Waiting for Godot* is a reflection (he calls it a distorted reflection) "of the impasse and disarray of Europe's present politics, ethic, and common way of life." Yet it is not only Europe the play refers to. *Waiting for Godot* sells even better in America than in France. The consciousness it mirrors may have come earlier to Europe than to America, but it is the consciousness that most "mature" societies arrive at when their successes in technological and economic systematization propel them into a time of examining the not-strictly-practical ends of culture. America is now joining Europe in this "mature" phase of development. Whether any of us remain in it long will depend on what happens as a result of the technological and economic revolutions now going on in the countries of Asia and Africa, and also of course on how long the cold war remains cold. At present no political party in Western Europe or America seems possessed of a philosophy of social change adequate to the pressures of current history.

In the Beckett plays, time does not go forward. We are always at the end, where events repeat themselves (*Waiting for Godot*), or hover at the edge of nothingness (*Endgame*), or turn back to the long-ago moment of genuine life (*Krapp's Last Tape*). This retreat from action may disappoint those of us who believe that the events of the objective world must still be dealt with. Yet it would be wrong to conclude that Beckett's work is "pessimistic." To say "perhaps," as the plays do, is not to say "no." The plays do not say that there is no future but that we do not see it, have no confidence about it, and approach it hopelessly. Apart from messianic Marxism, where is there today a faith asserting the contrary that succeeds in shaping a culture?

The walls that surround the characters of Beckett's plays are not walls that nature and history have built irrespective of the decisions of men. They are the walls of one's own attitude toward his situation. The plays are themselves evidence of a human capacity to see one's situation and by that very fact to transcend it. That is why Beckett can say that letting in "the mess" may bring with it a "chance of renovation." It is also why he is wrong, from philosophy's point of view, to say that there is only "the mess." If that were all there is, he could not recognize it as such. But the plays and the novels contain more, and that more is transcendence of the self and the situation.

In *Waiting for Godot* Beckett has a very simple and moving description of human self-transcendence. Vladimir and Estragon (Didi and Gogo) are discussing man, who bears his "little cross" until he dies and is forgotten. In a beautiful passage that is really a duet composed of short lines from first one pair of lips and then the other, the two tramps speak of their inability to keep silent. As Gogo says, "It's so we won't hear . . . all the dead voices." The voices of the dead make a noise like wings, sand, or leaves, all speaking at once, each one to itself, whispering, rustling, and murmuring.

> VLADIMIR. What do they say?
> ESTRAGON. They talk about their lives.
> VLADIMIR. To have lived is not enough for them.
> ESTRAGON. They have to talk about it.
> VLADIMIR. To be dead is not enough for them.
> ESTRAGON. It is not sufficient.
> [*Silence*]
> VLADIMIR. They make a noise like feathers.
> ESTRAGON. Like leaves.
> VLADIMIR. Like ashes.
> ESTRAGON. Like leaves.

In this passage, Didi and Gogo are like the dead, and the dead are like the living,

because all are incapable of keeping silent. The description of the dead voices is also a description of living voices. In either case, neither to live nor to die is "enough." One must talk about it. The human condition is self-reflection, self-transcendence. Beckett's plays are the whispering, rustling, and murmuring of man refusing merely to exist.

Is it not true that self-transcendence implies freedom, and that freedom is either the most glorious or the most terrifying of facts, depending on the vigor of the spirit that contemplates it? It is important to notice that the rebukes to Beckett's "despair" have mostly come from the dogmatists of humanist liberalism, who here reveal, as so often they do, that they desire the reassurance of certainty more than they love freedom. Having recognized that to live is not enough, they wish to fasten down in dogma the way that life ought to be lived. Beckett suggests something more free—that life is to be seen, to be talked about, and that the way it is to be lived cannot be stated unambiguously but must come as a response to that which one encounters in "the mess." He has devised his works in such a way that those who comment upon them actually comment upon themselves. One cannot say, "Beckett has said so and so," for Beckett has said, "Perhaps." If the critics and the public see only images of despair, one can only deduce that they are themselves despairing.

Beckett himself, or so I take it, has repented of the desire for certainty. There are therefore released in him qualities of affirmation that his interpreters often miss. That is why the laughter in his plays is warm, his concern for his characters affectionate. His warm humor and affection are not the attributes of defeatism but the consequences of what Paul Tillich has called "the courage to be."

Sergei
Eisenstein
1898–1948

Sergei Eisenstein, famed Soviet film director, was the son of an architect. Eisenstein too studied design and architecture but turned to theatre after serving in the Red Army during the civil war. For a time he was associated with a Workers' Theatre in Moscow. He also studied Oriental languages and theatre, and later attributed his innovative grasp of film montage to Oriental thought with its interior, affective logic. In 1923 Eisenstein turned to cinema as a more powerful medium than theatre. His early attempts dealt with revolutionary themes: *Strike* (1924) and the epoch-making *The Battleship Potemkin* (1925), which broke new ground in rhythmic montage, frame composition, dramatic crowd scenes, and expressive detail. Eisenstein's film aesthetic sought plastic values and visual effects through leitmotifs and metaphors and through assembling and counterpointing images. State support was lavished on the director, and after some lesser works, Eisenstein turned to re-creating heroic Russian history from a revolutionary standpoint. His choice fell upon the defense of Russia against foreign invaders during the Middle Ages and the unification of the Russian state under a powerful leader. *Alexander Nevsky* (1938) is an idealized, epic portrait of a Russian hero leading his people into victorious battle. Accompanied by the music of Prokofiev, the film achieved extraordinary beauty and excitement. Then at the height of the antifascist war, Eisenstein produced *Ivan the Terrible* (Part I, 1944; Part II, 1946), a celebration of the sixteenth-century czar, notorious for his cruelty, as the heroic defender of Russian unity and interests against the selfish and treacherous nobles (boyars). In conceiving the film Eisenstein decided to use Russian pictorial and literary art in realizing his scheme. He composed a scenario in stylized old Russian, with rhythmic lines approaching verse. When filmed, Part I was hailed and officially honored in the Soviet Union. Not so Part II, which was criticized for its treatment of Ivan and his private force, the *oprichniks*, and was not released until 1958. (It has been suggested that Part II was taken to reflect unfavorably on Stalin and the state security forces and so banned.) Eisenstein died before he could complete a projected third part.

IVAN THE TERRIBLE

The screenplay, part one

SERGEI EISENSTEIN

Translated by Ivor Montagu and Herbert Marshall

LIST OF PRINCIPAL CHARACTERS

Of the prologue:
IVAN IV, *Grand Prince of Muscovy*
HELENA GLINSKY, *his mother*
PRINCE TELEPNEV-OBOLENSKY
BOYAR SHUISKY
BOYAR BYELSKY
KASPAR VON OLDENBOCK, *the Ambassador of the Livonian Order*
HIS SECRETARY
THE AMBASSADOR OF THE HANSEATIC LEAGUE
IVAN'S NURSE

Of the story:
IVAN IV, *Tsar of Muscovy*
ANASTASIA ROMANOVNA [ZAKHARIN], *his wife*
MALYUTA SKURATOV-BYELSKY [GREGORY]
ALEXEY BASMANOV
FYODOR BASMANOV [FEDKA], *his son*
FOMA and YEROMA CHOKHOV, *plebeians*
OSIP NEPEYA, *the Tsar's Ambassador to the English Court*

PRINCE ANDREW KURBSKY
AMBROGIO, *his secretary*
BOYAR KOLYCHEV, *afterwards* PHILIP, *Metropolitan of Moscow*
EUSTACE, *his acolyte*
PIMEN, *at first Metropolitan of Moscow, later Archbishop of Novgorod*
PETER VOLYNETS, *his acolyte*
EUPHROSYNE STARITSKY, *Ivan's aunt*
VLADIMIR STARITSKY, *her son*
PENINSKY, *an old boyar, of the Staritsky faction*
DEMYAN TESHATA, *a Staritsky bondsman*
NIKOLA, *a beggar simpleton*
ENGINEER RASMUSSEN
HENRYK STADEN, *a German mercenary*
QUEEN ELIZABETH I OF ENGLAND
KING SIGISMUND OF POLAND
THE JESTER OF KING SIGISMUND, *German agent at his court*
KASPAR VON OLDENBOCK, *the Ambassador of the Livonian Order, now Vogt of Weissenstein Castle*

PROLOGUE

THE APPROACHING STORM

Clouds surge across the screen.

SOURCE: From *Ivan the Terrible*, by Sergei Eisenstein, translated by Ivor Montagu and Herbert Marshall. Copyright © 1962 by Simon and Schuster, Inc. Reprinted by permission of Simon and Schuster, Inc.

The film version is available from Brandon International Films, 221 West 57th Street, New York, N.Y.

Voices chant:
  Black clouds
  Are gathering,
  Crimson blood
  Bathes the dawn.
Lightning flashes.
Thunder roars.

Voices chant:
  Cunning treason—
  From the boyars—
  To royal power
  Offers battle.
Summoned by the lightning, the title of the film appears:

IVAN THE TERRIBLE.

The clouds billow.
Against the background of the clouds, the credits pass slowly across the screen.

Voices chant:
  Now comes the time
  Of dire conflict,
  Guard and save
  The soil of Rus[1]—
  A prize attracting
  Fierce plunderers—
  Spare neither sire nor mother
  For the sake of the great Russian realm.
The titles pass.

Voices chant:
  A cloud is risen
  Dread and black.
  Now the time is at hand
  To swear to Rus
  A weighty oath.
  A fearful oath.
Through pealing thunder the voices chant:
  Preserve the realm,
  Stand for Moscow,
  Guard the city.
  On the bones of its foes
  From the four corners of the earth
  The Russian realm shall rise.
An introductory title rises into view—
As it passes, there swells beneath it
Tsar Ivan's musical theme,
"The Approaching Storm"—

IN THAT SAME CENTURY THAT SAW IN EUROPE
CHARLES V AND PHILIP II,

---

[1] The name, in Ivan's time, for the Russian dominion. Among the petty Grand Dukedoms that composed it then, that of Muscovy gradually achieved ascendancy and became known as Moscow Rus, later as only Rus, and eventually as Russia. (Translators' notes.)

CATHERINE DE' MEDICI AND THE DUKE OF ALBA,
HENRY VIII AND BLOODY MARY,
THE FIRES OF THE INQUISITION AND THE NIGHT OF ST. BARTHOLOMEW,
TO THE THRONE OF THE GRAND PRINCES OF MUSCOVY
CAME HE WHO FIRST BECAME
TSAR AND AUTOCRAT OF ALL RUS
TSAR
IVAN THE TERRIBLE.

The theme of Ivan reaches its climax
Black clouds envelope the screen . . .
Through the darkness surge the voices:
    Black clouds are spreading,
    Crimson blood bathes the dawn.
    On the bones of its foes,
    In the hot ash of fires,
    Rus, one and united,
    Is welded together.
A sudden clap of thunder.
The music ceases abruptly.

QUICK FADE IN

THE HALL OF DARKNESS

In the gloom a bright spot of light picks out
an eight-year-old boy, crouching fearfully in a corner.

The camera approaches him swiftly.
CLOSE-UP—the frightened face of the boy.
OFF SCREEN—the anguished scream of a woman.
The boy creeps out of view.

The boy crouched on the floor.
Over the boy pass the shadows of people,
Walking by with tapers.

A low door opens suddenly.
A sharp ray of light cuts into the hall.
In the light comes running, then drops beside the boy,
a woman in the garb of a princess.

The Princess is beside the boy. She speaks in feverish haste:
I am dying . . . they've poisoned me . . . Beware poison! . . . Beware the boyars! . . .

Girls rush in, seize hold of the Princess.
They take her back into her chamber. The door slams to.

It is dark once more. The terrified boy.
A harsh voice in the darkness:
The Grand Princess Helena Glinsky is no more.
A hubbub of women's voices.

At the top of the staircase. A voice shouts in the darkness.
Seize Telepnev-Obolensky!
Feet running in the darkness.

Down the staircase is dragged handsome Telepnev-Obolensky.
Two or three men holding aloft tapers.

At the bottom of the stairs Telepnev-Obolensky wrenches himself free.
He rushes toward the door leading to the Princess' chamber.

Emerging bent, through the door, appears and then towers like a rock in his path
a boyar of gigantic stature (Andrew Shuisky).
Telepnev leaps aside, away from the boyar.

The voice out of the darkness:
Strangle the Princess' lover!
Telepnev flings himself to one side.
He sees the boy.
He throws himself down at the feet of the boy:
Save me, Grand Prince of Moscow!

Telepnev is seized and dragged away from the feet of Ivan.
Telepnev desperately clutching at the thin small legs
of the Grand Prince.

From above, the harsh voice—Andrew Shuisky's.
TAKE HIM AWAY!

Telepnev is dragged to a flight of stairs leading downward.
He is beaten and kicked.
His silk shirt is torn open.

Torches moving downward.
Telepnev being dragged to the dungeons.
The tapers disappear upstairs.
The torches downstairs . . .

The boy Ivan trembling alone in the darkness.

FADE OUT

FADE IN

THE HALL OF AUDIENCE

Many people. An atmosphere of solemn expectancy. Boyars.

Above the throne—a fresco:
the Angel of Wrath—from the Apocalypse—
trampling the universe underfoot.

The throne of the Grand Prince
as yet empty.

The boyars sitting in groups on low forms.
They are talking among themselves.
Explanations to the uninitiated:
The Grand Prince in person will receive the Ambassadors.
We shall hear which Moscow has decided to pay.
Hansa, or Livonia.

They glance sideways at the ambassadors.
They point them out to one another.

Apart, in two groups, stand the foreign embassies.
The representative of the Livonian Order—Kaspar von Oldenbock,
a knight in a white mantle that reaches to the floor.
Beside him his secretary, a Humanist,
looking like Erasmus of Rotterdam,
with an astute and cunning face.

Heading the other group—a red-bearded merchant,
looking like a sea robber,
the representative of the Hanseatic League
of German Merchant Cities.

Von Oldenbock and the red-bearded merchant
looking each other up and down with hostile glances.

The Humanist smiles to himself a thin-lipped smile.

The Hall of Audience is packed with people.
A general movement.
The embassies draw themselves up.

The door opens.
High-ranking boyars enter. Bodyguards.
Palace Guards.
PAN: from the door, through the hall,
toward the throne of the Grand Prince
in the midst of his suite comes the thin boy Ivan,
clad in full Grand Prince's robes.
He is thirteen years old.
His skinny neck protrudes from a massive gold collar.
His eyes are wide open. Fear lurks in them.
He walks timidly between the ranks of the boyars.
As he passes, all drop to their knees.

One on either side of the throne,
Andrew Shuisky and Byelsky,
make deep obeisance to him.

Ivan hesitatingly approaches the throne.
He is guided toward it.
He is seated on it.

At a sign the ambassadors approach.
Each bends the knee.

Everyone is kneeling before Ivan.

In fear and confusion the tiny Ivan gazes
at the assembled boyars prostrate at his feet.
At the ambassadors each with bended knee.

And, in mortal terror, he carefully and distinctly pronounces
—at a sign from Shuisky—the words of the ceremonial proclamation:
We, by the Grace of God, Ioannis Basildis,

Magnus Moscovitae Rerum Dux,
Voluntatem Nostrum Proclamemus . . .

As one, the boyars rise to their feet.
Their tall caps increase their stature.
The ambassadors stand up, bowing respectfully.

Ivan on the throne.
His skinny neck projects like a blade of grass through the heavy gold collar.

His child's eyes are opened wide.

But all the pomp is beginning to affect him:
gradually his timidity is leaving him.
The boy settles more firmly on the throne.

Byelsky solemnly announces:
Ivan son of Vasily, Grand Prince of Moscow . . .
All bow.
. . . deems it well to enter into a trading agreement with,
and to make payment for the right of passage of wares through the Baltic to,
the Hanseatic League of German Merchant Cities.

At a sign from Byelsky,
to the red-bearded Hansa merchant
there approaches a scribe
bearing a scroll and seal.

The Hansa merchant stretches out his hand for the scroll.
The movement is arrested by the rap of Andrew Shuisky's iron staff.

Shuisky announces loudly:
Ivan son of Vasily, Grand Prince of Moscow, has reconsidered:
the trading agreement will be entered into with the Livonian Order of Sword
    Bearers.

And at a sign from Shuisky there appears a second scribe,
with an identical scroll and seal,
who hastily goes over with it to Kaspar von Oldenbock.

The old Humanist beside him quickly takes the scroll
and hides it
in the folds of his black gown.

General astonishment.

Byelsky shouts excitedly at Shuisky:
Hansa! The German Hansa!
The Privy Council decided definitely on Hansa!

SHUISKY:
The will of the Grand Prince can alter even the decisions of the Privy Council!

BYELSKY:
But the Sovereign's word was actually given . . .

SHUISKY:
The Grand Prince is sole master of his word.
At his will it is given, at his will it is altered.
The Grand Prince's will is law!

Byelsky is furious.
Tears of rage stand in his eyes.
But the will of the Grand Prince gave the decision to the German Hansa!

The boy Ivan fidgets on his throne.
He evidently does not like others to speak in his name.
It is obvious that on this particular subject
he has an opinion of his own.

In the frightened boy the eaglet awakens.
He wishes to speak.

But Shuisky does not let him.
Again he speaks on the boy's behalf.
The will of the Grand Prince extends license to the Livonian Order.

From amongst the boyars a loud voice exclaims in envy:
Shuisky has been paid a high price! . . .

A cunning smile appears on the face of the secretary to the Livonian Ambassador.
A furious glare appears on the face of the Hansa merchant.

Byelsky splutters, choking with wrath.
Shrilly he tries to shout something.

Ivan wants to speak.

But Andrew Shuisky raps fiercely with his iron staff.
He solemnly declares:
Ivan son of Vasily, Grand Prince of Moscow,
is wearied by the affairs of embassy.
He therefore deems this audience at an end.

Byelsky attempts to protest.
But . . .
Shuisky outshouts him:
The Grand Prince's will is law!

Once more he raps with his iron staff.
And once more all prostrate themselves before Ivan.
All make humble obeisance to Ivan.

The legs of Ivan dangle helplessly from the throne.
They swing about:
they cannot reach the floor. . . .

They cannot reach until beneath the feet of the Grand Prince of Moscow
is placed the desired footstool.

And above the Prince of Moscow
the Angel of Wrath—

from the Apocalypse—
tramples the universe underfoot.

FADE OUT

FADE IN

IVAN'S APARTMENTS

Sing about the ocean! The ocean!—
cries Ivan merrily, running around in his bedchamber.

Lifting high the skirts of his Grand-Prince's robe,
he hops about on one leg.
He is all haste to divest himself of his robes, taking them off as he moves.

His old nurse and two nursemaids-of-the-bedchamber
help Ivan to disrobe.
The boy is impatient to get out of his gold collar.
In a cracked voice the old nurse sings:
 Ocean-sea,
 Azure sea,
 Azure sea,
 Glorious sea . . .

Ivan takes off his Grand-Prince's cap:
 Thy waters reach to the very Heavens,
 Thy waves roll up to the sun on high . . .
Ivan throws off the heavy collar of beaten gold.
He is listening.
And thinking.
 . . . the rivers of Rus
  they flow to thee.
 By thy shores
  stand mighty cities . . .
Thinking hard, Ivan stares in front of him.
He ceases disrobing.
The song has gripped him.
 The cities that stand there
  were ours of old.
 By black foes
  they're now enthralled . . .
A number of boyars enter noisily.
Fierce argument is in progress.

Byelsky leaps around Shuisky, snapping and snarling:
We must make a pact with the Hanseatic League!
Shuisky replies menacingly:
We shall make a pact with the Livonians!

The old woman continues disrobing Ivan.
Her song is barely audible:
 . . . Ocean-sea,
 Azure sea,
 Azure sea,
 Russian sea . . .

Shuisky roughly interrupts the song:
How dare you disturb the boy with that rubbish?
Get out!

The old woman hastily makes her exit through the private chapel.
Ivan gazes longingly after her.
He looks up frowningly at Shuisky.
Byelsky keeps pressing his point:
It would be better to pay the Hansa merchants!
Shuisky sticks to his:
We're going to pay the Livonians!

Ivan's disrobing is almost complete.
The nursemaids remove the last of his ceremonial attire.
Underneath—Ivan has on a simple shirt.
Almost poor.
But in the eyes of the listening Ivan
there lurks something
of that look that came to him upon the throne.

Shuisky and Byelsky never pause:
A deal with Hansa would be better for the State!
Better, not for the State—but for you!
And you've been bought by the Livonians!

Byelsky screams shrilly:
We must pay Hansa!

We shall pay the Livonians,—
answers Shuisky.

Amidst the richly-clad boyars
Ivan looks almost poverty-stricken.
But his voice rings out pridefully:
It's no obligation of ours to pay tribute to anyone!
Our grandsires built those cities on the coast.
That soil is properly part of our heritage—
they must belong to Moscow.

Shuisky says sneeringly:
Nobody's going to be stupid enough to give back those cities!
Possession is nine points of the law,—
Byelsky in servile fashion rallies to his opponent.

Says Ivan:
If they do not yield them willingly—we'll take them by force!

Everyone laughs.

SHUISKY:
By force?
BYELSKY:
Where's your force coming from?

The might of Rus, that you have squandered!
That has trickled away into boyar pockets!—
shouts Ivan.

All roar with laughter.

Shuisky, overcome with laughing,
drops into a low armchair:
I shall die! . . . God Almighty!
He flings his feet onto the bed.

Ivan jumps forward.
Panting with anger,
he shouts:
Take your feet off that bed!
Take them off, I say!
Take your feet off my mother's bed!
Between his teeth he adds:
. . . my mother, whom you curs worried to death!

I'm a cur, eh?—
Shuisky roars, rising from his chair like a wild beast:
She was a bitch herself!
That He-dog Telepnev and she were thick together;
no one knows who sired you!

The gigantic figure of Shuisky towers over Ivan,
brandishing his iron staff:
Son of a bitch!

Ivan covers his head with his arms to ward off the blow,
then suddenly,
unexpectedly even to himself,
he screams out hysterically:
ARREST HIM!

All,
and Ivan among them,
are staggered with surprise.
The other boyars shrink towards the door.
Shuisky stands as though petrified.

Ivan searches with his eyes.
At the entrance to his private chapel he notices his kennelmen.
They too are standing motionless.

And now with a voice of decision, Ivan commands:
Take him away!

And . . . the kennelmen take hold of the chief lord of the realm—Andrew Shuisky.
They hustle him from the apartment.

The rest of the boyars make themselves scarce, muttering fearfully:
The Elder Boyar given over to the kennel lackeys!
Ivan remains alone.

He is frightened by his own determination
and by the unexpectedness of everything that has happened.

His strength leaves him.
He is once more a weak, helpless little boy.

He presses his face against the covers on his mother's bed
and sobs as though his head lay on her breast.
His skinny shoulders shake.

Hurried footsteps are heard in the corridor.
The door creaks.

Ivan cowers, afraid to turn around.

Through the door, fearfully comes one of the kennelmen.
Cautiously he touches Ivan on the shoulder.

Ivan turns.

Shifting from foot to foot,
the kennelman says guiltily:
We got a bit overzealous . . . strangled the boyar . . .

CLOSE-UP of Ivan's face.
At first at a loss.
Then stern and concentrated.
The "royal" look in his eyes.
And in his glance—approval.

I'll rule myself . . . without the boyars . . .

The kennelman looks apprehensively at Ivan.

I'll be a Tsar! . . .

The eyes of Ivan gaze into the distance.

                                                    FADE OUT

THE CATHEDRAL OF THE ASSUMPTION

FADE IN

The frantic pealing of bells.

The coronation ceremony is taking place OFF SCREEN
Singing is heard.
But we cannot as yet see the ceremony itself.

The spectator sees pass before him various groups,
attentively gazing OFF SCREEN.

First we see, against a background of dark frescoes,
a group of indignant foreign ambassadors.

The foreigners grow heated:
Where has he suddenly sprung from—
this new—Moscow—Tsar?

The Prince of Muscovy has no right to style himself a Tsar!
The Pope won't recognize this as a coronation!
The Emperor will refuse to use the title in addressing him!
Europe will not recognize him as Tsar!

The voice of the Metropolitan, Pimen, speaking OFF SCREEN:
By our ancient title
I hereby crown with the royal crown
Grand Prince and Sovereign
Ivan son of Vasily . . .

Among the foreigners, prominently placed—a familiar figure:
it is the Humanist whom we saw with the Livonian embassy in an earlier scene.
The old man is not very much older—only four years have gone by.
But now he himself is the Ambassador of Livonia.
And by his side is a young secretary.

Pimen's voice is heard:
And proclaim him, divinely crowned,
Tsar of Muscovy
and, of all great Rus,
Autocrat.

Kyrie Eleison!—comes ecstatically from the choir on the right.
Kyrie Eleison!—responds ecstatically the choir on the left.

The Humanist-Ambassador follows the ceremony intently
and whispers to himself:
That fledgling has flown a long way . . .

Kyrie Eleison!—the two choirs sing in unison.

While, beneath the ecstatic chorus,
against the background of dark frescoes, rays of sunshine lighting them,
the foreign ambassadors give rein to their indignation:
The Pope won't recognize this as a coronation!
The Emperor will refuse to use the title in addressing him!
Europe will not recognize him as Tsar!

And only the Humanist-Ambassador,
talking to himself, barely whispers, thin-lipped:
If he's strong—they'll recognize him . . .

One of the foreigners says to another:
Incidentally, certain of his own subjects too are not particularly
enthusiastic about this coronation . . .

And we see a group of boyars headed by the Staritskys.

The group is patently displeased;
Especially is this noticeable in the face of a tall, elderly woman.
The figure next to her is evidently her son—
he wears on his face an indifferent expression
and in his eyes a faraway look.

The one foreigner explains to the other:
It's not difficult to understand why these nobles are not pleased.

The one over there is a cousin of the Grand Prince—
Waldemar Staritsky—and next to him his mother.

His words are heard over a shot
of the Princess Euphrosyne Staritsky
with her son Vladimir.
And it is obvious that they are thinking what the ambassador is saying:
John's coronation as Tsar will hinder their path
to the throne of Muscovy!

A third foreigner intervenes in the conversation:
But there are also, it seems, partisans of John . . .
And his words sound over a group including the Zakharins and the Glinskys.
Those are kinsfolk of the betrothed of the Grand Prince . . .
explains the first foreigner.

And we see Anastasia.
By the brightness of her attire and the silver of her ornaments
she gleams in the sunshine
amidst the kinsfolk surrounding her.
Her eyes sparkle with a joy more brilliant than the sun.

The Humanist-Ambassador of Livonia scathingly corrects
the first foreigner:
Not of the Grand Prince, but . . . of the Tsar!

The first foreigner snorts.
But the Livonian Ambassador reiterates:
Of the Tsar, now!

And at last we can see that now it has been concluded—the mystery
of anointment into Tsarship.

The venerable Metropolitan of Moscow, Pimen, completes the ritual.

In front of Pimen,
with his back to the spectator,
Ivan in the coronation mantle and full royal robes.
Around him—in billowing cloaks—
the bishops of the most important sees.

Pimen takes from a golden platter
the royal crown—the cap of Monomakh.
He gives it to Ivan to kiss.
He places it on Ivan's head.
He pronounces:
In the name of the Father, the Son and the Holy Ghost . . .

Ivan bows his head.

The words of Pimen:
Guard and preserve this crown!
Magnify it on the throne of truth,
fortify it with Thy might!
And subdue beneath Thy feet
every enemy and foe!

Ivan draws himself erect and turns round.

He is seventeen years old.

His mien is proud.
His eyes blaze.
Ivan stands rooted to the spot
while the invocation continues:

For Thine is the Kingdom,
the Power and the Glory,
in the name of the Father, the Son and the Holy Ghost . . .

Joyfully gazes Anastasia at Ivan.
Joyfully gaze the Glinskys and Zakharins.

. . . as it was in the beginning,
is now, and ever shall be,
world without end!

Gloomily the Staritskys frown.

Amen!—resoundingly sings the choir.

Ironically the foreigners watch.

Toward Ivan approach:
from the left—a young golden-haired prince,
from the right—an older black-browed boyar.

They take Ivan by the arms.
They lead him down the steps of the ambo before the altar.

Vessels filled with gold coins are brought to them.

And, raising high the vessels, in accordance with the ceremonial,
they pour over the young Tsar a golden shower.

The golden shower rings resoundingly.

Rings out the ecstatic
Kyrie Eleison!
of the Cathedral choir.
Rings out the joyous clamor of the bells.
Ring out the cries of greeting from the people. . . .

But, behold, the peal is silent.
The bells are stilled.

And soundlessly is spread before the feet of Ivan
a gold-embroidered carpet.

Stilled are the cries of the people.
All is stilled. . . .

And through the golden somnolence of the silent Cathedral
Ivan moves forward.

The retainers scarcely have time to unroll the carpet:
with such swift steps does Ivan advance towards them.

Like a young wild animal,
supple, shapely, sensuous,
he glides through the stillness up the eight steps
of the platform raised in the center—
"the prelatical ambo, denominated the theater."

In the rays of sunlight falling at the very center of the Cathedral he stands still.

He is submerged in the vastness of the Cathedral.
He glitters in the half-darkness like an emerald:
reflections from the play of the sun waver like fire.

His eye flashes from the eminence like that of a young snow leopard.

Young.
Pale.
His gaze piercing.
Slightly asymmetrical of visage.
Black locks falling to his shoulders.

Like an icon in its frame the Tsar is encased in golden garments.

Within all is seething.
The bonds of his will bind him tighter than golden chains.

Holding himself back, he strives to speak quietly.
Holding himself back, he strives to speak evenly.

But thought surges after thought.
Word presses on word.
And in an unchecked, passionate flood
the speech of the youthful Tsar pours forth.

At first his tone is low.
Ivan speaks of power:
Now, for the first time a Prince of Muscovy
takes the crown of Tsar of all Rus
upon himself.

But, see, into his words he suddenly inserts
the first sparks of wrath
and in a fiery stream they flow with the flood of his speech—
Ivan recalls the rule of the boyars:

And thereby forever
boyar power over Rus—
multifarious,
crafty—
is put to an end.

The faces of the boyars darken.

He lifts his hand against the boyar power!—
mutters the Staritsky group.

With growing force
Ivan goes on angrily:
But to hold the Russian land
in a single hand
strength is needed.

Anastasia's eyes are fixed warmly on Ivan.
The young golden-haired prince is pleased.
The black-browed boyar is thoughtful.

And therefore henceforward we shall establish
an army—paid, trained,
permanent . . .

Boyar anger, like an ocean wave,
mounts at these words . . .

Ivan continues
in a voice that hints a threat:
He who, in the ranks of these Royal troops,
does not fight in person,
shall yet, in the great campaigns of the Tsar,
participate with money . . .

In explosive rejoinders, the boyars' anger
bursts forth at these words.

Euphrosyne mutters:
Risk your own money on your own head!

Ivan continues
calmly,
as though he did not notice this anger:
Likewise, also, the holy monasteries
with their great incomes
shall participate henceforward in our military enterprises.
The monasteries have amassed both treasure and territory
of which the Russian land has reaped no benefit . . .

A stir amongst the clergy.
The archimandrites are at a loss.
The archpresbyters are perplexed.
The Metropolitan is astounded.
The bishops are shaken.

Pimen, in surprise, drops his crosier.
The black-browed boyar catches it in its fall,
He hands it back to Pimen.
His eyes and Pimen's eyes have met.
So, evidently, have their thoughts.

The thoughts of the clergy and the boyars meet.
In counter to the Tsar, a wave of fury sweeps through the clergy
and fuses with the anger of the boyars.

Ivan sees the rising fury.
Ivan sees the growing wrath.

He sees the displeasure.

He continues still more forcefully:
A stronger power is needed
in order to crush
all who oppose the unity of Russian rule . . .

From the Staritskys has come a muttering in answer.
Ivan's eyes have flashed toward the Staritskys.

Euphrosyne has sprung forward in a rage to answer.
The angry eyes of Euphrosyne are gleaming.
Vladimir holds his mother back.

The young golden-locked prince at the Tsar's right hand
gazes at him with enthusiasm.

On the Tsar's other side—the black-browed boyar
casts down his eyes, and his face darkens.

A murmur runs through the Cathedral.
An angry murmur of disapproval.

Only the foreigners look on detached, and derisive.
The issue appears not to concern them.
They are merely amused and mildly curious—
how will this discord between the young Tsar on the one hand,
and on the other the boyars and clergy,
work out in the end. . . .

Then, all of a sudden, the words of Ivan
have turned unexpectedly in their direction.
Quietly, barely audibly, Ivan continues:
. . . For only a united realm
strong,
welded within,
can likewise be firm without . . .

The foreigners have caught their breath.
The ambassadors are now on their guard.

Ivan continues, even more quietly.
And in his voice there seems to sound the distant echo of the song
that tells of the "Ocean-sea, Azure sea, Russian sea . . ."

And what does our fatherland now resemble
but a trunk,
severed at knee and elbow?
The upper reaches of our rivers—
the Volga, Dvina, Volkhov—
are beneath our rule,
but their outlets to the sea
are in alien hands . . .

Now still more clearly the Tsar's words seem to echo with the refrain
"Azure sea, Russian sea":

. . . the maritime lands of our fathers and grandfathers—on the Baltic—
have been rent from our soil . . .

The ambassadors have become worried.
Ivan sees their worry.

The ambassadors have become agitated.
Ivan sees their agitation.
And he proclaims, in loud and royal tones:
Therefore this day We crown Ourself
with dominion also over those lands, which now—temporarily—
lie beneath other sovereignties!

A fearful stir among the ambassadors.
The Livonian Ambassador raises his eyebrows:
A fledgling indeed!

A fledgling no longer—an eagle on the heights.
Like a mountain eagle, soaring above the storm,
So Ivan breasts the raging tide
of human breakers.

The song of the azure sea,
of the Russian sea,
rings high in the dome.

And, through the storm of wrath
of ambassadors,
boyars,
clergy—
tossed in the hurricane,
flung about in the whirlwind,
the medley of people,
passions,
songs,
fury—
Ivan hurls in conclusion:
Two Romes fell
but the third—
Moscow—
shall stand,
and a fourth shall never be!
And in that Third Rome—
as ruler of Muscovy—
as sole Master
from this day forth shall I reign
ALONE!

And with these words he suddenly breaks off.

Rising above the hurricane of passions,
the deacon chants:
   To the Grand Prince of Muscovy,
   I-o-a-nnis son of Vasily,
   Tsar and Autocrat of all Russia—
   Long life!

The storm in the Cathedral sweeps to a tempest.
People are cast about in raging confusion.

In the midst of the storm, pale, his eyes burning,
like a rock—
alone—
stands Ivan.

The choir ecstatically takes up:
Long life!
Long life!

The joy of the Glinskys and Zakharins,
The rage of the Staritskys,
The wrath of the ambassadors
and the church chanting
blend in a general din.
The Cathedral hums like a beehive.

Long life!
Long life!

Euphrosyne Staritsky hisses:
The wedding's fixed for tomorrow.
We'll celebrate this "Master's" wedding!
The Staritskys bunch together in a tighter huddle.

The chanting surges.
The bells clamor.

The foreigners:
The Pope won't permit it!
The Emperor won't agree to it!
Europe'll never recognize it!

The Livonian Ambassador says:
If he's strong—everyone'll recognize it!
And adds, to his secretary:
He mustn't be strong . . .

And while the rest grow heated,
the old diplomat says with a sigh:
The time has come to undo the purse strings . . .

And during this time when through the Cathedral rise
the Church-Slavonic chants
and the clamor of the bells,
the old diplomat and the young secretary
begin closely to scrutinize the entourage of Ivan:
on whom shall they place their stake?

THE CAMERA HALTS at the young prince on Ivan's right.
The young prince is gazing rapturously at Ivan.

And, unexpectedly, it is of him that the Ambassador speaks:
That one!

The secretary is astonished:
But he's the first man after Ivan.
The first friend of Ivan and the second man in the State!

But the Ambassador answers deliberately:
Ambition is more terrible than greed . . .
No man can be satisfied while he is first . . .
after another . . .

The young secretary is not convinced:
But he has everything!
He needs nothing!

Yet again the old man speaks:
No man knows the limits of human desire . . .
And his glance turns to the other side of the young prince.
There, too, has looked the secretary.

And we see that the young prince
has changed the direction of his gaze from Ivan to Anastasia.
And his look has grown sullen.

The Livonian Ambassador glances ironically at his secretary.
The secretary apologetically lowers his head.
And the old diplomat says, in businesslike style:
Occupy yourself with Prince Andrew Kurbsky.

And, beneath the incessant clangor of the bells, we see
the musing face of young Prince Kurbsky.
He is gazing at Anastasia.
And, from the expression on his face, we come to believe
that the Ambassador was not, maybe, quite so far wrong . . .

Long life!
Long life!—
clamors the choir.

FADE OUT

HEADFALL RING[2]

The frantic clamor of the bells merges
into a loud roaring of crowds.
The glittering interior of the Cathedral changes
to the dark streets of Moscow.
The streets are seething with people.
The roar rolls along with the hurrying crowds.

Staritsky kinsmen are scattered in the crowd.
They are stirring up the people.
They are urging the people to listen to a voice from Headfall Ring,
and pay heed.

[2] *Lobnoye Mesto*, a circular stone platform outside the Kremlin on the square now called Red Square, used in medieval times as a place of execution.

The people listen.
Listening—two brothers: Foma and Yeroma Chokhov.

The Tsar is bewitched!—
comes the voice from Headfall Ring:
Bewitched by the kin of the future Tsarina!
Bewitched by the Glinskys!

And we see the tall figure of an idiot beggar,
raving,
with foam on his lips,
crying out a message to the people—
calling on them to save the young Tsar from the spells of the Evil Ones:

He turns from his own kin, the Staritskys.
He oppresses his faithful boyars.
He lays hands upon the treasures of the monasteries and of the church!

Nikola the Simple cries, with foam on his lips:
For these offenses the Lord God will send down great woes upon the people!

Fire will come down from heaven!

And shouts rise above the crowd in response:
Down with the Glinskys!—cries Foma.
And it is patent that his cry is prompted by exclamations
cunningly flung out by partisans of the Staritskys.

The most excited of all among the crowd
is a stalwart ginger-haired lad named Gregory.

The din floats above the night square.
Torches flare.
Bells clang.

To the bell ringers on the belfry there climbs up
one of the retinue of the Staritsky group.
Together with him are the bondsmen Kozma and Demyan.
These latter conceal themselves at one side.

Down with the Glinskys!—
Everyone is shouting insistently.

The din floats above the night square.
The din merges with the clanging of the bells.
The black night-square seethes.

THE HALL OF GOLD

It is far from the square to the apartments of the Tsar.
The clangor reaches from far off to the nuptial hall.
It merges
with the shouts:
Bitter! Bitter! [3]

---

[3] The cry "Bitter! Bitter!" by guests at Russian weddings is, by ancient custom, an injunction to the bridegroom to kiss the bride. The implication: "Sweeten things up a bit!"

And, enveloped in the shouts of the revelers,
the Tsar,
from the lips of the Tsarina,
completing his kiss, breaks away . . .

Anastasia blushes.
The Tsar is delighted.
The guests shout.
The clangor is heard from far off.

The Tsar hears the pealing of the bells:
Why does Moscow
ring so resoundingly?

And, from her high place of nuptial godmother, to the Tsar
Euphrosyne Staritsky flatteringly replies:
The joy of the people of Moscow is flowing over . . .

With Pimen, who occupies a place of honor,
Staritsky exchanges glances.

Above Moscow—
the frantic pealing of the bells.

The old Glinsky witch—the Tsar's grandmother—practices sorcery!—
Nikola "Big-Fool," the simpleton, is at it as strongly as ever:
She tears the hearts out of human beings.
She sprinkles houses with human blood.
And, from that blood, fire is born—
houses burn!

Gripped by the speech, Gregory shouts:
Burn the Glinskys themselves!

And the Staritsky partisans piercingly take up the cry:
Cross over the river[4]*—and burn the Glinskys!*

The din floats above the square.
The din merges with the pealing of the bells.

The black night-square seethes . . .

In the nuptial Hall of Gold,
Ivan turns to Kurbsky and Kolychev with a question:
Why are my closest friends sad at this moment?

Kurbsky answers evasively:
Well, Sovereign-Tsar,
there is an apt saying among the people:
"when marriage begins—friendship ends . . ."

Anastasia has turned toward Kurbsky.
Kurbsky has averted his glance.

---

[4] The actual cry was "To Zamoskvorechiye"—the suburb of old Moscow on the other side
of the river.

Ivan laughs.
He turns to his other friend:
And what does Fyodor Kolychev answer?

Kolychev rises.
He bows to the Tsar.
Speaks:
Thou art breaking, Tsar, with the ancient customs;
great discord will arise therefrom . . .

And, as though underlining the words of Kolychev,
pouring like a tempestuous sea,
from the far square of Headfall Ring
the crowds of people surge forward.
Cries resound:
To the Tsar!

It is far from the square to the apartments of the Tsar—
the cry does not carry to the Tsar's apartments.

Kolychev continues:
Against the Tsar I dare not go.
With thee I cannot go . . .
He says, with a bow:
Permit me to retire to a monastery . . .

From her place of honor Euphrosyne
is listening to the distant hubbub with malicious joy.

Ivan is hurt.
He replies to Kolychev:
Thou wouldst change the earthly Tsar for the Tsar of Heaven?
Well, betwixt thee and the Tsar of Heaven
I shall not stand.
He waves his hand:
Go!
Pray for us—sinners . . .
With sorrow he looks into the eyes of Kolychev.
And speaks, deeply moved:
One thing only I ask:
When an ill time comes do not desert me—
in the hour of need return at our summons . . .

Fyodor Kolychev bows low to the Tsar . . .

A servitor approaches Euphrosyne—
as though to pour wine—
and whispers close in her ear—
disturbing news.
The eyes of Euphrosyne sparkle with pleasure.

Somewhere, far off, the clamor of bells is now a tocsin.
Somewhere, far off, the vague din is coming nearer.
It is heard through the wedding music.

The din is more audible.

Someone
who is near the windows
begins to listen to the far-off din.

The gaze of the Tsar is fixed on Anastasia—
he hears nothing . . .

Kolychev goes up to the Metropolitan Pimen.
The Metropolitan looks at the boyar with sympathy.
He blesses the boyar.
Speaks:
Go to Solovyets Monastery.
I ordain you abbot . . .

The roar is louder . . .
And, in order to drown the roar,
Euphrosyne gives a sign with her kerchief.

A wedding song rings out:
    In and round the city the Tsar wanders,
    Wanders, seeking for a bride,
    Into the attics of houses peering,
    Looking for a white, white swan. . . .

Outside the windows, the hubbub is growing louder.
Euphrosyne gives a second sign—
the song thunders more resoundingly.
    Open, gates,
    Open wide . . .
The doors swing open
The hubbub and the song are both drowned in cries of rejoicing—
down the wide staircase float dishes:
roast swans held aloft,
white swans
decorated with silver tiaras.
Beneath the cries is heard the song:
    The white swan swims,
    Plump-white,
    Desire-white,
    Crowned with light!
The chorus is sung a second time in honor of the Tsarina:
    Desire-white,
    Crowned with light!

And against the background of this general rejoicing,
triumphantly,
a cup in her hands,
rises from the table
·she who is to say the wedding benediction—
Euphrosyne.

The dishes with the swans float by.
The white swans float by the Tsarina.
Their silver tiaras gleam . . .

Euphrosyne pronounces,
in a loud voice

drowning all and everything:
A health to thee,
Tsar Ivan son of Vasily!
And a flourishing future
to thy works!
Glory!

Every cup has been raised.
The cups are carried to the lips.
The Tsar is glorified with wine.

All cry: *Glory!*

First to drain his cup is the Tsar's closest friend—
Kurbsky.
High he lifts his empty cup—in accordance with custom.
He has swung his arm:
Heigh— ...
His glance has lighted on Anastasia.
His brow has darkened.
In accordance with custom he has smashed his cup to pieces on the floor.
... —*ho!*

Only, just a little more strongly than prescribed by custom,
as though in anger,
as though consumed with jealousy.

Euphrosyne has smiled, a smile of irony, of understanding.
Among the others, none has noticed ...

All lift their empty cups.
They are ready to hurl them to the ground—
in accordance with custom.

They have swung their arms:
Heigh— ...
A deafening crash bursts.
Not of cups, smashing on the ground,
but of windows, smashed into bits by stones!

The pealing tocsin bursts through the broken windows.
The din of the crowd fills the hall with cries.
Through the broken windows the wind blows, howling,
snuffing out, in one breath, a hundred candles ...

The hall is plunged in darkness.
And, through that darkness, in ominous scarlet tongues,
creeps the distant glow of a fire ...

The guests have rushed to the windows.
Outside the windows is a conflagration:
Across the river—the houses burn!

In the courtyard murmur the angry people.
Outside the windows rage the flames.

Above the raging fire looms the bell tower.

The Staritskys' minions cast down the bells from the belfries.

The Staritskys' bondsman—
Demyan—
cuts the bell ropes with a knife.

Actively helping Demyan
is Nikola "Big-Fool," the Simpleton.
By all appearances, he is far from simple.

Below, into the flames plunges a bell—
the biggest—the "Harbinger of Blessings."
After it small bells rattle down like peas.

Through the broken windows the boyars watch the fire.

In the vast festive hall of the Tsar
only two are left together in the gloom:

the white dove—Anastasia;
by one unextinguished candle,
the last,
she is pallidly lit.

And Ivan, in the rays of the bloody glow,
towering like an angry giant.

You would rouse the people against me,
boyars!
Not peace but a sword you have asked for . . .

He draws himself up—
the shadow flits across the vaulted ceiling like a black phantom.
Fixedly the Tsar drinks in the glow with his eyes:
And the sword you shall get!

With a roar and a clatter the doors are flung open—
into the hall burst the people.

They light the hall with long torches.

They press against the guard.
They jostle.
They trample.

Kurbsky and Kolychev rush to the rescue of Ivan.
They wish to defend the Tsar from the people.

But Ivan orders:
Let the people pass!

The guards of the Tsar do not hearken—
with a forest of halberds they halt the people.

Angered, the people force back the guard.
Foremost of all—the ginger lad Gregory.

The tumult spreads.

Ivan throws himself forward to part the tumult.
At that moment, with a titanic wrench,
Gregory forces his way through the guard.

Having raised a club above his head with a titanic swing,
he hurls himself at Ivan.

With a cry Anastasia closes her eyes.
The club must surely crush Ivan . . .

But, at the last moment,
just in time, beneath it jumps
Kurbsky.

He covers Ivan with his body—
warding off the blow to one side.

Kolychev seizes Gregory.
Forces him to his knees before the Tsar.

Kurbsky and Kolychev glare fiercely at Gregory . . .

The guard swept aside, the people in their rush stand rooted.
They recognize the Tsar.
They fall on their knees before the Tsar.

Great Sovereign,
we come to make plaint against the Glinskys!
We ask justice!
The Glinskys have been practicing sorcery.

Foma Chokhov exclaims:
Dread omens threaten Moscow . . .

Yeroma Chokhov exclaims:
The bells fall by themselves from the belfries!

And, rising from their knees,
the people cry,
Yield, Tsar, to the sign from God!

Foremost of all, more than any other,
rages the ginger lad Gregory.

Not far behind are the Brothers Chokhov:
Foma and Yeroma.
The crowd seethes.

Tsar Ivan gazes long at the people.
He is separated from the people by his friends—
Kurbsky and Kolychev.

It is the first encounter of Ivan and the people
face to face.

With an imperious gesture Ivan parts the guard
standing between him and the common people.
He thrusts aside Kurbsky, clears out of the way Kolychev.
He approaches the excited giant—Gregory.

The people grow still.
Kurbsky has assumed a position to protect Anastasia.

IVAN:
Magic, you say? Bells have fallen?
He stretches out his hand:
Any head that believes in magic is, like a bell . . .
He taps his finger on the forehead of Gregory:
. . . empty.

Titters in the crowd.

IVAN:
Can a head fly off by itself?

There is already laughter in the crowd.
Gregory is flummoxed.

Ivan says gently:
To fly off—it must be cut off.
He has drawn his finger along Gregory's neck.
And then his eyes have given such a look
that cold sweat has broken out on Gregory's skin.
Something of the future "Terrible" blazed in that look
of the young Ivan.

But Ivan continues lightly:
With bells is it likewise.
Indeed, whosoever without the Tsar's permission has cut down a bell
shall speedily, by the Tsar's decree, have his head cut also.

The Tsar's speech pleases the people.
The Brothers Chokhov like the Tsar.

FOMA:
This Tsar fellow, it's plain, has a noddle on him!
YEROMA:
His eyes see right down to the root of things!

The people laugh approvingly.

After a pause, Gregory himself unexpectedly bursts into a loud guffaw,
having felt that the storm has passed over.

However, in the depths of the hall, Vladimir Staritsky
fearfully passes his hand over his own neck . . .
He has caught the stern glance of his mother on him.
He has felt embarrassed—hid his hand in his long sleeve.

The Staritskys' bondsman—Demyan—looks fearfully at Ivan . . .

Ivan speaks with heat to the people:

And We shall cut off heads ruthlessly!
Stamp out treason.
Tear out boyar treachery by the roots!

The crowd is pleased with the Tsar's speech.
The people exclaim approvingly.

Like one spellbound,
at the Tsar gazes
Anastasia.
In her excitement she involuntarily clutches at Kurbsky's hand.

Kurbsky presses her hand responsively.

Anastasia has looked round.
She has caught his glance fixed on her.
She has taken away her hand.
And curtly said:
Of that, Prince, you must not even dare think!
I stand devoted to a great service—
of the Tsar of Muscovy I am the loyal slave!

She has strained toward Ivan.
She looks at him in ecstasy.

Kurbsky's brow has darkened.
He bites his moustaches angrily.

And, some distance away, Ivan is speaking to the people.
He does not shout.
Nor grow heated.
Judiciously, commonsensically,
gradually
he speaks on to them:
Our lands are great and bountiful,
but of order there is little in them.
We shall not call in mercenaries.
We shall introduce order ourselves.
We shall stamp out sedition.
Working people, tradesmen, merchants—
We shall not let be harmed ...

So Ivan has spoken to his people in council,
to the many-headed council ...

The people hearken to the Tsar attentively.
Near the Tsar's feet
they seat themselves on the ground.

Not this did the Staritsky woman expect,
not this did she plan.

Up to the Staritsky woman runs
her bondsman Demyan;
excitedly he exclaims:
Three emissaries from Kazan to the Tsar ...

A flash lights the eyes of the old woman:
Let them in!—she bids.

Interrupting the Tsar's speech,
Insolently and noisily enter the three Kazan envoys.

The people turn toward the envoys.

The chief envoy speaks, without bowing to the Tsar:
Kazan breaks friendship with Moscow.
Alliance with Moscow ends.
War with Moscow starts!

The crowd has jumped up as one man.
Slowly Ivan has stood erect.
He has straightened his shoulders.

The envoy continues:
Kazan—big.
Moscow—small.

The second envoy clarifies:
KICHKINE . . .

The first says:
Moscow—finish.
The Great Khan . . .

The envoys bow.

. . . sends a knife.
Russian Tsar not wish have shame:
Then Russian Tsar end himself.

The third envoy shouts:
KUTARDY!

The first envoy holds out to Ivan
a rusty dagger.

But here too takes place that
which the Staritskys did not expect.

The people raise their staves with cries of wrath.

Ivan leaps to the envoy.
He grasps the rusty dagger.
He cries hotly:
God sees—We do not seek warfare.
But the time has passed when the usurper might dictate
to the Moscow Tsar.
And this dagger shall pierce those who have raised their hand against Muscovy!

He has shouted:
We shall finish with Kazan forever . . .
He has turned the dagger point against the envoy:
It is We who shall launch the campaign—against Kazan!

To Kazan!—
the call has been taken up with enthusiasm first by Gregory.
To Kazan!—the call has been taken up with enthusiasm by the people.

That same cry comes from the courtyard.
It bursts through the broken windows.

To Kazan!

Beneath the windows,
on the courtyard,
the people clamor.

Ivan, stirred and flushed with triumph,
looks round for Anastasia.

She, radiant with happiness,
is led to Ivan by Kurbsky.

Ivan embraces Kurbsky.
He proclaims:
I appoint you to lead the vanguard!

Kurbsky is proud.
He looks around grandly.

The three envoys stand in confusion.

Yet louder ring the cries:
To Kazan!
The music swells.
The crowd is in general movement.

Gregory rakes into his mighty embrace
the chief Kazan envoy.

The people run along passageways to the high staircase.
High above the people,
Gregory lifts the Kazan envoy,
and, from the high staircase, hurls him
down
into the crowd below.

Yet louder and in unison
the cry is heard:
To Kazan!

The long-drawn-out cry is changed into a song:
  Forge the copper cannon true,
    cannoneers,
  And trusty arquebuses too,
    cannoneers . . .
Pikes and axes being forged.

Foma and Yeroma are busy forging.
  There'll be sisters to the cannon,
    cannoneers,

> *Pikes and sabers sharp,*
>> *cannoneers.*

Cannon being cast.

The long-drawn-out singing rises:
> *Straight is the way,*
>> *'cross the Tartar steppe.*
> *Famed City of Kazan—*
>> *comes woe, bitter woe.*

To the sound of the singing,
out of the fire,
cannon being born.
New.
Huge . . .

A fine cannon!—the voice of Ivan is heard suddenly.
But what is it called?

Bully Boy!—quietly answers the chief gunsmith.
"Bully Boy" let it be! gaily says Ivan.
The remaining guns,
all old friends,
under the measured beat of the hammers,
are christened in turn:
Lion!
Wolf!
Singer!
Basilisk!
Bully Boy!—cries Foma.
The singing rings yet more heartily:
> *Lay true the cannon of the Tsar,*
>> *cannoneers . . .*
> *Move the siege towers to the wall,*
>> *cannoneers . . .*

Foma forging axes.

Yeroma casting cannon.

The song goes on.

> *Against Kazan's wall,*
>> *cannoneers . . .*
> *Good Muscovy lads all,*
>> *cannoneers . . .*

Cannon being cast.
YEROMA:
The lads are doing a good job . . .

Halberds being forged.
FOMA:
Wonderful fellows.

> *Straight is the way,*
>> *'cross the Tartar steppe.*

> *Famed city of Kazan—*
>   *'Tis hard, heavy toil . . .*

Guns being dragged along mushy roads.
Immense and unwieldy guns.

Muscles are straining,
ropes are being hauled—
the cannon "Basilisk" is being drawn by
twenty-five sweating horses . . .

Royal troops[5] march forward.
A forest of axes passes into the darkness.

Soon it is quite dark.
In the darkness some kind of movement is vaguely perceptible.
We hear the scraping sound of spades
and the heavy blows of pickaxes.

From the orchestra comes the sound of the gunners' song.
And heavily, in rhythm, strike the pickaxes . . .

KAZAN

Gradually, from the darkness, emerge the outlines of separate figures.
Spades, picks, and mattocks are being strenuously plied.
Among those digging, directing the labor, is a tall, sturdy lad.
He is the foreman.

Somewhere the work has bogged down.
The foreman has seized a pick from someone
and himself turned to the job.
The soil is excavated furiously.

The black earth is removed on sledges.
Simultaneously with the sledges, there emerges at the exit from the mine the
      sturdy lad.
It is Gregory.
He is black with dirt, sweating and hot,
but keen and eager.

Gregory crawls out of the pit.
He blinks in the light, like a ginger cat.
He opens his eyes wide.

In front of him, above the pit, stands Tsar Ivan.
Beside Ivan is Kurbsky.
And a foreigner—Engineer Rasmussen.
High personages.

Behind the Tsar—the endless Tartar steppe.

---

5 *Streltsi*—literally "sharpshooters"; first they were arquebusiers, later musketeers. Established by Ivan as the first State standing army, in contrast to levies supplied by nobles as a feudal duty.

Voices ring out in song:
  Oh, woe, bitter woe,
    thou Tartar steppe.
The Tsar's mail gleams against the coming dawn.
On his breast burns a golden sun.

The armor worn by Kurbsky shines silver,
bright.
  Hard work,
    Tsar's work . . .

Gregory reports:
The mine can now be packed with gunpowder.

Ivan is pleased:
We have waited a month.
Enough of waiting.
Long since time for the assault!

And we see, in the first light
of the approaching dawn,
that in front of us is not only the mine,
but the whole Russian camp, on the hilly side of the river.

Above the entrenchments stand cannon.

In the trenches are Royal troops;
two or three of the men we recognize as having been among those
who burst into the Tsar's hall.

On the other side of the river—in the foggy mist—
looms the outline
of besieged Kazan.
It grows lighter.
The fort of Kazan is still clad in morning mist.

Kurbsky causes Tartar prisoners to be led out above the entrenchments.
He has them tied, half naked, to palings in full view of the city.
Through interpreters, Kurbsky bids them shout
to the defenders of Kazan a proposal to surrender:
Cry: *"Kazan, surrender!"*

One, despairing, calls out
in Tartar.
One has lowered his gaze sullenly to the ground.
One is forced to cry out
in Tartar.

The cry carries to the walls of Kazan.
Several heads appear.
They listen.
Suddenly, above the walls, rises the figure of a tall old man
in a white turban.
By his side are some young princes—Tartar commanders.

And the old man in the turban shouts from the height of the Kazan citadel
to the bound Tartar prisoners:

Better you perish at our hands
than die
by those of uncircumcised giaours!

A flight of arrows has whistled from the walls of Kazan—
the dead prisoners droop from the palings.

Kurbsky spitefully waves his hand:
If they won't—now they needn't.

Kurbsky's signal has been caught,
and passed on.

Barrels of gunpowder are rolling into the mine.
The barrels roll with a rumble.

And as they rumble Ivan in a rage hastens
to Kurbsky, standing on the entrenchments.

Angrily Ivan upbraids Kurbsky
for purposeless cruelty:
Senseless savagery—stupidity.
Even an untaught beast when it bites has a purpose!

Kurbsky is stung to the quick. He boils up. Loses control of himself.
He grasps Ivan round the waist.
Ivan is astounded at the audacity of Kurbsky.

Gregory has run up with a report.
He sees what is happening.
He stands amazed.

Ivan strongly gripped by Kurbsky.
Kurbsky has realized that he has gone too far.

Between them as they quarrel there flies past an arrow.
Two more have stuck in the paling.

Quick as lightning Kurbsky presses Ivan to the paling.
Gregory is ready to hurl himself on Kurbsky.

But Kurbsky explains to Ivan that he was trying
to cover him from the arrow:
I sought to protect thee from the arrow . . .

Gregory glares furiously at Kurbsky.

The underground rumble of the rolling barrels grows louder.

Ivan says to Kurbsky:
If from the arrow . . . then thanks.
With a wave of the hand he dismisses him to the vanguard.

With hatred in his eyes Gregory glares after Kurbsky.

Kurbsky mounts his horse.
He speaks to himself:

The Livonian was right—he always treats me like a puppy.

Ivan catches Gregory's look at Kurbsky.
He sends Gregory back into the mine.
He himself gazes after his friend.

Kurbsky, mounted on a white horse,
is lost in the ranks of his troops.

Slowly, thoughtfully, Ivan says:
Some arrows fly timefully . . .

Alongside Ivan, a voice
as though speaking his thought aloud:
Worse than Tartar arrows
is boyar hatred . . .

The Tsar has turned round.
Before him, the chief gunner
speaks deliberately:
Not arrows—but boyar princes—
need fearing.

Your name?—Ivan casts his gaze upon him.

Alexey Basmanov—
the man says—*Daniel's son.*

A smile of approval
passes across the Tsar's face:
The name of a boyar-hater
shall not slip my memory . . .

He has turned.
He has gone off toward his tent.

Basmanov speaks
to a young lad—his lieutenant:
See there, Fyodor!
See, son—
the Tsar of all Russia . . .

The Tsar . . .
repeats Fyodor
in awe.

He looks after Ivan, without blinking.
He stares open-eyed.
He does not remove his eyes from the Tsar.

Ivan high up, in front of the tents,
above Kazan,
is silhouetted against the morning sky.

Gregory in the mine is surrounded by barrels of gunpowder.
The Brothers Chokhov, Foma and Yeroma, are there too.
Other gunners assisting, they stand a candle in the midst of the barrels.

To the base of the candle
Gregory fastens the fuses.

For the first time in their lives Foma and Yeroma are silent—
the importance of the moment overcomes them . . .

A similar candle,
where everyone can see it,
is put on the ground above
by the foreigner—Engineer Rasmussen.

The candle underground burns.
The candle on the surface burns.
Ivan looks at Kazan.
Kurbsky looks, stationed at the head of his troops.
The gunners watch . . .

The candle burns slowly.
Its flame wavers slightly in the wind.

The Royal troops are watching. Yeroma is watching.
Silence all round.
On the walls, the Tartars are watching.

Slowly the candle burns.

CLOSE-UP—Ivan by his tent.

CLOSE-UP—the flame.

CLOSE-UP—Kurbsky.

CLOSE-UP—the candle.

Already the candle is half burned down.

The giant Gregory, oil-smothered, dirty, breathes heavily—
tensely.

Nervously the flame wavers.

Another quarter of the candle is gone.
The Tsar watches, motionless as a statue.

The priests are dumb before their icons.

Kurbsky gnaws his moustache.

The flame starts guttering at the end of the candle.

Gregory's eyes are screwed up.

The candle has completely burned away.

Silence.
The Tsar holds his breath.

Kurbsky is taut.

The guns are motionless.

But no explosion comes . . .

The Tsar shouts:
What then has become of your underground thunders?

Gregory dashes off.
He runs to the mine.
The foreign engineer Rasmussen grabs him by the scruff.
He does not let him go.
He holds him by the arms.

Kurbsky has sent a derisive look at the Tsar.
The Tsar has drawn his brows together:
The gunners hither!

The gunners fling themselves down at the Tsar's feet.

The gunners have been dragged to the gallows.
The gunner's tunics have been torn off.
They have been left in their shirts.

Nooses have been laid round their necks.
Candles have been placed in their hands.

Gregory has wrenched himself away from Rasmussen.
He has thrown himself on his knees before the Tsar:
This is not treachery, Sovereign—
a candle burns faster in the open air;
underground it goes more gently.

The Tsar does not listen to him.
He bids the gunners be strung up.

Gregory hurls himself toward the gunners.
With his own hands he dons a noose.
Holy Cross!—
he bows.
Lord!—
he sinks to his knees.

The ropes are slowly hoisted over the gallows.

Underground, in the darkness, the candle has burned right down to the fuses.
The fire runs along the fuses.

Gregory raises his head.
The ropes have been drawn tight over the gallows.

An explosion has gone off—
the wall has staggered.

A second explosion—
the Kazan tower is crumbling.

A third explosion.

Gregory comes running up to the Tsar, just as he was, the noose round his neck.

Fifty rubles for the gunners!—
shouts Ivan, exalted.

Kurbsky has rushed forward to the assault.

The song has thundered:
 The black powder's vomited,
  cannoneers,
 The horsemen have charged,
  cannoneers . . .
The troops have leaped forward through the breach:
 The crows have flown on,
  cannoneers,
 The Warriors' prayers are said,
  cannoneers . . .
Not a shot greets them.
It is as though no one were left alive.

The siege ladders have surged forward.
Kurbsky in front.

Ivan turns away.
He cannot control himself—
he fears for his friend.
He hides his face in the folds of his tent.

Quite suddenly Kazan has burst forth
with a shower of arrows, of stones,
with a hail of burning pitch . . .
 Ah! Woe, bitter woe;
  thou Tartar steppe . . .
Every third man in the ranks has fallen . . .
 Hard work,
  Tsar's work . . .

Ivan has turned round.
Kurbsky is unharmed—
his armor glitters in the sun.

Ivan has given a signal:
To the aid of Kurbsky!

The cannon crash.

Ivan calls off
the pet names:
Lion!
Wolf!
Singer!
Bully Boy!
The cannon crash out in sequence.
They crash out together.

And behold, Kurbsky is already upon the walls—
he has been the first to reach them.

He waves aloft the standard.
On the wall, through the smoke,
like a bright dot,
shines his armor.

Ivan towers above the cannon:
Now indeed I'll be Tsar;
the Tsar of Muscovy shall be recognized everywhere!

The thunder of cannon,
bells,
fanfare,
music,
ring out in reply to the Tsar's pronouncement.

We see rise up the domes,
hard by Headfall Ring,
of the Cathedral of St. Basil the Blessed.
And in an endless procession the embassies flow forward
to glorify the Moscow Tsar.
They come to stand within the shadow of the Tsar of Muscovy.

An Astrakhan embassy.
A Cherkassian embassy.
Gifts sent from Siberia.

The herald proclaims their names
as they step into the Tsar's courtyard.

In the courtyard
are a lion and a lioness—
To the glorious Tsar of Muscovy,
from his sister,
a gift from England's Queen . . .

THE PALACE CORRIDORS

Into the clamor of the music there gradually blends
a melancholy bell.

And already the people stand silent by the Tsar's apartments.
On the staircases and in the corridors.
Rasmussen, distressed, stands with bended knee.
Nearby stands Vyrodkov.

The boyars stand silent in the hallways.

Beneath an arch, saddened, the merchant Stroganovs.

And some distance away, at the bottom of the stairs,
in the dark habit of a soldier—
the warrior-captain Alexey Basmanov.

In the Audience Chamber—the ambassadors.
Here mingle West and East:
England and Persia,
Siberia and Italy.

The foreigners whisper:
How fares the Tsar?
How is the health of the Tsar of Muscovy?
The Tsar is sick.

The word "Tsar" is pronounced by all with notable respect
and deference.

A young foreigner is explaining to someone:
While on the very way back from Kazan, the Tsar fell ill.

The Livonian Ambassador remarks sarcastically to him:
So even for you he has now started to be Tsar?

Piqued, the foreigner turns away.

A group of boyars. A little to one side—Kurbsky.
Among the boyars—Euphrosyne Staritsky.
With a sigh she says:
Just is the Lord,
Who raiseth on high above other princes the Prince of Muscovy,
And bringeth him also to the dust . . .

Pondering stands Kurbsky.
A voice beside him:
Well, Prince, always second? . . .
Kurbsky has turned around.

In front of him—Euphrosyne Staritsky.
She laughs soundlessly.

Thou didst love Anastasia
Ivan took her.
Thou didst win Kazan in battle—
yet Ivan is the victor.
To him the glory,
while to thee . . .
she venomously emphasizes:
. . . for service to the State
they'll cut thee off a tiny bit of land . . .
Abruptly altering her tone, she speaks swiftly:
Thou didst capture Kazan for Ivan
to the injury of the boyars,
on thine own head be it . . .

Kurbsky in displeasure has turned away.
But, OFF SCREEN, sounds the voice of Euphrosyne:
And that head of thine is not long for thy shoulders . . .
Kurbsky has suddenly become alert.

With emphasis Euphrosyne continues:
Not quickly will the Tsar forget the Kazan arrow . . .

Kurbsky has abruptly flamed with rage.

Euphrosyne has gripped him by the arm and,
staring him straight in the eye, says:
And should he forget . . . there'll always be someone to remind him!
Suddenly both start, and glance aside:

beside them on the staircase there has slowly passed
the shadow of Malyuta (of Gregory Skuratov-Byelsky).

Euphrosyne whispers in the ear of Kurbsky:
With Ivan living Kurbsky cannot live . . .

Malyuta has disappeared from view.

But God is merciful!—
Euphrosyne has added, pointing to the procession
that is entering the inner chamber of the Tsar.

At its head is the Metropolitan Pimen bearing the holy sacraments.
Behind him the black habit of a monk is borne
by seven priests.[6]
Then monks with lighted candles.

A clerk explains to the foreigners:
They come to give extreme unction to the Tsar . . .
One foreigner says to another foreigner:
It is a custom in this land just before death . . .

Dolefully tolls a single bell.
The monks sing the 51st Psalm:
  Have mercy upon me, O God!
The procession has disappeared into the inner apartments.
From afar is borne the prayer:
Once more, once more, pray for peace unto the Lord.

All is subdued:
the door has closed.
Complete silence.

Dolefully tolls the single bell.

Alone, amidst the luxury, all in darkness, sorrowing
stands Basmanov.

Euphrosyne has sternly questioned Kurbsky:
To whom wilt thou kiss the cross in fealty?

Kurbsky is astonished:
To the son of Ivan—his heir Dmitry . . .

And Anastasia?—
Euphrosyne breaks in:
Thy ambition is to play Telepnev to the widow?

[6] It was a tradition for Russian princes to abdicate temporal power, renounce the world and
become monks immediately before death, that they might die in the odor of sanctity.

Kurbsky has turned away offended.

Beware, Prince, don't hazard too highly!—

and, after a pause, she has added:
Kiss the cross to my son Vladimir!

Kurbsky looks at her questioningly,
then transfers his glance across the chamber.

In a corner sits Vladimir Staritsky.
In apparently profound bliss he is catching flies.
Not figuratively—
but in actual fact.
Only, by no means can he catch them:
he always grabs air.

Kurbsky transfers his mocking gaze
away from him and back to Euphrosyne.

Euphrosyne has grasped his thought.
She has spoken out crudely:
That's exactly why! . . .

She has added hotly:
Men like thee gold cannot buy.
To such as thee a kingdom must be given.
With Vladimir enthroned, thou'lt hold Moscow's reins . . .

More aggrieved than regretful, she has continued:
He is worse than a baby.
His mind is afflicted . . .

Vladimir has reached after a fly.
And again grabbed at air.

Euphrosyne has finished:
Complete master thou'dst be! . . .

In the bedchamber of Ivan
the unction pursues its course.
Pimen takes a Gospel,
opens it, straightens it out and
"lays its written pages upon the head of the ailing,
as though it were the hand of the Savior himself,
healing the sick by touch."

The face of Ivan, part covered by the Gospel.
The Gospel is held by the seven priests.
In their free hands burn seven candles.

The pallid lips of Ivan
ceaselessly mutter beneath the Gospel:
Lord, have mercy . . .
Lord, have mercy . . .
Lord, have mercy . . .
His hands are lain crosswise upon his breast.

In chorus the seven ecclesiastics chant . . .

Anastasia weeps.

In the depths of the chamber outside, Vladimir Staritsky is still trying to catch flies.
And always missing.
Beside him the boyar Peninsky
and the Chancellor Mikita Funikov.
Both are watching Euphrosyne and Kurbsky.
Is the old woman bringing him round? . . .
Eigh, that'd be good! After Kurbsky all would follow.
While as it is—their purpose wavers.

Euphrosyne is bending over Kurbsky:
Kiss the cross to Vladimir!
Both have turned round.

From behind a pillar of the staircase Malyuta is watching them.

Kurbsky has grabbed Euphrosyne by the arm.
Did he hear?
And Euphrosyne has replied soothingly:
He won't be able to report . . .

From the inner apartments emerge Pimen and the monks,
bearing the Holy Sacraments.

Malyuta calls the boyars to the Tsar:
The Tsar commands . . .

The boyars are on the move toward the inner apartments.
After them, her head raised royally, Euphrosyne,
the old Peninsky, Funikov, Vladimir Staritsky.

Her head flung back, Euphrosyne moves forward with royal stride.
Before her, as before a Tsarina,
the boyars obsequiously make way.
They allow her to precede.
Only one has not moved out of her path; the plain,
the dark-clad, semi-soldier—Basmanov.
Transfixed with sorrow, his eye never wavers from the Tsar's door.
Euphrosyne pays no heed to him.

The forceful old woman bears down upon him.
She contracts her brows in anger.
With her staff she has pushed away Basmanov:
in silence and respect Basmanov moves to one side.

From the gorgeous, golden, boyar flood he draws aside.

Suddenly next to Kurbsky
appears the dark figure of the Livonian Ambassador:
And should aught betide—King Sigismund would always be glad.
He is eager for talented military commanders . . .
The King has great plans . . .

Kurbsky has moved past him to the Tsar's bedchamber.

IVAN'S BEDCHAMBER

Ivan lies in a fever.
At his bedside, Anastasia.
To one side, a cradle containing the infant Dmitry.
In a corner, the grim Malyuta.
Beneath an icon case the monk's habit lies ready . . .
Seven candles burn, embedded in a seven-branched candlestick.
At the head of the bed is a tall monk from Solovyets.

The boyars enter.

Ivan, barely moving his lips, says with an effort:
. . . The end has come . . .
I am taking leave of the world . . .
Kiss the cross to my heir . . .
the lawful heir . . .
Dmitry . . .
Ivan weakens.

Anastasia weeps.

Defiantly gaze back at Ivan, Euphrosyne Staritsky
and her son Vladimir.

Ivan reads refusal in their eyes.
He raises himself on the bed.
Anastasia supports him.

Ivan demands:
Kiss the cross to my son Dmitry . . .

The boyars are silent.

Ivan implores:
Kiss the cross to my son . . .

The boyars are silent.

Ivan with tears in his eyes urges them:
Not for my sake.
Not for my son:
but for the Russian land I beg you.
Only a power united—
bound by ties of blood—
can protect Moscow.
From foes.
From carnage.
Else the Tartars again will encroach upon us.
The Polish-Livonian power advance against us! . . .

The boyars are silent.
Ivan rises from the bed.

Throws himself on his knees.
From his knees, his face streaming with tears,
he appeals to the boyars.

He appeals to each individually:
Ivan Shuisky . . .
Peter Shchenyatov . . .
Semyon Rostovsky . . .

The boyars turn away.

Yet more feverishly,
yet more desperately,
Ivan appeals to the boyars:
Ivan Turuntay-Pronsky,
set an example!

Turuntay answers not a word.

Nemoy-Obolensky!
Why are you silent?

Obolensky turns away.

Kurletov!
Funikov!

A terrible attack of fury chokes Ivan.
He raises himself to his feet.

He shouts at the boyars:
For this, for all time
accursed be!

He loses consciousness.
He falls.

No one goes to his aid.

Alone Anastasia busies herself about him.
Malyuta stretches out his feet upon the bed.

Ivan in a dead faint.

And suddenly,
forgetting her shyness,
pale,
Anastasia draws herself to her full height.
She turns to the boyars:
Only in Dmitry—his son—lies salvation.
If there is no united power above you,
then though you be strong,
be you also brave,
though you be wise,
yet shall your rule be as chaos:
hating one the other,
foreign governance you'll serve.

Anastasia's cheeks are burning.
Her face is lit with conviction.
The pallor has fled from her features.

For her fledgling the dove offers battle.
For the great work of her husband she stands like an eagle.

From the doorway, not hearkening to a word,
Kurbsky adores Anastasia . . .

Like a lioness aroused, Euphrosyne has quit her place.
Like a lioness aroused, she bears down on the dove.
Mother against mother,
to defend her offspring she has risen:
Never shall the boyars, glorious, of ancient lineage,
lie beneath a Glinsky heel!

And the boyars look on in agreement:
We must kiss the cross to Vladimir Staritsky!

Mother advances against mother.
Mother before mother retreats.
A mother glares hatred into a mother's eyes . . .

Anastasia protects with her body the cradle containing Dmitry.

Dmitry is sleeping peacefully.

Ivan lies motionless.

Vladimir simpers.
Louder grows the boyar murmur:
We must kiss the cross to Prince Vladimir.

Euphrosyne snarls. She bears down on the Tsarina.
Anastasia defensively protects Dmitry with her body.

A shudder runs through Ivan . . .

But he lies motionless . . .
Only his fingers move, digging deep into the blanket.

Kurbsky shifts in the doorway.
His eyes have met Anastasia's.
Anastasia looks at him imploringly;
with her gaze she begs protection.

Between the Tsarina and Euphrosyne stands Kurbsky.
His gaze is fixed on Ivan.

With eyes bloodshot, Malyuta follows Kurbsky's every motion.

Now cries out the old boyar Peninsky—
of the retinue of the Staritskys—
voicing the general verdict:
The power must pass to a boyar Tsar!
So that authority shall be shared with the boyars!
And the boyar will prevail!

The clumsy lubber
Prince Vladimir Staritsky
simpers with satisfaction.

And Euphrosyne cries:
All must kiss the cross to Tsar Vladimir!

Ivan shudders.
But Ivan lies like one dead.

Kurbsky with steady gaze looks into his face.
He bends over him.

The face of Ivan, stonelike, deathlike.
Only drops of cold sweat upon his brow.

Kurbsky's doubts are assuaged.
He tears away his gaze.
He breaks into the boyar hubbub.
Looking at Anastasia, he bids all go from the chamber.
Noisily the boyars go out.
Kurbsky after them.

As though stung, Tsar Ivan raises himself on his elbow.
He gazes after the boyars.
The Tsar is in a fever, but the life in his look
is, at the least measure, trebled.
Malyuta has jumped forward.

Anastasia has gone to Ivan.
She has laid him down.
Malyuta, calm again, is watching Ivan.

                                                                        FADE OUT

The door of the bedchamber suddenly opens.
Mightily enfeebled,
leaning on Anastasia and Malyuta,
appears Tsar Ivan:
The Holy Sacraments brought me succor . . .

The boyars are worried.
Ivan approaches Kurbsky,
Andrew stands in fear before the Tsar.

Ivan speaks:
You were as first before the Tsar. But yet higher shall you be exalted.
To you I assign the most notable duty of all.
With Kazan, with the East, it is finished,
and you, Kurbsky, shall lead the Russian forces . . .
to the West. To Livonia! To the sea!
He embraces Kurbsky.

And it is as though we can hear the voice of his old nurse:
   Ocean-sea,
   Azure sea,
   Azure sea,
   Russian sea . . .

Kurbsky over the shoulder of Ivan
meets the gaze of Anastasia.

Black is the gaze of her bright eyes:
she reads the soul of the Prince.

With a sharp turn of the head she averts her gaze.

Kurbsky has also turned away his head.
Eye to eye, his gaze has met that of Malyuta.
The face of Malyuta is laden with mistrust.
His eyes flash hatred.
Kurbsky lowers his glance.
And hastily bows before Ivan.

All shout to Kurbsky: *Glory!*

Ivan continues:
*And to guard our southern borders from the Crimean Khan
I appoint . . .*

All are holding their breath: to whom will he render this great honor?

Says Ivan:
. . . Alexey Basmanov . . .
Who's that? To whom?—is borne along the rows
of puzzled boyar corpulence.

In the doorway has modestly appeared Basmanov.
He is clad plainly: darkly, like a soldier . . .
All look at him with wonder.
Not looking aside at anyone, Basmanov has come up to Ivan.
He has kneeled down.

The Tsar has placed his hand on Basmanov's shoulder. He rests his weight upon it.
With heavy gaze Tsar Ivan encompasses those present.

SLOW FADE OUT

QUICK FADE IN

THE STARITSKYS' MANSION

The Tsar trusts no one!
The boyars close to the throne he thrusts aside!
Quite unknown people he draws close to him!
To them he shows trust!—

the boyars bewail to Euphrosyne.
Amidst them Euphrosyne
stands like a stone statue.
I know—she says.

Land from ancient patrimonies to new upstarts
he transfers.
He persecutes the boyars!
Shchenyatov has been imprisoned!
Kurletov arrested!

I know—says Euphrosyne.

I shall flee!—shrilly cries Turuntay-Pronsky.
I can't stand it. I'm afraid. I shall escape to Lithuania.

For shame, Ivan Turuntay—says Euphrosyne—
The Metropolitan has gone to the Tsar:
he is interceding . . .

The doors are flung open.
The Metropolitan himself is in the doorway.
Quickly he comes into the chamber.
He drops onto a low bench.

Euphrosyne has run to him.
The others cluster round.

Says Pimen, breathing heavily,
whether from running,
or whether from wrath:
He spares no one . . .
I, the intercessor,
he has deprived of office . . .
He is transferring me from Moscow to Novgorod . . .

I shall flee! . . .—cries Turuntay-Pronsky—
By the Holy Cross—I shall flee!

He dashes from the chamber.
Past the flabbergasted boyars.

Those who are cowards, let them run—
the old Staritsky woman screeches after him.
He who stays shall fight.

Two boyars have fled hurriedly in Turuntay's wake . . .
The remainder have closed in around Pimen.

Says Pimen hotly:
While Ivan's close friend—
Kurbsky—
is far off . . . the opportunity must be seized to deal with the Tsar.

An aside has dropped from Euphrosyne:
The value of Kurbsky's friendship we shall yet learn . . .

Pimen instructs:
As a first task,
Ivan must be deprived of Anastasia . . .

All have dropped their eyes.
They stare in front of them.

The task is mine—I'll take it on myself . . .
says Euphrosyne.

She places herself on her knees before the icon.
She crosses herself with a wide cross . . .

FADE OUT

IVAN'S APARTMENTS

A din.
Cursing.
Chinaware being broken.
Articles being smashed.

Ivan is seized with an access of wrath.
This is why they warily scamper away
into corners, tremble on staircases—
table servitors, bedchamber attendants, body servants of the Tsar.

Raging, foam on his lips, Ivan shouts:
The maritime cities, the Baltic cities. I must have them!

He runs over to a series of silver models of Riga, Narva, Reval.
Fixed on the models, the Swedish and Livonian arms
glitter brazenly.

Reval, Riga, Narva—I need them!
He is inflamed by the sight of the coats of arms.

Once more the Livonians,
Once more the Hansa traders,
have detained all wares from England.
Once more without lead, without sulphur, without tin, without trained craftsmen
my cannon have been left helpless.

Ivan has grasped the silver Reval:
Reval! Thou SHALT *be mine!*

The silver Reval has crashed to the ground.
It has shattered in fragments.
He has stamped upon the pieces.

Once again by a good Russian name—
Kolyvan—
shalt thou be known!

In her chamber hard by, Anastasia is indisposed:
burning fire wracks her; she lies in fever.

Euphrosyne Staritsky sits over her like a sable-hued bird.
She never moves her gaze from the sufferer.

Through cry and din the anger of Ivan reaches Anastasia.
Anastasia wants to rise,
to go to Ivan:
Let me to the Tsar. . . . He needs me . . .

Euphrosyne does not let her.
She makes her lie back.
Herself she listens.
The noise is dying down.

Ivan in his apartments.
He stands all moist with wrath.
He breathes heavily.
He throws himself down in a wide armchair.
He collects his breath.
He changes his voice.
He controls his anger.
To a shrewd-faced boyar, standing to one side,
he speaks thickly:
You see, Nepeya, how much this military alliance
is necessary to me . . .

He pushes over toward the boyar a luxurious set of chessmen:
Bear these as a gift
to our sweet sister Elizabeth
and, using them as pattern, you shall explain all to her . . .

Osip Nepeya enfolds the men in a silk handkerchief.

And you shall remind her that the Tsar Ivan at Moscow is the sole merchant.
To whom he wishes—he gives leave.
Whom he wishes not—he allows not in his State.
Whom he fancies—to him he will open the road to the East . . .

He goes up to the boyar, dismisses him and shouts after him:
Further, take care that you do not drink too much, Nepeya:
What the sober man keeps in his head, the drunkard lets out on his tongue . . .
Bowing deeply, Nepeya exits.

Behind the window—rain.
It is cold.
The Tsar shivers.
He wraps his fur cloak round himself.

In the chamber hard by, brooding over Anastasia, like a sable-hued bird,
sits Euphrosyne Staritsky.
Through the doorway she follows every movement of the Tsar.
She has recoiled with a start.
She has concealed herself on a stairway.

Ivan comes into the chamber.
Above Anastasia—eternal icon lamps in an arc.
Around—icon hangings embroidered by the Tsarina's own hands.
Ivan bends his head toward Anastasia . . .

Is Tsar Ivan worried?—says Anastasia.

She smooths Ivan's hair.
And, sick though she is, comforts the Tsar.

Says Ivan:
It is impossible to trust anyone.

Kurbsky is far: he fights in Livonia.
Kolychev is yet farther: he is praying in Solovyets.
You are all I have . . .

He bends lower.
He wishes to forget his troubles for a moment.

The Tsar is not allowed to forget,
The Tsar is not allowed to rest . . .
They run in with dispatches:
From Basmanov at Ryazan!

Ivan jumps up.
His eyes greedily devour the dispatch.
He takes in its contents:
THEY *again!*
He passionately complains to Anastasia:
Again the boyars set themselves to thwart our cause.
They are giving Basmanov and the people of Ryazan nothing for defense.
They are ready to surrender the city to the Crimean Khan!

Says Anastasia:
BE FIRM! . . .

Bitterly, Euphrosyne in the darkness hears the Tsarina's words.
Under the black kerchief on her bosom she fumbles.
She is groping for something . . .

Ivan rises. He says hotly:
I'll squeeze the boyars in this fist.
All land shall be allotted for service to the State!

The eyes of Euphrosyne have blazed with wrath.
With decision.
She slips out surreptitiously through a doorway . . .

Malyuta comes running in.
He speaks to the Tsar in a whisper:
Woeful news! The Russian army at Nevel is beaten.

He adds meaningly:
Kurbsky's been beaten . . .

Ivan lets fly.
Anastasia gives a cry.

Euphrosyne has stepped back into the apartment.

Anastasia feels suddenly ill.
She has been taken worse.

She twists on the bed.
She hangs over the bedside.
Near the floor she whispers:
. . . It cannot be . . .
It can't be . . .

Like a sable-hued shadow Euphrosyne stands in a corner.
In her hands she is holding a cup hidden by her kerchief . . .

Ivan rushes to Anastasia,
to give her a drink,
to bring her relief.
He turns to the beaker beside her.
The beaker is empty.
He stumbles, he twists—he seeks everywhere for water.

Carefully Euphrosyne stands her cup in the path of Ivan.

She looks out of the corner of her eye at Malyuta:
Malyuta notices nothing; he is plunged in deep thought.

Ivan snatches up the cup.
He carries it to the Tsarina.

Euphrosyne conceals herself in a corner. She watches from the corner.

Anastasia drinks thirstily from the cup.
Her eyes are wide open in fear.
Ivan holds the cup solicitously . . .

Euphrosyne crosses herself in her corner
with a tiny cross.
She whispers:
There is yet a God in Russia . . .

Hastily she hides an empty phial in her bosom.
In the darkness she noiselessly slips away . . .

FADE OUT

THE PALACE OF SIGISMUND

A luxurious tapestried hall.
A ceremonial atmosphere.
Fanfares.

The scene begins almost like the scene of Ivan's coronation.
Something is happening OFF SCREEN.
And various groups look OFF SCREEN.

Three German knights in armor.
A tall monk in a white robe.

A group of court ladies.
One of them—plump, in black velvet.
In widow's weeds.
Indistinguishable from a Gospel in a costly binding.
Her silhouette recalls that of Catherine de' Medici.
Such, most probably, was Anna Golshansky—
herself thrice a widow
and, in the future, the second wife of Kurbsky, widower.
Behind her—four pale ladies.

Two—in white.
Two—in black.
A pair of effeminate courtiers.

And above them, lit by reflections—
ponderous black figures of knights on horseback
woven in the tapestry.

In the foreground
a huge white and black ball.

Clustered around it—striped jesters.
The jesters keep glancing OFF SCREEN.
And tinkle their bells.

The jesters are mimicking what is happening in the background,
as yet invisible to the spectator.

Two jesters are balancing on the ball.
One of them—the chief, browless and moonfaced—
brandishes high his beribboned jester's wand.
A third bends the knee before the ball.
The first jester dangles in front of the kneeler his wand with the ribbon,
as though to invest the latter's neck with the decoration on its end.
He knocks the second jester off the ball by pushing him from behind.
The second jester falls.
A fourth jester takes a running leap over the ball.
The ball rolls.
The jesters fall in a heap one on top of the other. They freeze motionless.

The background has been revealed.
We see the throne of Sigismund II—Sigismund Augustus.

The King stands up.
He holds in his hand a ribbon with a glittering cross.

On his knees before the King—
Kurbsky with sword extended hilt foremost.
The King hangs the cross on Kurbsky.
He returns him his sword.

Close to Kurbsky—the Livonian Ambassador.
The old diplomat says unctuously:
Sometimes a defeat is a brilliant victory.
Kurbsky kisses the King's hand.

And triumphantly asserts:
In Moscow all are ready to come over to the side of Lithuania.
The defeat of the Russian troops at Nevel
will be the signal for revolt.
The Tsar's army is far to the south.
Tsar Ivan is like a bear
on all sides in his own den
surrounded.
It is possible to take him with one's bare hands . . .

The knights lean forward.
The monk listens intently.

Kurbsky continues:
The throne will be free,
For a new Tsar—
a friend of Poland . . .
The Prince looks at Sigismund expectantly.

Sigismund looks back at him enigmatically,
rises and proclaims:
On a Holy
Crusade
of all Christian States
we shall go up against Moscow!

A general *Vivat!*

The trumpets blare.

FADE OUT

A DARK CATHEDRAL INTERIOR. NIGHT

A coffin with the body of Anastasia.
A voice in the darkness is reading in whispers a psalm—
a Psalm of David, the 69th:
> *Save me, O God;*
> *for the waters are come in unto my soul . . .*
The coffin is not made from boards but hollowed out,
carved, from the whole trunk of an oak.
It is draped with a black pall.

The psalm is heard:
> *I sink in deep mire*
> *where there is no standing:*
> *I am come into deep waters,*
> *where the floods overflow me . . .*
Ivan in deep sorrow beside the coffin.
> *I am weary of my crying:*
> *my throat is dried:*
> *mine eyes fail . . .*
The psalm is intoned in a whisper by a monk standing behind the lectern.

The words of the psalm intermingle with words spoken by Malyuta.
Malyuta is reading a dispatch.

Ivan's eyes are fixed on Anastasia.
He has no ears for either the dispatch or the prayer.

But the dispatch is disturbing:
Prince Ivan Shuisky
has taken refuge on Lithuanian soil . . .

Prince Ivan Sheremetyev
has been captured in flight . . .

Boyar Ivan Tugoy Luk of Suzdal
has escaped to Livonian territory . . .

In a whisper, the monk:
   They that hate me without a cause
   are more than the hairs of mine head
Calm is the countenance of the dead
Ivan gazes at her with yearning.
In his misery he flings himself on the ground.

In a whisper, Ivan:
Am I right in what I am doing?
Am I right?
Is this not the chastisement of God?

The monk continues:
   I am become a stranger unto my brethren,
   and an alien unto my mother's children . . .
Malyuta continues:
Prince Ivan Turuntay-Pronsky
has been captured in flight.
He has been turned back . . .
He has been brought back here . . .

Ivan rises from the ground.
He fixes his gaze on the dead countenance.
Am I right in this hard struggle of mine?

The dead countenance of Anastasia is silent.
And Tsar Ivan strikes his forehead on the edge of the coffin.
   When I wept, and chastened my soul with fasting,
   that was to my reproach . . .
The elder Basmanov runs into the cathedral.
With him is his son Fyodor.
   I made sackcloth also my garment;
   and I became a proverb to them.
The Basmanovs run up to Malyuta.
They have whispered in his ear.
Malyuta is startled.

   They that sit in the gate speak against me;
   and I was the song of the drunkards.
Malyuta has fallen on his knees before Ivan.
The treachery of Kurbsky is reported:
Kurbsky has gone over to Sigismund . . .

Ivan has raised his head.
His eyes are fixed far off in an uncomprehending stare.

He has understood.
Swiftly, in a whisper, he speaks:
Andrew, my friend . . . why?
Did aught not suffice thee?
Or didst thou covet my Royal Cap? . . .

The monk, in a whisper:

Deliver me out of the mire,
and let me not sink:
let me be delivered from them that hate me,
and out of the deep waters . . .
But Malyuta whispers to Ivan of worse yet:
Against you the boyars afresh
are inciting the people.
The Livonian defeat
has resulted in confusion and bewilderment . . .

The monk, in a whisper:
Reproach hath broken my heart;
and I am full of heaviness . . .
And I looked for some to take pity,
but there was none;
and for comforters,
but I found none . . .
Ivan has turned his head.

And he roars, like a wounded beast, to the whole Cathedral:
Thou liest!

The monk who was saying the psalm has been startled.
He has upset the lectern.

Through the whole Cathedral rings the proclamation:
The Moscow Tsar is not broken yet!

At the shout there run to Ivan those
who remain of the ones most near to him.
They are few—they are lost in the emptiness of the Cathedral . . .

Ye are few!—cries Ivan.
And he bids:
Summon to me my true friend, the last, the only one—
Kolychev.
In the far Solovyets Monastery
he prays for us!

Tsar! Trust not Boyar Kolychev—
Alexey Basmanov, the taciturn one, passionately urges the Tsar:
Surround yourself with new people.
All beholden to you.
Forge from them around you an iron ring
with sharp spikes presented to your enemies!

Ivan listens eagerly.

Basmanov goes on:
Forge it from such as shall forswear
their kith and kin,
their sires and mothers,
know none but the Tsar,
obey no will but the Tsar's!

He has taken hold of his son—Fyodor.
He has pushed him down onto his knees in front of the Tsar:

As first to be part of that iron ring.
For that great cause,
my own-born son, my only son,
his mother's only child,
I give to you!
Ivan listens eagerly to Basmanov the father.
Basmanov the son trembles to the roots of his hair.

Fyodor is sturdy: rough he is, and tough.
Wide-open eyes gaze at Ivan:
they are burning in an ecstasy of devotion.

Alexey goes on:
With them alone you will maintain power.
With them alone you will break the boyars.
Crush the traitors.
Accomplish your great task.

Ivan hears him greedily:
Thou speakest truthfully, Alyoshka!
We shall girdle Ourself with an iron ring.
We shall gather round Ourself an iron brotherhood.
Except for these men, my own, apart.[7] I shall trust none.
And I to them shall be their iron abbot . . .

Ivan's eyes flash with a clever thought,
his mind flying ahead of Basmanov:
Moscow I'll quit.
I'll go from it.
I'll go to the Alexandrov Liberty[8] . . .

The eyes of Malyuta have flashed back in reply:
Launch a march on Moscow . . .

Return as conqueror—
Alexey Basmanov cries.

But Ivan bends towards his comrades-in-arms:
No, we shall not return by a march . . .

They stand dumbfounded.

The Tsar continues:
We shall not return by a march . . .
We shall come back summoned by the people!

Basmanov and Malyuta are both perplexed . . .
Where is the Tsar's mind taking him?

Basmanov objects energetically:
You cannot await a summons from the people!

---

[7] These were the *Oprichniki,* men of the *Oprichnina,* which was one of two estates of the realm into which Ivan at this time divided Muscovy. He retained the *Oprichnina*—the "estate apart"—for his absolute personal use and service.
[8] A "Liberty" in medieval times was a suburb outside the city walls where the population was exempted from various rules and taxes.

And Malyuta grumbles reproachfully:
You cannot listen to a mob.
Nor put your faith in ragged riffraff!

The anger of the Tsar has been roused:
Thou forgettest thyself, ginger cur!
Thou presumest to teach the Tsar
how he should act?!

He speaks in wrath:
. . . in that summons—
I shall find power unlimited.
A new anointing, that I shall use
for the great cause—
RELENTLESSLY!

Ivan seeks support for his unprecedented idea.
He finds none from his comrades-in-arms.
Gloomily Malyuta fixed his gaze on the ground.
Gloomily at the ground stares Basmanov.

The Tsar's nearest are far from him—
they do not agree with the Tsar.

Ivan seeks approval for his unheard-of plan.
He finds none from those most near to him.
To his true companion—
his counselor—
to Anastasia he turns.

But Anastasia's dead countenance is silent:
her eyelids lowered . . .

Only one gaze gleams in the darkness of the Cathedral.
Unwaveringly it is fixed upon the Tsar:
the gaze of Fyodor Basmanov.

"Speak then!"

Fyodor replies firmly:
"You are right!"

Malyuta and Alexey Basmanov have given an indignant start,
but Ivan has flown to the platform like an arrow.

He hangs suspended above the coffin.
He gazes into the dead features.

The lines of the dead face seem to soften.
The face of Anastasia seems to shine with approval.

And not with grief now, but with decision,
Ivan gazes at that face.

Basmanov whispers to his Fedka:
Swiftly indeed have you grown into a Tsar's Man,
heeding none other . . .

Fixedly Fyodor is gazing at the Tsar:
he does not hear his father . . .
Swiftly have you changed father for father . . .

Music rises:
the theme of Ivan The Terrible—
"The Approaching Storm . . ."

Ivan straightens himself above the coffin.
His eyes burn with a new strength,
with resolution.
His hand passes above Anastasia.
And he swears a great oath.

*In this summons from the people
I shall read the will of the Almighty.
Into my hands I shall take the Lord's avenging sword.
The great task I shall accomplish:
a Sovereign almighty upon earth shall I become!*

Broader in the orchestra grows the theme of The Terrible—
"The Approaching Storm."

The Cathedral has become alive with the blaze of torches.
The arches of the Cathedral are ringing with sound.
Through the Cathedral hurry torchbearers.
They are making ready for the Tsar's great cause.

High in the blaze of the light stands Ivan.
He speaks:
*Two Romes fell,
but the third—*
MOSCOW—
*shall stand.
And a fourth Rome
shall never be!*

The orchestra's trumpets blare the theme of The Terrible—
"The Approaching Storm" . . .

In the glare—Ivan.
Behind Ivan:
Malyuta, Basmanov.
Full of determination.
Fyodor.
Ivan kisses Anastasia on the forehead.

                                                        FADE OUT

FADE IN

THE OUTSKIRTS OF MOSCOW

The outskirts of Moscow are covered in snow.
Through the snow come sledge upon sledge in a train.
The runners creak.

But this train is no ordinary train—
it is an extraordinary one.
It bears not fish, nor salt, nor grain.
Under the matting covers gleam icon frames.
Under the matting are piled dishes.
Under the matting go coffers—
their beaten-metal sides glitter.

Mounted retainers escort the train on its flanks.

Retainers with halberds stand on the runners of the sledges;
the sledges are not ordinary ones—
they are the Tsar's.

In one of them the profile of the Tsar flashes by.
The profile of Tsar Ivan, muffled in a fur cloak.

The people run after the sledges.
They are perplexed.
They understand nothing of what has happened.

The Tsar's servants repeat only:
The Tsar is renouncing his kingdom . . .
He is leaving the boyar traitors—
Leaving the betrayers . . .

The sledges have passed beyond the outskirts.

The train of the Tsar has vanished in the distance.

The people are perplexed.
They whisper.

Abandoned Moscow is silent.

A whisper spreads through empty Moscow:
. . . The Tsar has abdicated . . .
The Tsar has gone . . .

THE ALEXANDROV LIBERTY

Beneath the gloomy vaults appears the face of Ivan.
A song resounds:
   Before God I swear
   A faithful oath,
   A weighty oath,
   A fearful oath.
Here beneath the vaulted ceilings of the Alexandrov Liberty
the Tsar's Men are gathered
to swear an oath.
In their hands they hold lighted candles.
They stand in a semicircle:
repeating after the elder Basmanov the words of the oath.
THE TSAR'S MEN:
   Before God I swear
   A fearful oath . . .

BASMANOV:
To serve the Sovereign of Russia like a dog.
THE TSAR'S MEN:
Its towns and villages to sweep with a broom.
BASMANOV:
Villainous scoundrels to tear with my teeth.
THE TSAR'S MEN:
At the Tsar's command to lay down my bones.
TOGETHER:
FOR THE SAKE OF THE GREAT RUSSIAN REALM . . .
The Tsar's Men stand in a semicircle.
With lighted candles.
Habited all in black . . .

Against a table, brooms are leaning.
On the table, heads of dogs.
In front of it the elder Basmanov
holds a cup.

Fyodor is the first to pronounce the words of the oath:
Before God I swear
A faithful oath:
To destroy the enemies of the State,
To renounce kith and kin,
Forget sire . . .
Steadily the Basmanovs look at each other:
father and son.
. . . and own mother,
True friend, blood brother,
FOR THE SAKE OF THE GREAT RUSSIAN REALM.
Ivan towers like a black shadow.
He does not hear the oath.
He is lost in thought.
He examines his thin fingers.

Are you waiting for a messenger from Moscow?—
Malyuta whispers to the Tsar.

The Tsar moves suddenly towards Malyuta.
He seems to be listening to far-off Moscow.
From the distance he hears nothing.

Only the oath reverberates under the vaulted ceilings:
Before God I swear
A weighty oath:
To execute throughout Russia the will of the Tsar,
To destroy throughout Russia savage robbers,
To shed throughout Russia the blood of the guilty,
To burn out treason with fire,
To cut out treachery with the sword,
Not self nor others sparing—
FOR THE SAKE OF THE GREAT RUSSIAN REALM.

The door has opened—
Boyar Nepeya
is at the feet of the Tsar:

Ships—
from England—
have sailed into the White Sea!

Ivan's eyes are shining with joy.
He has clenched his fists.
He has risen to his full height.

And from far, far off—
comes a sound like the singing of a church choir
in the distance.

As though reflecting the Tsar's delight,
the blades of the Tsar's Men are gleaming—
the Tsar's Men have drawn their daggers:
  If I should break this fearful oath,
  Then may my brother Tsar's Men pierce me
  Mercilessly with their sharp daggers . . .
BASMANOV THE SON:
  Then may I be overtaken by the penalty of death.
BASMANOV THE FATHER:
  And by curses, and the tortures of Hell.
BASMANOV THE SON:
  And by shame, and the torments of the damned.
THE TSAR'S MEN:
  Then may green mother earth reject me.
The echo rolls hollowly through the vaulted chambers.
With it, more clearly now, the far-off singing
of many voices
merges.
The Tsar hears the singing from afar.
Eagerly he listens to the singing.

Then the oath taken under the vaulted ceilings is finished.
It blends with the far chorus.
THE TSAR'S MEN
  May this my fearful oath before God
  Remain inviolable to the end of time,
  On earth as in Heaven—
  FOR THE SAKE OF THE GREAT RUSSIAN REALM.
The Tsar's Men have fallen silent . . .

Basmanov the father declares
against the background of the distant chorus
coming nearer:
  And may it stand for ages eternal
  Inviolable for ever and ever.
Amen!—
concludes the Tsar.

The door has been flung open.
Malyuta has rushed in.

A beam of light enters from the door
and the roar of the singing pilgrimage
bursts in.

Ivan goes out through the beam of light.
In the midst of a vast snowy expanse,
flooded by the sun,
he stands on the roof.

Before him in an endless stream
stretches the pilgrimage from Moscow . . .
With crosses,
with icons,
with sacred banners,
it glitters against the snow.

The people see the Tsar.

Their singing ceases.
They fall on their knees.

Return to thy kingdom!—
a voice cries beseechingly.

Dear father of ours!—
voices join in.

Ivan draws himself erect.
His nostrils dilate.

With heads bowed, there stand
Pimen,
Euphrosyne,
Vladimir,
and five more boyars.

All their voices as one:
RETURN!—
the people cry.
The theme of the "Terrible" expands in the music.

Suddenly, slyly,
to those nearest him—
to the Tsar's Men—
the Tsar smiles:
Saddle the horses
to gallop to Moscow!

From a swift MIX
cries of *Holla! Holla!*

Over the snowy hills
pours raven-hued lava:

In a black cloud tear along
riders fantastic.

Clad in long black tunics,
on their saddles, brooms and dogs' heads,
The "TSAR'S MEN."

In the orchestra the theme of The Terrible swells to a roar.
Among the riders, on horseback also,
the Tsar himself.

Terrible is the Tsar's aspect.
The Tsar has grown haggard.
He has aged.
His eyes blaze.
Behind him whirl the Basmanovs,
Malyuta.

Holla! Holla!
In a black cloud against the snow
the riders furiously tear forward . . .

                                                         FADE OUT

                                                    END OF PART ONE

Ivor Montagu

EISENSTEIN'S *IVAN*

1. THE SCREENPLAY

The screenplay of *Ivan the Terrible* was first published in 1943. At that time, as is clear from his arrangement of the text, Eisenstein planned to make the film in two parts.

The parts of the film were not made successively. They overlapped in the making, and sequences of both mingled in the floor schedule at Alma-Ata film studios. Part One, however, was finished first, at the end of 1944. It was released at once, and it won applause from the Soviet government and public. The author-director was decorated with the Order of Lenin.

With intensification of actual work the material had developed. At some point, Eisenstein decided to split what had originally been—and is still, of course, . . . —Part Two and to issue nearly the first half of it as a separate section ("Tale Two"—*The Boyars' Plot*), leaving the remainder, the later sequences, to form a third part. This second film, however, ready in 1946, was not well received by the authorities. A scathing comment on it was made in a Party decision published about another film, and the result was that "Tale Two" did not reach the public until thirteen years later.

Eisenstein was seriously ill in 1947. At the time of his death in 1948 he was working on the completion of the final section. He died of heart failure at the desk of the library in his home in Potilikha, the Moscow film suburb. Four reels of the last section are said to have been finished, but they have disappeared.

The screenplay is, therefore, the only form in which it is possible to appreciate the grand design of one of the most re-markable works ever conceived—and so nearly realized—in the cinema.

The *Ivan* screenplay has a double interest. On the one hand it is, in itself, an intensely exciting and vivid dramatic narrative. On the other it provides an opportunity to study an act of filmic creation; it sheds light not only on its author-director's method of working but on the "cinematic process" in general.

There are no other full Eisenstein scripts accessible to the reader at present. There are fragments, worked out for his classes at the State Institute of Cinematography, Moscow (G.I.K.). There are more elementary sketches, such as those of *Ferghana Canal* (abandoned) and the Mexican film (never finished). The script of *Nevsky* is said to have survived, but the booklet published in the U.S.S.R. as a script of *Potemkin* is nothing of the kind; it is only a transcript made afterward from the finished, edited film. The scenarios written in Hollywood for Paramount by Eisenstein, Grisha Alexandrov, and myself from Blaise Cendrars' *Sutter's Gold* and Theodore Dreiser's *An American Tragedy* could not be published at the time because of copyright obstacles; though they illuminate another aspect of the director's creative work, it should be remembered that they are not original film stories but adaptations from novels. The *Ivan* screenplay stands alone.

Eisenstein taught that a screenplay should be as readable as any other form of literature. He did not work from a scenario bespattered with technical instructions—C.U., pan, location—together with shot numbers. These things would appear finally on some copies, no doubt, but only as a part of the administrative schedule for those whom

SOURCE: From *Ivan the Terrible*, by Sergei Eisenstein, translated by Ivor Montagu and Herbert Marshall. Copyright © 1962 by Simon and Schuster, Inc. Reprinted by permission of Simon and Schuster, Inc. (Footnotes omitted.)

they directly concerned. He held that a scenario should vividly convey to a reader the feeling, the atmosphere, the emotion of each scene, exactly as these would be perceived and appreciated by the spectator of the finished film. "Literary" scripts without scene numbers are also to be found as a stage in the work of other film directors; indeed, a special term applies to them—the "line-by-line continuity." But in *Ivan* Eisenstein goes much further. Not only does each "scene" (the "scene" sometimes later being a single shot, sometimes an edited group of shots) appear as a separate paragraph, but the paragraphs themselves are scrupulously divided into lines, almost in the manner of free verse, and the order of the words within each line also has a deliberate significance. All this meticulous arrangement was designed to convey not only action and mood but even the future graphic style—to give the reader an inkling of the succession in which the various elements of the described action or scene must be apprehended by the spectator from the future visual composition in order that the dramatic development should fall exactly into place.

The prime object of such a scenario was, of course, to provide a means of complete understanding of the author-director's purpose on the part of his creative colleagues (the actors, cameramen, composer, sound recordist, set and costume designers, makeup men, and assistants in every technical branch). But an incidental by-product, as it were, of the process was that a work became available equally capable of appealing to the dramatic sensibility of the lay reader. This was why Eisenstein was able to publish the script as a piece of literature while shooting was in progress, and why it remains fascinating today.

Eisenstein also held that the director should possess a modicum of drawing ability. The director did not need, he told his pupils, to be a talented graphic artist. But what a director could not visualize sufficiently clearly himself to sketch, or show as a diagram indicating the essential even if only in conventional symbols, he would never be able to describe sufficiently clearly in words for the guidance of his colleagues. His own sketches . . . went far beyond this minimum. For *Ivan* he produced countless drawings. He himself describes how they arose, not as illustrations for an already thought-out scenario, but as part of the thinking-out, the creative process, itself. They arose before the writing, inspiring parts of it; simultaneously with the writing; and after it, contributing to the intensifying and polishing process. Many are well known. Selections have been published, and collections have been exhibited in Warsaw, Paris, and elsewhere. . . .

More drawings still, and innumerable jotted notes, appear on the reverse blank pages and in the margins of his own personal copy of the script. Their study brightly illumines the continuous process of perfecting with which Eisenstein, to the last moment and beyond, incessantly deepened the content of his treatment, loaded it with more and more significant detail, gilded refined gold. Once, when I was young and naïve, I put to Sergei Mikhailovich this question: Should a director complete his script precisely and then shoot exactly what is written, or should he write it approximately and then modify it on the floor? I say "naïve" because the answer I received now seems to me obvious: at every stage of his realization of the film he should be ready to make use of everything, even the unexpected, consistent with its idea. . . . That Eisenstein's creative demon never froze in preconceived positions but was ever alert to seize each happy "happenstance" is sufficiently attested by his felicitous decision in *Potemkin* to locate its massacre scene on the Odessa steps (where none of the massacres of those days actually happened, although he created it so vividly that it has now entered illegitimately into history) and by the wonderful use made by him, Grisha Alexandrov and Eduard Tisse, of the mist in Odessa roadstead in the same film.

Consistent with its idea—those are the crucial and difficult watchwords. To admit an improvisation, to improve safely by however painstaking an accretion and refinement of detail—these need the rigid will and unwavering power of visualization of a chess grand master. Where Eisenstein transgressed, with this very film, in respect to its general idea, we shall see below. To his visualizing power, nevertheless, this script and the two completed films bear conclusive witness. In sequence after sequence, scene after scene, the words of the scenario bring before our eyes exactly the drama and emotion we derive from sight of what is on the screen. For each of Dombrovsky's stills ... there is an appropriate script phrase that determined its "feeling" as faithfully as a gene prefigures a character.

2. THE STYLE

But if Eisenstein bade the director be ever-ready, like a captain on the battlefield, to suit his dispositions to the lie of the terrain and the sway of combat, like a good captain he was determined to leave the minimum to chance. Scientist no less than artist—or, rather, scientist in art, capable of extraordinary intuitions and sensitivities to form, he was nonetheless perpetually seeking, on his own behalf and that of his pupils, the means of increasing the *conscious* element, the deliberate, in artistic creation. Control must attain the maximum. No hair must lie out of place, unless foreseen and to order.

Unless this is understood, there is risk of missing the whole point of his lifework. Planning a tragedy on the grand scale, Eisenstein chose a form to suit it and plumbed the recesses of the form. When the reels of *Ivan*, Part One, were first screened, not a few admirers were astonished to see in this, the latest work of its director, a period piece, heavily stylized. Was this the master they worshiped, the great innovator who first used nature as the stuff of drama? The inspirer, through *Potemkin*, via Grierson and *Drifters*, of whole schools of "documentary"? The youthful realist who, impatient of theatrical bonds of bricks and mortar, burst out to stage a play of working-class struggle in a real factory and then to do the same on film? The conjuror who pinned and captured first the Russian, then the Mexican, landscape as his back cloth?

Especially, were these actor-puppets with their rolling eyes directed by the great exponent of "typage," the use of non-actors to seek greater realism?

Even to ask these questions is to go astray. The consistency in Eisenstein is

the perpetual search to increase the range of elements subject to artistic mastery and to discover the means by which these elements may be made to serve. Perhaps the clue that was forgotten is that the theater the young master and his companions sprang from was really a circus, with clowns' grins and acrobats, a circus of satire. When Eisenstein broke into cinema it was not to retreat into naturalism that he tried the factory setting but in an experiment to recruit the factory among the tractable materials capable of being included within the artist's repertoire. His realism was comprised of symbols whose impact was the greater because they were themselves real.

Eisenstein's recourse to natural settings and types was really antinatural, at the opposite pole from the contemporary (and therefore sometimes confused with his method) Dziga-Vertov theory of the Kino-Eye. Dziga-Vertov's idea was that the artist should interfere as little as possible with natural processes and use the camera only to observe. This is a principle as impossible in art as it is in science. Just as the scientist's observation inevitably interferes, if only by a beam of electrons or a stream of light, and therefore must be allowed for in seeking the truth of the processes he is trying to observe, so the artist, in reproducing nature, however abstemiously intended his interference, is inevitably creating and arbitrating by the act of selection. The Kino-Eye theory —which is but "documentary" taken to its logical limit—is a blind alley, negated by every attempt to explore it. Eisenstein, on the contrary, basing himself on the Engels' dictum that freedom is the awareness of necessity, sought the power to recreate a vivid reality by knowledge of the laws and processes of effect within his chosen art. He chose that art precisely because, of all the arts, it gives the possibility of the widest range of subjugable means—graphic composition not only spatially but in time, light, shade, color (in three reels of *Ivan*), music, sound, living beings (actors)—and of subjugating them most plastically—by preplanning and, afterward, by editorial scissors. When Eisenstein dealt with nature, it was not as worshiper but as some magician of old, triumphing over the forces of nature to weave his spells.

To Eisenstein the non-actor was a graphic image of infinite adaptability, with appearance more convincing than the makeup of a professional; editing was the means to use him without having to encounter the stubborn habits instilled by the professional's training. There was no principle about it, only practical advantage, and when he set himself the task of portraying the majesty and tragedy of power, he naturally turned to classicism and, as Bachelis acutely saw, "the resurrection of the Russian classical style of acting as practiced at the beginning of the 19th century, with its deliberate coldness and its contempt for internal fullness of emotion." It was a reaction against the naturalism—totally unsuited to this theme—of the Moscow Art Theater and a resurrection of that which the Moscow Art Theater had initially been a reaction against. To quote Bachelis again, "The magnificent Byzantine ceremonies portrayed are not merely the decorative luxury of an operatic-historical production; solemnity, pomp, majesty and picturesque wealth are the necessary concomitants of the very idea of the film."

3. THE THEME

"The very idea of the film . . ." This, chosen by Eisenstein, was no less than the birth of the Russian state, the attempt by a renaissance monarch to construct a unitary power for the nation, above and replacing the rulers of petty feudal princedoms—the boyars—among whom the Grand Duke had been hitherto but primus inter pares. Such a task required review of the traditional literary image of Ivan.

This is how Eisenstein himself wrote about Ivan:

> Making this film was an extremely complicated matter. The personality of Ivan the Terrible and his historic role had to be thoroughly reconsidered. Ivan the IV's principal aim was to create a strong centralized sovereign State in place of the scattered, mutually hostile feudal principalities of old Russia. He laid the foundations of a vast and mighty power. . . . The heirs to the feudal lords crushed by Ivan refused to accept the idea of a unified power and did

not scruple to resort to treachery and conspiracy. They secretly prepared the ground for an invasion of Russia by her western neighbors and it was they who cried to heaven about the cruelty and bloodthirstiness of the Moscow Tsar. They painted Ivan's harsh measures and relentless firmness in protecting the interests of the State against the self-interest and arbitrary power of the boyars as irrational malice and insane thirst for blood. . . . Their writings determined the past historical and artistic interpretation of the role and character of Ivan but they were far from being unbiased pictures of "things gone by." They were deliberate propaganda designed to incite hatred against the Moscow State and to discredit it among Western nations.

Is this idea of Ivan historical? Yes, certainly. No one, seeing the film, could conceive of it as a whitewashing operation. But Eisenstein's Ivan is no monster, no special "Thing from the Slav Renaissance." Just as at Paramount in Hollywood Eisenstein had accepted to be interested in the one modern American murder story—Dreiser's—that links the crime-committer through his growth, makeup and background to the social influences around him, so here he—in Grisha's words—"shows how Ivan's character was made 'terrible' by his environment," i.e., his role and situation. It is not only a Marxist interpretation but also nowadays a commonplace of academic historians that the unification of the State by monarchy was everywhere a progressive stage in national development. This story was always bloody. Bachelis does well to remind us that in Western Europe the classic authority for the prince's duty during this process was Machiavelli, and Eisenstein at the very outset of his script challengingly recalls the persons and events contemporary with the "Terrible" in other lands. It is known that Ivan was a milder man before he lost Anastasia. (Thereafter, his matrimonial adventures, spared to us in this film study, matched those of Henry VIII.) It is true also that the principal sources for the traditional image that has come down of Ivan are his lengthy correspondence with Kurbsky, the latter ever seeking to justify his betrayal; Staden, who spied on him for his enemies; and the scribes of those boyars who, on his death, returned to Moscow as puppets with the armies of the Polish King. Expect as well to find a balanced picture of Richard Crookshank in Shakespeare's "historie" written to do pleasure to a Tudor Queen, or, for that matter, of Henry VIII in a chronicle written by a dispossessed monk.

Shaw in *Saint Joan* depicts, intellectually, the birth among the masses of the national idea and embodies it in the argybargy of contrasting characters. Eisenstein in *Ivan* depicts the institutional conflicts attending national birth and embodies them in a graphic study of the torment within the monarch, a child of his times, his vision of duty warring with his ties of loyalty to kin and church. He personalizes this conflict in subtle, ingeniously interwoven relationships and seemingly fated developments, sometimes bloodcurdling, always grandiose.

Here is how the director explains the relation of theme and form:

> The grandeur of our subject called for monumental means of presentation. Details were pushed into the background and everything was subordinated to the principal idea of the might of Russia and the struggle to make it a great power. The principal conflicts in the general struggle, in which Ivan lost those who were nearest and dearest to him—some because, failing to understand his aims, they turned away from him, some because the mercenary nature of their own aims caused them to oppose him, and some because they perished at his side in the course of the struggle—called for the use of the forms of tragedy.
>
> This was how the style of the film was determined, a style that runs counter to many of the traditional methods to which we have grown accustomed on the screen both here and abroad. The general custom is to try to make the historical personage, the historical hero, "accessible," to portray him as an ordinary person showing the ordinary, human traits of other people, to show him, as it is said, "in dressing-gown and slippers."
>
> But with Ivan we wanted a different tone. In him we wished chiefly to convey a sense of majesty, and this led us to adopt majestic forms. Frequently the dialogue is accompanied by music, and choral singing intermingles with it.

> The principal idea—the formation of a strong State—governs the Tsar's whole conduct.
>
> Irrelevant details in the characters of the other personages are ignored, while their principal features—chiefly their hostility or loyalty to Ivan's cause—are drawn in bold relief. Because of this, when taken individually some of the characters may perhaps seem somewhat one-sided. But the point is that they must be taken together as a whole, in their general relationship to the cause for which Ivan stands. They cannot be taken separately, just as the part of one instrument cannot be singled out in judging a whole complex orchestrated score, for the meaning of their individual actions is disclosed only in their general interaction. Neither can they be considered outside the plastic setting and musical whole in which they are immersed.

The threads of the interrelationships of which Eisenstein speaks together form a dynamically developing, dramatic tapestry. Details, at the time appearing insignificant or else justified merely by service as color to an early scene, emerge later as in fact seeds of growth that powerfully determine the subsequent action. In the script, the theme is fully triumphant, Eisenstein's objective is attained.

Where the whole thing came a cropper in practice was through the circumstance of its conception as two films and, yet further, its development as three. Stubborn problems arise from the very nature of sequel presentation in the cinema. The audience cannot turn back a page, from Part Two to Part One, as a reader of the scenario can while it is printed as a book. Feature sequels in film viewing are known, if rarely, both in the U.S.S.R. and elsewhere, but the greatest success in this kind is with such as *Pather Panchali* and its successors and the Gorki or *Maxim* trilogies—or, for that matter, the adventures of Tarzan or the various offspring of *Dracula*—where each subject is independent in itself and the unifying factor is simply a character or characters, each time hopping onward into a quite separate locality or period. A continuous plot is just not possible.

When the sum of the projected series is a unity, the development and balance of the whole so carefully studied, as in *Ivan*, then obstacles of Himalayan magnitude immediately obstruct the separations. Examine here our screenplay. Has there ever been a more preposterous remark than that . . . introducing the Vogt of Weissenstein? "Sometime—long ago —he came with an embassy to the young Ivan, and spectators will remember him from the prologue of the film." Will they, indeed? Perhaps on rare occasions all three parts of the triple film might have been revived together for galas and festivals, so that hardy spectators with powerful *Sitzfleisch* might see the thing through as long as they could put up with it, like the Wagnerian "Ring," but 99 and a large decimal point of spectators would have been seeing in the Vogt a figure that last appeared to them (if ever) not merely 200 odd pages but two or three years before.

A similar lost echo would have been the reappearance of Foma and Yeroma, grown "handsome, bearded," toward the end of Part Three.

The script envisages one dramatic curtain at the end of Part One, and the obvious choice for an eventual second break was where Eisenstein finally put it, after the defeat of the Staritskys. Yet even this involved him in serious dramatic difficulties. To omit the Prologue from the beginning of Part One weakened our understanding there of Ivan's conduct; we had advance knowledge only by hearsay of the bitterness of the boyar struggle that conditioned its harshness; we did not see its origin with our own eyes, a proof so much stronger. Yet it had to be transferred to Part Two, where the separation of the family intrigue part of the story made it still more necessary and appropriate. The awful oprichnik oath at the end of Part One (in the script) is a perfect introduction to the Tsar's return at the start of Part Two, where he is embittered by betrayal and the loss of his loved one. But when the oath is removed as an excrescence to the film of Part One considered on its own, the opening venom of "Tale Two," now separated from its cause, comes as a shock to the spectator, who left Ivan noble and suffering and sees him suddenly return transformed and violent. Further, with the second curtain placed, as it was, after the defeat of the Staritskys, how could Eisenstein, having omitted from "Tale

Two" the there irrelevant beginning of the Eustace story, have built it up later so as to retain its climax in the Confession Sequence? Such questions can now never be answered; but is it not here, in the asperities consequent on the breaking of the whole into parts, in the consequent changes of proportion and balance, that we find the rock on which the project foundered?

Hindsight often gives the explanation nowadays that "Tale Two" contained topical allusions about ruthlessness that the authorities found too near the mark. But this leaves everything unexplained. Why swallow the script and not its embodiment? It is quite clear that a crude analogy may be drawn between Russia's problems in Ivan's day and Eisenstein's. The struggle to build a strong state, the pressure of external foes seeking to foment treasonous partnerships within and the consequent suspicions—these parallels were inherent in the subject. We know from Eisenstein's preliminary studies, and from the internal structure of the film itself, how scrupulously the author-director sought the essence of the *period* factors. Naturally, a creative artist interpreting the past to his contemporaries reflects, in proportion to his integrity, his own experience of the world and man. But that the task Eisenstein consciously set himself was in no sense a veiled (as Lenin called it, "Ethiopian") criticism but something quite different is attested by the dates. The film was made from 1943 to 1945, at the height of the war. It will forever be a wonder, a tribute to the tenacity and firmness of vision of the author-director on the one hand and the liberality of the authorities and administrators toward a never complaisant artist on the other, that, with the Nazis at the gates of Stalingrad, with the entire country mobilized to resist the frightful wounds inflicted upon it, facilities could be afforded for a lavish reconstruction of renaissance Moscow in the heart of Central Asia. *But this is because the film was a grand patriotic demonstration for the Great Patriotic War*—a film about "an heroic builder of our State," to use Eisenstein's own words. That Eisenstein so saw it, we know from his whole approach to the film and everything he wrote about it. The preparatory work was begun around 1940, all undoubtedly a part of that preparation of the Soviet people for the ordeal gathering against them in the west, of which *Nevsky* was likewise a part and in which many other talented film makers participated. Such modern parallels as may be detected between the strains and stresses of the times and those of Ivan's day were no bootleg introductions but always implicit in the parallels of the situation, explicit in the script—approved by the authorities and widely published beforehand. "Tale Two" is exactly as its author-director left it; that nothing was smuggled in can be confirmed at once by comparison of published text and finished film. The only fresh topical allusions are still further patriotic ones, e.g., the new opening title to Part One, the enlarged speech by King Sigismund of Poland to his court, and the new terminal color sequence to "Tale Two."

But if there were no new introductions to provoke objection, what then led to the fiasco?

H. G. Wells left us a brilliant short story about a rajah and a ranee, who loved each other with a love sung by poets, a perfect love. In the flower of their youth together, the princess was bitten in the foot by a serpent and she died. The rajah resolved to raise above her tomb a marble palace so majestic and so beautiful that it should outshine the Taj (unless, perchance, it was itself the Taj) and make his love for her immortal. For years and years he labored, with a regiment of architects and an army of artificers. At last the shrine was complete. Yet something was wrong; something—he could not tell what—marred the perfection of its symmetry. At last, head on one side, he decided. The culprit was an object in the corner. Pointing to the tomb, he cried: "Take that damn thing away!" This sad parable is an epitome of formalism.

Something like this happened with Eisenstein and *Ivan*. His critics—and this does not diminish him; it only defines him—have sometimes called him "the master of the episode." Meaning that he was apt to deepen and to polish the episode so thoroughly that, while in itself it became a thing of brilliance, it was apt to become hypertrophied in its rela-

tionship with the whole. It is noteworthy that the two most perfectly balanced unities among Eisenstein films—*Potemkin* and "Tale Two"—are both polished and inflated episodes, originally conceived as parts of greater wholes. The Party decision on *The Great Life*, with the back-handed swipe at Eisenstein, which so long delayed the release of "Tale Two," complained—among other things—that therein the director had shown the oprichniks as a band of degenerates similar to the Ku Klux Klan and Ivan as a waverer "something like Hamlet." Can anyone deny this? Ivan of the grand design, taken from start to finish of the original script, is a man of inflexible purpose, of iron will. The oprichniks are clearly the men of the people, rough and liable to corruption maybe, but plainly gathered by the Tsar to serve as his ring against feudal kin and external foe. But boiled down into "Tale Two"? Had the author not become so devoted to the polishing of his chip of diamond—till it shines as a deeply felt personal horror story of brilliance unparalleled—that he had compromised its functional role? He himself so described the trouble. He wrote (using a different simile): "Like a bad foundryman, we light-mindedly allowed the precious stream of creation to be poured out over sand and become disposed in private unessential sidelines." Even the title chosen—no longer *Ivan, Part II*, but a tale in itself, *The Boyars' Plot*—showed how much the master plan had narrowed.

The answer to a question that has puzzled many devotees of Eisenstein throws light on the way even graphic qualities enhanced this contraction. Why did Eisenstein modify his lifelong exclusive partnership with Tisse? Yurenyev tells us that he chose to use two cameramen, Eduard Tisse for exteriors only and Moskvin for interiors, precisely because he wished the plastic contrast of two visions, two entirely different seeing and composing eyes, to emphasize (unconsciously, graphically) the duality in Ivan's mind and conscience—the clear exteriors where the future dominated, his progressive role as the creator of the nation-state, reliant on the people for victory in the conflict; and the oppressive, cruel interiors, where the barbarism of the feudal past woke echoes in his own nature, kin of kin to the boyars. This duality is apparent in Part One, but all the scenes that were to have been Tisse's share in Part Two are in the latter half, or among the sections pared from *The Boyars' Plot*; with them even the visual associations displaying the social meaning of the conflict vanish and only the horrors of the internecine feud remain.

Why did he let this happen? Eisenstein was no fool, he was one of the most acute minds of his day. He must have foreseen the obstacles. But he was a man of boundless integrity, invincible courage, implacable stubbornness, wherever his passion for perfect presentation of what he saw as truth might lead.

So "Tale Two," no longer a cutting tool within the grand design but a dark jewel on its own, became his final masterpiece as *Potemkin* was his first. Timeous but untimely, for the times were out of joint. A legacy that lay hidden for thirteen years.

However, the grandeur of the original conception is still here, in the screenplay.

A
Peking
Opera

Peking opera (so named after its center in Peking) is a unique form of musical theatre evolved over centuries from song and acrobatics and incorporating dialogue, poetry, and acting. Originally an aristocratic entertainment, Peking opera, in the nineteenth century, developed a more popular audience, and with the fall of the Manchu dynasty in 1911 became independent of court patronage. In the 1930's, thanks to Westernizing influences and improved status for actors, women were allowed on the stage. Visual excitement in traditional Peking opera depended not on scenery but on brilliant costuming, elaborate women's hair-dos, and intense, expressive make-up, sometimes highly patterned and colorful. Props were often ornamental and symbolic; gestures and movements, stylized. An orchestra accompanied the performance, and singing followed certain basic styles. The plots of Peking opera, largely drawn from history and legend, dealt with emperors, warriors, lords and ladies, ghosts, and monsters. Inevitably, demands to modernize Peking opera and Chinese theatre arose in this century. With the triumph of the Chinese Revolution, two lines on culture emerged. One line called for imitating Soviet models; another, Chairman Mao's, demanded an indigenous proletarian art adapting traditional Chinese forms towards revolutionary ends. At first the Sovietizing line won out. Later, however, classical Chinese drama was revived. But now it was argued that Peking opera must be kept separate from modern forms and themes to preserve its classical perfection. This view—identified with ex-President Liu Shao-ch'i—was strongly challenged during the Great Cultural Revolution (1965–1969). Chiang Ching, Mao's wife, took the lead in organizing new operas based on contemporary revolutionary themes, collectively developed, discarding traditional heroes and legends, and adopting contemporary costumes and more natural make-up. The results were such works as *The Red Lantern, On the Docks, Red Detachment of Women, Taking the Bandits' Stronghold, Raid on the White Tiger Regiment,* and *The White-Haired Girl.*

THE RED LANTERN

A Peking opera

Adapted by WONG OU-HUNG and AH CHIA from the Shanghai Opera Version

Translated by Yang Hsien-yi and Gladys Yang

CHARACTERS

LI YU-HO, a switchman
TIEH-MEI, his daughter
GRANNY, Tieh-mei's grandmother
OLD CHOU, a worker
AUNT LIU, Li's neighbor
KUEI-LAN, her daughter
THE LIAISON MAN
THE KNIFE-GRINDER
GUERRILLA COMMANDER LIU
THE GRUEL-WOMAN
THE CIGARETTE-VENDOR

HATOYAMA, chief of the Japanese military police
HOU HSIEN-PU, his Chinese lieutenant
A JAPANESE SERGEANT
INSPECTOR WANG, underground agent for the guerrillas
THE PEDDLER, a spy for the Japanese
THE COBBLER, a spy for the Japanese
JAPANESE GENDARMES, THUGS, TOWNS-PEOPLE, GUERRILLAS, ETC.

SCENE ONE

THE LIAISON MAN IS RESCUED

[A late autumn night during the War of Resistance Against Japan. A siding near Lungtan Station in northeast China. It is dark and the wind is howling. Four Japanese gendarmes march past on a tour of inspection. There is a slope near by, with hills in the distance. A train passes on the other side of the slope.]

[Enter LI YU-HO, quietly, with a signal lantern.]

LI.
Red lantern in hand, I look round;
The Party is sending a man here from the north;

The time fixed is half past ten. [Looks at his watch.]
The next train should bring him.[1]
[Enter TIEH-MEI with a basket.]
TIEH-MEI. Dad!
LI. Well, Tieh-mei, how was business today?
TIEH-MEI [angrily]. The gendarmes and their thugs kept searching people and made them too jittery to buy anything.
LI. Those gangsters!
TIEH-MEI. Do be careful, Dad.
LI. Don't worry. Go home and tell Granny that an uncle is coming. Ask her to have a meal ready.
TIEH-MEI. Right.
LI. Come over here. [Wraps his scarf round her neck.]
TIEH-MEI. Dad, I'm not cold.
LI. No, you have it.

SOURCE: Reprinted from Chinese Literature (May 1965), pp. 3–48.
[1] Verse passages are sung according to various styles in Peking opera.

TIEH-MEI. Where's he from, this uncle?

LI [kindly]. Children shouldn't bother their heads about such things.

TIEH-MEI [to herself]. I'll go and ask Granny. Take good care of yourself, Dad. I'm off now. [Exit.]

LI. Our girl is doing all right.
She can peddle goods, collect cinders,
Carry water and chop wood.
A poor man's child soon learns to cope
With all tasks at home and outside.
Different trees bear different fruit,
Different seeds grow different flowers.

[Enter INSPECTOR WANG.]

WANG. Who's that?

LI. It's Li.

WANG. The Japanese are keeping a close watch today, Old Li. They must be up to something.

[Enter two Japanese soldiers. WANG and LI step apart. Exeunt the Japanese.]

WANG [taking out a cigarette]. Got a light?

LI. Here. [He goes over to light his cigarette, bending close to WANG.] Things are tense, Old Wang. We must take special care. Let's get in touch once every ten days from now on. I'll let you know where to meet.

WANG. Right.

[A whistle sounds in the distance and a train roars past. When it nears the station the LIAISON MAN jumps off. The Japanese police on the train fire two shots. LI and WANG step back.]

[The LIAISON MAN, wounded in the chest, staggers in and falls by the track. LI and WANG rush over to him.]

LI [helping him up]. Well, mate.

LIAISON [regaining consciousness, looks around]. What's this place?

LI. The fifty-first siding, Lungtan Station. You . . . .

[With an effort the LIAISON MAN puts a blue glove on his left hand and raises this. Then he faints.]

LI [to himself]. The left hand gloved. [To WANG.] He's our man. [Not far off Japanese yell and whistles are blown.]

WANG. Get him away, quick. I'll cover you.

LI [carrying off the man on his back].

Be careful, Old Wang. [Exit.] [The shouts and whistles come nearer.]

[WANG draws his pistol and fires two shots in the direction opposite to that taken by LI. Pounding footsteps can be heard and angry yells. To fox the enemy, WANG clenches his teeth and shoots himself in the arm. As he falls to the ground in come the Japanese sergeant, HOU HSIEN-PU and several gendarmes.]

SERGEANT [to WANG]. Where's the man from that train?

WANG [pointing towards the opposite direction and groaning]. Over there.

SERGEANT [in alarm]. Down! [All the Japanese flop to the ground.]

SCENE TWO

THE SECRET CODE

[The same evening. The road where LI's house stands. The house, in the center of the stage, has a door on the right and by the door a window. In the middle of the room is a square table with a lamp on it. Behind is a kang. The north wind howls. The room is dark. GRANNY strikes a match and lights the lamp. Wind rustles the window paper.]

GRANNY:
Fishermen brave the wind and waves,
Hunters fear neither tigers nor wolves;
The darkest night must end at last
In the bright blaze of revolution.

GRANNY [draws back the curtain and looks out. Shaking her head she mutters, "Still not back." She goes to the table and takes up her needlework. Enter TIEH-MEI with a basket].

TIEH-MEI. Granny.

GRANNY. You must be cold, child.

TIEH-MEI. I'm not. Granny, Dad told me to let you know there's an uncle coming. He wants you to get a meal ready. [Puts down the basket.]

GRANNY. Oh, just coming, are they? I've rice and dishes ready.

TIEH-MEI. Why do I have so many uncles, Granny?

GRANNY. Your father has so many sisters, of course you have lots of uncles.

TIEH-MEI. Which one is this coming today?

GRANNY. Why ask? You'll know when he arrives.

TIEH-MEI. Even if you won't tell me, Granny, I know.

GRANNY. What do you know?

TIEH-MEI. Listen.

I've more uncles than I can count;
They only come when there's important
    business.
Though we call them relatives we have
    never met,
Yet they're closer to us than our own
    family.
Both you and Dad call them your own
    folk;
Well, I can guess the secret—
They're all men like my dad,
Men with fine, loyal hearts.

GRANNY [smiling]. You smart girl.

[Sound of a police siren. Enter LI with the wounded man on his back. He pushes open the door and staggers in. GRANNY and TIEH-MEI hurry to help the LIAISON MAN to a chair.]

TIEH-MEI [frightened]. Oh!

LI [to TIEH-MEI]. Watch the street.

[With a sigh the girl goes to the window. GRANNY brings a towel. LI cleans the man's wound and gives him a drink of water.]

LIAISON. Can you tell me if there's a switchman here named Li?

LI. That's me.

[The LIAISON MAN's eye lights on GRANNY and he hesitates.]

LI. It's all right. You can speak.

LIAISON [using the password]. I sell wooden combs.

LI. Any made of peach-wood?

LIAISON [eagerly]. Yes, for cash down.

LI [with a pleased glance at GRANNY]. Fine.

[GRANNY lights the small square lantern to show the LIAISON MAN that one side is pasted with red paper.]

LIAISON [not seeing the right lantern, struggles to get up]. I must . . . go.

LI [holding high the other lantern]. Look, comrade!

LIAISON [grasping LI's hand]. Comrade, I've found you at last.

[He faints away.]

[TIEH-MEI is puzzled by this business with the lantern.]

LI. Comrade. . . .

GRANNY. Comrade, comrade. . . .

[The LIAISON MAN comes to.]

LIAISON. Comrade Li, I'm . . . the liaison man . . . sent . . . from the north. [With difficulty he tears open the lining of his padded jacket, produces the code and hands it to LI.] This is . . . a secret code. [Panting.] Send it . . . quickly . . . to the guerrillas in the north hills. [Gasping for breath.] Tomorrow afternoon, the gruel stall in the junk market. . . .

LI. Yes, comrade. What about the junk market?

LIAISON. A knife-grinder will get in touch with you there.

LI. So a knife-grinder will get in touch with me.

LIAISON. Same password as before.

LI. The same, yes.

LIAISON. The task must be carried out. . . . [He dies.]

[TIEH-MEI cries. GRANNY quickly stops her. LI takes off his cap and looks at the code in his hand. All three bow their heads before the dead man.]

LI. I swear to carry out the task.

[The siren of the police car wails. GRANNY hastily blows out the light.]

SCENE THREE

A COMMOTION AT THE GRUEL STALL

[The next afternoon. The gruel stall in the junk market. To the right of the shabby booth is a rickety table at which three men, A, B, and C are eating gruel. At the foot of the pillar on the left squats a woman selling cigarettes. As the curtain rises the market hums with noise.]

[Enter LI with his lantern in one hand and a canteen in the other.]

LI.

Come to find our man in the junk market
I have hidden the code in my canteen;
No obstacles can stop me,
I must send it up to the hills.

[He enters the booth and greets the people there.] A bowl of gruel, please, mum. [*Hangs his lantern on the right-hand pillar.*] How is business?

GRUEL-WOMAN. So-so [*She serves him.*]

[c *finishes his gruel and pays for it.*]

GRUEL-WOMAN. Another bowl, brother?

c. No more, thanks.

GRUEL-WOMAN. Is one bowl enough for you?

c. Enough? It's all I can afford. We work all day but don't earn enough to buy gruel. It's a hell of a life. [*Exit.*]

[*Enter another man,* D.]

D. A bowl of gruel, please.

[*The woman serves him.*]

D [*stirring the gruel with his chopsticks*]. This is thin, watery stuff.

A. It's government rice. What can we do?

[*With a sigh* D *takes the bowl to the left pillar to drink. He then squats down and buys a cigarette.*]

B. Hey, what's this in the gruel? Nearly broke one of my teeth.

A. It's full of stones.

GRUEL-WOMAN. You'd better put up with it.

B. The swine just don't treat us as human.

A. Keep quiet, or you'll find yourself in trouble.

B [*sighing*]. How are we to live?

LI. Let's have another bowl, mum.

Our people are fuming with discontent,

Trampled by iron hoofs they seethe with fury

And wait for the first rumble of spring thunder.

China's brave sons will never bow their heads;

May our guerrillas come soon from the north hills!

[*Enter the* KNIFE-GRINDER *with a carrying-pole.*]

KNIFE-GRINDER.

Glancing around in search of my man,

I see the red lantern hanging high to greet me.

[*Raising his gloved left hand to his ear he cries.*]

Any knives or scissors to grind?

LI.

The knife-grinder has his eye on my red lantern

And he raised his hand to accost me.

I shall casually give him the password.

[*Before* LI *can speak the siren wails and Japanese* GENDARMES *charge in.*]

GENDARMES. Don't move. This is a search.

[*The* KNIFE-GRINDER *deliberately drops his tools to divert the attention of the Japanese.*]

LI. Good man.

He draws their fire in order to cover me.

[*He empties his bowl of gruel into his canteen and asks for another helping. The* GENDARMES *finish searching the* KNIFE-GRINDER, *wave him angrily away and turn towards* LI. *He offers them his canteen and lantern but they push them aside.* LI *puts them on the table and lets himself be searched.*]

GENDARME A [*having searched him*]. Clear out.

[*Li picks up his canteen and lantern and goes out.*]

SCENE FOUR

WANG TURNS RENEGADE

[*The following afternoon.* HATOYAMA's *office. On his desk are a medal, a medical report and a telephone. Beside the desk stands a screen.*]

[*Enter* HOU HSIEN-PU *with* WANG's *file.*]

HOU.

The man from the train fired a shot

And wounded Inspector Wang's arm;

The damage done is not serious

But Hatoyama is making much of it.

No doubt he has his reasons.

[*The telephone rings.* HOU *takes the call.*]

HOU. Yes? [*Standing to attention.*] Yes, sir. [*He puts the receiver down.*] A call for you, Captain Hatoyama.

[*Enter* HATOYAMA *from behind the screen.*]

HATOYAMA. Where from?

HOU. From the commander.

HATOYAMA. You should have said so. [*Takes the phone.*] Hatoyama speaking.

What? Got away? Eh? Hmm.... Don't worry, sir, I promise to get the code. Yes, sir. What? An order from the Kwantung Army Headquarters. [*He stands to attention.*] The deadline for clearing this up ... Yes, sir. [*Rings off, muttering to himself.*] Those Reds are the devil. Headquarters discovered some clues in the north, but now they've covered their tracks again. The Communists are the very devil.

HOU. Report! Here is the dossier on Inspector Wang. [*Presents the file.*]

HATOYAMA. Good. [*He takes it and looks through it casually.*]

SERGEANT [*off*]. Report!

HATOYAMA. Come in.

[*Enter the* SERGEANT.]

HATOYAMA. Find him?

SERGEANT. We searched all the hotels, bath-houses, theaters and gambling dens but found no trace of the man from the train. We arrested a few suspects. Would you like to see them, sir?

HATOYAMA. What's the use of arresting suspects? This is urgent. Headquarters have just notified us that this man from the train is a liaison officer for the Communists in the north. He has a very important secret code with him.

HOU and SERGEANT [*standing at attention*]. Yes, sir.

HATOYAMA. This code has been sent from the Reds' headquarters in the north to the guerrillas in the northern hills, who are waiting for this to get in touch with them. If this code reaches the guerrillas it will be like fitting several thousand tigers with wings, and that would be most detrimental to our empire.

HOU and SERGEANT [*standing at attention*]. Most detrimental. Yes, sir.

HATOYAMA. How could you let such an important Red slip through your fingers? [*The* SERGEANT *and* HOU *look at each other.*]

HATOYAMA. Fools!

HOU and SERGEANT. Yes, sir.

HATOYAMA. How about Inspector Wang?

HOU. He was shot in the left arm, but the bone ...

HATOYAMA. That's not what I was asking. Tell me his background.

HOU. Very good, sir. His name is Wang Hung-chang, otherwise known as Wang Lien-chu. His grandfather used to sell opium, his father kept a tavern, and he was one of the first graduates from the Manchukuo police school. He has one wife, one son, and one father.

HATOYAMA. So he comes from a good family. This time he did his best. Bring him here.

HOU. Yes, sir. [*Calling.*] Inspector Wang.

[*Enter* WANG *with one arm in a sling. He salutes* HATOYAMA.]

WANG. Captain.

HATOYAMA. Well, young man.
You have paid for your courage, young fellow,
Stopping the enemy's bullet with your body
And fearlessly defending our great empire.
On behalf of headquarters I give you this medal, third class.

WANG [*surprised and pleased*]. Ah!
My ill luck has changed to good,
Hatoyama does not suspect me.
Thank you, sir, for your goodness,
This is too great an honor.

HATOYAMA. Young man,
Provided you serve the empire loyally
You have every chance to rise high;
One who repents can leave the sea of troubles,
The choice is up to you.

WANG. I don't follow you, sir.

HATOYAMA. You should understand. You are not an actor, so why try to fool me? I'm afraid I can't compliment you on your performance.

WANG. Sir ...

HATOYAMA. I don't suppose you have followed my career. Let me tell you that when you were still a baby I was already a surgeon of some reputation. Though you fired that shot accurately enough, you forgot one thing. How could the man from the train get within three centimeters of your arm to fire?

WANG. I'm sorry you should think such a thing, sir.

HATOYAMA [*chuckling*]. Sorry. I'm sure you are. Sorry that I wasn't taken in by your trick. You can't fox me so easily, young fellow. So now, out with the truth. Who was your accomplice?

WANG. Accomplice?

HATOYAMA. Does that word surprise you? It's obvious enough. That man who jumped off the train was badly wounded. Without an accomplice to help him and another to cover their escape, could he have grown wings and flown away?

WANG. Sir, you can investigate what happened. I was shot and fell to the ground. How could I know where that man went?

HATOYAMA. You knew all right. Why else should you shoot yourself? Don't try to outsmart me, young fellow. Tell me the truth. Who's in the underground Communist Party? Who were your accomplices? Where is the liaison man hiding? Who's got the secret code now? Make a clean breast of things and I have ready plenty of medals and rewards.

WANG. You're making my brain whirl, sir.

HATOYAMA [laughing derisively]. In that case we shall have to sober you up. Hou Hsien-pu!

HOU. Yes, sir.

HATOYAMA. Take this young man out and help to sober him.

HOU. Very good, sir. Guards!

[Enter two GENDARMES.]

WANG. I've done nothing, sir. Nothing wrong.

HATOYAMA. Take him away.

WANG. Don't punish an innocent man, sir.

[HATOYAMA jerks his head in dismissal.]

HOU. Come on.

[The GUARDS march WANG out, followed by HOU.]

HATOYAMA [smiling cynically after them].
Iron hoofs trample the whole northeast,
Human skulls are used for goblets;
The crack of whips, the sound of sobs
And drumming on bones make music.
No matter how tough the fellow,
[His singing is punctuated by the sound of blows and cries.]

He must break down under torture.

[Enter HOU.]

HOU. If you please, sir, he has confessed.

HATOYAMA. Who was his accomplice?

HOU. Li Yu-ho, the switchman of the No. 51 Siding.

HATOYAMA. Li Yu-ho! [He takes off his glasses.] Well, well . . .

SCENE FIVE

THE FAMILY'S REVOLUTIONARY HISTORY

[The next afternoon. LI's house. GRANNY is sewing and worrying about LI.]

GRANNY.
Already dusk, but my son is still not back.
[In the distance sound shouts and the wail of the siren. TIEH-MEI rushes fearfully in with her basket and locks the door.]
TIEH-MEI. It looks bad, Granny.
GRANNY. What's happening?
TIEH-MEI. Granny,
The streets are in confusion
With sentries at every crossroad;
They are searching and arresting men right and left,
It's even worse at the station.
I ran home because I'm worried about Dad.
GRANNY. Don't worry, child.
Your dad is brave and wary,
He knows the way to deal with the Japanese.
[She tries to calm herself.]
TIEH-MEI. Yes, of course, Granny.
[Enter LI with the red lantern and canteen.]
LI [knocking at the door]. Mother.
TIEH-MEI. It's Dad. [She quickly opens the door.] At last you're back, Dad.
LI. Yes. . . . Mother.
GRANNY. So you're back, son. You had me really worried.
LI. It was a near thing, Mother. [He walks towards the pillar by the bed and signs to her to take the canteen.] Let me have the thing in that, quick.
GRANNY [signing to TIEH-MEI to watch the street while she opens the canteen]. There's nothing here but gruel.
LI. It's underneath, Mother.
[She empties out the gruel, produces the code which is wrapped in cellophane and hands it to LI.]
GRANNY. What is this?
[TIEH-MEI, standing guard by the window, keeps an eye on her father.]
LI [hiding the code in a crack in the pillar by the bed]. Mother,
I'd just met the knife-grinder by the gruel stall

When a police car came and the Japanese
started a search;
They didn't find the code hidden under
the gruel,
I smiled calmly while they searched.

TIEH-MEI. Trust you, Dad. But what
are we to do with this?

LI. Don't worry. We'll think of some
way to send it, Tieh-mei. [He makes her
sit down opposite him and speaks gravely.]
You've seen everything. I can't keep this
from you any longer. This is something
more important than our own lives. We
must keep it a secret even if it costs us
our heads.

[GRANNY lights the paraffin lamp.]

TIEH-MEI [naïvely yet earnestly]. I understand.

LI. Hah, I suppose you think you're the
smartest girl in the world.

TIEH-MEI [pouting]. Dad!

GRANNY. Look at you both.

TIEH-MEI. Granny.

LI [consulting his watch]. It's getting
late. I must go out.

TIEH-MEI. Wait till you've had supper,
Dad.

LI. I'll eat when I come back.

GRANNY. Don't be too late.

LI. I won't. [He gets up to go.]

TIEH-MEI [giving him the scarf]. Take
this, Dad. [She wraps the scarf round his
neck.] Come back early.

LI. I will. [Exit.]

[GRANNY polishes the lantern with care.]

TIEH-MEI [struck by an idea]. Polishing
the red lantern again, Granny?

GRANNY [deciding to satisfy her curiosity.] Tieh-mei, the time has come to tell
you something. Sit down and listen to
the story of the red lantern.

TIEH-MEI. Yes.

GRANNY. We've had this lantern for
thirty years. For thirty years it has lighted
the way for us poor people, for workers.
Your granddad carried this lantern, and
now your dad carries it. It's bound up
with all that happened last night and to-
day, which you saw for yourself. I tell
you, the red lantern is our family treasure.

TIEH-MEI. Ah, the red lantern is our
family treasure. I'll remember that.

GRANNY. It's dark, time to get supper.
[She puts the lantern carefully down and
goes to the kitchen.]

[TIEH-MEI picks up the lantern to examine it carefully and then puts it
gently down. She pensively turns up
the paraffin lamp.]

TIEH-MEI.
Granny has told me the story of the red
lantern,
Only a few words, yet how much it means.
I have seen my father's courage,
My uncles' willingness to die for it.
What are they working for?
To save China, save the poor and defeat
the Japanese invaders.
I know they are in the right,
They are examples for the rest of us.
You are seventeen, Tieh-mei, no longer a
child,
You should lend your father a hand.
If his load weighs a thousand pounds,
You should carry eight hundred.

[Enter GRANNY. She calls TIEH-MEI,
who does not hear.]

GRANNY. What were you thinking
about, child?

TIEH-MEI. Nothing.

GRANNY. The food will soon be ready.
When your dad comes, we'll start.

TIEH-MEI. Right.

[The child next door cries.]

GRANNY. Listen, is that Lung-erh crying next door?

TIEH-MEI [looking towards the curtain
behind the kang]. Yes, it is.

GRANNY. Poor child, he's hungry I'll be
bound. Have we any of that acorn flour
left?

TIEH-MEI. Not much.

[The child cries again.]

TIEH-MEI [eager to help]. There's a little, Granny. Shall I take them a bowl?
[She gets the flour.]

GRANNY. Yes, do.

[Enter KUEI-LAN.]

KUEI-LAN [knocking at the door]. Aunty
Li.

TIEH-MEI. It's Sister Kuei-lan. [Opens
the door.] I was just going to call on you,
sister.

GRANNY. Is Lung-erh any better?

KUEI-LAN. Yes, but . . . we've nothing at
home to eat.

TIEH-MEI. Sister Kuei-lan, this is for
you. [Gives her the bowl of flour.]

KUEI-LAN [hesitating to accept it].
Well . . .

GRANNY. Take it. I heard Lung-erh crying and thought you probably had noth-

ing he could eat. Tieh-mei was just going to take this over.

TIEH-MEI [to KUEI-LAN]. Go on, take it.

KUEI-LAN [accepting the bowl]. I don't know what to say, Aunty. You're too good to us.

GRANNY. Well, with the wall between us we're two families. If we pulled the wall down we'd be one family, wouldn't we?

TIEH-MEI. We are one family even with the wall.

GRANNY. That's true.

[The child next door cries again.]

[Enter AUNT LIU and she opens the door.]

AUNT LIU. Kuei-lan, the child is crying. [Sees the bowl in her hand.] Aunty, Tieh-mei, you . . . How can we accept it? You haven't got much yourselves.

GRANNY. Never mind. In times like these we must help each other and make do as best we can. You'd better go and fix a meal for the child.

AUNT LIU. I don't know how to thank you. [She starts out with KUEI-LAN.]

GRANNY. It's nothing. [She sees them to the door.]

TIEH-MEI [closing the door]. Granny, look at Kuei-lan's family. Her husband out of work and the little boy ill. How are they going to manage?

GRANNY. We'll do our best to help them.

TIEH-MEI. Yes.

[An enemy agent posing as a PEDDLER comes to the door and knocks lightly three times.]

PEDDLER. Is Old Li in?

TIEH-MEI. Someone wants Dad.

GRANNY. Open the door.

TIEH-MEI. Right. [Opens the door.]

GRANNY. You want . . .

[Enter the PEDDLER. He looks around and closes the door behind him.]

PEDDLER. [raising his gloved left hand]. I sell wooden combs.

GRANNY [observing him carefully]. Have you any peach-wood combs?

PEDDLER. Yes, for cash down.

TIEH-MEI [eagerly]. Wait! [She turns to pick up the red lantern.]

[GRANNY coughs. TIEH-MEI stops. GRANNY strikes a match and lights the small square lantern while TIEH-

MEI, understanding, catches her breath.]

PEDDLER [raises the curtain and looks out as if on his guard. Then he eyes the small lantern]. Thank goodness, I've found you at last.

TIEH-MEI [realizing that this is a trick, angrily]. You . . .

GRANNY [throwing her a warning glance]. Well, let me see your combs.

PEDDLER [pretending to be in earnest]. This is no time for jokes, old lady. I've come for the code. That's important to the communist cause. The revolution depends on it. Every minute is more precious than gold to the revolution. Give it to me quickly, without any more delay.

TIEH-MEI [vehemently]. What nonsense are you talking? Get out.

PEDDLER. Now then . . .

TIEH-MEI. Are you going? [She pushes him.]

GRANNY. Tieh-mei, call the police.

TIEH-MEI. If you won't go, I'll call the police.

PEDDLER. Don't do that. I'll go, I'll go.

TIEH-MEI. Get out quickly.

[The spy gives her a dirty look and shuffles out. TIEH-MEI closes the door with a bang. Two plainclothes men enter, making signs to each other, and stand outside the door.]

TIEH-MEI. He nearly fooled me, Granny. Where did that mangy dog come from?

GRANNY. Child, this is a bad business. Never mind that mangy dog,
A poisonous snake will be following behind;
It's clear that someone
Has talked.

TIEH-MEI. We must send the secret code away at once.

GRANNY. It's too late. They'll have laid a trap.

TIEH-MEI. Ah! [Runs to the window and looks out.] Granny. [She comes back to her.] There's a man by the telegraph pole watching our door.

GRANNY. You see? Hurry up and paste the sign on the window.

TIEH-MEI. What sign?

GRANNY. The paper butterfly I told you to cut out.

TIEH-MEI. It's in the box of patterns.

GRANNY. Get it out then.

TIEH-MEI. Right. [*Hurries behind the bed-curtain and fetches the paper.*] How shall I paste it, Granny?

GRANNY. Open the door to keep the window dark before you start. I'll sweep the ground outside so that they can't see you.

[TIEH-MEI *opens the door and* GRANNY *gets a broom. Before she can go out* LI *enters and walks in.*]

TIEH-MEI [*startled*]. Why, Dad. [*The paper butterfly falls to the ground. The old woman drops her broom.*]

LI [*seeing the paper butterfly on the ground*]. Has something happened, Mother? [*Closes the door.*]

GRANNY. There are agents outside.

[*They fall silent.* GRANNY *is thinking hard.* TIEH-MEI *waits for her father to speak.* LI *paces thoughtfully up and down.*]

[*Enter* HOU HSIEN-PU *and he knocks at the door.*]

LI. Mother, they may be coming to arrest me. I went to look for Old Chou just now but couldn't find him. If you need any help, get in touch with Old Chou at No. 36 West Bank. You must be careful.

GRANNY. I know. Don't worry.

LI. Tieh-mei, open the door.

[LI *calmly sits down.* HOU *enters the room beaming.* GRANNY *makes a show of sweeping the floor.* TIEH-MEI *takes this chance to paste up the paper sign.*]

HOU. Are you Mr. Li?

LI. Yes, sir. Take a seat.

HOU [*with an awkward laugh presenting an invitation card*]. Mr. Li, Mr. Hatoyama is celebrating his birthday today. He wants you to go and have a cup of wine with him.

[GRANNY *and* TIEH-MEI *are startled.*]

LI [*calmly*]. What, is Mr. Hatoyama inviting me to a feast?

HOU. Just to be friendly.

LI. He wants to make friends with me?

HOU. You'll understand when you see him. Come along.

LI. All right. Mother, [*gravely*] I'm going now.

GRANNY. Wait. Tieh-mei, bring some wine.

TIEH-MEI. Yes. [*She fetches wine from the table.*]

HOU. There'll be plenty for him to drink at the feast, old lady.

GRANNY [*with a contemptuous glance*]. Pah.

The poor prefer their own wine,
Each drop of it warms the heart.

You like wine, son, but I don't usually encourage you to drink. Today I want you to drink up this bowl. [*She passes him the wine.*]

LI [*taking the bowl*]. Right. With this to put heart into me I can cope with whatever's coming. Watch me drink, Mother.

GRANNY. I'm watching you.

LI [*looking at her as if to reassure her with his strength. He grasps the bowl hard and drains it in one breath. His cheeks are flushed, his eyes gleam*]. Thank you, Mother.

GRANNY [*proudly*]. That's my fine son.

LI. Mother,

I drink your wine at parting
And it fills me with courage and strength.
The Japanese is offering me a feast,
Well, I can manage even a thousand cups.
This is stormy, treacherous weather,
Be ready for squalls.

TIEH-MEI. Dad. [*Clasps him and sobs.*]

LI. Tieh-mei.

Keep your weather eye open outside,
Don't forget our unsettled accounts;
Keep watch for wild dogs at the door,
And listen for the magpie's lucky cry.
You must help at home
And share your granny's troubles.

TIEH-MEI. Dad. [*Clasps him and sobs.*]

GRANNY. Don't cry, Tieh-mei. Our family has this rule: when one of us leaves, nobody must cry.

LI. Always do as Granny says, Tieh-mei. Don't cry.

TIEH-MEI [*wiping her tears*]. I won't.

GRANNY. Open the door, child, and let your father go to the feast.

LI. Mother, look after yourself.

[*Grasping* LI's *hands,* GRANNY *gazes at him while* TIEH-MEI *opens the door. A gust of wind.* LI *strides out into the wind. Huddled up in his coat* HOU *follows.* TIEH-MEI *runs after them with the scarf.*]

TIEH-MEI. Dad!

[*Four enemy* THUGS *bar her way.*]

THUG A. Go back. [*He forces her back*

through the door. Then he enters and tells GRANNY.] We're making a search.

[The THUGS give the place a professional going over. TIEH-MEI nestles up to GRANNY as they turn everything upside down. They discover an almanac and toss it away but fail to find anything incriminating.]

THUG A. Come on. [He signs to the others to leave. Exeunt.]

TIEH-MEI [closes the door, draws the curtain and looks at the chaos in the room]. Granny! [She falls into her arms and sobs.]

GRANNY [weeping despite herself]. All right, cry, child. Have a good cry.

TIEH-MEI. Granny, will Dad ever come back?

GRANNY [restraining her own tears. She knows there is little hope of his returning but does not want to say so. She takes up LI's scarf and strokes it]. Tears won't help him, child. [Looks at her.] Tieh-mei, the time has come to tell you about our family.

TIEH-MEI. Yes, Granny?

GRANNY. Sit down. I'll tell you.

TIEH-MEI. Yes. [Sits down on a stool.]

GRANNY. Tell me: Is your dad good?

TIEH-MEI. There's no one better in the whole wide world.

GRANNY. Well . . . he's not your real father.

TIEH-MEI [incredulously]. Ah! What do you mean, Granny?

GRANNY. Neither am I your real granny.

TIEH-MEI [startled]. What's come over you, Granny? Have you taken leave of your senses?

GRANNY. No, child. We don't belong to one family. Your surname is Chen, mine is Li and your dad's is Chang.

TIEH-MEI [blankly]. Oh.

GRANNY.

For seventeen storm-tossed years I held my peace,
Eager to speak but afraid you were not ready for the truth.

TIEH-MEI. You can tell me, Granny. I won't cry.

GRANNY.

Your father can hardly escape
And they may imprison me too;
Then the work for the revolution will fall to you.

When I tell you the truth, Tieh-mei,

Don't break down but take it bravely,
Like a girl of iron.

TIEH-MEI. Tell me. I won't cry.

GRANNY. It's a long story. When the railway was seized by the Japanese at the end of the Ching dynasty, my husband fled to the south and became a maintenance man in Kiangan. He had two apprentices. One was your real father, Chen Chih-hsing.

TIEH-MEI. My father, Chen Chih-hsing.

GRANNY. The other was your present dad, Chang Yu-ho.

TIEH-MEI. Chang Yu-ho.

GRANNY [standing up]. The country was torn by the fighting between warlords. But then the Chinese Communist Party was born to lead the Chinese people's revolution. In February, 1923, workers of the Peking-Hankow Railway set up a trade union in Chengchow. One of the warlords, Wu Pei-fu, was a stooge of the foreign invaders. When he tried to suppress the union, it called on all the workers on the line to strike. More than ten thousand men in Kiangan demonstrated. That was another cold, dark night. I was so worried about your grandfather that I couldn't rest or sleep. I was mending clothes by the lamp when I heard someone knocking at the door, calling, "Aunty, Aunty, quickly open the door." I opened the door, and he came in.

TIEH-MEI. Who was it?

GRANNY. Your dad.

TIEH-MEI [surprised]. My dad?

GRANNY. Yes, your present dad. Dripping with blood and all gashed with wounds, in his left hand he held this red lantern. . . .

TIEH-MEI. Ah, the red lantern.

GRANNY. In his right arm he held a baby.

TIEH-MEI. A baby?

GRANNY. A mite less than one year old.

TIEH-MEI. That baby . . .

GRANNY. That baby was none other . . .

TIEH-MEI. Than who?

GRANNY. Than you.

TIEH-MEI. Me . . .

GRANNY [quickly]. Hugging you tight to his chest, with tears in his eyes your dad stood before me and said, "Aunty, Aunty . . ." [TIEH-MEI gazes expectantly at her.]

GRANNY. For some minutes he just

stared at me and couldn't go on. In a panic, I begged him to speak. He said, "They've murdered . . . my master and brother. This is Brother Chen's child, a child of the revolution. I must bring her up to carry on our work." He said, "Aunty, from now on I am your son and this child is your granddaughter." Then I took you in my arms.

TIEH-MEI. Granny! [She buries her head in the old woman's lap.]

[GRANNY holds and comforts her.]

GRANNY. Ah! You mustn't cry. Take a grip on yourself and listen.

In the strike those devils murdered your father and mother,
Li Yu-ho went east and west for the revolution;
He swore to tread in their steps, keep the red lantern burning;
He staunched his wounds, buried the dead, and went back to the fight.
Now the Japanese brigands are burning, killing, and looting,
Before our eyes your dad was taken away;
Remember this debt of blood and tears,
Be brave and make up your mind to settle scores,
A debt of blood must be paid for with enemy blood.

TIEH-MEI.
Granny tells a stirring tale of the revolution,
They brought me up in wind and rain and storm,
How much I owe you, Granny, for all these years!
My mind is made up now, I see my way clear;
Blood must be shed for our blood,
I must carry on the task my father began.
Here I raise the red lantern, let its light shine far.
My father is as dauntless as the pine,
The Communist Party fears nothing under the sun,
I shall follow it and never, never waver.
The red lantern's light
Shines on my father fighting those wild beasts.
Generation shall fight on after generation,
Never leaving the field until the victory is won.

[GRANNY and TIEH-MEI hold high the red lantern.]

SCENE SIX

HATOYAMA IS DEFIED

[That evening, HATOYAMA's house. A sumptuous feast is spread. Through the lattice windows glittering lights can be seen. Jazz sounds and girls dance past the window.]

[Enter HOU with LI YU-HO.]

HOU. Please wait a minute. [He starts off to report LI's attitude to HATOYAMA.]

LI. As you like. [He stands there looking round, puffing his cigarette, disgusted by the surroundings.]

HOU [off]. Captain Hatoyama.

HATOYAMA [hurrying in]. Ah, my old friend, it's good to see you again. Have you been keeping well?

LI. How are you, Mr. Hatoyama?

HATOYAMA. So we meet again after all this time. Do you remember when we were both working on the railway in Harbin?

LI [drily]. You were a celebrated Japanese doctor while I was a poor Chinese worker. We were like two trains running on different tracks, not traveling the same road.

HATOYAMA. Well, brother, there's not all that difference between a surgeon and a worker. We're old friends, not strangers, right?

LI. In that case can I hope for good treatment from you?

HATOYAMA. That's why I asked you over for a chat. Do sit down, please. [They sit down.] Today is my birthday, friend, a time to celebrate. Suppose we just talk of friendship and leave politics out of it?

LI. I'm a switchman. I don't understand politics. You can say whatever you like.

HATOYAMA. Fine, I like your frankness. Come on. [Pours wine.] Just a cup of wine for friendship's sake. Now, drink up. [Raises the cup.]

LI. You are too polite, Mr. Hatoyama. Sorry, but I've given up drinking. [He pushes the cup away.]

HATOYAMA. Well, friend. [Taking up his own cup.] If you won't oblige me, I can't force you. [He drinks and then *starts his offensive.*] Why take things so seriously? There's an old Chinese saying, "Life is over in a flash like a dream. We should drink and sing, for who knows how soon life will end?"

LI. Yes, listening to songs and watching dances is living like an immortal. I wish you long life, Mr. Hatoyama, and all prosperity.

HATOYAMA [*frustrated, lamely*]. Thank you, thank you.

LI [*eyeing him contemptuously*]. You are too ceremonious. [*He laughs.*]

HATOYAMA [*with a hollow laugh*]. My friend, I am a believer in Buddhism. A Buddhist sutra tells us, "Boundless the sea of sorrow, yet a man who will turn back can reach the shore."

LI [*jokingly*]. For myself, I don't believe in Buddhism but I've heard the saying, "A butcher who lays down his knife can become a Buddha, too."

HATOYAMA. Good. [*On the defensive.*] Well said. But both add up to the same thing. In fact we can sum up all human beliefs in two words.

LI. What are they?

HATOYAMA. "For me."

LI. "For you," eh?

HATOYAMA. No. "Each for himself."

LI. "Each for himself." [*He laughs.*]

HATOYAMA [*earnestly*]. Old friend, you know the saying, "Heaven destroys men who won't look out for themselves."

LI. Oh? Heaven destroys men who won't look out for themselves?

HATOYAMA. That's the secret of life.

LI. So life has a secret. I'm afraid it's too difficult for a blockhead like me to grasp. [*He laughs.*]

HATOYAMA [*to himself*]. What a stubborn fool!
His heart is hard to fathom;
He parries my thrusts
With no thought of his own safety,
Impervious to both praise and flattery.
I must be patient.
With my experience and tact
I'll get hold of that secret code.
Let's stop this shadow-boxing, friend. I want your help.

LI [*with an air of surprise*]. What do you mean? How can a poor switchman help you?

HATOYAMA [*unable to keep his temper*]. Quit joking. Hand it over.

LI. What is it you want?

HATOYAMA [*coldly and distinctly*]. The secret code.

LI. What's that? All I can do is work switches. I've never used any such thing as a code.

HATOYAMA [*rising abruptly*]. If you choose to do things the hard way instead of the easy way, friend, don't blame me if we get rough.

LI. Do as you like.

HATOYAMA. All right. [*Beats his plate with a chopstick.*]

[*Enter* INSPECTOR WANG *in army uniform wearing his medal.*]

HATOYAMA. My old friend, look, who is this?

LI [*shocked by the sight of* WANG]. Ah!

WANG. Take my advice, brother . . .

LI. You shameless renegade!
Only a coward would bend his knees in surrender,
A cur afraid of death and clinging to life.
How often did I warn you
Against enemy threats and bribes?
You swore you would gladly die for the revolution;
How could you sell out and help the Japanese?
They are treating you like a dog,
Yet you count disgrace an honor.
Come here and look me in the eyes,
Shame on you, you sneaking slave.

[HATOYAMA *waves* WANG *away and he slinks out.*]

HATOYAMA. Steady on, my friend. I didn't want to play my trump card but you forced me to.

LI [*laughing derisively*]. I expected as much. Your trump card is nothing but a mangy dog with a broken back. You'll get no satisfaction out of me.

HATOYAMA. I can give you some satisfaction. Let's hear your terms.

LI. Terms?

HATOYAMA. Here's your chance to strike a good bargain.

LI. Bargain?

HATOYAMA. Yes, bargain. I understand you Communists very well; you have your beliefs. But beliefs can be bought or sold. The main thing is to make a profit.

LI. That's frank enough. It follows that there's nothing you wouldn't sell if you could make a profit. [*He laughs.*]

HATOYAMA [furious]. You ... [Fuming.] You go too far, friend. You must know my job. I'm the one who issues passes to Hell.

LI. You don't seem to know my job. I'm the one who takes your pass and destroys your Hell.

HATOYAMA. You know, my leg-screws are hungry for human flesh.

LI. I tried out that silly gadget of yours long ago.

HATOYAMA [impressed by LI's spirit, makes a show of sympathy]. Take my advice and recant before your bones are broken.

LI. I'd sooner have my bones broken than recant.

HATOYAMA. Our police are rough. They think nothing of killing people.

LI. We Communists are tough. We look on death as nothing.

HATOYAMA. Even if you are made of iron, I'll force you to speak.

LI. Even if you have hills of swords and a forest of knives, you'll get nothing out of me, Hatoyama.
The Japanese militarists are wolves
Hiding their savagery under a smile;
You kill our people and invade our land
In the name of "Co-prosperity in East
    Asia."
The Communists lead the people's revolution;
We have hundreds of millions of heroes
    in the resistance;
For you to rely on renegades
Is like fishing for the moon in the lake.

HATOYAMA.
I'll let you taste the leg-screws.
    [Enter the SERGEANT and two GENDARMES.]

LI.
I need to take the weight off my feet.

SERGEANT. Get moving.
    [The GENDARMES grasp LI's arms.]

LI. I can do without your help. [He throws them off and calmly picks up his cap, blows the dust off it, shakes it, and walks out with dignity.]
    [The SERGEANT and GENDARMES follow LI out.]

HATOYAMA [pacing to and fro, very put out, scratches his head and mutters]. Quite mad, these Reds.
My eyes are dim, my head is ready to burst;

My blood pressure has risen, my hands
    are cold;
The Reds are flesh and blood like us,
What makes them tougher than steel?
He refuses to say where the code is hidden, curse him!
What shall I do if I can't get hold of it?
    [The telephone rings.]

HATOYAMA [taking the call]. Hatoyama here. Yes, sir, we are still searching for the code. Quite so, sir. Certainly, certainly. Yes, sir. I'll stake my life on it. [He replaces the receiver and shouts.] Here. How are you doing?
    [Enter the SERGEANT.]

SERGEANT. We have tried all the tortures, but Li Yu-ho would rather die than speak.

HATOYAMA. Rather die than speak?

SERGEANT. Let me take some men to search his house, sir.

HATOYAMA. That's no use. Judging by my experience, ten thousand men can't find something which a Communist has hidden. Fetch him in.

SERGEANT. Bring Li Yu-ho here!
    [Two GENDARMES push LI in. Bloodstained and battered, he stands there defiantly.]

LI.
You cur with the heart of a wolf.

HATOYAMA. The code! Give me the code!

LI. Hatoyama!
You have tried every torture to break me;
Though my body is mangled I clench my
    teeth,
I shall never bow my head.
    [He laughs.]

SCENE SEVEN

THE CODE FINDS A NEW HIDING-PLACE

[One morning several days later. LI's house. By the telegraph pole not far from the door is an enemy agent disguised as a cobbler. While pretending to mend shoes he watches the house.]

TIEH-MEI [just out of bed and emerging from behind the curtain]. Why isn't Dad back yet, Granny?

Ever since Dad was arrested—

GRANNY.

We've been worrying and cannot rest.

[The KNIFE-GRINDER offstage cries, "Any knives or scissors to grind?"]

TIEH-MEI. Granny, listen.

[Enter the KNIFE-GRINDER.]

KNIFE-GRINDER. Any knives or scissors to grind?

[GRANNY pulls TIEH-MEI to the window and they look out.]

[The KNIFE-GRINDER comes up to the window and sees the butterfly sign. He hesitates, then nods and starts shouting again.]

COBBLER. There's no business for you in this poor part of town. Why do your caterwauling here?

KNIFE-GRINDER [in a loud, friendly voice]. You stick to your business, friend, and I'll stick to mine. We knife-grinders have to call out. If you make me keep quiet, how am I to find customers?

COBBLER. You clear out if you don't want to run into trouble.

KNIFE-GRINDER. All right, all right. I get it. I'll try my luck somewhere else. [As he leaves he raises his left hand to his ear and yells.] Any knives or scissors to grind? [Exit.]

COBBLER. Still caterwauling, blast him.

GRANNY [pulling TIEH-MEI close]. Did you hear that, child?

TIEH-MEI. What?

GRANNY. That knife-grinder probably came to make contact with us. He went away after seeing the sign on the window. Run after him quickly with the code and lantern and see whether he's our man or not. I'll get the code.

TIEH-MEI. All right. [Goes to the window.]

GRANNY. It won't do, child, not with those agents outside. You can't go.

TIEH-MEI. What shall we do, then?

I want to run after the knife-grinder,
But I can't leave the house and am worried.
I wish I could grow wings and fly like a bird.

[The child next door cries.]

TIEH-MEI. Granny, I have an idea.

GRANNY. What is it?

TIEH-MEI. Granny.

I know a way out.

Look. [Points to the kang.] There's only

a wall between this and the Liu's kang. I can make a hole and slip through.

GRANNY [pleased]. That's a good idea. Go ahead.

[TIEH-MEI disappears behind the curtain. GRANNY starts chopping cabbage to hide the noise she makes.]

TIEH-MEI [coming back]. It's done, Granny.

GRANNY [takes the code from the crack in the pillar and gives it to her with the red lantern. Solemnly]. Make sure he's the right man, Tieh-mei. He must get the password correct. Be very careful.

TIEH-MEI. I will. [She disappears behind the curtain.]

COBBLER [calling outside]. Open the door.

GRANNY. Who's that?

COBBLER. It's me. The cobbler.

GRANNY. Wait, I'll open the door. [Opens the door.]

COBBLER [sees the knife in her hand]. What are you doing?

GRANNY. Tomorrow is my son's birthday. We are going to have some vegetable rolls.

COBBLER. Ah, vegetable rolls.

GRANNY. What do you want?

COBBLER. I want to borrow a light.

GRANNY [indicating the match-box on the table]. Help yourself.

COBBLER. How many of you are there, old lady?

GRANNY. You've been squatting outside our door the last few days; you should know all about us. One has gone, there are two of us left.

COBBLER. Where's the girl?

GRANNY. She's not well.

COBBLER. Not well? Where is she?

GRANNY. She's lying down in bed.

COBBLER. Lying down, eh? [He walks towards the kang.]

GRANNY [stopping him]. Keep away. Don't frighten the child.

COBBLER [sniggering]. If she's ill, old lady, why isn't she whimpering?

GRANNY. My granddaughter never whimpers when she's ill.

COBBLER. That means she isn't ill. But perhaps you feel sick at heart?

GRANNY. Seems to me you're the one who is sick.

COBBLER. Me sick? How?

GRANNY. There's a canker gnawing at your bones—they're moldering.

COBBLER. That's nothing that a little sun won't cure.

GRANNY. You're too rotten to face the sun.

COBBLER. Never mind. Men's bones have got to rot some day, so let them be rotten. Tell your girl to sit up for a bit, old lady. It's no good lying down all the time. [He tries to lift the curtain.]

GRANNY. What d'you think you're doing? Asking all these foolish questions, throwing your weight about in other people's houses, and insulting women. What's the idea? Clear off. Get out!

COBBLER. All right, just wait. [Enter two ENEMY AGENTS. They whisper together and the agents open the door.]

GRANNY. Who are you?

AGENTS. We are checking up. How many people live here?

GRANNY. Three.

AGENTS. Where are the other two?

GRANNY. You should know where my son is now.

AGENTS. Where's your granddaughter?

GRANNY. She's ill.

AGENTS. Where is she? Where is she? [Goes to lift the curtain.]

[Voice from behind the curtain: "Granny. Who's there?"]

GRANNY. Police checking up.

[The AGENTS grunt, shrug and go out. GRANNY closes the door behind them.]

AGENTS [to the COBBLER]. What a fuss over nothing. She was on the kang all the time. She didn't go out.

COBBLER. All right. That old bitch tried to make a fool of me. [Exeunt.]

GRANNY. What a near thing! When did you come back, Tieh-mei? [She lifts the curtain and KUEI-LAN sits up.]

GRANNY. So it's you, Kuei-lan.

KUEI-LAN [getting off the kang to catch hold of GRANNY]. Granny Li.
After Tieh-mei slipped away from our house
My mother sent me to tell you.
When I heard those spies questioning you
I pretended to be Tieh-mei lying ill in bed.
When Tieh-mei comes, she can come through our house,
With me helping, you don't have to worry.

GRANNY. You've saved us. We shall never forget what you've done.

TIEH-MEI [emerging from behind the curtain]. Granny. Sister Kuei-lan.

GRANNY. So you're back at last.

KUEI-LAN. Your granny was worried about you.

GRANNY. My heart nearly jumped out of my mouth. If not for Kuei-lan we'd have been in serious trouble.

TIEH-MEI. Thank you, Sister Kuei-lan. What would we have done without you?

KUEI-LAN. It was nothing. Why thank me for such a little thing? It's good that you're back. I must be going now.

TIEH-MEI. Won't you stay a while?

GRANNY. You go and tidy up the kang.

TIEH-MEI. Yes.

[KUEI-LAN points at the door and they understand. She steps behind the curtain and leaves. TIEH-MEI straightens the bedding and pulls the curtain back.]

GRANNY. Did you find the knife-grinder?

TIEH-MEI [in a low voice]. I searched several streets but couldn't find him. Then I looked for Uncle Chou but he wasn't at home. So I hurried back for fear those spies might discover that I was out.

GRANNY. Where is the code?

TIEH-MEI. I left it outside.

GRANNY [disturbed]. But why?

TIEH-MEI. I thought it would be safer outside, so I hid it under a pier of Short Bridge.

GRANNY [relieved]. Ah, you made me break into a cold sweat, child. You've done right. I shan't worry provided the code's in a safe place.

[Enter HATOYAMA in a Chinese gown and hat with a walking stick. He is followed by HOU carrying two boxes of cakes. They knock at the door.]

GRANNY. Who's there?

HOU. Captain Hatoyama is paying you a visit.

GRANNY [grasping TIEH-MEI]. Child, if your granny is arrested now, you must find Uncle Chou and give him the code, then go to the north hills.

TIEH-MEI. Granny! [She cries.]

GRANNY. Don't cry. Go and open the door.

[TIEH-MEI *opens the door.*]

HATOYAMA [*entering with a show of sympathy*]. How are you, madam? I am Li Yu-ho's old friend, but I have been too busy to call before. [*Signs to* HOU *to leave after he has put the cakes on the table.*] This is a trifling present.

GRANNY. So you are Mr. Hatoyama?

HATOYAMA. Yes. I'm Hatoyama, Hatoyama.

GRANNY. Will you let me tidy up a bit before I come with you?

HATOYAMA. Don't misunderstand. That's not what I came for. Please sit down.

[GRANNY *ignores him.* HATOYAMA *takes a seat.*]

HATOYAMA. You must be longing to see your son, madam.

GRANNY. Of course, a mother naturally thinks of her son.

HATOYAMA. You needn't worry. He'll come back very soon safe and sound.

GRANNY. So much the better.

HATOYAMA. This wasn't our doing. We had orders from above. As a matter of fact we are looking after him very well.

GRANNY. Thank you.

HATOYAMA. We heard from Li, madam, that he left something with you.

GRANNY. Left what?

HATOYAMA [*casually*]. Some code.

GRANNY. I don't know what you mean. [*To* TIEH-MEI.] What does he mean, child?

HATOYAMA. A code. A book.

GRANNY. A book? My son can't read, Mr. Hatoyama. My granddaughter has never been to school and I can't tell one character from another. Our family has never bought books.

HATOYAMA. Since Li Yu-ho has told us about that book, old lady, why try to hide it?

GRANNY. If he told you, why not let him come and find it? Wouldn't that be simpler?

HATOYAMA [*to himself*]. She's a crafty old bitch. [*To* GRANNY.] Don't try to fool me, old lady. Let's make a bargain. You give me that book and I'll send your son straight back. If he wants a job, the railway can make him a vice-section-chief. If he wants money, he can have five thousand dollars.

GRANNY. Five thousand dollars and the job of a vice-section-chief? What book can be worth that much?

HATOYAMA. You have to sell to someone who knows its value.

GRANNY. If that book means so much to you, I'll have a look for it. Wait a minute. Tieh-mei, help me find it.

HATOYAMA. Take your time. There's no hurry.

[GRANNY *takes* TIEH-MEI *behind the curtain.*]

HATOYAMA [*waiting expectantly, to himself*]. So after all money can work miracles.

[GRANNY *comes back with* TIEH-MEI *carrying a bundle.*]

HATOYAMA [*very pleased*]. You've found it, madam?

GRANNY. Yes. This is what my son brought back.

HATOYAMA. Right, that must be it. That's it.

GRANNY. You can have it. [*Gives him an almanac.*]

HATOYAMA [*furiously*]. Bah, an almanac. [*He wants to throw it away but thinks better of it, fuming.*] I'll take it back anyway. Ah . . . You must be worried about your son. Suppose I take you to see him and find out about the book. We are bound to find it. There's no hurry.

GRANNY. That's very good of you. Thank you. [*To* TIEH-MEI.] Look after the house, child.

HATOYAMA. She had better come as well to see her father.

GRANNY [*startled*]. But she's only a child.

HATOYAMA [*beckoning*]. Come along.

TIEH-MEI. All right. I want to see my dad.

HATOYAMA. You'd like to help your father, wouldn't you?

TIEH-MEI. Yes.

HATOYAMA. Fine. Come on.

[*Enter* HOU *with several gendarmes.*]

HATOYAMA. Look after them well. [*He strides out. To the agents.*] Keep an eye on the house. [*Exit.*]

HOU [*to* GRANNY *and* TIEH-MEI *with a sinister smile*]. Come on, old lady. Come on, miss.

[*They leave the house together. The agents seal up the door.*]

TIEH-MEI [*upset to see the door sealed*]. Granny!

GRANNY [*putting one hand through* TIEH-MEI'S *arm and wrapping the scarf round her neck*]. Come on.

[*A gust of wind.*]

SCENE EIGHT

THE EXECUTION GROUNDS

[*Night. The Japanese police headquarters outside the prison. Enter* HATOYAMA, HOU HSIEN-PU *and the* SERGEANT.]

HATOYAMA. It doesn't look as if we shall get anywhere with our interrogation. Hurry up and get the tape recorder ready. We'll hear what the old woman says when she meets her son. We may find out something.

HOU and SERGEANT. Yes, sir.

HATOYAMA. Bring the old woman in.

HOU. Yes, sir. Fetch the old woman.

[*Two Japanese* GENDARMES *bring* GRANNY *in*.]

HATOYAMA. Do you know this place, madam?

GRANNY. It's the police headquarters.

HATOYAMA [*pointing*]. And over there?

[GRANNY *glances in that direction.*]

HATOYAMA [*with a menacing smile*]. That's the gate to paradise, where your son will mount to heaven.

[GRANNY *shivers.*]

HATOYAMA. When a man has committed a crime, madam, and his mother refuses to save his life, don't you think she is rather cruel?

GRANNY. What do you mean, Mr. Hatoyama? You've arrested my son for no reason and thrown him into prison. Now you want to kill him. You are the ones that are committing a crime. You are the ones that are cruel. How can you shift the blame for his murder on to me?

HATOYAMA. Have you thought what will come of talking like that, old lady?

GRANNY. The lives of our family are in your hands. You can do whatever you like.

HATOYAMA [*controlling himself*]. All right, go and see your son. [GRANNY *starts off*.] This is his last chance, old lady. I hope you will all decide to steer clear of trouble and be reunited as one family.

GRANNY. I know what's right.

HATOYAMA. Take her away.

[*Exit* HOU *with* GRANNY.]

HATOYAMA. Here. Take Li to the execution grounds.

SERGEANT. Bring Li Yu-ho.

[*The scene changes. On the left is the path to the prison. In the center is a stone. In the rear on the left a slope leading to the execution grounds is backed by a high wall covered with barbed wire. It is dark. Offstage the Japanese* GENDARMES *yell: "Fetch Li Yu-ho!" Chains clank.*]

[*Enter* LI.]

LI.

At the jailers' blood-thirsty cry I leave my cell;

Though my hands and feet are manacled and fettered

They cannot chain my soaring spirit.

Hatoyama has tortured me to get the code;

My bones are broken, my flesh torn, but firm my will.

Walking boldly to the execution grounds

I look up and see the red flag of revolution,

The flames of the resistance.

Not for long will these invaders lord it over us,

And once the storm is past fresh flowers will bloom;

New China will shine like the morning sun,

Red flags will flutter over all the country—

I smile through tears of joy at the thought of it.

I have done very little for the Party,

Worst of all, I failed to send the code to the hills;

That renegade Wang's only contact was with me,

The wretch can betray no one else;

And my mother and daughter are as staunch as steel,

So Hatoyama may search heaven and earth,

But he will never find the secret code.

[*Enter* GRANNY *and she looks round.*]

GRANNY [*seeing* LI, *cries*]. Yu-ho!

LI [*startled*]. Mother!

GRANNY. My son.

LI. Mother.

[GRANNY *runs over to put her arms around him.*]

Again I live through that day seventeen
　　years ago,
And burn with hate for the foe of my
　　class and country.
The cruel Japanese devils
Have beaten and tortured you, my son,
　　my son!
　　LI. Don't grieve for me, mother.
　　GRANNY.
I shouldn't grieve to have such a fine son.
　　LI.
Brought up in a hard school
I'll fight and never give ground;
Though they break every bone in my
　　body,
Though they lock me up until I wear
　　through my chains.
As long as our country is ravaged my
　　heart must bleed;
As long as the war lasts my family is in
　　danger;
However hard the road to revolution,
We must press on in the steps of the
　　glorious dead.
My one regret if I die today
Is the debt I have left unpaid.
I long to soar like an eagle through the
　　sky,
Borne on the wind above the mountain
　　passes
To rescue our millions of suffering
　　countrymen—
Then how gladly would I die for the
　　revolution!
　　GRANNY.
That unpaid debt is in good hands,
Cost what it may, we shall pay it.
　　[Enter HOU with the guards.]
　　HOU. I'll say this for you: You cer-
tainly know how to keep your mouths
shut and not give anything away. Come
on, old woman. Captain Hatoyama
wants you.
　　LI. Mother . . . .
　　GRANNY. Don't worry, son. I know
what he wants. [She goes out fearlessly,
followed by the guards.]
　　HOU. Bring Tieh-mei here! [Exit.]
　　LI [calling]. Tieh-mei!
　　TIEH-MEI [running in]. Dad!
　　LI. Tieh-mei.
　　TIEH-MEI. Dad.
I hoped day and night to see my dad
　　again,
Yet I hardly know you, so battered and
　　drenched with blood

I wish I could break your chains,
Dear father. . . .
　　LI [smiling]. Silly child.
　　TIEH-MEI [sobbing]. If you have any-
thing to say to me, Dad, tell me quickly.
　　LI. Child,
One thing I have wanted many times to
　　tell you,
It's been hidden in my heart for seven-
　　teen years. . . .
　　TIEH-MEI [quickly stopping him]. Don't
say it. You are my own true father.
Don't say it, Father,
I know the bitter tale of these seven-
　　teen years.
You are so good, our country needs you;
Why can't I die in your stead?
Ah, Dad.
　　[She kneels and clasps LI's knees,
　　sobbing.]
　　LI.
Nurse your hatred in your heart.
Men say that family love outweighs all
　　else,
But class love is greater yet.
Listen, child, your dad is a poor man,
With no money at home to leave you;
All I have is a red lantern,
I entrust it to your safe keeping.
　　TIEH-MEI.
You have left me a priceless treasure,
How can you speak of money?
You have left me your integrity
To help me stand firm as a rock;
You have left me your wisdom
To help me see clearly through the
　　enemy's wiles;
You have left me your courage
To help me fight those brutes;
This red lantern is our heirloom,
A treasure so great
That a thousand carts and boats
Could not hold it all.
I give you my word I shall keep the lan-
　　tern safe.
　　LI.
As wave follows wave in the great Yang-
　　tse River,
Our red lantern will be passed from hand
　　to hand.
If they let you go home,
Find friends to help settle that debt and
　　I'll be content.
　　TIEH-MEI. I will, father.
　　LI. Good child.
　　[Enter HOU.]

HOU [to TIEH-MEI]. What about the secret code, girl?

[She ignores him.]

HOU. Why don't you speak?

TIEH-MEI. My dad and my grandmother have said all there is to say. I've nothing to add.

HOU. Even this child is so pig-headed, confound her! Here. Bring that old woman back.

[Two GUARDS bring in GRANNY.]

HOU. Now your whole family is here. Think well. If you don't give us the code, not one of you will leave this place alive. [Exit.]

[LI and TIEH-MEI help GRANNY to the stone.]

LI. They've tortured you, mother. The swine!

GRANNY. It doesn't matter if my old bones ache a little, my heart is still sound.

[TIEH-MEI sobs with her head on GRANNY's lap. Enter the SERGEANT. TIEH-MEI looks up.]

SERGEANT. Captain Hatoyama gives you five more minutes to think it over. If you still won't give up the secret code, you will all be shot.

GRANNY [indignantly]. You brutes, won't you even let the child go?

SERGEANT. We'll spare no one.

[LI and GRANNY look at TIEH-MEI, who meets their eyes and straightens up.]

SERGEANT [dragging TIEH-MEI away]. Only five minutes left, girl. Give up the code and save your whole family. Speak!

[TIEH-MEI shakes off his hand and walks back to stand between GRANNY and LI.]

SERGEANT. Where is the code?

TIEH-MEI. I don't know.

SERGEANT [looking at his watch]. Firing squad!

LI. There's no need for such a commotion. This is nothing much.

GRANNY. That's right, child, let's go together, the three of us.

LI. Tieh-mei, take Granny's other arm.

TIEH-MEI. Right.

LI. Tieh-mei, mother, I'll lead the way. [He holds himself proudly.]

[They walk up the slope. Enter HATOYAMA.]

HATOYAMA. Wait! I want to give you every chance. You can have another minute to think it over.

LI. Hatoyama, you can never kill all the Chinese people or Chinese Communists. I advise you to think that over.

HATOYAMA [frustratedly to himself]. These Reds are the very devil. Carry out your orders. [Exit.]

SERGEANT. Shoot them!

[The three disappear from the slope followed by the SERGEANT and guards.]

LI [off]. Down with Japanese imperialism! Long live the Chinese Communist Party!

[Two shots are heard. Then two guards push TIEH-MEI back.]

TIEH-MEI [walking down the slope in a daze, turns to call]. Dad! Granny!

HATOYAMA [entering behind her, followed by HOU]. Where is the code book? Tell me quick.

[TIEH-MEI says nothing but stares at him with loathing.]

HATOYAMA. Here. Let her go.

HOU. What? Let her go? [He looks at HATOYAMA in surprise.]

HATOYAMA. Yes, let her go.

HOU. Very good, sir. [He grabs TIEH-MEI.] Get out, get out.

[He pushes her away. Exit TIEH-MEI.] Why are you letting her off, sir?

HATOYAMA [smiling coldly]. If I kill them all, how can I find the code? This is called using a long line to catch a big fish.

SCENE NINE

THE NEIGHBORS HELP

[Immediately after the last scene. LI's house. The door is sealed. The room is unchanged but wears an air of desolation.]

[TIEH-MEI walks slowly in. She stares at the house, quickens her steps and pushing the door open steps inside. She looks around, crying "Dad! Granny!" then rests her head on the table and sobs. Slowly rising, she sees the red lantern and picks it up.]

TIEH-MEI. Ah, red lantern, I've found you again but I shall never see Granny or Dad again. Granny, Dad, I know what you died for. I shall carry on your work. I've inherited the red lantern. That scoundrel Hatoyama has only let me go in the hope that I will lead them to the code. [Pause.] Never mind whether you arrest me or release me, you'll never get the code. [She puts down the red lantern and smooths her hair.]
My heart is bursting with anger,
I grind my teeth with rage;
Hatoyama has tried every trick to get the code,
He has killed my granny and dad.
In desperation he threatened me,
But I defy his threats,
Nursing hatred in my heart;
No cry shall escape me,
No tears wet my cheeks,
But the sparks of my smoldering fury
Will blaze up in flames of anger
To consume this black reign of night.
Nothing can daunt me now:
Arrest, release, torture, imprisonment. . . .
I shall guard the code with my life.
Wait, Hatoyama! This is Tieh-mei's answer.
[She polishes the red lantern and rearranges her peddler's basket. Sadly.] Granny, Dad, I'm leaving now. This isn't our home any more. Only the red lantern will be ours for ever. I promise to take the code to the north hills. I promise to avenge you. Don't you worry. [She puts on her scarf and picks up the lantern and basket.]

> [AUNT LIU and KUEI-LAN have heard TIEH-MEI's sobbing and slipped in through the hole in the wall.]

AUNT LIU. Tieh-mei!
TIEH-MEI. Aunty. Sister Kuei-lan.
AUNT LIU. Where are your dad and granny?
TIEH-MEI. Aunty . . . [She leans her head on AUNT LIU's shoulder and cries.]
AUNT LIU. I see. It'll soon be their turn, the devils. There's a spy outside, Tieh-mei, so you mustn't leave by the door. You can slip out again from our house. Hurry up now and change clothes with Kuei-lan.
KUEI-LAN. Yes, quick. [She takes off her jacket.]
TIEH-MEI. No, Aunty, Sister, I mustn't bring you into this.

AUNT LIU [helping TIEH-MEI to change]. Tieh-mei,
None but the poor will help the poor,
Two bitter gourds grow on a single vine;
We must save you from the tiger's jaws,
And then you can press on.
TIEH-MEI. But what if something happens to you?
AUNT LIU. Tieh-mei, your people were good people. I may not understand much, but that I know. No matter how risky it is, I must see you safely away. [She weeps.]
TIEH-MEI. Aunty. [Kneels.]
[AUNT LIU hastily helps her up.]
KUEI-LAN. Go quickly. [Gives her the red lantern.]
TIEH-MEI. I shall never forget you, sister.
AUNT LIU. Hurry, child. [TIEH-MEI slips behind the curtain.] Be very careful, Kuei-lan. [AUNT LIU in turn leaves from behind the curtain.]

> [KUEI-LAN wraps TIEH-MEI's scarf round her head and steps out of the door with the basket. Enemy AGENT C comes up and follows her. Enter the KNIFE-GRINDER. He is about to call out when he notices the agent trailing a girl who looks like TIEH-MEI. He follows them.]

SCENE TEN

THE END OF THE RENEGADE

> [Immediately after the last scene. The street.]
> [Enter INSPECTOR WANG with two agents. A THIRD AGENT comes in from the other side.]

THIRD AGENT. Inspector, I've lost Tieh-mei.
WANG. What?
THIRD AGENT. She got away.
WANG. You fool! [Slaps his face.] Well, she must be making for the north hills. Ring up Captain Hatoyama and ask him to send reinforcements to the road to the north hills. The rest of you come with me to catch her. I'll see that you don't escape me, Li Tieh-mei.
[Black-out. The scene changes to the

north suburb of Lungtan and the road to the hills. *Enter* CHOU *with three guerrillas.*]

[*Enter* TIEH-MEI *with the lantern. She greets the men.*]

TIEH-MEI. Uncle Chou!

CHOU. Tieh-mei!

TIEH-MEI. At last I've found you. [*Cries.*] My granny and dad . . .

CHOU. We know. [*Pause.*] Don't give way. Take a grip on yourself. Have you got the code with you?

TIEH-MEI. Yes, I took it from under Short Bridge where I'd hidden it.

CHOU. Good.

[*The* KNIFE-GRINDER *hurries in.*]

KNIFE-GRINDER. Old Chou. Ah, Tieh-mei, so you're here. How was it I missed you?

TIEH-MEI. It was thanks to the help of my neighbors, Uncle. Kuei-lan disguised herself as me and led the agent off on the wrong track so that I could get the code and bring it here.

KNIFE-GRINDER. So I was chasing the wrong girl.

CHOU. They'll start suspecting Kuei-lan's family now. [*To one of the guerrillas.*] Old Feng, go and help them move away at once.

FENG. Right. Just leave it to me. [*Exit.*]

[*The police car's siren is heard.*]

CHOU [*to the* KNIFE-GRINDER]. The enemy's coming, Old Chao. You deal with them while I take Tieh-mei to the north hills. [*Exit with* TIEH-MEI.]

KNIFE-GRINDER. Look, comrades, there aren't too many of them. I'll handle their leader. You take care of the rest.

GUERRILLAS. Right.

[*Enter* INSPECTOR WANG *with four enemy agents.*]

WANG. Now, where is Tieh-mei?

[*The* KNIFE-GRINDER *kicks the pistol out of* WANG's *hand and they start fighting.* WANG *and the agents are killed. The police siren wails in the distance.*]

SCENE ELEVEN

THE TASK IS ACCOMPLISHED

[*The north hills, which rise steep and sheer. The guerrillas have formed a line stretching behind the hills. Halfway up the slope is a big red flag and scouts there are keeping a lookout.*]

[LIU *and other guerrilla officers come up the slope. Enter the* KNIFE-GRINDER. *He salutes* LIU *and points behind him.* CHOU *comes in with* TIEH-MEI. *A bugle blows.* TIEH-MEI *salutes* LIU *and gives him the code.*]

CURTAIN

Mao Tse-tung

ON LITERATURE AND ART (1942)

... Literary and art criticism constitutes a major weapon which must be developed to carry on a struggle in literary and art circles. As many comrades have rightly pointed out, our past work has been inadequate in this respect.

Criticism of literature and art presents a complicated problem requiring special study. Here I shall discuss only the problem of basic standards of criticism. I shall also comment on various problems raised by comrades and the incorrect views expressed by some.

There are two standards for literary and art criticism. One is the political standard and the other, the artistic standard.

By the political standard, artistic production is good, or comparatively good, if it serves the interests of our war of resistance and unity, if it encourages solidarity among the masses, and if it opposes retrogression and promotes progress. Conversely, artistic production is bad, or comparatively bad, if it encourages dissension and division among the masses, if it impedes progress and holds the people back.

Shall we distinguish between the good and bad on the basis of the motives (subjective intention) or the effects (actual practice in society)? Idealists stress the motives and deny the effects; mechanical materialists stress the effects and deny the motives. We are opposed to both approaches.

We are dialectical materialists; we insist upon a synthesis of motive and effect. The motive of working for the masses cannot be separated from the effect which is welcomed by the masses. The motive and the effect must dovetail. A motive engendered by individual self-interest or narrow group-interest is not good. On the other hand, a good intention of working for the masses is of no value if it does not produce an effect which is welcomed by the masses and benefits them.

In examining the subjective intent of a writer, that is to say, in determining whether his motive is correct or good, we cannot depend upon his own declaration of intent; we must analyze the effect which his behavior (his creative product) has on society and the masses. The standard for examining a subjective intent is social practice; and the standard for examining a motive is the effect it produces.

Our criticism of literature and art must not be sectarian. Bearing in mind the general principles of the war of resistance and national unity, we must tolerate all works of literature and art expressing every kind and shade of political attitude. At the same time, we must be firm in principle and in our position when we criticize. This means that we must criticize severely all literary and artistic works which present viewpoints that are opposed to national, scientific, mass, and Communist interests because both the motives and the effects of this so-called literature and art jeopardize our war of resistance and wreck our national unity.

From the point of view of artistic standards, all works of higher artistic quality are good, or comparatively good while those of inferior artistic quality are bad, or comparatively bad. But this criterion also depends upon the effect a given work of art has on society. There are few writers and artists who do not consider their own works excellent.

Also, we must allow free competition of various types and shadings of artistic work. At the same time, we must criticize the work correctly, by scientific and

SOURCE: From *Talks at the Yenan Forum on Literature and Art*, in *Selected Works* by Mao Tse-tung, Peking, 1967.

artistic standards, in order gradually to raise art of a lower level to a higher level, and to change art which does not meet the requirements of the people's struggle (even when it is on a very high level) to art which does.

We know now that there is a political standard and an artistic standard. What then is the proper relation between them? Politics is not at the same time art. The world outlook in general is not at the same time the methods of artistic creation. Not only do we reject abstract and rigid political standards but we also reject abstract and rigid artistic standards. Different class societies have different political and artistic standards as do the various classes within a given class society. But in any class society or in any class within that society, political standards come first and artistic standards come second.

The bourgeois class rejects the literature and art of the proletariat, no matter how high their artistic quality. The proletariat must likewise reject the reactionary political essence of bourgeois literature and art, and extract their artistic quality very judiciously. It is possible for outright reactionary literature and art, the creative work of fascists, to have a certain measure of artistic quality. Since reactionary productions of high artistic quality, however, may do very great harm to the people, they must definitely be rejected. All literature and art of the exploiting classes in their decadent period have one characteristic in common— a contradiction between their reactionary political content and their artistic form.

We demand unity between politics and art; we demand harmony between content and form—the perfect blending of revolutionary political content with the highest possible level of artistic form. Works of art and literature without artistic quality are ineffectual no matter how progressive they are politically.

Thus we condemn not only works of art with a harmful reactionary content but also works done in the "poster-and-slogan style," which stresses content to the exclusion of form. It is on these two fronts that we must fight in the sphere of literature and art.

Many of our comrades suffer from both defects. Some tend to neglect artistic quality when they ought to be devoting much more attention to advancing artistic quality. But even more important at present is their lack of political quality. Many comrades lack fundamental political common sense, with the result that they entertain all sorts of confused notions. Let me give you a few examples of the notions entertained in Yenan.

1. "The theory of human nature"— is there such a thing as human nature? Yes, certainly, but only concrete human nature. In a class society human nature takes on class characteristics; there is no abstract human nature which stands above class distinctions.

We stand for the human nature of the proletariat, while the bourgeoisie and the petty-bourgeoisie advocate the human nature of their respective classes. And while they may not express it in so many words, they consider that theirs is the only kind of human nature. In their eyes, therefore, the human nature of the proletariat is contrary to human nature. There are in Yenan some who think along similar lines; they advocate the so-called theory of human nature as the basis for their theory of literature and art. This is absolutely wrong.

2. "The origin of all literature and art is love, love of mankind." Love may be a starting point, but there is still another even more basic starting point. Love is a concept which is the product of objective experience. Fundamentally we cannot start from an idea; we must start from objective experience.

The love that we writers and artists with our intellectual background bear for the proletariat stems from the fact that society has forced upon us the same destiny as it has forced upon the proletariat and that our lives have been integrated with the life of the proletariat. Our hatred of Japanese imperialism, on the other hand, is the result of our oppression by Japanese imperialists. Nowhere in the world does love exist without reason nor does hatred exist without reason.

As for love of mankind, there has been no such all-embracing love since the human race was divided into classes. The ruling classes have preached universal love. Confucius advocated it, as did Tolstoy. But no one has ever been able to practice it because it cannot be attained in a class society.

A true love of mankind is attainable, but only in the future when class distinctions will have been eliminated throughout the world. Classes serve to divide society; when classes are eliminated, society will be united again. At that time, the love of mankind will flourish but it cannot flourish now. Today we cannot love the fascists nor can we love our enemies. We cannot love all that is evil and ugly in society. It is our objective to eliminate all these evils. The people know that. Cannot our writers and artists understand it?

3. "Literature and art have always presented impartially and with equal emphasis the bright and dark sides, always as much of one as of the other."

This remark reflects a series of muddled ideas. Literature and art do not always present the bright and dark impartially. Many petty-bourgeois writers have never discovered the bright side; they depict only the dark side and call their work "exposé literature." They even produce works which are devoted entirely to spreading pessimism and defeatism.

During the period of socialist reconstruction the literature of the Soviet Union primarily described the bright side. Although shortcomings were admitted, they were presented as shadings against a background of over-all brightness. There was no equal emphasis of the bright and the dark.

During periods of reaction bourgeois writers and artists have characterized the revolutionary masses as bandits and gangsters but referred to themselves as god-like. Thus have they distorted the bright and the dark sides.

Only truly revolutionary writers and artists can correctly solve the problem of balance between praise and exposé. Every dark force which endangers the masses must be exposed while every revolutionary struggle of the masses must be praised. This is the fundamental task of revolutionary writers and artists.

4. "The function of literature and art has always been to expose." This kind of talk, just like the previous remark, shows a lack of understanding of the science of history and historical materialism.

As I have pointed out, to expose what is bad is not the only function of literature and art. Revolutionary writers and artists should limit the subject matter of their exposure to the aggressors, exploiters, and oppressors. The people, naturally enough, also have shortcomings, but their defects are produced in large measure by the rule of the aggressors, exploiters, and oppressors. Our revolutionary writers and artists must lay the blame for these shortcomings upon the crimes committed by the aggressors, exploiters, and oppressors, not expose the people themselves. As for the people, our only problem is how to educate them and raise their level. Only counter-revolutionary writers and artists consider the masses "born fools" and describe the revolutionary masses as "despotic mobs."

5. "This is still the period for essays. The style used by Lu Hsün still constitutes the right approach."

Essays in Lu Hsün's satirical style may be considered the correct means of attack only when dealing with the enemies of the people. Lu Hsün lived under the rule of the dark forces; he was not free to speak. He, therefore, fought back with very satirical essays and in this he was absolutely correct.

Of course, fascists and reactionary cliques in China must be attacked with bitter satire, but in the Shan-Kan-Ning Border Region and in the anti-Japanese bases in the enemy's rear, where all except counter-revolutionary elements and spies enjoy complete freedom and democracy, essayists do not need to adopt Lu Hsün's style. Here you can shout out loud, in plain language that holds nothing back, so that the masses may understand easily. When Lu Hsün was not dealing with the enemies of the people but with the people themselves, he never, even in his "essay period," directed his satire against the revolutionary people and the revolutionary parties. The style of his essays dealing with the people was entirely different from the style he used in attacking their enemies. As I have already pointed out, we should criticize the shortcomings of the people only from the standpoint of the people and with heartfelt sincerity, with a view to protecting and educating the people. If you treat your comrades in the same merciless manner that you use for the enemy, you are taking the very same position as the enemy.

Should we, then, discard satire entirely? There are several kinds of satire: one for dealing with the enemy, another for dealing with friends, and still another for dealing with the people in your own camp. Each of these three kinds of satire is entirely different from the others. We do not wish to discard satire as a whole but we must discard the abuse of it.

6. "I am not here to sing the praises of virtue and merit! To eulogize the good side does not necessarily make for great art and to expose the bad side does not necessarily make for inferior art."

If you are a writer or artist of the bourgeoisie it is quite natural that you will not extol the working class but you will eulogize the bourgeoisie. Similarly, if you are a writer or artist of the proletariat, it is quite natural that you will extol only the proletariat and the working people. But you must be either on one side or the other.

The writings which extol the bright side of bourgeois society are not necessarily superior nor are the writings which describe the dark side of that society necessarily inferior. The writings which praise the bright side of the proletariat are not necessarily inferior, but it is certainly reprehensible, to describe the so-called "darkness" of the proletariat. Has this fact not been established in the history of literature and art? Why should we not extol the people, the creators of history and civilization? Why should we not extol the proletariat, the Communist Party, the New Democracy, and socialism?

There are certain people who have no enthusiasm for the great cause of the masses. They act like aloof bystanders of the struggle and victories of the people as well as of the vanguard of the people. They are primarily concerned with and never tired of praising themselves or their admirers or perhaps a few others within their small coterie. These petty-bourgeois individualists are, of course, unwilling to praise the accomplishments and virtues of the people or to strengthen the courage of the revolutionary people for the struggle and increase their confidence in victory. These persons are maggots in the revolutionary camp and the revolutionary people have no use for their "eulogists."

7. "This is not a problem of our position, for our position is correct, our intentions good; we have grasped the idea; only our means of expression is not good and, therefore, the effect is bad."

I have already interpreted the problem of motive and effect in the light of dialectical materialism. Let us then see whether the problem of effect is not also a problem of position. When one approaches a task only with a motive, without ascertaining what the effect will be, he is like a doctor who prescribes without ascertaining whether the remedy will cure or kill his patient. Similarly, is it correct for a political party to issue a manifesto without ascertaining whether it can be carried out? Is that what you would call a good intention? We may err in estimating effects but can it be said that your intentions are good if you persist in using a method after it has been proved that that method produces undesirable results?

We judge a political party or a doctor by the practical results or the effects they achieve. We must judge a writer or artist in the same way.

Those who really have good intentions must consider the effect, take into account all past experience, and carefully examine their method or their so-called form of expression. If they really have good intentions, they must recognize the shortcomings and errors in their work, practice earnest self-criticism, and be determined to correct these mistakes. It is in this spirit that Communist Party members practice self-criticism. Then and then only can your position be called correct. At the same time, it is only by maintaining a serious and responsible attitude toward actual practice that you may get to understand what position is correct and get to grasp the correct viewpoint. If you do not move in this direction in actual practice but insist that you are always right, you actually understand nothing, despite anything you may say.

8. "Learning Marxism-Leninism is a mechanical repetition of dialectical materialism, which will stifle the creative spirit."

Learning Marxism-Leninism means only observing and studying the world, society, literature, and art from the point of view of dialectical and historical materialism. It does not mean that one must include an outline of philosophy in a work of literature or art.

Marxism-Leninism embraces but does not replace realism in creative literature and art, just as Marxism-Leninism can only embrace but not replace the theories of atoms and electrons in physics. Empty, dry dogmas truly stifle the creative spirit; furthermore, they destroy Marxism-Leninism. Dogmatic Marxism-Leninism is not Marxism-Leninism; it is contrary to Marxism-Leninism.

Will not Marxism-Leninism then destroy the creative spirit? Oh yes, it will. It will destroy the feudal, bourgeois, and petty-bourgeois creative spirit; the creative spirit that is rooted in liberalism, individualism, abstractionism; the creative spirit that stands for art-for-art's sake and is aristocratic, defeatist, and pessimistic. It will destroy any brand of creative spirit which is not of the masses and of the proletariat. And is it not right that these brands of creative spirit should be destroyed as far as proletarian writers and artists are concerned? I think so. They should be extirpated to make room for the new.

**The Revolutionary Committee of
the China Peking Opera Theatre**

LET HEROIC IMAGES OF THE PROLETARIAT SHINE ON THE PEKING OPERA STAGE!

In high spirit and with lofty aspirations, we revolutionary fighters in literature and art are most warmly celebrating the 25th anniversary of the publication of Chairman Mao's brilliant work the *Talks at the Yenan Forum on Literature and Art.* The celebration takes place at a time when the deep-going process of the great proletarian cultural revolution has reached a new high tide and when we are singing songs of one victory after another for Chairman Mao's revolutionary line.

By this illustrious work, our most respected and beloved great leader Chairman Mao has creatively formulated the most complete, thoroughgoing and correct proletarian revolutionary line on literature and art, and has opened up a brand-new road for the revolutionary literature and art of the proletariat.

This essential work of Chairman Mao's has illuminated the road for the revolution of Peking opera. It was under the radiance of this work that *The Red Lantern*, a prototype of the proletarian revolutionary Peking opera, came into being.

The Red Lantern, shining with Mao Tse-tung's thought, possesses a profound revolutionary content and a powerful artistic effect, with which it has attracted the broad sections of the workers, peasants and soldiers and the revolutionary masses, and received from them a warm welcome and high approbation.

The Red Lantern has created noble heroic images of the proletariat on the Peking opera stage. This is an achievement of the struggle in which Comrade Chiang Ching[1] has led us against the counter-revolutionary revisionist black line on literature and art. This is a significant victory for Chairman Mao's revolutionary line on literature and art.

I

With regard to literature and art Chairman Mao teaches us: "This question of 'for whom?' is fundamental; it is a question of principle." He added:

> All our literature and art are for the masses of the people, and in the first place for the workers, peasants and soldiers; they are created for the workers, peasants and soldiers and are for their use.

For a long period the sharp struggle between the two classes—the proletariat and the bourgeoisie—and the two lines on the literary and art front has centred on the fundamental question of "for whom?"

The proletariat strictly adhere to the teachings of Chairman Mao. They devote great efforts to creating and ardently singing the praises of the heroic characters of workers, peasants and soldiers so that Mao Tse-tung's thought will occupy all the positions in literature and art in the service of the political line of proletarian revolution and of the strengthening and consolidation of the political power already won by the proletariat. However, Chairman Mao constantly teaches us:

> The overthrown bourgeoisie is trying, by all methods, to use the position

SOURCE: From *On the Revolution of Peking Opera*, Peking, Foreign Language Press, 1968.
[1] Chairman Mao's wife.

of literature and art as a hotbed for corrupting the masses and preparing for the restoration of capitalism.

To carry out their plot for a capitalist restoration, the top capitalist roader in the Party,[2] together with a handful of counter-revolutionary revisionists, had long tolerated emperors, princes, generals, ministers, scholars, beauties, ghosts and monsters dominating the arena of literature and art, thus turning it into a position for preparing public opinion in favour of a capitalist restoration.

On the Peking opera stage these people eulogized emperors, princes, generals and ministers, and prettified scholars and beauties. They advocated the view that "it is right to oppress" and "exploitation has its merits." They advertised feudal and bourgeois ethics and morality and peddled wares which were vulgar and obscene. As a result, Peking opera theatre was replete with bad plays of all descriptions and in fantastic styles, which for years had corroded the minds of the people. What was worse was that several years ago when activities of the class enemy, both at home and abroad, aimed at a comeback had reached a peak, *Fourth Son Visits His Mother*, a poisonous opera propagating national and class capitulation, cropped up with direct support from the top capitalist roader in the Party. Backed by the same person, China's Khrushchov, the ghosts and monsters became still more unscrupulous and *Hsieh Yao-huan*, *Li Hui-niang*, *The Mouth of the Nine Streams*, *A Visit to Hades*, and other bad plays sprang up one after another. In our theatre the counter-revolutionary revisionists were prepared to stage *The Dragon Flirts with the Phoenix*, a play depicting the lustful, dissipated life of a feudal monarch. Peking opera stage was haunted by ill winds and shrouded in deadly mists. How arrogant were the counter-revolutionary revisionists who chanted elegies to landlords and the bourgeoisie and cast spells to summon the ghost of capitalism!

At the time of sharp class struggle between the two classes and the two lines on literature and art Chairman Mao issued important instructions on two occa-

sions to literary and art circles, one in December 1963 and the other in June 1964, with which he personally kindled the torch of revolution in literature and art. And Comrade Chiang Ching holding high the great red banner of Mao Tse-tung's thought sounded the battle-drum of the proletarian revolution in literature and art. After a thorough study and investigation for a long period, she took her place in the lead of a broad section of revolutionary literary and art workers. She used the invincible thought of Mao Tse-tung as a weapon to launch bold, persistent attacks on feudal, bourgeois and revisionist literature and art. She came to our theatre in 1963 and called on us to create works of literature and art in defence of our socialist economic base. She gave personal leadership during our creative and rehearsal work on *The Red Lantern*, fighting valiantly to seize control of the stage from the bourgeoisie.

II

Chairman Mao teaches us:

> If you are a bourgeois writer or artist, you will eulogize not the proletariat but the bourgeoisie, and if you are a proletarian writer or artist, you will eulogize not the bourgeoisie but the proletariat and working people: it must be one or the other.

To eulogize which class, create the heroes of which class, and allow the characters of which class to take the dominant place in literary and artistic works—this constitutes the focus of the class struggle between the proletariat and the bourgeoisie on the literary and art front. It also provides the criterion by which one is to judge to which class a literature and art belongs and the political line of which class it serves.

Comrade Chiang Ching has said:

> It is inconceivable that, in our socialist country led by the Communist Party, the dominant position on the stage is not occupied by the workers, peasants and soldiers, who are the real creators of history and the true masters of our country.

---

[2] Liu Shao-chi, former President of the People's Republic of China, now in disgrace.

The heroes springing up from among workers, peasants and soldiers who are nurtured by the thought of Mao Tse-tung are true heroes of our socialist era, and in their fine quality is reflected in concentrated form the class character of the proletariat. It is a fundamental task for the revolutionary literature and art of the proletariat to work enthusiastically for the characterization of heroes from among workers, peasants and soldiers who are armed with Mao Tse-tung's thought and to make them occupy the stage at all times. Only by so doing will it be possible to get to the roots of the task of the fundamental orientation in literature and art serving workers, peasants and soldiers, the orientation pointed out by Chairman Mao.

In the process of guiding the writing of The Red Lantern, Comrade Chiang Ching never failed to devote her energy to creating revolutionary heroic images of the proletariat. Besides, she had to wage resolute struggles against the handful of counter-revolutionary revisionists on a series of questions of principle, such as whether or not it was necessary to create heroic images of the proletariat and how to create them.

Thanks to the constant explanations and instructions by Comrade Chiang Ching we came to understand the essential significance of the characterization of the proletarian hero Li Yu-ho. She stressed the necessity of creating heroic images of the proletariat, specifically the image of Li Yu-ho. She demanded that The Red Lantern should have a distinctive type of character so that it not only would convince the domestic audience of the truth that the political power of the proletariat is not easily won in order to educate posterity, but would also be a contribution to all the people in the world who are fighting for liberation by providing them with a lesson. We have seen that the feudal landlord class in the past always devoted its energies to creating "heroes" like Huang Tien-pa, henchman of the feudal ruling class. To-day, why should we not exert the utmost effort to create the noble image of such a proletarian hero as Li Yu-ho for our socialist stage? Only among the proletariat armed with Mao Tse-tung's thought will be found the greatest and most brilliant

heroes in history who bear their country in mind, extend their view to embrace the world and set themselves the task of liberating the whole of mankind. On our stage there are not too many but too few heroes of this kind.

Chou Yang, Lin Mo-han and their lackeys who are extremely hostile to revolutionary contemporary opera were compelled to accept the work of revising The Red Lantern after their various schemes had gone bankrupt. However, they in one way or another resisted Comrade Chiang Ching's instructions by resorting to various kinds of disruption and obstructions. They relegated Li Yu-ho to a secondary role and deleted the scene "A Commotion at the Gruel Stall" in which Li Yu-ho was portrayed as courageous and resourceful. Particularly in the scene "A Fight in the Face of Death" they made Tieh-mei, Li's daughter, run about frantically at the sight of her grandmother and father being tortured by the enemy, in order to reveal her mental "conflict," "agony" and "vacillation." By emphasizing horror and suffering, they tried to upset and poison the audience with a touch of bourgeois sentimentality. On the other hand, the Japanese aggressor Hatoyama was shown in all his arrogance. The scene "Hatoyama Is Defied" highlighted this chief of the Japanese gendarmerie, who, while going off with the singsong girls in his train, laughed bombastically like a conqueror. In peddling the traitor's philosophy of the top capitalist roader in the Party, Chou Yang, Lin Mo-han and their followers did all they could to show the "mental suffering" of the traitor Wang Lien-chu in the act of betrayal. They vainly hoped to smuggle rubbish from feudalism, capitalism and revisionism into this revolutionary contemporary opera, divert it from serving proletarian politics on to the adverse road of serving bourgeois politics, and by covert means remove the heroic characters of workers, peasants and soldiers from the stage.

Comrade Chiang Ching sternly criticized them and repeated her express assertion about the necessity of creating revolutionary heroic images of the proletariat in The Red Lantern. She pointed out that the heroic character of Li Yu-ho as an ideal type of proletarian revolutionary fighter should be moulded in the light of the history of our Party's revolutionary struggles, and that in the person of Li Yu-ho the fine quality and thoroughgoing revolutionary spirit of the proletariat should be embodied.

Comrade Chiang Ching worked arduously with us on portraying the heroic character of Li Yu-ho, establishing the positions of the leading and minor roles, positive and negative characters and arranging episodes, music and songs, stage setting and scenery, costume, property and lighting. The opera develops with Li Yu-ho as the centre; negative characters yield ground to positive ones so that the latter have a decided superiority over the former. Given the best position and ample scope for movement, Li Yu-ho holds sway on the stage and gets the upper hand of the enemy.

We restored the scene "A Commotion at the Gruel Stall" because it shows Li Yu-ho's underground struggle, the sufferings of the labouring people under the heel of the Japanese invader and Li's deep class feeling for them, his self-possession, resourcefulness and courage in fighting the enemy, and things that inspire him with wisdom and strength. At the same time we resolutely struck out the part of the scene which depicts the arrogance of Hatoyama and the "mental suffering" of the traitor.

Comrade Chiang Ching also waged a firm struggle against the counter-revolutionary revisionists over the scene "A Fight in the Face of Death," the climax of the opera. Bearing Comrade Chiang Ching's views in mind, we highlighted Li Yu-ho and gave prominence to his revolutionary heroism and optimism by making him sing a moving song cycle of different airs so that he could give full expression to his broad vision and noble spirit. The Internationale played when the execution takes place rouses an emotion which is revolutionary and political. We also resolutely did away with the details of torturing Li Yu-ho and his mother on the stage because we simply reject naturalism and sensationalism.

Holding firm to Chairman Mao's revolutionary line on literature and art, Comrade Chiang Ching on the spot gave concrete guidance for rehearsal and persevered in the struggle by relying on the revolutionary masses. In the end she broke through all obstacles and disruption and made the image of Li Yu-ho, a proletarian of heroic stature, tower on the stage of our socialist land and for ever live in the hearts of the millions who have made up the audiences.

III

The struggle centring on the question of creating the brilliant image of the proletarian hero Li Yu-ho is one between the proletariat and the bourgeoisie and between the proletarian and bourgeois lines. The counter-revolutionary revisionists tried in a thousand and one ways to distort and smear proletarian heroes so as to remould the world according to their reactionary bourgeois world outlook. Comrade Chiang Ching led us in adhering to a proletarian world outlook which enabled us to create noble images of proletarian heroes. Anything detrimental to the characters of the revolutionaries of three generations in Li Yu-ho's family— be it an episode, an aria, a sentence, a minor movement, or even a costume or make-up which was found to be a little out of place—was altered over and over again till it came up to the required standard. Many of these changes relating to singing, words and movement were made by Comrade Chiang Ching herself. Holding high the great red banner of Mao Tse-tung's thought, she worked according to the policy of "making no concession on questions of principle and settling questions of art in practice." It was in this way that, together with us, she smashed the plots of the counter-revolutionary revisionists and created the noble image of Li Yu-ho, with the result that the revolutionary contemporary Peking opera The Red Lantern, which combines revolutionary political content with highly-developed artistic form, has won the warm approbation of the broad sections of workers, peasants and soldiers and the revolutionary masses, and the enthusiastic appreciation of many foreign friends as well. All revolutionary people, at home and abroad, have cheered this great victory for Chairman Mao's thinking on literature and art.

On the occasion of celebrating the 25th anniversary of the publication of the

Talks at the Yenan Forum on Literature and Art we cannot restrain our elation as we reminisce about the revolutionary road which we have opened up in our struggle through thick and thin, guided by Chairman Mao's thinking on literature and art. At the crucial juncture when Peking opera theatre was shrouded in the miasma of "emphasis on the ancient as against the contemporary" and "emphasis on the dead as against the living," it was Mao Tse-tung's thought which, like a lodestar, led us forward to blaze a trail! It was the invincible thought of Mao Tse-tung which encouraged us to wage a dauntless battle against the counter-revolutionary revisionist black line on literature and art, and defeat and smash the schemes of obstruction, disruption and attacks by the handful of counter-revolutionary revisionists.

We shall always remember those days of intense creative work and rehearsal on *The Red Lantern* when the amiable and endearing Comrade Chiang Ching often came into our midst, carefully listening to our views and earnestly giving us guidance. When we were in difficulties she never failed to urge us to be bold in creation and innovation. She ardently induced us to eulogize the workers, peasants and soldiers, and advance along Chairman Mao's line on literature and art. Who can tell how much energy she has expended on *The Red Lantern*! What outstanding contributions she has made to the great proletarian cultural revolution!

We are determined to devote our greatest effort to the creative study and application of Chairman Mao's works. Following Comrade Chiang Ching's example, we shall always be loyal to our great leader Chairman Mao, to the great thought of Mao Tse-tung, and to the revolutionary cause of the proletariat and be thorough revolutionaries! We are determined to keep to that orientation in literature and art serving the workers, peasants and soldiers as pointed out by Chairman Mao, to reverse what has been reversed on the old stage, restore the history of the people which has been distorted by the reactionary ruling classes to what it should be, send to the deepest pit of hell all those emperors, princes, generals, ministers, scholars and beauties who have dominated our stage for thousands of years, and let heroic images of the workers, peasants and soldiers, creators of the world, shine forth on the stage of Peking opera!

Charles
Gordone
1925–

Unknown until he was forty-three, actor-playwright Charles Gordone burst onto the theatrical scene in 1969 with *No Place to Be Somebody*, a passionate, tragi-comic melodrama of American racial and social dilemmas. Born in Cleveland—part black, Indian, Irish, and French—Gordone and his family moved to a small Midwest town, Elkhart, Indiana, when he was small. There, as he grew into adolescence, Gordone experienced the division and confusion about him. His mother was an evangelical Seventh Day Adventist; he was a light-skinned black of mixed ancestry living in a white neighborhood and unwelcome in the black community. In 1944 Gordone enlisted in the Air Force and after being discharged went to California where he worked at odd jobs and studied dramatic arts at Los Angeles State College. After graduating, Gordone did some acting and then left for New York. There he failed to make much headway as actor or producer and took up barkeeping at Johnny Romero's, the one bar in Greenwich Village run by a black. This experience forms the background for his play *No Place to Be Somebody*. In 1961 Gordone joined the company playing Jean Genêt's *The Blacks* and was compelled by this powerful work to confront the issues of race and color. The result was an astonishing first play—*No Place to Be Somebody*—a complex, divided, intense, an eloquent drama.

NO PLACE TO BE SOMEBODY

A black black comedy in three acts

CHARLES GORDONE

CAST

GABE GABRIEL, a young fairskinned Negro
SHANTY MULLIGAN, a young white man
JOHNNY WILLIAMS, a young Negro
DEE JACOBSON, a young white woman
EVIE AMES, a young Negro woman
CORA BEASELY, a young Negro woman
MELVIN SMELTZ, a young Negro man
MARY LOU BOLTON, a white girl
ELLEN, a white girl
SWEETS CRANE, an elderly Negro

MIKE MAFFUCCI, a young white man
TRUCK DRIVER, a young white man
JUDGE BOLTON, a middle-aged white man, father of Mary Lou
MACHINE DOG, a young Negro (in Johnny's imagination)
SERGEANT CAPPALETTI, a young white man
HARRY, a Negro detective
LOUIE, a young white man

ACT I

Scene One

[Time: The past fifteen years
Place: New York City
Setting: Johnny's Bar
At rise: GABE sits near jukebox, typing. Rips page from typewriter. Balls it up, flings it angrily at audience.]

GABE. Excuse me. Forgot you were out there. My name is Gabe. Gabe Gabriel, to be exact. I'm a writer. Didn't mean to lose my temper. Something I've been working on all my life. Not losing my temper. [Takes out marihuana cigarette. Lights it. Inhales it. Holds smoke in.] Right now I'm working on a play. They say if you wanna be a writer you gotta go out an' live. I don't believe that no more. Take my play for instance. Might not be- lieve it but I'm gonna make it all up in my head as I go along. Before I prove it to you, wanna warn you not to be thinkin' I'm tellin' you a bunch'a bare-faced lies. An' no matter how far out I git, don't want you goin' out'a here with the idea what you see happenin' is all a figment of my grassy imagination. 'Cause it ain't! [He picks up Bible from table. Raises it above his head. Without looking turns pages.] "And I heard a Voice between the banks of the U'Lai. And it called, Gabriel! Gabriel! Make this man understand the vision! So He came near where I stood! And when He came, I was frightened and fell upon my face!"

[He closes Bible. As he exits, lights dim out, then come up on SHANTY, at jukebox. Jazz is playing. SHANTY takes out his drumsticks. Begins to rap on bar. JOHNNY enters. Hangs up raincoat and umbrella.]

JOHNNY. Cool it, Shanty.

SOURCE: From No Place to Be Somebody. Copyright © 1969 by Charles Gordone. Reprinted by permission of the publisher, The Bobbs-Merrill Company, Inc.

SHANTY. Man, I'm practicing.

JOHNNY. Damned if that bar's anyplace for it. Git on that floor there.

SHANTY [puts drumsticks away. Takes broom]. Ever tell you 'bout the time I went to this jam session? Max Roach was there. Lemme sit in for him.

JOHNNY. Said you played jus' like a spade.

SHANTY. What's wrong with that? Ol' Red Taylor said wasn't nobody could hold a beat an' steady cook it like me. Said I had "the thing"! 'Member one time we played "Saints." For three hours, we played it.

JOHNNY. Had to git a bucket'a col' water an' throw it on you to git you to quit, huh?

SHANTY. One these days I'm gonna have me a boss set'a skins for my comeback. Me an' Cora was diggin' a set up on "Four-Six Street." Sump'm else ag'in. Bass drum, dis'pearin' spurs, snares, tom-toms. . . .

JOHNNY. Gon' steal 'em?

SHANTY. I been savin' up. Gonna git me them drums. Know what I'm gonna do then? I'm gonna quit you flat. Go for that. Sheee! I ain't no lifetime apron. That's for damned sure.

JOHNNY. Yeah, well meantime how 'bout finishin' up on that floor? Time to open the store. [DEE and EVIE enter. Hang coats up.] You broads let them two ripe apples git away from you, huh?

DEE. Don't look at me.

EVIE. Aw, later for you an' your rich Texas trade.

DEE. Just gettin' too damned sensitive.

EVIE. Sensitive my black behin'! Excuse me, I mean black ass. [Goes to jukebox. Punches up number.]

DEE. Last night we bring those two johns up to her pad. An' like, Jack? One with the cowboy hat? Stoned? Like out of his skull. And like out of nowhere he starts cryin'.

EVIE. All weekend it was "Nigger this an' Nigger that."

DEE. Never bothered you before. I didn't like it when he started sayin' things like "The black sons a'bitches are gettin' to be untouchables! Takin' over the country!"

EVIE. Bet he'll think twice before he says sump'm like that ag'in.

DEE. That lamp I gave her? One the senator brought me back from Russia? Evie goes an' breaks it over his head.

JOHNNY. What the hell'd you do that for?

EVIE. Sure hated to lose that lamp.

JOHNNY. Wouldn't care if they b'longed to the Ku Klux Klan long's they gimme the bread. [He goes into DEE's purse.]

SHANTY. Sure had plenty of it too! When they was in here, they kept buyin' me drinks. Thought I was the boss.

JOHNNY. Crackers cain't 'magine Niggers runnin' nothin' but elevators an' toilets.

DEE. Leave me somethin', please.

EVIE. Ain't gon' do nothin' with it nohow.

JOHNNY [finds pair of baby shoes in DEE's purse]. Thought I tole you to git rid'a these?

DEE. I forgot.

JOHNNY. Save you the trouble. [He starts to throw them away.]

DEE. Don't you do that, you black bastard. So help me, Johnny.

EVIE. Aw, let'er have them things, Nigger! Wha's the big deal?

JOHNNY. 'Tend to your own business, bitch. Ain't a minute off your ass for messin' it up las' night.

EVIE. Excuse me. Didn't know you was starvin' to death.

JOHNNY [goes for EVIE but quickly checks himself when she reaches for her purse. He turns back to DEE]. Look'a here, girl. I ain't gon' have no harness bulls knockin' down yo' door.

DEE. All of a sudden you worried about me.

JOHNNY. Jus' git rid'a that crap. Worrin' over sump'm pass, over an' done with.

[CORA enters. A wet newspaper covers her head.]

CORA. Lawd'a mercy! Now I gotta do this un'form all over ag'in. Bad as I hate to iron.

JOHNNY. Ironin' for them crackers. Cain't see why you cain't iron for yourself.

CORA. This ain't no maid's un'form as any fool kin see. I makes my livin' as a pract'cal nurse. I ain't nobody's maid.

JOHNNY. Somebody tole me they seen

you wheelin' a snotty nose, blue-eyed baby th'ough Washin'ton Square the other day.

CORA. They was a Wash'ton Square lie. Onlies' baby I wheel aroun' gon' be my own.

JOHNNY. Hell! By the time you an' Shanty git aroun' to somethin' like that ... you ain't gon' wheel nothin' roun' but a tray'a black-ass coffee.

[DEE and EVIE laugh.]

CORA. You cheap husslers don't hit the street, you gon' be sellin' yo' wares in'a home for the cripple an' infirm.

EVIE. Gon' have to bring ass to git ass.

[CORA comes off her stool. Jerks off shoe. EVIE comes up with a switchblade.]

JOHNNY. Hey! Hey! Git under the bed with that shit! [He races around bar. Comes between them.] What the hell's the matter with you, Cora? Cain't you take a little joke?

CORA. Don't know why every time I come in here, I gotta be insulted by you an' these here Harlows.

[EVIE still has her knife out.]

EVIE. Bet if that heifer messes with me, I'll carve her up like'a fat piece'a barbecue.

JOHNNY. Naw you won't neither. Not in here, you won't. Put it away! I said put it away.

[EVIE reluctantly puts knife away.]

DEE. Let's get out of here, Evie. She's always pickin' her nose about somethin'.

EVIE. She don't scare me none. Jus' smells bad, tha's all.

DEE [looks at her watch]. Well, I gotta date, and you gotta see your headshrinker, don't you?

JOHNNY. Headshrinker? Damned if Evie ain't gone an' got herself a pimp.

EVIE. He don't come as expensive as some pimps I know.

DEE [goes for the coats]. Now, don't you two start up again. [The two women start for the street doors.]

JOHNNY. Make money, baby. Make that money.

DEE. That's all you ever think about. Can't you just dig me for my soul?

JOHNNY. Wrong color be talkin' 'bout soul.

DEE. Negroes. Think you gotta corner on soul.

EVIE. Us has suffahd, das why.

[DEE and EVIE exit.]

CORA. Gimme a martini, Shangy. Gotta bad taste in my mouth.

JOHNNY. Make sure she pays for that drink.

CORA. I works an' I pays. I don't ask a livin' ass for nothin'.

JOHNNY. 'Member when you did.

CORA. I was broke. Couldn't fin' no work. 'Sides I had you to take care of! Like I p'omised yo' mama I would. 'Fore she died. Till you had to go git in trouble with that Eye-tralian boy.

JOHNNY. Maybe I jus' got tired'a all them col'-cuts an' fuck-ups.

CORA. When you got out'a that 'form school, I was ready to take care you ag'in! But that bad Nigger Sweets Crane got holt you an' ruint ya.

JOHNNY. Fixed it so's I didn't have to go to that orphan-house, didn't he? Took me in, treated me like I was his own son, didn't he? Damned sight more'n you or that drunken bitch of a mama'a mine did.

CORA. Jay Cee? Might God strike you dead. Maybe I ain't yo' flesh an' blood. But yo' mama? She couldn't he'p none'a the things she did.

JOHNNY. Do me one favor, bitch. Leave my mama on the outside. 'Nother thing, if you cain't say nothin' boss 'bout Sweets Crane, you don't have to come in here yo' dam-self. [He slaps her on the behind and exits to the kitchen.]

CORA. Well, fan me with a brick! Tha's one Nigro you jus' cain't be civil with. [She sips her drink as SHANTY finishes sweeping floor.] Eb'm as a chile—give him a piece'a candy, wudn't the kin' he wanted, he'd rare back an' th'ow it at you. An' he'd stan' there lookin' all slangeyed darin' you to touch him. [She watches SHANTY beat on the bar.] Never had no papa. 'Less you call that ol' dog Sweets Crane a father. His mama was always sickly an' she did drink. Never would give it out though, who it was did it to her. Carried that to her grave! [She downs her drink.] I knowed her ever since I was a li'l gal down South. You know, they was always sump'm funny 'bout her. Swore Jay Cee was born with a veil over his face.

SHANTY. A what?

CORA. A veil over his face. Ev'body knows babies born with veils over they faces is s'pose to see ghostes an' raise forty-one kin's'a hell.

SHANTY. Johnny? Sheee.

CORA. If I'm lyin', I'm flyin'!

SHANTY. Cora, you're superstishus as hell.

CORA. Cain't he'p but be, li'l bit. My peoples all had fogey-isms. Where I come from ev'body had 'em. One kin' or 'nother.

[MELVIN enters, hangs up knapsack and rain jacket, takes cap off. Knocks the wet from his pants. His head is almost clean-shaven.]

Chile! you sho' don't have to worry 'bout yo' head goin' back home!

MELVIN. My home, sweety, is in Saint Albans. You don't have to inform me as to where yours is. [He goes into a soft-shoe dance and sings.] "Where the people beat they feet on the Mississippi mud."

CORA. Now, ain't that jus' like you ig'orint Nigroes. If they cain't think'a nothin' to say, they starts slippin' you into the dozens.

JOHNNY [enters from kitchen]. You late, Mel.

MELVIN. Today was my dance class, remember? Anyway, who can get a cab in this weather?

JOHNNY. White folks, baby. Wheeeet folks!

MELVIN. Objectively speaking, plenty of them were passed up too. [He begins to stretch his leg muscles.]

JOHNNY. Dig? One these days we gon' see this on tee vee.

MELVIN. You got your people mixed. The dances they do on television is sterictly commercial.

JOHNNY. What hell's wrong with that? If you gon' run 'roun' wigglin' yo' tukus, mights well git paid for it.

MELVIN. I study with a great artist! He deplores that sort of thing.

JOHNNY. Whozis great artist you study with?

MELVIN. Victor Weiner! He teaches the Chenier method.

JOHNNY. This Shimmy-yay method you don't wiggle the tukus?

MELVIN. Why?

JOHNNY. Them turkeys on tee vee mus' make a whole lotta coins jus' for wigglin' they tukeruseys.

MELVIN. Prostitutes. All of them.

JOHNNY. Pros'tutes, huh? [He goes to jukebox. Punches up number. Classical music comes on.] Go with a little sample what you jokers is puttin' down.

MELVIN. Nothing doing. To appreciate true art, one must first be familiar with it.

CORA. Talk that talk, Mel. What do Jay Cee know 'bout bein' artistic?

JOHNNY [rejects the music]. This Wineberg you study with? He's a Jew, ain't he?

MELVIN. So what?

JOHNNY. Gotta give it to him. Connin' spades into thinkin' they gotta be taught how to dance.

MELVIN. You're just prejudiced, Johnny. That's why you have no appreciation.

JOHNNY. When you start teachin' him, maybe I'll git me some pre-she-a-shun. [A loud voice is heard offstage.]

VOICE. Inn keeper!

GABE [bursts in clad in army raincoat and Sou'wester. He brandishes an umbrella and briefcase]. Cock-a-doodle-doo!

[JOHNNY paws the floor with his feet.] "I am a ringtailed squeeler. I am that very infant that refused his milk before his eyes was opened an' called out for a bottle of old rye."

[They circle each other.]

JOHNNY. "This is me! Johnny Earthquake. I rassle with light'nin', put a cap on thunder. Set every mammy-jammer in the graveyard on a wonder."

GABE. "I grapple with lions! Put knots in they tails! Sleep on broken glass an' for breakfast, eat nails. I'm a ba-a-a-d mother-for-ya."

[JOHNNY goes behind the bar and takes down a bottle of whisky as GABE spies CORA.]

Eeeeeow! I feel like swallowin' a nappy-headed woman whole!

CORA [pushes him away playfully]. Better stay out'a my face, fool.

[JOHNNY moves around bar to center. Theatrically pours a waterglass half-full of whisky. Sets glass before GABE on table. GABE removes coat and hat. Hands them to CORA. He eyes the whisky. Sniffs. Picks up the glass.]

A-Lawd! Gabe you ain't. . . .

[GABE *puts the glass to his lips and begins to drink.*]

Ooooo!

[GABE *is emptying the glass.*]

Ooooo!

[*He finishes. Eyes crossed. Sets the glass down. Grimaces. Shakes his head.* JOHNNY *and* SHANTY *laugh.*] I swear! Y'all is sho' crazy. Ain't neither one'a ya got good sense.

GABE. Needed that. Needed that one bad. Gimme another one.

[SHANTY *reaches for the bottle.*]

CORA. Don't you do it, Shangy. Let that fool kill hisse'f. Ain't no call for you to he'p him.

JOHNNY. Dam, Gabe! You ain't done gone an' got alcoholic on us?

GABE. Don't you worry yo' li'l happy head 'bout me, sir. Matter fact, I'm cuttin' myself right out'a the herd.

JOHNNY. Tell me sump'm, baby? Is this herd pink? An' got snoots an' grea' big ears?

GABE. No they ain't. In color, they're black with big, thick, lip-pussys.

JOHNNY. Man! Them ain't elephants you been hangin' out with, them's hippo-bottom'-a-the-pot'a-muses!

[JOHNNY *and* GABE *give each other some skin.*]

CORA. Lawd! What in the devil an' Tom Walker you Nigros talkin' 'bout now?

JOHNNY. Keep her in the dark, Gabe. Keep that mulyan in the black.

MELVIN. They're talking about Gabe's audition, Cora. Gabe had an audition today.

GABE. I said it was a herd call, Melvino Rex!

MELVIN. Lots of actors there, huh?

GABE. Actors? Actors did you say? Well, yes! Every damned black actor in town.

CORA. Well, why didn't you say so in the first place? Lawd, chile! You ought'a lean up off this stuff.

[GABE *tries to put his arm around her.*] An' take yo' arm out from 'roun' my neck.

MELVIN. How'd you make out at that audition, Gabe?

GABE. Dig this. It was a musical! A musical about slavery.

MELVIN. Slavery? Well! It's about time.

JOHNNY. Gabe's gon' play'a ha'f-white house Nigger! An' they ain't no whiter, ha'f-white house Nigger in New Yawk than Gabe is, I'll bet'a fat man.

GABE. You jus'a-got-dat-wrong, John. Stage manager calls me over. Whispers they're auditionin' the white actors tomorrow. Baby! I refuse to see anything musical at all about slavery.

[*Everyone breaks up laughing.*]

CORA. Say, Gabe? How about doin' one o' them crazy po'm's'a your'n? Ain't heard none in a long time.

SHANTY. Yeah, Gabe! How 'bout it?

MELVIN. Might make you feel better.

JOHNNY. Git under the bed with that shit! Ain't runnin' no cabaret. Fixin' to git me a summons!

GABE. What you wanna hear?

CORA. Anythin'.

JOHNNY. If you jus' gotta. Knowin' you, you always jus' gotta. Make it sump'm you know.

GABE. Dig this one.

[*All except* JOHNNY *eagerly take seats.*]

They met on the banks of the Potomac, the rich, the great and the small!
It's impossible to tell you, should'a been there an' seen it all!
They came by train, by plane, by bus an' by car!
Bicycle an' tricycle from near an' very far!
On mule an' on horseback!
With greasy bag an' kroker sack!
Buckboard an' clapboard an' goats pullin' wagons!
Tin lizzies an' buggies an' trucks so weighted down with people, you could see the backends saggin'!
Carts with motors, an' trams!
Wheelchairs an' wheelbarrels an' women pushin' prams!
Little boys on scooters! Little girls on skates!
Beatnicks, hippies an' hoboes, most of them had come by freights!
We had walked in light-footed an' barefooted, had walked all out'a our shoes! Some hopped it on crutches for days!
An' then we got the news, some black power agitators was arrested along the way!
'Course they was a lotta Cadillacs an'

Buicks, rich people showin' off! I
  didn't pay that no min',
I jus' took comfort in the thought we
  needed people of every kin'!
An' if all America had been there or seen
  it on tee vee,
They would'a knowed we all meant business in gittin' our e-kwa-le-tee!
Well, we moved to the square with the
  pool in the middle!
While we waited, some strange young
  folk from New Yawk played a flute
  an' a fiddle!
Then somebody pro-nounced that reb'm
  somebody would pray!
An' by the settin' sun, we knelt in the
  dust'a that day!
Somebody else got up with a great loud
  voice!
Said they had on han' the speaker of our
  choice!
Said this black man was a black man of
  black deeds an' black fame!
(I'll be damned to hell, I disremember
  his name!)
Then a hush fell on all them people that
  night,
'Cause we was there for one thing, our
  civil right!
This black man, he rizzed up an' walked
  to the stan'! I could tell at a glance
  that he was the man!
An' he boomed out over that mickey-
  phone an' called for all black folk
  to unite an' not roam to other
  orguzashuns who jus' wanted to
  fight white people an' git what they
  can in a country that would soon
  give liberty an' 'quality to every
  man!
If we worked long an' hard, he admitted
  it'd be rough!
But he said, black unity an' solidarity
  would be enough!
Then he rizzed up his arms an' bobbled
  his head!
Best as I kin I'll try to remember what
  he said!

[GABE pretends he is skinning a team
of mules.]

Hya!
You, Afro-Americans!
Hya!
You, American Afros!

Hya!
You Muslims an' nay-cee-pees!
Hya!
You so-called Negroes!
Tan liberals!
Black radicals!
Hya!
You respec-rabble black boorwahzeees!
Hya!
Black Demos an' 'Publicans,
Git back on the track!
You Nash-na-lissys and Marx-a-sissies
Who all been pin-pointin' black!
Hya!
You half-white pro-fesh-nals!
Hya!
Civil rights pro-shesh-nals!
Hya!
You cursed sons-a-ham!
Don't rock no boat!
Don't cut ne'r th'oat!
Be a beacon for some black magazeen!
Come doctor!
Come lawyer!
Come teacher!
Black employer!
An' keepers of white latrines!
On Donner!
On Blitzen!
You black nick-surd-rich-ins!
On! On! With the soul kweezeen!
You inter-urbans!
Satisfied suburbans!
To you, I gotta say whoa!
What's needed to save us
Is not Some-a-Davus!
Or even Benjammer O.!
Giddy-up! Yippeee-ay! Or Kidney Pot-
  eeay!
They already got they dough!
Now, here are the bare facks,
Grab yo' selves by the bootblacks!
Leave Heroin Manderson on the side!
An' all you take notice,
You'll all git yo' lettuce!
You'll own the post office yet!
Off-springs off mixed couples
Who're more than a han'fu,
You'll make the cover of Jet!
We'll have invented a machine that
  delivers
A cream to make crackers pay the debt!
Now junkies don't dilly
You husslers don't dally!
Don't waste yo' time smokin' pot
In some park or some alley,
'Cause Cholly is watchin' you!"

Well, he would a'went that'a way
To this very day but his th'oat
It got too hoarse!
When he sat down wasn't a clap ne'r a
*   soun',*
Couldn't tell if he'd got to the end!
A cracker preacher there, then said a
*   prayer!*
Said civil rights you could not fo'ce!
By this time I was so confused my head
*   was in a spin!*
Somebody else got up with a grinnin'
*   face!*
Said to leave that place like we found it!
Tha's when I reached in my pocket an'
*   pulled out my packet an' before*
*   everybody took a sip'a my wine!*
Then we lef' that place without ne'r
*   trace!*
An' we didn't leave ne'r chit'lin' behin'!

[*Everyone laughs and claps his hands.*]

JOHNNY. If you ask me, it's all a big-ass waste'a time an' energy. Jus' how long you gon' keep this up? Ought'a be in some office makin'a white man's pay.

GABE. Sheee! Think I'd rather be hawkin' neckbones on a Hundred an' Twenty-Fifth Street.

CORA. Uh-aw! Better git out'a here 'fore you two start goin' at it agin. [*She gets newspaper and peers out of window.*] An' 'fore it starts up rainin' ag'in! Lawd knows I ain't prepared for neither one. [*She moves to* MELVIN *who is stirring something in a skillet. She sniffs.*] Shanty! If you want sump'm 'sides Mel's warmed-over chili better see you for supper.

GABE. Better watch it, Shanty. She's thinkin' the way to a man's heart is through his stomach.

CORA [*moves to street doors*]. Sho' ain't no way to stay there.

[*She exits.* MELVIN *exits to kitchen.* SHANTY *busies himself.* GABE *sits. Looks thoughtful.* JOHNNY *tosses him some bills.*]

GABE. What's this?

JOHNNY. Aw, take the bread, Nigger.

[GABE *does not pick up the money.*] Look'a here, Gabe. I know you think I'm all up 'side the wall. You hip to the books an' all like'a that. But ser-us-ly! Why ain't they doin' you no good?

GABE. Let's jus' say I ain't in no big rush.

JOHNNY. It's Charlie, ain't it?

GABE. What about Charlie?

JOHNNY. It's wrote all over you! Might be foolin' some people. Cock-a-doodle-dooin' an' comin' on with yo' funky po'try. . . .

GABE. When you git me some answers other than the one's you been handin' me, I'll git in the bed with you.

JOHNNY. One thing Sweets says to me, 'fore he got his time. He says. . . .

GABE. Screw it, John. When you start bringin' Sweets into the picture, I know exactly what's comin' next. The answer is still negative.

JOHNNY. Still wanna believe you kin sell papers an' become President, huh? Snowballs in Egypt.

GABE. I ain't lookin' to break no law.

JOHNNY. They ain't no law. They kill you an' me in the name'a the law. You an' me wouldn't be where we at, if it wasn't for the law. Even the laws they write for us makes us worse off.

GABE. From the git-go, they don't operate like Sweets anymore. Harlem's all caught up.

JOHNNY. Who's operatin' in Harlem?

GABE. You cain't be thinkin' about down here! It was branchin' out'a Harlem got Sweets where he's at right now.

JOHNNY. Man, what you think I been doin' the ten years Sweets been in the joint? I tell you the scheme is together. Me an' him gon' git us a piece'a this town.

GABE. An' end up on the bottom'a the East River with it tied aroun' your necks.

JOHNNY. Bet we'll have us a box'a crackers under each armpit if we do!

GABE. Well, I don't dig crackers that much.

JOHNNY. Okay, Hollywood! Keep knockin' on doors with yo' jeans at half-mast. Sellin' yo'self like some cheap-ass whore. If I know one thing about you, you ain't that good'a actor. Whitey knows right away you cain't even stan' to look at him.

[GABE *grins, picks money up. Pockets it.*]

BLACKOUT

Scene Two

[*Time: A week later*
Place: The same
Setting: The same
At rise: GABE *stands at center.*]

GABE. When I'm by myself like this, for days, weeks, even months at a time, it sort'a gets to me! I mean deep down inside things begin to happen. Lemme confess, sometimes I git to feelin'—like I get so vicious, I wanna go out an' commit mass murder. But don't misunderstand me. Because I call myself a black playwright, don't git the impression I'm hung up on crap like persecution an' hatred. 'Cause I ain't! I'm gonna leave that violence jazz to them cats who are better at it than me. I ain't been out of the house in over two months. Not because I been that busy, I just been too damned scared. I been imaginin' all kind'a things happenin' out there. An' they're waitin' just for me. All manner of treachery an' harm. But don't think because of it my play is about Negro self-pity. Or even that ol' "You-owe-me-whitey party line." 'Cause it ain't. In spite of what I learned in college, it did not give me that introduction to success, equality an' wealth, that to my parents were the most logical alternatives to heaven. Anyway, like I say, I'm gonna leave that social protest jive to them cats who are better equipped than me.

[*Lights dim out on* GABE *and come up on* JOHNNY, *who is asleep on the floor. One shoe is off and an empty bottle and glass lie nearby. A telegram is pushed under the door.* JOHNNY *rouses himself. Puts on his shoe and goes to the door. Picks up the telegram and studies it. Someone is heard trying the street doors. He hides the telegram and opens the door.* DEE *enters. Goes behind the bar. Makes a Bromo.* JOHNNY *takes out the telegram. Peers at it again.*]

DEE. What is it?

JOHNNY. Looks like a telegram from Sweets. [*He gives her the telegram.*] Read it.

[DEE *downs her Bromo.*]
Read it, I said.
[*She picks up the telegram.*]

DEE. It's from Sweets allright.

JOHNNY. Well, what does it say?

DEE. Says he's going to be released in three weeks.

[JOHNNY *snatches telegram.*]
Makes you pretty happy, doesn't it?

JOHNNY. Babeee! Happy ain't the word! I am dee-ler-russ! Yeeeeoweee!

DEE [*grabs her head*]. Hold it down, will ya?

JOHNNY. S'matter? Rough night?

DEE. What else?

JOHNNY. Go home! Cop some zees!

DEE. Just sit here for a while! If you don't mind.

JOHNNY. Dam'dest thing. Las' night I stayed here. Burnt one on. Fell asleep right here. Had this dream. 'Bout Sweets gittin' out. Man, tha's weird! Tha's damned weird.

DEE. Today's my birthday.

JOHNNY. Dam! Forgot all about it.

DEE. Wish to hell I could.

JOHNNY. Anybody'd think you was a wrinkled up ol' mulyan. [*He takes money from her purse. Tosses her a few bills, stuffs the rest into his pocket.*] Here. Go out an' buy yourself sump'm real nice.

DEE [*flinging the bills back at him*]. I don't want anything for my birthday.

JOHNNY. Now, lissen. Don't you start no shit this mornin'. I'm in too good'a humor.

DEE. Johnny. Let's you and me just take off for somewhere! For a couple of weeks.

JOHNNY. You off your wood, girl? With Sweets gittin' out?

DEE. I gotta bad feelin'.

JOHNNY. I don't give'a dam what kind'a feelin' you got. Sweets was like a father to me.

DEE. So you told me. A thousand times you told me.

JOHNNY. I know. That bitch Evie's been puttin' ideas into your head.

DEE. That's not true. You lay off her, Johnny.

JOHNNY. Lissen to her, she'll have you husslin' tables at Howard Johnson's.

DEE. Might be better off.

JOHNNY [*slaps her*]. Kiss me an' tell me you sorry.

DEE [*she kisses him*]. Sorry. [*She moves to street doors.*]

JOHNNY. Hey, girl. Gotta celebrate your birthday some way. Tomorrow mornin'. Bring over the Sunday papers an' a bottle'a my bes' wampole. "All day, all night, Mary Ann!"

[DEE *exits.* JOHNNY *peers at telegram. Goes to jukebox. Punches up number. Presently* CORA *and* SHANTY *enter.*]

CORA. Jay Cee? I know it ain't none'a my business, but that woman'a yours? She's out there in the car. Jus'a cryin' her eyeballs out.

JOHNNY [*getting his jacket, moving to street doors*]. Hol' down the store, Shanty. Be back in'a couple'a hours.

[*He exits.* SHANTY *goes to door. Locks it. Punches up number on jukebox.*]

CORA. Shangy? I been doin' some thinkin'. You heard anything from Gloria?

SHANTY. Heard what?

CORA. 'Bout yo' divorce! Tha's what.

SHANTY. Gloria ain't gonna give me no die-vo'ce.

CORA. Well, if she ain't that don't stop us from livin' together, do it?

SHANTY. What made you change your mind?

CORA. 'Nother thing. Ever since I knowed you, you been belly-achin' 'bout gittin' you some drums.

SHANTY. Gonna git 'em too!

CORA. Well, I'm willin' to do everything I kin to help you.

SHANTY. You mean—you mean, you'd help me git 'em? No jive?

CORA. Then you could quit ol' Jay Cee an' go back to playin' in them nightclubs like you said you used to.

SHANTY. You really mean it? You'd help me git my drums?

CORA. Ain't talkin' jus' to hear myse'f rattle.

SHANTY. Mama, you are the greatest. [*He hugs her.*]

CORA. Honey, hush.

SHANTY. Know what I'm gonna do, Cora? Soon's I git them drums I'm gonna bring 'em in here. Set 'em up an' play "the thing" for Johnny.

CORA. Lawd, Shangy! I wouldn't miss that for nothin' in this worl'.

[SHANTY *takes out marihuana cigarette. Wets, lights it. Smokes.*]

Lawd, Shangy! I done tole you 'bout smokin' them ol' nasty things.

[*He passes the cigarette to her. She grins.*]

Guess it won't hurt none once in a while. [*She inhales. Coughs.*]

SHANTY. I was just thinkin' about ol' Gloria. How much she hated jazz. Nigger music, she called it. Man, every time I'd set up my skins to practice, she'd take the kids an' go over to her mother's.

[*They begin to pass the cigarette back and forth.*]

Dig? One night after a gig, brought some cats over for a little game. Some spade cat grabs her between the legs when I wasn't lookin'.

CORA. Spent the bes' part'a my life on Nigros that won't no good. Had to baby an' take care all of 'em.

SHANTY. Never heard the last of it. You'd think he raped her or somethin'.

CORA. Cain't hol' no job! Take yo' money an' spen' it all on likker.

SHANTY. Got this job playin' the Borsh-Belt. My skins was shot! Had to borrow a set from Champ Jones.

CORA. Cain't make up their min's! Jus' be a man, I says.

SHANTY. Gone about a week. Come home. Shades all down. Key won't fit in the door.

CORA. Git evil. Nex' thing you know they goin' up 'side yo' head.

SHANTY. She's over at her mother's. Says she gonna sue me for desershun.

CORA. I thought you was a dif'rent kind'a Nigger. I'm gon' git me a white man, one that'll take care me. Or he'p me take care myse'f.

SHANTY. I never did nothin' to her.

CORA. Tha's when he went up 'side my head with the ash tray!

SHANTY. Said she needed some bread. Went to the bank. Cashed my check. Come back. Skins the cat loaned me are gone.

CORA. I loved him so much.

SHANTY. Grabbed a broom out'a the closet. Went to work on the bitch.

CORA. Them awful things he said to me.

SHANTY. Bitch never made a soun' or dropped a tear.

CORA. I cried sump'm ter'ble.

SHANTY. Says I'd never see my kids ag'in or the drums neither.

CORA. Wanted children so bad! Doctor said I couldn't have none.

SHANTY. Started chokin' her. Would'a killed her, if my kid hadn't jumped on my back.

CORA. Ain't hard to satisfy me. 'Cause Lawd knows I ain't never asked for much.

SHANTY. One thing I learned. Stay away from bitches like that. Just ain't got no soul. [He gets can of spray deodorant. Opens street doors and sprays the bar.]

CORA [rouses herself. Wipes tears]. Shangy! I sho' wanna see Jay Cee's face when he sees you play them drums.

BLACKOUT

Scene Three

[Time: Three weeks later
Place: The same
Setting: The same
At rise: MELVIN is doing his dance exercises. JOHNNY enters with white tablecloth and slip of paper. SHANTY busies himself behind the bar.]

JOHNNY. Sure we need all this, Mel?

MELVIN. You hired me to be a short order cook around here. That's exactly what that list is too. A short order.

JOHNNY. Jus' checkin'. Don't want you slippin' none'a that what-wuzzit over on me ag'in.

MELVIN. Po-tahge par-mun-teeay. Everybody else liked it.

JOHNNY. Been some chit'lin's, you'da been sayin' sump'm.

MELVIN. Chit'lin's? Sometimes I think you have the taste-buds of a slave.
[He snatches the slip of paper out of JOHNNY's hands and exits as MARY LOU BOLTON enters and goes to a table.]

JOHNNY. Sump'm I kin do for you?

MARY LOU. I'd like a daiquiri, please. . . .

JOHNNY. Got any identification?

MARY LOU. Really!

JOHNNY. Mary Lou Bo—

MARY LOU. Mary Lou Bolton.

JOHNNY. This the school you go to?

MARY LOU. Just graduated.

JOHNNY [goes behind the bar to mix drink]. Buddy'a mine come out'a there. . . .

MARY LOU. Elmira is an all-woman's school.

JOHNNY. I mean the slammers up there.

MARY LOU. Beg your pardon?

JOHNNY [sets drink before her]. Prison.

MARY LOU. Oh, yes! My father spent a lot of time up there.

JOHNNY. You kiddin'? Your father did?

MARY LOU [she laughs]. He was a criminal lawyer.

JOHNNY. He ain't no lawyer no more?

MARY LOU. He's a judge now.

JOHNNY. Must'a been a hell of a lawyer.

MARY LOU. Oh, I suppose so. . . .

JOHNNY. What you mean, you s'pose so?

MARY LOU. I'd rather not discuss it.

JOHNNY. Sorry.
[ELLEN enters. Carries a civil rights placard.]

ELLEN. C'mon, Mary! Everyone's waitin' on you.

MARY LOU. Be there in a second, Ellen. [She looks into her purse. ELLEN exits.] What do I owe you for the drink?

JOHNNY. Ain't you gonna finish it?

MARY LOU. I really shouldn't. But this is my first time out! Kind of nervous, you know?

JOHNNY. First time out?

MARY LOU. We're picketing the construction work up the street. The new hospital they're building.

JOHNNY. What for?

MARY LOU. Haven't you heard? The unions won't accept qualified Negroes.

JOHNNY. Why don't them qualified Nigroes do they own pickitin'?

MARY LOU. It's everyone's responsibility.

JOHNNY. You only git in the way.

MARY LOU. I'm glad all Negroes don't feel the way you do.

JOHNNY. You don't know how I feel.

MARY LOU [puts a bill on the table and prepares to leave]. I don't think I care to find out.

JOHNNY. Jus' happen to think somebody invented this civil rights jive to git a whole lotta people runnin' in the wrong direction.

MARY LOU [starts to move to street doors. JOHNNY catches her by the arm]. Would you mind?

JOHNNY. Know what's in that daiquiri, baby?

MARY LOU. Let me go, please.

JOHNNY. Jizzum juice. A triple dose of jizmistic juice. Any minute you gonna turn into a depraved sex maniac! A teen-age Jeckle an' Hide. Yo' head is gon' sprout fuzzy like somebody from the Fee-gee Eye-lan's. Yo' hot tongue'll roll out'a your mouth like'a fat snake. You'll pant like'a go-rilla in heat. Yo' buzzooms will blow up like gas balloons an' the nipples will swell an' hang like ripe purple plums. Yo' behin' will begin to work like the ol' gray mare an' you'll strut aroun' flappin' yo' wings like'a raped duck. Then you'll suck me up with one mighty slurp an' fly out'a here a scream-in' vampire. They'll finally subdue an' slay you on top'a the Empire State Build-in', with ray guns where you'll be at-temptin' to empale yo'self astride that giant antenna. An' nobody will ever know that you, li'l Mary Lou Bolton, who jus' graduated from Elmira College, was lookin' to lay down in front of a big, black bulldozer, to keep America safe for democracy.

MARY LOU. I think I get your point.

[ELLEN enters.]

ELLEN. Mary Lou! Are you coming or not? Everyone's leaving.

[MARY LOU and ELLEN exit. ELLEN scolding. CORA enters.]

CORA. Shangy! Movin' man's waitin'.

[SHANTY takes off his apron.]

JOHNNY. Where you think you goin'?

SHANTY. Movin' in with Cora today.

JOHNNY. Not on my time, you ain't! An' me 'spectin' Sweets any minute.

CORA. Wha's so 'portant 'bout that Crane Nigro Shangy's just gotta be here? Or maybe you 'spectin' standin' room for the 'casion?

JOHNNY. Ain't lettin' him off an' tha's it.

CORA. Jay Cee, why is you so bent'n boun' on breakin' up our li'l club?

JOHNNY. Somebody's gotta look out for Shangy if he don't.

CORA. What is you talkin' about? Shangy's free, white an' long pass twenty-one! It ain't none'a yo' business what he does outside this bucket'a blood.

JOHNNY. Well, bitch, I got news for you. I put him in here when none'a these other hunkies 'roun' here would hire him. Talkin' his up 'side the wall talk an' beatin' up they benches.

CORA. Wha's that gotta do with me?

JOHNNY. Ain't lettin' you or nobody else turn his head but so far. Jus' per-teckin' my interest.

CORA. Ain't gon' let you stan' in my way, Jay Cee. Me an' Shangy took a likin' for one 'nother from the day I walked in here an' foun' you runnin' this place. Up to now they ain't been much happiness in this worl' for neither one of us. But what li'l we got comin', figger we bes' jump on it with all fo' feet.

JOHNNY. That the way you feel 'bout it, Shanty?

SHANTY. Man, she's gonna help me git my drums.

JOHNNY. She ain't gon' do nothin' but turn you into sump'm you don't wanna be.

CORA. What is you talkin' 'bout, fool?

JOHNNY. This black bitch is gon' turn you into a real white man, Shanty.

SHANTY. What??

CORA. You kin quit this Nigger today, Honey. We'll manage.

JOHNNY. You wanna be a white man, Shanty?

SHANTY. Knock that stuff off, Johnny! I don't go for it.

JOHNNY. You think if you git with somebody like Cora, it'll make the whole thing complete, huh?

CORA. Hush up, Jay Cee.

JOHNNY. Well, it won't. She'll make you so damn white you won't be able to bang two spoons together.

CORA. I'm warnin' you, Jay Cee.

JOHNNY. An' play the drums? You'll never play no drums.

[CORA rushes at JOHNNY. He catches her arm and throws her to the floor. SHANTY is shocked by JOHNNY's cruelty. He makes a move to JOHNNY.]

SHANTY. Why you—you—you mother fucker!

[JOHNNY stands ready to throw a punch. SHANTY checks himself. Turns away. CORA gets to her feet and goes to him. Puts her arm around him. He shuns her. Exits slowly.]

CORA. Tha's alright, Jay Cee honey. Tha's all right! That day ain't long off, 'fore you gon' git yours. Honey, you gon' git a hurtin' put on you. You gon' git a hurtin' put on you in the place where you do wrong.

JOHNNY. Better wish all that hurtin' on all them Niggers that messed up yo' min'.

[CORA exits as GABE enters.]

GABE. Dam! What was all that smoke about?

JOHNNY. Them two ain't got sense nuff to pour piss out'a a boot if the directions was wrote on the heel.

GABE. You just don't wanna see anybody git any enjoyment out'a life.

JOHNNY. Bastard's movin' in with her. You dig that?

GABE. An' you tried to stop 'em, huh?

[JOHNNY doesn't answer. Takes bottle of champagne and bucket. Sets it on a table.]

Well, I see you're gettin' ready for the big homecomin', huh?

JOHNNY. That's right. An' I don't want you goin' into none'a yo' high'n mighty when Sweets git here. Tell you right now he don't go for none of that giddy-up-yippee-yaye shit!

GABE. Didn't come to stay. Lemme hold some coins! Lan'lord's on my tail.

JOHNNY. Good. [JOHNNY grins. Spreads bills over table. GABE picks them up.]

GABE. You'll git it all back soon's I git me a show.

JOHNNY. You keepin' a record?

[A black man enters.]

On yo' way, wine.

SWEETS. S'matter, Sonny Boy? Don't you know me?

JOHNNY. Sweets? Is it really you?

SWEETS. It's me, all right. [SWEETS coughs. JOHNNY rushes forward. Embraces SWEETS.]

JOHNNY. Lock the doors, Gabe. Don't want no innerrupshuns.

[GABE locks the street doors. JOHNNY and SWEETS box playfully.]

SWEETS. Minute there, was 'bout to go out an' come back in again.

JOHNNY. Reason I didn't rec'nize you at firs' was, well, I always remember you bein' 'bout as sharp as a skeeter's peter in the dead'a winter. Three hundred suits he had, Gabe. Nothin' but the fines' vines. Never seen so many kicks in one closet. Wasn't a cat in Harlem....

[SWEETS coughs violently.]

Dam! What you doin' 'bout that cough, Sweets?

SWEETS. Little souvenir I picked up at the jute mill.

JOHNNY. Jute mill?

SWEETS. Where they make burlap bags at.

JOHNNY. Pretty rough in Fedsville, huh?

[SWEETS coughs again.]

Meet my man, Gabe.

[GABE and SWEETS shake hands.]

GABE. Pleased to meet you, Mister Crane.

SWEETS. Jus' call me Sweets.

JOHNNY [brings bottle and two glasses]. Sweets, some'a Pete Zerroni's bes'.

SWEETS. Zerroni? You don't mean ol' big fat Pete from up there in the Bronx?

JOHNNY. Yeah. He's runnin' everything down here from soup to nuts! But we gon' change all that, ain't we, Sweets? [JOHNNY struggles with cork.]

SWEETS. Sonny Boy, we wasn't much on sendin' kites. Wha's been happenin' since I been in the joint?

JOHNNY. Jews, Irish an' the Ginees still runnin' things as usual.

SWEETS. No. I mean with you, Sonny Boy.

JOHNNY. Like you know I had a tough gaff gittin' my divorce. Whole thing started when I wanted her to do a little merchandizin' for me. Real Magdaleen, she was! One thing led to 'nother. Boom! Back to mama she went. Had a helluva time gittin' her to sign this joint over to me. Went into my act. Fell down on my duece'a benders. Gave her the ol' routine. Like how the worl' been treatin' us black folk an' everything.... [He pops cork. Pours. Holds his glass up. The two men clink their glasses.] Well, look here, Sweets, here's to our li'l piece'a this town.

SWEETS [looks into his glass. As JOHNNY sips]. Speakin'a hussslers, Sonny Boy. [He coughs. GABE goes to bar. Gets large glass and fills it with champagne.] You runnin' any kind'a stable?

JOHNNY. You kiddin', Sweets? [Gives GABE a dirty look.]

SWEETS. Pushin' or bookin'?

JOHNNY. Nay, that ain't my stick.

SWEETS. Sonny Boy, when I was yo' age, I was into some'a ev'thing.

JOHNNY. Wish you wouldn't call me that, Sweets! I ain't that little boy runnin' up an' down Saint Nicklas Avenue for you no more.

SWEETS. Jus' habit, Johnny. But I sort'a was hopin' you was into sump'm on yo' own, like.

JOHNNY. Hell! I been tryin' to stay clean. Waitin' on you, man! Like we planned.

SWEETS. Well, now! Tha's—tha's what I wanna talk to you 'bout, Sonny Boy.

JOHNNY. Yes, sir! You still the boss, Sweets. Didn't think you wanted to git into it jus' yet. Figgered we'd have us a few drinks. Talk 'bout ol' times. . . .

SWEETS. Sonny Boy!

JOHNNY. Sir?

SWEETS. Firs' off! I gotta tell you I'm th'ough. . . .

JOHNNY. Whatchu say?

SWEETS. Wrappin' it all up for good. . . .

JOHNNY. Wrappin' what up?

SWEETS. The rackets.

JOHNNY. You gotta be jokin'.

SWEETS. Never been no more ser'us in all my life. . . .

JOHNNY. Sweets, you jus' tired.

SWEETS. Don't need no res'. . . .

JOHNNY. Git you'self together. . . .

SWEETS. My min's made up.

JOHNNY. Waitin' on you this long, little more ain't gon' kill me.

SWEETS. Look, Sonny Boy, it's like this . . .

JOHNNY. Shut up with that Sonny Boy, shit! [*He tries to control himself.* GABE *laughs.*] Look, man. You ain't let the slammers psyche you out? That ain't like you. That ain't like you, at all. [*He reaches out to touch* SWEETS. SWEETS *jerks away.* JOHNNY *grabs* SWEETS *by the throat violently.*] Mother fucker! I been waitin' on you for ten long-ass years. You ain't gon' cop out on me like this.

GABE [*moves to contain* JOHNNY]. Cut it out, John! Let him alone. Cain't you see the man's sick?

[JOHNNY *hits* GABE *in the stomach.* GABE *doubles over. Goes to the floor.*]

JOHNNY [*to* SWEETS]. What the hell they do to you, huh?

SWEETS. What'd who do to me?

JOHNNY. In the bastille. They did sump'm to you.

SWEETS. Nothin' that wasn't already done to me. [SWEETS *moves to* GABE.] You all right, young fella?

GABE. Yeah—yeah—I—I'm okay.

SWEETS [*takes wallet from* GABE's *back pocket. Puts it into his own pocket*]. Shouldn'ta mixed in. [*He turns back to* JOHNNY.] You got the Charlie fever, Johnny. Tha's what you got. I gave it to you. Took yo' chile's min' an' filled it with the Charlie fever. Givin' you a education or teachin' you to dinner-pail, didn't seem to me to be no way for you to grow up an' be respected like'a man. Way we was raised, husslin' an' usin' yo' biscuit to pull quickies was the only way we could feel like we was men. Couldn't copy Charlie's good points an' live like men. So we copied his bad points. That was the way it was with my daddy an' his daddy before him. We just pissed away our lives tryin' to be like bad Charlie. With all our fine clothes an' big cars. All it did was make us hate him all the more an' ourselves too. Then I tried to go horse-to-horse with 'em up there in the Bronx. An' ended up with a ten. All because'a the Charlie fever. I gave you the Charlie fever, Johnny. An' I'm sorry! Seems to me, the worse sickness'a man kin have is the Charlie fever.

JOHNNY [*glares at* SWEETS]. Git out'a here, Sweets. Goddam you! Git out'a here. 'Fore I kill you.

[SWEETS *coughs and exits to the street.*
JOHNNY *looks after him.*]
They did sump'm to him. White sons'a bitches. They did sump'm to him. Sweets don't give up that easy. Charlie fever. Sheeee!

GABE. Ten years is a long time. An' the man's sick. Anyone kin see that.

JOHNNY. He could be fakin'. He's into sump'm! Don't want me in on it. He used to do that to me all the time. He better be fakin'. [*Brings his arm up to look at his watch.*]

GABE. What? What the hell. . . . [*He searches frantically in his pockets.*] I'll be goddam.

JOHNNY. Hell's matter with you?

GABE. My watch! It's gone.

JOHNNY. Hell with your watch!

GABE. It's gone! An' my wallet! The bread you loaned me! It's gone, too.

[JOHNNY *begins to laugh hysterically.*] What the hell's so goddam funny?

JOHNNY. It's Sweets! The bastard *is* fakin'. He snatched it!

BLACKOUT

ACT II

Scene One

[*Time: Two days later*
Place: The same
Setting: The same
At rise: GABE *sits at table. Whisky
bottle before him.*
*He is obviously drunk. He begins to
sing an old Protestant hymn.*]

GABE.

"Whiter than snow, yes!
Whiter than snow!
Now, wash me, and I shall be
Whiter than snow!"

[*He chants.*]

We moved out of that dirty-black slum!
Away from those dirty-black people!
Who live in those dirty-black hovels,
Amidst all of that garbage and filth!
Away from those dirty-black people,
Who in every way,
Prove daily
They are what they are!
Just dirty-black people!

We moved to a house with a fenced-in
    yard!
To a clean-white neighborhood!
It had clean-white sidewalks
And clean-white sheets
That hang from clean-white clotheslines
    to dry!
They were clean-white people!
Who in every way
Prove daily
They are what they are!
Just clean-white people!

Now those clean-white people thought
    we were
Dirty-black people!
And they treated us like we were
Dirty-black people!
But we stuck it out!
We weathered the storm!
We cleansed and bathed
And tried to be and probably were
Cleaner than most of those clean-white
    people!

[*He sings.*]

"Break down every idol, cast out every
    foe!
Oh, wash me and I shall be whiter than
    snow!"

[*He speaks again.*]

We went to schools that had clean-white
Rooms with clean-white teachers
Who taught us and all of the clean-white
Children how to be clean and white!

[*He laughs.*]

Now, those dirty-black people across
The tracks became angry, jealous and
    mean!
When they saw us running or skipping
    or
Hopping or learning with all of those
Clean-white children!

They would catch us alone
When the clean-white children weren't
    there!
And kick us or slap us and spit
On our clean-white clothes!
Call us dirty-black names
And say that we wanted to be like our
    clean-white
Neighbors!

But in spite of the kicking, the slapping
The spitting, we were exceedingly glad!
For we knew we weren't trying to be
    like
Our clean-white neighbors! Most of all,
We were certain we weren't like those
Dirty-black Niggers,
Who lived in hovels, far away across the
    tracks!

[*He sings.*]

"Whiter than snow! Oh, whiter than
    snow!
Please wash me, and I shall be whiter
    than snow!"

[*He speaks again.*]

So we grew up clean and keen!
And all of our clean-white neighbors
Said we had earned the right to go

Out into the clean-white world
And be accepted as clean-white people!
But we soon learned,
The world was not clean and white!
With all of its powders and soaps!
And we learned too that no matter how
Much the world scrubbed,
The world was getting no cleaner!

Most of all!
We saw that no matter how much or
  how
Hard we scrubbed,
It was only making us blacker!
So back we came to that dirty-black
  slum!
To the hovels, the filth and the garbage!
Came back to those dirty-black people!
Away from those clean-white people!
That clean, white anti-septic world!
That scrubs and scrubs and scrubs!

But those dirty-black people!
Those dirty-black people!
Were still angry, jealous and mean!
They kicked us and slapped us and spit
  again
On our clothes!
Denied us!
Disowned us
And cast us out!
And we still were exceedingly glad!

For at last they knew
We were not like our clean-white neigh-
  bors!
Most of all! We were safe!
Assured at last!
We could never more be
Like those dirty-black Niggers!
Those filthy, dirty-black Niggers!
Who live far away!
Far away, in hovels across the tracks!

[He bursts into song.]

"Whiter than snow! Yes! Whiter than
  snow!
Oh, wash me and I shall be whiter than
  snow!"

[GABE is on his knees. Hands stretched
  up to heaven. Lights slowly dim out
  on him, and come up on bar. SHANTY
  is behind the bar. MIKE MAFFUCCI
  stands at center, throwing darts into
  a dartboard. SWEETS CRANE enters.]

SHANTY. Hit the wind, Mac. This ain't
the place.

SWEETS. Johnny here?

SHANTY. What you want with Johnny?

SWEETS. I'm a frien'a his.

SHANTY. Yeah? Well, he ain't here.

SWEETS. Where's me a broom an' a
drop pan?

SHANTY. What for?

SWEETS. Need me a bucket an' some
rags too.

SHANTY. What do you want all that
shit for?

SWEETS. The floor, they don't look too
good an' the windas, it could stan'. . . .

SHANTY. Eighty-six, ol' timer! We ain't
hirin'.

SWEETS. Ain't askin' f'no pay.

SHANTY. What'a ya? Some kind'a nut?
C'mon! Out you go. Eighty-six.

SWEETS. Think you better wait till
Johnny gets here. Let him put me out.
[SWEETS pushes SHANTY roughly aside
and moves to kitchen.] Think I'll fin'
what I need back here.

SHANTY [looks incredulous. Scratches
his head and follows SWEETS to kitchen.
JOHNNY enters. SHANTY rushes in from
kitchen.] Hey, Johnny! Some ol' timer
just came in an'. . . .

MAFFUCCI. How you doin', Johnny
Cake?

JOHNNY [stops short]. Only one cat
usta call me that.

MAFFUCCI. Gettin' warm, Johnny
Cake.

JOHNNY [moves behind bar]. Little
snotty-nose wop kid, name Mike Maffucci.

MAFFUCCI. On the nose. [Sends a dart
in JOHNNY's direction. JOHNNY ducks.
The dart buries into the wood of the
back bar. Both men laugh. They shake
hands.] Long time no see, eh, Johnny
Cake?

JOHNNY. What you drinkin'?

MAFFUCCI. Little dago red. Gotta take
it easy on my stomach with the hard
stuff.

[JOHNNY snaps his fingers. SHANTY
  brings bottle.]

SHANTY. Dig, Johnny! Some ol'
goat. . . .

JOHNNY. Cool it, Shanty. Can't you
see I'm busy? How's your ol' man,
Footch?

MAFFUCCI [*makes the sign of the cross*]. My ol' man chalked out, Johnny. Heart attack. Right after you went to the nursery. You ain't still sore 'bout what happened, are you, Johnny Cake?

JOHNNY. Bygones is bygones, Footch!

MAFFUCCI. Glad'a hear ya say that, Johnny. Didn't know what happened to you after that. When they tole me you was runnin' this joint, had'a come over an' see ya.

[*He looks around. SWEETS enters with broom and rags. Proceeds to sweep the floor. JOHNNY registers surprise and anger. SHANTY starts to say something but JOHNNY puts his finger to his lips.*]

How ya doin' with the place, Johnny?

JOHNNY. Stabbin' horses to steal blankets. Jay Cee ag'inst the worl'.

MAFFUCCI. Joe Carneri used to say that. You ain't never forgot that huh, Johnny?

[*JOHNNY glances angrily at SWEETS.*] Remember the first time they busted him? There was this pitchure on the front page. Joe's standin' on the courthouse steps. Cops an' reporters all aroun'. Joe's yellin' "Jay Cee ag'inst the worl'! Jay Cee ag'inst the worl'!"

JOHNNY. He sho' was your hero all right.

MAFFUCCI. Too bad he had'a go an' git hit like that. Sittin' in a barber chair!

JOHNNY. Better'n the electric chair.

[*SWEETS is now dusting the chairs.*]

MAFFUCCI. You know, Johnny Cake, that was a groovy idea for a kid! Coppin' all that scrapiron from ol' Julio an' then sellin' it back to him. [*He breaks up laughing.*]

JOHNNY. Wasn't so pretty when I tried to tell the fuzz you was in on it with me.

MAFFUCCI. Awful sorry 'bout that, Johnny Cake.

[*MAFFUCCI puts his hand on JOHNNY's shoulder. JOHNNY knocks his hand off. MAFFUCCI comes down on JOHNNY's shoulder with a karate chop. JOHNNY punches MAFFUCCI in the stomach and shoves him away. Comes toward MAFFUCCI menacingly. SWEETS keeps sweeping.*]

JOHNNY. One thing I gotta give you Ginees credit for. Sho' know how to stick together when you wanna.

MAFFUCCI [*backs away*]. He was my father Johnny. Any father would'a done the same thing. If he had the connections.

JOHNNY. Who tole you I was runnin' this joint, Footch?

MAFFUCCI. To give you the works, Johnny, I'm one'a Pete Zerroni's local boys now.

[*SWEETS dusts near MAFFUCCI.*]

JOHNNY. No jive! Battin' in the big leagues, ain't you? Your ol' man was aroun', bet he'd be pretty proud'a you.

MAFFUCCI. Would you believe, my ol' man had ideas 'bout me bein' a lawyer or a doctor?

JOHNNY. What you doin' for Pete?

MAFFUCCI. Sort'a community relations like, Johnny.

JOHNNY [*laughs*]. I'm one'a Pete's customers! What kind'a community relashuns you got for me?

MAFFUCCI. Glad you opened that, Johnny Cake. Pete says you got him a little concerned.

JOHNNY. What is he, crazy? Ain't he got more 'portant things on his min'?

MAFFUCCI. Way we got it, first thing ol' Sweets Crane did when he got out was come see you.

JOHNNY. So what? Sweets was like'a father to me.

MAFFUCCI. So I hear. But before they shut the gate on him, he let some things drop. Like, he made a few threats. What I hear 'bout him, might be crazy enough to give 'em a try.

[*JOHNNY laughs.*]

What, am I throwin' zingers or sump'm? What's the joke?

JOHNNY. Sweets came 'roun' to tell me he's all caught up.

MAFFUCCI. Wouldn't promote me, would you, Johnny Cake? For ol' time's sake, let's not you an' me go horse-to-horse 'bout nothin'.

JOHNNY. On the up an' up, Footch. Sweets has wrapped it all up for good. Matter'a fack, right now he's doin' odd gigs an' singin' the straight an' narrow.

MAFFUCCI. Wanna believe you, Johnny. But just in case you an' this Sweets are thinkin' 'bout makin' a little noise, Pete wants me to give you the six-to-five!

[*SWEETS bumps into MAFFUCCI, spilling the wine down the front of MAF-FUCCI's suit.*]

Hey! Watch it there, pops!

SWEETS. Awful sorry 'bout that, mister! [*Attempts to wipe* MAFFUCCI's *suit with the rag.* MAFFUCCI *pushes him aside.*]

MAFFUCCI. That's okay, pops! [SWEETS *continues to wipe* MAFFUCCI's *vest.*] Okay, okay, I said! [SWEETS *stops, and continues with his work.*] Well, Johnny Cake. Like to stay an' rap with ya a little bit but you know how it is. Community relations.

JOHNNY. Sho' preshiate you lookin' out for me, Footch!

MAFFUCCI. Think nothin' of it, Johnny Cake. It's Pete. He don't like jigs. Says the minute they git a little somethin', they start actin' cute. You an' me, we was like brothers. Way I see it, was like you took a dive for me once. Figger I owe ya.

JOHNNY. You don't owe me a dam thing, Footch.

MAFFUCCI [*heads for the street doors. Turns back*]. You know, Johnny Cake, some reason I never been able to git you off my mind. After all these years. I think if you'da been a wop, you'da been a big man in the rackets.

[*Exits.* SWEETS *holds watch to ear.*]

JOHNNY. All right now, Sweets. Goddammit, wha's this game you playin'?

SHANTY. Sweets??? That's Sweets Crane?

JOHNNY. Shut up, Shanty. [*Snatches the rag out of* SWEETS' *hand. Gets broom. Gives both to* SHANTY.] Take this crap back to the kitchen. [SHANTY *takes them to kitchen.*] Man, you either gotta be stir-buggy or you puttin' on one helluva ack.

SWEETS [*checks the watch*]. Jus' tryin' to be helpful, Sonny Boy.

JOHNNY. Don't you be kickin' no more farts at me, man. Wha's with this pil'fin stuff off'a people an' makin' like'a dam lackey? You mus' be plumb kinky.

SWEETS. Cain't see no point in watchin' George Raff on tee vee ev'a night. All my life I been into things. Always active.

JOHNNY. This what you call bein' active? An' look at you! Look like you jus' come off the Bow'ry! Ain't they no pride lef' in you?

SWEETS. Pride? Sheee. Pride, Sonny Boy, is sump'm I ain't got no mo' use for.

JOHNNY. For the las' time, ol' man. You better tell me wha's happenin' with you. Don't you make me have to kill you.

SWEETS [*produces an envelope*]. I'm as good as dead right now! [*He hands* JOHNNY *the envelope.*]

JOHNNY. What the hell is it?

SWEETS. Guess you could call it my will.

JOHNNY [*turns it over*]. Yo' will??

SWEETS. Open it up.

JOHNNY. Shanty!

SHANTY [*enters*]. How ya doin', Sweets?

JOHNNY. Check this out, Shanty. I don't read this jive so good.

SHANTY [*reads will*]. It's legal stuff. Says here you're gonna inherit interest in barbershops, meat markets, stores an' a whole lotta Harlem real estate. Dam!

JOHNNY [*snatches the papers out of* SHANTY's *hands*]. You gotta be jokin'.

SWEETS. I'm leavin' it all to you, Sonny Boy. My lawyers will take care ev'thing.

JOHNNY. How come you ain't tole me nothin' 'bout this before?

SWEETS. Couldn't take no chance it gittin' out. Might'a strung me out on a tax rap too.

JOHNNY. You lookin' to take some kind'a back gate commute? Suicide?

SWEETS [*coughs*]. Doctors ain't gimme but six months to ride. Didn't wanna lay it on you till they made sho'.

JOHNNY. Six months, huh?

SWEETS. Mo' or less.

JOHNNY. Goddamit, Sweets. What the hell kin I say? I sho' been a real bastard. Guess it don't help none for me to say I'm sorry.

SWEETS. Might he'p some if you was to turn all this into sump'm worth while an' good. Maybe the Lawd will f'give me f'the way I got it. [*Bursts into laughter and coughs.*]

JOHNNY. Git off it, Sweets. Jus' 'cause you s'pose to chalk out on us don't mean you gotta go an' 'brace relijun.

SWEETS. Figure it won't hurt none if I do.

JOHNNY. Shit. That good Lawd you talkin' 'bout is jus' as white as that judge who sent yo' black ass to Fedsville.

SWEETS. How you know? You ever seen him? When I was down there in that prison, I reads a lot. Mos'ly the

Bible. Bible tells me, the Lawd was hard to look upon. Fack is, he was so hard to look upon that nobody eva looked at him an' lived. Well, I got to figgerin' on that. An' reasons that was so, 'cause he was so black. [*Goes into loud laughter and coughs again.*] Lawd knows! White's easy nuff to look at! [JOHNNY *throws the will on the floor.* SWEETS *goes to his knees and clutches the will.*] What you doin', Sonny Boy? My life is in them papers! [*Hits* JOHNNY *with hat.* JOHNNY *reaches under the bar and comes up with a revolver. Levels it at* SWEETS.]

JOHNNY. See this, Sweets? My firs' an' only pistol. You gave it to me long time ago when I was a lookout for you when you was pullin' them owl jobs in Queens. I worshipped the groun' you walked on. I thought the sun rose an' set in yo' ass. You showed me how to make thirteen straight passes without givin' up the dice. Stood behin' me an' nudged me when to play my ace. Hipped me how to make a gapers cut. How to handle myself in a pill joint. Taught me to trust no woman over six or under sixty. Turned me on to the best horse players an' number runners. Showed me how to keep my ass-pocket full'a coins without goin' to jail. Said the wors' crime I ever committed was comin' out'a my mama screamin' black. Tole me all about white folks an' what to expect from the best of 'em. You said as long as there was a single white man on this earth, the black man only had one free choice. That was the way he died. When you went to jail for shootin' Cholly you said, "Sonny Boy, git us a plan." Well, I got us a plan. Now, you come back here nutty an' half dead, dancin' all over me about me goin' through a change'a life. An' how you want me to help you git ready to meet yo' Lawd. Well, git ready, mother fucker. Tha's exactly what I'm gon' do. Help you to meet him. [JOHNNY *pulls back the hammer of the gun.* SWEETS *coughs and looks at the barrel of the gun.*]

SWEETS. You ain't gon' shoot me, Johnny. You cain't shoot me. They's a whole lotta you I ain't even touched.

[SWEETS *exits.*]

BLACKOUT

Scene Two

[*Time: Two weeks later*
Place: The same
Setting: The same
At rise: GABE *sits at a table. Glass of red wine before him, strumming a guitar.* MELVIN *stands next to him thumbing through a playscript.* SHANTY *is behind the bar as usual.*]

MELVIN. "The Tooth of a Red Tiger"? What part will you play, Gabe?

GABE. What you tryin' to do, Mel? Jinx me? I ain't got the part yet.

MELVIN. They gave you this script, didn't they?

GABE. The part calls for a guitar player. Cain't you hear these clinkers? [MELVIN *puts script on table.*] How was your recital?

MELVIN. Ugh! Don't remind me, Gabe. I have this solo in "variations and diversions." I have to do three tour jêtés? Well, ol' Mel fell! Would you believe it? I stumbled and fell! Victor, my teacher, he was there shaking! He was actually shaking.

GABE. What the hell, Mel. Always another recital.

MELVIN. I suppose you could look at it that way! Anyway, I was simply heartbroken. Gabe, do you like Carl Sandburg?

GABE. Ain't exactly in love with him.

MELVIN. I was thinking, since you do write poetry, maybe you'd like to go with me to hear some of his works. Peter Demeter is reading tomorrow night. . . .

GABE. Got somethin' I gotta do.

MELVIN. Well, maybe you'd like to hear some chamber music at the Brooklyn Academy over the weekend.

GABE. Don't dig chamber music, Mel.

MELVIN. I believe an artist should learn all he can about the other forms too.

[*Slaps* GABE *on his back and exits to kitchen.*]

DEE [*enters and goes to the bar*]. Squeeze the bar rag out, Shanty. [*She glances at* GABE.] Full of little surprises, aren't you?

GABE. Just fakin'.

[SHANTY *pours her drink. She takes*

bottle and glass to a table. Suddenly she catches GABE *staring at her.*]

DEE. What's with the fish eyes? I gotta new wrinkle or sump'm?

GABE. Sorry! Just thinkin'!

DEE [*downs drink*]. You think too much! Give it a rest!

GABE. Tell me somethin', Dee . . .

DEE. What'a ya? Writin' a book or sump'm?

GABE. How'd you meet up with John in the first place?

DEE [*doesn't answer. Pours another drink. Presently gets to her feet. Goes to window. Peers out*]. Got Evie to thank for that. She used to come in here a lot when the joint was really jumpin'. She'll never admit it but I think she had it for Johnny. She's never been much of a drinker but one night she got too looped to drive. Johnny brought her home. When they came in, I was in the process of having my face lifted by a boy friend. Johnny pulled him off.

GABE. Stop me if I'm bein' a little too personal.

DEE. Oh, you be as personal as you like, Gabe.

GABE. How do chicks like you an' Evie . . .

DEE. Get into the life? Is that what you're askin'? For me it was easy! Got a job as a sales girl! Rich Johns would come in propositioning the girls! One day I took one up on it, and here I am.

GABE. Was it for the money?

DEE. What cheap paperbacks you been readin', Gabe?

GABE. I get it! You hate your father.

DEE. That poor miserable bastard? That bum? He ain't worth hating.

GABE. You love John?

DEE. Johnny? Johnny's not the kind of man you love. I think I pity Johnny. Don't get me wrong. I don't mean the kind of pity you'd give to my father or some bum on the street. Somebody blindfolded him. Turned him around. Somewhere inside Johnny's got something. It just come out crooked! Comes out the wrong way. [*She takes drink and becomes theatrical.*] In a way, Johnny reminds me of a classmate of mine in high school.

GABE. Boyhood sweetheart, huh?

DEE. Got me pregnant. Nice decent boy. Only, he was black. Went to my folks. Said, "I'll marry her." The crazy bastard. They made his life miserable. I don't have to tell you.

GABE. Did you love this boy?

DEE. You mean, why didn't we run away together? We were too young and stupid.

GABE. And the baby?

DEE. Oh, they got rid of it for me. [*She almost appears to be improvising.*] Word got out somehow. My mother fled to Puerto Rico for a well needed vacation. I stayed around the house. [*She lapses into theatrical Southern dialect à la Tennessee Williams.*] For weeks I just read, listened to the radio or watched television. One night late my father came in dead drunk. Staggered into my room and got into bed with me. Week later, I came to New York. [*She giggles.*] Funny thing. When I first got into the life, I was always thinkin' about my father. He was always comin' into my mind. Like it was him I was screwin' over and over again. Like I was takin' him away from my mother and punishin' him for lettin' her rule his life.

GABE. You know? Just the way you're standin' there, you remind me of somebody?

DEE. Dame May Whitty?

GABE. Maxine.

DEE. Who?

GABE. Maxine.

DEE. Who's Maxine?

GABE. Probably every woman I've ever known.

DEE. I don't usually think of you with a woman.

GABE. Come on, Dee!

DEE. I didn't mean it like that, Gabe. I always think of you—well, sort'a like the intellectual type! For some reason people kind'a think intellectual types don't even use the toilet! So who's Maxine?

GABE. My mother.

DEE. Talking to you is like eatin' cotton candy.

GABE. She was the little girl who sat across from me.

DEE. In grade school?

GABE. I stole a quarter from her. It was in her inkwell. Teacher lined us up. Searched us. The quarter rolled out of the pocket of my hightop boots. I kin still hear them kids yellin' "Our theeefer!"

DEE. Pretty humiliatin', huh?

GABE. We sang duets together in the high school choir. Neck an' rub stomachs in dark alleys an' doorways. They kicked her out'a school when she got pregnant. Sent her away. They was sure I did it. Her mama was wild an' crazy. Turned tricks for a cat who owned a Cadillac. Didn't want me messin' aroun' with Maxine. Said I was a dirty Nigger an' jus' wanted Maxine's ass. When Maxine didn't make her period, her mama got drunk an' come lookin' for me with a razor. I hid out for a couple days. Heard later she slashed all the upholsterin' in her pimp's Cadillac. Ha! She was smart, Maxine was. An' Jewish too. Taught me social consciousness. Said I was a good lover. Said white boys got their virility in how much money they made an' the kind'a car they drove. Said I related better 'cause I was black an' had nothin' to offer but myself. So I quit my job. Used to hide in the closet when her folks came in from Connecticut. Listened to 'em degradin' her for livin' with an' supportin' a Nigger. Maxine got herself an Afro hair-do an' joined the Black Nationalists when I couldn't afford to get her hair straightened at Rose Meta's! Didn't really wanna marry me. Jus' wanted my baby so she could go on welfare. She is out there somewhere. Maxine is. She's out there, waitin' on me to come back to her, Maxine is.

DEE [laughs]. Gabe? Gabe, are you sure you're all right? [He grins.] You really loved Maxine, didn't you? [She puts her arms around his neck.]

GABE. I sure wanted to . . .

JOHNNY [enters]. What the hell's goin' on here?

GABE. You jealous?

JOHNNY. Depen's on yo' intenshuns.

[GABE puts guitar into case. Picks up script. Prepares to leave.]

JOHNNY. What, you done gone an' got yo'self a job an' ain't tole nobody?

GABE. It's only an audition.

DEE. Good luck, Gabe.

JOHNNY. Yeah. I'm lookin' forward to gettin' a few payments back on all them loans.

[GABE gives a razz-berry and exits.] You know, Dee? I been thinking. Maybe we ought'a take that trip after all.

DEE. Well now, you don't say? Sweets Crane wouldn't have anything to do with this sudden change of mind, would he? [She starts to pour another drink.]

JOHNNY [snatches bottle out of her hands]. Take it easy on that stuff, girl! Still wanna go, don't you?

DEE. Right now I got somethin' more important on my mind.

JOHNNY. Dump it on me.

DEE. I want out of the life, Johnny.

JOHNNY. Dam! You are stoned, ain't you?

DEE. I mean it, Johnny.

JOHNNY. Thought you an' me had a understandin'.

DEE. There's a hell of a lot more room for a better one.

JOHNNY. Like what, for instance?

DEE. I need some permanence.

JOHNNY. You mean git married?

DEE. Maybe.

JOHNNY. Thought you was down on all that housewife jazz.

DEE. I don't take tee vee commercials very seriously if that's what you mean.

JOHNNY. I gotta business here! Tough nuff time keepin' it perm'nant! Wasn't for the coins you bring in, I'd go under 'fore the week was out.

DEE. Let's build it back up, Johnny. Together. Together, Johnny.

JOHNNY. What the hell you know 'bout this business?

DEE. Teach me, Johnny! You could teach me.

JOHNNY. No good. Ain't no woman'a mine gon' be workin'. She b'long at home. [She laughs.] Look'a here, go on home. Git yo'self together. We'll talk 'bout it later.

DEE. I'll tie a string around my finger. [She gathers her things. Weaves to the street door.]

JOHNNY. Hey, girl! You still ain't said where you wanna go.

DEE [whirls]. I don't know. I hear the north pole's pretty swingin' these days.

JOHNNY. Keep it up. I'll break yo' damn chops yet.

DEE. Where thou goest, I will follow, Johnny baby.

JOHNNY. Thinkin' 'bout makin' the Bim'ni scene. Won't have to worry 'bout crackers doin' the bird with the long red neck. Split this weekend. You make res'vashuns.

DEE [*blows him a kiss. Bows theatrically*]. Yah suh, Boss! [*She exits.*]

JOHNNY. Bitches. Cain't please none of 'em.

Scene Three

[*Time: A day later*
Place: The same
Setting: The same
At rise: MELVIN *is arranging chairs and straightening tablecloths.* GABE *enters.*]

MELVIN. What happened, Gabe? Did you get the part?

GABE. Nah! Wasn't the right type after all.

MELVIN. What type did they want?

GABE. Whatever it was I wasn't it.

JOHNNY [*enters from kitchen. He is munching a sandwich.*] Nigra type.

MELVIN. What type is that?

JOHNNY. Whatever it is, tha's what he ain't.

MELVIN. Doesn't talent have anything to do with it?

JOHNNY. Prop'ganda, Mel! When whitey pick one'a y'all you gotta either be a clown, a freak or a Nigra type.

GABE. They do the same thing among themselves too.

JOHNNY. 'Mongst themselves, they ain't so damn choosey.

GABE. Should'a seen the cat they did pick. Hell, I'm as black as he is.

JOHNNY. Gabe, ain't they no mirrors in yo' house?

GABE. I mean black in here!

MELVIN. You people are more preoccupied with color than white people are.

JOHNNY. They won't let us be porcupined with nothin' else.

GABE. Don't make no difference what color I am. I'm still black.

JOHNNY. Yeah! But you ain't gon' git no chance to prove it. Not on no stage, you ain't. You remin' whitey'a too many things he don't wanna take'a look at. Figgers he's got nuff problems dealin' with Niggers who jus' look black, like me.

GABE. Aw, shut the fuck up, John.

JOHNNY. Who you talkin' to?

GABE. You, you bastard. I'm tellin' you to shut the fuck up. Jus' cool it with yo' shit.

JOHNNY. Jus' tryin' to tell you like it is, Gabe! You jus' don't b'lieve a hard head makes a sof' ass!

MELVIN [*pats* GABE *on the back*]. Like you told me, Gabe. Always another recital.

[MELVIN *exits to kitchen.* JOHNNY *tosses* GABE *some bills.*]

GABE. No more handouts, baby.

JOHNNY. This ain't no handout! Want you to do me a favor.

GABE. Yeah?

JOHNNY. Me an' Dee goin' on a little vacation. Want you to help Shanty an' Mel with the store while we gone.

GABE. When you leavin'?

JOHNNY. End'a the week. Makin' it to Bim'ni.

[CORA *and* SHANTY *enter. Carry black drum cases.*]

CORA. Give us a han' here, Gabe? They's more out there in the cab.

[GABE *exits to the street.*]

JOHNNY. What you bringin' this junk in here for?

CORA. We bringin' this junk in here as you call it on a purpose.

JOHNNY. Be damned if tha's so. Git out'a here, an' Shanty, let's git to work.

[GABE *returns with another case.*]

CORA. Look'a here, Jay Cee. Me an' Shangy swore when we got these here drums, we was gon' bring 'em in here for you to look at an' lissen to with yo' own eyes an' ears.

JOHNNY. All of a sudden I done gone deaf an' blin'. Now, git this hazarae out'a here.

CORA. Ain't gon' do ner such thing. Not till me an' Shangy has got som'a what we's set out to do.

GABE. Sure got a pretty good start.

CORA. Shangy! What is you doin' with the broom?

[JOHNNY *reaches for one of the drum cases.*]

Take yo' nasty, stinkin', filthy black han's off them drums!

[JOHNNY *recoils.*]

MELVIN [*comes out of the kitchen*]. What on earth is happening?

CORA. It ain't happenin' yet.

MELVIN. Well, I just never would have believed it. Isn't it wonderful?

CORA. 'Fore Shangy gits on these drums, they's sump'm you oughta know, Jay Cee.

JOHNNY. You runnin' the show.

CORA. Shangy is quittin' you today. Right now.

JOHNNY. Why the hell didn't you say that in the first place?

CORA. 'Cause you was so busy gittin' these drums out'a here. Tha's why.

MELVIN. You're really going to play for us, Shanty?

CORA. Tha's his intenchun, thank you. Shangy! Will you come on over here? Gabe don't know nothin' 'bout what he's doin'.

[SHANTY *hands* JOHNNY *the broom. Approaches the drums reluctantly.*]

JOHNNY. Some reason, Shangy, you don't look so happy. Now I want you to jump up there an' give ol' Jay Cee a little wham-bam-thank-ya-ma'm. Piece'a the funky nitty-gritty. Like the time they said you played like'a spade. Guess I kin risk gettin' a summons on that.

CORA. Ne' min', Jay Cee. Go 'head, honey! Git yo'se'f together. Take all the time you need.

GABE. Wail, baby.

[SHANTY *sits on the stool. Fumbles. Accidentally puts foot on pedal. Strikes pose. Taps cymbals. Moves to snares. Mixes. Pumps. Works. Gets loud.* CORA *fidgets. Anxious.* SHANTY *fakes. Can't cover up. Becomes frustrated. Louder. Stands. Begins to beat wildly. Moves around the drums banging for all he's worth.* CORA *is ashamed.* GABE *frowns.* CORA *grabs* SHANTY's *arm. He pushes her away. Becomes a windmill.*]

CORA. Stop it, Shangy! Stop it, I said!

[SHANTY *beats as if possessed.* CORA *is helpless.* JOHNNY *calmly reaches behind the bar. Gets pitcher of water. Pours it over* SHANTY's *head.*]

SHANTY. Ya-hoooo! [*Leaps into the air.*] I had it! I was on it! I was into it, babee! [*He moves around doing the pimp walk.*] Ol' Red Taylor said I had the thing. Said, "Shanty man! You got the thing!" [*Goes to* MEL.] Gimme some skin, mother fucker. [MEL *gives him some skin. Goes to* GABE.] Gimme some skin. [GABE *doesn't put his hand out.*] Ah, fuck you, man. Didn't I hip you to

my happenin's, Johnny? Didn't I show you where it's at?

JOHNNY. You burned, baby, you burned. [SHANTY *gives* JOHNNY *some skin.*]

CORA. Shangy! I—think you better start packin' up now.

SHANTY. Git away from me, you funky black bitch.

CORA. Shangy!

SHANTY. Just stay away from me—you evil piece'a chunky.

CORA. You ain't got no call to say nothin' like that to me.

SHANTY. Oh, no? You ain't jive timin' me, you just like Gloria.

CORA. What you sayin', Shangy?

SHANTY. You don't want me to play no drums.

CORA. You wrong, Shangy.

SHANTY. Thought you'd make a fool out'a me, did you? Gittin' me to bring these drums in here. You thought I'd mess it up. Well, I showed you where it was at. I showed all'a you.

CORA. Shangy, you crazy! You the one suggestid that!

SHANTY. Bitch, call the man. Have him come git these drums.

CORA. Come git the drums? Why, Shangy? Why?

SHANTY. I don't need you to help me get my drums. I get my own drums. Dig it?

CORA. This chile done clean los' his min'.

SHANTY. You an' me are through! Dig it? We are through. We've had it. Splitsville. [CORA *is numb.*] Now you believe me huh, Johnny? A bucket'a cold water an' throw it on me, huh?

JOHNNY. To git you to quit. Come on, baby. Let's git some dry clothes on you. [JOHNNY *leads* SHANTY *to the kitchen.*]

SHANTY. A bucket'a cold water like the night we played "Saints" . . .

[JOHNNY *and* SHANTY *exit to kitchen. For a moment* CORA *looks up at the clock.*]

CORA. What time is it, Gabe?

GABE. My watch was stolen . . .

CORA [*points to clock above cash register*]. What time do that clock say?

GABE. Quarter after three . . .

CORA. Know sump'm, Gabe? I ain't never learned how to tell time. Thirty years ol' an' I don't even know the time'a day. But when I gits up in the mornin', tha's the very firs' thing I'm gon' do. I'm gonna learn how to tell me some time.

[*She exits.*]

JOHNNY [*enters from kitchen*]. Go back there an' help Shanty, Mel! He don't feel so good. [MELVIN *goes to kitchen.*] Help me tear down this thing, Gabe. [JOHNNY *begins to dismantle drums.*]

GABE. Do it your damned-self. I ain't feelin' so hot either.

[*Exits hurriedly.*]

JOHNNY. Now, what in hell's matter with you? [*Busies himself with the drums.* MARY LOU BOLTON *enters.*]

MARY LOU. Hello . . .

JOHNNY [*his attention is still with the drums*]. Sump'm I kin do for you?

MARY LOU [*moves to table. Sits*]. I'd like a daiquiri, please.

JOHNNY [*looks up*]. Tha's one drink I ain't never been able to make right.

MARY LOU. Simple! Just go easy with the sugar.

JOHNNY [*goes behind bar. Begins to mix drink. Dumps in a lot of sugar*]. Never 'spected to see you back here ag'in.

MARY LOU. Let's just say, I don't scare so easy. By the way, what were you trying to prove anyway?

JOHNNY [*comes to her table and sets the drink before her*]. I was waitin' for you to ask sump'm like that.

MARY LOU. Really?

JOHNNY. You sho' didn't come back here for no drink.

MARY LOU. Pretty conceited, aren't you?

JOHNNY. Jus' hipt to yo' kin', tha's all.

MARY LOU. "My kind," huh?

JOHNNY. You don't like to be kept in the dark 'bout nothin'.

MARY LOU. That's the difference between man and beast.

JOHNNY. I kin see you ain't learned a damned thing in that college, neither.

MAFFUCCI [*enters with truck driver who carries case of whisky to kitchen*]. How you doin', Johnny Cake?

JOHNNY. Okay, Gumba. What'd Pete do? Demote you? Got you ridin' the truck.

MAFFUCCI. New kind'a community relations, Johnny Cake. Ride aroun' with the boys, see if the customers are happy. You happy, Johnny Cake?

[TRUCK DRIVER *comes out of kitchen, exits.*]

JOHNNY. Dee-leer-iuss.

MAFFUCCI [*spies* MARY LOU]. Good, good. Makes me happy too. [*He moves to* MARY LOU.] Say! Ain't you Judge Bolton's kid?

MARY LOU. Why, yes. Yes I am.

MAFFUCCI [*takes her in his arms. Handles her. She resists, to no avail*]. Never forget a face. Turned out to be a real nice tomata, huh? Don't mind me, kid. [*He releases her.*] Next time you see your ol' man, tell him Mike Maffucci says "Hello!" [*He pats her on the behind.*] See you aroun', Johnny Cake! [*Looks at drums. Taps them.*] Didn't know you was rhythmical.

JOHNNY [JOHNNY *reacts playfully by toying with the drum sticks*]. Chow, Footch. [MAFFUCCI *exits.*] Okay. How does he know yo' ol' man?

MARY LOU [*visibly shaken*]. They were clients of his.

JOHNNY. They? They who? You mean Footch?

MARY LOU [*nods*]. Something about bribing a city official. And someone was murdered.

JOHNNY. Mary. Does the name Pete Zerroni ring a bell?

MARY LOU. Yes! He was one of the defendants. My father won the case.

JOHNNY. I don't care what nobody say. Your father was a damn good lawyer.

MARY LOU. What's your interest? You know this Pete Zerroni?

JOHNNY. Not personal.

MARY LOU. He's not a very good person to know.

JOHNNY. With Pete, sometimes you ain't got no choice. [*She prepares to leave.*] Here! Lemme freshen up yo' drink.

MARY LOU. No thanks. I'm getting— I'm getting a headache. [*She moves to the street doors.*] Goodbye, mister . . .

JOHNNY. Johnny. Johnny Williams.

MARY LOU. Goodbye, Johnny. . . .

[*She exits, leaving her purse.*]

JOHNNY [*picks her purse up. Thinks for a moment. Goes to phone, dials.*] Hey, Dee? Cancel them reservashuns. Sump'm important jus' came up. Won't be able

to after all. Now don't hand me no crap.
Just cancel.

BLACKOUT

ACT THREE

Scene One

[Time: Two weeks later
Place: The same
Setting: The same
At rise: Table at center has a folded
newspaper leaning against a large Molotov
cocktail. Its headline reads: "Negroes
Riot!" A banner resembling the American flag dangles from a flagstand. Next to
the Molotov cocktail is a plate, on which
rests a large black automatic pistol. Beside the plate are a knife and fork. A toilet
is heard flushing. GABE comes on stage
zipping his pants. His attitude is ceremonial.]

GABE.

"They's mo' to bein' black than meets
    the
    Eye!
Bein' black, is like the way ya walk an'
    Talk!
It's a way'a lookin' at life!
Bein' black, is like sayin', "Wha's hap-
    penin',
    Babeee!"
An' bein' understood!
Bein' black has a way'a makin' ya call
    some-
Body a mu-tha-fuc-kah, an' really meanin'
    it!
An' namin' eva'body broh-thah, even if
    you don't!
Bein' black, is eatin' chit'lins an' wah-
    tah-
Melon, an' to hell with anybody, if they
    don't
Like it!
Bein' black has a way'a makin' ya wear
    bright
Colors an' knowin' what a fine hat or a
    good
Pair'a shoes look like an' then—an'
    then—

It has a way'a makin' ya finger pop! In-
    vent a
New dance! Sing the blues! Drink good
    Scotch!
Smoke a big seegar while pushin' a black
    Cadil-
lac with white sidewall tires! It's conkin'
    yo'
Head! Wearin' a black rag to keep the
    wave!
Carryin' a razor! Smokin' boo an' lis-
    tenin' to
Gut-bucket jazz!
Yes! They's mo' to bein' black than
    meets the eye!
Bein' black is gittin' down loud an'
    wrong! Uh-huh!
It's makin' love without no hangups!
    Uh-huh! Or
Gittin' sanctified an' holy an' grabbin' a
    han'ful'a
The sistah nex' to ya when she starts
    speakin' in
Tongues!
Bein' black is havin' yo' palm read!
    Hittin' the
Numbers! Workin' long an' hard an'
    gittin' the
Short end'a the stick an' no glory! It's
Knowin' they ain't no dif'rence 'tween
White trash an' white quality! Uh-huh!
Bein' black is huggin' a fat mama an'
    hav-
in' her smell like ham-fat, hot biscuits
An' black-eyed peas!
Yes! They's mo' to bein' black than
    meets
The eye!
Bein' black has a way'a makin' ya mad
    mos'
Of the time, hurt all the time an' havin'
So many hangups, the problem'a soo-side
Don't even enter yo' min'! It's buyin'
What you don't want, beggin' what
    you don't
Need! An' stealin' what is yo's by rights!
Yes! They's mo' to bein' black than
    meets the
Eye!
It's all the stuff that nobody wants but
Cain't live without!
It's the body that keeps us standin'! The
Soul that keeps us goin'! An' the spirit
That'll take us thooo!
Yes! They's mo' to bein' black than
    meets
The eye!"

[GABE *sits at table. Cuts into gun with knife and fork. Finally picks gun up. Bites into it. Chews and swallows. Takes drink from Molotov cocktail. Wipes mouth.*]

Bru-thas an' sistahs! Will ya jine me!

[*Blackout on* GABE. *Lights come up on* DEE *and* SHANTY. *She sits at table, bottle of whisky in front of her.* SHANTY *sits on stool reading copy of* Downbeat.]

DEE. Ain't like him to stay away from the joint like this. Can't reach him at his apartment either.

SHANTY. He don't come in but about once a day. Just to check things out—

DEE. It's a woman he's with, isn't it?

SHANTY. Huh?

DEE. Hello?

SHANTY. What you say? Eh, *que pasa?*

DEE. He's with a woman—it's a woman he's with . . .

SHANTY. Uh—it's uh—Mel's day off, Dee—gotta go clean up the kitchen . . .

DEE. Shanty, come here a second . . . [*He comes to her reluctantly.*] Thanks, huh? [*She stuffs a bill into the pocket of his apron.*] For nothing!

[*He shrugs. Exits to kitchen. She goes back to drinking.*]

EVIE [*enters. Spies* DEE. *Moves to juke-box*]. Hey.

DEE. Hey, yourself! [*Music comes on.*] How does it feel to be on your way to good citizenship?

EVIE. Yeah, huh? Imagine me doin' it to an IBM machine.

DEE. It ain't hard.

EVIE. That bottle ain't doin' you a damn bit'a good.

DEE. Tha's debatable.

EVIE. How 'bout a nice hot cup'a black coffee?

DEE. Uh-uh! Gotta stay here an' wait for Johnny.

EVIE. Pretty soon you'll be waitin' for him flat on the floor.

DEE. Drunk or sober, it doesn't matter anyway.

EVIE. Why you doin' this? Sheee! He ain't worth the powder it'd take to blow him up.

DEE. Tha's mah business.

EVIE. It's my business you was up at Jack's last night.

DEE. Where'd you hear that?

EVIE. Jack. He called me. Now, if you wanna kill yourself, or git killed—go right ahead! But I wanna warn you 'bout one thing. Stay out'a Jack's, you hear me? A lotta Niggers in there, jus' waitin' for somebody like you! 'Nother thing! Jack's my uncle—don't want'a see him lose his license—on account'a some bitch like you!

DEE. Okay, so I was up at Jack's!

EVIE. What was you lookin' for anyway? Way off yo' beat! Ain't nobody up there got your price!

DEE. I wasn't sellin'—I was buyin'.

EVIE. You was what?

DEE. The biggest blackest cat you ever saw picked me up.

EVIE. You just lookin' to git yourself hurt, girl.

DEE. Oh, he was polite. Too polite. Took me to his room. Smelled like that greasy pomade an' hair straightener you smell sometimes on those pretties in the subway. An' when he put on his silk stocking-cap—I just about cracked. Kept the light on so he could watch.

EVIE. Git yourself together, girl. Drunk as you are—you liable to tell Johnny 'bout this an' he'd have to kill you.

DEE. When it got good to him he started singin', "Black an' white together —black an' white together!" An' the toilet down the hall was flushing over and over again.

EVIE. Bitch, did you hear what I said?

DEE. No! I ain't goin' anyplace! I'm stayin' right here . . . [*She sits at table. Goes into purse. Takes out can of shoe polish.*] If I have to stage a sit-in to do it. [*She puts mirror before her. Begins to apply polish to her face.*]

EVIE. Girl, what are you doin' . . .

DEE [*knocks* EVIE's *hand away*]. Take your hands off me, you stinkin' cunt! Dirty black sow!

EVIE [*slaps* DEE *viciously*]. All right, you crazy, uptight, drunken whore! Sure as shit you gon' end up in Bellvue or git your ass sliced up an' thrown to the rats in some alley . . .

[JOHNNY *enters.* DEE *sing-songs him.*]

DEE. Where you been keepin' yo'se'f, Johnneee, babeee!

JOHNNY. Git that crap off your face an' git the hell out'a here!

DEE [snaps her fingers]. I's black an' I's proud!

EVIE. Listen here, Johnny! This girl is in trouble!

JOHNNY. She's free, white an' always right!

[DEE laughs. He goes to her, wipes the black from her face, forcing her to relent. DEE begins to weep. He is almost tender with her.]

EVIE. She ain't free a'you—Dee, if you got an ounce a sense left in yo' head you'll git on up and come on out with me now.

DEE. Hit the wind, sugar! Git on back to your stupid analyst an' your fuckin' IBM machine! Hit da win', sugar.

[EVIE shakes her head, moves quickly to the door.]

JOHNNY. Hey! Pussy! [She turns angrily.] I know what's eatin' yo' ass. You don't like it 'cause I went for her an' not you! That's it, ain't it?

EVIE [moves quickly to the two of them. Takes DEE by the shoulders. Pulls her up and draws her to her roughly. Plants a hard kiss upon DEE's mouth. She shoves DEE into the arms of JOHNNY who quickly puts DEE aside. He faces EVIE furiously. SHANTY enters]. Darlin', you way off base. I've known Niggers like you all my life! Think everything's'a game. I wouldn't piss on you if yo' ass was on fire. Lef' to me, I'd give you a needle— let you sit in a corner like little Jackie Horner, jerkin' off all by yourself!

[JOHNNY raises his hand. EVIE beats him to the punch, clubs him with her forefinger between the legs. He winces and doubles over. EVIE exits quickly. DEE laughs hysterically. MARY LOU BOLTON enters. DEE is lying on the floor.]

MARY LOU. Johnny, I . . .

JOHNNY. Stay where you at, Mary.

MARY LOU. Johnny, maybe I'd better . . .

DEE. Well, well, well. And just might who you be, Miss Baby Cakes?

MARY LOU. Johnny!

JOHNNY. I said stay where you at!

DEE [struggles to her feet. Gathers her belongings]. Baby Cakes, let me give you the best advice you ever had in your whole little life. Run away from here fast. Run for your life.

[She goes into her purse. Comes up with baby shoes. Drops them on the floor. Exits.]

MARY LOU. Who is she, Johnny?

JOHNNY. Some chick with a problem.

MARY LOU. She—she looked . . .

JOHNNY. She was wiped out.

MARY LOU [picks up the baby shoes]. Who do these belong to . . .

JOHNNY [snatches them out of her hands and throws them into the waste basket]. Don't ask me! Never had no kid'a mine if tha's what you're thinkin'!

MARY LOU. I don't think you'll be seeing me anymore, Johnny.

JOHNNY. Why the hell not, Mary?

MARY LOU. Are you in any trouble, Johnny?

JOHNNY. Trouble? What kind'a trouble?

MARY LOU. My father! Someone called him about us!

JOHNNY. What about?

MARY LOU. Whoever it was said if he didn't stop me from seeing you, they would.

[He grins.]

Are you in some kind of trouble?

JOHNNY. That depen's, Mary. Take off, Shanty!

SHANTY. Man, I still got . . .

JOHNNY. I said, take off!

[SHANTY takes off apron. Gets hat. Exits. JOHNNY locks doors behind him.]

'Member when we was talkin' 'bout Pete Zerroni?

MARY LOU. Yes . . .

JOHNNY. Pete don't like it if a Nigger's got a place'a business in his ter'tory.

MARY LOU. You gotta be kidding.

JOHNNY. Ain't you learned nothin' from all that civil rights?

MARY LOU. What proof do you have?

JOHNNY. Baby, this ain't no ord'nary type 'scrimunashun. They give you the signal. You ignore it. Place burns down.

MARY LOU. But why don't they want me to see you?

JOHNNY. Your ol' man was Zerroni's lawyer. Think maybe I might try to work you. . . .

MARY LOU. Work me?

JOHNNY. Yo' ol' man might have somethin' on Zerroni an' his boys in his records or files.

MARY LOU. That's silly! It could never be used as any real evidence.

JOHNNY. Sho' could make it hot for a whole lotta people if the D.A. happened to get a few tips.

MARY LOU. What are you getting at?

JOHNNY. Nothin'. You wanted to know why they didn't want you to see me, didn't you? 'Les yo' ol' man's prege'dice.

MARY LOU. He knows I've dated Negroes before. [She thinks for a moment.] You really believe if you got this information it would keep Zerroni off your back?

JOHNNY. Well, they still don't know who killed Rep'senative Mahoney. . . .

MARY LOU. Well, you know I couldn't do anything like that. I mean take that information. My father would never forgive me.

JOHNNY. Like I say. Tha's the only reason I kin figger why they don't want you to be seein' me.

MARY LOU. Anyway, he keeps that sort of thing locked in a safe! In his office.

JOHNNY [comes to her. Takes her by the hand and pulls her to him. He kisses her gently. She responds]. Queer, ain't it? Yo' ol' man's a judge. Sworn to uphol' justice. We cain't even go to him for help.

MARY LOU. I'll speak to him about it, Johnny.

JOHNNY. Don't you do that, Mary. Don't you do nothin' like that.

MARY LOU. But why, Johnny? He could probably help you.

JOHNNY. For all we know, he might be in with Zerroni.

MARY LOU. Don't you say that.

JOHNNY. Funny, after that rotten bunch'a Ginees got off he got to be judge right away.

MARY LOU. I think I'd better leave now.

JOHNNY. Why'd you come back here, Mary? Make like you wanted a daiquiri. Think I'd be a sucker for some white missionary pussy?

MARY LOU. That is a terrible thing to say.

JOHNNY. You don't give a dam about civil rights. What about my civil rights? Don't I git any?

MARY LOU. There are ways to stop Zerroni. There are people we can go to for help.

JOHNNY. Yeah? An' they'll go over to Zerroni's an' picket!

MARY LOU. That's not funny.

JOHNNY. You liberal-ass white people kill me! All the time know more 'bout wha's bes' for Niggers'n Niggers do.

MARY LOU. You don't have to make the world any worse.

JOHNNY. Never had no chance to make it no better neither.

[There is pounding on street doors. JOHNNY unlocks them. MARY LOU rushes out as GABE hurries in.]

GABE. Git your coat, John. Quick!

JOHNNY. What the hell for?

GABE. It's Dee! She's dead.

JOHNNY. Dead?

GABE. Can't figger how they got my number. She slit her wrists. Why'd they call me?

JOHNNY. Where is she?

GABE. The ladies' room. Hotel Theresa.

BLACKOUT

Scene Two

[Time: Three days later
Place: The same
Setting: The same
At rise: Music from jukebox is going full blast. SHANTY is seated on a barstool. Beats on the next stool with drumsticks.]

SHANTY. Aw, blow it, baby! Workout! Yeah! I hear ya! Swing it! Work yo' show!

[JOHNNY and GABE enter dressed in suits. GABE as usual carries briefcase.]

JOHNNY. Goddamit, Shanty! Git under the bed with that shit. Ain't you got no respect for the dead? [Pulls cord out of socket. SHANTY puts sticks away. MELVIN comes out of kitchen.]

MELVIN. How was the funeral?

GABE. How is any funeral, Mel?

JOHNNY [goes behind bar. Mixes drinks]. Every damned whore in town showed up! Think they'd have a little respeck an' stay home!

MELVIN. Was her people there?

GABE. Only us!

SHANTY [picks up newspaper]. Paper sure gave you hell, Johnny!

JOHNNY. Who the hell asked ya? [He comes around bar.] Comin' on like some bitch in a cheap-ass movie! Writin' all that jive on the shithouse wall with lipstick!

SHANTY. I always liked Dee! Good tipper.

JOHNNY [bangs on bar]. Anybody'd think I killed her! Blamin' me for everything! Hell, I never did nothin' to her!

GABE. Nothin' for her neither!

CORA [enters. Dressed to kill. Wears white rose corsage.] Hello, ev'body.

GABE. Hello Cora. . . .

CORA. Wha's ev'body lookin' so down in the mouth about? Like you jus' come from a funeral.

JOHNNY. Is that yo' idea of some kind'a damn joke?

MELVIN. Ain't you heard, Cora?

CORA. Heard what?

MELVIN. It's been in all the papers! Johnny's friend, Dee. She committed suicide a couple of days ago.

CORA. Lawd have mercy! I'm so sorry! I—I haven't exactly been keepin' up with the news lately! You see I—I jus' got married this morning.

MELVIN. Married? I hope you'll be very happy, Cora.

GABE. Congratulations, Cora.

CORA. Oh, thank you! Thank you so much.

JOHNNY. Must'a been a whirlwin' co't-ship.

CORA. Ack-shully, I been knowin' him f'quite some time! He's a heart speshlis' I met at the hospital.

JOHNNY. From the looks of you, he mus' be a pretty good'n.

CORA. He's jus' aroun' the corner gittin' the car checked over! It's a good distance to Kwee-beck.

GABE. Quebec?

CORA. Our honeymoon! Wants me to meet his peoples! 'Cause they's French, you know. Jay Cee? [She goes to JOHNNY.]

JOHNNY. What?

CORA. Awful sorry 'bout what happened.

JOHNNY. Yeah! Sure, Cora!

CORA. Sump'm ter'ble must'a happen to drive her to do a thing like that!

JOHNNY. Good luck with the married bag, huh?

CORA. Why, thank you, Jay Cee! Thank you. You know me an' you knowed each other a lotta years. Some reason, I could never do nothin' to suit you. No matter how hard I tried. Sometimes you make me so mad I ha'f wanna kill you! But I was fool 'nuff to care sump'm 'bout you anyway. 'Cause to me you always been that li'l bad boy who was lef' all alone in the worl' with nobody to take care him!

JOHNNY. Guess it'll always be "Jay Cee ag'inst the worl'!"

CORA [tries to touch him. He jerks away. She looks at SHANTY]. Ain't you gon' wish me good luck too, Shangy Mulligans?

[SHANTY remains silent. Stares out of the window. She shrugs. Moves to street doors.]

Well, o-re-vo-ree, ev'body! O-re-vo-ree! [She giggles.] Tha's French, you know! That means, "Bye, y'all!"

[She exits happily.]

SHANTY. Se-la-goddam-vee.

MELVIN. She sure was happy!

GABE. Different too.

JOHNNY. Married a doctor! Ain't that a bitch? Say one thing for her! That number don't give up! She . . .

SHANTY. Shut up, man!

JOHNNY. What you say?

SHANTY. I said shut up, Nigger.

JOHNNY. Now, look. I know you upset 'bout Cora, but . . .

SHANTY. Will you cool it! Big man! Mister hot daddy! Think you know everything in the whole goddam world, don't you? Well, lemme tell you somethin', man. You don't know a mu-thah-fuc-kun thing. [He rips off his apron and flings it into JOHNNY's face.] Here! Do your own dirty Nigger work! I've done all I'm gonna do! Took all I'm gonna take! [He pulls out his drumsticks. Boldly beats on the bar.] Stood behind this bar! Let you put me down for the last time 'cause my skin is white. [He beats harder on the bar.] Yeah, baby. I'm white. An' I'm proud of it. Pretty an' white. Dynamite. Eh, mothah fuckah. Know what else I got that you ain't got? I got soul. You ain't got no soul. Mothahfuckah's black an' ain't got no soul. If you're an example of what the white race is ag'inst, then baby, I'm gittin' with 'em. They are gonna need a cat like me. Somebody that really knows where you black sons-a-bitches are at. [*He picks up the butcher knife. Plunges it into the top of the bar.*] That's what I think of this ol' piece'a kindlin'! Take it an' stick it up you black, rusty, dusty!

[*He moves quickly to the street doors. Turns. Gives* JOHNNY *the finger and exits quickly.*]

JOHNNY. Well, looks like ol' Corabelle Beasely done turned Shanty into a real white man, after all. Now, what about you, Mel?

MELVIN. Huh?

JOHNNY. Don't you wanna cuss me out an' split too?

MELVIN. I ain't got nothin' against you, Johnny.

JOHNNY. Tha's too dam bad. [*Tosses* MELVIN *some bills.*]

MELVIN. What's this for, Johnny?

JOHNNY. Cain't afford to keep the kitchen open no more. Business all aroun' ain't worth lickin' the lead on a pencil.

MELVIN. Let me stay on, Johnny, please? Shanty's gone. I can tend bar and still do whatever short orders there are. Please, Johnny, don't let me go.

JOHNNY. Dam, Mel. Didn't know you liked it aroun' here that much.

GABE. What about your dancin', Mel? You wanna work in a bar the rest of your life?

MELVIN. I—I quit my dancin', Gabe. . . .

GABE. Why'd you do that?

MELVIN. Well, I—I went to this party Victor gave at his penthouse. A lot of celebrities were there. And Gabe, you just wouldn't have believed it.

GABE. What happened?

MELVIN. I'm ashamed to tell you!

JOHNNY. Aw, go on, Mel. We big boys.

MELVIN. Well, they all got plastered! They were smoking marihuana, too! Even the women! Can you imagine? And then they started taking off their clothes.

JOHNNY. Didn't you know where these turkeys was at before you went?

MELVIN. I don't go to parties much. I don't drink. You know that.

JOHNNY. Did you take your clothes off too?

MELVIN. Are you kidding?

GABE. So you left.

MELVIN. They wouldn't let me leave. So I ran into that bathroom and locked that door. But they jimmied the door open.

JOHNNY. An' then what happened?

MELVIN. They—they held me down and took all my clothes off. It was awful. I said if that's what you gotta do to be a dancer then . . .

JOHNNY. Mel, yo' mama must'a gave you too many hot baths when you was a baby.

MARY LOU [*enters. She carries a paper bag*]. Helped my father at the office yesterday. Must have watched him dial the combination to that safe at least twenty times.

[JOHNNY *snatches bag. Locks doors. Comes behind bar.* MARY LOU *follows.*]

Didn't get a chance to hear the tapes. Glanced through some of the other stuff, though. Looks pretty explosive.

JOHNNY. Don't read so good, Mary. What's this stuff say?

MARY LOU. Zerroni admits that he had Joseph Mahoney killed! Muffucci did it. And here it says that he was in on several bribes . . .

JOHNNY. Mary, this is it. This is the stuff I need!

MARY LOU. I—I thought about it a long time. There just wasn't any other solution.

[JOHNNY *stuffs papers back into bag.*] Johnny, I—I . . . [*She peers at* GABE *and* MELVIN.]

JOHNNY. Go 'head! You kin say anything in front'a them.

MARY LOU. Well, it's not the kind of thing you would say in front of . . .

JOHNNY. Mary, I don't think it's wise for you to be seen aroun' here. I want you to lay low for a while.

MARY LOU. I can't go home, Johnny. Daddy will know I . . .

JOHNNY. Ain't they some girlfri'n you kin stay with?

MARY LOU. I—I suppose so. But I thought we . . .

GABE. What's this all about, John?

MARY LOU. It's to keep Pete Zerroni from forcing Johnny out of business. Don't you know about it?

MELVIN. First time I've heard about it.

GABE. What's your father got to do with it?

MARY LOU. He was Zerroni's lawyer.

GABE. And you stole that material from your father?

MARY LOU. Yes, I stole that material from my father. There was nothing else we could do.

GABE. Why, you stupid, naive little bitch. Don't you know what he wants that stuff for?

MARY LOU. To keep Zerroni from forcing him out of business.

GABE. That's a lie! He wants it so he kin blackmail his way into his own dirty racket.

MARY LOU. That's not true! Tell him, Johnny.

GABE. A black Mafia. That's what he wants. [GABE laughs.]

MARY LOU. You're crazy. Johnny, are you going to stand there and . . .

JOHNNY. I gotta right to my own game. Just like they do.

MARY LOU. What?

JOHNNY. My own game!

MARY LOU. Johnny!

GABE. What did you do it for, Mary? For love? Sheee! He hates you, you bitch. Hates everything you stand for. Nice little suffering white girl.

[MARY LOU slaps GABE. He throws her into a chair. She begins to weep.]

Lemme tell you something. Before he kin lay one hot hand on you, you gonna have to git out there on that street an' hussle your ass off.

[GABE moves to JOHNNY.]

Gimme that file, John.

[JOHNNY reaches under bar. Comes up with revolver. Levels it at GABE. MELVIN gasps. Falls to floor.]

JOHNNY. I don't wanna kill you, Gabe. This is the one break I been waitin' on. It ain't much but it's gon' have to do.

GABE. You kill me that file ain't gonna do you no good anyway. I'm tellin' you. Gimme that file.

[JOHNNY finally lowers gun. GABE puts bag into briefcase. Starts to move to street doors. MAFFUCCI and JUDGE BOLTON enter.]

BOLTON. Get in the car, Mary Lou.

MARY LOU. Daddy, I . . .

BOLTON. I said get in the car!

[MARY LOU rushes out, followed by MAFFUCCI.]

You know what I'm here for, Williams.

JOHNNY. Just like that, huh?

BOLTON. Just like that.

[MAFFUCCI reenters.]

JOHNNY. I wanna talk to Pete Zerroni.

MAFFUCCI. Pete ain't got nothin' to say to you, Johnny Cake.

BOLTON. Those notes belong to me. Not to Zerroni.

JOHNNY. I ain't budgin' till I see Pete, personal. He's got to come here an' go horse-to-horse with me. Ain't gon' wait too long neither. 'Lection's comin' up. Li'l phone call to the D.A. could make him very happy 'bout his future.

[MAFFUCCI suddenly pulls gun on JOHNNY.]

BOLTON. Put that away, you fool!

[MAFFUCCI returns gun to shoulder holster.]

JOHNNY. Footch, don't think Pete or the Judge here wanna see me git hit jus' yet.

BOLTON. What is it, Williams? Money? [Produces an envelope.]

JOHNNY. You ofays sho' think money's the root'a all evil, don't you, Judge?

MAFFUCCI. Let's go, Frank. We're just wastin' time.

BOLTON. Williams, you'd better listen to me and listen good. You're in dangerous trouble. If you don't hand over that material, I'm not going to be responsible for what happens to you.

JOHNNY. An' I sho' ain't gon' be responsible for what happens to you neither, Judge. [Both JOHNNY and the JUDGE laugh. BOLTON starts to exit.] Judge?

[BOLTON turns. JOHNNY tosses him MARY LOU's purse. BOLTON exits.]

MAFFUCCI. Johnny Cake?

JOHNNY. What?

MAFFUCCI. Right now, your life ain't worth a plug nickel.

JOHNNY. Footch?

[Puts his thumbnail under his upper teeth and flicks it at MAFFUCCI. MAFFUCCI exits.]

JOHNNY. Gabe-ree-el. How come you didn't hand over the file?

GABE. I couldn't! When I saw those two bastards together, I just couldn't bring myself to do it! [GABE removes bag *from briefcase. Hands it to* JOHNNY.]

JOHNNY. Mel, take this over to the drugstore. Get copies made, quick! Move!

[MELVIN *exits quickly.*]

GABE. You know they're gonna git you.

JOHNNY. Gabe, we was got the day we was born! Where you been? Jus' bein' black ain't never been no real reason for livin'.

GABE. If I thought that I'd probably go crazy or commit suicide.

BLACKOUT

Scene Three

[*Time: A day later*
Place: The same
Setting: The same
At rise: JOHNNY *is seated on a barstool, checking his gun.* GABE *exits to kitchen.* MACHINE DOG *appears wearing a shabby military uniform.*]

MACHINE DOG. I don't work at the garage no more, brother.

JOHNNY. You jive. You don't know nothin' else.

MACHINE DOG. They's other work to be done. They's other mo' important things to be worked on and fixed. Like my black brothers. They needs fixin' bad. Tha's when I got to thinkin'a you, Brother Williams.

JOHNNY. Yea, well you can just kick them farts at somebody else.

MACHINE DOG. On yo' feet, mothah fuckah!

[JOHNNY *comes to his feet militarily.* MACHINE DOG *presents a Nazi-like salute.*]

By the powers invested in me by the brothers I hereby deliver to you the edick!

[JOHNNY *and* MACHINE DOG *give each other some skin.* MACHINE DOG *goes back to his salute.*]

Brother Williams. The brothers have jus' sennunced an' condemned you to death. Now, repeat after me. I have been chosen to be the nex' brother to live on in the hearts an' min's'a the enemy host.

JOHNNY. I have been chosen to be the nex' brother to live on in the hearts an' min's'a the enemy host.

MACHINE DOG. My duty will be to ha'nt they cripple an' sore min's.

JOHNNY. My duty will be to haunt they cripple an' sore min's.

MACHINE DOG. I will cling to the innermos' closets'a they brains an' agonize them.

JOHNNY. I will cling to the innermos' closets'a they brains an' agonize them.

MACHINE DOG [*breaks his salute and gives an aside*]. Maniacks though they is already! [*He goes back into his salute.*] The more they will try to cas' me out, the mo' they torment will be.

JOHNNY. The more they will try to cast me out, the more they torment will be!

MACHINE DOG. Se la an' ayman! [MA-CHINE DOG *shakes* JOHNNY's *hand.*] You will have plen'y'a he'p, Brother Williams. All them brothers that went before you an' all them tha's comin' after you.

JOHNNY. I gladly accept the condemna-shun, Gen'ral Sheen. Tell the brothers I won't let 'em down. Tell 'em I look forward to meetin' 'em all in par'dise.

MACHINE DOG. Se la! An' ayman!

[*They salute each other.*]

JOHNNY. Se la an' ay-man!

[MACHINE DOG *goes into kitchen as* JUDGE BOLTON *and two plainclothesmen,* CAPPALETTI *and* HARRY, *enter.*]

BOLTON. This is the man, Al!

[CAPPALETTI *flashes his badge.*]

CAPPALETTI. Cappaletti. Vice squad.

JOHNNY. Big deal!

CAPPALETTI. Judge Bolton, here. His daughter was picked up this afternoon.

JOHNNY. So what?

CAPPALETTI. She tried to solicit this officer here.

JOHNNY. What's that got to do with me?

CAPPALETTI. Said she was workin' for you.

JOHNNY. Tha's a lie. Tha's a goddam lie. Lemme hear her say that to my face.

CAPPALETTI. Plenty of time for that.

JOHNNY. What the hell you tryin' to pull, Bolton?

CAPPALETTI. Now, why would the Judge wanna pull anything on you, Johnny?

JOHNNY. He—he don't want his daughter seein' me. 'Cause I'm a Nigger.

I'll lay odds she don't know nothin' about this.

CAPPALETTI. Go get Miss Bolton, Harry.

[*Harry moves to street doors.*]

JOHNNY. Hurry, Harry!

[HARRY *grins. Exits.*]

CAPPALETTI. By the way. Ain't you the guy this girl killed herself about a few days ago? She was a call girl?

JOHNNY. Tell you like I tole them other fuzzys. What she did was her own business.

CAPPALETTI. Just the same you kin see how we kin believe Miss Bolton's story. [HARRY *leads* MARY LOU *into bar.* CAPPALETTI *seats her.*] Now, Miss Bolton. We'll ask you again. Who did you say you was workin' for when you was picked up?

MARY LOU. I—I . . .

CAPPALETTI. Speak up, Miss Bolton. We can't hear you.

MARY LOU. Daddy, I . . .

BOLTON. All you have to do is identify him. Is he the man?

[CAPPALETTI *puts his hand on* MARY LOU'S *head.*]

Take your hands off her!

[HARRY *laughs.*]

Mary Lou! Is he or isn't he?

MARY LOU [*forces herself to face* JOHNNY]. Yes! This is the man! Johnny Williams! I was working for him!

[MARY LOU *rushes from bar followed by* HARRY.]

JOHNNY. Dirty lyin' bitch.

BOLTON. Now, see here, Williams!

CAPPALETTI. You're gonna have to come with me, Johnny.

JOHNNY. What is this, a pinch? You gonna book me? I'm gonna call my lawyer!

CAPPALETTI. Shut up! You're not callin' nobody right now. Let's go.

BOLTON. Just a minute, Al. I want a few words with him before you take him down.

CAPPALETTI. Okay, Frank, but make it snappy.

BOLTON. Williams, I've worked too long and too hard to get where I am. I'm giving you one last chance to give back those notes and tape. If you don't, it's on the bottom of the woodpile for you. Even if I have to sacrifice my own daughter to do it. I want that file.

JOHNNY. Okay, Judge. Okay. You win.

[JOHNNY *goes behind bar. Brings out paper bag.* JUDGE *checks it. Nods to* CAPPALETTI *and exits.*]

CAPPALETTI. All right, Johnny. All of a sudden the Judge wants me to forget the whole thing. Lucky we didn't get you down to the precinct. Would have busted you up on general principles.

[CAPPALETTI *exits. Quickly* JOHNNY *puts his revolver into his back pocket. Goes behind the bar.*]

JOHNNY. Better split, Gabe. While the gittin's good.

GABE. Don't think so, John. I'm gonna stick aroun'.

JOHNNY. Suit yo'self!

[*Doors open.* JOHNNY *goes for his gun.* SWEETS CRANE *enters. He is practically in tatters. He carries a shopping bag. Goes to table and begins to take out various articles of food. He coughs and rubs his hands together.*]

SWEETS. I got fried chicken! Ham! Candied yams! Got me some hot chit'-lin's! Blackeyed peas an' rice! Cornbread! Mustard greens an' macaroni salit! [*Coughs.*] Top ev'thing off I got me'a thermos full'a—full'a—lemme see now. How'd my gran'daddy used to call it? Chassy San'burg coffee! [*Laughs.*] An' a big chunk'a pee-kan pie. Y'all fellas is welcomed to join me.

JOHNNY. Wouldn't touch it if it was blessed by the pope!

SWEETS. Well, now tha's a dam shame. 'Member when I couldn't pull you away from my cookin'.

GABE. You don't mind if I join him, do you, John?

JOHNNY. Be my guest.

SWEETS. He'p yo'se'f, young fella. they's plen'y here. Have some'a these here chit'lin's!

GABE. Ain't never had none before.

SWEETS. Then let this be the day you start.

[GABE *takes a sniff.*]

Go 'head! Go 'head! You don't eat the smell.

GABE. Lemme ask you sump'm, Sweets.

SWEETS. Hope I kin answer it.

GABE. How come you took my watch an' wallet?

SWEETS. Son, all my life I been one kind'a thief or 'nother. It's jus' in me. 'Course I don't have to steal. But I steals for the pure enjoyment of it. Jus' the other day I stole a rat'la from a baby. [*Laughs.*] When you steals for fun it don't matter who you steals from! [*Goes into his pocket. Comes up with* GABE's *watch and wallet.*]

GABE. It's all here!

SWEETS. 'Co'se it is! Gave the baby back his rat'la too.

JOHNNY. You ain't gon' make the white man's heaven this way.

SWEETS. The Lawd died 'tween two thieves.

MAFFUCCI [*enters with* LOUIE]. Wouldn't listen to me, would you, Johnny Cake?

JOHNNY. What Pete say? Give a jig a half'a chance . . .

SWEETS. This the fella work for big fat Pete, Sonny Boy?

MAFFUCCI. What's it to ya, Pops? You an' this other joker better get the hell out'a here before you catch cold.

SWEETS. I ain't never got up from a meal in my life 'fore I was finished . . .

MAFFUCCI. Look, Pops! Don't make me have to . . . [*Glances at food.*] What's that? Macaroni salad you got there?

SWEETS. Matter fack it is!

MAFFUCCI [*dips into it*]. Ummm! Not bad. Who made it?

SWEETS. I did.

MAFFUCCI. No kiddin'? Knew it didn't taste like dela-ga-tes. Mama used to make macaroni salad.

SWEETS. Have'a piece'a my fried chicken to go with it.

JOHNNY. If Zerroni could see you now, Footch.

MAFFUCCI. How's that, Johnny Cake?

JOHNNY. Tha's the great Sweets Crane you eatin' with.

MAFFUCCI. Pops, here? He's Sweets Crane?

SWEETS. What's lef' of me.

MAFFUCCI. You'd'a made out better as a cook, Pops. Mama couldn't beat that macaroni salad!

SWEETS [*produces* MAFFUCCI's *watch*]. I think this b'longs to you.

MAFFUCCI. My watch! I been lookin' all over for it. Pops, you copped my watch? [*Laughs.*] How come you're givin' it back? This watch is worth a lotta bread.

SWEETS. Figger you need it wors'n I do.

MAFFUCCI. Say, Johnny Cake, you sure Pops here is Sweets Crane?

JOHNNY. You don't know how much I wish he wasn't.

MAFFUCCI. Too bad Johnny didn't learn a lesson after what happened to you, Pops. Gotta give him credit though. Takes a lotta balls to try to put the bleed on Pete Zerroni.

SWEETS. You was tryin' to blackmail ol' big fat Pete, Sonny Boy?

JOHNNY. What the hell. Couldn't pull it off. Don't matter much now.

MAFFUCCI. That's where you're wrong, Johnny Cake. Matters a helluva lot to me. Pete now, he's willin' to forget the whole thing. Says the trick is not to take you jigs too serious. I can't do nothin' like that, Johnny. Don't look good on my record.

JOHNNY. What you gonna do about it, Footch?

[MAFFUCCI *quickly pulls his gun. Levels it at* JOHNNY. *Backs to street doors. Locks them. Pulls shades. Takes a large sign from his pocket. It reads, "CLOSED." He puts it on the bar in front of* JOHNNY.]

The sign in both hands, Johnny Cake. [JOHNNY *slowly picks up sign.*] Pops, you an' that other joker stay put!

[MAFFUCCI *nods to* LOUIE *who moves behind* SWEETS *and* GABE. JOHNNY *starts to tear sign.*]

Ah-ah! I want you to lick that sign an' paste it right up there on the door. Start lickin', Johnny Cake! [JOHNNY *begins to wet sign with his tongue.*] That's it! Wet it up a little more! That's enough! Now start walkin' real careful like! [JOHNNY *moves to street door with sign.*] Now, paste it up there! [JOHNNY *does so.*] Now, back up! Real slow! [JOHNNY *backs up.* MAFFUCCI *seats* JOHNNY *on a barstool.*]

SWEETS. You don't have to do that, Sonny Boy. [*Goes to the door with knife he has been eating with.*] You don't have to do nothin' like that. [*He pulls the sign from the window and tears it up.*]

MAFFUCCI. What are you doin', Pops? Look, if you don't want hi-call-it to get hit . . .

JOHNNY. Keep out'a this, Sweets. This is my game.

SWEETS. Not any more, it ain't. You don't have to do nothin' like that.

[*Advances to* MAFFUCCI.]

MAFFUCCI. What'a ya, crazy, Pops? Put that ax away.

JOHNNY. Lay out of it, Sweets. Lay out of it, I said!

MAFFUCCI. I'm warnin' you, Pops! Take another step an' . . .

[SWEETS *lunges at* MAFFUCCI *as* MAF-FUCCI *fires. Knife penetrates* MAF-FUCCI's *heart.* JOHNNY *kills* LOUIE. *Whirls and fires three shots into* MAFFUCCI. *Rushes to* SWEETS.]

JOHNNY. Goddamit, Sweets! I tole you I could handle it!

GABE. I'll call a doctor!

SWEETS. Fuck a doctor! Cain't you see I'm dead? [*Coughs. Winces in pain.*] Lissen to me, Sonny Boy! You—you gotta promise me one thing . . .

JOHNNY. What is it, Sweets?

SWEETS. The—the will! It's here in—in my pocket.

[JOHNNY *finds will.*] If—if you git out'a this. Promise you'll git straightened out. [*He grabs* JOHNNY's *arm.*] Promise!

JOHNNY. I—I promise.

SWEETS. Swear!

JOHNNY. Yeah! Yeah! I swear, Sweets!

SWEETS. Git—git rid'a the—the Ch-Cholly fever—[SWEETS *goes limp.*]

GABE. He did it for you, John . . .

JOHNNY. Look, Gabe. We gotta git our story together. When the fuzz gits here we gotta have us a story.

GABE. We tell 'em the truth, John . . .

JOHNNY. What you say?

GABE. We tell the police the truth!

JOHNNY. Shit. The truth is I'm alive! I got a copy'a that file an' Sweets' will.

GABE. But you tole Sweets you was gonna throw them ideas out'a your head.

JOHNNY. Come on, man, you didn't think I meant that shit, did you?

GABE. With his last dyin' breath, you gave that ol' man your word. You swore.

JOHNNY. What good is anybody's word to that ol' bastard? He's dead an' cain't remember.

GABE. You are mad.

JOHNNY. I'm goin' ahead with my plans. [*He holds up will.*] An' he's still gon' help me do it.

GABE. Naw, naw! That ain't the way it's s'pose to be!

JOHNNY. You in this as deep as I am. It's our word ag'inst these dead turkeys.

You gave me back that file, remember?

GABE. That's where I got off. I ain't got no stomach for this personal war you got ag'inst the white man.

JOHNNY. It's your war too, Nigger. Why can't you see that? You wanna go on believin' in the lie? We at war, Gabe! Black ag'inst white.

GABE. You're wrong, John. You're so goddam wrong.

[JOHNNY *picks up gun. Puts it into* GABE's *hand.*]

JOHNNY. Take this gun in yo' han'. Feel that col' hard steel. Bet you ain't never held a heater in yo' han' like that in yo' life. Well, you gon' have to, Gabe. They gon' make you do it. 'Cause we at war, Gabe. Black ag'inst white.

GABE. I—I don't wanna—kill—you . . .

JOHNNY. You ain't got the guts! You wanna believe you kin sell papers an' become President! You're a coward, Gabe! A lousy, yellow, screamin' faggot coward!

[*Enraged,* GABE *fires at* JOHNNY, JOHNNY *tumbles backward and then forward into* GABE's *arms.* GABE *eases* JOHNNY *to the floor.* JOHNNY *goes limp.* MACHINE DOG *enters.*]

GABE [*startled*]. Who're you? Where did you come from?

MACHINE DOG. The Brothers call me Machine Dog! It is written: "He that slays a true brother, he hisse'f shall how-someever be perished!"

GABE. He made me kill him! He . . .

[*During* MACHINE DOG's *speech,* GABE *takes gun. Wipes it off. Places it in* JOHNNY's *hand. Covers* JOHNNY *with tablecloth. Exits.*]

MACHINE DOG. Hush yo' lyin', trait-ious tongue! Ver'ly, ver'ly, I says into you! You has kilt all them li'l innusunt cherbs'a the ghetto! Them li'l rams who been hatin' 'thorty eb'm from the cradle! All them holy de-lin-cunts who been the true creators'a unsolved thef's an' killin's! You has slewn an' slaughtered them young goateed billygoats who been ded-cated to that sanctified an' precious art'a lootin' the destruction'a private public poverty! You has hung an' lynched the black angels'a color who went by that high code'a rooftops an' been baptized in the stink of urine scented hallways! You has burnt an' melted down a million switchblade knives an' razors an' broke preshus bottles'a communion upon the empty white-paved streets'a the enemy host! An' lef' the brothers thirsty an' col' to bang the doors'a the guilty white Samaritan! You has crushed the very life fum black an' profane souls! Hordes'a un-re-gen-rants! An' smashed the spirit an' holy ghost fum rollers an' dancers who founded they faith on black, human sufferin'! Burnt an' tortured souls who knew th'ough the power of love that they trials an' trib'lashuns could not be leg'slated away by no co't, no congruss, not eb'm God Hisse'f! You has scortched an' scalded them black Moheekans an' stuffed them in the very stoves they cooked on! Se la! An' ay-man!

BLACKOUT

EPILOGUE

[GABE *enters dressed as a woman in mourning. A black shawl is draped over his head.*]

GABE. Like my costume? You like it?

You don't like it! I know what I am by what I see in your faces. You are my mirrors. But unlike a metallic reflection, you will not hold my image for very long. Your capacity for attention is very short. Therefore, I must try to provoke you. Provoke your attention. Change my part over and over again. I am rehearsing at the moment. For tomorrow, I will go out amongst you, "The Black Lady in Mourning." I will weep, I will wail, and I will mourn. But my cries will not be heard. No one will wipe away my bitter tears. My black anguish will fall upon deaf ears. I will mourn a passing! Yes. The passing and the ending of a people dying. Of a people dying into that new life. A people whose identity could only be measured by the struggle, the dehumanization, the degradation they suffered. Or allowed themselves to suffer perhaps. I will mourn the ending of those years. I will mourn the death of a people dying. Of a people dying into that new life.

BLACKOUT

THE END

Walter Kerr

NOT SINCE EDWARD ALBEE

Let's be simple about this. Charles Gordone is the most astonishing new American playwright to come along since Edward Albee, and with *No Place to Be Somebody*, now running in the Public Theater's downstairs tryout room, he lurches at us not like the younger Albee or the one-act Albee but like the already ripe and roaring Albee of *Who's Afraid of Virginia Woolf?*

This time the milieu is black, this time the malice can't be made to crumple and die at dawn but must see its way to as many sprawled corpses as *Hamlet* has, this time the work is called comedy but plunges straight through the paper hoop of comedy to land upside down and splattered all over with an ugliness that won't wipe off, this time the tongue lashings shade away regularly into a thumping or a reflective poetry. The construction of the play is complex, rich, garish, improbable, overburdened, defiant and successful.

Mr. Gordone wishes to keep every observable, every conceivable aspect of the black-white love-hate relationship alive in his head and alive in ours, without cant, without bias, without coming to any absolute conclusion except that terrifying contraries exist simultaneously. To do the job, and to keep the violent survey in some kind of control, he presents us with a man—a writer and actor so nearly white that he can't get a job as a black—who carries a whole boiling world of the race hatreds and race lusts in his head, who conceives of them all as coming face to face, grinning and snarling, as part of a single crisscrossed action in a single Village bar.

He drops into his imagined bar as he wishes, always to overhear the world at knife's edge. He can, in effect, make the bar vanish when he wishes, reducing the whole world to himself, his race—remembered dance steps, his sharp chanted "heahs!" that seem to function as a rein on the universe, his quiet recollection of what it was like to get out of the ghetto and away from those "dirty black people" only to discover that his new friends, "those clean white people," somehow or other imagined that he was one of the dirty black people, too. (Showering and showering, he was cleaner than anybody, but nobody noticed.)

Functioning as a tribal god to the play, and also as one of its sacrificial participants, he is insider and outsider, all-knowing and unknowing, cynically curled lip and damaged psyche at once. Ron O'Neal, an actor who must have the most expressive eyes since Ronald Colman, plays both the poet and the poem superbly. (The adjective sounds conventional; you will have to see for youself that Mr. O'Neal is better than that.)

What goes on inside the tough, tawdry, bluntly melodramatic poem, which is to say inside Johnny's Bar? Johnny, played with a nasty vigor and unerring skill by Nathan George, is a black man who means to become his own Mafia. He has cut out from "goodness," cut out from whites (though he doesn't in the least mind making use of two white mistresses before the last clatter of gunfire is sounded), cut out from all the promises in which no urgent man could possibly believe. He is race in a rage, on the rise, ready for triumph or for martyrdom, which would amount to a win either way.

In Johnny's Bar there are white and black whores, competing with one an-

SOURCE: From *The New York Times*, May 18, 1969. Copyright © 1969 by The New York Times Company. Reprinted by permission.

other. There are white and black liberals, jointly guilty in their innocence. There is, to pave the way for an entirely characteristic scene of Mr. Gordone's, a reefer-crazed white handyman (Ronnie Thompson) who boasts, between twitches, of his earlier glories as a musician. He is loved by a simple, a too-simple, black girl; she buys him the drums he had yearned for. Once he has the drums, he must play them, play them before the blacks to whom he has boasted. The blacks surround him, waiting. Mouth working spastically, fingers trembling apprehensively, he begins to perform. He gains confidence, gains speed, loses himself altogether in the rising rattle, finishes maniacally triumphant —unaware that he has, in the act, exposed himself cruelly for the nonentity he is, an untalented child caught showing off before his stern, embarrassed betters.

It is Mr. Gordone's habit—an excellent one because it is the fundamental stuff of drama—to press his confrontations until they become reversals, until the roles are changed. If on-the-make Johnny is turning himself into his kind of white man, the bad white man who gets everything he wants, so the white drummer is trying—and failing hideously—to make himself musically black. The humiliation that comes of the failed inversion is rammed home—hard—in what is probably the evening's ugliest, prickliest sequence. Johnny's white whore (Susan G. Pearson) is being discarded by Johnny. Too shrewd not to know what is happening, too drunk to do anything about its happening, Miss Pearson begins brazenly to black her own face, smearing grease wantonly and bitterly while shocked, angry and sorrowing blacks try to stop her.

The moment is vicious in every way, it hurts everyone participating in it. It also summarizes absolutely the double thrust of the play, the terrible effort at adaptation on both sides that ends just now in grotesquerie. We have not got through the cruel comedy of adaptation yet; this play is the situation's unforgettable weather report.

Not everything in it is harsh or harshly funny. The author has a great gift for dropping from intense heat to a pleasant chill, from importance to how-do-y'do.

An Italian thug who went to school with Johnny is now going to destroy Johnny —he will get to it in a minute—pauses to savor a delicious macaroni salad made, to the thug's astonishment, by a filthy, dying black. The girl who has wasted herself on the drummer asks someone to read the clock on the wall for her, then falls into earnest hushed thought. She decides that she will go home and, first thing tomorrow morning, begin to learn how to tell time. (Mr. Gordone's touch here is so light that what might become obtrusively symbolic is instead personal and touching).

And for Mr. O'Neal he has written not only act-prologues that expand like areas but at least one passage of deliberate verse that begins at doggerel beat and then climbs beyond simple tempo to full orchestration. (Listening to it is to have one's hope renewed that verse theater, clamoring and contemporary, may be possible after all.) Everything under Ted Cornell's strict and vigorous stage direction, is extremely well performed, the cast has been immaculately selected, the interplay is the easiest and most effective since Boys in the Band.

There are flaws, as there are bound to be in any genuinely original play, though the title is almost the worst of these, sounding moralizing and familiar as it does. (If you have any feeling that you've seen all this before or that No Place to Be Somebody is just one more Negro protest play, forget it; you haven't felt any of it at this precise temperature, and the play is—in its complexity—miles above the bleat of routine propaganda.) Mr. Gordone writes a bit sentimentally at times ("Somewhere inside, Johnny's got something, only it comes out crooked"). Occasionally he makes a dramatic gesture that seems schematically planned, unspontaneous: the drummer's turning on his girl after he has failed, for instance. And at the very end of the evening, he puts Mr. O'Neal through a sudden "camp" bit in widow's weeds, giddily standing in for all the mourning women of the world, that is false to the play's tone; it is too thin and obvious in its humor for the weight and wiliness of the text as a whole and should, I think, be dropped.

But what is important is that a writer

has turned up who has the nerve of his talent. The overfull play does not sprawl, is never embarrassed by its own appetite. The melodrama belongs to the materials at the same time that it is being theatrically arresting, the bar talk and the imagery relieve each other readily, the inside of a man's head and the outside, outsize, roiling world fuse. We have come all the way down to the end of the season and been rewarded for our patience: here's a playwright.

SELECTIVE BIBLIOGRAPHY

I. PERIODICALS

The Drama Review
Educational Theatre Journal
Gambit
Modern Drama

Plays and Players
Theatre Quarterly
Yale/Theatre

II. REFERENCE WORKS

ADELMAN, IRVING and R. DWORKIN. *Modern Drama: A Checklist of Critical Literature on Twentieth Century Plays.* Metuchen: Scarecrow Press, 1967.

ANDERSON, MICHAEL et al. *Crowell's Handbook of Contemporary Drama.* New York: Thomas Y. Crowell Co., 1971.

BREED, PAUL and F. SNIDERMAN. *Dramatic Criticism Index.* Detroit: Gale Research Co., 1972.

COLEMAN, ARTHUR and G. TYLER, eds. *Drama Criticism.* Denver: Swallow Press, 1966.

GASSNER, JOHN and E. QUINN, eds. *The Reader's Encyclopedia of World Drama.* New York: Thomas Y. Crowell Co., 1969.

HALLIWELL, LESLIE. *The Filmgoer's Companion.* New York: Hill & Wang, 1965.

HARTNOLL, PHYLLIS. *Oxford Companion to the Theatre.* 3d ed. New York: Oxford University Press, 1967.

MATLAW, MYRON. *Modern World Drama: An Encyclopedia.* New York: E. P. Dutton & Co., 1972.

PALMER, HELEN and ANNE J. DYSON. *American Drama Criticism, 1890–1965.* Hamden, Conn.: Shoe String Press, 1967.

———. *European Drama Criticism.* Hamden, Conn.: Shoe String Press, 1968.

WEST, DOROTHY and D. PEAKE. *Play Index.* New York: H. W. Wilson Co., 1953.

III. GENERAL WORKS ON DRAMA AND THEATRE

BENTLEY, ERIC. *The Life of the Drama.* New York: Atheneum Publishers, 1964.

CORRIGAN, ROBERT, ed. *Comedy: Meaning and Form.* San Francisco: Chandler Publishing Co., 1965.

————, ed. *Tragedy: Vision and Form.* San Francisco: Chandler Publishing Co., 1965.

FERGUSSON, FRANCIS. *The Idea of a Theater.* Princeton: Princeton University Press, 1949.

GASSNER, JOHN. *Masters of the Drama.* 3d ed., rev. & enl. New York: Dover Publications, 1954.

MACGOWAN, KENNETH and W. MELNITZ. *The Living Stage.* New York: Prentice-Hall, 1955.

PEACOCK, RONALD. *The Art of Drama.* London: Routledge and Kegan Paul, Inc., 1967.

STYAN, J. L. *The Elements of Drama.* Cambridge, Cambridge University Press, 1960.

IV. WORKS ON MODERN DRAMA

ARTAUD, ANTONIN. *The Theatre and Its Double.* Translated by Mary C. Richards. New York: Grove Press, 1958.

BRUSTEIN, ROBERT. *The Theatre of Revolt.* Boston: Atlantic Monthly Press, 1964.

COHN, RUBY. *Currents in Contemporary Drama.* Bloomington: Indiana University Press, 1969.

ESSLIN, MARTIN. *The Theatre of the Absurd.* Garden City: Doubleday & Co., 1961.

GASSNER, JOHN. *Form and Idea in Modern Theatre.* New York: Dryden Press, 1956.

GORELIK, MORDECAI. *New Theatres for Old.* New York: Samuel French, 1940.

PEACOCK, RONALD. *The Poet in the Theatre.* New York: Harcourt, Brace & Co., 1946.

TAYLOR, JOHN RUSSELL. *Anger and After.* London: Methuen & Co., 1969.

WILLIAMS, RAYMOND. *Modern Tragedy.* Stanford: Stanford University Press, 1966.

V. COLLECTIONS OF ESSAYS AND REVIEWS

BENTLEY, ERIC. *The Dramatic Event.* New York: Horizon Press, 1954.

————. *In Search of Theater.* New York: Alfred A. Knopf, 1953.

————. *The Theatre of Commitment and Other Essays.* New York: Atheneum Publishers, 1967.

————, ed. *The Theory of the Modern Stage.* Baltimore: Penguin Books, Pelican Original, 1968.

————. *What Is Theatre?* New York: Atheneum Publishers, 1968.

BLOCK, HASKELL and H. SALINGER, eds. *The Creative Vision.* New York: Grove Press, 1960.

BOGARD, TRAVIS and W. OLIVER, eds. *Modern Drama.* New York: Oxford University Press, 1965.

BROWN, JOHN RUSSELL, ed. *Modern British Dramatists.* Twentieth Century Views. Englewood Cliffs: Prentice-Hall, 1968.

BRUSTEIN, ROBERT. *Seasons of Discontent.* New York: Simon & Schuster, 1967.

COLE, TOBY, ed. *Playwrights on Playwriting,* New York: Hill & Wang, 1960.

CORRIGAN, ROBERT, ed. *Theatre in the Twentieth Century.* New York: Grove Press, 1963.

GASSNER, JOHN. *Theatre at the Crossroads.* New York: Holt, Rinehart & Winston, 1960.

————. *Theatre in Our Times.* New York: Crown Publishers, 1954.

GILMAN, RICHARD. *Common and Uncommon Masks.* New York: Random House, 1971.

McCARTHY, MARY. *Sights and Spectacles.* New York: Farrar, Straus & Cudahy, 1956.

MAROWITZ, CHARLES, ed. *The Encore Reader.* London: Methuen & Co., 1965.

———— and S. TRUSSLER, eds. *Theatre at Work.* London: Methuen & Co., 1967.

TYNAN, KENNETH. *Curtains.* New York: Atheneum Publishers, 1961.

————. *Tynan Right and Left.* New York: Atheneum Publishers, 1967.

WAGER, WALTER, ed. *The Playwrights Speak.* New York: Dial Press, 1967.

YOUNG, STARK. *Immortal Shadows.* New York: Charles Scribner's Sons, 1948.

VI. INDIVIDUAL AUTHORS

SAMUEL BECKETT

BARNARD, GUY. *Samuel Beckett.* London: Dent, 1970.

COE, RICHARD. *Samuel Beckett.* New York: Grove Press, 1970.

COHN, RUBY. *Samuel Beckett.* New Brunswick, N. J.: Rutgers University Press, 1962.

ESSLIN, MARTIN. *The Theatre of the Absurd.* Garden City: Doubleday & Co., 1961.

———, ed. *Samuel Beckett.* Twentieth Century Views. Englewood Cliffs: Prentice-Hall, 1965.

HASSAN, IHAB. *The Literature of Silence.* New York: Random House, 1967.

JACOBSEN, JOSEPHINE and W. MUELLER. *The Testament of Samuel Beckett.* London: Faber & Faber, 1966.

KENNER, HUGH. *Samuel Beckett.* New York: Grove Press, 1962.

ROBINSON, MICHAEL. *The Long Sonata of the Dead.* London: Rupert Hart-Davis, 1969.

BERTOLT BRECHT

Brecht Issue of *Tulane Drama Review* 6 (September 1961).

BENTLEY, ERIC. *Playwright as Thinker.* New York: Meridian Books, 1955.

BRUSTEIN, ROBERT. *The Theatre of Revolt.* Boston: Atlantic Monthly Press, 1964.

DEMETZ, PETER, ed. *Brecht.* Twentieth Century Views. Englewood Cliffs: Prentice-Hall, 1962.

ESSLIN, MARTIN. *Brecht.* Garden City: Doubleday & Co., 1960.

EWEN, FREDERIC. *Bertolt Brecht.* New York: Citadel Press, 1967.

LYONS, CHARLES. *Bertolt Brecht.* Carbondale: Southern Illinois University Press, 1968.

WEIDELI, WALTER. *The Art of Bertolt Brecht.* New York: New York University Press, 1963.

WILLET, JOHN. *The Theatre of Bertolt Brecht.* London: Methuen & Co., 1959.

———, ed. *Brecht on Theatre.* New York: Hill & Wang, 1964.

ANTON CHEKHOV

BRUFORD, W. H. *Chekhov and His Russia.* Hamden, Conn.: Shoe String Press, 1971 repr. of 1947 ed.

BRUSTEIN, ROBERT. *The Theatre of Revolt.* Boston: Atlantic Monthly Press, 1964.

CHEKHOV, ANTON. *Selected Letters.* New York: Farrar, Straus & Cudahy, 1955.

JACKSON, ROBERT L., ed. *Chekhov.* Twentieth Century Views. Englewood Cliffs: Prentice-Hall, 1967.

LUCAS, F. L. *The Drama of Chekhov, Synge, Yeats, and Pirandello.* London: Cassell & Co., 1963.

MAGARSHACK, DAVID. *Chekhov the Dramatist.* Gloucester, Mass.: Peter Smith, 1960.

SIMMONS, ERNEST. *Chekhov: A Biography.* Boston: Atlantic Monthly Press, 1962.

VALENCY, MAURICE. *The Breaking String.* New York: Oxford University Press, 1966.

YERMILOV, V. *A. P. Chekhov.* Translated by Ivy Litvinov. Moscow: Foreign Languages Publishing House, 195–(?).

SERGEI EISENSTEIN

CHERKASOV, N. *Notes of a Soviet Actor.* Translated by G. Ivanov-Mumjiev and S. Rosenberg. Moscow: Foreign Languages Publishing House, 1957.

EISENSTEIN, S. *Drawings.* Moscow: Iskusstvo, 1961.

———. *Film Essays and a Lecture.* Translated by Jay Leyda. New York: Frederick A. Praeger, 1970.

———. *Film Form.* New York: Harcourt Brace Jovanovich, 1969.

————. *Film Sense*. New York: Harcourt Brace Jovanovich, 1969.

————. *Ivan the Terrible*. Translated by I. Montagu and H. Marshall, with appendices and illustrations. New York: Simon & Schuster, 1962.

————. "Notes from a Director's Laboratory," *Film Form*. Edited by Jay Leyda. New York: Harcourt, Brace & Co., 1949.

————. *Notes of a Film Director*. New York: Dover Publications, 1970.

SETON, M. *Eisenstein*. New York: Grove Press, 1960.

STEPHENSON, RALPH and J. DEBRIX. *The Cinema as Art*. Baltimore: Penguin Books, 1965.

FEDERICO GARCÍA LORCA

BAREA, ARTURO. *Lorca: The Poet and His People*. New York: Harcourt, Brace & Co., 1949.

DURAN, MANUEL, ed. *Lorca*. Twentieth Century Views. Englewood Cliffs: Prentice-Hall, 1962.

HONIG, EDWIN. *García Lorca*. New York: New Directions, 1948.

LIMA, ROBERT. *The Theatre of García Lorca*. New York: Las Americas Publishers, 1963.

SALINAS, PEDRO. "Lorca and the Poetry of Death." In *Theater in the Twentieth Century*. Edited by R. Corrigan. New York: Grove Press, 1963.

CHARLES GORDONE

BOSWORTH, PATRICIA. "From Nowhere to 'No Place,' " *The New York Times*, June 8, 1969, II, 1, 11.

GORDONE, CHARLES. "From the Muthah Lode," *Newsweek*, May 25, 1970, p. 95.

————. "Quiet Talk with Myself," *Esquire*, January 1970.

HENRIK IBSEN

BENTLEY, ERIC. "Ibsen, Pro and Con," *In Search of Theater*. New York: Alfred A. Knopf, 1953.

BRADBROOK, MURIEL. *Ibsen, the Norwegian*. London: Chatto & Windus, 1946.

BRUSTEIN, ROBERT. *The Theatre of Re-*

volt. Boston: Atlantic Monthly Press, 1964.

IBSEN, HENRIK. *Letters and Speeches*. Edited by Evert Sprinchorn. New York: Hill & Wang, 1964.

LUCAS, F. L. *Ibsen and Strindberg*. New York: Macmillan, 1962.

McFARLANE, JAMES W., ed. *Henrik Ibsen*. Baltimore: Penguin Books, 1970.

————, ed. *Discussions of Henrik Ibsen*. Boston: D. C. Heath, 1962.

MEYER, MICHAEL. *Henrik Ibsen*. London: Rupert Hart-Davis, 1967.

SHAW, GEORGE BERNARD. *The Quintessence of Ibsenism*. New York: Hill & Wang, 1913.

WEIGAND, HERMANN. *The Modern Ibsen*. New York: E. P. Dutton & Co., 1960.

EUGENE IONESCO

BONNEFOY, CLAUDE. *Conversations with Eugène Ionesco*. New York: Holt, Rinehart & Winston, 1971.

COE, RICHARD. *Eugène Ionesco*. New York: Grove Press, 1961.

ESSLIN, MARTIN. *The Theatre of the Absurd*. Garden City: Doubleday & Co., 1961.

IONESCO, EUGENE. *Fragments of a Journal*. Translated by Jean Pace. New York: Grove Press, 1968.

————. *Notes and Counternotes*. Translated by Donald Watson. New York: Grove Press, 1964.

JACOBSEN, JOSEPHINE and WILLIAM MUELLER. *Ionesco and Genêt*. New York: Hill & Wang, 1968.

MORRIS, KELLY, ed. *Genêt/Ionesco*. New York: Bantam Books, 1969.

EUGENE O'NEILL

ALEXANDER, DORIS. *The Tempering of Eugene O'Neill*. New York: Harcourt, Brace & World, 1962.

BRUSTEIN, ROBERT. *The Theatre of Revolt*. Boston: Atlantic Monthly Press, 1964.

CARGILL, OSCAR et al., eds. *O'Neill and His Plays*. New York: New York University Press, 1961.

ENGEL, EDWIN. *The Haunted Heroes of Eugene O'Neill*. Cambridge, Mass.: Harvard University Press, 1953.

GASSNER, JOHN, ed. *O'Neill*. Twentieth Century Views. Englewood Cliffs: Prentice-Hall, 1964.

GELB, BARBARA and ARTHUR GELB. *O'Neill*. New York: Harper & Row, 1962.

LEECH, CLIFFORD. *O'Neill*. New York: Barnes & Noble, 1965.

WINTHER, SOPHUS. *Eugene O'Neill*. Rev. & enl. ed. New York: Russell & Russell, 1961.

PEKING OPERA

CHIANG CHING. *On the Revolution of Peking Opera*. San Francisco: China Books and Periodicals, 1968.

HALSON, ELIZABETH. *Peking Opera*. New York: Oxford University Press, 1966.

LEVENSON, JOSEPH. *Revolution and Cosmopolitanism*. Berkeley: University of California Press, 1971.

SNOW, LOIS. *China on Stage*. New York: Random House, 1972.

LUIGI PIRANDELLO

BENTLEY, ERIC. *Playwright as Thinker*. New York: Meridian Books, 1955.

BRUSTEIN, ROBERT. *The Theatre of Revolt*. Boston: Atlantic Monthly Press, 1964.

BUDEL, OSCAR. *Pirandello*. Reprint of 1966 ed. New York: Hillary House Publishers, 1969.

CAMBON, G., ed. *Pirandello*. Twentieth Century Views. Englewood Cliffs: Prentice-Hall, 1967.

HEFFNER, HUBERT. "Pirandello and the Nature of Man." In *Modern Drama*, edited by T. Bogard and W. Oliver. New York: Oxford University Press, 1965.

LUCAS, F. L. *The Drama of Chekhov, Synge, Yeats and Pirandello*. London: Cassell & Co., 1963.

STARKIE, WALTER. *Luigi Pirandello*. 2d ed., rev. & enl. New York: E. P. Dutton & Co., 1937.

STYAN, J. L. *The Dark Comedy*. London: Cambridge University Press, 1962.

VITTORINI, DOMENICO. *The Drama of Luigi Pirandello*. Philadelphia: University of Pennsylvania Press, 1935.

ARTHUR SCHNITZLER

APSLER, ALFRED. "A Sociological View of Arthur Schnitzler," *Germanic Review* 18 (April 1943): 90–106.

DUKES, ASHLEY. *Modern Dramatists*. Folcroft, Pa.: Folcroft Press, Inc., 1911.

GARTEN, H. F. *Modern German Drama*. New York: Evergreen-Grove, 1962.

SCHNITZLER, ARTHUR. *My Youth in Vienna*. New York: Holt, Rinehart & Winston, 1970.

SWALES, MARTIN. *Arthur Schnitzler*. Oxford: Oxford University Press, 1971.

GEORGE BERNARD SHAW

BENTLEY, ERIC. *Bernard Shaw*. New York: New Directions, 1957.

CHESTERTON, G. K. *George Bernard Shaw*. London: Cambridge University Press, 1909.

CROMPTON, LOUIS. *Shaw the Dramatist*. Lincoln: University of Nebraska Press, 1969.

HENDERSON, ARCHIBALD. *George Bernard Shaw*. New York: Appleton-Century-Crofts, 1956.

IRVINE, WILLIAM. *The Universe of G. B. S.* New York: McGraw-Hill Book Co., 1949.

KAUFFMANN, R. J., ed. *G. B. Shaw*. Twentieth Century Views. Englewood Cliffs: Prentice-Hall, 1965.

MANDER, RAYMOND and JOE MITCHESON. *Theatrical Companion to Shaw*. New York: Pitman Publishing Corp., 1955.

MEISEL, MARTIN. *Shaw and the Nineteenth Century Theatre*. Princeton: Princeton University Press, 1963.

MORGAN, MARGERY. *The Shavian Playground*. London: Methuen & Co., 1972.

NETHERCOT, ARTHUR. *Men and Supermen*. Cambridge, Mass.: Harvard University Press, 1954.

PEARSON, HESKETH. *George Bernard Shaw*. New York: Harper & Brothers, 1942.

VALENCY, MAURICE. *The Cart and the Trumpet*. New York: Oxford University Press, 1973.

WATSON, BARBARA. *A Shavian Guide to the Intelligent Woman*. London: Chatto & Windus, 1964.

WEST, ALICK. *George Bernard Shaw.* New York: International Publishers Co., 1950.

WINSTEN, STEPHEN, ed. *G. B. S. 90.* New York: Dodd, Mead & Co., 1946.

AUGUST STRINDBERG

Strindberg Issue of *Modern Drama* 5 (December 1962).

BRUSTEIN, ROBERT. *The Theatre of Revolt.* Boston: Atlantic Monthly Press, 1964.

McGILL, V. J. *August Strindberg.* New York: Coward-McCann, 1930.

MORTENSEN, BRITA and BRIAN DOWNS. *Strindberg.* Cambridge: Cambridge University Press, 1965.

SPRIGGE, ELIZABETH. *The Strange Life of August Strindberg.* New York: Macmillan Co., 1949.

VALENCY, MAURICE. *The Flower and the Castle.* New York: Macmillan Co., London: Collier-Macmillan, 1963.

JOHN MILLINGTON SYNGE

BOURGEOIS, MAURICE. *John Millington Synge.* New York: Benjamin Blom, Inc., 1913.

CORKERY, DANIEL. *Synge and Anglo-Irish Literature.* Oxford: Oxford University Press, 1947.

ELLIS-FERMOR, UNA. *The Irish Dramatic Movement.* London: Methuen & Co., 1954.

GREENE, DAVID and E. STEPHENS. *J. M. Synge.* New York: Crowell Collier & Macmillan, 1961.

LUCAS, F. L. *Drama of Chekhov, Synge, Yeats and Pirandello.* London: Cassell & Co., 1963.

PEACOCK, RONALD. *The Poet in the Theatre.* New York: Harcourt, Brace & Co., 1946.

PRICE, ALAN. *Synge and Anglo-Irish Drama.* London: Methuen & Co., 1961.

SKELTON, ROBIN. *J. M. Synge and His World.* New York: Studio Publications, 1971.

————. *The Writings of J. M. Synge.* Indianapolis: Bobbs-Merrill Co., 1971.